Catalogue of the Neotropical Squamata

Catalogue of the Neotropical Squamata

JAMES A. PETERS *and* BRAULIO OREJAS-MIRANDA

with the collaboration of
ROBERTO DONOSO-BARROS

Part I

Snakes

new material by P.E. VANZOLINI

JAMES A. PETERS *and* ROBERTO DONOSO-BARROS

with the collaboration of
BRAULIO OREJAS-MIRANDA

Part II

Lizards and Amphisbaenians

new material by P.E. VANZOLINI

SMITHSONIAN INSTITUTION PRESS

Washington, D.C., and London

Originally published 1970
Revised edition 1986

Library of Congress
Cataloging-in-Publication Data

Peters, James Arthur, 1922-
Catalogue of the neotropical squamata.
English and Spanish.
"With new material by P.E. Vanzolini."
"Originally published 1970."
Contents: Snakes/James A. Peters, Braulio
Orejas-Miranda—Lizards and amphisbaenians/
James A. Peters, Roberto Donoso-Barros.
Includes indexes.
1. Snakes—Latin America. 2. Lizards—Latin
America. 3. Amphisbaenia—Latin America.
4. Reptiles—Latin America. I. Orejas-
Miranda, Braulio. II. Donoso-Barros, Roberto.
III. Vanzolini, P.E. (Paulo Emílio) IV. Title
QL666.L19P48   1986   597.95′0972
86-600220
ISBN 0-87474-757-0

This reprint edition is made possible by a
generous grant from the Artherton Seidell
Endowment Fund.

Contents

Publisher's Note

This is a reprint of *United States National Museum Bulletin 297*, originally published in 1970. This edition presents the two parts in one volume, with new material by P.E. Vanzolini, J. Cadle, R. Crombie, and G. Zug.

The scientific publications of the United States National Museum included two series, *Proceedings of the United States National Museum* and *United States National Museum Bulletin*.

In these series were published original articles and monographs dealing with the collections and work of the Museum and setting forth newly acquired facts in the fields of anthropology, biology, geology, history, and technology. Copies of each publication were distributed to libraries and scientific organizations and to specialists and others interested in the various subjects.

The *Proceedings*, begun in 1878, were intended for the publication, in separate form, of shorter papers. These were gathered in volumes, octavo in size, with the publication date of each paper recorded in the table of contents of the volume.

In the *Bulletin* series, the first of which was issued in 1875, appeared longer, separate publications consisting of monographs (occasionally in several parts) and volumes in which were collected works on related subjects. *Bulletins* were either octavo or quarto in size, depending on the needs of the presentation. Since 1902, papers relating to the botanical collections of the Museum were published in the *Bulletin* series under the heading *Contributions from the United States National Herbarium*.

Part I Snakes

The "Catalogue of Neotropical Squamata" has proved a most useful contribution to zoologists working in Central and South America. As with all taxonomic lists and keys, new studies of the fauna soon make the contents outdated. The reprinting of this catalogue offers an opportunity to add the new species and taxonomic arrangements described since the original publication, to correct errors, and to comment on the accuracy of the keys.

The following corrections, additions, and comments concerning the South American fauna derive principally from P.E. Vanzolini; however, other corrections and additions have been taken from the notes of John E. Cadle and Ronald I. Crombie. The following lists include only those genera in which we are aware of recent (1969-84) taxonomic changes. For the sake of brevity, literature citations to the older (<1970) name are generally not included unless a correction is presented; readers are advised to use the Catalogue indices to locate the name and the citation (G. Zug, ed.)

Addenda and Corrigenda to Part I Snakes

P. E. Vanzolini

Key to Genera of Snakes

Couplet 47 <u>Sibynomorphus</u>, which has 15 rows, will key here as having 17.
Couplet 101 <u>Rhadinaea</u> has a diastema, but will key here as not having one.
Couplet 128 <u>Lampropeltis</u> of mountainous area of Costa Rica and low lands of eastern Panama, Colombia, Ecuador, and Venezuela have a single anterior temporal.
Couplet 138 <u>Rachidelus</u>, not <u>Rachedelis</u>.
Couplet 140 Some <u>Dendrophidion</u> with a divided anal will key here as single anal.

Genera and Species

<u>Adelphicos</u> Jan, 1862.
Key to all species in Campbell & Ford, 1982, Occas. Pap. Mus. Nat. Hist. Univ. Kansas 100:1-22.
1982 <u>A. daryi</u> Campbell & Ford, Ibid. 100:3. Type-locality: Guatemala, Guatemala, San Jorge Muxbal, 5.5 km W San Jose Pinula.

<u>Apostolepis</u> Cope, 1862.
The key has been tried and found unsatisfactory. Specimens should be checked against the descriptions of geographically plausible species, also see key in Lema, 1978, Comun. Mus. Cienc. Pontif Univ. Catol. Rio G. Sul, 18/19:1-49.
    <u>A. ambinigra</u> (W. Peters). See Peters & Orejas-Miranda, 1972, Copeia 1972:588-90.
1978 <u>A. barrioi</u> Lema, Ibid. 18/19:30 Type-locality: Paraguay, San

Pedro, Cororo, Rio Ypane.

A. niceforoi Amaral. Correct type-locality: Colombia, Caqueta,
La Pedrera.

A. pymi Boulenger. Placed in synonymy of coronata (Sauvage,
1877) but probably a good species, extensively
distributed in Amazonia (P.E.V.).

A. rondoni Amaral. Distribution: Brasil, Rondonia, ?Mato
Grosso. Explanation: When the species was described
there was no Rondonia, it was all Mato Grosso, but most
of the work of the Rondon expedition was in present
Rondonia, from where I have one specimen (first one
after the type, P.E.V.).

A. tenuis Ruthven. See Peters & Orejas-Miranda, 1972, Copeia
1972(3):588-90.

1978 A. ventrimaculata Lema, Ibid. 18/19:34. Type-locality:
Paraguay, no further data.

1978 A. villaricae Lema, Ibid. 18/18:32. Type-locality: Paraguay,
Guaira, Villarrica.

A. vittata (Cope). See Peters & Orejas-Miranda, 1972, Ibid.
(3):588-90.

Atractus Wagler, 1829.
Peters & Orejas-Miranda present a matrix key, that should be used
jointly with geographic information.

1983 A. albuquerquei Cunha and Nascimento, Bol. Mus. Paraense
Emilio Goeldi (Zool.) 123:6. Type-locality: Brasil,
Para, Vila Nova, on Highway PA-256, near Timboteua.
Distribution: Brasil, Eastern Para, Rondonia.

1983 A. alphonsehogei Cunha and Nascimento, Ibid. 123:25.
Type-locality: Brasil, Para, Bela Vista, km 75 Hwy
PA-242 (Braganca to Vizeu). Distribution: Brasil,
eastern Para.

A. elaps (Gunther). See Dixon, Thomas & Greene, 1976,
Herpetologica 32:221-27.

1971 A. emigdioi Gonzales-Sponga, Monogr. Cient."Augusto Pi Suner"
Inst. Pedag. Caracas, 3:3. Type-locality: Venezuela,
Trujillo, 19 km Bocono on Valera-Trujillo road.

A. emmeli (Boettger). See McCoy, 1971, Herpetologica
27(3):314-16.

A. favae (Filippi), fide Hoogmoed, 1980, Zool. Verh. Leiden
175:16.

1840 Calamaria favae Filippi, Bibl. Ital. 99:16.
Type-locality: unknown.

1862 Rabdosoma longicaudatum Jan, Arch. Zool. Anat. Fisiol.
2:15. Type-locality: Java ?.
Atractus favae, Boulenger, 1894.
Distribution: the Guianas.

A. flammigerus flammigerus (Boie), fide Hoogmoed, 1980, Ibid.
175:20.

1827 Brachyorrhos flammigerus Boie, Isis von Oken 20:540.
Type-locality: unknown.
Rabdosoma badium var. B. Dumeril, Bibron & Dumeril, 1854.
Atractus badius var. E. Boulenger, 1894.

1979 Geophis alasukai Gasc & Rodriques, Bull. Mus. Nat. Hist.

Nat. Paris (4)1(4):1122. Type-locality: Trois Sauts,
French Guiana. Synonym fide Hoogmoed, 1983, Mem. Inst.
Butantan [1982] 42:227.
Distribution: the Guianas.
A. flammigerus snethlageae Cunha & Nascimento.
1983 Atractus flammigerus snethlageae Cunha & Nascimento, Bol.
Mus. Paraense Emilio Goeldi (Zool.) 123:19.
Type-locality: Brasil, Para, Colonia Nova, on Highway
BR-316, 10 km before the Rio Gurupi.
Distribution: Brasil, eastern Para.
A. gaigeae Savage. Type-locality: Santiago-Zamora, not
Santiago-Zaruma.
A. guentheri (Wucherer). Type-locality: Brasil, Bahia,
Canavieiras. Distribution: forests of eastern Brasil.
A. latifrons (Gunther). Distribution: also known from Surinam
(Hoogmoed, 1980, Ibid. 175:20) and French Guiana (Gasc &
Rodriques, 1980 Ibid. 1(4):1122).
1969 A. mariselae Lancini Publ Ocas. Mus. Cien. Nat. Caracas
Zool. 15:1-6. Type-locality: Venezuela, Trujillo,
Bocono
A. microrhynchus (Cope) = A. badius (Boie), fide Dixon &
Soini, 1977, Milwaukee Publ. Mus. Contrib. Biol. Geol.
12:1-91.
A. obesus Marx. Distribution: Valle del Cauca, not Valle and
Carca.
A. occipitoalbus (Jan). Distribution: also Bolivia (USNM
specimen).
A. poeppigi (Jan). Revalidated by Dixon, Thomas & Greene,
1976, Ibid. 32:221-27.
A. roulei Despax. Distribution: elevation range listed as
1200-1600 m, type-locality at 2350 m.
A. schach (Boie), fide Hoogmoed, Ibid. 175:31.
1827 Brachyorrhos schach Boie, Isis von Oken 20:540.
Type-locality: unknown.
Atractus badius var. E Boulenger, 1894.
Distribution: Guianas and eastern Para, Brasil.
A. subbicinctum (Jan) = A. badius, fide Hoogmoed, 1980, Ibid.
175:1-47.
A. taeniatus Griffin = A. boettgeri Boulenger, fide McCoy,
1971, Ibid. 27(3):314-16.
A. torquatus (D.,B.& D.) Distribution: includes Surinam,
Guianas Peru, Bolivia (Hoogmoed, 1980, Ibid. 175:1-47).
A. trilineatus Wagler.
1820 Coluber brachyurus Kuhl, Beitr. Zool. Vergl. Anat., Erste
Abt.:89 (not C. brachiurus Shaw, 1802). Type-locality:
Java, fide Hoogmoed, 1982, Zool. Med. Leiden 56(10):131.
1826 Brachyorrhos Kuhli Schlegel, Bull. Sci. Nat. Geol. 9:236
(nomen novum for Coluber brachyurus Kuhl).
1828 Atractus trilineatus Wagler, Isis von Oken 21:742.
Type-locality: none given.
1862 Rabdosoma trivirgatum Jan, Arch. Zool. Anat. Fisiol.
2:17. Type-locality: unknown.
1862 Rabdosoma punctatovittatum Jan, Ibid. 2:17.
Type-locality: Antilles.

Distribution: Trinidad, the Guianas, and eastern Venezuela.
A. ventrimaculatus Boulenger. Type-locality: Fuqueros, Estado
de Merida, fide Roze, 1966, Taxon. Zoogeog. Ofid.
Venezuela. Distribution: Venezuela, fide Roze, op. cit.
1979 A. zidoki Gasc & Rodrigues, Bull. Mus. Nat. Hist. Nat. (Paris)
(4,A)1(2):548. Type-locality: French Guiana:
Trois-Sauts, Haut Oyapock. Distribution: French Guiana
and eastern Para, Brasil.

Boa Linnaeus, 1758.
B. constrictor sabogae (Barbour). Type-locality: Panama, Pearl
Island group, Saboga Island, incorrectly changed by
Peters & Orejas-Miranda.

Bothrops Wagler, 1824.
Identification of South American Bothrops frequently depends on
color pattern; reliably identified specimens and good photographs
should be used to check identification. New checklist provided by
Hoge & Romano-Hoge, 1981, Mem. Inst. Butantan [1978/79] 42/43:
179-310. Matrix error: B. brazili, 26 dorsal scalerows in holotype.
B. atrox (Linnaeus).
1845 Trigonocephalus colombiensis Hallowell, Proc. Acad. Nat.
Sci. Philadelphia 1845:246. Type-locality: "Republic of
Colombia, within two hundred miles of Caracas".
Comment: Sandner-Montilla (1979, Mem. Cient. Ofidiol.
3:1-7). reduced B. colombiensis to synonymy of
lanceolatus and described B. lanceolatus aidae; Johnson
& Dixon 1984, J. Herpetol. 18(3):329-332 reduced
colombiensis to synonymy of atrox.
B. brazili Hoge. Distribution: also Ecuador (USNM) and
northern Peru (MVZ, USNM).
B. castelnaudi castelnaudi D.,B. & D. Comment: Hoogmoed &
Gruber, 1983, Spixiana Suppl. 9:337, synonymized
castelnaudi with taeniatus Wagler, a species for which
no holotype is extant.
Distribution: equatorial forest of Brazil, Venezuela,
Colombia, Ecuador, Peru and Bolivia; also French Guiana,
fide Gasc and Rodrigues, 1980, Bull. MNHN, Paris
(4)2:559-98.
B. castelnaudi lichenosus Roze.
1958 Bothrops lichenosus Roze, Acta Biol. Venezuela 2:308.
Type-locality: Chimanta Tepui, Estado Bolivar,
Venezuela.
Bothrops castelnaudi Sandner-Montilla, 1976, Mem. Cien.
Ofidiol. 2:1.
Bothrops castelnaudi lichenosus Hoge and Romano-Hoge,
1981, Mem. Inst. Butantan [1978/79] 42/43:205.
Distribution: Known only from type locality.
B. colombiensis (Hallowell) = B. atrox.
1976 B. eneydae Sandner-Montilla, Mem. Cien. Ofidiol. 1:1.
Type-locality: Kavanayen, Estado Bolivar, Venezuela.
Distribution: known only from type locality.
1979 B. isabelae Sandner-Montilla, Mem. Cien. Ofidiol. 4:3.
Type-locality: 7 km SE Guanare, Estado Portuguesa,

Venezuela. Distribution: only from the type locality.

<u>B</u>. <u>jararaca</u> (Wied). Hoogmoed & Gruber, 1983, Ibid. 9:336, removed <u>B</u>. <u>leucostigma</u> from the synonymy of <u>jararaca</u>.

<u>B</u>. <u>jararacussu</u> Lacerda. Distribution: also eastern Brasil from Bahia to Santa Catarina (Lema & Araujo, 1980, Iheringia 56:63-70).

<u>B</u>. <u>lanceolatus</u> (Lacepede).

1981 <u>B</u>. <u>lanceolatus</u> <u>aidae</u> Sandner-Montilla, Mem. Cien. Ofidiol. 6:4. Type-locality: Agua Blanca, en las selvas de Guatopo, Estado Miranda, 25 km en via recta de Altagracia de Orituco. Distribution: only type locality.
Comment: <u>B</u>. <u>lanceolatus</u> (sensu stricto) is restricted to Lesser Antillean island of Martinique, thus <u>B</u>. <u>atrox</u> <u>aidae</u> would be correct citation.

<u>B</u>. <u>leucurus</u> Wagler, 1824. Revalidated by Hoge & Romano, 1971, in Bucherl & Buckley (eds.) Venomous Animals and Their Venoms. Vol. 2.

<u>B</u>. <u>lichenosus</u> Roze = <u>B</u>. <u>castelnaudi</u> <u>lichenosus</u>.

<u>B</u>. <u>moojeni</u> Hoge. Distribution: central and southeastern Brasil to Misiones, Argentina.

<u>B</u>. <u>nasutus</u>. See recent review by Wilson et al., 1981, Tulane Stud. Zool. Bot. 22:85-107

<u>B</u>. <u>neuwiedi</u> Wagler. Distribution: east of Andes and south of 10 S in South America.

<u>B</u>. <u>picadoi</u>. See recent review by Werman, 1984, J. Herpetol. 18:207-10.

<u>B</u>. <u>roedingeri</u> Mertens. Type-locality: Huayuri, not Huayri, (Titschak).

<u>B</u>. <u>supraciliaris</u> Taylor = <u>B</u>. <u>schlegelii</u>, fide Werman, 1984, J. Herpetol. 18:484-86.

<u>Cercophis</u> Fitzinger, 1843, Syst. Rept. :26. Type-species: Dendrophis aurata Schlegel.
<u>Cercophis</u> <u>auratus</u> (Schlegel)
1837 Dendrophis aurata Schlegel, Essai Phys. Serp. :227. Type-locality: Paramaribo, Surinam.
<u>Cercophis</u> <u>auratus</u> Fitzinger, 1843, Syst. Rept. :26.
<u>Cercophis</u> <u>auratus</u> Hoogmoed, 1983, Mem. Inst. Butantan [1982] 42:225.

<u>Chironius</u> Fitzinger, 1843.
1969 <u>C</u>. <u>barrioi</u> Donoso-Barros, Bol. Soc. Biol. Concepcion 41:191. Type-locality: Bolivia, Beni, Laguna Suarez, near Trinidad.
1970 <u>C</u>. <u>cochranae</u> Hoge & Romano, Mem. Inst. Butantan [1969] 34:93. Type-locality: Brasil, Para, Agua Preta, Utinga, Belem. Comment: Cunha & Nascimento, 1982, Bol. Mus. Paraense Emilio Goeldi (Zool.) 119:9, synonymized <u>cochranae</u> with <u>multiventris</u>.
<u>C</u>. <u>exoletus</u> (Linnaeus). Revalidated by Hoge, Romano & Cordeiro 1978, Mem. Inst. Butantan [1976/77] 40/41:37-52.
<u>C</u>. <u>holochlorus</u> (Cope). Revalidated by Donoso-Barros, 1969, maintained by Hoge, Romano & Cordeiro, 1978, Ibid 40/41:37-52

<u>C</u>. <u>spixii</u> (Hallowell). Comment: Valid, fide Freiberg, 1982, Snakes S. Amer. :92, but with no explanation.

<u>Clelia</u> Fitzinger, 1826.
Color patterns used in key are quite variable.
<u>C</u>. <u>bicolor</u> (Peracca). Distribution: also Peru, vicinity of Iquitos (Dixon & Soini, 1977) and Huanuco (USNM).
<u>C</u>. <u>equatoriana</u> (Amaral). Distribution: also Amazonian Ecuador (USNM).

<u>Conophis</u> Peters, 1960.
<u>C</u>. <u>nevermanni</u> Dunn = <u>Crisantophis</u> <u>nevermanni</u>, fide Villa, 1971, J. Herpetol 5:173-177.

<u>Corallus</u> Daudin, 1803.
<u>C</u>. <u>enydris</u>. Subspecific key has couplets reversed, <u>cooki</u> fewer than 50 scale rows.

<u>Crisantophis</u> Villa, 1971, Ibid. 5:173. Type-species: <u>Conophis</u> <u>nevermanni</u> Dunn. Monotypic.

<u>Crotalus</u> Linnaeus, 1758.
The identification of the subspecies of <u>C</u>. <u>durissus</u> is largely based on color pattern and should be checked against specimens or photographs.
<u>C</u>. <u>durissus</u> Linnaeus.
1978 <u>Crotalus</u> <u>durissus</u> <u>trigonicus</u> Harris & Simmons, Bull. Maryland Herpetol. Soc. 14(3):112. Nomen nudum.
1978 <u>C</u>. <u>durissus</u> <u>trigonicus</u> Harris & Simmons, Mem. Inst. Butantan [1976/77] 40/41 306. Type locality, Guyana, Rupununi Savanna. Distribution: Rupununi Savanna.
1980 <u>C</u>. <u>pifanorum</u> Sandner-Montilla, Mem. Cien. Ofidiol. 5:3. Type-locality: 68 km S Espino, en direccion a Puerto Parmana, Parcelamiento de Agrotecnicos "Dr. Gonzalo Ledesma", entre los nacientes de los Rios Otocuao (Este) y Carapa (Oeste), Distrito Infante, Estado Guarico, Venezuela. Distribution: known only from type locality.

<u>Cyclagras</u> Cope, 1885 = <u>Hydrodynastes</u> Fitzinger, 1843, fide Hoge, 1966, Cien. Cult. 18(2):143.

<u>Dendrophidion</u> Fitzinger, 1843.
The key has been tested and is unreliable. Specimens should be checked against descriptions of geographically suitable species.
<u>D</u>. <u>brunneus</u> (Gunther). Distribution: also Peru, Depto. Cajamarca (MVZ).

<u>Dipsas</u> Laurenti, 1768
<u>D</u>. <u>elegans</u> (Boulenger), fide Kofron, 1982, Copeia (1):46.
1896 <u>Leptognathus</u> <u>elegans</u> Boulenger, Cat. Sn. British. Mus. 3:452. Type-locality: Isthmus of Tehuantepec.
1898 <u>Leptognathus</u> <u>ellipsifera</u> Boulenger, Proc. Zool. Soc. London 1898:117. Type-locality: Ibarra, western Ecuador. Distribution: Andes of western Ecuador.

Dipsas ellipsifera = D. elegans, fide Kofron, 1982, op. cit.
D indica bucephala (Shaw).
1976 D. indica petersi Hoge & Romano. Type-locality: Brasil,
        Sao Paulo, Pedro de Toledo.
D. neivai Amaral, 1923, Arch. Mus. Nat. Brasil 26:108.
D. oreas (Cope), fide Kofron, 1982, Ibid. (1):48.
1868 Leptognathus oreas Cope.
1884 Leptognathus andrei Sauvage, Bull. Soc. Philomath.
        (7)8:146. Type-locality: Nouvelle Grenade (Andre coll.).
        Leptognathus andiana Boulenger, 1896.

Drepanoides Dunn, 1928.
        D. anomalus (Jan). Distribution: also Brasil, Para (Cunha &
            Nascimento, 1978) and Rondonia (MZUSP).

Dromicus Bibron, 1843, sensu Peters & Orejas-Miranda 1970 =
            Alsophis Cope, 1862, sensu Maglio, 1970 = Philodryas
            Wagler, 1830, fide Thomas, 1977, Copeia 1977(4):648-52.
        D. angustilineatus Schmidt & Walker = Philodryas simonsii
            Boulenger, 1900, fide Thomas 1977, Ibid. (4):648-52.
        D. chamissonis (Wiegmann) = Philodryas chamissonis, fide
            Thomas, 1977, Ibid. (4):648-52.
        D. inca Schmidt & Walker = Philodryas simonsii Boulenger,
            1900, fide Thomas, 1977, Ibid. (4):648-52.
        D. tachymenoides Schmidt & Walker = Philodryas tachymenoides,
            fide Thomas, 1977, Ibid. (4):648-52.

Drymobius Fitzinger, 1843.
        D. chloroticus (Cope). See review by Wilson, 1970, J.
            Herpetol. 4:155-63.
        D. rhombifer (Gunther). Distribution: also Bolivia (Vaeth &
            Rossman, 1984, Herpetol. Rev. 15:78) and eastern
            Venezuela (MVZ).

Drymoluber Amaral, 1929.
        Herpetodryas occipitalis Gunther, 1868, Ann. Mag. Nat. Hist.
            1:420.

Elapomorphus Wiegmann, 1843.
Key to all species in Lema, 1979, Rev. Brasil. Biol. 39:835-53.
        E. bilineatus suspectus Amaral. Revalidated by Lema, 1978,
            Comun. Mus. Cienc. Pontif. Univ. Catol. Rio Grande Do
            Sul 16/17:1-10.
        E. nasutus Gomes. Type-locality: Brasil, Minas Gerais,
            Paineiras (= Peiropolis). Distribution: "Triangulo
            Mineiro", Minas Gerais, Brasil.
1979 E. punctatus Lema, Rev. Brasil. Biol. 39:836. Type-locality:
            Argentina, Salta, Rosario de la Frontera. Distribution:
            northern Argentina.

Emmochliophis Fritts & Smith, 1969, Trans. Kansas Acad. Sci.
            72(1):60. Type-species: E. fugleri Fritts & Smith.
1969 E. fugleri Fritts & Smith, Ibid. 72(1):60. Type-locality:
            Ecuador, Pichincha, 24 km S Santo Domingo de los

7

Colorados, 4 km E Rio Baba Bridge, ca 600 m.

Epicrates Wagler, 1830.
    1816 _Draco ocellatus_ Oken, Lehrb. Naturg. 3:272.

Erythrolamprus Wagler, 1830.
    Erythrolamprus aesculapii aesculapii (Linnaeus), fide Cunha &
        Nascimento, 1980, Bol. Mus. Paraense Emilio Goeldi
        (Zool.) 102:5.
    1863 _Erythrolamprus Aesculapii_ [Aesculapii] Jan.
    1854 _Erythrolamprus baupertuisii_ D., B. & D.
    1959 _Erythrolamprus baileyi_ Roze, Acta Biol. Venezuela 2:526.
        Type-locality: Caripito, Estado Monagas, Venezuela.
      Distribution: northern South America from coastal Venezuela
        to Amazonia.
    Erythrolamprus baupertuisii = _E. a. aesculapii_.

Eunectes Wagler, 1830.
    E. deschauenseei Dunn & Conant. Distribution: also French
        Guiana (Hoogmoed, 1982, Mem. Inst. Butantan 46:219-54).

Ficimia Gray.
Key, descriptions and distributions of all species in Hardy, 1975,
J. Herpetol. 9:133-168.
    Distribution: southern Texas through eastern Mexico to Yucatan
        Peninsula, Guatemala, Belize and northern Honduras.
    Content: six species, five extralimital.

Geophis Wagler, 1830.
Key to Costa Rican and Panamanian species in Savage, 1981, Ibid.
(3):549-553.
1979 _G. alasukai_ Gasc & Rodrigues, Bull. Mus. Nat. Hist. Nat.
        (Paris)(4)1(4):1122. Type-locality: French Guiana, Trois
        Sauts. Comment: junior synonym of _Atractus flammigerus_,
        fide Hoogmoed, 1980, Ibid. 175:20.
1981 _G. downsi_ Savage, Copeia (3):549. Type-locality: Costa Rica,
        Puntarenas, 4 km S San Vito de Joba, 1200 m.
        Distribution: premontane rain forest of Cordillera
        Costena, Costa Rica, 1100-1200m.
    G. cancellatus Smith. Distribution: also Guatemala (MVZ).

Helicops Wagler, 1830.
Key couplet substitutions, fide Rossman, 1973, HISS News 1:189-191.

      4. Dorsum striped...5
        Dorsum spotted or blotched...6
      5. Venter heavily pigmented..._carinicaudus_
        Venter light or with faint flecks..._modestus_
      6. Dorsum $>$ 4 rows of blotches...7
        Dorsum 3 rows of large spots..._gomesi_

    H. hagmanni Roux. Distribution: Colombia, Brasil and probably
        Peru (Rossman, 1975, Herpetologica 31:414-18).
    H. pastazae Shreve. Distribution: also Peru and Venezuela

(Rossman, 1976, Occ. Pap. Mus. Zool. LSU 50:1-15).
1976 H. petersi Rossman, Occ. Pap. Mus. Zool. Louisiana St. Univ.
     50:2. Type-locality: Ecuador, Napo, E. bank Rio
     Misahualli, 1 mi NE Tena. Distribution: eastern Andean
     foothills, Ecuador.
1975 H. yacu Rossman & Dixon, Herpetologica 31(4):412.
     Type-locality: Peru, Loreto, Moropon. Probably = H.
     pastazae, fide Rossman & Abe, 1979, Proc. Louisiana
     Acad. Sci. 42:7-9. Distribution: only from type locality

Hydrodynastes Fitzinger, 1843, includes Cyclagras Cope, 1885, fide
     Hoge, 1966, Cien. Cult. 18(2):143.

Hydrops Wagler, 1830.
     H. triangularis bolivianus Roze. Distribution: northeastern
          Bolivia to Corrientes, Argentina.

Hypsiglena Cope.
Not included in Costa Rican fauna by Savage, 1980, Handlist Key
Herpetofauna Costa Rica.

Imantodes A. Dumeril, 1853.
Recently revised with the addition of a new species, updated
synonymies and a key, Myers, 1982, Amer. Mus. Novit. 2738:1-50.
     I. cenchoa (Linnaeus). No subspecies recognized; combine
          synonymies of leucomelas & semifasciatus with cenchoa.
          Distribution: from Veracruz, Mexico, to northern
          Argentina.
     I. gemmistratus (Cope). Question the validity of subspecies,
          hence have omitted names in Zweifel and Stuart cited by
          Myers, op. cit (P.E.V.). Combine synonymies and add:
     1899 Himatodes hemigenius Cope, Bull. Philadelphia Sci. Mus.
          1:16. Type-locality: Santa Clara, Costa Rica.
          Distribution: from Sonora and Veracruz, Mexico, to
          northern Colombia.
     I. inornatus (Boulenger). Distribution: Nicaragua to
          northwestern Ecuador.
     I. lentiferus (Cope). Distribution: Amazonian South America
          and Guianas.
     1982 I. phantasma Myers, Ibid. 2738:3. Type-locality: "southeastern
          slope of Cerro Cituro, a peak on the northern end of the
          Serrania de Pirre, Province of Darien, Republic of
          Panama", 1030 m. Distribution: only from type-locality.

Incaspis Donoso-Barros, 1974, Neotropica 20(16):14. Type-species:
     I. cercostropha Donoso-Barros, 1974, op. cit. =
     Philodryas Wagler, 1830, fide Thomas, 1977,
     Copeia(4):648-52.
1974 Incaspis cercostropha Donoso-Barros, Ibid. 20(16):14 =
     Philodryas simonsii Boulenger, fide Thomas, 1977,
     Ibid. (4):648-52.

Lachesis Daudin, 1803.
     L. muta noctivaga Hoge = L. m. rhombeata Wied, fide Hoge &

Romano, 1978, Mem. Inst. Butantan [1976/77] 40/41:53-54.

Lampropeltis Fitzinger, 1843.
Williams, 1978, Milwaukee Public Mus. Publ. Biol. Geol. (2):1-258, revised L. triangulum with new subspecies descriptions, complete synonymies and key to all subspecies.
    L. triangulum (Lacepede).
    1978 L. triangulum andesiana Williams, Ibid. (2):231.
        Type-locality: "near Cali, Colombia, Valle."
        Distribution: Andes of northwestern Colombia.
    1978 L. triangulum hondurensis Williams, Ibid. (2):212.
        Type-locality: "Cukra, Departmento de Zelaya, Nicaragua." Distribution: Caribbean versant of Honduras (except the northwestern corner) and Nicaragua.
    1978 L. triangulum stuarti Williams, Ibid. (2):217.
        Type-locality: "Finca Los Cedros (100 m), Tecla, Departmento La Libertad, El Salvador." Distribution: Pacific versant of El Salvador, Honduras, Nicaragua and northwestern Costa Rica.

Leimadophis Fitzinger, 1843, sensu Peters & Orejas-Miranda, 1970 = Liophis Wagler, except for the following species:
    L. atahuallpae (Steindachner) = Saphenophis atahuallpae (Steindachner), fide Myers, 1973, Amer. Mus. Novit. 2522:1-37.
    L. simonsii (Boulenger) = Philodryas simonsii Boulenger, fide Thomas, 1977, Ibid. (4):648-52.
    L. pygmaeus (Cope) = Umbrivaga pygmaea (Cope), fide Markezich & Dixon, 1979, Copeia (4):698-701.

Leptodeira Fitzinger, 1843.
The key to the Brasilian subspecies of L. annulata does not work properly.

Leptomicrurus Schmidt, 1937 = Micrurus Wagler, 1824, fide Romano, 1972, Mem. Inst. Butantan [1971] 35:111-15.
    L. schmidti Hoge & Romano = Micrurus karlschmidti (nomen novum) Romano, 1972, Ibid. 35:111-15.

Leptophis Bell, 1824.
Key to all species in Mertens, 1973, Stud. Neotrop. Fauna 8:141-54.
    L. ahaetulla chocoensis Oliver = L. a. urostictus (W. Peters), fide Mertens, 1973, op. cit.
    L. modestus (Gunther). Revalidated by Mertens, 1973, op. cit. Distribution: southern Mexico to El Salvador.

Leptotyphlops Fitzinger, 1843.
    L. albifrons (Wagler).
    1824 Stenostoma albifrons Wagler.
        Leptotyphlops albifrons Stejneger.
        Leptotyphlops tenella Klauber = L. albifrons fide Hoogmoed & Gruber, 1983, Spixiana Suppl. 9:339.
        Distribution: Trinidad, Guianas and eastern Amazonia.
  1969 Leptotyphlops amazonicus Orejas-Miranda, Comun. Zool. Mus.

Hist. Natur. Montevideo 10:1. Type-locality: Esmeralda,
Territorio Federal de Amazonas, Venezuela. = L.
signatus, fide Hahn, 1979, Herpetologica 35:57.
1977 L. collaris Hoogmoed, Zool. Med. (Leiden) 51:100. Type
locality: Surinam, Marowijne, Base Camp Nassau Mts.
Distribution: Surinam and French Guiana.
L. cupinensis Bailey & Carvalho. See Hoogmoed, 1977, Ibid.
51:99-123.
1970 L. guayaquilensis Orejas-Miranda & Peters, Mitt. Zool. Mus.
Berlin 46:439. Type-locality: Ecuador, Guayas,
Guayaquil.
L. rubrolineatus (Werner). See Orejas-Miranda & Zug, 1974,
Proc. Biol. Soc. Washington 87:167-74.
L. rufidorsus Taylor. See Orejas-Miranda & Zug, 1974, Ibid.
87:167-74.
L. septemstriatus (Schneider). See Hoogmoed, 1977, Ibid.
51:99-123.
L. signatus (Jan).
1861 Stenostoma signatum Jan, Arch. Zool. Anat. Fisiol. 1:188.
Type-locality: unknown; restricted to "northern
Amazonian region of South America.", fide Hahn, 1979,
Herpetologica 35:57.
L. striatula Smith & Laufe. Resurrected by Laurent, 1984, Acta
Zool. Lilloana 38:33.
1974 L. tricolor Orejas-Miranda & Zug, Ibid. 87:167. Type-locality:
Peru, Ancash, Yunca Pampa, Huaylas. Distribution: Peru,
from Cajamarca to Ancash, 2700-3300 m (Zug, 1977, Copeia
(4):744).
1984 L. vellardi Laurent, Acta Zool. Lilloana 38:30. Type-locality:
Argentina, Formosa, Ciudad de Formosa. Distribution:
known only from type locality.

Liophis Wagler, 1830.
1830 Liophis Wagler, Nat. Syst. Amph. :187. Type-species: Coluber
cobella Linnaeus.
1843 Dromicus Bibron, in la Sagra, Hist. Fis. Pol. Nat. Cuba
4:133. Type-species: Dromicus angulifer Bibron.
1843 Pariopeltis Fitzinger, Syst. Rept. :25. Type-species: Coluber
triscalis Linnaeus.
1843 Opheomorphus Fitzinger.
1843 Leimadophis Fitzinger, Ibid. :26. Type-species· Coronella
almadensis, Fitzinger (= Natrix almadensis Wagler).
1843 Pseudophis Fitzinger, Ibid. :26. Type-species: Xenodon
schottii, Boie (= Coluber schottii Fitzinger).
1843 Lygophis Fitzinger, Ibid. :26. Type species: Herpetodryas
lineatus, Schlegel (= Coluber lineatus Linnaeus).
1847 Limadophis Agassiz, Nomencl. Zool. Index Univ. :210;
emendation for Leimadophis Fitzinger.
1862 Ophiomorphus Cope.
1878 Aporophis Cope, Proc. Amer. Philos. Soc. 17:34; substitute
name for Lygophis.
1894 Echinanthera Cope, Amer. Nat. 28:241. Type-species: Aporophis
cyanopleurus Cope.
1895 Taeniophallus Cope.

11

In key, insignissimus (couplet 24) is listed under Rhadinaea, not Liophis.

L. almadensis (Wagler).
1824 Natrix almada Wagler, Spec. Nov. Serp. Brasil :30.
     Type-locality: Almada, Bahia, Brasil.
     Natrix almadensis Wagler, 1824, Ibid. :pl. 10.
1858 Liophis conirostris Guenther, Cat. Colubr. Sn. British
     Mus. :46. Type-locality: Bahia, Brasil.
1863 Liophis verecundus Jan, Arch. Zool. Anat. Fisiol. 2:300.
     Type-locality: none given.
     Liophis wagleri (part) Jan, 1863, Ibid. 2:297; based on
     Natrix almadensis Wagler.
1882 Liophis (Lygophis) Ygraecum Peters, Sitzber. Ges.
     Naturf. Fr. Berlin 1882:129. Type locality:
     Guaratingueta, Sao Paulo, Brasil.
1906 Trigonocephalus scolecomorphus Bacque, Rev. Mus. La
     Plata 12:116. Type-locality: Asuncion, Paraquay.
L. albiceps (Amaral) = Rhadinaea decipiens (Gunther, 1893),
     fide Myers, 1974, Bull. Amer. Mus. Nat. Hist.
     153:1-262.
L. almadensis (Wagler), fide Dixon, 1980, Ibid. 31:4.
     Leimadophis almadensis Hoogmoed & Gruber, 1983, Spixiana
     Suppl. 9:331; designation of lectotype.
     Distribution: Atlantic forests of Brasil, southeastern
     Bolivia, Uruguay, Paraguay, and northern Argentina.
L. amarali Wettstein. Incertae sedis, fide Dixon, 1980, Ibid.
     31:4. Distribution: Bahia and Minas Gerais to Santa
     Catarina, Brasil.
L. amoenus (Jan). Incertae sedis, fide Dixon, 1980, Ibid.
     31:5. Distribution: Atlantic forest of Brasil.
1983 L. andinus Dixon, Ann. Carnegie Mus. 52:129.
     Type-locality:Bolivia, Cochabamba, Incachaca, 2500 m.
     Distribution: known only from type locality.
L. breviceps breviceps Cope.
1861 Liophis breviceps Cope, Proc. Acad. Nat. Sci.
     Philadelphia 1860:252. Type-locality: Surinam.
     Liophis breviceps breviceps, Dixon, 1983, J. Herpetol.
     17:153.
     Distribution: forested parts of the Amazon basin in
     Bolivia, Brasil, Colombia, Peru, and similar areas of
     French Guiana, Guyana, Surinam and Venezuela.
L. breviceps canaima Roze.
1957 Liophis canaima Roze, Bol. Mus. Cien. Nat. Caracas
     [1955] 1:188. Type-locality: Ugueto, Territorio Federal
     de Amazonas, Venezuela.
     Liophis breviceps canaimus Dixon, 1983, Ibid. 17:153.
     Distribution: region of Rio Ugueto, Amazonas, Venezuela.
L. chrysostomus (Cope, 1868). Revalidated by Dixon & Soini,
     1977, Milwaukee Public Mus. Contrib. Biol. Geol.
     12:1-91 = Dromicus amazonicus Dunn, 1922 incertae sedis
     fide Peters & Orejas-Miranda, 1970. = L. miliaris
     chrysostomus, fide Dixon, 1983, Ibid. (3):800.
L. cobella cobella (Linnaeus, 1758).
     Liophis cobella cobella Dixon, 1983, Ibid. 17:159.

Distribution: eastern area of Guiana Shield exclusive of Venezuelan tepui region.

L. cobella dyticus Dixon.

1983 L. cobella dyticus Dixon, Ibid. 17:159. Type-locality: Peru, Loreto, Monte Carmelo (= Requena). Distribution: western Amazon basin, from Lomalinda, Colombia, south to Buenavista, Bolivia, & east to Porto Velho, Brasil.

L. cobella taeniogaster Jan.

1863 Liophis taeniogaster Jan, Ibid. 2:292. Type-locality: Brasil.
    Liophis cobella taeniogaster Dixon, 1983, Ibid. 17:159.
    Distribution: Brasil, south of Amazon, to central Brasil and coastal Bahia (a re-interpretation of Dixon's text - PEV).

L. cobella trebbaui Roze.

1958 Liophis trebbaui Roze, Acta Biol. Venezuela 2:262. Type-locality: Auyantepui, Estado Bolivar, Venezuela.

1958 Liophis ingeri Roze, Ibid. 2:303. Type-locality: Chimanta Tepui, Estado Bolivar, Venezuela, 1900 m.
    Liophis cobella trebbaui Dixon, 1983, Ibid. 17:159.
    Distribution: Chimanta and Auyan Tepuis, and Km marker 144 El Dorado-Santa Elena [de Uairen] Hwy, Bolivar, Venezuela.

L. coralliventris (Boulenger). Distribution: lower valley of Rio Paraguay.

L. dilepis Cope, fide Hoge, Russo, Santos & Furtado, 1981, Mem. Inst. Butantan [1978/79] 42/43:89. Distribution: open formations of Brasil, Bolivia, Paraguay, and northern Argentina.

L. epinephelus epinephelus Cope. Distribution: lower elevations of mountains of western Panama east to Colombian lowlands and most of Colombian inter-Andean valleys to elevations of 1500 m; also south to extreme northern Ecuador along Pacific coast.

L. epinephelus albiventris Jan, fide Dixon, 1983, In Rhodin & Miyata (eds.), Advanc. Herpetol. Evol. Biol. :138.

1863 Liophis reginae var. albiventris Jan.

1863 Liophis reginae var. quadrilineata Jan, Ibid. 2:295. Type-locality: Ecuador & Colombia.

1868 Opheomorphus alticolus Cope.

1872 Zamenis ater Gunther, Ann. Mag. Nat. Hist. (4) 9:2. Type-locality: Biscra, Algeria.
    Distribution: western Ecuador from sea level to 2600 m in Andean valleys.

L. epinephelus bimaculatus Cope, fide Dixon, 1983, Ibid.:138.

1899 Liophis bimaculatus Cope.

1903 Liophis bipraeocularis Boulenger.

1984 Leimadophis epinephelus ecuadoriensis Laurent, Bull. Inst. Roy. Hist. Nat. Belgique 25:8. Type-locality: Ecuador.
    Distribution: high (2600-3300 m) Andean valleys of western Venezuela, central Colombia, south to northern Peru.

L. epinephelus fraseri Boulenger, fide Dixon, 1983, Ibid. :138. Distribution: middle elevations of eastern and

13

eastern Andean slopes of southern Ecuador, south to
central Peru.

L. epinephelus lamonae Dunn, fide Dixon, 1983, Ibid. :139.
Distribution: eastern slopes of Andes of Colombia from
1500-2600 m, south to east-central Ecuador.

L. epinephelus opisthotaenia Boulenger, fide Dixon, 1983,
Ibid. :139. Distribution: Merida region of Venezuela
and Paramo de Tama region of Venezuela and Colombia.

L. epinephelus pseudocobella Peracca, fide Dixon, 1983, Ibid.
139. Distribution: middle elevations of central and
western areas of Colombian Andes south to Ecuador.

L. flavifrenatus (Cope). Distribution: southern Brasil,
Uruguay, Paraguay and northern Argentina.

L. fraseri Boulenger. Distribution: also Peru, Huancabamba
Depression (Duellman, 1979).

L. frenatus (Werner), fide Dixon, Ibid. 17:161.
1909 Rhadinaea frenata Werner.
1923 Rhadinaea brazili Amaral, Proc. New England Zool. Club
7:87. Type-locality: Julio Pontes, SP.
Distribution: southeastern Brasil and Paraguay.

L. jaegeri (Gunther). Distribution: central & southern
Brasil, Uruguay, Paraguay, and northern Argentina.

L. joberti (Sauvage). Incertae sedis, fide Dixon, 1980, Ibid.
31:9.

L. lineatus (Linnaeus). No subspecies, fide Dixon, 1980,
Ibid.31:10.
1758 Coluber lineatus Linnaeus.
1758 Coluber minervae Linnaeus.
1766 Coluber jaculatrix Linnaeus.
1789 Coluber jaculus Lacepede, Hist. Nat. Serp. :104, 297;
nomen novum for Coluber jaculatrix.
1826 Coluber terlineatus Lacepede.
Distribution: Panama to Amazonia.

L. longiventris Amaral. Distribution: Rio Manjuru, Amazonas,
Brasil; camp at 12 51´S, 51 46´W, Mato Grosso.

L. melanauchen (Jan). Distribution: known from only type
locality.

L. melanostigma (Wagler). Incertae sedis, fide Dixon, 1980,
Ibid. 31:7.
1824 Natix melanostigma Wagler.
1868 Lygophis nicagus Cope, Proc. Acad. Nat. Sci.
Philadelphia 1868:132; based on Enicognathus
melanocephalus Jan in Jan & Sordelli, Icon. Gen.
Ophid. 16:1:4.
1885 Aporophis cyanopleurus Cope.
Distribution: Atlantic forest of Brasil from Minas Gerais
and Espirito Santo to Rio Grande do Sul.

L. melanotus (Shaw). Distribution: Colombia, Venezuela,
Trinidad and Tobago.

L. meridionalis (Schenkel).
1902 Aporophis lineatus var. meridionalis Schenkel.
Distribution: central Brasil to Paraguay and northern
Argentina.

L. miliaris (Linnaeus).

<u>L</u>. <u>miliaris miliaris</u> (Linnaeus), fide Dixon, 1983, Copeia
   (3):799.
1785 <u>Coluber miliaris</u> Linnaeus. Type-locality: restricted to
   Surinam by Dixon, 1983, Ibid. (3):799.
1854 <u>Ablabes purpurans</u> D. B. & D.
1863 <u>Liophis cobella collaris</u> Jan.
1864 <u>Coronella orientalis</u> Gunther.
   Distribution: the Guianas.
<u>L</u>. <u>miliaris amazonicus</u> (Dunn), fide Dixon, 1983, Ibid.
   (3):800.
1922 <u>Dromicus amazonicus</u> Dunn, Proc. Biol. Soc. Washington
   31:219. Type-locality: Santarem, Brasil.
   Distribution: from Santarem southwest to Rio Itenez in
   Bolivia and to Mato Grosso in Brasil.
<u>L</u>. <u>miliaris chrysostoma</u> (Cope), fide Dixon, 1983, Ibid.
   (3):800.
1868 <u>Rhadinaea chrysostoma</u> Cope.
1872 <u>Coronella poecilolemus</u> Gunther, Ann. Mag. Nat. Hist.
   (4)7:19. Type-locality: Napo or Maranon, Ecuador.
   Distribution: dense forests of lowland Amazonian parts of
   Brasil, Colombia, Ecuador and Peru.
<u>L</u>. <u>miliaris merremii</u> (Wied), fide Dixon 1983, Ibid. (3):800.
1821 <u>Coluber merremii</u> Wied.
1824 <u>Coluber dyctiodes</u> Wied.
1834 <u>Coluber bicolor</u> Reuss.
1858 <u>Coronella australis</u> Gunther.
   Distribution: Atlantic forests of Brasil from Pernambuco
   to Rio de Janeiro.
<u>L</u>. <u>miliaris mossoroensis</u> Hoge & Lima-Verde, fide Dixon, 1983,
   Ibid. (3):801.
1973 <u>Liophis mossoroensis</u> Hoge & Lima-Verde, Mem. Inst.
   Butantan [1972] 36:215. Type-locality: Mossoro, Rio
   Grande do Norte, Brasil.
   Distribution: northeastern Brasil.
<u>L</u>. <u>miliaris orinus</u> (Griffin), fide Dixon, 1983, Ibid.
   (3):800.
1916 <u>Rhadinaea orina</u> Griffin.
1926 <u>Rhadinaea merremii natricoides</u> Werner, Sitzber. Akad.
   Wiss. Wien 135:246. Type-locality: unknown.
   Distribution: southeastern Brasil from southern Minas
   Gerais south through Sao Paulo, Parana, Santa Catarina
   and northern third of Rio Grande do Sul.
<u>L</u>. <u>miliaris semiaureus</u> (Cope), fide Dixon, 1983 Ibid.
   (3):800.
1862 <u>Opheomorphus merremii</u> var. <u>semiaureus</u> Cope.
1863 <u>Liophis reginae ornata</u> Jan.
1885 <u>Opheomorphus fuscus</u> Cope.
   Distribution: Paraguay, west and south of Iguazu Falls,
   northeastern Argentina, southern and eastern Uruguay,
   and southern half of Rio Grande do Sul, Brasil.
<u>L</u>. <u>occipitalis</u> (Jan) = <u>Rhadinaea occipitalis</u> (Jan 1863), fide
   Myers, 1974, Ibid. 153:1-262.
<u>L</u>. <u>sagittifer sagittifer</u> (Jan), fide Dixon & Thomas, 1982,
   Herpetologica 38:394.

1863 Liopeltis sagittifer Jan.
1867 Liophis pulcher Steindachner.
1917 Zamenis argentinus Brethes, Physis 3(13):93.
    Type-locality: La Banda, Santiago del Estero,
    Argentina.
  Distribution: Monte vegetation from Tucuman to Chubut,
    Argentina.
L. sagittifer modestus (Koslowsky), fide Dixon & Thomas,
    1982, Ibid. 38:394.
1896 Rhadinaea modesta Koslowsky.
1899 Liophis trifasciatus Werner.
  Distribution: southern Bolivia, northern Argentina,
    Uruguay, and Rio Grande do Sul, Brasil.
L. steinbachi (Boulenger). Incertae sedis, fide Dixon, Ibid.
    31:15. Distribution: southeastern Bolivia.
L. taeniurus Tschudi, fide Dixon, 1980, Ibid. 31:16.
    Distribution: eastern Andean slopes of Ecuador & Peru.
L. triscalis (Linnaeus), fide Dixon, 1981, Copeia (2):302.
    Distribution: Curacao. South American records doubtful.
L. typhlus (Linnaeus). No subspecies, fide Dixon, 1980, Ibid.
    31:17. Distribution: Cis-Andean South America south to
    northern Argentina.
L. undulatus (Wied). Incertae sedis, fide Dixon, 1980, Ibid.
    31:17. Distribution: Cis-Andean South America south to
    northern Argentina.
L. viridis Gunther. Distribution: northeastern Brasil and
    Atlantic forests, south to northern Argentina.
L. williamsi (Roze). Distribution: Cordillera de la Costa
    Venezuela.
L. zweifeli (Roze) = L. reginae, fide Dixon, 1983, Ibid.
    52:113-138.

Liotyphlops W. Peters, 1881.
Key to all species in Dixon & Kofron, 1985, Amphibia-Reptilia
[1983] 4:241-164.
    L. albirostris Peters.
1857 Rhinotyphlops albirostris Peters.
1883 Typhlops (Idiotyphlops) emunctus Garman.
1889 Helminthophis petersii Boulenger.
1903 Helminthophis Canellei Mocquard.
1916 Helminthophis bondensis Griffin.
1944 Liotyphlops cucutae Dunn.
1952 Liotyphlops caracasensis Roze.
1958 Liotyphlops rowani Smith & Grant.
    Liotyphlops albirostris Dixon & Kofron, 1985, Ibid.
      [1983] 4:246.
  Distribution: Costa Rica to Venezuela and Ecuador.
L. anops (Cope)
1899 Helminthophis anops Cope.
1944 Liotyphlops metae Dunn.
    Liotyphlops anops Dixon & Kofron, 1983, Ibid. 4:259.
  Distribution: known with certainty only from Villavicencio.
1985 L. argaleus Dixon & Kofron, Ibid. [1983] 4:261. Type-
    locality: La Selva, Cundinamarca, Colombia.

Distribution: Colombia, Cundinamarca.

L. beui (Amaral), fide Dixon & Kofron, 1985, Ibid. [1985]
4:258. Distribution: Brasil, Mato Grosso to Parana, and
Brasilian border of Paraguay.

L. guentheri (Boulenger) = L. wilderi (Garman), fide Dixon &
Kofron, 1985, Ibid. [1983] 4:251.

L. incertus (Amaral) = L. ternetzii (Boulenger), fide Dixon &
Kofron, 1985, Ibid. [1983] 4:255.

L. schubarti Vanzolini. Distribution: known from the type
locality and from Sapucai, Sao Paulo (22 19´S 46 42´W).

L. ternetzii (Boulenger). Distribution: central Brasil and
Paraguay. Comment: specimens from Para, Brasil (Cunha &
Nascimento, 1975, Bol. Mus. Paraense Emilio Goeldi
(Zool.) 82:1) are closer to beui than to ternetizii,
but seem to represent still another species, perhaps
incertus.

L. wilderi (Garman). Distribution: Brasil, states of Minas
Gerais and Rio de Janeiro.

Lygophis Fitzinger, 1843 = Liophis Wagler, fide Dixon, 1980,
Milwaukee Publ. Mus. Contrib. Biol. Geol. (31):1-40.
The key contains disabling errors, e.g. L. coralliventris has 17
dorsal scale rows. Specimens should be checked against the
descriptions of geographically plausible species, after exclusion
of the forms listed below.

L. antioquiensis (Dunn) = Saphenophis antioquiensis (Dunn,
1943), fide Myers, 1973, Amer. Mus. Novit. 2522:1-37.

L. boursieri (Jan) = Saphenophis boursieri (Jan, 1867), fide
Myers, 1973, Ibid. 2522:1-37.

L. lineatus dilepis Cope, 1862, Proc. Acad. Nat. Sci.
Philadelphia 1862:81.

L. tristriatus (Rendahl & Vestergren) = Saphenophis
tristriatus (Rendahl & Vestergren), fide Myers, 1973,
Ibid. 2522:1-37.

Lystrophis Cope, 1826.

L. nattereri (Steindachner). Revalidated by Hoge, Cordeiro &
Romano, 1976, Mem. Inst. Butantan [1975] 39:37-50.

Masticophis Baird & Girard, 1853.

M. mentovarius D., B & D. See Johnson, 1977, J. Herpetol.
11(3):287-309, for a key to all subspecies.

Mastigodryas Amaral, 1935.

M. bifossatus subspecies do not seem biologically sound.

M. dorsalis (Bocourt). Distribution: also Baja Verapaz,
Atlantic versant of Guatemala (MVZ).

Micrurus Wagler, 1824. Includes Leptomicrurus Schmidt, 1937, fide
Romano, 1972, Mem. Inst. Butantan [1971] 35:111-15. Number of bands
is often more variable than range given in key. List of all
species in Roze, 2983, Ibid. [1982] 46:305-38.

M. albicinctus Amaral = M. ornatissimus, fide Cunha &
Nascimento, 1982, Bol. Mus. Paraense Emilio Goeldi

(Zool.) 116:8.

<u>M</u>. <u>annellatus annellatus</u> (Peters).

1871 <u>Elaps annellatus</u> Peters.

1954 <u>Micrurus annellatus montanus</u> Schmidt.
<u>Micrurus annellatus annellatus</u> Roze, 1983, Mem. Inst.
Butantan [1982] 46:315.
Distribution: Amazonian slope of Andes from Ecuador to
central Bolivia.

<u>M</u>. <u>a</u>. <u>bolivianus</u>. Distribution: also Amazonas, Brasil (Hoge &
Romano-Hoge, 1981, Ibid. 42/43)

<u>M</u>. <u>averyi</u>. Distribution: also Manaus region, Brasil. (Hoge &
Romano-Hoge, 1981, op. cit.).

<u>M</u>. <u>bocourti</u> (Jan). No subspecies, fide Roze, 1983, Ibid.
46:316.

<u>M</u>. <u>bocourti sangilensis</u> = <u>M</u>. <u>sangilensis</u>, fide Roze, 1983,
Ibid. 46:334.
Distribution: western Ecuador and northern Peru.

1976 <u>M</u>. <u>donosoi</u> Hoge, Cordeiro & Romano, Cien. Cult. supl.
28(7):417. Type-locality: Brasil, Para, Mineracao Serra
do Sul, 60 km N Sao Felix do Xingu. = <u>M</u>. <u>psyches donosoi</u>
fide Roze, 1983, Ibid. 46:335.

<u>M</u>. <u>filiformis</u> (Gunther). No subspecies, fide Cunha &
Nascimento, 1982, Ibid. 112:1.

1859 <u>Elaps filiformis</u> Gunther.

1967 <u>Micrurus filiformis subtilis</u> Roze.
Distribution: northern and eastern Amazonia.

<u>M</u>. <u>frontalis frontalis</u> (D. B. & D.). Distribution: from
northern Sao Paulo and western Mato Grosso in Brasil to
Paraguay.

<u>M</u>. <u>frontalis altirostris</u> (Cope).

1860 <u>Elaps altirostris</u> Cope.

1887 <u>Elaps heterochilus</u> Mocquard.
<u>Micrurus frontalis altirostris</u> Roze, 1983, Ibid. 46:323.
Distribution: Rio Grande do Sul, Brasil, Uruguay, and
probably northeastern Argentina.

<u>M</u>. <u>frontalis baliocoryphus</u> (Cope).

1859 <u>Elaps baliocoryphus</u> Cope, Proc. Acad. Nat. Sci.
Philadelphia 1859:346. Type-locality: Buenos Aires;
restricted to Villa Federal, Entre Rios, Argentina, by
Roze, 1983, Ibid. 46:323.
<u>Micrurus frontalis baliocoryphus</u> Roze, op. cit.
Distribution: Entre Rios, Corrientes and Missiones,
Argentina.

<u>M</u>. <u>frontalis diana</u> Roze.

1983 <u>Micrurus frontalis diana</u> Roze, Ibid. 46:324.
Type-locality: Santiago, Provincia de Chiquiticos
[mistake for Chiquitos], Depto. Santa Cruz, Bolivia,
700m.

<u>M</u>. <u>frontalis multicinctus</u> Amaral.

1944 <u>Micrurus lemniscatus multicinctus</u> Amarl.
<u>Micrurus frontalis multicinctus</u> Roze, 1983, Ibid. 46:325.
Distribution: probably from southern Sao Paulo to northern
Rio Grande do Sul, Brasil.

<u>M</u>. <u>frontalis pyrrhocryptus</u> (Cope).

1862 *Elaps pyrrhocryptus* Cope.
1902 *Elaps simonsii* Boulenger.
   Micrurus frontalis pyrrhocryptus Roze, 1983, Ibid.46:326.
   Distribution: northern Argentina.
M. frontalis tricolor Hoge.
1957 *Micrurus tricolor* Hoge. Type-locality: Garandazal
   [mistake for Carandazal], Mato Grosso do Sul, Brasil.
   Micrurus frontalis tricolor Roze, 1983, Ibid. 46:326.
   Distribution: southern Mato Grosso do Sul, Brasil, and
   adjacent Paraguay.
M. frontifasciatus (Werner).
1927 *Elaps frontifasciatus* Werner.
   Micrurus lemniscatus frontifaciatus Roze, 1967.
   Micrurus frontifasciatus Roze, 1983, Ibid. 46:326.
   Distribution: eastern Andean slopes in Bolivia.
M. ibiboboca (Merrem, 1820). See Vanzolini, Ramos-Costa &
   Vitt, 1980, Repteis Caatingas, Acad. Brasileira Cien.
1972 *M. karlschmidti* Romano, Mem. Inst. Butantan [1971] 35:111-15.
   Nomen novum for *Leptomicrurus schmidti* Hoge & Romano,
   1966.
M. langsdorffi Wagler. No subspecies, fide Cunha &
   Nascimento, 1982, Ibid. 116:8.
1824 *Micrurus langsdorffi* Wagler.
1868 *Elaps imperator* Cope, Proc. Acad. Nat. Sci. Philadelphia
   1868:110. Type-locality: Napo and Maranon.
1868 *Elaps batesi* Gunther.
1935 *Micrurus mimosus* Amaral.
   Micrurus langsdorffi langsdorffi Roze, 1967.
   Distribution: western Amazonia.
M. lemniscatus carvalhoi Roze, 1967. Distribution: eastern
   Brasil, not "Amazon Basin of Brasil."
M. lemniscatus frontifasciatus = *M. frontifasciatus*, fide
   Roze, 1983, Ibid. 46:326.
M. mipartitus decussatus (D., B. & D. 1854).
M. nigrocinctus nigrocinctus (Girard).
1854 *Elaps nigrocinctus* Girard.
1860 *Elaps melanocephalus* Hallowell.
1951 *Micrurus pachecoi* Taylor.
   Micrurus nigrocinctus nigrocinctus Roze, 1983, Ibid.
   46:331.
   Distribution: Pacific side of Central America from
   Nicaragua to Panama, and Colombian Choco.
M. nigrocinctus melanocephalus = *M. n. nigrocinctus*, fide
   Roze, 1983, Ibid. 46:331.
M. ornatissimus (Jan).
1858 *Elaps ornatissimus* Jan.
1896 *Elaps buckleyi* Boulenger.
1925 *Micrurus albicinctus* Amaral. Type-locality: Mato Grosso
   (now probably in Rondonia).
   Micrurus ornatissimus Cunha & Nascimento, 1982, Ibid.
   116:8.
   Distribution: western Amazonia.
M. paraensis Cunha & Nascimento, fide Hoge & Romano-Hoge,
   1981, Mem. Inst. Butantan [1978/79] 42/43:400.

1973 <u>Micrurus psyches paraensis</u> Cunha & Nascimento, Publ.
   Avuls. Mus. Paraense Emilio Goeldi 20:276.
   Type-locality: Icoaraci, Belem, Para. Distribution:
   eastern Para, Brasil.
<u>M</u>. <u>petersi</u> Roze, fide Roze, 1983, Ibid. 46:332. Distribution:
   southeastern Ecuador.
<u>M</u>. <u>psyches donosoi</u> Hoge, Cordeiro & Romano-Hoge, fide Roze,
   1983, Ibid. [1982] 46:335. Distribution: known only from
   type locality.
1973 <u>M</u>. <u>psyches paraensis</u> Cunha & Nascimento, Publ. Avuls. Mus.
   Paraense Emilio Goeldi 20:276. Type-locality: Brasil,
   Para, Icoaraci.
<u>M</u>. <u>sangilensis</u> Niceforo-Maria, fide Roze, 1983, Ibid. 46:334.
   Distribution: northern Colombia, between Cordilleras
   Central and Oriental.
<u>M</u>. <u>spurrelli</u> (Boulenger, 1914), not <u>M</u>. <u>spurelli</u>.
<u>M</u>. <u>steindachneri petersi</u> = <u>M</u>. <u>petersi</u>, fide Roze, 1983, Ibid.
   46:332.
<u>M</u>. <u>tricolor</u> = <u>M</u>. <u>frontalis tricolor</u>, fide Roze, 1983, Ibid.
   46:326.

<u>Ninia</u> Baird & Girard, 1853.
   <u>N</u>. <u>hudsoni</u> Parker. Distribution: also Acre, Brasil (P.E.V.).

<u>Oxyrhopus</u> Wagler, 1830.
Extensive ontogenetic and geographic variation of color pattern
makes the key largely unusable; available descriptions are not much
help. Identifications should be based on comparison with reliably
identified specimens.
   <u>O</u>. <u>melanogenys melanogenys</u> (Tschudi), fide Cunha & Nascimento,
      1983, Bol. Mus. Paraense Emilio Goeldi (Zool.) 122:1-42.
   <u>O</u>. <u>melanogenys orientalis</u> Cunha & Nascimento, 1983, Ibid.
      122:6. Type-locality: Santa Rosa, Estrada da Vigia,
      Para, Brasil. Distribution: easternmost Para and
      adjacent Maranhao, Brasil.
   <u>O</u>. <u>occipitalis</u> (Wagler). Revalidated by Hoge et al., 1973,
      Mem. Inst. Butantan [1972] 36:221-32.
   <u>O</u>. <u>trigeminus</u> D., B. & D. Distribution: also Paraguay
      (Bailey, 1939).
1978 <u>O</u>. <u>trigeminus guibei</u> Hoge & Romano, Mem. Inst. Butantan
      [1976/77] 40/41:58. Type-locality: Brasil, Parana,
      Londrina.

<u>Paraptychophis</u> Lema, 1967 = <u>Ptychophis</u> Gomes, 1915, fide Hoge &
      Romano, 1969, Cien. Cult. 21(2):453.
   <u>P</u>. <u>meyeri</u> Lema = <u>Ptychophis flavovirgatus</u> Gomes, fide Hoge &
      Romano, 1969, Ibid. 21(2):453.

<u>Paroxyrhopus</u> Schenkel, 1900 = <u>Xenopholis</u> W. Peters, 1869, fide Hoge
      & Federsoni, 1975, Mem. Inst. Butantan [1974] 38:137-46.
   <u>P</u>. <u>reticulatus</u> Schenskel = <u>Xenopholis undulatus</u> (Jensen), fide
      Hoge & Federsoni, 1975, Ibid. 38:137-46.
   <u>P</u>. <u>undulatus</u> (Jensen). Distribution: specimen from Amazonian
      Colombia is misidentified (Hoge & Federsoni, 1975, op.

cit.)

Philodryas Wagler, 1830. Includes Alsophis sensu Maglio, 1970 =
     Dromicus sensu Peters & Orejas-Miranda, 1970.
     P. aestivus subcarinatus Boulenger. Revalidated by Barrio,
          Laurent & Thomas, 1977, J. Herpetol. 11(2):230-31.
     P. aestivus manegarzoni Orejas-Miranda = P. a. subcarinatus
          Boulenger, fide Barrio, Laurent & Thomas, 1977, Ibid.
          11(2):230-311.
     P. borellii Peracca. Revalidated by Barrio, Laurent & Thomas,
          1977, Herpetologica 33:82-86. Now = P. varius, fide
          Thomas & Johnson, 1984, J. Herpetol. 18:80.
     P. chamissonis (Wiegmann), fide Thomas, 1977, Copeia
          1977(4):648-52.
     P. elegans rufodorsatus (Gunther), not rufidorsatus.
     P. pseudoserra Amaral = Tropidodryas striaticeps (Cope), fide
          Thomas & Dixon, 1977, Pearce-Sellards Ser. 27:1-20.
     P. serra (Schlegel) = Tropidodryas serra (Schlegel), fide
          Thomas & Dixon, 1977, Ibid. 27:1-20.
     P. simonsii Boulenger. Reinstated by Thomas, 1977, Ibid.
          (4):648-52.
     P. tachymenoides (Schmidt & Walker), fide Thomas, 1977, Ibid.
          (4):648-52.
     P. varius (Jan).
     1863 Liophis wagleri var. varia Jan, Arch. Zool. Anat. Fisiol.
          2:301. Type-locality: Veracruz.
     1897 Philodryas borellii Peracca.
     1925 Philodryas werneri Muller.
          Philodryas varius Thomas & Johnson, 1984, Ibid. 18:80.
     Distribution: puna region of Bolivia and Argentina.

Phimophis Cope, 1860.
     P. guerini (D.,B. & D.). Distribution: also Guianan region
          (Hoogmoed, 1982).
     P. guianensis (Troschel). Distribution: also French Guiana
          (Gasc & Rodrigues, 1980).

Platyinion Amaral, 1923, not Platynion.
     P. lividum Amaral. Type-locality: Brasil, Mato Grosso do Sul,
          Guiacurus, fide Amaral, 1926, Arch. Mus. Nac. (Rio de
          Janeiro) 26:95-127.

Pseudoboa Schneider, 1801.
     P. haasi (Boettger). Distribution: also Rio de Janeiro region
          (USNM).

Pseudoeryx Fitzinger, 1826.
1965 P. plicatilis ecuadorensis Mertens, Senckenberg. Biol.
          46(4):281. Type-locality: Ecuador, no further data.

Pseustes Fitzinger, 1843
     P. shropshirei (Barbour & Amaral). Distribution: not Costa
          Rica, fide Savage, 1980, Handlist key...Costa Rica.
     P. sulphureus (Wagler). Distribution: also Venezuela (Roze,

1966).
P. sulphureus dieperinkii (Schlegel). Revalidated by Hoge &
Romano, 1970, Mem. Inst. Butantan [1969] 34:89-92.

Rhadinaea Cope, 1863. Reviewed by Myers, 1974, Bull. Amer. Mus.
Nat. Hist. 153:1-262.
R. beui Prado = R. persimilis (Cope), fide Myers, 1974, op.
cit.
R. bilineata (Fischer). Revalidated by Myers, 1974, op.cit.
R. dumerilli (Bibron). Revalidated by Myers, 1974, op. cit.
R. godmani (Gunther). Distribution: also Honduras (Wilson,
1972, Bull. S. California Acad Sci 71:50-52).
R. insignissimus (Amaral) = R. persimilis (Cope), fide Myers,
1974, op. cit.
R. lateristriga multilineata (W. Peters) = R. multilineata (W.
Peters), fide Myers, 1974, op. cit.
R. montecristi Mertens. Distribution: also Honduras (1979,
Herpetol. Rev. 20:62).
R. pachyura fulviceps Cope = R. fulviceps Cope, fide, Myers,
1974, op. cit.

Rhinobothryum Wagler, 1830.
Distribution: Guatemala and Honduras through...

Saphenophis Myers, 1973, Amer. Mus. Novit. 2522:2. Type species,
Dromicus boursieri Jan. & Sordelli, by original
designation. Contains also:
Liophis atahuallpae Steindachner.
Rhadinaea antioquiensis Dunn.
Rhadinaea tristriata Rendahl & Vestergren.
1973 Saphenophis sneiderni Myers, Ibid. 2522:22. Type-locality:
Colombia, Cauca, El Tambo. Distribution: type locality.

Scaphiodontophis Taylor & Smith, 1943.
1969 S. dugandi Roze, Caldasia 10(48):355. Type-locality: Colombia,
Antioquia, Rio Currulao, Uraba, near Turbo.

Sibon Fitzinger, 1826.
Includes Tropidodipsas, fide Kofron, 1985, J. Herpetol. 19:84-92;
key to all species and subspecies in Kofron, 1985, op. cit.
1977 S. neilli Henderson, Hoevers & Wilson, J. Herpetol. 11:77.
Type-locality: Belize, vicinity of Belize = S. sanniola
neilli, fide Kofron, 1985, op. cit.
S. anthracops (Cope). Distribution: also El Salvador (Hidalgo,
1979, Herpetol. Rev. 10:103).

Sibynomorphus Fitzinger, 1843.
S. mikanii mikanii (Schlegel).
1837 Dipsas mikanii Schlegel.
1884 Leptognathus andrei Sauvage.
1887 Leptognathus garmani Cope. Correct type-locality: Sao
Joao do Montenegro, Rio Grande do Sul, Brasil, fide
Vanzolini, 1953, Copeia (2):124.
Distribution: Brasil south of Amazon basin.

<u>S</u>. <u>mikanii</u> <u>neuwiedi</u> = <u>S</u>. <u>neuwiedi</u>, fide Hoge, Laporta &
    Romano-Hoge, 1981, Mem. Inst. Butantan [1978/79]
    42/43:176.
<u>S</u>. <u>mikanii</u> <u>septentrionalis</u> Cunha, Nascimento & Hoge, Bol. Mus.
    Paraense Emilio Goeldi (Zool.) 103:2. Type-locality:
    Puraqueu, on Hwy. BR-222, Maranhao, Brasil.
    Distribution: Maranhao, Brasil.
<u>S</u>. <u>neuwiedi</u> (Ihering).
1911 <u>Cochliophagus</u> <u>mikani</u> <u>neuwiedi</u> R.V. Ihering.
1930 <u>Sibynomophus</u> <u>mikanii</u> <u>fasciatus</u> Amaral.
    <u>Sibynomorphus</u> <u>neuwiedii</u> Hoge, Laporta & Romano-Hoge,
    1981, Ibid. 42/42:176.
    Distribution: southeastern and southern Brasil.
1979 <u>S</u>. <u>oneilli</u> Rossman & Thomas, Occ. Pap. Mus. Zool. Louisiana
    St. Mus. 54:1. Type-locality: Peru, Amazonas, NNE
    Balsas, road to Abra Chanchillo.
1974 <u>S</u>. <u>williamsi</u> Carrillo de Espinoza, Publ. Mus. Hist. Nat.
    "Javier Prado" 24:3. Type-locality: Peru, Lima,
    Jicamarca.

<u>Synophis</u> Peracca, 1896.
    <u>S</u>. <u>lasallei</u> (Maria). Distribution: lowlands, but
        type-locality is 2200 m.

<u>Tachymenis</u> Wiegmann, 1835
    <u>T</u>. <u>peruviana</u> <u>assimilis</u> (Jan) = <u>T</u>. <u>chilensis</u> <u>coronellina</u>
        (Werner), fide Ortiz, 1973, Ibid. 146:1021-39.
    <u>T</u>. <u>peruviana</u> <u>chilensis</u> (Schlegel) = <u>T</u>. <u>c</u>. <u>chilensis</u>
        (Schlegel), fide Ortiz, 1973, Bull. Mus. Nat. Hist. Nat.
        (3)146:1021-39.
    <u>T</u>. <u>peruviana</u> <u>yutoensis</u> Miranda & Couturier.
    1981 <u>Tachymenis</u> <u>peruviana</u> <u>yutoensis</u> Miranda & Couturier, Com.
        Mus. Argentina Cien. Nat. Bernardino Rivadavia (zool.)
        4(10):80. Type-locality: Yuto, Jujuy, Argentina.
        Distribution: northwestern Argentina.
    <u>T</u>. <u>surinamensis</u> Dunn = <u>Philodryas</u> <u>elegans</u>, fide Myers &
        Hoogmoed, 1974, Zool. Med. 48:187-94.

<u>Tantilla</u> Baird & Girard, 1853
Error in key; couplet 17 refers to nonexistent couplet 26. Key to
all species in Wilson, 1982, Catalog. Amer. Amphib. Rept. 307:1-4.
1980 <u>T</u>. <u>andinista</u> Wilson & Mena, Mem. San Diego Soc. Nat. Hist.
        11:21. Type-locality: 5 km E Alausi, Prov. Chimborazo,
        Ecuador, 2600-2750 m. Distribution: only type locality.
    <u>T</u>. <u>annulata</u> Boettger, 1892. Distribution: also in South
        America, (Wilson, McCranie & Porras, 1977, Bull. S.
        California Acad. Sci. 6:49-56).
    <u>T</u>. <u>alticola</u> (Boulenger). Distribution: also Costa Rica (Wilson
        et al., 1977, Ibid. 6:49-56).
    <u>T</u>. <u>brevicauda</u> Mertens. Distribution: also Chimaltenango,
        Guatemala (Wilson, 1970, Bull. S. California Acad. Sci.
        69:228-120).
    <u>T</u>. <u>capistrata</u> Cope, fide Wilson & Mena, 1980, Ibid. 11:1-58.
        Distribution: northwestern Peru.

1982 T. cuesta Wilson, Milwaukee Pub. Mus. Contrib. Biol. Geol.
        52:29. Type-locality 1.5 km E San Rafael Pie de la
        Cuesta, 1050 m. Distribution: only from type locality.
1980 T. equatoriana Wilson & Mena, Ibid. 11:23. Type-locality: San
        Lorenzo, Provincia Esmeraldas, Ecuador. Distribution:
        known only from type locality.
1980 T. insulamontana Wilson & Mena, Ibid. 11:24. Type-locality:
        Rio Minas, 15.1 km W Santa Isabel, Provincia Azuay,
        Ecuador, ca. 1250 m. Distribution: intermediate
        elevations of Rio Jubones valley, Ecuador.
1980 T. lempira Wilsom & Mena, Ibid. 11:25. Type-locality:
        Honduras, Francisco Morazan, 41 km NW Tegucigalpa.
        Distribution: moderate elevations of Pacific versant of
        Honduras.
     T. melanocephala capistrata = T. capistrata, fide Wilson &
        Mena, 1980, Ibid. 11:1-58.
1979 T. petersi Wilson, Herpetologica 35(3):274. Type-locality:
        Ecuador, Imbabura, San Nicolas, Pimampiro.
     T. reticulata Cope. Distribution: Caribbean versant from
        southeastern Nicaragua to Panama and northwestern
        Colombia (Wilson, 1985, Catal. Amer. Amphib. Rept. 370).
     T. ruficeps (Cope) = T. melanocephala, fide Wilson & Mena,
        1980, Ibid. 11:26.
     T. semicincta (D..B. & D.). Distribution: not Panama (Wilson,
        1976, Bull. S. Calif. Acad. Sci. 75:42-48).
     T. taeniata (Bocourt). Distribution: also El Salvador
        (Wilson, 1974, Bull. S. Calif. Acad. Sci. 73:53-54).
     T. vermiformis (Hallowell). Distribution: low elevations of
        Pacific versant from northwestern Nicaragua to
        northwestern Costa Rica.

Tantillita Smith, 1941.
     Content: two species, T. brevissima in Mexico.
     T. lintoni (Smith). Distribution: also Peten, Guatamala (MVZ).

Thamnodynastes Wagler, 1830.
Identifications in this genus should be considered provisional,
since there are many new species awaiting description.

Tretanorhinus Dumeril, Bibron & Dumeril, 1854.
     T. n. nigroluteus Cope, 1862. Distribution also in South
        America (Alarcon-Pardo, 1978, Lozania (Bogota) 27:1-4).

Trimetopon Cope, 1885.
     T. hannsteini Stuart = Rhadinaea hannsteini, fide Myers, 1974,
        Ibid. 153:1-262.
     T. pilonaorum Stuart = R. pilonaorum, fide Myers, 1974, op.cit.
     T. posadasi Slevin = R. posadasi, fide Myers, 1974, op. cit.
     T. veraepacis (Stuart & Bailey) = R. kinkelini, fide Myers,
        1974, op. cit.

Tropidodipsas Gunther, 1858 = Sibon, fide Kofron, 1985, Ibid.
        19:84-92.

Tropidodryas Fitzinger, 1843. Revalidated by Thomas & Dixon, 1977,
        Pearce-Sellards Ser. 27:1-20. Contains:
    T. serra (Schlegel).
    T. striaticeps (Cope).

Typhlops Oppel, 1811.
Key to continental Neotropical species in Dixon & Hendricks, 1979,
Zool. Verh. Rijksm. Nat. Hist. 73:1-39.
1976 T. brongersmianus Vanzolini, Pap. Avul. Zool. (Sao Paulo)
        29:247. Nomen novum for T. brongersmai Vanzolini, 1972,
        Zool. Med. (Leiden) 47:27. Type-locality: Brasil, Bahia,
        Barra de Itaipe, Ilheus.
    T. costaricensis Jimenez & Savage. Distribution: Costa Rica
        and Nicaragua.
    T. microstomus Cope. Distritution: Merida, Mexico, to El
        Paso, Guatemala.
1979 T. minuisquamus Dixon & Hendricks, Ibid. 73:21. Type-locality:
        Peru, Loreto, Mishana. Distribution: Amazon basin from
        Iquitos area and Manaus area northward to Moroa,
        Venezuela, and on north edge of Guyana Shield, Guyana.
1979 T. paucisquamus Dixon & Hendricks, Ibid. 173:23.
        Type-locality: Brasil, Pernambuco.
    T. reticulatus (Linnaeus). Distribution: Cis-andean South
        America between 12 N & 14 S, and coastal Ecuador.
    T. stadelmani Schmidt = T. tenuis, fide Dixon & Hendricks,
        1979, op. cit.
    T. tenuis Salvin. Distribution: also Honduras.
    T. unilineatus (D.&B.). Distribution: not Neotropical,
        possibly Oriental.

Umbrivaga Roze, 1964.
1979 U. pyburni Markezich & Dixon, Copeia (4):698. Type-locality:
        Colombia, Meta, Loma Linda. Distribution: type locality.
    U. pygmaea (Cope, 1868), fide Markezich & Dixon, 1979, Ibid.
        (4):698-701.

Uromacerina Amaral, 1929.
    U. ricardinii (Peracca). Distribution: Brasil, Sao Paulo to
        Rio Grande do Sul; one isolated population in Para
        (Cunha & Nascimento, 1982, Ibid. 113:1).

Waglerophis Romano & Hoge, 1973, Mem. Inst. Butantan [1972] 36:209.
        Type-species: Ophis merremii Wagler, 1824, monotypic.

Xenodon Boie, 1824.
Comment: X. werneri listed as part of French Guiana fauna, fide
Gasc & Rodrigues, 1980, Bull. Mus. Nat. Hist. Nat., Paris
(4)2:559-98.
    X. merremii (Wagler) = Waglerophis merremii (Wagler), fide
        Romano & Hoge, 1973, Ibid. 36:209-14.
    X. rabdocephalus rabdocephalus (Wied), fide Dixon, 1983, Texas
        J. Sci. 35:257.
    1824 Coluber rabdocephalus Wied.
    1858 Xenodon colubrinus Gunther.

1864 _Xenodon_ _angustrirostris_ Peters.
1868 _Xenodon_ _suspectus_ Cope.
1885 _Xenodon_ _bipraeoculis_ Cope.
    Distribution: Amazonia.
_X_. _suspectus_ Cope = _X_. _r_. _rabdocephalus_, fide Dixon 1983,
      Ibid. 35:257.

Xenopholis W. Peters, 1869. Includes _Paroxyrhopus_ Schenkel, 1900,
    fide Hoge & Federsoni, 1975, Ibid. 38:137-46.

INTRODUCTION

This catalogue represents an attempt to make it possible for participants in the International Biological Program working in Latin America to identify the snakes encountered in the field. It was originally planned to include information on the ecology and ethology of the reptilian species, to permit field investigators to distinguish the unusual ecological event from the commonplace occurrence, but time has not permitted the inclusion of that degree of detail. We have instead focussed our attentions on the construction of a workable field manual with keys designed to help identification without laboratory facilities. We have not been entirely successful, because a few taxa cannot be separated without the use of a dissecting microscope or the checking of internal characteristics, but for the most part the keys can be used with little more than a hand lens for specimen examination.

The limits we have established for the area covered by this work are from the border between Mexico and Guatemala south throughout continental South America and all off-shore islands within the continental shelf. The Galapagos and the islands of the Caribbean are not included.

The synonymies presented for the taxa are very abbreviated. Within each genus we include only those generic synonyms whose type species are considered to belong to the genus under discussion. Only the original description for each genus is included, with no attempt made to document changes in the "generic concept". The type species, when given, has always been previously designated as such, unless we clearly indicate that we are taking such an action at this time. We apologize for our failure to indicate the method of type designation, but time did not permit us to undertake this difficult task. For each species we have included the original citation to it, its first assignment to its current generic position if other than as originally assigned, all "absolute" synonyms (i.e., those in which the holotype, lectotype, or neotype belongs to the species in which the synonym occurs), and, whenever possible, a citation to a recent work which includes a modern description and/or a figure, to aid the user in identification. No other generic shifts, no misidentifications, and no "in part" references are included. The author's name is not separated in any way from the binomial in the citations to original descriptions. In all other citations, the author's name is separated from the binomial by a dash. Each citation includes the actual date of publication; the name exactly as it was spelled by the original author, including capitalization of specific names; the author; the journal; the volume or the number, which stands alone if possible but which is qualified by material in parentheses if necessary; the page on which the taxon is first named; illustrations; and finally the type locality, with summaries of any restrictions or later clarifications of it.

Este catálogo representa un intento de posibilitar la identificación de serpientes encontradas en el campo a los participantes del International Biological Program que trabajan en Sudamérica. Originariamente se había planeado la inclusión de información ecológica y etológica de las especies de reptiles, para permitir al investigador de campaña la distinción entre acontecimientos ecológicos desusados y los que son lugar común, pero la falta de tiempo impidió la inclusión de tal grado de detalles. En cambio hemos concentrado nuestra atención en la elaboración de un manual de campaña funcional con claves diseñadas para ayudar a la identificación sin las facilidades de un laboratorio. No hemos tenido éxito en todo porque unos pocos taxones no pueden ser separados sin usar el microscopio de disección o sin examinar las características internas, pero en su mayoría las claves se pueden usar con poco más que un lente de aumento con que examinar el ejemplar.

Los límites que hemos establecido para el área cubierta por este trabajo son desde la frontera entre Méjico y Guatemala hasta el extremo sur de Sudamérica continental y todas las islas costeras dentro de la plataforma continental. Las islas Galápagos y del Caribe no han sido incluidas.

Los sinónimos de los taxones presentados están muy abreviados. En cada género se incluyen solamente aquellos sinónimos genéricos cuya especie tipo es considerada como perteneciente al género en discusión. Se incluye solamente la descripción original de cada género, no hemos intentado documentar cambios en el "concepto genérico". Siempre que damos la especie tipo es porque ha sido designada como tal previamente, a menos que indiquemos claramente que hemos tomado aquí tal medida. Lamentamos no poder indicar el método de designación de tipos, pero la falta de tiempo no nos permite emprender tal difícil tarea. En cada especie hemos incluido su cita original, su primera asignación a la posición genérica corriente si es que se le ha asignado otra distinta que la original, todos los sinónimos "absolutos" (ej.: aquéllos en que el holotipo o neotipo pertenece a la especie en que ocurre el sinónimo) y, cuando posible, una cita de un trabajo reciente que incluye una descripción moderna y/o una figura, para ayudar al usuario en la identificación. No se incluye ninguna otra transferencia genérica, identificación falsa o referencia "parcial". El nombre del autor no ha sido separado de ningún modo del binomio en las citas de las descripciones originales. En todas las otras citas el nombre del autor está separado del binomio por un guión. Cada cita incluye la fecha efectiva de la publicación; el nombre con la misma ortografía que usó autor, incluyendo nombres específicos con mayúscula; el autor; la revista; el volumen o el número, por sí solos si es posible o con material aclaratorio entre paréntesis si es necesario; la página en que se nombra al taxón por primera vez; ilustraciones y, finalmente la localidad tipo con resúmenes de cualquier restricción o aclaración posterior.

INTRODUCTION

We have attempted to avoid any non-documented taxonomic changes in this catalogue, although it has proven necessary to make a few modifications in some taxa. When we have made such changes, we indicate it by the words "new combination" after the species heading, and we have given our reasons for so doing in the "Comments". In those genera prepared by cooperating herpetologists, however, we have not prevented the presentation of his concepts of the alignment of species within the genus, even though documentation has not been published elsewhere. In every instance we have ascertained that prompt publication of documentation is anticipated before including the changes, but we cannot guarantee that it will be done. In all cases where material has been furnished by a cooperator, his name and address will be found at the beginning of the generic discussion, and he should be given full credit in any citations of that material.

The date of publication is always the actual date, insofar as we could determine it, and it does not always agree with the date given in the publication itself. When there is a difference, the latter date is given in parentheses after the volume number. The only exception to this is volume 4 of the Memorias do Instituto Butantan. We learned too late to modify all of the many citations to this volume that it actually appeared in 1930, not 1929, as stated on the cover. All other volumes in the Memorias are cited here by actual year of publication, which is usually one or two years later than indicated on the publication.

The distribution given for each taxon is based on information in the literature, with additions and extensions from specimens we have been able to find in various collections. Some of our changes in known distribution have been documented, but we have made no attempt to do so for every modification we have included.

The names of all political and geographic units within any country have been given as spelled by that country, but country names have been given in English usage, so that "Brasil" is "Brazil" and "Panamá" is "Panama". Where names but not boundaries have been changed, we use the modern name, even in the citation of type localities. Thus, all localities in "British Guiana" are here given as "Guyana". We have corrected errors in orthography throughout, if we could successfully document the error. Our primary source has been the series of gazetteers prepared by the United States Board on Geographic Names, although many additional sources have been checked.

Most of the keys presented here are the standard dichotomous type, although occasionally we have found it useful to include "trichotomies" and the user should watch for this possibility. In such instances, of course, a choice is made from three possibilities rather than two. In the case of very large genera, however, we have intro-

Hemos tratado de evitar en este catálogo todos los cambios taxonómicos que no estuvieran documentados, si bien fue necesario hacer unas pocas modificaciones en algunos taxones. Cuando se han hecho tales cambios lo indicamos con las palabras "new combination" después del título de la especie y explicamos nuestra razones para el cambio en "Comments". Sin embargo en aquellos géneros preparados por nuestros colaboradores herpetólogos no hemos impedido la presentación de sus conceptos en el ordenamiento de las especies dentro del género, aun cuando no hubiera documentación previamente publicada. En cada caso hemos solicitado la pronta publicación de documentación antes de introducir tales cambios, pero no podemos garantizar que así se haga. En todos los casos en que un colaborador ha proporcionado material hemos puesto su nombre y dirección al comienzo de la discusión del género y a él le corresponde todo el crédito cuando dicho material sea citado.

La fecha de publicación es siempre la fecha real en la medida en que se pueda determinar ésta y no siempre coincide con la fecha dada por la publicación misma. En tales casos esta última aparece entre paréntesis después del número del volumen. Una excepción es el volumen 4 de las Memorias do Instituto Butantan. Cuando era demasiado tarde para modificar las numerosas citas de este volumen descubrimos que en realidad había aparecido en 1930, no en 1929. Los demás volúmenes de las Memorias son citados aquí con el año efectivo de de la publicación, que es usualmente uno o dos años más tarde del indicado en la portada.

La distribución dada en cada taxón se basa en información sacada de la literatura con adiciones y agregados basados en ejemplares que hemos encontrado en varias colecciones. Algunos de nuestros cambios en la distribución conocida han sido documentados, pero no hemos intentado documentar todas las modificaciones incluidas por nosotros.

Se dan los nombres de todas las unidades políticas y geográficas dentro de cada país de acuerdo a la ortografía de ese país, pero los nombres de los países se han escrito según la ortografía inglesa, así "Brasil" es "Brazil" y "Panamá" es "Panama". Donde los nombres han cambiado, pero no las fronteras, usamos el nombre moderno, aún al citar localidades tipo. Así aquí nos referimos a todos las localidades en "British Guiana" como "Guyana". Hemos corregido todos los errores ortográficos que pudieran ser documentados debidamente. Nuestra principal fuente de información ha sido la serie de gacetas preparadas por Board on Geographic Names del gobierno de los Estados Unidos, aunque también hemos consultado muchas otras fuentes.

La mayoría de las claves aquí presentadas son del tipo dicotómico común, aunque ocasionalmente ha sido conveniente incluir "tricotomías", y el usuario debe estar al tanto de esta posibilidad. En tales ocasiones, naturalmente, hay que elegir entre tres posibilidades en vez de dos. No obstante en el caso de géneros muy grandes se ha

duced a different concept. Any attempt at writing keys for poorly known, large genera is likely to be futile, and we have avoided this by presenting as much data as possible in the form of a matrix. This permits "random entry" identification, for the user can select any character in the matrix he wishes to check, and eliminate all taxa that do not possess that character, finally arriving at a considerably reduced number of taxa (hopefully, only one) after checking a series of characters. This concept has formed the basis of computer identification, since the machine can do such sorting more rapidly and efficiently than the human, and the random entry matrices presented here are organized in such a way that they can be incorporated in the computer programs now available for such machine sorting. It is our assumption that this method of identification will be used more and more in the future, and we hope that presenting these matrices will encourage others to begin to organize their data similarly, thus anticipating the day when computer keys are available to all users.

A work of this magnitude becomes very dependent upon the cooperation and collaboration of many people. We wish to express our gratitude to all those who have helped us in any way. The following list indicates the number of individuals who have contributed to the work. While we have tried to make the list inclusive, the omission of anyone who has aided us should be regarded solely as the consequence of the faulty nature of our "disc storage", rather than failure to recognize the help.

introducido un concepto diferente. Probablemente resultaría inútil intentar escribir una clave de un género grande, poco conocido, hemos evitado esto al presentar la mayor cantidad de datos posibles en forma de una matriz. Esto permite la identificación de "entradas al azar", por que el usuario puede seleccionar dentro de la matriz cualquier carácter que desee poner a prueba y eliminar todos los taxones que no posean tal carácter, llegando finalmente a un número sumamente reducido de taxones (es de esperar que sea uno solo) después de revisar una serie de caracteres. Este concepto constituye la base de la identificación por computadora, ya que esta máquina puede seleccionar más rápida y eficazmente que el ser humano y las matrices de entradas al azar presentadas aquí están organizadas en tal forma que se las puede incorporar en los programas para computadoras ahora disponibles para tal selección automática. Suponemos que este método de identificación se usará cada vez más en el futuro y esperamos que la presentación de estas matrices alentará a otros a empezar a organizar sus datos en forma similar, previendo así el día en que haya claves para computadoras disponibles para todos los usuarios.

Un trabajo de esta magnitud depende en alto grado de la cooperación y colaboración de mucha gente. La siguiente lista indica el número de personas que han contribuido a esta obra. Aunque hemos tratado de incluir a todos en esta lista, la omisión de alguno de los que nos ayudaron debe ser considerada solamente como consecuencia de la naturaleza defectuosa de nuestra memoria, pero no como una inhabilidad de apreciar la ayuda recibida.

(In alphabetical order): Jorge Abalos, Fernando Achaval, Joseph Bailey, Avelino Barrio, Charles Bogert, Werner Bokermann, Simon Campden-Main, Nelly Carrillo de Espinoza, Antenor de Carvalho, Ronald Crombie, Marcos Freiberg, Howard Gloyd, Jose Gallardo, Alphonse Hoge, Robert Inger, George Jacobs, Edward Keiser, Miguel Klappenbach, Abdem Lancini, Clarence McCoy, Nicéforo María, Oswaldo Mineses, Marta Miranda, Charles Myers, Gustavo Orcés-V., Donald Owens, Neil Richmond, Carlos Rivero-Blanco, Douglas Rossman, Janis Roze, Richard Sage, Jay Savage, Wade Sherbrooke, Hobart Smith, Richard Timmerman, Robert Tuck, Paulo Vanzolini, Jaime Villa, Warren Walker, Larry Wilson, George Zug.

In addition to the above, we also wish to acknowledge several specific contributions to the work involved in the production of this volume. By far the bulk of the typing work was done by Jean Middleton, and the overall appearance of the text owes a great deal to her attention to detail, layout, arrangement, and so on. She functioned as a general manager of the entire project, and we cannot overestimate the magnitude of her contribution. Beatriz Moisset Peters spent many hours translating and correcting the spanish versions of the text after one of us (Orejas) returned to South America, and she also has contributed greatly to our overall accuracy. Additional typing assistance came from Gladys Banks and Dolores Icarangal. The text figures, unless otherwise acknowledged, were done by Thomas Yuskiw.

We wish finally to record our debt to Roberto Donoso Barros, who worked with us on this catalogue. He perhaps should have been recorded as an author rather than as a collaborator, since all three of us have worked closely together on the entire project.

Además de los mencionados, deseamos expresar nuestro reconocimiento por varias contribuciones específicas referentes a la producción de este volumen. Jean Middleton mecanografió la mayor parte de este trabajo y la apariencia general del texto ganó mucho gracias a su interés en los detalles. Ella operó como administradora general de todo el proyecto y no es posible sobreestimar el valor de su contribución. Beatriz Moisset Peters dedicó muchas horas a la traducción y corrección de la versión en español después que uno de nosotros (Orejas) regresara a Sudamérica. También contribuyó en gran medida a la exactitud del trabajo. Gladys Banks y Dolores Icarangal mecanografiaron el resto del trabajo. Las figuras del texto fueron hechas por Thomas Yuskiw a menos que se especfique otra cosa.

Finalmente deseamos expresar nuestra deuda para con Roberto Donoso Barros, que trabajó con nosotros en este catálogo. Talvez se lo debería incluir como uno de los autores en vez de colaborador, ya que los tres trabajamos en estrecho contacto a través de todo el proyecto.

INTRODUCTION

We are concerned that the users of this catalogue may regard everything presented as of equal value and significance, since there are considerable differences in the comparative reliability of the information given from one genus to another. In order to forestall assumptions of equivalent reliability, we have devised a code to indicate an evaluation of the information presented for each genus. The user will note one to four stars in the heading line for every genus. These stars have the following significance:

One Star: Low reliability. Keys and synonymies prepared by us from existing literature; difficulties encountered by us because of insufficient descriptions, non-availability of critical specimens, or other reasons; manuscript not checked by outside reviewer, since no one is currently engaged in revisionary study of the genus, to our knowledge. In the case of monotypic genera, one star means we have reasons to doubt its validity as a distinct genus.

Two Stars: Moderate reliability. Keys and synonymies prepared almost entirely by us, but usually checked against specimens and adequate information in the literature; manuscript often reviewed externally, although not necessarily by specialist actively studying genus. Further study needed to give better understanding of genus.

Three stars. Good reliability. Keys and synonymies prepared either by us in consultation with a specialist or by the expert himself, or modified from monographs, checklists, or regional studies. Added work is usually in progress on the genus by the specialist, and we anticipate early publication by him to improve our understanding even more.

Four Stars. High reliability. Manuscript either prepared externally, in which case the author is acknowledged in the heading material; or taken by us from a very recent generic monograph summarizing the literature and including all available specimens for study.

We have submitted this "reliability" list to all external authors and asked for their opinion before assigning the code, so it can be considered an indication of the author's personal evaluation, rather than ours.

Nos preocupa la posibilidad de que los usuarios de este catálogo vayan a dar igual valor o significado a las distintas partes del mismo, ya que la seguridad de la información suministrada varía considerablemente de unos géneros a otros. Para evitar que se llegue a la conclusión de que toda la información es igualmente digna de confianza hemos ideado un código que valore la calidad de la información presentada en cada género. El usuario verá de una a cuatro estrellas en el encabezamiento de cada género. Estas tienen el siguiente significado:

Una Estrella: Poca confianza. Claves y sinónimos preparados exclusivamente por nosotros a partir de la literatura existente; dificultades halladas por nosotros a causa de descripciones insuficientes, especímenes críticos no disponibles u otras razones; el manuscrito no ha sido revisado por nadie de afuera ya que no sabemos de nadie que esté ocupado en hacer un estudio de revisión del género en el momento actual. En el caso de géneros monotípicos una estrella significa que tenemos motivos para dudar de su validez como género aparte.

Dos Estrellas: Moderada confianza. Claves y sinónimos preparados casi totalmente por nosotros, pero usualmente confrontados con especímenes e información adecuada en la literatura; manuscrito a menudo revisado por alquien de afuera, aunque no necesariamente por un especialista en ese género. Se necesita más estudio para comprender mejor ese género.

Tres Estrellas: Bastante confianza. Claves y sinónimos preparados por nosotros en consulta con un especialista o por el experto mismo o modificados de monografías, listas de especies o estudios regionales. Usualmente hay trabajo adicional en marcha del especialista en el género, y anticipamos su pronta publicación para mejorar aun más nuestra comprensión del mismo.

Cuatro Estrellas. Mucha confianza. Manuscrito o bien preparado afuera en cuyo caso se nombra al autor en el encabezamiento o preparado por nosotros a partir de una monografía muy reciente que resume la literatura e incluye todos los especímenes disponibles para estudio.

Hemos presentado esta lista de "dignidad de confianza" a todos los autores de afuera y pedido su opinión antes de asignar el código, así que se la puede considerar como indicación de una valoración del autor antes que nuestra.

The work on this catalogue was supported by a Smithsonian Research Award to the senior author. The catalogue is listed as project no. 2 in the U.S.A. section of Section CT (Conservation Terrestrial) of the International Biological Program.

El trabajo del catálogo fue sufragado por Smithsonian Research Award al autor principal. El catálogo figura como proyecto no. 2 en la parte de los Estados Unidos de la Sección CT (Conservación Terrestre) del Programa Biológico Internacional.

KEY TO THE GENERA OF SNAKES

1. Ventrals and dorsals equal in size, or ventrals feebly enlarged, only slightly larger than dorsal scales, do not extend clear across venter------------------------------------173
   Ventrals considerably enlarged, much larger than dorsal scales, extend across entire venter--------------------------------------2

2. Large, deep pit in loreal region between eye and nostril--------------------------------181
   Loreal region without deep pit---------------- 3

3. Scale rows at midbody fewer than 30-------------
   --4
   Scale rows at midbody more than 30----------165

4. Tail not compressed----------------------------5
   Tail compressed, oarlike--------------Laticauda

5. Dorsal scale rows about one head length anterior to anus at least two less than count at midbody--------------------------------------6
   Dorsal scale rows same number throughout body, no dorsal reductions-------------------------8

6. Scales in odd number of rows-----------------69
   Scales in even number of rows, vertebral row missing---------------------------------------7

7. Scale rows 12 or fewer-----------------Chironius
   Scale rows 14 or more-------------------Spilotes

8. Number of dorsal scale rows at midbody more than 18--------------------------------------67
   Number of dorsal scale rows at midbody fewer than 18--------------------------------------9

9. Anal single-----------------------------------47
   Anal divided-----------------------------------10

10. Dorsal scale rows at midbody 17--------------32
    Dorsal scale rows at midbody fewer than 17-----
    ---11

11. Body pattern of complete rings of color around body-------------------------------------29
    Body pattern without complete rings----------12

12. Anteriormost tooth on maxillary (often only tooth on bone) with venom canal (Fig. 1)-----
    ---------------------------------Leptomicrurus
    Anteriormost teeth on maxillary without canal or otherwise differentiated from other maxillary teeth---------------------------------13

13. Loreal present--------------------------------20
    Loreal absent----------------------------------14

14. Parietal in contact with labials-------------15
    Parietal separated from labials by temporals-16

15. Internasals fused with prefrontals-------------
    --------------------------------------Apostolepis
    Internasals distinct from prefrontals, which may be fused into single scale or not---------
    --------------------------------------Elapomorphus

1. Ventrales y dorsales de igual tamaño, o ventrales sólo ligeramente mayores que dorsales, no se extienden a través de todo el vientre---
   --173
   Ventrales considerablemente dilatadas, mucho mayores que dorsales, se extienden a través de todo el vientre------------------------------2

2. Con una fosa grande, profunda en región loreal entre ojo y narina--------------------------181
   Sin fosa profunda en región loreal------------3

3. Hileras de escamas a través del medio cuerpo menos de 30---------------------------------- 4
   Hileras de escamas a través del medio cuerpo más de 30---------------------------------165

4. Cola no comprimida---------------------------5
   Cola comprimida, en forma de remo-------------
   --------------------------------------Laticauda

5. Hileras de escamas dorsales a una cabeza de longitud antes del ano por lo menos dos menos que la cuenta del medio cuerpo--------------6
   Hileras de escamas dorsales en igual número a lo largo de todo el cuerpo, sin reducciones--8

6. Escamas en número impar de hileras----------69
   Escamas en número par de hileras, sin hilera vertebral-------------------------------------7

7. Hileras de escamas 12 o menos---------Chironius
   Hileras de escamas 14 o más-----------Spilotes

8. Número de hileras de escamas dorsales del medio cuerpo más de 18--------------------------67
   Número de hileras de escamas dorsales del medio cuerpo menos de 18--------------------------9

9. Anal única-----------------------------------47
   Anal dividida-----------------------------------10

10. Hileras de escamas dorsales del medio cuerpo 17
    ---32
    Hileras de escamas dorsales del medio cuerpo menos de 17------------------------------------11

11. Diseño del cuerpo con anillos completos de color alrededor del cuerpo--------------------29
    Diseño del cuerpo sin anillos completos------12

12. Diente más anterior del maxilar (a menudo el único diente en este hueso) con canal de veneno (Fig. 1)------------------Leptomicrurus
    Diente más anterior del maxilar sin canal u otra diferenciación de demás dientes maxilares
    ---13

13. Con loreal------------------------------------20
    Sin loreal-------------------------------------14

14. Parietal en contacto con labiales-----------15
    Parietal separado de labiales por temporales-16

15. Internasales fusionadas con prefrontales-------
    --------------------------------------Apostolepis
    Internasales distintas de prefrontales, que pueden estar fusionadas en una sola escama o no--------------------------------Elapomorphus

Fig. 1. Maxillary of elapid snake, showing fixed fang on anterior end of bone

Fig. 2. Colubrid maxillary, all teeth uniform, no diastema, no grooved teeth

Fig. 3. Colubrid maxillary, last two teeth enlarged, no diastema, no grooves

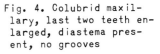

Fig. 4. Colubrid maxillary, last two teeth enlarged, diastema present, no grooves

Fig. 5. Colubrid maxillary, diastema present, last two teeth enlarged and grooved

16. Internasals normal, not fused----------------17
    Internasals fused, single plate----------------
    ----------------------------------Pseudoeryx

17. Ventrals more than 120----------------------18
    Ventrals fewer than 120----------------------19

18. Ventrals fewer than 170; maxillary teeth anter-
    ior to fangs 12-15---------------------Tantilla
    Ventrals more than 170; maxillary teeth anter-
    ior to fangs 3-5-----------------Elapomorphus

19. Total maxillary teeth 22-25; last two without
    grooves---------------------------Tantillita
    Total maxillary teeth fewer than 21; last two
    with grooves-----------------------Tantilla

20. Scale rows at midbody more than thirteen-------
    --------------------------------------21
    Scales at midbody thirteen---------------------
    -----------------------------Pseudablabes

21. Prefrontals two or three--------------------22
    Prefrontals fused into single scale------------
    --------------------------------Trimetopon

22. Two prefrontals----------------------------23
    Three prefrontals-----------------Hydromorphus

23. Internasals and prefrontals distinct----------
    --------------------------------------24
    Internasals fused with prefrontals, but still
    paired----------------------------Elapomojus

24. Anterior temporals more than one--------------
    --------------------------------Mastigodryas
    One anterior temporal----------------------25

25. Preocular absent; both loreal and prefrontal
    enter orbit------------------------------27
    Preocular present; prefrontal does not enter
    orbit----------------------------------26

26. Chinshields large; striped-----------Adelphicos
    Chinshields small; unicolor------------Enulius

16. Internasales normales, no fusionadas-----------
    --17
    Internasales fusionadas, una sola lámina-------
    ----------------------------------Pseudoeryx

17. Ventrales más de 120------------------------18
    Ventrales menos de 120----------------------19

18. Ventrales menos de 170; dientes maxilares ante-
    riores a colmillos 12-15--------------Tantilla
    Ventrales más de 170; dientes maxilares ante-
    riores a colmillos 3-5-----------Elapomorphus

19. Total de dientes maxilares 22-25; los dos últi-
    mos sin surcos---------------------Tantillita
    Total de dientes maxilares menos de 21; los dos
    últimos con surcos--------------------Tantilla

20. Hileras de escamas del medio cuerpo más de
    trece----------------------------------21
    Hileras de escamas del medio cuerpo trece------
    ----------------------------------Pseudablabes

21. Prefrontales dos o tres---------------------22
    Prefrontales fusionadas en una sola escama-----
    --------------------------------Trimetopon

22. Dos prefrontales----------------------------23
    Tres prefrontales------------------Hydromorphus

23. Internasales y prefrontales distintas----------
    --24
    Internasales fusionadas con prefrontales, pero
    aún en pares----------------------Elapomojus

24. Temporales anteriores más de una--------------
    ----------------------------------Mastigodryas
    Una temporal anterior----------------------25

25. Sin preocular; loreal y prefrontal entran en la
    órbita----------------------------------27
    Con preocular; prefrontal no entra en la órbita
    --26

26. Escudos geniales grandes, a rayas-------------
    ----------------------------------Adelphicos
    Escudos geniales chicos, unicolores-----------
    ----------------------------------Enulius

27. Body striped----------------------------------28
    Body with dark blotches dorsally--------------
    ----------------------------Calamodontophis

28. Apical pits absent on dorsal scales-----------
    ------------------------------------Liophis
    Single apical pit present------------Trimetopon

29. Loreal present-------------------------------31
    Loreal absent--------------------------------30

30. Fixed fang with venom canal on maxillary bone
    (Fig. 1)----------------------------Micrurus
    No fixed fang with venom canal----------Hydrops

31. Apical pits present on dorsal scales-----------
    --------------------------------Scolecophis
    Apical pits absent--------------Erythrolamprus

32. Two prefrontals present, may be fused with
    internasals----------------------------------33
    Prefrontals fused into single scale------------
    ------------------------------------Trimetopon

33. Parietals separated from labials by temporals--
    --34
    Parietals in contact with labials-------------
    ----------------------------Parapostolepis

34. Rostral does not separate internasals and/or
    prefrontals which are in contact on middorsal
    line---35
    Rostral separates internasals and/or prefron-
    tals, and contacts frontal------------Ficimia

35. Scales smooth--------------------------------37
    Scales keeled on all or only posterior part of
    body---36

36. Entire body with keeled scales---------Storeria
    Keels only on scales on posterior part of body,
    most prominent near anus-----------Amastridium

37. Nasal not fused with internasal--------------38
    Anterior nasal fused with internasal----------
    ----------------------------------Stenorrhina

38. Body round; head not distinctly broader than
    neck; vertebral scale row approximately same
    width as paravertebral row-------------------39
    Body strongly compressed; head distinctly
    broader than neck; vertebral scale row wider
    than paravertebral rows-------------Imantodes

39. One anterior temporal-----------------------41
    Two anterior temporals----------------------40

40. Ventrals fewer than 160--------Scaphiodontophis
    Ventrals more than 159------------Mastigodryas

41. Body with "coral snake" pattern, may or may not
    be complete ventrally--------------------42
    Body without "coral snake" pattern----------43

27. Cuerpo rayado----------------------------------28
    Cuerpo con manchas oscuras a dorsal-----------
    ----------------------------Calamodontophis

28. Sin fosetas apicales en escamas dorsales-------
    ------------------------------------Liophis
    Con fosetas apicales en escamas dorsales------
    ------------------------------------Trimetopon

29. Con loreal-----------------------------------31
    Sin loreal--------------------------------30

30. Colmillo fijo con canal del veneno en maxilar
    (Fig. 1)----------------------------Micrurus
    Sin colmillo fijo con canal del veneno--------
    --------------------------------------Hydrops

31. Con fosetas apicales en escamas dorsales-------
    --------------------------------Scolecophis
    Sin fosetas apicales------------Erythrolamprus

32. Con dos prefrontales, pueden estar fusionadas
    con internasales----------------------------33
    Prefrontales fusionadas en una sola escama-----
    ------------------------------------Trimetopon

33. Parietales separadas de labiales por temporales
    --34
    Parietales en contacto con labiales-----------
    ----------------------------Parapostolepis

34. Rostral no separa las internasales y/o prefron-
    tales que contactan en línea media dorsal-----
    --35
    Rostral separa las internasales y/o prefron-
    tales y contacta la frontal-----------Ficimia

35. Escamas lisas--------------------------------37
    Escamas quilladas en todo el cuerpo o sólo en
    parte posterior-----------------------------36

36. Todo el cuerpo con escamas quilladas-----------
    --------------------------------------Storeria
    Quillas sólo en escamas de parte posterior del
    cuerpo, más prominentes cerca del ano---------
    --------------------------------Amastridium

37. Nasal no fusionada con internasal-----------38
    Nasal anterior fusionada con internasal-------
    ----------------------------------Stenorrhina

38. Cuerpo redondo; cabeza no distintamente más
    ancha que el cuello; hilera vertebral de esca-
    mas aproximadamente tan ancha como hilera
    paravertebral-------------------------------39
    Cuerpo fuertemente comprimido; cabeza clara-
    mente más ancha que el cuello; hilera verte-
    bral de escamas más ancha que hileras paraver-
    tebrales----------------------------Imantodes

39. Una temporal anterior-----------------------41
    Dos temporales anteriores-------------------40

40. Ventrales menos de 160--------Scaphiodontophis
    Ventrales más de 159------------Mastigodryas

41. Cuerpo con diseño de "serpiente de coral",
    puede ser completo a ventral o no----------42
    Cuerpo sin diseño de "serpiente de coral"----43

42. Maxillary teeth normal---------------Pliocercus
    Maxillary teeth with spatulate tip, arranged in
    groups of three, each group including one
    short, one medium, and one long tooth---------
    ----------------------------Scaphiodontophis

43. Loreal and preocular both present, two plates
    between nasal and orbit--------------------44
    Loreal or preocular absent, only one plate
    between nasal and orbit---------------Enulius

44. Apical pits absent on dorsal scales (Fig. 6)---
    --102
    Apical pits present (Fig. 7)-----------------45

42. Dientes maxilares normales-----------Pliocercus
    Dientes maxilares con ápice espatulado, dispues-
    tas en grupos de tres, cada grupo incluye un
    diente corto, mediano y largo-----------------
    ----------------------------Scaphiodontophis

43. Con loreal y preocular; dos láminas entre nasal
    y órbita-----------------------------------44
    Sin loreal o sin preocular, sólo una lámina
    entre nasal y órbita-------------------Enulius

44. Sin fosetas apicales en escamas dorsales (Fig.
    6)---102
    Con fosetas apicales (Fig. 7)----------------45

Fig. 6. Dorsal scales, without apical
pits. Anterior end of scale at top in
this figure and Figure 7.

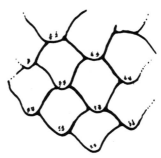

Fig. 7. Double apical pits on dorsal
scales. May also be single. Usually
outer layer of scale must be removed
and examined dry under high magnifi-
cation to see pits.

45. No nuchal collar or band across back of head;
    size generally large-----------------------46
    With nuchal collar or band across back of head;
    size diminutive--------------------Trimetopon

46. Posteriormost maxillary teeth enlarged (Fig. 4)
    ----------------------------------Leimadophis
    All maxillary teeth about same size (Fig. 2)---
    ----------------------------------Sordellina

47. Dorsals at midbody 17----------------------58
    Dorsals at midbody fewer than 17------------48

48. Vertebral and paravertebral rows subequal------
    --51
    Vertebral scale row distinctly larger than
    paravertebrals----------------------------49

49. Mental groove absent (Fig. 8)-----------Dipsas
    Mental groove present----------------------50

45. Sin banda o collar nucal a través del dorso de
    la cabeza; generalmente de gran tamaño------
    --46
    Con collar o banda nucal a través del dorso de
    la cabeza; tamaño diminuto---------Trimetopon

46. Dientes maxilares posteriores dilatados (Fig.4)
    ----------------------------------Leimadophis
    Todos los dientes maxilares aproximadamente del
    mismo tamaño (Fig. 2)--------------Sordellina

47. Dorsales del medio cuerpo 17-----------------58
    Dorsales del medio cuerpo menos de 17--------48

48. Hileras vertebral y paravertebral casi iguales-
    --51
    Hilera vertebral distintamente más grande que
    paravertebrales---------------------------49

49. Sin surco mental (Fig. 8)--------------Dipsas
    Con surco mental---------------------------50

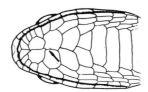

Fig. 8. Dipsas latifrontalis, showing absence of mental groove (from Peters, 1960)

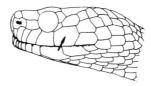

Fig. 9. Sibon nebulata, showing enlarged
sixth labial (from Peters, 1960)

50. Labial below anterior temporal enlarged and in contact with postocular, anterior and posterior temporal, much higher than neighboring labials (Fig. 9)----------------------Sibon
No one labial in contact with postocular, anterior and posterior temporal----------------
-----------------------------------Imantodes

51. Parietals separated from labials by temporals--
--54
Parietals in contact with labials-----------52

52. Internasals and prefrontals distinct---------
-------------------------------------Geophis
Internasals and prefrontals fused-----------53

53. Loreal absent----------------------Apostolepis
Loreal present-----------------------Geophis

54. Apical pits absent on dorsal scales (Fig. 6)---
---55
Apical pits present (Fig. 7)---------Drymoluber

55. No tooth on maxillary either with groove or closed canal--------------------------------57
Tooth on maxillary either with groove or closed canal------------------------------------56

56. Anteriormost, often only, tooth on maxilla with closed canal (Fig. 1)-----------------Micrurus
Posteriormost, never only, tooth on maxilla with open groove (Fig. 5)---------Apostolepis

57. Loreal plate present------------------------60
Loreal plate absent----------------Drepanoides

58. Prefrontals fused into single scale------------
---66
Prefrontals normal-------------------------59

59. Subcaudals double---------------------------60
Subcaudals single--------------------Pseudoboa

60. Parietal separated from labials by temporals---
---61
Parietal in contact with at least one upper labial------------------------------Geophis

61. Scales keeled------------------------------62
Scales smooth-----------------------------63

62. Ventrals fewer than 170--------------------Ninia
Ventrals more than 170-----------Tropidodipsas

63. Mental groove present----------------------64
Mental groove absent-------------Sibynomorphus

64. Labial below anterior temporal enlarged, considerably higher than neighboring labials, and in contact with postocular, anterior and posterior temporals (Fig. 9)----------------Sibon
All labials about same size, not as described above--------------------------------------65

65. Ventrals more than 200------------------Clelia
Ventrals fewer than 200---------------Atractus

50. Labial debajo de temporal anterior agrandado y en contacto con postocular, temporal anterior y posterior mucho más altas que labiales vecinas (Fig. 9)----------------------Sibon
Ninguna labial en contacto con postocular, temporal anterior y posterior-----------------
-----------------------------------Imantodes

51. Parietales separadas de labiales por temporales
--54
Parietales en contacto con labiales---------52

52. Internasales y prefrontales distintas--------
-------------------------------------Geophis
Internasales y prefrontales fusionadas-------53

53. Sin loreal----------------------Apostolepis
Con loreal-----------------------------Geophis

54. Sin fosetas apicales en escamas dorsales (Fig. 6)---55
Con fosetas apicales (Fig. 7)--------Drymoluber

55. Ningun diente del maxilar con surco o canal cerrado-----------------------------------57
Diente en maxilar con surco o con canal cerrado
---56

56. Diente anterior (a menudo el único) del maxilar con canal cerrado (Fig. 1)-----------Micrurus
Diente posterior (nunca el único) del maxilar con surco (Fig. 5)-----------------Apostolepis

57. Con lámina loreal------------------------60
Sin lámina loreal-----------------Drepanoides

58. Prefrontales fusionadas en una sola lámina-----
---66
Prefrontales normales-----------------------59

59. Subcaudales dobles---------------------------60
Subcaudales de a una-----------------Pseudoboa

60. Parietales separadas de labiales por temporales
---61
Parietales en contacto con una labial superior por lo menos--------------------------Geophis

61. Escamas quilladas---------------------------62
Escamas lisas------------------------------63

62. Ventrales menos de 170--------------------Ninia
Ventrales más de 170-------------Tropidodipsas

63. Con surco mental----------------------------64
Sin surco mental------------------Sibynomorphus

64. Labiales debajo de temporal anterior agrandadas, considerablemente más altas que labiales vecinas y en contacto con postocular, temporales anterior y posterior (Fig. 9)-----------Sibon
Todas las labiales aproximadamente del mismo tamaño, no como el anterior----------------65

65. Ventrales más de 200--------------------Clelia
Ventrales menos de 200----------------Atractus

66. Scales keeled---------------------Chersodromus
    Scales smooth---------------------Xenopholis

67. Prefrontals normal----------------------68
    Prefrontals fused to form single scale --------
    ------------------------------------Synophis

68. Ventrals fewer than 200------------------Ninia
    Ventrals more than 200------------------Clelia

69. Some or all dorsal scales keeled------------140
    Dorsal scales smooth-----------------------70

70. Anal single--------------------------------116
    Anal divided-------------------------------71

71. Rostral normal-----------------------------73
    Rostral modified, either raised, pointed, and
    keeled dorsally, or flattened, with hori-
    zontal edge-------------------------------72

72. Scales in 15-17 rows-------------------Simophis
    Scales in 19-21 rows-----------------Lystrophis

73. Vertebral row of scales greatly enlarged, dis-
    tinctly larger than neighboring rows of scales
    ---74
    Vertebral row of scales approximately same as
    neighboring scales-------------------------75

74. Ventrals fewer than 200------------Uromacerina
    Ventrals more than 200---------------Imantodes

75. Two loreal plates between nasal and preocular--
    ------------------------------Trimorphodon
    One or no loreal plates present------------- 76

76. Fewer than 26 midbody scale rows------------77
    More than 26 midbody scale rows---------Elaphe

77. Loreal plate present---------------------81
    Loreal plate absent-----------------------78

78. Maxillary lacks diastema in tooth row, last
    teeth distinctly larger than others (Fig. 3)--
    ---------------------------------------Hydrops
    Not as above-----------------------------79

79. Head short, wide; snout rounded--------------80
    Head elongated, slender: snout pointed-Oxybelis

80. Maxillary bone extremely reduced, without teeth
    anterior to enlarged, grooved fangs-----------
    ------------------------------------Opisthoplus
    Maxillary not reduced, teeth present anterior
    to enlarged, grooved fangs (Fig. 5)----Tomodon

81. Anterior temporals two or more--------------103
    One anterior temporal or none---------------82

82. Midbody scale rows 17 or fewer---------------93
    Midbody scale rows more than 17-------------83

66. Escamas quilladas------------------Chersodromus
    Escamas lisas----------------------Xenopholis

67. Prefrontales normales-----------------------68
    Prefrontales fusionadas formando una sola
    escama----------------------------Synophis

68. Ventrales menos de 200--------------------Ninia
    Ventrales más de 200--------------------Clelia

69. Algunas o todas las escamas dorsales quilladas-
    --140
    Escamas dorsales lisas-----------------------70

70. Anal única---------------------------------116
    Anal dividida------------------------------71

71. Rostral normal-----------------------------73
    Rostral modificada, o bien elevada, puntuda y
    quillada dorsalmente o aplanada con borde
    horizontal--------------------------------72

72. Escamas en 15-17 hileras--------------Simophis
    Escamas en 19-21 hileras------------Lystrophis

73. Hilera vertebral de escamas muy agrandadas,
    claramente mayores que hileras de escamas
    vecinas-----------------------------------74
    Hilera vertebral de escamas del mismo tamaño
    aproximado que escamas vecinas--------------75

74. Ventrales menos de 200--------------Uromacerina
    Ventrales más de 200-----------------Imantodes

75. Dos láminas loreales entre nasal y preocular---
    ---------------------------------Trimorphodon
    Con una o ninguna lámina loreal-------------- 76

76. Menos de 26 hileras de escamas del medio cuerpo
    ---77
    Más de 26 hileras de escamas del medio cuerpo--
    ------------------------------------Elaphe

77. Con lámina loreal--------------------------81
    Sin lámina loreal---------------------------78

78. Maxilar sin diastema en la hilera de dientes,
    últimos dientes mucho mayores que los otros
    (Fig. 3)--------------------------------Hydrops
    No como el anterior-------------------------79

79. Cabeza corta, ancha; hocico redondeado-------80
    Cabeza alargada, fina; hocico puntudo--Oxybelis

80. Hueso maxilar extremadamente reducido; sin
    dientes anteriores a colmillos grandes
    ----------------------------------Opisthoplus
    Maxilar no reducido; con dientes anteriores a
    colmillos grandes surcados (Fig. 5)----Tomodon

81. Temporales anteriores dos o más-------------103
    Temporal anterior uno o ninguno-------------82

82. Hileras de escamas del medio cuerpo 17 o menos-
    ---93
    Hileras de escamas del medio cuerpo más de 17--
    ---83

83.Dorsal scales normal (Fig. 10)---------------**84**
   Dorsal scales in oblique rows (Fig. 11)-------
   -------------------------------------**Xenodon**

83.Escamas dorsales normales (Fig. 10)----------84
   Escamas dorsales en hileras oblicuas (Fig. 11)-
   -------------------------------------**Xenodon**

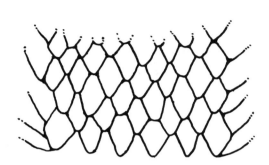

Fig. 10. Normal arrangement of dorsal
scale rows. Anterior end of snake is
toward top of page in this and Fig. 11.

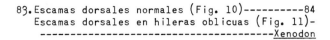
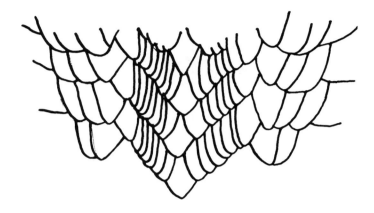

Fig. 11. Dorsal scales arranged in
oblique rows, as seen in **Xenodon**.

84.Apical pits present (Fig. 7)------------------85
   Apical pits absent (Fig. 6)-------------------89

84.Con fosetas apicales (Fig. 7)----------------85
   Sin fosetas apicales (Fig. 6)----------------89

85.Maxillary with diastema, teeth posterior to
   diastema enlarged, not grooved (Fig. 4)-----86
   Not as above---------------------------------88

85.Maxilar con diastema, dientes posteriores a
   diastema agrandados, no acanalados (Fig. 4)-86
   No como el anterior--------------------------88

86.Dorsal scales 19 at midbody------------------87
   Dorsal scales 21 at midbody----------**Hypsiglena**

86.Hileras de escamas del medio cuerpo 19-------87
   Hileras de escamas del medio cuerpo 17--------
   -------------------------------------**Hypsiglena**

87.Subcaudals fewer than 80-----------**Leimadophis**
   Subcaudals more than 80----------------**Dromicus**

87.Subcaudales menos de 80-------------**Leimadophis**
   Subcaudales más de 80-----------------**Dromicus**

88.Pupil vertically elliptic--------------------97
   Pupil round------------------------**Philodryas**

88.Pupila verticalmente elíptica---------------97
   Pupila redonda----------------------**Philodryas**

89.Body striped throughout its length-----------91
   Body not striped throughout its length-------90

89.Cuerpo rayado a todo lo largo----------------91
   Cuerpo no rayado a todo lo largo-------------90

90.Diastema present in maxillary tooth row (Fig.
   4)------------------------------**Lioheterophis**
   Diastema absent (Fig. 3)--------------**Liophis**

90.Con diastema en hilera de dientes maxilares
   (Fig. 4)------------------------**Lioheterophis**
   Sin diastema (Fig. 3)-----------------**Liophis**

91.No grooves on posteriormost maxillary teeth--92
   With grooves on posteriormost maxillary teeth--
   ------------------------------------**Coniophanes**

91.Sin surcos en dientes maxilares posteriores--92
   Con surcos en dientes maxilares posteriores----
   ------------------------------------**Coniophanes**

92.Pale brown above, with dark brown vertebral and
   single lateral stripe----------------**Liophis**
   Not as above--------------------------**Lygophis**

92.Castaño claro arriba, con cinta vertebral y una
   sola cinta lateral, ambos parda oscura-**Liophis**
   No como el anterior--------------------**Lygophis**

93.Prefrontals paired--------------------------94
   Single prefrontal scale-----------**Hydromorphus**

93.Prefrontales en par--------------------------94
   Una sola escama prefrontal--------**Hydromorphus**

94.Apical pits present (Fig. 7)-----------------95
   Apical pits absent (Fig. 6)------------------98

94.Con fosetas apicales (Fig. 7)---------------95
   Sin fosetas apicales (Fig. 6)----------------98

95.Maxillary with diastema, last teeth enlarged
   but not grooved (Fig. 4)-----------**Leimadophis**
   Not as above---------------------------------96

95.Maxilar con diastema, últimos dientes agrandados pero sin surco (Fig. 4)--------**Leimadophis**
   No como el anterior--------------------------96

GENERIC KEY

96.Spotted or blotched dorsally, not unicolor,
without black margins on scales------------97
Bluish gray dorsally, scales usually with black
margins, uniform yellow below--------Platynion

97.Maxillary teeth gradually and feebly increasing
in length (Fig. 3); usually without dark line
from eye to corner of mouth---------Leptodeira
Maxillary teeth subequal (Fig. 2); head usually
light with oblique dark streak from eye to
corner of mouth---------------------Tachymenis

98.Ventrals more than 131-----------------------99
Ventrals fewer than 131--------------Umbrivaga

99.Body striped throughout length-------------100
Body not striped throughout length------Liophis

100.Without grooves or canals on posteriormost
maxillary teeth---------------------------101
Last maxillary teeth grooved (Fig. 5)-Ditaxodon

101.No diastema in row of maxillary teeth-------102
Diastema present----------------------Lygophis

102.Hemipenis single; tip capitate--------Rhadinaea
Hemipenis bifurcate; tip disked---------Liophis

103.Posteriormost maxillary teeth grooved (Fig. 5)-
---104
Without grooved teeth----------------------112

104.Apical pits present (Fig. 7)----------------105
Apical pits absent (Fig. 6)-----------------110

105.Anterior mandibular teeth longest-----------106
All mandibular teeth subequal---------------108

106.Maxillary fang rather small, weak; maxillary
teeth usually more than ten (in a few species
of Tachymenis as few as six)---------------107
Maxillary fang large, strong; maxillary teeth
6-8-----------------------------Pseudotomodon

107.Pupil round; pterygoid teeth 20-24, extend
anteriorly beyond articulation of pterygoid
with ectopterygoid-----------------Gomesophis
Pupil vertical; pterygoid teeth fewer than 20,
do not extend anteriorly beyond articulation
of pterygoid with ectopterygoid---------------
----------------------------------Tachymenis

108.More than ten maxillary teeth anterior to two
enlarged teeth----------------------------109
Fewer than ten maxillary teeth anterior to two
enlarged teeth, maxillary may be completely
edentulous except for enlarged fang-like teeth
(Fig. 5)----------------------------Tomodon

109.Pupil round-----------------------Philodryas
Pupil vertical----------------Thamnodynastes

96.Con borrones o manchas dorsales, no unicolor,
escamas sin bordes negros------------------97
Gris azulado a dorsal, escamas usualmente con
borde negro, amarillo uniforme a ventral------
--Platynion

97.Dientes maxilares que aumentan de longitud
gradualmente (Fig. 3); usualmente sin línea
oscura desde el ojo accomisura de la boca-----
--Leptodeira
Dientes maxilares casi iguales (Fig. 2); cabeza
usualmente clara con línea oscura oblicua
desde el ojo a comisura de la boca--Tachymenis

98.Ventrales más de 131-------------------------99
Ventrales menos de 131---------------Umbrivaga

99.Cuerpo rayado a todo lo largo---------------100
Cuerpo no rayado a todo lo largo--------Liophis

100.Sin surcos ni canales en dientes maxilares
posteriores-------------------------------101
Últimos dientes maxilares con surcos (Fig. 5)--
--Ditaxodon

101.Sin diastema en hilera de dientes maxilares-102
Con diastema--------------------------Lygophis

102.Hemipene simple, ápice capitado-------Rhadinaea
Hemipene bifurcado, ápice discado------Liophis

103.Dientes maxilares posteriores con surcos (Fig.
5)---104
Sin dientes con surcos---------------------112

104.Con fosetas apicales (Fig. 7)---------------105
Sin fosetas apicales (Fig. 6)---------------110

105.Dientes mandibulares anteriores son los más
largos------------------------------------106
Todos los dientes mandibulares aproximadamente
iguales-----------------------------------108

106.Colmillo maxilar más bien chico, débil; dientes
maxilares usualmente más de diez (en unas
especies de Tachymenis nada más que seis)--107
Colmillo maxilar grande, fuerte; dientes
maxilares 6-8--------------------Pseudotomodon

107.Pupila redonda; dientes pterygoideos 20-24, se
extienden anteriormente más allá de la articulación del pterygoides con ectopterygoides----
--Gomesophis
Pupila vertical; dientes pterygoideos menos de
20, no se extienden anteriormente más allá de
la articulación del pterygoides con ectoptery-
goides----------------------------Tachymenis

108.Más de diez dientes maxilares anteriores a dos
dientes agrandados------------------------109
Menos de diez dientes maxilares anteriores a
dos dientes agrandados, maxilar puede ser completamente desdentado excepto por dientes
agrandados, como colmillos (Fig. 5)----Tomodon

109.Pupila redonda-----------------------Philodryas
Pupila vertical-----------------Thamnodynastes

110.Head and anterior part of body not longitudinally striped------------------------------111
Head and anterior part of body with very pronounced, strongly contrasting stripes--------
------------------------------------Conophis

111.Mandibular teeth subequal-------Thamnodynastes
Anterior mandibular teeth longest------------
-----------------------------------Tachymenis

112.Dorsal scale rows 19 at midbody-------------113
Dorsal scale rows 17 at midbody-------------114

113.Hemipenis single, capitate tip--------Rhadinaea
Hemipenis bifurcate, tip normal--------Dromicus

114.Small presubocular below preocular----------115
No presubocular below preocular--------------
------------------------------Mastigodryas

115.Ventrals more than 180-------------Masticophis
Ventrals fewer than 180----------------Coluber

116.Temporal region covered by small scales--------
-----------------------------------Ungaliophis
Not as above--------------------------------117

117.Parietal separated from labials by temporal
scales---------------------------------118
Parietal in contact with labials-------------
----------------------------------Paroxyrhopus

118.Scale rows at midbody 17 or more------------120
Scale rows at midbody fewer than 17----------
--119

119.Body strongly compressed----------------Dipsas
Body cylindrical----------------Sibynomorphus

120.Dorsals at midbody 19 or more---------------127
Dorsals at midbody 17-----------------------121

121.Body striped--------------------------------122
Body not striped----------------------------123

122.Ventrals more than 175----------Thamnodynastes
Ventrals fewer than 175------------Leptodrymus

123.Mental groove present-----------------------124
Mental groove absent (Fig. 8)------------Dipsas

124.Posterior maxillary teeth grooved----------126
Posterior maxillary teeth not grooved-------125

125.Ventrals more than 180--------------Drymarchon
Ventrals fewer than 180------------Drymoluber

126.Subcaudals single--------------------Pseudoboa
Subcaudals paired----------------------Clelia

127.Rostral normal------------------------------128
Rostral tip turned up into sharp point--------
-----------------------------------Phimophis

128.Anterior temporal single--------------------129
More than one anterior temporal-------------131

110.Cabeza y parte anterior del cuerpo no rayada
longitudinalmente-------------------------111
Cabeza y parte anterior del cuerpo con rayas
muy pronunciadas, que contrastan intensamente--
------------------------------------Conophis

111.Dientes mandibulares casi iguales-------------
----------------------------Thamnodynastes
Dientes mandibulares anteriores son los más
largos-----------------------------Tachymenis

112.Hileras de escamas del medio cuerpo 19------113
Hileras de escamas del medio cuerpo 17------114

113.Hemipene simple, ápice capitado-------Rhadinaea
Hemipene bifurcado, ápice normal-------Dromicus

114.Con presubocular chico debajo del preocular----
--115
Sin presubocular debajo del preocular---------
-------------------------------Mastigodryas

115.Ventrales más de 180----------------Masticophis
Ventrales menos de 180-----------------Coluber

116.Región temporal cubierta de escamas chicas-----
------------------------------------Ungaliophis
No como el anterior-------------------------117

117.Parietal separada de labiales por escamas tem-
porales---------------------------------118
Parietal en contacto con labiales------------
----------------------------------Paroxyrhopus

118.Hileras de escamas del medio cuerpo 17 o más---
--120
Hileras de escamas del medio cuerpo menos de 17
--119

119.Cuerpo fuertemente comprimido-----------Dipsas
Cuerpo cilíndrico----------------Sibynomorphus

120.Dorsales del medio cuerpo 19 o más---------127
Dorsales del medio cuerpo 17-----------------121

121.Cuerpo rayado-------------------------------122
Cuerpo no rayado----------------------------123

122.Ventrales más de 175------------Thamnodynastes
Ventrales menos de 175--------------Leptodrymus

123.Con surco mental---------------------------124
Sin surco mental (Fig. 8)----------------Dipsas

124.Dientes maxilares posteriores acanalados-------
--126
Dientes maxilares posteriores no acanalados-125

125.Ventrales más de 180----------------Drymarchon
Ventrales menos de 180--------------Drymoluber

126.Subcaudales de a una-----------------Pseudoboa
Subcaudales en pares---------------------Clelia

127.Rostral normal------------------------------128
Apice de la rostral se levanta formando una
punta aguda------------------------Phimophis

128.Temporal anterior única---------------------129
Más de una temporal anterior----------------131

129.Last maxillary teeth enlarged, not grooved;
    diastema present (Fig. 4)----------------130
    Not as above------------------------Oxyrhopus

130.Apical pits absent on dorsal scales-----------
    -----------------------------------Paroxyrhopus
    Apical pits present--------------------Xenodon

131.One or more labials enter orbit------------132
    Row of suboculars separates all labials from
    orbit------------------------------Cyclagras

132.Body pattern of complete rings----------------
    -------------------------------Lampropeltis
    Body pattern without complete rings--------133

133.Posteriormost maxillary teeth with grooves (Fig.
    5)-------------------------------------134
    Not as above-------------------------------138

134.Vertebral scales about same size as scales in
    paravertebral rows------------------------135
    Scales in vertebral row distinctly larger than
    paravertebral row scales-----------Tripanurgos

135.All subcaudals paired or mixed, with some single
    single, most paired-----------------------136
    Subcaudals all single----------------Pseudoboa

136.Anterior mandibular teeth somewhat enlarged,
    but length decreases gradually posteriorly-137
    Third to fifth anterior mandibular teeth very
    much enlarged, contrasting sharply with other
    mandibular teeth--------------------Siphlophis

137.Color pattern usually of dark and light cross-
    bands which do not extend across venter------
    -----------------------------------Oxyrhopus
    Juvenile color pattern of dark head and light
    collar, with variable pattern on rest of body
    but never with regular crossbands, adults
    usually melanistic, obscuring all juvenile
    pattern----------------------------------Clelia

138.Dorsal scale rows at midbody **fewer** than 25-----
    ---139
    Dorsal scale rows at midbody more than 24------
    -----------------------------------Rhachedelis

139.Apical pits present on dorsal scales-----------
    -------------------------------------Pseustes
    Apical pits absent----------------Hydrodynastes

140.Anal single---------------------------------152
    Anal divided--------------------------------141

141.Dorsal scale rows at midbody more than 17------
    ---142
    Dorsal scale rows at midbody 17 or fewer-------
    ---146

142.Apical pits present on dorsal scales(Fig. 7)---
    ---144
    Apical pits absent (Fig. 6)----------------143

129.Ultimos dientes maxilares agrandados, no acana-
    lados; con diastema (Fig. 4)---------------130
    No como el anterior-------------------Oxyrhopus

130.Sin fosetas apicales en escamas dorsales-------
    -----------------------------------Paroxyrhopus
    Con fosetas apicales--------------------Xenodon

131.Una o más labiales entra la órbita---------132
    Hilera de suboculares separa todas las labiales
    de la órbita-------------------------Cyclagras

132.Diseño del cuerpo con anillos completos--------
    -------------------------------Lampropeltis
    Diseño del cuerpo sin anillos completos-----133

133.Dientes maxilares posteriores con surcos (Fig.
    5)---134
    No como el anterior------------------------138

134.Escamas vertebrales aproximadamente del mismo
    tamaño que escamas de hileras paravertebrales-
    ---135
    Escamas de hilera vertebral mucho mayores que
    escamas de hileras paravertebrales------------
    -----------------------------------Tripanurgos

135.Todas las subcaudales en pares o mezcladas,
    algunas de a una, la mayoría pares---------136
    Subcaudales todas de a una------------Pseudoboa

136.Dientes mandibulares alteriores algo agranda-
    dos, la longitud decrece gradualmente hacia
    posterior----------------------------------137
    Tercero al quinto dientes mandibulares anteri-
    ores mucho más grandes, en agudo contraste con
    los otros dientes mandibulares------Siphlophis

137.Usualmente con diseño de bandas transversales
    claras y oscuras que no se extienden a través
    del vientre-------------------------Oxyrhopus
    Diseño de los juveniles de cabeza oscura y
    collar claro con diseño variable en el resto
    del cuerpo pero nunca con bandas transversales
    regulares, adultos usualmente melanísticos,
    eclipsando todo el diseño juvenil-------Clelia

138.Hileras de escamas dorsales del medio cuerpo
    menos de 25--------------------------------139
    Hileras de escamas dorsales del medio cuerpo
    más de 24---------------------------Rhachedelis

139.Con fosetas apicales en escamas dorsales-------
    -------------------------------------Pseustes
    Sin fosetas apicales--------------Hydrodynastes

140.Anal única---------------------------------152
    Anal dividida------------------------------141

141.Hileras de escamas dorsales del medio cuerpo
    más de 17----------------------------------142
    Hileras de escamas dorsales del medio cuerpo 17
    o menos------------------------------------146

142.Con fosetas apicales en escamas dorsales (Fig.
    7)---144
    Sin fosetas apicales (Fig. 6)--------------143

143.Two internasals; usually single anterior
      temporal----------------------Tretanorhinus
      Single internasal; usually but not always more
      than one anterior temporal-----------Helicops

144.Body pattern of complete rings-----------------
      ----------------------------------Rhinobothryum
      Body without rings------------------------145

145.Ventrals 160 or more----------------Philodryas
      Ventrals fewer than 160---------Thamnodynastes

146.Dorsal scale rows at midbody 17-------------147
      Dorsal scale rows at midbody fewer than 17-----
      --164

v147.Loreal present---------------------------148
      Loreal absent------------------------Oxybelis

148.Ventrals more than 135--------------------149
      Ventrals fewer than 135-------------------151

149.Posterior maxillary teeth grooved (Fig. 5)--150
      Posterior maxillary teeth not grooved---------
      -------------------------------Drymobius

150.Dorsum with some pattern----------------------
      ----------------------------Thamnodynastes
      Dorsum unicolor--------------------Philodryas

151.Diastema on maxillary absent (Fig. 3)----------
      ----------------------------Paraptychophis
      Diastema on maxillary present (Fig. 4)--------
      --------------------------------Ptychophis

152.Prefrontals fused or replaced by many small
      scales------------------------------153
      Prefrontals normal------------------------156

153.Subcaudals in pairs---------------------154
      Subcaudals single--------------------Trachyboa

154.Scale rows 25 or more----------------Nothopsis
      Scale rows fewer than 25--------------------155

155.One keel on each scale in vertebral row-------
      ----------------------------------Synophis
      Two keels on each scale in vertebral row------
      ----------------------------Diaphorolepis

156.Dorsal scale rows more than 15-------------157
      Dorsal scale rows 15----------------------164

157.Dorsal scale rows more than 17-------------158
      Dorsal scale rows 17-------------Dendrophidion

158.Dorsal scale rows 19-----------------------159
      Dorsal scale rows more than 19-------------160

159.Vertebral scales with single keel----Thamnophis
      Vertebral scales with two keels---Diaphorolepis

160.Subcaudals in pairs-----------------------161
      Subcaudals single------------------Tropidophis

161.Loreal plate present----------------------162
      Loreal plate absent------------------Pseustes

143.Dos internasales; usualmente temporal anterior
      única---------------------------Tretanorhinus
      Internasal única; usualmente, pero no siempre
      más de una temporal anterior---------Helicops

144.Diseño del cuerpo de anillos completos---------
      ----------------------------------Rhinobothryum
      Cuerpo sin anillos------------------------145

145.Ventrales 160 o más------------------Philodryas
      Ventrales menos de 160-----------Thamnodynastes

146.Hileras de escamas dorsales del medio cuerpo 17
      ---147
      Hileras de escamas dorsales del medio cuerpo
      menos de 17-------------------------------164

147.Con loreal-------------------------------148
      Sin loreal--------------------------Oxybelis

148.Ventrales más de 135----------------------149
      Ventrales menos de 135--------------------151

149.Dientes maxilares posteriores acanalados (Fig.
      5)---150
      Dientes maxilares posteriores no acanalados----
      -------------------------------Drymobius

150.Dorso con algún diseño------------------------
      ----------------------------Thamnodynastes
      Dorso unicolor--------------------Philodryas

151.Sin diastema en maxilar (Fig. 3)--------------
      ----------------------------Paraptychophis
      Con diastema en maxilar (Fig. 4)-----Ptychophis

152.Prefrontales fusionados o reemplazados por mu-
      chas escamas chicas-----------------------153
      Prefrontales normales----------------------156

153.Subcaudales en pares-----------------------154
      Subcaudales únicas------------------Trachyboa

154.Hileras de escamas 25 o más-----------Nothopsis
      Hileras de escamas menos de 25-------------155

155.Una quilla en cada escama de hilera vertebral--
      ----------------------------------Synophis
      Dos quillas en cada escama de hilera vertebral-
      ----------------------------Diaphorolepis

156.Hileras de escamas dorsales más de 15-------157
      Hileras de escamas dorsales 15--------------164

157.Hileras de escamas dorsales más de 17-------158
      Hileras de escamas dorsales 17----Dendrophidion

158.Hileras de escamas dorsales 19-------------159
      Hileras de escamas dorsales más de 19-------160

159.Escamas vertebrales con una quilla---Thamnophis
      Escamas vertebrales con dos quillas-----------
      ----------------------------Diaphorolepis

160.Subcaudales pares-------------------------161
      Subcaudales de a una---------------Tropidophis

161.Con lámina loreal-------------------------162
      Sin lámina loreal------------------Pseustes

162. Dorsal scale rows fewer than 27------------163
 Dorsal scale rows 27 or more---------Pituophis

163. Ventrals fewer than 175-------------Thamnophis
 Ventrals more than 175----------------Pseustes

164. Posteriormost maxillary teeth enlarged but
 without grooves----------------------Leptophis
 Posteriormost maxillary teeth not or slightly
 enlarged, with groove present but located
 laterally on tooth-------------------Oxybelis

165. Area behind eye covered by many small scales---
 --166
 Area behind eye covered by several large plates
 --Elaphe

166. Deep sensory pits in most if not all upper
 labials-----------------------------------171
 No sensory pits in labials-----------------167

167. Subcaudals single-------------------------168
 Subcaudals paired-------------------Loxocemus

168. Scales smooth-----------------------------169
 Some or all scales keeled-----------Trachyboa

169. Dorsum of head with some enlarged plates----170
 Dorsum of head covered by small scales, no
 enlarged plates on snout------------------Boa

170. No shields posterior to paired internasals and
 paired prefrontals; body scale rows more than
 40---------------------------------Epicrates
 Dorsum of head with regular plates, including
 azygous prefrontal, frontal and parietal;
 scale rows fewer than 40---------Ungaliophis

171. Midbody scale rows fewer than 36-------Xenoboa
 Midbody scale rows more than 36------------172

162. Hileras de escamas dorsales menos de 27-----163
 Hileras de escamas dorsales 27 o más--Pituophis

163. Ventrales menos de 175---------------Thamnophis
 Ventrales más de 175-------------------Pseustes

164. Dientes maxilares posteriores agrandados pero
 sin surcos---------------------------Leptophis
 Dientes maxilares posteriores no o ligeramente
 agrandados, con surco situado a lateral del
 diente-------------------------------Oxybelis

165. Area detrás del ojo cubierta de muchas escamas
 chicas-------------------------------------166
 Area detrás del ojo cubierta de varias láminas
 grandes-----------------------------------Elaphe

166. Fosetas sensoriales profundas en la mayoría o
 en todas las labiales superiores-----------171
 Sin fosetas sensoriales en labiales---------167

167. Subcaudales de a una-----------------------168
 Subcaudales en pares-----------------Loxocemus

168. Escamas lisas------------------------------169
 Algunas o todas las escamas quilladas----------
 ------------------------------------Trachyboa

169. Dorso de la cabeza con algunas láminas
 agrandadas---------------------------------170
 Dorso de la cabeza cubierto de pequeñas escamas
 sin láminas agrandadas en el hocico--------Boa

170. Sin escudos a posterior de internasales pares y
 prefrontales pares; hileras de escamas más de
 40---------------------------------Epicrates
 Dorso de la cabeza con láminas regulares, incluyendo prefrontal, frontal y parietal
 azygos; hileras de escamas menos de 40-------
 ------------------------------------Ungaliophis

171. Hileras de escamas menos de 36----------Xenoboa
 Hileras de escamas más de 36----------------172

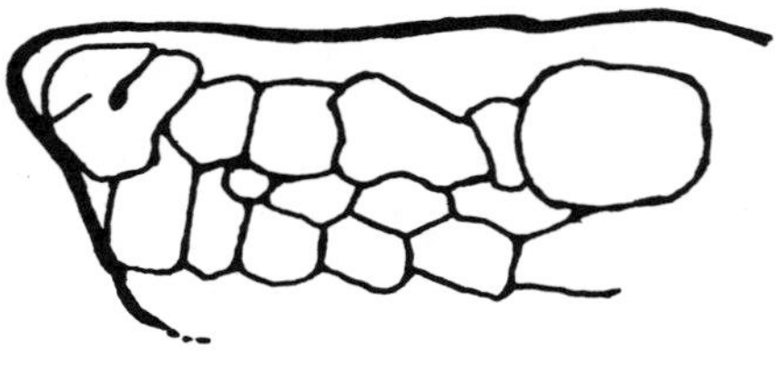

Fig. 12. Corallus, lateral view
of snout

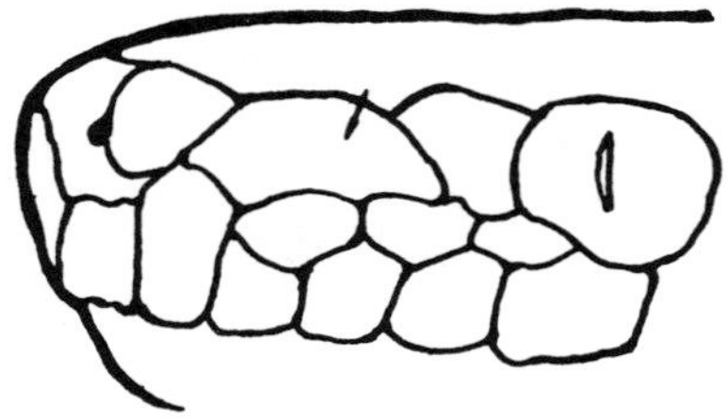

Fig. 13. Epicrates, lateral view
of snout

172. Loreal plate absent (Fig. 12); usually more
 than 50 scale rows at midbody; usually more
 than 65 subcaudals--------------------Corallus
 Loreal plate present (Fig.13); usually fewer
 than 52 scale rows at midbody; usually fewer
 than 66 subcaudals-------------------Epicrates

173. Tail not compressed------------------------174
 Tail compressed, oarlike----------------Pelamis

172. Sin lámina loreal (Fig. 12); usualmente más de
 50 hileras de escamas en el medio cuerpo;
 usualmente más de 65 subcaudales--------------
 ------------------------------------Corallus
 Con lámina loreal (Fig. 13); usualmente menos
 de 52 hileras de escamas en el medio cuerpo;
 usualmente menos de 66 subcaudales------------
 ------------------------------------Epicrates

173. Cola no comprimida--------------------------174
 Cola comprimida, en forma de remo--------------
 ------------------------------------Pelamis

174. Ventrals feebly enlarged but recognizably
distinct from dorsals---------------------175
Ventrals same size as dorsals--------------176

174. Ventrales ligeramente agrandadas pero
reconociblemente distintas de dorsales-----175
Ventrales de igual tamaño que dorsales------176

175. Body pattern of complete rings---------<u>Anilius</u>
No rings encircling body-------------<u>Eunectes</u>

175. Diseño del cuerpo de anillos completos--<u>Anilius</u>
Sin anillos alrededor del cuerpo-------<u>Eunectes</u>

176. Body scale rows 15 or more------------------177
Body scale rows 14----------------<u>Leptotyphlops</u>

176. Hileras de escamas 15 o más------------------177
Hileras de escamas 14------------<u>Leptotyphlops</u>

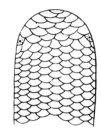
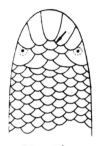
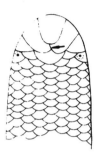

Fig. 14.   Fig. 15.   Fig. 16.   Fig. 17.   Fig. 18.
<u>Anomalepis</u>   <u>Typhlophis</u>   <u>Typhlops</u>   <u>Helminthophis</u>   <u>Liotyphlops</u>

Figs. 14-18. Dorsum of head in genera of worm snakes. Figs. 14-17 from Jan and Sordelli, Icon.
Gén. Ophid., various dates; Fig. 18 from Boulenger, 1893.

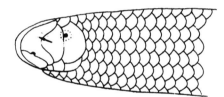

Fig. 19. Lateral view of head in
<u>Typhlops</u>, showing fusion of nasal
and prefrontal, from Jan and Sordelli.

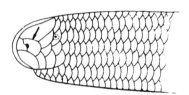

Fig. 20. Lateral view of head in
<u>Helminthophis</u>, with nasal and pre-
frontal distinct, from Jan and
Sordelli.

177. Scales on dorsum of head behind rostral highly
modified, usually similar in appearance to
body scales, although larger---------------178
Pair of polygonal prefrontals in contact on
midline behind rostral, followed by pentagonal
frontal (Fig. 14)------------------<u>Anomalepis</u>

177. Escamas del dorso de la cabeza detrás del
rostral muy modificados, usualmente de aspecto
similar a las del cuerpo, pero más grandes-178
Par de prefrontales poligonales en contacto en
la línea media detrás del rostral, seguidas de
frontal pentagonal (Fig. 14)--------<u>Anomalepis</u>

178. Head with plates larger than scales of body-179
Head covered with small scales indistinguishable from those of body (Fig. 15)----<u>Typhlophis</u>

178. Cabeza con láminas más grandes que las escamas
del cuerpo------------------------------------179
Cabeza cubierta de escamas chicas indiferenciadas de las del cuerpo (Fig. 15)--<u>Typhlophis</u>

179. Prefrontals present above nasals (Fig. 20), in
contact with frontal-----------------------180
Prefrontals absent, fused with nasals (Fig.
19), which contact frontal behind rostral
(Fig. 16)----------------------------<u>Typhlops</u>

179. Con prefrontales encima de nasales (Fig. 20),
en contacto con frontal--------------------180
Sin prefrontales, fusionadas con nasal (Fig.
19), la cual contact con frontal detrás de la
rostral (Fig. 16)--------------------<u>Typhlops</u>

180. Prefrontals in contact behind rostral, separating latter from frontal (Fig. 17)-------------
-------------------------------<u>Helminthophis</u>
Rostral in contact with frontal, preventing
contact between prefrontals on dorsum of head
(Fig. 18)-------------------------<u>Liotyphlops</u>

180. Prefrontales en contacto detrás de rostral,
separando a ésta de la rostral (Fig. 17)------
-------------------------------<u>Helminthophis</u>
Rostral en contacto con prefrontal, impidiendo
el contacto entre prefrontales sur el dorso de
la cabeza (Fig. 18)---------------<u>Liotyphlops</u>

GENERIC KEY

181. Tip of tail without rattle------------------182
     Tip of tail with rattle---------------Crotalus

182. Posterior subcaudals finely divided------------
     -------------------------------------Lachesis
     Posterior subcaudals normal----------------183

183. Dorsum of head posteriorly with large, regular
     plates---------------------------Agkistrodon
     Dorsum of head covered posteriorly by small,
     irregular scales---------------------Bothrops

181. Punta de la cola sin cascabel---------------182
     Punta de la cola con cascabel----------Crotalus

182. Subcaudales posteriores finamente divididas----
     -------------------------------------Lachesis
     Subcaudales posteriores normales------------183

183. Parte dorsal posterior de la cabeza con láminas
     regulares, grandes----------------Agkistrodon
     Parte dorsal posterior de la cabeza cubierta de
     escamas irregulares, chicas-----------Bothrops

ADELPHICOS Jan

1862 _Adelphicos_ Jan, Arch. Zool. Anat. Fis., 2: 18. Type-species: _Adelphicos quadrivirgatum_ Jan.
1866 _Rhegnops_ Cope, Proc. Acad. Nat. Sci. Phila., 1866: 128. Type-species: _Rhegnops visoninus_ Cope.

Distribution: Atlantic slopes from central Honduras through British Honduras (apparently not in
Yucatán) to central Veracruz; on Pacific slopes from central Guatemala to central Oaxaca; interior
valleys of Guatemala and Chiapas.

Content: Two species.

Key to the species

1. Third infralabial nearly as broad as long, subequal in size to second; chinshields not
greatly expanded toward lip (Fig. 1)----------
-------------------------------------_veraepacis_
Third infralabial absent, or greatly reduced in
size and confined to labial border; chinshields greatly expanded toward lip (Figs.
2-3)-----------------------_quadrivirgatus_

Clave de especies

1. Tercera infralabial aproximadamente tan ancha
como larga, de tamaño subigual a la segunda;
escudos mentales no expandidos notablemente
hacia el borde labial (Fig. 1)------_veraepacis_
Tercera infralabial ausente o muy reducida en
tamaño y confinada al borde labial; escudos
mentales muy expandidos hacia el borde labial
(Figs. 2-3)--------------------_quadrivirgatus_

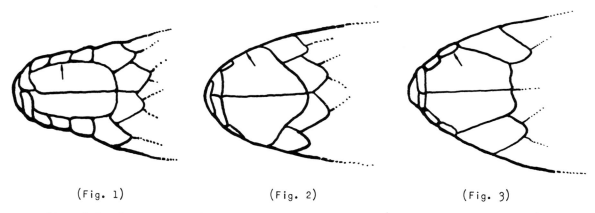

(Fig. 1)   (Fig. 2)   (Fig. 3)

Figs. 1-3. Arrangement of scales on chin of _Adelphicos_ (adapted from Smith, 1942).

ADELPHICOS QUADRIVIRGATUS Jan

1862 _Adelphicos quadrivirgatum_ Jan, Arch. Zool. Anat. Fis., 2: 18, pl. 8. Type-locality: "Mexico".

Distribution: Chiapas, Mexico through British Honduras to Guatemala.

Content: Three subspecies, one (_quadrivirgatus_ Jan) extralimital.

Key to the subspecies

1. Third infralabial absent; chinshields bordering lip (Fig. 2); belly not or slightly
pigmented-------------------------_sargii_
Very narrow third infralabial separates
chinshield from lip (Fig. 3); belly frequently heavily pigmented--------_visoninus_

Clave de subespecies

1. Tercera infralabial ausente; escudos mentales formando el labio (Fig. 2); vientre
sin o con muy poca pigmentación (Fig. 2)--
--------------------------------_sargii_
Una tercera infralabial muy angosta separa
los escudos mentales del labio (Fig. 3);
vientre frecuentement muy pigmentado------
--------------------------------_visoninus_

Adelphicos quadrivirgatus sargii (Fischer)

1885 _Rhegnops sargii_ Fischer, Jahrb. Hamb. Wiss. Anst., 2: 92. Type-locality: Guatemala.
1887 _Adelphicos sargii_—Cope, Bull. U.S. Nat. Mus., 32: 85.
1942 _Adelphicos quadrivirgatus sargii_—Smith, Proc. Rochester Acad. Sci., 8: 192.

Distribution: Foothills on Pacific slopes from southern Chiapas to central Guatemala.

Adelphicos quadrivirgatus visoninus (Cope)

1866 Rhegnops visoninus Cope, Proc. Acad. Nat. Sci. Phila., 1866: 128. Type-locality: Honduras.
1887 Adelphicos visoninus—Cope, Bull. U.S. Nat. Mus., 32: 85.
1942 Adelphicos quadrivirgatus visoninus—Smith, Proc. Rochester Acad. Sci., 8: 186.

Distribution: Foothills on Atlantic slopes from Tabasco, Mexico, south and east to central Honduras.

ADELPHICOS VERAEPACIS Stuart

1941 Adelphicos veraepacis Stuart, Occ. Pap. Mus. Zool. Univ. Mich., 452: 5. Type-locality: Finca Samac, 7 km west of Coban, Alta Verapaz, Guatemala.

Distribution: Alta Verapaz, Guatemala and San Cristobal, Mexico.

Content: Three subspecies, two (latifasciatus Lynch and Smith and nigrilatus Smith) extralimital.

Adelphicos veraepacis veraepacis Stuart

1942 Adelphicos veraepacis veraepacis—Smith, Proc. Rochester Acad. Sci., 8: 180.

Distribution: Intermediate elevations of Alta Verapaz and Sierra de los Cuchumatanes of Guatemala.

REPTILIA: SERPENTES: CROTALIDAE AGKISTRODON

Prepared by Howard K. Gloyd, University of Arizona, Tucson, Arizona

<u>AGKISTRODON</u> Palisot de Beauvois

1799 <u>Agkistrodon</u> Palisot de Beauvois, Trans. Amer. Phil. Soc., 4: 381. Type-species: <u>Agkistrodon</u>
   <u>mokasen</u> Palisot de Beauvois.
1799 <u>Agkishodon</u> Palisot de Beauvois (typographical error), Trans. Amer. Phil. Soc., 4: 370.
1802 <u>Scytale</u> Latreille, in Sonnini and Latreille, Hist. Nat. Rept., 3: 158. Type-species: <u>Boa</u>
   <u>contortrix</u> Linnaeus.
1803 <u>Cenchris</u> Daudin, Hist. Nat. Rept., 5: 356. Type-species: <u>Cenchris</u> <u>mokeson</u> Daudin.
1819 <u>Scytalus</u> Rafinesque (emendation of <u>Scytale</u> Latreille), Amer. Jour. Sci., 1: 84.
1826 <u>Tisiphone</u> Fitzinger, Neue Classification der Reptilien: 34. Type-species: <u>Tisiphone</u> <u>cuprea</u>
   Fitzinger.
1830 <u>Ancistrodon</u> Wagler (emendation of <u>Agkistrodon</u> Palisot de Beauvois), Nat. Syst. Amphib.: 176.
1836 <u>Acontias</u> Troost (preoccupied by <u>Acontias</u> Cuvier, 1829), Ann. Lyc. Nat. Hist. New York, 3: 176.
   Type-species: <u>Acontias</u> <u>leucostoma</u> Troost.
1836 <u>Toxicophis</u> Troost (substitute name for <u>Acontias</u> Troost, 1836), Ann. Lyc. Nat. Hist. New York, 3:
   190.
1843 <u>Hypnale</u> Fitzinger, Systema Reptilium: 28. Type-species: <u>Cophias</u> <u>hypnale</u> Merrem.
1849 <u>Halys</u> Gray, Cat. Sn. Brit. Mus.: 14. Type-species: <u>Trigonocephalus</u> <u>halys</u> Boie.

   Distribution: Central and southern Asia south of 54th Parallel, from Caspian Sea to and including
      Sakhalin, Japan and islands to south, and Taiwan (but not Hainan); south to northern Iran,
      Peninsular India and Ceylon, and Tonkin (North Vietnam). United States from southeastern
      Nebraska and southeastern Iowa southwest to Trans-Pecos Texas and south to Gulf of Mexico near
      Corpus Christi Bay and northern Florida, northeast to Massachusetts; Mexico and Central America,
      from southern Sonora and Nuevo Leon south to Yucatán, Guatemala, and Pacific Coast of Nicaragua.

   Content: Approximately eleven species; about eight in Asia and three in New World, of which all but
      one are extralimital.

<u>AGKISTRODON BILINEATUS</u> (Günther)

1863 <u>Ancistrodon</u> <u>bilineatus</u> Günther, Ann. Mag. Nat. Hist., (3) 12: 364. Type-locality: Pacific coast
   of Guatemala.
1899 <u>Agkistrodon</u> <u>bilineatus</u>—Stejneger, North American Fauna, 14: 71.
1943 <u>Agkistrodon</u> <u>bilineatus</u>—Gloyd and Conant, Bull. Chicago Acad. Sci., 7: 163, figs. 4, 11-12.

   Distribution: Tamaulipas, Mexico on Atlantic slope and southern Sonora on Pacific slope to
      Nicaragua. Records in British Honduras have been questioned by Allen and Neill, Herpetologica,
      15, 1959, 229.

   Content: Two subspecies, one of which (<u>taylori</u> Burger and Robertson) is extralimital.

<u>Agkistrodon bilineatus bilineatus</u> (Günther)

   1951 <u>Agkistrodon</u> <u>bilineatus</u> <u>bilineatus</u>—Burger and Robertson, Univ. Kansas Sci. Bull., 34: 214,
      pl. 25, fig. 3.

      Distribution: Nicaragua, Guatemala, and possibly British Honduras to southern Sonora on
         Pacific slope and to Campeche and Yucatán Peninsula on Atlantic slope of Mexico; Tres Marias
         Islands.

Prepared by Larry David Wilson, University of Southwestern Louisiana, Lafayette, Louisiana

AMASTRIDIUM Cope

  1861 <u>Amastridium</u> Cope, Proc. Acad. Nat. Sci. Phila., 1860: 370. Type-species: <u>Amastridium</u> <u>veliferum</u>
     Cope.
  1898 <u>Fleischmannia</u> Boettger, Katalog der Reptilien-Sammlung im Museum der Senckenbergischen
     Naturforschenden Gesellschaft in Frankfurt am Main, 2: 69. Type-species: <u>Fleischmannia</u>
     <u>obscura</u> Boettger.
  1903 <u>Mimometopon</u> Werner, Abh. Bayer. Akad. Wiss., 22: 349, pl. 1, figs. 3-5. Type-species:
     <u>Mimometopon</u> <u>sapperi</u> Werner.
  1905 <u>Phrydops</u> Boulenger, Ann. Mag. Nat. Hist., (7) 15: 453. Type-species: <u>Phrydops</u> <u>melas</u> Boulenger.

  Distribution: As for single known species.

  Content: One species.

AMASTRIDIUM VELIFERUM Cope

  1861 <u>Amastridium</u> <u>veliferum</u> Cope, Proc. Acad. Nat. Sci. Phila., 1860: 370. Type-locality: Cocuyas de
     Veraguas, N. Grenada, which is Cocuyas, Panama.
  1898 <u>Fleischmannia</u> <u>obscura</u> Boettger, Katalog der Reptilien-Sammlung im Museum der Senckenbergischen
     Naturforschenden Gesellschaft in Frankfurt am Main, 2: 69. Type-locality: San José, Costa
     Rica.
  1903 <u>Mimometopon</u> <u>sapperi</u> Werner, Abh. Bayer. Akad. Wiss., 22: 349, pl. 1, figs. 3-5. Type-locality:
     Guatemala.
  1905 <u>Phrydops</u> <u>melas</u> Boulenger, Ann. Mag. Nat. Hist., (7) 15: 454. Type-locality: Cariblanco, Costa
     Rica.
  1925 <u>Amastridium</u> <u>sapperi</u>—Dunn, Proc. U.S. Nat. Mus., 65: 1.
  1931 <u>Phydrops</u> [sic] <u>melas</u>—Dunn, Copeia, 1931: 163.

  Distribution: Atlantic and Pacific slopes from Nuevo Leon and Chiapas, Mexico, through Guatemala,
    Honduras, Nicaragua, Costa Rica and Panama.

ANILIUS Oken

1811 Tortrix Oppel (preoccupied by Tortrix Denis and Schiffermüller, 1775), Die Ordnungen, Familien, und Gattungen der Reptilien: 55. Type-species: None indicated.
1816 Anilius Oken, Lehrb. Naturgesch., 3: 283. Type-species: Anguis scytale Linnaeus.
1820 Elysia Hemprich (new name for Tortrix Oppel, preoccupied by Elysia Risso, 1818), Grundriss der Naturgeschichte, 1820: 119.
1820 Helison Goldfuss (new name for Tortrix Oppel, 1811), Handbuch der Zoologie, 2: 146.
1823 Ilysia Lichtenstein (emendation of Elysia Hemprich), Verzeichniss der Doubletten des Zoologischen Museums der Königl. Universität zu Berlin: 104.
1825 Torquatrix Haworth (new name for Tortrix Oppel), Phil. Mag., 65: table opposite p. 372.
1833 Illisia Schinz (emendation of Ilysia Lichtenstein), Naturgeschichte und Abbildungen der Reptilien: 131.
1844 Anileus Agassiz (emendation of Anilius Oken), Nomenclatoris Zoologici Index Universalis: 23.

   Distribution: As for single species.

   Content: One species.

ANILIUS SCYTALE (Linnaeus)

1758 Anguis Scytale Linnaeus, Systema Naturae, Ed. 10: 228. Type-locality: "Indiis".
1816 Anilius scytale—Oken, Lehrb. Naturgesch., 3: 283.

   Distribution: Guianas; northern Brazil; Venezuela; Amazonian drainage of Colombia, Ecuador and Peru.

   Content: Two subspecies.

              Key to the subspecies   Clave de subespecies

1. Ventrals fewer than 225; black bands   1. Ventrales menos de 225; bandas transversas
   broader than red---------------phelpsorum   negras más anchas que las rojas-phelpsorum
   Ventrals more than 225; black bands   Ventrales más de 225; bandas transversas
   narrower than red-----------------scytale   negras más angostas que las rojas--scytale

Anilius scytale scytale (Linnaeus)

   1768 Anguis annulata Laurenti, Synopsin Reptilium: 69. Type-locality: None given.
   1768 Anguis fasciata Laurenti, Synopsin Reptilium: 70. Type-locality: None given.
   1768 Anguis caerulea Laurenti, Synopsin Reptilium: 71. Type-locality: Surinam.
   1768 Anguis corallina Laurenti, Synopsin Reptilium: 71. Type-locality: Brazil.
   1768 Anguis atra Laurenti, Synopsin Reptilium: 71. Type-locality: Ceylon.
   1958 A.[nilius] scytale [scytale]—Roze, Acta Biol. Venezuélica, 2: 261.

      Distribution: Amazonian Peru, Ecuador and Colombia; northern Brazil; Guianas; southeastern Venezuela.

Anilius scytale phelpsorum Roze

   1958 Anilius scytale phelpsorum Roze, Acta Biol. Venezuélica, 2: 258. Type-locality: Auyantepui, Estado Bolívar, Venezuela.

      Distribution: Eastern and southern Venezuela.

ANOMALEPIS Jan

1860 Anomalepis Jan, Icon. Gén. Ophid., Livr. 1: pl. 5, fig. 1; pl. 6, fig. 1. Type-species:
Anomalepis mexicanus Jan.
1893 Anomalolepis Günther (substitute name for Anomalepis Jan), Biol. Cent. Amer., Rept.: 87.

Distribution: Mexico through Central America to Peru and Ecuador.

Content: Four species.

Key to the species

1. Head and tip of tail brown--------------------2
Head and tip of tail yellowish white----------
------------------------------------flavapices

2. Dorsal scales at midbody in more than 22 rows;
more than 300 dorsals from head to tip of
tail--3
Dorsal scales at midbody in 22 rows; less than
300 dorsals from head to tip of tail----------
------------------------------------mexicanus

3. Dorsal scales at midbody in 24-26 rows; less
than 350 total dorsals (320-343)-----aspinosus
Dorsal scales in 28 rows at midbody; total
dorsals 365--------------------------colombia

Clave de especies

1. Cabeza y porción terminal de la cola pardos---2
Cabeza y porción terminal de la cola blanco
amarillentos-----------------------flavapices

2. Escamas dorsales en el medio cuerpo más de 22
filas; más de 300 dorsales totales-----------3
Escamas dorsales en el medio cuerpo en 22
filas; menos de 300 dorsales totales---------
------------------------------------mexicanus

3. Escamas dorsales en el medio del cuerpo 24-26
filas; menos de 350 dorsales (320-343)-------
------------------------------------aspinosus
Escamas dorsales en el medio del cuerpo en 28
filas; dorsales totales 365-----------colombia

ANOMALEPIS ASPINOSUS Taylor

1939 Anomalepis aspinosus Taylor, Proc. New England Zool. Club, 17: 92, pl. 5, figs. 5-7. Type-
locality: Perico, Peru.

Distribution: Known only from type locality.

ANOMALEPIS COLOMBIA Marx

1953 Anomalepis colombia Marx, Fieldiana: Zool., 34: 197. Type-locality: La Selva, Pueblo Rico,
Department of Caldas, Colombia.

Distribution: Known only from type locality.

ANOMALEPIS FLAVAPICES Peters

1957 Anomalepis flavapices Peters, Amer. Mus. Novitates, 1851: 3. Type-locality: Esmeraldas,
Esmeraldas Province, Ecuador.

Distribution: Lowlands of northwestern Ecuador.

ANOMALEPIS MEXICANUS Jan

1861 Anomalepis mexicanus Jan, Icon. Gén. Ophid., Livr. 1: pl. 5, fig. 1, pl. 6, fig. 1. Type-
locality: Mexico.
1939 Anomalepis dentatus Taylor, Proc. New England Zool. Club, 17: 90, pl. 5, figs. 1-3. Type-locality:
Barro Colorado, Canal Zone, Panama.

Distribution: Known only from Mexico and Panama.

APOSTOLEPIS Cope

1862 *Apostolepis* Cope, Proc. Acad. Nat. Sci. Phila., 1861: 524. Type-species: *Elapomorphus flavo-*
    torquatus Duméril, Bibron and Duméril.
1869 *Rhynchonyx* Peters, Monats. Akad. Wiss. Berlin, 1869: 437. Type-species: *Rhynchonyx ambiniger*
    Peters.

Distribution: Guyana and eastern Peru south to Argentinian, Paraguayan and Bolivian Chaco.

Content: Fourteen species.

Key to the species

1. Nasal in contact with preocular----------------2
   Nasal not in contact with preocular----------4

2. One postocular-------------------------------3
   Two postoculars---------------------*coronata*

3. Less than 35 subcaudals; four or five labials
   in contact with anterior pair of chinshields--
   --12
   More than 45 subcaudals; four labials in contact with anterior pair of chinshields-------
   ------------------------------*longicaudata*

4. Six supralabials-----------------------------5
   Five supralabials--------------------*goiasensis*

5. Fifth upper labial only in contact with parie-
   tal---6
   Fifth and sixth upper labials in contact with
   parietal-----------------------------------8

6. Dorsal pattern other than five stripes--------7
   Dorsal pattern with five stripes-------*rondoni*

7. Four lower labials in contact with anterior
   chinshields-------------------------*cearensis*
   Five lower labials in contact with anterior
   chinshields-------------------------*assimilis*

8. No stripes dorsally--------------------------9
   Dorsum striped-----------------------------10

9. Without double row of ventral spots---------11
   With double row of ventral spots----*erythronota*

10. Five lower labials in contact with anterior
    chinshields-------------------------*ambiniger*
    Four lower labials in contact with anterior
    chinshields-------------------------*dorbignyi*

11. Three or four lower labials in contact with
    anterior chinshields----------------*intermedia*
    Five lower labials in contact with anterior
    chinshields--------------------*nigroterminata*

12. More than 230 ventrals---------------------13
    Less than 230 ventrals----------*quinquelineata*

13. Body striped; no black-bordered collar---------
    ------------------------------------*niceforoi*
    Body not striped; black-bordered red collar
    present------------------------*flavotorquata*

Clave de especies

1. Nasal contacta con la preocular---------------2
   Nasal no contacta con la preocular------------4

2. Con una postocular--------------------------3
   Con dos postoculares------------------*coronata*

3. Menos de 35 escamas caudales; cuatro o cinco
   labiales en contacto con el par anterior de
   geneiales-----------------------------------12
   Más de 45 escamas caudales; cuatro labiales en
   contacto con el par anterior de geneiales-----
   ------------------------------*longicaudata*

4. Con seis supralabiales-----------------------5
   Con cinco supralabiales-------------*goiasensis*

5. Unicamente la quinta supralabial contacta con
   la parietal----------------------------------6
   Quinta y sexta supralabial en contacto con la
   parietal-----------------------------------8

6. Sin diseño dorsal con cinco líneas longitudi-
   nales--7
   Diseño dorsal con cinco líneas longitudinales--
   ------------------------------------*rondoni*

7. Cuatro labiales inferiores en contacto con
   geneiales anteriores----------------*cearensis*
   Cinco labiales inferiores en contacto con
   geneiales anteriores----------------*assimilis*

8. Diseño dorsal no lineado---------------------9
   Diseño dorsal lineado------------------------10

9. Sin doble hilera de manchas ventrales--------11
   Con doble hilera de manchas-------------------
   ------------------------------------*erythronota*

10. Cinco labiales inferiores en contacto con
    geneiales anteriores----------------*ambiniger*
    Cuatro labiales inferiores en contacto con
    geneiales anteriores----------------*dorbignyi*

11. Tres o cuatro labiales inferiores en contacto
    con geneiales anteriores-----------*intermedia*
    Cinco labiales inferiores en contacto con
    geneiales anteriores-----------*nigroterminata*

12. Más de 230 ventrales-----------------------13
    Menos de 230 ventrales----------*quinquelineata*

13. Diseño dorsal lineado; sin collar bordeado de
    negro------------------------------*niceforoi*
    Diseño dorsal no lineado; con collar rojo bor-
    deado de negro-----------------*flavotorquata*

APOSTOLEPIS <u>AMBINIGER</u> (Peters)

    1869 <u>Rhynchonyx ambiniger</u> Peters, Monats. Akad. Wiss. Berlin, 1869: 438, fig. 2. Type-locality:
        Paraguay.
    1887 <u>Rhynchonyx ambiniger vittatus</u> Cope, Proc. Amer. Phil. Soc., 24: 56. Type-locality: Mato
        Grosso, Brazil.
    1896 <u>Apostolepis ambinigra</u>—Boulenger (unjustified emendation), Cat. Sn. Brit. Mus., 3: 237.
    1927 <u>Apostolepis tenuis</u> Ruthven, Occ. Pap. Mus. Zool. Univ. Mich., 188: 1. Type-locality: Buena
        Vista, Santa Cruz, Bolivia.

    Distribution: Western Brazil, Bolivia and Paraguay.

APOSTOLEPIS <u>ASSIMILIS</u> (Reinhardt)

    1861 <u>Elapomorphus assimilis</u> Reinhardt, Vid. Meddel. Naturh. For. Kjöbenhavn, 1860: 235, pl. 4, figs.
        1-5. Type-locality: Minas Gerais, Brazil.
    1896 <u>Apostolepis assimilis</u>—Boulenger, Cat. Sn. Brit. Mus., 3: 234.

    Distribution: Central and southwestern Brazil, Argentinian Chaco.

APOSTOLEPIS <u>CEARENSIS</u> Gomes

    1915 <u>Apostolepis cearensis</u> Gomes, Ann. Paulistas Med. Cirurg., 4: 122, pl. 3, figs. 4-8. Type-
        locality: Ceará, Brazil.
    1925 <u>Apostolepis amarali</u> Werner, Sitz. Akad. Wiss. Wien, 134: 62. Type-locality: unknown.

    Distribution: Northeastern Brazil.

APOSTOLEPIS <u>CORONATA</u> (Sauvage)

    1877 <u>Elapomorphus (Elapomorphus) coronatus</u> Sauvage, Bull. Soc. Philom.,(7) 1: 110. Type-locality:
        South America.
    1896 <u>Apostolepis coronata</u>—Boulenger, Cat. Sn. Brit. Mus., 3: 233.
    1903 <u>Apostolepis Pymi</u> Boulenger, Ann. Mag. Nat. Hist.,(7) 12: 353. Type-locality: Brazil.

    Distribution: Known only from Teresópolis, Estado de Rio de Janeiro, Brazil.

APOSTOLEPIS <u>DORBIGNYI</u> (Schlegel)

    1837 <u>Calamaria d'Orbignyi</u> Schlegel, Essai Physion. Serpens, 2: 30. Type-locality: Chile.
    1896 <u>Apostolepis dorbignyi</u>—Boulenger, Cat. Sn. Brit. Mus., 3: 236.

    Distribution: Southwestern Brazil, Paraguay and Bolivia.

APOSTOLEPIS <u>ERYTHRONOTA</u> (Peters)

    1880 <u>Elapomorphus erythronotus</u> Peters, Monats. Akad. Wiss. Berlin, 1880: 222. Type-locality: São
        Paulo, Brazil.
    1887 <u>Apostolepis erythronotus lineatus</u> Cope, Proc. Amer. Philos. Soc., 24: 56. Type-locality: Mato
        Grosso, Brazil.
    1897 <u>Apostolepis nigriceps</u> Werner, Sitz. Akad. Wiss. München, 1897: 207. Type-locality: São Paulo,
        Brazil.

    Distribution: Central and southwestern Brazil, northern Argentina and Paraguay.

APOSTOLEPIS <u>FLAVOTORQUATA</u> (Duméril, Bibron and Duméril)

    1854 <u>Elapomorphus flavo-torquatus</u> Duméril, Bibron and Duméril, Erp. Gén., 8: 836. Type-locality:
        "Amérique Méridional".
    1862 <u>Apostolepis flavotorquata</u>—Cope, Proc. Acad. Nat. Sci. Phila., 1861: 524.
    1869 <u>Elapomorphus nigrolineatus</u> Peters, Monats. Akad. Wiss. Berlin, 1869: 439. Type-locality: Given
        as "Guinea", but assumed by Peters to be South America.
    1924 <u>Apostolepis sanctae-ritae</u> Werner, Sitz. Akad. Wiss. Wien, 133: 43. Type-locality: Santa Rita,
        Brazil. (Probably Santa Rita do Araguaia, Estado de Goiás).

    Distribution: Central Brazil.

APOSTOLEPIS GOIASENSIS Prado

  1942 Apostolepis goiasensis Prado, Mem. Inst. Butantan, 16: 7, pl. 1. Type-locality: Rio Verde,
      Goiás, Brazil.

  Distribution: Estado de Goiás, Brazil.

APOSTOLEPIS INTERMEDIA Koslowsky

  1898 Apostolepis intermedia Koslowsky, Rev. Mus. La Plata, 8: 30, pl. 1, figs. 4-7. Type-locality:
      Mato Grosso, Brazil.

  Distribution: Estado de Mato Grosso, Brazil.

APOSTOLEPIS LONGICAUDATA Gomes

  1921 Apostolepis longicaudata Gomes, in Amaral, Ann. Paulistas Med. Cirurg., 9 (7-8): 3, pl. A,
      figs. 4-7. Type-locality: Municipio de Santa Philomena, Estado de Piauhy, Brazil.

  Distribution: Known only from type locality.

APOSTOLEPIS NICEFOROI Amaral

  1935 Apostolepis niceforoi Amaral, Mem. Inst. Butantan, 9: 221, fig. 5. Type-locality: La
      Pedrera, Bajo Caquetá, Amazonas, Brazil.

  Distribution: Known only from type-locality.

APOSTOLEPIS NIGROTERMINATA Boulenger

  1896 Apostolepis nigroterminata Boulenger, Cat. Sn. Brit. Mus., 3: 235, pl. 10, fig. 2.
      Type-locality: Cayaria, Northeastern Peru.
  1904 Apostolepis borellii Peracca, Bol. Mus. Zool. Anat. Comp. Univ. Torino, 19 (460): 9. Type-
      locality: Urucum (probably Mato Grosso, Brazil).

  Distribution: Eastern Peru, western Brazil.

APOSTOLEPIS QUINQUELINEATA Boulenger

  1896 Apostolepis quinquelineata Boulenger, Cat. Sn. Brit. Mus., 3: 235, pl. 10, fig. 1. Type-
      locality: Demerara, Guyana.

  Distribution: Guyana.

APOSTOLEPIS RONDONI Amaral

  1925 Apostolepis Rondoni Amaral, Comm. L.T.E. Matto-Grosso-Amazonas, 84: 25, figs. 4-6. Type-
      locality: Mato Grosso, Brazil.

  Distribution: Known only from the type locality.

ATRACTUS Wagler

1828 *Atractus* Wagler, Isis von Oken, 21: 741. Type-species: *Atractus trilineatus* Wagler.
1843 *Urobrachys* Fitzinger, Systema Reptilium: 24. Type-species: *Brachyorrhos flammigerus* Boie.
1858 *Isoscelis* Günther, Cat. Sn. Brit. Mus.: 204. Type-species: *Isoscelis maculata* Günther.
1910 *Atractopsis* Despax, Bull. Mus. Hist. Nat. Paris, 16: 372. Type-species: *Atractus* (*Atractopsis*) *paucidens* Despax.

Distribution: Panama; South America as far south as Amazonian Bolivia and southern Brazil, east of Andes and northwestern Ecuador west of Andes; slopes and highlands of Andes in Colombia, Ecuador and Peru.

Content: Approximately 70 species.

Comment: *Atractus subbicinctum* Jan is omitted from the data matrix below, because there was insufficient information in the original description.

Matrix for Identification of Species   Matriz para identificación de especies

	SEX[1]	R/P	I/P	No L.L.	L PN	UPPER LABIALS	DORSAL ROWS	MAXILLARY TEETH	VENTRALS	CAUDALS	PATTERN[1]	NUMBER OF POSTOCULARS
ANDINUS	2	0	0	3	1	7	17	---	174	37	1	2
ARANGOI	2	0	0	3	1	7	17	---	159	---	1	2
BADIUS	0	0	3	3	1	7	17	---	143-160	20-47	1	2
BALZANI	0	0	0	3	1	6	17	---	159	32	4	1
BISERIATUS	1	0	0	3	1	7	15	---	148	18	1	2
BOCKI	0	0	0	3	1	6	17	---	164	50	1	2
BOCOURTI	0	0	0	3	1	7	17	---	175-191	25-39	1	2
BOETTGERI	0	0	0	3	1	6	15	---	177	20	4	2
BOULENGERII	1	0	0	3	1	7	17	---	189	44	1	2
CARRIONI	1	3	3	1	4	6	15	8-9	145-149	29-34	4	1
CARRIONI	2	3	3	1	4	6	15	8-9	152-159	21-27	4	1
CLARKI	2	0	0	3	1	7	17	---	185	33	4	2
COLLARIS	1	3	3	3	1	7-8	17	5-5	163	31	2	2
COLLARIS	2	3	3	3	1	7-8	17	5-5	175	21	2	2

[1]Significance of values:

Sex
0 = Unknown
1 = Male
2 = Female
3 = Juvenile

Pattern
1 = Spotted or incompletely banded
2 = Longitudinal lines
3 = Completely ringed
4 = Unicolor
0 = Unknown
X = Combinations of above

Abbreviations*
R/P = Rostral larger than prefrontals.
I/P = Width of internasals larger than half length of prefrontal suture.
No L. = No loreal.
L/PN = Loreal larger than postnasal.

[1]Significado de valores:

Sexo
0 = Desconocido
1 = Macho
2 = Hembra
3 = Juvenil

Diseño
1 = Con manchas o bandas incompletas
2 = Líneas longitudinales
3 = Con anillos completos
4 = Unicolor
0 = Desconocido
X = Combinaciones de los otros

Abreviaturas*
R/P = Rostral más grande que prefrontales.
I/P = Ancho de internasales mayor que la mitad de la longitud de la sutura prefrontal.
No L. = Loreal ausente.
L/PN = Loreal más grande que postnasal.

*(See Savage, Misc. Publ. Mus. Zool. Univ. Mich., 112, 1960, 16, for discussion of these characters in *Atractus*).

	SEX	R/P	I/P	No L.	L/PN	UPPER LABIALS	DORSAL ROWS	MAXILLARY TEETH	VENTRALS	CAUDALS	PATTERN	NUMBER OF POSTOCULARS
		0=Unknown 1=True 2=Variable 3=False 4=Inapplic.				ACTUAL COUNTS						
CRASSICAUDATUS	0	0	3	3	1	6-7	17	---	139-161	16-29	1	2
DUIDENSIS	1	0	3	3	1	7	17	8-8	156	35	4	2
DUIDENSIS	2	0	3	3	1	7	17	8-9	173	35	4	2
DUNNI	2	3	3	3	1	7	17	---	144	20	2	2
ECUADORENSIS	1	3	3	3	1	7	17	8-8	144	41	2	2
ELAPS	1	1	1	3	3	6	15	6-8	135-154	28-37	3	1-2
ELAPS	2	1	1	3	3	6	15	6-8	141-161	16-24	3	1-2
EMMELI	0	0	3	3	1	7	15	---	167-170	28-30	4	2
EMMELI	2	0	0	3	1	7	17	---	188	22	4	2
ERYTHROMELAS	0	0	3	3	1	7	15	---	159-181	23-34	1	2
FULIGINOSUS	0	0	3	3	1	6-7	17	9-9	157-161	26-29	4	2
GAIGEAE	1	3	3	3	1	7	17	5-6	187-198	35-39	2	2
GAIGEAE	2	3	3	3	1	7	17	5-6	207-213	25-27	2	2
GUENTHERI	0	0	3	3	1	7-8	17	---	143-161	18-33	4	2
INDISTINCTUS	2	0	0	3	1	---	17	---	170	35	4	2
INSIPIDUS	1	0	3	3	1	7	15	7-7	154	36	1	2
IRIDESCENS	1	0	3	3	1	7	17	---	135	40	1	2
LANCINII	2	0	3	3	1	8	17	9-9	174	27	1	2
LASALLEI	1	0	3	3	1	6-7	17	---	161-166	22-24	4	2-3
LATIFRONS	0	1	1	3	3	6	17	---	142-150	35-42	3	1
LEHMANNI	1	3	3	3	1	7	17	8-8	141-144	25-28	4	2
LEHMANNI	2	3	3	3	1	7	17	8-8	148-153	20-21	4	2
LIMITANEUS	1	0	0	3	3	6	17	---	146	30	2	2
LOVERIDGEI	1	0	0	3	1	7	17	---	149-165	21-30	2	2
LOVERIDGEI	2	0	0	3	1	7	17	---	161-174	14-22	2	2
MACULATUS	0	0	3	3	1	7	17	---	148-159	21-26	1	2
MAJOR	1	3	3	3	1	7-8	17	5-7	148-172	31-49	1	1-2
MAJOR	2	3	3	3	1	7-8	17	5-7	157-181	27-37	1	1-2
MANIZALESENSIS	1	0	0	3	1	7	15	---	152	20	1	2
MANIZALESENSIS	2	0	0	3	1	7	15	---	154	18	1	2
MELANOGASTER	2	0	0	0	0	8	17	---	174	18	1	X
MELAS	1	0	0	3	1	7	17	---	157	24	4	2
MELAS	2	0	0	3	1	7	17	---	146	25	4	2
MICHELI	1	0	0	3	1	7	17	---	146	46	1	2
MICRORHYNCHUS	0	0	0	3	1	7	17	---	---	--	0	1-2
MODESTUS	1	3	3	3	3	6	17	9-9	173	38	4	2
MULTICINCTUS	1	3	3	3	1	7	17	5-6	168-183	40-43	1	2
MULTICINCTUS	2	3	3	3	1	7	17	5-6	177-184	31-36	1	2
NICEFORI	1	0	0	3	1	7	15	---	146-155	22	4	2
NICEFORI	2	0	0	3	1	7	15	---	152	20	4	2
NIGRICAUDUS	2	0	3	3	1	7	17	---	157-158	17-19	2	2

368-492 O—70——3

0=Unknown
1=True
2=Variable
3=False
4=Inapplic.

	SEX	R/P	I/P	No L.	L/PN	UPPER LABIALS	DORSAL ROWS	MAXILLARY TEETH	VENTRALS	CAUDALS	PATTERN	NUMBER OF POSTOCULARS
						ACTUAL COUNTS						
NIGRIVENTRIS	2	0	0	3	1	7	17	---	175	26	4	2
OBESUS	2	3	3	3	1	7	17	---	171-183	26-30	3	2
OBTUSIROSTRIS	1	0	0	0	0	7-8	17	---	149-160	33-42	1	X
OBTUSIROSTRIS	2	0	0	0	0	7-8	17	---	155-167	17-33	1	X
OCCIDENTALIS	1	3	3	3	1	7	17	6-7	153	39	2	2-3
OCCIDENTALIS	2	3	3	3	1	7	17	6-7	162	26-27	2	2-3
OCCIPITOALBUS	1	3	3	3	1	7-8	15	7-8	137-153	21-32	4	1-2
OCCIPITOALBUS	2	3	3	3	1	7-8	15	7-8	150-171	9-19	4	1-2
OCULOTEMPORALIS	1	0	0	3	1	7	15	---	142-147	27-31	1	0
OCULOTEMPORALIS	2	0	0	3	1	7	15	---	145-152	23-28	1	0
PAMPLONENSIS	1	0	0	3	1	7	17	---	174-183	28-30	1	1-2
PAMPLONENSIS	2	0	0	3	1	7	17	---	172-184	23-24	1	1-2
PAUCIDENS	2	3	3	3	1	6-7	17	5-6	169-186	31-37	4	2
PAUCISCUTATUS	2	0	3	3	1	6-7	17	---	146	18	2	2
PERUVIANUS	0	0	0	3	1	6	17	---	140	31	1	2
PUNCTIVENTRIS	1	0	0	3	1	7	15	---	157-158	28-33	1	2
RESPLENDENS	1	3	3	3	1	7-9	17	7-7	157-174	25-31	4	0-2
RESPLENDENS	2	3	3	3	1	7-9	17	7-7	170-185	14-19	4	0-2
RETICULATUS	0	0	3	3	1	7	15	---	156-166	24-26	4	2
RIVEROI	1	0	3	3	0	8	17	7-7	153	37-41	1	2
ROULEI	1	3	3	3	1	6	15	10-11	140-145	20-26	4	1
ROULEI	2	3	3	3	1	6	15	10-11	145-149	14-23	4	1
SANCTAEMARTAE	1	0	0	3	1	7	17	---	152-159	33-36	1	1-3
SANCTAEMARTAE	2	0	0	3	1	7	17	---	148-171	22-28	1	1-3
SANGUINEUS	1	0	0	3	1	7	17	---	179	43	1	2
SERRANUS	0	0	0	3	1	7	17	8-8	171	21	4	2
STEYERMARKI	0	0	0	3	1	7	17	6-6	160-177	30-37	4	2
TAENIATUS	1	0	0	3	1	6	15	8-8	152	24	2	2
TORQUATUS	0	0	3	3	1	8	17	---	140-165	35-47	1	1
TRILINEATUS	0	0	3	3	1	7-8	15	---	125-150	11-19	2	2
TRIVITTATUS	1	0	0	3	1	8	17	---	176	33	1	2
UNIVITTATUS	0	0	3	3	1	6-7	17	---	151-158	33	2	2
VARIEGATUS	1	0	0	3	1	6	17	---	157	27	1	2
VENTRIMACULATUS	1	0	0	3	1	8	15	---	145-157	19-20	X	2
VENTRIMACULATUS	2	0	0	3	1	8	15	---	158-159	14-15	X	2
VERTEBRALIS	1	0	0	3	1	7-8	17	---	170	32	1	2
VERTEBRALIS	2	0	0	3	1	7-8	17	---	173-175	21-24	1	2
VERTEBROLINEATUS	1	0	0	3	1	7	17	---	159	46	2	2
WAGLERI	2	0	0	3	1	7	17	---	174	43	1	2
WERNERI	0	0	0	3	1	7	17	---	161	18	2	1
WERNERI	1	0	0	3	1	7	17	---	144-153	27-29	2	2

ATRACTUS ANDINUS Prado

1944 Atractus andinus Prado, Ciencia (Mexico), 5: 111, fig. 1. Type-locality: Andes, Antioquia, Colombia.
1945 Atractus andinus—Prado, Mem. Inst. Butantan, 18 (1944-45): 109, fig.

Distribution: Known only from type locality.

ATRACTUS ARANGOI Prado

1939 Atractus arangoi Prado, Mem. Inst. Butantan, 13: 15, fig. 1. Type-locality: Colombia.

Distribution: Known only from Puerto Asís, Putumayo, Colombia.

ATRACTUS BADIUS (Boie)

1827 Brachyorrhos badius Boie, Isis von Oken, 20: 540. Type-locality: Java?
1827 Brachyorrhos flammigerus Boie, Isis von Oken, 20: 540. Type-locality: Java?
1837 Calamaria badius Schlegel, Essai Physiog. Serpens, 2: 35. Type-locality: French Guiana.
?1862 Rabdosoma badium var. Rubinianum Jan, Arch. Zool. Anat. Fis., 2: 14. Type-locality: Venezuela.
?1862 R. abdosoma dubium Jan, Arch. Zool. Anat. Fis., 2: 18. Type-locality: Bogotá, Colombia.
1894 Atractus badius—Boulenger, Cat. Sn. Brit. Mus., 2: 308.

Distribution: Northern South America east of Andes and south to northern Argentina.

ATRACTUS BALZANI Boulenger

1898 Atractus balzani Boulenger, Ann. Mus. Civ. Storia Nat. Genova, (2) 19: 129. Type-locality: Missiones Mosetenes, northwest Bolivia.

Distribution: Known only from type locality.

ATRACTUS BISERIATUS Prado

1941 Atractus biseriatus Prado, Mem. Inst. Butantan, 14 (1940): 26, fig. Type-locality: Manizales, Departamento de Caldas, Colombia; Villamaria, Departamento de Caldas, according to E. R. Dunn, in Savage, Misc. Publ. Mus. Zool. Univ. Mich., 112, 1960, 80.

Distribution: Known only from type locality.

ATRACTUS BOCKI Werner

1909 Atractus bocki Werner, Mitt. Naturhist. Mus. Hamburg, 26: 228, fig. 5. Type-locality: Cochabamba, Departamento de Cochabamba, Bolivia.

Distribution: Known only from type locality.

Comment: Amaral, Mem. Inst. Butantan, 4, 1929, 26, indicated that this was a synonym of A. modestus Boulenger, which is known only from western Ecuador.

ATRACTUS BOCOURTI Boulenger

1894 Atractus bocourti Boulenger, Cat. Sn. Brit. Mus., 2: 306. Type-locality: Acomayo, Departamento de Huanuco, Peru.

Distribution: Northern Peru; Ecuador.

ATRACTUS BOETTGERI Boulenger

1896 Atractus boettgeri Boulenger, Cat. Sn. Brit. Mus., 3: 645. Type-locality: Yungas, Sierra de las Yungas, Departamento de Cochabamba, Bolivia.

Distribution: Known only from type locality.

ATRACTUS BOULENGERII Peracca

    1896 Atractus Boulengerii Peracca, Bol. Mus. Zool. Anat. Comp. Univ. Torino, 11 (252): 1, fig. Type-locality: South America.

      Distribution: Unknown.

ATRACTUS CARRIONI Parker

    1930 Atractus carrioni Parker, Ann. Mag. Nat. Hist., (10) 5: 208, figs. Type-locality: Loja, Ecuador, 2200 m.
    1960 Atractus carrioni—Savage, Misc. Publ. Mus. Zool. Univ. Mich., 112: 32.

      Distribution: Intermontane valley of Loja, Ecuador.

ATRACTUS CLARKI Dunn and Bailey

    1939 Atractus clarki Dunn and Bailey, Bull. Mus. Comp. Zool., 86: 8. Type-locality: Mine at Santa Cruz de Cana, Provincia de Darién, Panama.

      Distribution: Known only from type locality.

ATRACTUS COLLARIS Peracca

    1897 Atractus collaris Peracca, Bol. Mus. Zool. Anat. Comp. Univ. Torino, 12 (284): 4. Type-locality: Río Cononaco, Provincia Pastaza, Ecuador.
    1960 Atractus collaris—Savage, Misc. Publ. Mus. Zool. Univ. Mich., 112: 34.

      Distribution: Amazonian Ecuador and northeastern Peru, 300-600 ft.

ATRACTUS CRASSICAUDATUS (Duméril, Bibron and Duméril)

    1854 Rabdosoma crassicaudatum Duméril, Bibron and Duméril, Erp. Gén., 7: 103. Type-locality: Bogotá, Departamento de Cundinamarca, Colombia.
    1894 Atractus crassicaudatus—Boulenger, Cat. Sn. Brit. Mus., 2: 310.
    1914 Atractus Fuhrmanni Peracca, Mem. Soc. Neuchatel Sci. Nat., 5: 100. Type-locality: Bogotá, Departamento de Cundinamarca, Colombia.

      Distribution: Highlands of Colombia.

ATRACTUS DUIDENSIS Roze

    1961 Atractus duidensis Roze, Acta Biol. Venezuelica, 3: 110. Type-locality: Cumbre del Cerro Duida, Territorio Federal Amazonas, Venezuela, 2050 m.

      Distribution: Region of Cerro Duida, Venezuela.

ATRACTUS DUNNI Savage

    1883 Rabdosoma maculatum Bocourt (preoccupied by maculata Günther, 1858), Miss. Sci. Mex., Rept., 3: 539, pl. 34, figs. 2-2e; pl. 35, fig. 1. Type-locality: Ecuador.
    1955 Atractus dunni Savage (substitute name for Rabdosoma maculatum Bocourt), Proc. Biol. Soc. Washington, 68: 14.

      Distribution: Peru and Ecuador.

ATRACTUS ECUADORENSIS Savage

    1955 Atractus ecuadorensis Savage, Proc. Biol. Soc. Washington, 68: 15. Type-locality: "Llangate area"; probably Llanganate Range, Provincia Tunguruhua, Ecuador.

      Distribution: Known only from type locality.

ATRACTUS ELAPS (Günther)

1858 Rhabdosoma elaps Günther, Cat. Sn. Brit. Mus.: 241. Type-locality: Guayaquil, Ecuador (probably
       in error).
1862 R.[abdosoma] brevifrenum Jan, Arch. Zool. Anat. Fis., 2: 12. Type-locality: Brazil.
1862 R.[abdosoma] Pöppigi Jan, Arch. Zool. Anat. Fis., 2: 11. Type-locality: Brazil.
1931 Atractus elaps tetrazonus Amaral, Bull. Antivenin Inst. Amer., 4: 87. Type-locality: Guaicaramo,
       east of Bogotá, Colombia.
1943 Geophis diplozeugus Schmidt and Walker, Zool. Ser. Chicago Nat. Hist. Mus., 24: 286. Type-
       locality: Departamento de Madre de Dios, Peru.
1960 Atractus elaps—Savage, Misc. Publ. Mus. Zool. Univ. Mich., 112: 39.

   Distribution: Oriente and interandean highlands of Ecuador, northern Peru, eastern Colombia, and
       Amazonas, Brazil.

ATRACTUS EMMELI (Boettger)

1888 Geophis Emmeli Boettger, Ber. Senckenberg Naturforsch. Ges., 1888: 192, figs. Type-locality:
       Río Mapiri, Departamento de La Paz, Bolivia.
1894 Atractus emmeli—Boulenger, Cat. Sn. Brit. Mus., 2: 311.

   Distribution: Bolivia and Peru.

ATRACTUS ERYTHROMELAS Boulenger

1903 Atractus erythromelas Boulenger, Ann. Mag. Nat. Hist., (7) 11: 483. Type-locality: Mérida,
       Estado de Mérida, Venezuela, 1600 m.
1966 Atractus erythromelas—Roze, Ofidios de Venezuela: 80.

   Distribution: Andes of Mérida, Venezuela, above 1000 m.

ATRACTUS FULIGINOSUS (Hallowell)

1845 Coluber fuliginosus Hallowell, Proc. Acad. Nat. Sci. Phila., 1845: 243. Type-locality: Given as
       "within 200 miles of Caracas", in Colombia; indicated as Venezuela by Roze (below).
1958 Atractus fuliginosus—Roze, Notulae Naturae, 309: 3.
1966 Atractus fuliginosus—Roze, Ofidios de Venezuela: 81.

   Distribution: Northern Venezuela.

ATRACTUS GAIGEAE Savage

1955 Atractus gaigeae Savage, Proc. Biol. Soc. Washington, 68: 12. Type-locality: Santiago-Zaruma or
       Morona-Chinchipe Provinces, Ecuador.

   Distribution: Amazonian lowlands of Ecuador.

ATRACTUS GUENTHERI (Wucherer)

1861 Geophis Güntheri Wucherer, Proc. Zool. Soc. London, 1861: 115, pl. 19, fig. 1. Type-locality:
       Cañavieras, south of Bahia (São Salvador), Estado do Bahia, Brazil.
1894 Atractus guentheri—Boulenger, Cat. Sn. Brit. Mus., 2: 305.

   Distribution: Amazonian Colombia and Brazil.

ATRACTUS INDISTINCTUS Prado

1940 Atractus indistinctus Prado, Mem. Inst. Butantan, 13 (1939): 16, fig. 2. Type-locality: Ocaña,
       Departamento de Norte de Santander, Colombia.

   Distribution: Known only from type locality.

A RACTUS INSIPIDUS Roze

> 1961 Atractus insipidus Roze, Acta Biol. Venezuelica, 3: 106. Type-locality: Poste M-1, cerca de Río Uraricapará, Venezuela-Brazil border, 400 m.

> Distribution: Venezuela-Brazil border.

ATRACTUS IRIDESCENS Peracca

> 1896 Atractus iridescens Peracca, Bol. Mus. Zool. Anat. Comp. Univ. Torino, 11 (252): 2, fig. Type-locality: South America.

> Distribution: Unknown.

ATRACTUS LANCINII Roze

> 1961 Atractus lancinii Roze, Acta Biol. Venezuelica, 3: 112. Type-locality: El Junquito, Distrito Federal, Venezuela, 1900 m.

> Distribution: Known only from type locality.

ATRACTUS LASALLEI Amaral

> 1931 Atractus lasallei Amaral, Bull. Antivenin Inst. Amer., 4: 87. Type-locality: San Pedro, north of Medellín, Departamento de Antioquia, Colombia.

> Distribution: Highlands of northern Colombia.

ATRACTUS LATIFRONS (Günther)

> 1868 Geophis latifrons Günther, Ann. Mag. Nat. Hist., (4) 1: 415, pl. 19, fig. B. Type-locality: Pébas, Departamento de Loreto, Peru.
> 1896 Atractus latifrons—Boulenger, Cat. Sn. Brit. Mus., 2: 303.
> 1927 Elaps herthae Ahl, Zool. Anz., 70: 252. Type-locality: Mundurucú, Rio Manacapurú, Estado do Amazonas, Brazil.

> Distribution: Western Brazil; eastern Peru; eastern Colombia.

ATRACTUS LEHMANNI Boettger

> 1898 Atractus lehmanni Boettger, Katal. Rept. Mus. Senckenberg, 2: 80. Type-locality: Cuenca, Provincia Azuay, Ecuador.
> 1960 Atractus lehmanni—Savage, Misc. Publ. Mus. Zool. Univ. Mich., 112: 45.

> Distribution: Known only from type locality.

ATRACTUS LIMITANEUS (Amaral)

> 1935 Leptocalamus limitaneus Amaral, Mem. Inst. Butantan, 9: 219, figs. 1-3. Type-locality: La Pedrera, Río Caquetá, Comisaria de Amazonas, Colombia.
> 1960 [Atractus] limitaneus—Savage, Misc. Publ. Mus. Zool. Univ. Mich., 112: 81.

> Distribution: Known only from type locality.

ATRACTUS LOVERIDGEI Amaral

> 1930 Atractus loveridgei Amaral, Bull. Antivenin Inst. Amer., 4: 28. Type-locality: Jericó, Departamento de Antioquia, Colombia.

> Distribution: Highlands of northern Colombia.

ATRACTUS MACULATUS (Günther)

1858 Isoscelis maculata Günther, Cat. Sn. Brit. Mus., 1858: 204. Type-locality: Unknown.
1862 R. [abdosoma] zebrinum Jan, Arch. Zool. Anat. Fis., 2: 15. Type-locality: None given.
1894 Atractus maculatus—Boulenger, Cat. Sn. Brit. Mus., 2: 306, pl. 14, fig. 3.

   Distribution: Espirito Santo and Rio de Janeiro, Brazil.

ATRACTUS MAJOR Boulenger

1893 Atractus major Boulenger, Cat. Sn. Brit. Mus., 2: 307. Type-locality: Pallatanga, Canelos, and
   Intac, Ecuador; restricted by lectotype designation to Canelos, Provincia Pastaza, Ecuador, by
   Savage, Misc. Publ. Mus. Zool. Univ. Mich., 112, 1960, 50.
1960 Atractus major—Savage, Misc. Publ. Mus. Zool. Univ. Mich., 112: 47.

   Distribution: Ecuador and Colombia on Amazonian slopes; Venezuela; Brazil.

ATRACTUS MANIZALESENSIS Prado

1940 Atractus manizalesensis Prado, Mem. Inst. Butantan, 13 (1939): 17, fig. 4. Type-locality:
   Colombia; actually from Villamaria, Departamento de Caldas, according to E. R. Dunn, in Savage,
   Misc. Publ. Mus. Zool., 112, 1960, 82.

   Distribution: Known only from type locality.

ATRACTUS MELANOGASTER Werner

1916 Atractus melanogaster Werner, Zool. Anz., 47: 308. Type-locality: Cañon del Tolima,
   Departamento de Tolima, Colombia.

   Distribution: Departamentos de Tolima and Antioquia, Colombia.

ATRACTUS MELAS Boulenger

1908 Atractus melas Boulenger, Ann. Mag. Nat. Hist., (8) 1: 114. Type-locality: Los Mangos,
   Departamento Valles, Colombia, 300 m.

   Distribution: Known only from type locality.

ATRACTUS MICHELI Mocquard

1904 Atractus Micheli Mocquard, Bull. Mus. Hist. Nat. Paris, 1904: 301. Type-locality: French Guiana.

   Distribution: Known only from type specimen.

ATRACTUS MICRORHYNCHUS (Cope)

1868 Rhabdosoma microrhynchum Cope, Proc. Acad. Nat. Sci. Phila., 1868: 102. Type-locality:
   Guayaquil, Ecuador.
1960 Atractus microrhynchum—Savage, Misc. Publ. Mus. Zool. Univ. Mich., 112: 52.

   Distribution: Lower Andean slopes in northwestern Ecuador.

ATRACTUS MODESTUS Boulenger

1894 Atractus modestus Boulenger, Cat. Sn. Brit. Mus., 2: 304, pl. 15, fig. 1. Type-locality: Western
   Ecuador.
1960 Atractus modestus—Savage, Misc. Publ. Mus. Zool. Univ. Mich., 112: 53.

   Distribution: Western Ecuador.

ATRACTUS MULTICINCTUS (Jan)

1865 Rabdosoma badium var. multicinctum Jan, in Jan and Sordelli, Icon. Gén. Ophidiens, Livr. 10: pl. 4, fig. 5. Type-locality: Lima, Peru (in error).
1898 Atractus multicinctus—Boulenger, Proc. Zool. Soc. London, 1898: 116.
1960 Atractus multicinctus—Savage, Misc. Publ. Mus. Zool. Univ. Mich., 112: 54.

Distribution: Northwestern Ecuador into Chocó of Colombia.

ATRACTUS NICEFORI Amaral

1930 Atractus nicefori Amaral, Bull. Antivenin Inst. Amer., 4: 28. Type-locality: Jericó, Departamento de Antioquia, Colombia.

Distribution: Highlands of northern Colombia.

ATRACTUS NIGRICAUDUS Schmidt and Walker

1943 Atractus nigricaudus Schmidt and Walker, Zool. Ser. Chicago Nat. Hist. Mus., 24: 327. Type-locality: Huachon, east of Cerro de Pasco, Departamento de Junín, Peru, 10,000 ft.

Distribution: Known only from type locality.

ATRACTUS NIGRIVENTRIS Amaral

1933 Atractus nigriventris Amaral, Mem. Inst. Butantan, 7 (1932): 116. Type-locality: Chita, southeast of San Gil, Departamento de Santander, Colombia.

Distribution: Known only from type locality.

ATRACTUS OBESUS Marx

1960 Atractus obesus Marx, Fieldiana: Zool., 39: 411, fig. 71. Type-locality: Santa Bárbara, at base of Cerro Frontimo, upper Río Urrao, a tributary of Río Penserisco, Cordillera Occidental, Antioquia, Colombia.

Distribution: Known from type locality and El Roblal, Río Pichinadé, tributary of Río Cali, Los Farallones, Valle and Carca Colombia, 700-800 air miles south of type locality.

ATRACTUS OBTUSIROSTRIS Werner

1916 Atractus obtusirostris Werner, Zool. Anz., 47: 308. Type-locality: Cañon del Tolima, Departamento de Tolima, Colombia.

Distribution: Known from type locality and from Pensilvania, Colombia.

ATRACTUS OCCIDENTALIS Savage

1955 Atractus occidentalis Savage, Proc. Biol. Soc. Washington, 68: 16. Type-locality: Mindo, Provincia Pichincha, Ecuador.

Distribution: Pacific slopes of Andes in northwestern Ecuador, 800-1200 m.

ATRACTUS OCCIPITOALBUS (Jan)

1862 Rhabdosoma occipitoalbum Jan, Arch. Zool. Anat. Fis., 2: 16. Type-locality: Andes of Ecuador, 4000 ft.
1880 Rabdosoma Duboisi Boulenger, Bull. Soc. Zool. France, 1880: 44. Type-locality: Andes of Ecuador.
1894 Atractus occipitoalbus—Boulenger, Cat. Sn. Brit. Mus., 2: 310.
1955 Atractus orcesi Savage, Proc. Biol. Soc. Washington, 68: 17. Type-locality: Loreto, Provincia Pastaza, Ecuador.

Distribution: Eastern slopes of Andes in Ecuador.

ATRACTUS OCULOTEMPORALIS Amaral

　　1932 Atractus oculo-temporalis Amaral, Bull. Antivenin Inst. Amer., 5: 67. Type-locality: Jericó,
　　　　Departamento de Antioquia, Colombia.

　　　Distribution: Known only from type locality.

ATRACTUS PAMPLONENSIS Amaral

　　1937 Atractus pamplonensis Amaral, Compte Rendu 12th Congress Internat. Zool., Lisbon, Vol. 3: 1763,
　　　　fig. 2. Type-locality: Pamplona, Departamento de Norte de Santander, Colombia.

　　　Distribution: Departamento de Norte de Santander, Colombia.

ATRACTUS PAUCIDENS Despax

　　1910 Atractus (Atractopsis) paucidens Despax, Bull. Mus. Hist. Nat. Paris, 16: 372. Type-locality:
　　　　Santo Domingo de los Colorados, Provincia Pichincha, Ecuador.
　　1960 Atractus paucidens—Savage, Misc. Publ. Mus. Zool. Univ. Mich., 112: 62.

　　　Distribution: Northwestern Ecuador in tropical rain forest.

ATRACTUS PAUCISCUTATUS Schmidt and Walker

　　1943 Atractus pauciscutatus Schmidt and Walker, Zool. Ser. Chicago Nat. Hist. Mus., 24: 326. Type-
　　　　locality: Carpapata, upper Chanchamayo Valley, northeast of Tarma, Departamento de Junín, Peru.

　　　Distribution: Known only from type locality.

ATRACTUS PERUVIANUS (Jan)

　　1862 R.[abdosoma] peruvianum Jan, Arch. Zool. Anat. Fis., 2: 12. Type-locality: Peru.
　　1894 Atractus peruvianus—Boulenger, Cat. Sn. Brit. Mus., 2: 305.

　　　Distribution: Known only from type specimen.

ATRACTUS PUNCTIVENTRIS Amaral

　　1933 Atractus punctiventris Amaral, Mem. Inst. Butantan, 7 (1932): 117. Type-locality: Villavicencio,
　　　　Intendencia de Meta, Colombia.

　　　Distribution: Known only from type locality.

ATRACTUS RESPLENDENS Werner

　　1901 Atractus torquatus var. resplendens Werner, Ver. Zool.-Bot. Ges. Wien, 51: 598. Type-locality:
　　　　Ecuador.
　　1960 Atractus resplendens—Savage, Misc. Publ. Mus. Zool. Univ. Mich., 112: 64.

　　　Distribution: Amazonian slopes of Ecuador.

ATRACTUS RETICULATUS (Boulenger)

　　1885 Geophis reticulatus Boulenger, Ann. Mag. Nat. Hist., (5) 16: 87. Type-locality: São Lourenço,
　　　　Estado do Rio Grande do Sul, Brazil.
　　1894 Atractus reticulatus—Boulenger, Cat. Sn. Brit. Mus., 2: 311, pl. 15, fig. 3.

　　　Distribution: Paraguay and southern Brazil.

　　　Content: Two subspecies.

ATRACTUS

<table>
<tr><td>Key to the subspecies</td><td>Clave de subespecies</td></tr>
<tr>
<td>1. Two postoculars----------------<u>reticulatus</u>
   One postocular----------------<u>paraguayensis</u></td>
<td>1. Dos postoculares----------------<u>reticulatus</u>
   Un postocular------------------<u>paraguayensis</u></td>
</tr>
</table>

<u>Atractus</u> <u>reticulatus</u> <u>reticulatus</u> (Boulenger)

   1929 <u>Atractus</u> <u>reticulatus</u> <u>reticulatus</u>—Amaral, Mem. Inst. Butantan, 4: 27.

     Distribution: Southern Brazil.

<u>Atractus</u> <u>reticulatus</u> <u>paraguayensis</u> Werner

   1924 <u>Atractus</u> <u>paraguayensis</u> Werner, Sitz. Akad. Wiss. Wien, 133 (1): 40. Type-locality:
      Paraguay.
   1929 <u>Atractus</u> <u>reticulatus</u> <u>paraguayensis</u>—Amaral, Mem. Inst. Butantan, 4: 27.

     Distribution: Paraguay.

ATRACTUS RIVEROI Roze

   1961 <u>Atractus</u> <u>riveroi</u> Roze, Acta Biol. Venezuelica, 3: 114. Type-locality: Cerro Duida, Territorio
     Federal Amazonas, Venezuela, 1800 m.

     Distribution: Territorio Federal Amazonas, Venezuela.

ATRACTUS ROULEI Despax

   1910 <u>Atractus</u> <u>Roulei</u> Despax, Bull. Mus. Hist. Nat. Paris, 16: 370. Type-locality: Alausi, Ecuador,
     2350 m.
   1960 <u>Atractus</u> <u>roulei</u>—Savage, Misc. Publ. Mus. Zool. Univ. Mich., 112: 67.

     Distribution: Western slopes in southwestern Ecuador, 1200-1600 m.

ATRACTUS SANCTAEMARTAE Dunn

   1946 <u>Atractus</u> <u>sanctaemartae</u> Dunn, Occ. Pap. Mus. Zool. Univ. Mich., 493: 2. Type-locality: San
     Sebastián, Departamento de Magdalena, Colombia.

     Distribution: Sierra Nevada de Santa Marta, Colombia.

ATRACTUS SANGUINEUS Prado

   1944 <u>Atractus</u> <u>sanguineus</u> Prado, Ciencia (Mexico), 5: 111, fig. 2. Type-locality: Yarumal,
     Departamento de Antioquia, Colombia.
   1945 <u>Atractus</u> <u>sanguineus</u>—Prado, Mem. Inst. Butantan, 18 (1944-45): 110, fig.

     Distribution: Known only from type locality.

ATRACTUS SERRANUS Amaral

   1930 <u>Atractus</u> <u>serranus</u> Amaral, Bull. Antivenin Inst. Amer., 4: 65. Type-locality: Serra de
     Paranapiacaba, Estado do São Paulo, Brazil.

     Distribution: Estado do São Paulo, Brazil.

ATRACTUS STEYERMARKI Roze

   1958 <u>Atractus</u> <u>steyermarki</u> Roze, Acta Biol. Venezuelica, 2: 301. Type-locality: Chimantá Tepui, Estado
     de Bolivar, Venezuela.

     Distribution: Savannas of Estado de Bolivar, Venezuela.

ATRACTUS SUBBICINCTUM (Jan)

1862 [Rabdosoma badium] subbicinctum Jan, Arch. Zool. Anat. Fis., 2: 14. Type-locality: Surinam and French Guiana.
1960 [Atractus] subbicinctum—Savage, Misc. Publ. Mus. Zool. Univ. Mich., 112: 83.

Distribution: Known only from type material.

Comment: This taxon was not mentioned in the literature until Savage, loc. cit., included it in his list of the nominal species of Atractus. No author discussing A. badius has indicated that subspecies are recognized, so it would appear to be necessary to list the taxon here as a species, although it has never been so defined in the literature.

ATRACTUS TAENIATUS Griffin

1916 Atractus taeniatus Griffin, Mem. Carnegie Mus., 7 (1915): 173. Type-locality: Santa Cruz de la Sierra, Departamento de Santa Cruz, Bolivia.

Distribution: Known only from type locality.

ATRACTUS TORQUATUS (Duméril, Bibron and Duméril)

1854 Rabdosoma torquatum Duméril, Bibron and Duméril, Erp. Gén., 7: 101. Santa Cruz de la Sierra, Departamento de Santa Cruz, Bolivia.
1862 R.[abdosoma] varium Jan, Arch. Zool. Anat. Fis., 2: 18. Type-locality: "Santa Cruz", without country.
1894 Atractus torquatus—Boulenger, Cat. Sn. Brit. Mus., 2: 309.

Distribution: Amazonian Colombia and Bolivia; Amazonas, Brazil.

ATRACTUS TRILINEATUS Wagler

1828 Atractus trilineatus Wagler, Isis von Oken, 21: 742, pl. 10, figs. 1-4. Type-locality: None given.
1862 R.[abdosoma] trivirgatum Jan, Arch. Zool. Anat. Fis., 2: 17. Type-locality: Unknown.
1862 Rabdosoma punctatovittatum Jan, Arch. Zool. Anat. Fis., 2: 17. Type-locality: Antilles.

Distribution: Trinidad, Guianas, eastern Venezuela.

ATRACTUS TRIVITTATUS Amaral

1933 Atractus trivittatus Amaral, Mem. Inst. Butantan, 7 (1932): 118. Type-locality: Chita, Departamento de Santander, Colombia.

Distribution: Known only from type locality.

ATRACTUS UNIVITTATUS (Jan)

1862 R.[abdosoma] univittatum Jan, Arch. Zool. Anat. Fis., 2: 15. Type-locality: Caracas, Distrito Federal, Venezuela.
1961 Atractus univittatus—Roze, Acta Biol. Venezuelica, 3: 117.

Distribution: Cordillera de la Costa, Venezuela.

ATRACTUS VARIEGATUS Prado

1942 Atractus variegatus Prado, Mem. Inst. Butantan, 15 (1941): 379, fig. Type-locality: La Uvita, Departamento de Boyacá, Colombia.

Distribution: Known only from type locality.

ATRACTUS VENTRIMACULATUS Boulenger

    1905 *Atractus ventrimaculatus* Boulenger, Ann. Mag. Nat. Hist., (7) 15: 455. Type-locality: Mérida, Estado de Mérida, and Fuqueros (Estado desconocido), Venezuela.

    Distribution: Known only from type material.

ATRACTUS VERTEBRALIS Boulenger

    1904 *Atractus vertebralis* Boulenger, Ann. Mag. Nat. Hist., (7) 13: 451. Type-locality: Santo Domingo, Cordillera de Carabaya, Departamento de Puno, Peru, 6000 ft.

    Distribution: Known only from type locality.

ATRACTUS VERTEBROLINEATUS Prado

    1941 *Atractus vertebrolineatus* Prado, Mem. Inst. Butantan, 14 (1940): 25, fig. Type-locality: Ocaña, Departamento de Norte de Santander, Colombia.

    Distribution: Known only from type locality.

ATRACTUS WAGLERI Prado

    1945 *Atractus wagleri* Prado, Ciencia (Mexico), 6: 61, fig. 1. Type-locality: Humbo, Departamento de Boyacá, Colombia.
    1945 *Atractus wagleri*—Prado, Mem. Inst. Butantan, 18 (1944-45): 110, fig.

    Distribution: Known only from type locality.

ATRACTUS WERNERI Peracca

    1914 *Atractus Werneri* Peracca, Mem. Soc. Neuchatel Sci. Nat., 5: 102. Type-locality: Viotá, Departamento de Cundinamarca, Colombia, 1830 m.
    1940 *Atractus longimaculatus* Prado, Mem. Inst. Butantan, 13 (1939): 17, fig. 3. Type-locality: Region of Quindío, Colombia; in error for Pacho, Departamento de Cundinamarca, Colombia, according to E. R. Dunn, Rev. Acad. Colombiana Cien. Exactas Fis. Nat., 6, 1944, 77.
    1940 *Atractus colombianus* Prado, Mem. Inst. Butantan, 13 (1939): 18, fig. 5. Type-locality: Chocontá, Departamento de Cundinamarca, Colombia.

    Distribution: Highlands of Colombia.

BOA Linnaeus

1758 Boa Linnaeus, Systema Naturae, Ed. 10: 214. Type-species: Boa Constrictor Linnaeus
1768 Constrictor Laurenti, Synopsin Reptilium: 106. Type-species: Constrictor formosissimus Laurenti.

Distribution: Mexico to Argentina; Antilles.

Content: One species.

BOA CONSTRICTOR Linnaeus

1758 Boa Constrictor Linnaeus, Systema Naturae, Ed. 10: 215. Type-locality: India (in error).
1768 Constrictor rex serpentum Laurenti (unavailable because not binomial), Synopsin Reptilium: 107. Type-locality: Madagascar; Java.
1768 Constrictor auspex Laurenti, Synopsin Reptilium: 108. Type-locality: America.
1801 [Boa] constrictrix Schneider (unjustified emendation of constrictor Linnaeus), Hist. Amphib., 2: 247.

Distribution: Mexico to Argentina; Antilles.

Content: Eight subspecies, two of which (nebulosus Lazell and orophias Linnaeus) are extra-limital.

Key to the subspecies	Clave de subespecies
1. Conspicuous dorsal pattern always present-2 Dorsal pattern pale or dark, but always inconspicuous or even absent-------------5	1. Diseño dorsal conspícuo siempre presente--2 Diseño dorsal pálido u oscuro, pero siempre inconspícuo o ausente--------------------5
2. Longitudinal middorsal band on head without lateral projections----------------------3 Longitudinal middorsal band on head sends lateral projections to eyes------imperator	2. Una banda longitudinal supracefálica sin proyecciones laterales--------------------3 Una banda longitudinal supracefálica emite proyecciones hacia los ojos------imperator
3. Dorsal pattern of yellow spots bordered by black rings which are connected to each other-------------------------------------4 Black rings around yellow dorsal spots not in contact with each other----occidentalis	3. Diseño dorsal de manchas amarillas rodeadas por anillos negros conectados entre sí---4 Diseño dorsal de manchas amarillas rodeadas por anillos negros independientes entre sí----------------------------occidentalis
4. More than 21 saddle-shaped dorsal spots; ventrals 226-237--------------------amarali Fewer than 20 rounded dorsal spots; 234-250 ventrals----------------------constrictor	4. Manchas dorsales en forma de silla de montar, con prolongación anterior y posterior, en número de 22 o más; ventrales 226-237---------------------------amarali Manchas dorsales rodeadas, sin prolongaciones, en número menor de 20; ventrales 234-250-----------------------constrictor
5. Dorsal color pale, light, sandy-----ortonii Dorsal color dark reddish brown-----sabogae	5. Color dorsal arenoso, pálido, claro-ortonii Color dorsal pardo rojizo oscuro----sabogae

Boa constrictor constrictor Linnaeus

1768 Constrictor formosissimus Laurenti, Synopsin Reptilium: 107. Type-locality: America.
1768 Constrictor diviniloquus Laurenti, Synopsin Reptilium: 108. Type-locality: Mexico and Peru.
1960 Boa constrictor constrictor—Forcart, Herpetologica, 7: 199.

Distribution: Amazonian South America to Argentina and Paraguay; Trinidad; Tobago.

Boa constrictor amarali (Stull)

1932 Constrictor constrictor amarali Stull, Occ. Pap. Boston Soc. Nat. Hist., 8: 27. Type-locality: São Paulo, Brazil.
1951 Boa constrictor amarali—Forcart, Herpetologica, 7: 199.

Distribution: Southern and southwestern Brazil; southeastern Bolivia.

Boa constrictor imperator Daudin

1803 Boa imperator Daudin, Hist. Nat. Rept., 5: 150. Type-locality: Mexico; restricted to Córdoba, Veracruz, Mexico, by Smith and Taylor, Univ. Kansas Sci. Bull., 33, 1950, 350, also restricted to Chocó of Colombia by Dunn and Saxe, Proc. Acad. Nat. Sci. Phila., 102, 1950, 161, in a rather offhand fashion.

1842 Boa eques Eydoux and Souleyet, Voyage La Bonite, Zoology, 1: 144. Type-locality: Paita, Peru [original citation not verified by us].

1863 Boa diviniloquax var. mexicana Jan, Elenco Sistema Ofidi: 23. Type-locality: Mexico.

1883 Boa constrictor var. isthmica Garman, Mem. Mus. Comp. Zool., 8 (3): 9. Type-locality: Given as Central America; further specified, from the syntypes, as Bas Obispo, Panama, and Turbo, Colombia, by Barbour and Loveridge, Bull. Mus. Comp. Zool., 69, 1929, 227.

1943 Constrictor constrictor sigma Smith, Proc. U. S. Nat. Mus., 93: 411. Type-locality: María Madré Island, Tres Marías, Mexico.

1951 Boa constrictor imperator—Forcart, Herpetologica, 7: 199.

Distribution: Mexico to northwestern South America, west of Andes, in Colombia, Ecuador, and Peru.

Boa constrictor occidentalis Philippi

1873 Boa occidentalis Philippi Zeitsch. Gesammte Naturwiss., 41: 128, pl. 3. Type-locality: Argentina; indicated as Provincias de Mendoza and San Juan, Argentina, by Stimson, Das Tierreich, 89, 1969, 3.

1951 Boa constrictor occidentalis—Forcart, Herpetologica, 7: 199.

Distribution: Argentina and Paraguay.

Boa constrictor ortonii Cope

1878 Boa ortonii Cope, Proc. Amer. Phil. Soc., 17 (1877): 35. Type-locality: Chilete, near Pacasmayo, Peru, 3000 ft.

1951 Boa constrictor ortonii—Stimson, Das Tierreich, 89, 1969, 4.

Distribution: Northwestern Peru.

Boa constrictor sabogae (Barbour)

1906 Epicrates sabogae Barbour, Bull. Mus. Comp. Zool., 46: 226. Type-locality: Saboga Island, Panama, which is now spelled Taboga Island.

1951 Boa constrictor sabogae—Forcart, Herpetologica, 7: 199.

Distribution: Taboga Island, Panama.

BOTHROPS Wagler

1824 Bothrops Wagler, in Spix, Sp. Nov. Serp. Bras.: 50. Type-species: Coluber lanceolatus Lacépède.
1859 Bothriechis Peters, Monats. Akad. Wiss. Berlin, 1859: 278. Type-species: Bothriechis nigroviridis Peters.
1860 Teleuraspis Cope, Proc. Acad. Nat. Sci. Phila., 1859: 338. Type-species: Trigonocephalus schlegelii Berthold.
1860 Thamnocenchris Salvin, Proc. Zool. Soc. London, 1860: 459. Type-species: Thamnocenchris aurifer Salvin.
1861 Bothriopsis Peters, Monats. Akad. Wiss. Berlin, 1861: 359. Type-species: Bothriopsis quadriscutatus Peters.
1871 Porthidium Cope, Proc. Acad. Nat. Sci. Phila., 1871: 207. Type-species: Trigonocephalus lansbergii Schlegel.
1881 Rhinocerophis Garman, Bull. Mus. Comp. Zool., 8: 85. Type-species: Rhinocerophis nasus Garman.
1887 Ophryacus Cope, Bull. U. S. Nat. Mus., 32: 88. Type-species: Atropos undulatus Jan.
1889 Thanatophis Posada-Arango, Bull. Soc. Zool. France, 14: 343. Type-species: Thanatophis torvus Posada-Arango.

Distribution: Mexico; Central America; almost all of South America except southernmost parts, Lesser Antilles as far north as Martinique.

Content: 59 species, of which 51 are found within limits set for this work, following the most recent list of species by Hoge, Mem. Inst. Butantan, 32, 1965 (1966), 109.

Matrix for identification of species   Matriz para identificación de especies

	SNOUT NORMAL[1]	HEAD SCALES KEELED	INTERNASALS IN CONTACT	SUPRAOCULAR LARGE	UPPER LABIAL IN PIT	WITH POSTOCULAR STRIPE	KEEL SHORTER THAN SCALE	TAIL PREHENSILE	SUBCAUDALS MOSTLY PAIRED	SCALES BETWEEN SUPRA-OCULARS	UPPER LABIALS	DORSAL SCALE ROWS	VENTRALS	CAUDALS	DORSAL COLOR[1]	VENTRAL COLOR[1]
ALBOCARINATUS	1	1	3	3	1	1	3	1	2	6	8-9	21	181	-----	X	4
ALTERNATUS M	1	1	1	3	3	3	3	3	1	8-13	8-10	24-37	155-185	34-48	3	2
ALTERNATUS F												26-37	156-190	30-46		
ALTICOLUS		1	1	1	1	1	1	3	1	3	5	7	19	178	-----	5	4
AMMODYTOIDES	3	1	0	1	3	1	3	3	1	8-9	9-10	23-25	149-160	30-38	4	4

ACTUAL COUNTS (spanning UPPER LABIALS, DORSAL SCALE ROWS, VENTRALS, CAUDALS)

[1]Significance of various values
  Symbols for first nine characters:
  0=Unknown; 1=True; 2=Variable; 3=False;
  4=Inapplicable.
  Symbols for color patterns: (0=Unknown)
  Dorsal color (X=Combinations)
  1=Greenish, with or without black spotting
    and ventrolateral light stripe
  2=Triangular blotches
  3=Hollow, "C" shaped blotches
  4=Large, squarish blotches
  5=Round or rhomboidal spots
  Ventral color
  1=Immaculate or lightly spotted
  2=Checkered; with light and dark spots
  3=Dark with lighter spots or blotches
  4=Light with darker spotting

[1]Significado de los distintos valores
  Símbolos de los primeros nueve caracteres:
  0=Desconocido; 1=Verdadero; 2=Variable;
  3=Falso; 4=Inaplicable.
  Símbolos de los diseños de color: (0=Desconocido)
  Color dorsal (X=Combinaciones)
  1=Verdoso, con o sin manchas negras y cinta
    clara ventrolateral
  2=Bloques triangulares
  3=Bloques huecos, en forma de "C"
  4=Bloques grandes, cuadriláteros
  5=Manchas redondas o romboidales
  Color ventral
  1=Inmaculado o ligeramente manchado
  2=Cuadriculado, con manchas claras y oscuras
  3=Oscuro con manchas claras
  4=Claro con manchas oscuras

BOTHROPS

	SNOUT NORMAL	HEAD SCALES KEELED	INTERNASALS IN CONTACT	SUPRAOCULAR LARGE	UPPER LABIAL IN PIT	WITH POSTOCULAR STRIPE	KEEL SHORTER THAN SCALE	TAIL PREHENSILE	SUBCAUDALS MOSTLY PAIRED	ACTUAL COUNTS					DORSAL COLOR	VENTRAL COLOR
										SCALES BETWEEN SUPRA-OCULARS	UPPER LABIALS	DORSAL SCALE ROWS	VENTRALS	CAUDALS		
ANDIANUS	1	2	1	0	1	1	3	3	1	3-6	7	21	157-161	50-55	2	1
ASPER	1	1	0,1	1	0	0	3	1		6-7	7	27	188-199	63-74	2	0
ATROX	1	1	1	1	1	1	1	3	1	5-11	7-8	23-33	169-231	47-75	X	4
BARNETTI	1	1	1	1	1	3	3	3	1	6	7-9	23-25	172-179	42-46	3	1
BICOLOR	1	1	3	3	1	3	0	1	3	10-11	10-11	21	164-167	62-67	1	1
BILINEATUS	1	1	1	1	1	2	0	1	1	5-8	7-8	23-35	192-220	55-71	1	1
BRAZILI	1	1	1	1	1	3	0	3	1	8	8-9	23-25	159-179	48-64	2	3
CASTELNAUDI	1	2	1	1	1	1	0	3	3	5	7	25-27	211-253	71-91	4	3
COTIARA M	1	1	2	3	3	1	3	1	1	11-14	8-9	27	156-166	34-51	3	3
COTIARA F													164-173	34-44		
COLUMBIENSIS	1	0	0	1	0	0	0	0	1	------	7	-----	207	70	2	4
ERYTHROMELAS	1	1	1	0	3	3	3	0	1	5	7-8	19-21	144-155	33-42	2	4
FONSECAI M	1	1	0	1	3	1	0	3	1	10	8	-----	165-173	45-57	3	3
FONSECAI F													165-179	39-51		
GODMANI	1	1	0	1	3	1	0	3	3	5-7	9-10	21	135-146	22-36	5	4
HYOPRORUS	3	1	3	1	3	1	1	3	3	4-6	7	23	125-134	44-50	2	4
IGLESIASI	1	1	1	0	3	0	3	3	1	-----	8-9	21-25	160-170	35-43	4	4
INSULARIS M	1	1	1	3	2	3	3	2	1	5-9	8-9	23-27	171-188	52-64	X	1
INSULARIS F													182-195	51-61		
INSULARIS I													178-194	48-65		
ITAPETININGAE	1	1	1	1	3	1	0	3	0	7-9	8	25	150-152	28-29	X	4

	SNOUT NORMAL[1]	HEAD SCALES KEELED	INTERNASALS IN CONTACT	SUPRAOCULAR LARGE	UPPER LABIAL IN PIT	WITH POSTOCULAR STRIPE	KEEL SHORTER THAN SCALE	TAIL PREHENSILE	SUBCAUDALS MOSTLY PAIRED	SCALES BETWEEN SUPRA-OCULARS	ACTUAL COUNTS — UPPER LABIALS	ACTUAL COUNTS — DORSAL SCALE ROWS	ACTUAL COUNTS — VENTRALS	ACTUAL COUNTS — CAUDALS	DORSAL COLOR[1]	VENTRAL COLOR[1]
JARARACA	1	1	3	1	1	1	3	3	1	6-12	6-9	21-27	175-216	52-70	2	4
JARARACUSSU	1	1	1	1	1	1	3	3	1	4-8	8	23-27	181-185	60-66	4	4
LANSBERGI	3	1	1	1	3	3	0	3	3	5-7	8-10	23-27	139-159	27-35	X	4
LATERALIS	1	1	3	3	1	0	0	1	3	7	9-11	21-23	155-171	58-66	1	1
LICHENOSUS	1	2	1	1	1	1	0	2	3	7-8	7	25	205	66	5	2
LOJANUS	1	2	1	1	1	1	3	3	1	3	7	21-23	144-155	37-45	5	4
MARAJOENSIS M	1	0	0	0	1	1	0	3	1	-----	7-8	-----	176-188	60	0	0
MARAJOENSIS F													178-194			
MEDUSA	1	2	3	1	1	1	0	3	3	2-5	7	21	254-168	46-62	4	4
MICROPHTHALMUS	3	2	3	1	3	1	1	3	1	5-8	7	23	144-161	49-55	2	3
MOOJENI M	3	1	3	0	1	1	3	3	1	-----	7	23-27	182-197	57-70	3	1
MOOJENI F												25-29	187-210	51-66		
NASUTUS	3	1	0	1	3	0	0	3	3	5-7	9-11	23-27	130-145	24-36	X	3
NEUWIEDI	1	1	1	1	3	1	3	3	1	6-9	8-9	21-27	168-185	41-53	5	4
NIGROVIRIDIS	1	3	3	1	2	1	0	1	3	4-10	9-11	19	134-158	49-57	1	4
NUMMIFER	1	1	3	3	3	1	0	3	3	7-10	9-11	23-27	121-134	26-36	5	1
OLIGOLEPIS	1	1	0	1	1	1	0	1	1	5-6	7-8	23-25	178-191	41-63	X	4
OPHRYOMEGAS	1	1	0	1	0	1	0	3	3	6	9-10	25-27	160-173	32-42	5	4
PERUVIANUS	1	1	0	1	1	1	3	1	1	7	7-8	23	188	66	1	4
PESSOAI	3	1	3	1	3	0	1	3	3	4	7	23	128	57	5	4
PICADOI	1	1	3	3	3	1	3	3	3	10-11	9-10	25	146-152	32-40	5	1
PICTUS	1	2	1	1	1	1	3	3	1	5-7	8-9	21-25	157-172	40-74	5	1

BOTHROPS

	SNOUT NORMAL	HEAD SCALES KEELED	INTERNASALS IN CONTACT	SUPRAOCULAR LARGE	UPPER LABIAL IN PIT	WITH POSTOCULAR STRIPE	KEEL SHORTER THAN SCALE	TAIL PREHENSILE	SUBCAUDALS MOSTLY PAIRED	ACTUAL COUNTS SCALES BETWEEN SUPRA-OCULARS	UPPER LABIALS	DORSAL SCALE ROWS	VENTRALS	CAUDALS	DORSAL COLOR	VENTRAL COLOR
PIRAJAI	1	1	2	1	1	3	3	3	1	5-7	8	23-27	155-164	43-52	4	4
PRADOI	1	1	0	1	1	1	3	3	1	10	7	23-25	191-207	56-70	X	2
PULCHER	1	2	0	1	1	3	1	3	1	5-7	7	21-23	156-174	47-64	X	4
PUNCTATUS	1	1	2	1	1	1	3	1	1	7	7	27	202-203	82-88	5	1
ROEDINGERI	1	2	1	1	3	1	3	3	1	6-7	11-12	23-25	179-185	43-48	5	1
SANCTAECRUCIS	1	1	1	1	1	3	0	3	1	6	8	25	182	57	2	1
SCHLEGELII	1	2	3	1	1	3	0	1	3	5-9	8-9	19-25	138-166	47-62	1	X
SUPRACILIARIS	1	1	3	3	1	1	0	1	3	10	9-10	23	146	46	1	X
VENEZUELENSIS	1	1	1	1	2	1	3	3	1	8-14	7-9	21-25	179-203	48-63	X	3
XANTHOGRAMMUS	1	3	0	1	·1	1	0	3	1	9-10	7	27	196	54	2	3

BOTHROPS ALBOCARINATUS Shreve

> 1934 Bothrops albocarinata Shreve, Occ. Pap. Boston Soc. Nat. Hist., 8: 130. Type-locality: Río Pastaza, from Canelos to Río Marañón, Ecuador.

> Distribution: Río Pastaza drainage, Ecuador.

BOTHROPS ALTERNATUS Duméril, Bibron and Duméril

> 1854 Bothrops alternatus Duméril, Bibron and Duméril, Erp. Gén., 7: 1512, pl. 82 bis, figs. 1-1a. Type-locality: Paraguay and South America.
> 1925 Lachesis inaequalis Magalhães, Mem. Inst. Oswaldo Cruz, 18: 153, pls. 7-12. Type-locality: Vila de São Lourenço, Lago a Dos Patos, Estado do Rio Grande do Sul, Brazil.

> Distribution: Northern Argentina, Uruguay, Paraguay, and southeastern Brazil.

BOTHROPS ALTICOLUS Parker

> 1934 Bothrops alticola Parker, Ann. Mag. Nat. Hist., (10) 14: 272. Type-locality: Five km east of Loja, Ecuador, 9200 ft.

> Distribution: Known only from type locality.

BOTHROPS AMMODYTOIDES Leybold

> 1873 Bothrops ammodytoides Leybold, Escursión a las Pampas Arjentinas; Hojas de mi Diario: 80. Type-locality: Northern Argentina.
> 1881 Rhinocerophis nasus Garman, Bull. Mus. Comp. Zool., 8: 85. Type-locality: Puerto San Antonio, Argentina.
> 1885 Bothrops patagonicus Müller, Verh. Naturforsch. Ges. Basel, 7: 697. Type-locality: Bahía Blanca, Argentina.
> 1895 Bothrops burmeisteri Koslowsky, Rev. Mus. La Plata, 6: 369, pl. 4. Type-locality: Chilecito, La Rioja, Argentina.

> Distribution: Provincia Tucumán to Provincia Chubut, Argentina.

BOTHROPS ANDIANUS Amaral

> 1923 Bothrops andiana Amaral, Proc. New England Zool. Club, 8: 103. Type-locality: Machu Picchu, Departamento Cuzco, Peru, 8000-10,000 ft.

> Distribution: Known only from Departamento Cuzco, Peru.

BOTHROPS ASPER (Garman)

> 1883 Trigonocephalus asper Garman, Mem. Mus. Comp. Zool., 8: 124. Type-locality: Obispo, Darién, Panama.
> 1885 Bothrops atrox septentrionalis Müller, Verh. Naturforsch. Ges. Basel, 7: 699. Type-locality: None given; recorded as Costa Grande, Guatemala, by Stuart, Misc. Publ. Mus. Zool. Univ. Mich., 122, 1963, 129.
> 1966 Bothrops asper—Hoge, Mem. Inst. Butantan, 32 (1965): 113.

> Distribution: Isthmus of Tehuantepec, Mexico south on both Atlantic and Pacific slopes at lower elevations throughout Central America and Pacific slopes of Colombia and Ecuador.

BOTHROPS ATROX (Linnaeus)

1758 Coluber atrox Linnaeus, Systema Naturae, Ed. 10: 222. Type-locality: "Asia"; restricted to Surinam, according to Hoge, Mem. Inst. Butantan, 32, 1965 (1966), 113.
1824 Bothrops furia Wagler, in Spix, Sp. Nov. Serp. Bras.: 52, pl. 20. Type-locality: Rio Amazon, Brazil?
1842 Bothrops Sabinii Gray, Zoological Miscellany: 47. Type-locality: Demerara, Guyana.
1842 Bothrops subscutatus Gray, Zoological Miscellany: 47. Type-locality: Demerara, Guyana.
1849 Bothrops affinis Gray, Cat. Sn. Brit. Mus.: 7. Type-locality: Berbice; Demarara; Tropical America.
1934 B.[othrops] Neuvoiedii Venezuelenzi Briceño, Bol. Ministerio Salubr. Agríc. Cria, Venezuela, 1 (15): 46. Type-locality: Río de Oro region, Venezuela.

Distribution: Tropical forests of Guianas, Venezuela, Brazil, Colombia, Ecuador, Peru and Bolivia; also Misiones, Argentina.

BOTHROPS BARNETTI Parker

1938 Bothrops barnetti Parker, Ann. Mag. Nat. Hist., (11) 2: 447. Type-locality: From mouths of Quebradas Honda and Perines, between Lobitos and Talara, northern Peru.

Distribution: Coast of northern Peru.

BOTHROPS BICOLOR Bocourt

1868 Bothrops bicolor Bocourt, Ann. Sci. Nat. Paris (5) 10: 202. Type-locality: Forests of St. Augustin, on western slope of Cordillera, Departamento de Sololá, Guatemala, 610 m.
1878 Bothrops (Bothriechis) Bernoullii Müller, Verh. Nat. Ges. Basel, 6: 399, pl. 3, fig. A. Type-locality: Volcán Atitlan, Guatemala.

Distribution: Pacific foothills of Guatemala and Chiapas, Mexico.

BOTHROPS BILINEATUS (Wied)

1825 C.[ophias] bilineatus Wied, Beiträge zur Naturgeschichte von Brasilien, 1: 483. Type-locality: Villa Viçoza, = Marobá, according to Hoge and Lancini, Publ. Oc. Mus. Cien. Nat. Caracas, Zool., 11, 1962, 17, on Rio Peruhype, Estado da Bahía, Brazil.
1854 Bothrops bilineatus—Duméril, Bibron and Duméril, Erp. Gén., 7: 1514.

Distribution: Amazonian South America; an isolated Atlantic slope population in Brazil.

Content: Two subspecies.

Key to the subspecies	Clave de subespecies
1. Dorsum ground color green, with all scales of head and back heavily dark-spotted; no vertical dark bars on upper labials--smaragdinus Color not as above--------------bilineatus	1. Dorso coloreado en verde, todas las escamas de la cabeza y el dorso densamente mancha-das de oscuro; sin barras verticales oscu-ras en las labiales superiores-smaragdinus Coloración no como el anterior---bilineatus

Bothrops bilineatus bilineatus (Wied)

1869 Trigonocephalus (Bothrops) arboreus Cope, Proc. Amer. Phil. Soc., 11: 157. Type-locality: Bahía, Brazil.
1966 Bothrops bilineatus bilineatus—Hoge, Mem. Inst. Butantan, 32 (1965): 114, pl. 1, fig. 1.

Distribution: Equatorial forests of Venezuela and Guianas; Territorio Federal Amapá, Brazil; and isolated population in forests of Atlantic slope from Bahía to Rio de Janeiro, Brazil.

Bothrops bilineatus smaragdinus Hoge

    1966 Bothrops bilineatus smaragdinus Hoge, Mem. Inst. Butantan, 32 (1965): 114, pl. 1, figs.
        2a-b. Type-locality: Upper Rio Perús, Estado do Amazonas, Brazil.

      Distribution: Amazonian Colombia, Ecuador, Peru, Bolivia and Brazil; one specimen in
        Universidad Central, Caracas, from Territorio Amazonas, Venezuela, fits description
        of this subspecies, according to Abdem Lancini.

BOTHROPS BRAZILI Hoge

    1953 Bothrops brazili Hoge, Mem. Inst. Butantan, 25: 15, figs. 1-6 and 7b. Type-locality: Tomé Assú
        on Rio Acará-Mirim, Estado do Pará, Brazil.

      Distribution: Probably throughout equatorial forests; known from Venezuela, Guianas, and Colombia,
        as well as Pará, Amazonas, and extreme northern Mato Grosso, Brazil.

BOTHROPS CASTELNAUDI Duméril, Bibron and Duméril

    1854 Bothrops Castelnaudi Duméril, Bibron and Duméril, Erp. Gén., 7: 1511. Type-locality: Not
        designated; Guichenot, in Castelnau, Expédition dans les Parties Centrales de l'Amerique du
        Sud, Reptiles, 1855, 76, gave type locality as "Province du Goyaz", now Estado de Goiás,
        Brazil.
    1854 Atropos Castelnautii—Duméril, Bibron and Duméril (in error for castelnaudi Duméril, Bibron and
        Duméril), Erp. Gén., 9: 388.
    1860 Bothriechis Castelnaui—Cope (in error for castelnaudi Duméril, Bibron and Duméril), Proc. Acad.
        Nat. Sci. Phila., 1860: 345.
    1861 Bothriopsis quadriscutatus Peters, Monats. Akad. Wiss. Berlin, 1861: 359. Type-locality: Quito,
        Ecuador; in error, according to Peters, Rev. Ecuat. Ent. Parasit., 2, 1955, 347.
    1871 Bothriopsis castelnavii—Cope (in error for castelnaudi Duméril, Bibron and Duméril), Proc. Acad.
        Nat. Sci. Phila., 1871: 209.
    1889 Thanatophis montanus Posada-Arango, Bull. Soc. Zool. France, 1889: 344. Type-locality: Mountains
        of Antioquia, Colombia, 2200 m.
    1966 [Bothrops] quadricarinatus Hoge (in error for quadriscutatus Peters), Mem. Inst. Butantan, 32
        (1965): 118.

      Distribution: Equatorial forests of Brazil, Colombia, Ecuador and Peru.

BOTHROPS COLOMBIENSIS (Hallowell)

    1845 Trigonocephalus Colombiensis Hallowell, Proc. Acad. Nat. Sci. Phila., 1845: 246. Type-locality:
        "Republic of Colombia, within two hundred miles of Caracas".
    1966 Bothrops colombiensis—Hoge, Mem. Inst. Butantan, 32 (1965): 164.

      Distribution: Northern Venezuela except altitudes above 2500 m.

BOTHROPS COTIARA (Gomes)

    1913 Lachesis cotiara Gomes, Ann. Paulistas Med. Cirurg., 1: 65, pl. 8, figs. 1-6. Type-locality:
        Nucleo Colonial Cruz Machado, Marechal Mallet, Estado do Paraná, Brazil.
    1925 Bothrops cotiara—Amaral, Contrib. Harvard Inst. Trop. Biol. Med., 2: 53.
    1959 Bothrops cotiara—Hoge and Belluomini, Mem. Inst. Butantan, 28 (1957-1958): 196, figs. 3-8.

      Distribution: Araucaria forests of Argentina and Brazil.

BOTHROPS ERYTHROMELAS Amaral

    1923 Bothrops erythromelas Amaral, Proc. New England Zool. Club, 8: 96. Type-locality: Near
        Joazeiro, Estado da Bahia, Brazil.

      Distribution: Areas of Caatinga vegetation en Brazil.

BOTHROPS

BOTHROPS FONSECAI Hoge and Belluomini

1959 Bothrops fonsecai Hoge and Belluomini, Mem. Inst. Butantan, 28 (1957-1958): 195, figs. 1-5 and 9. Type-locality: Santo Antonio do Capivary, Estado do Rio de Janeiro, Brazil.

Distribution: Northeastern São Paulo, southern Rio de Janeiro and extreme southern Minas Gerais, Brazil.

BOTHROPS GODMANI (Günther)

1863 Bothriechis godmanni Günther, Ann. Mag. Nat. Hist., (3) 12: 364, pl. 6, fig. G. Type-locality: Duenas and other parts of tableland of Guatemala.
1868 Bothrops Brammianus Bocourt, Ann. Sci. Nat. Paris, (5) 10: 201. Type-locality: San Lucas, Guatemala, 1558 m.
1878 Bothrops (Bothriopsis) godmanni—Müller, Verh. Naturforsch. Ges. Basel, 6: 402, pl. 3, fig. B.
1880 Bothriechis scutigera Fischer, Arch. für Naturg., 46 (1): 218, pl. 8, figs. 8-9. Type-locality: Guatemala.
1883 Bothriechis trianguligera Fischer, Oster-Programm Akad. Gymnasiums Hamburg, 1833: 13. Type-locality: Guatemala.

Distribution: Oaxaca and Chiapas, Mexico to Panama at moderate to high elevations.

BOTHROPS HYOPRORUS Amaral

1935 Bothrops hyoprora Amaral, Mem. Inst. Butantan, 9: 222, figs. 7-8. Type-locality: La Pedrera, Colombia.

Distribution: Equatorial forests of Colombia, Ecuador, Peru and western Brazil.

BOTHROPS IGLESIASI Amaral

1923 Bothrops iglesiasi Amaral, Proc. New England Zool. Club, 8: 97. Type-locality: Near Fazenda Grande on right bank of Rio Gurgueia, Estado do Piauí, Brazil.

Distribution: Known only from northern Piauí, Brazil.

BOTHROPS INSULARIS (Amaral)

1921 Lachesis insularis Amaral, Anex. Mem. Inst. Butantan, 1: 18, pls. 3-4, figs. 1-5. Type-locality: Isla Queimada Grande, Estado de São Paulo, Brazil.
1929 Bothrops insularis—Amaral, Mem. Inst. Butantan, 4: 114.

Distribution: Queimada Grande Island, Brazil.

BOTHROPS ITAPETININGAE (Boulenger)

1907 Lachesis itapetiningae Boulenger, Ann. Mag. Nat. Hist., (7) 20: 338. Type-locality: Itapetininga, Estado de São Paulo, Brazil.
1929 Bothrops itapetiningae—Amaral, Mem. Inst. Butantan, 4: 235.

Distribution: Southeastern Brazil.

BOTHROPS JARARACA (Wied)

1824 Cophias jajaraca Wied (later emended to jararaca), Isis von Oken, 15: 1103. Type-locality: None mentioned; later given as Mucurí, Lagoa d'Arara, Brazil, by Wied, Beiträge zur Naturgeschichte von Brasilien, 1, 1825, 481.
1824 Bothrops Megaera Wagler (preoccupied by Bothrops megaera Shaw, 1802), in Spix, Sp. Nov. Serp. Bras.: 50, pl. 19. Type-locality: Bahía, Brazil.

BOTHROPS JARARACA (Wied), continued

1824 Bothrops leucostigma Wagler, in Spix, Sp. Nov. Serp. Bras.: 53, pl. 21, fig. 1. Type-locality: Bahía, Brazil.
1824 Bothrops tessellatus Wagler, in Spix, Sp. Nov. Serp. Bras.: 54, pl. 21, fig. 2. Type-locality: Rio San Francisco, Brazil.
1824 Bothrops taeniatus Wagler, in Spix, Sp. Nov. Serp. Bras.: 55, pl. 21, fig. 3. Type-locality: Rio Amazonas, Brazil.
1825 C.[ophias] Jararakka Wied, Beiträge zur Naturgeschichte von Brasilien, 1: 470. Type-locality: Not mentioned.
1830 [Bothrops] Jararaca—Wagler, Nat. Syst. Amph.: 174.
1925 Bothrops jararaca—Amaral, Cont. Harvard Inst. Trop. Biol. Med., 2: 42; pl. 2; pl. 4, figs. 2-2'; pl. 6A, figs. 2-2'; pl. 7, figs. 2-2'.

   Distribution: Brazil from central Minas Gerais south; Paraguay; Misiones, Argentina.

BOTHROPS JARARACUSSU Lacerda

1884 Bothrops jararacussu Lacerda, Léçons sur le Venin des Serpents du Brésil: 8. Type-locality: Province of Rio de Janeiro, Brazil.
1925 Bothrops jararacussu—Amaral, Cont. Harvard Inst. Trop. Biol. Med., 2: 43, pl. 3; pl. 4, figs. 3-3'; pl. 6A, figs. 3-3'; pl. 7, figs. 3-3'.

   Distribution: Northeastern Argentina in Misiones, southern Bolivia, Paraguay and Brazil from southern Minas Gerais southward.

BOTHROPS LANSBERGII (Schlegel)

1841 Trigonocephalus lansbergii Schlegel, Mag. Zool. Rept., (1-3), pl. 1. Type-locality: Turbaco, Colombia.
1860 T.[eleuraspis] Castelnaui var. brachystoma Cope, Proc. Acad. Nat. Sci. Phila., 1859: 339. Type-locality: Unknown.
1863 B.[othrops] Lansbergi—Jan, Elenco Sist. Ofidi: 127.
1889 Thanatophis sutus Posada Arango, Bull. Soc. Zool. France, 1889: 344. Type-locality: Zea, Colombia.

   Distribution: Discontinuous; Caribbean Venezuela and Colombia; Honduras.

   Content: Three subspecies.

   Comment: No recent author has indicated with which subspecies should be associated the synonyms here listed.

Key to the subspecies

1. Ventrals more than 146--------------------2
   Ventrals menos de 146----------------rozei

2. Snout raised sharply upward------lansbergii
   Snout not at all turned up in front--------
   ------------------------------annectens

Clave de subespecies

1. Ventrales más de 146-----------------------2
   Ventrales menos de 146----------------rozei

2. Hocico levantado bruscamente hacia arriba--
   --------------------------------lansbergii
   Hocico no levantado hacia arriba--annectens

Bothrops lansbergii lansbergii (Schlegel)

1959 B.[othrops] l.[ansbergii] lansbergii—Roze, Amer. Mus. Novitates, 1934: 11.

   Distribution: Arid and semi-arid regions of Caribbean coast in Colombia.

Bothrops lansbergii annectens (Schmidt)

1936 Trimeresurus lansbergii annectens Schmidt, Proc. Biol. Soc. Washington, 49: 50. Type-
   locality: Subirana Valley, Yoro, Honduras, 2800 ft.
1966 Bothrops lansbergii annectens—Hoge, Mem. Inst. Butantan, 32 (1955): 123.

   Distribution: Honduras.

Bothrops lansbergii rozei Peters

1959 Bothrops lansbergii venezuelensis Roze (preoccupied by Bothrops venezuelensis Sandner),
   Amer. Mus. Novitates, 1934: 11. Type-locality: Caripito, Monagas, Venezuela, 50.
1968 Bothrops lansbergii rozei Peters (replacement name for Bothrops venezuelensis Roze), Proc.
   Biol. Soc. Washington, 81: 320.

   Distribution: Northern Venezuela.

BOTHROPS LATERALIS (Peters)

1863 Bothriechis lateralis Peters, Monats. Akad. Wiss. Berlin, 1862: 674. Type-locality: Veragua
   and Volcán Barba, Costa Rica.
1878 Bothrops (Bothriechis) lateralis—Müller, Verh. Naturforsch. Ges. Basel, 6: 401.
1951 Bothrops lateralis—Taylor, Univ. Kansas Sci. Bull., 34: 175.

   Distribution: Costa Rica and Panama.

BOTHROPS LICHENOSUS Roze

1958 Bothrops lichenosa Roze, Acta. Biol. Venezuélica, 2: 308, three figs. Type-locality: Chimanta
   Tepui, Estado Bolívar, Venezuela.

   Distribution: Known only from type locality.

BOTHROPS LOJANUS Parker

1930 Bothrops lojana Parker, Ann. Mag. Nat. Hist., 5 (10 : 568. Type-locality: Loja, Provincia de
   Loja, Ecuador, 2200 m.

   Distribution: Known only from vicinity of type locality.

BOTHROPS MARAJOENSIS Hoge

1966 Bothrops marajoensis Hoge, Mem. Inst. Butantan, 32 (1965): 123. Type-locality: Severino, Marajó
   Island, Estado do Pará, Brazil.

   Distribution: Known only from savannah of Marajó, Brazil.

BOTHROPS MEDUSA (Sternfeld)

1920 Lachesis medusa Sternfeld, Senckenbergiana, 2: 180, figs. 1-2. Type-locality: Caracas,
   Venezuela.
1929 Bothrops medusa—Amaral, Mem. Inst. Butantan, 4: 236.

   Distribution: Cordillera de la Costa, Distrito Federal and Estados de Aragua and Carabubo,
   Venezuela.

BOTHROPS MICROPHTHALMUS Cope

1876 Bothrops microphthalmus Cope, Jour. Acad. Nat. Sci. Phila., (2) 8 (1875): 182. Type-locality:
Between Balso Puerto and Moyabamba, Peru.

Distribution: Amazonian lowlands of Ecuador, Peru, and Bolivia; Pacific slopes of Colombia.

Content: Two subspecies.

<table>
<tr><td>Key to the subspecies</td><td>Clave de subespecies</td></tr>
<tr><td>1. Ventrals more than 165; scale rows 25 or
   or more----------------------colombianus
   Ventrals fewer than 165; scale rows fewer
   than 25--------------------microphthalmus</td><td>1. Ventrales más de 165; hileras de escamas
   25 o más----------------------colombianus
   Ventrales menos de 165; hileras de escamas
   menos de 25----------------microphthalmus</td></tr>
</table>

Bothrops microphthalmus microphthalmus Cope

1912 Lachesis pleuroxanthus Boulenger, Ann. Mag. Nat. Hist., (8) 10: 423. Type-locality:
Alpayaca, Río Pastaza, eastern Ecuador, 3600 ft.
1940 [Bothrops microphthalmus microphthalmus]—Rendahl and Vestergren (by inference), Ark.
för Zool., 33A: 15.

Distribution: Amazonian lowlands of Ecuador, Peru, and one locality in Bolivia.

Bothrops microphthalmus colombianus Rendahl and Vestergren

1940 Bothrops microphthalmus colombianus Rendahl and Vestergren, Ark. för Zool., 33A: 15.
Type-locality: La Costa, Cauca, Colombia.

Distribution: Pacific slope of Colombia.

BOTHROPS MOOJENI Hoge

1966 Bothrops moojeni Hoge, Mem. Inst. Butantan, 32 (1965): 126, pl. 4; pl. 5, fig. 2. Type-locality:
Brasília, Distrito Federal, Brazil.

Distribution: Known only from type locality.

BOTHROPS NASUTUS Bocourt

1868 Bothrops nasutus Bocourt, Ann. Sci. Nat. Paris (5) 10: 202. Type-locality: Panzos, on banks of
Río Polochic, Guatemala.
1876 Bothriopsis proboscideus Cope, Jour. Acad. Nat. Sci. Phila., (2) 8 (1875): 150, pl. 27, fig. 3.
Type-locality: Sipurio, Costa Rica.

Distribution: Vera Cruz, Mexico, south on east coast of Central America to Pacific Colombia and
Ecuador.

BOTHROPS NEUWIEDI Wagler

1824 Bothrops neuwiedi Wagler, in Spix, Sp. Nov. Serp. Bras.: 56, pl. 22, fig. 1. Type-locality:
Estado da Bahía, Brazil.
1824 Bothrops leucurus Wagler, in Spix, Sp. Nov. Serp. Bras.: 57, pl. 22, fig. 2. Type-locality:
Bahia, Brazil.

Distribution: East of Andes and north of 10°S in South America.

Content: Twelve subspecies.

Comment: We have not been able to devise a satisfactory key to the subspecies, and the user will
have to consult the original descriptions of the taxa to make an identification.

Bothrops neuwiedi neuwiedi Wagler

   1925 Bothrops neuwiedii neuwiedii—Amaral, Contr. Harvard Inst. Trop. Biol. Med., 2: 57.

    Distribution: Southern Bahia, Brazil.

Bothrops neuwiedi bolivianus Amaral

   1927 Bothrops neuwiedii boliviana Amaral, Bull. Antivenin Inst. America, 1: 6, fig. 2. Type-locality: Buenavista, Provincia del Sara, Departamento Santa Cruz de la Sierra, Bolivia.

    Distribution: Departamento Santa Cruz de la Sierra, Bolivia; extreme western part of Estado de Mato Grosso, Brazil.

Bothrops neuwiedi diporus Cope

   1862 Bothrops diporus Cope, Proc. Acad. Nat. Sci. Phila., 14: 347. Type-locality: Vermejo River region; given as region of Río Vermejo, on boundary of Paraguay and Argentina, by Cochran, Bull. U.S. Nat. Mus., 220, 1961, 151.
   1930 Bothrops neuwiedii meridionalis Amaral (preoccupied by Bothrops neuwiedii meridionalis Müller), Bull. Antivenin Inst. America, 4 (3): 66, fig. 1. Type-locality: Embarcación, Salta, Argentina.
   1961 Bothrops neuwiedii diporus—Cochran, Bull. U.S. Nat. Mus., 220: 151.

    Distribution: Central and northern Argentina, southern Paraguay and Estado do Paraná, Brazil.

Bothrops neuwiedi goyazensis Amaral

   1925 Bothrops neuwiedii goyazensis Amaral, Contr. Harvard Inst. Trop. Biol. Med., 2: 58, pl. 14, fig. 3; pl. 15, fig. 3. Type-locality: Ipamery, Goiás, Brazil.

    Distribution: Known only from type locality.

Bothrops neuwiedi lutzi (Miranda-Ribeiro)

   1915 Lachesis lutzi Miranda-Ribeiro, Arch. Mus. Nac. Rio de Janeiro, 17: 4, pl. Type-locality: Rio São Francisco, Bahía, Brazil.
   1925 Bothrops neuwiedii bahiensis Amaral, Contr. Harvard Inst. Trop. Biol. Med., 2: 57, pl. 14, fig. 1, and pl. 15, fig. 1. Type-locality: Itiuba, Bahía, Brazil.
   1929 Bothrops neuwiedii lutzi—Amaral, Mem. Inst. Butantan, 4: 238.

    Distribution: Dry regions of Bahía, Brazil.

Bothrops neuwiedi mattogrossensis Amaral

   1925 Bothrops neuwiedii mattogrossensis Amaral, Contr. Harvard Inst. Trop. Biol. Med., 2: 60, pl. 14, fig. 6; pl. 16, fig. 6. Type-locality: Miranda, Estado de Mato Grosso, Brazil.

    Distribution: Southern Mato Grosso, Brazil.

Bothrops neuwiedi meridionalis Müller

   1885 Bothrops atrox meridionalis Müller, Verh. Naturforsch. Ges. Basel, 7: 699. Type-locality: Andaraí, Estado do Rio de Janeiro, Brazil.
   1933 Bothrops neuwiedii fluminensis Amaral, Mem. Inst. Butantan, 7 (1932): 97, fig. 1. Type-locality: Easternmost section of Rio de Janeiro, near Cabo São Thomé, Brazil.
   1966 Bothrops neuwidi meridionalis—Hoge, Mem. Inst. Butantan, 32 (1965): 128.

    Distribution: Rio de Janeiro, Guanabara and Espirito Santo, Brazil.

Bothrops neuwiedi paranaensis Amaral

1925 Bothrops neuwiedii paranaensis Amaral, Contr. Harvard Inst. Trop. Biol. Med., 2: 61, pl. 14, fig. 7; pl. 16, fig. 7. Type-locality: Castro, Paraná, Brazil.

   Distribution: Estado do Paraná, Brazil.

Bothrops neuwiedi pauloensis Amaral

1925 Bothrops neuwiedii pauloensis Amaral, Contr. Harvard Inst. Trop. Biol. Med., 2: 59, pl. 14, fig. 5; pl. 16, fig. 5. Type-locality: Leme, São Paulo, Brazil.

   Distribution: Southern parts of Estado de São Paulo, Brazil.

Bothrops neuwiedi piauhyensis Amaral

1925 Bothrops neuwiedii piauhyensis Amaral, Contr. Harvard Inst. Trop. Biol. Med., 2: 58, pl. 14, fig. 2; pl. 15, fig. 2. Type-locality: Fazenda Grande, Piauí, Brazil.

   Distribution: Piauí, Pernambuco, Estado do Ceará and southern Maranhão, Brazil.

Bothrops neuwiedi pubescens (Cope)

1870 Trigonocephalus (Bothrops) pubescens Cope, Proc. Amer. Phil. Soc., 11 (1869): 157. Type-locality: Rio Grande do Sul, Brazil.
1925 Bothrops neuwiedii riograndensis Amaral, Contr. Harvard Inst. Trop. Biol. Med., 2: 61, pl. 14, fig. 8; pl. 16, fig. 8. Type-locality: Itaquy, Rio Grande do Sul, Brazil.
1959 Bothrops neuwiedii pubescens—Hoge, Mem. Inst. Butantan, 28 (1957-1958): 84.

   Distribution: Estado do Rio Grande do Sul, Brazil; Uruguay.

Bothrops neuwiedi urutu Lacerda

1884 Bothrops urutu Lacerda, Lec. Ven. Serp. Brésil: 11, pl. 3. Type-locality: Provincia de Minas Gerais, now Estado de Minas Gerais, Brazil.
1937 Bothrops neuwiedii urutu—Amaral, Mem. Inst. Butantan, 10 (1936): 160.

   Distribution: Southern Minas Gerais and northern São Paulo, Brazil.

BOTHROPS NIGROVIRIDIS (Peters)

1859 Bothriechis nigroviridis Peters, Monats. Akad. Wiss. Berlin, 1859: 278, fig. 4. Type-locality: Volcán Barba, Costa Rica.
1878 Bothrops (Bothriechis) nigroviridis—Müller, Verh. Naturforsch. Ges. Basel, 6: 401.

Distribution: Chiapas, Mexico to Panama.

Content: Three subspecies.

Key to the subspecies	Clave de subespecies

1. Ventrals more than 150--------------------2
   Ventrals fewer than 150--------nigroviridis
	1. Ventrales más de 150----------------------2
	   Ventrales menos de 150---------nigroviridis

2. Dorsum uniform, scales with narrow black
   edges; no temporal streak---------marchii
   Dorsum green with scattered yellow spots;
   black streak on temporal----------aurifer
	2. Dorso uniforme, escamas con bordes negros
	   angostos; sin estría temporal------marchii
	   Dorso verde con manchas amarillas dispersas;
	   con estría negra en el temporal----aurifer

Bothrops nigroviridis nigroviridis (Peters)

   1929 Bothrops nigroviridis nigroviridis—Barbour and Loveridge, Bull. Antivenin Inst. America, 3: 1.

   Distribution: Costa Rica to Panama.

Bothrops nigroviridis aurifer (Salvin)

   1860 Thamnocenchris aurifer Salvin, Proc. Zool. Soc. London, 1860: 459, pl. 32, fig. 1. Type-locality: Cobán, Alta Verapaz, Guatemala.
   1878 Bothrops aurifer—Müller, Verh. Naturforsch. Ges. Basel, 6: 401.
   1929 Bothrops nigroviridis aurifera—Barbour and Loveridge, Bull. Antivenin Inst. America, 3: 1.

   Distribution: Caribbean slope from Chiapas, Mexico to Guatemala.

Bothrops nigroviridis marchii Barbour and Loveridge

   1929 Bothrops nigroviridis marchii Barbour and Loveridge, Bull. Antivenin Inst. America, 3: 2, fig. 1. Type-locality: Quimistan, Santa Barbara, Honduras.

   Distribution: Vicinity of type locality.

   Comment: Although not listed by Hoge as a valid subspecies of nigroviridis by Hoge, Mem. Inst. Butantan, 32, 1965 (1966), 129, neither is it given as a synonym of any other taxon. Since it apparently has not been synonymized with any existing taxon, we list it here.

BOTHROPS NUMMIFER (Rüppell)

   1845 Atropos nummifer Rüppell, Verh. Mus. Senckenberg, 3: 313. Type-locality: Mexico; restricted to Teapa, Tabasco, Mexico, by Burger, Bull. Chicago Acad. Sci., 9, 1950, 65.
   1863 B. [othrops] nummifer—Jan, Elenco Sist. Ofidi: 126.

   Distribution: Southeastern edge of Mexican Plateau in San Luis Potosí and Oaxaca to Costa Rica.

   Content: Three subspecies, one of which (the nominate subspecies) is extralimital.

Key to the subspecies	Clave de subespecies
1. Lateral spots vertically elongate and many fused with dorsal blotches-------mexicanus Lateral spots rounded, very few fused with dorsal blotches------------------occiduus	1. Manchas laterales alargadas verticalmente y muchas fusionadas con los bloques dorsales------------------------mexicanus Manchas laterales redondeadas, muy pocas fusionadas con los bloques dorsales------- ---------------------------------occiduus

Bothrops nummifer mexicanus (Duméril, Bibron and Duméril)

   1854 Atropos Mexicanus Duméril, Bibron and Duméril, Erp. Gén., 7 (part 2): 1521, pl. 83 bis, figs. 1-2. Type-locality: Cobán, Alta Verapaz, Guatemala.
   1880 Bothriechis nummifer var. notata Fischer, Arch. für Naturg., 46: 222, pl. 8, figs. 10-12. Type locality: Cobán, Alta Verapaz, Guatemala.
   1882 Bothrops mexicanus—Müller, Verh. Naturforsch. Ges. Basel, 7: 154.
   1952 Bothrops nummifer mexicanus—Mertens, Abh. Senckenberg Naturforsch. Ges., 487: 79.

   Distribution: Lower elevations on Caribbean slope from extreme southern Mexico to Panama.

Bothrops nummifer occiduus Hoge

1868 Bothrops affinis Bocourt (preoccupied by Bothrops affinis Gray, 1849), Ann. Sci. Nat.
Paris, (5) 10: 201. Type-locality: San Augustin, on south slope of mountains,
in Guatemala, 610 m.
1963 Bothrops nummifer affinis—Stuart, Misc. Publ. Mus. Zool. Univ. Mich., 122: 130.
1966 Bothrops nummifer occiduus Hoge (replacement name for Bothrops affinis Bocourt), Mem.
Inst. Butantan, 32 (1965): 130.

Distribution: Pacific slope, Guatemala to El Salvador; possibly in Chiapas, Mexico.

BOTHROPS OLIGOLEPIS (Werner)

1901 Lachesis bilineatus var. oligolepis Werner, Abh. Ber. Mus. Dresden, 9 (2): 13. Type-locality:
Bolivia.
1912 Lachesis chloromelas Boulenger, Ann. Mag. Nat. Hist., (8) 10: 423. Type-locality: Huancabamba,
eastern Peru, above 3000 ft.
1926 Bothrops chrysomelas Amaral (in error for chloromelas Boulenger), Ann. Carnegie Mus., 16: 320.

Distribution: Peru and Bolivia.

BOTHROPS OPHRYOMEGAS Bocourt

1868 Bothrops ophryomegas Bocourt, Ann. Sci. Nat. Paris, (5) 10: 201. Type-locality: Warm regions
on western (actually southern) slope of Cordillera, Escuintla, Guatemala.

Distribution: Pacific slope of Central America from western Guatemala to Panama.

BOTHROPS PERUVIANUS (Boulenger)

1903 Lachesis peruvianus Boulenger, Ann. Mag. Nat. Hist., (7) 12: 354. Type-locality: La Oroya and
Carabaya, southeastern Peru.
1929 Bothrops peruviana—Amaral, Mem. Inst. Butantan, 4: 240.

Distribution: Southeastern Peru.

BOTHROPS PESSOAI Prado

1939 Bothrops pessoai Prado, Mem. Inst. Butantan, 12 (1938-1939): 2. Type-locality: Rio Parauary,
Estado do Amazonas, Brazil.
1948 Trimeresurus pessoai—Hoge, Bol. Mus. Paraense E. Goeldi, 10: 325.

Distribution: Known only from type locality.

BOTHROPS PICADOI (Dunn)

1939 Trimeresurus nummifer picadoi Dunn, Proc. Biol. Soc. Washington, 52: 165. Type-locality: La
Palma, Costa Rica, 4500 ft.
1945 Bothrops picadoi—Smith and Taylor, Bull. U.S. Nat. Mus., 187: 183.
1951 Bothrops picadoi—Taylor, Univ. Kansas Sci. Bull., 34: 180.

Distribution: Central Plateau of Costa Rica and surrounding mountains.

BOTHROPS PICTUS (Tschudi)

1845 L.[achesis] picta Tschudi, Arch. für Naturg., 11: 166 (fig. 10 in Fauna Peruana, 1845). Type-
locality: High mountains of Peru.
1863 B.[othrops] pictus—Jan, Elenco Sist. Ofidi: 126.

Distribution: Coastal region of Peru to 1800 m.

BOTHROPS PIRAJAI Amaral

1923 Bothrops pirajai Amaral, Proc. New England Zool. Club, 8: 99. Type-locality: Ilhéus, Estado da
    Bahía, Brazil.
1923 Bothrops neglecta Amaral, Proc. New England Zool. Club, 8: 100. Type-locality: Bahía, Brazil.

   Distribution: Known only from southern Bahía, Brazil.

BOTHROPS PRADOI (Hoge)

1948 Trimeresurus pradoi Hoge, Mem. Inst. Butantan, 20 (1947): 193. Type-locality: Pau Gigante,
    Estado do Espírito Santo, Brazil.
1966 Bothrops pradoi—Hoge, Mem. Inst. Butantan, 32 (1965): 132, pl. 8.

   Distribution: Espírito Santo to southern Bahía, Brazil.

BOTHROPS PULCHER (Peters)

1862 Trigonocephalus pulcher Peters, Monats Akad. Wiss. Berlin, 1862: 672. Type-locality: Quito,
    Ecuador; in error, according to Peters, Rev. Ecuat. Ent. Parasit., 2, 1955, 347.
1929 Bothrops pulchra—Amaral, Mem. Inst. Butantan, 4: 240.

   Distribution: Equatorial forests in Amazonian lowlands of Ecuador and Peru.

BOTHROPS PUNCTATUS (García)

1896 Lachesis punctata García, Los Ofidios Venenosas de Cauca, Cali, Colombia: 31, fig. 8. Type-
    locality: Las Montañas de Dagua, Colombia.
1910 Lachesis Monticellii Peracca, An. Mus. Napoli, 3 (12): 2. Type-locality: Unknown; "America
    tropicale".
1923 Bothrops leptura Amaral, Proc. New England Zool. Club, 8: 102. Type-locality: Cana, eastern
    Panama, 3000 ft.
1944 Bothrops punctatus—Dunn, Caldasia, 3: 215.

   Distribution: Darién of Panama to northwestern Ecuador.

BOTHROPS ROEDINGERI Mertens

1942 Bothrops roedingeri Mertens, Beiträge zur Fauna Perus, 11: 284. Type-locality: Hacienda Huayri,
    Peru.

   Distribution: Desert region, Pacific coast of Peru.

BOTHROPS SANCTAECRUCIS Hoge

1966 Bothrops sanctaecrucis Hoge, Mem. Inst. Butantan, 32 (1965): 133, pl. 9. Type-locality: Oromomo,
    Río Secure, upper Río Beni, Bolivia.

   Distribution: Amazonian lowlands of Bolivia.

BOTHROPS SCHLEGELII (Berthold)

1846 Trigonocephalus schlegelii Berthold, Nachr. Univ. Ges. Wiss. Göttingen: 147. Type-locality:
    Popayan; indicated to be Popayan, Colombia by Dunn and Stuart, Copeia, 1954, 56.
1859 Lachesis nitidus Günther, Proc. Zool. Soc. London, 1859: 414, pl. 20, fig. C. Type-locality:
    Western Andes of Ecuador.
1863 B. [othrops] Schlegeli—Jan, Elenco Sist. Ofidi: 127.
1870 Bothrops (Teleuraspis) nigroadspersus Steindachner, Sitz. Math.-Natur. Cl. Akad. Wiss. Wien, 62:
    348, pl. 8. Type-locality: Central America.
1889 Thanatophis torvus Posada Arango, Bull. Soc. Zool. France, 1889: 345. Type-locality: Antioquia,
    Colombia.
1951 Bothrops schlegeli—Taylor, Univ. Kansas Sci. Bull., 34: 173.
1966 Bothrops schlegelii—Hoge (in error for schlegelii Berthold), Mem. Inst. Butantan, 32 (1965): 134.

   Distribution: Southern Mexico to Pacific Ecuador; mountains of Ureña, Estado de Táchira, Caribbean
    Venezuela.

BOTHROPS SUPRACILIARIS Taylor

1954 Bothrops schlegelii supraciliaris Taylor, Univ. Kansas Sci. Bull., 36: 791, fig. 39. Type-
     locality: Mountains near San Isidro del General, San José Province, Costa Rica.
1963 [Bothrops supraciliaris]—Stuart, Misc. Publ. Mus. Zool. Univ. Mich., 122: 131.

   Distribution: Known only from type locality.

BOTHROPS VENEZUELENSIS Sandner Montilla

1952 Bothrops venezuelensis Sandner Montilla, Mon. Cien. Inst. Terap. Exp. Lab. "Veros" Ltda., 21 (9):
     4. Type-locality: "Boca de Tigre", Serranía de El Avila, Distrito Federal al Norte de Caracas,
     Venezuela.
1961 Bothrops pifanoi Sandner Montilla and Romer, Nov. Cien. Contr. Ocas. Mus. Hist. Nat. La Salle,
     29: 3, figs. 1-4. Type-locality: Serranía de el Avila, El Papelón, Venezuela.
1961 Bothrops venezuelae Sandner Montilla, Mon. Cien. Centr. Ocas. Mus. Hist. Nat. La Salle, Caracas,
     Zool., 30: 3. Type-locality: Serranía de El Avila, Venezuela.

   Distribution: Northern and central part of Venezuela, including Avila Mountain, western mountains
      of los Tigres, forests of Rancho Grande and Fila Miranda, Estado de Aragua and forests of Guatopo,
      Estado Miranda; Estados Trujillo and Sucre.

BOTHROPS XANTHOGRAMMUS (Cope)

1868 Trigonocephalus xanthogrammus Cope, Proc. Acad. Nat. Sci. Phila., 1868: 110. Type-locality:
     Pallatanga, Ecuador.
1889 Bothrops quadriscutatus Posada Arango (preoccupied by quadriscutatus Peters, 1861), Bull. Soc.
     Zool. France, 1889: 345. Type-locality: Antioquia, Colombia.
1929 Bothrops xanthogramma—Amaral, Mem. Inst. Butantan, 4: 241.
1966 Bothrops xantogrammus—Hoge (in error for xanthogrammus Cope), Mem. Inst. Butantan, 32 (1965):
     135.

   Distribution: Highlands of Ecuador; doubtful in Colombia.

INCERTAE SEDIS

   Comment: The following taxa have not been included by Klemmer or Hoge in their recent lists of
      Neotropical Viperids. Boulenger, Cat. Sn. Brit. Mus., 3, 1896, 535, included all in the synonymy of
      his composite species Lachesis lanceolatus, a taxon now regarded as endemic to Martinique. These
      taxa are probably all synonymous with one of following: atrox, jararaca, jararacussu, and some
      could take priority over the latter two.

1788 Coluber ambiguus Gmelin, Systema Naturae, Ed. 12: 1104. Type-locality: America.
1789 C.[oluber] Tigrinus Lacépède, Hist. Nat. Serp., 2: 82. Type-locality: Unknown.
1789 C.[oluber] Brasiliensis Lacépède, Hist. Nat. Serp., 2: 98. Type-locality: Brazil.
1802 Vipera brasiliniana Latreille (emendation of brasiliensis Lacépède), Hist. Nat. Rept., 4: 7.
1803 Vipera Weigeli Daudin (substitute name for Coluber ambiguus Gmelin), Hist. Nat. Rept., 6: 60.
     Type-locality: America.
1821 Cophias holosericeus Wied, Reise nach Brasilien, 2: 243. Type-locality: None given.
1842 Bothrops cinereus Gray, Zoological Miscellany: 47. Type-locality: America.
1863 B.[othrops] atrox var. dirus Jan, Elenco Sist. Ofidi: 126. Type-locality: Buenos Aires, Mexico,
     and Orizaba; restricted to Buenos Aires, Argentina, by Smith and Taylor, Bull. U.S. Nat. Mus.
     187, 1945, 180.

CALAMODONTOPHIS Amaral

    1935 Calamodon Amaral (preoccupied by Calamodon Cope, 1875), Mem. Inst. Butantan, 9: 203. Type-
        species: Calamodon paucidens Amaral.
    1963 Calamodontophis Amaral (substitute name for Calamodon Amaral), Copeia, 1963: 580.

   Distribution: As for single known species.

   Content: One species.

CALAMODONTOPHIS PAUCIDENS (Amaral)

    1935 Calamodon paudicens Amaral, Mem. Inst. Butantan, 9: 204, fig. 1. Type-locality: S. Simão, Río
        Grande do Sul, Brazil.
    1963 [Calamodontophis] paucidens—Amaral, Copeia, 1963: 580.

   Distribution: Known only from Estado do Rio Grande do Sul, Brazil.

CHERSODROMUS Reinhardt

1860 *Chersodromus Reinhardt*, Vidensk. Medd. Naturhist. Foren. Kjöbenhavn, 1860: 242. Type-species *Chersodromus Liebmanni* Reinhardt.
1861 *Opisthiodon* Peters, Monats. Akad. Wiss. Berlin, 1861: 460. Type-species: *Opisthiodon torquatus* Peters.

Distribution: Mexico to Guatemala.

Content: Two species, one (*annulatus* Zweifel) extralimital. Scott, Copeia, 1967, 281, considered *annulatus* to be synonymous with *Tropidodipsas annulifera* Boulenger.

CHERSODROMUS LIEBMANNI Reinhardt

1860 *Chersodromus Liebmanni* Reinhardt, Vidensk. Medd. Naturhist. Foren. Kjöbenhavn, 1860: 243. Type-locality: Mexico; restricted to Cuautlapán, Veracruz, Mexico by Smith and Taylor, Univ. Kansas Sci. Bull., 33, 1950, 347.
1860 *Chersodromus nigricans* Reinhardt, Vidensk. Medd. Naturhist. Foren. Kjöbenhavn, 1860: 245. Type-locality: Mexico; restricted to Cuautlapán, Veracruz, Mexico by Smith and Taylor, Univ. Kansas Sci. Bull., 33, 1950, 347.
1861 *Opisthiodon torquatus* Peters, Monats. Akad. Wiss. Berlin, 1861: 461. Type-locality: Huanusco, in error for Huatusco, Veracruz, Mexico.
1900 *Dirosema collare* Werner, Zool. Anz., 23: 197, Figs. 3-5. Type-locality: Mexico; restricted to Cuautlapán, Veracruz, Mexico by Smith and Taylor, Univ. Kansas Sci. Bull., 33, 1950, 347.

Distribution: Mexico to Guatemala.

<u>CHIRONIUS</u> Fitzinger

   1826 <u>Chironius</u> Fitzinger, Neue Classification der Reptilien, 31. Type-species: <u>Coluber</u> <u>carinatus</u>
        Linnaeus.
   1826 <u>Erpetodryas</u> Boie, in Férussac, Bull. Sci. Nat. Geol., Paris, 9: 237. Type-species: Not desig-
        nated.
   1830 <u>Herpetodryas</u> Wagler (emendation of <u>Erpetodryas</u> Boie), Nat. Syst. Amph.: 180.
   1830 <u>Macrops</u> Wagler, Nat. Syst. Amph.: 182. Type-species: <u>Coluber</u> <u>saturninus</u> Linnaeus.
   1843 <u>Hylophis</u> Fitzinger, Systema Reptilium: 26. Type-species: <u>Coluber</u> <u>Laevicollis</u> Wied.
   1862 <u>Phyllosira</u> Cope, Proc. Acad. Nat. Sci. Phila., 1862: 349. Type-species: <u>Phyllosira</u> <u>flavescens</u>
        Cope.

   Distribution: Nicaragua to southern Brazil and Argentina.

   Content: Sixteen species.

Key to the species	Clave de especies

1. With ten scale rows at midbody----------------2
   With twelve scale rows at midbody-----------11
	1. Con diez filas de escamas en el medio cuerpo--2
	   Con doce filas de escamas en el medio cuerpo-11

2. Anal single----------------------------------3
   Anal divided---------------------------------6
	2. Anal entera---------------------------------3
	   Anal dividida--------------------------------6

3. Ground color reddish, brownish or yellowish---4
   Ground color green, blue or black--------<u>fuscus</u>
	3. Color general pardo, rojizo o amarillento-----4
	   Color general verde, azul o negro--------<u>fuscus</u>

4. Dorsal scales smooth; fewer than 40 maxillary
   teeth---5
   At least two rows of dorsal scales keeled;
   41-45 maxillary teeth-------------------<u>fuscus</u>
	4. Escamas dorsales lisas, menos de 40 dientes
	   maxilares------------------------------------5
	   Por lo menos dos hileras de dorsales carenadas;
	   41-45 dientes maxilares-----------------<u>fuscus</u>

5. Ground color reddish cinnamon; light supra-
   labials; eight scale rows at level of anus----
   --------------------------------------<u>cinnamomeus</u>
   Ground color brownish-yellow; dark supra-
   labials; ten scale rows at level of anus------
   --<u>scurrulus</u>
	5. Color canela rojizo; supralabiales claras; ocho
	   hileras dorsales a nivel del ano---<u>cinnamomeus</u>
	   Color pardo amarillento; supralabiales oscuras;
	   diez hileras sobre el ano-----------<u>scurrulus</u>

6. Paravertebral scales lack pits throughout
   length of body--------------------------------7
   Paravertebral scales with prominent apical pits
   throughout length of body------------<u>foveatus</u>
	6. Hileras de escamas paravertebrales sin fosetas
	   en toda la longitud del animal---------------7
	   Hileras de escamas paravertebrales con fosetas
	   en toda la longitud del animal--------<u>foveatus</u>

7. Caudals fewer than 135------------------------8
   Caudals more than 136------------------------9
	7. Menos de 135 caudales-------------------------8
	   Más de 136 caudales--------------------------9

8. Temporals 2 + 2; all dorsal scales keeled with
   exception of paravertebrals and lowermost row-
   --------------------------------<u>grandisquamis</u>
   Temporals 1 + 2; only two paravertebral rows
   keeled------------------------------<u>schlueteri</u>
	8. Todas las dorsales carenadas con la excepción
	   de las paravertebrales y la fila exterior;
	   2 + 2 temporales----------------<u>grandisquamis</u>
	   Sólo las dos filas paravertebrales carenadas;
	   1 + 2 temporales--------------------<u>schlueteri</u>

9. Not black dorsally; lower surface of tail not
   same color as dorsum; usually two secondary
   temporals-----------------------------------10
   Dorsum black; lower surface of tail also black,
   same color as dorsum; usually one secondary
   temporal----------------------------------<u>melas</u>
	9. No negro a dorsal; superficie ventral de la
	   cola de distinto color que el dorso; usualmente
	   dos temporales secundarios------------------10
	   Dorso negro; superficie ventral de la cola
	   también negra; usualmente un temporal
	   secundario-------------------------------<u>melas</u>

10.Dorsal scale rows ten immediately anterior to
   vent; 30-41 maxillary teeth; 153-172 ventrals;
   outer tips of subcaudals black, contrasting
   with ventral tail color------------<u>bicarinatus</u>
   Dorsal scale rows eight immediately anterior to
   vent; 24-28 maxillary teeth; 137-157 ventrals;
   outer tips of subcaudals not sharply contrasting
   with ventral tail color------------<u>pyrrhopogon</u>
	10.Filas de escamas dorsales diez inmediatamente
	   anterior al ano; 30-41 dientes maxilares;
	   153-172 ventrales; ápices externos de sub-
	   caudales negros, en contraste con el color
	   ventral de la cola----------------<u>bicarinatus</u>
	   Filas de escamas dorsales ocho inmediatamente
	   anterior al ano; 24-28 dientes maxilares;
	   137-157 ventrales; ápices externos de sub-
	   caudales no contrastan fuertemente con color
	   ventral de la cola-----------------<u>pyrrhopogon</u>

11. Lacking lateral dark stripe on tail----------12
    With lateral black stripe on tail-----monticola

12. Fewer than 180 caudals-----------------------13
    More than 190 caudals-------------multiventris

13. Anal divided--------------------------------14
    Anal single-----------------------laevicollis

14. Head not brownish red; lacks median yellowish
    stripe-----------------------------------15
    Head brownish red with median yellowish stripe-
    -------------------------------flavolineata

15. Light vertebral stripe present----------------16
    Light vertebral stripe absent----------------17

16. Fewer than four rows of keeled scales in both
    sexes--------------------------------carinatus
    At least four scale rows keeled in both sexes--
    ---------------------------quadricarinatus

17. Keeled scales with light spot at base, giving
    appearance of yellow vertebral line; no zig-zag
    line down median ventral surface of tail;
    subcaudals 108-120------------------flavopictus
    Light vertebral line continuous, not made up of
    yellow spots; zig-zag line down median ventral
    surface of tail; subcaudals 128-154--bicarinatus

11. Sin cinta oscura laterocaudal----------------12
    Con cinta negra a los lados de la cola---------
    --------------------------------------monticola

12. Menos de 180 caudales------------------------13
    Más de 190 caudales---------------multiventris

13. Anal dividida------------------------------14
    Anal entera-----------------------laevicollis

14. Cabeza no pardo rojiza sin cinta mediana
    amarillenta------------------------------15
    Cabeza pardo rojiza con una cinta mediana
    amarillenta---------------------flavolineata

15. Con cinta clara vertebral--------------------16
    Sin cinta clara vertebral--------------------17

16. Menos de cuatro hileras de escamas quilladas en
    ambos sexos--------------------------carinatus
    Por lo menos cuatro hileras de escamas qui-
    lladas en ambos sexos----------quadricarinatus

17. Escamas quilladas con mancha clara en la base,
    con aspecto de línea vertebral amarilla; sin
    línea en zigzag a lo largo de la superficie
    media ventral de la cola; subcaudales 108-120
    ------------------------------------flavopictus
    Línea vertebral clara continua, no formada por
    manchas amarillas; con línea en zigzag a lo
    largo de la superficie media ventral de la cola;
    subcaudales 128-154-----------------bicarinatus

CHIRONIUS BICARINATUS (Wied)

1820 Coluber bicarinatus Wied, Reise nach Brasilien, 1: 181. Type-locality: Lake near Rio Jucú, five
     leagues south of Cidade Espirito Santo, Espirito Santo, Brazil.
1955 Chironius bicarinatus—Bailey, Occ. Pap. Mus. Zool. Univ. Mich., 571: 8.

   Distribution: Espirito Santo and eastern Minas Gerais, Brazil, southwest of Misiones and Río
   Uruguay, Provincias Chaco, Corrientes, Salta, Formosa, and Entre Rios, Argentina; northwestern
   Uruguay.

CHIRONIUS CARINATUS (Linnaeus)

1758 Coluber carinatus Linnaeus, Systema Naturae, Ed. 10: 223. Type-locality: "Indiis".
1798 Coluber (Chironius) Donndorff, Zoologische Beyträge, 3—Amphibien und Fische: 209. Type-
     locality: Not given.
1845 Coluber Spixii Hallowell, Proc. Acad. Nat. Sci. Phila, 1845: 241. Type-locality: South America.
1845 Coluber Pickeringii Hallowell, Proc. Acad. Nat. Sci. Phila., 1845: 242. Type-locality: South
     America.
1891 Herpetodryas carinatus var. vincenti Boulenger, Proc. Zool. Soc. London, 1891: 355.
     Type-locality: Saint Vincent Island.
1896 Zaocys tornieri Werner, Verh. Zool.-Bot. Ges. Wien, 46: 15, pl. 1, fig. 1. Type-locality:
     Sumatra.
1922 Chironius carinatus—Ruthven, Misc. Publ. Mus. Zool. Univ. Mich., 8: 65.

   Distribution: Central America; tropical South America; Trinidad; Guadalupe; San Vicente I.

CHIRONIUS CINNAMOMEUS (Wagler)

1824 Natrix cinnamomea Wagler, in Spix, Sp. Nov. Serp. Bras.: 20, pl. 6, fig. 1. Type-locality:
     Amazonian forest, Brazil.
1964 Chironius cinnamomeus—Hoge, Mem. Inst. Butantan, 30 (1960-62): 53.

   Distribution: Surinam and Lower Amazonian region of Brazil.

CHIRONIUS

CHIRONIUS FLAVOLINEATUS (Boettger)

1885 Herpetodryas flavolineatus Boettger, Zeits. für Naturwiss., 58: 234. Type-locality: Paraguay.
1955 Chironius flavolineatus—Bailey, Occ. Pap. Mus. Zool. Univ. Mich., 571: 13.

   Distribution: Savannas of central and western Bahia, northeastern Mato Grosso, and São Paulo, Brazil; Paraguay; central Bolivia.

CHIRONIUS FLAVOPICTUS (Werner)

1909 Herpetodryas carinatus L. var. flavopicta Werner, Mitt. Naturhist. Mus. Hamburg, 26: 220. Type-locality: Ecuador, and Guayaquil, Ecuador.
1960 Chironius flavopictus—Peters, Bull. Mus. Comp. Zool., 122: 511.

   Distribution: Known under this name only from type-locality and Cabeceras de Río Congo, Ecuador; possibly occurs in northwestern Peru.

CHIRONIUS FOVEATUS

1955 Chironius foveatus Bailey, Occ. Pap. Mus. Zool. Univ. Mich., 571: 10, fig. 1. Type-locality: Rio Fortuna, Ilhéus, Bahia, Brazil.

   Distribution: Bahia to Santa Catarina, on Brazilian coast.

CHIRONIUS FUSCUS (Linnaeus)

1758 Coluber fuscus Linnaeus, Systema Naturae, Ed. 10: 222. Type-locality: Asia (in error).
1758 Coluber saturninus Linnaeus, Systema Naturae, Ed. 10: 223. Type-locality: Indiis.
1854 Dendrophis viridis Duméril, Bibron and Duméril, Erp. Gén., 7: 202. Type-locality: unknown.
1860 Herpetodryas sebastus Cope, Proc. Acad. Nat. Sci. Phila., 1860: 562. Type-locality: unknown.
1876 Herpetodryas holochlorus Cope, Jour. Acad. Nat. Sci. Phila., (2) 8 (1875): 178. Type-locality: Río Marañón, Peru.
1915 Herpetodryas vicinus Boulenger, Proc. Zool. Soc. London, 1915: 660. Type-locality: Andagoya, Colombia.
1929 Chironius fuscus—Amaral, Mem. Inst. Butantan, 4: 161.

   Distribution: Panama, Colombia, Venezuela, Guianas, central Brazil, Peru.

CHIRONIUS GRANDISQUAMIS (Peters)

1868 Spilotes grandisquamis Peters, Monats. Akad. Wiss. Berlin, 1868: 451. Type-locality: Costa Rica.
1951 Chironius grandisquamis—Taylor, Univ. Kansas Sci. Bull., 34: 96.

   Distribution: Costa Rica, Panama, northwestern Ecuador.

CHIRONIUS LAEVICOLLIS (Wied)

1824 Coluber laevicollis Wied, Isis von Oken, 1824, heft 6: 666. Type-locality: None given; Wied, Beitr. Naturges. Bras., 1825, 299, said Fazenda of Muribeca on lower Rio Itabapoana, on boundary between Espirito Santo and Rio de Janeiro, Brazil.
1955 Chironius laevicollis—Bailey, Occ. Pap. Mus. Zool. Univ. Mich., 571: 18.

   Distribution: Central Espirito Santo to Paraná, Brazil.

CHIRONIUS MELAS (Cope)

1886 Herpetodryas melas Cope, Proc. Amer. Phil. Soc., 23: 278. Type-locality: Nicaragua.
1951 Chironius melas—Taylor, Univ. Kansas Sci. Bull., 34: 97.

   Distribution: Honduras, Nicaragua and Costa Rica.

CHIRONIUS <u>MONTICOLA</u> Roze

> 1952 <u>Chironius monticola</u> Roze, Acta Biol. Venezuelica, 1: 100, figs. Type-locality: El Junquito, Distrito Federal, Venezuela.

> Distribution: Coastal Cordillera from Caracas, to Andes of Táchira, above 1,200 m in Venezuela; Colombia; also recorded from Bolivia by Roze, Ofidios de Venezuela, 1966, 101.

CHIRONIUS <u>MULTIVENTRIS</u> Schmidt and Walker

> 1943 <u>Chironius multiventris</u> Schmidt and Walker, Zool. Ser. Field Mus. Nat. Hist., 24: 282. Type-locality: Departamento Madre de Dios, Peru.

> Distribution: Known from type-locality; also recorded from Onverwacht, Surinam by Hoge, Mem. Inst. Butantan, 30, 1964, 54; Museo Nacional of Brazil has specimen from Benjamin Constant, Brazil.

CHIRONIUS <u>PYRRHOPOGON</u> (Wied)

> 1824 <u>Coluber pyrrhopogon</u> Wied, Isis von Oken, 1824, heft 6: 666. Type-locality: None given; Wied, Beitr. Naturges. Bras., 1825, 296, gave great forests of Rio Iritiba or Benevente, Espirito Santo, Brazil.
> 1955 <u>Chironius pyrrhopogon</u>—Bailey, Occ. Pap. Mus. Zool. Univ. Mich., 571: 12.

> Distribution: Bahia to Santa Catarina, Brazil, along coast; Bailey, loc. cit., recorded the same or a closely related form from western Mato Grosso.

CHIRONIUS <u>QUADRICARINATUS</u> (Boie)

> 1827 <u>Erpetodryas 4-dricarinatus</u> Boie, Isis von Oken, 20 (1): 548. Type-locality: None given, restricted to Asunción, Paraguay by Bailey, Occ. Pap. Mus. Zool. Univ. Mich., 571: 15.
> 1862 <u>Phyllosira flavescens</u> Cope, Proc. Acad. Nat. Sci. Phila., 1862: 349. Type-locality: Paraguay or northern Argentina.
> 1955 <u>Chironius quadricarinatus</u>—Bailey, Occ. Pap. Mus. Zool. Univ. Mich., 571: 15.

> Distribution: Savanna areas of northern Mato Grosso, Brazil, and central Bolivia; central Paraguay; vicinity of São Paulo city, Brazil.

CHIRONIUS <u>SCHLUETERI</u> (Werner)

> 1899 <u>Herpetodryas Schlüteri</u> Werner, Zool. Anz., 22: 115. Type-locality: Napo, Ecuador.
> 1960 <u>Chironius schlüteri</u>—Peters, Bull. Mus. Comp. Zool., 122: 512.

> Distribution: Amazonian slopes of Ecuador.

CHIRONIUS <u>SCURRULUS</u> (Wagler)

> 1824 <u>Natrix Scurrula</u> Wagler, in Spix, Sp. Nov. Serp. Bras.: 24, pl. 8. Type-locality: Rio Japura, Brazil.
> 1964 <u>Chironius scurrulus</u>—Hoge, Mem. Inst. Butantan, 30 (1960-62): 72.

> Distribution: Amazonas, Minas Gerais, Rondônia, and Pará, Brazil; southeastern Colombia; Moyobamba and Xeberos, Peru.

Prepared by Joseph R. Bailey, Duke University, Durham, North Carolina

CLELIA Fitzinger

1826 <u>Clelia</u> Fitzinger, Neue Classification der Reptilien: 29. Type-species: <u>Coluber</u> <u>clelia</u> Daudin.
1830 <u>Cloelia</u> Wagler (emendation of <u>Clelia</u> Fitzinger), Nat. Syst. Amphib.: 187.
?1843 <u>Rhinoscytale</u> Fitzinger, Systema Reptilium: 25. Type-species: <u>Rhinoscytale</u> <u>Cloelia</u>, nomen nudum,
    which may be same as <u>Coluber</u> <u>clelia</u> Daudin.
1843 <u>Deiropeda</u> Fitzinger, Systema Reptilium: 25. Type-species: <u>Coluber</u> <u>clelia</u> Daudin.
1843 <u>Hydroscopus</u> Fitzinger, Systema Reptilium: 25. Type-species: <u>Coluber</u> <u>plumbeus</u> Wied.
1853 <u>Brachyrruton</u> Duméril, Mém. Acad. Sci. Paris, 23: 502. Type-species: None given.
1924 <u>Barbourina</u> Amaral, Jour. Washington Acad. Sci., 14: 201. Type-species: <u>Barbourina</u> <u>equatoriana</u>
    Amaral.

    Distribution: Tropical Mexico to about 35°S latitude east of Andes and to northwestern Ecuador west
    of Andes in South America; lesser Antilles.

    Content: Six species currently known, plus several undescribed taxa.

Key to the species

1. Dorsal scales in 19 rows at midbody-----------2
   Dorsal scales in 17 rows at midbody-----------5

2. Upper labials usually seven (rarely eight),
   lower labials eight; if eight upper and eight
   or nine lower, subcaudals fewer than 60 in
   males, 54 in females; solid maxillary teeth
   usually thirteen or fewer; loreal smaller than
   preocular and squarish-----------------------3
   Upper labials eight, lower labials usually
   nine; solid maxillary teeth 15-17; loreal
   long, about equal to preocular in size--------
   --<u>bicolor</u>

3. Subcaudals fewer than 80 in males, 70 in
   females; if overlapping range given above,
   belly prominently smudged (in juveniles) or all
   dark; juvenile with dark middorsal stripe
   continuous with nape blotch or nearly uniform
   including head pattern-----------------------4
   Subcaudals over 75 in males, 64 in females;
   belly immaculate except for dorsal pigment
   encroaching on tips of ventrals; juvenile
   coral red with dark crown and nape blotch
   separated by cream collar--------------<u>clelia</u>

4. Subcaudals 53-62 in males, 42-54 in females,
   all paired; dorsum dark olive; venter immaculate or with dark pigment arranged in transverse patterns; juveniles usually lack
   distinct light occipital collar; if present,
   median dark stripe less than five scales wide-
   --------------------------------------<u>rustica</u>
   Subcaudals 59-79 in males, 51-69 in females,
   frequently some basal ones single; dorsum dark
   brown or black; venter irregularly smudged
   with dark in juveniles, often almost solid
   black in adults; juveniles always with distinct light occipital collar and middorsal
   dark stripe more than five scale rows wide----
   ---------------------------------<u>occipitolutea</u>

Clave de especies

1. Escamas dorsales en 19 filas al medio del
   cuerpo---2
   Escamas dorsales en 17 filas al medio del
   cuerpo---5

2. Usualmente siete supralabiales (raramente ocho),
   ocho infralabiales; con ocho supralabiales y
   ocho o nueve infralabiales, las subcaudales
   son menos de 60 en machos y 54 en hembras;
   usualmente trece o menos dientes maxilares sin
   canal; loreal rectangular y más pequeña que la
   preocular--------------------------------------3
   Ocho supralabiales, usualmente nueve infralabiales; normalmente 15-17 dientes maxilares
   sin canal; loreal alargada, aproximadamente de
   igual tamaño que la preocular----------<u>bicolor</u>

3. Subcaudales menos de 80 en machos, 70 en hembras; si estos números se sobremontan, vientre
   prominentemente tiznado (en juveniles) o todo
   oscuro; juveniles con una banda oscura mediodorsal continuo con la mancha nucal o casi
   uniforme incluyendo diseño de la cabeza------4
   Más de 75 subcaudales en machos, 64 en hembras;
   vientre inmaculado excepto por la pigmentación
   dorsal que invade los lados de las placas
   ventrales; juveniles con rojo coral, parte superior de la cabeza y nuca con manchas oscuras
   separadas por collar crema-------------<u>clelia</u>

4. Subcaudales 53-62 en machos, 42-54 en hembras,
   todas pares; dorso oliva oscuro; vientre inmaculado o con pigmento oscuro dispuesto en
   diseños transversales; usualmente juveniles
   sin collar occipital claro distinto; cuando
   está presente la banda oscura mediodorsal es
   de menos de cinco escamas de ancho-----<u>rustica</u>
   Subcaudales en machos 59-79, en hembras 51-69,
   frecuentemente algunas de las basales no divi-
   didas; dorso pardo oscuro o negro; vientre
   irregularmente tiznado de oscuro en juveniles,
   frecuentemente negro casi uniforme en adultos;
   juveniles con collar claro occipital siempre
   presente y banda mediodorsal oscura de más de
   cinco filas de ancho-------------<u>occipitolutea</u>

5. Subcaudals 78-92 in males, 70-81 in females; ventrals 202-212 in males, 216-228 in females; apical scale pits paired; solid maxillary teeth 13-14; middorsal row and head scales normal--------------------------------scytalina

Subcaudals 60-82 in males, 56-78 in females; ventrals 185-208 in males, 202-223 in females; apical pits often lacking, but numerous tiny pits centrally located on scale usually present; solid maxillary teeth 11-13; middorsal row frequently widened; also anterior or posterior reduction from 17 dorsal rows common; head scales frequently reduced by absence of loreal, fewer than 1+2 oculars, or 2+3 temporals---------------------equatoriana

5. Subcaudales en machos 78-92, en hembras 70-81; ventrales en machos 202-212, en hembras 216-228; hoyuelos apicales pares; dientes maxilares sin canal 13-14; fila mediodorsal y placas de la cabeza normales---------scytalina

Subcaudales 60-82 en machos, en hembras 56-78; ventrales 185-208 en machos, en hembras 202-223, frecuentemente sin hoyuelos apicales, aunque usualmente hay numerosos hoyuelos diminutos situados en el centro de la escama; dientes maxilares sin canal 11-13; fila mediodorsal frecuentemente ensanchada; también es común reducción de 17 filas dorsales posterior y anterior; placas cefálicas frecuentemente reducidas por ausencia de loreal, menos de 1+2 oculares o 2+3 temporales---equatoriana

CLELIA BICOLOR (Peracca), new combination
   bicolor group

   1904 Oxyrhopus bicolor Peracca, Rev. Suisse Zool., 12: 667. Type-locality: North of Santa Fé, Argentina.

   Distribution: Southern Mato Grosso, Brazil, south to San Luis and Santa Fé, Argentina. An old specimen from Pelotas, Rio Grande do Sul, Brazil, may be an error.

CLELIA CLELIA (Daudin)
   clelia group

   1803 Coluber clelia Daudin, Hist. Nat. Rept., 6: 330, pl. 78. Type-locality: Surinam.
   1826 [Clelia clelia]—Fitzinger, Neue Classification der Reptilien: 31.

   Distribution: All of Central America to northwestern Ecuador west of Andes and to northern Argentina east of Andes.

   Content: Two subspecies.

               Key to the subspecies

   1. Hemipenis lacks spines; loreal frequently minute or absent-------------------plumbea
      Hemipenis spinose; loreal seldom abnormal-----------------------------------clelia

               Clave de subespecies

   1. Hemipenis sin espinas; loreal frecuentemente muy pequeña o ausente--------plumbea
      Hemipenis espinosos; loreal raramente anormal----------------------------clelia

Clelia clelia clelia (Daudin)

   1826 C.[lelia] Daudinii Fitzinger (substitute name for Coluber clelia Daudin), Neue Classification der Reptilien: 55.
   1944 Clelia clelia clelia Dunn, Caldasia, 3 (12): 201.
   1965 Clelia clelia groomei Greer, Breviora, 223: 1, fig. 1a-c. Type-locality: Beausejour, Grenada Island, Lesser Antilles.

   Distribution: Guatemala and British Honduras to northwestern Ecuador west of Andes, and to Uruguay and northern Argentina east of Andes.

Clelia clelia plumbea (Wied), new combination

   1820 Coluber plumbeus Wied, Reise nach Brasilien, 1: 25. Type-locality: Between Cabo Frio and Rio São João, Brazil.

   Distribution: Mouth of Rio Amazonas to Maranhão and forested areas from Espirito Santo to Santa Catarina, southeastern Brazil, and Misiones, Argentina.

CLELIA EQUATORIANA (Amaral), new combination
     scytalina group

  1924 Barbourina equatoriana Amaral, Jour. Washington Acad. Sci., 14: 201. Type-locality: Guayaquil,
       Ecuador.
  1944 Clelia clelia scytalina—Dunn, Caldasia, 3 (12): 201.

    Distribution: Pirri Range in eastern Panama through Cauca Valley of Colombia to northwestern
       Ecuador.

CLELIA OCCIPITOLUTEA (Duméril, Bibron and Duméril), new combination
     occipitolutea group

  1854 Brachyruton occipito-luteum Duméril, Bibron and Duméril, Erp. Gén., 7: 1009. Type-locality:
       Unknown.
  1896 Oxyrhopus maculatus Boulenger, Cat. Sn. Brit. Mus., 3: 110, pl. 6, fig. 2. Type-locality:
       Uruguay.

    Distribution: Southern Brazil to Uruguay and central Argentina.

CLELIA RUSTICA (Cope), new combination
     rustica group

  1878 Oxyrrhopus rusticus Cope, Proc. Amer. Phil. Soc., 17 (1877): 92. Type-locality: Argentina?

    Distribution: Southern Minas Gerais and Rio de Janeiro, Brazil south to Uruguay and Buenos Aires;
       west to Tucumán and Jujuy in Argentina.

CLELIA SCYTALINA (Cope)
     scytalina group

  1867 Scolecophis scytalinus Cope, Proc. Acad. Nat. Sci. Phila., 1866: 320. Type-locality: Near
       Tabasco, Mexico.
  1897 Oxyrhopus proximus Bocourt, Miss. Sci. Mex., Rept.: 856, pl. 67, figs. 3-4. Type-locality:
       Western [southern] slope of Volcán Atitlan, Guatemala.
  1942 Clelia clelia immaculata Smith, Proc. U.S. Nat. Mus., 92: 394. Type-locality: "Guadalajara",
       Mexico; see Zweifel, Amer. Mus. Novitates, no. 1949, 1959, 1-9, for comments on this type
       locality.
  1963 Clelia scytalina—Stuart, Misc. Publ. Mus. Zool. Univ. Mich., 122: 90.

    Distribution: Veracruz, Mexico on Atlantic slope and Colima on Pacific slope along Pacific highlands
       to Costa Rica.

COLUBER Linnaeus

1758 Coluber Linnaeus, Systema Naturae, Ed. 10: 216. Type-species: Coluber constrictor Linnaeus.
1818 Scoliophis Lesueur, J. Phys. Chim. Hist. Nat., 86: 297. Type-species: Scoliophis atlanticus Lesueur.
1826 Hemorrhois Boie, Isis von Oken, 19: 982. Type-species: Coluber hippocrepis Linnaeus.
1826 Tyria Fitzinger, Neue Classification der Reptilien: 29. Type-species: none given.
1827 Haemorrhois Boie, Isis von Oken, 20: 538. Type-species: Coluber trabalis Pallas = Coluber jugularis Linnaeus.
1830 Periops Wagler, Nat. Syst. Amphib.: 189. Type-species: Coluber hippocrepis Linnaeus.
1843 Eremiophis Fitzinger, Systema Reptilium: 25. Type-species: Coluber trabalis Boie (? = Coluber jugularis Linnaeus).
1853 Bascanion Baird and Girard, Cat. N. Amer. Rept.: 93. Type-species: Coluber constrictor Linnaeus.
1854 Coryphodon Duméril, Bibron and Duméril, Erp. Gén., 7: 180. Type-species: Coluber capistratus Lichtenstein.
1860 Platyceps Blyth, Jour. Asiatic Soc. Bengal, 29: 114. Type-species: Platyceps semifasciatus Blyth.
1862 Bascanium Cope (emendation of Bascanion Baird and Girard), Proc. Acad. Nat. Sci. Phila., 1862: 338.
1865 Megablabes Günther, Ann. Mag. Nat. Hist., (3) 15: 92. Type-species: Megablabes olivaceus Günther.
1868 Dolichophis Gistl, Blicke Leben U. Natur, 155. [Paper not seen; synonymy according to Romer, Osteology of the Reptiles, 1956, 576.]
1895 Acanthocalyx Cope, Trans. Amer. Phil. Soc., 18: 204. Type-species: Coluber ventromaculatus Gray.
1924 Argyrogena Werner, Sitz. Math.-Naturwiss. K. Akad. Wiss. Wien, 133, abt. 1: 50, fig. 4. Type-species: Argyrogena rostrata Werner = Coluber fasciolatus (Russell).

  Distribution: Central America, North America, Europe, North Africa, Asia, East Indies.

  Content: As few as four or as many as 25, depending upon whether the partition of the genus suggested by Clark and Inger, Copeia, 1943, 141-145, is accepted or not. Some recent authors have accepted it (Smith, Taylor, Auffenberg) but others continue to use Coluber in the older sense (Mertens, Minton, Wermuth). Only one species is found within limits of this work.

COLUBER CONSTRICTOR Linnaeus

1758 Coluber Constrictor Linnaeus, Systema Naturae, Ed. 10: 216. Type-locality: Canada.

  Distribution: Parts of southern Canada, all of United States, eastern Mexico to northern Guatemala.

  Content: Eight subspecies, according to Auffenberg, Tulane Stud. Zool., 2, 1955, 146, of which only one is found within limits of this work.

  Coluber constrictor stejnegerianus (Cope)

1895 Zamenis stejnegerianus Cope, Amer. Nat., 29: 678. Type-locality: Cameron County, Texas.
1934 Coluber ortenburgeri Stuart, Occ. Pap. Mus. Zool. Univ. Mich., 284: 1. Type-locality: Kalto Sabana, 3 mi west of La Libertad, El Péten, Guatemala.
1942 Coluber constrictor stejnegerianus—Muliak and Muliak, Copeia, 1942: 14.

  Distribution: Low elevations, southern Texas through Gulf coastal plain of Mexico to northern Guatemala.

CONIOPHANES Hallowell

1860 <u>Coniophanes</u> Hallowell, in Cope, Proc. Acad. Nat. Sci. Phila., 1860: 248. Type-species:
     <u>Coronella fissidens</u> Günther.
1863 <u>Glaphyrophis</u> Jan, Arch. Zool. Anat. Fis., 2: 304. Type-species: <u>Glaphyrophis pictus</u> Jan.
1885 <u>Hydrocalamus</u> Cope, Proc. Amer. Phil. Soc., 22 (1884): 176. Type-species: <u>Homalopsis</u>
     <u>quinquevittatus</u> Duméril, Bibron and Duméri.

   Distribution: Extreme southern Texas through Mexico and Central America to Pacific Colombia,
     Ecuador and Peru.

   Content: Twelve species, of which four (<u>andresensis</u> Bailey, <u>frangivirgatus</u> Peters, <u>lateritius</u> Cope,
     and <u>meridanus</u> Schmidt and Andrews) are extralimital.

   Comment: <u>Coniophanes brevifrons</u> Bailey, Occ. Pap. Mus. Zool. Univ. Mich., 362, 1937, 3, has been
     shown to be a synonym of <u>Coniophanes andresensis</u> by Dunn and Saxe, Proc. Acad. Nat. Sci. Phila.,
     102, 1950, 162. The latter is confined to San Andres Island, Colombia.

                    Key to the species   Clave de especies

1. Dorsal scales in 21 or fewer rows------------2   1. Escamas dorsales en no más de 21 hileras
   Dorsal scales in 23-25 rows-----------------8   longitudinales como máximo------------------2
                                                            Escamas dorsales dispuestas en 23 a 25 hileras
2. Dorsal scales in 21 rows--------------------3   longitudinales-----------------------------8
   Dorsal scales in 19 or fewer rows-----------5
                                                        2. Escamas dorsales dispuestas en 21 hileras
3. Large, dark, rounded spot on external border   longitudinales-----------------------------3
   of each ventral----------------------------4   Escamas dorsales dispuestas en 19 hileras
   Ventrals immaculate, lightly bordered by dorsal   longitudinales como máximo------------------5
   ground color, or with very fine punctate spot-
   ting; if spots are present, they are small----   3. Una mancha grande oscura redondeada en el borde
   ---------------------------------<u>fissidens</u>   externo de cada placa abdominal------------4
                                                            Escudos abdominales inmaculados o ligeramente
4. Ventrals more than 150---------<u>quinquevittatus</u>   bordeados por el tono general del cuerpo, o
   Ventrals fewer than 150-------------<u>bipunctatus</u>   muy finas punteaciones oscuras, si hay manchas
                                                            laterales, son muy pequeñas----------<u>fissidens</u>
5. Dorsal scales in 19 rows--------------------6
   Dorsal scales in 17 rows----------------<u>joanae</u>   4. Más de 150 ventrales------------<u>quinquevittatus</u>
                                                            Menos de 150 ventrales-------------<u>bipunctatus</u>
6. Middorsal stripe one scale row wide, either
   continuous or broken, may be absent entirely-7   5. Escamas dorsales dispuestas en 19 hileras-----6
   Middorsal stripe five scale rows wide, always   Escamas dorsales dispuestas en 19 hileras---<u>joanae</u>
   continuous----------------------<u>dromiciformis</u>
                                                        6. Una banda dorsal contínua o quebrada, del ancho
7. No light temporal stripe through eye; hemipenis   de una escama-------------------------------7
   unifurcate, spinose, capitate--------<u>fissidens</u>   Una banda dorsal contínua, nunca quebrada, de
   Light temporal stripe through top of eye; hemi-   cinco escamas de ancho----------<u>dromiciformis</u>
   penis bifurcate, spineless----------<u>imperialis</u>
                                                        7. Sin línea clara temporal a través del ojo;
8. Lateral dark stripes four to five scale rows   hemipenes unifurcados, espinosos y capitados--
   wide, sharply defined on longer edge----------   --<u>fissidens</u>
   ---------------------------------<u>piceivittis</u>   Línea clara temporal a través de la parte
   Lateral dark stripes 1/2 - 1-1/2 scale rows   superior del ojo; hemipenes bifurcados, no
   wide, shading gradually to ventrals---<u>schmidti</u>   espinosos---------------------------<u>imperialis</u>

                                                        8. Bandas oscuras laterales ocupan cuatro a cinco
                                                           filas de escamas con borde bien definido------
                                                           ----------------------------------<u>piceivittis</u>
                                                           Bandas oscuras laterales ocupan entre un medio
                                                           y una y media filas de escamas; esfumándose
                                                           gradualmente hacia los ventrales------<u>schmidti</u>

CONIOPHANES BIPUNCTATUS (Günther)

   1858 <u>Coronella bipunctata</u> Günther, Cat. Sn. Brit. Mus.: 36. Type-locality: Unknown; suggested as
        British Honduras by Schmidt, Zool. Ser. Field Mus. Nat. Hist., 22, 1941, 504.
   1866 <u>Coniophanes bipunctatus</u>—Cope, Proc. Acad. Nat. Sci. Phila., 1866: 128.

     Distribution: Tehuantepec and southern Veracruz, Mexico through Central America to northwestern
       Panama.

     Content: Two subspecies, of which one (<u>biseriatus</u> Smith) is extralimital.

Coniophanes bipunctatus bipunctatus (Günther)

1863 G.[laphyrophis] pictus Jan, Arch. Zool. Anat. Fis., 2: 305. Type-locality: None given.
1940 [Coniophanes bipunctatus] bipunctatus—Smith, Proc. Biol. Soc. Washington, 53: 59.

Distribution: Humid lowlands; southern Veracruz, Mexico, east through northern El Petén, Guatemala, into British Honduras, northern Honduras, Nicaragua, and northwestern Panama.

CONIOPHANES DROMICIFORMIS (Peters)

1863 Tachymenis dromiciformis Peters, Monats. Akad. Wiss. Berlin, 1863: 273. Type-locality: Guayaquil, Ecuador.
1866 C.[oniophanes] dromiciformis—Cope, Proc. Acad. Nat. Sci. Phila., 1866: 128.
1892 Coniophanes signatus Garman, Bull. Essex Inst., 24: 91. Type-locality: Guayaquil, Ecuador.
1939 Coniophanes dromiciformis—Bailey, Pap. Mich. Acad. Sci., 24 (1938): 32.

Distribution: Pacific coastal areas of southern Ecuador and northern Peru.

CONIOPHANES FISSIDENS (Günther)

1858 Coronella fissidens Günther, Cat. Sn. Brit. Mus.: 36. Type-locality: Mexico; restricted to San Andres Tuxtla, Veracruz, Mexico, by Smith and Taylor, Univ. Kansas Sci. Bull., 33, 1950, 350.
1860 C.[oniophanes] fissidens—Cope, Proc. Acad. Nat. Sci. Phila., 1860: 248.

Distribution: Both slopes in Mexico, from Nayarit and Veracruz throughout Central America to northwestern Ecuador.

Content: Six subspecies, of which three (convergens Shannon and Smith, dispersus Smith, and proterops Cope) are extralimital.

Key to the subspecies	Clave de subespecies
1. No dorsolateral white stripe on neck------2 Dorsolateral white stripe extending posteriorly a considerable distance on neck----------------------------------fissidens	1. Sin línea blanca dorsolateral en la nuca--2 Con banda blanca dorsolateral que se extiende posteriormente a considerable distancia de la nuca----------------fissidens
2. With distinctive dark paravertebral spots----------------------------punctigularis Lacking dark paravertebral spots--obsoletus	2. Con manchas oscuras paravertebrales distintas----------------------punctigularis Sin manchas oscuras paravertebrales--------------------------------------obsoletus

Coniophanes fissidens fissidens (Gunther)

1937 [Coniophanes] fissidens fissidens—Bailey, Occ. Pap. Mus. Zool. Univ. Mich., 362: 5.

Distribution: Central Veracruz south on Atlantic coast of Central America to northwestern Ecuador, avoiding high mountains and Yucatán Peninsula.

Coniophanes fissidens obsoletus Minton and Smith

1962 Coniophanes fissidens obsoletus Minton and Smith, Herpetologica, 16: 108, fig. 1. Type-locality: Max Cone Finca, 1 mi east of Volcán de Buenos Aires, Puntarenas Province, Costa Rica.

Distribution: Known from type locality and Turrialba, Costa Rica.

Coniophanes fissidens punctigularis Cope

1860 C.[oniophanes] punctigularis Cope, Proc. Acad. Nat. Sci. Phila., 1860: 248. Type-locality: Honduras.
1878 Dromicus chitalonensis Müller, Verh. Naturforsch. Ges. Basel, 6: 407. Type-locality: Hacienda Chitalón, near Mazatenango, Guatemala.
1941 Coniophanes fissidens punctigularis—Smith, Proc. U.S. Nat. Mus., 91: 107.

Distribution: Low and moderate elevations of Pacific slope in Tehuantepec, Mexico, to Costa Rica.

CONIOPHANES IMPERIALIS (Baird and Girard)

1859 _Taeniophis imperialis_ Baird and Girard, in Baird, Reptiles of the Boundary: 23, pl. 19, fig. 1.
    Type-locality: Given as Brownsville, Texas, but recorded as Matamoros, Tamaulipas, Mexico in
    USNM Catalogue, according to Cochran, Bull. U.S. Nat. Mus., 220, 1961, 216.
1861 [Coniophanes] imperialis—Cope, Proc. Acad. Nat. Sci. Phila., 1861: 74.

  Distribution: Southern Texas to northern Honduras on Caribbean slope.

  Content: Three subspecies, of which two (_imperialis_ Baird and Girard and _copei_ Hartweg and Oliver)
  are extralimital.

  Coniophanes imperialis clavatus (Peters)

    1864 _Dromicus (Dromicus) clavatus_ Peters, Monats. Akad. Wiss. Berlin, 1864: 388. Type-
        locality: Mexico.
    1937 _Coniophanes imperialis clavatus_—Bailey, Occ. Pap. Mus. Zool. Univ. Mich., 362: 6.

      Distribution: Low elevations of Caribbean slope, Veracruz, Mexico, to northern Honduras.

CONIOPHANES JOANAE Myers

  1966 _Coniophanes joanae_ Myers, Copeia, 1966: 665, figs. 1-2. Type-locality: Cerro Pirre, Serranía
      de Pirre, Darién, Panama, 1440 m.

  Distribution: Highlands of eastern Panama.

CONIOPHANES PICEIVITTIS Cope

  1870 _Coniophanes piceivittis_ Cope, Proc. Amer. Phil. Soc., 11 (1869): 149. Type-locality: Chihuitan,
      Oaxaca, Mexico.
  1870 _T.[achymenis] taeniata_ Peters, Monats. Akad. Wiss. Berlin, 1869: 876. Type-locality: Mexico.

  Distribution: Guerrero, Mexico to Costa Rica on Pacific slope; central Honduras. Not yet recorded
  in Guatemala.

  Content: Two subspecies, of which one (_taylori_ Hall) is extralimital.

  Coniophanes piceivittis piceivittis Cope

    1951 _Coniophanes piceivittis piceivittis_—Hall, Univ. Kansas Sci. Bull., 34: 208, fig. 3.

      Distribution: As for species, except Guerrero, Mexico.

CONIOPHANES QUINQUEVITTATUS (Duméril, Bibron and Duméril)

  1854 _Homalopsis quinque-vittatus_ Duméril, Bibron and Duméril, Erp. Gén., 7: 975. Type-locality:
      Unknown.
  1865 _C.[alopisma] quinquevittatum_ var. _mexicana_ Jan, Arch. Zool. Anat. Fis., 3: 55. Type-locality:
      Mexico.
  1871 _Hydrops lubricus_ Cope, Proc. Acad. Nat. Sci. Phila., 1871: 217. Type-locality: Río Coatzacoalcos,
      Veracruz, Mexico.
  1939 _Coniophanes quinquevittatus_—Bailey, Pap. Mich. Acad. Sci., 24 (1938): 26, pl. 1, fig. 6.

  Distribution: Caribbean lowlands; southern Veracruz, Mexico, to northern Guatemala.

CONIOPHANES SCHMIDTI Bailey

  1937 _Coniophanes schmidti_ Bailey, Occ. Pap. Mus. Zool. Univ. Mich., 362: 1. Type-locality: Chichen
      Itzá, Yucatán, Mexico.

  Distribution: Lowlands of Yucatán Peninsula to British Honduras and central El Petén, Guatemala.

<u>CONOPHIS</u> Peters

    1860 <u>Conophis</u> Peters, Monats. Akad. Wiss. Berlin, 1860: 519, fig. 3. Type-species: <u>Conophis</u>
        <u>vittatus</u> Peters.

    Distribution: Semiarid regions of southern Mexico and Central America to Costa Rica.

    Content: Four species, according to the most recent revision by Wellman, Univ. Kansas Publ. Mus.
    Nat. Hist., 15, 1963. One species (<u>vittatus</u> Peters) is extralimital.

Key to the species	Clave de especies
1. Supralabials immaculate or having dark borders below; head and body usually pale with dark stripes, or without stripes-----------------2 Supralabials having black borders above; head and body generally black with two or four white lines running length of body (fig. 1)----------------------------------<u>nevermanni</u>	1. Supralabiales inmaculadas o con bordes inferiores oscuros; cabeza y cuerpo usualmente claros con o sin líneas oscuras----------------2 Bordes superiores de supralabiales negros; cabeza y cuerpo generalmente negros con dos o cuatro líneas blancas a lo largo del cuerpo (fig. 1)---------------------------<u>nevermanni</u>

    (Fig. 1)   (Fig. 2)   (Fig. 3)

Figs. 1-3. Color patterns in <u>Conophis</u> (1 and 2 from Wellman, 1963).

2. Lateral dark stripe through eye involving upper half of second scale-row (fig. 2); dark stripe on paravertebral row at least posteriorly--<u>pulcher</u> Lateral dark stripe becoming indistinct on body, or restricted to fourth or third and fourth rows anteriorly, not involving second scale-row on anterior first third of body; an auxiliary lateral stripe sometimes present involving second row; no paravertebral stripes----------------------------------<u>lineatus</u>	2. Línea oscura lateral a través del ojo ocupa la mitad superior de la segunda fila de escamas (fig. 2); a lo menos posteriormente hay una línea oscura paravertebral------------<u>pulcher</u> Línea oscura lateral indistinta sobre el cuerpo o restringida anteriormente a la cuarta, o tercera y cuarta fila de escamas; no presente en la segunda fila, en el primer tercio del cuerpo; ocasionalmente una línea auxiliar presente en la segunda fila; no hay línea paravertebral -------------------------<u>lineatus</u>

<u>CONOPHIS LINEATUS</u> (Duméril, Bibron and Duméril)

    1854 <u>Tomodon lineatum</u> Duméril, Bibron and Duméril, Erp. Gén. 7: 936, pl. 73. Type-locality: Mexico.
    1871 <u>Conophis lineatus</u>—Cope, Third Ann. Rep. Peabody Acad. Sci., 1869: 8.
    1963 <u>Conophis lineatus</u>—Wellman, Univ. Kansas Publ. Mus. Nat. Hist., 15: 262.

    Distribution: From Veracruz and Yucatán, Mexico to Costa Rica.

    Content: Three subspecies, one (<u>lineatus</u> Duméril, Bibron and Duméril) extralimital.

Key to the subspecies	Clave de subespecies
1. Stripes disappearing posteriorly (except for small spots of pigment on scale-row four or seven); first scale-row unpigmented (fig. 3)-------------------<u>concolor</u> Stripes present posteriorly; first scale-row pigmented (fig. 4)---------------<u>dunni</u>	1. Posteriormente, lineado dorsal ausente (excepto pequeños puntos sobre la hilera cuarta o séptima); primera hilera no pigmentada (fig. 3)------------------<u>concolor</u> Posteriormente, lineado dorsal presente; primera hilera pigmentada (fig. 4)---<u>dunni</u>

Conophis lineatus concolor Cope

1867 Conophis concolor Cope, Proc. Acad. Nat. Sci. Phila., 1866: 318. Type-locality: "Yucatan", restricted to Chichén Itzá, Yucatán, Mexico, by Smith and Taylor, Univ. Kansas Sci. Bull., 33, 1950, 352.
1900 Conophis lineaticeps Cope, Ann. Rept. U. S. Nat. Mus., 1898: 1094. Type-locality: Petén, Guatemala.
1941 Conophis lineatus concolor—Smith, Jour. Wash. Acad. Sci., 31: 122.
1963 Conophis lineatus concolor—Wellman, Univ. Kansas Publ. Mus. Nat. Hist., 15: 270.

 Distribution: Yucatán Peninsula, northern Guatemala, northern third of British Honduras, and questionable record for northeastern Honduras.

Conophis lineatus dunni Smith

1941 Conophis lineatus similis Smith (preoccupied by similis Bocourt, 1886), Jour. Wash. Acad. Sci., 31: 123. Type-locality: Managua, Nicaragua.
1942 Conophis lineatus dunni Smith (substitute name for similis Smith), Proc. U. S. Nat. Mus., 92: 395. Type-locality: Managua, Nicaragua.
1963 Conophis lineatus dunni—Wellman, Univ. Kansas Publ. Mus. Nat. Hist., 15: 262.

 Distribution: Semiarid habitats from sea level to 1000 m from Cuilco Valley in western Guatemala, El Petén, and British Honduras to northeastern and southern Honduras, western Nicaragua and northwestern Costa Rica.

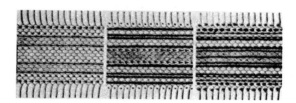

Fig. 4. Variations in color pattern of C. l. dunni from different parts of its range (from Wellman, 1963).

CONOPHIS NEVERMANNI Dunn

1937 Conophis nevermanni Dunn, Copeia, 1937: 214. Type-locality: Río Poas de Aserri (a few mi south of San José), Costa Rica.
1963 Conophis nevermanni—Wellman, Univ. Kansas Publ. Mus. Nat. Hist., 15, 272.

 Distribution: Pacific coast of Honduras and northwestern Costa Rica; Meseta Central of Costa Rica.

CONOPHIS PULCHER Cope

1869 Conophis pulcher Cope, Proc. Acad. Nat. Sci. Phila., 1869: 308. Type-locality: Petén or Verapaz, Guatemala.
1886 Conophis pulcher var similis Bocourt, Miss. Sci. Mex., Rept.: 647, pl. 38, fig. 6. Type-locality: unknown; restricted to Tonalá, Chiapas, by Smith and Taylor, Univ. Kansas Sci. Bull., 33, 1950, 326.
1941 Conophis pulcher plagosus Smith, Jour. Wash. Acad. Sci., 31: 121. Type-locality: Tonalá, Chiapas.
1963 Conophis pulcher—Wellman, Univ. Kansas Publ. Mus. Nat. Hist., 15: 274.

 Distribution: Pacific coastal region of Chiapas, Mexico, into Guatemala; southeastern highlands and dry valley of central and eastern Guatemala; Caribbean lowlands of Honduras south to region of Tegucigalpa.

CORALLUS Daudin

1803 Corallus Daudin, Hist. Nat. Rept., 5: 256. Type-species: Corallus obtusirostris Daudin.
1824 Xiphosoma Wagler, In Spix, Sp. Nov. Serp. Brasil: 40. Type-species: Boa canina Linnaeus.
1860 Chrysenis Gray, Proc. Zool. Soc. London, 1860: 132. Type-species: Chrysenis batesii Gray.

Distribution: Nicaragua to Amazonian South America; Windward Islands.

Content: Three species.

Key to the species

1. Nasals separated; fewer than 85 subcaudals----2
   Nasals in contact; more than 100 subcaudals----
   ---------------------------------------enydris

2. Dorsals in 61 or more rows; ventrals fewer than
   225---------------------------------caninus
   Dorsals in fewer than 60 rows; ventrals more
   than 230----------------------------annulatus

Clave de especies

1. Nasales separados; menos de 85 subcaudales----2
   Nasales en contacto; más de 100 subcaudales----
   ---------------------------------------enydris

2. Escamas dorsales en 61 o más hileras; ventrales
   menos de 225--------------------------caninus
   Escamas dorsales en menos de 60 hileras;
   ventrales más de 230----------------annulatus

CORALLUS ANNULATUS (Cope)

1876 Xiphosoma annulatum Cope, Jour. Acad. Nat. Sci. Phila., (2) 8 (1875): 129, pl. 28, fig. 6.
     Type-locality: Costa Rica.
1893 Corallus annulatus—Boulenger, Cat. Sn. Brit. Mus., 1: 102.

Distribution: Nicaragua to Ecuador.

Content: Three subspecies.

Key to the subspecies

1. With one pair of internasals--------------2
   More than one pair of internasals; anterior
   lateral internasals in contact; posterior
   internasals separated by single median
   scale (Fig. 1)------------------annulatus

Clave de subespecies

1. Con un par de internasales---------------2
   Más de un par de internasales; internasales
   anteriores en contacto, posteriores separadas por una escama mediana (Fig. 1)--------
   ---------------------------------annulatus

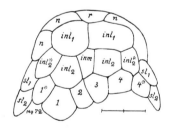 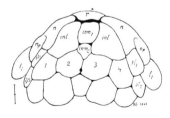 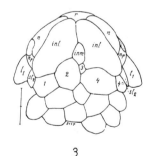

1   2   3

Tip of snout as viewed from above in subspecies of Corallus annulatus (taken from Rendahl and Vester-gren, 1941). Abbreviations used are: INL1-anterior lateral nasal; INL2-posterior lateral nasal; INM-medial internasal; N-nasal; R-rostral; SL-supraloreals; Nos. 1 to 4 represent a series of scales considered by Rendahl and Vestergren to be same in all three subspecies. Fig. 1, a. annulatus. Fig. 2, a. blombergi. Fig. 3, a. colombianus.

2. Two medium-sized lateral internasals
   separated by two median scales arranged
   one behind other (Fig. 2)----------------
   --------------------------------blombergi
   Large pair of lateral internasals which are
   in contact anteriorly but separated
   posteriorly by single median internasal
   (Fig. 3)----------------------colombianus

2. Dos internasales laterales de tamaño medio,
   separadas por dos escamas medianas
   ubicadas una detrás de la otra (Fig. 2)---
   --------------------------------blombergi
   Dos grandes internasales laterales, en
   contacto anteriormente y separadas
   posteriormente por una escama mediana
   (Fig. 3)----------------------colombianus

Corallus annulatus annulatus (Cope)

1940 [Boa annulata annulata]—Rendahl and Vestergren, Ark. för Zool., 33A (1): 2.
1957 [Corallus] a.[nnulata] annulata—Peters, Amer. Mus. Novitates, 1851: 2.

   Distribution: Nicaragua to Colombia.

Corallus annulatus blombergi (Rendahl and Vestergren)

1941 Boa annulata blombergi Rendahl and Vestergren, Ark. för Zool., 33A (5): 1, figs. 6-7.
      Type-locality: Río Zamora, eastern Ecuador.
   1957 [Corallus annulatus] blombergi—Peters, Amer. Mus. Novitates, 1851: 2.

   Distribution: Known only from type locality.

Corallus annulatus colombianus (Rendahl and Vestergren)

   1940 Boa annulata colombiana Rendahl and Vestergren, Ark. för Zool., 33A (1): 2, fig. 1.
         Type-locality: Cabeceras, Chocó, Colombia.
   1957 Corallus annulata colombiana—Peters, Amer. Mus. Novitates, 1851: 1.

   Distribution: Pacific lowlands of Colombia and northwestern Ecuador.

CORALLUS CANINUS (Linnaeus)

1758 Boa canina Linnaeus, Systema Naturae, Ed. 10: 215. Type-locality: America.
1758 Boa Hipnale Linnaeus, Systema Naturae, Ed. 10: 215. Type-locality: Asia.
1768 Boa thalassina Laurenti (substitute name for Boa canina Linnaeus), Synopsin Reptilium: 89.
1768 Boa aurantiaca Laurenti, Synopsin Reptilium: 89. Type-locality: America.
1768 Boa exigua Laurenti (substitute name for Boa Hipnale Linnaeus), Synopsin Reptilium: 89.
1824 Xiphosoma araramboya Wagler, in Spix, Sp. Nov. Serp. Brasil.: 45, pl. 16. Type-locality:
      the rio Negro, Amazonas, Brazil.
1860 Chrysenis batesii Gray, Proc. Zool. Soc. London, 1860: 132, pl. 24. Type-locality: Upper Amazon.
1893 Corallus caninus—Boulenger, Cat. Sn. Brit. Mus., 1: 102.

   Distribution: Amazonian Basin of Colombia, Venezuela, Brazil, Ecuador, Peru, Bolivia; also Guianas.

CORALLUS ENYDRIS (Linnaeus)

1758 Boa Enydris Linnaeus, Systema Naturae, Ed. 10: 215. Type-locality: America.
1951 Corallus enydris—Forcart, Herpetologica, 7: 197.

   Distribution: Nicaragua to Ecuador and Peru; Windward Islands.

   Content: Two subspecies.

   Comment: Authors since Boulenger's Catalogues have used hortulanus Linnaeus and enydris Linnaeus
   equally as often for this taxon. We follow the latest check list of the Boidae by Stimson,
   Das Tierreich, 89, 1969, in the use of enydris.

Key to the subspecies	Clave de subespecies
1. Rounded dorsal and lateral blotches; more than 50 scale rows-----------------cookii Rhomboid dorsal and lateral blotches; fewer than 50 scale rows----------------enydris	1. Manchas dorsales y laterales redondeadas; más de 50 filas de escamas---------cookii Manchas dorsales y laterales romboidales; menos de 50 filas de escamas-------enydris

Corallus enydris enydris (Linnaeus)

1758 Boa Hortulana Linnaeus, Systema Naturae, Ed. 10: 215. Type-locality: America.
1768 Vipera bitis Laurenti, Synopsin Reptilium: 102. Type-locality: Brazil.
1768 Vipera madarensis Laurenti, Synopsin Reptilium: 102. Type-locality: "Isle Madère."
1796 Boa Merremii Sentzen, in Meyer, Zool. Arch., 2: 53. Type-locality: unknown.
1798 Boa Ambleocephala Donndorff, Zoologische Beyträge, 3: 149. Type-locality: none given.
1802 Boa obtusiceps Bechstein, in Lacépède's Naturgesch. Amphibien, 5: 46. Type-locality: none given.
1803 Corallus obtusirostris Daudin (substitute name for Boa Merremii Sentzen), Hist. Nat. Rept., 5: 259.
1824 Xiphosoma ornatum Wagler, in Spix, Sp. Nov. Serp. Brasil.: 40, pl. 14, fig. 2. Type-locality: Rio Solimões, Brazil.
1824 Xiphosoma dorsuale Wagler (substitute name for Boa hortulana Linnaeus), in Spix, Sp. Nov. Serp. Brasil.: 43, pl. 15.
1834 Boa modesta Reuss, Abh. Mus. Senckenbergianum, 1: 129. Type-locality: Ilheus, Bahia, Brazil.
1842 Corallus maculatus Gray, Zoological Miscellany, 1842: 42. Type-locality: Berbice, Guyana.
1951 Corallus enydris enydris—Forcart, Herpetologica, 7: 197.

   Distribution: Northern and western Brazil, southern Venezuela, Guianas; Amazonian Ecuador, Peru, and Bolivia.

Corallus enydris cookii Gray

1842 Corallus Cookii Gray, Zoological Miscellany, 1842: 42. Type-locality: America.
1876 Xiphosoma ruschenbergii Cope, Jour. Acad. Nat. Sci. Phila., (2) 8 (1875): 129. Type-locality: Panama.
1914 Boa grenadensis Barbour, Mem. Mus. Comp. Zool., 44: 327. Type locality: St. George's, Grenada Island, West Indies.
1934 Boa salmonidia Briceño, Bol. Minist. Salubr. Agric. Cría, Venezuela, 1 (14): 1141. Type-locality: Río de Oro, on Colombian frontier, Distrito Colon, Estado de Zulia, Venezuela.
1951 Corallus enydris cookii—Forcart, Herpetologica, 7: 197.

   Distribution: Nicaragua to Colombia; northern and central Venezuela; Trinidad; Windward Islands.

CROTALUS Linnaeus

1758 Crotalus Linnaeus, Systema Naturae, Ed. 10: 214. Type-species: Crotalus horridus Linnaeus, confirmed by Opinion 92, Int. Comm. Zool. Nomen.
1764 Crotalophorus Houttuyn, Natuur. Hist., 6, part 1: 290. Type-species: Crotalus horridus Linnaeus.
1768 Caudisona Laurenti, Synopsin Reptilium: 92. Type-species: Caudisona terrificus Laurenti.
1818 Crotalinus Rafinesque, Amer. Month. Mag. Crit. Rev., 3: 446. Type-speeies: Crotalinus cyanurus Rafinesque = Crotalus horridus Linnaeus.
1822 Crotalus Fleming (not of Linnaeus, 1758), Philos. of Zool., 2: 294. Type-species: Crotalus miliaris Linnaeus.
1825 Crotalophorus Gray (not of Houttuyn, 1764), Ann. Philos., 10: 205. Type-species: Crotalus miliaris Linnaeus.
1826 Caudisona Fitzinger (not of Laurenti, 1768), Neue Classification der Reptilien: 63. Type-species: Crotalus miliaris Linnaeus.
1830 Uropsophus Wagler, Nat. Syst. Amph.: 176. Type-species: Uropsophus triseriatus Wiegmann.
1843 Urocrotalon Fitzinger, Systema Reptilium: 29. Type-species: Crotalus durissus Linnaeus.
1867 Aploaspis Cope, Proc. Acad. Nat. Sci. Phila., 1866: 310. Type-species: Caudisona lepida Kennicott.
1875 Aechmophrys Coues, in Wheeler, Rept. Explor. and Surv. West of 100th Mer., 5: 609. Type-species: Crotalus cerastes Hallowell.
1883 Sistrurus Garman, Mem. Mus. Comp. Zool., 8: 118. Type-species: Crotalus miliarius Linnaeus.
1883 Haploaspis Cope (emendation of Aploaspis Cope), Proc. Acad. Nat. Sci. Phila., 1883: 13.

Distribution: The Americas.

Content: About 26 species, of which only two occur within the limits of this work, according to latest revision, by Klauber, Rattlesnakes, 1956. Hoge, Mem. Inst. Butantan, 32, 1965 (1966), is followed, as the most recent summary of the genus, in using Crotalus and Sistrurus as subgenera.

Key to the species

1. Pattern obsolete; never conspicuous-----------2
   Pattern well-defined, always conspicuous--durissus

2. With scattered white spots or streaks on some but not all scales------------------vegrandis
   No scattered white streaks on scales---durissus

Clave de especies

1. Diseño obsoleto; nuca conspícuo---------------2
   Diseño definido, siempre conspícuo-----durissus

2. Con algunas escamas salpicadas de puntos o líneas blancas----------------------vegrandis
   Escamas no salpicadas de líneas blancas--durissus

CROTALUS (CROTALUS) DURISSUS Linnaeus

1758 Crotalus Durissus Linnaeus, Systema Naturae, Ed. 10: 214. Type-locality: America; restricted to Jalapa, Veracruz, Mexico, by Smith. and Taylor, Univ. Kansas Sci. Bull., 33, 1950, 348.

Distribution: Discontinuous; Mexico to Costa Rica; savannas of South America. See map in Hoge, Mem Inst. Butantan, 32, 1965 (1966), 138.

Content: Twelve subspecies, of which two (culminatus Klauber and totonacus Gloyd and Kauffeld) are extralimital.

Key to the subspecies

1. Conspicuous pattern of longitudinal bands on neck, followed by rhomboid blotches strongly contrasting with ground color---2
   No conspicuous pattern (except in juveniles), no strongly contrasting colors--unicolor

2. Centers of rhomboid blotches light, conspicuous in contrast to rest of blotch-------------------------------------3
   Centers of rhomboid blotches not light, only slightly lighter than rest of blotch-------------------------------terrificus

Clave de subespecies

1. Diseño conspícuo de bandas longitudinales en la nuca, seguido de manchas romboidales contrastantes con el color de fondo------2
   Diseño no conspícuo (excepto en juveniles), no acentuado por contraste entre colores claros y oscuros----------------unicolor

2. Centros de manchas romboidales claros, destacándose en contraste con el resto del rombo------------------------------------3
   Centros de manchas romboidales no claros o muy ligeramente más claros que el resto del rombo-----------------------terrificus

3. Paravertebral nuchal stripes of uniform
   color, center not lighter than borders---4
   Paravertebral nuchal stripes very broad
   (four scale rows) with lighter borders and
   center lighter than borders--------ruruima

4. Paravertebral nuchal stripes wider than
   single scale---------------------------5
   Paravertebral nuchal stripes one scale row
   wide-----------------------------dryinus

5. Paravertebral nuchal stripes long, usually
   longer than one head length-------------6
   Paravertebral nuchal stripes short, less
   than one head length------------cascavella

6. Paravertebral nuchal stripes lack accessory
   stripes below---------------------------7
   Paravertebral nuchal stripes with continuous or interrupted stripes beneath them,
   never with single accessory spot---------8

7. With single, simple accessory spot beneath
   paravertebral nuchal stripe-------durissus
   Lacking any accessory spots beneath paravertebral nuchal stripe------------tzabcan

8. Paravertebral nuchal stripes with continuous dark stripe below-------------------9
   Paravertebral nuchal stripes with series of
   dark spots below--------------marajoensis

9. Loreal indistinguishable from other lateral
   head scales----------------collilineatus
   Loreal clearly distinguishable from other
   lateral head scales------------cumanensis

3. Cintas paravertebrales nucales de color
   uniforme; con centro no más claro que los
   bordes----------------------------------4
   Cintas paravertebrales nucales muy anchas
   (cuatro escamas) limitadas de claro exter-
   iormente; con el centro más claro que los
   bordes---------------------------ruruima

4. Cintas paravertebrales nucales más anchas
   que una escama--------------------------5
   Cintas paravertebrales nucales de una
   escama de ancho-------------------dryinus

5. Cintas nucales paravertebrales largas;
   normalmente más largas sobre la nuca que
   la longitud de la cabeza----------------6
   Cintas nucales paravertebrales cortas;
   menores que la longitud de la cabeza------
   ---------------------------------cascavella

6. Cintas paravertebrales nucales sin cintas
   accesorias debajo-----------------------7
   Cintas paravertebrales nucales con cintas
   contínuas o interrumpidas debajo; nunca
   una simple mancha accesoria-------------8

7. Con sólo una simple mancha suplementaria
   debajo de la cinta paravertebral nucal----
   -----------------------------------durissus
   Sin manchas ni cintas suplementarias debajo
   de la cinta paravertebral nucal----tzabcan

8. Bandas nucales paravertebrales acompañadas
   por líneas no interrumpidas debajo-------9
   Bandas nucales paravertebrales acompañadas
   por una serie de puntos oscuros debajo----
   -------------------------------marajoensis

9. Loreal que no se destaca del resto de las
   escamas látero-cefálicas-----collilineatus
   Loreal muy clara que se destaca del resto
   de las escamas látero-cefálicas-cumanensis

Crotalus (Crotalus) durissus durissus Linnaeus

   1802 Crotalus simus Latreille, in Sonnini and Latreille, Hist. Nat. Rept., 3: 202. Type-
        locality: "Ceylan".
   1936 Crotalus durissus durissus—Klauber, Occ. Pap. San Diego Soc. Nat. Hist., 1: 4.

      Distribution: Veracruz and Oaxaca, Mexico south to Costa Rica, avoiding Caribbean slope in
      Central America.

Crotalus (Crotalus) durissus cascavella Wagler

   1824 Crotalus cascavella Wagler, in Spix, Sp. Nov. Serp. Bras.: 60, pl. 24. Type-locality:
        Bahia, Brazil; restricted through neotype designation to Mina Caraiba, Bahia, Brazil,
        by Hoge, Mem. Inst. Butantan, 32, 1965 (1966), 139.
   1926 Crotalus terrificus var. collirhombeatus Amaral, Rev. Mus. Paulista, 15: 90, pl. 1. Type-
        locality: Northeastern Brazil.
   1966 Crotalus durissus cascavella—Hoge, Mem. Inst. Butantan, 32 (1965): 139, pl. 12.

      Distribution: Caatinga regions of northeastern Brazil.

Crotalus (Crotalus) durissus collilineatus Amaral

    1926 Crotalus terrificus var. collilineatus Amaral, Rev. Mus. Paulista, 15: 90. Type-locality:
        None specified in original description; restricted through neotype designation to
        Estado de Mato Grosso, Brazil by Amaral and Hoge, in Hoge, Mem. Inst. Butantan, 32, 1965
        (1966), 139.
    1966 Crotalus durissus collilineatus—Hoge, Mem. Inst. Butantan, 32 (1965): 139, pl. 13.

      Distribution: Goiás, Distrito Federal, Minas Gerais, northeastern São Paulo, and south-
      western Mato Grosso, Brazil.

Crotalus (Crotalus) durissus cumanensis Humboldt

    1833 Crotalus cumanensis Humboldt, in Humboldt and Bonpland, Recueil d'Obs. Zool. Anat. Comp.,
        2: 6. Type-locality: Cumaná, Venezuela.
    1833 Crotalus loefflingii Humboldt, in Humboldt and Bonpland, Recueil d'Obs. Zool. Anat. Comp.,
        2: 6. Type-locality: Cumaná, Venezuela.
    1966 Crotalus durissus cumanensis—Hoge, Mem. Inst. Butantan, 32 (1965): 142.

      Distribution: Venezuela except high mountains of Andes, savannas of Monagas, and savannas of
      Bolivar and Amazonas.

Crotalus (Crotalus) durissus dryinus Linnaeus

    1758 Crotalus Dryinas Linnaeus, Systema Naturae, Ed. 10: 214. Type-locality: America;
        restricted to Paramaribo, Surinam, by Hoge, Mem. Inst. Butantan, 32, 1965 (1966), 143.
    1966 Crotalus durissus dryinus—Hoge, Mem. Inst. Butantan, 32 (1965): 142, pl. 14.

      Distribution: Guianas.

Crotalus (Crotalus) durissus marajoensis Hoge

    1966 Crotalus durissus marajoensis Hoge, Mem. Inst. Butantan, 32 (1965): 143, pl. 15. Type-
        locality: Tuiuiu, Ilha de Marajó, Estado do Pará, Brazil.

      Distribution: Marajó Island, Brazil.

Crotalus (Crotalus) durissus ruruima Hoge

    1966 Crotalus durissus ruruima Hoge, Mem. Inst. Butantan, 32 (1965): 145, pl. 16. Type-
        locality: Paulo Camp, Mt. Roraima, Venezuela, 4000 ft.

      Distribution: Mt. Roraima, Venezuela; may extend over isolated savannas of southern
      Venezuela, according to Hoge, loc. cit., p. 147.

Crotalus (Crotalus) durissus terrificus (Laurenti)

    1768 Caudisona terrifica Laurenti, Systema Reptilium: 93. Type-locality: "Habitat in America
        infra graduum elev. 45"; restricted through neotype designation to Julio de Castilho,
        Município Taquari, Estado Rio Grande do Sul, Brazil, by Hoge, Mem. Inst. Butantan, 32,
        1965 (1966), 147.
    1936 Crotalus durissus terrificus—Klauber, Rattlesnakes, 1: 32.
    1957 Crotalus terrificus crotaminicus Moura Conçalves, An. Acad. Bras. Cienc., 28: 365. Type-
        locality: Uncertain (original publication unseen by authors).

      Distribution: Rio Grande do Sul, Santa Catarina, Paraná, and São Paulo, Brazil; northern
      Argentina, Paraguay and Uruguay.

Crotalus (Crotalus) durissus tzabcan Klauber

    1952 Crotalus durissus tzabcan Klauber, Bull. Zool. Soc. San Diego, 26: 71. Type-locality:
        Kantunil, Yucatán, Mexico.

      Distribution: Yucatán, Mexico to northern El Petén, Guatemala and British Honduras.

Crotalus (Crotalus) durissus unicolor van Lidth

1887 Crotalus horridus var. unicolor van Lidth, Notes Leyden Mus., 2 (8): 133. Type-locality: Aruba Island, Dutch West Indies.

1905 Crotalus pulvis Ditmars, Ann. Rept. N. Y. Zool. Soc., 9 (1904): 199, pl. Type-locality: 20 mi inland from Managua, Nicaragua; "probably based on a specimen with erroneous locality", according to Hoge, Mem. Inst. Butantan, 32, 1965 (1966), 149.

1940 Crotalus durissus unicolor—Brongersma, in Hummelinck, Studies on the Fauna of Curaçao, Aruba, Bonaire and Venezuelan Islands, 2: 131, pl. 12.

Distribution: Aruba Island, Dutch West Indies.

CROTALUS (CROTALUS) VEGRANDIS Klauber

1941 Crotalus vegrandis Klauber, Trans. San Diego Soc. Nat. Hist., 9 (30): 334. Type-locality: Maturin Savannah, near Uracoa, Sotillo District, Monagas, Venezuela.

Distribution: Southern parts of Estados Monagas and Anzoategui, Venezuela.

CYCLAGRAS Cope

1885 Cyclagras Cope, Proc. Amer. Phil. Soc., 22: 185. Type-species: Xenodon gigas Duméril, Bibron and Duméril.

Distribution: As for single species.

Content: One species.

Comment: Hoge, Pap. Avul. Dept. Zool. São Paulo, 13, 1958, 221, has used Lejosophis Jan for this taxon. Reasons for using Cyclagras in preference to Lejosophis are elaborated in a paper by one of us (Peters) to appear elsewhere.

CYCLAGRAS GIGAS (Duméril, Bibron and Duméril)

1854 Xenodon gigas Duméril, Bibron and Duméril, Erp. Gén., 7: 761. Type-locality: Provincia de Corrientes, Argentina.
1885 Cyclagras gigas—Cope, Proc. Amer. Phil. Soc., 22: 185.

Distribution: Southern Brazil, eastern Bolivia, Paraguay and northern Argentina.

DENDROPHIDION Fitzinger

1843 Dendrophidion Fitzinger, Systema Reptilium: 26. Type-species: Herpetodryas dendrophis Schlegel.
1861 Dendrophidium Cope (in error for Dendrophidion Fitzinger), Proc. Acad. Nat. Sci. Phila., 1860: 561.
1895 Cacocalyx Cope, Trans. Amer. Phil. Soc., 18: 205. Type-species: Drymobius percarinatus Cope.

   Distribution: Mexico; Central America; northern South America.

   Content: Eight species.

   Comment: This genus is currently under revision by one of us (Peters), and the arrangement shown here, which reflects the current state of the literature, will be rather thoroughly changed upon completion of the review.

                    Key to the species   Clave de especies

1. Subcaudals fewer than 175---------------------2   1. Subcaudales menos de 175----------------------2
   Subcaudals more than 175------------dendrophis   Subcaudales más de 175--------------dendrophis

2. Dorsal pattern of stripes, spots or cross-   2. Dibujo dorsal con cintas, manchas, o barras
   bands---3   transversales-------------------------------3
   Dorsum generally unicolor--------------------6   Tono general unicolor, sin dibujo------------6

3. Without broad, dark paravertebral stripes-----4   3. Sin cintas paravertebrales anchas y oscuras---4
   With broad, dark, paravertebral stripes--------   Con cintas paravertebrales anchas y oscuras----
   ----------------------------------bivittatus   -----------------------------------bivittatus

4. Distinct transverse dark bands----------------5   4. Con barras transversales, oscuras y anchas----5
   Double row of dark spots on each side of mid-   Con una serie doble de manchas oscuras en cada
   dorsal line--------------------------boshelli   lado de la línea vertebral------------boshelli

5. Anal divided----------------------percarinatus   5. Placa anal dividida----------------percarinatus
   Anal entire---------------------------vinitor   Placa anal entera-----------------------vinitor

6. Keels on more than middorsal scale row--------7   6. Escamas quilladas en más filas que la fila
   Only middorsal scales with keel, and only   mediodorsal----------------------------------7
   posteriorly on body-------------paucicarinatus   Sólo la fila mediodorsal es quillada en la
                                                          parte posterior del cuerpo------paucicarinatus

7. No keels on first three rows of dorsals--------   7. Sin quillas en las primeras tres filas de
   ------------------------------------brunneus   dorsales---------------------------brunneus
   All dorsals keeled, weakly on first row--------   Todas las filas quilladas, débilmente la
   ------------------------------------clarkii   primera----------------------------------clarkii

DENDROPHIDION BIVITTATUS (Duméril, Bibron and Duméril)

1854 Leptophis bi-vittatus Duméril, Bibron and Duméril, Erp. Gén., 7: 540. Type-locality: "New Grenada".
1865 T.[ropidonotus] subradiatus Jan, Arch. Zool. Anat. Fis., 3: 227. Type-locality: Colombia.
1872 Herpetodryas tetrataenia Günther, Ann. Mag. Nat. Hist., (4) 9: 23. Type-locality: Bogotá, Colombia.

   Distribution: Highlands of Colombia.

DENDROPHIDION BOSHELLI Dunn

1944 Dendrophidion boshelli Dunn, Caldasia, 2 (10): 475. Type-locality: Volcanes, Municipio de Caparrapi, Cundinamarca, Colombia, 250 m.

   Distribution: Known only from type locality.

DENDROPHIDION

DENDROPHIDION BRUNNEUS (Günther)

1858 Herpetodryas brunneus Günther, Cat. Sn. Brit. Mus.: 116. Type-locality: Guayaquil, Ecuador.
1960 Dendrophidion brunneum—Peters, Bull. Mus. Comp. Zool., 122: 514.

Distribution: Interandean valleys of Ecuador.

DENDROPHIDION CLARKII Dunn

1933 Dendrophidion clarkii Dunn, Occ. Pap. Boston Soc. Nat. Hist., 8: 78. Type-locality: El Valle de Anton, Panama.

Distribution: Panama.

DENDROPHIDION DENDROPHIS (Schlegel)

1837 Herpetodryas dendrophis Schlegel, Essai Physion. Serpens, 2: 196. Type-locality: "Cayenne".
1843 Dendrophidion dendrophis—Fitzinger, Systema Reptilium: 26.
1847 Herpetodryas aestivus Berthold, Abh. K. Ges. Wiss. Göttingen, 3: 11. Type-locality: Provincia Popayan, Colombia.
1854 Herpetodryas Poitei Duméril, Bibron and Duméril, Erp. Gén., 7: 208. Type-locality: Cayenne and El Petén, Guatemala.
1863 Herpetodryas nuchalis Peters, Monats. Akad. Wiss. Berlin, 1863: 285. Type-locality: Caracas, Venezuela.

Distribution: Southern Central America and northern South America.

DENDROPHIDION PAUCICARINATUS (Cope)

1894 Drymobius paucicarinatus Cope, Proc. Acad. Nat. Sci. Phila., 1894: 202. Type-locality: La Candelaria, Bruno Carranza, Costa Rica.
1933 Dendrophidion paucicarinatus—Stuart, Copeia, 1933: 9.

Distribution: Southern Costa Rica and western Panama.

DENDROPHIDION PERCARINATUS (Cope)

1893 Drymobius percarinatus Cope, Proc. Amer. Phil. Soc., 31: 344. Type-locality: Boruca and Buenos Aires, Costa Rica.
1941 [Dendrophidion] percarinatus—Smith, Proc. Biol. Soc. Washington, 54: 73.

Distribution: Honduras, Costa Rica, Panama.

DENDROPHIDION VINITOR Smith

1941 Dendrophidion vinitor Smith, Proc. Biol. Soc. Washington, 54: 74. Type-locality: Piedras Negras, Guatemala.

Distribution: Low and moderate elevations of Caribbean slope, Veracruz, Mexico, to Panama.

DIAPHOROLEPIS Jan

1863 Diaphorolepis Jan, Elenco Sistema Ofidi: 94. Type-species: Diaphorolepis Wagneri Jan.

Distribution: Panama to Ecuador.

Content: Two species, according to most recent revision, by Bogert, Senckenbergiana Biol., 45, 1964.

Key to the species	Clave de especies
1. Dorsal scales keeled; vertebral row bicarinate--------------------------wagneri Dorsal scales smooth-------------------laevis	1. Escamas dorsales quilladas; fila vertebral bicarenada-----------------------------wagneri Escamas dorsales lisas-------------------laevis

DIAPHOROLEPIS LAEVIS Werner

1923 Diaphorolepis laevis Werner, Ann. Naturhist. Mus. Wien, 36: 160. Type-locality: Colombia.

Distribution: Species still known only from holotype, which lacks precise locality data.

DIAPHOROLEPIS WAGNERI Jan

1863 Diaphorolepis Wagneri Jan, Elenco Sistema Ofidi: 98. Type-locality: Andes of Ecuador.
1964 Diaphorolepis wagneri—Bogert, Senckenbergiana Biol., 45: 513, figs. 1, 3-7.

Distribution: Darien region of Panama to western Ecuador; one doubtful record from "Eastern Ecuador."

DIPSAS Laurenti

1768 Dipsas Laurenti, Synops. Rept.: 89. Type-species: Dipsas indica Laurenti.
1810 Bungarus Oppel (partim; non Bungarus Daudin 1803), Ann. Mus. Hist. Nat. Paris, 13: 391.
   Type-species: none designated.
1843 Pholidolaemus Fitzinger, Syst. Rept., 1: 27. Type-species: Coluber bucephala Shaw.
1853 Dipsadomorus Duméril, Mém. Acad. Sci., Paris, 23: 467. Type-species: Dipsas indica Laurenti.
1853 Leptognathus Duméril (non Leptognathus Swainson 1839), Mém. Acad. Sci. Paris, 23: 467.
   Type-species: none designated.
1853 Stremmatognathus Duméril, Mém. Acad. Sci. Paris, 23: 468. Type-species: Coluber catesbeji
   Sentzen.
1895 Neopareas Günther, Biol. Centr. Amer. Rept.: 178. Type-species: Neopareas bicolor Günther.
1923 Heterorhachis Amaral, Proc. New Engl. Zool. Club, 8: 94. Type-species: Heterorhachis
   poecilolepis Amaral.

  Distribution: Tropical Mexico, Central America and South America.

  Content: 31 species, of which three (elegans (Boulenger), gaigeae (Oliver), and maxillaris Werner)
  are extralimital, according to the most recent revision, by Peters, Misc. Publ. Mus. Zool. Univ.
  Mich., 114, 1960.

Key to the species	Clave de especies
1. Scale rows on body 17 or more (polylepis group)--2 Scale rows on body 15 or less-----------------4	1. Escamas en 17 o más filas (grupo polylepis)---2 Escamas en 15 o menos filas------------------4
2. Scale rows extremely variable over entire body--3 Scale rows consistent number from head to anus--------------------------------polylepis	2. Filas de escamas en número extremadamente variable a lo largo del cuerpo--------------3 Filas de escamas constantes en número de la cabeza al ano-----------------------polylepis
3. Ventrals 153----------------------poecilolepis Ventrals 193----------------------perijanensis	3. Ventrales 153---------------------poecilolepis Ventrales 193---------------------perijanensis

Fig. 1. Dipsas brevifacies, illustrative
of articulata group.

4. Dorsal pattern of broad, dark-brown or black bands that are much wider than interspaces, and are complete (except in temporalis and viguieri) across venter over length of body; interspaces pink or red in life, yellow in preservative (articulata group, Fig. 1)------5 Dorsal pattern not as above------------------11	4. Diseño dorsal de anchas bandas transversas pardo oscuras o negras, más anchas que los interespacios, completas (excepto en temporalis y viguieri) como anillos a lo largo del cuerpo; interespacios rosa o rojo en vida, amarillo en preservados (grupo articulata, Fig. 1)------------------------------------5 Diseño dorsal no como el anterior-----------11
5. Paired chin shields present------------------6 All chin shields posterior to labials in contact single--------------------------bicolor	5. Con geniales pares-------------------------6 Geniales, posteriores al primer par labial en contacto, simples---------------------bicolor
6. Subcaudals 100 or more----------------------7 Subcaudals 99 or less--------------brevifacies	6. Subcaudales 100 o más----------------------7 Subcaudales 99 o menos-------------brevifacies
7. At least one pair of labials in contact behind mental------------------------------------8 Mental in contact with paired chin shields---------------------------------------temporalis	7. A lo menos un par de labiales contacta atrás de la mentoneana----------------------------8 Mentoneana en contacto con el par anterior geneial---------------------------temporalis

8. No preocular; usually two postoculars; posterior interspaces not or lightly spotted---9
One preocular; usually three postoculars; posterior interspaces heavily streaked and spotted------------------------------------10

9. Bands on posterior part of body twice as wide as interspaces-----------------------gracilis
Bands on posterior part of body approximately equal to interspaces---~-----------articulata

10. Dorsum of head unicolor dark brown; upper labials eight-------------------------tenuissima
Dorsum of head spotted with white; upper labials nine or ten---------------------viguieri

11. Dorsal pattern of rounded, dark-brown or black blotches or saddles, interspaces tawny brown (catesbyi group, Fig. 2)---------------------12
Dorsal pattern not as above-----------------15

12. Dorsal scale rows 13------------------------13
Dorsal scale rows 15---------------------copei

13. Prefrontals two; dorsum of head unicolor-----14
Prefrontals usually fused; dorsum of head variegated and streaked with white------------
-----------------------------------vermiculata

14. Blotches narrower at vertebral row than laterally; loreal does not enter eye--catesbyi
Blotches saddle-shaped, wider at vertebral row than laterally; loreal enters eye-----pavonina

15. Dorsal blotches triangular or lozenge-shaped, usually widest at ventrals, with yellow spot between corners of blotches at ventrals (indica group, Fig. 3)----------------------16
Dorsal pattern not as above------------------17

8. Preocular ausente; usualmente dos postoculares; interespacios posteriores no manchados o muy levemente---------------------------------9
Una preocular; usualmente tres postoculares; interespacios posteriores densamente manchados y lineados----------------------------------10

9. Parte posterior del cuerpo con bandas dos veces más anchas que los interespacios------gracilis
Parte posterior del cuerpo con bandas de aproximadamente igual ancho que los interespacios---------------------------articulata

10. Cabeza dorsalmente unicolor, en pardo oscuro; ocho supralabiales------------------tenuissima
Cabeza dorsalmente manchada de blanco; nueve o diez supralabiales-------------------viguieri

11. Diseño dorsal de manchas redondeadas o en forma de silla de montar, pardo oscuras o negras, interespacios en pardo tostado (grupo catesbyi, Fig. 2)-----------------------12
Diseño dorsal no como el anterior-----------15

12. Dorsales en 13 filas-----------------------13
Dorsales en 15 filas--------------------copei

13. Dos prefrontales; cabeza dorsalmente unicolor--14
Prefrontales normalmente fusionadas; cabeza dorsalmente variegada y lineada en blanco-----
-----------------------------------vermiculata

14. Manchas más angostas a nivel de la línea vertebral que lateralmente; loreal no llega el ojo-----------------------------------catesbyi
Manchas en forma de silla de montar, más anchas a nivel de la linea vertebral que lateralmente; loreal llega al ojo-----------pavonina

15. Manchas dorsales triangulares o romboidales usualmente más anchas a nivel ventral, con mancha amarilla entre ellas, a ese nivel (grupo indica, Fig. 3)----------------------16
Diseño dorsal no como el anterior-----------17

Fig. 2. Dipsas catesbyi, illustrative of catesbyi group.

Fig. 3. Dipsas indica cisticeps, illustrative of indica group.

16. Scale rows 15---------------------------neivai
Scale rows 13, often reducing to 11------indica

17. Dorsal ground color of light browns and tans, with narrow blotches that are higher than wide, and much narrower than interspaces (at least posteriorly), interspaces streaked, spotted or stippled throughout (variegata group, Fig. 4)-----------------------------18
Dorsal pattern not as above------------------21

16. Dorsales en 15 filas--------------------neivai
Dorsales en 13 filas; frecuentemente con reducción a 11---------------------------indica

17. Dorsalmente pardo claro bronceado, con manchas angostas, más altas que anchas, mucho más angostas que los interespacios (por lo menos posteriormente), interespacios lineados, manchados o punteados (grupo variegata, Fig. 4)-18
Diseño dorsal no como el anterior-----------21

Fig. 4. Dipsas albifrons, illustrative
of variegata group.

Fig. 5. Dipsas ellipsifera, illustrative
of oreas group.

18.Two or more pairs of labials in contact
   mental----------------------------------19
   Single pair of labials in contact behind
   mental-----------------------------------incerta

19.Dorsum of head unicolor light tan or with
   poorly defined darker spots on parietals-----
   --20
   Dorsum of head with dark-brown spot clearly
   defined on parietal and occipital region,
   sutures of head scales outlined in brown------
   ----------------------------------variegata

20.Small brown spot present on tips of ventrals
   and first scale rows, alternating with dorsal
   blotches----------------------------------variegata
   Spots in interspaces absent or poorly defined,
   never prominent----------------------albifrons

21.Dorsal blotches wider than interspaces, little
   contrast between them, centers of blotches
   often considerably lightened, so that blotch
   resembles paired ellipses (oreas group, Fig.
   5)--22
   Color not as above (pratti group)------------23

22.Centers of dorsal blotches very light, so that
   blotch resembles paired ellipses on all individuals; chin heavily spotted; venter with
   two parallel dark streaks; ventrals often less
   than 170, subcaudals less than 80--ellipsifera
   Centers of dorsal blotches lightened only in
   adults, not in juveniles, and never so light
   that the blotch resembles paired ellipses;
   chin not or sparsely spotted; venter with
   large rectangular blotches between ends of
   neighboring dorsal blotches; ventrals more
   than 175; subcaudals more than 79--------oreas

23.Loreal enters orbit; no suboculars-----------24
   Loreal does not enter orbit; suboculars pre-
   sent-----------------------------sanctijoannis

24.Ventrals 177 or more------------------------25
   Ventrals 176 or less----------------------pratti

25.Dorsum of head not unicolor, spotted---------26
   Dorsum of head unicolor, not spotted---------27

26.Dorsum of head reddish-brown with black spot-
   ting------------------------------------boettgeri
   Dorsum of head black with yellow spotting-----
   ---------------------------------------schunkii

18.Dos o más pares de labiales en contacto detrás
   de mentoneana-----------------------------19
   Un único par de labiales en contacto detrás de
   mentoneana-------------------------------incerta

19.Cabeza dorsalmente unicolor en bronceado pálido
   o con manchas oscuras poco definidas en parie-
   tales--------------------------------------20
   Cabeza dorsalmente con manchas pardo-oscuras
   bien definidas sobre la región parietal y
   occipital, suturas de escamas cefálicas
   lineadas en pardo--------------------variegata

20.Con pequeñas manchas pardas en el límite
   lateral de las ventrales y primeras filas de
   escamas, alternando con las manchas dorsales--
   -------------------------------------variegata
   Manchas de los interespacios ausentes o pobremente definidas, nunca prominentes---albifrons

21.Manchas dorsales más anchas que los interespacios, con poco contraste entre sí; centros
   de las manchas frecuentemente considerablemente más claros, con manchas que recuerdan un
   par de paréntesis (grupo oreas, Fig. 5)-----22
   Coloración no como la anterior (grupo pratti)--
   --23

22.Manchas dorsales con centros muy claros; que
   recuerdan un par de paréntesis; geneiales
   densamente manchados; vientre con dos bandas
   oscuras y paralelas; ventrales frecuentemente
   menos de 170, subcaudales menos de 80---------
   ----------------------------------ellipsifera
   Centros de manchas dorsales claros sólo en
   adultos, no en juveniles, nunca tan claros
   como en las manchas que recuerdan un par de
   paréntesis; geneiales no manchadas o con manchas esparcidas; vientre con grandes manchas
   rectangulares ubicadas entre los nacimientos de
   las dorsales; ventrales más de 175; subcaudales más de 179-----------------------------oreas

23.Loreal conforma la órbita; sin suboculares---24
   Loreal no conforma la órbita; con suboculares--
   ---------------------------------sanctijoannis

24.Ventrales 177 o más------------------------25
   Ventrales 176 o menos--------------------pratti

25.Cabeza dorsalmente no unicolor, manchada----26
   Cabeza dorsalmente unicolor, no manchada-----27

26.Cabeza dorsalmente pardo rojiza con manchas
   negras-----------------------------------boettgeri
   Cabeza dorsalmente negra con manchas amarillas-
   ---------------------------------------schunkii

27.All dorsal blotches fail to meet on venter;
   usually less than two pairs of labials in contact behind mental-------------------------28
   First few dorsal blotches fused ventrally;
   usually two pairs of labials in contact behind
   mental-----------------------------latifasciata

28.Anterior body blotches twice as wide as
   lighter interblotch area---------latifrontalis
   Anterior body blotches approximately the same
   width as light interblotch areas-------peruana

27.Ninguna mancha dorsal se fusiona ventralmente;
   frecuentemente menos de dos pares de labiales
   en contacto detrás de la mentoneana---------28
   Pocas de las primeras manchas dorsales fusionadas ventralmente; frecuentemente dos pares
   de labiales en contacto detrás de la men-
   toneana-------------------------latifasciata

28.Manchas anteriores doblemente anchas que interespacios claros------------------latifrontalis
   Manchas anteriores de aproximadamente igual
   ancho al de los interespacios claros---peruana

DIPSAS ALBIFRONS (Sauvage)
variegata group

1884 Dipsadomorus albifrons Sauvage, Bull. Soc. Philom. Paris, (7) 8: 145. Type-locality: Brazil.
1908 Dipsas albifrons—Mocquard in Duméril & Bocourt, Miss. Sci. Mex. 3: 897.
1950 Dipsas albifrons cavalheiroi Hoge, Mem. Inst. Butantan, 22: 154. Type-locality: Ilha da
      Queimada Grande, São Paulo, Brazil.
1960 Dipsas albifrons—Peters, Misc. Publ. Mus. Zool. Univ. Mich., 114: 121.

   Distribution: Known from Estados de Santa Catarina and São Paulo, Brazil; also reported from
   Paraguay and Mato Grosso, Brazil.

DIPSAS ARTICULATA (Cope)
articulata group

1868 Leptognathus articulata Cope, Proc. Acad. Nat. Sci. Phila., 1868: 135. Type-locality: Veraguas,
      "Costa Rica" (actually in Panama).
1926 [Dipsas articulata]—Parker, Ann. Mag. Nat. Hist., (9) 18: 206.
1960 Dipsas articulata—Peters, Misc. Publ. Mus. Zool. Univ. Mich., 114: 33.

   Distribution: Lower elevations on Atlantic and Pacific slopes, Costa Rica and Panama.

DIPSAS BICOLOR (Günther)
articulata group

1895 Neopareas bicolor Günther, Biol. Centr. Amer., Rept.: 178. Type-locality: Chontales mine,
      Nicaragua.
1926 [Dipsas bicolor]—Parker, Ann. Mag. Nat. Hist., (9) 18: 206.
1954 Neopareas tricolor Brattstrom and Howell, Herpetologica, 10: 120. Type-locality: Jalapa, Nueva
      Segovia, Nicaragua.
1960 Dipsas bicolor—Peters, Misc. Publ. Mus. Zool. Univ. Mich., 114: 36.

   Distribution: Pacific slopes of southern Nicaragua and northern Costa Rica.

DIPSAS BOETTGERI (Werner)
pratti group

1901 Leptognathus boettgeri Werner, Abh. Ber. Königl. Zool. Anthropol.-Ethnol. Mus. Dresden, 9: 11.
      Type-locality: Chanchamayo, Peru.
1909 Leptognathus boliviana Werner, Mitt. Naturhist. Mus. Hamburg, 26: 240. Type-locality: Beni
      River, Bolivia.
1960 Dipsas boettgeri—Peters, Misc. Publ. Mus. Zool. Univ. Mich., 114: 98.

   Distribution: Andean slopes of southern Peru and northern Bolivia.

DIPSAS BREVIFACIES (Cope)
    articulata group

1866 Tropidodipsas brevifacies Cope, Proc. Acad. Nat. Sci. Phila., 1866: 127. Type-locality: Yucatán.
1884 Dipsadomorus fasciatus Bocourt, Bull. Soc. Philom. Paris, (7) 8: 135. Type-locality: Yucatán.
1885 Leptognathus torquatus Cope (substitute name for Dipsadomorus fasciatus Bocourt), Proc. Amer.
    Philos. Soc., 22: 172.
1926 [Dipsas brevifacies]—Parker, Ann. Mag. Hat. Hist., (9) 18: 206.
1960 Dipsas brevifacies—Peters, Misc. Publ. Mus. Zool. Univ. Mich., 114: 38.

  Distribution: Yucatán Peninsula to British Honduras on east and Carmen Island on west.

DIPSAS CATESBYI (Sentzen)
    catesbyi group

1796 Coluber catesbeji Sentzen (typographical error), Meyer's Zool. Arch., 2: 66. Type-locality:
    "Wahrscheinlich Amerika".
1827 Dipsas catesbyi—Boie, Isis von Oken, 20: 560.
?1947 Sibynomorphus macedoi Prado & Hoge, Ciencia, Mexico, 8:180. Type-locality: Pucallpa, Loreto
    Province, Peru.
1956 Dipsas catesbyi—Peters, Amer. Mus. Novitates, 1783: 2.

  Distribution: Amazonas region of South America, from Andean slopes of Bolivia, Peru, Ecuador,
    and Colombia to coast of Venezuela and British Guiana, and through northern half of Brazil.

DIPSAS COPEI (Günther)
    catesbyi group

1872 Leptognathus Copei Günther, Ann. Mag. Nat. Hist., (4) 9: 30. Type-locality: "Probably from
    Surinam".
1960 Dipsas copei—Peters, Misc. Publ. Mus. Zool. Univ. Mich., 114: 58.

  Distribution: Guianas and southern Venezuela.

DIPSAS ELLIPSIFERA (Boulenger)
    oreas group

1898 Leptognathus ellipsifera Boulenger, Proc. Zool. Soc. London, 1898: 117. Type-locality: Ibarra,
    Ecuador.
1960 Dipsas ellipsifera—Peters, Misc. Publ. Mus. Zool. Univ. Mich. 114: 87.

  Distribution: Known only from higher Andean slopes, western Ecuador.

DIPSAS GRACILIS (Boulenger)
    articulata group

1902 Leptognathus gracilis Boulenger, Ann. Mag. Nat. Hist., (7) 9: 57. Type-locality: San Javier,
    Ecuador.
1920 Leptognathus hammondii Boulenger, Ann. Mag. Nat. Hist., (9) 6: 110. Type-locality: Guatea,
    western Ecuador.
1925 Sibynomorphus macrostomus Amaral, Proc. U. S. Nat. Mus. 67: 9. Type-locality: Ecuador.
1960 Dipsas gracilis—Peters, Misc. Publ. Mus. Zool. Univ. Mich., 114: 44.

  Distribution: Northwestern Ecuador.

DIPSAS INCERTA (Jan)
    variegata group

1863 Leptognathus incertus Jan, Elenco Sist. Ofid.: 101. Type-locality: French Guiana.
1885 Leptognathus alternans Fischer, Jahrb. Wiss. Anat. Hamburg, 2: 105. Type-locality: "Angeblich
    aus Santos".
1923 Sibynomorphus barbouri Amaral, Proc. New Engl. Zool. Club, 8: 92. Type-locality: Utinga,
    Alagoas, Brazil.
1923 Sibynomorphus garbei Amaral, Proc. New Engl. Zool. Club, 8: 93. Type-locality: Colonia Hansa,
    Santa Catarina, Brazil.
1935 Dipsas incerta—Parker, Proc. Zool. Soc. London, 1935: 527.
1960 Dipsas incerta—Peters, Misc. Publ. Mus. Zool. Univ. Mich., 114: 127.

  Distribution: Southeastern coastal area of Brazil, from Espírito Santo to Santa Catarina.

<u>DIPSAS</u> <u>INDICA</u> Laurenti
   <u>indica</u> group

1768 <u>Dipsas</u> <u>indica</u> Laurenti, Synops. Rept.: 90. Type-locality: "Ceylon"; designated by Peters,
    Misc. Publ. Mus. Zool. Univ. Mich., 114: 68, as the Amazonian region of South America.

  Distribution: South America north of the Tropic of Capricorn.

  Content: Four subspecies, according to the latest revision by Peters, Misc. Publ. Mus. Zool. Univ.
    Mich., 114, 1960.

              Key to the subspecies

1. Dorsum of head unicolor light brown, or
   with three or four dark brown spots on
   posterior head shields (frontals,
   parietals, and occipitals)---------------2
   Dorsum of head darker brown, strongly variegated with black and yellow or white----3

2. Spots on posterior head plates absent or
   small, occupying less than one quarter of
   each scale---------------------<u>bucephala</u>
   Spots on posterior head plates large, occupying almost entire area of each scale--
   ------------------------------<u>cisticeps</u>

3. Occipital region not streaked, may be
   spotted, first dorsal blotch broadly
   fused along middorsal line---------<u>indica</u>
   Occipital region longitudinally streaked,
   first dorsal blotch separated by light
   line at vertebrals-----------<u>ecuadorensis</u>

              Clave de subespecies

1. Cabeza dorsalmente unicolor en pardo claro,
   o con tres o cuatro manchas pardo oscuras
   sobre los escudos posteriores (frontal,
   parietales y occipitales)----------------2
   Dorso de la cabeza pardo oscuro, fuertemente manchado en negro y amarillo o
   blanco-----------------------------------3

2. Manchas de placas posteriores de la cabeza,
   ausentes o pequeñas, ocupando menos de un
   cuarto de cada escama-----------<u>bucephala</u>
   Manchas de placas posteriores de la cabeza
   ocupando casi enteramente la superficie de
   cada escama---------------------<u>cisticeps</u>

3. Región occipital no lineada, aunque puede
   ser punteada, primera mancha dorsal ampliamente fusionada al nivel de la línea
   vertebral-------------------------<u>indica</u>
   Región occipital lineada longitudinalmente,
   primera mancha dorsal separada a nivel
   vertebral por una línea clara-<u>ecuadorensis</u>

<u>Dipsas</u> <u>indica</u> <u>indica</u> Laurenti

  1960 <u>Dipsas</u> <u>indica</u> <u>indica</u>—Peters, Misc. Publ. Mus. Zool. Univ. Mich., 114: 67.

    Distribution: Amazon drainage in Brazil, Colombia, British Guiana, Ecuador and Peru.

<u>Dipsas</u> <u>indica</u> <u>bucephala</u> (Boettger)

  1802 <u>Coluber</u> <u>bucephalus</u> Shaw, Gen. Zool., 3: 422. Type-locality: Ceylon; restricted by
    Peters, Misc. Publ. Mus. Zool. Univ. Mich., 114: 73, to Brazil.
  1960 <u>Dipsas</u> <u>indica</u> <u>bucephala</u>—Peters, Misc. Publ. Mus. Zool. Univ. Mich., 114: 73.

    Distribution: Southeastern Brazil; Misiones, Argentina.

<u>Dipsas</u> <u>indica</u> <u>cisticeps</u> (Boettger)

  1885 <u>Leptognathus</u> (<u>Dipsadomorus</u>) <u>cisticeps</u> Boettger, Zeit. Naturwiss., 58: 237. Type-
    locality: Paraguay.
  1914 <u>Dipsas</u> <u>cisticeps</u>—Bertoni, Descr. Fis. Econom. Paraguay, 59: 29.
  1960 <u>Dipsas</u> <u>indica</u> <u>cisticeps</u>—Peters, Misc. Publ. Mus. Zool. Univ. Mich., 114: 78.

    Distribution: Bolivia and Paraguay.

<u>Dipsas</u> <u>indica</u> <u>ecuadorensis</u> Peters

  1960 <u>Dipsas</u> <u>indica</u> <u>ecuadorensis</u> Peters, Misc. Publ. Mus. Zool. Univ. Mich., 114: 81. Type-
    locality: Río Solis, Cabeceras del Río Bobonaza, 14 km east southeast of Puyo, Pastaza
    Province, Ecuador.

    Distribution: Amazonian drainage of Ecuador.

DIPSAS LATIFASCIATA (Boulenger)
pratti group

1913 Leptognathus latifasciatus Boulenger, Ann. Mag. Nat. Hist., (8) 12: 72. Type-locality: Upper Marañon, Eastern Peru.
1960 Dipsas latifasciata—Peters, Misc. Publ. Mus. Zool. Univ. Mich., 114: 100.

Distribution: Amazonian slopes of Andes of northern Peru and extreme southern Ecuador.

DIPSAS LATIFRONTALIS (Boulenger)
pratti group

1905 Leptognathus latifrontalis Boulenger, Ann. Mag. Nat. Hist. (7) 15: 561. Type-locality: Aricagua, Estado Mérida, Venezuela, 1000 m.
1909 Leptognathus praeornata Werner, Mitt. Naturhist. Mus. Hamburg, 26: 240. Type-locality: Venezuela.
1912 Leptognathus palmeri Boulenger, Ann. Mag. Nat. Hist., (8) 10: 422. Type-locality: El Topo, Río Pastaza, Ecuador.
1960 Dipsas latifrontalis—Peters, Misc. Publ. Mus. Zool. Univ. Mich., 114: 109.

Distribution: Lower Amazonian slopes from Venezuela to southern Ecuador.

DIPSAS NEIVAI Amaral
indica group

1926 Dipsas neivai Amaral, Arch. Mus. Nac. Brasil, 26: 14. Type-locality: Caratinga, Minas Geraes, Brazil.
1960 Dipsas neivai—Peters, Misc. Publ. Mus. Zool. Univ. Mich., 114: 85.

Distribution: Caratinga (Minas Geraes) and Catú (Bahia) Brazil.

DIPSAS OREAS (Cope)
oreas group

1868 Leptognathus oreas Cope, Proc. Acad. Nat. Sci. Phila. 1868: 109. Type-locality: "From the elevated valley of Quito," Ecuador; locality questioned by Peters, Rev. Ecuat. Entom. Parasit., 2, 1955, 347.
1896 Leptognathus andiana Boulenger, Cat. Sn. Brit. Mus., 3: 452. Type-locality: Quito, Ecuador; (locality questioned by Peters, Rev. Ecuat. Entom. Parasit., 2, 1955, 347.
1934 Dipsas mikanii oreas—Parker, Ann. Mag. Nat. Hist., (10) 14: 271.
1960 Dipsas oreas—Peters, Misc. Publ. Mus. Zool. Univ. Mich., 114: 92.

Distribution: Higher parts and western slopes of Ecuadorian Andes.

DIPSAS PAVONINA Schlegel
catesbyi group

1837 Dipsas pavonina Schlegel, Essai Physion. Serpens, 2: 280. Type-locality: apparently from "Guyanes".
1960 Dipsas pavonina—Peters, Misc. Publ. Mus. Zool. Univ. Mich., 114: 61.

Distribution: Guianas and Venezuela to Pará, Brazil, and to Amazonian slopes of Andes; Colombia to Bolivia on eastern slope.

DIPSAS PERIJANENSIS Alemán, new combination

1953 Tropidodipsas perijanensis Alemán, Mem. Soc. Cien. Nat. La Salle, 13 (35): 217, fig. Type-locality: Jamayaujaina, Sierra de Perijá, Estado Zulia, Venezuela, 1700 m.

Distribution: Region of Perijá, Zulia, Venezuela.

DIPSAS PERUANA (Boettger)
    pratti group

  1898 Leptognathus peruana Boettger, Kat. Rept.-Samml. Mus. Senck. Nat. Ges., 2: 128. Type-locality:
        Santa Ana, Cuzco Province, Peru.
  1943 Dipsas mikanii peruanus—Schmidt & Walker, Zool. Ser. Field Mus. Nat. Hist., 24: 288.
  1960 Dipsas peruana—Peters, Misc. Publ. Mus. Zool. Univ. Mich., 114: 110.

    Distribution: Eastern slopes of Andes in southern Peru.

DIPSAS POECILOLEPIS (Amaral)
    polylepis group

  1923 Heterorhachis poecilolepsis Amaral (typographical error), Proc. New England Zool. Club, 8: 94.
        Type-locality: Villa Bomfim, Estado de São Paulo, Brazil.
  1960 Dipsas poecilolepis—Peters, Misc. Publ. Mus. Zool. Univ. Mich., 114: 95.

    Distribution: Known only from the type locality.

DIPSAS POLYLEPIS (Boulenger)
    polylepis group

  1912 Leptognathus polylepis Boulenger, Ann. Mag. Nat. Hist., (8) 10: 422. Type-locality:
        Huancabamba, Peru, above 3000 ft.
  1960 Dipsas polylepis—Peters, Misc. Publ. Mus. Zool. Univ. Mich., 114: 96.

    Distribution: Known only from the type locality.

DIPSAS PRATTI (Boulenger)
    pratti group

  1897 Leptognathus Pratti Boulenger, Ann. Mag. Nat. Hist., (6) 20: 523. Type-locality: Medellín,
        Colombia.
  1899 Leptognathus triseriatus Cope, Mus. Sci. Bull., 1: 13. Type-locality: Colombia.
  1916 Leptognathus nigriceps Werner, Zool. Anz., 47: 309. Type-locality: Cañón del Tolima, Colombia.
  1926 [Dipsas pratti]—Parker, Ann. Mag. Nat. Hist., (9) 18: 206.
  1940 Dipsas niceforoi Prado, Mem. Inst. Butantan, 14: 14. Type-locality: Quindío, Colombia.
  1941 Dipsas tolimensis Prado, Ciencia, México, 2: 345. Type-locality: Tolima, Líbano, Colombia.
  1960 Dipsas pratti—Peters, Misc. Publ. Mus. Zool. Univ. Mich., 114: 112.

    Distribution: Cordillera Central in Colombia.

DIPSAS SANCTIJOANNIS (Boulenger)
    pratti group

  1911 Leptognathus sancti-joannis Boulenger, Ann. Mag. Nat. Hist., (8) 7: 24. Type-locality: Pueblo
        Rico, slopes of San Juan River, Chocó, Colombia, 5200 ft.
  1916 Leptognathus sancti-johannis Werner (substitute name for Leptognathus sancti-joannis Boulenger),
        Zool. Anz., 47: 310.
  1941 Sibynomorphus caucanus Rendahl & Vestergren, Ark. för Zool., (A) 33: 11. Type-locality:
        Munchique, Cauca, Colombia.
  1960 Dipsas sanctijoannis—Peters, Misc. Publ. Mus. Zool. Univ. Mich., 114: 115.

    Distribution: Slopes of Cordillera Occidental in Colombia; also recorded from Medellín.

DIPSAS SCHUNKII (Boulenger)
    pratti group

  1908 Leptognathus schunkii Boulenger, Ann. Mag. Nat. Hist., (8) 1: 115. Type-locality: Chanchamayo,
        Peru.
  1922 Leptognathus schunckii Werner (substitute name for Leptognathus schunkii Boulenger), Arch.
        Naturgesch., (A) 8: 197.
  1926 [Dipsas schunkii]—Parker, Ann. Mag. Nat. Hist., (9) 18: 206.
  1960 Dipsas schunkei—Peters, Misc. Publ., Mus. Zool. Univ. Mich., 114: 119.

    Distribution: Amazonian slopes of Andes in Peru.

DIPSAS TEMPORALIS (Werner)
    articulata group

1909 Leptognathus temporalis Werner, Mitt. Naturhist. Mus. Hamburg, 26: 241. Type-locality: Esmeraldas, Ecuador.
1913 Leptognathus spurrelli Boulenger, Proc. Zool. Soc. London, 1913: 1036. Type-locality: Condoto, Peña Lisa, Chocó, Colombia.
1960 Dipsas temporalis—Peters, Misc. Publ. Mus. Zool. Univ. Mich., 114: 50.

   Distribution: Pacific coast of South America in Ecuador and Colombia; Atlantic coast of Panama.

DIPSAS TENUISSIMA Taylor
    articulata group

1954 Dipsas tenuissima Taylor, Univ. Kansas Sci. Bull., 26: 771. Type-locality: On Dominical Road in swamp , approximately 15 km WSW of San Isidro del General, Costa Rica.
1960 Dipsas tenuissima—Peters, Misc. Publ. Mus. Zool. Univ. Mich., 114: 52.

   Distribution: Panama and Costa Rica.

DIPSAS VARIEGATA (Duméril, Bibron and Duméril)
    variegata group

1854 Leptognathus variegatus Duméril, Bibron and Duméril, Erp. Gén., 7: 477. Type-locality: Surinam.
1918 Dipsas variegata—Gomes, Rev. Mus. Paulista, 10: 525.

   Distribution: Panama and northern South America.

   Content: Three subspecies, according to Peters, 1960, Misc. Pub. Mus. Zool. Univ. Mich., 114.

Key to the subspecies

1. Dorsum of head with dark-brown spot clearly defined on parietal and occipital region, sutures of head scales outlined in brown-2
Dorsum of head unicolor light or with poor-ly defined darker spots on parietals------
----------------------------------trinitatis

2. Dark-brown spots on head unite on frontals to form U-shaped mark, posterior tips of "U" often fused to first dorsal blotch----
--------------------------------nicholsi
Dark-brown spots on head not fused on frontal, do not extend to first dorsal blotch------------------------variegata

Clave de subespecies

1. Dorso de la cabeza con manchas pardo oscuras claramente definidas sobre la región parie-tal y occipital; suturas de escamas cefáli-cas lineadas en pardo--------------------2
Dorso de la cabeza unicolor en tostado claro, o con puntos oscuros pobremente definidos sobre las parietales--trinitatis

2. Manchas pardo oscura dorso cefálicas unidas, formando sobre la zona frontal, una U, cuya parte posterior frecuentemente se fusiona a la primera mancha dorsal-----
------------------------------------nicholsi
Manchas pardo oscuras, dorso cefálicas no unidas sobre la zona frontal y no exten-diéndose hasta la primera mancha dorsal---
------------------------------variegata

Dipsas variegata variegata (Duméril, Bibron and Duméril)

1923 Leptognathus robusta L. Müller, Zool. Anz., 57: 155. Type-locality: East Ecuador.
1960 Dipsas variegata variegata—Peters, Misc. Publ. Mus. Zool. Univ. Mich., 114: 132.

   Distribution: Venezuela, Guianas, Ecuador, and Peru.

Dipsas variegata nicholsi (Dunn)

1933 Sibynomorphus nicholsi Dunn, Copeia, 1933: 193. Type-locality: mid-basin of Chagres River and mouth of Pequeni River, Panama.
1960 Dipsas variegata nicholsi—Peters, Misc. Publ. Mus. Zool. Univ. Mich., 114: 137.

   Distribution: Atlantic side of Panama to northwestern Ecuador.

Dipsas variegata trinitatis Parker

1926 Dipsas trinitatis Parker, Ann. Mag. Nat. Hist., (9) 18: 206. Type-locality: Trinity
Hill Reserve, Trinidad.
1960 Dipsas variegata trinitatis—Peters, Misc. Publ. Mus. Zool. Univ. Mich., 114: 139.

Distribution: Island of Trinidad.

DIPSAS VERMICULATA Peters
catesbyi group

1960 Dipsas vermiculata Peters, Misc. Publ. Mus. Zool. Univ. Mich., 114: 65. Type-locality:
Chichirota, Lower Río Bobonaza, Pastaza Province, Ecuador.

Distribution: Amazonian Ecuador and northeastern Peru.

DIPSAS VIGUIERI (Bocourt)
articulata group

1884 Leptognathus viguieri Bocourt, Bull. Soc. Philom. Paris, (7) 8: 136. Type-locality: Isthmus of
Darién, Panama.
1926 [Dipsas viguieri]—Parker, Ann. Mag. Nat. Hist., (9) 18: 206.
1960 Dipsas viguieri—Peters, Misc. Publ. Mus. Zool. Univ. Mich., 114: 54.

Distribution: Pacific coast of Panama.

DITAXODON Hoge

    1958 Ditaxodon Hoge, Mitt. Zool. Mus. Berlin, 34 (1): 54, figs. 5-7. Type-species: Philodryas
        taeniatus Hensel.

   Distribution: Southern Brazil.

   Content: One species.

DITAXODON TAENIATUS (Hensel)

    1868 Philodryas taeniatus Hensel, Arch. für Naturg., 1868: 331. Type-locality: Porto Alegre, Rio
        Grande do Sul, Brazil.

    1958 Ditaxodon taeniatus—Hoge, Mitt. Zool. Mus. Berlin, 34 (1): 54, figs. 5-7.

   Distribution: Southern Brazil.

REPTILIA: SERPENTES: COLUBRIDAE  DREPANOIDES

Prepared by Joseph R. Bailey, Duke University, Durham, North Carolina

DREPANOIDES Dunn

1896 _Drepanodon_ Peracca (preoccupied by _Drepanodon_ Nesti, 1826), Boll. Mus. Zool. Anat. Comp. Univ. Torino, 11 (231): 3. Type-species: _Cloelia anomala_ Jan.
1928 _Drepanoides_ Dunn (substitute name for _Drepanodon_ Peracca), Bull. Antivenin Inst. Amer., 2: 22. Type-species: _Cloelia anomala_ Jan.
1941 _Pseudoclelia_ Rendahl and Vestergren, Ark. för Zool., 33A (5): 10. Type-species: _Pseudoclelia guttata_ Rendahl and Vestergren.

Distribution: As for single species.

Content: One species.

Comment: There is a possibility that the species _Arrhyton quenselii_ Andersson, 1901, belongs here, but it is omitted until additional information on the species is available. _Drepanodon eatoni_ Ruthven is a synonym of _Oxyrhopus marcapatae_ Boulenger.

DREPANOIDES ANOMALUS (Jan)

1863 _Cloelia anomala_ Jan, Elenco Sist. Ofidi, 1863: 92. Type-locality: Originally given by Jan as "Amer. Merid." and "Brasile", but modified to "Amer. Merid." only by Jan, Icon. Gén. Ophid., 1870, Livr. 35, pl. 1, fig. 4; Peracca, Boll. Mus. Zool. Anat. Comp. Univ. Torino, 1896, 11 (231), 5, states that the bottle containing the type at Neuchâtel includes a label saying "Perou-Voyage Tschudi".
1896 _Drepanodon anomalus_—Peracca, Boll. Mus. Zool. Anat. Comp. Univ. Torino, 11 (231): 3.
1896 _Drepanodon astigmaticus_ Peracca, Boll. Mus. Zool. Anat. Comp. Univ. Torino, 11 (231): 5. Type-locality: Iquitos, Peru.
1941 _Pseudoclelia guttata_ Rendahl and Vestergren, Ark. för Zool., 33A (5): 10. Type-locality: Río Pastaza between Río Puyo and Río Copataza, Ecuador.

Distribution: Central Bolivia north to southern Colombia along Andean front.

DROMICUS Bibron

1843 Dromicus Bibron, in de la Sagra, Hist. Fis. Pol. Nat. Cuba, Spanish Ed., 4: 133. Type-species: Dromicus angulifer Bibron.
1854 Taeniophis Girard, Proc. Acad. Nat. Sci. Phila., 1854: 227. Type-species: Taeniophis tantillus Girard.
1899 Pachyurus Philippi, An. Univ. Chile, 104: 721. Type-species: None given.

Distribution: Pacific slopes of South America, between Peru and Chile, possibly Ecuador, Galapagos Islands and Antilles.

Content: About 20 species, several of them with large numbers of subspecies; most extralimital in Antilles and Galapagos Islands; only four species occur in the area covered by this work.

Key to the species

1. Dorsal pattern not made up of two longitudinal series of dark spots fused anteriorly--------2
Dorsal pattern of two longitudinal series of dark spots, fused anteriorly-----tachymenoides

2. Dorsal pattern with a middorsal black stripe only one scale row wide---------------------3
Dorsal pattern with one longitudinal dark band at least five scale rows wide------chamissonis

3. Fewer than 195 ventrals--------------------inca
More than 195 ventrals---------angustilineatus

Clave de especies

1. Diseño no formado por dos hileras de manchas oscuras dorsales fusionadas anteriormente----2
Diseño dorsal con dos hileras de manchas oscuras fusionadas anteriormente-tachymenoides

2. Diseño dorsal con cinta negra media del ancho de una escama--------------------------------3
Diseño dorsal con una cinta parda que ocupa por lo menos cinco filas de escamas---chamissonis

3. Menos de 195 ventrales--------------------inca
Más de 195 ventrales-----------angustilineatus

DROMICUS ANGUSTILINEATUS Schmidt and Walker

1943 Dromicus angustilineatus Schmidt and Walker, Zool. Ser. Field. Mus. Nat. Hist., 24: 308. Type-locality: Toquepala, Tacna, Peru.
1966 Dromicus angustilineatus—Donoso-Barros, Reptiles de Chile: 419.

Distribution: Arica valley, Chile; southwestern Peru, from near sea level to about 10,000 ft.

DROMICUS CHAMISSONIS (Wiegmann)

1835 Coronella Chamissonis Wiegmann, Nova Acta Acad. Caes. Leop. Carol., 17: 246, pl. 19. Type-locality: Tollo, Chile.
1837 Psammophis temminckii Schlegel, Essai Physiog. Serpens, 2: 218, pl. 8, figs. 14-15. Type-locality: Valparaíso, Chile.
1854 Taeniophis tantillus Girard, Proc. Acad. Nat. Sci. Phila., 1854: 227. Type-locality: Santiago, Chile.
1867 Dromicus chamissonis—Steindachner, Reise Novara, Rept.: 65.
1899 Liophis luctuosa Philippi, An. Univ. Chile, 104: 723. Type-locality: None given.
1966 Dromicus chamissonis—Donoso-Barros, Reptiles de Chile: 415, pl. 32.

Distribution: Between 27°S and 41°S in Chile.

DROMICUS INCA Schmidt and Walker

1943 Dromicus inca Schmidt and Walker, Zool. Ser. Field Mus. Nat. Hist., 24: 325. Type-locality: Cajamarca, Departamento de Cajamarca, Peru.

Distribution: Known from type locality only.

DROMICUS TACHYMENOIDES Schmidt and Walker

1943 Dromicus tachymenoides Schmidt and Walker, Zool. Ser. Field Mus. Nat. Hist., 24: 309. Type-
    locality: Chucurapí, near Mollendo, Departamento Arequipa, Peru.
1966 Dromicus tachymenoides—Donoso-Barros, Reptiles de Chile: 421, pl. 32.

   Distribution: Extreme northern Chile and southern coastal Peru, from sea level to 10,000 ft.

DRYMARCHON Fitzinger

1843 Drymarchon Fitzinger, Syst. Rept.: 26. Type-species: Coluber corais Boie.
1853 Georgia Baird and Girard, Cat. N. Amer. Rept.: 92. Type-species: Coluber couperi Holbrook.
1867 Geoptyas Steindachner, Sitz. Math.-Naturwiss. Kl.Akad. Wiss. Wien, 55 (1): 271, pl. 3, figs. 4-7.
      Type-species: None designated.

Distribution: From southern United States to northern Argentina.

Content: One widely ranging species.

DRYMARCHON CORAIS (Boie)

1827 Coluber corais Boie, Isis, von Oken, 1827: 537. Type-locality: America.
1899 [Drymarchon corais]—Stejneger, North Amer. Fauna, 14: 70.

Distribution: From United States to northern Argentina.

Content: Eight subspecies, three (erebennus Cope, couperi Holbrook and orizabensis Dugés) extra-
      limital.

Key to the subspecies	Clave de subespecies

1. Dorsal pattern uniformly black------------2
   Dorsum with some pattern, not uniformly
      black----------------------------------3

2. Tail and venter not reddish----------corais
   Tail and venter reddish-----------rubidus

3. Dorsal pattern light brown at least
      anteriorly---------------------------4
   Dorsal pattern black with irregular grey
      transverse bands, dim or indistinct
      anteriorly, more prominent posteriorly
      and on tail--------------------margaritae

4. Dorsal pattern uniform light brownish------
   ---------------------------------unicolor
   Dorsal pattern in dark brown more intensive
      on posterior third of body and entire
      tail---------------------------melanurus

1. Dorso enteramante negro--------------------2
   Dorso no enteramente negro---------------3

2. Cola y vientre no rojizos-----------corais
   Cola y vientre rojizos-------------rubidus

3. Diseño dorsal pardo claro por lo menos
      anteriormente--------------------------4
   Diseño dorsal negro con bandas transversas
      irregulares grises, difusa o indistinta
      anteriormente, más prominente en la parte
      posterior y en la cola----------margaritae

4. Diseño dorsal en pardo claro uniforme------
   ---------------------------------unicolor
   Diseño dorsal en pardo oscuro más intenso
      en el tercio posterior del cuerpo y toda
      la cola--------------------------melanurus

Drymarchon corais corais (Boie)

1867 Geoptyas flaviventris Steindachner, Sitz. Math.-Naturwiss. Kl. Akad. Wiss. Wien, 55 (1):
      272, pl. 4, figs. 1-4. Type-localities: Cüyaba, Mato Grosso, Brazil, and Rio Vaupés,
      which may be either Colombia or Brazil (where it is spelled Uaupés).
1899 [Drymarchon corais corais]—Stejneger, North Amer. Fauna, 14: 70.
1923 Phrynonax angulifer Werner, Ann. Naturhist. Mus. Wien, 36: 162. Type-locality: Joinville,
      Brazil.

   Distribution: Amazonian and Paraguayan basins; from Venezuela to Argentina; Trinidad and
      Tobago.

Drymarchon corais margaritae Roze

1959 Drymarchon margaritae Roze, Nov. Cient. Mus. Hist. Nat. La Salle, Venezuela, Ser. Zool.,
      25: 1. Type-locality: Near San Francisco de Macanao, Isla Margarita, Venezuela.
1964 Drymarchon corais margaritae—Roze, Mem. Soc. Cien. Nat. La Salle, Venezuela, 69: 222.

   Distribution: Known only from western Margarita Island, Venezuela.

Drymarchon corais melanurus (Duméril, Bibron and Duméril)

1854 Spilotes melanurus Duméril, Bibron and Duméril, Erp. Gén., 7: 224. Type-locality: Mexico.
1867 Geoptyas collaris Steindachner, Sitz. Math.-Naturwiss. Kl. Akad. Wiss. Wien, 55 (1); 271, pl. 3, figs. 4-7. Type-locality: Brazil.
1899 Drymarchon corais melanurus—Stejneger, North Amer. Fauna, 14: 70.
1941 Drymarchon corais melanocercus Smith (substitute name for melanurus Duméril, Bibron and Duméril), Jour. Washington Acad. Sci., 31: 473.

   Distribution: Pacific slopes of Colombia and Ecuador; Northern Venezuela; Central America to Veracruz, Mexico, on Atlantic Slope and to Nicaragua on Pacific Slope.

Drymarchon corais rubidus Smith

1941 Drymarchon corais rubidus Smith, Jour. Washington Acad. Sci., 31: 474. Type-locality: Rosario, Sinaloa, Mexico.
1942 Drymarchon corais cleofae Brock, Copeia, 1942: 249. Type-locality: Isla Maria Cleofa, Tres Marias Islands, Mexico.

   Distribution: Low and moderate elevations of Pacific coast from Sinaloa, Mexico, south to Isthmus of Tehuantepec and apparently through valley of Río Grijalva, Chiapas into extreme southwestern Guatemala.

Drymarchon corais unicolor Smith

1941 Drymarchon corais unicolor Smith, Jour. Washington Acad. Sci., 31: 470. Type-locality: La Esperanza, near Escuintla, Chiapas, Mexico.

   Distribution: Low and moderate elevations from Chiapas, Mexico along Pacific coast into Nicaragua.

DRYMOBIUS Fitzinger

1843 Drymobius Fitzinger, Systema Reptilium: 26. Type-species: Herpetodryas margaritiferus Schlegel.
1893 Crossanthera Cope, American Naturalist, 1893: 481. Type-species: Dendrophidium melanotropis Cope.

Distribution: Texas on Atlantic slope and Chiapas, Mexico on Pacific slope through Central America to Ecuador, Peru and Venezuela.

Content: Four species.

Key to the species

1. Dorsal pattern not reticulate; individual scales not green surrounded by black---------2
   Dorsal pattern reticulate; each scale green surrounded by black------------margaritiferus

2. Dorsal pattern without rhomboid blotches, more or less uniform green-----------------------3
   Dorsal pattern of rhomboid blotches---rhombifer

3. Keels on middorsal scale rows not blackish--chloroticus
   Keels on three middorsal scale rows blackish---------------------------------------melanotropis

Clave de especies

1. Diseño dorsal no reticulado; escamas individualmente no verdes rodeadas de negro--------2
   Diseño dorsal reticulado; cada escama verde, rodeada de negro---------------margaritiferus

2. Diseño dorsal sin manchas romboidales, más o menos uniformemente verde--------------------3
   Diseño dorsal de manchas romboidales--rhombifer

3. Quillas de las filas mediodorsales no negras--chloroticus
   Quillas de las tres filas mediodorsales negras---melanotropis

DRYMOBIUS CHLOROTICUS (Cope)

1886 Dendrophidium chloroticum Cope, Proc. Amer. Phil. Soc., 23 (1885): 278. Type-locality: Guatemala; restricted by Cope, Bull. U.S. Nat. Mus., 32, 1887, 69, to Cobán, [Alta Verapaz], Guatemala.
1887 Drymobius chloroticus—Cope, Bull. U.S. Nat. Mus., 32: 69.

Distribution: Moderate and intermediate elevations; San Luis de Potosí, Mexico, along Caribbean coast to Honduras, and Isthmus of Tehuantepec, Mexico to Costa Rica on Pacific slope.

DRYMOBIUS MARGARITIFERUS (Schlegel)[1]

1837 Herpetodryas margaritiferus Schlegel, Essai Physion. Serpens, 2: 184. Type-locality: New Orleans (in error); restricted by Smith, Proc. U.S. Nat. Mus., 92, 1942, 383, to Veracruz, Mexico; further restricted to Córdoba, Veracruz, by Smith and Taylor, Univ. Kansas Sci. Bull., 33, 1950, 347.
1878 D.[rymobius] margaritiferus—Cope, Proc. Amer. Phil. Soc., 17 (1877): 35.

Distribution: Texas through Central America to South America.

Content: Four subspecies, one (fistulosus Smith) extralimital.

Key to the subspecies

1. Anterior margins of median dorsal scales blue in adults, white in faded specimens, gray in juveniles; well differentiated from black scale tip--------------------2
   Color not as above------------occidentalis

Clave de subespecies

1. Borde anterior de escamas dorsales medianas azul en adultos, claro en especímenes marchitados, gris en juveniles; bien diferenciado de ápices negros de escama----2
   Diseño dorsal no como el anterior----------------------------occidentalis

---

[1]A petition currently before the International Commission for Zoological Nomenclature [Z.N.(S.) 1704] would set aside Coluber Chiametla Shaw, Gen. Zool., Amphib., 2, 1802, 440, in favor of its younger synonym, margaritiferus Schlegel. The rules direct the retention of the status quo until a decision is reached, so we retain the junior synonym here. The name chiametla would apparently be allocated to subspecies fistulosus, if used.

2. Adults retaining juvenile pattern of 35-45 diffuse dorsal blotches or bands, 2-3 scale rows wide, more conspicuous anteriorly; ground color turquoise-green in life (dull or bluish-gray in preservative), dorsal scales almost entirely black (on dark blotches) to almost entirely turquoise-green (on lighter areas), bordered with gray or black, always black-tipped------------------------------------maydis
Not as above-----------------margaritiferus

2. Adultos reteniendo el patrón juvenil de unas 35-45 manchas o bandas dorsales que se extienden hasta el origen de las ventrales; color de fondo verde-turquesa en vida (gris opaco o azulado en líquido preservativo), dorsales color verde-turquesa con grados variables de pigmentación negra o gris oscura; ápice de las dorsales siempre negro----------------------maydis
No como el anterior----------margaritiferus

Drymobius margaritiferus margaritiferus (Schlegel)

1855 Zamenis tricolor Hallowell, Jour. Acad. Nat. Sci. Phila., (2) 3: 34, pl. 3. Type-locality: Honduras.
1890 Drymobius margaritiferus [margaritiferus]—Bocourt, Miss. Sci. Mex., Reptiles: 718.

Distribution: Low and moderate elevations from Texas south along Caribbean coast to northern South America.

Drymobius margaritiferus maydis Villa

1968 Drymobius margaritiferus maydis Villa, Rev. Biol. Trop. Costa Rica, 15: 117, figs. 2-4. Type-locality: Great Corn Island, Departamento de Zelaya, Nicaragua.

Distribution: Known only from Great Corn Island, Nicaragua.

Drymobius margaritiferus occidentalis Bocourt

1890 Drymobius margaritiferus var. occidentalis Bocourt, Miss. Sci. Mex., Rept.: 718. Type-locality: Near Volcán Atitlán, Guatemala.

Distribution: Low and moderate elevations on Pacific coast of Chiapas, Mexico east to El Salvador.

DRYMOBIUS MELANOTROPIS (Cope)

1876 Dendrophidium melanotropis Cope, Jour. Acad. Nat. Sci. Phila., (2) 8 (1875): 134, pl. 26, fig. 1. Type-locality: Costa Rica.
1933 Drymobius melanotropis—Stuart, Copeia, 1933: 10.

Distribution: Nicaragua to Panama.

DRYMOBIUS RHOMBIFER (Günther)

1860 Coryphodon rhombifer Günther, Proc. Zool. Soc. London, 1860: 236. Type-locality: Esmeraldas, Ecuador.
1888 Drymobius rhombifer—Bocourt, Miss. Sci. Mex., Rept., pl. 43, fig. 1.

Distribution: From Nicaragua to Peru, Venezuela, Colombia, and Ecuador.

DRYMOLUBER Amaral

1929 Drymoluber Amaral, Mem. Inst. Butantan, 4: 335, fig. Type-species: Herpetodryas dichroa Peters.

Distribution: Tropical South America, from northeastern Brazil and Guianas through Amazonian region to Colombia, Ecuador and Peru.

Content: Two species.

Key to the species

1. Dorsal scales in 15 rows---------------dichrous
   Dorsal scales in 17 rows---------------brazili

Clave de especies

1. Escamas dorsales en 15 filas----------dichrous
   Escamas dorsales en 17 filas----------brazili

DRYMOLUBER BRAZILI (Gomes)

1918 Drymobius Brazili Gomes, Mem. Inst. Butantan, 1: 81, pl. 14, fig. 2. Type-locality: Estação de Engenheiro Lisbôa, near Uberaba, Estado de Minas Gerais, Brazil.
1923 Drymobius rubriceps Amaral, Proc. New England Zool. Club , 8: 85. Type-locality: Estado de São Paulo, Brazil.
1932 Drymoluber brazili—Stuart, Occ. Pap. Mus. Zool. Univ. Mich., 236: 3.

Distribution: South central Brazil.

DRYMOLUBER DICHROUS (Peters)

1863 Herpetodryas dichroa Peters, Monats. Akad. Wiss. Berlin, 1863: 284. Type-locality: Brazil; Surinam.
1868 Herpetodryas occipitalis Günther, Ann. Mag. Nat. Hist., (4) 1: 430. Type-locality: Pebas, Ecuador.
1868 Spilotes piceus Cope, Proc. Acad. Nat. Sci. Phila., 1868: 105. Type-locality: Napo or Upper Marañón, Ecuador.
1930 Drymoluber dichrous—Amaral, Mem. Inst. Butantan, 4: 82.

Distribution: Colombia, Ecuador, eastern Peru, northern Brazil, Amazonian Venezuela.

ELAPHE Fitzinger

1833 Elaphe Fitzinger, in Wagler, Descrip. Icon. Amphib., 3: text for pl. 27. Type-species: Elaphe
parreysii Fitzinger = Coluber quatuorlineatus Lacépède.
1843 Pantherophis Fitzinger, Syst. Rept.: 25. Type-species: Coluber guttatus Linnaeus.
1853 Scotophis Baird and Girard, Cat. N. Amer. Rept.: 73. Type-species: Coluber alleghaniensis
Holbrook = C. obsoletus Say.
1943 Pseudelaphe Mertens and Rosenberg (subgenus novum), Wochenschrift (Blätter) für Aquarien and
Terrarienkunde, 3: 61. Type-species: Coluber flavirufus Cope.

Distribution: United States through Central America to Panama and Costa Rica.

Content: Eight species, six of which (guttata Linnaeus, vulpina Baird and Girard, obsoleta Say
phaescens Dowling, rosaliae Mocquard and subocularis Brown) are extralimital, according to
Dowling, Occ. Pap. Mus. Zool. Univ. Mich., 541, 1952.

Key to the species	Clave de especies
1. With three dark bands on parietal region, one on midline between parietals and one one outer margin of each parietal; usually eight upper labials--------------------------------triaspis	1. Con tres bandas oscuras en la región parietal, una en la línea media entre parietales y una en borde externo de cada parietal; usualmente ocho labiales superiores-------------triaspis
Lacking three more or less continuous bands on parietals; usually nine upper labials--flavirufa	Sin tres bandas más o menos continuas en los parietales; usualmente nueve labiales superiores--------------------------flavirufa

ELAPHE FLAVIRUFA (Cope)

1867 Coluber flavirufus Cope, Proc. Acad. Nat. Sci. Phila., 1867: 319. Type-locality: Yucatán;
restricted to vincinty of Campeche, Campeche, by Dowling, Occ.Pap. Mus. Zool. Univ. Mich.,
542, 1952, 3.
1936 Elaphe flavirufa—Gaige, Carnegie Inst. Washington Publ., 547: 299.

Distribution: Mexico and Guatemala on Caribbean Coast to Corn Island, Nicaragua.

Content: Four subspecies, two of which (flavirufa Cope and matudai Smith) are extralimital.

Key to the subspecies	Clave de subespecies
1. Maximum 34 (usually 33) scale rows; posterior minimum 23 scale rows----polysticha Maximum 31 scale rows; posterior minimum 21 scale rows--------------------pardalina	1. Máximo 34 (usualmente 33) filas de escamas; mínimo posterior 23 filas-------polysticha Máximo 31 filas de escamas; mínimo posterior 21 filas-----------------pardalina

Elaphe flavirufa pardalina (Peters)

1868 Elaphis pardalinus Peters, Monats. Akad. Wiss. Berlin, 1868: 642. Type-locality:
Unknown.
1887 Elaphis rodriguezii Bocourt, le Naturaliste, (2) 14: 168. Type-locality: Panzos, Alta
Verapaz, Guatemala.
1952 Elaphe flavirufa pardalina—Dowling, Occ. Pap. Mus. Zool. Univ. Mich., 540: 9.

Distribution: Alta Verapaz, Guatemala through Honduras to Corn Island, Nicaragua.

Elaphe flavirufa polysticha Smith and Williams

1966 Elaphe flavirufa polysticha Smith and Williams, Nat. Hist. Misc. Chicago Acad. Sci., 185:
1. Type-locality: Ruatán Island, Islas de la Bahía, Honduras.

Distribution: Known only from type locality.

ELAPHE TRIASPIS (Cope)

1866 Coluber triaspis Cope, Proc. Acad. Nat. Sci. Phila., 1866: 128. Type-locality: Belize;
      restricted to vicinity of the town of Belize, British Honduras, by Smith and Taylor, Univ.
      Kansas Sci. Bull., 33, 1950, 316.
1929 Elaphe triaspis—Amaral, Mem. Inst. Butantan, 4: 159.

   Distribution: Arizona through Mexico and Central America to Costa Rica.

   Content: Three subspecies, one of which (intermedia Boettger) is extralimital, according to most
      recent revision by Dowling, Zoologica, 45, 1960, 53-80.

Key to the subspecies	Clave de subespecies
1. Median frontoparietal band with small rounded opening at about middle of suture between parietals; band not open anteriorly----------------------------triaspis Median frontoparietal band with elongate opening along suture between parietals; band usually opening anteriorly, thus forming a "Y"--------------------mutabilis	1. Una banda frontoparietal mediana, con una abertura pequeña y redonda aproximadamente en el medio de la sutura entre parietales; banda no abierta anteriormente----triaspis Una banda frontoparietal con abertura alargada sobre la sutura interparietal; banda generalmente abierta anteriormente formando una "Y"--------------------------mutabilis

Elaphe triaspis triaspis (Cope)

1948 [Elaphe triaspis triaspis]—Stuart, Misc. Publ. Mus. Zool. Univ. Mich., 69: 68.
1960 Elaphe triaspis triaspis—Dowling, Zoologica, 45: 71, figs. 1, 9a.

   Distribution: Yucatán Peninsula, from Chichén Itzá and Mérida south to Uaxactún, in Petén,
      Guatemala.

Elaphe triaspis mutabilis (Cope)

1885 Coluber mutabilis Cope, Proc. Amer. Phil. Soc., 1884: 175. Type-locality: Verapaz,
      Guatemala and Costa Rica.
1948 Elaphe triaspis mutabilis—Stuart, Misc. Publ. Mus. Zool. Univ. Mich., 69: 68.
1960 Elaphe triaspis mutabilis—Dowling, Zoologica, 45: 72, fig. 9b.

   Distribution: Highlands of Guatemala south to vicinity of San José, Costa Rica.

ELAPOMOJUS Jan

   1862 <u>Elapomojus</u> Jan, Arch. Zool. Anat. Fis., 2: 42. Type-species: <u>Elapomorphus</u> (<u>Elapomojus</u>)
      <u>dimidiatus</u> Jan.
   1896 <u>Elapomoius</u> Boulenger (emendation of <u>Elapomojus</u>), Cat. Sn. Brit. Mus., 3: 238.
   1898 <u>Elapohomoeus</u> Berg (emendation of <u>Elapomojus</u>), An. Mus. Nac. Buenos Aires, 6: 28.

   Distribution: As for single known species.

   Content: One species.

ELAPOMOJUS DIMIDIATUS Jan

   1862 <u>E</u>.[<u>lapomorphus</u> (<u>Elapomojus</u>)] <u>dimidiatus</u> Jan, Arch. Zool. Anat. Fis., 2: 47. Type-locality:
      Brazil.
   1896 <u>Elapomoius</u> <u>dimidiatus</u>—Boulenger, Cat. Sn. Brit. Mus., 3: 238.

   Distribution: Known only from type specimen, which is no longer extant.

ELAPOMORPHUS Wiegmann

1843 _Elapomorphus_ Wiegmann, Fitzinger, Syst. Rept.: 25. Type-species: _Calamaria_ _Blumii_ Schlegel.
1858 _Elapocephalus_ Günther, Cat. Sn. Brit. Mus.: 276. Type-species: _Elapocephalus_ _taeniatus_ Günther.
1862 _Phalotris_ Cope, Proc. Acad. Nat. Sci. Phila., 1861: 524. Type-species: _Elapomorphus_ _tricolor_
        Duméril, Bibron and Duméril.

   Distribution: Tropical and subtropical South America; from northeastern Brazil to Argentina.

   Content: Eight species.

Key to the species

1. Two prefrontals--------------------------------2
   One prefrontal---------------------------------4

2. Dorsal pattern with three longitudinal stripes-
   --3
   Dorsal pattern with five longitudinal stripes--
   ------------------------------------_quinquelineatus_

3. Parietals at least twice as long as broad;
   ventrals 176-184--------------------_wuchereri_
   Parietals not twice as long as broad; ventrals
   190-234------------------------------_lepidus_

4. Parietals separated from labials by
   temporals-------------------------------------5
   Parietals in contact with labials; anterior
   temporal absent------------------------_nasutus_

5. Dorsal pattern not lineate--------------------6
   Dorsum with lineate pattern---------_bilineatus_

6. Dorsal scales spotted with black on posterior
   tip; nuchal collar three scales wide; ventrals
   more than 223--------------------------_mertensi_
   Dorsal scales without black spotting; nuchal
   collar six scales wide; fewer than 217
   ventrals-------------------------------_tricolor_

7. With fourth labial in contact with parietal----
   --------------------------------------_bollei_
   With fifth labial in contact with parietal-----
   --------------------------------------_nasutus_

Clave de especies

1. Dos prefrontales----------------------------2
   Una prefrontal-----------------------------4

2. Diseño dorsal con tres líneas longitudinales--3
   Diseño dorsal con cinco líneas longitudinales--
   ----------------------------------_quinquelineatus_

3. Parietales por lo menos doblemente más largas
   que anchas; ventrales 176-184--------_wuchereri_
   Parietales no doblemente largas que anchas;
   ventrales 190-234----------------------_lepidus_

4. Parietales separadas de labiales por
   temporales-----------------------------------5
   Parietales en contacto con labiales; sin
   temporal anterior----------------------_nasutus_

5. Diseño dorsal no lineado---------------------6
   Diseño dorsal lineado----------------_bilineatus_

6. Escamas dorsales manchados de negro en el
   ápice; collar nucal estrecho de tres escamas
   de ancho; ventrales más de 223-------_mertensi_
   Escamas dorsales sin manchas negras; ancho
   collar nucal que ocupa seis escamas; menos de
   217 ventrals-------------------------_tricolor_

7. Con cuarta labial en contacto con parietal-----
   -------------------------------------_bollei_
   Con quinta labial en contacto con parietal-----
   --------------------------------------_nasutus_

ELAPOMORPHUS _BILINEATUS_ Duméril, Bibron and Duméril

1854 _Elapomorphus_ _bilineatus_ Duméril, Bibron and Duméril, Erp. Gén., 7: 839. Type-locality:
        Corrientes, Argentina.
1854 _Elapomorphus_ _lemniscatus_ Duméril, Bibron and Duméril, Erp. Gén., 7: 840. Type-locality:
        "Amérique du Sud".
1860 _Elapomorphus_ _reticulatus_ Peters, Monats. Akad. Wiss. Berlin, 1860: 518, pl., fig. 2.
        Type-locality: "Brazil?"
1884 _Elapomorphus_ _Iheringi_ Strauch, Bull. Acad. Imp. Sci. Saint Petersbourg, 29: 571. Type-locality:
        Mundo Novo, Rio Grande do Sul, Brazil.
1885 _Phalotris_ _melanopleurus_ Cope, Proc. Amer. Phil. Soc., 22: 189. Type-locality: Rio Grande do
        Sul, Brazil.
1889 _Elapomorphus_ _trilineatus_ Boulenger, Ann. Mag. Nat. Hist., (6) 4: 265. Type-locality: Camaquam
        River District, Rio Grande do Sul, Brazil.
1913 _Elapomorphus_ _spegazzinii_ Boulenger, Ann. Mus. Civ. Stor. Nat. Genova, (3) 6: 49. Type-locality:
        La Plata, Argentina.
1924 _Elapomorphus_ _suspectus_ Amaral, Jour. Washington Acad. Sci., 14: 202. Type-locality: Pilar, near
        Córdoba, Argentina.

   Distribution: Southern Brazil, Uruguay, Paraguay and Argentina.

ELAPOMORPHUS BOLLEI Mertens

 1934 _Elapomorphus bollei_ Mertens, Senckenbergiana, 34: 183, fig. 1. Type-locality: Tandil, about 350
    km south of Buenos Aires and about 150 km from coast, Provincia de Buenos Aires, Argentina.

  Distribution: Known only from type locality.

ELAPOMORPHUS LEPIDUS Reinhardt

 1861 _Elapomorphus Lepidus_ Reinhardt, Vidensk. Medd. Naturhist. Foren. Kjöbenhavn, 2 (1860): 239,
    pl. 4, fig. 6-9. Type-locality: "Arrayal de Bicudo near Rio da casca, Minas, Brazil".
 1896 _Elapomorphus lepidus_—Boulenger, Cat. Sn. Brit. Mus., 3: 241.

  Distribution: Estados do Minas Gerais, Bahia, Espirito Santo, and Rio de Janeiro, Brazil.

ELAPOMORPHUS MERTENSI Hoge

 1955 _Elapomorphus mertensi_ Hoge, Senckenbergiana Biol., 36: 301, pl. 27 and pl. 29, fig. 3.
    Type-locality: Serra Azul, São Paulo, Brazil.

  Distribution: São Paulo, Mato Grosso, Minas Gerais, and Paraná, Brazil.

ELAPOMORPHUS NASUTUS Gomes

 1915 _Elapomorphus nasutus_ Gomes, Ann. Paulistas Med. Cirurg., 4: 121, pl. 3, fig. 1-3. Type-locality:
    Paineiras, near Uberaba, Estado de Minas Gerais, Brazil.
 1949 _Elapomorphus nasutus_—Hoge, Mem. Inst. Butantan, 21 (1948): 67, 4 figs.

  Distribution: "Triângulo Mineiro", Estado de São Paulo; also Minas Gerais and Santa Catarina,
    Brazil.

ELAPOMORPHUS QUINQUELINEATUS (Raddi)

 1820 _Coluber 5—Lineatus_ Raddi, Mem. Soc. Italiana Sci. Modena, 18, (Mem. 2, Fisica): 339, pl.
    Type-locality: Near Rio de Janeiro, Brazil.
 1837 _Calamaria Blumii_ Schlegel, Essai Phys. Serp.,2:45. Type-locality: Estado do São Paulo, Brazil.
 1858 _Elapocephalus taeniatus_ Günther, Cat. Sn. Brit. Mus.: 276. Type-locality: "America" ("North
    America", according to Gray, Cat. Sn. Brit. Mus., 1849, 78, referring to same specimen).
 1959 _Elapomorphus quinquelineatus_—Hoge, Mem. Inst. Butantan, 28 (1957-58): 270.

  Distribution: Eastern and Central Brazil.

ELAPOMORPHUS TRICOLOR Duméril, Bibron and Duméril

 1854 _Elapomorphus tricolor_ Duméril, Bibron and Duméril, Erp. Gén., 7: 837. Type-locality: Santa Cruz
    "Santa Cruz de la Sierra à Chuquisaca, en Bolivia", according to Vanzolini, Rev. Bras. Biol.,
    8, 1948, 383.
 1955 _Elapomorphus tricolor_—Hoge, Senckenbergiana Biol., 36: 301, pls. 28 and 29, fig. 4.

  Distribution: Southern and western Brazil, Bolivia, Uruguay, Argentina and Paraguay.

ELAPOMORPHUS WUCHERERI Günther

 1861 _Elapomorphus wuchereri_ Günther, Ann. Mag. Nat. Hist., (3) 7: 415, fig. Type-locality: Bahia,
    Brazil (according to Boulenger, Cat. Sn. Brit. Mus., 3, 1896, 240, who recognized the composite
    nature of Günther's type series, and fixed the name using two female syntypes from Bahia).
 1861 _Elapomorphus accedens_ Jan, Arch. Zool. Anat. Fis., 2: 46. Type-locality: Bahia, Brazil.
 1896 _Elapomorphus wuchereri_—Boulenger, Cat. Sn. Brit. Mus., 3: 240.

  Distribution: Known from Bahia and Espirito Santo, Brazil.

ENULIUS Cope

1871 <u>Enulius</u> Cope, Proc. Amer. Philos. Soc., 11: 558. Type-species: <u>Enulius</u> <u>murinus</u> Cope.
1872 <u>Leptocalamus</u> Günther, Ann. Mag. Nat. Hist., (4) 9: 16. Type-species: <u>Leptocalamus</u> <u>torquatus</u> Günther.

Distribution: Western and southern Mexico through Central America to Colombia.

Content: Three species, one of which (<u>oligostichus</u> Smith, Ardnt and Sherbrooke) is extralimital, according to latest summary of genus, by Smith, Ardnt and Sherbrooke, Nat. Hist. Misc. Chicago Acad. Sci., 186, 1967.

Key to the species	Clave de especies
1. Rostral pointed; 17 scale rows at midbody--<u>flavitorques</u> Rostral not pointed; 15 scale rows at midbody--<u>sclateri</u>	1. Rostral puntiaguda; 17 filas de escamas en el medio cuerpo---------------------<u>flavitorques</u> Rostral no puntiaguda; 15 filas de escamas en el medio cuerpo----------------------<u>sclateri</u>

ENULIUS FLAVITORQUES (Cope)

1869 <u>Liophis</u> <u>flavitorques</u> Cope, Proc. Acad. Nat. Sci. Phila., 1868: 307. Type-locality: Río Magdalena, Colombia.
1938 <u>Enulius</u> <u>flavitorques</u>—Dunn, Proc. Acad. Nat. Sci. Phila., 89: 415.

Distribution: Southern Mexico through Central America to Colombia.

Content: Three subspecies, two of which (<u>sumichrasti</u> Bocourt and <u>unicolor</u> Fischer) are extralimital.

Enulius flavitorques flavitorques (Cope)

1871 <u>Enulius</u> <u>murinus</u> Cope, Proc. Amer. Philos. Soc., 11: 558. Type-locality: Chinandega, Nicaragua (this new genus and species were also described by Cope in second and third Ann. Rept. Peabody Acad. Sci., 1869-1870 [1871], 80. It is uncertain which paper was published first, according to Osborne, Biog. Mem. Nat. Acad. Sci., 13, 1930, 193-195).
1872 <u>Leptocalamus</u> <u>torquatus</u> Günther, Ann. Mag. Nat. Hist., (4) 9: 17. Type-locality: South America.
1967 [<u>Enulius</u>] f[<u>lavitorques</u>] <u>flavitorques</u>—Smith, Ardnt and Sherbrooke, Nat. Hist. Misc. Chicago Acad. Sci., 186: 4.

Distribution: Guatemala to Colombia.

ENULIUS SCLATERI (Boulenger)

1894 <u>Leptocalamus</u> <u>sclateri</u> Boulenger, Cat. Sn. Brit. Mus., 2: 251, pl. 12, fig. 1. Type-locality: South America.
1938 <u>Enulius</u> <u>slateri</u> (sic)—Dunn, Proc. Acad. Nat. Sci. Phila., 89: 417.

Distribution: Nicaragua, Panama, Colombia.

EPICRATES Wagler

1830 <u>Epicrates</u> Wagler, Nat. Syst. Amphib.: 168.   Type-species: <u>Boa</u> <u>Cenchria</u> Linnaeus.
1844 <u>Chilabothrus</u> Duméril and Bibron, Erp. Gén., 6: 562.   Type-species: <u>Boa</u> <u>inornatus</u>
     Reinhardt.
1849 <u>Cliftia</u> Gray, Cat. Sn. Brit. Mus.: 99.   Type-species: <u>Cliftia</u> <u>fusca</u> Gray.
1856 <u>Epicarsius</u> Fischer, Abh. Nat. Ver. Hamburg., 3: 94.   Type-species: <u>Epicarsius</u> <u>cupreus</u> Fischer.
1856 <u>Homalochilus</u> Fischer, Abh. Nat. Ver. Hamburg., 3: 100.   Type-species: <u>Homalochilus</u> <u>striatus</u>
     Fischer.
1881 <u>Piesigaster</u> Seoane, Abh. Senck. Ges., 12: 217.   Type-species: <u>Piesigaster</u> <u>Boettgeri</u> Seoane.

   Distribution: From Costa Rica to Argentina; Antilles.

   Content: Seven species, six of which (<u>angulifer</u> Bibron, <u>exsul</u> Netting and Goin, <u>gracilis</u> Fischer,
     <u>inornatus</u> Reinhardt, <u>striatus</u> Fischer, and <u>subflavus</u> Stejneger) are extralimital.

EPICRATES CENCHRIA (Linnaeus)

1758 <u>Boa</u> <u>Cenchria</u> Linnaeus, Systema Naturae, Ed. 10: 215.   Type-locality: Surinam.
1766 <u>Boa</u> <u>Cenchris</u> Gmelin, Systema Naturae, Ed. 13: 1083.   Type-locality: Surinam.
1788 <u>Coluber</u> <u>tamachia</u> Scopoli, Delicia Florae et Faunae Insubricae etc., 3: 38, pl. 19, fig. 1.
     Type-locality: none given.
1803 <u>Boa</u> <u>ternatea</u> Daudin, Hist. Nat. Rept., 5: 153.   Type-locality: none given.
1803 <u>Boa</u> <u>Aboma</u> Daudin, Hist. Nat. Rept., 5: 132, pl. 62, fig. 2.   Type-locality: Surinam and Guiana.
1803 <u>Boa</u> <u>annulifer</u> Daudin, Hist. Nat. Rept., 5: 202, pl. 63, fig. 3.   Type-locality: South America.
1816 <u>Draco</u> <u>ocellatus</u> Oken, Lehrb. Naturg., 3: 227.   We have been unable to verify this citation from
     Boulenger, Cat. Sn. Brit. Mus., 1, 1893, 94.
1830 [<u>Epicrates</u>] <u>Cenchria</u>—Wagler, Nat. Syst. Amphib.: 168.
1849 <u>Cliftia</u> <u>fusca</u> Gray, Cat. Sn. Brit. Mus.: 99.   Type-locality: India.
1854 <u>Boa</u> <u>liberiensis</u> Hallowell, Proc. Acad. Nat. Sci. Phila., 1854: 100.   Type-locality: Liberia;
     in error, corrected to South America by Hallowell, Proc. Acad. Nat. Sci. Phila., 1857, 66.
1856 <u>Epicarsius</u> <u>cupreus</u> Fischer, Abh. Nat. Ver. Hamburg, 3: 96, pl. 2, figs. 1a-1b.   Type-locality:
     Puerto Cabello, Venezuela.

   Distribution: Costa Rica to Argentina; Trinidad and Tobago.

   Comment: Recent authors who have described subspecies of this species have not indicated where
     they thought the synonyms listed above should be assigned.   Some of them could easily be prior
     names for currently recognized taxa.   We cannot attempt to make any allocations at this time,
     but some future worker will need to do so.

   Content: Nine subspecies.

Key to the subspecies

1. Dorsal pattern always including some con-
    spicuous dorsal spots--------------------2
    Dorsum uniformly colored------------<u>maurus</u>

2. Lateral ocelli, located in interspaces be-
    tween median distal spots, without outer
    ring of light color---------------------3
    Same ocelli bordered by light ring-------5

3. Lateral ocelli uniform, without lighter
    center-----------------------------------4
    Lateral ocelli with central area lighter
    than rest of spot------------------<u>gaigei</u>

4. Ventrals with dark spotting on lateral mar-
    gins-----------------------------<u>cenchria</u>
    Ventrals not spotted laterally--<u>hygrophilus</u>

Clave de subespecies

1. Coloración dorsal no uniforme, manchas
    bien conspicuas--------------------------2
    Coloración dorsal uniforme, manchas obso-
    letas o del mismo color del cuerpo--<u>maurus</u>

2. Ocelos laterales múltiples, ubicados en los
    intervalos de las manchas medio dorsales,
    no circundados de color claro-----------3
    Ocelos laterales múltiples, ubicados en los
    intervalos de las manchas medio dorsales,
    circundados de color claro---------------5

3. Ocelos laterales oscuros sin el centro
    blanco-----------------------------------4
    Ocelos laterales oscuros con el centro
    blanco----------------------------<u>gaigei</u>

4. Cara ventral manchada de oscuro en su mar-
    gen lateral----------------------<u>cenchria</u>
    Cara ventral no manchada de oscuro ni aun
    lateralmente------------------<u>hygrophilus</u>

5. Median dorsal spots bordered by black area which does not contact border of neighboring blotch----------------------------6
   Median dorsal spots fused laterally by broad dark band--------------------------8

6. Median dorsal spots not saddle-shaped-----7
   Median dorsal spots saddle-shaped--barbouri

7. Median dorsal stripe on head broken by a circumnuchal stripe; more than 245 ventrals----------------------------assisi
   Median dorsal stripe on head fused with circumnuchal stripe; fewer than 240 ventrals-----------------------polylepis

8. More than 47 scale rows at midbody; 47-55 caudals--------------------------alvarezi
   Fewer than 47 scale rows at midbody; 34-45 caudals---------------------------crassus

5. Manchas medio dorsales aisladas por bordes negros que no contactan entre sí---------6
   Manchas medio dorsales fusionadas lateralmente por ancha banda oscura------------8

6. Sin manchas medio dorsales en forma de silla de montar-------------------------7
   Manchas medio dorsales en forma de silla de montar---------------------------barbouri

7. Estría medio cefálica separada de la estría circunnucal; más de 245 ventrales---assisi
   Estría medio cefálica fusionada con la circunnucal, menos de 240 ventrales-polylepis

8. Más de 47 hileras medio dorsales; 47-55 caudales---------------------------alvarezi
   Menos de 47 hileras medio dorsales; 34-45 caudales----------------------------crassus

Epicrates cenchria cenchria Linnaeus

  1929 Epicrates cenchria cenchria—Amaral, Mem. Inst. Butantan, 4: 77.

    Distribution: Amazonian Basin; southern Venezuela and coastal Guianas.

Epicrates cenchria alvarezi Abalos, Baez and Nader

  1964 Epicrates cenchria alvarezi Abalos, Baez and Nader, Acta. Zool. Lilloana, 20: 218, fig. 3.
    Type-locality: Forres, Depto. Robles, Santiago del Estero, Argentina.

    Distribution: Provincia de Santiago del Estero, Argentina.

Epicrates cenchria assisi Machado

  1945 Epicrates cenchria assisi Machado, Bol. Inst. Vital Brazil, 27: 61, fig. Type-locality:
    Campina Grande, Poraiba do Norte, NE Brazil.
  1954 Epicrates cenchria xerophilus Amaral, Mem. Inst. Butantan, 26: 237. Type-locality: Rio
    Branco, Pernambuco, Brazil.

    Distribution: Piaui to northern Bahia in Caatinga region of Brazil.

Epicrates cenchria barbouri Stull

  1938 Epicrates cenchria barbouri Stull, Occ. Pap. Boston Soc. Nat. Hist., 8: 300. Type-
    locality: Marajó Island, Para, Brazil.

    Distribution: Known only from type locality.

Epicrates cenchria crassus (Cope)

  1862 Epicrates crassus Cope, Proc. Acad. Nat. Sci. Phila., 1862: 349. Type-locality: Cadosa,
    Parana River, Paraguay.
  1929 Epicrates cenchria crassus—Amaral, Mem. Inst. Butantan, 4: 140.

    Distribution: Southern Brazil, Paraguay and northern Argentina.

Epicrates cenchria gaigei Stull

  1938 Epicrates cenchria gaigei Stull, Occ. Pap. Boston Soc. Nat. Hist., 8: 298. Type-locality:
    Buenavista, Santa Cruz, Bolivia.

    Distribution: Eastern lowlands of Bolivia and Peru.

Epicrates cenchria hygrophilus Amaral

1954 Epicrates cenchria hygrophilus Amaral, Mem. Inst. Butantan, 26: 239. Type-locality:
Baixo Guandú, Rio Doce, Espíritu Santo, Brazil.

Distribution: Estado do Amazonas and region of Rio Doce, Estado do Espíritu Santo, Brazil.
Restricted on west by Serra do Espinhaço, according to Amaral, loc. cit.

Epicrates cenchria maurus Gray

1849 Epicrates maurus Gray, Cat. Sn. Brit. Mus.: 96. Type-locality: Venezuela.
1863 Epicrates cupreus var. concolor Jan, Elenco Sist. Ofid.: 24. Type-locality: Costa Rica.
1935 Epicrates cenchria maurus—Stull, Proc. Boston Soc. Nat. Hist., 40: 396.

Distribution: From Costa Rica to northern Colombia and Venezuela, probably northern
Guianas; Trinidad, Tobago and Margarita Islands.

Epicrates cenchria polylepis Amaral

1935 Epicrates cenchria polylepis Amaral, Mem. Inst. Butantan, 9: 236. Type-locality: None
given by Amaral, specimens included came from Rio Pandeiro, Minas Gerais, and "Canna
Brava" (later called Rio Canabrava), in Goiás, Brazil. In 1954 (below) Amaral selected
a neotype from among the syntypes (calling it a "holotype"), thus restricting the type-
locality to Rio Pandeiro.
1954 Epicrates cenchria polylepis—Amaral, Mem. Inst. Butantan, 26: 241.

Distribution: Region of rios Canabrava and Pandeiro in western Bahia and eastern Goiás; also
Distrito Federal, Brazil.

ERYTHROLAMPRUS Wagler

1830 Erythrolamprus Wagler, Nat. Syst. Amph.: 187. Type-species: Coluber agilis Linnaeus.
1843 Erythrophis Fitzinger, Systema Reptilium: 25. Type-species: Erythrolamprus venustissimus Wagler.

Distribution: Nicaragua to southern Brazil and Peru east of Andes, and to northwestern Ecuador on Pacific slope.

Content: Six species.

Key to the species	Clave de especies
1. Body with complete black rings----------------2 Body reddish, without rings; 25-26 black dorsal spots with light centers-----------aesculapii	1. Cuerpo con anillos negros completos-----------2 Cuerpo rojizo sin anillos; 25-26 manchas negras dorsales con el centro claro--------aesculapii
2. Each dorsal ring equidistant from others------3 Dorsal rings arranged in pairs---------------6	2. Anillos dorsales aislados---------------------3 Anillos dorsales en parejas-------------------6
3. Lacking black rings bordered by white rings of equal width------------------------------------4 Black rings with white borders of equal width--------------------------------------guentheri	3. Sin anillos negros bordeados de blancos de igual ancho---------------------------------4 Con anillos negros con borde blanco de igual ancho al de ellos--------------------guentheri
4. Red areas less than three times as wide as black rings; lacking light band between eyes--5 Red areas at least three times as wide as black rings; with light band between eyes-aesculapii	4. Espacios rojos de menor extensión que tres anillos negros; sin banda clara sobre los ojos---5 Espacios rojos por lo menos tres veces al ancho de los anillos negros; con banda clara sobre los ojos---------------------------aesculapii
5. Posterior maxillary teeth strongly grooved; more than 50 subcaudals---------pseudocorallus Posterior maxillary teeth not grooved, may be weakly striated; subcaudals fewer than 52---------------------------------------mimus	5. Dientes posteriores fuertemente acanalados; subcaudales más de 50-----------pseudocorallus Dientes posteriores no acanalados o con suaves estrías; subcaudales menos de 52---------mimus
6. Black rings in pairs; distance between pairs equal to width of pair-----------------------7 Black rings in pairs; distance between pairs reduced by extension of red interspaces--aesculapii	6. Anillos negros dispuestos en parejas que equidistan entre sí-----------------------------7 Anillos negros dispuestos en parejas; cada dos parejas, interespacio entre sí menor, por extensión de interespacio rojo------aesculapii
7. Black rings not divided dorsally--------------8 Black rings divided dorsally, giving appearance of tetrad formation-------------bauperthuisii	7. Sin anillos negros con fisura dorsal que se asemejan a tétradas-------------------------8 Con anillos negros con fisura dorsal que se asemejan a tétradas-------------bauperthuisii
8. Fewer than 45 caudals---------------aesculapii More than 45 caudals--------------------bizona	8. Menos de 45 caudales-----------------aesculapii Más de 45 caudales----------------------bizona

ERYTHROLAMPRUS AESCULAPII (Linnaeus)

1766 Coluber Aesculapii Linnaeus, Systema Naturae, Ed. 12: 380. Type-locality: "Indiis".
1766 Coluber agilis Linnaeus, Systema Naturae, Ed. 12: 381. Type-locality: "Indiis".
1789 C[oluber] nigrofasciatus Lacépède, Histoire Naturelle des Serpens, 2: 98. Type-locality: None given.
1803 Coluber atro-cinctus Daudin, Hist. Nat. Rept., 6: 389. Type-locality: None given.
1823 C[oluber] binatus Lichtenstein, Verzeichniss der Doubletten des Zoologischen Museums der Königl. Universität zu Berlin: 105. Type-locality: Brazil.
1854 Erythrolamprus Aesculapii—Duméril, Bibron and Duméril, Erp. Gén., 7: 845.
1854 Erytolamprus (sic) Milberti Duméril, Bibron and Duméril, Erp. Gén., 7: 854. Type-locality: "New Yorck".
1854 Erythrolamprus intricatus Duméril, Bibron and Duméril, Erp. Gén., 7: 855. Type-locality: Unknown.
1860 Erythrolamprus albostulatus Cope, Proc. Acad. Nat. Sci. Phila., 1860: 259. Type-locality: "Jijuca" = Tijuca, Rio de Janeiro, Brazil.

ERYTHROLAMPRUS AESCULAPII (Linnaeus), continued

1863 Erythrolamprus Aesculapii dicranta Jan, Arch. Zool. Anat. Fis., 2: 314. Type-locality: "Brasile, Bahia, Popayan".
1863 Erythrolamprus Aesculapii confluentus Jan, Arch. Zool. Anat. Fis., 2: 315. Type-locality: "America".

Distribution: Amazonian South America to central Brazil and Bolivia; Tobago Island.

Content: Five subspecies.

Comment: None of the recent authors who have recognized subspecies within this species has discussed the proper subspecific allocation of the taxa listed above under the species name. We are not able to assign them at this time.

Key to the subspecies	Clave de subespecies
1. Body with complete black rings------------2 Body without rings; 25-26 black dorsal spots, each with light center----ocellatus	1. Cuerpo con anillos negros completos-------2 Cuerpo sin anillos; 25-26 manchas negras dorsales con el centro claro-----ocellatus
2. Red interspaces less than three times as wide as black rings; no light band between eyes-------------------------------------3 Red interspaces at least three times as wide as black rings; light band between eyes-----------------------------monozona	2. Interespacios rojos, entre anillos negros, menos de tres veces más anchos que aquéllos; sin banda clara sobre los ojos-3 Interespacios rojos, por lo menos tres veces más anchos que anillos negros; con banda clara sobre los ojos-------monozona
3. Black rings in equidistant pairs----------4 Black rings not in equidistant pairs, but forming groups of four, with wider red interspaces between such groups----------- -------------------------------tetrazona	3. Anillos negros dispuestos en parejas que equidistan entre sí----------------------4 Parejas de anillos negros no equidistantes; cada dos de ellas con mayor extensión del interespacio rojo entre sí------tetrazona
4. Head light with dark band across eyes; red interspaces equal in width to black bands- -------------------------------aesculapii Head black with light band between eyes; red space twice as wide as black rings---- ----------------------------venustissimus	4. Cabeza clara con banda oscura através de los ojos; espacios rojos iguales a anillos negros------------------------aesculapii Cabeza negra con banda clara através de los ojos; espacios rojos dos veces mayores que anillos negros--------------venustissimus

Erythrolamprus aesculapii aesculapii (Linnaeus)

1863 Erythrolamprus Aesculapii [Aesculapii]—Jan, Arch. Zool. Anat. Fis., 2: 314.

Distribution: Amazonian South America.

Erythrolamprus aesculapii monozona Jan

1863 [Erythrolamprus Aesculapii] monozona Jan, Arch. Zool. Anat. Fis., 2: 312. Type-locality: "Bahia", (Brazil).
1945 Erythrolamprus aesculapii monozona—Machado, Bol. Inst. Vital Brazil, 5: 77, one pl., one fig.

Distribution: Bahia to Rio de Janeiro, Brazil.

Erythrolamprus aesculapii ocellatus Peters

1868 Erythrolamprus ocellatus Peters, Monats. Akad. Wiss. Berlin, 1868: 642. Type-locality: None given.
1966 Erythrolamprus aesculapii [ocellatus]—Emsley, Copeia, 1966: 129.

Distribution: Trinidad and Tobago Island.

Erythrolamprus aesculapii tetrazona Jan

1863 [Erythrolamprus Aesculapii] tetrazona Jan, Arch. Zool. Anat. Fis., 2: 315. Type-locality:
Bolivia.
1956 Erythrolamprus aesculapii tetrazona—Mertens, Zool. Jahrb., Abt. Syst. Oekol. Geog.
Tiere, 84: 544, pl. 14, fig. 38.

Distribution: Southwestern Bolivia.

Erythrolamprus aesculapii venustissimus (Wied)

1821 Coluber venustissimus Wied, Reise nach Brasilien, 2: 75. Type-locality: None given.
1945 Erythrolamprus aesculapii venustissima—Machado, Bol. Inst. Vital Brazil, 5: 77.

Distribution: Minas Gerais and Rio de Janeiro, Brazil to eastern Bolivia; Misiones, Argentina.

ERYTHROLAMPRUS BAUPERTHUISII Duméril, Bibron and Duméril

1854 Erythrolamprus Bauperthuisii Duméril, Bibron and Duméril, Erp. Gén., 7: 850. Type-locality:
"Côte ferme"; restricted by Hoge and Lancini, Bol. Mus. Cien. Nat. Caracas, 6-7, 1960, 61, to
vicinity of Cumaná, Estado Sucre, Venezuela.
1959 Erythrolamprus baileyi Roze, Acta Biol. Venezuélica, 2: 526, fig. 1. Type-locality: Caripito,
Estado Monagas, Venezuela.

Distribution: Monagas, Sucre, Bolívar, and Territorio Federal Delta Amacuro, Venezuela.

ERYTHROLAMPRUS BIZONA Jan

1863 [Erythrolamprus Aesculapii] bizona Jan, Arch. Zool. Anat. Fis., 2: 314. Type-locality: "Bahia,
Messico, Popayan, Cayenne, Brasile, Montevideo, Colombia"; restricted to Colombia, by Dunn and
Bailey, Bull. Mus. Comp. Zool., 86, 1939, 12.
1939 Erythrolamprus bizona—Dunn and Bailey, Bull. Mus. Comp. Zool., 86: 12.

Distribution: Costa Rica to Colombia and northern Venezuela.

ERYTHROLAMPRUS GUENTHERI Garman

1883 Erythrolamprus guentheri Garman, Mem. Mus. Comp. Zool., 8 (3): 154. Type-locality: "Mexico?"
(based on Erythrolamprus venustissimus var. D., Gunther, Cat. Sn. Brit. Mus., 1848, 48).

Distribution: Amazonian slopes of Ecuador.

ERYTHROLAMPRUS MIMUS (Cope)

1868 Opheomorphus mimus Cope, Proc. Acad. Nat. Sci. Phila., 1868: 307. Type-locality: "High regions
of Ecuador or New Grenada".
1939 Erythrolamprus mimus—Dunn and Bailey, Bull. Mus. Comp. Zool., 86: 12.

Distribution: Honduras and Nicaragua to Peru and Ecuador.

Content: Three subspecies.

Key to the subspecies	Clave de subespecies
1. Black collar covering posterior tips of parietals and at least three scales on midline of neck------------------------2 Black collar either absent, represented by spots, or only about one scale wide on midline, diverging to about three scales on sides of neck--------------------mimus	1. Collar negro cubriendo porción posterior de parietales y por lo menos tres escamas medialmente en la nuca-------------------2 Collar negro ausente, representado por puntos o sólo de una escama de ancho medialmente, divergiendo aproximadamente tres escamas en los lados de la nuca------mimus

2. Body rings 12-15, with light centers later-
    ally; ventrals 171-183--------------impar
    Body rings 9-12 (rarely more); usually
    solid, but occasionally split ventrally on
    posterior part of body; ventrals 178-199--
    ------------------------------micrurus

2. Con 12-15 anillos sobre el cuerpo, con
    centros claros lateralmente; ventrales
    171-183------------------------------impar
    Con 9-12 (raramente más) anillos sobre el
    cuerpo, usualmente sólidos, aunque ocas-
    ionalmente pueden dividirse ventralmente
    en la parte posterior del cuerpo;
    ventrales 178-199----------------micrurus

Erythrolamprus mimus mimus (Cope)

1939 [Erythrolamprus mimus] mimus—Dunn and Bailey, Bull. Mus. Comp. Zool., 86: 14.

   Distribution: Eastern Peru and Ecuador.

Erythrolamprus mimus impar Schmidt

1936 Erythrolamprus aesculapii impar Schmidt, Proc. Biol. Soc. Washington, 49: 49. Type-
   locality: Yoro, Mataderos Mts., Honduras, 3300 ft.
1939 [Erythrolamprus mimus] impar—Dunn and Bailey, Bull. Mus. Comp. Zool., 86: 13.

   Distribution: Nicaragua and Honduras.

Erythrolamprus mimus micrurus Dunn and Bailey

1939 Erythrolamprus mimus micrurus Dunn and Bailey, Bull. Mus. Comp. Zool., 86: 12. Type-
   locality: Mine at Santa Cruz de Caña, Darién, Panama, 2000 ft.

   Distribution: Atlantic Panama to Pacific Colombia and Ecuador.

ERYTHROLAMPRUS PSEUDOCORALLUS Roze

1959 Erythrolamprus pseudocorallus Roze, Acta Biol. Venezuélica, 2: 530. Type-locality: In mountainous areas near Maracaibo, Estado Zulia, Venezuela.

   Distribution: Perijá region and Maracaibo, Zulia, Venezuela.

EUNECTES Wagler

   1830 Eunectes Wagler, Nat. Syst. Amphib.: 167. Type-species: Boa murina Linnaeus.

    Distribution: Venezuela and Colombia to Argentina.

    Content: Four species.

Key to the species	Clave de especies

1. Scale rows at midbody 40-50-------------------2
   Scale rows at midbody 55-80-------------------3
	1. Filas dorsales al medio del cuerpo, entre
	   40-50--2
	   Filas dorsales al medio del cuerpo, entre
	   55-80--3

2. Dorsal pattern with single series of large uni-
   formly black vertebral spots and with smaller
   lateral black spots-------------deschauenseei
   Dorsal pattern with two series of black verte-
   bral blotches with lighter centers; vertical
   black bands laterally------------------notaeus
	2. Diseño dorsal con una hilera de grandes manchas
	   negras vertebrales y con manchas laterales
	   negras, pequeñas-----------------deschauenseei
	   Diseño dorsal en dos hileras de manchas negras
	   con el centro no melánico; lateralmente fajas
	   verticales negras---------------------notaeus

3. Dorsal spots with lighter centers------barbouri
   Dorsal spots uniformly black-----------murinus
	3. Manchas dorsales con centros claros----barbouri
	   Manchas dorsales uniformemente oscuras--murinus

EUNECTES BARBOURI Dunn and Conant

   1936 Eunectes barbouri Dunn and Conant, Proc. Acad. Nat. Sci. Phila., 88: 504, pl. 14, fig. 1. Type-
     locality: Marajó Island, mouth of Amazon River, Brazil.

    Distribution: Marajó Island, Brazil.

EUNECTES DESCHAUENSEEI Dunn and Conant

   1936 Eunectes deschauenseei Dunn and Conant, Proc. Acad. Nat. Sci. Phila., 88: 505, pl. 14, fig. 2.
     Type-locality: Marajó Island, mouth of Amazon River, Brazil.

    Distribution: Marajó Island, Brazil.

EUNECTES MURINUS (Linnaeus)

   1758 Boa murina Linnaeus, Systema Naturae, Ed. 10: 215. Type-locality: "America".
   1831 Eunectes murina—Gray, Synopsis Species Class Reptilia, in Griffith, Cuvier's Animal Kingdom,
     9: 96.

    Distribution: Venezuela and Colombia to Bolivia.

    Content: Two subspecies.

Key to the subspecies	Clave de subspecies

1. Postocular area enclosed in two dark
   stripes same color as ground color of
   body-----------------------------murinus
   Postocular area enclosed in two dark
   stripes markedly lighter than ground color
   of body----------------------------gigas
	1. Area posocular entre dos líneas oscuras
	   del mismo color que el cuerpo------murinus
	   Area posocular entre dos líneas oscuras
	   marcadamente más clara que el cuerpo------
	   ------------------------------------gigas

Eunectes murinus murinus (Linnaeus)

    1758 Eunectes scytale Linnaeus, Systema Naturae, Ed. 10: 214. Type-locality: Americas.
    1824 Boa aquatica Wied, Isis von Oken, 6: 664. Type-locality: Brazil.
    1936 [Eunectes murinus] murinus—Dunn and Conant, Proc. Acad. Nat. Sci. Phila., 88: 503.

     Distribution: Amazonian drainage.

Eunectes murinus gigas (Latreille)

    1802 _Boa gigas_ Latreille, in Sonnini and Latreille, Hist. Nat. Rept., 3: 136. Type-locality: Guiana.

    1803 _Boa anacondo_ Daudin (substitute name for _Boa gigas_ Latreille), Hist. Nat. Rept., 5: 161, pl. 63, fig. 2.

    1936 [_Eunectes murinus_] _gigas_—Dunn and Conant, Proc. Acad. Nat. Sci. Phila., 88: 503.

      Distribution: Colombia, Venezuela, Guianas and Trinidad.

EUNECTES NOTAEUS Cope

    1862 _Eunectes notaeus_ Cope, Proc. Acad. Nat. Sci. Phila., 1862: 70. Type-locality: Paraguay River and its tributaries.

    1903 _Epicrates wieningeri_ Steindachner, Sitz. Math-Naturwiss. Kl. Akad. Wiss. Wien, 112, Abt. 1: 15. Type-locality: Altos, Paraguay.

      Distribution: Bolivia, Paraguay, Uruguay, western Brazil, and northeastern Argentina.

FICIMIA Gray

  1849 Ficimia Gray, Cat. Sn. Brit. Mus., 1849: 80. Type-species: Ficimia olivacea Gray.
  1858 Amblymetopon Günther, Cat. Sn. Brit. Mus., 1858: 7. Type-species: Amblymetopon variegatum
      Günther.

  Distribution: Mexico to Guatemala and Honduras.

  Content: Five species, four of which are extralimital.

FICIMIA PUBLIA Cope

  1866 Ficimia publia Cope, Proc. Acad. Nat. Sci. Phila. 18: 126. Type-locality: Yucatán; restricted
      to Chichen Itzá, Yucatán, Mexico, by Smith and Taylor, Univ. Kansas Sci. Bull., 33, 1950, 352.

  Distribution: From the Isthmus of Tehuantepec to Honduras on the Atlantic and to southern Guatemala
    on the Pacific.

  Content: Two subspecies, one (taylori Smith) extralimital.

  Ficimia publia publia Cope

    1883 Ficimia ornata Bocourt, Miss. Sci. Mex., 1883: 571. Type-locality: Mexico; restricted
        to Chichen Itzá, Yucatán, Mexico by Smith and Taylor, Univ. Kansas Sci. Bull., 33, 1950,
        352.
    1947 [Ficimia publia publia]—Smith, Jour. Wash. Acad. Sci., 37: 411.

    Distribution: Southern Veracruz to Honduras on Atlantic, from Guerrero to Guatemala on
      Pacific slope.

GEOPHIS Wagler

1830 Catostoma Wagler, Nat. Syst. Amphib.: 194. Type-species: Catostoma chalybeum Wagler.
1830 Geophis Wagler, Nat. Syst. Amphib.: 342. Substitute name for Catostoma Wagler, 1830, to prevent
     confusion with Catostomus Lesueur, 1817, a fish; Type-species: Catostoma chalybeum Wagler.
1853 Rabdosoma Duméril, Mem. Acad. Sci., 23: 440. Type-species: Rabdosoma semidoliatum Duméril,
     Bibron, and Duméril.
1859 Colobognathus Peters, Monats. Akad. Wiss. Berlin, 1859: 275. Type-species: Colobognathus
     Hoffmanni Peters.
1861 Geophidium Peters, Monats. Akad. Wiss. Berlin, 1861: 923. Type-species: Geophidium dubium
     Peters.
1868 Colophrys Cope, Proc. Acad. Nat. Sci. Phila., 1868: 130. Type-species: Colophrys rhodogaster
     Cope.
1883 Parageophis Bocourt, Miss. Sci. Mex., Rept.: 534. Type-species: Rabdosoma semidoliatum Duméril,
     Bibron, and Duméril.
1894 Dirosema Boulenger, Cat. Sn. Brit. Mus., 2: 298. Type-species: Geophis bicolor Günther.

     Distribution: Tamaulipas and Chihuahua, Mexico to northwestern Colombia.

     Content: 34 species arranged in seven species-groups, according to the most recent revision by
     Downs, Misc. Publ. Mus. Zool. Univ. Mich., 131, 1967. 22 species are extralimital, all in
     Mexico.

Key to the species	Clave de especies
1. Dorsal scales in 17 rows----------------------2 Dorsal scales in 15 rows----------------------6	1. Escamas dorsales en 17 filas------------------2 Escamas dorsales en 15 filas------------------6
2. Dorsal scales distinctly keeled on at least posterior half of body----------------------3 Dorsal scales smooth, or keeled only above the vent region--------------------------------4	2. Escamas dorsales distintamente quilladas a lo menos en la mitad posterior del cuerpo-------3 Escamas dorsales lisas, o quilladas sólo sobre la región anal------------------------------4
3. Dorsum unicolor brownish to blackish----nasalis Dorsum light with dark blotches or saddles----- ---dunni	3. Dorso unicolor pardo o negruzco---------nasalis Dorso claro con manchas oscuras, con o sin forma de silla de montar----------------dunni
4. Supraocular present, frontal not in orbit-----5 Supraocular absent, frontal in orbit (Fig. 1)-- ----------------------------------rhodogaster	4. Supraoculares presentes; frontal no conforma la órbita---------------------------------5 Supraoculares ausentes; frontal conforma la órbita (Fig. 1)--------------------rhodogaster

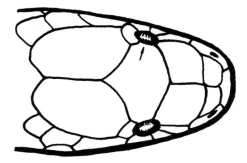

Fig. 1. G. rhodogaster (all figures in Geophis after Downs, 1967)

5. Dorsum unicolor--------------------immaculatus Dorsum with light lateral blotches on dark ground color--------------------fulvoguttatus	5. Dorso unicolor----------------------immaculatus Dorso con manchas claras lateralmente, sobre fondo oscuro--------------------fulvoguttatus
6. Supraocular present; parietal not in orbit (Fig. 2); color of rostral and prenasals similar to adjacent scales------------------7 Supraocular absent; parietal enters orbit (Fig. 3); rostral and prenasals whitish, contrasting with adjacent head scales--------- --godmani	6. Supraocular presente; parietal no conforma la órbita (Fig. 2); rostral y prenasales de color similar al de las escamas adyacentes---------7 Supraocular ausente; parietal conforma la órbita (Fig. 3); rostral y prenasales blanque- cinas, contrastando con las escamas adyacentes----------------------------godmani

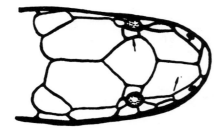

Fig. 2. _G. cancellatus_

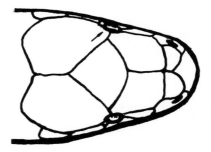

Fig. 3. _G. godmani_

7. Six supralabials; venter light or not---------8
   Five supralabials; venter mostly light---------
   --hoffmanni

8. Internasals not fused with prefrontals;
   coloration not as in following---------------9
   Internasals fused with prefrontals (Fig. 2);
   dark dorsal saddles separated by narrow light
   interspaces; ventrals light and immaculate----
   -----------------------------------cancellatus

9. Dorsal scales smooth, or faintly keeled above
   the vent region-----------------------------10
   Dorsal scales keeled on at least the posterior
   half of the body----------------------------11

10. Sum of ventrals and caudals more than 170;
    snout bluntly rounded------------------zeledoni
    Sum of ventrals and caudals less than 170;
    snout acuminose--------------------championi

11. Loreal longer than combined nasals; greatest
    internasal length less than half as long as
    prefrontal suture; frontal one-third longer
    than parietal suture (Fig. 4)---brachycephalus
    Loreal shorter than combined nasals; greatest
    internasal length as long as prefrontal su-
    ture; frontal twice as long as parietal su-
    ture (Fig. 5)------------------------ruthveni

7. Seis supralabiales; vientre claro o no--------8
   Cinco supralabiales; vientre en su mayor parte
   claro-----------------------------------hoffmanni

8. Internasales no fusionadas con prefrontales;
   coloración no como el siguiente--------------9
   Internasales fusionadas con prefrontales (Fig.
   2); dorso con manchas oscuras en forma de
   silla de montar, separadas por interspacios
   angostos claros; ventrales clares,
   inmaculadas-----------------------cancellatus

9. Escamas dorsales lisas, o débilmente quilladas
   sobre la región anal------------------------10
   Escamas dorsales quilladas, por lo menos en la
   mitad posterior del cuerpo------------------11

10. Suma de ventrales y caudales más de 170; ho-
    cico redondeado-----------------------zeledoni
    Suma de ventrales y caudales menos de 170; ho-
    cico acuminado--------------------championi

11. Loreal más larga que la suma de nasales; la
    mayor longitud internasal equivale a menos de
    la mitad del largo de la sutura prefrontal;
    frontal igual a un tercio del largo de la
    sutura parietal (Fig. 4)--------brachycephalus
    Loreal más corta que la suma de nasales; la
    mayor longitud internasal es igual a la sutura
    prefrontal; frontal dos veces el largo de la
    sutura parietal (Fig. 5)--------------ruthveni

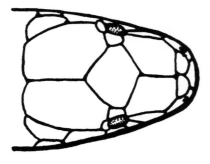

Fig. 4. _G. brachycephalus_

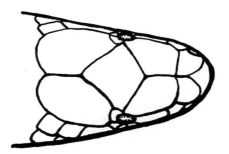

Fig. 5. _G. ruthveni_

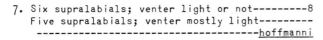

GEOPHIS BRACHYCEPHALUS (Cope)
    sieboldi group

  1871 Colobognathus brachycephalus Cope, Proc. Acad. Nat. Sci. Phila., 1871: 211. Type-locality: Near
      San José, Costa Rica.
  1871 Colobognathus dolichocephalus Cope, Proc. Acad. Nat. Sci. Phila., 1871: 211. Type-locality: San
      José, Costa Rica.
  1872 Geophis moestus Günther, Ann. Mag. Nat. Hist., (4) 9: 15. Type-locality: Near Cartago, Costa
      Rica.
  1908 Geophis nigroalbus Boulenger, Ann. Mag. Nat. Hist., (8) 2: 522. Type-locality: Pavas, Colombia.[1]
  1942 Geophis brachycephalus—Dunn (in part), Notulae Nat., 108: 4.
  1954 Geophis bakeri Taylor, Univ. Kansas Sci. Bull., 36: 689. Type-locality: Isla Bonita, Cinchona,
      Costa Rica.
  1967 Geophis brachycephalus—Downs, Misc. Publ. Mus. Zool. Univ. Mich., 131: 146, fig. 19.

    Distribution: Cordillera Central, Costa Rica south to Colombia; 250-2000 m.

GEOPHIS CANCELLATUS Smith
    semidoliatus group

  1941 Geophis cancellatus Smith, Smithsonian Misc. Coll., 99 (19): 1. Type-locality: Chicharras,
      Chiapas, Mexico, 1035 m.
  1967 Geophis cancellatus—Downs, Misc. Publ. Mus. Zool. Univ. Mich., 131: 129, fig. 16.

    Distribution: Known only from the type locality; probably west to the Isthmus of Tehuantepec and
      east into Guatemala. Landy et al, Jour. Ohio Herp. Soc., 5, 1966, 95, add a specimen from a
      questioned locality, near Unión Juárez, Chiapas, Mexico.

GEOPHIS CHAMPIONI Boulenger
    championi group

  1894 Geophis championi Boulenger, Cat. Sn. Brit. Mus. 2: 321, pl.16, fig. 3. Type-locality: Chiriqui,
      Panama.
  1967 Geophis championi—Downs, Misc. Publ. Mus. Zool. Univ. Mich., 131: 70, fig. 15.

    Distribution: Known only from the type locality and Boquete, eastern slopes of Volcán Chiriqui,
      Chiriqui Prov., Panama.

GEOPHIS DUNNI Schmidt
    sieboldi group

  1932 Geophis dunni Schmidt, Copeia, 1932: 8. Type-locality: Matagalpa, Nicaragua, 705 m.
  1967 Geophis dunni—Downs, Misc. Publ. Mus. Zool. Univ. Mich., 131: 153, fig. 19.

    Distribution: Known only from type locality.

GEOPHIS FULVOGUTTATUS Mertens
    dubius group

  1952 Geophis fulvoguttatus Mertens, Zool. Anz., 149: 134. Type-locality: Hacienda Monte Cristo,
      Sierra de Metapan, Dept. Santa Ana, El Salvador.
  1967 Geophis fulvoguttatus—Downs, Misc. Publ. Mus. Zool. Univ. Mich., 131: 88, fig. 7.

    Distribution: Known only from the type locality; in a cloud forest at 2200 m.

GEOPHIS GODMANI Boulenger
    championi group

  1894 Geophis godmani Boulenger, Cat. Sn. Brit. Mus., 2: 322, pl.16, fig.4. Type-locality: Irazú,
      Costa Rica.
  1967 Geophis godmani—Downs, Misc. Publ. Mus. Zool. Univ. Mich., 131: 72, fig. 5.

    Distribution: Caribbean and Pacific slopes of central Costa Rica south to Canal Zone of Panama,
      between 1300-2100 m.

---

[1]Downs, Misc. Publ. Mus. Zool. Univ. Mich., 131, 1967, 146, indicated that a specimen from eastern
  Panama may demonstrate that nigroalbus is a valid taxon.

GEOPHIS

GEOPHIS HOFFMANNI (Peters)
    sieboldi group

  1859 *Colobognathus Hoffmanni* Peters, Monats. Akad. Wiss. Berlin, 1859: 276, 4 figs. Type-locality:
      Costa Rica and Puerto Caballo, Costa Rica; fixed as Costa Rica by lectotype designation in
      Downs, Misc. Publ. Mus. Zool. Univ. Mich., 131, 1967, 155.
  1883 *Geophis hoffmanni*—Bocourt, Miss. Sci. Mex., Reptiles: 529.
  1954 *Geophis bartholomewi* Brattstrom and Howell, Herpetologica, 10: 120. Type-locality: Arenal,
      25 mi east of Jalapa, Nueva Segovia, Nicaragua, 1200 ft.
  1954 *Geophis acutirostris* Taylor, Univ. Kansas Sci. Bull., 36: 391, fig. 3. Type-locality: Cot,
      Volcán Irazú, Provincia Cartago, Costa Rica, about 5500 ft.
  1967 *Geophis hoffmanni*—Downs, Misc. Publ. Mus. Zool. Univ. Mich., 131: 155, fig. 19.
  Distribution: Low and moderate elevations in Honduras and Nicaragua on both slopes to Panama.

GEOPHIS IMMACULATUS Downs
    dubius group

  1967 *Geophis immaculatus* Downs, Misc. Publ. Mus. Zool. Univ. Mich., 131: 90, fig.7. Type-locality:
      Finca Lorena, Quetzaltenango, Guatemala, about 1700 m.

    Distribution: Known only from the type locality; Pacific slope of Guatemala.

GEOPHIS NASALIS (Cope)
    sieboldi group

  1868 *Catostoma nasale* Cope, Proc. Acad. Nat. Sci. Phila., 1868: 160. Type-locality: near the city
      of Guatemala, Guatemala.
  1941 *Geophis nasalis*—Smith, Smithsonian Misc. Coll., 99 (19): 4.
  1967 *Geophis nasalis*—Downs, Misc. Publ. Mus. Zool. Univ. Mich., 131: 160, fig. 19.

    Distribution: Pacific slope of Chiapas, and Guatemala, and adjacent parts of Guatemalan Plateau and
      South-eastern highlands in eastern Guatemala; 600-1500 m; in "coffee zone".

GEOPHIS RHODOGASTER (Cope)
    dubius group

  1868 *Colophrys rhodogaster* Cope, Proc. Acad. Nat. Sci. Phila., 1868: 130. Type-locality: "the ele-
      vated country in the neighborhood of the city of Guatemala."
  1883 *Geophis rhodogaster*—Bocourt, Miss. Sci. Mex., Rept.: 531.
  1967 *Geophis rhodogaster*—Downs, Misc. Publ. Mus. Zool. Univ. Mich., 131: 92, fig. 7.

    Distribution: Western part of Guatemalan Plateau, east through southeastern highlands of Guatemala
      and El Salvador; generally from oak-pine associations between 1500-2500 m.

GEOPHIS RUTHVENI Werner
    championi group

  1925 *Geophis ruthveni* Werner, Sitz. Akad. Wiss. Wien, 134 (1): 60. Type-locality: Sarapigui, Brazil;
      in error for Sarapiqui, Provincia Heredia, Costa Rica, according to Downs, Misc. Publ. Mus.
      Zool. Univ. Mich., 131, 1967, 75.
  1967 *Geophis ruthveni*—Downs, Misc. Publ. Mus. Zool. Univ. Mich., 131: 75, fig. 5.

    Distribution: Caribbean slopes of western end of Cordillera Central and Pacific slopes of
      Cordillera Guanacaste, Costa Rica, 550-1600 m.

GEOPHIS ZELEDONI Taylor
    sieboldi group

  1954 *Geophis zeledoni* Taylor, Univ. Kansas Sci. Bull., 36: 693, fig. 4. Type-locality: Finca
      Zeledón, between Volcán Barba and Volcán Poás, Costa Rica, about 6000 ft.
  1967 *Geophis zeledoni*—Downs, Misc. Publ. Mus. Zool. Univ. Mich., 131: 174, fig. 19.

    Distribution: Slopes of Volcán Poás between 1600 and 2000 m, Cordillera Central of Costa Rica.

GOMESOPHIS Hoge and Mertens

   1959 Gomesophis Hoge and Mertens, Senck. Biol., 40: 242. Type-species: Tachymenis brasiliensis Gomes.

    Distribution: Estados de Minas Gerais, São Paulo, Paraná, and Rio Grande do Sul, Brazil.

    Content: One species.

GOMESOPHIS BRASILIENSIS (Gomes)

   1918 Tachymenis Brasiliensis Gomes, Mem. Inst. Butantan, 1 (1): 78, pl. 14, fig. 1. Type-locality:
      Pindamonhangaba, São Paulo, Brazil.
   1959 Gomesophis brasiliensis——Hoge and Mertens, Senck. Biol., 40: 242, figs. 1-2.

    Distribution: Estados de Minas Gerais, São Paulo, Paraná and Rio Grande do Sul, Brazil.

REPTILIA: SERPENTES: COLUBRIDAE ★ ★ ★ HELICOPS

Prepared by Douglas A. Rossman, Museum of Zoology, Louisiana State University, Baton Rouge, Louisiana

HELICOPS Wagler

1830 Helicops Wagler, Nat. Syst. Amph.: 170. Type-species: Coluber carinicaudus Wied.
1843 Tachynectes Fitzinger, Systema Reptilium: 25. Type-species: Homalopsis Leopardina Schlegel.
1843 Uranops Fitzinger, Systema Reptilium: 25. Type-species: Coluber angulatus Linnaeus.

Distribution: Colombia throughout South America to Argentina.

Content: Thirteen species.

Comment: Helicops wettsteini Amaral, Bull. Antivenin Inst. Amer., 3, 1929, 40, described from San Juan de Viñas, base of Volcán Turrialba, Costa Rica, has been shown to be a synonym of Enhydris plumbea (Boie), an Asian species, by Rossman and Scott, Herpetologica, 24, 1968, 262 who concluded the locality data were erroneous.

Key to the species

1. More than 17 scale rows at midbody-----------2
   With 17 scale rows at midbody------pictiventris

2. With 19 scale rows at midbody-----------------3
   More than 19 scale rows at midbody-----------8

3. Subcaudals not keeled----------------------4
   Subcaudals keeled--------------------angulatus

4. Scale ornamentation uniform throughout body---5
   Scale ornamentation not uniform throughout
   body; anterior scales smooth or feebly keeled,
   posterior scales strongly keeled--carinicaudus

5. Dorsum striped, or with at least four rows of
   spots or blotches---------------------------6
   Dorsum with three rows of large spots or
   blotches---------------------------------gomesi

6. Dorsum spotted or blotched--------------------7
   Dorsum striped------------------------modestus

7. Belly whitish with two series of black spots---
   --danieli
   Belly pattern of narrow, interconnected black
   and white crossbands--------------leopardinus

8. Dorsal scales in 21 rows at midbody-----------9
   More than 21 dorsal scale rows at midbody----11

9. Single preocular----------------------------10
   Two preoculars-----------------------trivittatus

10. Dorsum without stripes--------------leopardinus
    Three dark stripes on neck------------scalaris

11. Dorsum striped--------------------------------12
    Dorsum spotted or blotched-----------------13

12. Single preocular-------------------------hogei
    Two preoculars---------------------trivittatus

13. Subcaudals more than 60---------------------14
    Subcaudals fewer than 60--------------hagmanni

Clave de especies

1. Más de 17 filas de escamas en el medio del
   cuerpo---------------------------------------2
   Con 17 filas de escamas en el medio del cuerpo-
   ------------------------------------pictiventris

2. Con 19 filas de escamas en el medio del cuerpo-
   ---3
   Más de 19 filas de escamas en el medio del
   cuerpo---------------------------------------8

3. Subcaudales no quilladas--------------------4
   Subcaudales quilladas----------------angulatus

4. Ornamentación de escamas uniforme a lo largo
   del cuerpo-----------------------------------5
   Ornamentación de escamas no uniforme a lo largo
   del cuerpo; escamas anteriores lisas o débilmente quilladas posteriores fuertemente
   quilladas----------------------carinicaudus

5. Diseño dorsal lineado o con cuatro o más
   hileras de manchas--------------------------6
   Diseño dorsal con tres hileras de manchas------
   -------------------------------------gomesi

6. Diseño dorsal con manchas--------------------7
   Diseño dorsal lineado-----------------modestus

7. Vientre blanquecino con dos series de manchas
   negras-------------------------------danieli
   Diseño ventral de bandas angostas, negras y
   blancas conectados entre sí--------leopardinus

8. Con 21 filas de escamas dorsales en el medio
   del cuerpo----------------------------------9
   Más de 21 filas de escamas dorsales en el
   medio del cuerpo---------------------------11

9. Una preocular------------------------------10
   Dos preoculares---------------------trivittatus

10. Diseño dorsal sin línea-------------leopardinus
    Tres líneas oscuras en la nuca---------scalaris

11. Diseño dorsal lineado------------------------12
    Diseño dorsal con manchas------------------13

12. Con una preocular------------------------hogei
    Con dos preoculares----------------trivittatus

13. Subcaudales más de 60----------------------14
    Subcaudales menos de 60--------------hagmanni

14. Paravertebral spots less than three scales long--------------------------------polylepis
    Paravertebral spots more than three scales long--------------------------------pastazae

14. Manchas paravertebrales de menor extensión que tres escamas dorsales----------------polylepis
    Manchas paravertebrales de major extensión que tres escamas dorsales----------------pastazae

HELICOPS ANGULATUS (Linnaeus)

1758 Coluber angulatus Linnaeus, Systema Naturae, Ed. 10: 217. Type-locality: "Asia".
1802 Coluber Surinamensis Shaw, Gen. Zool., Amphib., 3: 460, pl. 118. Type-locality: "Said to be a native of Surinam".
1824 Natrix aspera Wagler, in Spix, Sp. Nov. Serp. Bras.: 37, pl. 13. Type-locality: Bahia, Brazil.
1830 Helicops angulatus—Wagler, Nat. Syst. Amphib.: 171.
1869 Helicops cyclops Cope, Proc. Acad. Nat. Sci. Phila., 1868: 309. Type-locality: Bahia, Brazil.
1869 Helicops fumigatus Cope, Proc. Acad. Nat. Sci. Phila., 1868: 308. Type-locality: Surinam.

Distribution: Venezuela and Colombia throughout South America to Bolivia; Trinidad, Ecuador and Peru.

HELICOPS CARINICAUDUS (Wied)

1825 Coluber carinicaudus Wied, Beitr. Naturgesch. Bras., 1: 300. Type-locality: "Brazil, Estado do Espirito Santo, Rio Itapémirim" (from label in bottle containing holotype at AMNH).
1830 [Helicops] carinicaudus—Wagler, Nat. Syst. Amphib.: 170.

Distribution: From Espirito Santo, Brazil to Uruguay and Argentina.

Content: Two subspecies.

Key to the subspecies

1. Venter with two longitudinal series of black spots along midline, occasionally with single series of small black spots forming a finer midventral row which usually begins at end of first third or beginning of second third of body; ground color yellowish-white--------carinicaudus
   Venter with three narrow black stripes on yellowish-white, pinkish, or red ground color, or anteriorly yellow with red from second third of body on; stripes may be fused with each other by lateral extensions as wide as single ventral, which extend toward central stripe but not beyond it unless two such extensions meet; these extensions may be so abundant on some individuals that venter appears black with yellow, pink or red streaks-------------------------------infrataeniatus

Clave de subespecies

1. Vientre con dos series de puntos negros longitudinales situados en el centro del vientre, pudiendo haber una serie de puntos negros menores formando una fila central más fina que en general reinicia en el fin del primer tercio o principio del segundo; coloración de fondo blanco amarillenta--------------------carinicaudus
   Vientre con estrías negras sobre fondo blanco amarillento, rosado, rojo o anteriormente amarillo y desde el segundo tercio en adelante rojo; estas estrías son en número de tres y pueden estar unidas entre sí por fajas transversales del ancho de un escudo ventral que llegan hasta la estría central no pasando adelante, con excepción de cuando dos fajas se encuentran y se sueldan a la central luciendo entonces como una faja ventral entera; estas fajas son tan frecuentes en algunos ejemplares que el vientre se torna melánico con pequeñas fajas amarillas, rosadas o rojas (de acuerdo al color dominante de fondo del ejemplar)--------------------infrataeniatus

Helicops carinicaudus carinicaudus (Wied)

1958 Helicops carinicauda carinicauda—Lema, Iheringia, Mus. Rio-Grandense, Cien. Nat. Zool., 10: 20.

Distribution: São Paulo, Rio de Janeiro, and Espirito Santo, southeastern Brazil.

Helicops carinicaudus infrataeniatus (Jan)

1865 H.[elicops] infrataeniatus Jan, Arch. Zool. Anat. Fis., 3: 253. Type-locality: "Surinam" and "Brasile".
1865 Helicops carinicaudus var. gastrosticta Jan, Arch. Zool. Anat. Fis., 3: 253. Type-locality: "Brasile".
1878 Helicops trivittatus Cope, Proc. Amer. Phil. Soc., 17 (1877): 92. Type-locality: "Unknown, supposed to be Argentine Confederation".
1885 Helicops baliogaster Cope, Proc. Amer. Phila. Soc., 22 (1884): 193. Type-locality: Rio Grande do Sul Brazil (possibly São Joao do Monte Negro).
1916 Helicops carinicauda var. infrataeniata—Griffin, Mem. Carnegie Mus., 7: 179.

Distribution: Santa Catarina and Rio Grande do Sul, southern Brazil; Uruguay and Argentina.

HELICOPS DANIELI Amaral

1938 Helicops danieli Amaral, Mem. Inst. Butantan, 11: 232. Type-locality: Carare, Santander, Colombia.

Distribution: Atrato and Magdalena valleys, from Barranquilla to Barrancabermeja, Colombia.

HELICOPS GOMESI Amaral

1921 Helicops gomesi Amaral, Anex. Mem. Inst. Butantan, 1 (1): 7, pl. 1, figs. 1-4. Type-locality: Estação Costa Pinto, Sorocabana Railway, Estado de São Paulo, Brazil.

Distribution: Rio Tieté basin, São Paulo, Brazil.

HELICOPS HAGMANNI Roux

1910 Helicops hagmanni Roux, Zool. Anz., 36: 439. Type-locality: Santarem, northern Brazil.

Distribution: Northern Brazil.

HELICOPS HOGEI Lancini

1964 Helicops hogei Lancini, Publ. Oc. Mus. Cienc. Nat. Venezuela, Zool., 7: 2. Type-locality: Río Autana, Territorio Federal Amazonas, Venezuela.

Distribution: Known from type locality and Territorio Federal de Tamacuro, Venezuela.

HELICOPS LEOPARDINUS (Schlegel)

1837 Homalopsis leopardina Schlegel, Essai Physion. Serp., 2: 358. Type-locality: Unknown.
1854 Helicops Leprieurii Duméril, Bibron and Duméril, Erp. Gén., 7: 750, pl. 68. Type-locality: Bahia, Brazil and Cayenne, Guianas.
1865 H.[elicops] leopardinus—Jan, Arch. Zool. Anat. Fis., 3: 251.

Distribution: Guianas and Brazil to northern Argentina.

HELICOPS MODESTUS Günther

1861 Helicops modestus Günther, Ann. Mag. Nat. Hist., (3) 7: 425, fig. Type-locality: "Tropical America?"
1866 Helicops assimilis Reinhardt, Vidensk, Medd. Naturhist. Foren. Kjöbenhavn, 1866: 156. Type-locality: Minas Gerais, Brazil.

Distribution: Central and southern Brazil.

HELICOPS PASTAZAE Shreve

    1934 Helicops pastazae Shreve, Occ. Pap. Boston Soc. Nat. Hist., 8: 129. Type-locality: Pastaza
        River, from Canelos to Marañón River, Ecuador.

   Distribution: Amazonian Ecuador and Colombia.

HELICOPS PICTIVENTRIS Werner

    1897 Helicops pictiventris Werner, Sitz. Math.-Phys. Cl. Akad. Wiss. Munich, 27 (2): 205. Type-
        locality: Porto Alegre, Brazil.

   Distribution: Southern Brazil.

HELICOPS POLYLEPIS Günther

    1861 Helicops polylepis Günther, Ann. Mag. Nat. Hist., (3) 7: 426. Type-locality: Upper Amazon.
    1862 Tachynectes chrysostictus Cope, Proc. Acad. Nat. Sci. Phila., 1862: 71. Type-locality: "Amazon".
    1865 H.[elicops] spixii Jan, Arch. Zool. Anat. Fis., 3: 249. Type-locality: Brazil.

   Distribution: Amazonian Brazil, Colombia, Peru and Bolivia.

HELICOPS SCALARIS Jan

    1865 H.[elicops] scalaris Jan, Arch. Zool. Anat. Fis., 3: 250. Type-locality: Venezuela.

   Distribution: Maracaibo Basin, Venezuela, and adjacent Colombia.

HELICOPS TRIVITTATUS (Gray)

    1849 Myron trivittatus Gray, Cat. Sn. Brit. Mus.: 70. Type-locality: India?
    1863 Helicops trivittatus—Boulenger, Cat. Sn. Brit. Mus., 1: 276, pl. 18, fig. 2.

   Distribution: Equatorial Brazil.

H:LMINTHOPHIS Peters

1860 Helminthophis Peters, Monats. Akad. Wiss. Berlin, 1860: 518. Type-species: Typhlops
(Helminthophis) frontalis Peters.
1861 Idiotyphlops Jan, Arch. für Naturg., 27: 6. Type-species: Typhlops flavoterminatus Peters.

Distribution: Central America, northern and central South America.

Content: Three species, according to most recent review, by Dunn, Caldasia, 3, 1944, 47.

Key to the species   Clave de especies

1. Body scales in 20 rows-------------praeocularis   1. Escamas del cuerpo en 20 hileras---praeocularis
   Body scales in 22 rows----------------frontalis   Escamas del cuerpo en 22 hileras------frontalis
   Body scales in 24 rows----------flavoterminatus   Escamas del cuerpo en 24 hileras--------------
                                                         ------------------------------flavoterminatus

HELMINTHOPHIS FLAVOTERMINATUS (Peters)

1857 Typhlops flavoterminatus Peters, Monats. Akad. Wiss. Berlin, 1857: 402. Type-locality: Caracas,
Venezuela.
1873 Helminthophis flavoterminatus—Bocage, Jour. Sci. Math. Phys. Nat. Acad. Lisbon, 4: 252.

Distribution: Venezuela and Colombia.

HELMINTHOPHIS FRONTALIS (Peters)

1860 Typhlops (Helminthophis) frontalis Peters, Monats. Akad. Wiss. Berlin, 1860: 517, pl., figs. 1-1c.
Type-locality: Costa Rica.
1881 H.[elminthophis] frontalis—Peters, Sitz. Ges. Naturforsch. Freunde Berlin, 1881: 69.

Distribution: Costa Rica.

HELMINTHOPHIS PRAEOCULARIS Amaral

1924 Helminthophis praeocularis Amaral, Proc. New England Zool. Club, 9: 28. Type-locality: Honda,
upper valley of Río Magdalena, Colombia.
1944 Helminthophis praeocularis—Dunn, Caldasia, 3: 47, figs. 1-2.

Distribution: Interandean area of northern Colombia, in Tolima, Santander and Norte de Santander,
from 200 to 1200 m.

HYDRODYNASTES Fitzinger

1843 Hydrodynastes Fitzinger, Systema Reptilium: 25. Type-species: Elaps Schrankii Wagler.
1863 Lejosophis Jan, Arch. Zool. Anat. Fis., 2: 320. Type-species: Coluber bicinctus Herrmann.
1944 Dugandia Dunn, Caldasia, 3: 70. Type-species: Coluber bicinctus Herrmann.

Distribution: As for single known species.

Content: One species.

HYDRODYNASTES BICINCTUS (Herrmann)

1804 Coluber bicinctus Herrmann, Observationes Zoologicae: 276. Type-locality: none given.
1958 Hydrodynastes bicinctus—Hoge, Pap. Avul. Depto. Zool. São Paulo, 13: 222.

Distribution: Guianas; Amazonian region of Brazil, Colombia and Venezuela.

Content: Two subspecies.

Key to the subspecies

1. First dorsal blotch enlarged; belly
   checkered with black and white-----schultzi
   First dorsal blotch not enlarged; black
   spots on belly arranged in cross bars------
   ---------------------------------bicinctus

Clave de subespecies

1. Primera mancha dorsal agrandada; vientre
   salpicado en negro y blanco------------schultzi
   Primera mancha dorsal no agrandada; manchas
   negras del vientre ordenadas en barras
   transversas--------------------------bicinctus

Hydrodynastes bicinctus bicinctus (Herrmann)

1824 Elaps Schrankii Wagler, in Spix, Sp. Nov. Serp. Bras.: 1, pl. 1. Type-locality: Rio Japurá,
     Brazil.
1966 Hydrodynastes bicinctus bicinctus—Hoge, Ciência e Cultura, São Paulo, 18: 143.

Distribution: Uncertain, not defined by Hoge.

Hydrodynastes bicinctus schultzi Hoge

1966 Hydrodynastes bicinctus Schultzi Hoge, Ciência e Cultura, São Paulo, 18: 143. Type-locality:
     Presidenté Epitácio, Estado de São Paulo, Brazil.

Distribution: Uncertain, not defined by Hoge.

HYDROMORPHUS Peters

> 1859 <u>Hydromorphus</u> Peters, Monats. Akad. Wiss. Berlin, 1859: 276. Type-species: <u>Hydromorphus</u> <u>concolor</u>
> Peters.
>
> Distribution: Costa Rica and Panama.
>
> Content: Three species, according to most recent review of genus, by Nelson, Texas Jour. Sci.,
> 18, 1966, 365-371.

<table>
<tr><td>Key to the species</td><td>Clave de especies</td></tr>
</table>

1. Dorsal pigmentation extending to ends of
   ventrals; anterior temporal excluded from
   orbit--2
   Dorsal pigmentation ends on third scale row,
   ventral color begins at that level; anterior
   temporal enters orbit below single postocular-
   --<u>clarki</u>

2. Three prefrontals; scales in 15 rows at mid-
   body--------------------------------------<u>dunni</u>
   One prefrontal; scales in 17 rows at midbody---
   ------------------------------------<u>concolor</u>

1. Pigmentación dorsal se extiende al extremo de
   los ventrales; temporal anterior excluido de
   la órbita--------------------------------------2
   Pigmentación dorsal términa en la tercera
   hilera de escamas, color ventral empieza a ese
   nivel; temporal anterior entra la órbita
   debajo del único postocular------------<u>clarki</u>

2. Tres prefrontales; escamas en 15 hileras al
   medio del cuerpo--------------------------<u>dunni</u>
   Un prefrontal; escamas en 17 hileras al medio
   del cuerpo----------------------------<u>concolor</u>

<u>HYDROMORPHUS</u> <u>CLARKI</u> Dunn

> 1942 <u>Hydromorphus</u> <u>clarki</u> Dunn, Notulae Naturae, Acad. Nat. Sci. Phila., 108: 2. Type-locality: Agua
> Clara village, near Chagres River, Panama.
> 1966 <u>Hydromorphus</u> <u>clarki</u>—Nelson, Texas Jour. Sci., 18: 368.
>
> Distribution: Known only from type-locality.

<u>HYDROMORPHUS</u> <u>CONCOLOR</u> Peters

> 1859 <u>Hydromorphus</u> <u>concolor</u> Peters, Monats. Akad. Wiss. Berlin, 1859: 277, text-fig. 3. Type-locality:
> Costa Rica.
> 1966 <u>Hydromorphus</u> <u>concolor</u>—Nelson, Texas Jour. Sci., 18: 368, figs. 2-3, 5-9.
>
> Distribution: Honduras and Costa Rica; not yet recorded from Nicaragua.

<u>HYDROMORPHUS</u> <u>DUNNI</u> Slevin

> 1942 <u>Hydromorphus</u> <u>dunni</u> Slevin, Proc. Calif. Acad. Sci., 23: 474. Type-locality: Vicinity north of
> Boquete, Provincia Chiriquí, Panama, 3800 ft.
> 1966 <u>Hydromorphus</u> <u>dunni</u>—Nelson, Texas Jour. Sci., 18: 367, fig. 4.
>
> Distribution: Known only from type locality.

HYDROPS Wagler

1830 Hydrops Wagler, Nat. Syst. Amph.: 170. Type-species: Elaps martii Wagler.
1842 Higina Gray, Zoological Miscellany: 67. Type-species: Higina fasciata Gray.

  Distribution: South America east of Andes and north of 15°S.

  Content: Two species, according to most recent revision by Roze, Acta Biol. Venezuelica, 2,
    1957.

              Key to the species   Clave de especies

1. With 15 scale rows at midbody------triangularis   1. Con 15 filas de escamas en la mitad del
                                                          cuerpo----------------------------triangularis
   With 17 scale rows at midbody-----------martii   Con 17 filas de escamas en la mitad del
                                                          cuerpo----------------------------------martii

HYDROPS MARTII (Wagler)

  1824 Elaps Martii Wagler, in Spix, Sp. Nov. Serp. Bras.: 3, pl. 2, fig. 2. Type-locality: Provincia
      Maranhao, Rio Itapicuru, Brazil.
  1830 Hydrops [Martii]—Wagler, Nat. Syst. Amph.: 170.

    Distribution: Amazonian region of Peru, Colombia and Brazil.

    Content: Two subspecies, according to most recent revision, by Roze, Acta Biol. Venezuelica, 2,
      1957, 69.

            Key to the subspecies   Clave de subespecies

  1. Ventrals 175-180; total ventrals 239-258;   1. Ventrales 175-180; ventrales totales 239-
     68-88 black cross bands crossing venter,   258; 68-88 bandas transversas negras com-
     fused or alternating at midline-----martii   pletas, unidas o alternas sobre el vientre
     Ventrals 162-175; total ventrals 226-241;   ----------------------------------martii
     51-70 black cross bands, generally not in   Ventrales 162-175; ventrales totales 226-
     contact on midventral line---------------   241; 51-70 bandas negras transversas,
     ----------------------------callostictus   frecuentemente incompletas, no cubren todo
                                                         el vientre-------------------callostictus

Hydrops martii martii (Wagler)

  1957 Hydrops martii martii—Roze, Acta Biol. Venezuelica, 2: 69.

    Distribution: Amazonian region, from Colombia to Maranhao, Brazil.

Hydrops martii callostictus Günther

  1868 Hydrops callostictus Günther, Ann. Mag. Nat. Hist., (4) 1: 421, pl. 17, fig. B. Type-
      locality: Chyavetas, Upper Amazon, Peru.
  1957 Hydrops martii callostictus—Roze, Acta Biol. Venezuelica, 2: 71.

    Distribution: Northeastern Peru in drainage areas of Río Ucayali and Río Marañón.

HYDROPS TRIANGULARIS (Wagler)

  1824 Elaps triangularis Wagler, in Spix, Sp. Nov. Serp. Bras.: 5, pl. 2a, fig. 1. Type-locality: Ega
      (= Tefé) Lago Tefé, at confluence with Rio Amazon, Brazil.
  1830 Hydrops [triangularis]—Wagler, Nat. Syst. Amph.: 170.

    Distribution: From Venezuela, Guianas and Trinidad to eastern Peru and northern Bolivia.

    Content: Six subspecies, according to most recent revision, by Roze, Acta Biol. Venezuelica, 2,
      1957, 74.

Key to the subspecies[1]

1. Black dorsal bands reach vertebral line,
   where they are not noticeably narrower
   than on sides--------------------------2
   Black dorsal bands often do not reach
   vertebral line, always distinctly narrower
   dorsally than laterally---------fasciatus

2. Black bands without extensions posteriorly;
   fewer than 69 subcaudals------------------3
   Black bands have distinct projections or
   protuberances on posterior edge at dorsal
   end; 69 subcaudals-----------venezuelensis

3. More than 50 subcaudals-------------------4
   Subcaudals 47-51; black bands of equal
   width but with very irregular borders-----
   --------------------------------neglectus

4. Fewer than 164 ventrals (fewer than 163 in
   females)----------------------------------5
   Ventrals 162-191 (169-191 in females)------
   --------------------------------bassleri

5. Black bands narrower on fourth row of
   dorsals than either above or below--------
   --------------------------------bolivianus
   Black bands not narrower in fourth row of
   scales, about same size throughout--------
   --------------------------------triangularis

Clave de subespecies[1]

1. Bandas negras siempre alcanzan la línea
   vertebral y no son a este nivel más
   angostas que lateralmente----------------2
   Bandas negras más angostas sobre la línea
   vertebral que lateralmente, o no la alcanzan del todo--------------------fasciatus

2. Bandas negras sin protuberancias negras;
   menos de 69 subcaudales------------------3
   Bandas negras en su límite posterior dorsal
   con protuberancias negras irregulares; 69
   subcaudales-----------------venezuelensis

3. Más de 50 subcaudales--------------------4
   Subcaudales 47-51; bandas negras de igual
   ancho sobre el cuerpo, con bordes bastante
   irregulares---------------------neglectus

4. Menos de 164 ventrales (menos de 163 para
   las hembras)-----------------------------5
   Ventrales 162-191 (169-191 para las
   hembras)-------------------------bassleri

5. Bandas negras más angostas sobre la cuarta
   hilera dorsal que sobre las otras---------
   --------------------------------bolivianus
   Bandas negras no más angostas sobre la
   cuarta hilera dorsal, y aproximadamente
   del mismo tamaño sobre el cuerpo----------
   --------------------------------triangularis

Hydrops triangularis triangularis (Wagler)

   1929 Hydrops triangularis triangularis—Amaral, Mem. Inst. Butantan, 4: 92.
   1957 Hydrops triangularis triangularis—Roze, Acta Biol. Venezuelica, 2: 74.

   Distribution: Amazonian basin of Brazil, to Belem, Pará.

Hydrops triangularis bassleri Roze

   1957 Hydrops triangularis bassleri Roze, Acta Biol. Venezuelica, 2: 83, fig. 14e. Type-
   locality: Iquitos, Peru.

   Distribution: Northeastern Peru, in drainage areas of Río Ucayali and Río Marañón.

Hydrops triangularis bolivianus Roze

   1957 Hydrops triangularis bolivianus Roze, Acta Biol. Venezuelica, 2: 86, fig. 14f. Type-
   locality: Puerto Sucre, Río Mamoré, Bolivia.

   Distribution: Northern Bolivia.

[1]Taken directly from Roze, Acta Biol.
Venezuelica, 2, 1957, 68-69. We have exper-
ienced difficulty in running specimens,
including paratypes, through this key.

[1]Tomado directament de Roze, Acta Biol.
Venezuelica, 2, 1957, 68-69. Hemos tenido
alguna dificultad en el uso de esta clave,
incluso con paratipos de las subespecies que
incluye.

Hydrops triangularis fasciatus (Gray)

1849 Higina fasciata Gray, Zoological Miscellany: 67. Type-locality: Demerara, Guyana.
1894 Pseuderyx inagnitus Bocourt, Le Naturaliste, (2) 16: 155. Type-locality: Cayenne.
1957 Hydrops triangularis fasciatus—Roze, Acta Biol. Venezuelica, 2: 76.

   Distribution: Essequibo, Guyana, to Dutch Guiana.

Hydrops triangularis neglectus Roze

1957 Hydrops triangularis neglectus Roze, Acta Biol. Venezuelica, 2: 81, fig. 13d. Type-locality: Trinidad.

   Distribution: Trinidad and western Guyana.

Hydrops triangularis venezuelensis Roze

1957 Hydrops triangularis venezuelensis Roze, Acta Biol. Venezuelica, 2: 78, fig. 13c. Type-locality: San Fernando de Apure, Estado Apure, Venezuela, 250 m.

   Distribution: Río Orinoco basin, Venezuela, and southern llanos of Colombia, to Río Vaupés.

HYPSIGLENA Cope

1860 <u>Hypsiglena</u> Cope, Proc. Acad. Nat. Sci. Phila., 1860: 246. Type-species: <u>Hypsiglena</u>
    <u>ochrorhynchus</u> Cope.
1863 <u>Comastes</u> Jan, Elenco Sist. Ofidi: 102. Type-species: <u>Comastes</u> <u>quincunciatus</u> Jan.

   Distribution: Southwestern United States through Mexico and Central America. No valid records of
      occurrence in South America exist.

   Content: Three species, two of which (<u>affinis</u> Boulenger and <u>dunklei</u> Taylor) are extralimital.

   Comment: The generic name <u>Pseudodipsas</u> Peters, 1860, as published was based on a nomen nudum. It
      is not available under the International Rules of Zoological Nomenclature.

HYPSIGLENA TORQUATA (Günther)

1860 <u>Leptodeira</u> <u>torquata</u> Günther, Ann. Mag. Nat. Hist., (3) 5: 170, pl. 10, fig. A. Type-locality:
    Laguna Island, Nicaragua.
1894 <u>Hypsiglena</u> <u>torquata</u>—Boulenger, Cat. Sn. Brit. Mus., 2: 210.

   Distribution: Southwestern United States through Mexico and Baja California to Costa Rica.

   Content: About twelve subspecies, of which only one has been recorded within limits of this work.

   Hypsiglena torquata torquata (Günther)

   1871 <u>Comastes</u> <u>quincunciatus</u> Jan, Icon. Gén. Ophid., Livr. 38: pl. 1, fig. 1. Type-locality:
       Caracas, Venezuela.
   1939 <u>Hypsiglena</u> <u>torquata</u> <u>torquata</u>—Taylor, Univ. Kansas Sci. Bull., 25 (1938): 371, pl. 37, fig.
       3.

      Distribution: Nayarit, Mexico south on Pacific slope to Costa Rica.

      Comment: Although this species has been recorded from South America several times, it
         appears that all records are erroneous. Roze, Ofidios de Venezuela, 1966, 205, excludes
         it from Venezuela. Peters, Copeia, 1956, 57, eliminates it from Ecuador and also removes
         the name <u>Pseudodipsas</u> <u>fallax</u> Peters, 1860, from its synonymy.

IMANTODES Duméril

  1853 Imantodes Duméril, Mém. Acad. Sci. Paris, 23: 507. Type-species: Coluber cenchoa Linnaeus.
  1860 Himantodes Cope (emendation of Imantodes Duméril), Proc. Acad. Nat. Sci. Phila., 1860: 264.

   Distribution: Mexico through Central America to northwestern Ecuador west of Andes to Paraguay,
   Argentina, and Bolivia east of Andes.

   Content: Five species, of which only one (tenuissimus Cope) is extralimital.

   Comment: According to Stuart, Misc. Publ. Mus. Zool. Univ. Mich., 122, 1963, 100, two varieties of
   Imantodes described by Müller, Verh. Naturforsch. Ges. Basel, 7, 1882, 151, as Dipsas cenchoa var.
   rhombeata and Dipsas cenchoa var. reticulata, cannot be properly determined because of inadequate
   descriptions. Type locality for both is "Guatemala".

                  Key to the species   Clave de especies

  1. Scale rows at midbody 17----------------------2   1. Con 17 filas de escamas en el medio del cuerpo-
     Scale rows at midbody 15-------------lentiferus   --2
                                                              Con 15 filas de escamas en el medio del cuerpo-
                                                              -----------------------------------lentiferus

  2. Vertebral scales not three to four times larger   2. Escamas vertebrales no tres o cuatro veces
     than lateral rows; caudals fewer than 140-----3   mayores que las laterales; caudales menos de
     Vertebral scales three to four times larger   140--3
     than lateral rows; caudals more than 140------   Escamas vertebrales tres o cuatro veces mayores
     -------------------------------------cenchoa   que las laterales; caudales más de 140-cenchoa

  3. Dorsal pattern of inconspicuous spots on back;   3. Diseño dorsal de manchas inconspícuas sobre la
     ventrals fewer than 223--------------inornatus   hilera mediana; ventrales menos de 223-------
     Dorsal pattern of large dark blotches; ventrals   ------------------------------------inornatus
     more than 223---------------------gemmistratus   Diseño dorsal con manchas oscuras diferenciadas;
                                                              ventrales más de 223--------------gemmistratus

IMANTODES CENCHOA (Linnaeus)

  1758 Coluber Cenchoa Linnaeus, Systema Naturae, Ed. 10: 226. Type-locality: America.
  1810 Bungarus cencoalt Oppel (error for cenchoa Linnaeus), Ann. Mus. Hist. Nat. Paris, 16: 392.
  1826 D.[ipsas] Weigelii Fitzinger (substitute name for cenchoa Wied, which is same as cenchoa
       Linnaeus), Neue Classification der Reptilien: 59.
  1853 I.[mantodes] cenchoa—Duméril, Mém. Acad. Sci. Paris, 23: 507.

   Distribution: Isthmus of Tehuantepec region of Mexico through Central America and South America to
   Paraguay and Bolivia.

   Content: Three subspecies.

                  Key to the subspecies   Clave de subespecies

  1. More than 248 ventrals--------------------2   1. Más de 248 ventrales---------------------2
     Fewer than 245 ventrals----------leucomelas   Menos de 245 ventrales-----------leucomelas

  2. Venter light, dotted and spotted with dark-   2. Vientre claro punteado y manchado de
     er pigment-------------------------cenchoa   oscuro-----------------------------cenchoa
     Venter light, no darker pigmentation at all   Vientre claro, sin punteado ni manchado----
     ---------------------------semifasciatus   ---------------------------semifasciatus

Imantodes cenchoa cenchoa Linnaeus

   1899 Himantodes platycephalus Cope, Phila. Mus. Sci. Bull., 1: 15, pl. 4, fig. 4a-d. Type-
        locality: "Colombia; presumably near Bogotá" [from label with type].
   1942 [Imantodes cenchoa] cenchoa—Smith, Proc. U.S. Nat. Mus., 92: 384.

   Distribution: Panama; northern South America, to Paraguay, Bolivia and Argentina; Trinidad.

Imantodes cenchoa leucomelas (Cope)

1861 Himantodes leucomelas Cope, Proc. Acad. Nat. Sci. Phila., 1861: 296. Type-locality: Mirador, Veracruz, Mexico.
1942 Imantodes cenchoa leucomelas—Smith, Proc. U.S. Nat. Mus., 92: 384, pl. 37, fig. 1.

Distribution: Low and moderate elevations from Veracruz, Mexico, to northern Honduras on the Caribbean slope and from eastern Chiapas, Mexico, into southern Guatemala along the Pacific.

Imantodes cenchoa semifasciatus (Cope)

1894 Himantodes semifasciatus Cope, Amer. Nat., 28: 614. Type-locality: Paso Azul, Santa Clara, Carillo, Alajuela, Monte Aguacate, and San José, Costa Rica.
1894 Himantodes anisolepis Cope, Amer. Nat., 28: 614. Type-locality: Monte Aguacate, Costa Rica.
1899 Himantodes hemigenius Cope, Phila. Mus. Sci. Bull., 1: 16. Type-locality: Santa Clara, Costa Rica.
1942 [Imantodes cenchoa] semifasciatus—Smith, Proc. U.S. Nat. Mus., 92: 385.

Distribution: Central America; Guatemala to Panama.

IMANTODES GEMMISTRATUS (Cope)

1861 Himantodes gemmistratus Cope, Proc. Acad. Nat. Sci. Phila., 1861: 296. Type-locality: Originally given as San Salvador, Central America, but cited as "near Isalco, San Salvador", by Cope, Proc. Acad. Nat. Sci. Phila., 1860, 265.
1942 Imantodes gemmistratus—Smith, Proc. U.S. Nat. Mus., 92: 385.

Distribution: Southern Sonora in Pacific Mexico and central Veracruz in Caribbean Mexico south to Panama.

Content: Six subspecies, four of which (gracillimus Günther, latistratus Cope, luciodorsus Oliver and splendidus Günther) are extralimital.

Key to the subspecies

1. Dorsal spots fewer than 45, of which at least 50% are continuous laterally--------------------------------------gemmistratus
Dorsal spots more than 45, of which more than 50% are interrupted laterally--oliveri

Clave de subespecies

1. Manchas dorsales en número menor de 45, por lo menos el 50% se continúa lateralmente----------------------------------gemmistratus
Manchas dorsales en número mayor de 45, de las cuales más del 50% se interrumpen lateralmente----------------------oliveri

Imantodes gemmistratus gemmistratus (Cope)

1871 Himantodes cenchoa var. elegans Jan, Icon. Gén. Ophid., Livr. 38: pl. 2, fig. 1. Type-locality: Central America.
1886 Leptognathus stratissima Cope, Proc. Amer. Phil. Soc., 23 (1885): 280. Type-locality: Panama.
1954 [Imantodes] g[emmistratus] gemmistratus—Peters, Occ. Pap. Mus. Zool. Univ. Mich., 554: 24.

Distribution: Low and moderate elevations of Pacific slope from eastern Guatemala south to Panama; Motagua Valley on Caribbean slope of Guatemala; where it may also extend across southeastern highlands.

Imantodes gemmistratus oliveri Smith

1942 Imantodes splendidus oliveri Smith, Proc. U.S. Nat. Mus., 92: 388. Type-locality: Tapanatepec, Oaxaca, Mexico.
1954 Imantodes gemmistratus oliveri—Peters, Occ. Pap. Mus. Zool. Univ. Mich., 554: 23.

Distribution: Low and moderate elevations from Oaxaca, Mexico, into western Guatemala.

IMANTODES INORNATUS (Boulenger)

    1896 Himantodes inornatus Boulenger, Cat. Sn. Brit. Mus., 3: 88, pl. 5, fig. 1. Type-locality:
        Hacienda Rosa de Jericho, Nicaragua, 3250 ft.
    1951 Imantodes inornatus—Taylor, Univ. Kansas Sci. Bull., 34: 130, pl. 14.

    Distribution: Nicaragua, Costa Rica, Panama, western Colombia and northwestern Ecuador.

IMANTODES LENTIFERUS (Cope)

    1894 Himantodes lentiferus Cope, Amer. Nat., 28: 613. Type-locality: Pebas "Ecuador" (= Peru), and
        "E. Ecuador".
    1929 Imantodes lentiferus—Amaral, Mem. Inst. Butantan, 4: 203.

    Distribution: Amazonas, Brazil; Amazonian Colombia, Ecuador and Peru.

<u>LACHESIS</u> Daudin

    1803 <u>Lachesis</u> Daudin, Hist. Nat. Rept., 5: 349. Type-species: <u>Crotalus</u> <u>mutus</u> Linnaeus.

    Distribution: As for only known species.

    Content: One species.

<u>LACHESIS</u> <u>MUTA</u> (Linnaeus)

    1766 [<u>Crotalus</u>] <u>mutus</u> Linnaeus, Systema Naturae, Ed. 12: 373. Type-locality: Surinam.
    1803 <u>Lachesis</u> <u>mutus</u>—Daudin, Hist. Nat. Rept., 5: 351.

    Distribution: Costa Rica and Panama; Pacific slope of Colombia and Ecuador; equatorial forests east of Andes.

    Content: Three subspecies.

Key to the subspecies	Clave de subespecies
1. Ventrals more than 214 in males, 226 in females----------------------------------2 Ventrals less than 214 in males, 226 in females------------------------stenophrys	1. Ventrales más de 214 en machos, 226 en hembras---------------------------------2 Ventrales menos de 214 en machos, 226 en hembras------------------------stenophrys
2. Large and distinct spots on head; wide postocular stripe, not bordered by light stripe above; triangular rostral shield; bright reddish ground color; color of supraoculars contrasts strongly with surrounding black spots-------------noctivaga Small spots on head; narrow black postocular bordered with white above; trapezoidal rostral; greyish ground color; color of supraoculars not strongly contrasting with surrounding black spots--muta	2. Puntos grandes y distintos en la cabeza; ancha banda postocular, no bordeada de claro por encima; rostral triangular; color de fondo rojizo brillante; supraoculares fuertemente contrastados con manchas negras que los rodean----noctivaga Pequeños puntos sobre la cabeza; angosta banda negra postocular bordeada de blanco por encima; rostral trapezoidal; color de fondo grisáceo; supraoculares no contrastados fuertemente por manchas negras que las rodean---------------------------muta

<u>Lachesis</u> <u>muta</u> <u>muta</u> (Linnaeus)

    1788 <u>Coluber</u> <u>crotalinus</u> Gmelin, Systema Naturae, Ed. 13, 1: 1094. Type-locality: None given.
    1802 <u>Coluber</u> <u>alecto</u> Shaw, General Zoology, Amphibians, 3: 405. Type-locality: Ceylon.
    1802 <u>Scytale</u> <u>catenatus</u> Latreille, in Sonnini and Latreille, Hist. Nat. Rept., 3: 162. Type-locality: Surinam.
    1802 <u>Scytale</u> <u>ammodytes</u> Latreille, in Sonnini and Latreille, Hist. Nat. Rept., 3: 165. Type-locality: Ceylon.
    1824 <u>Bothrops</u> <u>Surucucu</u> Wagler, in Spix, Sp. Nov. Serp. Brasil: 59, pl. 23. Type-locality: Brazil.
    1824 <u>Lachesis</u> <u>rhombeata</u> Wied, Abbild. Nat. Brasil, pt. 5: pl. 5 and 5a. Type-locality: Brazil.
    1896 <u>Bothrops</u> <u>achrochordus</u> Garcia, Ofidios Venenosos del Cauca: 23, pl. 4. Type-locality: None specified; statement of distribution only.
    1951 <u>Lachesis</u> <u>muta</u> <u>muta</u>—Taylor, Univ. Kansas Sci. Bull., 34: 184.

    Distribution: Equatorial forests of Brazil, Guianas, Venezuela, Trinidad, Bolivia, Peru, Ecuador and Colombia; Pacific slopes of Ecuador and Colombia.

<u>Lachesis</u> <u>muta</u> <u>noctivaga</u> Hoge

    1966 <u>Lachesis</u> <u>muta</u> <u>noctivaga</u> Hoge, Mem. Inst. Butantan, 32 (1965): 162, pl. 20. Type-locality: Vitória, Espírito Santo, Brazil.

    Distribution: Forests of Atlantic slope in Brazil, from Estado de Alagoas to Estado do Rio de Janeiro.

Lachesis muta stenophrys Cope

    1876 Lachesis stenophrys Cope, Jour. Acad. Nat. Sci. Phila., (2) 8 (1875): 152. Type-locality:
        Sipurio, Costa Rica.
    1951 Lachesis muta stenophrys—Taylor, Univ. Kansas Sci. Bull., 34: 184.

    Distribution: Forests of Costa Rica and Panama.

<u>LAMPROPELTIS</u> Fitzinger

1843 <u>Lampropeltis</u> Fitzinger, Systema Reptilium: 25. Type-species: <u>Herpetodryas</u> <u>getulus</u> Schlegel.
1843 <u>Sphenophis</u> Fitzinger, Systema Reptilium: 25. Type-species: <u>Coronella</u> <u>coccinea</u> Schlegel, not of
     Blumenbach, = <u>Lampropeltis</u> <u>triangulum</u> (Lacépède).
1853 <u>Ophibolus</u> Baird and Girard, Cat. N. Amer. Rept., Serp.: 82. Type-species: <u>Ophibolus</u> <u>Sayi</u> Baird
     and Girard.
1876 <u>Bellophis</u> Lockington, Proc. California Acad. Sci., 7: 52. Type-species: <u>Bellophis</u> <u>zonatus</u>
     Lockington = <u>Coluber</u> <u>zonatus</u> Blainville.
1897 <u>Oreophis</u> Dugès, Proc. Zool. Soc. London, 1897: 284. Type-species: <u>Oreophis</u> <u>boulengeri</u> Dugès =
     <u>Ophibolus</u> <u>triangulus</u> <u>mexicanus</u> Garman.
1924 <u>Triaenopholis</u> Werner, Sitz. Math.-Naturwiss. Kl. Akad. Wiss. Wien, 133, abt. 1: 50. Type-species:
     <u>Triaenopholis</u> <u>arenarius</u> Werner.

   Distribution: Southwestern Canada through United States, Mexico and Central America into extreme
   northwestern South America.

   Content: About 16 species, only one of which occurs within limits of this work.

<u>LAMPROPELTIS</u> <u>TRIANGULUM</u> (Lacépède)

   1789 <u>Coluber Triangulum</u> Lacépède, Hist. Nat. Quadr. Ovip. Serp., 2: 86. Type-locality: America.
   1860 L⎡ampropeltis⎤ triangula—Cope, Proc. Acad. Nat. Sci. Phila., 1860: 256.

      Distribution: Most of continental United States to Panama and northwestern Colombia and Ecuador.

      Comment: Opinion 804, Bull. Zool. Nomen., 24, 1967, fixes the trivial name of this taxon as
      "<u>triangulum</u>", which must therefore be used rather than "<u>doliata</u>".

      Content: About 15 subspecies, of which five occur within limits of this work.

Key to the subspecies	Clave de subespecies
1. Body with ringed pattern in adults--------2 Body in adults uniformly black------<u>gaigae</u>	1. Diseño de adultos anillado----------------2 Diseño de adultos uniformemente negro------ --------------------------------------<u>gaigae</u>
2. Black annuli not expanded middorsally; light annuli complete middorsally--------3 Black annuli expanded middorsally to pinch out intervening light annuli-------<u>abnorma</u>	2. Anillos negros no expandidos mediodorsal- mente; anillos claros completos en el medio dorso------------------------------3 Anillos negros expandidos mediodorsalmente, invaden comprimiendo los claros---<u>abnorma</u>
3. Less than 180 ventrals--------------------4 More than 210 ventrals---------<u>micropholis</u>	3. Menos de 180 ventrales--------------------4 Más de 210 ventrales-----------<u>micropholis</u>
4. Light annuli numbering more than 18 on body; scales in red annuli with darker tips in adults---------------------<u>polyzona</u> Light annuli on body numbering 17 or less; scales in red annuli without darker tips-- ------------------------------<u>oligozona</u>	4. Anillos claros en número mayor a 18 en el cuerpo; escamas de los anillos rojos con marcas oscuras en adultos---------<u>polyzona</u> Anillos claros en número de 17 o menos sobre el cuerpo; escamas de los anillos rojos sin marcas oscuras---------<u>oligozona</u>

<u>Lampropeltis</u> <u>triangulum</u> <u>abnorma</u> (Bocourt)

   1886 ⎡<u>Coronella</u> <u>formosa</u>⎤ var. <u>anomala</u> Bocourt (preoccupied by <u>Coronella</u> <u>anomala</u> Günther, 1858),
        Miss. Sci. Mex., Rept.: 614. Type-locality: Alta Verapaz, Guatemala.
   1886 <u>Coronella</u> <u>formosa</u> <u>abnorma</u> Bocourt (substitute name for <u>Coronella</u> <u>anomala</u> Bocourt, 1886),
        Miss. Sci. Mex., Rept., 1886: pl. 39, figs. 4-4e.
   1942 ⎡<u>Lampropeltis</u>⎤ t⎡riangulum⎤ abnorma—Smith, Proc. Rochester Acad. Sci., 8: 246.

      Distribution: Low and moderate elevations in central Guatemala.

<u>Lampropeltis</u> <u>triangulum</u> <u>gaigae</u> Dunn

   1937 <u>Lampropeltis</u> <u>triangulum</u> <u>gaigae</u> Dunn, Occ. Pap. Mus. Zool. Univ. Mich., 353: 9. Type-
        locality: Boquete, Chiriqui, Panama.

      Distribution: Mountains of western Panama and eastern Costa Rica.

<u>Lampropeltis</u> <u>triangulum</u> <u>micropholis</u> Cope

1860 <u>Lampropeltis</u> <u>micropholis</u> Cope, Proc. Acad. Nat. Sci. Phila., 1860: 257. Type-locality:
    Panama.
1937 [<u>Lampropeltis</u> <u>triangulum</u>] <u>micropholis</u>—Dunn, Occ. Pap. Mus. Zool. Univ. Mich., 353: 3.

   Distribution: Costa Rica and Panama; northwestern and Caribbean Colombia; northwestern Ecuador;
   northwestern Venezuela.

<u>Lampropeltis</u> <u>triangulum</u> <u>oligozona</u> (Bocourt)

1886 <u>Coronella</u> <u>formosa</u> <u>oligozona</u> Bocourt, Miss. Sci. Mex., Rept.: 614, pl. 39, figs. 8-8d.
    Type-locality: Western slope of Guatemala to Isthmus of Tehuantepec; corrected to
    "southern slope of . . . .", by Stuart, Misc. Publ. Mus. Zool. Univ. Mich., 122, 1963,
    102.
1945 <u>Lampropeltis</u> <u>triangulum</u> <u>oligozona</u>—Smith, Proc. Rochester Acad. Sci. 8: 202.

   Distribution: Low and moderate elevations of Pacific coast from Isthmus of Tehuantepec,
   Mexico, south through El Salvador.

<u>Lampropeltis</u> <u>triangulum</u> <u>polyzona</u> Cope

1860 <u>Lampropeltis</u> <u>polyzona</u> Cope, Proc. Acad. Nat. Sci. Phila., 1860: 258. Type-locality:
    Jalapa; and Quatupe, near Jalapa, Mexico (= Cuatupe, according to Stuart, Misc. Publ.
    Mus. Zool. Univ. Mich., 122, 1963, 102).
1945 <u>Lampropeltis</u> <u>triangulum</u> <u>polyzona</u>—Smith, Proc. Rochester Acad. Sci., 8: 200.

   Distribution: Veracruz, Mexico through Nicaragua, except outer end of Yucatan Peninsula and
   mountains of central Guatemala.

LATICAUDA Laurenti

1768 <u>Laticauda</u> Laurenti, Synopsin Reptilium: 109. Type-species: <u>Laticauda</u> <u>scutata</u> Laurenti, which is synonymous with <u>Laticauda</u> <u>laticaudata</u> (Linnaeus).
1802 <u>Platurus</u> Latreille, in Sonnini and Latreille, Hist. Nat. Rept., 4: 183. Type-species: <u>Platurus</u> <u>fasciatus</u> Latreille, which is synonymous with <u>Laticauda</u> <u>laticaudata</u> (Linnaeus).
1847 <u>Platyurus</u> Agassiz (substitute name for <u>Platurus</u> Latreille), Nomenclator Zoologici Index Universalis: 297.

Distribution: Bay of Bengal to southern Japan; north coast of Australia; Oceania; west coast of Nicaragua.

Content: Four species, according to last generic summary, by Smith, Monograph of the Sea Snakes (Hydrophiidae), 1926. Only one occurs within limits of this work.

LATICAUDA COLUBRINA (Schneider)

1799 [<u>Hydrus</u>] <u>colubrinus</u> Schneider, Hist. Amphib.: 238. Type-locality: Unknown.
1905 <u>Platurus</u> <u>frontalis</u> DeVis, Ann. Queensland Mus., 6: 48. Type-locality: New Guinea.
1907 <u>Laticauda</u> <u>colubrina</u>—Stejneger, Bull. U.S. Nat. Mus., 58: 406.
1926 <u>Laticauda</u> <u>colubrina</u>—Smith, Monograph of the Sea Snakes: 6.

Distribution: Bay of Bengal to southern Japan, Australia, New Zealand and Oceania; west coast of Nicaragua.

Comment: This species is reported from Nicaragua by Jaime Villa, "Las Serpientes Venenosas de Nicaragua", 1962, 29.

LEIMADOPHIS Fitzinger

1843 Leimadophis Fitzinger, Systema Reptilium: 26. Type-species: Coronella almadensis Wagler.
1843 Pariopeltis Fitzinger, Systema Reptilium: 25. Type-species: Coluber triscalis Linnaeus.
1843 Pseudophis Fitzinger, Systema Reptilium: 26. Type-species: Xenodon schottii Schlegel.
1843 Calophis Fitzinger, Systema Reptilium: 26. Type-species: Herpetodryas cursor Schlegel.
1847 Limadophis Agassiz (emendation of Leimadophis Fitzinger), Nomenclatoris Zoologici Index Universalis: 210.
1894 Echinanthera Cope, Amer. Nat., 28: 841. Type-species: Aporophis cyanopleurus Cope.

Distribution: Southern Central America; most of South America; Caribbean Islands.

Content: About 40 species, of which about 20 are extralimital.

Key to the species[1]

1. Scale rows at midbody more than 15----------2
   Scale rows at midbody 15------------oligolepis

2. Scale rows at midbody 19---------------------3
   Scale rows at midbody 17---------------------9

3. Temporals 1 + 2-----------------------------4
   Temporals 2 + 3-----------------------simonsi

4. Dorsum uniform green; venter uniformly light colored (occasionally with scattered black spotting)----------------------------------5
   Not as above--------------------------------6

5. Caudals 60-78--------------------------viridis
   Fewer than 59 caudals-------------------typhlus

6. Lower surfaces of tail not uniformly black----7
   Lower surfaces of tail uniformly black--------
   -----------------------------------taeniurus

7. Fewer than 68 caudals-----------------------8
   More than 75 caudals----------------sagittifer

8. Head with irregular, whitish, U- or Y-shaped marking----------------------------almadensis
   No such head pattern--------------poecilogyrus

9. Two upper labials in orbit--------------------10
   Three upper labials in orbit------melanostigma

10. More than 48 caudals-----------------------11
    Fewer than 45 caudals-----------------pygmaeus

11. Two preoculars-----------------------------12
    One preocular------------------------------13

12. Four lower labials in contact with first chin-shields---------------------------bimaculatus
    Five lower labials in contact with first chin-shields------------------------------triscalis

13. Ventral part of tail not black--------------14
    Ventral part of tail uniformly black--taeniurus

14. Fewer than 165 ventrals--------------------15
    More than 165 ventrals---------------triscalis

[1]atahuallpae is not included in this key.

Clave de especies[1]

1. Más de quince escamas en el medio del cuerpo--2
   Quince escamas en el medio del cuerpo---------
   -----------------------------------oligolepis

2. Escamas en el medio del cuerpo 19------------3
   Escamas en el medio del cuerpo 17------------9

3. Temporales 1 + 2----------------------------4
   Temporales 2 + 3----------------------simonsi

4. Dorso verde uniforme; vientre claro homogeneo (ocasionalmente con puntos negros dispersos)--
   --5
   No como el anterior--------------------------6

5. Caudales 60-78-------------------------viridis
   Menos de 57 caudales--------------------typhlus

6. Cola no uniformemente negra-------------------7
   Cola, en normal ventral, uniformemente negra---
   -----------------------------------taeniurus

7. Menos de 68 caudales------------------------8
   Más de 75 caudales-----------------sagittifer

8. Cabeza con un diseño blanquecino irregular en U o Y-----------------------------almadensis
   Sin diseño cefálico como el anterior----------
   -----------------------------------poecilogyrus

9. Dos supralabiales formando la órbita---------10
   Tres supralabiales formando la órbita----------
   -----------------------------------melanostigma

10. Más de 48 caudales------------------------11
    Menos de 45 caudales-----------------pygmaeus

11. Con dos preoculares------------------------12
    Con una preocular---------------------------13

12. Cuatro labiales inferiores en contacto con la primera geneial---------------------bimaculatus
    Cinco labiales inferiores en contacto con la primera geneial-----------------------triscalis

13. Norma ventral de la cola no negra------------14
    Norma ventral de la cola uniformemente negra---
    -----------------------------------taeniurus

14. Placas ventrales menos de 165----------------15
    Placas ventrales más de 165-----------triscalis

[1]En esta clave no se incluye atahuallpae.

15. Vertebral region black, well marked on middle
of body----------------------------------16
Not colored as above------------------------17

16. Venter light, without spots----------melanotus
Venter with transverse black spotting----------
------------------------------------pseudocobella

17. More than 155 ventrals----------------------18
Fewer than 155 ventrals--------------------19

18. Venter uniformly light----------------------22
Venter black spotted--------------------fraseri

19. Fewer than 65 subcaudals--------------------20
More than 70 subcaudals--------------zweifeli

20. No black stripe along tail and posterior part
of body-----------------------------------21
Distinct black stripe along tail and posterior
part of body----------------------bimaculatus

21. Dorsum reticulate, without transverse spots;
tail more than 1/4 total length--------reginae
Dorsum without reticulation; with large transverse spots; tail less than 1/4 total length--
----------------------------------epinephelus

22. Ventrals more than 185--------------epinephelus
Ventrals fewer than 185-------------albiventris

15. Región dorso vertebral negra, bien manifiesta
en el centro del cuerpo----------------------16
No como el anterior-------------------------17

16. Vientre claro, sin manchas------------melanotus
Vientre con fajas negras transversas----------
--------------------------------pseudocobella

17. Más de 155 ventrales-------------------------18
Menos de 155 ventrales----------------------19

18. Vientre uniformemente claro------------------22
Vientre manchado de negro---------------fraseri

19. Menos de 65 subcaudales----------------------20
Más de 70 subcaudales-----------------zweifeli

20. Sin línea negra longitudinal en la cola y parte
posterior del cuerpo-----------------------21
Con línea negra longitudinal en la cola y parte
posterior del cuerpo--------------bimaculatus

21. Diseño reticulado sin manchas transversas; cola
no más de cuatro veces en la longitud total---
---reginae
Diseño sin retículo, con manchas transversas
grandes; cola más de cuatro veces y media en
la longitud total------------------epinephelus

22. Más de 185 ventrales----------------epinephelus
Menos de 185 ventrales--------------albiventris

LEIMADOPHIS ALBIVENTRIS (Jan)

1863 [Liophis reginae] var. albiventris Jan, Arch. Zool. Anat. Fis., 2: 294. Type-locality: Western
Andes of Ecuador and "fra Lacutunga e Guayaquil", Ecuador.
1868 Opheomorphus alticolus Cope, Proc. Acad. Nat. Sci. Phila., 1868: 102. Valley of Quito, Ecuador.
1944 [Leimadophis] albiventris—Dunn, Caldasia, 2: 481.

Distribution: Found in lowlands on both sides of Andes in Ecuador. Its range elsewhere in South
America is obscured at present by erroneous use of name in literature.

LEIMADOPHIS ALMADENSIS (Wagler)

1824 Natrix Almada Wagler, in Spix, Sp. Nov. Serp. Bras.: 30. Type-locality: Proximity of Bahia,
Brazil.
1824 Natrix Almadensis Wagler, in Spix, Sp. Nov. Serp. Bras.: pl. 10. Type-locality: Proximity of
Bahia, Brazil.
1858 Liophis conirostris Günther, Cat. Sn. Brit. Mus.: 46. Type-locality: Bahia, Brazil.
?1863 L.[iophis] verecundus Jan, Arch. Zool. Anat. Fis., 2: 300. Type-locality: Unknown.
1882 Liophis (Lygophis) y-graecum Peters, Sitz. Ges. Naturforsch. Freunde, Berlin, 1882: 129. Type-
locality:
1906 Trigonocephalus scolecomorphus Bacqué, Rev. Mus. La Plata, 12: 116. Type-locality: Asunción,
Paraguay.
1926 [Leimadophis] almadensis—Amaral, Rev. Mus. Paulista, 15: 78.

Distribution: Central, western and southern Brazil, Paraguay, Argentina and Uruguay.

Comment: Wagler used two names in the original description of this species, almada and almadensis.
Vanzolini, Pap. Avul. Depto. Zool. São Paulo, 8, 1947, 255, argues that almada must be used, but very
few authors have done so. Since the use of almadensis has been widely accepted, and the rule of the
first revisor would seem to be applicable, we see no reason to change a name long established in the
literature.

LEIMADOPHIS ATAHUALLPAE (Steindachner)

1901 Liophis atahuallpae Steindachner, Anz. Akad. Wiss. Wien, 38: 195. Type-locality: Las Palmas,
    W. spur of Andes between Babahoyo and Guaranda, Ecuador, 2500 m.
1969 Leimadophis atahuallpae—Myers, Amer. Mus. Novitates, 2385: 21.

  Distribution: Known only from type locality.

LEIMADOPHIS BIMACULATUS (Cope)

1899 Liophis bimaculatus Cope, Sci. Bull. Mus. Phila., 1: 11, pl. 4, fig. 2a-e. Type-locality:
    Colombia. "Presumably from the vicinity of Bogotá", according to Dunn, Caldasia, 2, 1944, 484.
1944 Leimadophis bimaculatus—Dunn, Caldasia, 2: 484.

  Distribution: Colombia, Venezuela and Ecuador.

  Content: Three subspecies.

Key to the subspecies	Clave de subespecies
1. Venter distinctly spotted with black------2 Venter immaculate or with small, indistinct spotting--------------------opisthotaenia	1. Vientre manchado en negro distintamente---2 Vientre inmaculado o con pequeñas manchas obsoletas--------------------opisthotaenia
2. Ventrals 154 or fewer; caudals fewer than 60-------------------------------lamonae Ventrals 165 or more; caudals 60 or more--- -----------------------------bimaculatus	2. Ventrales 154 o menos; caudales menos de 60 -----------------------------------lamonae Ventrales 165 o más; caudales 60 o más----- -----------------------------bimaculatus

Leimadophis bimaculatus bimaculatus (Cope)

1903 Liophis bipraeocularis Boulenger, Ann. Mag. Nat. Hist., (7) 12: 351. Type-locality:
    Facatativa, Colombia, 8000 m.
1944 Leimadophis bimaculatus bimaculatus—Dunn, Caldasia, 2: 484.

  Distribution: Eastern Andes of Colombia.

Leimadophis bimaculatus lamonae Dunn

1944 Leimadophis bimaculatus lamonae Dunn, Caldasia, 2: 486. Type-locality: Sonsón,
    Antioquia, Colombia, 2410 m.

  Distribution: Provincias Antioquia and Caldas, in central and western Andes, Colombia;
    Laurent, Bull. Inst. Roy. Sci. Nat. Belgique, 25 (9), 1949, 8, reports a specimen from
    Ecuador.

Leimadophis bimaculatus opisthotaenia (Boulenger)

1908 Liophis opisthotaenia Boulenger, Ann. Mag. Nat. Hist., (8) 1: 114. Type-locality:
    Mérida, Venezuela, 1600 m.
1966 Leimadophis bimaculatus opisthotaenia—Roze, Ofidios de Venezuela: 157.

  Distribution: Andes of Mérida, Venezuela.

LEIMADOPHIS EPINEPHELUS (Cope)

1862 Liophis epinephalus Cope (corrected in errata sheet to epinephelus), Proc. Acad. Nat. Sci. Phila.,
    1862: 78. Type-locality: Truando, Colombia.
1929 Leimadophis epinephelus—Amaral, Mem. Inst. Butantan, 4: 165.

  Distribution: Costa Rica to northwestern Ecuador.

  Content: Three subspecies.

Key to the subspecies

1. Ventrals fewer than 175------------------2
   Ventrals more than 175---------ecuadorensis

2. Venter white--------------------epinephelus
   Venter red with black blotches----juvenalis

Clave de subespecies

1. Menos de 175 ventrales--------------------2
   Más de 175 ventrales-----------ecuadorensis

2. Vientre blanco------------------epinephelus
   Vientre rojo con manchas negras---juvenalis

Leimadophis epinephelus epinephelus (Cope)

   1944 Leimadophis epinephalus epinephalus—Dunn, Caldasia, 2: 483.

      Distribution: Canal Zone, Panama to western Ecuador.

Leimadophis epinephelus ecuadorensis Laurent

   1949 Leimadophis epinephalus ecuadorensis Laurent, Bull. Inst. Roy. Hist. Nat. Belgique, 25
      (9): 8. Type-locality: Ecuador.

      Distribution: Known only from type specimen.

Leimadophis epinephelus juvenalis Dunn

   1937 Leimadophis taeniurus juvenalis Dunn, Copeia, 1937: 213. Type-locality: San José, Costa
      Rica.
   1944 [Leimadophis] epinephalus juvenalis—Dunn, Caldasia, 2: 483.
   1951 Leimadophis taeniurus juvenalis— Taylor, Univ. Kansas Sci. Bull., 34: 102.

      Distribution: Costa Rica to western Panama.

LEIMADOPHIS FRASERI (Boulenger)

   1894 Liophis fraseri Boulenger, Cat. Sn. Brit. Mus., 2: 131, pl. 6, fig. 2. Type-locality: Western
      Ecuador.
   1929 Leimadophis fraseri—Amaral, Mem. Inst. Butantan, 4: 166.

      Distribution: Western Ecuador.

LEIMADOPHIS MELANOSTIGMA (Wagler)

   1824 Natrix melanostigma Wagler, in Spix. Sp. Nov. Serp. Bras.: 17, pl. 4, fig. 2. Type-locality:
      Bahia, Brazil.
   1885 Aporophis cyanopleurus Cope, Proc. Amer. Phil. Soc., 22: 191. Type-locality: Rio Grande do Sul,
      Brazil, probably São João do Monte Negro, according to Cope, loc. cit., p. 185.
   1929 Leimadophis melanostigma—Amaral, Mem. Inst. Butantan, 4: 166.

      Distribution: Brazil.

LEIMADOPHIS MELANOTUS (Shaw)

   1802 Coluber Melanotus Shaw, General Zoology, 3: 534. Type-locality: Cape of Good Hope, Africa.
   1820 [Coluber (Natrix)] raninus Merrem, Tentamen Systematis Amphibiorum: 106. Type-locality: None
      given.
   1845 Coluber vittatus Hallowell, Proc. Acad. Nat. Sci. Phila., 1845: 242. Type-locality: Within 200
      mi of Caracas, "Colombia"; actually in Venezuela.
   1860 Liophis melanonotus Cope,(replacement name for melanotus Shaw), Proc. Acad. Nat. Sci. Phila.,
      1860: 253.
   1929 Leimadophis melanotus—Amaral, Mem. Inst. Butantan, 4: 166.
   1966 Leimadophis melanotus—Roze, Ofidios de Venezuela: 159, fig. 38.

      Distribution: Colombia, Venezuela, Trinidad, Tobago and Grenada.

LEIMADOPHIS OLIGOLEPIS (Boulenger)

1905 Liophis oligolepis Boulenger, Ann. Mag. Nat. Hist., (7) 15: 455. Type-locality: Igapé-Assu, Pará, Brazil.
1929 Leimadophis oligolepis—Amaral, Mem. Inst. Butantan, 4: 86.

Distribution: Estado do Pará, Brazil.

LEIMADOPHIS POECILOGYRUS (Wied)

?1823 C.[oluber] alternans Lichtenstein, Verzeichniss der Doubletten Des Zoologischen Museums, Berlin: 104. Type-locality: Brazil.
1825 C.[oluber] poecilogyrus Wied, Beiträge zur Naturgeschichte von Brasilien, 1: 371. Type-locality: Barra de Jucú, Rio Espirito Santo, Brazil.
1825 C.[oluber] doliatus Wied, Beiträge zur Naturgeschichte von Brasilien, 1: 368. Type-locality: Barra de Jucú, Rio Espirito Santo, Brazil.
1860 [Liophis Merremii] var. sublineatus Cope, Proc. Acad. Nat. Sci. Phila., 1860: 252. Type-locality: Buenos Aires, Argentina.
1866 L.[iophis] reginae var. viridicyanea Jan, Icon. Gén. Ophid., livr. 18: pl. 2, fig. 1. Type-locality: Paraná, Brazil.
1909 Rhadinaea praeornata Werner, Jahrb. Ver. Naturk. Stuttgart, 65: 58. Type-locality: Central Brazil.
1927 [Leimadophis] poecilogyrus—Amaral, Rev. Mus. Paulista, 15: 78.

Distribution: Argentina and Uruguay north to Amazonian Brazil and Ecuador.

Content: Twelve subspecies.

Comment: Amaral did not mention any of the synonyms listed above in his review of variation in this taxon (Pap. Avul. Depto. Zool. São Paulo, 5, 1944), and further study will be necessary to determine the proper place of each within the system. All are listed as synonyms of poecilogyrus by Boulenger, Cat. Sn. Brit. Mus., 2, 1894, 131.

Key to the subspecies

1. Belly without spots-----------------------2
   Belly spotted-----------------------------4

2. Not as below-----------------------------3
   Dorsum pinkish-brown with very fine reticulation, usually lacking bands or stripes-----------------------------pinetincola

3. Dorsum uniform brown or with numerous transverse dark bands resulting from fusion of dark spotting, or, occasionally, a zig-zag pattern formed of elongated and fused spots-------------------subfasciatus
   Not as above--------------------reticulatus

4. Head uniformly colored--------------------5
   Head with spots or markings---------------8

5. Dorsum not reddish-brown with black spotting on scales--------------------------6
   Dorsum reddish-brown with black spotting on scales------------------------amazonicus

6. Dorsum not olive-brown with faint traces of dark bands-----------------------------7
   Dorsum olive-brown with faint traces of dark bands---------------------xerophilus

Clave de subespecies

1. Vientre sin manchas---------------------2
   Vientre manchado-------------------------4

2. No como el siguiente---------------------3
   Dorso rosado-parduzco con retículo muy fino, usualmente sin bandas o estrías----------------------------pinetincola

3. Dorso pardo uniforme o con numerosas bandas transversales oscuras que resultan de la fusión de manchas oscuras, y ocasionalmente un dibujo en zig-zag formado por manchas alargadas y fusionadas-----------------------------------subfasciatus
   No como el anterior------------reticulatus

4. Cabeza de color uniforme----------------5
   Cabeza con manchas o marcas--------------8

5. Dorso no pardo rojizo, sin manchas negras en escamas-------------------------------6
   Dorso pardo rojizo con manchas negras en escamas------------------------amazonicus

6. Dorso no pardo oliváceo con débiles trazas de bandas oscuras-----------------------7
   Dorso pardo oliváceo con débiles trazas de bandas oscuras------------------xerophilus

7. Dorsum olive-green stippled with black on borders of scales; no trace of light transverse stripes; stippling occasionally agglomerated into transverse or zig-zag spotting--------------------pictostriatus
Not as above-------------------poecilogyrus

8. Dorsum not brown with dark transverse bands which tend to form into groups of three--9
Dorsum brown with poorly marked dark trans-verse bands, which tend to form groups of three, posteriorly becoming three longitu-dinal stripes separated by lighter stripe-------------------------------franciscanus

9. Dorsum not greenish-brown; no cream spot-ting on dorsal scales; no black tips on scales----------------------------------10
Dorsum greenish-brown; cream-colored spots on dorsal scales, some of which have black apices-------------------------intermedius

10.Dorsum not bottle-green with yellow spots in centers of scales-----------------------11
Dorsum bottle-green, with yellow spots in centers of scales, spots may be confluent into transverse light bands with inter-calated blocks of dark color-----platensis

11.Dorsum with olive reticulations, and with narrow black and white transverse bands made up of white specks and black spots, posteriorly forming a dark paraventral stripe bordered above by a light stripe with a dark line on vertebral area------------------------------------montanus
Not as above----------------------schottii

7. Dorso verde oliváceo, con bordes de las escamas negros; sin rastros de bandas transversales claras; los puntos negros se aglomeran a veces en manchas transversales o en zig zag-----------------pictostriatus
No como el anterior-----------poecilogyrus

8. Dorso no pardo con bandas transversas oscu-ras que tienden a agruparse de a tres----9
Dorso pardo con bandas transversas oscu-ras débilmente marcadas que tienden a for-mar grupos de tres hacia posterior que se transforman en tres cintas longitudinales separadas por cintas claras---franciscanus

9. Dorso no pardo verdoso, escamas dorsales sin manchas crema, sin ápices negros----10
Dorso pardo verdoso; escamas dorsales con manchas crema, algunas con ápices negros----------------------------------intermedius

10.Dorso no verde botella con manchas amari-llas en el centro de las escamas--------11
Dorso verde botella, con manchas amarillas en el centro de las escamas, las manchas puede confluir en bandas transversales claras intercaladas con bloques de pigmento oscuro------------------platensis

11.Dorso oliváceo reticulado, con bandas transversales angostas blancas y negras formadas por estrías blancas y manchas ne-gras que forman hacia posterior una cinta oscura paraventral bordeada por una cinta clara con una línea oscura en la región vertebral-------------------------montanus
No como el anterior---------------schottii

Leimadophis poecilogyrus poecilogyrus (Wied)

1944 L.[eimadophis] poecilogyrus poecilogyrus—Amaral, Pap. Avul. Dept. Zool. São Paulo, 5: 79.

Distribution: Espirito Santo to Bahia, Rio de Janeiro, Minas Gerais, and São Paulo, Brazil.

Leimadophis poecilogyrus amazonicus Amaral

1944 L.[eimadophis] poecilogyrus amazonicus Amaral, Pap. Avul. Depto. Zool. São Paulo, 5: 81. Type-locality: Probably Pará, Brazil; not clearly stated as such.

Distribution: Estados do Amazonas and Pará, Brazil.

Leimadophis poecilogyrus franciscanus Amaral

1944 L.[eimadophis] poecilogyrus franciscanus Amaral, Pap. Avul. Depto. Zool. São Paulo, 5: 80. Type-locality: Pirapora, Minas Gerais, Brazil.

Distribution: Region of Rio São Francisco, in northern Minas Gerais, central and western Bahia, Goiás and southwestern Pernambuco, Brazil.

Leimadophis poecilogyrus intermedius Amaral

1944 L.[eimadophis] poecilogyrus intermedius Amaral, Pap. Avul. Depto. Zool. São Paulo, 5: 81. Type-locality: Goiás, Brazil.
1952 Leimadophis poecilogyrus intermedius—Hoge, Mem. Inst. Butantan, 24 (2): 188.

Distribution: Goiás and Mato Grosso, Brazil.

<u>Leimadophis</u> <u>poecilogyrus</u> <u>montanus</u> Amaral

1944 <u>L.</u>[<u>eimadophis</u>] <u>poecilogyrus</u> <u>montanus</u> Amaral, Pap. Avul. Depto. Zool. São Paulo, 5: 79. Type-locality: Piquete, São Paulo, Brazil.

Distribution: Region of type locality.

<u>Leimadophis</u> <u>poecilogyrus</u> <u>pictostriatus</u> Amaral

1944 <u>L.</u>[<u>eimadophis</u>] <u>poecilogyrus</u> <u>pictostriatus</u> Amaral, Pap. Avul. Depto. Zool. São Paulo, 5: 77. Type-locality: São Lourenço, Brazil.

Distribution: Central and southern Rio Grande do Sul to coastal Santa Catarina, Brazil and Uruguay.

<u>Leimadophis</u> <u>poecilogyrus</u> <u>pinetincola</u> Amaral

1944 <u>L.</u>[<u>eimadophis</u>] <u>poecilogyrus</u> <u>pinetincola</u> Amaral, Pap. Avul. Depto. Zool. São Paulo, 5: 78. Type-locality: Central Paraná, Brazil.

Distribution: Central highlands of Estado do Paraná, to Santa Catarina and São Paulo, Brazil.

<u>Leimadophis</u> <u>poecilogyrus</u> <u>platensis</u> Amaral

1944 <u>L.</u>[<u>eimadophis</u>] <u>poecilogyrus</u> <u>platensis</u> Amaral, Pap. Avul. Depto. Zool. São Paulo, 5: 77. Type-locality: La Plata, Argentina.

Distribution: Eastern and central Argentina.

<u>Leimadophis</u> <u>poecilogyrus</u> <u>reticulatus</u> Parker

1931 <u>Leimadophis</u> (<u>Liophis</u>) <u>poecilogyrus</u> <u>reticulatus</u> Parker, Jour. Linn. Soc. London Zool., 37: 285. Type-locality: Makthlawaiya, Paraguayan Chaco, 23°25'S and 58°19'W.
1944 <u>L.</u>[<u>eimadophis</u>] <u>poecilogyrus</u> <u>reticulatus</u>—Amaral, Pap. Avul. Depto. Zool. São Paulo, 5: 76.

Distribution: Bolivia, northern Argentina, Paraguay, and Mato Grosso, Brazil.

<u>Leimadophis</u> <u>poecilogyrus</u> <u>schottii</u> (Schlegel)

1837 <u>X.</u>[<u>enodon</u>] <u>Schottii</u> Schegel, Essai Physion. Serpens, 2: 91. Type-locality: South America; restricted to Estado de São Paulo, Brazil, by Hoge, Mem. Inst. Butantan, 30, 1960-62 (1964), 68.
1944 <u>Leimadophis</u> <u>poecilogyrus</u> <u>albadspersus</u> Amaral, Pap. Avul. Depto. Zool. São Paulo, 5: 78. Type-locality: Piracicaba, São Paulo, Brazil.
1964 <u>Leimadophis</u> <u>poecilogyrus</u> <u>schottii</u>—Hoge, Mem. Inst. Butantan, 30 (1960-62): 67.

Distribution: São Paulo, Brazil.

<u>Leimadophis</u> <u>poecilogyrus</u> <u>subfasciatus</u> (Cope)

1862 <u>Liophis</u> <u>subfasciatus</u> Cope, Proc. Acad. Nat. Sci. Phila., 1862: 77. Type-locality: Paraguay.
1862 <u>Opheomorphus</u> <u>doliatus</u> var. <u>caesius</u> Cope, Proc. Acad. Nat. Sci. Phila., 1862: 348. Type-locality: Santa Fé, Paraguay.
1944 <u>L.</u>[<u>eimadophis</u>] <u>poecilogyrus</u> <u>subfasciatus</u>—Amaral, Pap. Avul. Depto. Zool. São Paulo, 5: 76.

Distribution: Paraguay and Entre Ríos, Argentina.

Leimadophis poecilogyrus xerophilus Amaral

   1944 L.[eimadophis] poecilogyrus xerophilus Amaral, Pap. Avul. Depto. Zool. São Paulo, 5: 81.
      Type-locality: Not clearly stated; perhaps Ceará, Brazil.

     Distribution: Semi-arid regions, Pernambuco to Piauí, northeastern Brazil.

LEIMADOPHIS PSEUDOCOBELLA (Peracca)

   1914 Liophis pseudocobella Peracca, Mem. Soc. Neuchatel Sci. Nat., 5: 99. Type-locality: Angelópolis,
     Colombia.
   1929 Leimadophis pseudocobella—Amaral, Mem. Inst. Butantan, 4: 167.
   1931 Liophis cobella alticolus Amaral, Bull. Antivenin Inst. America, 4: 87. Type-locality: Jericó,
     Colombia.
   1944 Leimadophis pseudocobella—Dunn, Caldasia, 2: 484.

     Distribution: Central and western Andes of Colombia.

LEIMADOPHIS PYGMAEUS (Cope)

   1868 Liophis pygmaeus Cope, Proc. Acad. Nat. Sci. Phila., 1868: 103. Type-locality: Napo or neighbor-
     ing part of Marañón, Ecuador
   1894 Liophis pygmaeus—Boulenger, Cat. Sn. Brit. Mus., 2: 129.
   1929 Leimadophis pygmaeus—Amaral, Mem. Inst. Butantan, 4: 167.
   1944 Leimadophis pygmaeus—Dunn, Caldasia, 2: 488.

     Distribution: Upper Amazonian region of Colombia and Ecuador.

LEIMADOPHIS REGINAE (Linnaeus)

   1758 Coluber Reginae Linnaeus, Systema Naturae, Ed. 10: 219. Type-locality: Indiis; in error,
     according to Hoge, Mem. inst. Butantan, 30, 1960-62 (1964), 57, who designated it as Surinam.
?1789 Coluber Violaceus Lacépède, Histoire Naturelle des Serpens, 2 (1): 116, pl. 8, fig. 1. Type-
     locality: None given.
   1802 Coluber Graphicus Shaw, General Zoology, 3: 474. Type-locality: America.
   1824 Natrix semilineata Wagler, in Spix, Sp. Nov. Serp. Bras.: 33, pl. 11, fig. 2. Type-locality: Rio
     Solimões, Brazil.
   1863 [Liophis reginae] var. quadrilineata Jan, Arch. Zool. Anat. Fis., 2: 295. Type-locality:
     Ecuador.
   1863 [Liophis reginae] var. ornata Jan, Arch. Zool. Anat. Fis., 2: 295. Type-locality: Buenos Aires,
     Argentina.

     Distribution: Northern South America, east of Andes; Goiás and São Paulo, Brazil.

     Content: Two subspecies.

     Comment: Neither Amaral, in his description of macrosoma, nor Hoge, in the description of
     maculicauda, discussed the position of the many synonyms listed above. It is appropriate here
     only to suggest that full review of the species with proper allocation of the synonyms and
     detailed statement of ranges needs to be made.

Key to the subspecies	Clave de subespecies
1. Caudal scales with dark spots; no lateral spots on body anteriorly; body light; tail long--------------------------macrosoma Caudal scales without dark spots; body with lateral spots anteriorly; body dark; tail short-------------------------------reginae	1. Escamas caudales con manchas oscuras; sin manchas laterales en el parte anterior del del cuerpo; cuerpo claro; cola larga------ --------------------------------macrosoma Escamas caudales sin manchas oscuras; cuerpo con manchas laterales anteriormente; cuerpo oscuro; cola corta----------reginae

Leimadophis reginae reginae (Linnaeus)

  1935 Leimadophis reginae [reginae]—Amaral, Mem. Inst. Butantan, 9: 238.

    Distribution: As for species, except for Goiás and São Paulo, Brazil.

Leimadophis reginae macrosoma Amaral

  1935 Leimadophis reginae macrosoma Amaral, Mem. Inst. Butantan, 9: 238. Type-locality:
      Canna Brava, Goiás, Brazil.
  1954 Leimadophis reginae maculicauda Hoge, Mem. Inst. Butantan, 24 (2) (1952): 241. Type-
      locality: Not given.
  1959 Leimadophis reginae macrosoma—Hoge, Mem. Inst. Butantan, 28 (1957-58): 69.

    Distribution: Goiás and São Paulo, Brazil.

LEIMADOPHIS SAGITTIFER (Jan)

  1863 L.[iopeltis] sagittifer Jan, Elenco Sistematico Degli Ofidi: 82. Type-locality: Mendoza,
      Argentina.
  1867 Liophis pulcher Steindachner, Sitz. Akad. Wiss. Wien, 55: 267, pl. 2, figs. 1-3.
  1894 Rhadinaea sagittifera—Boulenger, Cat. Sn. Brit. Mus., 2: 165.
  1896 Rhadinaea modesta Koslowsky, Rev. Mus. La Plata, 7: 453, pl. 3. Type-locality: Provincia de
      Salta, Argentina.
  1926 Leimadophis sagittifer—Amaral, Rev. Mus. Paulista, 14: 19.
  1964 Leimadophis sagittifer—Abalos, Baez, and Nader, Acta Zool. Lilloana, 20: 227, fig. 5.

    Distribution: Northwestern Argentina; southern Brazil.

LEIMADOPHIS SIMONSII (Boulenger)

  1900 Philodryas Simonsii Boulenger, Ann. Mag. Nat. Hist., (7) 6: 185. Type-locality: Cajamarca, Peru,
      9000 ft.
  1932 Leimadophis simonsii—Parker, Ann. Mag. Nat. Hist., (10) 9: 22.

    Distribution: Higher elevations in northern Peru and southern Ecuador.

    Comment: Schmidt and Walker, Zool. Ser. Field Mus. Nat. Hist., 24, 1943, 315, put this species in
      the synonymy of Philodryas elegans rufidorsatus, but they do not refer to Parker's paper (above),
      in which the species is re-validated, and it is not certain whether they had seen it.

LEIMADOPHIS TAENIURUS (Tschudi)

  1845 L.[iophis] taeniurus Tschudi, Arch. für Naturg., 11 (1): 164. Type-locality: Peru; "in der
      heissen Waldregion," Peru, according to Tschudi, Fauna Peruana, Rept., 1846, 51.
  1894 Liophis taeniurus—Boulenger, Cat. Sn. Brit. Mus., 2: 130.
  1944 [Leimadophis] taeniurus—Dunn, Caldasia, 2: 481.

    Distribution: Amazonian Peru and Ecuador.

LEIMADOPHIS TRISCALIS (Linnaeus)

  1758 Coluber Triscalis Linnaeus, Systema Naturae, Ed. 10: 224. Type-locality: Indiis.
  1758 Coluber corallinus Linnaeus, Systema Naturae, Ed. 10: 223. Type-locality: Asia.
 ?1863 L.[iophis] rufus Jan, Arch. Zool. Anat. Fis., 2: 301. Type-locality: Unknown.
  1894 Liophis triscalis—Boulenger, Cat. Sn. Brit. Mus., 2: 129.
  1929 Leimadophis triscalis—Amaral, Mem. Inst. Butantan, 4: 168.

    Distribution: Caribbean South America; Curaçao. A record from Paraguay, by Gatti, 1955, is probably
      an erroneous identification. Roze, Ofidios de Venezuela, 1966, 163, also questions validity of
      records from Venezuela.

LEIMADOPHIS TYPHLUS (Linnaeus)

1758 Coluber Typhlus Linnaeus, Systema Naturae, Ed. 10: 218. Type-locality: Indiis.
1870 Xenodon isolepis Cope, Proc. Amer. Phil. Soc., 11 (1869): 155. Type-locality: Pebas, Peru.
1887 Opheomorphus brachyurus Cope, Proc. Amer. Phil. Soc., 24: 57. Type-locality: Near Chapada, Mato Grosso, Brazil.
1897 Liophis Guentheri Peracca, Bol. Mus. Zool. Anat. Comp. Univ. Torino, 12 (274): 11. Type-locality: Caiza, Chaco of Bolivia.
1916 Liophis elaeoides Griffin, Mem. Carnegie Mus., 7 (1915): 187. Type-locality: Santa Cruz de la Sierra, Provincia del Sara, Bolivia.
1925 Liophis macrops Werner, Sitz. Akad. Wiss. Wien, 134 (1): 57. Type-locality: Paramaribo, Surinam.
1926 Leimadophis typhlus—Amaral, Ann. Carnegie Mus., 16: 322.

Distribution: South America east of Andes and north of about 35°S latitude.

Content: Two subspecies.

Comment: Hoge, Mem. Inst. Butantan, 30, 1960-62 (1964), did not comment on any of the above synonyms when he revived the taxon forsteri Wagler, and we cannot place them in their proper positions below. This must await a review of their status by future workers.

Key to the subspecies	Clave de subespecies
1. Ventrals 136-148--------------------typhlus	1. Ventrales 136-148-------------------typhlus
Ventrals 155-169--------------------forsteri	Ventrales 155-169------------------forsteri

Leimadophis typhlus typhlus (Linnaeus)

1964 Leimadophis typhlus typhlus—Hoge, Mem. Inst. Butantan, 30 (1960-62): 58.

Distribution: Uncertain; not defined by Hoge, loc. cit.

Leimadophis typhlus forsteri (Wagler)

1824 Natrix G. Forsteri Wagler, in Spix, Sp. Nov. Serp. Bras.: 16, pl. 4, fig. 1. Type-locality: Bahia, Brazil.
1964 Leimadophis typhlus forsteri—Hoge, Mem. Inst. Butantan, 30 (1960-62): 59.

Distribution: Uncertain; not defined by Hoge, loc. cit., when he revalidated this taxon.

LEIMADOPHIS VIRIDIS (Günther)

1862 Liophis viridis Günther, Ann. Mag. Nat. Hist., (3) 9: 58, pl. 9, fig. 2. Type-locality: Pernambuco, Brazil; and South America.
1863 Liophis typhlus var. prasina Jan, Icon Gén. Ophid., Livr. 18: pl. 4, fig. 3. Type-locality: Brazil.
1894 Liophis viridis—Boulenger, Cat. Sn. Brit. Mus., 2: 135.
1926 [Leimadophis] viridis—Amaral, Rev. Mus. Paulista, 15: (78? Taken from reprint).

Distribution: Southern and eastern Brazil; Paraguay.

LEIMADOPHIS ZWEIFELI Roze

1959 Leimadophis zweifeli Roze, Amer. Mus. Novitates, 1934: 4, fig. 1. Type-locality: Rancho Grande, Estado de Aragua, Venezuela, 1100 m.
1966 Leimadophis zweifeli—Roze, Ofidios de Venezuela: 164, fig. 39.

Distribution: Central part of Cordillera de la Costa, Venezuela.

INCERTAE SEDIS

1820 Coluber M-nigrum Raddi, Mem. Nat. Fis. Soc. Ital. Sci. Modena, 18: 338. Type-locality: Rio
de Janeiro, Brazil.

Comment: Boulenger, Cat. Sn. Brit. Mus., 2, 1894, 131, listed this as a synonym of poecilogyrus.
It was not mentioned by Amaral in his review of that species. If considered synonymous with
poecilogyrus, it will take priority over that name.

1863 L.[iophis] poecilogyrus var. californica Jan, Arch. Zool. Anat. Fis., 2: 292. Type-locality:
California.

Comment: Neither Boulenger nor Amaral mention this taxon. Since Jan considered it to belong in
poecilogyrus, we presume it is a Leimadophis, but we are uncertain of this.

LEPTODEIRA Fitzinger

1843 _Leptodeira_ Fitzinger, Syst. Rept.: 27. Type-species: _Coluber_ _annulatus_ Linnaeus.
1861 _Megalops_ Hallowell, Proc. Acad. Nat. Sci. Phila., 1860: 488. Type-species: _Megalops_ _maculatus_
    Hallowell.
1893 _Anoplophallus_ Cope, Amer. Natur., 27: 480. Substitute name for _Megalops_ Hallowell, pre-
    occupied. Type-species: _Megalops_ _maculatus_ Hallowell.
1938 _Pseudoleptodeira_ Taylor, Univ. Kansas Sci. Bull., 25: 343. Type-species: _Hypsiglena_ _lati-_
    fasciata Günther.

Distribution: Southern Sonora, Mexico, and Río Grande in southern Texas to northern Argentina
and Paraguay, except in the high Andes and the coastal deserts of Peru and Chile.

Content: Nine species arranged in four species groups, according to the most recent revision of
the genus by Duellman, Bull. Amer. Mus. Nat. Hist., 114, 1958, of which four (_latifasciata_
Günther, _maculata_ Hallowell, _punctata_ Peters, and _splendida_ Günther) are extralimital.

Key to the species

1. Maxillary teeth 14 or fewer, including those
    posterior to diastema----------------------2
    Maxillary teeth 16 or more, including those
    posterior to diastema----------------------3

2. More than 20 dark blotches on dorsum----_frenata_
    Less than 20 dark dorsal blotches-_nigrofasciata_

3. With 19 or fewer body scale rows at midbody---4
    With more than 19 body scale rows at midbody--5

4. Large dorsal spots which extend to margins of
    ventrals-------------------------------_bakeri_
    Dorsal spots extend to level of third or
    fourth scale row---------------------_annulata_

5. With median stripe on nuchal region----------6
    Without median nuchal stripe, or if present,
    bordered on either side by a longitudinal
    bar----------------------------------_annulata_

6. Ventrals less than 186; body rounded; no paired
    nuchal blotches; nape stripe may or may not
    touch nuchal blotch------------------------7
    Ventrals 186 or more; body slender; two lateral
    nuchal blotches that may be fused to form
    U-shaped blotch; nape stripe not touching
    nuchal blotch-----------------_septentrionalis_

7. Nape stripe laterally expanded anteriorly to
    form butterfly-shaped mark on postparietals
    and posttemporals; 34-49 (average 42) dorsal
    blotches---------------------_septentrionalis_
    Nape stripe not expanded to form butterfly
    pattern; 23-56 (average 36) dorsal blotches---
    -------------------------------------_annulata_

Clave de especies

1. Dientes maxilares 14 o menos incluyendo los
    posteriores al diastema--------------------2
    Dientes maxilares 16 o más, incluyendo los
    posteriores al diastema--------------------3

2. Más de 20 manchas oscuras dorsales------_frenata_
    Menos de 20 manchas oscuras-------_nigrofasciata_

3. Con 17 a 19 filas de escamas al medio del
    cuerpo-------------------------------------4
    Con más de 19 filas de escamas al medio del
    cuerpo-------------------------------------5

4. Manchas dorsales grandes extendidas hasta las
    proximidades de las ventrales----------_bakeri_
    Manchas dorsales no muy grandes extendidas sólo
    hasta la tercera o cuarta fila de escamas
    dorsales-----------------------------_annulata_

5. Con una cinta nucal mediana------------------6
    Sin cinta nucal mediana, si la hay, bordeada
    por una barra longitudinal a cada lado -------
    -------------------------------------_annulata_

6. Ventrales menos de 186; cuerpo redondeado; no
    hay manchas nucales apareadas; cinta nucal
    contacta con la primer mancha o no----------7
    Ventrales 186 o más, cuerpo delgado; dos
    bloques nucales laterales que pueden
    fusionarse constituyendo una mancha en U;
    cinta nucal no contacta con la mancha
    nucal-------------------------_septentrionalis_

7. Cinta nucal lateralmente expandida anterior-
    mente forma un contorno en mariposa en las
    posparietales y postemporales; 34-49 (42 pro-
    medio) manchas dorsales-------_septentrionalis_
    Cinta nucal no expandida lateralmente para
    formar contorno en mariposa; 23-56 (36 pro-
    medio) manchas dorsales--------------_annulata_

LEPTODEIRA ANNULATA (Linnaeus)
annulata group

1758 _Coluber_ _annulatus_ Linnaeus, Syst. Nat., ed. 10: 224. Type-locality: Amazon Basin; restricted by
    Duellman, Bull. Amer. Mus. Nat. Hist., 114, 1958, 48, to lower Rio Amazon, Pará, Brazil.
1843 _Leptodeira_ _annulata_—Fitzinger, Syst. Rept.: 27.

Distribution: Mexico to Argentina.

Content: Six subspecies, two (_cussiliris_ Duellman and _maculata_ Hallowell) extralimital.

Key to the subspecies	Clave de subespecies

1. Body rounded; vertebral row normal; nape
   pattern present------------------------2
   Body compressed; vertebral row enlarged;
   no stripes on nape---------------<u>annulata</u>

2. Two bars laterally on nape----------------3
   One stripe middorsally on nape---<u>rhombifera</u>

3. Neither longitudinal stripes on parietals
   or temporals, nor Y-shaped mark on parie-
   tals---------------------------<u>ashmeadi</u>
   Either longitudinal dark stripes on parietals or temporals, or a Y-shaped mark on
   parietals--------------------<u>pulchriceps</u>

1. Cuerpo redondeado; fila vertebral normal;
   diseño nucal presente-------------------2
   Cuerpo comprimido; fila vertebral agrandada; sin diseño nucal-----------<u>annulata</u>

2. Diseño nucal con dos bandas longitudi-
   nales-----------------------------------3
   Diseño nucal con una banda longitudinal----
   -----------------------------<u>rhombifera</u>

3. Parietales y temporales sin líneas oscuras
   o marca en forma de Y------------<u>ashmeadi</u>
   Parietales o temporales con líneas oscuras
   o con una marca en forma de Y sobre parie-
   tales----------------------<u>pulchriceps</u>

<u>Leptodeira annulata annulata</u> (Linnaeus)

1789 <u>Coluber albofuscus</u> Lacépède, Hist. Nat. Serp., 2: 312. Type-locality: America.
1863 <u>Eteirodipsas annulata</u> var. <u>rhomboidalis</u> Jan, Elenco Syst. Ofidi: 105. Type-locality:
    Brasil.
1872 <u>Dipsas approximans</u> Günther, Ann. Mag. Nat. Hist., (4) 9: 32. Type-locality: Chyavetas,
    Peru.
1884 <u>Eteirodipsas Wieneri</u> Sauvage, Bull. Soc. Philom. Paris, (7) 8: 146. Type-locality:
    Ecuador.
1901 <u>Leptodira nycthemera</u> Werner, Verh. Zool. Bot. Ges. Wien, 1901: 598. Type-locality:
    Ecuador.
1929 <u>Leptodeira annulata annulata</u>—Amaral, Mem. Inst. Butantan, 4: 78.
1958 <u>Leptodeira annulata annulata</u>—Duellman, Bull. Amer. Mus. Nat. Hist., 114: 47.

    Distribution: Amazon Basin from below 1100 m in southern Venezuela, Ecuador, Peru, and
    Bolivia, to mouth of Amazon; along Atlantic coast south to São Paulo.

<u>Leptodeira annulata ashmeadi</u> (Hallowell)

1845 <u>Coluber ashmeadi</u> Hallowell, Proc. Acad. Nat. Sci. Phila., 1845: 244. Type-locality:
    "200 miles of Caracas, Venezuela" restricted by Duellman, Bull. Amer. Mus. Nat. Hist.,
    114, 1958, 44, to vicinity of Caracas, Distrito Federal, Venezuela.
1947 <u>Leptodeira rhombifera kugleri</u> Shreve, Bull. Mus. Comp. Zool., 99: 531. Type-locality:
    Riecito, Acosta District, Falcón, Venezuela.
1958 <u>Leptodeira annulata ashmeadi</u>—Duellman, Bull. Amer. Mus. Nat. Hist., 114: 43.

    Distribution: East of Santa Marta Mountains, Colombia, through coastal northern Venezuela,
    to Río Orinoco; Tobago, Trinidad, and Isla Margarita, Venezuela.

<u>Leptodeira annulata pulchriceps</u> Duellman

1958 <u>Leptodeira annulata pulchriceps</u> Duellman, Bull. Amer. Mus. Nat. Hist., 114: 51. Type-
    locality: Bodoquena, Mato Grosso, Brazil.

    Distribution: Southern Mato Grosso to vicinity of Santa Cruz de la Sierra, Bolivia, and
    Asunción, Paraguay; Chaco region, Argentina.

<u>Leptodeira annulata rhombifera</u> Gunther

1872 <u>Leptodeira rhombifera</u> Gunther, Ann. Mag. Nat. Hist., (4) 9: 32. Type-locality: Río
    Chisoy, near Cubulco, Guatemala.
1893 <u>Sibon septentrionale</u> Kenn., subsp. <u>rubricatum</u> Cope, Proc. Amer. Phil. Soc., 31: 347.
    Type-locality: Boca Mala, Costa Rica.
1895 <u>Leptodeira ocellata</u> Günther, Biol. Cent. Amer., Rept.: 172, pl. 55, fig. B. Type-
    localities: Chontales Mines, Nicaragua, and Costa Rica.
1958 <u>Leptodeira annulata rhombifera</u>—Duellman, Bull. Amer. Mus. Nat. Hist., 114: 39.

    Distribution: Central and southeastern Guatemala to Panama in subhumid habitats; Archipiélago
    de las Perlas, Panama.

LEPTODEIRA BAKERI Ruthven
   annulata group

   1936 Leptodeira bakeri Ruthven, Occ. Pap. Mus. Zool. Univ. Mich., 330: 1. Type-locality: Aruba
       Island, Dutch West Indies.
   1958 Leptodeira bakeri——Duellman, Bull. Amer. Mus. Nat. Hist., 114: 51.

   Distribution: Aruba Island.

LEPTODEIRA FRENATA (Cope)
   annulata group

   1886 Sibon frenatum Cope, in Ferrari-Perez, Proc. U. S. Nat. Mus., 9: 184. Type-locality: Jalapa,
       Veracruz, Mexico.
   1891 Leptodeira frenatum——Cope, Proc. U. S. Nat. Mus., 14: 677.

   Distribution: Veracruz, Tabasco, and Chiapas, throughout Yucatán Península, El Petén, Guatemala
   and British Honduras.

   Content: Three subspecies, according to the most recent revision, by Duellman, Bull. Amer. Mus.
   Nat. Hist., 114, 1958, 58, of which two (frenata Cope and yucatanensis Cope) are extralimital.

   Leptodeira frenata malleisi Dunn and Stuart

      1935 Leptodeira yucatanensis malleisi Dunn and Stuart, Occ. Pap. Mus. Zool. Univ. Mich., 313:
          1. Type-locality: Tuxpena, Campeche, Mexico.
      1955 Leptodeira frenata malleisi——Duellman and Werler, Occ. Pap. Mus. Zool. Univ. Mich., 570:
          1, pl. 1.
      1958 Leptodeira frenata malleisi——Duellman, Bull. Amer. Mus. Nat. Hist., 114: 62.

      Distribution: Northern Chiapas, El Petén, Guatemala and British Honduras.

LEPTODEIRA NIGROFASCIATA Günther
   nigrofasciata group

   1868 Leptodeira nigrofasciata Günther, Ann. Mag. Nat. Hist. (4) 1: 425. Type-locality: Nicaragua.
   1869 Leptodeira mystacina Cope, Proc. Amer. Phil. Soc., 11: 151. Type-locality: Western Mexico,
       Isthmus of Tehuantepec; restricted to Tehuantepec city by Smith and Taylor, Univ. Kansas Sci.
       Bull., 33, 1950, 340.
   1958 Leptodeira nigrofasciata——Duellman, Bull. Amer. Mus. Nat. Hist., 114: 87.

   Distribution: Pacific lowlands of Guerrero, Mexico to Guatemala, Honduras, Nicaragua and Costa
   Rica.

LEPTODEIRA SEPTENTRIONALIS (Kennicott)
   septentrionalis group

   1859 Dipsas septentrionalis Kennicott, in Baird, Rept. of the Boundary, 2: 16, pl. 8, fig. 1. Type-
       locality: Matamoras, Tamaulipas, Mexico; restricted by Smith and Taylor, Univ. Kansas Sci.
       Bull., 33, 1950, 361, to Brownsville, Texas.
   1891 Leptodeira septentrionalis——Stejneger Proc. U. S. Nat. Mus., 14: 505.

   Distribution: From Texas on east and central Nayarit on west, south along both coasts to
   Caribbean Colombia, Pacific slope of South America to northern Peru, and in upper Río Marañón
   Valley, Peru.

   Content: Four subspecies, one (septentrionalis Kennicott) extralimital, according to the
   latest revision by Duellman, Bull. Amer. Mus. Nat. Hist., 114: 1958. Shannon and Humphrey,
   Herpetologica, 19, 1963 (1964), 262, include taylori Smith, 1941, as a subspecies of
   septentrionalis.

Key to the subspecies

1. Dorsal scales in 21-25 rows, with vertebral
   and paravertebral rows not noticeably enlarged; body rounded or only slightly com-
   pressed--------------------------------2
   Dorsal scales in 21 rows, with vertebral
   and paravertebral rows noticeably enlarged; body laterally compressed---ornata

2. Ventrals 186 or more; body slender; two
   lateral nuchal blotches that may be fused
   to form U-shaped blotch; nape stripe not
   touching nuchal blotch; 38-70 (average 54)
   small dorsal blotches as wide as or wider
   than long; usually three preoculars-------
   -----------------------------polysticta
   Ventrals fewer than 186; body rounded; no
   paired nuchal blotches; nape stripe may or
   may not touch first body blotch; 56 or
   fewer large dorsal blotches, longer than
   interspaces; usually two preoculars-------
   ------------------------------larcorum

Clave de subespecies

1. Dorsales en 21-25 filas, vertebral y paravertebral no notoriamente agrandadas;
   cuerpo redondeado o muy poco comprimido
   lateralmente----------------------------2
   Dorsales en 21 filas, vertebral y paravertebral notoriamente agrandadas; cuerpo
   comprimido lateralmente------------ornata

2. Ventrales 186 o más; cuerpo delgado; dos
   manchas látero-nucales que pueden fusio-
   narse en una con forma de U; banda nucal
   no contacta con mancha nucal; 38-70 (pro-
   medio 54) manchas dorsales tan anchas o
   más anchas que largas; normalmente tres
   preoculares--------------------polysticta
   Ventrales menos de 186; cuerpo redondeado;
   sin par de manchas nucales; banda nucal
   contacta la primer mancha nucal o no; manchas grandes, en número de 56 o menos
   mayores que los interespacios; normalmente dos preoculares------------larcorum

Leptodeira septentrionalis larcorum Schmidt and Walker

1943 Leptodeira larcorum Schmidt and Walker, Zool. Ser. Field Mus. Nat. Hist., 24: 311. Type-
    locality: Chiclin, Libertad, Peru.
1958 Leptodeira septentrionalis larcorum—Duellman, Bull. Amer. Mus. Nat. Hist., 114: 77.

Distribution: Northern coastal Peru and upper Río Marañón Valley, Peru.

Leptodeira septentrionalis ornata (Bocourt)

1884 Comastes ornatus Bocourt, Bull. Soc. Philom. Paris, (7) 8: 141. Type-locality: Isthmus
    of Darién, Panama.
1895 Leptodeira affinis Günther, Biol. Cent. Amer., Rept.: 170. Type-locality: Central
    America.
1913 Leptodeira dunckeri Werner, Mitt. Nat. Hist. Mus. Hamburg, 30: 28. Type-locality:
    "Mexico or Venezuela".
1958 Leptodeira septentrionalis ornata—Duellman, Bull. Amer. Mus. Nat. Hist., 114: 75.

Distribution: Southern Costa Rica to Caribbean Panama, Colombia, and western Venezuela, also
    Pacific Colombia and Ecuador.

Leptodeira septentrionalis polysticta Günther

1895 Leptodeira polysticta Günther, Biol. Cent. Amer., Rept.: 172, pl. 55. Type-locality:
    Mexico and Central America; restricted by Smith and Taylor, Univ. Kansas Sci. Bull.,
    33, 1950, 316, to Belize, British Honduras.
1941 Leptodeira annulata taylori Smith, Proc. Biol. Soc. Wash., 54: 115. Type-locality:
    Orizaba, Veracruz, Mexico.
1958 Leptodeira septentrionalis polysticta—Duellman, Bull. Amer. Mus. Nat. Hist., 114: 72.

Distribution: Both slopes below 2000 m from Nayarit and southern Veracruz, south to central
    Costa Rica, in local mesic habitats only on dry Pacific coast from El Salvador to Costa
    Rica.

LEPTODRYMUS Amaral

    1927 <u>Leptodrymus</u> Amaral, Bull. Antivenin Inst. Amer., 1: 28. Type-species: <u>Leptodrymus</u> <u>clarki</u>
        Amaral.

    Distribution: As for only known species.

    Content: One species.

LEPTODRYMUS PULCHERRIMUS (Cope)

    1874 <u>Masticophis</u> <u>pulcherrimus</u> Cope, Proc. Acad. Nat. Sci. Phila., 1874: 65. Type-locality: Western
        side of central America.
    1898 <u>Zamenis</u> <u>bitaeniatus</u> Boettger, Katalog der Reptilien-Sammlung im Mus. Senckenbergischen
        Naturforsch. Ges., pt. 2: 42. Type-locality: Retalhuleu, Guatemala.
    1927 <u>Leptodrymus</u> <u>clarki</u> Amaral, Bull. Antivenin Inst. Amer., 1: 29, fig. 10a-b. Type-locality: Taloa
        Creek, Tela, Honduras.
    1931 <u>Leptodrymus</u> <u>pulcherrimus</u>—Dunn, Copeia, 1931: 163.

    Distribution: Low elevations on Pacific coast of Guatemala to Nicaragua; Caribbean coast of Honduras
      to Costa Rica.

REPTILIA: SERPENTES: ELAPIDAE

LEPTOMICRURUS Schmidt

1937 *Leptomicrurus* Schmidt, Zool. Ser. Field Mus. Nat. Hist., 20: 363. Type-species: *Elaps collaris* Schlegel.

Distribution: Tropical South America, east of Andes in Colombia, Ecuador, Peru and Bolivia; also Guianas, southern Venezuela and northern Brazil.

Content: Three species, according to most recent revision, by Hoge and Romano, Mem. Inst. Butantan, 32, 1965 (1966).

Key to the species	Clave de especies

1. Temporal formula 1 + 1; white nuchal collar crosses parietals (Fig. 1)------------------2
   Temporal formula 0 + 1; white nuchal collar entirely behind parietals------------*collaris*

1. Fórmula temporal 1 + 1; collar nucal blanco sobre las parietales (Fig. 1)----------------2
   Fórmula temporal 0 + 1; collar nucal blanco atrás de parietales-------------------*collaris*

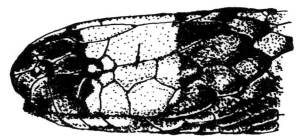

Fig. 1. *Leptomicrurus narduccii*, showing single anterior temporal and white nuchal collar.

2. Ventrals more than 231----------------*narduccii*
   Ventrals fewer than 225----------------*schmidti*

2. Ventrales más de 231------------------*narduccii*
   Ventrales menos de 225------------------*schmidti*

LEPTOMICRURUS COLLARIS (Schlegel)

1837 *Elaps collaris* Schlegel, Essai Physion. Serpens, 2: 448. Type-locality: unknown; designated as Guianas by Hoge and Romano, Mem. Inst. Butantan, 32, 1965 (1966), 4.
1854 *Elaps gastrodelus* Duméril, Bibron and Duméril, Erp. Gén., 7: 1212. Type-locality: unknown.
1937 *Leptomicrurus collaris*—Schmidt, Zool. Ser. Field Mus. Nat. Hist., 20: 261.
1966 *Leptomicrurus collaris*—Hoge and Romano, Mem. Inst. Butantan, 32 (1965): 4, figs. 3, 3a-c.

Distribution: Guyana; southeastern Venezuela.

LEPTOMICRURUS NARDUCCII (Jan)

1863 *Elaps Narduccii* Jan, Arch. Zool. Anat. Fis., 2: 222. Type-locality: Bolivia. There is some doubt about this type locality. Schmidt, Zool. Ser. Field Mus. Nat. Hist., 20, 1936, 190, cited it as "Ecuador". Peters, Bull. Mus. Comp. Zool., 122, 1960, 525, felt it was unknown. Klemmer, in Behringwerk-Mitteilungen, Die Giftschlangen der Erde, 1963, 299, gave it as "Bolivien und Peru". Roze, Amer. Mus. Novitates, 2287, 1967, 3, gives it as Bolivia. Jan, in the original description, said the type was in a shipment received in very fresh condition from Narducci, sent during his trip through Bolivia, and in the Icon. Gen., Ophid., Livr. 42, pl. 6, fig. 5, says Bolivia.
1870 *Elaps scutiventris* Cope, Proc. Amer. Phil. Soc., 11 (1869): 156. Type-locality: Pebas, Peru.
1881 *Elaps melanotus* Peters, Sitz. Ges. Naturforsch. Freunde Berlin, 1881: 51. Type-locality: Sarayacú, Ecuador.
1937 *Leptomicrurus narduccii*—Schmidt, Zool. Ser. Field Mus. Nat. Hist., 20: 363.
1966 *Leptomicrurus narduccii*—Hoge and Romano, Mem. Inst. Butantan, 32 (1965): 5, figs. 1, 1a-c.

Distribution: Amazonian slopes of Andes in southern Colombia, Ecuador, Peru and Bolivia; Estado do Acre, Brazil.

LEPTOMICRURUS SCHMIDTI Hoge and Romano

    1966 Leptomicrurus Schmidti Hoge and Romano, Mem. Inst. Butantan, 32 (1965): 1, figs. 2, 2a-c.
        Type-locality: Tapurucuara, M. Uaupés, Estado do Amazonas, Brazil.

    Distribution: Known only from type locality.

LEPTOPHIS Bell

1825 Leptophis Bell, Zool. Jour., 2: 328. Type-species: Coluber ahaetulla Linnaeus.
1825 Ahaetulla Gray, Ann. Phil., new ser., 10: 208. Type-species: Coluber ahaetulla Linnaeus.
1826 Dendrophis Boie, in Fitzinger, Neue Classification der Reptilien: 29. Type-species: Coluber ahaetulla Linnaeus.
1831 Ahoetula Gray (substitute name for Leptophis Bell), Synopsis Species Class Reptilia, in Griffith, Cuvier's Animal Kingdom, 9: 93.
1872 Diplotropis Günther, Ann. Mag. Nat. Hist., (4) 9: 24. Type-species: Diplotropis bilineata Günther.
1947 Thalerophis Oliver, Copeia, 1947: 64. Type-species: Coluber richardi Bory St. Vincent.

   Distribution: Mexico; Central America, South America west of Andes to Ecuador, east of Andes to central Argentina.

   Content: Seven species, including six recognized in most recent generic revision by Oliver, Bull. Amer. Mus. Nat. Hist., 92, 1948, and one other (cupreus) more recently revived. One species (diplotropis Günther) is extralimital.

   Comment: Romer, Osteology of the Reptiles, 1956, 579, includes Leptophina Bonaparte, 1831 as a generic synonym of Leptophis. Neave, Nomenclator Zoologicus, 2, 1939, 916, gives Leptophina Bonaparte, 1831, Sagg. An. Vert., p. 74, as a replacement name for Leptophis. There is no such name on p. 74, however, and Leptophis Bell is cited without comment on p. 80, both in Bonaparte.

Key to the species	Clave de especies
1. Loreal present--------------------------------2 Loreal absent----------------------------------3	1. Loreal presente------------------------------2 Loreal ausente--------------------------------3
2. Keels present only on paravertebral row and occasionally on adjacent rows; no keels on dorsal caudal scales-----------depressirostris Keels present on all dorsal scales except first row; keels on most dorsal caudal scales---mexicanus	2. Quillas presentes sólo en la fila paravertebral y ocasionalmente, en las adyacentes; escamas dorsocaudales no quilladas-----depressirostris Quillas presentes en todas las escamas dorsales excepto en la primera fila; la mayoría de las escamas dorsocaudales quilladas------mexicanus
3. Ventrals usually more than 149; adults lack dark oblique bands on body; no keels on first dorsal row----------------------------------4 Ventrals 133-149; adults with dark oblique bands on body; all dorsal scales keeled---riveti	3. Usualmente más de 149 ventrales; adultos sin bandas oscuras oblicuas en el cuerpo; primera fila dorsal no quillada---------------------4 Ventrales 133-149; adultos con bandas oscuras oblicuas sobre el cuerpo; todas las filas dorsales quilladas------------------------riveti
4. Dorsum usually uniform green or blue or with stripes; ventral color contrasts with dorsal color---5 Dorsum with strong coppery tint; venter also coppery, but slightly darker, with dark brown and white streaking-------------------cupreus	4. Usualmente, dorso en verde o azul, uniforme o lineado; coloración dorsal en contraste con la ventral----------------------------------5 Dorso pigmentado en tinte cobre fuerte; vientre semejante aunque ligeramente más oscuro, con lineado en pardo oscuro y blanco-------cupreus
5. Adult color pattern with broad greenish blue or blue dorsolateral stripe anteriorly on second and third or third and fourth rows; Central America---------------------------nebulosus Adult color pattern not as above, if greenish blue or dark blue stripe is present anteriorly, it covers more than rows three, four, and five; Central and South America, with striped forms only in latter----------------ahaetulla	5. Diseño de adultos con ancha banda dorsolateral anterior, sobre segunda y tercera o tercera y cuarta filas, en azul o azul verdoso; América Central----------------------------nebulosus Diseño de adultos no como el anterior, si hay banda azul verdosa o azul oscura anteriormente, ocupa más que la tercera, cuarta y quinta filas; América Central y del Sur; formas con diseño lineado sólo en la última-----ahaetulla

LEPTOPHIS AHAETULLA (Linnaeus)

1758 Coluber Ahaetulla Linnaeus, Systema Naturae, Ed. 10: 225. Type-locality: "Asia, America".
1825 Leptophis Ahaetulla—Bell, Zool. Jour., 2: 328.
1958 Leptophis ahaetulla—Int. Comm. Zool. Nomen., Op. 524: 270.

Distribution: Southern Mexico through Central America to northwestern Ecuador west of Andes and central Argentina east of Andes.

Content: Twelve subspecies.

Key to the subspecies

1. Adult pattern not of two dark dorsolateral
   stripes separated by light vertebral
   stripe----------------------------------2
   Adult color pattern consisting of a broad
   greenish blue or dark blue dorsolateral
   stripe anteriorly on rows three to seven,
   separated by light vertebral stripe on row
   eight---------------------------ahaetulla

2. Adult color pattern of predominantly uniform greenish blue occupying scales of all
   dorsal rows-----------------------------3
   Adult color pattern not as above, or, if
   predominantly uniform greenish blue, not
   occupying scales of all dorsal rows------8

3. Black postocular stripe present; dorsal
   body pattern without narrow, white,
   chevron-shaped bands--------------------4
   No black postocular stripe; dorsal body
   pattern with narrow, white, chevron-shaped
   transverse bands that may not be apparent
   until dorsal scales have been spread
   apart---------------------------praestans

4. Black postocular stripe narrow, occupying
   only lower edges of anterior temporal and
   lower posterior temporal; if black marks
   present on keels of dorsal scales, marks
   are narrow and well defined--------------5
   Black postocular stripe very broad,
   occupying all or nearly all of anterior
   temporal and lower posterior temporal;
   heavy, irregularly defined black marks on
   keels of scales on median dorsal rows-----
   -------------------------------chocoensis

5. Head plates margined with black and with
   numerous small black spots or with prominent large black spot on each parietal and
   supraocular----------------------------6
   Head plates rarely margined with black; if
   narrow black margin is present, head
   plates never marked with numerous small
   black spots or with prominent large black
   spot on each parietal and supraocular-----
   -----------------------------occidentalis

Clave de subespecies

1. Diseño de adultos sin dos bandas dorsolaterales oscuras separadas por una vertebral clara-----------------------------2
   Diseño de adultos con una ancha banda
   dorsolateral azul oscura o azul verdosa,
   anteriormente, en las filas tercera a
   séptima, separada por una banda clara
   vertebral, sobre la fila octava--ahaetulla

2. Diseño de adulto predominantemente uniforme
   en color azul verdoso sobre la totalidad
   de las filas dorsales--------------------3
   Diseño dorsal en adultos no como el anterior; si la coloración es uniforme en azul
   verdosa no ocupa la totalidad de las filas
   dorsales-------------------------------8

3. Banda negra postocular presente; diseño
   dorsal del cuerpo sin bandas angostas blancas paralelas en forma de V (cheurón)---- 4
   Banda negra postocular ausente; diseño dorsal del cuerpo con bandas angostas, blancas y paralelas en forma de V (cheurón);
   las bandas transversas pueden no ser aparentes hasta que las escamas dorsales
   hayan sido extendidas aparte-----praestans

4. Banda postocular angosta que ocupa sólo los
   bordes inferiores de las temporales anterior e ínferoposterior; si hay marcas negras sobre las quillas de las escamas
   dorsales, son angostas y bien definidas--5
   Banda postocular muy ancha, que ocupa toda
   o casi toda la temporal anterior así como
   la ínferoposterior; marcas negras sobre
   las quillas de escamas de la fila dorsal
   mediana irregulares y densas----chocoensis

5. Placas de la cabeza marginadas de negro,
   con pequeños y numerosos puntos negros o
   con una prominente mancha negra sobre cada
   parietal y supraocular------------------6
   Placas de la cabeza raramente marginadas de
   negro; si los márgenes negros están presentes, nunca ofrecen pequeños y numerosos
   puntos negros o prominentes manchas sobre
   parietales y supraoculares----occidentalis

6. Head plates and dorsal scales not marked as below, but with prominent large spot on each parietal and supraocular------------7
Head plates and dorsal scales with numerous small, irregularly shaped black spots, also present on extreme outer edge of ventrals anteriorly--------------bocourti

7. Dorsal scales without, or with only a narrow black margin, but with distinct narrow black line along keel of each dorsal scale; ventrals in males 156-169, in females 162-173--------------bolivianus
Dorsal scales with heavy prominent black margins, no black on keels; ventrals in males 147-165, in females 150-166---------
-------------------------nigromarginatus

8. Ventrals fewer than 172-------------------9
Ventrals more than 172--------------copei

9. Dorsal coloration of head and anterior body region persisting throughout length of body although sometimes reduced in distri-bution; north and central South America-10
Dorsal coloration of head and anterior body distinctly different from that of poster-ior half of body; southern South America--
---11

10.Dorsal coloration on body occupies pro-portionately same width throughout entire body length; ventral plates margined anteriorly and laterally with dark green-ish blue; maxillary teeth 24-28----ortoni
Dorsal coloration on body reduced in dis-tribution posteriorly; ventrals not mar-gined; maxillary teeth 21-23--------------
-------------------------coeruleodorsus

11.Plates on top of head heavily margined with black, postparietal scales five to eight, temporals frequently 1+1-------marginatus
Plates on top of head not or but slightly margined with black; postparietal scales seven to eleven, temporals typically 1+2--
----------------------------------liocercus

6. Placas de la cabeza y escamas dorsales sin manchas irregulares, pequeñas y negras; con mancha negra prominente sobre cada parietal y supraocular--------------------7
Placas de la cabeza y escamas dorsales con manchas irregulares, pequeñas y negras, también presentes sobre el borde exterior de las ventrales anteriores-------bocourti

7. Escamas dorsales con sólo un angosto margen negro o sin él; con una conspícua línea angosta negra, sobre las quillas de cada escama dorsal; ventrales en machos 156-169, en hembras 162-173--------------bolivianus
Escamas dorsales con densos y prominentes márgenes negros no hay negro sobre las quillas; ventrales en machos 147-165, en hembras 150-166------------nigromarginatus

8. Ventrales menos de 172---------------------9
Ventrales más de 172-----------------copei

9. Coloración de la cabeza y parte anterior del cuerpo que persiste a lo largo de todo el cuerpo, aunque a veces se reduce su distribución; Sur América norte y central-10
Coloración de la cabeza y parte anterior del cuerpo sustancialmente diferente de la mitad posterior del cuerpo; sur de Sur América----------------------------------11

10.Coloración dorsal del cuerpo ocupa pro-porcionalmente el mismo ancho a lo largo de todo el cuerpo; placas ventrales mar-ginadas anterior y lateralmente con azul grisáceo oscuro; dientes maxilares 24-28--
-------------------------------------ortoni
Coloración dorsal del cuerpo que reduce posteriormente su distribución; ventrales no marginadas; dientes maxilares 21-23----
-------------------------coeruleodorsus

11.Placas de la parte superior de la cabeza densamente marginadas en negro; cinco a ocho escamas postparietales, temporales frecuentemente 1+1-------------marginatus
Placas de la parte superior de la cabeza no marginadas o levemente marginadas de negro; siete a once escamas postparietales, temporales típicamente 1+2------liocercus

Leptophis ahaetulla ahaetulla (Linnaeus)

1823 Coluber Richardi Bory de Saint Vincent, Dictionnaire Classique d'Histoire Naturelle, Paris, 4: 588. Type-locality: Guiana.
1831 Ahoe.[tula] Linnei Gray (substitute name for Coluber ahaetulla Linnaeus), Synopsis Species Class Reptilia, in Griffith, Cuvier's Animal Kingdom, 9: 93.
1942 Leptophis ahaetulla ahaetulla—Oliver, Occ. Pap. Mus. Zool. Univ. Mich., 462: 1.
1948 Thalerophis richardi richardi—Oliver, Bull. Amer. Mus. Nat. Hist., 92: 219, fig. 4.

Distribution: British Guiana to Estado da Bahia, Brazil, along Atlantic coast.

Leptophis ahaetulla bocourti Boulenger

1898 Leptophis bocourti Boulenger, Proc. Zool. Soc. London, 1898: 116. Type-locality:
     Paramba and Cachabé, Ecuador.
1905 Leptophis occidentalis insularis Barbour, Bull. Mus. Comp. Zool., 46: 101. Type-locality:
     Isla de Gorgona, Colombia.
1948 Thalerophis richardi bocourti—Oliver, Bull. Amer. Mus. Nat. Hist., 92: 223, pl. 19.
1958 Leptophis ahaetulla [bocourti]—Int. Comm. Zool. Nomen., Op. 524: 270.

   Distribution: Northwestern Ecuador; Gorgona Island, Colombia.

Leptophis ahaetulla bolivianus Oliver

1942 Leptophis ahaetulla bolivianus Oliver, Occ. Pap. Mus. Zool. Univ. Mich., 462: 1. Type-
     locality: Buenavista, Departamento Santa Cruz, Bolivia.
1948 Thalerophis richardi bolivianus—Oliver, Bull. Amer. Mus. Nat. Hist., 92: 225, fig. 6
     and pl. 18, fig. 2.

   Distribution: Departamentos Beni and Santa Cruz, Bolivia.

Leptophis ahaetulla chocoensis Oliver

1942 Leptophis occidentalis chocoensis Oliver, Occ. Pap. Mus. Zool. Univ. Mich., 462: 15.
     Type-locality: Peña Lisa, Río Condoto, Chocó, Colombia.
1948 Thalerophis richardi chocoensis—Oliver, Bull. Amer. Mus. Nat. Hist., 92: 227.
1958 Leptophis ahaetulla [chocoensis]—Int. Comm. Zool. Nomen., Op. 524: 270.

   Distribution: Colombian Chocó.

Leptophis ahaetulla coeruleodorsus Oliver

1942 Leptophis coeruleodorsus Oliver, Occ. Pap. Mus. Zool. Univ. Mich., 462: 4. Type-locality:
     Trinidad.
1948 Thalerophis richardi coeruleodorsus—Oliver, Bull. Amer. Mus. Nat. Hist., 92: 228.
1958 Leptophis ahaetulla [coeruleodorsus]—Int. Comm. Zool. Nomen., Op. 524: 270.

   Distribution: Coast of northeastern Venezuela; Trinidad and Tobago Islands.

Leptophis ahaetulla copei Oliver

1942 Leptophis copei Oliver, Occ. Pap. Mus. Zool. Univ. Mich., 462: 7. Type-locality: Salto
     do Huá, Brazil - Venezuela boundary.
1948 Thalerophis richardi copei—Oliver, Bull. Amer. Mus. Nat. Hist., 92: 230.
1958 Leptophis ahaetulla [copei]—Int. Comm. Zool. Nomen., Op. 524: 270.

   Distribution: Area of divide between Río Orinoco and Río Negro in Venezuela, Brazil and
    Colombia.

Leptophis ahaetulla liocercus (Wied)

1824 Coluber liocercus Wied, Abbildungen zur Naturgeschichte von Brasilien: section 14, pl. 3
    [also numbered as pl. 58] and accompanying unnumbered page of text. Type-locality:
    Wied mentions material from Cabo Frio, Parahiba, Marica, Sagoarema, [lake?] Araruama,
    Ponta Negra, Lagoa Freia, and Espirito Santo, Brazil.
1901 Leptophis flagellum Andersson, Bihang Till K. Svenska Vet.-Akad. Handlingar, 27 (4, No.
    5): 13. Type-locality: Rio de Janeiro, Brazil.
1909 Leptophis vertebralis Werner, Mitt. Naturhist. Mus. Hamburg, 26: 221. Type-locality:
    Petropolis, Brazil.
1948 Thalerophis richardi liocercus—Oliver, Bull. Amer. Mus. Nat. Hist., 92: 232, fig. 4.
1958 Leptophis ahaetulla [liocercus]—Int. Comm. Zool. Nomen., Op. 524: 270.

   Distribution: Atlantic drainage of southeastern Brazil.

Leptophis ahaetulla marginatus (Cope)

1862 Thrasops marginatus Cope, Proc. Acad. Nat. Sci. Phila., 1862: 349. Type-locality:
 Paraguay.
1870 Herpetodryas affinis Steindachner, Sitz. Math.-Naturwiss. Cl. Akad. Wiss. Wien, 62: 348,
 pl. 7, figs. 4-5. Type-locality: Brazil.
1902 Leptophis rostralis Lönnberg, Ann. Mag. Nat. Hist., (7) 10: 458. Type-locality: San
 Miguel, Chaco, Argentina.
1903 Leptophis argentinus Werner, Abh. K. Bayer. Akad. Wiss. München, 22 (2): 384. Type-
 locality: Rosario, Argentina.
1948 Thalerophis richardi marginatus—Oliver, Bull. Amer. Mus. Nat. Hist., 92: 235, fig. 4
 and pl. 18, fig. 3.
1958 Leptophis ahaetulla [marginatus]—Int. Comm. Zool. Nomen., Op. 524: 270.

 Distribution: Southeastern Bolivia to western Estado de São Paulo, Brazil south to
 Paraguay and northern Argentina.

Leptophis ahaetulla nigromarginatus (Günther)

1866 Ahaetulla nigromarginata Günther, Ann. Mag. Nat. Hist., (3) 18: 28. Type-locality:
 "Upper Amazons".
1915 Leptophis nigromarginatus—Griffin, Mem. Carnegie Mus., 7 (3): 185.
1942 Leptophis ahaetulla nigromarginatus—Oliver, Occ. Pap. Mus. Zool. Univ. Mich., 462: 4.
1948 Thalerophis richardi nigromarginatus—Oliver, Bull. Amer. Mus. Nat. Hist., 92: 238, figs.
 4 and 6; pl. 18, fig. 1.

 Distribution: Western Brazil; Amazonian lowlands of Colombia, Ecuador, and Peru.

Leptophis ahaetulla occidentalis (Günther)

1859 Ahaetulla occidentalis Günther, Proc. Zool. Soc. London, 1859: 412. Type-locality:
 Guayaquil and western Ecuador.
1873 Ahaetulla urosticta Peters, Monats. Akad. Wiss. Berlin, 1873: 606. Type-locality:
 Bogotá, Colombia.
1894 Leptophis ultramarinus Cope, Proc. Acad. Nat. Sci. Phila., 1894: 203. Type-locality:
 Pazo Azul, Costa Rica.
1948 Thalerophis richardi occidentalis—Oliver, Bull. Amer. Mus. Nat. Hist., 92: 241.
1958 Leptophis ahaetulla [occidentalis]—Int. Comm. Zool. Nomen., Op. 524: 270.

 Distribution: Central America from Nicaragua on Caribbean coast and Costa Rica on Pacific
 coast to coast of western Venezuela and to Pacific Colombia and Ecuador. Not known from
 Chocó of Colombia.

Leptophis ahaetulla ortonii Cope

1876 Leptophis ortonii Cope, Jour. Acad. Nat. Sci. Phila., (2) 8 (1875): 177. Type-locality:
 Solimões or middle Amazon, Brazil.
1942 Leptophis ahaetulla ortoni—Oliver, Occ. Pap. Mus. Zool. Univ. Mich., 462: 4.
1948 Thalerophis richardi ortoni—Oliver, Bull. Amer. Mus. Nat. Hist., 92: 245.

 Distribution: Amazon Valley of southeastern Colombia, middle Amazon region of Brazil, and
 extreme northern Bolivia.

Leptophis ahaetulla praestans (Cope)

1869 Thrasops praestans Cope, Proc. Acad. Nat. Sci. Phila., 1868: 309. Type-locality: Near
 El Petén, Guatemala.
1881 Thrasops (Ahaetulla) sargii Fischer, Arch. für Naturg., 47 (1): 229, pl. 11, figs. 7-9.
 Type-locality: Cobán, Guatemala.
1930 Leptophis maximus Weller, Proc. Jr. Soc. Nat. Hist. Cincinnati, 1: 7. Type-locality:
 Unknown.
1948 Thalerophis richardi praestans—Oliver, Bull. Amer. Mus. Nat. Hist., 92: 248, fig. 5.
1958 Leptophis ahaetulla [praestans]—Int. Comm. Zool. Nomen., Op. 524: 270.

 Distribution: Low and moderate elevations from central Veracruz, Mexico, south on Caribbean
 slope into northern Honduras.

LEPTOPHIS CUPREUS (Cope)

    1868 Thrasops cupreus Cope, Proc. Acad. Nat. Sci. Phila., 1868: 106. Type-locality: From Napo and
         Marañón, Ecuador.
    1960 Leptophis cupreus—Peters and Orcés, Beitr. Neotrop. Fauna, 2: 139.

       Distribution: Amazonian lowlands of Ecuador.

LEPTOPHIS DEPRESSIROSTRIS (Cope)

    1861 P.[hilothamnus] depressirostris Cope, Proc. Acad. Nat. Sci. Phila., 1860: 557. Type-locality:
         Cocuyas de Veraguas, New Grenada; actually in Panama.
    1872 Diplotropis bilineata Günther, Ann. Mag. Nat. Hist., (4) 9: 24, pl. 6, fig. B. Type-locality:
         Costa Rica.
    1876 Leptophis aeruginosus Cope, Jour. Acad. Nat. Sci. Phila., (2) 8 (1875): 132. Type-locality:
         Costa Rica.
    1876 Leptophis saturatus Cope, Jour. Acad. Nat. Sci. Phila., (2) 8 (1875): 133. Type-locality:
         Sipurio, Costa Rica.
    1937 Leptophis depressirostris—Gaige, Hartweg, and Stuart, Occ. Pap. Mus. Zool. Univ. Mich., 357: 14.
    1948 Thalerophis depressirostris—Oliver, Bull. Amer. Mus. Nat. Hist., 92: 203, fig. 4.

       Distribution: Atlantic slopes of Nicaragua, Costa Rica and Panama; Pacific slopes of Colombia and
       Ecuador. A questionable record from Peru.

LEPTOPHIS MEXICANUS Duméril, Bibron and Duméril

    1854 Leptophis mexicanus Duméril, Bibron and Duméril, Erp. Gén., 7: 536. Type-locality: Mexico.

       Distribution: Southern Mexico from Veracruz and Oaxaca south to Costa Rica.

       Content: Two subspecies, one of which (yucatanensis Oliver) is extralimital.

    Leptophis mexicanus mexicanus Duméril, Bibron and Duméril

       1872 Ahaetulla modesta Günther, Ann. Mag. Nat. Hist., (4) 9: 26, pl. 6, fig. C. Type-locality:
            Río Chisoy (= Chixoy or Negro), below town of Cubulco, Baja Verapaz, Guatemala.
       1942 Leptophis mexicanus mexicanus—Oliver, Occ. Pap. Mus. Zool., Univ. Mich., 462: 10.
       1948 Thalerophis mexicanus mexicanus—Oliver, Bull. Amer. Mus. Nat. Hist., 92: 211, figs. 4
            and 7.

          Distribution: Low and moderate elevations from Tamaulipas, Mexico, into Costa Rica (except
          outer end of Yucatán Peninsula) on Caribbean slope and from Isthmus of Tehuantepec,
          Mexico, into Guatemala along Pacific slope.

LEPTOPHIS NEBULOSUS Oliver

    1942 Leptophis nebulosus Oliver, Occ. Pap. Mus. Zool. Univ. Mich., 462: 12. Type-locality:
         Cariblanca, Costa Rica.
    1948 Thalerophis nebulosus—Oliver, Bull. Amer. Mus. Nat. Hist., 92: 217, fig. 4.

       Distribution: Patuca, Honduras, to Cariblanco, Costa Rica.

LEPTOPHIS RIVETI Despax

    1910 Leptophis Riveti Despax, Bull. Mus. Hist. Nat. Paris, 1910: 368. Type-locality: Gualaquiza,
         Ecuador, 730 m.
    1914 Leptophis brevior Boulenger, Proc. Zool. Soc. London, 1914: 815. Type-locality: Near Peña Lisa,
         Condoto, Chocó, Colombia.
    1948 Thalerophis riveti—Oliver, Bull. Amer. Mus. Nat. Hist., 92: 250, figs. 4-5.

       Distribution: Higher altitudes to 5000 ft on both sides of Andes in Ecuador; Amazonian Peru;
       Western and north central Colombia; Panama. A single record from Trinidad.

REPTILIA: SERPENTES: LEPTOTYPHLOPIDAE ★ ★ ★ LEPTOTYPHLOPS

Prepared by Braulio Orejas-Miranda, Museo Nacional de Uruguay

LEPTOTYPHLOPS Fitzinger

1824 _Stenostoma_ Wagler (preoccupied by _Stenostoma_ Latreille, 1810), in Spix, Sp. Nov. Serp. Bras.: 68, pl. 25, fig. 3. Type-species: _Stenostoma albifrons_ Wagler.

1843 _Leptotyphlops_ Fitzinger, Systema Reptilium: 24. Type-species: _Typhlops nigricans_ Schlegel.

1843 _Eucephalus_ Fitzinger, Systema Reptilium: 24. Type-species: _Typhlops bilineatus_ Schlegel.

1844 _Catodon_ Duméril and Bibron (preoccupied by _Catodon_ Linnaeus, 1761), Erp. Gén., 6: 318. Type-species: _Typhlops septem-striatus_ Schneider.

1845 _Epictia_ Gray, Cat. Liz. Brit. Mus.: 139. Type-species: None designated.

1845 _Glauconia_ Gray, Cat. Liz. Brit. Mus.: 139. Type-species: _Typhlops nigricans_ Schlegel.

1853 _Rena_ Baird and Girard, Cat. N. Amer. Rept., 1: 142. Type-species: None indicated.

1857 _Sabrina_ Girard, Proc. Acad. Nat. Sci. Phila., 1857: 181. Type-species: _Typhlops tesselatum_ Tschudi.

1861 _Rhamphostoma_ Jan (preoccupied by _Rhamphostoma_ Wagler, 1830), Arch. Zool. Anat. Fis., 1: 190. Type-species: _Stenostoma macrorhynchum_ Jan.

1861 _Tricheilostoma_ Jan, Arch. Zool. Anat. Fis., 1: 190. Type-species: None indicated.

1861 _Tetracheilostoma_ Jan, Arch. Zool. Anat. Fis., 1: 191. Type-species: _Typhlops bilineatus_ Schlegel.

1863 _Ramphostoma_ Jan (emendation of _Rhamphostoma_ Jan), Elenco Sist. Ofidi: 16.

1881 _Siagonodon_ Peters, Sitz. Ges. Naturforsch. Freunde Berlin, 1881: 71. Type-species: _Typhlops septemstriatus_ Schneider.

1885 _Stenostomophis_ Rochebrune (substitute name for _Stenostoma_ Wagler), Faune de la Sénégambie, Rept.: 141.

Distribution: Southeastern Asia; Africa; southwestern United States; most of Central and South America.

Content: About 95 species, of which 31 are found within limits of this work.

Key to the species[1]

1. Supraoculars absent---------------------------2
   Supraoculars present------------------------6

2. Rostral lacks sharp horizontal cutting edge
      anteriorly---------------------------------3
   Rostral with sharp horizontal cutting edge
      anteriorly----------------------_borrichianus_

3. Ten or twelve rows of scales around central
      part of tail-------------------------------4
   Fourteen rows of scales around central part of
      tail-----------------------------_cupinensis_

4. Dorsum uniform, without lineate pattern-------5
   Dorsum with conspicuous lineate pattern, dark
      brown on light ground color-----_septemstriatus_

5. Prefrontal present; nasals normally developed,
      not elongated past line connecting posterior
      border of eyes-------------------_brasiliensis_
   Prefrontal absent; nasals elongated posteriorly,
      passing through line between posterior border
      of eyes--------------------------------_nasalis_

6. Supraoculars in contact with supralabials-----7
   Supraoculars not in contact with supralabials--
      ---10

7. Venter not uniform black; dorsal coloration
      reddish brown with longitudinal stripes of
      same width---------------------------------8
   Venter uniform deep black; dorsal coloration of
      red and black, with longitudinal stripes of
      unequal width------------------------------9

Clave de especies[1]

1. Sin supraoculares----------------------------2
   Con supraoculares---------------------------6

2. Rostral sin agudo filo cortante horizontal
      anterior-----------------------------------3
   Rostral con agudo filo cortante horizontal
      anterior-----------------------_borrichianus_

3. Filas de escamas en diez o doce series alre-
      dedor de la parte media de la cola----------4
   Filas de escamas en 14 series alrededor de la
      parte media de la cola------------_cupinensis_

4. Dorso sin diseño lineado conspícuo, de colora-
      ción uniforme------------------------------5
   Dorso con diseño lineado conspícuo, en pardo
      oscuro sobre fondo claro--------_septemstriatus_

5. Prefrontal presente; nasales de normal desarro-
      llo, que no se prolongan hacia atrás de una
      línea que pasara por el borde posterior de los
      ojos-----------------------------_brasiliensis_
   Prefrontal ausente; nasales prolongadas hacia
      atrás, que sobrepasan el nivel de una línea
      que pasara por el borde posterior de los
      ojos-----------------------------------_nasalis_

6. Supraoculares en contacto con supralabiales---7
   Supraoculares no en contacto con supralabiales-
      ---10

7. Vientre no negro uniforme; coloración dorsal en
      pardo rojizo con diseño en bandas longitudi-
      nales de semejante ancho--------------------8
   Vientre negro intenso uniforme; coloración
      dorsal en rojo y negro con diseño de bandas
      longitudinales de ancho desigual------------9

---

[1] _L. undecimstriatus_ is not included in this key.

[1] _L. undecimstriatus_ no se incluye en esta clave.

8. More than 250 total dorsals; very small size;
   total length/diameter greater than 55---------
   ------------------------------------tesselatus
   Fewer than 240 total dorsals; size medium to
   large; total length/diameter less than 49----
   ---------------------------------------tenella

9. Four reddish stripes dorsally, two wide white
   bands laterally-----------------------teaguei
   Five red stripes dorsally, no lateral white
   bands----------------------------rubrolineatus

10. Supraoculars large, larger than prefrontal and
    frontal--11
    Supraoculars small, smaller than prefrontal and
    frontal--21

11. Twelve rows of scales around central part of
    tail---12
    Ten rows of scales around central part of
    tail---14

12. Lacking dorsal striping; uniform coloration--13
    Longitudinal striping present------melanotermus

13. Dorsals more than 240; ventrals spotted along
    free edge----------------------------weyrauchi
    Dorsals fewer than 220; ventrals spotted at
    base--------------------------------albipuncta

14. Rostral normal, does not extend past line con-
    necting eyes; with prefrontal---------------15
    Rostral elongated dorsally, extends beyond line
    connecting eyes; prefrontal absent----goudotii

15. First supralabial low, never reaches level of
    center of eye; always separated from supra-
    ocular by at least twice its width----------16
    First supralabial high, reaches point as high
    as or higher than center of eye, approaches
    supraocular by distance equal to or less than
    its width--------------------------rufidorsus

16. More than 290 total dorsals------------------17
    Fewer than 280 total dorsals-----------------18

17. Fewer than 350 total dorsals------subcrotillus
    More than 370 total dorsals-----------melanurus

18. Lineate dorsal pattern----------------------19
    Uniform dorsal pattern------------------nicefori

19. Light and dark stripes of equal size, at least
    on the median dorsal area-------------------20
    Dorsum with wide dark bands separated by very
    inconspicuous, much narrower light lines that
    may or may not be absent laterally; never with
    light lines as wide as dark---------albifrons

20. Dorsum with seven dark and eight light stripes,
    all equal in width, at least on posterior half
    of body-------------------------------------30
    Dorsum with three dark and four light stripes,
    equal in width; laterally with two wider
    dorsal stripes which may or may not be divided
    by narrow light stripe, at least in posterior
    half of body-------------------------goudotii

8. Más de 250 dorsales totales; tamaño muy pequeño; relación longitud total diámetro mayor
   de 55------------------------------tesselatus
   Menos de 240 dorsales totales; tamaño medio o
   mayor; relación longitud total diámetro menor
   de 49-------------------------------tenella

9. Cuatro bandas rojizas sobre el dorso, dos
   anchas bandas blancas laterales--------teaguei
   Cinco bandas rojas sobre el dorso, sin bandas
   blancas laterales----------------rubrolineatus

10. Supraoculares grandes, mayores que la pre-
    frontal y frontal con que limitan----------11
    Supraoculares pequeñas, menores que la pre-
    frontal y frontal con que limitan----------21

11. Con doce escamas alrededor de la parte media de
    la cola-------------------------------------12
    Con diez escamas alrededor de la parte media de
    la cola-------------------------------------14

12. Sin diseño longitudinal; coloración dorsal
    uniforme------------------------------------13
    Diseño longitudinal presente-------melanotermus

13. Dorsales más de 240, escamas ventrales man-
    chadas en el borde libre-------------weyrauchi
    Dorsales menos de 220, escamas ventrales man-
    chadas en la base-------------------albipuncta

14. Rostral normal, que en su desarrollo dorsal no
    sobrepasa el nivel de una línea que pasara por
    detrás de los ojos; con prefrontal----------15
    Rostral prolongada, que en su desarrollo dorsal
    sobrepasa el nivel de una línea que pasara por
    detrás de los ojos; sin prefrontal----goudotii

15. Primera supralabial baja, nunca llega a la
    mitad del ojo; siempre distante de la supra-
    ocular por lo menos dos veces su ancho------16
    Primera supralabial alta, que llega por lo
    menos hasta la mitad del ojo o sobrepasa ese
    nivel; próxima a la supraocular una distancia
    igual o menor a la de su ancho------rufidorsus

16. Más de 290 dorsales totales------------------17
    Menos de 280 dorsales totales----------------18

17. Menos de 350 dorsales totales------subcrotillus
    Más de 370 dorsales totales----------melanurus

18. Dorso con diseño lineado--------------------19
    Dorso con pigmentación uniforme--------nicefori

19. Bandas oscuras y claras de igual ancho, por lo
    menos en el medio dorso---------------------20
    Diseño dorsal de bandas oscuras muy anchas,
    limitadas por poco conspícuas líneas claras
    mucho más angostas, que pueden o no estar pre-
    sentes lateralmente; nunca líneas claras de
    igual ancho a las oscuras-----------albifrons

20. Diseño dorsal de siete bandas oscuras y ocho
    claras todas de semejante ancho, a lo menos
    en la mitad posterior del cuerpo------------30
    Diseño dorsal de tres bandas oscuras y cuatro
    claras de semejante ancho; lateralmente dos
    bandas anchas oscuras divididas o no por
    angostas claras, a lo menos en la mitad
    posterior del cuerpo-----------------goudotii

21. With ten rows of scales around middle of tail---22
    With twelve rows of scales around middle of tail---------------------------------joshuai

22. Rostral lacks sharp cutting edge anteriorly--23
    Rostral with sharp cutting edge projecting forward------------------------unguirostris

23. With two supralabials, four scales plus rostral form border of upper lip on each side-------24
    With three supralabials, five scales plus rostral form border of upper lip on each side--25

24. Labial border of first supralabial equal to or smaller than labial border of ocular--dimidiatus
    Labial border of first supralabial much larger than labial border of ocular-----------affinis

25. Venter uniformly pigmented, without reticulate pattern---26
    Ventral scales densely pigmented centrally, lightly pigmented peripherally, making conspicuous reticulate pattern---------macrolepis

26. No longitudinal stripes----------------------27
    With longitudinal stripes, seven dark and eight light lines length of body------------dugandi

27. Dorsum uniform, violet-black or dark brown---28
    Dorsum uniform, light brown------------------29

28. Dorsum violet-black; total dorsals more than 170----------------------------------anthracinus
    Dorsum reddish-brown; total dorsals fewer than 170------------------------------brevissimus

29. Fewer than 200 total dorsals; interoccipital neither enlarged nor surrounded by smaller scales----------------------------------koppesi
    More than 200 total dorsals; interoccipital enlarged and surrounded by small scales--salgueiroi

30. More than 230 total dorsals; conspicuous black ring around posterior half of tail---australis
    Fewer than 230 total dorsals; no black rings on tail----------------------------------munoai

21. Con diez filas de escamas alrededor de la parte media de la cola----------------------------22
    Con doce filas de escamas alrededor de la parte media de la cola----------------------joshuai

22. Rostral sin borde cortante anterior proyectado hacia adelante-----------------------------23
    Rostral con borde cortante anterior proyectado hacia adelante-------------------unguirostris

23. Con dos supralabiales, cuatro escamas más la rostral formando el borde labial superior---24
    Con tres supralabiales, cinco escamas más la rostral formando el borde labial superior---25

24. Borde labial de primera supralabial subigual o menor que el de ocular--------------dimidiatus
    Borde labial de primera supralabial mucho mayor que el de ocular----------------------affinis

25. Vientre pigmentado uniformemente, sin diseño reticulado--------------------------------26
    Vientre con escamas pigmentadas densamente en sus centros y claras en la periferia, ofreciendo un conspícuo diseño reticulado--macrolepis

26. Sin diseño dorsal longitudinal----------------27
    Con diseño dorsal longitudinal; siete líneas oscuras y ocho claras a lo largo del dorso--------------------------------------dugandi

27. Dorso coloreado en negro violáceo o pardo oscuro uniforme----------------------------28
    Dorso coloreado en pardo claro uniforme------29

28. Dorso negro violáceo; dorsales totales más de 170------------------------------------anthracinus
    Dorso pardo rojizo; dorsales totales menos de 170------------------------------------brevissimus

29. Menos de 200 dorsales totales; interoccipital no agrandada ni rodeada de pequeñas escamas---------------------------------------koppesi
    Más de 200 dorsales totales; interoccipital agrandada rodeada de pequeñas escamas--------------------------------------salgueiroi

30. Más de 230 dorsales totales; anillo negro conspícuo en la mitad terminal de la cola-------------------------------------australis
    Menos de 230 dorsales totales; sin anillo negro en la mitad terminal caudal------------munoai

LEPTOTYPHLOPS AFFINIS (Boulenger)
    dulcis group

    1884 Stenostoma affine Boulenger, Ann. Mag. Nat. Hist., (5) 13: 396. Type-locality: Táchira, Venezuela.
    1929 Leptotyphlops affinis—Amaral, Mem. Inst. Butantan, 4: 138.

    Distribution: Known only from type locality.

LEPTOTYPHLOPS ALBIFRONS (Wagler)
    albifrons group

    1824 Stenostoma albifrons Wagler, in Spix, Sp. Nov. Serp. Bras.: 68, pl. 25, fig. 3. Type-locality: Vicinity of Belem, Pará, Brazil.
    1929 Leptotyphlops albifrons—Amaral, Mem. Inst. Butantan, 4: 76.

    Distribution: Known only from type locality and Rio Grande do Norte, Brazil.

LEPTOTYPHLOPS ALBIPUNCTA (Jan)
    melanotermus group

    1861 Stenostoma albifrons var. albipuncta Jan, Icon. Gén. Ophid., Livr. 2: pl. 5, fig. 1*. Type-locality: Tucumán, Argentina.

    Distribution: Known only from type specimen.

    Comment: Earlier authors have regarded this as synonymous with Leptotyphlops albifrons but reasons for its recognition here will be published elsewhere.

LEPTOTYPHLOPS ANTHRACINUS Bailey
    dulcis group

    1946 Leptotyphlops anthracinus Bailey, Occ. Pap. Mus. Zool. Univ. Mich., 492: 1. Type-locality: Baños, Provincia Pastaza, Ecuador.
    1967 Leptotyphlops anthracinus—Orejas-Miranda, Atas Simp. Biota Amaz., 5: 432.

    Distribution: Baños and Abituagua in eastern lowlands of Ecuador, and one record from Balzapamba, in western Ecuadorian lowlands.

LEPTOTYPHLOPS AUSTRALIS Freiberg and Orejas-Miranda
    albifrons group

    1968 Leptotyphlops australis Freiberg and Orejas-Miranda, Physis, Soc. Arg. Cien. Nat., 28: 145, figs. 1-2. Type-locality: Valcheta, Río Negro, Argentina.

    Distribution: Río Negro to Córdoba, Argentina.

LEPTOTYPHLOPS BORRICHIANUS (Degerbøl)
    septemstriatus group

    1923 Glauconia borrichiana Degerbøl, Vidensk. Medd. Naturhist. Foren. Kjöbenhavn, 76: 113. Type-locality: Santa Rosa, Mendoza, Argentina.
    1929 Leptotyphlops borrichiana—Amaral, Mem. Inst. Butantan, 4: 139.
    1951 Leptotyphlops borrichiana—Freiberg, Physis, Rev. Asoc. Arg. Cien. Nat., 20: 259, figs. 1-2.

    Distribution: Mendoza to Río Negro, western Argentina.

LEPTOTYPHLOPS BRASILIENSIS Laurent
    septemstriatus group

    1949 Leptotyphlops brasiliensis Laurent, Bull. Inst. Roy. Sci. Nat. Belgique, 25 (9): 4, figs. 7-9. Type-locality: Brazil.

    Distribution: Known from type specimen and another from Barrieras, Bahia, Brazil.

LEPTOTYPHLOPS BREVISSIMUS Shreve
    dulcis group

    1964 Leptotyphlops brevissima Shreve, Breviora, Mus. Comp. Zool., 211: 1. Type-locality: Florencia, Caquetá, Colombia.
    1967 Leptotyphlops brevissima—Orejas-Miranda, Atas Simp. Biota Amaz., 5: 433.

    Distribution: Known only from type locality.

LEPTOTYPHLOPS CUPINENSIS Bailey and Carvalho
    septemstriatus group

    1946 Leptotyphlops cupinensis Bailey and Carvalho, Bol. Mus. Nac. Brazil, Nova Ser., Zool., 52: 1, figs. 1-3. Type-locality: Rio Tapirapé (tributary of Rio Araguaia), Mato Grosso, Brazil.
    1966 Leptotyphlops cupinensis—Orejas-Miranda, Com. Zool. Mus. Hist. Nat. Montevideo, 9 (108): 1.

    Distribution: Known from type locality and Serra do Navio, Amapá, Brazil.

LEPTOTYPHLOPS DIMIDIATUS (Jan)
    dulcis group

1861 Stenostoma dimidiatum Jan, Arch. Zool. Anat. Fis., 1: 188. Type-locality: Brazil; herewith
    restricted to São Marcos, near confluence of Rios Uriracuera and Tacutu, both tributaries of
    Rio Branco, Territorio de Roraima, Brazil.
1929 Leptotyphlops dimidiata—Amaral, Mem. Inst. Butantan, 4: 76.
1967 Leptotyphlops dimidiatus—Orejas-Miranda, Atas Simp. Biota Amaz., 5: 433.

    Distribution: Guianas, northern Brazil and southeastern Venezuela.

LEPTOTYPHLOPS DUGANDI Dunn
    dulcis group

    1944 Leptotyphlops dugandi Dunn, Caldasia, 3 (11): 52. Type-locality: Juanamina, 20 m, about 11 km
        SW of Barranquilla, Departamento Atlántico, Colombia.

    Distribution: Known only from type locality.

LEPTOTYPHLOPS GOUDOTII (Duméril and Bibron)
    albifrons group

    1844 Stenostoma Goudotii Duméril and Bibron, Erp. Gén., 6: 330. Type-locality: Valley of Río
        Magdalena, Colombia.
    1857 Stenostoma fallax Peters, Monats. Akad. Wiss. Berlin, 1857: 402. Type-locality: La Guaira,
        Venezuela.
    1929 Leptotyphlops goudotii—Amaral, Mem. Inst. Butantan, 4: 139.

    Distribution: Colima on Pacific coast and Tehuantepec on Atlantic coast of Mexico throughout
        Central America; Caribbean Colombia and Venezuela; many offshore islands.

    Content: Five subspecies, one of which (bakewelli Oliver) is extralimital.

Key to the subspecies

1. Rostral normal, does not extend dorsally
   beyond line connecting eyes; prefrontal
   present--------------------------------2
   Rostral elongated dorsally, extending
   beyond line drawn between eyes; prefrontal
   absent-------------------------------ater

2. Light caudal spot about equal in size dorsally and ventrally---------------------3
   Light caudal spot at least twice as large
   ventrally than dorsally-----------phenops

3. With strongly contrasting pattern; dorsal
   spot on head usually very conspicuous and
   large; total length/diameter 43-58; total
   dorsal scales 233-253-------magnamaculatus
   Weakly contrasting dorsal pattern; dorsal
   spot on head, if present, usually inconspicuous and small; total length/diameter
   56-66; total dorsals 217-248 (less than
   230 in Panama)--------------------goudotii

Clave de subespecies

1. Rostral normal, que en su desarrollo dorsal
   no sobrepasa el nivel de una línea que
   pasara por detrás de los ojos; prefrontal
   presente--------------------------------2
   Rostral prolongada, que en su desarrollo
   dorsal sobrepasa el nivel de una línea que
   pasara por detrás de los ojos; sin pre-
   frontal------------------------------ater

2. Mancha clara caudal de semejante superficie
   dorso y ventralmente--------------------3
   Mancha clara caudal por lo menos dos veces
   mayor ventral que dorsalmente------phenops

3. Diseño de vívido contraste, mancha dorso
   cefálica generalmente muy conspícua y
   grande; relación longitud total diámetro
   43-58; dorsales totales 233-253----------
   --------------------------magnamaculatus
   Diseño de poco contraste; mancha dorso
   cefálica, si existe, generalmente poco
   conspícua y pequeña; relación longitud total diámetro 56-66; dorsales totales 217-
   248 (menos de 230 en Panamá)------goudotii

Leptotyphlops goudotii goudotii (Duméril and Bibron), new combination

    1952 Leptotyphlops albifrons margaritae Roze, Mem. Soc. Cien. Nat. La Salle, Venezuela, 12:
        154, figs. 6-7. Type-locality: San Francisco de Macanao, Isla Margarita, Venezuela.

    Distribution: Panama and Colombia to Caribbean coast of Venezuela; Trinidad, Bonaire and
        Margarita Islands.

Leptotyphlops goudotii ater Taylor, new combination

   1940 Leptotyphlops ater Taylor, Univ. Kansas Sci. Bull., 26: 536, text-fig. 4. Type-locality:
        Managua, Nicaragua.
   1955 Leptotyphlops ater—Taylor, Univ. Kansas Sci. Bull., 37: 562.

     Distribution: Nicaragua and Costa Rica; possibly Honduras and southern El Salvador.

Leptotyphlops goudotii magnamaculatus Taylor, new combination

   1940 Leptotyphlops magnamaculata Taylor, Univ. Kansas Sci. Bull., 26: 532, text-fig. 1. Type-
        locality: Isla Utilla, Islas de la Bahía, Honduras.

     Distribution: Bay islands of Honduras; San Andrés and Providence Islands.

Leptotyphlops goudotii phenops (Cope), new combination

   1876 Stenostoma phenops Cope, Jour. Acad. Nat. Sci. Phila., (2) 8 (1875): 128. Type-locality:
        Tehuantepec, Mexico and Cobán, Guatemala.
   1939 Leptotyphlops phenops—Smith, Zool. Ser. Field Mus. Nat. Hist., 24: 28.

     Distribution: Tehuantepec and Yucatán, Mexico to Guatemala, Honduras, Nicaragua, and El
        Salvador; Suma Islands.

LEPTOTYPHLOPS JOSHUAI Dunn
        dulcis group

   1944 Leptotyphlops joshuai Dunn, Caldasia, 3 (11): 53, figs. 9-10. Type-locality: Jericó, Antioquia,
        Colombia, 1967 m.

     Distribution: Central and western Andes, in Provincias Antioquia and Caldas, Colombia.

LEPTOTYPHLOPS KOPPESI Amaral
        dulcis group

   1955 Leptotyphlops koppesi Amaral, Mem. Inst. Butantan, 26 (1954): 203, figs. 4-6. Type-locality:
        Terenos, Mato Grosso, Brazil.

     Distribution: Known only from type locality.

LEPTOTYPHLOPS MACROLEPIS (Peters)
        dulcis group

   1857 Stenostoma macrolepis Peters, Monats. Akad. Wiss. Berlin, 1857: 402. Type-locality: Caracas and
        Puerto Cabello, Venezuela; restricted to Puerto Cabello, Venezuela, by Orejas-Miranda, Atas
        Simp. Biota Amaz., 5, 1967, 430.
   1922 Leptotyphlops macrolepis—Ruthven, Misc. Publ. Mus. Zool. Univ. Mich., 8: 64.
   1933 Leptotyphlops ihlei Brongersma, Zool. Meded., 15: 175, figs. 1-2. Type-locality: Toegoemoetoe,
        Surinam.
   1967 Leptotyphlops macrolepis—Orejas-Miranda, Atas Simp. Biota Amaz., 5: 430.

     Distribution: Panama to Colombia, Venezuela, Guianas and northern Brazil.

LEPTOTYPHLOPS MELANOTERMUS (Cope)
    melanotermus group

1862 Stenostoma melanoterma Cope, Proc. Acad. Nat. Sci. Phila., 1862: 350. Type-locality: Corrientes,
    Argentina.
1876 Stenostoma flavifrons Weyenbergh, in Napp, Die Argentinische Republik, Buenos Aires: 164. Type-
    locality: Argentina.
1893 Stenostoma melanostoma—Günther (in error for melanoterma Cope), Biol. Cent. Amer., Rept.: 85.
1893 Stenostoma melanosterna—Boulenger (in error for melanoterma Cope), Cat. Sn. Brit. Mus., 1: 63.
1945 Leptotyphlops striatula Smith and Laufe, Proc. Biol. Soc. Washington, 58: 29, figs. A and B, and
    pl. 5, figs. A and B. Type-locality: "Yamachi" = Yanacachi, Sur de Yungas, Bolivia.
1964 L.[eptotyphlops] melanotermus—Orejas-Miranda, Com. Zool. Mus. Hist. Nat. Montevideo, 8 (103): 4.

    Distribution: Extreme southern Peru, through Bolivia and northern Argentina to Santa Fé; possibly
    western and southern Paraguay and southwestern Brazil.

LEPTOTYPHLOPS MELANURUS Schmidt and Walker
    albifrons group

1943 Leptotyphlops melanurus Schmidt and Walker, Zool. Ser. Field Mus. Nat. Hist., 24: 303. Type-
    locality: Chiclín, Libertad, Peru.

    Distribution: Known only from type-locality.

LEPTOTYPHLOPS MUNOAI Orejas-Miranda
    albifrons group

1961 Leptotyphlops muñoai Orejas-Miranda, Act. Biol. Venezuelica, 3: 85, figs. la-c. Type-locality:
    Pozo Hondo, Tambores, Departamento de Tacuarembó, Uruguay.

    Distribution: Northern Argentina, Uruguay and Rio Grande do Sul, Brazil.

LEPTOTYPHLOPS NASALIS Taylor
    septemstriatus group

1940 Leptotyphlops nasalis Taylor, Univ. Kansas Sci. Bull., 26: 535, text-fig. 3. Type-locality:
    Managua, Nicaragua.

    Distribution: Known only from type locality.

    Comment: Dunn and Saxe, Proc. Acad. Nat. Sci. Phila., 102, 1950, 161, considered this a synonym
    of Leptotyphlops ater, but this is rejected here.

LEPTOTYPHLOPS NICEFORI Dunn
    albifrons group

1946 Leptotyphlops nicefori Dunn, Caldasia, 4 (17): 121. Type-locality: Mogotes, Santander, Colombia,
    1746 m.

    Distribution: Known only from type locality.

LEPTOTYPHLOPS RUBROLINEATUS (Werner)
    tesselatus group

1901 Glauconia albifrons rubrolineata Werner, Abh. Ber. Zool. Anthro.-Ethno. Mus. Dresden, 9 (2): 6.
    Type-locality: Lima, Peru.

    Distribution: Known only from type locality.

    Comment: This species has been considered a synonym of Leptotyphlops albifrons
    by previous authors, but is restored here, reasons to be amplified elsewhere.

LEPTOTYPHLOPS RUFIDORSUS Taylor
      albifrons group

   1940 Leptotyphlops rufidorsum Taylor, Univ. Kansas Sci. Bull., 26: 533, text-fig. 2. Type-locality:
        Lima, Peru.
   1943 Leptotyphlops rufidorsus—Schmidt and Walker, Zool. Ser. Field Mus. Nat. Hist., 24: 302.

      Distribution: Known only from type locality and Chiclín, Libertad, Peru.

LEPTOTYPHLOPS SALGUEIROI Amaral
      dulcis group

   1955 Leptotyphlops salgueiroi Amaral, Mem. Inst. Butantan, 26 (1954): 203, figs. 1-3. Type-locality:
        Itá, Espirito Santo, Brazil

      Distribution: Known only from type locality.

LEPTOTYPHLOPS SEPTEMSTRIATUS (Schneider)
      septemstriatus group

   1801 [Typhlops] Septemstriatus Schneider, Hist. Amphib., 2: 341. Type-locality: Unknown.
   1925 Leptotyphlops septemstriatus—Mertens, Senckenbergiana, 7: 78.
   ?1934 Leptotyphlos tatacuá, Briceño-Rossi, Bol. Min. Salub. Agri. Cría, Venezuela, 1: 1133. Type-
        locality: Río de Oro, Distrito Colón, Estado Zulia, Venezuela.
   1967 Leptotyphlops septemstriatus—Orejas-Miranda, Atas Simp. Biota Amaz., 5: 426.

      Distribution: Northern Brazil, Guiana and southeastern Venezuela.

LEPTOTYPHLOPS SUBCROTILLUS Klauber
      albifrons group

   1939 Leptotyphlops subcrotilla Klauber, Trans. San Diego Soc. Nat. Hist., 9: 61, figs. 2a-b. Type-
        locality: Grau Tombes, northern Peru; in error, according to Schmidt and Walker, Zool. Ser.
        Field Mus. Nat. Hist., 24, 1943, 303, who correct it to Grau, Tumbez, Peru.
   1943 Leptotyphlops subcrotillus—Schmidt and Walker, Zool. Ser. Field Mus. Nat. Hist., 24: 303.

      Distribution: Chiclín, Libertad, Peru to Pacific lowlands of southwestern Ecuador.

LEPTOTYPHLOPS TEAGUEI Orejas-Miranda
      tesselatus group

   1964 Leptotyphlops teaguei Orejas-Miranda, Com. Zool. Mus. Hist. Nat. Montevideo, 8 (103): 4, pls. 2-3.
        Type-locality: Río Chotano, between Chota and Cutervo, northern Peru, 2350 m.

      Distribution: Known only from type locality.

LEPTOTYPHLOPS TENELLA Klauber
      tesselatus group

   1939 Leptotyphlops tenella Klauber, Trans. San Diego Soc. Nat. Hist., 9: 59, figs. 1a-1b. Type-
        locality: Kartabo, Guyana.
   1967 Leptotyphlops tenella—Orejas-Miranda, Atas Simp. Biota Amaz., 5: 435.

      Distribution: Guianas, Trinidad, southeastern Venezuela, Amazonian Brazil; possibly Ecuador and
        Peru.

LEPTOTYPHLOPS TESSELATUS (Tschudi)
      tesselatus group

   1845 Typhlops (Stenostoma) tesselatum Tschudi, Arch. für Naturg., 11: 162. Type-locality: Peru; more
        precisely stated as Lima, Peru, by Tschudi, Fauna Peruana, Herp., 1846, 46.
   1943 Leptotyphlops tessellatus—Schmidt and Walker, Zool. Ser. Field Mus. Nat. Hist., 24: 304.

      Distribution: Known only from vicinity of Lima, Peru.

LEPTOTYPHLOPS UNDECIMSTRIATUS (Schlegel)
      melanotermus group

   1839 Typhlops undecimstriatus Schlegel, Abbildungen Amphibien, text: 36. Type-locality: Santa Cruz,
         Bolivia (= Santa Cruz de la Sierra).

      Distribution: Known only from type locality.

LEPTOTYPHLOPS UNGUIROSTRIS (Boulenger)
      dulcis group

   1902 Glauconia unguirostris Boulenger, Ann. Mag. Nat. Hist., (7) 9: 338. Type-locality: Cruz del
         Eje, Córdoba, Argentina.
   1921 Leptotyphlops unguirostris—Serié, An. Soc. Cien. Argentina, 92: 148.

      Distribution: San Juan to Santiago del Estero, Argentina; southern Paraguay.

LEPTOTYPHLOPS WEYRAUCHI Orejas-Miranda
      melanotermus group

   1964 Leptotyphlops weyrauchi Orejas-Miranda, Com. Zool. Mus. Hist. Nat. Montevideo, 8 (103): 1, pl. 1.
         Type-locality: Ciudad de Tucumán, Provincia de Tucumán, Argentina.

      Distribution: Provincias Tucumán, Santiago del Estero, Chaco, and Córdoba, Argentina.

LEPTOTYPHLOPS AMAZONICUS Orejas-Miranda[1]
      albifrons group

   1969 Leptotyphlops amazonicus Orejas-Miranda, Comun. Zool. Mus. Hist. Nat. Montevideo, 10 (124): 1,
         fig. 1. Type-locality: Esmeralda, Territorio Federal Amazonas, Venezuela.

      Distribution: Estado Bolívar to Territorio Federal Amazonas, Venezuela; possibly in Amazonian
         lowlands of Ecuador.

LEPTOTYPHLOPS DIAPLOCIUS Orejas-Miranda[1]
      albifrons group

   1969 Leptotyphlops diaplocius Orejas-Miranda, Comun. Zool. Mus. Hist. Nat. Montevideo, 10 (124): 5,
         fig. 2. Type-locality: Requena, Montecarmelo, Peru.

      Distribution: Lower parts of valleys of Ríos Ucayali and Huallaga, northeastern Peru.

LEPTOTYPHLOPS PERUVIANUS Orejas-Miranda[1]
      albifrons group

   1969 Leptotyphlops peruvianus Orejas-Miranda, Comun. Zool. Mus. Hist. Nat. Montevideo, 10(124): 9,
         pl. 2, fig. 1. Type-locality: Chanchamayo, Departamento Junín, Peru.

      Distribution: Known only from type locality.

[1]The descriptions of these new species were received too late to permit including them in the key,
putting them in proper alphabetical order, or inserting them in the index.

LIOHETEROPHIS Amaral

    1935 <u>Lioheterophis</u> Amaral, Mem. Inst. Butantan, 8 (1934): 187. Type-species: <u>Lioheterophis iheringi</u> Amaral.

    Distribution: As for only known species.

    Content: One species.

LIOHETEROPHIS IHERINGI Amaral

    1935 <u>Lioheterophis iheringi</u> Amaral, Mem. Inst. Butantan, 8 (1934): 187. Type-locality: Campina Grande, Estado da Parahyba, Brazil.

    Distribution: Still known only from type specimen.

REPTILIA: SERPENTES: COLUBRIDAE

LIOPHIS Wagler

1830 *Liophis* Wagler, Nat. Syst. Amphib.: 187. Type-species: *Coluber cobella* Linnaeus.
1843 *Opheomorphus* Fitzinger, Systema Reptilium: 25. Type-species: *Coluber miliaris* Linnaeus.
1862 *Ophiomorphus* Cope (emendation of *Opheomorphus* Fitzinger), Proc. Acad. Nat. Sci. Phila., 1862: 75.
1895 *Taeniophallus* Cope, Trans. Amer. Phil. Soc., 18: 201. Type-species: *Taeniophallus nicagus* Cope.

Distribution: South America.

Content: Twenty-five species.

Key to the species	Clave de especies

1. With 15 scale rows at midbody------------------2
   More than 15 scale rows at midbody------------3

2. Fewer than 150 ventrals----------------------22
   More than 152 ventrals--------------occipitalis

3. With 19 scale rows at midbody-----------------4
   With 17 scale rows at midbody-----------------7

4. Single preocular-----------------------------5
   Two preoculars--------------------------festae

5. Fewer than 168 ventrals----------------------6
   Ventrals more than 170-----------------obtusus

6. Dorsum uniform green (occasionally reddish
   dorsal stripe)------------------------jaegeri
   Dorsal pattern profusely spotted and streaked--
   -------------------------------------anomalus

7. Loreal absent--------------------------------8
   Loreal present-------------------------------9

8. Anal single---------------------------frenata
   Anal divided---------------------------amarali

9. Preocular single----------------------------10
   Two preoculars--------------------subocularis

10. Eight supralabials--------------------------11
    Six or seven supralabials-------------------20

11. Caudals fewer than 100; ventrals more than 130-
    ---12
    Caudals more than 100; ventrals fewer than 130-
    -------------------------------------albiceps

12. Two supralabials entering orbit-------------13
    Three supralabials entering orbit-----undulatus

13. Ventrals more than 189----------------------14
    Ventrals fewer than 189----------------------15

14. Dorsal pattern with three longitudinal stripes-
    --------------------------------------joberti
    Dorsal pattern with cross bands anteriorly,
    posteriorly uniformly black------------brazili

15. Dorsal pattern other than salt and pepper (dark
    scales with lighter base)-------------------16
    Salt and pepper dorsal pattern (dark scales
    with lighter base)--------------------miliaris

16. Lacking laterocaudal black stripe-----------17
    With laterocaudal black stripe-------purpurans

1. Con 15 filas de escamas al medio del cuerpo---2
   Más de 15 filas al medio del cuerpo-----------3

2. Menos de 150 ventrales---------------------22
   Más de 152 ventrales---------------occipitalis

3. Con 19 filas de escamas al medio del cuerpo---4
   Con 17 filas de escamas al medio del cuerpo---7

4. Una preocular-------------------------------5
   Dos preoculares-------------------------festae

5. Menos de 168 ventrales----------------------6
   Más de 170 ventrales-------------------obtusus

6. Dorso verde uniforme (ocasionalmente una banda
   dorsal rojiza)------------------------jaegeri
   Dorso profusamente diseñado, con manchas y
   líneas-------------------------------anomalus

7. Loreal ausente------------------------------8
   Loreal presente------------------------------9

8. Anal entera---------------------------frenata
   Anal dividida--------------------------amarali

9. Una preocular------------------------------10
   Dos preoculares-------------------subocularis

10. Ocho supralabiales--------------------------11
    Seis o siete supralabiales------------------20

11. Menos de 100 caudales; más de 130 ventrales--12
    Más de 100 caudales; menos de 130 ventrales----
    -------------------------------------albiceps

12. Dos supralabiales entran en la órbita--------13
    Tres supralabiales entran en la órbita---------
    -------------------------------------undulatus

13. Más de 189 ventrales-----------------------14
    Menos de 189 ventrales-----------------------15

14. Diseño dorsal con tres líneas longitudinales---
    --------------------------------------joberti
    Diseño dorsal con bandas transversas; poster-
    iormente uniformemente negra----------brazili

15. Diseño dorsal no en sal y pimienta (escamas
    oscuras con la base clara)------------------16
    Diseño dorsal uniforme en sal y pimienta
    (escamas oscuras con la base clara)---miliaris

16. Sin cinta laterocaudal negra----------------17
    Con cinta laterocaudal negra---------purpurans

17. Ventrals more than 170----------------------18
    Ventrals fewer than 170----------------------19

18. Dorsal pattern reticulate (occasionally uni-
      form black)-----------------------------ingeri
    Uniform olive grayish or with dark and light
    crossbands------------------------------trebbaui

19. Uniform green, with or without brick-red
      vertebral stripe-----------------------jaegeri
    Other than uniform green, with or without
    brick-red vertebral stripe------------cobella

20. Preocular not higher than eye----------------21
    Preocular higher than eye--------------canaima

21. Dorsal pattern other than three longitudinal
      stripes---------------------------------------23
    Dorsal pattern of three longitudinal stripes---
    ---------------------------------------poecilopogon

22. Reddish brown above, with blackish cross bands-
    -----------------------------------melanauchen
    Gray above, anterior part of body with broad
    dark vertebral band and narrower lateral band-
    -----------------------------------steinbachi

23. Ventrals fewer than 170---------------------24
    Ventrals more than 170------------longiventris

24. With crossbands------------------------------25
    Lacking crossbands---------------insignissimus

25. More than 150 ventrals----------------breviceps
    Fewer than 150 ventrals------------leucogaster

17. Ventrales más de 170------------------------18
    Ventrales menos de 170----------------------19

18. Diseño dorsal reticulado (a veces uniforme-
      mente negro)-----------------------------ingeri
    Coloración gris-oliva uniforme o con bandas
    transversales claro-oscuras-----------trebbaui

19. Coloración verde uniforme con o sin una banda
      vertebral rojo ladrillo----------------jaegeri
    Coloración no verde uniforme con o sin una
    banda vertebral rojo ladrillo----------cobella

20. Preocular no mas alta que el ojo------------21
    Preocular más alta que el ojo----------canaima

21. Diseño dorsal sin tres líneas longitudinales-23
    Diseño dorsal con tres líneas longitudinales---
    ---------------------------------------poecilopogon

22. Dorso pardo rojizo con bandas transversales
      negruzcas-----------------------------melanauchen
    Dorso gris, parte anterior del cuerpo con
    banda vertebral oscura y bandas laterales
    más angostas-----------------------steinbachi

23. Ventrales menos de 170---------------------24
    Ventrales más de 170-------------longiventris

24. Con bandas transversas--------------------25
    Sin bandas transversas-----------insignissimus

25. Más de 150 ventrales------------------breviceps
    Menos de 150 ventrales-------------leucogaster

LIOPHIS ALBICEPS (Amaral)

1924 Rhadinaea albiceps Amaral, Jour. Washington Acad. Sci., 14: 200. Type-locality: "Probably from
     Ecuador".
1929.Liophis albiceps—Amaral, Mem. Inst. Butantan, 4: 170.

   Distribution: Known only from type specimen.

LIOPHIS AMARALI Wettstein

1930 Liophis amarali Wettstein, Zool. Anz., 88: 93. Type-locality: Bello Horizonte, Minas Gerais,
     Brazil.

   Distribution: Bahia, Minas Gerais, Paraná and Santa Catarina, Brazil.

LIOPHIS ANOMALUS (Günther)

1858 Coronella anomala Günther, Cat. Sn. Brit. Mus.: 37. Type-locality: "Banks of the Parana"
     (=Río Paraná?, country unknown).
1862 Lygophis rutilus Cope, Proc. Acad. Nat. Sci. Phila., 1862: 80. Type-locality: Río Tigre and
     Río Paraná, Paraguay.
1863 C.[oronella] pulchella Jan, Arch. Zool. Anat. Fis., 2: 251. Type-locality: Buenos Aires,
     Argentina.
1895 Rhadinaea elegantissima Koslowsky, Rev. Mus. La Plata, 7: 155, pl. 1. Type-locality:
     Sierra de la Ventana, Provincia de Buenos Aires, Argentina.
1925 Liophis anomala—Amaral, Proc. U. S. Nat. Mus., 67 (24): 7.

   Distribution: Southern Brazil, Northern Argentina, Uruguay and Paraguay.

   Comment: Cranwell, Rev. Argentina Zoogeog., 2, 1942, 143, suggested that elegantissima Koslowsky
      is recognizable, but did not revalidate it. Specimens in the Instituto Malbran, Buenos Aires,
      Argentina, support this suggestion.

LIOPHIS BRAZILI (Amaral)

1923 Rhadinaea brazili Amaral, Proc. New England Zool. Club, 7: 87. Type-locality: Julio Pontes,
     São Paulo, Brazil.
1926 Liophis brazili—Amaral, Arch. Mus. Nacional Brazil, 26: 9, pl. 1, figs. 4-6.

   Distribution: Mato Grosso and São Paulo, Brazil.

LIOPHIS BREVICEPS Cope

1861 Liophis breviceps Cope, Proc. Acad. Nat. Sci. Phila., 1860: 252. Type-locality: Surinam.

   Distribution: Surinam, northwestern Brazil and Ecuador.

LIOPHIS CANAIMA Roze

1957 Liophis canaima Roze, Bol. Mus. Cien. Nat. Venezuela, 1 (1955): 188, fig. Type-locality:
     Ugueto, Territorio Federal Amazonas, Venezuela.

   Distribution: Known only from type-locality.

LIOPHIS COBELLA (Linnaeus)

1758 Coluber Cobella Linnaeus, Systema Naturae, Ed. 10: 218. Type-locality: America.
1803 Coluber serpentinus Daudin, Hist. Nat. Rept., 7: 87. Type-locality: none given.
1803 Coluber cenchrus Daudin, Hist. Nat. Rept., 7: 139. Type-locality: Asia.
1863 Liophis taeniogaster Jan, Arch. Zool. Anat. Fis., 2: 292. Type-locality: Brazil and South
     America.
1866 Liophis cobella var. flaviventris Jan, Icon. Gén. Ophid., livr. 16: pl. 5, fig. 2.
     Type-locality: South America.
1894 Rhadinaea cobella—Boulenger, Cat. Sn. Brit. Mus., 2: 166.
1925 Liophis cobella—Amaral, Proc. U. S. Nat. Mus., 67 (24): 7.

   Distribution: Northern South America east of Andes.

LIOPHIS FESTAE (Peracca)

1897 Rhadinaea festae Peracca, Bol. Mus. Zool. Anat. Comp. Torino, 12 (300): 16. Type-locality:
     Valley of Río Santiago, Ecuador.
1929 Liophis festae—Amaral, Mem. Inst. Butantan, 4: 171.

   Distribution: Known only from type locality.

LIOPHIS FRENATA (Werner)

1909 Rhadinaea frenata Werner, Mitt. Naturhist. Mus. Hamburg, 26: 224. Type-locality: Paraguay.

   Distribution: Paraguay.

   Comment: Amaral, Mem. Inst. Butantan, 4, 1929, 23, suggested that this taxon is probably identical
     with Liophis brazili Amaral, 1925, but he has continued to use the latter name. He did not use
     frenata for the taxon in his list of Neotropical Ophidia (l.c., 171), although he put it in the
     genus Liophis and also in the synonymy of brazili, with a question mark.

LIOPHIS INGERI Roze

1958 Liophis ingeri Roze, Acta Biol. Venezuélica, 2 (25): 303. Type-locality: Chimantá Tepui, Estado
     Bolivar, Venezuela, 1900 m.

   Distribution: Known only from type locality.

LIOPHIS

LIOPHIS JAEGERI (Günther)

1858 Coronella jaegeri Günther, Cat. Sn. Brit. Mus.: 37. Type-locality: Brazil.
1863 Liophis (Ophiomorphus) dorsalis Peters, Monats. Akad. Wiss. Berlin, 1863: 283. Type-locality: Brazil.
1899 Rhadinaea dichroa Werner, Zool. Anz., 22: 115. Type-locality: Argentina.
1900 Rhadinaea lineata Jensen, Vidensk. Medd. Naturhist. Foren. Kjöbenhavn, 1900: 105, fig. 1. Type-locality: Lagoa Santa, Minas Gerais, Brazil.
1929 Liophis jaegeri—Amaral, Mem. Inst. Butantan, 4: 172.

Distribution: Brazil, Uruguay, Paraguay and Argentina.

LIOPHIS JOBERTI (Sauvage)

1884 Enicognathus Joberti Sauvage, Bull. Soc. Philom. Paris, (7) 8: 146. Type-locality: Marajó Island, Pará, Brazil.
1885 Liophis (Lygophis) genimaculata Boettger, Zeitsch. für Naturwiss., 58: 229. Type-locality: Paraguay.
1958 Liophis joberti—Hoge, Pap. Avul. Depto. Zool., São Paulo, 13: 223.

Distribution: Central and coastal Brazil from Pará to Rio de Janeiro and from Mato Grosso to Ceará; Bolivia and Paraguay.

LIOPHIS LEUCOGASTER Jan

1863 Liophis leucogaster Jan, Arch. Zool. Anat. Fis., 2: 289. Type-locality: Unknown.

Distribution: Known only from type specimen.

LIOPHIS LONGIVENTRIS Amaral

1925 Liophis longiventris Amaral, Commissão de Linhas Telegráficas Estratégicas de Mato Grosso ao Amazonas, publ. 84, Anex. 5: 16, pl. 1-3. Type-locality: None given.

Distribution: Mato Grosso, Brazil.

LIOPHIS MELANAUCHEN (Jan)

1863 Enicognathus melanauchen Jan, Arch. Zool. Anat. Fis., 2: 267. Type-locality: Bahia, Brazil.
1894 Rhadinaea melanauchen—Boulenger, Cat. Sn. Brit. Mus., 2: 175.
1929 Liophis melanauchen—Amaral, Mem. Inst. Butantan, 4: 173.

Distribution: Bahia, Brazil.

LIOPHIS MILIARIS (Linnaeus)

1758 Coluber miliaris Linnaeus, Systema Naturae, Ed. 10: 220. Type-locality: "Indiis"; restricted to Santos, São Paulo, Brazil, by Gans, Amer. Mus. Novitates, 2178, 1964, 39.
1821 Coluber merremii Wied, Reise nach Brasil, 2: 121. Type-locality: São Pedro d'Alcantara, Bahia, Brazil; = Itabuna, according to Gans, Amer. Mus. Novitates, 2178, 1964, 39.
1824 C.[oluber] dictyodes Wied, Isis von Oken, 6: 668. Type-locality: None given; according to Wied, Beitr. Naturges. Bras., 1825, 343, it is Cabo Frio, Rio de Janeiro, Brazil.
1834 Coluber bicolor Reuss, Abh. Senckenberg. Naturforsch. Ges., 1: 145, pl. 8, fig. 1. Type-locality: Ilheos, Bahia, Brazil.
1858 Coronella australis Günther, Cat. Sn. Brit. Mus.: 40. Type-locality: Australia; restricted to southern Bahia, Brazil, by Gans, Amer. Mus. Novitates, 2178, 1964, 39.
1862 Opheomorphus merremii var. semiaureus Cope, Proc. Acad. Nat. Sci. Phila., 1862: 348. Type-locality: Paraguay; probably lower Paraguay River, according to Gans, Amer. Mus. Novitates, 2178, 1964, 39.
1885 Opheomorphus fuscus Cope, Proc. Amer. Phil. Soc., 22 (1884): 190. São João de Monte Negro, Rio Grande do Sul, Brazil.
1915 Rhadinaea orina Griffin, Mem. Carnegie Mus., 7: 195. Type-locality: Sierras of Bolivia, restricted to São Paulo, São Paulo, Brazil, by Gans, Amer. Mus. Novitates, 2178, 1964, 39.

Distribution: Brazil, from Rio Negro, Amazonas (Hoge and Gans, Copeia, 1965, 511) south to Uruguay, Argentina, Paraguay and Bolivia.

LIOPHIS OBTUSUS (Cope)

1863 Rhadinaea obtusa Cope, Proc. Acad. Nat. Sci. Phila., 1863: 101. Type-locality: Paysondu,
Uruguay, = Paysandú, Uruguay, according to Vaz Ferreira and Sierra de Soriano, Rev. Fac. Hum.
Cienc. Montevideo, 18, 1960, 35.
1929 Liophis obtusus—Amaral, Mem. Inst. Butantan, 4: 89.

Distribution: Southern Brazil, Uruguay and Argentina.

LIOPHIS OCCIPITALIS (Jan)

1863 E.[nicognathus] occipitalis Jan, Arch. Zool. Anat. Fis., 2: 267. Type-locality: Bahia, Brazil.
1864 Dromicus (Lygophis) wuchereri Günther, Ann. Mag. Nat. Hist., (3) 12: 225, fig. Type-locality:
Bahia, Brazil.
1891 Dromicus miolepis Boettger, Zool. Anz., 1891: 346. Type-locality: Sorata, Bolivia.
1929 Liophis occipitalis—Amaral, Mem. Inst. Butantan, 4: 89.

Distribution: Brazil, Uruguay, Argentina, Paraguay, Bolivia and eastern Peru.

LIOPHIS PURPURANS (Duméril, Bibron and Duméril)

1854 Ablabes purpurans Duméril, Bibron and Duméril), Erp. Gén., 7: 312. Type-locality: Mana, French
Guiana.
1864 Coronella orientalis Günther, Reptiles of British India: 236. Type-locality: "Dekkan;" stated
by Boulenger, Cat. Sn. Brit. Mus., 2, 1894, 168, to be unknown.
?1866 Liophis cobella var. collaris Jan, Arch. Zool. Anat. Fis., 2: 293. Type-locality: South
America.
1868 Rhadinaea chrysostoma Cope, Proc. Acad. Nat. Sci. Phila., 1868: 104. Type-locality: Napo or
Marañón, Ecuador.
1872 Coronella poecilolaemus Günther, Ann. Mag. Nat. Hist., (4) 9: 19. Type-locality: Upper Rio
Amazonas.
1872 Liophis purpurans—Günther, Ann. Mag. Nat. Hist., (4) 9: 19.

Distribution: Guianas; Upper Amazonian region of Colombia, Ecuador and Peru.

LIOPHIS STEINBACHI (Boulenger)

1905 Rhadinaea Steinbachi Boulenger, Ann. Mag. Nat. Hist., (7) 15: 454. Type-locality: Provincia
Sara, Departamento Santa Cruz de la Sierra, Bolivia.
1915 Aporophis melanocephalus Griffin, Mem. Carnegie Mus., 7: 171. Type-locality: Las Juntas,
Bolivia, 250 m.
1929 Liophis steinbachi—Amaral, Mem. Inst. Butantan, 4: 174.

Distribution: Eastern Bolivia.

LIOPHIS SUBOCULARIS Boulenger

1902 Rhadinaea subocularis Boulenger, Ann. Mag. Nat. Hist., (7) 9: 56. Type-locality: Paramba,
Ecuador, 3500 ft.
1929 Liophis subocularis—Amaral, Mem. Inst. Butantan, 4: 174.

Distribution: Western Ecuador.

LIOPHIS TREBBAUI Roze

1958 Liophis trebbaui Roze, Acta Biol. Venezuélica, 2: 262, fig. 11. Type-locality: Auyantepui,
Estado Bolívar, Venezuela.

Distribution: Region of Auyantepui, Estado Bolivar, Venezuela.

LIOPHIS UNDULATUS (Wied)

1824 C.[oluber] undulatus Wied, Isis von Oken, 6: 667. Type locality: none given.
1863 E.[nicognathus] taeniolatus Jan, Arch. Zool. Anat. Fis., 2: 272. Type-locality: Brazil.
1895 Taeniophallus nicagus Cope, Trans. Amer. Phil. Soc., 18: 201. Type-locality: Brazil.
1909 Rhadinaea binotata Werner, Mitt. Naturhist. Mus. Hamburg, 26: 223. Type-locality:
       Novo Friburgo, Brazil.
1929 Liophis undulatus—Amaral, Mem. Inst. Butantan, 4: 174.

   Distribution: Brazil, Ecuador and Guianas.

LIOTYPHLOPS **Peters**

1857 Rhinotyphlops Peters (preoccupied by Rhinotyphlops Fitzinger), Monats. Akad. Wiss. Berlin,
    1857: 402. Type-species: Rhinotyphlops albirostris Peters.
1881 Liotyphlops Peters, Sitz. Ges. Naturforsch. Freiburg, 1881: 69. Type-species: Rhinotyphlops
    albirostris Peters.

Distribution: Costa Rica to Paraguay.

Content: Twelve species.

Key to the species

1. Either dark dorsally and lighter ventrally or
  entire body dark, never uniformly light------2
  Entire body nearly uniform pale greenish-slate
  color---------------------------------rowani

2. Three upper labials---------------------------3
  Four upper labials (Fig. 1)--------------------5

3. Ocular separated from labials by subocular----4
  Ocular in contact with labial; one preocular
  (Fig. 2)-------------------------------wilderi

4. One preocular (Fig. 3)----------------schubarti
  Two preoculars--------------------------incertus

1. O bien oscuro dorsalmente y claro ventralmente
  o todo el cuerpo oscuro, nunca uniformemente
  claro---2
  Todo el cuerpo de color pizarra verdoso pálido
  casi uniforme------------------------------rowani

2. Tres labiales superiores----------------------3
  Cuatro labiales superiores (Fig. 1)-----------5

3. Ocular separado de labiales por subocular-----4
  Ocular en contacto con labial, un preocular
  (Fig. 2)-------------------------------wilderi

4. Un preocular (Fig. 3)-----------------schubarti
  Dos preoculars--------------------------incertus

    1   2   3   4   5

    Lateral view of head in Liotyphlops species. Fig. 1, L. anops, after Cope, 1899. Fig. 2, L.
wilderi, after Hammar, 1908. Fig. 3, L. schubarti, after Vanzolini, 1948. Fig. 4, L. metae, after
Dunn, 1944. Fig. 5, L. caracasensis, after Roze, 1952.

5. Scale rows 24 or fewer-----------------------6
  Scale rows 26 or more--------------------anops

6. Two scales in contact with posterior margin of
  prefrontal between frontal and nasal--------7
  Three scales in contact with prefrontal between
  frontal and nasal (Fig. 4)--------------metae

7. Ocular separated from labial by subocular-----8
  Ocular in contact with labial row------------10

8. Prefrontal in contact with anterior half of
  nasal (Figs. 5, 6)---------------------------9
  Prefrontal not in contact with anterior half of
  nasal; posterior half of nasal contacts
  rostral (Fig. 7)--------------------petersii

5. Hileras de escamas 24 o menos------------------6
  Hileras de escamas 26 o más---------------anops

6. Dos escamas en contacto con margen posterior de
  prefrontal entre frontal y nasal------------7
  Tres escamas en contacto con prefrontal entre
  frontal y nasal (Fig. 4)-----------------metae

7. Ocular separado de labial por subocular-------8
  Ocular en contacto con hilera labial---------10

8. Prefrontal en contacto con mitad anterior de
  nasal (Figs. 5, 6)---------------------------9
  Prefrontal no contacta la mitad anterior de
  nasal, mitad posterior del nasal contacta con
  rostral (Fig. 7)--------------------petersii

    6   7   8   9

    Lateral view of head of Liotyphlops species. Fig. 6, L. ternetzii, after Parker, 1928 (holotype of
collenettei). Fig. 7, L. petersii, after Boulenger, 1893. Fig. 8, L. cucutae, after Dunn, 1944.
Fig. 9, L. guentheri, after Boulenger, 1893.

9. Uniform dark brown-----------------<u>caracasensis</u>
   Brown above, lighter beneath----------<u>ternetzii</u>

10. Two preoculars (Fig. 8)----------------------11
    One preocular (Fig. 9)----------------<u>guentheri</u>

11. Scale rows 24; scales light with dark dot at
    base; length/diameter ratio 41---------<u>cucutae</u>
    Scale rows 22; scales uniform dark; length/
    diameter ratio 65------------------<u>albirostris</u>

9. Castaño oscuro uniforme------------<u>caracasensis</u>
   Arriba castaño, claro abajo-----------<u>ternetzii</u>

10. Dos preoculares (Fig. 8)--------------------11
    Un preocular--------------------------<u>guentheri</u>

11. Hileras de escamas 24; escamas claras con punto
    negro en la base; proporción largo/diámetro
    41--------------------------------------<u>cucutae</u>
    Hileras de escamas 22; escamas oscuras unifor-
    mes; proporción largo/diámetro 65--<u>albirostris</u>

<u>LIOTYPHLOPS</u> <u>ALBIROSTRIS</u> (Peters)

1857 <u>Rh.</u>[<u>inotyphlops</u>] <u>albirostris</u> Peters, Monats. Akad. Wiss. Berlin, 1857: 402. Type-locality:
      "Veragua," Panama.
1881 <u>Liotyphlops</u> <u>albirostris</u>—Peters, Sitz. Ges. Naturforsch. Freunde Freiburg, 1881: 69.
1883 <u>Typhlops</u> (<u>Idiotyphlops</u>) <u>emunctus</u> Garman, Mem. Mus. Comp. Zool., 8 (3): 3. Type-locality: Panama.
1903 <u>Helminthophis</u> <u>Canellei</u> Mocquard, Bull. Mus. Hist. Nat. Paris, 1903: 211. Type-locality: Isthmus
      of Panama.
1916 <u>Helminthophis</u> <u>bondensis</u> Griffin, Mem. Carnegie Mus., 7 (1915): 165. Type-locality: Bonda,
      Colombia.
1932 <u>Liotyphlops</u> <u>albirostris</u>—Dunn, Proc. Biol. Soc. Washington, 45: 176.

   Distribution: Southern Central America and northern South America, including Costa Rica, Panama,
   Colombia, Venezuela, and Curaçao.

   Comment: Dunn, Proc. Biol. Soc. Washington, 45, 1932, 174, placed <u>emunctus</u> Garman as a synonym of
   <u>albirostris</u> after examining both types. Taylor, Univ. Kansas Sci. Bull., 34, 1951, 25, indicated
   that he thought <u>emunctus</u> was a valid species, but he did not document this sufficiently to permit
   the two species to be distinguished, so we follow Dunn until further information is presented.

<u>LIOTYPHLOPS</u> <u>ANOPS</u> (Cope)

1899 <u>Helminthophis</u> <u>anops</u> Cope, Phila. Mus. Sci. Bull., 1: 10, pl. 4, figs. 1a-1f. Type-locality:
      "New Grenada," which is Colombia; Dunn, Caldasia, 3, 1944, 8, says "near Bogotá."
1944 <u>Liotyphlops</u> <u>anops</u>—Dunn, Caldasia, 3: 48.

   Distribution: Provincias Santander and Cundinamarca, Colombia.

<u>LIOTYPHLOPS</u> <u>CARACASENSIS</u> Roze

1952 <u>Liotyphlops</u> <u>caracasensis</u> Roze, Mem. Soc. Cien. Nat. La Salle, Caracas, 12 (32): 150, figs. 1-2.
      Type-locality: Cuartel Urdaneta, Caracas, Venezuela.

   Distribution: North central Venezuela.

<u>LIOTYPHLOPS</u> <u>CUCUTAE</u> Dunn

1944 <u>Liotyphlops</u> <u>cucutae</u> Dunn, Caldasia, 3: 49, figs. 5-6. Type-locality: Cúcuta, Norte de Santander,
      Colombia, 215 m.

   Distribution: Known only from type locality.

<u>LIOTYPHLOPS</u> <u>GUENTHERI</u> (Boulenger), new combination

1889 <u>Helminthophis</u> <u>guentheri</u> Boulenger, Ann. Mag. Nat. Hist., (6) 4: 361. Type-locality: Porto Real,
      Rio de Janeiro, Brazil.
1893 <u>Helminthophis</u> <u>guentheri</u>—Boulenger, Cat. Sn. Brit. Mus., 1: 6, pl. 1, fig. 2.

   Distribution: Estado do Rio de Janeiro, Brazil.

LIOTYPHLOPS INCERTUS (Amaral)

1924 Helminthophis incertus Amaral, Proc. New England Zool. Club, 9: 29. Type-locality: Surinam.
1948 L.[iotyphlops] incertus—Vanzolini, Rev. Brasil. Biol., 8: 380.

   Distribution: Surinam.

LIOTYPHLOPS METAE Dunn

1944 Liotyphlops metae Dunn, Caldasia, 3: 49, figs. 3-4. Type-locality: Villavicencio, Meta,
     Colombia, 498 m.

   Distribution: Known only from type locality.

LIOTYPHLOPS PETERSII (Boulenger)

1889 Helminthophis petersii Boulenger, Ann. Mag. Nat. Hist., (6) 4: 360. Type-locality: Guayaquil,
     Ecuador.
1893 Helminthophis petersii—Boulenger, Cat. Sn. Brit. Mus., 1: 6, pl. 1, fig. 1.
1944 [Liotyphlops] petersii—Dunn. Proc. Biol. Soc. Washington, 45: 175.

   Distribution: Northwestern Ecuador.

LIOTYPHLOPS ROWANI Smith and Grant

1958 Liotyphlops rowani Smith and Grant, Herpetologica, 14: 207. Type-locality: Pacific shoreline,
     Ft. Clayton Reservation, Panama Canal Zone, Panama.

   Distribution: Known only from type locality.

LIOTYPHLOPS SCHUBARTI Vanzolini

1948 Liotyphlops schubarti Vanzolini, Rev. Brasil. Biol., 8: 379, figs. 1-2. Type-locality:
     Cachoeira de Emas, São Paulo, Brazil.

   Distribution: Known only from type locality.

LIOTYPHLOPS TERNETZII (Boulenger)

1896 Helminthophis ternetzii Boulenger, Cat. Sn. Brit. Mus., 3: 584. Type-locality: Paraguay.
1924 Helminthophis beui Amaral, Proc. New England Zool. Club, 9: 29. Type-locality: São Paulo, Brazil.
1928 Helminthophis collenettei Parker, Ann. Mag. Nat. Hist., (10) 2: 97, fig. Type-locality: Burity,
     30 mi northeast of Coyaba, Mato Grosso, Brazil.
1955 Helminthophis ternetzii—Amaral, Mem. Inst. Butantan, 26 (1954): 191, figs. 1-2.
1958 [Liotyphlops] ternetzi—Smith and Grant, Herpetologica, 14: 207.

   Distribution: São Paulo and Mato Grosso, Brazil; northern Argentina.

LIOTYPHLOPS WILDERI (Garman)

1883 Typhlops Wilderi Garman, Science Observer, Boston, 4 (5/6): 48. Type-locality: São Cyriaco,
     Brazil; noted as Cyriaco, near Serra Providencia, Minas Gerais, Brazil, by Hammar, Ann. Mag.
     Nat. Hist., (8) 1, 1908, 334; corrected by Marx, Fieldiana: Zool., 36, 1958, 496, to São
     Cyprião, Minas Gerais, Brazil.
1908 Helminthophis wilderi—Hammar, Ann. Mag. Nat. Hist., (8) 1: 334, figs. a-c.
1948 L.[iotyphlops] wilderi—Vanzolini, Rev. Brasil. Biol., 8: 380.

   Distribution: Minas Gerais, Brazil; Paraguay.

LOXOCEMUS Cope

    1861 <u>Loxocemus</u> Cope, Proc. Acad. Nat. Sci. Phila., 1861: 76. Type-species: <u>Loxocemus bicolor</u> Cope.
    1862 <u>Plastoseryx</u> Jan, Arch. für Naturg., 28 (1): 244. Type-species: <u>Plastoseryx Bronni</u> Jan.

    Distribution: Nayarit, western Mexico to Costa Rica.

    Content: One species.

LOXOCEMUS BICOLOR Cope

    1861 <u>Loxocemus bicolor</u> Cope, Proc. Acad. Nat. Sci. Phila., 1861: 77. Type-locality: Unknown; re-
        stricted to La Unión, El Salvador, by Smith and Taylor, Univ. Kansas Sci. Bull., 33, 1950, 316.
    1862 <u>Plastoseryx Bronni</u> Jan, Arch. für Naturg., 28 (1): 244. Type-locality: America.
    1876 <u>Loxocemus sumichrasti</u> Bocourt, Ann. Sci. Nat. Zool. Paris, (6) 4 (7): 1. Type-locality: Tehuante-
        pec, Mexico.
    1967 <u>Loxocemus bicolor</u>—Nelson and Meyer, SW Nat., 12: 439.

Distribution: On Pacific coast from Nayarit, Mexico to Costa Rica; Atlantic coast in northwestern
Honduras.

LYGOPHIS Fitzinger

1843 Lygophis Fitzinger, Systema Reptilium: 26. Type-species: Given as Herpetodryas lineatus
    Schlegel, which is Coluber lineatus Linnaeus.
1878 Aporophis Cope, Proc. Amer. Phil. Soc., 17: 34. Type-species: Coluber lineatus Linnaeus.

Distribution: Northern and central South America.

Content: Eight species.

<table>
<tr><td colspan="2">Key to the species</td><td colspan="2">Clave de especies</td></tr>
</table>

1. Seventeen scale rows at midbody---------------2
   Nineteen scale rows at midbody---------------6

2. More than 14 maxillary teeth------------------3
   Fewer than 15 maxillary teeth--------paucidens

3. More than 152 ventrals-----------------------4
   Fewer than 152 ventrals----------------amoenus

4. Dorsal pattern without two yellow lines beginning on snout------------------------------5
   Two yellow lines beginning on snout-----------
   -----------------------------flavifrenatus

5. Dark vertebral and lateral lines broken or
   absent anteriorly, occasionally also posteriorly; scale edges usually dark; hemipenis
   one-half bilobated------------------boursieri
   Dark lines continuous anteriorly; dorsal
   ground color uniform brown or gray without
   dark edges on scales; hemipenis one-third
   bilobated------------------------tristriatus

6. Not as below--------------------------------7
   Venter totally or partially red; tail red
   ventrally with black border on individual
   ventrals----------------------coralliventris

7. Head and body dark brown---------antioquiensis
   Head and body with prominent, contrasting
   stripes----------------------------lineatus

1. Diecisiete filas de escamas en el medio del
   cuerpo--2
   Diecinueve filas de escamas en el medio del
   cuerpo--6

2. Más de 14 dientes maxilares-------------------3
   Menos de 15 dientes maxilares--------paucidens

3. Más de 152 ventrales-------------------------4
   Menos de 152 ventrales----------------amoenus

4. Diseño sin dos líneas amarillas desde el hocico
   --5
   Diseño con dos líneas amarillas desde el hocico
   ---------------------------------flavifrenatus

5. Líneas oscuras vertebral y laterales discon-
   tinuas o ausentes a anterior; ocasionalmente
   también a posterior; bordes de las escamas
   usualmente oscuro; hemipene bilobulado hasta
   la mitad----------------------------boursieri
   Líneas oscuras continuas a anterior; dorso con
   color de fondo uniforme castaño o gris sin
   bordes oscuros en las escamas; un tercio del
   hemipene bilobulado---------------tristriatus

6. No como el siguiente-------------------------7
   Vientre (total o parcialmente) rojo; cola
   ventralmente roja con bordes de placas en
   negro-------------------------coralliventris

7. Cabeza y cuerpo castaño oscuro----antioquiensis
   Cabeza y cuerpo con cintas en marcado
   contraste---------------------------lineatus

LYGOPHIS AMOENUS (Jan)

1863 E.[nicognathus] amoenus Jan, Arch. Zool. Anat. Fis., 2: 270. Type-locality: Unknown.
1929 Lygophis amoenus—Amaral, Mem. Inst. Butantan, 4: 169.

Distribution: Estado do Paraná through São Paulo as far north as Estado do Rio de Janeiro, Brazil.

LYGOPHIS ANTIOQUIENSIS (Dunn)

1943 Rhadinaea antioquiensis Dunn, Caldasia, 2: 307. Type-locality: San Pedro, Antioquia, Colombia,
    2560 m.
1969 Lygophis antioquiensis—Myers, Amer. Mus. Novitates, 2385: 2, figs. 1-3.

Distribution: Known only from type locality.

LYGOPHIS BOURSIERI (Jan)

1867 Dromicus Boursieri Jan, Icon, Gén. Ophid., Livr. 25: pl. 2, fig. 2. Type-locality: Quito, Ecuador.
1882 Coronella Whymperi Boulenger, Ann. Mag. Nat. Hist., (5) 9: 460, fig. Type-locality: Milligalli, Ecuador.
1934 Lygophis boursieri—Shreve, Occ. Pap. Boston Soc. Nat. Hist., 8: 125.

Distribution: Río Pastaza region, Amazonian slopes and western slopes above 1000 m, Ecuador; southwestern Colombia.

LYGOPHIS CORALLIVENTRIS (Boulenger)

1894 Aporophis coralliventris Boulenger, Ann. Mag. Nat. Hist., (6) 13: 346. Type-locality: An island north of Concepción, near San Salvador, north Paraguay.
1929 Lygophis coralliventris—Amaral, Mem. Inst. Butantan, 4: 169.

Distribution: Paraguay; Rio Grande do Sul, Brazil.

LYGOPHIS FLAVIFRENATUS Cope

1862 Lygophis flavifrenatus Cope, Proc. Acad. Nat. Sci. Phila., 1862: 80. Type-locality: Río Vermejo region, Paraguay, according to Cope; Cochran, Bull. U.S. Nat. Mus., 224, 1961, 196, says Buenos Aires, Argentina.
1867 Dromicus amabilis Jan, Icon. Gén. Ophid., Livr. 24: pl. 5, fig. 2. Type-locality: Brazil.

Distribution: Paraguay; Argentina; southern Brazil as far north as Estado de São Paulo.

LYGOPHIS LINEATUS (Linnaeus)

1758 Coluber lineatus Linnaeus, Systema Naturae, Ed. 10: 221. Type-locality: Asia.
1843 [Lygophis] lineatus—Fitzinger, Systema Reptilium: 26.

Distribution: Panama; north and middle South America from northern Argentina; to northwestern Ecuador west of Andes.

Content: Three subspecies.

Key to the subspecies

1. Three distinct dark stripes not interrupted on neck; first through fourth series of dorsal scales white or nearly white------2
Three indistinct dark stripes, interrupted on neck; lateral scales heavily dotted with black; ventrals with lateral series of black spots---------------meridionalis

2. Lateral stripe about one scale wide on body (much larger on head)-------------lineatus
Lateral stripe three or more scales wide------------------------------------dilepis

Clave de subespecies

1. Diseño dorsal con tres bandas longitudinales no interrumpidas en la nuca; primera a cuarta fila latero-dorsal blancas o casi blancas----------------------------------2
Diseño dorsal con tres bandas longitudinales interrumpidas en la nuca; primera a cuarta fila latero-dorsal manchada de negro------------------------meridionalis

2. Banda lateral del grosor de una escama o ligeramente mayor-----------------lineatus
Banda lateral del grosor de tres o más escamas----------------------------dilepis

Lygophis lineatus lineatus (Linnaeus)

1758 Coluber minervae Linnaeus, Systema Naturae, Ed. 10: 226. Type-locality: "Indiis".
?1766 Coluber jaculatrix Linnaeus, Systema Naturae, Ed. 12: 381. Type-locality: Surinam.
1826 Coluber terlineatus Lacépède, Hist. Nat. Quad., Serp., New Ed., 4: 106 [not seen]. Type-locality: None given.
1953 Lygophis lineatus lineatus—Hoge, Mem. Inst. Butantan, 24 (1952): 249, fig. 1; pl. 1.

Distribution: Panama; northern South America; to northwestern Ecuador west of Andes.

Comment: It is not certain that Coluber jaculatrix Linnaeus belongs in this synonymy, but Hoge, loc. cit., included in his species synonymy citations to Lacépède and Latreille which mentioned the Linnaean species. Boulenger does not mention jaculatrix at all, and we have found no other discussion in the literature of its status.

Lygophis lineatus dilepis Cope

    1862 Lygophis dilepis Cope, Proc. Acad. Nat. Sci. Phila., 1862: 348. Type-locality: Paraguay.
    1928 Aporophis lineatus lativittatus Müller, Zool. Anz., 77: 74. Type-locality: San Fermin
      (Chiquitos), Bolivia.
    1953 Lygophis lineatus dilepis—Hoge, Mem. Inst. Butantan, 24 (1952): 251, fig. 2.

      Distribution: Rio Grande do Norte, Brazil through Mato Grosso and Paraguay to northern
        Argentina, according to Hoge, loc. cit.

Lygophis lineatus meridionalis (Schenkel)

    1901 Aporophis lineatus var. meridionalis Schenkel, Verh. Naturforsch. Ges. Basel, 13 (1900):
        160. Type-locality: "Mte. Sociedad", Bemalcue, Paraguay.
    1952 Lygophis lineatus meridionalis—Hoge, Mem. Inst. Butantan, 24 (1952): 252, fig. 3.

      Distribution: Southern Brazil, Paraguay, northern Argentina, according to Hoge, loc. cit.

LYGOPHIS PAUCIDENS Hoge

    1953 Lygophis paucidens Hoge, Mem. Inst. Butantan, 24 (1952): 189. Type-locality: Mato Verde, Estado
      de Goiás, Brazil.

    Distribution: Known only from type locality.

LYGOPHIS TRISTRIATUS (Rendahl and Vestergren)

    1941 Rhadinaea tristriata Rendahl and Vestergren, Ark. för Zool., 33A (1): 5. Type-locality: Cauca,
      Colombia.
    1969 Lygophis tristriatus—Myers, Amer. Mus. Novitates, 2385: 6.

    Distribution: Known only from type locality.

LYSTROPHIS Cope

1826 Rhinostoma Fitzinger, Neue Classification der Reptilien: 56. Type-species: Vipera nasua Wagler.
Suppressed by Int. Comm. Zool. Nomen., Op. 698, 1964, 101.
1885 Lystrophis Cope, Proc. Amer. Phil. Soc., 1884: 193. Type-species: Heterodon Dorbignyi
Duméril, Bibron and Duméril.

Distribution: South and southeastern Brazil, Paraguay, Bolivia, north and central Argentina, and
Uruguay.

Content: Three species.

Key to the species

1. Dorsals in 21 rows----------------------------2
Dorsals in 19 rows--------------------histricus

2. Tip of tail very rounded; dorsum with succes-
sive rings of black, yellow, black, red; venter predominantly black; ventrals more than
148-------------------------------semicinctus
Tail ending in point; dorsal pattern of rounded
black blotches or irregular transverse bands,
usually bordered by yellow; coloration between
spots usually red; venter with equal amounts
of red and black; ventrals fewer than 148-----
--------------------------------------dorbignyi

Clave de especies

1. Dorsales en 21 filas------------------------2
Dorsales en 19 filas-----------------histricus

2. Punta de la cola muy redondeada; coloración
dorsal en anillos negros, amarillos, negros y
rojos; vientre predominantemente negro; ventrales más de 148----------------semicinctus
Cola puntiaguda; coloración dorsal de manchas
circulares o bandas transversas irregulares
negras usualmente bordeadas de amarillo; coloración entre las manchas usualmente roja;
vientre con igual cantidad de rojo y negro;
ventrales menos de 148--------------dorbignyi

LYSTROPHIS DORBIGNYI (Dumeril, Bibron, and Dumeril)

1830 Vipera (Rhinostoma) nasua Wagler, Nat. Syst. Amphib.: 171. Type-locality: America. Suppressed
by Int. Comm. Zool. Nomen., Op. 698, 1964, 101.
1854 Heterodon Dorbignyi Duméril, Bibron, and Dumeril, Erp. Gén., 7: 772. Type-locality: The series
of syntypes apparently came from four areas, including Buenos Aires, Montevideo, Santa Catarina, and "Bresil", without more precise data. No restrictions have been made.
1885 Lystrophis dorbignyi---Cope, Proc. Amer. Phil. Soc., 1884: 193.
1966 Lystrophis dorbignyi—Orejas Miranda, Copeia, 1966: 196, figs. 8a b, 9a-d.

Distribution: Between 25° and 40° S: southeastern and southern Paraguay, southern Brazil, central
Argentina east of the Andes, and Uruguay.

LYSTROPHIS HISTRICUS (Jan)

1863 Heterodon histricus Jan, Arch. Zool. Anat. Fis., 2: 224. Type-locality: unknown.
1867 Heterodon nattereri Steindachner, Reise der Osterreichischen Fregatte Novara, Zool., Reptiles:
90. Type-locality: Brazil.
1894 Lystrophis histricus—Boulenger, Cat. Sn. Brit. Mus., 2: 152.
1966 Lystrophis histricus—Orejas Miranda, Copeia, 1966: 203, figs. 8e-f, 9f.

Distribution: Between 15° and 34° S: southern and southeastern Brazil, northeastern Argentina,
Paraguay, and northeastern Uruguay.

LYSTROPHIS SEMICINCTUS (Duméril, Bibron, and Duméril)

1854 Heterodon semi-cinctus Duméril, Bibron, and Duméril, Erp. Gen., 7: 774. Type-locality: "á
Buenos Ayres et Santa-Cruz" (see note under Lystrophis dorbignyi).
1863 Heterodon pulcher Jan, Arch. Zool. Anat. Fis., 2: 222. Type-locality: Bolivia.
1894 Lystrophis semicinctus—Boulenger, Cat. Sn. Brit. Mus., 2: 153.
1928 Lystrophis semicinctus weiseri Müller, Zool. Anz., 77: 72. Type-locality: Catamarca, Argentina.
1966 Lystrophis semicinctus—Orejas Miranda, Copeia, 1966: 202, figs. 8c-d, 9e.

Distribution: Between 20° and 30° S: central and northern Argentina, southwestern Brazil,
southern Bolivia, and probably northern Paraguay.

MASTICOPHIS Baird and Girard

  1853 Masticophis Baird and Girard, Cat. N. Amer. Rept.: 98. Type-species: Masticophis ornatus Baird and Girard.

    Distribution: Southern and western United States to northern Colombia and Venezuela.

    Content: Eight species, of which only one is found within limits of this work.

MASTICOPHIS MENTOVARIUS Duméril, Bibron and Duméril

  1854 C[oryphodon] Mento-varius Duméril, Bibron and Duméril, Erp. Gén., 7: 187. Type-locality: Mexico.
  1923 Masticophis mentovarius—Ortenburger, Occ. Pap. Mus. Zool. Univ. Mich., 139: 2.

    Distribution: San Luis Potosi and Guerrero, Mexico through Central America to Colombia and Venezuela.

    Content: Three subspecies.

Key to the subspecies	Clave de subespecies
1. Juveniles with longitudinal stripes, adults may show stripes or be unicolor; nasal divided--------------------------------2 Juveniles with irregular transverse dorsal bands; adult color unknown; nasal entire---------------------------------centralis	1. Juveniles con cintas longitudinales, los adultos pueden presentar bandas o ser unicolor; nasal dividida--------------------2 Juveniles con bandas dorsales, transversales, irregulares; color del adulto desconocido; nasal entera-------centralis
2. Juveniles with two lateral light stripes, head in adults heavily mottled and spotted----------------------mentovarius Juveniles with four or more light stripes, head in adults immaculate-----suborbitalis	2. Juveniles con dos cintas laterales claras, cabeza del adulto intensamente moteada y manchada----------------------mentovarius Juveniles con cuatro o más cintas claras, cabeza del adulto inmaculada--suborbitalis

Masticophis mentovarius mentovarius Duméril, Bibron and Duméril

  1867 Bascanion suboculare Cope, Proc. Acad. Nat. Sci. Phila., 1866: 319. Type-locality: Between Coban and Clusec (corrected to Chisec by Stuart, 1966), Guatemala.
  1942 Masticophis m[entovarius] mentovarius—Smith, Copeia, 1942: 87.

    Distribution: Low and moderate elevations from San Luis Potosi, Mexico, to Honduras on Caribbean slope and from Guerrero, Mexico, to Costa Rica along Pacific.

Masticophis mentovarius centralis (Roze)

  1953 Coluber (Masticophis) mentovarius centralis Roze, Herpetológica, 9: 117. Type-locality: Maicao, Guajira, Colombia.

    Distribution: Panama and northern Colombia to northwest Venezuela.

Masticophis mentovarius suborbitalis (Peters)

  1868 Spilotes corais var. suborbitalis Peters, Monats. Akad. Wiss. Berlin: 641. Type-locality: Caracas, Venezuela.
  1942 Masticophis mentovarius suborbitalis—Smith, Copeia, 1942: 86.

    Distribution: Northern and southeastern Venezuela; Isla Margarita.

M. STIGODRYAS Amaral

1843 _Eudryas_ Fitzinger (preoccupied by _Eudryas_ Boisduval, 1836), Systema Reptilium: 26. Type-species: _Coluber Boddaerti_ Sentzen.
1935 _Mastigodryas_ Amaral, Mem. Inst. Butantan, 8 (1933-34): 157. Type-species: _Mastigodryas danieli_ Amaral.
1939 _Dryadophis_ Stuart (substitute name for _Eudryas_ Fitzinger), Copeia, 1939: 55.

Distribution: Mexico through Central and South America to Argentina.

Content: Eleven species arranged in four species groups; one (_bruesi_ Barbour) extralimital.

Comment: Romer, Osteology of the Reptiles, 1956, pointed out that _Mastigodryas_ and _Dryadophis_ were synonymous. He did not use _Mastigodryas_ for the taxon. It is the prior name, however, and one of us (Peters) has examined the type, which clearly indicates the synonymy of the two taxa, so the earlier name is used here.

Key to the species

1. With 17 scale rows at midbody------------------2
   With 15 scale rows at midbody--------_bifossatus_

2. Usually nine supralabials; dorsal pattern lacks alternate lateral and dorsal rectangular dark blotches-------------------------------------3
   Usually eight supralabials; dorsal pattern with alternate lateral and dorsal rectangular dark blotches-------------------------_pulchriceps_

3. With vertebral stripe at least anteriorly-----4
   Without vertebral stripe anteriorly-----------6

4. Lacking lateral stripes, or if present, never fused with vertebral stripe posteriorly------5
   Two dorsolateral stripes anteriorly which fuse with vertebral stripe on posterior part of body; lateral dark stripe present--------_plee_

5. Light lateral line on part of fourth and fifth rows----------------------------_sanguiventris_
   Light lateral line on third row--------_dorsalis_

6. Dorsum unicolor------------------------------7
   Some indication of dorsal pattern------------8

7. Subcaudals fewer than 100--------------_danieli_
   Subcaudals more than 100-----------_melanolomus_

8. Pattern reticulate, each scale with distinct black borders--------------------_melanolomus_
   Pattern not reticulate, each scale may have slightly darker borders---------------------9

9. One or more light lateral stripes on body----10
   No lateral light stripes-----------_melanolomus_

10. Dorsal pattern with one light stripe dorsolaterally-----------------------------------11
    Dorsal pattern with two lateral light lines--12

11. Dorsolateral light line on fourth, fifth and sixth rows---------------------------_heathii_
    Dorsolateral light line on fourth and fifth rows--------------------------------_boddaerti_

Clave de especies

1. Con 17 filas de escamas en el medio cuerpo----2
   Con 15 filas de escamas en el medio cuerpo-----
   -------------------------------------_bifossatus_

2. Normalmente nueve supralabiales; diseño dorsal sin manchas rectangulares laterales y dorsales oscuras alternadas--------------------------3
   Normalmente ocho supralabiales; diseño dorsal con manchas rectangulares laterales y dorsales oscuras alternadas----------------_pulchriceps_

3. Con línea vertebral por lo menos anteriormente-
   --4
   Sin línea vertebral anteriormente------------6

4. Líneas laterales ausentes, o si están presentes nunca fusionadas con la línea vertebral posteriormente-------------------------------------5
   Dos líneas dorsolaterales anteriores que se fusionan con la vertebral posteriormente; línea oscura lateral presente-----------_pleei_

5. Línea clara lateral sobre parte de la cuarta y quinta filas---------------------_sanguiventris_
   Línea clara lateral sobre tercera fila-_dorsalis_

6. Dorso unicolor-------------------------------7
   Con por lo menos alguna indicación de diseño dorsal--8

7. Subcaudales menos de 100---------------_danieli_
   Subcaudales más de 100-------------_melanolomus_

8. Diseño reticulado, cada escama con conspícuo borde negro----------------------_melanolomus_
   Diseño no reticulado, cada escama puede tener bordes ligeramente oscuros------------------9

9. Una o más cintas laterales claras en el cuerpo-
   --10
   Sin cintas laterales claras---------_melanolomus_

10. Diseño dorsal con una línea dorsolateral clara-
    --11
    Diseño dorsal con dos líneas claras laterales--
    --12

11. Línea dorsolateral clara sobre cuarta, quinta y sexta filas---------------------------_heathii_
    Línea dorsolateral clara sobre cuarta y quinta filas--------------------------------_boddaerti_

12. Upper lateral light stripe on scale rows four and five only---------------------------13
    Upper lateral light stripe on scale rows three, four and five-------------------------amarali

13. More than 110 subcaudals--------------------14
    Fewer than 110 subcaudals-----------melanolomus

14. Upper light stripe without border------------15
    Upper light stripe with prominent dark border---------------------------------boddaerti

15. Lateral light stripes prominent-------boddaerti
    Lateral light stripes obscure------melanolomus

12. Cinta clara lateral superior en hileras de escamas cuatro y cinco solamente------------13
    Cinta clara lateral superior en hileras de escamas tres, cuatro y cinco----------amarali

13. Más de 110 subcaudales-----------------------14
    Menos de 110 subcaudales------------melanolomus

14. Cinta clara superior sin borde---------------15
    Cinta clara superior con borde oscuro prominente---------------------------------boddaerti

15. Cintas claras laterales prominentes---boddaerti
    Cintas claras laterales confusas----melanolomus

MASTIGODRYAS AMARALI (Stuart), new combination
    pleei group

1938 Eudryas amarali Stuart, Copeia, 1938: 7. Type-locality: Margarita Island, Venezuela.
1941 Dryadophis amarali—Stuart, Misc. Publ. Mus. Zool. Univ. Mich., 49: 57, pl. 3, fig. 3.
1966 Dryadophis amarali—Roze, La Taxonomía y Zoogeografía de Los Ofidios en Venezuela: 116, Map 24.

Distribution: Margarita Island and dry areas in northeastern Venezuela; Tobago Island.

MASTIGODRYAS BIFOSSATUS (Raddi), new combination
    bifossatus group

1820 Coluber bifossatus Raddi, Mem. Soc. Italiana Sci. Modena, 18: 333. Type-locality: Rio de Janeiro, Brazil.
1939 Dryadophis [bifossatus]—Stuart, Copeia, 1939: 55.

Distribution: From northern South America in Venezuela and Colombia to southern Brazil, Bolivia, Paraguay and northeastern Argentina.

Content: Four subspecies; three according to latest revision by Stuart, Misc. Publ. Mus. Zool. Univ. Mich., 1941, 49, and one described by Hoge, 1952.

Key to the subspecies

1. Body pattern of less than 48 constricted, broad, dark crossbands, or series of dark dorsal and lateral blotches; total ventrals less than 278--------------------2
   Body pattern of 50-62 continuous dark crossbands; total ventrals more than 278--------------------------------striatus

2. Body pattern of dark crossbands unbroken laterally--------------------------------3
   Body pattern of series of dark, dorsal blotches separated from lateral series of similar blotches--------------triseriatus

3. Broad crossbands, with lateral constriction but at least four scale rows wide at middorsum------------------------bifossatus
   Crossbands triangular, very constricted middorsally, never more than two scale rows wide at middorsum-----------villelai

Clave de subespecies

1. Diseño de bandas transversas anchas, oscuras y constreñidas, en número menor de 48, o series de manchas oscuras dorsales y laterales; ventrales totales menos de 278-------------------------------------2
   Diseño de bandas transversas angostas, continuas y oscuras; en número mayor de 49; ventrales totales más de 278------striatus

2. Diseño de bandas transversas oscuras, no interrumpidas lateralmente--------------3
   Diseño de series de manchas oscuras dorsales, separadas de series laterales similares------------------------triseriatus

3. Anchas bandas transversas con constricción lateral, por lo menos de cuatro escamas de ancho en el medio dorso---------bifossatus
   Bandas transversas triangulares, muy constreñidas medio dorsalmente, donde nunca alcanzan más de dos escamas de ancho------------------------------------villelai

Mastigodryas <u>bifossatus</u> <u>bifossatus</u> (Raddi), new combination

   1823 <u>Coluber</u> <u>capistratus</u> Lichtenstein, Verzeichniss der Doubletten des Zoologischen Museums
         der Königl. Universität zu Berlin: 104. Type-locality: Brazil.
   1825 <u>Coluber</u> <u>Lichtensteinii</u> Wied, Nova Acta Acad. Leop.-Carol., 12 (2): 493. Type-locality:
         Brazil.
   1837 <u>Coluber</u> <u>pantherinus</u> Schlegel (not of Daudin), Essai Physion. Serpens, 2: 143, pl. 5,
         figs. 13-14. Type-locality: "St. Paul" [São Paulo], Brazil.
   1941 <u>Dryadophis</u> <u>bifossatus</u> <u>bifossatus</u>—Stuart, Misc. Publ. Mus. Zool. Univ. Mich., 49: 39, pl.
         2, fig. 5.

      Distribution: From Rio Grande do Sul to Rio de Janeiro and Minas Gerais, Brazil; Uruguay.

Mastigodryas <u>bifossatus</u> <u>striatus</u> (Amaral), new combination

   1931 <u>Drymobius</u> <u>bifossatus</u> <u>striatus</u> Amaral, Bull. Antivenin Inst. Amer., 4: 86. Type-locality:
         Villavicencio, Colombia.
   1941 <u>Dryadophis</u> <u>bifossatus</u> <u>striatus</u>—Stuart, Misc. Publ. Mus. Zool. Univ. Mich., 49, pl. 2,
         fig. 4.

      Distribution: Eastern Colombia, southern Venezuela, northern Brazil.

Mastigodryas <u>bifossatus</u> <u>triseriatus</u> (Amaral), new combination

   1931 <u>Drymobius</u> <u>bifossatus</u> <u>triseriatus</u> Amaral, Bull. Antivenin Inst. Amer., 4: 86. Type-
         locality: Taunay, Mato Grosso, Brazil.
   1941 <u>Dryadophis</u> <u>bifossatus</u> <u>triseriatus</u>—Stuart, Misc. Publ. Mus. Zool. Univ. Mich., 49: 43,
         pl. 2, fig. 2.

      Distribution: Northern Argentina, Bolivia; Mato Grosso, Goiás and Ceará, Brazil.

Mastigodryas <u>bifossatus</u> <u>villelai</u> (Hoge), new combination

   1952 <u>Dryadophis</u> <u>bifossatus</u> <u>villelai</u> Hoge, Mem. Inst. Butantan, 24: 184, pl. 1-3, fig. Type-
         locality: Santa Izabel, Ilha do Bananal, Estado de Goiás, Brazil.

      Distribution: Known from Goiás, Para, and Mato Grosso, Brazil; Bananal Island and
      vicinity.

MASTIGODRYAS BODDAERTI (Sentzen), new combination
     <u>boddaerti</u> group

   1796 <u>Coluber</u> <u>Boddaerti</u> Sentzen, Ophiologische Fragmente, Meyer's Zool. Arch., 2: 59. Type-locality:
         Unknown.
   1939 <u>Dryadophis</u> [<u>boddaerti</u>]—Stuart, Copeia, 1939: 55.

      Distribution: Tropical South America, from Colombia and Venezuela to Bolivia and western Brazil.

      Content: Three subspecies, according to latest revision by Stuart, Misc. Publ. Mus. Zool. Univ.
      Mich., 1949, 49.

              Key to the subspecies   Clave de subespecies

   1. Upper light stripe not bordered by darker   1. Banda clara superior no marginada---------2
        color----------------------------------2   Banda clara superior con conspícuos **bordes**
      Upper light stripe with prominent dark   oscuros--------------------------**ruthveni**
      borders-------------------------<u>ruthveni</u>

                                                       2. Con dos bandas claras laterales-------<u>dunni</u>
   2. Two lateral light stripes------------<u>dunni</u>   Con una banda clara lateral-------<u>boddaerti</u>
      Single light lateral stripe-------<u>boddaerti</u>

Mastigodryas boddaerti boddaerti (Sentzen), new combination

1845 Coluber fuscus Hallowell, Proc. Acad. Nat. Sci. Phila., 1845: 241. Type-locality: 200
mi of Caracas, Republic of Colombia [Venezuela].
1858 Herpetodryas rappii Günther, Cat. Col. Sn. Brit. Mus., 116. Type-locality: Many localities in South America.
?1863 Herpetodryas reticulata Peters, Monats. Akad. Wiss. Berlin, 1863: 285. Type-locality:
Guayaquil, Ecuador (Questionably synonymized with boddaerti by Stuart, 1941).
1941 Dryadophis boddaerti boddaerti—Stuart, Misc. Publ. Mus. Zool. Univ. Mich., 49: 66, pl.
4, fig. 1.

Distribution: Amazon basin from lower slopes of Andes to mouth of Amazon River; from
Bolivia to Colombia, except Santa Marta region; extreme western Venezuela west of Andes on
Pacific slope of Colombia and Ecuador; an isolated colony in Bahía, Brazil is cited by
Stuart, 1941.

Mastigodryas boddaerti dunni (Stuart), new combination

1933 Eudryas dunni Stuart, Occ. Pap. Mus. Zool. Univ. Mich., 254: 5. Type-locality: Tobago
Island, British West Indies.
1939 Dryadophis [dunni]—Stuart, Copeia, 1939: 55.
1941 Dryadophis boddaerti dunni—Stuart, Misc. Publ. Mus. Zool. Univ. Mich., 49: 76, pl. 3,
fig. 6.

Distribution: Known only from type locality.

Mastigodryas boddaerti ruthveni (Stuart), new combination

1933 Eudryas ruthveni Stuart, Occ. Pap. Mus. Zool. Univ. Mich., 254: 4. Type-locality:
slopes of San Lorenzo, Sierra Nevada, Santa Marta, Colombia, 5000 ft.
1939 Dryadophis [ruthveni]—Stuart, Copeia, 1939: 55.
1941 Dryadophis boddaerti ruthveni—Stuart, Misc. Publ. Mus. Zool. Univ. Mich., 49: 4, pl. 3,
fig. 5.

Distribution: Known only from Sierra Nevada of Santa Marta, Colombia, above 2200 ft.

MASTIGODRYAS DANIELI Amaral
group unknown

1935 Mastigodryas danieli Amaral, Mem. Inst. Butantan, 8 (1933-34): 158. Type-locality: Medellín,
Colombia.
1935 Mastigodryas unicolor Amaral (lapsus for danieli Amaral), Mem. Inst. Butantan, 8 (1933-34):
159.

Distribution: Known only from type locality.

MASTIGODRYAS DORSALIS (Bocourt), new combination
melanolomus group

1890 Drymobius (Eudryas) dorsalis Bocourt, Miss. Sci. Mex., Rept.: 724, pl. 51, fig. 2a-d. Type-
locality: Guatemala.
1939 Dryadophis [dorsalis]—Stuart, Copeia, 1939: 55.
1941 Dryadophis dorsalis—Stuart, Misc. Publ. Mus. Zool. Univ. Mich., 49: 95, pl. 4, fig. 5.

Distribution: Highlands of western and southern Guatemala; Honduran uplands.

Comment: Lynch and Smith, Trans. Kansas Acad. Sci., 69, 1966, 69, considered this a subspecies
of M. melanolomus.

MASTIGODRYAS HEATHII (Cope), new combination
    boddaerti group

  1876 Drymobius heathii Cope, Jour. Acad. Nat. Sci. Phila., (2) 8 (1875): 179. Type-locality: Valley
       of Jequetepeque, Peru.
  1939 Dryadophis [heathii]—Stuart, Copeia, 1939: 55.
  1941 Dryadophis heathii—Stuart, Misc. Publ. Mus. Zool. Univ. Mich., 49, pl. 4, fig. 2.

    Distribution: Coastal Peru.

MASTIGODRYAS MELANOLOMUS (Cope), new combination
    melanolomus group

  1868 Masticophis melanolomus Cope, Proc. Acad. Nat. Sci. Phila., 1868: 134. Type-locality: Yucatán,
       Mexico.
  1939 Dryadophis [melanolomus]—Stuart, Copeia, 1939: 55.

    Distribution: Mexico through Central America to Panama.

    Content: Seven subspecies (five discussed in most recent revision by Stuart, Misc. Publ. Mus. Zool.
    Univ. Mich., 1941, 49, plus two described by Smith, 1943). Three (veraecrucis Stuart, slevini
    Stuart, and stuarti Smith) extralimital; slevini Stuart, was mentioned from Volcán Zunil, Guate-
    mala, by Stuart, 1941, loc. cit., but Stuart, Misc. Publ. Mus. Zool. Univ. Mich., 122, 1963, does
    not include slevini as a Guatemalan form.

Key to the subspecies	Clave de subespecies

1. Dorsal pattern not uniform----------------2
   Dorsal pattern uniform olive-------tehuanae
	1. Diseño dorsal no uniforme-----------------2
	   Diseño oliva uniforme-------------tehuanae

2. Pattern not reticulate--------------------3
   Pattern reticulate-------------melanolomus
	2. Diseño no reticulado----------------------3
	   Diseño reticulado--------------melanolomus

3. Two light longitudinal bands on each side--
   ----------------------------alternatus
   Body pattern of narrow, light crossbands
   anteriorly------------------------laevis
	3. Dos bandas longitudinales claras a cada
	   lado del cuerpo----------------alternatus
	   Diseño de bandas claras transversas, sobre
	   la parte anterior del cuerpo--------laevis

Mastigodryas melanolomus melanolomus (Cope), new combination

  1941 Dryadophis melanolomus melanolomus—Stuart, Misc. Publ. Mus. Zool. Univ. Mich., 49: 88,
       pl. 4, fig. 4.

    Distribution: Lowlands of Yucatán Peninsula south to central El Petén, Guatemala.

Mastigodryas melanolomus alternatus (Bocourt), new combination

  1884 Coryphodon alternatus Bocourt, Bull. Soc. Philom. Paris, (7) 8: 133. Type-locality:
       Isthmus de Darién, Panama.
  1933 Eudryas boddaerti gaigae Stuart, Occ. Pap. Mus. Zool. Univ. Mich., 254: 7. Type-locality:
       Wright's ranch, Boquete, Chiriquí Province, Panama.

    Distribution: Costa Rica, Honduras, Nicaragua and Panama.

Mastigodryas melanolomus laevis (Fischer), new combination

  1881 Herpetodryas Laevis Fischer, Arch. für Naturg.: 227. Type-locality: Guatemala.
  1885 Dromicus coeruleus Fischer, Jahrb. Wiss. Anst. Hamburg, 2, 1884: 103, pl. 4, fig. 7.
       Type-locality: Cobán, Guatemala.
  1903 Drymobius boddaerti var modesta Werner, Abh. K. Bayer. Akad. Wiss. München, (2) 24: 346.
       Type-locality: Cobán, Guatemala.
  1941 Dryadophis melanolomus laevis—Stuart, Misc. Publ. Mus. Zool. Univ. Mich., 49: 86.

    Distribution: Low and moderate elevations in mountains of Alta Verapaz, Guatemala.

Mastigodryas melanolomus tehuanae (Smith), new combination

   1943 Dryadophis melanolomus tehuanae Smith, Proc. U. S. Nat. Mus., 93: 420. Type-locality:
       Cerro Guengola, Oaxaca, Mexico.

     Distribution: Low and moderate elevations from Nayarit, Mexico, along Pacific slope south
      to western Guatemala.

MASTIGODRYAS PLEEI (Duméril, Bibron and Duméril), new combination
    pleei group

   1854 Dryadophis Pleei Duméril, Bibron and Duméril, Erp. Gén., 7: 661. Type-locality: Venezuela.
   1870 Herpetodryas quinquelineatus Steindachner, Sitz. Math.-Naturwiss. Kl. Akad. Wiss. Wien, 61: 340.
      Type-locality: Rio Vaupés, [Brazil or Colombia].
   1877 Dromicus (Alsophis) maculivittis Peters, Monats. Akad. Wiss. Berlin, 1877: 458. Type-locality:
      Calabozo, Venezuela.
   1887 Alsophis pulcher Garman, Proc. Amer. Phil. Soc., 24: 283. Type-locality: Testigos Islands.
   1939 Dryadophis [pleei]—Stuart, Copeia, 1939: 55.
   1941 Dryadophis pleei—Stuart, Misc. Publ. Mus. Zool. Univ. Mich., 49: 53, pl. 3, figs. 1-2.

     Distribution: Arid parts of Panama, Colombia, and Venezuela; also Margarita and Testigos Islands.

MASTIGODRYAS PULGHRICEPS (Cope), new combination
   group unknown

   1868 Masticophis pulchriceps Cope, Proc. Acad. Nat. Sci. Phila., 1868: 105. Type-locality: Plateau
      Valley of Quito, Ecuador.
   1905 Coluber fasciatus Rosen, Ann. Mag. Nat. Hist. (7) 15: 172, pl. 11, fig. 2. Type-locality:
      Ecuador.
   1939 Dryadophis [pulchriceps]—Stuart, Copeia, 1939: 55.
   1941 Dryadophis pulchriceps—Stuart, Misc. Publ. Mus. Zool. Univ. Mich., 49: 50, pl. 2, fig. 3.

     Distribution: Guaymas Basin and more humid habitats of west central Ecuador.

MASTIGODRYAS SANGUIVENTRIS (Taylor), new combination
    melanolomus group

   1954 Dryadophis sanguiventris Taylor, Univ. Kansas Sci. Bull., 36: 722. Type-locality: Esquinas,
      Forest Reserve, Las Esquinas (between Palmar and Golfito), Punta Arenas Province, Costa Rica.

     Distribution: Known from type locality and Los Diamantes, near Guápiles, Costa Rica.

Prepared by Janis Roze, American Museum of Natural History, New York, New York

MICRURUS Wagler

1824 Micrurus Wagler, in Spix, Sp. Nov. Serp. Bras.: 48. Type-species: Micrurus spixii Wagler.

Distribution: Southern United States throughout neotropical region to northern Argentina.

Content: Forty-six species, eight of which are extralimital.

Key to the species

1. Pattern of triads of black bands (black-white-
   black-white-black) separated by red bands on
   body--2
   Color pattern not forming triads------------16

2. Anal plate divided--------------------------3
   Anal plate undivided----------------hemprichii

3. First triad represented by more than one band--
   --4
   Only last black band of first body triad present
   (first two black bands are absent)-dissoleucus

4. First triad represented by two bands----------5
   First triad complete, consisting of three
   black bands---------------------------------9

5. More than nine triads on body----------------6
   Fewer than ten triads on body------------spixii

6. Dorsum of head black, including parietals-----7
   Some light bands present on head------------8

7. Supra-anal tubercles present in males; fewer
   than 14 triads on body--------------dumerilii
   No supra-anal tubercles present; 14 or more
   triads on body-----------------------bocourti

8. Temporals usually 0-1; white bands without
   black spots------------------------decoratus
   Temporals 1-1; white bands with abundant black
   spots--------------------------------elegans

9. Several supracephalic scales black, not outlined by black; frontal wider than supraocular
   --10
   All supracephalic scales red, outlined by
   black; frontal not wider than supraocular; 6-9
   complete triads on body----------surinamensis

10.First triad normal; first white band not
   oblique-------------------------------------11
   First two black bands in first triad anchor
   shaped, outlining oblique first white band,
   which is interrupted or nearly interrupted on
   middorsal line; 12-21 black triads---ancoralis

Clave de especies

1. Coloración de triadas de bandas negras (negro-
   blanco-negro-blanco-negro), separadas por
   bandas rojas, cubre todo el cuerpo----------2
   Bandas negras no forman triadas-------------16

2. Placa anal dividida-------------------------3
   Placa anal entera-------------------hemprichii

3. Primera triada representada por más de una
   banda negra---------------------------------4
   En primera triada solamente última banda negra
   presente (dos bandas negras anteriores
   ausentes)--------------------------dissoleucus

4. Primera triada representada por dos bandas
   negras--------------------------------------5
   Primera triada completa, formada por tres
   bandas negras-------------------------------9

5. Más de nueve triadas sobre el cuerpo----------6
   Menos de diez triadas sobre el cuerpo----spixii

6. Toda la parte superior de la cabeza negra,
   incluyendo parietales-----------------------7
   Bandas claras presentes en la parte superior de
   la cabeza-----------------------------------8

7. Tubérculos supraanales presentes en machos;
   menos de 14 triadas sobre el cuerpo--dumerilii
   No hay tubérculos supraanales presentes
   sobre el cuerpo----------------------bocourti

8. Temporales usualmente 0-1; bandas blancas sin
   manchas negras--------------------decoratus
   Temporales 1-1; bandas blancas con abundantes
   manchas negras------------------------elegans

9. Varias escamas supracefálicas negras, sin
   bordes negros; frontal más ancha que
   supraocular---------------------------------10
   Todas las escamas supracefálicas rojas con
   bordes negros; frontal no más ancha que supraocular; 6-9 triadas completas sobre el cuerpo
   ----------------------------------surinamensis

10.Primera triada normal; primera banda blanca no
   oblicua-------------------------------------11
   Primeras dos bandas negras de primera triada
   forman una figura de ancla, primera banda
   blanca oblicua, interrumpida o casi interrumpida sobre linea media dorsal; 12-21 triadas
   negras sobre el cuerpo--------------ancoralis

11.No red band, or red and white bands present on supracephalic scales; first nuchal black band usually does not cover parietal tips--------12
Single red band or spot present on parietals; some light spots occasionally present on snout; first nuchal black band usually reaches and covers parietal tips---------------------52

12.Fewer than 269 ventrals in both sexes--------13
More than 270 ventrals in both sexes; 14-20 triads on body----------------------filiformis

13.Snout all black; white internasal band present, well outlined and regular; black supraocular band of different width followed by red that covers posterior part of parietals, posterior temporals and first dorsal scales-----------14
No white internasal band, or when present, irregular, narrow and with black spots; parietals all black or with some light, irregular spots at least anteriorly-------------------15

14.Subcaudals fewer than 28, usually below 25; 7-9 black triads in males and 7-10 in females-----
-----------------------------------ibiboboca
Subcaudals 27 or more, usually over 30; exceptionally 8, usually more triads in both sexes-
-----------------------------------lemniscatus

15.Snout black; irregular white internasal band includes anterior part of frontal and supraoculars; all or at least posterior part of parietals, temporals and at least first three rows of dorsals red, latter without or with barely visible black tips; 7-10 triads on body-------------------------------ibiboboca
Snout usually with some white spots; usually no internasal band, when present irregular and narrow, spotted with black and covering part of prefrontal; all or at least posterior part of parietals black; first dorsals usually red with large black tips; usually more than 10 triads-------------------------------frontalis

16.At least some bands present------------------17
Body black with more than 130 rows of transverse white spots; no bands distinguishable---
-------------------------------margaritiferus

17.More than nine black bands present-----------18
Fewer than 10 black bands on body--------------
-----------------------------------latifasciatus

18.Head black (black cap present), including part or all of parietals; no light band interrupts black cap----------------------------------19
Black reduced on head, not or barely reaching parietals, or at least one light band crosses head on or anterior to parietals-----------34

11.Sin banda roja o con bandas rojas y blancas en las escamas supracefálicas; primera banda negra nucal usualmente no cubre los ápices parietales-----------------------------------12
Con una sola banda o mancha roja en parietales, ocasionalmente con algunas manchas claras en el hocico; primera banda negra nucal usualmente llega hasta y cubre los ápices parietales---52

12.Menos de 269 ventrales en ambos sexos--------13
Más de 270 ventrales en ambos sexos; 14-20 triadas sobre el cuerpo-------------filiformis

13.Todo el hocico negro; una banda internasal blanca presente, nítidamente formada y regular; banda supraocular negra de diferente ancho seguida por rojo que cubre la parte posterior de parietales, temporales posteriores y las primeras escamas dorsales-------14
Sin banda blanca internasal o, cuando presente, irregular, angosta y con manchas negras; todas las parietales negras o con algunas manchas claras irregulares por lo menos anteriormente-
---15

14.Subcaudales menos de 28, usualmente menos de 25; 7-9 triadas negras en machos y 7-10 en hembras-------------------------------ibiboboca
Subcaudales 27 o más, usualmente más de 30; excepcionalmente 8, usualmente más triadas en ambos sexos------------------------lemniscatus

15.Hocico negro; con banda internasal blanca irregular que incluye la parte anterior de frontal y supraoculares; todas o por lo menos la parte posterior de las parietales rojas como también las temporales y por lo menos las tres primeras dorsales que no poseen ápices negros o ápices negros apenas perceptibles; 7-10 triadas sobre el cuerpo---------ibiboboca
Hocico usualmente con algunas manchas blancas; sin banda internasal o cuando presente, irregular, angosta y manchada de negro, cubre parte de prefrontales; todas o por lo menos la parte posterior de parietales negras; las primeras dorsales usualmente rojas con ápices de escamas conspícuamente negros; usualmente más de 10 triadas-----------------------frontalis

16.Por lo menos algunas bandas presentes--------17
Cuerpo negro con más de 130 hileras de manchas blancas transversales; no hay bandas regulares sobre el cuerpo-----------------margaritiferus

17.Más de nueve bandas negras presentes---------18
Menos de 10 bandas negras sobre el cuerpo------
-----------------------------------latifasciatus

18.Cabeza negra (con casquete negro), incluyendo parte o todas las parietales; ninguna banda clara interrumpe el casquete negro---------19
Color negro sobre la cabeza reducido, sin llegar o apenas llegando a parietales, o por lo menos una banda clara cruza las parietales o delante de ellas--------------------------34

19. Solid black color reachs beyond parietals, including one or more dorsal scale rows, all temporals and almost all supralabials---20
Black usually does not cover all temporals, or with some light spots on supracephalic scales, or black on posterior part of parietals reduced; only few supralabials black; black tips on red scales present or absent--------21

20. Black bands cover 10 or more dorsal scales; red scales with black tips--------_putumayensis_
Black bands cover fewer than 10 dorsals; no black tips on red scales---------------_averyi_

21. Fewer than 70 black bands in males; fewer than 80 in females----------------------------22
More than 74 black bands in males; more than 84 in females----------------------_albicinctus_

22. Some infracephalic scales always black, particularly infralabials-----------------------23
All infracephalic scales white, some outlined with salt and pepper borders; 13-20 black body bands in both sexes----------------_clarki_

23. More than 31 black bands in males; more than 33 in females--------------------------------24
Fewer than 32 black bands in males; fewer than 32 in females--------------------------------26

24. Narrow white bands usually present on body, delimiting black bands; no small white supracephalic spots, but snout occasionally lighter than rest of head; usually not more than 30 black bands in males (occasionally up to 38), fewer than 35 in females (occasionally up to 42)--------------------------------------25
Black bands delimited by transverse rows of white spots; red bands either present or replaced by black; some small white spots usually present on supracephalic scales, particularly supraoculars; 32-67 black bands in males, 35-79 in females------------_langsdorffi_

25. Ventrals 200-216 in males, 225-234 in females; 24-38 black bands in males, 30-42 in females----------------------------------_steindachneri_
Ventrals 180-200 in males, 192-218 in females; 15-22 black bands in males, 22-41 in females--_psyches_

26. Black cap does not cover all of parietals; posterior border of black cap usually angular--27
Black head cap covers all of parietals-------29

27. Subcaudals 31 or more in females, 46 or more in males; supra-anal tubercles present at least in males----------------------------28
Subcaudals 26-31 in females, 41-47 in males; no supra-anal tubercles present--------_corallinus_

19. Color negro sólido llega más allá de parietales, incluyendo una o más dorsales, todas las temporales y casi todas las supralabiales--20
El negro usualmente no cubre todas las temporales, o existen manchas claras sobre las escamas supracefálicas, o el negro está reducido sobre la parte posterior de las parietales; sólo unas pocas supralabiales negras; ápices negros sobre las escamas rojas presentes o ausentes------------------------21

20. Las bandas negras ocupan diez o más escamas dorsales; escamas rojas con ápices negros-----------------------------------_putumayensis_
Las bandas negras ocupan menos de diez escamas dorsales; sin ápices negros------------_averyi_

21. Menos de 70 bandas negras en machos, y menos de 80 en hembras----------------------------22
Más de 74 bandas negras en machos, y más de 84 en hembras------------------------_albicinctus_

22. Algunas escamas infracefálicas siempre negras, sobre todo las infralabiales----------------23
Todas las escamas infracefálicas blancas, algunas delimitadas por un borde salpicado negruzco; 13-20 bandas negras en ambos sexos---------------------------------------_clarki_

23. Más de 31 bandas negras en machos; más de 33 en hembras--------------------------------24
Menos de 32 bandas negras en machos; menos de 32 en hembras--------------------------------26

24. Con bandas blancas angostas sobre el cuerpo, separando las negras; sin manchas claras supracefálicas, pero el hocico ocasionalmente más claro que el resto de la cabeza; usualmente menos de 30 bandas negras en machos (ocasionalmente hasta 38), menos de 35 en hembras (ocasionalmente hasta 42)-----------25
Bandas negras delimitadas por hileras transversales de manchas blancas; bandas rojas presentes o reemplazadas por negras; algunas manchas claras usualmente presentes sobre escamas supracefálicas, particularmente las supraoculares; 32-67 bandas negras en machos, 35-79 en hembras--------------------_langsdorffi_

25. Ventrales 200-216 en machos, 225-234 en hembras; 24-38 bandas negras en machos, 30-42 en hembras-------------------------_steindachneri_
Ventrales 180-200 en machos, 192-218 en hembras; 15-22 bandas negras en machos, 22-41 en hembras------------------------------_psyches_

26. Casquete negro no cubre todas las parietales; borde posterior de casquete usualmente angular-------------------------------------27
Casquete negro cubre todas las parietales----29

27. Subcaudales 31 o más en hembras, 46 o más en machos; tubérculos supraanales presentes por lo menos en machos-------------------------28
Subcaudales 26-31 en hembras, 41-47 en machos; sin tubérculos supraanales---------_corallinus_

28. Supra-anal tubercles present only in males; ventrals 177-204 in males, 194-217 in females------------------------------------dumerilii
    Supra-anal tubercles present in both sexes; 209-224 ventrals in males, 221-237 in females---------------------------------------alleni

29. Supra-anal tubercles present in either both sexes or in males only----------------------30
    No supra-anal tubercles present--------------31

30. Supra-anal tubercles present in both sexes; 209-224 ventrals in males and 221-237 in females------------------------------alleni
    Supra-anal tubercles present only in males; 177-204 ventrals in males and 194-217 in females------------------------------dumerilii

31. More than 21 black bands in males, 200 or more ventrals in males, or when fewer than 200, then more than 24 black bands--------------32
    Fewer than 23 black bands in males, 180-200 ventrals in males, and 192-218 in females--psyches

32. Ventrals 206 or more in both sexes, or when fewer than 206, then 30 or more black bands in females------------------------------------33
    Ventrals 205 or fewer in both sexes; 18-27 black bands in females--------------------peruvianus

33. Red bands usually melanistic, dark purple or nearly black; 30-42 black bands in females, 24-38 in males------------------steindachneri
    Red bands not melanistic, with regular black tips; 26-31 black bands in females and 22-28 in males-----------------------------mertensi

34. Only one light band crosses dorsal head scales, separating black of snout from first black nuchal band---------------------------------35
    At least two light bands cross dorsal head scales anterior to first nuchal black band; ocular-frontal band or spot very irregular with sinuous outline------------------spurelli

35. More than 190 ventrals in males, more than 208 in females, or if fewer in either sex, then fewer than 17 black bands-------------------36
    Ventrals 180-187 in males, 200-205 in females; 29-45 black bands in both sexes-------ruatanus

36. More than 38 subcaudals in males, usually more than 31 subcaudals in females, or if fewer, then fewer than 221 ventrals----------------37
    Subcaudals 27-38 in males, 23-30 in females; 37-80 black bands in both sexes; 222-335 ventrals in females----------------mipartitus

37. Bands of only two colors present on body, either black-white (yellow) or black-red----38
    Black, red, and white (yellow) bands present on body--------------------------------------41

28. Tubérculos supraanales presentes sólo en machos; 177-204 ventrales en machos, 194-217 en hembras---------------------------dumerilii
    Tubérculos supraanales presentes en ambos sexos; 209-224 ventrales en machos, 221-237 en hembras--------------------------------alleni

29. Tubérculos supraanales presentes en ambos sexos o sólo en machos----------------------------30
    Sin tubérculos supraanales------------------31

30. Tubérculos supraanales presentes en ambos sexos; 209-224 ventrales en machos, 221-237 en hembras--------------------------------alleni
    Tubérculos supraanales presentes sólo en machos; 177-204 ventrales en machos, 194-217 en hembras-------------------------dumerilii

31. Bandas negras 22 o más en machos; 200 o más ventrales en machos, o, cuando menos, entonces más de 24 bandas negras----------------32
    Bandas negras 22 o menos en machos; 180-200 ventrales en machos, 192-218 en hembras--psyches

32. Ventrales 206 o más en ambos sexos, o, cuando menos, entonces 30 o más bandas negras en hembras--------------------------------------33
    Ventrales 205 o menos en ambos sexos; 18-27 bandas negras en hembras------------peruvianus

33. Bandas rojas usualmente melanísticas, morado oscuro o casi negras; 30-42 bandas negras en hembras, 24-38 en machos---------steindachneri
    Bandas rojas no melanísticas, pero con ápices negros regulares; 26-31 bandas negras en hembras--------------mertensi

34. Sólo una banda clara cruza las escamas supracefálicas, separando la coloración negra del hocico de la primera banda nucal negra------35
    Por lo menos dos bandas claras cruzan las escamas supracefálicas hasta los ápices parietales y delante de la primera banda nucal negra; banda o mancha ocular-frontal muy irregular con borde sinuoso----------spurelli

35. Más de 190 ventrales en machos, más de 208 en hembras, o, cuando menos en ambos sexos, entonces menos de 17 bandas negras------------36
    Ventrales 180-187 en machos, 200-205 en hembras; 29-45 bandas negras en ambos sexos--ruatanus

36. Más de 38 subcaudales en machos, usualmente más de 31 subcaudales en hembras, o cuando menos, entonces menos de 221 ventrales en hembras--37
    Subcaudales 27-38 en machos, 23-30 en hembras; 37-80 bandas negras en ambos sexos; 222-335 ventrales en hembras---------------mipartitus

37. Solamente bandas de dos colores presentes sobre el cuerpo, negro-blanco (amarillo) o negro-rojo--------------------------------------38
    Bandas negras, rojas y blancas (amarillas) presentes sobre el cuerpo------------------41

38.All or most of parietals red; red and black
   bands on body--------------------------------39
   Narrow white band covers part of parietals,
   rest of head black; more than 20 black bands
   on body, separated by white---------annellatus

39.Black bands shorter than or as wide as red---40
   Black bands dorsally two or more times wider
   than red; 224 or more ventrals in males; 13-21
   black bands in both sexes------------stewarti

40.More than 39 black bands on body-------diastema
   Fewer than 30 black bands----------nigrocinctus

41.Posterior border of black snout color without
   posterior extension along parietal suture;
   supra-anal tubercles absent or present in
   males only----------------------------------42
   Black snout color extends back into point along
   parietal suture; supra-anal tubercles present
   in both sexes; 209-224 ventrals in males, 221-
   237 in females--------------------------alleni

42.More than 23 black bands in both sexes-------43
   Fewer than 24 black bands in both sexes------46

43.Usually fewer than 224 ventrals in females and
   usually fewer than 206 ventrals in males, or
   if more, then more than 27 black bands on
   body--44
   Ventrals 224 or more in females, 206-215 in
   males; not more than 27 black bands on body---
   ---browni

44.No supra-anal tubercles in males; usually more
   than 24 black bands in both sexes-----------45
   Supra-anal tubercles present in males; fewer
   than 26 black bands on body-------nigrocinctus

45.Subcaudals 38-48 in males, 26-35 in females----
   --------------------------------------annellatus
   Subcaudals 48-57 in males, 37-43 in females----
   ---------------------------------------diastema

46.Fewer than 206 ventrals in males, 221 in
   females---------------------------------------47
   More than 205 ventrals in males, 221 in
   females---------------------------------------49

47.No supra-anal tubercles; usually 1-2 temporals;
   black tips on red scales absent or present--48
   Supra-anal tubercles present in males; usually
   1-1 temporals; black tips on red scales
   usually present------------------nigrocinctus

48.Black bands 12-16 in both sexes; no black tips
   or hardly any on red scales--------hippocrepis
   Black bands 19 or more in both sexes; conspicuous black tips always present-------annellatus

49.Ventrals 206 or more in males, more than 223
   in females-----------------------------------50
   Ventrals 180-205 in males, 197-223 in females--
   --------------------------------nigrocinctus

38.Todas o mayor parte de parietales rojas;
   bandas rojas y negras sobre el cuerpo-------39
   Una banda blanca angosta presente sobre parte
   de las parietales, resto de la cabeza negro;
   más de 20 bandas negras sobre el cuerpo,
   separadas por bandas blancas--------annellatus

39.Bandas negras iguales o más angostas que las
   rojas---40
   Dorsalmente, las bandas negras dos o más veces
   más anchas que las rojas; 224 o más ventrales
   en hembras, 13-21 bandas negras en ambos
   sexos-----------------------------------stewarti
40.Más de 39 bandas negras sobre el cuerpo--------
   --diastema
   Menos de 30 bandas negras-----------nigrocinctus

41.Borde posterior de la coloración negra del
   hocico recto o sinuoso no llega hasta parietales; tubérculos ausentes o presentes solamente en machos-----------------------------42
   Coloración negra del hocico se proyecta a lo
   largo de sutura parietal en ángulo; tubérculos
   supraanales presentes en ambos sexos; 209-224
   ventrales en machos, 221-237 en hembras-alleni

42.Más de 23 bandas negras en ambos sexos-------43
   Menos de 24 bandas negras en ambos sexos-----46

43.Usualmente menos de 224 ventrales en hembras,
   usualmente menos de 206 en machos, o, cuando
   más, entonces más de 27 bandas negras sobre el
   cuerpo--44
   Ventrales 224 o más en hembras, 206-215 ventrales en machos; no más de 27 bandas negras
   sobre el cuerpo--------------------------browni

44.Sin tubérculos supraanales en machos; usualmente más de 24 bandas negras en ambos sexos--
   ---45
   Tubérculos supraanales presentes en machos; no
   más de 26 bandas negras en machos, no más de
   26 en hembras--------------------nigrocinctus

45.Subcaudales 38-48 en machos, 26-35 en hembras--
   --------------------------------------annellatus
   Subcaudales 48-57 en machos, 37-43 en hembras--
   ---------------------------------------diastema

46.Menos de 206 ventrales en machos y menos de 221
   en hembras------------------------------------47
   Más de 205 ventrales en machos y más de 221 en
   hembras---------------------------------------49

47.Sin tubérculos supraanales; usualmente 1-2 temporales; ápices negros sobre escamas rojas
   presentes o ausentes------------------------48
   Tubérculos supraanales presentes en machos,
   usualmente 1-1 temporales; usualmente hay
   ápices negros sobre las escamas rojas---------
   -----------------------------------nigrocinctus

48.Bandas negras 12-16 en ambos sexos; sin ápices
   negros sobre las escamas rojas, o ápices
   negros apenas perceptibles---------hippocrepis
   Bandas negras 19 o más en ambos sexos; ápices
   negros conspícuos siempre presentes-annellatus

49.Ventrales 206 o más en machos, más de 223 en
   hembras---------------------------------------50
   Ventrales 180-205 en machos, 197-223 en hem-
   bras-----------------------------------nigrocinctus

50. Black bands 15 or more on body, four or more on
tail in males; 17-27 black body bands, usually
more than four on tail in females; usually 1-1
sometimes 1-2 temporals--------------------51
Black bands 13-14 on body, four on tail in
males; 16-19 on body, 3-4 on tail in females;
usually 1-2 temporals------------------stuarti

51. Ventrals 213-217 in males; 31-35 subcaudals in
females; some irregular black tips always
present on red scales; belly usually with some
dark spots; 1-1 temporals--------nigrocinctus
Ventrals 206-213 in males; 34-38 subcaudals in
females; no black tips or few and small present on red scales; belly without black spots
usually; frequently 1-2, sometimes 1-1
temporals-----------------------------browni

52. White (yellow) bands as wide as or usually
wider than black body bands-----------isozonus
White (yellow) bands narrower than black body
bands--------------------------------tschudii

50. Bandas negras 15 o más sobre el cuerpo, cuatro
o más sobre la cola en machos; 17-27 bandas
negras sobre el cuerpo y, usualmente, más de
cuatro sobre la cola en hembras; usualmente
1-1, ocasionalmente 1-2 temporales----------51
Bandas negras 13-14 sobre el cuerpo, cuatro
sobre la cola en machos; 16-19 sobre el cuerpo, 3-4 sobre la cola en hembras; usualmente
1-2 temporales-------------------------stuarti

51. Ventrales 213-217 en machos; 31-35 subcaudales
en hembras; algunos ápices negros irregulares
siempre presentes sobre las escamas rojas;
vientre usualmente con algunas manchas oscuras;
1-1 temporales-------------------nigrocinctus
Ventrales 206-213 en machos; 34-38 subcaudales
en hembras; sin ápices negros o con ápices
negros pequeños y pocos; vientre usualmente
sin manchas oscuras; frecuentemente hay 1-2,
ocasionalmente 1-1 temporales----------browni

52. Bandas blancas (amarillas) tan anchas como o,
usualmente, más anchas que las bandas negras
del cuerpo---------------------------isozonus
Bandas blancas (amarillas) más angostas que
las bandas negras del cuerpo---------tschudii

MICRURUS ALBICINCTUS Amaral

1926 Micrurus albicinctus Amaral, Comm. Linh. Telegr. Mato Grosso, Publ. 84, annex 5: 26, figs. 7-10.
Type-locality: None given; collection containing type came from northern and central Mato
Grosso, Brazil.
1938 Micrurus waehnerorum Meise, Zool. Anz., 123: 20. Type-locality: São Paulo de Olivença, Brazil.

Distribution: From Mato Grosso to region of São Paulo de Olivença, Brazil.

MICRURUS ALLENI Schmidt

1936 Micrurus nigrocinctus alleni Schmidt, Zool. Ser. Field Mus. Nat. Hist., 20: 209, fig. 25. Type-
locality: Río Mico, seven mi above Rama, Siquía District, Nicaragua.
1951 [Micrurus alleni]—Taylor, Univ. Kansas Sci. Bull., 34: 172.

Distribution: Nicaragua, Costa Rica, and Panama.

Content: Two subspecies.

Key to the subspecies

1. Ventrals 229-237 in females, 214-224 in
males; black bands 15-20 in females; subcaudals 50-55 in males--------------alleni
Ventrals 221-230 in females, 209-215 in
males; black bands 20-28 in females; subcaudals 48-50 in males-------------yatesi

Clave de subespecies

1. Ventrales 229-237 en hembras, 214-224 en
machos; bandas negras 15-20 en hembras;
subcaudales 50-55 en machos----------alleni
Ventrales 221-230 en hembras, 209-215 en
machos; bandas negras 20-28 en hembras;
subcaudales 48-50 en machos----------yatesi

Micrurus alleni alleni Schmidt

1951 [Micrurus] alleni alleni—Taylor, Univ. Kansas Sci. Bull., 34: 172.
1951 Micrurus alleni richardi Taylor, Univ. Kansas Sci. Bull., 34: 169, pl. 23, fig. 7. Type-
locality: Los Diamantes, 2 km south of Guápiles, Costa Rica.

Distribution: Atlantic slopes of Nicaragua, Costa Rica, and northwestern Panama.

Micrurus alleni yatesi Dunn

1942 Micrurus nigrocinctus yatesi Dunn, Notulae Nat., 108: 8. Type-locality: Farm Two,
Chiriquí Land Co., near Puerto Armuelles, Chiriquí, Panama.
1967 Micrurus alleni yatesi—Roze, Amer. Mus. Novitates, 2287: 6.

Distribution: Pacific slopes of southeastern Costa Rica and southwestern Panama.

MICRURUS ANCORALIS (Jan)

1872 Elaps marcgravii var. ancoralis Jan, in Jan and Sordelli, Icon. Gén. Ophid., Livr. 42: pl. 4, fig. 2. Type-locality: Ecuador
1925 Micrurus ancoralis—Amaral, Proc. U.S. Nat. Mus., 67: 19.

Distribution: Eastern Panama to northwestern Ecuador, west of Andes.

Content: Two subspecies.

Key to the subspecies	Clave de subespecies

1. Black body bands 16-20 in males, 17-21 in females------------------------ancoralis
   Black bands 12-15 in males, 14-16 in females-----------------------------jani
	1. Bandas negras sobre el cuerpo 16-20 en machos, 17-21 en hembras---------ancoralis
	   Bandas negras sobre el cuerpo 12-15 en machos, 14-16 en hembras--------------jani

Micrurus ancoralis ancoralis (Jan)

1898 Elaps rosenbergi Boulenger, Proc. Zool. Soc. London, 1898: 117, pl. 13. Type-locality: Paramba, Esmeraldas Province, Ecuador.
1936 Micrurus ancoralis ancoralis—Schmidt, Zool. Ser. Field Mus. Nat. Hist., 20: 197.

Distribution: Rain forests of northwestern Ecuador.

Micrurus ancoralis jani Schmidt

1936 Micrurus ancoralis jani Schmidt, Zool. Ser. Field Mus. Nat. Hist., 20: 197. Type-locality: Andagoya, Chocó, Colombia.

Distribution: Eastern Panama to Chocó region of western Colombia.

MICRURUS ANNELLATUS (Peters)

1871 Elaps annellatus Peters, Monats. Akad. Wiss. Berlin, 1871: 402. Type-locality: Pozuzo, Peru.
1929 Micrurus annellatus—Amaral, Mem. Inst. Butantan, 4: 228.

Distribution: Moderate elevations on Amazonian slopes of Andes, from Ecuador to Bolivia.

Content: Four subspecies.

Key to the subspecies	Clave de subespecies

1. Black body bands fewer than 41 in males and 49 in females---------------------------2
   Black body bands 41-61 in males, 49-83 in females-----------------------annellatus
	1. Bandas negras sobre el cuerpo menos de 41 en machos, menos de 49 en hembras--------2
	   Bandas negras sobre el cuerpo 41-61 en machos, 49-83 en hembras--------annellatus

2. Two postoculars----------------------------3
   One postocular---------------------balzani
	2. Dos postoculares-------------------------3
	   Un postocular---------------------balzani

3. Usually 1-2 temporals; light band covers more than 50% of parietals------bolivianus
   Usually 1-1 temporals; light band covers less than 50% of parietals--------montanus
	3. Temporales usualmente 1-2; banda clara cubre más de 50% de parietales--bolivianus
	   Temporales usualmente 1-1; banda clara cubre menos de 50% de parietales--montanus

Micrurus annellatus annellatus (Peters)

1954 Micrurus annellatus annellatus—Schmidt, Fieldiana: Zool., 34: 322, fig. 62.

Distribution: Southern Ecuador to central Peru.

Micrurus annellatus balzani (Boulenger)

1898 Elaps balzani Boulenger, Ann. Mus. Stor. Nat. Genova, (2) 19: 130. Type-locality:
      Yungas, Bolivia.
1902 Elaps regularis Boulenger, Ann. Mag. Nat. Hist., (7) 10: 402. Type-locality: Chulumani,
      Bolivia, 2000 m.
1936 Micrurus balzani——Schmidt, Zool. Ser. Field Mus. Nat. Hist., 20: 192.
1967 Micrurus annellatus balzani——Roze, Amer. Mus. Novitates, 2287: 6.

   Distribution: Western Bolivia.

Micrurus annellatus bolivianus Roze

1967 Micrurus annellatus bolivianus Roze, Amer. Mus. Novitates, 2287: 7, fig. 2. Type-
      locality: Río Charobamba, about 50 km northeast of Zudañez, Chuquisaca, Bolivia.

   Distribution: Western Bolivia, south of area occupied by M. a. balzani.

Micrurus annellatus montanus Schmidt

1954 Micrurus annellatus montanus Schmidt, Fieldiana: Zool., 34: 322. Type-locality: Camp
      Four, about ten km north of Santo Domingo Mine, Puno, Peru, 2000 m.

   Distribution: Southeastern Peru to central Bolivia.

MICRURUS AVERYI Schmidt

1939 Micrurus averyi Schmidt, Zool. Ser. Field Mus. Nat. Hist., 24: 45, fig. 5. Type-locality: At
      head of Itabu Creek, Courantyne District, Guyana, 2000 ft (near Brazilian border, at Lat.
      1°40' N and Long. 58° W).

   Distribution: Known only from type-locality.

MICRURUS BOCOURTI (Jan)

1872 Elaps Bocourti Jan, in Jan and Sordelli, Icon. Gén. Ophid., Livr. 42: pl. 6, fig. 2. Type-
      locality: Unknown, restricted to Río Daule, Guayas Province, Ecuador, by Roze, Amer. Mus.
      Novitates, 2287, 1967, 8.
1967 [Micrurus bocourti]——Roze, Amer. Mus. Novitates, 2287: 8.

   Distribution: A disjunct distribution; known from western Ecuador and northern Colombia.

   Content: Two subspecies.

              Key to the subspecies   Clave de subespecies

1. Ventrals 197-206 in males, 32-35 subcaudals   1. Ventrales 197-206 en machos; subcaudales
   in females----------------------bocourti   32-35 en hembras------------------bocourti
   Ventrals 190-196 in males, 35-37 subcaudals   Ventrales 190-196 en machos; subcaudales
   in females-------------------sangilensis   35-37 en hembras--------------sangilensis

Micrurus bocourti bocourti (Jan)

1936 Micrurus ecuadorianus Schmidt, Zool. Ser. Field Mus. Nat. Hist., 20: 196. Type-locality:
      Río Daule, Guayas Province, Ecuador.
1967 Micrurus bocourti bocourti——Roze, Amer. Mus. Novitates, 2287: 8.

   Distribution: Western Ecuador.

Micrurus bocourti sangilensis Nicéforo-María

1942 Micrurus ecuadorianus sangilensis Nicéforo-María, Rev. Acad. Colomb. Cien. Exact. Fis.
      Nat., 5: 98, pl. 3, fig. 10. Type-locality: San Gil, Santander, Colombia.
1967 Micrurus bocourti sangilensis——Roze, Amer. Mus. Novitates, 2287: 8.

   Distribution: Region between Cordilleras Central and Oriental, northern Colombia.

MICRURUS BROWNI Schmidt and Smith

1943 *Micrurus browni* Schmidt and Smith, Zool. Ser. Field Mus. Nat. Hist., 29: 29. Type-locality: Chilpancingo, Guerrero, Mexico.

Distribution: Pacific Mexico from Guerrero south to western Guatemala.

Content: Three subspecies, one of which (*taylori* Schmidt and Smith) is extralimital.

Key to the subspecies	Clave de subespecies
1. Subcaudals 51-58----------------importunus	1. Subcaudales 51-58----------------importunus
Subcaudals 46-51--------------------browni	Subcaudales 46-51--------------------browni

Micrurus browni browni Schmidt and Smith

1967 *Micrurus browni browni*—Roze, Amer. Mus. Novitates, 2287: 11.

Distribution: Sierra Madre del Sur of central Guerrero south to mountains of western Guatemala.

Micururs browni importunus Roze

1967 *Micrurus browni importunus* Roze, Amer. Mus. Novitates, 2287: 11, fig. 4. Type-locality: Dueñas, about 25 km west-southwest of Guatemala City, in Antigua Basin, Sacatepequez, Guatemala.

Distribution: Known only from type locality.

MICRURUS CLARKI Schmidt

1936 *Micrurus clarki* Schmidt, Zool. Ser. Field Mus. Nat. Hist., 20: 211. Type-locality: Yavisa, Darién, Panama.

Distribution: Eastern Costa Rica to western Colombia.

MICRURUS CORALLINUS (Merrem)

1820 *Elaps corallinus* Merrem, Tentamen Systematis Amphibiorum: 144. Type-locality: Brazil; given as Rio de Janeiro, Cabo Frio, Brazil, by Roze, Amer. Mus. Novitates, 2287, 1967, 13.
1925 *Micrurus corallinus*—Amaral, Proc. U.S. Nat. Mus., 67: 20.

Distribution: Brazil south of Amazon Basin to Uruguay and northeastern Misiones, Argentina.

MICRURUS DECORATUS (Jan)

1858 *Elaps decoratus* Jan, Rev. Mag. Zool., (2) 10: 525, pl. B. Type-locality: Mexico (in error).
1921 *Elaps fischeri* Amaral, Anex. Mem. Inst. Butantan, 1: 59, pl. 2, figs. 1-5. Type-locality: Fazenda Bonito, Serra Bocaina, São Paulo, Brazil.
1923 *Elaps ezequieli* Lutz and Mello, Folha Medica, 4: 2. Type-locality: Caxambú, Serra da Mantiqueira, Minas Gerais, Brazil.
1926 *Micrurus decoratus*—Amaral, Rev. Mus. Paulista, 14: 32.

Distribution: Eastern Brazil, from Rio de Janeiro to Santa Catarina.

MICRURUS DIASTEMA (Duméril, Bibron and Duméril)

1854 *Elaps Diastema* Duméril, Bibron and Duméril, Erp. Gén., 7: 1222. Type-locality: Mexico (restricted to Colima, Mexico, by Schmidt, Zool. Ser. Field Mus. Nat. Hist., 20, 1933, 39; Roze, Amer. Mus. Novitates, 2287, 1967, 14 points out that this locality is far outside the range of the typical subspecies).
1933 *Micrurus diastema*—Schmidt, Zool. Ser. Field Mus. Nat. Hist., 20: 36.

Distribution: Caribbean slopes from Veracruz to Honduras, including Yucatán Peninsula.

Content: Seven subspecies, of which four (the nominate subspecies, *affinis* Jan, *alienus* Werner, and *macdougalli* Roze) are extralimital.

Key to the subspecies

Clave de subespecies

1. Fewer than 40 black bands in both sexes---2
   Black bands 40-59 in males, 44-61 in
   females----------------------------apiatus

1. Menos de 40 bandas negras en ambos sexos--2
   Bandas negras 40-59 en machos, 44-61 en
   hembras---------------------------apiatus

2. More or less perfect narrow black central
   band present between two regular black
   body bands, dividing red band in two and
   formed by concentration of black tips;
   black bands 31-34 in females------aglaeope
   No central black band within red band;
   occasionally black tips concentrated
   around middle of red band; black bands 24-
   33 in females, usually fewer than 30------
   ----------------------------------sapperi

2. Con banda central negra angosta más o menos
   perfecta entre dos bandas negras regulares
   del cuerpo, dividiendo la banda roja en
   dos y formada por concentración de ápices
   negros; 31-34 bandas negras en hembras----
   --------------------------------aglaeope
   Sin banda negra central en el rojo, ocasionalmente ápices negros se concentran
   aproximadamente en el medio de la banda
   roja; 24-33 bandas negras en hembras,
   usualmente menos de 30------------sapperi

Micrurus diastema aglaeope (Cope)

1860 Elaps aglaeope Cope, Proc. Acad. Nat. Sci. Phila., 1859: 344. Type-locality: Honduras.
1967 Micrurus diastema aglaeope—Roze, Amer. Mus. Novitates, 2287: 15.

Distribution: Mountains of northwestern Honduras.

Micrurus diastema apiatus (Jan)

1858 Elaps apiatus Jan, Rev. Mag. Zool., (2) 10: 522. Type-locality: Veracruz, Mexico (shown to
     be a lapsus for Verapaz, Guatemala, by Schmidt, Zool. Ser. Field Mus. Nat. Hist., 20, 1933,
     38; later restricted to Cobán, Guatemala, by Smith and Taylor, Univ. Kansas Sci. Bull., 33,
     1950, 317).
1967 Micrurus diastema apiatus—Roze, Amer. Mus. Novitates, 2287: 15.

Distribution: Caribbean slope from Chiapas, Mexico, to central Guatemala; may also occur in
Tabasco and Veracruz, Mexico, according to Roze, l.c.

Micrurus diastema sapperi (Werner)

1903 Elaps fulvius var. sapperi Werner, Zool. Anz., 26: 350. Type-locality: Guatemala.
1927 Elaps guatemalensis Ahl, Zool. Anz., 70: 251. Type-locality: Guatemala.
1933 Micrurus affinis stantoni Schmidt, Zool. Ser. Field Mus. Nat. Hist., 20: 36. Type-locality:
     Belize, British Honduras.
1967 Micrurus diastema sapperi—Roze, Amer. Mus. Novitates, 2287: 17.

Distribution: Southern Veracruz to lowlands of northern Guatemala and British Honduras,
omitting Yucatán Peninsula.

MICRURUS DISSOLEUCUS (Cope)

1860 Elaps dissoleucus Cope, Proc. Acad. Nat. Sci. Phila., 1859: 345. Type-locality: Venezuela
     (restricted to Maracaibo, Zulia, Venezuela, by Roze, Acta Biol. Venezuelica, 1, 1955, 478).
1925 Micrurus dissoleucus—Amaral, Proc. U.S. Nat. Mus., 47: 18.

Distribution: Caribbean slopes from Panama Canal Zone to eastern Venezuela.

Content: Four subspecies.

Key to the subspecies

Clave de subespecies

1. Subcaudals more than 22 in males; usually
   more than 18 in females-----------------2
   Subcaudals 21-22 in males, 17-19 in females
   ----------------------------melanogenys

1. Subcaudales más de 22 en machos; usualmente
   más de 18 en hembras--------------------2
   Subcaudales 21-22 en machos; 17-19 en
   hembras---------------------melanogenys

2. Usually eight or more triads in both sexes-
   --3
   Triads 6-8 in both sexes-------nigrirostris

2. Usualmente ocho o más triadas en ambos
   sexos-----------------------------------3
   Triadas 6-8 en ambos sexos-----nigrirostris

3. Subcaudals fewer than 20 in females; ventrals usually more than 212 in females----
------------------------------------dunni
  Subcaudals more than 20 in females; ventrals 201-212 in females-------dissoleucus

3. Subcaudales menos de 20 en hembras; generalmente más de 212 ventrales en hembras---
------------------------------------dunni
  Más de 20 subcaudales en hembras; 201-212
  ventrales en hembras-----------dissoleucus

Micrurus dissoleucus dissoleucus (Cope)

1936 Micrurus dissoleucus dissoleucus—Schmidt, Zool. Ser. Field Mus. Nat. Hist., 20: 202.

Distribution: Northeastern Colombia to eastern Venezuela.

Micrurus dissoleucus dunni Barbour

1923 Micrurus dunni Barbour, Occ. Pap. Mus. Zool. Univ. Mich., 129: 15. Type-locality: Ancón,
  Panama Canal Zone, Panama.
1936 Micrurus dissoleucus dunni—Schmidt, Zool. Ser. Field Mus. Nat. Hist., 20: 203.

Distribution: Canal Zone to eastern Panama.

Micrurus dissoleucus melanogenys (Cope)

1860 Elaps melanogenys Cope, Proc. Acad. Nat. Sci. Phila., 1860: 72. Type-locality: Unknown;
  restricted to Santa Marta region, Colombia, by Schmidt, Fieldiana, Zool., 34, 1955, 355.
1916 Elaps hollandi Griffin, Mem. Carnegie Mus., 7: 218, pl. 28, figs. 10-12. Type-locality:
  Bonda, Colombia.
1936 Micrurus dissoleucus melanogenys—Schmidt, Zool. Ser. Field Mus. Nat. Hist., 20: 203.

Distribution: Santa Marta region of Colombia.

Micrurus dissoleucus nigrirostris Schmidt

1858 Elaps gravenhorsti Jan, Rev. Mag. Zool., (2) 10: 523. Type-locality: Brazil (in error).[1]
1955 Micrurus dissoleucus nigrirostris Schmidt, Fieldiana, Zool., 34: 355. Type-locality:
  Barranquilla, Colombia.

Distribution: Lower Magdalena region, northern Colombia.

MICRURUS DUMERILII (Jan)

1858 Elaps dumerilii Jan, Rev. Mag. Zool., (2) 10: 522. Type-locality: Cartagena, Colombia.
1922 Micrurus dumerilii—Ruthven, Misc. Publ. Mus. Zool. Univ. Mich., 8: 68.

Distribution: Northern Venezuela around northern end of Andes in Colombia and south along Pacific
  slope to Ecuador.

Content: Five subspecies.

Comment: The oldest available name for this species is dumerilii Jan, and it replaces carinicaudus
  Schmidt, used by Roze, Amer. Mus. Novitates, 2287, 1967, 13.

Key to the subspecies

1. Black bands not in triads----------------2
   Black bands in triads--------------------4

2. First black nuchal band usually complete;
   most infracephalic scales light----------3
   First black nuchal band absent or reduced;
   usually most infracephalic scales
   blackened-------------------antioquiensis

Clave de subespecies

1. Bandas negras no en triadas---------------2
   Bandas negras en triadas------------------4

2. Primera banda nucal negra usualmente completa; mayoría de escamas infracefálicas
   claras------------------------------------3
   Primera banda nucal negra ausente o reducida; usualmente mayoría de escamas infracefálicas negruzcas----------antioquiensis

[1] Roze, Amer. Mus. Novitates, 2287, 1967, 18, suspects that this species probably belongs within this
taxon, but he plans to petition to the International Commission on Zoological Nomenclature, asking that
it be set aside.

3. Black bands 11-16 in males and 15-21 in
   females; yellow (white) and red bands
   among black bands on tail-----transandinus
   Black bands 15-24 in males and 19-25 in
   females; usually only yellow (white) and
   black bands on tail-----------carinicauda

4. Fewer than 187 ventrals in males, fewer
   than 208 in females------------colombianus
   More than 189 ventrals in males, more than
   208 in females------------------dumerilii

3. Bandas negras 11-16 en machos, 15-21 en
   hembras; bandas amarillas (blancas) y
   rojas entre las bandas negras de la cola--
   ------------------------------transandinus
   Bandas negras 15-24 en machos y 19-25 en
   hembras; usualmente sólo bandas amarillas
   (blancas) y negras en la cola--carinicauda

4. Menos de 187 ventrales en machos, menos de
   208 en hembras-----------------colombianus
   Más de 189 ventrales en machos, más de 208
   en hembras----------------------dumerilii

Micrurus dumerilii dumerilii (Jan), new combination

   1967 Micrurus carinicauda dumerilii—Roze, Amer. Mus. Novitates, 2287: 13.

   Distribution: Lower Magdalena River region to Norte de Santander, Colombia.

Micrurus dumerilii antioquiensis Schmidt, new combination

   1936 Micrurus antioquiensis Schmidt, Zool. Ser. Field Mus. Nat. Hist., 20: 195. Type-
        locality: Santa Rita, north of Medellín, Antioquia, Colombia.
   1955 Micrurus carinicaudus antioquiensis—Schmidt, Fieldiana, Zool., 34: 343.

   Distribution: Cauca Valley, Colombia.

Micrurus dumerilii carinicauda Schmidt, new combination

   1936 Micrurus carinicauda Schmidt, Zool. Ser. Field Mus. Nat. Hist., 20: 194. Type-locality:
        Orope, Zulia, Venezuela.
   1955 Micrurus carinicaudus carinicaudus—Schmidt, Fieldiana, Zool., 34: 343.

   Distribution: Northern Venezuela to Norte de Santander, Colombia.

Micrurus dumerilii colombianus (Griffin), new combination

   1916 Elaps colombianus Griffin, Mem. Carnegie Mus., 7: 216. Type-locality: Minca, Colombia.
   1967 Micrurus carinicauda colombianus—Roze, Amer. Mus. Novitates, 2287: 13.

   Distribution: Santa Marta region of northern Colombia.

Micrurus dumerilii transandinus Schmidt, new combination

   1936 Micrurus transandinus Schmidt, Zool. Ser. Field Mus. Nat. Hist., 20: 195. Type-locality:
        Andagoya, Chocó, Colombia.
   1955 Micrurus carinicaudus transandinus—Schmidt, Fieldiana, Zool., 34: 343.

   Distribution: Pacific lowlands of Colombia and northwestern Ecuador.

MICRURUS ELEGANS (Jan)

   1858 Elaps elegans Jan, Rev. Mag. Zool., (2) 10: 524. Type-locality: Mexico (restricted to Jalapa,
        Veracruz, Mexico, by Smith and Taylor, Univ. Kansas Sci. Bull., 33, 1950, 348).
   1929 Micrurus elegans—Amaral, Mem. Inst. Butantan, 4: 229.

   Distribution: Central Veracruz to Alta Verapaz, Guatemala.

   Content: Two subspecies, one (elegans Jan) extralimital.

Micrurus elegans veraepacis Schmidt

    1933 Micrurus elegans verae-pacis Schmidt, Zool. Ser. Field Mus. Nat. Hist., 20: 32.
        Type-locality: Campur, Alta Verapaz, Guatemala.

    Distribution: Chiapas and southern Tabasco, Mexico, to Alta Verapaz, Guatemala.

MICRURUS FILIFORMIS (Günther)

  1859 Elaps filiformis Günther, Proc. Zool. Soc. London, 1859: 86, pl. 18, fig. b. Type-locality:
      Pará, Brazil.
  1925 Micrurus filiformis—Amaral, Proc. U.S. Nat. Mus., 67: 19.

    Distribution: Northern Amazon region, extreme southern Colombia to northern Peru.

    Content: Two subspecies.

Key to the subspecies	Clave de subespecies
1. Two postoculars; ventral counts in males 274-279------------------------subtilis Usually one postocular; ventral counts in males 283-309------------------filiformis	1. Dos postoculares; ventrales en machos 274-279--------------------------subtilis Usualmente una postocular; ventrales en machos 283-309------------------filiformis

Micrurus filiformis filiformis (Günther)

    1967 Micrurus filiformis filiformis—Roze, Amer. Mus. Novitates, 2287: 22.

    Distribution: Northern Amazon region, extreme southern Colombia to northern Peru.

Micrurus filiformis subtilis Roze

    1967 Micrurus filiformis subtilis Roze, Amer. Mus. Novitates, 2287: 22, fig. 8. Type-
      locality: Carurú, Río Vaupés, Colombia-Brazil boundary.

    Distribution: Provinces of Vaupés and Amazonas, Colombia.

MICRURUS FRONTALIS (Duméril, Bibron and Duméril)

  1854 Elaps Frontalis Duméril, Bibron and Duméril, Erp. Gén., 7: 1223. Type-locality: Corrientes and
      Misiones, Argentina.
  1925 Micrurus frontalis—Amaral, Proc. U.S. Nat. Mus., 67: 19.

    Distribution: South America east of Andes, between 10°S and 35°S.

    Content: Four subspecies.

Key to the subspecies	Clave de subespecies
1. More than nine triads--------------------2 Six to nine triads in both sexes----------------------------------pyrrhocryptus	1. Más de nueve triadas----------------------2 Triadas seis a nueve en ambos sexos--------------------------------pyrrhocryptus
2. Subcaudals more than 18 in females; ventrals usually fewer than 223 in males----3 Subcaudals 16-18 in females; ventrals 223-242 in males------------------brasiliensis	2. Más de 18 subcaudales en hembras; usualmente menos de 223 ventrales en machos---3 Subcaudales 16-18 en hembras; ventrales 223-242 en machos------------brasiliensis
3. Ventrals usually more than 215 in males; parietals all black or with narrow light band inferiorly, head with some black spots only--------------------------------4 Ventrals 192-216 in males; anterior part of parietals with irregular light spot; inferiorly, head blackened-----altirostris	3. Usualmente más de 215 ventrales en machos; parietales totalmente negras o con banda clara angosta que las atraviesa; inferiormente cabeza con sólo algunas manchas negras----------------------------------4 Ventrales 192-216 en machos; parte anterior de parietales con mancha irregular clara; cabeza negruzca inferiormente-altirostris

4. Ventrals 215-222. in females; median black band of triad much wider than outer ones; head black with narrow light crossband----

-------------------------------mesopotamicus

Ventrals 222-242 in females; median black band not or slightly wider than outer ones; head nearly or all black---frontalis

4. Ventrales 215-222 en hembras; banda negra media de la triada mucho más ancha que las externas; cabeza negra con banda transversal clara angosta---------mesopotamicus

Ventrales 222-242 en hembras; banda negra media igual o ligeramente más ancha que las externas; cabeza negra o casi totalmente negra----------------------frontalis

Micrurus frontalis frontalis (Duméril, Bibron and Duméril)

1859 Elaps baliocoryphus Cope, Proc. Acad. Nat. Sci. Phila., 1859: 346. Type-locality: Buenos Aires, Argentina.
1936 Micrurus frontalis frontalis—Schmidt, Zool. Ser. Field Mus. Nat. Hist., 20: 199.

Distribution: Southern Brazil and southern Paraguay, including adjacent Argentina.

Micrurus frontalis altirostris (Cope)

1860 Elaps altirostris Cope, Proc. Acad. Nat. Sci. Phila., 1859: 345. Type-locality: South America.
1887 Elaps heterochilus Mocquard, Bull. Soc. Philom. Paris, (7) 11: 39. Type-locality: Brazil.
1936 Micrurus frontalis altirostris—Schmidt, Zool. Ser. Field Mus. Nat. Hist., 20: 199.
1944 Micrurus lemniscatus multicinctus Amaral, Pap. Avul. Dept. Zool. São Paulo, 5: 91. Type-locality: Texeira Soares, Paraná, Brazil.

Distribution: Southern Brazil, Uruguay, and northeastern part of Provincia de Misiones, Argentina.

Micrurus frontalis brasiliensis Roze

1967 Micrurus frontalis brasiliensis Roze, Amer. Mus. Novitates, 2287: 25, fig. 9. Type-locality: Barreiras, Bahia, Brazil.

Distribution: Southeastern Brazil.

Micrurus frontalis mesopotamicus Barrio and Miranda

1968 Micrurus frontalis mesopotamicus Barrio and Miranda, Mem. Inst. Butantan, 33 (1966): 872. Type-locality: Villa Federal, Entre Ríos, Argentina.

Distribution: Provincias de Entre Ríos, Corrientes and southwestern Misiones, Argentina.

Micrurus frontalis pyrrhocryptus (Cope)

1862 Elaps pyrrhocryptus Cope, Proc. Acad. Nat. Sci. Phila., 1862: 347. Type-locality: Vermejo River, Argentina (Roze says "Argentine Chocó").
1902 Elaps Simonsii Boulenger, Ann. Mag. Nat. Hist., (7) 9: 338. Type-locality: Cruz del Eje, Córdoba, Argentina.
1953 Micrurus frontalis pyrrhocryptus—Shreve, Breviora, 16: 5.
1956 Micrurus tricolor Hoge, Mem. Inst. Butantan, 27: 67, figs. 1-4, 6. Type-locality: Garandazal, Mato Grosso, Brazil.

Distribution: Southwestern Mato Grosso in Brazil, western and southwestern Bolivia and adjacent Paraguay, south to Mendoza and Santa Fé, Argentina.

MICRURUS HEMPRICHII (Jan)

1858 Elaps hemprichii Jan, Rev. Mag. Zool, (2) 10: 523. Type-locality: Colombia.
1929 Micrurus hemprichii—Amaral, Mem. Inst. Butantan, 4: 230.

Distribution: Northern South America east of the Andes.

Content: Two subspecies.

1. Triads 5-6 in both sexes; ventrals 184-191
   in males--------------------------ortoni
   Triads 7-10 in both sexes; ventrals 159-184
   in males----------------------hémprichii

1. Triadas 5-6 en ambos sexos; ventrales 184-
   191 en machos----------------------ortoni
   Triadas 7-10; ventrales 159-184 en machos--
   ----------------------------hemprichii

Micrurus hemprichii hemprichii (Jan)

1953 Micrurus hemprichii hemprichii—Schmidt, Fieldiana, Zool., 34: 166.

Distribution: Eastern Colombia and southern Venezuela to Guianas.

Micrurus hemprichii ortoni Schmidt

1953 Micrurus hemprichii ortoni Schmidt, Fieldiana, Zool., 34: 166. Type-locality: Pebas, Peru.

Distribution: Amazonian slopes of Colombia, Ecuador, and Peru; also recorded from Pará, Brazil.

MICRURUS HIPPOCREPIS (Peters)

1862 Elaps hippocrepis Peters, Monats. Akad. Wiss. Berlin, 1861: 925. Type-locality: Santo Tomás
   (=Puerto Matias de Galvez), Guatemala.
1933 Micrurus hippocrepis—Schmidt, Zool. Ser. Field Mus. Nat. Hist., 20: 36.

Distribution: Caribbean lowlands of British Honduras and Guatemala.

MICRURUS IBIBOBOCA (Merrem)

1820 Elaps ibiboboca Merrem, Tentamen Systematis Amphibiorum: 142. Type-locality: Brazil.
1820 Elaps marcgravii Wied, Nova Acta Acad. Leop.-Carol., 10: 109. Type-locality: Brazil; noted as
   mouth of Río Belmente in Wied, Beiträge zur Naturgeschichte von Brazilien, 1, 1825, 420.
1925 Micrurus ibiboboca—Amaral, Rev. Mus. Paulista, 15: 29.

Distribution: Eastern Brazil.

MICRURUS ISOZONUS (Cope)

1860 E[laps] isozonus Cope, Proc. Acad. Nat. Sci. Phila., 1860: 73. Type-locality: South America;
   restricted to Caracas, Venezuela, by Roze, Acta Biol. Venez., 1, 1955, 486.
1920 Elaps omissus Boulenger, Ann. Mag. Nat. Hist., (9) 6: 109. Type-locality: Venezuela.
1936 Micrurus isozonus—Schmidt, Zool. Ser. Field Mus. Nat. Hist., 20: 198.

Distribution: Northern and central Venezuela to Intendencia Meta, Colombia.

MICRURUS LANGSDORFFI Wagler

1824 Micrurus Langsdorffi Wagler in Spix, Sp. Nov. Serp. Bras.: 10, pl. 2, fig. 2. Type-locality:
   Rio Japurá, Amazonas, Brazil.

Distribution: Headwaters of Amazonian basin, from southern Colombia to northern Peru.

Content: Two subspecies.

Key to the subspecies

1. More than 40 black bands on body----------
   ----------------------------ornatissimus
   Fewer than 36 black bands on body----------
   ----------------------------langsdorffi

Clave de subespecies

1. Más de 40 bandas negras sobre el cuerpo----
   ----------------------------ornatissimus
   Menos de 36 bandas negras sobre el cuerpo--
   ----------------------------langsdorffi

Micrurus langsdorffi langsdorffi Wagler

1868 Elaps imperator Cope, Proc. Acad. Nat. Sci. Phila., 1868: 110. Type-locality: Napo and Marañón, Peru.
1868 Elaps batesi Günther, Ann. Mag. Nat. Hist., (4) 1: 428, pl. 17-1. Type-locality: Pebas, Peru.
1935 Micrurus mimosus Amaral, Mem. Inst. Butantan, 9: 221. fig. 6. Type-locality: Río Putumayo, Colombia.
1967 Micrurus langsdorffi langsdorffi—Roze, Amer. Mus. Novitates, 2287: 30.

Distribution: Upper Amazonian region from southern Colombia to northern Peru, including north-western Brazil and adjacent Ecuador.

Micrurus langsdorffi ornatissimus

1858 Elaps ornatissimus Jan, Rev. Mag. Zool., (2) 10: 521. Type-locality: Mexico (in error).
1896 Elaps buckleyi Boulenger, Cat. Sn. Brit. Mus., 3: 416, pl. 22-1. Type-locality: Canelos, Ecuador, and Pará, Brazil.
1936 Micrurus ornatissimus—Schmidt, Zool. Ser. Field Mus. Nat. Hist., 20: 191.
1967 Micrurus langsdorffi ornatissimus—Roze, Amer. Mus. Novitates, 2287: 30.

Distribution: Amazonian slopes in eastern Ecuador and northern Peru.

MICRURUS LATIFASCIATUS Schmidt

1933 Micrurus latifasciatus Schmidt, Zool. Ser. Field Mus. Nat. Hist., 20: 35. Type-locality: Finca El Ciprés, Volcán Zunil, Suchitepequez, Guatemala.

Distribution: Pacific slopes from southern Chiapas to western Guatemala.

MICRURUS LEMNISCATUS (Linnaeus)

1758 Elaps lemniscatus Linnaeus, Systema Naturae, Ed. 10: 224. Type-locality: Asia; restricted to Belém, Pará, Brazil, by Schmidt and Walker, Zool. Ser. Field Mus. Nat. Hist., 24, 1943, 294; subsequent restriction considered invalid by Roze, Amer. Mus. Novitates, 2287, 1967, 32, because the locality lies outside known distribution of M. l. lemniscatus.
1919 Micrurus lemniscatus—Beebe, Zoologica, 2: 216.

Distribution: Trinidad, eastern Venezuela, Guianas, and Amazon Basin.

Content: Five subspecies.

Key to the subspecies

1. Ventrals fewer than 226 in males; usually fewer than 243 in females----------------2
   Ventrales more than 226 in males; more than 243 in females------------------------3

2. Practically all infralabials white; subcaudals 30-34 in females---frontifasciatus
   Some infralabials black; subcaudals 32-41 in females----------------------diutius

3. Subcaudals usually more than 33 in females; no black spots, only regular black tips on red scales; white bands usually more than two scales long------------------------4
   Subcaudals 27-33 in females; few and irregular black spots or tips on red scales; white bands one to two scales long--------------------------------carvalhoi

4. Black triads 9-11 in both sexes-----helleri
   Black triads 12-14 in both sexes (occasionally 11 in females)------------lemniscatus

Clave de subespecies

1. Menos de 226 ventrales en machos; usualmente menos de 243 en hembras------------2
   Más de 226 ventrales en machos; más de 243 en hembras-------------------------3

2. Prácticamente todas las infralabiales blancas; 30-34 subcaudales en hembras-----
   ------------------------frontifasciatus
   Algunas infralabiales negras; 32-41 subcaudales en hembras---------------diutius

3. Usualmente más de 33 subcaudales en hembras; escamas rojas sin manchas o sólo con ápices negros regulares; bandas blancas usualmente más de dos escamas de largo---4
   Subcaudales 27-33 en hembras; escamas rojas con pocos ápices o manchas negras irregulares; bandas blancas de una o dos escamas de largo----------------carvalhoi

4. Triadas negras 9-11 en ambos sexos--helleri
   Triadas negras 12-14 en ambos sexos (ocasionalmente 11 en hembras)------lemniscatus

Micrurus lemniscatus lemniscatus (Linnaeus)

1955 [Micrurus] lemniscatus lemniscatus—Burger, Bol. Mus. Cien. Nat. Caracas, 1: 40.

Distribution: Northern parts of Guyana, Surinam, and French Guiana.

Micrurus lemniscatus carvalhoi Roze

1967 Micrurus lemniscatus carvalhoi Roze, Amer. Mus. Novitates, 2287: 33, fig. 11. Type-locality: Catanduva, São Paulo, Brazil.

Distribution: Amazon Basin of Brazil.

Micrurus lemniscatus diutius Burger

1955 Micrurus lemniscatus diutius Burger, Bol. Mus. Cien. Nat., Caracas, 1: 8. Type-locality: Tunapuna, Trinidad.

Distribution: Trinidad, eastern Venezuela, and central areas of Guyana, Surinam, and French Guiana.

Micrurus lemniscatus frontifasciatus (Werner)

1927 Elaps frontifasciatus Werner, Sitz. Akad. Wiss. Vienna, 135: 250. Type-locality: Bolivia.
1967 Micrurus lemniscatus frontifasciatus—Roze, Amer. Mus. Novitates, 2287: 34.

Distribution: Eastern Andean slopes in Bolivia.

Micrurus lemniscatus helleri Schmidt and Schmidt

1925 Micrurus helleri Schmidt and Schmidt, Zool. Ser. Field Mus. Nat. Hist., 12: 129. Type-locality: Pozuzo, Huanuco, Peru.
1967 Micrurus lemniscatus helleri—Roze, Amer. Mus. Novitates, 2287: 35.

Distribution: Northern Brazil, southern Venezuela and Colombia to Amazonian foothills of Ecuador, Peru, and Bolivia.

MICRURUS MARGARITIFERUS Roze

1967 Micrurus margaritiferus Roze, Amer. Mus. Novitates, 2287: 35, fig. 12. Type-locality: Boca Río Santiago-Río Marañón, Peru.

Distribution: Known only from type-locality.

MICRURUS MERTENSI Schmidt

1936 Micrurus mertensi Schmidt, Zool. Ser. Field Must. Nat. Hist., 20: 192. Type-locality: Pacasmayo, Peru.

Distribution: Lowlands of southwestern Ecuador to central Peruvian coastal areas.

MICRURUS MIPARTITUS (Duméril, Bibron and Duméril)

1854 Elaps mipartitus Duméril, Bibron and Duméril, Erp. Gén., 7: 1220. Type-locality: "Col. rio-sucio ou senio."; Roze, Amer. Mus. Novitates, 2287, 1967, 36, suggested that this might be the same as "Sinú," Colombia.
1926 Micrurus mipartitus—Amaral, Proc. New England Zool. Club, 9: 66.

Distribution: Caribbean Central America from Nicaragua to northern South America on both sides of Andes; coastal mountains of Venezuela.

Content: Six subspecies.

Key to the subspecies	Clave de subespecies

1. Ventrals more than 223 in males; usually more than 251 in females----------------2
   Ventrals 197-220 in males; 222-251 in females----------------------semipartitus
	1. Ventrales más de 223 en machos; usualmente más de 251 en hembras--------------------2
	   Ventrales 197-220 en machos; 222-251 en hembras----------------------semipartitus

2. Subcaudals usually 25 or more in females; black-red or black-white on body---------3
   Subcaudals 23-25 in females; black-white (yellow) on body----------------mipartitus
	2. Usualmente 25 o más subcaudales en hembras; negro-rojo o negro-blanco en el cuerpo---3
	   Subcaudales 23-25 en hembras; negro-blanco (amarillo) en el cuerpo--mipartitus

3. Black-white (yellow) on body-------------4
   Black-red on body------------------------5
	3. Negro-blanco (amarillo) en el cuerpo------4
	   Negro-rojo en el cuerpo-------------------5

4. Ventrals 224-247 in males, 244-287 in females--------------------------anomalus
   Ventrals 254-275 in males, 276-335 in females-----------------------decussatus
	4. Ventrales 224-247 en machos; 244-287 en hembras-------------------------anomalus
	   Ventrales 254-275 en machos; 276-335 en hembras-----------------------decussatus

5. Ventrals 237-244 in males, 256-269 in females---------------------------hertwigi
   Ventrals 247-265 in males, 278-311 in females--------------------multifasciatus
	5. Ventrales 237-244 en machos; 256-269 en hembras--------------------------hertwigi
	   Ventrales 247-265 en machos, 278-311 en hembras--------------------multifasciatus

Micrurus mipartitus mipartitus (Duméril, Bibron and Duméril)

?1903 **Elaps aequicinctus** Werner, Zool. Anz., **26**: 249. Type-locality: Unknown, supposedly Venezuela or Ecuador.
 1955 Micrurus mipartitus mipartitus—Rendahl and Vestergren, Ark. för Zool., 33A (1): 9.

 Distribution: Darien of Panama to Pacific lowlands of Colombia.

Micrurus mipartitus anomalus (Boulenger)

 1896 Elaps anomalus Boulenger, Cat. Sn. Brit. Mus., 3: 417, pl. 22, fig. 2. Type-locality: Colombia.
 1929 Micrurus anomalus—Amaral, Mem. Inst. Butantan, 4: 228.
 1967 Micrurus mipartitus anomalus—Roze, Amer. Mus. Novitates, 2287: 37.

 Distribution: Santa Marta Mountains and Cordillera Oriental, east of Magdalena River, Colombia, and of Andes in western Venezuela.

Micrurus mipartitus decussatus (Duméril, Bibron and Duméril)

 1845 Elaps decussatus Duméril, Bibron and Duméril, Erp. Gén., 7: 1221. Type-locality: Probably Colombia.
 1896 Elaps fraseri Boulenger, Cat. Sn. Brit. Mus., 3: 432, pl. 22, fig. 3. Type-locality: West Ecuador.
 1896 Elaps mentalis Boulenger, Cat. Sn. Brit. Mus., 3: 432, pl. 22, fig. 4. Type-locality: Pallatanga, Ecuador, and Cali, Colombia.
 1902 Elaps calamus Boulenger, Ann. Mag. Nat. Hist., (7) 9: 57. Type-locality: San Javier, north-western Ecuador.
 1913 Elaps microps Boulenger, Proc. Zool. Soc. London, 1913: 1036, pl. 108, fig. 2. Type-locality: Peña Lisa, Condoto, Chocó, Colombia.
 1940 Micrurus mipartitus multiscutatus Rendahl and Vestergren, Ark. för Zool., 33A (1): 9, fig. 3. Type-locality: El Tambo, Cauca, Colombia.
 1967 Micrurus mipartitus decussatus—Roze, Amer. Mus. Novitates, 2287: 37.

 Distribution: Western and central Andes and southern part of eastern Andes in Colombia; western Ecuador; possibly Peru.

Micrurus mipartitus hertwigi (Werner)

1897 *Elaps hertwigi* Werner, Sitz. Akad. Wiss. Munich, 27: 354. Type-locality: Central America.
1967 *Micrurus mipartitus hertwigi*—Roze, Amer. Mus. Novitates, 2287: 37.

Distribution: Caribbean slopes of Nicaragua, Costa Rica and Panama.

Micrurus mipartitus multifasciatus (Jan)

1858 *Elaps multifasciatus* Jan, Rev. Mag. Zool., (2) 10: 521. Type-locality: Central America.
1955 *Micrurus mipartitus multifasciatus*—Roze, Acta Biol. Venez., 1: 467.

Distribution: Central Panama, including Canal Zone.

Micrurus mipartitus semipartitus (Jan)

1858 *Elaps semipartitus* Jan, Rev. Mag. Zool., (2) 10: 113. Type-locality: Cayenne; restricted to Caracas, Venezuela by Roze, Acta Biol. Venez., 1, 1955, 467.
1955 *Micrurus mipartitus semipartitus*—Roze, Acta Biol. Venez., 1: 466.

Distribution: Cordillera de la Costa in Northern Venezuela.

MICRURUS NIGROCINCTUS (Girard)

1854 *Elaps nigrocinctus* Girard, Proc. Acad. Nat. Sci. Phila., 1854: 226. Type-locality: Taboga Island, Bay of Panama.
1927 *Micrurus nigrocinctus*—Amaral, Bull. Antivenin Inst. Amer., 1: 34.

Distribution: Chiapas, Mexico through Central America to Pacific Colombia.

Content: Seven subspecies, according to the latest review by Roze, Amer. Mus. Novitates, 2287, 1967, 38.

Key to the subspecies	Clave de subespecies

1. First black nuchal band does not cover parietals---------------------------------2
   First black nuchal band covers at least tips of parietals-----------------------3

2. Ventrals 180-192 in males; 192-211 in females---------------------*mosquitensis*
   Ventrals 195-210 in males; 205-220 in females-----------------------*divaricatus*

3. Ventrals fewer than 213 in males, fewer than 228 in females--------------------4
   Ventrals 213-217 in males, 228-230 in females-------------------------*coibensis*

4. Ventrals usually fewer than 193 in males and more than 205 in females-------------5
   Ventrals approximately 193 in males, 205-209 in females; black bands 21-23 in females-------------------------*babaspul*

5. At least some black tips present; white bands present; usually more than 14 black bands---------------------------------6
   Usually no black tips on red scales; no white band or barely visible white bands on body (when well developed, then no more than 14 black bands on body)----*zunilensis*

1. Primera banda nucal negra no cubre parietales------------------------------------2
   Primera banda nucal negra cubre al menos ápices de las parietales-----------------3

2. Ventrales 180-192 en machos; 192-211 en hembras---------------------*mosquitensis*
   Ventrales 195-210 en machos; 205-220 en hembras-----------------------*divaricatus*

3. Ventrales menos de 213 en machos; menos de 228 en hembras---------------------------4
   Ventrales 213-217 en machos; 228-230 en hembras-------------------------*coibensis*

4. Ventrales usualmente menos de 193 en machos; más de 205 en hembras-----------5
   Ventrales aproximadamente 193 en machos; 205-209 en hembras; 21-23 bandas negras en hembras-------------------------*babaspul*

5. Al menos algunos apices negros presentes; bandas blancas presentes; usualmente más de 14 bandas negras----------------------6
   Usualmente escamas rojas sin ápices negros; bandas blancas ausentes o apenas visibles en el cuerpo (cuando bien desarrolladas entonces no más de 14 bandas negras en el cuerpo)-------------------------*zunilensis*

6. Black covers only parietal tips; white or
   light parietal band wide-----------------7
   Black covers anterior and posterior part of
   parietals; white parietal band narrow or
   nearly absent (when black does not cover
   anterior part of parietals, then usually
   black spots present on parietals; black
   frequently projects on chin shields)------
   ---------------------------melanocephalus

7. Black bands 13-21 in both sexes; usually
   black tips on all red scales--nigrocinctus
   Black bands usually more than 19, up to 26
   in both sexes; only few, irregular black
   tips present on red------------divaricatus

6. El negro cubre sólo los ápices parietales;
   ancha banda parietal blanca o clara------7
   Color negro cubre parte anterior y posterior
   de parietales; banda parietal blanca angosta o casi ausente (cuando el negro no
   cubre parte anterior de parietales, entonces usualmente hay manchas negras en
   parietales; el negro frecuentemente se
   proyecta en geniales)-------melanocephalus

7. Bandas negras 13-21 en ambos sexos; usualmente ápices negros en todas las escamas
   rojas------------------------nigrocinctus
   Usualmente más de 19, hasta 26 bandas
   negras en ambos sexos; sólo pocos ápices
   negros irregulares en escamas rojas------
   ----------------------------divaricatus

Micrurus nigrocinctus nigrocinctus (Girard)

1933 Micrurus nigrocinctus nigrocinctus—Schmidt, Zool. Ser. Field Mus. Nat. Hist., 20: 33.

Distribution: Pacific slope of southeastern Costa Rica and Panama to adjacent Colombia.

Micrurus nigrocinctus babaspul Roze

1967 Micrurus nigrocinctus babaspul Roze, Amer. Mus. Novitates, 2287: 38, fig. 13. Type-locality:
Little Hill, Great Corn Island, about 55 km east-northeast of Bluefields, Nicaragua.

Distribution: Corn and Great Corn Islands, Nicaragua.

Micrurus nigrocinctus coibensis Schmidt

1936 Micrurus nigrocinctus coibensis Schmidt, Zool. Ser. Field Mus. Nat. Hist., 20: 209.
Type-locality: Coiba Island, Panama.

Distribution: Coiba Island, Panama.

Micrurus nigrocinctus divaricatus (Hallowell)

1855 Elaps divaricatus Hallowell, Jour. Acad. Nat. Sci. Phila., (2) 3: 36. Type-locality:
Honduras.
1933 Micrurus nigrocinctus divaricatus—Schmidt, Zool. Ser. Field Mus. Nat. Hist., 20: 33.

Distribution: Northern and central Honduras to British Honduras.

Micrurus nigrocinctus melanocephalus (Hallowell)

1860 Elaps melanocephalus Hallowell, Proc. Acad. Nat. Sci. Phila., 1860: 226. Type-locality:
Ometepec, Nicaragua.
1951 Micrurus pachecoi Taylor, Univ. Kansas Sci. Bull., 34: 165, pl. 22, fig. 6. Type-locality:
Guanacaste, Costa Rica.
1967 Micrurus nigrocinctus melanocephalus—Roze, Amer. Mus. Novitates, 2287: 39.

Distribution: Pacific slope of Nicaragua and southwestern Costa Rica.

Micrurus nigrocinctus mosquitensis Schmidt

1933 Micrurus nigrocinctus mosquitensis Schmidt, Zool. Ser. Field Mus. Nat. Hist., 20: 33.
Type-locality: Limón, Costa Rica.

Distribution: Atlantic slopes of eastern and southern Nicaragua to northwestern Panama.

<u>Micrurus nigrocinctus zunilensis</u> Schmidt

   1932 <u>Micrurus nigrocinctus zunilensis</u> Schmidt, Proc. Calif. Acad. Sci., (4) 20: 266.
       Type-locality: Finca El Ciprés, lower slopes of Volcán Zunil, Suchitepequez Province, near
       Samayac and Mazatenango, Guatemala.
   1941 <u>Micrurus nigrocinctus wagneri</u> Mertens, Senckenbergiana, 23: 216. Type-locality: Finca
       Germania, Sierra Madre, Chiapas, Mexico, 400-1300 m.
   1943 <u>Micrurus nigrocinctus ovandoensis</u> Schmidt and Smith, Zool. Ser. Field Mus. Nat. Hist.,
       29: 26. Type-locality: Salto de Agua, Mount Ovando, about 15 mi northeast of Escuintla,
       Chiapas, Mexico.

    Distribution: Pacific slopes of Chiapas, Mexico to El Salvador and southern Honduras.

MICRURUS PERUVIANUS Schmidt

   1936 <u>Micrurus peruvianus</u> Schmidt, Zool. Ser. Field Mus. Nat. Hist., 20: 193. Type-locality: Perico,
       Departamento de Cajamarca, Peru.

    Distribution: Andes of northeastern Peru.

MICRURUS PSYCHES (Daudin)

   1803 <u>Vipera psyches</u> Daudin, Hist. Nat. Rept., 8: 320, pl. 100, fig. 1. Type-locality: Surinam.
   1919 <u>Micrurus psyches</u>—Beebe, Zoologica, 2: 216.

    Distribution: Northern South America from Colombia to Guianas; Trinidad.

    Content: Three subspecies.

Key to the subspecies	Clave de subespecies
1. Black bands usually more than 22 in males; ventrals usually fewer than 193 in males and usually fewer than 211 in females----2 Black bands 15-22 in males; ventrals 193-210 in males and 211-218 in females---<u>medemi</u>	1. Usualmente más de 22 bandas negras en machos; usualmente menos de 193 ventrales en machos y menos de 211 en hembras------2 Bandas negras 15-22 en machos; ventrales 193-210 en machos; 211-218 en hembras-------------------------------------<u>medemi</u>
2. Red bands usually melanistic; ventrals 188-195 in males, and 203-213 in females------------------------------<u>psyches</u> Red bands not melanistic; ventrals 180-191 in males and 192-205 in females-<u>circinalis</u>	2. Bandas rojas usualmente melanísticas; ventrales 188-195 en machos; 203-213 en hembras--------------------------<u>psyches</u> Bandas rojas no melanísticas; ventrales 180-191 en machos; 192-205 en hembras----------------------------------<u>circinalis</u>

<u>Micrurus psyches psyches</u> (Daudin)

   1931 <u>Micrurus psyches psyches</u>—Amaral, Bull. Antivenin Inst., 4: 89.

    Distribution: Guianas, eastern and southern Venezuela, and extreme southern part of Colombia.

<u>Micrurus psyches circinalis</u> (Duméril, Bibron and Duméril)

   1854 <u>Elaps circinalis</u> Duméril, Bibron and Duméril, Erp. Gén., 7: 1210. Type-locality: Martinique
       (in error, according to Roze, Amer. Mus. Novitates, 2287, 1967, 41).
   1858 <u>Elaps riisei</u> Jan, Rev. Mag. Zool., (2) 10: 525. Type-locality: Ile Saint Thomas, Antilles.
   1967 <u>Micrurus psyches circinalis</u>—Roze, Amer. Mus. Novitates, 2287: 40.

    Distribution: Trinidad and adjacent mainland of Venezuela.

Micrurus *psyches* *medemi* Roze

1967 *Micrurus* *psyches* *medemi* Roze, Amer. Mus. Novitates, 2287: 41. Type-locality: Villavicencio, Meta, Colombia.

Distribution: Known only from immediate vicinity of Villavicencio.

MICRURUS PUTUMAYENSIS Lancini

1962 *Micrurus* *schmidti* Lancini (preoccupied by *Micrurus* *schmidti* Dunn, 1940), Publ. Ocas. Mus. Cien. Nat. Caracas, Zool., 2: 1, fig. 1. Type-locality: Puerto Socorro, 270 km northeast of Iquitos, Río Putumayo, Depto. de Loreto, Peru.
1963 *Micrurus* *putumayensis* Lancini (replacement name for *Micrurus* *schmidti* Lancini, 1962), Publ. Ocas. Mus. Cien. Nat. Caracas, Zool., 3: 1.

Distribution: Known only from type locality.

MICRURUS RUATANUS (Günther)

1895 *Elaps* *ruatanus* Günther, Biol. Centr. Amer., Rept.: 185, pl. 57-b. Type-locality: Roatán Island, Honduras.
1933 *Micrurus* *ruatanus*—Schmidt, Zool. Ser. Field Mus. Nat. Hist., 20: 34.

Distribution: Roatán Island and adjacent mainland in Honduras.

MICRURUS SPIXII Wagler

1824 *Micrurus* *spixii* Wagler, in Spix, Sp. Nov. Serp. Bras.: 48, pl. 18. Type-locality: Rio Solimões, Brazil.

Distribution: Amazonian Basin, from mouth to Andean foothills.

Content: Four subspecies.

Key to the subspecies

1. First nuchal black band not projecting forward, covering fewer than eight dorsals --2
   First nuchal black band elongated and projecting forward, covering eight or more dorsal rows----------------------obscurus

2. Head all black or with small white spots; parietals black-------------------------3
   Head with large light spots; sometimes nearly all parietals white; usually 2/3 plus 7 triads on body-----------princeps

3. Black triads 2/3 plus 4-6 on body; ventrals 212-224 in females------------------spixii
   Triads usually more than 2/3 plus 6; ventrals approximately 226 in females----- ----------------------------------martiusi

Clave de subespecies

1. Primera banda nucal negra no se proyecta hacia adelante, cubre menos de ocho hileras dorsales-----------------------------2
   Primera banda nucal negra alargada, se proyecta hacia adelante cubriendo ocho o más hileras dorsales-------------obscurus

2. Cabeza toda negra o con pequeñas manchas blancas, parietales negras---------------3
   Cabeza con manchas claras, grandes; a veces casi todas las parietales blancas; usualmente 2/3 más 7 triadas en cuerpo-princeps

3. Triadas negras en cuerpo 2/3 más 4-6; ventrales 212-224 en hembras--------spixii
   Usualmente más de 2/3 más 6 triadas; ventrales aproximadamente 226 en hembras-- ----------------------------------martiusi

Micrurus *spixii* *spixii* Wagler

1926 *Elaps* *ehrhardti* Müller, Zool. Anz., 7/8: 198. Type-locality: Manacapurú, Rio Solimões, Brazil.
1943 [*Micrurus*] *spixii* *spixii*—Schmidt and Walker, Zool. Ser. Field Mus. Nat. Hist., 24: 294.

Distribution: Middle Amazonian region of Brazil.

Micrurus spixii martiusi Schmidt

1953 Micrurus spixi martiusi Schmidt, Fieldiana, Zool., 34: 175, figs. 33-34. Type-locality:
    Santarem, Pará, Brazil.

   Distribution: Amazonian drainage of Pará and Mato Grosso, Brazil.

Micrurus spixii obscurus (Jan)

1872 Elaps corallinus var. obscura Jan, in Jan and Sordelli, Icon. Gén. Ophid., Livr. 41: pl. 6, fig. 3.
    Type-locality: Lima (corrected and restricted to eastern Peru by Schmidt and Walker, Zool.
    Ser. Field Mus. Nat. Hist., 24, 1943, 294; apparently further designated as Iquitos, Peru,
    by Schmidt, Fieldiana, Zool., 34, 1953, 175).
1881 Elaps heterozonus Peters, Sitz. Ges. Naturforsch. Freunde Berlin, 1881: 52. Type-locality:
    Sarayacu, Ecuador.
1943 Micrurus spixii obscura—Schmidt and Walker, Zool. Ser. Field Mus. Nat. Hist., 24: 294.

   Distribution: Periphery of Amazon Basin, from southern Venezuela and Colombia to southern Peru.

Micrurus spixii princeps (Boulenger)

1905 Elaps princeps Boulenger, Ann. Mag. Nat. Hist., (7) 15: 456. Type-locality: Provincia Sara,
    Departamento Santa Cruz de la Sierra, Bolivia.
1953 Micrurus spixi princeps—Schmidt, Fieldiana, Zool., 34: 175.

   Distribution: Northwestern and central Bolivia.

MICRURUS SPURELLI (Boulenger)

1914 Elaps spurelli Boulenger, Proc. Zool. Soc. London, 1914: 817. Type-locality: Peña Lisa, Río
    Condoto, Colombia.
1955 Micrurus nicefori Schmidt, Fieldiana, Zool., 34: 346, fig. 65. Type-locality: Villavicencio,
    Cundinamarca, Colombia.

   Distribution: Western and central Colombia.

MICRURUS STEINDACHNERI (Werner)

1901 Elaps Steindachneri Werner, Verh. Zool. Bot. Ges. Vienna, 51: 599. Type-locality: Ecuador.
1967 Micrurus steindachneri—Roze, Amer. Mus. Novitates, 2287: 43.

   Distribution: Eastern slopes of Andes in Ecuador.

   Content: Three subspecies.

Key to the subspecies	Clave de subespecies
1. Subcaudals more than 29 in females; snout usually black------------------------2 Subcaudals 21 in females; snout with light spots----------------------------petersi	1. Subcaudales más de 29 en hembras; hocico usualmente negro-----------------------2 Subcaudales 21 en hembras; hocico con manchas claras--------------------petersi
2. Ventrals 200-207 in males; subcaudals 35-36 in females----------------steindachneri Ventrals 214-216 in males; subcaudals 29-33 in females-----------------------orcesi	2. Ventrales 200-207 en machos; subcaudales 35-36 en hembras------------steindachneri Ventrales 214-216 en machos; subcaudales 29-33 en hembras--------------------orcesi

Micrurus steindachneri steindachneri (Werner)

1926 Elaps fassli Werner, Sitz. Math.-Naturwiss. Kl. Akad. Wiss. Wien, 135 (abt. 1): 249.
1967 Micrurus steindachneri steindachneri—Roze, Amer. Mus. Novitates, 2287: 43.

   Distribution: Eastern slopes of Andes in Macas-Mendez region, southern Ecuador.

Micrurus steindachneri orcesi Roze

  1967 Micrurus steindachneri orcesi Roze, Amer. Mus. Novitates, 2287: 43, fig. 15. Type-locality: Meta trail, Baños, Ecuador, 1200 m.

   Distribution: Higher elevations, from 1000 to 1800 m, in valley of Río Pastaza, Pastaza Province, Ecuador.

Micrurus steindachneri petersi Roze

  1967 Micrurus steindachneri petersi Roze, Amer. Mus. Novitates, 2287: 45, fig. 16. Type-locality: One mi south of Plan de Milagro on trail to Pan de Azúcar, Morona-Santiago Province, Ecuador, 5600 ft.

   Distribution: Known only from type-locality.

MICRURUS STEWARTI Barbour and Amaral

  1928 Micrurus stewarti Barbour and Amaral, Bull. Antivenin Inst. Amer., 1: 100. Type-locality: Nombre de Dios, Sierra de la Bruja, Panama.
  1940 Micrurus schmidti Dunn, Proc. Acad. Nat. Sci. Phila., 92: 119, pl. 2. Type-locality: Valle de Antón, 50 mi west of Canal Zone, Panama, 2000 ft.

   Distribution: Intermediate elevations east and west of Canal Zone, Panama.

MICRURUS STUARTI Roze

  1967 Micrurus stuarti Roze, Amer. Mus. Novitates, 2287: 47, fig. 17. Type-locality: Finca La Paz, San Marcos, Guatemala, 1345 m.

   Distribution: Known only from type locality and Finca El Naranjo, Volcán Santa Clara, Suchitepequez, Guatemala.

MICRURUS SURINAMENSIS (Cuvier)

  1817 Elaps surinamensis Cuvier, Le Règne Animal, Paris, 2: 84. Type-locality: Surinam.
  1919 Micrurus surinamensis—Beebe, Zoologica, 2: 216.

   Distribution: Northern South America east of Andes.

   Content: Two subspecies.

Key to the subspecies	Clave de subespecies
1. Ventrals 162-174 in males; 173-187 in females----------------------surinamensis Ventrals 186-193 in males; 197-206 in females------------------------nattereri	1. Ventrales 162-174 en machos; 173-187 en hembras----------------------surinamensis Ventrales 186-193 en machos; 197-206 en hembras--------------------------nattereri

Micrurus surinamensis surinamensis (Cuvier)

  1952 Micrurus surinamensis surinamensis—Schmidt, Fieldiana, Zool., 34: 29, figs. 4-5.

   Distribution: Guianas and Amazonian region, including Colombia, Ecuador, Peru, Brazil, and Bolivia.

Micrurus surinamensis nattereri Schmidt

  1952 Micrurus surinamensis nattereri Schmidt, Fieldiana, Zool., 34: 27. Type-locality: Between Guaramoca and San Fernando, Venezuela.

   Distribution: Upper Río Orinoco and Río Negro region of southern Venezuela and northern Brazil.

MICRURUS TSCHUDII (Jan)

1858 Elaps tschudii Jan, Rev. Mag. Zool., (2) 10: 524. Type-locality: Peru.
1925 Micrurus tschudii—Schmidt and Schmidt, Zool. Ser. Field Mus. Nat. Hist., 12: 132, pl. 12.

Distribution: Pacific slopes from southern Ecuador to southern Peru and possibly northwestern Bolivia.

Content: Two subspecies.

Key to the subspecies

1. Black triads 13-19 (usually more than 13) in males; ventrals 206-230 in females--------------------------------------tschudii
   Black triads 10-13 in males; ventrals 197-210 in females--------------------olssoni

Clave de subespecies

1. Triadas negras 13-19 (usualmente más de 13) en machos; ventrales 206-230 en hembras------------------------------------tschudii
   Triadas negras 10-13 en machos; ventrales 197-210 en hembras-----------------olssoni

Micrurus tschudii tschudii (Jan)

1936 Micrurus tschudii tschudii—Schmidt, Zool. Ser. Field Mus. Nat. Hist., 20: 202.

Distribution: Pacific slopes of Peru from Departamento de Libertad probably to northwestern Bolivia.

Micrurus tschudii olssoni Schmidt and Schmidt

1925 Micrurus olssoni Schmidt and Schmidt, Zool. Ser. Field Mus. Nat. Hist., 12: 130, pl. 11. Type-locality: Negritos, Piura, Peru.
1936 Micrurus tschudii olssoni—Schmidt, Zool. Ser. Field Mus. Nat. Hist., 20: 202.

Distribution: Pacific slopes from southern Ecuador to northwestern Peru.

NINIA Baird and Girard

1853 <u>Ninia</u> Baird and Girard, Catalogue of North American Reptiles: 49. Type-species: <u>Ninia</u>
<u>diademata</u> Baird and Girard.
1854 <u>Streptophorus</u> Duméril, Bibron and Duméril, Erp. Gén., 7: 514. Type-species: <u>Streptophorus</u>
<u>bifasciatus</u> Duméril, Bibron and Duméril.

Distribution: Mexico through Central America to Venezuela, Colombia and Ecuador.

Content: Eight species.

Key to the species

1. Fewer than 21 scale rows at midbody-----------2
   With 21 scale rows at midbody-----------<u>hudsoni</u>

2. Scale rows at midbody 19----------------------3
   Scale rows at midbody 17----------------------6

3. Fewer than 75 subcaudals----------------------4
   More than 70 subcaudals-------------<u>diademata</u>

4. Venter usually immaculate, not variegated with
   yellow and black----------------------------5
   Venter never immaculate, variegated with yellow
   and black----------------------------<u>maculata</u>

5. Dorsum reddish, with black collar---------<u>sebae</u>
   Dorsum black, no collar------------------<u>atrata</u>

6. Dorsum not unicolor, at least a nuchal collar
   present--------------------------------------7
   Dorsum uniform black-------------------<u>psephota</u>

7. Dorsum blackish with 54-64 light crossbars; no
   nuchal collar-------------------------<u>oxynota</u>
   Dorsum dark blue, without crossbars; yellow
   nuchal collar----------------------<u>cerroensis</u>

Clave de especies

1. Menos de 21 filas de escamas al medio del
   cuerpo---------------------------------------2
   Filas de escamas al medio del cuerpo 21-<u>hudsoni</u>

2. Escamas en 19 filas al medio del cuerpo-------3
   Escamas en 17 filas al medio del cuerpo-------6

3. Menos de 75 escamas subcaudales---------------4
   Más de 70 escamas subcaudales--------<u>diademata</u>

4. Vientre generalmente inmaculado, no variegado
   de negro o amarillo-------------------------5
   Vientre nunca inmaculado, variegado de negro
   y amarillo---------------------------<u>maculata</u>

5. Dorso rojo, con collar negro--------------<u>sebae</u>
   Dorso negro, sin collar------------------<u>atrata</u>

6. Dorso no unicolor, al menos collar nucal
   presente-------------------------------------7
   Dorso negro uniforme-------------------<u>psephota</u>

7. Dorso pardo negruzco, atravesado por 54-64
   bandas grises claras; collar nucal ausente----
   -------------------------------------<u>oxynota</u>
   Dorso azul oscuro, no atravesado por bandas
   grises claras; collar nucal presente, de color
   amarillento------------------------<u>cerroensis</u>

NINIA <u>ATRATA</u> (Hallowell)

1845 <u>Coluber atratus</u> Hallowell, Proc. Acad. Nat. Sci. Phila., 1845: 245. Type-locality: within 200
miles of Caracas, Venezuela.
1854 <u>Streptophorus Lansbergi</u> Duméril, Bibron and Duméril, Erp. Gén., 7: 518. Type-locality: Caracas,
Venezuela.
1854 <u>Streptophorus Drozii</u> Duméril, Bibron and Duméril, Erp. Gén., 7: 518. Type-locality: New
Orleans; in error.
1860 <u>Ninia atrata</u>—Cope, Proc. Acad. Nat. Sci. Phila., 1860: 340.
1862 <u>Streptophorus sebae Schmidti</u> Jan, Arch. Zool. Anat. Fis., 2: 27. Type-locality: Guayaquil,
Ecuador.
1881 <u>Ninia spilogaster</u> Peters, Sitz. Ges. Naturforsch. Freunde Berlin, 1881: 49. Type-locality:
Ecuador.

Distribution: Southern Central America in Panama and Costa Rica to Ecuador, Venezuela and Trinidad.

Comment: This taxon is a primary homonym of <u>Coluber atratus</u> Gmelin, 1788, but it has been validated
by the International Commission of Zoological Nomenclature, Op. 644, Bull. Zool. Nomencl., 20,
1963, 26.

NINIA <u>CERROENSIS</u> Taylor

1954 <u>Ninia cerroensis</u> Taylor, Univ. Kansas Sci. Bull., 36: 699. Type-locality: Pacific slope of
Cerro de la Muerte, on Pan-American Highway, Costa Rica, at approximately 7500 ft.

Distribution: Known only from type locality.

NINIA DIADEMATA Baird and Girard

1853 *Ninia diademata* Baird and Girard, Cat. N. Amer. Rept.: 49. Type-locality: Orizaba, Mexico.

Distribution: Mexico, Honduras, Guatemala.

Content: Four subspecies, two (*diademata* Baird and Girard and *plorator* Smith) extralimital.

Key to the subspecies	Clave de subespecies
1. Rounded dark spots on belly; ventrals 132-145 in males, 138-150 in females------------------------------------*labiosa*	1. Manchas oscuras medioventrales redondeadas; ventrales 132-145 (machos) y 138-150 (hembras)--------------------------*labiosa*
Crescent-shaped spots on belly; ventrals 127-131 in males, 130-137 in females------------------------------------*nietoi*	Manchas oscuras en forma de crecientes; ventrales 127-131 (machos) y 130-137 (hembras)--------------------------*nietoi*

Ninia diademata labiosa (Bocourt)

1883 *Streptophorus labiosus* Bocourt, Miss. Sci. Mex., Rept.: 550, pl. 32, fig. 6-6f. Type-locality: Guatemala.
1930 *Ninia diademata labiosa*—Amaral, Mem. Inst. Butantan, 4: 151.

Distribution: Moderate elevations of Pacific slope from Oaxaca to Guatemala.

Ninia diademata nietoi Burger and Werler

1954 *Ninia diademata nietoi* Burger and Werler, Univ. Kansas Sci. Bull., 36: 657, fig. 1. Type-locality: San Andres Tuxtla, Veracruz, Mexico.

Distribution: Caribbean slope from southern Veracruz to Honduras; not on northern part of Yucatán Peninsula.

NINIA HUDSONI Parker

1940 *Ninia hudsoni* Parker, Ann. Mag. Nat. Hist., (11) 5: 270. Type-locality: New River, British Guiana.

Distribution: British Guiana; Amazonian Ecuador.

NINIA MACULATA (Peters)

1940 *Streptophorus maculata* Peters, Monats. Akad. Wiss. Berlin, 1861: 924. Type-locality: Costa Rica.
1935 *Ninia maculata*—Dunn, Proc. Nat. Acad. Sci., 21: 11.

Distribution: Alta Verapaz, Guatemala to Darién region in Panama.

Content: Three subspecies.

Key to the subspecies	Clave de subespecies
1. Fewer than 65 subcaudals------------------2	1. Menos de 65 subcaudales--------------------2
More than 65 subcaudals--------*pavimentata*	Más de 65 subcaudales----------*pavimentata*
2. More than 49 light grey cross bands---------------------------------------*tessellata*	2. Bandas transversales de color gris pálido en número de 50 o más-----------*tessellata*
Fewer than 25 light grey cross bands---------------------------------------*maculata*	Bandas transversales de color gris pálido en número de 25 o menos-----------*maculata*

Ninia maculata maculata (Peters)

  1948 Ninia maculata maculata—Stuart, Misc. Publ. Mus. Zool. Univ. Mich., 69: 75.

   Distribution: Pacific slopes of Darién and Panama Canal Zone to central Costa Rica; Caribbean drainage of Costa Rica.

Ninia maculata pavimentata (Bocourt)

  1883 Streptophorus maculatus pavimentatus Bocourt, Miss. Sci. Mex., Rept.: 549, pl. 32, figs. 8-8d, pl. 33, fig. 2. Type-locality: Alta Verapaz, Guatemala.
  1948 Ninia maculata pavimentata—Stuart, Misc. Publ. Mus. Zool. Univ. Mich., 69: 75.

   Distribution: Moderate elevations in mountains of Alta Verapaz, Guatemala.

Ninia maculata tessellata Cope

  1876 Ninia sebae tessellata Cope, Jour. Acad. Nat. Sci. Phila.,(2) 8, 1875: 145. Type-locality: Costa Rica.
  1910 Streptophorus subtessellatus Werner, Mitt. Nat. Hist. Mus. Hamburg, 26: 215. Type-locality: Cariblanco, Costa Rica.
  1954 Ninia maculata tessellata—Burger, Univ. Kansas Sci. Bull., 36: 653.

   Distribution: Caribbean slope of southern Nicaragua, Costa Rica, and probably of Panama.

NINIA OXYNOTA (Werner)

  1910 Streptophorus oxynotus Werner, Mitt. Nat. Hist. Mus. Hamburg, 26: 216. Type-locality: Cariblanco, Costa Rica.
  1951 Ninia oxynota—Taylor, Univ. Kansas Sci. Bull., 34: 56.

  Distribution: Subtropical zone of Cordillera Central, Costa Rica, above 4000 ft.

NINIA PSEPHOTA (Cope)

  1876 Catostoma psephotum Cope, Jour. Acad. Nat. Sci. Phila., (2) 8, 1875: 146. Type-locality: Higher points on Pico Blanco, chiefly in rainy zone from 5000-7000 ft, Costa Rica.
  1935 Ninia psephota—Dunn, Proc. Nat. Acad. Sci., 21: 12.

   Distribution: Subtropical zone, Volcán de Chiriquí, Panama, and adjacent Cordillera de Talamanca, eastern Costa Rica, above 4000 ft.

NINIA SEBAE (Duméril, Bibron and Duméril)

  1854 Streptophorus sebae Duméril, Bibron and Duméril, Erp. Gén., 7: 515. Type-locality: Mexico; restricted to state of Veracruz, Mexico, by Schmidt and Andrews, Zool. Ser. Field Mus. Nat. Hist., 20, 1936, 171, and to Veracruz, State of Veracruz, Mexico, by Smith and Taylor, Univ. Kansas Sci. Bull., 33, 1950, 351.
  1935 Ninia sebae—Dunn, Proc. Nat. Acad. Sci., 21: 11.

   Distribution: Oaxaca and Veracruz, Mexico, including dryer part of Yucatán Peninsula south to Costa Rica.

   Content: Four subspecies, according to the most recent revision of the species by Schmidt and Rand, Fieldiana: Zool., 39, 1957, 73-84.

Key to the subspecies

1. Black dorsal spots in the form of well-defined transverse bars, often reduced in both size and number or absent (nuchal black saddle invariable)----------------2
Dorsal markings of small spots rather than vertical bars, very numerous, never reduced in number or absent------punctulata

Clave de subespecies

1. Diseño dorsal de barras transversas, negras frecuentemente reducidas en número y tamaño, o ausentes; mancha nucal negra, en forma de silla de montar, constante------2
Diseño dorsal pequeñas manchas muy numerosas, nunca ausentes----------punctulata

2. Dorsal crossbars usually present, occasionally reduced or absent; loreal rectangular; caudals in males 41-72, in females
   37-61----------------------------------3
   No dorsal crossbars; loreal usually narrowed posteriorly; caudals in males 64-74, in
   females 53-65-------------------immaculata

3. Ventrals in males 139-151, in females 142-
   156; caudals in males 41-57, in females
   37-49; about 50 per cent of specimens with
   much reduced body spots, or without spots-
   ----------------------------------morleyi
   Ventrals in males 131-151, in females 134-
   152; caudals in males 41-72, in females
   40-61; majority of specimens boldly black-
   marked-----------------------------sebae

2. Barras dorsales usualmente presentes,
   occasionalmente reducidas o ausentes;
   loreal rectangular; subcaudales en machos
   41-72, en hembras 37-61------------------3
   Sin barras dorsales transversas; usualmente
   loreal angosta posteriormente; subcaudales
   en machos 64-74, en hembras 53-65---------
   -------------------------------immaculata

3. Ventrales en machos 139-151, en hembras
   142-156; subcaudales en machos 41-57, en
   hembras 37-49; alrededor del 50 por ciento
   de los ejemplares con manchas muy reducidas o sin ellas--------------------morleyi
   Ventrales en machos 131-151, en hembras 40-
   61; mayoría de ejemplares con manchas
   negras prominentes------------------sebae

Ninia sebae sebae (Duméril, Bibron and Duméril)

   1855 Elapoides fasciatus Hallowell, Jour. Acad. Nat. Sci. Phila., (2) 3: 35, pl. 4. Type-
         locality: Honduras.
   1862 Streptophorus sebae collaris Jan, Arch. Zool. Anat. Fis., 2: 27. Type-locality: Mexico.
   1883 Streptophorus sebae var dorsalis Bocourt, Miss. Sci. Mex., Rept.: 547. Type-locality:
         Belize, Honduras.
   1936 Ninia sebae sebae—Schmidt and Andrews, Zool. Ser. Field Mus. Nat. Hist., 20: 170.

   Distribution: Caribbean slopes except Yucatán Peninsula, from Veracruz to Guatemala; also
      El Salvador and Honduras.

Ninia sebae immaculata Schmidt and Rand

   1957 Ninia sebae immaculata Schmidt and Rand, Fieldiana: Zool., 39: 81. Type-locality: Río
         Escondido (or Bluefields River), southeastern Nicaragua.

   Distribution: Nicaragua.

Ninia sebae morleyi Schmidt and Andrews

   1936 Ninia sebae morleyi Schmidt and Andrews, Zool. Ser. Field Mus. Nat. Hist., 20: 169.
         Type-locality: Chichen Itzá, Yucatán, Mexico.

   Distribution: Northern half of Yucatán Peninsula; Petén, Guatemala.

Ninia sebae punctulata (Bocourt)

   1883 Streptophorus sebae var punctulata Bocourt, Miss. Sci. Mex., Rept.: 547. Type-locality:
         Guatemala; restricted to vicinity of Quezaltenango, Pacific slope, southern Guatemala,
         by Schmidt and Rand, Fieldiana: Zool., 39, 1957, 79.
   1957 Ninia sebae punctulata—Schmidt and Rand, Fieldiana: Zool., 39: 79.

   Distribution: Pacific slope of Guatemala and contiguous Chiapas, between 500 and 2000 m.

REPTILIA: SERPENTES: COLUBRIDAE ★ ★ ★ ★

NOTHOPSIS Cope

1871 Nothopsis Cope, Proc. Acad. Nat. Sci. Phila., 1871: 201. Type-species: Nothopsis rugosus Cope.

   Distribution: Atlantic coast of Nicaragua, Costa Rica, and Panama; Pacific coast of Colombia and Ecuador.

NOTHOPSIS RUGOSUS Cope

1871 Nothopsis rugosus Cope, Proc. Acad. Nat. Sci. Phila., 1871: 201. Type-locality: Darien, Panama.
1905 Nothopsis affinis Boulenger, Ann. Mag. Nat. Hist., (7) 15: 453. Type-locality: Salidero, Ecuador.
1951 Nothopsis torresi Taylor, Univ. Kansas Sci. Bull., 34: 31, pl. 1. Type-locality: Morehouse Finca, five mi southwest of Turrialba, Costa Rica.
1957 Nothopsis rugosus Dunn and Dowling, Copeia, 1957: 255, pl. 1.

   Distribution: Atlantic coast of Nicaragua, Costa Rica, and Panama; Pacific coast of Colombia and Ecuador.

OPISTHOPLUS Peters

   1882 Opisthoplus Peters, Sitz. Akad. Wiss. Berlin, 52: 1148. Type-species: Opisthoplus degener
       Peters.
   1947 Aproterodon Vanzolini, Pap. Avul. Depto. Zool. São Paulo, 8: 181. Type-species: Aproterodon
      clementei Vanzolini.

    Distribution: As for only known species.

    Content: One species.

OPISTHOPLUS DEGENER Peters

   1882 Opisthoplus degener Peters, Sitz. Akad. Wiss. Berlin, 52: 1149, figs. 1-4. Type-locality: Not
      indicated; restricted by Hoge, Mem. Inst. Butantan 28, 1959, 68, to Estado Rio Grande do Sul,
      Brazil.
   1947 Aproterodon clementei Vanzolini, Pap. Avul. Depto. Zool. São Paulo, 8, 183. Type-locality: Rio
      Grande do Sul, Brazil.
   1959 Opisthoplus degener—Hoge, Mem. Inst. Butantan (1957-1958), 28: 68.

    Distribution: Known only from Quinta, Carazinho and vicinity of Porto Alegre, Rio Grande do Sul,
    Brazil.

REPTILIA: SERPENTES: COLUBRIDAE   ★ ★ ★ ★   OXYBELIS

Prepared by E. D. Keiser, University of Southwestern Louisiana, Lafayette, Louisiana

OXYBELIS Wagler

1826 Dryophis Fitzinger (preoccupied by Dryophis Dalman, 1823), Neue Classification der Amphibien: 60.
    Type-species: Coluber fulgidus Daudin.
1830 Oxybelis Wagler, Nat. Syst. Amphib.: 183. Type-species: Dryinus aeneus Wagler.
1848 Plastor Gistl (substitute name for Oxybelis Wagler), Naturgeschichte des Thierreichs: x.

    Distribution: Extreme southwestern United States, tropical Mexico and South America to Brazil,
        Bolivia, and Peru.

    Content: Four species.

                Key to the species   Clave de especies

1. Lateral and vertebral dark stripes lacking----2   1. Sin líneas oscuras laterales y vertebrales----2
   Prominent lateral and vertebral dark stripes   Con líneas oscuras laterales y vertebrales-----
   present----------------------------argenteus   -----------------------------------argenteus

2. Anal plate divided; supralabials usually eight   2. Placa anal dividida; ocho o más supralabiales-3
   or more-----------------------------------3   Placa anal entera; seis supralabiales----------
   Anal plate single; supralabials usually six----   --------------------------------brevirostris
   --------------------------------brevirostris

3. Paired white or yellow lateral stripes on   3. Par de líneas blancas o amarillas prominente a
   venter prominent on full length of body-------   lo largo de todo el vientre-----------fulgidus
   ------------------------------------fulgidus   Par de líneas ventrales blancas o amarillas
   Paired white or yellow ventral stripes absent,   ausente; si está presente, las líneas son
   or if present, weak and restricted to extreme   pálidas y restrictas a los extremos de los
   lateral edges of ventrals on anterior half of   márgenes laterales, en la mitad anterior
   body---------------------------------aeneus   ventral del cuerpo---------------------aeneus

OXYBELIS AENEUS (Wagler)

1824 Dryinus aeneus Wagler, in Spix, Sp. Nov. Serp. Bras.: 12, pl. 3. Type-locality: "Habitat in
        sylvis adjacentibus flumini Solimoens, prope Ega." Ega is an older name for Tefé, Amazonas,
        Brazil.
1824 C.[oluber] acuminatus Wied, Isis von Oken, 6: 667. Type-locality: None stated; but Wied,
        Beiträge Naturgesch. Bras., 1825, 326, wrote: "Sie kommt besonders in der Gegend des Flusses
        Espirito Santo vor."
1825 Dryinus auratus Bell, Zool. Jour., London, 2: 325, pl. 12. Type-locality: Mexico.
1830 Oxybelis aeneus—Wagler, Nat. Syst. Amphib.: 183.
1854 Dryophis vittatus Girard, Proc. Acad. Nat. Sci. Phila., 1854: 226. Type-locality: Taboga, Bay
        of Panama.
1926 Oxybelis microphthalmus Barbour and Amaral, Proc. New England Zool. Club, 9: 80. Type-locality:
        Calabasas Canyon, Arizona.
1941 Oxybelis potosiensis Taylor, Univ. Kansas Sci. Bull., 27: 128, pl. 6, figs. 4-6. Type-locality:
        Km 192, 38 km northwest of Ciudad Maiz, San Luis Potosi, Mexico.

    Distribution: Low to moderate and occasionally intermediate elevations from southern Arizona south
        along eastern and western coasts of Mexico, throughout Central America, and east and west of Andes
        in northern half of South America.

OXYBELIS ARGENTEUS (Daudin)

1803 Coluber argenteus Daudin, Hist. Nat. Rept., 6: 336. Type-locality: Unknown.
1853 O.[xybelis] argenteus—Duméril, Mém. Acad. Sci. Paris, 23: 487.
1923 Oxybelis boulengeri Procter, Proc. Zool. Soc. London, 1923: 1062, fig. 1a-c. Type-locality:
        Trinidad, Río Mamoré, Bolivia.

    Distribution: Lowlands of northern South America east of Andes.

OXYBELIS BREVIROSTRIS (Cope)

1861 D.[ryophis] brevirostris Cope, Proc. Acad. Nat. Sci. Phila., 1860: 555. Type-locality: "Veraguas, New Grenada".
1863 O.[xybelis] coerulescens Jan, Elenco Sist. Degli Ofidi: 88. Type-locality: Costa Rica.
1896 Oxybelis brevirostris—Boulenger, Cat. Sn. Brit. Mus., 3: 190.

Distribution: Caribbean lowlands of Central America from Nicaragua through Panama to Pacific lowlands of Colombia and Ecuador.

OXYBELIS FULGIDUS (Daudin)

1803 Coluber fulgidus Daudin, Hist. Nat. Rept., 6: 352, pl. 80. Type-locality: In neighborhood of Port-au-Prince, Santo Domingo (presumably in error); suggested as Surinam by Schmidt, Zool. Ser. Field Mus. Nat. Hist., 22, 1941, 506; restricted to Chichen Itzá, Yucatán, Mexico, by Smith and Taylor, Univ. Kansas Sci. Bull., 33, 1950, 352.
1837 D.[ryiophis] catesbyi Schlegel, Essai Physion. Serp., 252. Type-locality: Uncertain.
1853 O.[xybelis] fulgidus—Duméril, Mém. Acad. Sci. Paris, 23: 487.

Distribution: Low to moderate elevations of Mexico, Central America, and tropical South America east of Andes.

Prepared by Joseph R. Bailey, Duke University, Durham, North Carolina

OXYRHOPUS Wagler

  1830 Oxyrhopus Wagler, Nat. Syst. Amphib.: 185. Type-species: Oxyrhopus petola Linnaeus (by sub-
    sequent restriction. This species not mentioned in Wagler).
  1843 Sphenocephalus Fitzinger, Systema Reptilium: 25. Type-species: Lycodon formosus Schlegel.
  1847 Oxyrrhopus Agassiz (emendation of Oxyrhopus Wagler), Nomenclator Zoologici Index Universalis:
    268.
  1913 Erythroxyrhopus Thompson, Proc. Acad. Nat. Sci. Phila., 1913: 80. Type-species: Oxyrhopus
    trigeminus Duméril, Bibron and Duméril.

    Distribution: Southern Mexico to about 35°S latitude east of Andes and to just north of Lima, Peru,
    west of Andes, in South America.

    Content: Six species groups containing eleven species for which names are currently available in
    the literature, plus several as yet undescribed taxa.

            Key to the species   Clave de especies

1. Preocular usually in contact with frontal;
   hemipenis with sulcus opening on terminal
   clear space or disc; usually ten lower labials
   with six in contact with chin shields (often
   nine with five contacting chin shields in
   rhombifer group); dark body bands only on
   outer quarter of ventrals posteriorly, unless
   in triads---------------------------------2
   Preocular usually well separated from frontal;
   hemipenis with calyces at tips; lower labials
   nine, five or fewer in contact with chin
   shields (clathratus has ten, six in about
   16%); body bands often reaching midventral
   line posteriorly-----------------------------6

2. Dorsal body bands either include outer edges of
   ventrals or are completely absent posteriorly-
   --3
   Dorsal body bands throughout body not extending
   laterally to ventrals---------------rhombifer

3. Dorsal bands arranged in triads at least in
   anal region, extending well onto ventrals
   (some individuals of melanogenys may lose some
   or all triads from posterior part of body, but
   retain a pair of dark bands on nape unless
   coalesced through ontogenetic melanism)------4
   Dorsal bands (unless obscured by ontogenetic
   melanism) not arranged in triads, and extend
   only onto outer tips of ventrals posteriorly--
   --petola

4. Distinct triads present throughout body (rarely
   obscured by ontogenetic melanism)------------5
   Triads absent posteriorly or incompletely
   developed at least anteriorly------melanogenys

1. Preocular usualmente en contacto con frontal;
   hemipenis cuyo sulcus se abre en espacio terminal o disco; frecuentemente diez infralabiales con seis en contact con geneiales (a
   menudo nueve infralabiales, cinco en contacto
   con las genèiales en el grupo rhombifer);
   bandas oscuras posteriores del cuerpo sólo en
   los cuartos exteriores de las ventrales, si no
   hay tríadas----------------------------------2
   Preocular usualmente bien separada de frontal;
   hemipenis con cálices en los ápices; infralabiales nueve, cinco o menos en contacto con
   geneiales (clathratus tiene diez, seis en contacto en alrededor del 16%); las bandas del
   cuerpo frecuentemente llegan al medioviente
   posteriormente-------------------------------6

2. Bandas dorsales del cuerpo u ocupan bordes
   exteriores de ventrales o están ausentes
   completamente en la zona posterior----------3
   Bandas dorsales sobre todo el cuerpo que no se
   extienden lateralmente hasta las ventrales----
   -------------------------------------rhombifer

3. Bandas dorsales dispuestas en tríadas a lo
   menos en la región anal, bien extendidas hasta
   las ventrales (algunos individuos de
   melanogenys pueden perder algunas o todas las
   tríadas de la parte posterior del cuerpo,
   reteniendo un par de bandas oscuras sobre la
   nuca a no ser que se suelden en casos de
   melanismo ontogénico)----------------------4
   Bandas dorsales (a menos estén oscurecidas por
   melanismo ontogenético) no dispuestas en
   tríadas, extendidas hasta alcanzar las ventrales sólo posteriormente-------------petola

4. Tríadas distintas presentes a lo largo de todo
   el cuerpo (raramente oscurecidas por melanismo
   ontogénico)----------------------------------5
   Tríadas ausentes posteriormente o incompleta-
   mente desarrolladas a lo menos anteriormente--
   -----------------------------------melanogenys

5. Scales along middorsal row from parietal notch to posterior edge of second dark band on neck 10-23, usually thirteen or more; triads much longer than interspaces; snout frequently light spotted----------------------_trigeminus_
   Scales from parietal notch to end of second dark band 6-14, usually ten or fewer; triads generally equal to or shorter than interspaces; snout dark-----------------_melanogenys_

6. Black body bands extending well onto ventrals and light interspaces, unless modified by ontogenetic change, in which case snout may be light and body scales tipped with dark, or snout dark and considerable dorsal pigment extending onto ventrals---------------------7
   Body color (in alcohol) dark brown and yellow or white irregularly spotted, each scale generally of a single color; venter immaculate; juvenile with light collar followed by dark nape blotch--------------------_fitzingeri_

7. Snout and crown dark anterior to parietals; body with dark and light bands, no ontogenetic fading of dark bands------------------------8
   Head red (white in alcohol); body with dark and light bands; in some populations, dark bands may fade while light interspaces and crown may darken, leaving unpatterned snake with dark scale tips and with dark brown crown and nape; snout always light--------------------_formosus_

8. Dorsal scales in 19 rows at midbody-----------9
   Dorsal scales in 17 or 15 rows at midbody----11

9. Body bands fewer, 25-36, nearly or quite complete posteriorly; light interspaces wider posteriorly than anteriorly and considerably wider on lower sides; ontogenetic melanism incomplete--------------------------------10
   Body bands generally more numerous, over 30 in south, 40 in north; bands usually not continuous across belly; light interspaces about one scale wide throughout length of body and not widening appreciably on sides; larger specimens frequently completely melanistic except midventrally------------------------_clathratus_

10. Posteriorly light interspaces 2-1/2 to 3 times length of dark bands; dark bands on body 25-29; light collar covers three to six scales along median row-----------------_venezuelanus_
    Posteriorly light interspaces usually less than twice length of dark bands; dark bands on body 27-36; light collar covers 1 to 2-1/2 scales along median row--------------_doliatus_

5. Con 10-23, usualmente trece o más, escamas en la fila mediodorsal, desde la muesca parietal al borde posterior de la segunda banda oscura sobre la nuca; tríadas mayores que interespacios; hocico frecuentemente manchado en claro------------------------------_trigeminus_
   Con 6-14, usualmente diez o menos, escamas en la fila mediodorsal, desde la muesca parietal hasta el borde posterior de la segunda banda oscura sobre la nuca; tríadas generalmente iguales o más cortas que los interespacios; hocico oscuro----------------------_melanogenys_

6. Bandas negras bien extendidas sobre ventrales conjuntament con interespacios claros a menos que hayan sido modificados por cambios ontogénicos, en cuyo caso el hocico puede ser claro y las escamas del cuerpo salpicadas de oscuro o el hocico oscuro y considerable pigmento dorsal se extiende por las ventrales---7
   Color del cuerpo (en alcohol) pardo oscuro manchado irregularmente con amarillo o blanco, cada escama generalmente de un solo tono; vientre inmaculado; juveniles con collar claro seguido de mancha nucal oscura------_fitzingeri_

7. Hocico y parte superior de la cabeza anteriormente a las parietales oscura; cuerpo con bandas claras y oscuras, no hay decoloración ontogenética de las bandas oscuras-----------8
   Cabeza roja (blanca en alcohol); cuerpo con bandas oscuras y claras; en algunas poblaciones, las bandas oscuras pueden decolorarse mientras los interespacios claros y la parte superior de la cabeza puede oscurecerse, dando una ausencia de diseño con escamas oscuras en los ápices y pardo oscuro sobre la parte superior de la cabeza y la nuca; hocico siempre claro------------------------_formosus_

8. Escamas dorsales en 19 filas al medio del cuerpo------------------------------------9
   Escamas dorsales en 17 o 15 filas al medio del cuerpo-----------------------------------11

9. Bandas del cuerpo menos de 25-36, casi completas posteriormente; interespacios claros más anchos posterior que anteriormente, considerablemente más anchos sobre los lado inferiormente; melanismo ontogénico incompleto------10
   Bandas del cuerpo generalmente más numerosas, sobre 30 en el sur, 40 en el norte; usualmente las bandas no son contínuas a través del vientre; interespacios claros alrededor de una escama de ancho a lo largo de todo el cuerpo no ensanchándose apreciablemente en los lados; grandes ejemplares frecuentemente totalmente melánicos excepto medioventralmente-_clathratus_

10. Interespacios claros posteriores 2-1/2 a 3 veces la longitud de las bandas oscuras; bandas oscuras sobre el cuerpo 25-29; collar claro que cubre tres a seis escamas sobre la fila mediana----------------------_venezuelanus_
    Interespacios claros posteriores menos del doble de la longitud de las bandas oscuras; bandas oscuras sobre el cuerpo 27-36; collar claro que cubre 1 a 2-1/2 escamas sobre la fila mediana-------------------------_doliatus_

11.Dorsals in 17 rows; usually eight upper
    labials, fourth and fifth in orbit; subcaudals
    more than 75----------------------leucomelas
    Dorsals in 15 rows; seven upper labials, third
    and fourth in orbit; subcaudals fewer than
    55----------------------------------marcapatae

11.Dorsales en 17 filas; usualmente ocho supra-
    labiales, cuarta y quinta en la órbita; sub-
    caudales más de 75------------------leucomelas
    Dorsales en 15 filas; siete supralabiales, ter-
    cera y cuarta en la órbita; subcaudales menos
    de 55-------------------------------marcapatae

OXYRHOPUS CLATHRATUS Duméril, Bibron and Duméril
    doliatus group

1854 Oxyrhopus clathratus Duméril, Bibron and Duméril, Erp. Gén., 7: 1026. Type-locality: Brazil.
1903 Oxyrhopus doliatus var. viperina Werner, Zool. Anz., 26: 250. Type-locality: Brazil.
1923 Clelia clathrata pulcherrima Müller, Zool. Anz., 57: 153. Type-locality: Humboldt, Santa
    Catarina, Brazil.

    Distribution: Southeastern Brazil from southern Minas Gerais to Rio Grande do Sul and Misiones,
    Argentina.

OXYRHOPUS DOLIATUS Duméril, Bibron and Duméril
    doliatus group

1854 Oxyrhopus doliatus Duméril, Bibron and Duméril, Erp. Gén., 7: 1020. Type-locality: Brazil?
1913 Drepanodon erdisii Barbour, Proc. Acad. Nat. Sci. Phila., 1913: 506, pl. 17, figs. 3-4. Type-
    locality: Machu Picchu, Peru.

    Distribution: Definitely known only from Cuzco Province, Peru.

OXYRHOPUS FITZINGERI (Tschudi)
    fitzingeri group

1845 Siphlophis Fitzingeri Tschudi, Arch. für Naturg., 11 (1): 165. Type-locality: Peru; further
    stated as coastal region of Peru by Tschudi, Fauna Peruana, Rept., 1846, 57, pl. 8.
1863 O.[xyrhopus] Fitzingeri—Jan, Elenco Sist. Ofidi: 93.

    Distribution: Coastal areas of Ecuador and Peru.

    Content: Two subspecies.

                    Key to the subspecies   Clave de subespecies

    1. More than 220 ventrals-----------fitzingeri   1. Ventrales más de 220-------------fitzingeri
       Fewer than 210 ventrals-----------frizzelli   Ventrales menos de 210-----------frizzelli

Oxyrhopus fitzingeri fitzingeri (Tschudi)

    1943 Oxyrhopus fitzingeri fitzingeri—Schmidt and Walker, Zool. Ser. Field Mus. Nat. Hist.,
        24: 312.

        Distribution: Coast of southern Peru.

Oxyrhopus fitzingeri frizzelli Schmidt and Walker

    1943 Oxyrhopus fitzingeri frizzelli Schmidt and Walker, Zool. Ser. Field Mus. Nat. Hist.,
        24: 313. Type-locality: Negritos, Piura, Peru.

        Distribution: Dry Pacific lowlands of Ecuador and Peru.

OXYRHOPUS FORMOSUS (Wied)

1820 Coluber formosus Wied, Nova Acta Acad. Leop. Carol., 10 (1): 109. Type-locality: Lagoa d'Arara, Rio Mucuri, Bahia, Brazil.
1824 Natrix occipitalis Wagler, in Spix, Sp. Nov. Serp. Bras.: 21, pl. 6, fig. 2. Type-locality: Rio Solimões, Brazil.
1854 Oxyrhopus leucocephalus Duméril, Bibron and Duméril, Erp. Gén., 7: 1038. Type-locality: Unknown.
1863 O.[xyrhopus] labialis Jan, Elenco Sist. Ofidi: 93, and Jan and Sordelli,1870, Icon. Gén. Ophidiens, Livr. 35: pl. 2, fig. 2. Type-locality: South America.
1871 Oxyrhopus submarginatus Peters, Monats. Akad. Wiss. Berlin, 1871: 401. Type-locality: Pozuzu, Peru.
1916 Clelia peruviana Griffin, Mem. Carnegie Mus., 7: 204. Type-locality: Tarma, Peru.
1927 Oxyrhopus iridescens Werner, Sitz. Math.-Naturwiss. Kl. Acad. Wiss. Wien, 135: 248. Type-locality: Huancàbamba, Peru.

Distribution: Forested South America north of about 20°S latitude.

Comment: This is obviously a complex of forms, and much more material than is presently available will be required to study it satisfactorily. The eastern Brazilian and the westernmost Peruvian material, along with a few other specimens, retain the characteristic orange head and banded pattern throughout life with only some darkening of the crown. Most of the specimens from the Amazon watershed and Colombia lose the dark bands with maturity, and the head behind the snout darkens to resemble closely unbanded specimens of Oxyrhopus melanogenys, with which these specimens have usually been confused.

OXYRHOPUS LEUCOMELAS (Werner), new combination
    doliatus group

1916 Tropidodipsas leucomelas Werner, Zool. Anz., 47: 309. Type-locality: Cañon de Tolima, Colombia.
1961 Tripanurgos leucomelas—Downs, Copeia, 1961: 386, fig. 1.

Distribution: Amazonian slopes of Ecuador and Peru; headwater areas of Cauca and Magdalena river valleys.

OXYRHOPUS MARCAPATAE (Boulenger), new combination
    doliatus group

1902 Homalocranium marcapatae Boulenger, Ann. Mag. Nat. Hist., (7) 10: 401. Type-locality: Marcapata Valley, eastern Peru.
1914 Drepanodon eatoni Ruthven, in Barbour, Proc. Acad. Nat. Sci. Phila., 1913: 506. Type-locality: Machu Picchu, Peru.

Distribution: Marcapata and Urubamba valleys in Peruvian highlands.

OXYRHOPUS MELANOGENYS (Tschudi)
    melanogenys group

.1845 Sphenocephalus melanogenys Tschudi, Arch für Naturg., 11 (1): 163. Type-locality: Peru; further specified as Chanchamayo region, Peru, by Tschudi, Fauna Peruana, Rept., 1846, 49, pl. 4.
1872 Tachymenis bitorquata Günther, Ann. Mag. Nat. Hist., (4) 9: 19. Type-locality: Peruvian Amazon.
1896 Oxyrhopus melanogenys—Boulenger, Cat. Sn. Brit. Mus., 3: 105.

Distribution: Amazonian watershed of Bolivia, Peru, Brazil and Ecuador.

OXYRHOPUS PETOLA (Linnaeus)
    petola group

1758 Coluber petola Linnaeus, Systema Naturae, Ed. 10: 225. Type-locality: Africa.
1896 [Oxyrrhopus] Petola—Lönnberg, Bihang till K. Svenska Vet.-Akad. Handlingar, 22 (4): 7.

Distribution: Mexico through Central America to northwestern Ecuador west of Andes and to Amazonian Bolivia and Brazil east of Andes.

Content: Three subspecies.

Key to the subspecies

1. Dorsal bands on body 17-59, usually more
   than 20; if fewer than 25, then more widely spaced, especially posteriorly; little
   or no ontogenetic melanism---------------2
   Dorsal bands on body few and long, 10-24,
   but usually fewer than 20, and distinctly
   wider than light interspaces posteriorly;
   large individuals often completely
   melanistic----------------------digitalis

2. Bands on body 24-59, usually more than 35,
   approximately equal in length, separated
   by interspaces about one scale wide-------
   -------------------------------------petola
   Bands on body 19-36, more widely spaced; in
   interior Colombia posterior bands frequently very short and widely spaced; in
   middle America, preoculars usually not in
   contact with prefrontal--------------sebae

Clave de subespecies

1. Bandas dorsales en el cuerpo 17-59, usualmente más de 20; si son menos de 25 son
   más espaciadas, particularmente posteriormente; melanismo ontogénico pequeño o
   ausente----------------------------------2
   Bandas dorsales en el cuerpo pocas y largas, 10-24, usualmente menos de 20, distintamente más anchas que los interespacios claros posteriormente; grandes individuos frecuentemente completamente
   melánicos------------------------digitalis

2. Bandas en el cuerpo 24-59, usualmente más
   de 35, aproximadamente iguales en largo,
   separadas por interespacios de una escama
   de ancho---------------------------petola
   Bandas en el cuerpo 19-36, más anchamente
   espaciadas; en el interior de Colombia
   bandas posteriores frecuentemente muy cortas y anchamente espaciadas; en América
   Central usualmente las preoculares no contactan con prefrontal---------------sebae

Oxyrhopus petola petola (Linnaeus)

1758 Coluber petolarius Linnaeus, Systema Naturae, Ed. 10: 225. Type-locality: "Indiis".
1766 Coluber Pethola Linnaeus (emendation of Coluber Petola Linnaeus), Systema Naturae, Ed. 12:
     387.
1766 Coluber petalarius Linnaeus (emendation of Coluber petolarius Linnaeus), Systema Naturae,
     Ed. 12: 387.
1854 Oxyrhopus multifasciatus Duméril, Bibron and Duméril, Erp. Gén., 7: 1019. Type-locality:
     Brazil or Cayenne; herewith restricted to Cayenne.
1854 Oxyrhopus spadiceus Duméril, Bibron and Duméril, Erp. Gén., 7: 1028. Type-locality:
     "Cote-Ferme"; which is determined as Cumaná and vicinity by Hoge and Lancini, Bol. Mus.
     Hist. Nat. Caracas, 6-7, 1960, 59.
1854 Oxyrhopus bi-prae-ocularis Duméril, Bibron and Duméril, Erp. Gén., 7: 1030. Type-locality:
     Cayenne.
1928 Clelia cornelii Müller, Zool. Anz., 77: 76. Type-locality: Maracay, Venezuela.
1946 Oxyrhopus petola petola—Beebe, Zoologica, 31: 37.

   Distribution: Villavicencio, Colombia east probably to French Guiana; Trinidad.

Oxyrhopus petola digitalis (Reuss), new combination

1834 Coluber digitalis Reuss, Mitgleid. Senckenb. Naturforsch. Ges., 1: 148, pl. 9, fig. 1.
     Type-locality: Ilheos, Brazil.
1854 Lycodon (Oxyrrhopus) semifasciatus Tschudi, Arch. für Naturg., 11 (1): 165. Type-
     locality: Peru; further specified as forest regions of middle Peru by Tschudi,
     Fauna Peruana, Rept., 1846, 55, pl. 7.
1854 Oxyrhopus immaculatus Duméril, Bibron, and Duméril, Erp. Gen., 7: 1029. Type-locality:
     Unknown.
1899 Oxyrrhopus intermedius Werner, Zool. Anz., 22: 481. Type-locality: Southern Brazil.

   Distribution: Amazonian parts of northern Bolivia, Peru and Ecuador; coastal and central
   Brazil in forested areas; Chocó region of Colombia and eastern Panama, intergrading with
   petola petola along the Amazon-Orinoco divide.

Oxyrhopus petola sebae Duméril, Bibron and Duméril

1854 Oxyrhopus Sebae Duméril, Bibron, and Duméril, Erp. Gén., 7: 1036. Type-locality:
    Colombia, New Grenada, Cayenne, Brazil, and Mexico; herewith restricted to Colombia.
1887 Oxyrrhopus doliatus semicinctus Cope, Bull. U.S. Nat. Mus., 32: 76. Type-locality:
    Eastern Costa Rica.
1909 Oxyrhopus doliatus var. aequifasciata Werner, Mitt. Naturhist. Mus. Hamburg, 26: 231.
    Type-locality: Coban, Guatemala.
1942 Clelia baileyi Smith, Proc. U.S. Nat. Mus., 92: 391. Type-locality: Potrero Viejo,
    Veracruz, Mexico.
1944 O.[xyrhopus] petola sebae—Dunn, Caldasia, 3 (12): 201.

Distribution: Western Ecuador and interior Colombia north to Veracruz, Mexico; intergrading with digitalis in eastern Panama and Chocó of Colombia.

OXYRHOPUS RHOMBIFER Duméril, Bibron and Duméril
    rhombifer group

1854 Oxyrhopus rhombifer Duméril, Bibron and Duméril, Erp. Gén., 7: 1018. Type-locality: Provincia
    Corrientes, Argentina.

Distribution: Amazon River south to central Argentina.

Content: Four subspecies.

Key to the subspecies

1. Dark bands black, about same shade centrally
   as on edges; sutures of head scales not
   distinctively colored except sometimes on
   snout; dark pigment in light interspaces
   usually confined to scale tips; subcaudals
   usually fewer than 72 in males, 62 in
   females (except in Mato Grosso and Goiás)-
   --2
   Dark bands brown, usually lighter in tone
   centrally; head scales all with light
   sutures giving pied appearance; dark
   dorsal pigment usually not confined to
   scale tips in light interspaces; subcaudals usually more than 71 in males, 61
   in females-----------------------------3

2. Dark dorsal bands numerous, about 30-60,
   anterior slightly longer than posterior,
   second band three to six scales long------
   ---------------------------------rhombifer
   Dark dorsal bands fewer, 16-30, anterior
   much longer than posterior, second band
   seven to twelve scales in length---------
   --------------------------septentrionalis

3. Anterior bands much longer than posterior,
   second band about 10-16 scales in length;
   ventrals plus subcaudals usually more than
   269---------------------inaequifasciatus
   Anterior bands slightly longer than
   posterior, second band fewer than ten
   scales in length; ventrals plus subcaudals
   usually fewer than 270-----------bachmanni

Clave de subespecies

1. Bandas oscuras negras, de igual intensidad
   en el centro que en los bordes; suturas
   entre placas cefálicas no coloreadas distintamente excepto a veces sobre el hocico;
   pigmento oscuro en los interespacios
   claros sólo confinado usualmente a los
   ápices de escamas; subcaudales normalmente
   menos de 72 en machos, 62 en hembras
   (excepto en Mato Grosso y Goiás)---------2
   Bandas oscuras pardas, usualmente más claras
   en el centro; suturas entre placas cefálicas claras dando el aspecto de manchas;
   pigmento oscuro dorsal no confinado a los
   ápices de escamas en los interespacios
   claros; subcaudales normalmente más de
   71 en machos, 61 en hembras-------------3

2. Bandas dorsales oscuras numerosas, alrededor de 30-60, anteriormente algo más
   largas que posteriormente, segunda banda
   de tres a seis escamas de largo--rhombifer
   Bandas dorsales oscuras poco numerosas, 16-
   30, anteriormente mucho más largas que
   posteriormente, segunda banda de siete a
   doce escamas de largo------septentrionalis

3. Bandas anteriores más largas que posteriores, segunda banda alrededor de 10-16
   escamas de largo; ventrales más subcaudales usualmente más de 269--------------
   ---------------------------inaequifasciatus
   Bandas anteriores ligeramente más largas
   que posteriores, segunda banda menos de
   diez escamas de largo; ventrales más subcaudales usualmente menos de 270----bachmanni

Oxyrhopus rhombifer rhombifer Duméril, Bibron and Duméril

1854 Oxyrhopus sub-punctatus Duméril, Bibron and Duméril, Erp. Gén., 7: 1016. Type-locality: Brazil.
1854 Oxyrhopus D'Orbignyi Duméril, Bibron and Duméril, Erp. Gén., 7: 1024. Type-locality: Buenos Aires, Argentina.
1909 Oxyrhopus rhombifer [rhombifer]—Werner, Mitt. Naturhist. Mus. Hamburg, 26: 230.

Distribution: Provincia de Buenos Aires to east of Río Paraná in Argentina and Uruguay; north to southern Minas Gerais and Rio de Janeiro, Brazil.

Oxyrhopus rhombifer bachmanni (Weyenbergh), new combination

1876 Coronella Bachmanni Weyenbergh, Period. Zool. Córdoba, 2 (1875): 193. Type-locality: Córdoba, Argentina.
1923 Leptodira weiseri Müller, Zool. Anz., 57: 152. Type-locality: Caspinchango, Valle Cachaqué, Catamarca, Argentina.

Distribution: West of Río Paraná and south to Mendoza and Córdoba, Argentina.

Oxyrhopus rhombifer inaequifasciatus Werner

1909 Oxyrhopus rhombifer var. inaequifasciata Werner, Mitt. Naturhist. Mus. Hamburg, 26: 230. Type-locality: Estancia Postillon, Puerto Max, Paraguay.
1955 Pseudoboa ornata Hoge and Mertens, Senckenbergiana Biol., 36: 305, pls. 30-31. Type-locality: Forte de Coimbra, Pôrto Esperança, Mato Grosso, Brazil.

Distribution: Salta and Jujuy, Argentina through Bolivian Chaco and Brazilian Pantanal.

Oxyrhopus rhombifer septentrionalis Vellard

1943 Oxyrhopus rhombifer septentrionalis Vellard, Acta. Zool. Lilloana, 1: 89, pl. Type-locality: Campos de Vilhena, northern Mato Grosso, Brazil.

Distribution: Central Planalto of Brazil; Mato Grosso (except Pantanal), Goiás, and north to Rio Amazonas in region of Santarem, Brazil.

OXYRHOPUS TRIGEMINUS Duméril, Bibron and Duméril
    melanogenys group

1854 Oxyrhopus trigeminus Duméril, Bibron and Duméril, Erp. Gén., 7: 1013. Type-locality: Bahia and Rio de Janeiro, Brazil; restricted to Distrito Federal, Brazil, by Vanzolini, Rev. Brasil. Biol., 8: 382; restriction here rejected, for reasons to be published elsewhere.
1913 Oxyrhopus trigeminus—Thompson, Proc. Acad. Nat. Sci. Phila., 1913: 79.

Distribution: Most of Brazil north of Rio de Janeiro, to Rio Amazonas and west into Mato Grosso; Marajó Island.

OXYRHOPUS VENEZUELANUS Shreve
    doliatus group

1947 Oxyrhopus venezuelanus Shreve, Bull. Mus. Comp. Zool., 99: 532. Type-locality: Pauji, Distrito Acosta, Estado de Falcón, Venezuela.

Distribution: Andes of north central Venezuela.

PARAPOSTOLEPIS Amaral

  1930 Parapostolepis Amaral, Mem. Inst. Butantan, 4 (1929): 51. Type-species: Apostolepis polylepis
       Amaral.

    Distribution: As for only known species.

    Content: One species.

PARAPOSTOLEPIS POLYLEPIS (Amaral)

  1921 Apostolepis polylepis Amaral, Anex. Mem. Inst. Butantan, 1 (1): 13, pl. 1, figs. 5-8.
       Type-locality: Eng. Dodt, Município de Santa Filomena, Estado do Piauí, Brazil.
  1930 Parapostolepis polylepis—Amaral, Mem. Inst. Butantan, 4 (1929): 51.

    Distribution: Known only from type locality.

PARAPTYCHOPHIS Lema

   1967 Paraptychophis Lema, Iheringia, Zool., no. 35: 62. Type-species: Paraptychophis meyeri Lema.

   Distribution: Known only from type locality of species.

   Content: One species.

PARAPTYCHOPHIS MEYERI Lema

   1967 Paraptychophis meyeri Lema, Iheringia, Zool., no. 35: 63, figs. 1-10. Type-locality:
      Pôrto Alegre, Estado do Rio Grande do Sul, Brazil.

   Distribution: Known only from type locality.

PAROXYRHOPUS Schenkel

> 1900 Paroxyrhopus Schenkel, Verh. Naturforsch. Ges. Basel, 13: 168. Type-species: Paroxyrhopus
> reticulatus Schenkel.

  Distribution: Southern Brazil, Paraguay, Colombia.

  Content: Two species.

Key to the species	Clave de especies
1. Two postoculars; supraocular not turned down behind orbit; unicolor dorsally, sides variegated with small spots or reddish color----------------------------------undulatus One postocular; supraocular has downward projecting extension behind orbit; dorsum with large, brownish-black spots--------reticulatus	1. Dos postoculares; supraocular no contorneando atrás y hacia abajo la órbita; dorsalmente unicolor, lados variegados con pequeñas manchas o en color rojizo---------------undulatus Una postocular; supraocular con una extensión que proyecta atrás y hacia abajo de la órbita; dorso con grandes manchas pardo negras--------------------------------------reticulatus

PAROXYRHOPUS UNDULATUS (Jensen), new combination

> 1900 Oxyrhopus undulatus Jensen, Vidensk. Medd. Naturhist. Foren. Kjöbenhavn, 1899 (1900): 106, fig. 2.
>   Type-locality: Lagoa Santa, Minas Gerais, Brazil.
> 1913 Oxyrhopus latifrontalis Werner, Mitt. Naturhist. Mus. Hamburg, 30: 30. Type-locality: Eastern
>   part of Estado de Minas Gerias, Brazil.
> 1923 Paroxyrhopus atropurpureus Amaral, Proc. New England Zool. Club, 8: 90. Type-locality: Nova
>   Baden, Estado do Minas Gerais, Brazil.
> 1929 Paroxyrhopus latifrontalis—Amaral, Mem. Inst. Butantan, 4: 208.

  Distribution: Mato Grosso, São Paulo, Minas Gerais, and Goiás, Brazil; Instituto Butantan, São
  Paulo, Brazil, has a specimen identified as this species from Amazonian Colombia.

  Comment: Dr. Joseph R. Bailey has pointed out this prior name for the species called Paroxyrhopus
  latifrontalis by earlier authors. He also thinks it likely that the two species are not
  distinguishable, but we retain both at this time.

PAROXYRHOPUS RETICULATUS Schenkel

> 1900 Paroxyrhopus reticulatus Schenkel, Verh. Naturforsch. Ges. Basel, 13: 169, figs. 5-5e. Type-
>   locality: Bemalcue, Paraguay.

  Distribution: Paraguay.

PELAMIS Daudin

1803 Pelamis Daudin, Hist. Nat. Rept., 7: 357. Type-species: Anguis platura Linnaeus.
1816 Pelamys Oken (emendation of Pelamis Daudin), Okens Lehrbuch der Naturgeschichte, 3 (2): 279.
1817 Ophinectes Rafinesque, Amer. Month. Mag. Crit. Rev., 1: 432. Type-species: None designated.
1848 Elaphrodytes Gistl (substitute name for Hydrus Daudin), Naturgeschichte des Tierreichs: ix.
1910 Pelamydrus Stejneger, Proc. U.S. Nat. Mus., 38: 111. Type-species: Anguis platura Linnaeus.

Distribution: As for single known species.

Content: One species.

PELAMIS PLATURUS (Linnaeus)

1766 Anguis platura Linnaeus, Systema Naturae, Ed. 12: 391. Type-locality: None given.
1799 [Hydrus] bicolor Schneider, Hist. Amphib. Nat., 1: 242. Type-locality: None given.
1803 [Pelamis] platuros—Daudin (in error for platurus), Hist. Nat. Rept., 7: 361.
1817 Pelamis schneideri Rafinesque (substitute name for Pelamis bicolor var. Daudin), Amer. Month.
   Mag. Crit. Rev., 1: 432.
1842 Pelamis ornata Gray, Zool. Misc., 1842: 60. Type-locality: "India".
1854 Pelamis variegata Duméril, Bibron and Duméril, Erp. Gén., 7: 1337. Type-locality: Macassar,
   Célébes.
1854 [Pelamis bicolor] var. Sinuata Duméril, Bibron and Duméril, Erp. Gén., 7: 1338. Type-locality:
   Unknown.
1856 [Hydrophis (Pelamis) bicolor] var. alternatus Fischer (substitute name for Pelamis variegata
   Duméril, Bibron and Duméril), Abh. Naturwiss. Ver. Hamburg, 3: 63.
1872 Hydrophis bicolor var. maculata Jan, Icon. Gen. Ophid., Livr. 40: pl. 3, fig. 3. Type-locality:
   "Mer des Indes" (Indian Ocean?); coast of China.

Distribution: Indo-Australian seas from Siberia to Tasmania; Pacific Ocean; west coast of Americas
   from Mexico to Ecuador; one unverified report on Gulf Coast of Central America.

PHILODRYAS Wagler

1830 <u>Philodryas</u> Wagler, Nat. Syst. Amphib.: 185. Type-species: <u>Coluber</u> <u>Olfersii</u> Lichtenstein.
1830 <u>Chlorosoma</u> Wagler, Nat. Syst. Amphib.: 185. Type-species: <u>Coluber</u> <u>viridissimum</u> Linnaeus.
1843 <u>Tropidodryas</u> Fitzinger, Systema Reptilium: 26. Type-species: <u>Herpetodryas</u> <u>Serra</u> Schlegel.
1857 <u>Callirhinus</u> Girard (preoccupied by <u>Callirhinus</u> Cuvier), Proc. Acad. Nat. Sci. Phila., 1857: 181.
     Type-species: <u>Callirhinus</u> <u>patagoniensis</u> Girard.
1858 <u>Euophrys</u> Günther, Cat. Sn. Brit. Mus.: 139. Type-species: <u>Euophrys</u> <u>modestus</u> Günther.
1859 <u>Galeophis</u> Berthold, Nach. Univ. K. Ges. Wiss. Göttingen, 17: 181. Type-species: <u>Galeophis</u> <u>Jani</u>
     Berthold.
1870 <u>Teleolepis</u> Cope, Proc. Amer. Phil. Soc., 11 (1869): 153. Type-species: <u>Teleolepis</u> <u>striaticeps</u>
     Cope.
1887 <u>Agratomus</u> Cope, Bull. U.S. Nat. Mus., 32: 93. Type-species: <u>Philodryas</u> <u>burmeisteri</u> Jan.
1887 <u>Dirrhox</u> Cope (substitute name for <u>Callirhinus</u> Girard), Proc. Amer. Phil. Soc., 24: 58.
1887 <u>Atomophis</u> Cope, Proc. Amer. Phil. Soc., 24: 58. Type-species: <u>Philodryas</u> <u>burmeisteri</u> Jan.
1903 <u>Rhinodryas</u> Werner, Abh. Bayerischen Akad., 22: 384, fig. Type-species: <u>Rhinodryas</u> <u>Königi</u> Werner.
1924 <u>Pseuduromacer</u> Werner, Sitz. Math.-Naturwiss. Kl. Akad. Wiss. Wien, 133, abt. 1: 52. Type-
     species: <u>Pseuduromacer</u> <u>lugubris</u> Werner.

Distribution: South America.

Content: Fifteen species.

·Key to the species

1. Normal rostral, without accessory scales------2
   Rostral prominent, with accessory scales-------
   --<u>baroni</u>

2. More than 15 scale rows at midbody-----------3
   With 15 scale rows at midbody--------<u>oligolepis</u>

3. More than 17 scale rows at midbody-----------4
   With 17 scale rows at midbody--------<u>carbonelli</u>

4. More than 19 scale rows at midbody-----------5
   With 19 scale rows at midbody----------------9

5. With 21 scale rows at midbody----------------6
   With 23 scale rows at midbody-------<u>burmeisteri</u>

6. Scales keeled--------------------------------7
   Scales not keeled----------------------------8

7. Belly immaculate; dorsal pattern uniform
   green---------------------------------<u>aestivus</u>
   Dark belly with yellow stripes; dorsal pattern
   brown spotted---------------------------<u>serra</u>

8. Belly brownish with yellow spotting; end of
   tail hispid----------------------<u>pseudoserra</u>
   Belly not spotted; end of tail not hispid------
   ---------------------------------------<u>nattereri</u>

9. Lacking dark, zig-zag vertebral stripe-------10
   With a dark, zig-zag vertebral stripe---<u>elegans</u>

10.Ventrals edged with black-------------------11
   Ventrals not black bordered-----------------12

Clave de especies

1. Rostral normal, sin escudos accesorios--------2
   Rostral prominente con escudos accesorios------
   --<u>baroni</u>

2. Más de 15 filas de escamas al medio del
   cuerpo---------------------------------------3
   Con 15 filas de escamas al medio del cuerpo----
   ---------------------------------------<u>oligolepis</u>

3. Con más de 17 filas de escamas al medio del
   cuerpo---------------------------------------4
   Con 17 filas de escamas al medio del cuerpo----
   ---------------------------------------<u>carbonelli</u>

4. Con más de 19 filas de escamas al medio del
   cuerpo---------------------------------------5
   Con 19 filas de escamas al medio del cuerpo---9

5. Con 21 filas de escamas al medio del cuerpo---6
   Con 23 filas de escamas al medio del cuerpo----
   ---------------------------------------<u>burmeisteri</u>

6. Escamas carenadas----------------------------7
   Escamas no carenadas-------------------------8

7. Vientre inmaculado; dorso verde uniforme-------
   ---------------------------------------<u>aestivus</u>
   Vientre oscuro con líneas amarillas; dorso
   manchado--------------------------------<u>serra</u>

8. Vientre pardo con punteado amarillo; porción
   final de la cola híspida----------<u>pseudoserra</u>
   Vientre sin manchas; porción final de la cola
   no híspida----------------------------<u>nattereri</u>

9. Sin banda oscura vertebral en zig-zag--------10
   Con banda oscura vertebral en zig-zag---<u>elegans</u>

10.Ventrales bordeadas de negro----------------11
   Ventrales no bordeadas de negro-------------12

11. Sharp <u>canthus</u> <u>rostralis</u>, 11 + 2 maxillary
teeth; 15 mandibular teeth------<u>patagoniensis</u>
<u>Canthus</u> <u>rostralis</u> inconspicuous; 15 + 2
teeth; 21 mandibular teeth-----------<u>arnaldoi</u>

12. Dorsal pattern uniformly green---------------13
Dorsal pattern not uniformly green-----------14

13. Ventrals fewer than 205---------------------16
Ventrals more than 205------------<u>viridissimus</u>

14. Lacking dark vertebral stripe, 3-5 scales wide-
---15
With dark vertebral stripe 3-5 scales wide-----
--------------------------------<u>psammophideus</u>

15. Ventrals more than 200; deep green dorsally,
posteriorly reddish------------<u>mattogrossensis</u>
Fewer than 200 ventrals; yellowish-green dorsally, often with scales streaked with black
and white----------------------<u>patagoniensis</u>

16. Dorsal scales smooth; usually fewer than 120
subcaudals---------------------------<u>olfersii</u>
Dorsal scales keeled; usually more than 120
subcaudals---------------------------<u>aestivus</u>

11. <u>Canthus</u> <u>rostralis</u> saliente y nítido; 11 + 2
dientes maxilares; 15 dientes mandibulares----
-------------------------------<u>patagoniensis</u>
<u>Canthus</u> <u>rostralis</u> imperceptible; 15 + 2 dientes
maxilares; 21 dientes mandibulares----<u>arnaldoi</u>

12. Dorso verde uniforme------------------------13
Dorso no verde uniforme----------------------14

13. Ventrales menos de 205----------------------16
Ventrales más de 205--------------<u>viridissimus</u>

14. Sin cinta vertebral oscura de tres a cinco
escamas de ancho---------------------------15
Con cinta vertebral oscura de tres a cinco
escamas de ancho----------------<u>psammophideus</u>

15. Más de 200 ventrales; dorso oliva oscura,
rojizo posteriormente---------<u>mattogrossensis</u>
Menos de 200 ventrales; dorso verde amarillento
con escamas frecuentemente líneadas de negro y
blanco--------------------------<u>patagoniensis</u>

16. Escamas dorsales lisas; usualmente menos de
120 subcaudales----------------------<u>olfersii</u>
Escamas dorsales quilladas; usualmente más de
120 subcaudales----------------------<u>aestivus</u>

<u>PHILODRYAS</u> <u>AESTIVUS</u> (Duméril, Bibron and Duméril)

1854 <u>Dryophylax</u> <u>aestivus</u> Duméril, Bibron and Duméril, Erp. Gén., 7: 1111. Type-locality: South
America.
1896 <u>Philodryas</u> <u>aestivus</u>—Boulenger, Cat. Sn. Brit. Mus., 3: 128.

Distribution: Southwestern and southern Brazil; Amazonian Bolivia; Paraguay, Uruguay and northern
Argentina.

Comment: The composite nature of <u>Herpetodryas</u> <u>aestivus</u> Schlegel (Essai Physion. Serp., 1837, 186)
was noted by Duméril, Bibron and Duméril, in Erp. Gén., 7, 1854, who restricted Schlegel's name to
the Asian material (p. 209), and gave a new name to the American material (p. 1111).
Unfortunately, they chose the same specific epithet for the latter that Schlegel gave to the
former (<u>aestivus</u>), and this has led to considerable confusion in later literature concerning the
authorship of the names. It is clear that they were dealing with two distinct taxa, and by
indicating the American species as <u>Dryophylas</u> <u>aestivus</u> Nobis they intended this to be a newly
coined name. We so use it here.

Content: Two subspecies.

Key to the subspecies

1. With 21 scale rows, strongly keeled except
outer row; black line behind eye----------
----------------------------------<u>manegarzoni</u>
With 19 moderately keeled scale rows,
lacking black line behind eye-----<u>aestivus</u>

Clave de subespecies

1. Con 21 filas de escamas fuertemente quilladas excepto la fila exterior; una línea
negra detrás del ojo----------<u>manegarzoni</u>
Con 19 filas de escamas moderadamente quilladas; sin línea negra atrás del ojo-----
----------------------------------<u>aestivus</u>

<u>Philodryas</u> <u>aestivus</u> <u>aestivus</u> (Duméril, Bibron and Duméril)

1900 <u>Philodryas</u> <u>campicola</u> Jensen, Vidensk. Medd. Naturhist. Foren. Kjöbnhavn, 1900: 108. Type-
locality: Lagoa Santa, Minas Gerais, Brazil.
1902 <u>Philodryas</u> <u>subcarinatus</u> Boulenger, Ann. Mag. Nat. Hist., (7) 9: 287. Type-locality: Colonia
Benítez, Paraguay.
1924 <u>P.</u>[<u>seuduromacer</u>] <u>lugubris</u> Werner, Sitz. Math.-Naturwiss. Kl. Akad. Wiss. Wien, 133, abt.
1: 53. Type-locality: São Paulo, Brazil.
1959 <u>Philodryas</u> <u>aestivus</u> [<u>aestivus</u>]—Orejas-Miranda, Com. Zool. Mus. Hist. Nat. Montevideo, 4
(82): 2.

Distribution: São Paulo, Brazil to Bolivia, Paraguay and northern Argentina.

Philodryas aestivus manegarzoni Orejas-Miranda

   1959 Philodryas aestivus manegarzoni Orejas-Miranda, Com. Zool. Mus. Hist. Nat. Montevideo, 4
     (82): 2. Type-locality: Near Zapicán, Departamento Lavalleja, Uruguay.

     Distribution: Uruguay.

PHILODRYAS ARNALDOI (Amaral)

   1932 Chlorosoma arnaldoi Amaral, Mem. Inst. Butantan, 7: 100, figs. 2-4. Type-locality: São Bento,
     Santa Catharina, Brazil.
   1936 Philodryas arnaldoi—Amaral, Mem. Inst. Butantan, 10: 140.

     Distribution: São Paulo, Paraná, Rio Grande do Sul, and Santa Catarina, Brazil.

PHILODRYAS BARONI Berg

   1895 Philodryas Baroni Berg, An. Mus. Nac. Buenos Aires, 4: 189. Type-locality: Tucumán, Argentina.
   1903 Rhinodryas Königi Werner, Abh. Bayerischen Akad., 22: 384, fig. Type-locality: Rosario,
     Argentina (province not mentioned).

     Distribution: Chaco, Santiago de Estero, Salta, Tucumán and Catamarca, Argentina.

     Comment: Serié described Philodryas baroni var. fusco-flavescens (An. Mus. Nac. Buenos Aires, 26,
     1914, 228, pl.), with the type-locality Salta, Argentina, and a paratype from Tucumán, Argentina.
     Insofar as we can determine, the range of the variety is the same as the nominate form, both as
     given by Serié in later papers, and in Abalos et al, Acta Zool. Lilloana, 20, 1964, 261. It seems
     clear that this does not represent a subspecies as usually recognized by herpetologists.

PHILODRYAS BURMEISTERI Jan

   1861 Herpetodryas trilineatus Burmeister (nomen nudum), Reise Durch die La Plata-Staaten, 1: 309.
   1861 Dr.[yophylax] burmeisteri Burmeister (nomen nudum), Reise Durch die La Plata-Staaten, 2: 529.
   1863 P.[hilodryas] Burmeisteri Jan, Elenco Sistema Ofidi: 84. Type-locality: Mendoza, Argentina.
   1898 Philodryas arenarius Andersson, Ofv. K. Vet.-Akad. Förh. Stockholm, 7: 458, 4 figs. Type-
     locality: Puerto Madryn, Patagonia, Argentina.

     Distribution: Northwestern Argentina to Patagonia.

PHILODRYAS CARBONELLI Roze

   1957 Philodryas carbonelli Roze, Bol. Mus. Cien. Nat. Caracas, 1 (1955): 186, figs. 2-3. Type-
     locality: Maroa, Territorio Federal Amazonas, Venezuela.

     Distribution: Southern Venezuela.

PHILODRYAS ELEGANS (Tschudi)

   1845 L.[ygophis (Lygophis)] elegans Tschudi, Archiv. für Naturg., 2: 164. Type-locality: Peru; more
     precisely stated later by Tschudi, Fauna Peruviana, Herp., 1845, 53, pl. 6, as Montañas de
     Urubamba and vicinity of Lima, Peru; restricted to Lima, Peru, by Schmidt and Walker, Zool.
     Ser. Field Mus. Nat. Hist., 24, 1943, 317.
   1896 Philodryas elegans—Boulenger, Cat. Sn. Brit. Mus., 3: 133.

     Distribution: Ecuador to Chile.

     Content: Two subspecies.

Key to the subspecies

1. Dark vertebral band broken anteriorly into
   paired or alternating spots, or into
   crossbands------------------rufidorsatus
   Dark vertebral band continuous anteriorly--
   ---------------------------------elegans

Clave de subespecies

1. Banda vertebral oscura interrumpida
   anteriormente, generando puntos apareados
   o alternos o bandas transversales---------
   ------------------------------rufidorsatus
   Banda vertebral oscura anteriormente
   contínua--------------------------elegans

Philodryas elegans elegans (Tschudi)

1854 Dryophylax freminvillei Duméril, Bibron and Duméril, Erp. Gén., 7: 1115. Type-locality:
   Guiana and Callao, Peru; restricted to Callao by Schmidt and Walker, Zool. Ser. Field
   Mus. Nat. Hist., 24, 1943, 317.
1943 Philodryas elegans elegans—Schmidt and Walker, Zool. Ser. Field Mus. Nat. Hist., 24:
   317.

Distribution: Rimac Valley in Peru to northern Chile.

Philodryas elegans rufidorsatus (Günther)

1858 Dromicus rufidorsatus Günther, Cat. Sn. Brit. Mus.: 130. Type-locality: America;
   restricted to coastal Peru by Schmidt and Walker, Zool. Ser. Field Mus. Nat. Hist., 24,
   1943, 315.
1868 Tachymenis canilatus Cope, Proc. Acad. Nat. Sci. Phila., 1868: 104. Type-locality:
   Guayaquil, Ecuador.
1876 Lygophis poecilostomus Cope, Jour. Acad. Nat. Sci. Phila., (2) 8 (1875): 180. Type-
   locality: Valley of Jequetepeque, Peru.
1878 Dryophylax vitellinus Cope, Proc. Amer. Phil. Soc., 17: 33. Type-locality: Pacasmayo,
   Peru.
1943 Philodryas elegans rufidorsatus—Schmidt and Walker, Zool. Ser. Field Mus. Nat. Hist.,
   24: 315.

Distribution: Guayaquil, Ecuador, to Departamento Libertad, Peru.

PHILODRYAS MATTOGROSSENSIS Koslowsky

1898 Philodryas mattogrossensis Koslowsky, Rev. Mus. La Plata, 8: 29, pl. 1, figs. 1-3. Type-
   locality: Miranda, Mato Grosso, Brazil.
1901 Philodryas ternetzii Schenkel, Verh. Naturforsch. Ges. Basel, 13 (1900): 170, fig. 6. Type-
   locality: Bemalcue, Paraguay.
1902 Philodryas Erlandi Lönnberg, Ann. Mag. Nat. Hist., (7) 10: 460. Type-locality: Crevaux and
   Tatarenda, Bolivian Chaco, Bolivia.
1909 Philodryas boulengeri Werner, Mitt. Naturhist. Mus. Hamburg, 26: 232, fig. 7. Type-locality:
   Unknown (Werner added "angeblich 'Indien'").

Distribution: Southwestern Brazil, Paraguay and Bolivia.

PHILODRYAS NATTERERI (Steindachner)

1870 Philodryas Nattereri Steindachner, Sitz. Math.-Naturwiss. Kl. Akad. Wiss. Wien, 62: 345, pl. 7,
   figs. 1-3. Type-locality: Mato Grosso, Brazil.
1896 Philodryas nattereri—Boulenger, Cat. Sn. Brit. Mus., 3: 134.

Distribution: Paraguay and western central Brazil.

PHILODRYAS OLFERSII (Lichtenstein)

1823 Coluber Olfersii Lichtenstein, Verzeichniss der Doubletten des Zoologischen Museums der Königl. Universität zu Berlin: 104. Type-locality: Brazil.

1825 C.[oluber] pileatus Wied, Beiträge zur Naturgeschichte von Brasilien, 1: 344. Type-locality: Rio Itabapuana, Brazil.

1825 C.[oluber] herbeus Wied, Beiträge zur Naturgeschichte von Brasilien, 1: 349. Type-locality: Capitania da Bahia, Brazil.

1862 Philodryas Reinhardtii Günther, Ann. Mag. Nat. Hist., (3) 9: 127, pl. 9, fig. 7. Type-locality: Bahia, Brazil, and Brazil.

1862 Philodryas latirostris Cope, Proc. Acad. Nat. Sci. Phila., 1862: 73. Type-locality: Paraguay.

1896 Philodryas olfersii—Boulenger, Cat. Sn. Brit. Mus., 3: 129.

1900 Philodryas laticeps Werner, Zool. Anz., 23: 198. Type-locality: Santa Catharina, Brazil.

1924 Philodryas argentinus Müller, Mitt. Zool. Mus. Berlin, 11: 90. Type-locality: Provincia Salta, Argentina.

Distribution: Western Brazil and eastern Peru through Bolivia and Paraguay to Uruguay and Argentina.

PHILODRYAS OLIGOLEPIS Gomes

1921 Philodryas oligolepis Gomes, in Amaral, Ann. Paulistas Med. Cirurg., 9: 4, pl. A, figs. 1-3. Type-locality: Mariana, Estado de Minas Gerais, Brazil.

Distribution: Minas Gerais, Brazil.

PHILODRYAS PATAGONIENSIS (Girard)

1857 Callirhinus patagoniensis Girard, Proc. Acad. Nat. Sci. Phila., 1857: 182. Type-locality: Mouth of Río Negro, Patagonia, Argentina.

1858 Euophrys modestus Günther, Cat. Sn. Brit. Mus.: 139. Type-locality: "Canton, China".

1863 L.[iophis] poecilostictus Jan, Arch. Zool. Anat. Fis., 2: 289. Type-locality: Uruguay.

1964 Philodryas patagoniensis—Hoge, Mem. Inst. Butantan, 30: 67.

Distribution: Brazil, Bolivia, Paraguay, Argentina and Uruguay.

PHILODRYAS PSAMMOPHIDEUS Günther

1872 Philodryas psammophideus Günther, Ann. Mag. Nat. Hist., (4) 9: 23, pl. 4, fig. A. Type-locality: Tucumán, Argentina.

1896 Philodryas bolivianus Boulenger, Cat. Sn. Brit. Mus., 3: 132, pl. 9, fig. 1. Type-locality: Charobamba, Bolivia.

1897 Philodryas Borellii Peracca, Bol. Mus. Zool. Anat. Comp. Torino, 12 (274): 14. Type-locality: "Las Concas fra Tala e Gnaichipá, prov. di Salta Argentina, la ♀ da San Paolo".

1899 Liophis trifasciatus Werner, Zool. Anz., 22: 114. Type-locality: Paraguay.

1909 Liophis bolivianus Werner, Mitt. Naturhist. Mus. Hamburg, 26: 222. Type-locality: Charobamba, Bolivia.

1909 Philodryas lineatus Werner, Mitt. Naturhist. Mus. Hamburg, 26: 233, fig. 8. Type-locality: Argentina.

1925 Philodryas werneri Müller, Mitt. Zool. Mus. Berlin, 12: 103. Type-locality: Sierra de Curumalan, Argentina.

1926 Philodryas pallidus Werner, Sitz. Math.-Naturwiss. Kl. Akad. Wiss. Wien, 135, abt. 1: 247. Type-locality: Montevideo, Uruguay.

Distribution: Western and southern Brazil, eastern Bolivia, Paraguay, Uruguay and Argentina.

PHILODRYAS PSEUDOSERRA Amaral

1938 Philodryas pseudo-serra Amaral, Mem. Inst. Butantan, 11 (1937): 207. Type-locality: Porto Martins, Estado de São Paulo, Brazil.

Distribution: Rio de Janeiro, Paraná, Sao Paulo, Minas Gerais and Santa Catharina, Brazil.

PHILODRYAS SERRA (Schlegel)

1837 Herp.[etodryas] Serra Schlegel, Essai Physion. Serpens, 2: 180, pl. 7, figs. 1-2. Type-locality: Brazil.
1858 Philodryas serra—Gunther, Cat. Sn. Brit. Mus.: 125.
?1859 Geleophis (sic) Jani Berthold, Nach. Univ. K. Ges. Wiss. Göttingen, 17: 181. Type-locality: Bahia, Brazil.
1870 Teleolepis striaticeps Cope, Proc. Amer. Phil. Soc., 11: 153. Type-locality: Brazil.
1896 Philodryas serra—Boulenger, Cat. Sn. Brit. Mus., 3: 134.

Distribution: Northeastern, central and south central Brazil.

PHILODRYAS VIRIDISSIMUS (Linnaeus)

1758 Coluber viridissimus Linnaeus, Systema Naturae, Ed. 10: 226. Type-locality: Surinam.
1803 Coluber janthinus Daudin, Hist. Nat. Rept., 6: 273. Type-locality: America.
?1861 P.[hilodryas] crassifrons Cope, Proc. Acad. Nat. Sci. Phila., 1860: 559. Type-locality: Cayenne.
1896 Philodryas viridissimus—Boulenger, Cat. Sn. Brit. Mus., 3: 129.
1928 Philodryas affinis Müller, Zool. Anz., 77: 77. Type-locality: Buenavista, 80 km northwest of Santa Cruz de la Sierra, Bolivia.

Distribution: Amazonas and Paraguay valleys, from southern Venezuela and Guianas to Argentina.

Prepared by Joseph R. Bailey, Duke University, Durham, North Carolina

PHIMOPHIS Cope

> 1854 Rhinosimus Duméril, Bibron and Duméril (preoccupied by Rhinosimus Latreille, 1802-03), Erp. Gén.,
>   7: 991. Type-species: Rhinosimus Guerini Duméril, Bibron and Duméril.
> 1860 Phimophis Cope (substitute name for Rhinosimus Duméril, Bibron and Duméril), Proc. Acad. Nat.
>   Sci. Phila., 1860: 79. Type-species: Rhinosimus Guerini Duméril, Bibron and Duméril.

>   Distribution: Panama to central Argentina in grassland regions.

>   Content: Four species.

Key to the species

1. Loreal present--------------------------------2
   Loreal absent------------------------iglesiasi

2. Ventrals more than 196-----------------------3
   Ventrals fewer than 195--------------guianensis

3. Two wide, longitudinal, dark brown bands-------
   ------------------------------------vittatum
   Without longitudinal bands-------------guerini

Clave de especies

1. Loreal presente-------------------------------2
   Loreal ausente------------------------iglesiasi

2. Más de 196 ventrales--------------------------3
   Menos de 195 ventrales---------------guianensis

3. Con dos bandas anchas longitudinales pardo
   oscuras-------------------------------vittatum
   Sin bandas longitudinales--------------guerini

PHIMOPHIS GUERINI (Duméril, Bibron and Duméril)

> 1854 Rhinosimus guerini Duméril, Bibron and Duméril, Erp. Gén., 7: 991, pl. 72. Type-locality:
>   Unknown; Duméril, Bibron and Duméril mentioned a second specimen, from Bahia, Brazil, in the
>   original description.
> 1913 Rhinostoma scytaloides Werner, Mitt. Naturhist. Mus. Hamburg, 30: 31. Type-locality: Eastern
>   Minas Gerais, Brazil.
> 1926 Rhinosimus amarali Mello, Mem. Inst. Oswaldo Cruz, 19: 128, figs. 1-11. Type-locality: Beltrão,
>   Minas Gerais, Brazil.
> 1962 Phimophis guerini—Bailey, Bull. Zool. Nomen., 19: 164.

>   Distribution: Southern Piauí, Brazil, south to Estado de São Paulo and southwest to Córdoba,
>   Argentina.

PHIMOPHIS GUIANENSIS (Troschel)

> 1848 Heterodon guianensis Troschel, in Schomburgk, Reise in Britisch-Guiana: 653. Type-locality:
>   Savannah near Pirara, Guyana.
> 1860 R.[hinostoma] Guntheri Cope, Proc. Acad. Nat. Sci. Phila., 1860: 243. Type-locality: Interior
>   Venezuela.
> 1944 Phimophis guianensis—Dunn, Caldasia, 3: 202.

>   Distribution: Cocle Province, Panama, to Surinam, in savannah and scrub areas.

PHIMOPHIS IGLESIASI (Gomes)

> 1915 Rhinostoma Iglesiasi Gomes, Ann. Paulistas Med. Cirurg., 4: 126. Type-locality: Piauí, Brazil.
> 1923 Rhinostoma bimaculatum Lutz and Mello, Folha Medica, 4: 3. Type-locality: Pirapora, Minas
>   Gerais, Brazil.
> 1967 Phimophis iglesiasi—Bailey, Herpetologica, 23: 159.

>   Distribution: Interior east central Brazil from Pirapora, Minas Gerais, to Piaui.

PHIMOPHIS VITTATUS (Boulenger), new combination

> 1896 Rhinostoma vittatum Boulenger, Cat. Sn. Brit. Mus., 3: 115. Type-locality: Buenos Aires,
>   Argentina (probably in error).

>   Distribution: Santa Fé and Entre Rios, Argentina, to southern Bolivia.

PITUOPHIS Holbrook

1842 *Pituophis* Holbrook, North American Herpetology, Ed. 2, 4: 7. Type-species: *Coluber melanoleucus* Daudin.

Distribution: United States to Central Guatemala.

Content: About thirteen species, all except one of which are extralimital.

PITUOPHIS LINEATICOLLIS (Cope)

1861 *Arizona lineaticollis* Cope, Proc. Acad. Nat. Sci. Phila., 1861: 300. Type-locality: Given as "Mexico" in original description, but Cope later (Ann. Rept. U. S. Nat. Mus., 1898 [1900], 861) said it came from "Jalapa". Stull, Bull. U. S. Nat. Mus., 175, 1940, 52, said this was probably Jalapa, Oaxaca, but Smith and Taylor, Bull. U. S. Nat. Mus., 187, 1945, 108, gave it as Jalapa, Veracruz, with no explanation. Duellman, Univ. Kansas Publ. Mus. Nat. Hist., 10, 1960, 607, designated a neotype, thus fixing the type locality as 24 km northwest of Ciudad Oaxaca, Oaxaca, Mexico.
1894 *Pituophis lineaticollis*—Günther, Biol. Cent. Amer., Rept.: 124, pl. 47.

Distribution: Mexico and Guatemala.

Content: Two subspecies, one of which (*lineaticollis* Cope) is extralimital.

Pituophis lineaticollis gibsoni Stuart

1954 *Pituophis deppei gibsoni* Stuart, Proc. Biol. Soc. Washington, 67: 172. Type locality: Vicinity of Yepocapa, Departamento Chimaltenango, Guatemala, 1430 m.
1960 *Pituophis lineaticollis gibsoni*—Duellman, Publ. Mus. Nat. Hist. Univ. Kansas, 10: 608.

Distribution: Moderate and intermediate elevations on Pacific coast of western Guatemala and Caribbean coast of Sierra de los Cuchumatanes, Guatemala.

PLATYNION Amaral

    1923 _Platynion_ Amaral, Proc. New England Zool. Club, 8: 91. Type-species: _Platynion lividum_ Amaral

      Distribution: As for only known species.

      Content: One species.

PLATYNION LIVIDUM Amaral

    1923 _Platynion lividum_ Amaral, Proc. New England Zool. Club, 8: 91. Type-locality: Dorizon, Paraná, Brazil.

      Distribution: Mato Grosso, Paraná and São Paulo, Brazil.

PLIOCERCUS Cope

1860 Pliocercus Cope, Proc. Acad. Nat. Sci. Phila., 1860: 253. Type-species: Pliocercus elapoides
        Cope.
1860 Elapochrus Peters, Monats. Akad. Wiss. Berlin, 1860: 293. Type-species: Elapochrus Deppei
        Peters.
1861 Pleiocercus Salvin (emendation of Pliocercus Cope), Proc. Zool. Soc. London, 1861: 227.
1862 Pleiokerkos Cope (emendation of Pliocercus Cope), Proc. Acad. Nat. Sci. Phila., 1862: 72.
1863 Cosmiosophis Jan, Arch. Zool. Anat. Phys., 2: 289. Type-species: Not designated.

    Distribution: Tropical Mexico through Central America to Amazonian South America.

    Content: Seven species, two of which (andrewsi Smith and bicolor Smith) are extralimital.

Key to the species

1. Scale rows at midbody 17----------------------2
   Scale rows at midbody 19--------------arubricus

2. One or two preoculars------------------------3
   Three preoculars--------------------dimidiatus

3. Body rings alternating red and black, not disposed in triads-----------------------------4
   Body rings alternating red, black, and yellow,
   with black rings frequently arranged in
   triads-----------------------------elapoides

4. More than 40 black rings--------------euryzonus
   Fewer than 40 black rings-----------annellatus

Clave de especies

1. Con 17 filas de escamas al medio del cuerpo---2
   Con 19 filas de escamas al medio del cuerop----
   --------------------------------------arubricus

2. Con dos o menos preoculares------------------3
   Con tres preoculares----------------dimidiatus

3. Anillos del cuerpo con alternancia de rojo y
   negro, no hay disposición en triadas---------4
   Anillos del cuerpo con alternancia de rojo,
   negro y amarillo, los anillos negros frecuentemente dispuestos en triadas-------elapoides

4. Más de 40 anillos negros dorsales-----euryzonus
   Menos de 40 anillos negros dorsales--annellatus

PLIOCERCUS ANNELLATUS Taylor

1951 Pliocercus annellatus Taylor, Univ. Kansas Sci. Bull., 34: 107, pl. 10; fig. 4. Type-locality:
        Morehouse Finca, 5 mi southwest of Turrialba, Costa Rica.

    Distribution: Known only from type locality.

PLIOCERCUS ARUBRICUS Taylor

1954 Pliocercus arubricus Taylor, Univ. Kansas Sci. Bull., 36: 734, fig. 14. Type-locality: Isla
        Bonita, southeastern slope of Volcán Poás, Costa Rica, about 5500 ft.

    Distribution: Atlantic slope of Costa Rica; known from type locality and Boca de Río Colorado.

PLIOCERCUS DIMIDIATUS Cope

1865 Pliocercus dimidiatus Cope, Proc. Acad. Nat. Sci. Phila., 1865: 190. Type-locality: Arriba,
        Costa Rica.
1951 Pliocercus dimidiatus—Taylor, Univ. Kansas Sci. Bull., 34: 106.

    Distribution: Nicaragua, Costa Rica, Panama.

PLIOCERCUS ELAPOIDES Cope

1860 Pliocercus elapoides Cope, Proc. Acad. Nat. Sci. Phila., 1860: 253. Type-locality: Near Jalapa,
        Veracruz.

    Distribution: Tropical Mexico to Guatemala and Honduras.

    Content: Nine subspecies, of which five (celatus Smith, elapoides Cope, hobartsmithi Liner,
        occidentalis Smith and Landy and schmidti Smith) are extralimital.

Key to the subspecies	Clave de subespecies
1. All primary black rings complete around body------------------------------------2 Most primary black rings incomplete ventrally--------------------laticollaris	1. Todos los anillos negros primarios completos alrededor del cuerpo-----------2 La mayoría de los anillos negros primarios incompletos a ventral--------laticollaris
2. Black rings on body fewer than 14---------3 Black rings on body more than 13---salvinii	2. Anillos negros del cuerpo menos de 14-----3 Anillos negros del cuerpo más de 13-------- ------------------------------------salvinii
3. Dark margin present between yellow and red rings---------------------------diastemus No dark margin between yellow and red rings ---------------------------salvadorensis	3. Con margen oscuro entre anillos amarillos y rojos----------------------------diastemus Sin margen oscuro entre anillos amarillos y rojos-----------------------salvadorensis

Pliocercus elapoides diastemus (Bocourt)

1886 Liophis elapoides var. diastema Bocourt, Miss. Sci. Mex., Rept.: 636, pl. 41, fig. 8.
Type-locality: Plateau of Guatemala.
1941 Pliocercus elapoides diastemus—Smith, Proc. Biol. Soc. Washington, 54: 120.

Distribution: Pacific slope of Chiapas, Mexico to El Salvador.

Pliocercus elapoides laticollaris Smith

1941 Pliocercus elapoides laticollaris Smith, Proc. Biol. Soc. Washington, 54: 122. Type-
locality: Tenosique, Tabasco, Mexico.
1941 Pliocercus elapoides semicinctus Schmidt, Zool. Ser. Field Mus. Nat. Hist., 22: 502.
Type-locality: Double Falls, west of Stann Creek, British Honduras.

Distribution: Tabasco, Mexico to British Honduras, excluding Yucatán Peninsula.

Comment: Stuart, Misc. Publ. Mus. Zool. Univ. Mich., 122, 1963, 110, does not regard
this subspecies as valid.

Pliocercus elapoides salvadorensis Mertens

1952 Pliocercus elapoides salvadorensis Mertens, Zool. Anz., 148: 91. Type-locality: Finca
San José, Santa Tecla, Departamento La Libertad, El Salvador, 1150 m.

Distribution: Departamento La Libertad, El Salvador.

Pliocercus elapoides salvinii Müller

1878 Pliocercus Salvinii Müller, Verh. Naturforsch. Ges. Basel, 6: 709, pl. 2A. Type-locality:
Verapaz, Guatemala.
1948 Pliocercus elapoides salvinii—Stuart, Misc. Publ. Mus. Zool. Univ. Mich., 69: 71.

Distribution: Low and moderate elevations in central and northern Guatemala.

PLIOCERCUS EURYZONUS Cope

1862 Pliocercus euryzonus Cope, Proc. Acad. Nat. Sci. Phila., 1862: 72. Type-locality: Region of
the Truando, New Grenada; this is now Colombia.

Distribution: Colombia, Ecuador, and equatorial Brazil to Guatemala.

Content: Three subspecies, one of which (bicolor Smith) is extralimital.

Key to the subspecies	Clave de subespecies
1. Red rings half scale row wide-----euryzonus Red rings more than two scale rows wide---- ---------------------------------aequalis	1. Anillos rojos del ancho de media escala---- --------------------------------euryzonus Anillos rojos de ancho mayor de dos escamas---------------------------aequalis

Pliocercus euryzonus euryzonus Cope

1863 L.[iophis] splendens Jan, Arch. Zool. Anat. Fis., 2: 302. Type-locality: Santa Fe de Bogotá, Colombia.
1948 Pliocercus euryzonus [euryzonus]—Stuart, Misc. Publ. Mus. Zool. Univ. Mich., 69: 72.

   Distribution: Amazonian Brazil, Colombia and Ecuador; Panama.

Pliocercus euryzonus aequalis Salvin

1861 Pliocercus aequalis Salvin, Proc. Zool. Soc. London, 1861: 227. Type-locality: San Gerónimo and neighboring mountains of Baja Verapaz, Guatemala.
1881 Pliocercus sargii Fischer, Arch. für Naturg., 47 (1): 225, pl. 11, figs. 1-3. Type-locality: Cobán, Guatemala.
1948 Pliocercus euryzonus aequalis—Stuart, Misc. Publ. Mus. Zool. Univ. Mich., 69: 72.

   Distribution: Known only from low and moderate elevations of Caribbean slope of central Guatemala.

PSEUDABLABES Boulenger

   1896 Pseudablabes Boulenger, Cat. Sn. Brit. Mus., 3: 126. Type-species: Eiremis agassizii Jan.

   Distribution: South and southwest Brazil, northeastern Argentina, Uruguay.

   Content: One species.

PSEUDABLABES AGASSIZII (Jan)

   1863 Eiremis Agassizii Jan, Arch. Zool. Anat. Fis., 2: 260. Type locality: Uruguay.
   1863 Philodryas paucisquamis Peters, Monats. Akad. Wiss. Berlin, 1863: 286. Type-locality: Brazil.
   1863 L. iopeltis brevicauda Jan, Elenco Sist. Ofidi: 82. Type-locality: unknown.
   1896 Pseudablabes agassizii—Boulenger, Cat. Sn. Brit. Mus., 3: 126.

   Distribution: South and southwest Brazil, northeastern Argentina, Uruguay.

REPTILIA: SERPENTES: COLUBRIDAE　　★ ★ ★ ★　　PSEUDOBOA

Prepared by Joseph R. Bailey, Duke University, Durham, North Carolina

PSEUDOBOA Schneider

1801 Pseudoboa Schneider, Hist. Amphib., 2: 286. Type-species: Pseudoboa coronata Schneider.
1859 Olisthenes Cope, Proc. Acad. Nat. Sci. Phila., 1859: 296. Type-species: Olisthenes euphaeus
　　　Cope.

Distribution: South America east of Andes to Santa Catarina, Brazil and central Bolivia; west of
　Andes in Colombia and western Panama; Tobago and Grenada Islands.

Content: Two species groups, containing a total of four currently recognized species, as well as
　several as yet undescribed taxa.

Key to the species

1. Dorsal scales in 19 rows; upper labials usually
　eight (except seven in haasi)----------------2
　Dorsal scales in 17 rows; upper labials seven--
　-------------------------------------coronata

2. Upper labials usually eight; body lighter
　dorsally than dark nape blotch or with rostral
　scale modified; subcaudals 79-109 in males,
　66-97 in females (counts overlapping those of
　haasi occur only in northern South America)--3
　Upper labials usually seven; body dark brown
　dorsally even in juveniles; rostral scale
　normal; subcaudals 83 in one male, 73 or fewer
　in females------------------------------haasi

3. Loreal short, highest posteriorly; rostral
　elevated from adjacent scales at edges, blunt
　as viewed from above; body coloration
　variable, wholly dark dorsally, with large
　irregular white blotches, or with no dark
　markings behind nape blotch; nasal bones fused
　along midline---------------------------nigra
　Loreal long with parallel horizontal edges;
　rostral normal (or prominent and pointed in
　large adults); body coloration fairly
　constant; salmon red above in juveniles becom-
　ing brown dorsally in adults, but remaining
　lighter than nape blotch; nasal bones separa-
　ted by suture-----------------------neuwiedii

Clave de especies

1. Escamas dorsales en 19 filas; usualmente ocho
　labiales superiores (excepto en haasi que
　tiene siete)--------------------------------2
　Escamas dorsales en 17 filas; siete labiales
　superiores---------------------------coronata

2. Usualmente ocho labiales superiores; cuerpo más
　claro dorsalmente que la mancha nucal o con la
　escama rostral modificada; subcaudales 79-109
　en machos, 66-97 en hembras (las cifras que
　sobremontan éstas son de haasi y sólo en el
　norte de América del Sur)-------------------3
　Usualmente siete labiales superiores; cuerpo
　dorsalmente pardo oscuro, aún en juveniles;
　escama rostral normal; 83 subcaudales en un
　macho y 73 o menos en hembras-----------haasi

3. Loreal corta, más alta posteriormente; rostral
　elevada en los bordes de las escamas adya-
　centes, redondeado como se ve de encima; colo-
　ración del cuerpo variable; totalmente oscuro
　dorsalmente con grandes e irregulares manchas
　blancas o sin ninguna marca detrás de la nu-
　cal; huesos nasales fusionados en la línea
　media-----------------------------------nigra
　Loreal larga con bordes horizontales paralelos;
　rostral normal (o prominente y puntiaguda en
　adultos); coloración del cuerpo más o menos
　constante; rojo salmón arriba en juveniles, en
　adultos pardo manteniendo la clara mancha
　nucal; huesos nasales separados por sutura----
　-----------------------------------neuwiedii

PSEUDOBOA CORONATA Schneider

1801 Pseudoboa coronata Schneider, Hist. Amphib., 2: 286. Type-locality: America.
1896 Oxyrhopus coronatus—Boulenger, Cat. Sn. Brit. Mus., 3: 111.

　Distribution: Guianas; Amazonian watershed in Brazil, Colombia, Ecuador, Peru and Bolivia.

PSEUDOBOA HAASI (Boettger)
　　coronata group

1905 Oxyrhopus haasi Boettger, Zool. Anz., 29: 374. Type-locality: Campos de Palmas, Paraná, Brazil.
1926 Pseudoboa haasi—Amaral, Rev. Mus. Paulista, 15: 105.

　Distribution: Arucaria forests of Paraná and northern Santa Catarina, Brazil.

PSEUDOBOA NEUWIEDII (Duméril, Bibron and Duméril)
    neuwiedii group

1854 Scytale neuwiedii Duméril, Bibron and Duméril, Erp. Gén., 7: 1001. Type-locality: Côte Ferme
    and Brazil; restricted to Cumaná, Venezuela through lectotype selection by Hoge and Lancini,
    Bol. Mus. Cien. Nat. Caracas, 6-7, 1960, 59.
1859 Olisthenes euphaeus Cope, Proc. Acad. Nat. Sci. Phila., 1859: 296. Type-locality: "Probably
    South America".
1887 Rhinocheilus thominoti Bocourt, Le Naturaliste, (2) 9: 45, figs. 1-4. Type-locality: Venezuela.
1901 Pseudoboa robinsoni Stejneger, Proc. U.S. Nat. Mus., 24: 190, fig. Type-locality: La Guaira,
    Venezuela.
1901 Pseudoboa neuwiedii—Stejneger, Proc. U.S. Nat. Mus., 24: 189.

    Distribution: Pacific Panama from just west of Canal Zone through northern and interior Colombia to
    Surinam; south to Brazil, along Amazon River; Trinidad and Tobago Islands.

PSEUDOBOA NIGRA (Duméril, Bibron and Duméril)
    neuwiedii group

1854 Scytale neuwiedii var. Nigrum Duméril, Bibron and Duméril, Erp. Gén., 7: 1002. Type-locality:
    Bahia, Brazil.
1926 Pseudoboa albimaculata Mello, Mem. Inst. Oswaldo Cruz, 19: 129. Type-locality: Minas Gerais,
    Brazil.
1962 Pseudoboa nigra—Bailey, Bull. Zool. Nomen., 19 (3): 164.

    Distribution: Northeastern Brazil to eastern Pará, south to Estado do Rio de Janeiro and São Paulo,
    thence west to northwestern Mato Grosso and central Bolivia and south to northern Corrientes,
    Argentina. Primarily, but not exclusively, a savanna species.

PSEUDOERYX Fitzinger

1826 Pseudoeryx Fitzinger, Neue Classification der Reptilien: 55. Type-species: Coluber plicatilis Linnaeus.
1838 Pseudoerix Thon (emendation of Pseudoeryx Fitzinger), in Ersch and Gruber, Enc. 2 (12): 387 (citation from Roze, Acta Biol. Venezuélica, 2, 1957, 20; not seen by us).
1843 Pseuderyx Fitzinger (emendation of Pseudoeryx Fitzinger), Systema Reptilium: 25.
1849 Dimades Gray, Cat. Sn. Brit. Mus.: 76. Type-species: Coluber plicatilis Linnaeus.

Distribution: As for single known species.

Content: One species.

PSEUDOERYX PLICATILIS (Linnaeus)

1758 Coluber plicatilis Linnaeus, Systema Naturae, Ed. 10: 217. Type-locality: "Ternataeis".
1826 Pseudoeryx plicatilis—Fitzinger, Neue Classification der Reptilien: 55.

Distribution: Colombia and Guianas to Bolivia, Paraguay and northern Argentina.

Content: Two subspecies, according to latest revision, by Hoge, Mem. Inst. Butantan, 30 (1960-62), 1964, 80.

Key to the subspecies	Clave de subespecies
1. Labials black with yellow spotting; 151-163 ventrals----------------------mimeticus	1. Labios negros manchados de amarillo; 151-163 ventrales--------------------mimeticus
Labials yellow with brown spotting; 129-142 ventrals----------------------plicatilis	Labios amarillos manchados de castaño; 129-142 ventrales------------------plicatilis

Pseudoeryx plicatilis plicatilis (Linnaeus)

1826 Pseudoeryx Daudinii Fitzinger, Neue Classification der Reptilien: 55. Type-locality: Unknown.
1895 Pseuderyx plicatilis var. anomalolepis Bocourt, Miss. Sci. Mex., Rept.: 804, pl. 60, figs. 6-6d. Type-locality: Colombia.
1944 Hydrops lehmanni Dunn, Caldasia, 3 (11): 71. Type-locality: Popayán, Cauca, Colombia, 1760 m.
1964 Pseudoeryx plicatilis plicatilis—Hoge, Mem. Inst. Butantan, 30 (1960-62): 80, figs. 28, 30-31.

Distribution: Colombia, Venezuela and Guianas to Brazil, Paraguay and northern Argentina.

Pseudoeryx plicatilis mimeticus Cope

1885 Pseuderyx mimeticus Cope, Proc. Amer. Phil. Soc., 23: 94. Type-locality: Río Mamoré, eastern Bolivia.
1957 Pseudoeryx mimeticus—Roze, Acta Biol. Venezuélica, 2: 23.
1964 Pseudoeryx plicatilis mimeticus—Hoge, Mem. Inst. Butantan, 30 (1960-62): 82, figs. 27, 29, 32.

Distribution: Amazonian Bolivia.

Prepared by Joseph R. Bailey, Duke University, Durham, North Carolina

PSEUDOTOMODON Koslowsky

   1896 Pseudotomodon Koslowsky, Rev. Mus. La Plata, 7: 454. Type-species: Pseudotomodon mendozinus
        Koslowsky.
   1897 Pseudotomodon Peracca, Bol. Mus. Zool. Anat. Comp. Univ. Torino, 12 (278): 1. Type-species:
        Pseudotomodon Crivellii Peracca.

   Distribution: As for single known species.

   Content: One species.

PSEUDOTOMODON TRIGONATUS (Leybold)

   1873 Pelias trigonatus Leybold, Excursión á las Pampas Argentinas, Hojas de mi Diario, 1873: 82.
        Type-locality: Mendoza Province, Argentina.
   1896 Pseudotomodon mendozinus Koslowsky, Rev. Mus. La Plata, 7: 455, pl. 4. Type-locality: Río
        Diamante, Departamento 25 de Mayo, Provincia Mendoza, Argentina.
   1897 Pseudotomodon Crivellii Peracca, Bol. Mus. Zool. Anat. Comp. Univ. Torino, 12 (278): 1. Type-
        locality: Las Chimbas, about 90 km northwest of San Luis, Argentina.

   Distribution: Western Argentina.

   Comment: This species has most recently been considered a subspecies of Tomodon ocellatus Duméril,
        Bibron and Duméril, but both it and the genus Pseudotomodon are clearly distinct from Tomodon.
        The author will publish full substantiation of this at a later date.

PSEUSTES Fitzinger

1843 Thamnobius Fitzinger (preoccupied by Thamnobius Schoenherr, 1836), Systema Reptilium: 26. Type-species: Coluber poëcilostoma Wied.
1843 Pseustes Fitzinger, Systema Reptilium: 27. Type-species: Dipsas Dieperinkii Schlegel.
1862 Phrynonax Cope, Proc. Acad. Nat. Sci. Phila., 1862: 348. Type-species: Tropidodipsas lunulata Cope.
1922 Paraphrynonax Lutz and Mello, Folha Medica, 3 (1920):97. Type-species: Paraphrynonax versicolor Lutz and Mello.

Distribution: Central America; northern and central South America.

Content: Four species.

Key to the species	Clave de especies
1. Lower rows of dorsal scales usually without keels; usually two postoculars; no subocular scales------------------------------------2 All dorsals keeled except first row; usually three postoculars; suboculars present or absent----------------------------sulphureus	1. Las hileras más bajas de escamas dorsales usualmente sin quillas; usualmente dos post-oculares; sin escamas suboculares------------2 Todas las dorsales quilladas excepto la primera hilera; usualmente tres postoculares; con o sin suboculares--------------sulphureus
2. Ventrals weakly angulate; no longitudinal line of color on ventrals-------------------------3 Ventrals strongly angulate; longitudinal dark line along angles of ventrals-----sexcarinatus	2. Ventrales ligeramente angulados; sin línea longitudinal coloreada en ventrales----------3 Ventrales fuertemente angulados; línea longi-tudinal oscura a lo largo de las ventrales-------------------------------------sexcarinatus
3. Dorsum irregularly barred with yellow, or each scale with yellow center and black margin--------------------------------------shropshirei Dorsum other than above description---poecilonotus	3. Dorso con barras irregulares amarillas o cada escama con centro amarillo y borde negro--shropshirei Dorso distinto del descripto-------poecilonotus

PSEUSTES POECILONOTUS (Günther)

1858 Spilotes poecilonotus Günther, Cat. Sn. Brit. Mus.: 100. Type-locality: Honduras and Mexico; restricted to Honduras through lectotype selection by Boulenger, Cat. Sn. Brit. Mus., 2, 1894, 20.
1937 Pseustes [poecilonotus]—Brongersma, Zool. Meded., 20: 6.

Distribution: Isthmus of Tehuantepec and Yucatán Peninsula, Mexico through all of Central America and northern South America into Amazonian drainage of Brazil, Ecuador, Peru and Bolivia; Trinidad.

Content: Four subspecies.

Key to the subspecies	Clave de subespecies
1. No paravertebral stripes on body----------2 Pair of paravertebral stripes on body-------------------------------poecilonotus	1. Sin cintas paravertebrales en el cuerpo---2 Par de cintas paravertebrales en el cuerpo-------------------------------poecilonotus
2. Head and neck same color as rest of body---------------------------------------3 Head and neck coal black, rest of body with transverse markings--------chrysobronchus	2. Color de cabeza y cuello igual que el resto del cuerpo------------------------------3 Cabeza y cuello negro carbón, resto del cuerpo con marcas transversales---------------------------------chrysobronchus
3. Body unicolor, dull brown in adults; series of brown bands on light brown ground color in juveniles--------------------polylepis Body markings of scattered dark spots and oblique lines----------------------argus	3. Cuerpo unicolor, pardo opaco en adultos; serie de bandas pardas en fondo pardo claro en juveniles--------------polylepis Cuerpo marcado por manchas oscuras dispersas y líneas oblicuas----------argus

Pseustes poecilonotus poecilonotus (Günther)

1861 Tropidodipsas lunulata Cope, Proc. Acad. Nat. Sci. Phila., 1860: 517. Type-locality: Honduras.
1929 Phrynonax poecilonotus poecilonotus—Amaral, Mem. Inst. Butantan, 4: 311, fig. 2.
1937 Pseustes [poecilonotus poecilonotus]—Brongersma, Zool. Meded., 20: 6.

   Distribution: Yucatán, Mexico through El Petén, Guatemala and British Honduras to Honduras.

Pseustes poecilonotus argus (Bocourt)

1888 Spilotes argus Bocourt, Miss. Sci. Mex., Rept.: 692, pl. 48, figs. 10-10f. Type-locality: Mexico.
1894 Phrynonax guentheri Boulenger, Cat. Sn. Brit. Mus., 2: 20. Type-locality: Atoyac, Veracruz, Mexico.
1929 Phrynonax poecilonotus argus—Amaral, Mem. Inst. Butantan, 4: 313, fig. 3.
1937 Pseustes [poecilonotus argus]—Brongersma, Zool. Meded., 20: 6.

   Distribution: San Luis Potosi, Mexico, south on Atlantic slopes to El Petén, Guatemala; also on Pacific slope in region of Isthmus of Tehuantepec, Mexico.

Pseustes poecilonotus chrysobronchus (Cope)

1876 Spilotes chrysobronchus Cope, Jour. Acad. Nat. Sci. Phila., (2) 8 (1875): 136, pl. 28, figs. 11a-b.
1893 Synchalinus corallioides Cope, Proc. Amer. Phil. Soc., 31: 345. Type-locality: Buenos Aires, Costa Rica.
1929 Phrynonax poecilonotus chrysobronchus—Amaral, Mem. Inst. Butantan, 4: 315.
1937 Pseustes [poecilonotus chrysobronchus]—Brongersma, Zool. Meded, 20: 6.

   Distribution: Costa Rica and Nicaragua.

Pseustes poecilonotus polylepis (Peters)

1867 Ahaetulla polylepis Peters, Monats. Akad. Wiss. Berlin, 1867: 709. Type-locality: Surinam.
1869 Spilotes fasciatus Peters, Monats. Akad. Wiss. Berlin, 1869: 443. Type-locality: Maroni, Surinam; Amaral, Mem. Inst. Butantan, 4, 1929 (1930), 302, suggests that this locality is in French Guiana.
1894 Phrynonax eutropis Boulenger, Cat. Sn. Brit. Mus., 2: 22, pl. 1, fig. 1. Type-locality: Unknown.
1901 Phrynonax lyoni Stejneger, Proc. U.S. Nat. Mus., 24: 185. Type-locality: Macuto, Venezuela.
1913 Phrynonax atriceps Werner, Mitt. Naturhist. Mus. Hamburg, 30: 22. Type-locality: None given.
1929 Phrynonax poecilonotus polylepis—Amaral, Mem. Inst. Butantan, 4: 313.
1937 Pseustes [poecilonotus polylepis]—Brongersma, Zool. Meded., 20: 6.

   Distribution: Amazonian region of Brazil, Ecuador, Peru, and Bolivia; also from Venezuela, Trinidad and Guianas.

PSEUSTES SEXCARINATUS (Wagler)

1824 Natrix sexcarinatus Wagler, in Spix, Sp. Nov. Serp. Brasil: 35. Type-locality: Rio Amazonas, Brazil.
1964 Pseustes sexcarinatus—Hoge, Mem. Inst. Butantan, 30 (1960-62): 28, 2 figs.

   Distribution: Estado do Pará, Brazil; Misiones, Argentina.

   Comment: The specimen described by Hoge, loc. cit., is very similar to specimens of poecilonotus as described by Amaral, Mem. Inst. Butantan, 4, 1929, 308, and we are not sure our key will suffice to distinguish the two taxa.

PSEUSTES SHROPSHIREI (Barbour and Amaral)

1924 Phrynonax shropshirei Barbour and Amaral, Occ. Pap. Boston Soc. Nat. Hist., 5: 131. Type-
    locality: Fort Sherman, Canal Zone, Panama.
1937 Pseustes [shropshirei]—Brongersma, Zool. Meded., 20: 6.

   Distribution: Costa Rica; Panama; Pacific Colombia and Ecuador.

PSEUSTES SULPHUREUS (Wagler)

1824 Natrix sulphurea Wagler, in Spix, Sp. Nov. Serp. Brasil: 26, pl. 9. Type-locality: Shoreline
    forests along Rio Japura, Brazil.
1937 Pseustes [sulphureus]—Brongersma, Zool. Meded., 20: 6.

   Distribution: Peru; Ecuador; Brazil; Guianas; Trinidad.

   Content: Two subspecies.

   Comment: Boulenger, Cat. Sn. Brit. Mus., 3, 1896, 626, questioned whether Coluber caracaras
   Gmelin, Systema Naturae, Ed. 13, 1766, 1117, should be synonymized with this species. If this
   were to be demonstrated, Gmelin's name would have priority over sulphureus.

Key to the subspecies	Clave de subespecies
1. Subocular absent; anterior chinshields longer than posterior; 205-227 ventrals----------------------------sulphureus Subocular present; anterior chinshields shorter than posterior; 199-215 ventrals----------------------------poecilostoma	1. Subocular ausente; escudos mentales anteriores más largos que posteriores; 205-227 ventrales--------------sulphureus Subocular presente; escudos mentales anteriores más cortos que posteriores; 199-215 ventrales--------------------poecilostoma

Pseustes sulphureus sulphureus (Wagler)

1837 Dipsas Dieperinkii Schlegel, Essai Physion. Serpens, 2: 282. Type-locality: Paramaribo,
    Surinam
1903 Phrynonax Faucherei Mocquard, Bull. Mus. Nat. Hist. Paris, 1903: 212. Type-locality:
    Suriname.
1929 Phrynonax sulphureus sulphureus—Amaral, Mem. Inst. Butantan, 4: 306.
1937 Pseustes sulphureus sulphureus—Brongersma, Zool. Meded., 20: 6, figs. 1a-b.

   Distribution: Equatorial Brazil, Peru, Ecuador, Guianas, and Trinidad.

Pseustes sulphureus poecilostoma (Wied)

1824 C.[oluber] poecilostoma Wied, Isis von Oken, 6: 665. Type-locality: Brazil; Wied, Beiträge zur
    Naturgeschichte von Brasilien, 1, 1825, 263, mentions specimens from Rio de Janeiro, Cabo
    Frio, Marica, Sagoarema and Parahyba, Brazil.
1922 Paraphrynonax versicolor Lutz and Mello, Folha Medica, 3 (1920): 97. Type-locality:
    Cataguazes, Minas Gerais, Brazil.
1929 Phrynonax sulphureus poecilostoma—Amaral, Mem. Inst. Butantan, 4: 308, fig. 1.
1937 Pseustes [sulphureus poecilostoma]—Brongersma, Zool. Meded., 20: 6.

   Distribution: Southeastern Brazil.

PTYCHOPHIS Gomes

    1915 Ptychophis Gomes, Ann. Paulistas Med. Cirurg., 4: 127. Type-species: Ptychophis flavovirgatus Gomes.

      Distribution: As for single species.

      Content: One species.

PTYCHOPHIS FLAVOVIRGATUS Gomes

    1915 Ptychophis flavovirgatus Gomes, Ann. Paulistas Med. Cirurg., 4: 128, pl. 4, figs. 4-6. Type-locality: São Bento, Estado de Santa Catharina, Brazil.

      Distribution: Santa Catherina and Paraná, Brazil.

RHACHIDELUS Boulenger

    1908 *Rhachidelus* Boulenger, Ann. Mag. Nat. Hist., (8) 2: 31. Type-species: *Rhachidelus brazili*
        Boulenger.

    Distribution: As for single species.

    Content: One species.

RHACHIDELUS BRAZILI Boulenger

    1908 *Rhachidelus brazili* Boulenger, Ann. Mag. Nat. Hist., (8) 2: 31. Type-locality: Near São Paulo,
        Brazil.

    Distribution: Southern Brazil and Misiones, Argentina.

RHADINAEA Cope

1863 <u>Rhadinaea</u> Cope, Proc. Acad. Nat. Sci. Phila., 1863: 101. Type-species: <u>Taeniophis vermiculaticeps</u> Cope.

Distribution: Southeastern United States through Mexico and Central America to Uruguay and northern Argentina.

Content: About 40 species, of which 24 are found within limits of this work.

Comment: Boulenger, Cat. Sn. Brit. Mus., 2, 1894, 160, synonymized <u>Calonotus</u> Jan, 1863 (proccupied by <u>Calonotus</u> Agassiz, 1846), with <u>Rhadinaea</u> Cope, and was followed in this synonymy by Romer, Osteology of the Reptiles, 1956, 581. Both of the African species included in <u>Calonotus</u> by Jan were considered by Boulenger, l.c., p. 196, to belong to <u>Coronella</u>, however, and there is no valid reason to include <u>Calonotus</u> Jan in this generic synonymy. Romer, l.c., also gave <u>Rhadinella</u> Smith, 1941, as a synonym of <u>Rhadinaea</u>, but we know of no published documentation of this action.
    This genus is currently being revised by C. W. Myers, and will be considerably changed from the arrangement seen here upon completion of his work.

Key to the species

1. Scale rows at midbody 21----------------------2
   Scale rows at midbody 19----------------------3
   Scale rows at midbody 17----------------------6

2. Dorsum with longitudinal stripes--------<u>godmani</u>
   Dorsum unicolor---------------------<u>altamontana</u>

3. Broad lateral dark stripe occupies all of
   fourth and adjacent halves of third and fifth
   scale rows-----------------------------------4
   Not as above---------------------------------5

4. With dark stripe occupying adjacent halves of
   first and second scale rows--------<u>serperaster</u>
   No dark stripe below broad stripe on fourth and
   adjacent rows----------------------<u>hempsteadae</u>

5. Lateral dark stripe broad, occupying all of
   third and neighboring halves of second and
   fourth scale rows------------------<u>montecristi</u>
   Lateral dark stripe narrow, occupying only
   contiguous halves of third and fourth scale
   rows-------------------------------<u>stadelmani</u>

6. Subcaudals fewer than 75----------------------7
   Subcaudals more than 75---------------------16

7. Upper labials eight--------------------------8
   Upper labials seven--------------------------12

8. Fourth and fifth labials in orbit; usually 17
   scale rows immediately anterior to vent------9
   Third, fourth and fifth labials in orbit;
   usually with reduction to 15 anterior to
   vent----------------------------<u>brevirostris</u>

9. More than 130 ventrals----------------------10
   Fewer than 130 ventrals----------------<u>sargenti</u>

10.Two posterior temporals----------------------11
   One posterior temporal----------------<u>pachyura</u>

Clave de especies

1. Filas de escamas al medio del cuerpo 21-------2
   Filas de escamas al medio del cuerpo 19-------3
   Filas de escamas al medio del cuerpo 17-------6

2. Diseño dorsal con líneas longitudinales-<u>godmani</u>
   Dorso uniforme---------------------<u>altamontana</u>

3. Cinta lateral ancha y oscura ocupa toda la
   cuarta hilera de escamas y las mitades adyacentes de la tercera y quinta----------------4
   No como el anterior--------------------------5

4. Cinta oscura ocupa las mitades adyacentes de
   primera y segunda hilera de escamas-------
   -----------------------------------<u>serperaster</u>
   Sin cinta oscura debajo de la cinta ancha en
   cuarta hilera de escamas y adyacentes--------
   -----------------------------------<u>hempsteadae</u>

5. Cinta lateral oscura, ancha ocupa toda la tercera hilera de escamas y las mitades adyacentes de la segunda y cuarta hileras-<u>montecristi</u>
   Cinta lateral oscura, angosta ocupa solamente
   las mitades contiguas de tercera y cuarta
   hileras de escamas------------------<u>stadelmani</u>

6. Subcaudales menos de 75-----------------------7
   Subcaudales más de 75-----------------------16

7. Labiales superiores ocho----------------------8
   Labiales superiores siete--------------------12

8. Cuarta y quinta labiales en órbita; usualmente
   17 hileras inmediatamente anterior al ano----9
   Tercera, cuarta y quinta labiales en órbita;
   usualmente con reducción a 15 delante del
   ano-----------------------------<u>brevirostris</u>

9. Más de 130 ventrales------------------------10
   Menos de 130 ventrales----------------<u>sargenti</u>

10.Dos temporales posteriores-------------------11
   Una temporal posterior----------------<u>pachyura</u>

11. Anterior chinshields longer than posterior--kinkelini
    Anterior chinshields shorter than posterior-------------------------------pulveriventris

12. Ventrals more than 140-----------------------13
    Ventrals fewer than 135--------------------beui

13. Midline area of individual ventral scale usually immaculate; outer tips of ventral usually with black spot or line------------14
    Black crescent shaped spon on midline of most ventrals, outer tips of ventrals usually entirely black---------------------calligaster

14. No light spots on dorsum of head------------15
    Triangular light spot behind eye and two roundish spots on parietals immediately behind frontal---------------------------------affinis

15. Temporal formula 1 + 1----------------pachyura
    Temporal formula 1 + 2------------poecilopogon

16. Upper labials seven--------------------------17
    Upper labials eight--------------------------19

17. Ventrals fewer than 160; anterior temporal present----------------------------------18
    Ventrals more than 160; anterior temporal may be fused with sixth labial, which then contacts parietal----------------------guentheri

18. Light occipital collar across posterior tips of parietals; edged anteriorly with black; no light spots on head-----------------decipiens
    No light occipital collar; light spot on each parietal and posterior temporal, larger light spot between temporal and lateral line----------------------------------persimilis

19. Temporal formula 1 + 2----------------------20
    Temporal formula 1 + 1------------lateristriga

20. Ventrals fewer than 152---------------------21
    Ventrals more than 152--------------lachrymans

21. Subcaudals fewer than 90--------------------22
    Subcaudals more than 90---------------------23

22. Dorsum of head vermiculated with yellow--------------------------------vermiculaticeps
    Dorsum of head unicolor---------------pinicola

23. Ventrals usually more than 135-------persimilis
    Ventrals usually fewer than 135--------decorata

11. Escudos geniales anteriores más largos que los posteriores----------------------kinkelini
    Escudos geniales anteriores más cortos que los posteriores----------------pulveriventris

12. Ventrales más de 140------------------------13
    Ventrales menos de 135---------------------beui

13. Zona de la línea media de cada escama ventral usualmente inmaculada; ápices externos usualmente con mancha o línea negra--------------14
    Con mancha negra en forma de media luna en la línea media de la mayoría de las ventrales; ápices externos usualmente todo negros---calligaster

14. Sin manchas claras en el dorso de la cabeza--15
    Con mancha clara triangular detrás del ojo y dos manchas redondeadas en parietales inmediatamente detrás de frontal-------------affinis

15. Fórmula temporal 1 + 1----------------pachyura
    Fórmula temporal 1 + 2------------poecilopogon

16. Labiales superiores siete--------------------17
    Labiales superiores ocho---------------------19

17. Ventrales menos de 160; con temporal anterior--18
    Ventrales más de 160; temporal anterior puede estar fusionada con sexta labial, que entonces contacta con parietal----------------guentheri

18. Collar occipital claro a través de los ápices posteriores de parietales, bordeada anteriormente de negro; sin manchas claras en la cabeza----------------------------------decipiens
    Sin collar occipital claro; mancha clara en cada parietal y temporal posterior, mancha clara más grande entre temporal y línea lateral----------------------------persimilis

19. Fórmula temporal 1 + 2----------------------20
    Fórmula temporal 1 + 1------------lateristriga

20. Ventrales menos de 152---------------------21
    Ventrales más de 152----------------lachrymans

21. Subcaudales menos de 90--------------------22
    Subcaudales más de 90----------------------23

22. Dorso de la cabeza vermiculado de amarillo-------------------------------vermiculaticeps
    Dorso de la cabeza unicolor-----------pinicola

23. Ventrales usualmente más de 135------persimilis
    Ventrales usualmente menos de 135------decorata

RHADINAEA AFFINIS (Günther)

1858 Dromicus affinis Günther, Cat. Sn. Brit. Mus.: 128. Type-locality: Rio de Janeiro and Brazil; restricted to Rio de Janeiro, Brazil, by Boulenger, Cat. Sn. Brit. Mus., 2, 1894, 173.
1885 Coronella Iheringii Boulenger, Ann. Mag. Nat. Hist., (5) 15: 194. Type-locality: Rio Grande do Sul, Brazil.
1943 Rhadinaea affinis—Prado, Mem. Inst. Butantan, 17: 12.

Distribution: Southern and southeastern Brazil.

RHADINAEA ALTAMONTANA Taylor

1954 Rhadinaea altamontana Taylor, Univ. Kansas Sci. Bull., 36: 740, fig. 16a-c. Type-locality:
    Edge of Costa Rican National Forest Reserve, Pan-American Highway, Talamanca Range, Costa
    Rica, 7000-8000 ft.

   Distribution: Known only from type locality.

RHADINAEA BEUI Prado

1943 Rhadinaea beui Prado, Mem. Inst. Butantan, 17: 13, two figs. Type-locality: Curitiba, Estado do
    Paraná, Brazil.

   Distribution: Known only from type locality.

RHADINAEA BREVIROSTRIS (Peters)

1863 Dromicus brevirostris Peters, Monats. Akad. Wiss. Berlin, 1863: 280. Type-locality: Apparently
    from Quito, Ecuador, purchased; probably erroneous, according to Peters, Rev. Ecuat. Ent.
    Parasit., 2, 1955, 347.
1868 Dromicus viperinus Günther, Ann. Mag. Nat. Hist., (4) 1: 418. Type-locality: Pebas, Peru.
1944 Rhadinaea brevirostris—Dunn, Caldasia, 2: 493.

   Distribution: Amazonian Basin, Guianas to Bolivia.

RHADINAEA CALLIGASTER (Cope)

1876 Contia calligaster Cope, Jour. Acad. Nat. Sci. Phila., (2) 8 (1875): 146, pl. 28, fig. 12. Type-
    locality: Pico Blanco, Costa Rica.
1894 Rhadinaea calligaster—Boulenger, Cat. Sn. Brit. Mus., 2: 164.

   Distribution: Costa Rica and Panama.

RHADINAEA DECIPIENS (Günther)

1893 Ablabes decipiens Günther, Biol. Cent. Amer., Reptiles: 105, pl. 37, fig. A. Type-locality:
    Irazú, Costa Rica.
1938 Rhadinaea pachyura decipiens—Dunn, Copeia, 1938: 198.
1954 Rhadinaea decipiens—Taylor, Univ. Kansas Sci. Bull., 36: 740.

   Distribution: Costa Rica.

   Content: Two subspecies.

Key to the subspecies	Clave de subespecies
1. Ventrals 130; subcaudals 125; total ventrals plus subcaudals 256---rubricollis Ventrals 133-157; subcaudals 110; total ventrals plus subcaudals 243-----decipiens	1. Ventrales 130; subcaudales 125; ventrales y subcaudales en total 256-------rubricollis Ventrales 133-157; subcaudales 110; ventrales y subcaudales en total 243--decipiens

Rhadinaea decipiens decipiens (Günther)

   1954 Rhadinaea decipiens decipiens—Taylor, Univ. Kansas Sci. Bull., 36: 740.

      Distribution: Costa Rica except for area occupied by R. d. rubricollis.

Rhadinaea decipiens rubricollis Taylor

   1954 Rhadinaea decipiens rubricollis Taylor, Univ. Kansas Sci. Bull., 36: 739. Type-
       locality: Cinchona, Volcán Poás, Costa Rica, about 5500 ft.

      Distribution: Known only from type locality.

RHADINAEA DECORATA (Günther)

1858 Coronella decorata Günther, Cat. Sn. Brit. Mus.: 35. Type-locality: Mexico.
1863 [Rhadinaea] decorata—Cope, Proc. Acad. Nat. Sci. Phila., 1863: 101.
1903 Erythrolamprus longicaudus Werner, Abh. Bayerische Akad. Wiss., 22 (2): 348. Type-locality:
    Guatemala.
1951 Rhadinaea decorata decorata—Taylor, Univ. Kansas Sci. Bull., 34: 113, pl. 11.

  Distribution: Low and moderate elevations, Veracruz, Mexico to Panama on Caribbean slope and
    locally on Pacific side in western Chiapas, Mexico.

RHADINAEA GODMANI Günther

1865 Dromicus godmanni Günther, Ann. Mag. Nat. Hist., (3) 15: 94. Type-locality: Duenas, Guatemala.
1876 R.[hadinaea] godmanji, Cope, Jour, Acad. Nat. Sci. Phila., (2) 8 (1875): 139.

  Distribution: Intermediate elevations on the southwestern highlands of Guatemala into El Salvador.

  Content: Two subspecies.

  Comment: Günther corrected the spelling of this taxon to godmani in Biol. Cent. Amer., Reptiles,
    1893, 110, a justified emendation.

Key to the subspecies	Clave de subespecies
1. Adult males with supra-anal keels; lateral black stripe on fifth and neighboring edges of fourth and sixth scale rows--zilchi Adult males lack supra-anal keels; lateral black stripe on second through fourth rows----------------------------------godmani	1. Machos adultos con quillas supra-anales; cinta lateral negra en la quinta hilera de escamas y en los bordes vecinos de cuarta y sexta hileras--------------------zilchi Machos adultos sin quillas supra-anales; cinta lateral negra de la segunda a la cuarta hilera---------------------godmani

Rhadinaea godmani godmani Günther

  1952 [Rhadinaea godmani] godmani—Mertens, Abh. Senckenb. Naturforsch. Ges., 487: 71.

    Distribution: Southwestern Guatemala to El Salvador.

Rhadinaea godmani zilchi Mertens

  1952 Rhadinaea zilchi Mertens, Zool. Anz., 148: 92. Type-locality: Laguna de las Ninfas
       (= Laguna de Apaneca), Volcán de la Lagunita, Departamento Sonsonate, El Salvador, 1630 m.
  1952 Rhadinaea godmani zilchi—Mertens, Abh. Senckenb. Naturforsch. Ges., 487: 70, pl. 6, fig.
       23.

    Distribution: Known only from region of type locality.

RHADINAEA GUENTHERI Dunn

  1895 Tachymenis decipiens Günther (preoccupied in this genus by Ablabes decipiens Günther), Biol.
       Cent. Amer., Rept.: 163, pl. 53, fig. A. Type-locality: Irazú, Costa Rica.
  1938 Rhadinaea güntheri Dunn (replacement name for Tachymenis decipiens Günther), Copeia, 1938: 198.

    Distribution: Costa Rica.

RHADINAEA HEMPSTEADAE Stuart and Bailey

  1941 Rhadinaea hempsteadae Stuart and Bailey, Occ. Pap. Mus. Zool., Univ. Mich., 442: 2. Type-
       locality: Cloud forest zone, above Finca Chichén, Alta Verapaz, Guatemala, about 5700 ft.

    Distribution: Intermediate elevations in mountains of Alta Verapaz, Guatemala.

RHADINAEA INSIGNISSIMUS (Amaral), new combination

  1926 Liophis insignissimus Amaral, Arch. Mus. Nacional Brazil, 26: 103, pl. 1, figs. 7-9. Type-
       locality: Estação Biologica, Serra de Cubatão, Estado de São Paulo, Brazil.

   Distribution: São Paulo and Espirito Santo, Brazil.

   Comment: One of us (Peters) has seen the holotype of this species in the Instituto Butantan, São
   Paulo, Brazil, and it seems unquestionably a Rhadinaea. Amaral used Liophis as a generic name for
   members of both taxa.

RHADINAEA KINKELINI Boettger

  1898 Rhadinaea kinkelini Boettger, Katalog der Reptilien-Sammlung im Museum der Senckenbergischen
       Naturforschende Gesellschaft im Frankfurt am Main, 2: 68. Type-locality: Matagalpa,
       Nicaragua.

   Distribution: Nicaragua to Guatemala.

RHADINAEA LACHRYMANS (Cope)

  1870 Lygophis lachrymans Cope, Proc. Amer. Phil. Soc., 11 (1869): 154. Type-locality: Unknown;
       Bailey, Occ. Pap. Mus. Zool. Univ. Mich., 412, 1940, 7, suggested Chiapas, Mexico.
  1846 R.[hadinaea] lachrymans—Cope, Jour. Acad. Nat. Sci. Phila., (2) 8 (1875): 140.

   Distribution: Moderate and intermediate elevations of Pacific slope, Chiapas, Mexico to Guatemala.

RHADINAEA LATERISTRIGA (Berthold)

  1859 Liophis lateristriga Berthold, Anz. Göttingen Gehlert., 3: 180. Type-locality: Popayan,
       Colombia.
  1867 Dromicus nuntius Jan, Icon. Gén. Ophid., livr. 24: pl. 6, fig. 1. Type-locality: Andes of
       Ecuador.
  1944 Rhadinaea lateristriga—Dunn, Caldasia, 2: 493.

   Distribution: Caribbean South America; Pacific slope of Colombia and Ecuador.

   Content: Two subspecies.

Key to the subspecies	Clave de subespecies
1. Single light spot on each parietal--------- ------------------------------lateristriga	1. Una sola mancha clara en cada parietal----- ------------------------------lateristriga
Light line on each parietal----multilineata	Línea clara en cada parietal---multilineata

Rhadinaea lateristriga lateristriga Berthold

  1863 Dromicus frenatus Peters, Monats. Akad. Wiss. Berlin, 1863: 218. Type-locality:
       Guayaquil, Ecuador.
  1901 Urotheca coronata Steindachner, Anz. Akad. Wiss. Wien, 1901: 106, pl. 1, figs. 3-3a.
       Type-locality: Region of Babahoyo, Ecuador.
  1909 Erythrolamprus labialis Werner, Mitt. Naturhist. Mus. Hamburg, 26: 237, fig. 10. Type-
       locality: Ecuador.
  1944 Rhadinaea lateristriga lateristriga—Dunn, Caldasia, 2: 493.

    Distribution: Pacific slope, central Colombia to Ecuador.

Rhadinaea lateristriga multilineata (Peters)

  1859 Dromicus multilineatus Peters, Monats. Akad. Wiss. Berlin, 1863: 279. Type-locality: var.
       A from Puerto Cabello and Caracas, Venezuela, and var. B from Bogotá, Colombia; name restrict-
       ed to var. A by Dunn, below.
  1944 Rhadinaea lateristriga multilineata—Dunn, Caldasia, 2: 439.

    Distribution: Caribbean Colombia and Venezuela.

RHADINAEA MONTECRISTI Mertens

   1952 Rhadinaea montecristi Mertens, Zool. Anz., 149: 136. Type-locality: Hacienda Monte Cristo,
      Metapán (Mountain?), Departamento Santa Ana, El Salvador, 2200 m.

    Distribution: Known only from type locality.

RHADINAEA PACHYURA (Cope)

   1876 Contia pachyura Cope, Jour. Acad. Nat. Sci. Phila., (2) 8 (1875): 145. Type-locality: Sipurio,
      Costa Rica.
   1938 Rhadinaea pachyura—Dunn, Copeia, 1938: 198.

    Distribution: Costa Rica to Pacific Ecuador.

    Content: Two subspecies.

Key to the subspecies	Clave de subespecies

1. Subcaudals 102-117---------------fulviceps
   Subcaudals fewer than 75----------pachyura
	1. Subcaudales 102-117---------------fulviceps
	   Subcaudales menos de 75-----------pachyura

   Rhadinaea pachyura pachyura (Cope)

     1944 [Rhadinaea pachyura] pachyura—Dunn, Caldasia, 2: 493.

      Distribution: Costa Rica and western Panama.

   Rhadinaea pachyura fulviceps Cope

     1886 Rhadinaea fulviceps Cope, Proc. Amer. Phil. Soc., 23: 279. Type-locality: Panama.
     1944 Rhadinata pachyura fulviceps—Dunn, Caldasia, 2: 492.

      Distribution: Panama; Pacific Colombia and Ecuador.

RHADINAEA PERSIMILIS Dunn

   1938 Rhadinaea persimilis Dunn, Copeia, 1938: 197. Type-locality: La Loma, Provincia Bocas del Toro,
      Panama, 1500 ft.
   1951 Rhadinaea persimilis—Taylor, Univ. Kansas Sci. Bull., 34: 117.

    Distribution: Costa Rica.

    Comment: Boulenger, Cat. Sn. Brit. Mus., 2, 1894, 173, tentatively synonymized Liophis persimilis
      Cope, 1868, with Rhadinaea poecilopogon Cope, 1863. If this synonymy is demonstrated to be
      valid, Rhadinaea persimilis Dunn, 1938, will require a new name.

RHADINAEA PINICOLA Mertens

   1952 Rhadinaea pinicola Mertens, Zool. Anz., 149: 135. Type-locality: Hacienda San José, Metapán
      (Mountain?), Departamento Santa Ana, El Salvador, 1500 m.

    Distribution: Known only from type locality.

RHADINAEA POECILOPOGON Cope

   1863 Rhadinaea poecilopogon Cope, Proc. Acad. Nat. Sci. Phila., 1863: 100. Type-locality: Paysondu,
      Uruguay; actually Paysandú, Uruguay, according to Vaz Ferreira and Sierra de Soriano, Rev.
      Fac. Hum. Cien., Montevideo, 18, 1960, 36.
   1863 E.[nicognathus] elegans Jan, Arch. Zool. Anat. Fis., 2: 268. Type-locality: Montevideo and
      Buenos Aires.
   1863 Dromicus melanocephalus Peters, Monats. Akad. Wiss. Berlin, 1863: 277. Type-locality:
      apparently São Paulo, Brazil.
 ?1869 Liophis persimilis Cope, Proc. Acad. Nat. Sci. Phila., 1868: 308. Type-locality: Rio de
      Janeiro, Brazil.
   1885 Enicognathus bilineatus Fischer, Jahr. Wiss. Anst. Hamburg, 2: 98, pl. 3, fig. 5. Type-locality:
      Santos, Brazil.
   1943 Rhadinaea poecilopogon—Prado, Mem. Inst. Butantan, 17: 13.

    Distribution: Southern Brazil, Uruguay and Argentina.

RHADINAEA POECILOPOGON Cope

1863 Rhadinaea poecilopogon Cope, Proc. Acad. Nat. Sci. Phila., 1863: 100. Type-locality: Paysondu, Uruguay, = Paysandú, Uruguay, according to Vaz Ferreira and Sierra de Soriano, Rev. Fac. Hum. Cien. Montevideo, 18, 1960, 36.
1943 Rhadinaea poecilopogon—Prado, Mem. Inst. Butantan, 17: 13.

Distribution: Southern Brazil, Uruguay and Argentina.

RHADINAEA PULVERIVENTRIS Boulenger

1896 Rhadinaea pulveriventris Boulenger, Cat. Sn. Brit. Mus., 3: 635. Type-locality: Azahar de Cartago, Costa Rica.
1951 Rhadinaea pulveriventris—Taylor, Univ. Kansas Sci. Bull., 31: 116.

Distribution: Costa Rica and western Panama.

RHADINAEA SARGENTI Dunn and Bailey

1939 Rhadinaea sargenti Dunn and Bailey, Bull. Mus. Comp. Zool., 86: 10. Type-locality: Pequeni-Esperanza Ridge, near head of Río Pequeni, Panama, 1800 ft.

Distribution: Hills east of Canal Zone, Panama.

RHADINAEA SERPERASTER Cope

1871 Rhadinaea serperaster Cope, Proc. Acad. Nat. Sci. Phila., 1871: 212. Type-locality: Near San José, Costa Rica.
1894 Rhadinaea serperastra—Boulenger, Cat. Sn. Brit. Mus., 2: 172.
1951 Rhadinaea serperastra—Taylor, Univ. Kansas Sci. Bull., 34: 112.

Distribution: Costa Rica and Panama.

RHADINAEA STADELMANI Stuart and Bailey

1941 Rhadinaea stadelmani Stuart and Bailey, Occ. Pap. Mus. Zool. Univ. Mich., 442: 4. Type-locality: Todos Santos, Huehuetenango, Guatemala, 8000 ft.

Distribution: Intermediate elevations on eastern and western flanks of Sierra de los Cuchumatanes, Guatemala.

RHADINAEA VERMICULATICEPS (Cope)

1860 T.[aeniophis] vermiculaticeps Cope, Proc. Acad. Nat. Sci. Phila., 1860: 249. Type-locality: Veragua, Panama.
1863 [Rhadinaea] vermiculaticeps—Cope, Proc. Acad. Nat. Sci. Phila., 1863: 101.
1929 Liophis vermimaculaticeps—Amaral (in error for vermiculaticeps Cope), Mem. Inst. Butantan, 4: 175.
1951 Rhadinaea vermiculaticeps—Taylor, Univ. Kansas Sci. Bull., 34: 116.

Distribution: West central Panama.

RHINOBOTHRYUM Wagler

 1830 Rhinobothryum Wagler, Nat. Syst. Amph.: 186. Type-species: Coluber macrorhinus Wagler.

 Distribution: Panama and Costa Rica through tropical South America to valley of Río Paraguay.

 Content: Two species.

<table>
<tr><td>Key to the species</td><td>Clave de especies</td></tr>
<tr><td>1. Wide red and black rings separated by narrow yellow rings------------------------bovallii
No yellow ring between neighboring red and black rings----------------------lentiginosum</td><td>1. Anchos anillos rojos y negros separados por finas bandas amarillas----------------bovallii
Anchos anillos rojos y negros no separados por finas bandas amarillas--------lentiginosum</td></tr>
</table>

RHINOBOTHRYUM BOVALLII Andersson

 1916 Rhinobothrium bovallii Andersson, Medd. Göteborgs Mus. Zool. Afd., 9: 32, fig. 4. Type-locality: Siquirres, Costa Rica.
 1965 Rhinobothryum Bovallii—Pons, Kasmera, Univ. Zulia, Maracaibo, Venezuela, 2: 99, figs.

 Distribution: Honduras, Costa Rica, Panama, northwestern Colombia and Ecuador, northwestern Venezuela.

RHINOBOTHRYUM LENTIGINOSUM (Scopoli)

 1785 Coluber Lentiginosus Scopoli, Deliciae Florae et Faunae Insubricae, 3: 41, pl. 20, fig. 2. Type-locality: None given.
 1830 Coluber macrorhinus Wagler, Nat. Syst. Amph.: 186. Type-locality: "America?" [This name was credited to Boie by Wagler ("H. Boie in Mus. Lugd."), and served as type species of Rhinobothryum, but we find no evidence that Boie ever published a description of the species, so it must be assigned to Wagler].
 1854 Rhinobothryum lentiginosum—Duméril, Bibron and Duméril, Erp. Gén., 7: 1061.

 Distribution: Basins of Ríos Amazon and Paraguay in tropical South America.

SCAPHIODONTOPHIS Taylor and Smith

1943 <u>Scaphiodontophis</u> Taylor and Smith, Univ. Kansas Sci. Bull., 29: 302. Type-species: <u>Enicognathus</u> <u>annulatus</u> Duméril, Bibron and Duméril.

Distribution: Southern Mexico through Central America to Panama.

Content: Five species, one of which (<u>sumichrasti</u> Bocourt) is extralimital.

Key to the species

1. Triads composed of two black bands enclosing
   one white (yellow)-------------------------2
   Triads composed of two yellow bands enclosing
   one black, on body and tail------<u>venustissimus</u>

2. Black head cap followed by red area (sometimes
   narrow), then a pair of black bands
   enclosing a white band----------------------3
   Black head cap followed by one white band,
   one black band, and a longer red band--------
   --------------------------------------<u>zeteki</u>

3. Black bands few, no more than three sets on
   anterior part of body------------<u>carpicinctus</u>
   Black bands numerous, five or more sets on
   anterior part of body---------------<u>annulatus</u>

Clave de especies

1. Tríadas de dos bandas negras encerrando una
   blanca (amarilla)--------------------------2
   Tríadas de dos bandas amarillas encerrando una
   negra, sobre el cuerpo y la cola-<u>venustissimus</u>

2. Cabeza negra dorsoanteriormente seguida en
   sucesión por un área roja (aveces angosta) y
   un par de bandas negras encerrando una
   blanca---3
   Cabeza negra dorsoanteriormente seguida en
   sucesión por una banda blanca, una negra y una
   ancha roja-----------------------------<u>zeteki</u>

3. Pocas bandas negras, no más de tres grupos en
   la porción anterior del cuerpo----<u>carpicinctus</u>
   Bandas negras numerosas, cinco o más grupos en
   la porción anterior del cuerpo-------<u>annulatus</u>

SCAPHIODONTOPHIS ANNULATUS (Duméril, Bibron and Duméril)

1854 <u>Enicognathus</u> <u>annulatus</u> Duméril, Bibron and Duméril, Erp. Gén., 7: 335, pl. 80. Type-locality:
     Cobán, Alta Verapaz, Guatemala.
1943 <u>Scaphiodontophis</u> <u>annulatus</u>—Taylor and Smith, Univ. Kansas Sci. Bull., 29: 311.

Distribution: Yucatán Peninsula to Guatemala and Honduras.

Content: Two subspecies.

Key to the subspecies

1. No black spots on scales of red inter-
   spaces-------------------------<u>hondurensis</u>
   Black spots on scales of red inter-
   spaces----------------------------<u>annulatus</u>

Clave de subespecies

1. Sin puntos negros en las escamas de los
   interespacios rojos-----------<u>hondurensis</u>
   Puntos negros en las escamas de los interespacios rojos-------------------<u>annulatus</u>

Scaphiodontophis annulatus annulatus (Duméril, Bibron and Duméril)

1943 <u>Scaphiodontophis</u> <u>annulatus</u> <u>annulatus</u>—Taylor and Smith, Univ. Kansas Sci. Bull., 29: 311.

Distribution: El Petén, Guatemala, and British Honduras south to Alta Verapaz, Guatemala.

Scaphiodontophis annulatus hondurensis (Schmidt)

1936 <u>Sibynophis</u> <u>annulatus</u> <u>hondurensis</u> Schmidt, Proc. Biol. Soc. Washington, 49: 48. Type-
     locality: Portillo Grande, Yoro, Honduras, 4100 ft.
1943 <u>Scaphiodontophis</u> <u>annulatus</u> <u>hondurensis</u>—Taylor and Smith, Univ. Kansas Sci. Bull., 29:
     314.

Distribution: Known from type-locality; Subirana Valley at 2800 ft; and Tela, Honduras.

SCAPHIODONTOPHIS CARPICINCTUS Taylor and Smith

1943 Scaphiodontophis carpicinctus Taylor and Smith, Univ. Kansas Sci. Bull., 29: 315. Type-locality:
Piedras Negras, Guatemala.

Distribution: Known only from type-locality and Tikal, El Petén, Guatemala; probably restricted to
forests of base of Yucatán Peninsula.

Comment: Neill and Allen, Publ. Res. Div. Ross Allen's Rept. Inst., 2, 1959, 47, suggested
that this should be considered a subspecies of annulatus. Smith, in Smith and Taylor,
Herpetology of Mexico, Preface, 1966, 26, indicated that it perhaps should be a junior
synonym of annulatus. Stuart, Misc. Publ. Mus. Zool. Univ. Mich., 122, 1963, 114,
recognized this as a full species. We do not know what the status of this taxon really is.

SCAPHIODONTOPHIS VENUSTISSIMUS (Günther)

1894 Henicognathus venustissimus Günther, Biol. Cent. Amer., Rept.: 144, pl. 51, fig. c. Type-
locality: Hacienda Santa Rosa de Jericó, Matagalpa, Nicaragua, 3250 ft.
1943 Scaphiodontophis venustissimus—Taylor and Smith, Univ. Kansas Sci. Bull., 29: 309, fig. 5.

Distribution: Nicaragua and Costa Rica.

SCAPHIODONTOPHIS ZETEKI (Dunn)

1930 Sibynophis zeteki Dunn, Occ. Pap. Boston Soc. Nat. Hist., 5: 329. Type-locality: Ancón, Canal
Zone, Panama.
1943 Scaphiodontophis zeteki—Taylor and Smith, Univ. Kansas Sci. Bull., 29: 317.

Distribution: Southern Mexico to Panama.

Content: Two subspecies.

Key to the subspecies	Clave de subespecies
1. Snout white------------------------zeteki	1. Hocico blanco------------------------zeteki
Snout not white--------------------nothus	Hocico no blanco----------------------nothus

Scaphiodontophis zeteki zeteki (Dunn)

1958 Scaphiodontophis zeteki zeteki—Alvarez del Toro and Smith, Herpetologica, 14: 17.

Distribution: Panama.

Scaphiodontophis zeteki nothus Taylor and Smith

1943 Scaphiodontophis nothus Taylor and Smith, Univ. Kansas Sci. Bull., 29: 320, pl. 23, fig.
2 and text fig. 8. Type-locality: Potrero Viejo, Veracruz, Mexico.
1943 Scaphiodontophis cyclurus Taylor and Smith, Univ. Kansas Sci. Bull., 29: 318, pl. 22,
fig. 2, text fig. 7. Type-locality: Cuautlapán, Veracruz, Mexico.
1943 Scaphiodontophis albonuchalis Taylor and Smith, Univ. Kansas Sci. Bull., 29: 323, pl. 23,
fig. 1; pl. 24; pl. 25, figs. 1-2; text fig. 9. Type-locality: La Esperanza, near
Escuintla, Chiapas, Mexico.
1958 Scaphiodontophis zeteki nothus—Alvarez del Toro and Smith, Herpetologica, 14: 17.

Distribution: Isthmus of Tehuantepec, Mexico, through Guatemala to Nicaragua, and Veracruz
to Tabasco, Mexico.

SCOLECOPHIS Fitzinger

> 1843 Scolecophis Fitzinger, Systema Reptilium: 25. Type-species: Calamaria atrocincta Schlegel.
> 1863 Platycranion Jan, Elenco Systema Ofidi: 40. Type-species: Calamaria atrocincta Schlegel.

> Distribution: As for single known species.

> Content: One species.

SCOLECOPHIS ATROCINCTUS (Schlegel)

> 1837 Calamaria atrocincta Schlegel, Essai Phys. Serp., 2: 47. Type-locality: Chile (in error).
> 1843 Scolecophis atrocincta—Fitzinger, Systema Reptilium: 25.
> 1855 Elaps zonatus Hallowell, Jour. Acad. Nat. Sci. Phila., (2) 3: 35. Type-locality: Honduras.

> Distribution: Moderate elevations along Pacific slope from El Salvador to Costa Rica.

SIBON Fitzinger

1826 *Sibon* Fitzinger, Neue Classification der Reptilien: 31. Type-species: *Coluber nebulatus* Linnaeus.
1843 *Sibynon* Fitzinger, Systema Reptilium: 27. Type-species: *Coluber nebulatus* Linnaeus.
1853 *Petalognathus* Duméril, Mem. Acad. Sci., Paris, 23: 466. Type-species: *Coluber nebulatus* Linnaeus.
1866 *Mesopeltis* Cope, Proc. Acad. Nat. Sci. Phila., 1866: 318. Type-species: *Mesopeltis sanniolus* Cope.
1884 *Asthenognathus* Bocourt, Bull. Soc. Philom. Paris, (7) 8: 141. Type-species: *Petalognathus multifasciatus* Jan.

Distribution: Southern Mexico, Central America and northern South America.

Content: Nine species arranged in three species groups, according to the most recent revision of the genus, by Peters, Misc. Publ. Mus. Zool. Univ. Mich., 114, 1960.

Key to the species

1. With 15 rows of scales-------------------------2
   With 13 rows of scales-------------------------11

2. No lower labials in contact behind mental------
   --3
   One pair of lower labials in contact behind
   mental---10

3. An azygous chin shield between paired chin
   shields and mental-------------------------4
   No azygous chin shields, or an extremely tiny
   one---8

4. Subcaudals more than 105----------------------5
   Subcaudals fewer than 100----------------------7

5. Dorsal blotches unicolor, not lighter toward
   centers--6
   Centers of dorsal blotches in adults considerably lighter than outer parts--------*dimidiata*

6. Ventrals 192 or fewer-----------------*annulata*
   Ventrals 193 or more-----------------*dimidiata*

7. Dorsal pattern of a series of vertebral
   blotches, small and numerous---------*sanniola*
   Dorsal pattern of large ocelli, which extend
   low on sides----------------------*longifrenis*

8. Ventrals fewer than 195-----------------------9
   Ventrals 195 or more---------------------*argus*

9. Extremely small pair of chin shields behind
   mental-------------------------------*annulata*
   First pair of chin shields larger than
   second pair-----------------------*longifrenis*

10. Ventrals fewer than 150-------------------*dunni*
    Ventrals more than 155----------------*nebulata*

11. No primary temporal, fifth upper labial in
    contact with parietal-------------------*carri*
    One primary temporal, no upper labial in con-
    tact with parietal-----------------*anthracops*

Clave de especies

1. Con 15 filas de escamas-----------------------2
   Con 13 filas de escamas-----------------------11

2. Sin labiales inferiores en contacto detrás de
   mentoneana------------------------------------3
   Con un par de labiales inferiores en contacto
   detrás de mentoneana---------------------------10

3. Un escudo geneial (azygus) entre el par geneial
   y la mentoneana-------------------------------4
   Sin escudo geneial (azygus), o con uno extremadamente pequeño-------------------------------8

4. Más de 105 subcaudales------------------------5
   Menos de 100 subcaudales----------------------7

5. Manchas dorsales uniformes, sin centros
   claros--6
   Centros de manchas dorsales, considerablemente
   más claros que la periferia, en adultos-------
   -----------------------------------*dimidiata*

6. Ventrales 192 o menos----------------*annulata*
   Ventrales 193 o más------------------*dimidiata*

7. Diseño dorsal formado par serie de pequeñas y
   numerosas manchas vertebrales--------*sanniola*
   Diseño dorsal formado por grandes ocelos vertebrales que se extienden lateralmente----------
   ---------------------------------*longifrenis*

8. Menos de 195 ventrales-----------------------9
   Más de 195 ventrales---------------------*argus*

9. Primer par geneial extremamente pequeño-------
   ------------------------------------*annulata*
   Primer par geneial mayor que el segundo--------
   --------------------------------*longifrenis*

10. Ventrales menos de 150----------------*dunni*
    Ventrales más de 155------------------*nebulata*

11. Sin temporal primaria, quinto labial superior
    en contacto con parietal---------------*carri*
    Una temporal primaria, sin supralabiales en
    contacto con parietal-------------*anthracops*

SIBON ANNULATA (Günther)
    annulata group

1872 Leptognathus annulatus Günther, Ann. Mag. Nat. Hist., (4) 9: 30. Type-locality: Near Cartago,
    Costa Rica.
1876 Leptognathus pictiventris Cope, Jour. Acad. Nat. Sci. Phila., 8 (2): 130. Type-locality: Costa
    Rica.
1939 S[ibon] annulata——Dunn and Bailey, Bull. Mus. Comp. Zool., Harvard, 86: 9.
1960 Sibon annulata——Peters, Misc. Publ. Mus. Zool. Univ. Mich., 114: 176.

    Distribution: Atlantic slopes of Costa Rica and Panama.

SIBON ANTHRACOPS (Cope)
    annulata group

1868 Leptognathus anthracops Cope, Proc. Acad. Nat. Sci. Phila., 1868: 136. Type-locality: Central
    America.
1921 Sibynomorphus ruthveni Barbour and Dunn, Proc. Biol. Soc. Wash., 34: 158. Type-locality:
    Aguacate Mountains, Costa Rica.
1960 Sibon anthracops——Peters, Misc. Publ. Mus. Zool. Univ. Mich., 114: 180, pl. 7c.

    Distribution: Pacific slopes of Costa Rica, Nicaragua, and Honduras.

SIBON ARGUS (Cope)
    argus group

1876 Leptognathus argus Cope, Jour. Acad. Nat. Sci. Phila., 8 (2): 130. Type-locality: Costa Rica.
1960 Sibon argus——Peters, Misc. Publ. Mus. Zool. Univ. Mich., 114: 189.

    Distribution: Known only from type locality.

SIBON CARRI (Shreve)
    nebulata group

1951 Tropidodipsas carri Shreve, Copeia, 1951: 52. Type-locality: Escuela Agrícola Panamericana,
    near Tegucigalpa, Honduras.
1960 Sibon carri——Peters, Misc. Publ. Mus. Zool. Univ. Mich., 114: 194.

    Distribution: Pacific slopes of Honduras; El Salvador.

SIBON DIMIDIATA (Günther)
    annulata group

1872 Leptognathus dimidiatus Günther, Ann. Mag. Nat. Hist., (4) 9: 31. Type-locality: Mexico.
1943 Sibon dimidiatus——Smith, Proc. U. S. Nat. Mus., 93: 470.

    Distribution: Southern Mexico and Central America.

    Content: Two subspecies.

Key to the subspecies	Clave de subespecies
1. Centers of dorsal blotches in adults considerably lighter than outer parts----------------------------------dimidiata Dorsal blotches unicolor, not lighter toward centers------------------grandoculis	1. Centros de manchas dorsales considerablemente más claros que la periferia, en adultos------------------------dimidiata Manchas dorsales uniformes sin centro claro----------------------------grandoculis

Sibon dimidiata dimidiata (Günther)

  1884 Petalognathus multifasciatus Jan, in Bocourt, Bull. Soc. Philom. Paris, (7) 8: 182. Type-
      locality: Verapaz, Guatemala.
  1960 Sibon dimidiata dimidiata——Peters, Misc. Publ. Mus. Zool. Univ. Mich., 114: 182, pl. 7b.

  Distribution: Atlantic coast of central America from Veracruz to Nicaragua, excluding the
  Yucatán Peninsula.

Sibon dimidiata grandoculis (Müller)

  1890 Leptognathus (Asthenognathus) grandoculis Müller, Verh. Nat. Ges. Basel, 8: 271. Type-
      locality: Mazatenango, Guatemala.
  1960 Sibon dimidiata grandoculis——Peters, Misc. Publ. Mus. Zool. Univ. Mich., 114: 185, pl. 7a.

  Distribution: Pacific slope of Guatemala.

SIBON DUNNI Peters
    nebulata group

  1957 Sibon dunni Peters, Copeia, 1957: 110. Type-locality: Pimanpiro, San Nicholas, Imbabura
      Province, Ecuador.
  1960 Sibon dunni——Peters, Misc. Publ. Mus. Zool. Univ. Mich., 114: 196, pl. 7d.

  Distribution: Known only from type locality.

SIBON LONGIFRENIS (Stejneger)
    argus group

  1909 Mesopeltis longifrenis Stejneger, Proc. U. S. Nat. Mus., 36: 457. Type-locality: Bocas del
      Toro, Panama.
  1951 Dipsas costaricensis Taylor, Univ. Kansas Sci. Bull., 34: 63. Type-locality: 5 mi southwest
      of Turrialba, Morehead Finca, Costa Rica.
  1960 Sibon longifrenis——Peters, Misc. Publ. Mus. Zool. Univ. Mich., 114: 192.

  Distribution: Atlantic slopes of Panama (a single locality) and Costa Rica (two localities).

SIBON NEBULATA (Linnaeus)
    nebulata group

  1758 Coluber nebulatus Linnaeus, Syst. Nat., Ed. 10: 222. Type-locality: America.
  1826 Sibon nebulatus——Fitzinger, Neue Classif. Rept.: 31.

  Distribution: Southeastern Mexico, Central America and northern South America.

  Content: Four subspecies.

Key to the subspecies

1. First dorsal blotches not different from
   rest of body blotches--------------------2
   First dorsal blotches wide, well-marked----
   ----------------------------------hartwegi

2. Dorsal pattern often obscured by heavy
   deposition of black pigment, belly heavily
   spotted with dark brown, or may be completely black---------------------------3
   Dorsal pattern of chocolate or reddish-
   brown blotches, contrasting strongly with
   light-brown or grayish interblotch areas--
   ----------------------------------nebulata

Clave de subespecies

1. Primeras manchas dorsales no diferentes
   del resto de manchas del cuerpo----------2
   Primeras manchas dorsales anchas, bien
   marcadas--------------------------hartwegi

2. Diseño dorsal frecuentemente oscurecido por
   mayor depósito de pigmento negro, vientre
   densamente manchado de pardo oscuro,
   pudiendo ser completamente negro---------3
   Diseño dorsal con manchas de color chocolate o pardo rojizo que contraste fuertemente con los interespacios grises o
   pardo claros----------------------nebulata

3. Ventrals fewer than 175 in both sexes; subcaudals fewer than 85 in males, fewer than
   75 in females----------------popayanensis
   Ventrals more than 175 in both sexes; subcaudals more than 90 in males, more than
   80 in females------------------leucomelas

3. Ventrales menos de 175 en ambos sexos; subcaudales menos de 85 en machos, y de 75 en
   hembras-----------------------popayanensis
   Ventrales más de 175 en ambos sexos; subcaudales más de 90 en machos, más de 80 en
   hembras------------------------leucomelas

Sibon nebulata nebulata (Linnaeus)

1758 Coluber sibon Linnaeus, Systema Naturae, Ed. 10: 222. Type-locality: Africa.
1845 Coluber variegatus Hallowell, Proc. Acad. Nat. Sci. Phila., 1845: 244. Type-locality:
     within 200 mi of Caracas, Venezuela.
1879 Leptognathus affinis Fischer, Verh. Naturwiss. Ver. Hamburg, (2) 3: 78, pl. 1, figs. 1a-c.
     Type-locality: Sabanna Larga, Colombia.
1960 Sibon nebulata nebulata—Peters, Misc. Publ. Mus. Zool. Univ. Mich., 114: 199.

   Distribution: Nayarit on west and Veracruz on east in Mexico, through lowlands of Central
   America, including Yucatán Peninsula, to extreme northern South America east and north
   of Andean Chain; Trinidad and Tobago Islands; an isolated population in northwestern
   Ecuador below range of S. n. leucomelas.

Sibon nebulata hartwegi Peters

1960 Sibon nebulata hartwegi Peters, Misc. Publ. Mus. Zool. Univ. Mich., 114: 200, pl. 8, figs.
     d-e. Type-locality: Barrancabermeja, Provincia Santander, Colombia.

   Distribution: Upper reaches of Río Magdalena and tributaries, valley of Río Porce (Medellín),
   Colombia.

Sibon nebulata leucomelas (Boulenger)

1896 Leptognathus leucomelas Boulenger, Ann. Mag. Nat. Hist., (6) 17: 18. Type-locality:
     Buenaventura, Colombia.
1960 Sibon nebulata leucomelas—Peters, Misc. Publ. Mus. Zool. Univ. Mich., 114: 202, pl. 8,
     fig. c.

   Distribution: Panama-Colombia border, including all coastal Colombia to northwestern Ecuador.

Sibon nebulata popayanensis Peters

1960 Sibon nebulata popayanensis Peters, Misc. Publ. Mus. Zool. Univ. Mich., 114: 203, pl. 8,
     figs. a-b. Type-locality: Popayan, Provincia Cauca, Colombia.

   Distribution: Upper reaches of Río Cauca, Colombia.

SIBON SANNIOLA (Cope)
annulata group

1866 Mesopeltis sanniolus Cope, Proc. Acad. Nat. Sci. Phila., 1866: 318. Type-locality: Yucatán,
     Mexico; restricted to Chichén Itzá, Yucatán, by Smith and Taylor, Univ. Kansas Sci. Bull.,
     33, 1950, 352.
1943 Sibon sanniolus—Smith, Proc. U. S. Nat. Mus., 93: 470.
1960 Sibon sanniola—Peters, Misc. Publ. Mus. Zool. Univ. Mich., 114: 187.

   Distribution: Northern and eastern parts of Yucatán Peninsula; British Honduras.

SIBYNOMORPHUS Fitzinger

1843 <u>Sibynomorphus</u> Fitzinger, Syst. Rept.: 27. Type-species: <u>Sibynomorphus mikanii</u> Schlegel.
1854 <u>Anholodon</u> Duméril, Bibron and Duméril, Erp. Gén., 7: 1165. Type-species: <u>Sibynomorphus mikanii</u> Schlegel.
1854 <u>Cochliophagus</u> Duméril, Bibron and Duméril, Erp. Gén., 7: 478. Type-species: <u>Sibynomorphus inaequifasciatus</u> Duméril and Bibron.
1896 <u>Pseudopareas</u> Boulenger, Cat. Sn. Brit. Mus., 3: 462. Type-species: <u>Sibynomorphus vagus</u> Jan.

Distribution: South America, south of the equator.

Content: Six species, according to the most recent revision of the genus, by Peters, Misc. Publ. Mus. Zool. Univ. Mich., 114, 1960.

Key to the species

1. Color pattern of clearly defined dorsal blotch-es or spots over entire body----------------2
   Lacking clearly defined dorsal blotches; narrow lateral spots anteriorly, jagged broken streaks on scales posteriorly-----------<u>vagus</u>

2. Subcaudals 60 or more-----------------------3
   Subcaudals 59 or fewer-----------------------5

3. Ventrals more than 163; dorsal blotches narrow posteriorly but reaching to first row of dorsal scales-------------------------------4
   Ventrals fewer than 162; dorsal blotches reduced posteriorly to vertebral spots---------<u>vagrans</u>

4. Upper labials ten-------------<u>inaequifasciatus</u>
   Upper labials nine or fewer------------<u>mikanii</u>

5. Upper labials usually seven or more; blotches only slightly wider than or equal to inter-spaces posteriorly on body------------------6
   Upper labials usually six; blotches much wider than interspaces on posterior part of body----
   --------------------------------<u>ventrimaculatus</u>

6. Blotches on posterior part of body reach only fourth or fifth row of scales---------<u>turgidus</u>
   Blotches on posterior part of body reach first or second row of scales---------------<u>mikanii</u>

Clave de especies

1. Diseño dorsal de manchas claramente definidas sobre todo el cuerpo-------------------------2
   Sin manchas dorsales claramente definidas; an-teriormente manchas angostas laterales; pos-teriormente, las escamas con líneas quebradas zigzagueantes---------------------------<u>vagus</u>

2. Subcaudales 60 o más-------------------------3
   Subcaudales 59 o menos-----------------------5

3. Ventrales más de 163; manchas dorsales pos-teriormente angostas, alcanzando la primer hilera de escamas dorsales--------------------4
   Ventrales menos de 162; manchas dorsales pos-teriormente reducidas a puntos vertebrales----
   -----------------------------------<u>vagrans</u>

4. Supralabiales diez-------------<u>inaequifasciatus</u>
   Supralabiales nueve o menos------------<u>mikanii</u>

5. Supralabiales frecuentemente siete o más; manchas ligeramente más anchas o iguales a los interespacios en la parte posterior del cuerpo--------------------------------------6
   Supralabiales frecuentemente seis; manchas mucho más anchas que las interespacios en la parte posterior del cuerpo-----<u>ventrimaculatus</u>

6. Manchas que en la mitad posterior del cuerpo alcanzan sólo la cuarta o quinta fila de escamas-------------------------------<u>turgidus</u>
   Manchas que en la mitad posterior del cuerpo alcanzan la primera o segunda fila de escamas-------------------------------<u>mikanii</u>

SIBYNOMORPHUS INAEQUIFASCIATUS (Duméril, Bibron and Duméril)

1854 <u>Cochliophagus inaequifasciatus</u> Duméril, Bibron and Duméril, Erp. Gén., 7: 480. Type-locality: South America, "Doubtfully from Brazil".
1960 <u>Sibynomorphus inaequifasciatus</u> Peters, Misc. Publ. Mus. Zool. Univ. Mich., 114: 146.

Distribution: Unknown.

SIBYNOMORPHUS MIKANII (Schlegel)

1837 <u>Dipsas mikanii</u> Schlegel, Essai Physion. Serpens, 2: 277. Type-locality: Brazil.
1843 <u>Sibynomorphus mikani</u>—Fitzinger, Systema Reptilium: 27.

Distribution: Southeastern Brazil.

Content: Two subspecies.

SIBYNOMORPHUS

1. Subcaudals 60 or more--------------neuwiedi   1. Subcaudales 60 o más---------------neuwiedi
   Subcaudals 59 or fewer -------------mikanii   Subcaudales 59 o menos-------------mikanii

Sibynomorphus mikanii mikanii (Schlegel)

   1887 Leptognathus garmani Cope, Proc. Amer. Philos. Soc., 24: 60. Type-locality: São Paulo,
        Brazil.
   1929 Sibynomorphus mikanii mikanii—Amaral, Mem. Inst. Butantan, 4: 198.
   1960 Sibynomorphus mikani mikani—Peters, Misc. Publ. Mus. Zool. Univ. Mich., 114: 148.

      Distribution: Internal drainage areas of southeastern Brazil, not including coastal areas
         except in north, in states of Mato Grosso, Minas Gerais, Paraná, Río Grande do Norte, Río
         Grande do Sul, and São Paulo.

Sibynomorphus mikanii neuwiedi (Ihering)

   1910 Cochliophagus mikani neuwiedi Ihering, Rev. Mus. Paulista, 8: 333. Type-localities:
        States of São Paulo and Espírito Santo.
   1930 Sibynomorphus mikanii fasciatus Amaral, Bull. Antivenin Inst. Amer., 4: 28. Type-
        localities: Pernambuco, Bahia, Río de Janeiro, and Porto Real in Brazil.
   1960 Sibynomorphus mikani neuwiedi—Peters, Misc. Publ. Mus. Zool. Univ. Mich., 114: 154.

      Distribution: Southeastern coastal strip of Brazil, from Bahia to Río Grande do Sul.

SIBYNOMORPHUS TURGIDUS (Cope)

   1868 Leptognathus turgida Cope, Proc. Acad. Nat. Sci. Phila., 1868: 136. Type-locality: Northern
        part of the Paraguay River.
   1874 Leptognathus atypicus Cope, Proc. Acad. Nat. Sci. Phila., 1874: 65. Type-locality: Peruvian
        Andes; questioned by Peters, Misc. Publ. Mus. Zool. Univ. Mich., 114, 1960, 160.
   1915 Tropidodipsas spilogaster Griffin, Mem. Carnegie Mus., 7: 197. Type-locality: Sara Province,
        Bolivia, 350 m.
   1926 Sibynomorphus turgidus—Amaral, Comm. Linh. Telegr. Estrat. Matto Grosso ao Amazonas São Paulo,
        84 annex 5, Hist. Nat. Zool.: 5.
   1960 Sibynomorphus turgidus—Peters, Misc. Publ. Mus. Zool. Univ. Mich., 114: 158.

      Distribution: Northern Paraguay; southeastern Bolivia; Mato Grosso, Brazil.

SIBYNOMORPHUS VAGRANS (Dunn)

   1923 Pseudopareas vagrans Dunn, Proc. Biol. Soc. Wash., 36: 187. Type-locality: Bellavista, Peru.
   1960 Sibynomorphus vagrans—Peters, Misc. Publ. Mus. Zool. Univ. Mich., 114: 161.

      Distribution: Known only from type locality.

SIBYNOMORPHUS VAGUS (Jan)

   1863 Leptognathus vagus Jan, Elenco Sist. Ofidi : 100. Type-locality: Hong Kong, designated as South
        America by Dunn, Proc. Biol. Soc. Wash., 36, 1923, 187.
   1960 Sibynomorphus vagus—Peters, Misc. Publ. Mus. Zool. Univ. Mich., 114: 164.

      Distribution: Known only from Huancabamba, Peru.

SIBYNOMORPHUS VENTRIMACULATUS (Boulenger)

   1885 Leptognathus ventrimaculatus Boulenger, Ann. Mag. Nat. Hist., (5) 16: 87. Type-locality: São
        Lorenço, Serra dos Tapes, Río Grande do Sul, Brazil.
   1903 Leptognathus intermedia Steindachner, Sitz. Math.-Naturwiss. Kl. Akad. Wiss. Wien, 112, abt. 1:
        16. Type-locality: Altos, Paraguay.
   1929 Sibynomorphus ventrimaculatus—Amaral, Mem. Inst. Butantan, 4: 200.
   1960 Sibynomorphus ventrimaculatus—Peters, Misc. Publ. Mus. Zool. Univ. Mich., 114: 165.

      Distribution: Southern Paraguay; northeastern Argentina; Río Grande do Sul, Brazil; Uruguay.

<u>SIMOPHIS</u> Peters

1860 <u>Simophis</u> Peters, Monats. Akad. Wiss. Berlin, 1860: 521. Type-species: <u>Heterodon</u> <u>rhinostoma</u>
    Schlegel.
1863 <u>Rhinaspis</u> Jan, Arch. Zool. Anat. Fis., 2: 215. Type-species: <u>Rhinaspis</u> <u>proboscideus</u> Jan.

   Distribution: Brazil and Paraguay.

   Content: Two species.

<table>
<tr><td>Key to the species</td><td>Clave de especies</td></tr>
<tr><td>1. Seven upper labials, dorsals in 15 rows at
  midbody----------------------------<u>rhinostoma</u>
  Eight upper labials, dorsals in 17 rows at
  midbody-------------------------------<u>rohdei</u></td><td>1. Siete labiales superiores; con 15 filas de
  escamas al medio del cuerpo--------<u>rhinostoma</u>
  Ocho labiales superiores; con 17 filas de
  escamas al medio del cuerpo------------<u>rohdei</u></td></tr>
</table>

<u>SIMOPHIS</u> <u>RHINOSTOMA</u> (Schlegel)

1837 <u>Heterodon</u> <u>rhinostoma</u> Schlegel, Essai Physion. Serpens, 2: 100, pl. 3, figs. 17-19. Type-
    locality: Interior of Brazil.
1858 <u>Rhinostoma</u> <u>schlegelii</u> Günther, Cat. Sn. Brit. Mus.: 8. Type-locality: North America.
1860 <u>Simophis</u> <u>Rhinostoma</u>—Peters, Monats. Akad. Wiss. Berlin, 1860: 521.
1863 <u>Rhinaspis</u> <u>proboscideus</u> Jan, Arch. Zool. Anat. Fis., 2: 215. Type-locality: Brazil.

   Distribution: Brazil.

<u>SIMOPHIS</u> <u>ROHDEI</u> (Boettger)

1885 <u>Rhinaspis</u> <u>Rohdei</u> Boettger, Zeits. für Naturwiss., 58: 231. Type-locality: Paraguay.
1894 <u>Simophis</u> <u>rohdii</u>—Boulenger, Cat. Sn. Brit. Mus., 2: 254.

   Distribution: Paraguay.

Prepared by Joseph R. Bailey, Duke University, Durham, North Carolina

SIPHLOPHIS Fitzinger

1843 Siphlophis Fitzinger, Systema Reptilium: 27. Type-species: Given as Lycodon audax Boie, which same as Coluber audax Daudin.
1853 Lycognathus Duméril, Mém. Acad. Sci. Paris, 23: 495. Type-species: Coluber audax Daudin.
1935 Callopistria Amaral, Mem. Inst. Butantan, 9: 204. Type-species: Callopistria rubrovertebralis Amaral.
1939 Alleidophis Prado, Mem. Inst. Butantan, 13: 5. Type-species: Alleidophis worontzowi Prado.

Distribution: Panama to Brazil and Bolivia.

Content: Five species.

Key to the species	Clave de especies
1. Body pattern series of distinct dorsal or paired dorsolateral spots not extending onto ventrals, although lower series of smaller alternating spots may touch them; venter without pigment or suffused with brownish; third upper labial usually excluded from orbit-----2 Body pattern of somewhat to very irregular light and dark markings, latter extending onto ventrals at least posteriorly; third upper labial usually entering orbit----------------3	1. Diseño del cuerpo de manchas nítidas dorsales o dorsolaterales pares que no se extienden dentro de las ventrales, aunque las series más bajas de manchas alternadas menores pueden tocarlas; vientre sin pigmento o parduzco difuso; tercer labial superior generalmente excluido de la órbita-----------------------2 Diseño del cuerpo con manchas claras y oscuras ligeramente o muy irregulares, las oscuras se extienden dentro de las ventrales, al menos a posterior; tercer labial superior generalmente entra la órbita------------------------------3
2. Dorsal pattern of 40-62 large brown spots, sometimes more or less offset on midline; head with scattered brown spots; solid maxillary teeth 13-16; anterior mandibular teeth moderately enlarged, gradually decreasing posteriorly; ventrals 230 or fewer-----longicaudatus Dorsal pattern of 60-72 black spots on either side separated or joined across back into dumbbells; head with black markings; solid maxillary teeth 16-18; fifth and sixth mandibular teeth greatly enlarged, followed by diastema and much smaller posterior mandibular teeth; ventrals 229 or more---------geminatus	2. Diseño dorsal con 40-62 manchas pardas grandes, a veces no coinciden en la línea media; cabeza con manchas pardas dispersas; dientes maxilares sólidos 13-16; dientes mandibulares anteriores moderadamente ensanchados, decreciendo gradualmente a posterior; ventrales 230 o menos--------------------------longicaudatus Diseño dorsal con 60-72 manchas negras a cada lado separadas o unidas a través del dorso por una banda angosta; cabeza con marcas negras; dientes maxilares sólidos 16-18; quinto y sexto dientes mandibulares muy ensanchados, seguidos de diastema y de dientes mandibulares posteriores mucho menores; ventrales 229 o más------------------------------------geminatus
3. Dorsal pattern with fewer than 25 light or dark spots or bands; head scales without light centers--4 Dorsal pattern of 55-103 irregular black and white vertical bars; venter with distinct black checks; top of head variegated light and dark; larger head scales light on margins and centers------------------------------cervinus	3. Diseño dorsal con menos de 25 manchas o bandas claras u oscuras; escamas de la cabeza sin centros claros------------------------------4 Diseño dorsal con 55-103 barras verticales irregulares negras y blancas; vientre con cuadrados negros nítidos; dorso de cabeza variegado claro y oscuro; escamas mayores de la cabeza claras en bordes y centros--cervinus
4. Dorsum dark (in preservative) except for pair of light nape spots and 16-19 light lateral bars or spots; venter uniformly dark except when adjacent to light spots; solid maxillary teeth 16-19; three postoculars; 15 rows of scales anterior to vent-------------worontzowi Dorsum with about 18 large dark spots or saddles extending about half way across venter; head and collar for four scales light with dark round spots; solid maxillary teeth thirteen; two postoculars; 17 rows of scales anterior to vent----------------leucocephalus	4. Dorso oscuro (en preservativo) excepto por un par de manchas nucales y 16-19 barras o manchas laterales claras; vientre uniformemente oscuro excepto en adyacencias a manchas claras; dientes maxilares sólidos 16-19; tres postoculares; 15 hileras de escamas anteriores al ano------------------------------worontzowi Dorso con aproximadamente 18 manchas o monturas que se extienden aproximadamente a mitad de camino a través del vientre; cabeza y collar claros con manchas redondas oscuras en las cuatro primeras líneas de escamas; dientes maxilares sólidos trece; dos postoculares; 17 hileras de escamas anteriores al ano--leucocephalus

SIPHLOPHIS CERVINUS (Laurenti)

1768 Coronella cervina Laurenti, Synopsin Reptilium: 88. Type-locality: "America".
1803 Coluber audax Daudin, Hist. Nat. Rept., 6: 345, pl. 79. Type-locality: None given.
1820 Coluber (Natrix) Maximiliani Merrem, Tentamen Systematis Amphibiorum: 105. Type-locality: None given.
1854 Lycognathus scolopax Duméril, Bibron and Duméril (replacement name for Coluber audax Daudin), Erp. Gén., 7: 919.
1916 Clelia euprepa Griffin, Mem. Carnegie Mus., 7 (1915): 203, pl. 28, figs. 7-9. Type-locality: Santa Cruz de la Sierra, Bolivia.
1920 Drepanodon attenuatus Barbour and Noble, Proc. U.S. Nat. Mus., 58: 619. Type-locality: San Fernando, Río Cosireni, Cusco, Peru, 3000 ft.
1964 Siphlophis cervinus—Hoge, Mem. Inst. Butantan, 30 (1960-62): 43.

Distribution: Central Bolivia and Maranhão to the Canal Zone and Trinidad.

SIPHLOPHIS LEUCOCEPHALUS (Günther), new combination

1863 Leptodira leucocephala Günther, Ann. Mag. Nat. Hist., (3) 11: 23. Type-locality: Bahia, Brazil.
1896 Lycognathus rhombeatus—Boulenger, Cat. Sn. Brit. Mus., 3: 58.

Distribution: "Bahia" and Canna Brava, Goiás on border of Goiás and Minas Gerais, Brazil.

SIPHLOPHIS LONGICAUDATUS (Andersson)

1907 Tropidodipsas Longicaudata Andersson, Bihang Till K. Svenska Vet.-Akad. Handlingar, 27 (4): 17, pl. 2, figs. 9-11. Type-locality: Brazil.
1964 Siphlophis longicaudatus—Hoge, Mem. Inst. Butantan, 30 (1960-62): 43.
1964 Siphlophis cinereus Lema, Rev. Bras. Biol., 24: 222, figs. 1-13. Type-locality: Colônia de São Padro, Torres, Rio Grande do Sul, Brazil.

Distribution: Espirito Santo to Rio Grande do Sul, Brazil.

SIPHLOPHIS PULCHER Raddi

1820 Coluber pulcher Raddi, Mem. Soc. Italiana Sci. Modena, 18: 537. Type-locality: Rio de Janeiro, Brazil.
1854 Lycognathus geminatus Duméril, Bibron and Duméril, Erp. Gén., 7: 922. Type-locality: Brazil.
1863 Oxyrhopus rhombeatus Peters, Monats. Akad. Wiss. Berlin, 1863: 288. Type-locality: Unknown.
1935 Callopistria rubrovertebralis Amaral, Mem. Inst. Butantan, 9: 205. Type-locality: Morro Azul, Estado do Rio de Janeiro, Brazil.
1964 Siphlophis pulcher—Hoge, Mem. Inst. Butantan, 30 (1960-62): 40, figs. 2, 8, 11, 13-14, 21.

Distribution: Guanabara and southern Minas Gerais to Rio Grande do Sul, Brazil.

Comment: Although Hoge, Mem. Inst. Butantan, 30, 1960-62 (1964), 40, invoked the nomen oblitum rule to eliminate pulcher Raddi as the proper name for this species, it seems appropriate to use Raddi's name in preference to geminatus Duméril, Bibron and Duméril, which has had a history of misinterpretation and erroneous usage.

SIPHLOPHIS WORONTZOWI (Prado), new combination

1940 Alleidophis worontzowi Prado, Mem. Inst. Butantan, 13 (1939): 5, pl., p. 7. Type-locality: Rio Amana, Estado do Amazonas, Brazil.
1964 Alleidophis worontzowi—Hoge, Mem. Inst. Butantan, 30 (1960-62): 40, figs. 4, 6, 10.

Distribution: Known only from type locality.

SORDELLINA Procter

1923 Sordellina Procter, Ann. Mag. Nat. Hist., (9) 11: 228, figs. 1-3. Type-species: Sordellina brandon-jonesii Procter.

Distribution: As for single known species.

Content: One species, according to Hoge, Mitt. Zool. Mus. Berlin, 34, 1958, 52.

SORDELLINA PUNCTATA (Peters)

1880 Xenodon punctatus Peters, Monats. Akad. Wiss. Berlin, 1880: 221, fig. 3. Type-locality: Brazil.
1909 Liophis rehi Werner, Mitt. Naturhist. Mus. Hamburg, 26: 223. Type-locality: Ypiranga, São Paulo, Brazil.
1923 Sordellina brandon-jonesii Procter, Ann. Mag. Nat. Hist., (9) 11: 229. Type-locality: Near Castro, Rio de Tiberia, Paraná, Brazil.
1923 Sordellina pauloensis Amaral, Proc. New England Zool. Club, 8: 88. Type-locality: Poa, São Paulo, Brazil.
1958 Sordellina punctata Hoge, Mitt. Zool. Mus. Berlin, 34: 52, figs. 1-3.

Distribution: Rio de Janeiro, Santa Catarina, São Paulo and Paraná, Brazil.

SPILOTES Wagler

1830 Spilotes Wagler, Nat. Syst. Amph.: 179. Type-species: Coluber pullatas Linnaeus.
1863 Agriotes Jan, Elenco Sist. Ofidi: 81. Type-species: Herpetodryas incertus Jan.

Distribution: As for single known species.

Comment: It is unclear to us that Jan intended Agriotes as a new generic or subgeneric name. His technique for handling such names is clear, with the genera within a family numbered, and the subgenera centered on the page in parentheses and the species listed below with the initial letter of the genus. Neither method is used for Agriotes, which is given in the same fashion used elsewhere by Jan to indicate prior synonymic placement of the species. It has been cited as a genus by Smith and Taylor, Bull. U.S. Nat. Mus., 187, 1945, 131.

Content: One species.

SPILOTES PULLATUS (Linnaeus)

1758 Coluber pullatas Linnaeus, Systema Naturae, Ed. 10: 225. Type-locality: Asia; in error.
1830 Spilotes pullat.[us]—Wagler, Nat. Syst. Amph.: 179.

Distribution: Southern Mexico through Central and South America to Argentina.

Content: Five subspecies.

Key to the subspecies

1. Without reticulate pattern---------------2
   Pattern reticulate in black and yellow----
   -----------------------------argusiformis

2. Dorsum yellow with black streaks and/or
   spots----------------------------------3
   Dorsum black with oblique yellow streaks,
   posteriorly less conspicuous or becoming
   rings--------------------------pullatus

3. Loreal absent----------------------------4
   Loreal present------------------mexicanus

4. Regular, subrectangular, transverse
   spots-------------------------maculatus
   Irregular spots, sometimes broken,
   occasionally forming rings-----anomalepis

Clave de subespecies

1. Diseño no reticulado----------------------2
   Diseño reticulado en negro y amarillo------
   -----------------------------argusiformis

2. Dorso amarillo con fajas o manchas negras--
   ---3
   Dorso negro con fajas oblícuas amarillas,
   poco conspícuas posteriormente o trans-
   formadas en anillos--------------pullatus

3. Loreal ausente---------------------------4
   Loreal presente------------------mexicanus

4. Manchas transversas regulares subrectan-
   gulares-------------------------maculatus
   Manchas irregulares, interrumpidas o no,
   a veces formando anillos--------anomalepis

Spilotes pullatus pullatus (Linnaeus)

1788 Cerastes coronatus Laurenti, Synopsin Reptilium: 83. Type-locality: Nova Hispania.
1790 Coluber variabilis Merrem, Beitr., 2: 40, pl. 12. Type-locality; not known. We have not been able to verify this citation taken from Boulenger, Cat. Sn. Brit. Mus., 2, 1894, 23.
1803 Coluber plutonius Daudin, Hist. Nat. Rept., 6: 324. Type-locality: unknown.
1820 Coluber (Natrix) Caninana Merrem, Tentamen Systematis Amphibiorum: 121. Type-locality: Mexico, Brazil, and other regions of South America.
1825 C.[oluber] variabilis Kuhlii Wied, Beiträge zur Naturgeschichte von Brasilien, 1: 271.
1865 Spilotes megalolepis Günther, Ann. Mag. Nat. Hist., (3) 15: 93. Type-locality: South America.
1920 Spilotes pullatus var. ater Sternfeld, Senckenbergiana, 2: 185. Type-locality: Tobago.
1929 Spilotes pullatus pullatus—Amaral, Mem. Inst. Butantan, 4: 277, fig. 1.

Distribution: Costa Rica and Panama to Paraguay and northern Argentina; Trinidad and Tobago Islands.

Spilotes pullatus anomalepis Bocourt

1888 Spilotes pullatus var. anomalepis Bocourt, Miss. Sci. Mex., Rept.: 685, pl. 44, figs. 3-4.
Type-locality: Brazil.
1929 Spilotes pullatus anomalepis—Amaral, Mem. Inst. Butantan, 4: 284, fig. 3.

Distribution: Bahia to Rio Grande do Sul, southeastern Brazil.

Spilotes pullatus argusiformis Amaral

1929 Spilotes pullatus argusiformis Amaral, Mem. Inst. Butantan, 4: 291, fig. 5. Type-
locality: Río Ulua, Tela, Honduras.

Distribution: Honduras to Nicaragua.

Spilotes pullatus maculatus Amaral

1929 Spilotes pullatus maculatus Amaral, Mem. Inst. Butantan, 4: 289, fig. 4. Type-locality:
São Paulo, São Paulo, Brazil.

Distribution: Vicinity of Serra Paranapiacaba and Serra do Mar, São Paulo, Brazil.

Spilotes pullatus mexicanus (Laurenti)

1768 Cerastes mexicanus Laurenti, Synopsin Reptilium: 83. Type-locality: Mexico (based on
plate in Seba).
1788 Coluber novae Hispaniae Gmelin (unavailable, because not binomial), Systema Naturae,
Ed. 13: 1088. Type-locality: New Spain.
1861 [Spilotes pullatus] auribundus Cope, Proc. Acad. Nat. Sci. Phila., 1861: 300. Type-
locality: Mirador, Veracruz, Mexico.
1862 Spilotes Salvini Günther, Ann. Mag. Nat. Hist., (3) 9: 125, pl. 9, fig. 5. Type-locality:
Izabal, British Honduras.
1863 Herpetodryas incertus Jan, Elenco Sist. Ofidi: 81. Type-locality: Belize, British
Honduras.
1894 Coluber novae-hispaniae Boulenger (first binomial use), Cat. Sn. Brit. Mus., 2: 33.
1903 Spilotes microlepis Werner, Abh. K. Bayer. Akad. Wiss. München, 1903: 346. Type-locality:
Guatemala.
1929 Spilotes pullatus mexicanus—Amaral, Mem. Inst. Butantan, 4: 272, fig. 2.

Distribution: Tamaulipas on Atlantic slope and Oaxaca on Pacific Slope of Mexico to Guatemala
and Honduras.

STENORRHINA Duméril

1853 <u>Stenorrhina</u> Duméril, Mem. Acad. Sci. Paris, 23: 490. Type-species: <u>Stenorhina ventralis</u>
   Duméril, Bibron and Duméril, 1854 (nomen nudum in original description of genus).
1854 <u>Microphis</u> Hallowell, Proc. Acad. Nat. Sci. Phila., 1854: 97. Type-species: <u>Microphis</u>
   <u>quinqueliniatus</u> Hallowell.
1854 <u>Stenorhina</u> Duméril, Bibron and Duméril (emendation of <u>Stenorrhina</u> Duméril), Erp. Gén., 7: 865.
   Type-species: <u>Stenorhina ventralis</u> Duméril, Bibron and Duméril.
1867 <u>Bergenia</u> Steindachner, Reise der Österreichischen Fregatte Novara, Zool., Rept.: 92. Type-
   species: <u>Bergenia mexicana</u> Steindachner.

   Distribution: Central Veracruz and Guerrero, Mexico, through Central America to Colombia, Venezuela
   and Pacific Ecuador.

   Content: Two species.

Key to the species	Clave de especies

1. Ventrals more than 160------------<u>freminvillii</u>
   Ventrals less than 160------------<u>degenhardtii</u>
	1. Ventrales más de 160--------------<u>freminvillii</u>
	   Ventrales menos de 160------------<u>degenhardtii</u>

STENORRHINA DEGENHARDTII (Berthold)

1846 <u>Calamaria Degenhardtii</u> Berthold, Abh. K. Ges. Wiss. Göttingen, 3: 8, pl. 1, figs. 3-4. Type-
   locality: "Etwa 2° N.B. und 301° L.," Popayán Province, Colombia.
1876 S[tenorrhina] degenhardtii—Cope, Jour. Acad. Nat. Sci. Phila., (2) 8 (1875): 142.

   Distribution: Mexico to Venezuela and Pacific Ecuador.

   Content: Three subspecies.

Key to the subspecies	Clave de subespecies

1. Without temporal stripe------------------2
   With temporal stripe---------<u>degenhardtii</u>
	1. Sin línea temporal------------------------2
	   Con línea temporal------------<u>degenhardtii</u>

2. Dorsum uniform grey in adults; belly with
   light spots on greyish ground color------
   -------------------------------<u>ocellata</u>
   Dorsum brownish in adults; belly with
   black spots--------------------<u>mexicana</u>
	2. Dorso gris uniforme en los adultos; vientre
	   con manchas claras sobre fondo gris-------
	   --------------------------------<u>ocellata</u>
	   Pardo encima en adultos; vientre con
	   manchas negras--------------------<u>mexicana</u>

<u>Stenorrhina degenhardtii degenhardtii</u> (Berthold)

1854 <u>Stenorhina ventralis</u> Duméril, Bibron and Duméril, Erp. Gén., 7: 867. Type-locality:
   Cobán, Alta Verapaz, Guatemala.
1860 <u>Stenorhina Kennicottiana</u> Cope, Proc. Acad. Nat. Sci. Phila., 1860: 242. Type-locality:
   Isthmus of Panama.
1876 <u>Stenorhina degenhardtii</u> [<u>degenhardtii</u>]—Jan, Icon. Gén. Ophid.: Liv. 48, pl. 2, figs. 5-6.

   Distribution: Panama to Pacific Colombia and Ecuador.

<u>Stenorrhina degenhardtii mexicana</u> (Steindachner)

1867 <u>Bergenia mexicana</u> Steindachner, Reise der Österreichischen Fregatte Novara, Zool., Rept.:
   92, 3 figs. Type-locality: Mexico; restricted by Smith and Taylor, Univ. Kansas Sci.
   Bull., 33, 1950, 347, to Córdoba, Veracruz, Mexico.
1941 <u>Stenorhina mexicana</u>—Taylor, Univ. Kansas Sci. Bull., 27: 122.
1943 <u>Stenorhina degenhardtii mexicana</u>—Smith, Proc. U.S. Nat. Mus., 93: 472.

   Distribution: Central Veracruz south to Guatemala.

Stenorrhina degenhardtii ocellata Jan

   1876 Stenorhina Degenhardtii var. ocellata Jan, Icon. Gén. Ophid.: Liv. 48, pl. 2, fig. 5.
      Type-locality: Puerto Cabello, Venezuela.
   1959 Stenorhina degenhardtii ocellata—Roze, Amer. Mus. Novitates, 1934: 11.

   Distribution: North central and northwestern Venezuela; possibly Colombia.

STENORRHINA FREMINVILLII Duméril, Bibron and Duméril

   1854 Stenorhina Freminvillii Duméril, Bibron and Duméril, Erp. Gén., 7: 868, pl. 70, figs. 1-2.
      Type-locality: Mexico; restricted to Totolapam, Oaxaca, Mexico, by Smith and Taylor, Univ.
      Kansas Sci. Bull., 33, 1950, 341.
   1855 Microphis quinqueliniatus Hallowell, Proc. Acad. Nat. Sci. Phila., 1854, 7: 97. Type-locality:
      Honduras; restricted to Totolapam, Oaxaca, Mexico by Smith and Taylor, Univ. Kansas Sci. Bull.,
      33, 1950, 341.
   1861 Stenorhina lactea Cope, Proc. Acad. Nat. Sci. Phila., 1861: 303. Type-locality: La Unión,
      Guatemala; restricted to La Unión, El Salvador, by Smith and Taylor, Univ. Kansas Sci. Bull.,
      33, 1950, 316.
   1876 S[tenorhina] d[egenhardtii] apiata Cope, Jour. Acad. Nat. Sci. Phila., (2) 8 (1875): 142.
      Type-locality: El Barrio, Oaxaca, Mexico.
   1906 Geophis multitorques yucatanensis Barbour and Cole, Bull. Mus. Comp. Zool., 50: 153. Type-
      locality: Chichen Itzá, Yucatán.

   Distribution: Guerrero, Mexico, to Panama.

   Content: Although several subspecies have been recognized in this species, Stuart (Misc. Publ. Mus.
   Zool. Univ. Mich., 122, 1963, 117) points out the difficulties in defining them, and recommends
   use of the specific name only. We follow this until a thorough review is available.

STORERIA Baird and Girard

1853 *Storeria* Baird and Girard, Cat. N. Amer. Rept.: 135. Type-species: *Tropidonotus Dekayi* Holbrook.

Distribution: North America and Mexico into Guatemala and Honduras.

Content: Two species, one of which (*occipitomaculata* Storer) is extralimital.

STORERIA DEKAYI (Holbrook)

1842 *Tropidonotus Dekayi* Holbrook, North American Herpetology, Ed. 2, 4: 53, pl. 14. Type-locality:
Massachusetts and New York; restricted to Cambridge, Massachusetts, according to Schmidt,
Checklist of North American Amphibians and Reptiles, Ed. 6, 1953, 165.
1853 *Storeria Dekayi*—Baird and Girard, Cat. N. Amer. Rept.: 135.

Distribution: Eastern North America west to Kansas, south through Mexico into Guatemala and
Honduras.

Content: Eight subspecies, seven of which (*anomala* Dugés, *dekayi* Holbrook, *limnetes* Anderson,
temporalineata Trapido, *texana* Trapido, *victa* Hay, and *wrightorum* Trapido) are extralimital.

Storeria dekayi tropica Cope

1885 *Storeria tropica* Cope, Proc. Amer. Phil. Soc., 22 (1884): 175. Type-locality: El Petén,
Guatemala.
1969 *Storeria dekayi tropica*—Sabath and Sabath, Amer. Midl. Nat., 81: 154.

Distribution: Low and moderate elevations of Caribbean slope of northern and central
Guatemala to northern Honduras.

SYNOPHIS Peracca

    1896 <u>Synophis</u> Peracca, Boll. Mus. Zool. Anat. Comp. Torino, 11 (266): 1. Type-species: <u>Synophis</u>
        <u>bicolor</u> Peracca.

    Distribution: Ecuador and Colombia.

    Content: Three species, according to the most recent revision by Bogert, Senck. Biol., 45, 1964.

	Key to the species	Clave de especies

1. Scales in 19 rows at midbody------------------2
   Scales in 21 to 23 rows at midbody-----<u>lasallei</u>

2. One postocular; no loreal----------------<u>miops</u>
   Two postoculars; loreal present--------<u>bicolor</u>

1. Escamas en 19 filas al medio del cuerpo-------2
   Escamas en 21 a 23 filas en el medio del
   cuerpo---------------------------------<u>lasallei</u>

2. Una posocular; sin loreal----------------<u>miops</u>
   Dos posoculares; loreal present--------<u>bicolor</u>

SYNOPHIS <u>BICOLOR</u> Peracca

    1896 <u>Synophis bicolor</u> Peracca, Boll. Mus. Zool. Anat. Comp. Torino, 11 (266): 1. Type-locality:
        South America.
    1964 <u>Synophis bicolor</u>—Bogert, Senck. Biol., 45: 515.

    Distribution: Amazonian Ecuador.

SYNOPHIS <u>LASALLEI</u> (María)

    1950 <u>Diaphorolepis lasallei</u> María, Rev. Acad. Colomb. Cien., 7: 149, fig. 1, 2 figs. in text. Type-
        locality: northwest of Albán, Prov. Cundinamarca, Colombia, 2200 m.
    1964 <u>Synophis lasallei</u>—Bogert, Senck. Biol., 45: 518.

    Distribution: Amazonian lowlands of Colombia and Ecuador.

SYNOPHIS <u>MIOPS</u> Boulenger

    1898 <u>Synophis miops</u> Boulenger, Proc. Zool. Soc. London, 1898: 115, pl. 12, fig. 1. Type-locality:
        Paramba, western Ecuador.

    Distribution: Known only from type locality.

TACHYMENIS Wiegmann

1835 Tachymenis Wiegmann, Nova Acta Acad. Caes.-Leop. Carol., 17: 251. Type-species: Tachymenis
peruviana Wiegmann.
1860 Zacholomorphus Fitzinger, Sitzb. Math.-Nat. Kl. Akad. Wiss. Wien, 42: 407. Type-species: None
designated.

Distribution: Pacific Peru and Chile; Amazonian Peru and Bolivia; Surinam.

Content: Six species. In the most recent revision of genus, Walker, Bull. Mus. Comp. Zool., 96,
1945, suggested that peruviana and its allies may represent a distinct genus or subgenus, and
pointed out two species of very uncertain status (elongata Despax, and surinamensis Dunn).

Key to the species

1. Caudals fewer than 60; ratio of tail length/
total length less than 0.22------------------2
Caudals 60 or more; ratio of tail length/total
length 0.22 or more------------------------4

2. Midbody scale rows 19------------------------3
Midbody scale rows 17--------------------affinis

3. Dorsal scales with single apical pits, may be
poorly developed; spotted dorsal ground color;
female caudals 50 or fewer; six to ten solid
maxillary teeth----------------------peruviana
Dorsal scales lacking apical pits; dorsum unicolor grayish brown, with no or only slight
trace of darker spots; female caudals more
than 50; twelve solid maxillary teeth--------
------------------------------------tarmensis

4. Ventrals more than 185-----------------------5
Ventrals fewer than 160--------------attenuata

5. Scales with apical pits; parietal as long as
frontal; temporals 1-2---------------elongata
Scales lack apical pits; parietal shorter than
frontal; temporals 1-1-----------surinamensis

Clave de especies

1. Caudales menos de 60; relación largo cola/
longitud total menos de 0.22----------------2
Caudales 60 o más; relación largo cola/longitud
total 0.22 o más----------------------------4

2. Con 19 filas al medio del cuerpo--------------3
Con 17 filas al medio del cuerpo--------affinis

3. Escamas dorsales con un solo hoyuelo apical,
que puede ser pobremente desarrollado; dorsalmente manchado; 50 o menos caudales en
hembras; seis a diez dientes maxilares sin
surco--------------------------------peruviana
Escamas dorsales sin hoyuelos apicales; dorso
unicolor en pardo grisáceo; sin manchas
oscuras o con muy débiles; más de 50 caudales
en hembras; doce dientes maxilares sin surco--
------------------------------------tarmensis

4. Más de 185 ventrales-------------------------5
Menos de 160 ventrales----------------attenuata

5. Escamas con hoyuelos apicales; parietales tan
largas como frontal; temporales 1-2---elongata
Escamas sin hoyuelos apicales; parietales más
cortas que frontal; temporales 1-1-----------
------------------------------------surinamensis

TACHYMENIS AFFINIS Boulenger

1896 Tachymenis affinis Boulenger, Cat. Sn. Brit. Mus., 3: 119, pl. 7, fig. 1. Type-locality: Muña,
Peru; Walker, Bull. Mus. Comp. Zool., 96, 1945, 22, suggests this is on upper Río Huallaga,
Huanuco, Peru.
1945 Tachymenis affinis—Walker, Bull. Mus. Comp. Zool., 96: 22, pl. 4, fig. 12.

Distribution: Highland valleys of Peru.

TACHYMENIS ATTENUATA Walker

1945 Tachymenis attenuata Walker, Bull. Mus. Comp. Zool., 96: 24. Type-locality: Peru; thought to
be Departamento Madre de Dios by Walker, loc. cit.

Distribution: Eastern Andean slopes of Bolivia and southern Peru.

Content: Two subspecies.

Key to the subspecies	Clave de subespecies
1. Maxillary teeth 12-14; black-speckled body pattern obscuring any other pattern; 148-150 ventrals; 60-64 caudals--<u>attenuata</u> Maxillary teeth 14-16; checkered body pattern; 152 ventrals; 69 caudals--------------------------------------<u>boliviana</u>	1. Dientes maxilares 12-14; cuerpo salpicado de negro; 148-150 ventrales; 60-64 caudales-------------------------<u>attenuata</u> Dientes maxilares 14-16; diseño en manchas cuadradas blancas y negras; 152 ventrales; 69 caudales----------------------<u>boliviana</u>

<u>Tachymenis attenuata attenuata</u> Walker

>   1945 <u>Tachymenis attenuata attenuata</u> Walker, Bull. Mus. Comp. Zool., 96: 24, pl. 2, fig. 3; pl. 4, figs. 13-15.

>   Distribution: Departamento Madre de Dios, Peru and Departamento Cochabamba, Bolivia.

<u>Tachymenis attenuata boliviana</u> Walker

>   1945 <u>Tachymenis attenuata boliviana</u> Walker, Bull. Mus. Comp. Zool., 96: 26, fig. 16. Type-locality: Incachaca, Departamento Cochabamba, Bolivia, 2500 m.

>   Distribution: Edge of Amazonian basin, Bolivia.

<u>TACHYMENIS</u> <u>ELONGATA</u> Despax

>   1910 <u>Tachymenis elongata</u> Despax, Bull. Mus. Nat. Hist. Nat. Paris, 1910: 373. Type-locality: Tablazo de Payta, Peru, 30 m.

>   Distribution: Still known only from type locality.

<u>TACHYMENIS</u> <u>PERUVIANA</u> Wiegmann

>   1835 <u>Tachymenis peruviana</u> Wiegmann, Nova Acta Acad. Caes.-Leop. Carol., 17: 252, pl. 20, fig. 1. Type-locality: None given.

>   Distribution: Coastal Peru and Chile.

>   Content: Four subspecies.

Key to the subspecies	Clave de subespecies
1. Not heavily melanistic dorsally-----------2 Heavily melanistic dorsally; may be without discernible pattern---------------<u>melanura</u>	1. Dorso no densamente melánico--------------2 Dorso densamente melánico; puede no presentar diseño definido---------<u>melanura</u>
2. With paravertebral stripes----------------3 With row of spots on either side of vertebral line----------------------<u>peruviana</u>	2. Con líneas paravertebrales----------------3 Con fila de puntos a cada lado de la línea vertebral-----------------------<u>peruviana</u>
3. Ground color yellowish ochre------<u>assimilis</u> Ground color brown with reddish tints---------------------------------<u>chilensis</u>	3. Color de fondo amarillo ocre------<u>assimilis</u> Color de fondo pardo con tinte rojizo-------------------------------------<u>chilensis</u>

<u>Tachymenis peruviana peruviana</u> Wiegmann

>   1901 [<u>Tachymenis peruviana</u>] var. <u>dorsalis</u> Werner, Abh. Ber. K. Zool. Anthro.-Ethn. Mus. Dresden, 9: 9. Type-locality: Bolivia.
>   1915 <u>Leimadophis andicolus</u> Barbour, Proc. Biol. Soc. Washington, 28: 149. Type-locality: Huispang, Andes of southern Peru.
>   1962 <u>Tachymenis peruviana peruviana</u>—Donoso-Barros, Not. Mens. Mus. Nac. Hist. Nat. Chile, 6 (66): 1.

>   Distribution: Coastal Peru to Antofagasta region of Chile.

Tachymenis peruviana assimilis (Jan)

1863 P[sammophylax] assimilis Jan, Arch. Zool. Anat. Fis., 2: 311. Type-locality: Unknown;
      given as Chile by Jan, Icon. Gen. Ophid., Livr. 19, pl. 1, fig. 2; given as Valparaiso,
      Chile, by Donoso-Barros, Reptiles de Chile, 1966, 403.
1898 [Tachymenis peruviana] var. coronellina Werner, Zool. Jahrb., suppl. 4: 259, pl. 13, fig.
      9b. Type-locality: Coquimbo, Chile.
1898 [Tachymenis peruviana] var. catenata Werner, Zool. Jahrb., suppl. 4: 259, pl. 13, fig.
      9a. Type-locality: Coquimbo, Chile.
1961 Tachymenis peruviana assimilis—Donoso-Barros, Copeia, 1961: 487.

   Distribution: From about 26°S to 34°S in coastal Chile.

Tachymenis peruviana chilensis (Schlegel)

1837 C.[oronella] chilensis Schlegel, Essai Physion. Serpens, 2: 70. Type-locality:
      Chile.
1854 Tachymenis chilensis—Girard, Proc. Acad. Nat. Sci. Phila., 1854: 226.
1898 Tachymenis peruviana var. vittata Werner, Zool. Jahrb., suppl. 4: 259, pl. 13, fig. 9c.
      Type-locality: Frutillar, Chile.
1962 Tachymenis peruviana chilensis—Donoso-Barros, Not. Mens. Mus. Nac. Hist. Nat. Chile, 6
      (66): 1.

   Distribution: From about 34°S to about 42°S, in coastal Chile.

Tachymenis peruviana melanura Walker

1945 Tachymenis chilensis melanura Walker, Bull. Mus. Comp. Zool., 96: 35, fig. 32. Type-
      locality: Mafil, Provincia Valdivia, Chile.
1962 Tachymenis peruviana melanura—Donoso-Barros, Not. Mens. Mus. Nac. Hist. Nat. Chile, 6
      (66): 1.

   Distribution: From about 42°S to about 44°S in coastal Chile; Islas de Chiloé and Calbuco.

TACHYMENIS SURINAMENSIS Dunn

   1922 Tachymenis surinamensis Dunn, Proc. Biol. Soc. Washington, 35: 220. Type-locality: Surinam.

   Distribution: Still known only from type specimen.

TACHYMENIS TARMENSIS Walker

   1945 Tachymenis tarmensis Walker, Bull. Mus. Comp. Zool., 96: 21, pl. 4, figs. 10-11. Type-locality:
      Tarma, Departamento Junin, Peru.

   Distribution: Known only from type locality.

<u>TANTILLA</u> Baird and Girard

1853 <u>Tantilla</u> Baird and Girard, Cat. N. Amer. Rept.: 131. Type-species: <u>Tantilla</u> <u>coronata</u> Baird and Girard.
1854 <u>Homalocranion</u> Duméril, Mem. Acad. Sci. Paris, 23: 490. Type-species: None given.
1860 <u>Lioninia</u> Hallowell, Proc. Acad. Nat. Sci. Phila., 1860: 484. Type-species: <u>Lioninia</u> <u>vermiformis</u> Hallowell.
1863 <u>Homalocranium</u> Günther,(emendation of <u>Homalocranion</u> Duméril), Ann. Mag. Nat. Hist., (3) 12: 352.
1872 <u>Microdromus</u> Günther, Ann. Mag. Nat. Hist., (4) 9: 17. Type-species: <u>Microdromus</u> <u>virgatus</u> Günther.
1894 <u>Pogonaspis</u> Cope, Proc. Acad. Nat. Sci. Phila., 1894: 204. Type-species: <u>Pogonaspis</u> <u>ruficeps</u> Cope.

Distribution: Southern United States through Central America and South America to northern Argentina.

Content: About 47 species, of which 25 occur within limits defined for this work.

Key to the species

1. With two pairs of chinshields-----------------2
   With one pair of chinshields----------<u>ruficeps</u>

2. Without white collar on neck------------------3
   With white neck collar, about six scale rows wide--------------------------------<u>supracincta</u>

3. Lacking two longitudinal black stripes ventrally----------------------------------4
   With two longitudinal black stripes on venter--------------------------------<u>virgata</u>

4. Some combination of labials other than fourth and fifth entering orbit, usually third and fourth------------------------------------5
   Fourth and fifth supralabials in orbit-------------------------------------<u>tritaeniata</u>

5. Dorsal pattern not made up of transverse, alternating light and dark bands------------6
   Dorsal pattern entirely of alternating, transverse, light and dark bands----<u>semicincta</u>

6. First pair of infralabials mot in contact on midline---------------------------------7
   First pair of infralabials in contact on midline--------------------------------15

7. Dorsum not olive, head and neck not ivory-----8
   Dorsum uniform olive; head and neck ivory color----------------------------<u>albiceps</u>

8. Dorsum not white with small black spots-------9
   Dorsum white with small black spots-<u>vermiformis</u>

9. With fewer than 50 caudals--------------------10
   With more than 50 caudals--------------------13

10.Fewer than 120 ventrals----------------------11
   More than 120 ventrals----------------------12

11.Head shields with light borders and centers--------------------------------------<u>canula</u>
   Head shields without light borders and centers--------------------------------<u>brevis</u>

12.Maxillary teeth anterior to diastema 12--<u>bairdi</u>
   Maxillary teeth anterior to diastema 14--<u>schistosa</u>

Clave de especies

1. Con dos pares geneiales----------------------2
   Con un par geneial--------------------<u>ruficeps</u>

2. Sin collar nucal blanco del ancho de seis escamas-------------------------------------3
   Con collar nucal blanco del ancho de seis escamas-----------------------------<u>supracincta</u>

3. Sin dos cintas longitudinales ventrales negras--------------------------------------4
   Con dos cintas longitudinales ventrales negras-------------------------------<u>virgata</u>

4. Otra combinación de supralabiales, no cuarta y quinta entrando en la órbita, generalmente, tercera y cuarta----------------------------5
   Cuarta y quinta supralabial entran en la órbita-----------------------------<u>tritaeniata</u>

5. Sin diseño dorsal formado por cintas claras y negras transversas, alternas----------------6
   Diseño dorsal formado totalmente por cintas claras y negras transversas alternas--------------------------------------<u>semicincta</u>

6. Primer par de infralabiales no contacta entre sí--7
   Primer par de infralabiales contacta entre sí--------------------------------------15

7. Sin dorso oliva ni cabeza y nuca en color marfil------------------------------------8
   Dorso oliva; cabeza y nuca en color marfil------------------------------------<u>albiceps</u>

8. Dorso no blanco con pequeñas manchas negras---9
   Dorso blanco con pequeñas manchas negras--------------------------------<u>vermiformis</u>

9. Con menos de 50 caudales----------------------10
   Con más de 50 caudales-----------------------13

10.Menos de 120 ventrales-----------------------11
   Más de 120 ventrales-------------------------12

11.Escudos cefálicos con bordes y centros claros--------------------------------<u>canula</u>
   Escudos cefálicos sin bordes ni centros claros--------------------------------------<u>brevis</u>

13. No dorsal reticulation; no light vertebral
    stripe--14
    Dorsum with reticulate pattern; a light verte-
    bral stripe------------------------reticulata

14. Venter yellowish white-----------------alticola
    Venter blackish brown-------------------moesta

15. First third of body lacks either transverse
    yellow spots or irregular bands bordered with
    black---16
    First third of body with transverse yellow
    spots or irregular bands bordered with black--
    -----------------------------------annulata

16. Not uniformly black---------------------17
    Uniformly black above and below----------nigra

17. Nuchal collar present---------------------18
    No nuchal collar-----------------------------26

18. Frontal not twice as long as wide-----------19
    Frontal twice as long as wide----longifrontalis

19. With light stripes dorsally------------------20
    No light stripes on dorsum------------------23

20. Fewer than three light dorsal stripes; fewer
    than 60 caudals----------------------------21
    With three light dorsal stripes; more than 60
    caudals-------------------------------taeniata

21. Caudals more than 35, single light vertebral
    line at least anteriorly--------------------22
    Caudals 21-27; two light paravertebral stripes-
    -----------------------------------brevicauda

22. Nuchal collar four scales wide-------trilineata
    Nuchal collar one scale wide or less-------jani

23. Postnasal not in contact with preocular------24
    Postnasal in contact with preocular------------
    ---------------------------------melanocephala

24. Without dark stripes on sides of body--------25
    With dark stripes on sides of body----armillata

25. Chinshields approximately equal in length------
    ---------------------------------------mexicana
    Anterior chinshields much larger than posterior
    ---------------------------------------fraseri

12. Dientes maxilares anteriores al diastema 12----
    -------------------------------------bairdi
    Dientes maxilares anteriores al diastema 14----
    -------------------------------------schistosa

13. Sin diseño dorsal reticulado; ni cinta verte-
    bral clara------------------------------------14
    Con diseño dorsal reticulado y cinta vertebral
    clara--------------------------------reticulata

14. Vientre blanco amarillento------------alticola
    Vientre pardo negruzco-------------------moesta

15. Primer tercio del cuerpo sin manchas transver-
    sales amarillas ni cintas irregulares bordea-
    das de negro---------------------------------16
    Primer tercio del cuerpo con manchas transver-
    sales amarillas o cintas irregulares bordeadas
    de negro-----------------------------annulata

16. No negra dorsal y ventralmente---------------17
    Dorsal y ventralmente negra---------------nigra

17. Collar nucal presente-----------------------18
    Collar nucal ausente------------------------26

18. Frontal no dos veces más larga que ancha-----19
    Frontal dos veces más larga que ancha----------
    ------------------------------longifrontalis

19. Con líneas dorsales longitudinales claras----20
    Sin líneas dorsales longitudinales claras----23

20. Con menos de tres líneas claras dorsales y
    menos de 60 caudales-----------------------21
    Con tres líneas claras dorsales, más de 60
    caudales-----------------------------taeniata

21. Caudales más de 35, una línea clara mediana por
    lo menos anteriormente--------------------22
    Caudales 21-27, dos líneas claras paraverte-
    brales------------------------------brevicauda

22. Collar nucal de cuatro escamas de ancho--------
    -----------------------------------trilineata
    Collar nucal del ancho de una escama o menos---
    ---------------------------------------jani

23. Posnasal no contacta con la preocular--------24
    Posnasal contacta con la preocular------------
    ---------------------------------melanocephala

24. Sin cintas oscuras a los lados del cuerpo----25
    Con cintas oscuras a los lados del cuerpo------
    -----------------------------------armillata

25. Geneiales subiguales--------------------mexicana
    Geneiales anteriores más largas que posteriores
    ---------------------------------------fraseri

TANTILLA ALBICEPS Barbour

1925 Tantilla albiceps Barbour, Occ. Pap. Boston Soc. Nat. Hist., No. 5: 156. Type-locality: Barro
     Colorado Island, Gatun Lake, Canal Zone of Panama.

   Distribution: Known only from type locality.

TANTILLA ALTICOLA (Boulenger)

1903 Homalocranium alticola Boulenger, Ann. Mag. Nat. Hist., (7) 12: 353. Type-locality: Santa Rita,
northern Medellín, Colombia.
1913 Homalocranium coralliventre Boulenger, Proc. Zool. Soc. London, 1913: 1035, pl. 108, fig. 1.
Type-locality: Peña Lisa, Río Condoto, Chocó, Colombia.
1929 Tantilla alticola—Amaral, Mem. Inst. Butantan, 4: 219.

Distribution: Chocó region of Colombia.

TANTILLA ANNULATA Boettger

1892 Tantilla annulata Boettger, Zool. Anz., 1892: 419. Type-locality: Nicaragua.

Distribution: Nicaragua to Costa Rica.

TANTILLA ARMILLATA Cope

1876 Tantilla armillatum Cope, Jour. Acad. Nat. Sci. Phila., (2) 8 (1875): 143. Type-locality:
Middle Costa Rica.

Distribution: Costa Rica, Honduras and El Salvador.

TANTILLA BAIRDI Stuart

1941 Tantilla bairdi Stuart, Occ. Pap. Mus. Zool. Univ. Mich., 452: 1. Type-locality: Two km northeast of Finca Chichen (10 km south of Coban, airline) on Chemelco trail, Alta Verapaz,
Guatemala, about 1550 m.

Distribution: Known only from type-locality.

TANTILLA BREVICAUDA Mertens

1952 Tantilla brevicauda Mertens, Zool. Anz., 149: 137. Type-locality: El Grito, Los Angeles,
Depto. La Libertad, El Salvador, 1510 m.

Distribution: Known only from La Libertad and San Vicente, El Salvador.

TANTILLA BREVIS (Günther)

1895 Homalocranium breve Günther, Biol. Centr.Amer., Rept.: 150. Type-locality: British Honduras.
1929 Tantilla brevis—Amaral, Mem. Inst. Butantan, 4: 220.

Distribution: British Honduras.

TANTILLA CANULA Cope

1876 Tantilla canula Cope, Jour. Acad. Nat. Sci. Phila., (2) 8 (1875): 144. Type-locality:
Yucatán, Mexico; restricted to Chichén Itzá, Yucatán, by Smith and Taylor, Univ. Kansas
Sci. Bull., 33, 1950, 352.

Distribution: Lowlands of Yucatán Peninsula south to El Petén, Guatemala and British Honduras.

Comment: Neill and Allen, Herpetologica, 17, 1961, 90, indicated that brevis Günther should
probably be considered a subspecies of canula. We noted this too late to add it to this list.

TANTILLA FRASERI (Günther)

1895 Homalocranium melanocephalum fraseri Günther, Biol. Centr. Amer., Rept.: 148. Type-locality:
Quito, Ecuador and "W. Ecuador."
1960 Tantilla fraseri—Peters, Bull. Mus. Comp. Zool., 122: 539.

Distribution: High western slopes of Andes in Ecuador, perhaps in Quito valley.

TANTILLA JANI (Günther)

1895 Homalocranium jani Günther, Biol. Centr. Amer., Rept.: 148, pl. 52, fig. D. Type-locality:
     Guatemala and Nicaragua; restricted to Guatemala, by Smith, Zoologica, 27, 1942, 37.
1942 Tantilla jani—Smith, Zoologica, 27: 36.

   Distribution: Low and moderate elevations of Pacific coast from Isthmus of Tehuantepec, Mexico, to
   Guatemala.

TANTILLA LONGIFRONTALIS Boulenger

1896 Homalocranium longifrontale Boulenger, Ann. Mag. Nat. Hist., (6) 17: 17. Type-locality: Cali,
     Colombia.
1929 Tantilla longifrontalis—Amaral, Mem. Inst. Butantan, 4: 220.

   Distribution: Eastern slopes of Andes, at lower altitudes, in Colombia and Ecuador.

TANTILLA MELANOCEPHALA (Linnaeus)

1758 Coluber melanocephalus Linnaeus, Syst. Nat., Ed. 10: 218. Type-locality: "America".
1861 [Tantilla] melanocephala—Cope, Proc. Acad. Nat. Sci. Phila., 1861: 74.

   Distribution: Central America through South America to northern Argentina.

   Content: Two subspecies.

Key to the subspecies	Clave de subespecies
1. Tip of snout white; prefrontals contact labials------------------------capistrata Tip of snout dark brown; prefrontals and labials not in contact-------melanocephala	1. Punta del hocico blanca; prefrontales en contacto con labiales----------capistrata Punta del hocico pardo oscura; prefrontales y labiales no contactan------melanocephala

Tantilla melanocephala melanocephala (Linnaeus)

1887 Tantilla pallida Cope, Proc. Amer. Phil. Soc., 24: 56. Type-locality: Mato Grosso, Brazil.
1895 [Homalocranium melanocephalum] var. pernambucense Günther, Biol. Centr. Amer., Reptiles:
     148. Type-locality: Pernambuco, Brazil.
1909 Homalocranium hoffmanni Werner, Mitt. Nat. Hist. Mus. Hamburg, 26: 239. Type-locality:
     Guatemala.
1914 Elapomorphus nuchalis Barbour, Proc. Biol. Soc. Washington, 27: 199. Type-locality: Villa Bella,
     Estado do Pará, Brazil.
1943 Tantilla melanocephala melanocephala—Schmidt and Walker, Zool. Ser. Field Mus. Nat. Hist.,
     24: 318.

   Distribution: Central America throughout South America east of Andes, including northern
   Argentina and Uruguay.

Tantilla melanocephala capistrata Cope

1876 Tantilla capistrata Cope, Jour. Acad. Nat. Sci. Phila., (2) 8 (1875): 181. Type-
     locality: Valley of Jequetepeque (Libertad), Peru.
1943 Tantilla melanocephala capistrata—Schmidt and Walker, Zool. Ser. Field Mus. Nat. Hist.,
     24: 318.

   Distribution: Northern coastal Peru to arid valley of Río Marañón; Catamayo and Malacatos
   Valleys in southern Ecuador.

TANTILLA MEXICANA (Günther)

1862 Elapomorphus mexicana Günther, Ann. Mag. Nat. Hist., (3) 9: 57, pl. 9, fig. 1. Type-locality: Mexico.
1883 [Homalocranion melanocephalum] var. fuscum Bocourt, Miss. Sci. Mex., Rept.: 589. Type-locality: Guatemala.
1942 Tantilla mexicana—Smith, Zoologica, 27: 37.

Distribution: Moderate elevations on Pacific slope from Chiapas, Mexico, to Guatemala.

TANTILLA MOESTA (Günther)

1863 Homalocranium moestum Günther, Ann. Mag. Nat. Hist., (3) 12: 352. Type-locality: El Petén, Guatemala.
1866 Tantilla moesta—Cope, Proc. Acad. Nat. Sci. Phila., 1866: 126.

Distribution: Lowlands of Yucatán Peninsula south to central El Petén, Guatemala.

TANTILLA NIGRA (Boulenger)

1914 Homalocranium nigrum Boulenger, Proc. Zool. Soc. London, 1914: 816, pl. 2, figs. 2-2a. Type-locality: Chocó of Colombia.
1929 Tantilla nigra—Amaral, Mem. Inst. Butantan, 4: 221.

Distribution: Chocó of Colombia.

TANTILLA RETICULATA Cope

1860 T[antilla] reticulata Cope, Proc. Acad. Nat. Sci. Phila., 1860: 77. Type-locality: Cocuyas de Veragua, "New Grenada".

Distribution: Costa Rica; Instituto Butantan has one specimen identified as this species from Río San Juan, Colombia.

TANTILLA RUFICEPS (Cope)

1894 Pogonaspis ruficeps Cope, Proc. Acad. Nat. Sci. Phila., 1894: 204. Type-locality: Costa Rica.
1929 Tantilla ruficeps—Amaral, Mem. Inst. Butantan, 4: 221.

Distribution: Still known only from type specimen.

TANTILLA SCHISTOSA (Bocourt)

1883 Homalocranion schistosum Bocourt, Miss. Sci. Mex., Rept.: 584, pl. 36, figs. 10-10e. Type-locality: Alta Verapaz, Guatemala, and Mexico. Restricted to Alta Verapaz, Guatemala, by Smith, Zoologica, 27, 1942, 39.
1942 [Tantilla] schistosa—Smith, Zoologica, 27: 39.

Distribution: Mexico to Costa Rica.

Content: Four subspecies, one (phrenitica Smith) extralimital.

Key to the subspecies	Clave de subespecies

1. More than 121 ventrals--------------------2
   Fewer than 120 ventrals-------------taylori
	1. Más de 121 ventrales----------------------2
	   Menos de 120 ventrales-------------taylori

2. Males with fewer than 136 ventrals; ventrals plus caudals fewer than 169 in females----------------------------------schistosa
   Males with more than 137 ventrals; ventrals plus caudals more than 172 in females----------------------------------costaricensis
	2. Machos con menos de 136 ventrales; hembras menos de 169 ventrales totales (ventrales más caudals)--------------------schistosa
	   Machos con más de 137 ventrales; hembras con más de 172 ventrales totales (ventrales más caudals)---------costaricensis

Tantilla schistosa schistosa (Bocourt)

1962 Tantilla schistosa schistosa—Smith, Herpetologica, 18: 15.

Distribution: Moderate elevations from southern Veracruz, Mexico, to Panama.

Tantilla schistosa costaricensis Taylor

1954 Tantilla costaricensis Taylor, Univ. Kansas Sci. Bull., 36: 766, fig. 25a. Type-locality:
    Cervantes, Cartago Province, Costa Rica, 4200 ft.
1962 Tantilla schistosa costaricensis—Smith, Herpetologica, 18: 16.

Distribution: Known only from Cervantes and Cinchona, Costa Rica.

Tantilla schistosa taylori Smith

1962 Tantilla schistosa taylori Smith, Herpetologica, 18: 17. Type-locality: Suretka, Costa
    Rica.

Distribution: Known only from type locality.

TANTILLA SEMICINCTA (Duméril, Bibron and Duméril)

1854 Homalocranion semi-cinctum Duméril, Bibron and Duméril, Erp. Gén., 7: 862. Type-locality:
    Colombia.
1860 Tantilla laticeps Günther, Proc. Zool. Soc. London, 1860: 240. Type-locality: Cartagena,
    Colombia.
1861 [Tantilla] semicincta—Cope, Proc. Acad. Nat. Sci. Phila., 1861: 74.
1883 Homalocranion lineatum Fischer, Oster-Programm Akad. Gymn. Hamburg, 1883: 6, figs. 6-8.
    Type-locality: Maracaibo, Venezuela.

Distribution: Panama to Venezuela and Colombia.

TANTILLA SUPRACINCTA Peters

1863 Homalocranion supracinctum Peters, Monats. Akad. Wiss. Berlin, 1863: 272. Type-locality:
    Guayaquil, Ecuador.
1960 Tantilla supracincta—Peters, Bull. Mus. Comp. Zool., 122: 539.

Distribution: Ecuador, probably on coastal plain from Guayaquil northward.

TANTILLA TAENIATA (Bocourt)

1883 Homalocranion taeniatum Bocourt, Miss. Sci. Mex., Rept.: 587, pl. 37, figs. 3-3e. Type-locality:
    Guatemala.
1885 Homalocranium trivittatum Müller, Verh. Naturforsch. Ges. Basel, 7: 678. Type-locality:
    Guatemala.
1887 Tantilla taeniata—Cope, Bull. U.S. Nat. Mus., 32: 83.

Distribution: Known from Guatemala and Honduras.

TANTILLA TRILINEATA (Peters)

1880 Leptocalamus trilineatus Peters, Monats. Akad. Wiss. Berlin, 1880: 221, fig. 2. Type-locality:
    Brazil; in error, according to Smith and Williams, Southwestern Nat., 11, 1966, 485, who
    indicate it "presumably came actually from some locality in Central America or Mexico".
1929 Tantilla trilineata—Amaral, Mem. Inst. Butantan, 4: 222.

Distribution: Unknown.

TANTILLA TRITAENIATA Smith and Williams

1967 Tantilla tritaeniata Smith and Williams, Southwestern Nat., 11 (1966): 483. Type-locality: Bonacca Island, Bay Islands, Honduras.

   Distribution: Known only from type-locality.

TANTILLA VERMIFORMIS (Hallowell)

1860 Lioninia vermiformis Hallowell, Proc. Acad. Nat. Sci. Phila., 1860: 484. Type-locality: Nicaragua.
1861 [Tantilla] vermiformis—Cope, Proc. Acad. Nat. Sci. Phila., 1861: 74.

   Distribution: Nicaragua.

TANTILLA VIRGATA (Günther)

1873 Microdromus virgatus Günther, Ann. Mag. Nat. Hist., (4) 9: 17, pl. 4, fig. B. Type-locality: Near Cartago, Costa Rica.
1881 Homalocranium sexfasciatum Fischer, Abh. Naturwiss. Vereins Bremen, 7: 225, pl. 14, figs. 8-10. Type-locality: Costa Rica.
1887 Tantilla virgata—Cope, Bull. U.S. Nat. Mus., 32: 84.

   Distribution: Known from Cartago, Costa Rica only.

TANTILLITA Smith

1941 _Tantillita_ Smith, Jour. Wash. Acad. Sci., 31: 117. Type-species: _Tantilla lintoni_ Smith.

Distribution: As for only known species.

Content: One species.

TANTILLITA LINTONI (Smith)

1940 _Tantilla lintoni_ Smith, Proc. Biol. Soc. Wash., 53: 61, fig. 1. Type-locality: Piedras Negras, El Petén, Guatemala.
1941 _Tantillita lintoni_—Smith, Jour. Wash. Acad. Sci., 31: 117.

Distribution: Known only from type locality.

THAMNODYNASTES Wagler

1830 Thamnodynastes Wagler, Nat. Syst. Amphib., 182. Type-species: Natrix punctatissimus Wagler.
1830 Dryophylax Wagler, Nat. Syst. Amphib.: 181. Type-species: Coluber nattereri Mikan.
1863 Mesotes Jan, Arch. Zool. Anat. Fis., 2: 306 Type-species: Mesotes obtrusus Jan (by present restriction).

Distribution: Caribbean coast of South America to northern Argentina.

Content: Five species. Peters, Bull. Mus. Comp. Zool., 122, 1960, 539, erroneously used T. nattereri (Mikan) for a specimen catalogued from Guayaquil, Ecuador, which may represent an undescribed species.

Key to the species	Clave de especies
1. Dorsal scales in 17 rows----------------------2 Dorsal scales in 19 rows----------------------3	1. Escamas dorsales en 17 hileras----------------2 Escamas dorsales en 19 hileras----------------3
2. Ventrals 144-159; subcaudals 90-97-----pallidus Ventrals 125-129; subcaudals 56-58-----chimanta	2. Ventrales 144-159; subcaudales 90-97---pallidus Ventrales 125-129; subcaudales 56-58---chimanta
3. Ventrals more than 136-----------------------4 Ventrals fewer than 136-----------------rutilus	3. Ventrales más de 136------------------------4 Ventrales menos de 136-----------------rutilus
4. Dorsals keeled; supra-anal tubercles absent in males--------------------------------strigilis Dorsals smooth; supra-anal tubercles present in males--------------------------------strigatus	4. Dorsales quilladas; tubérculos supranales ausentes en los machos--------------strigilis Dorsales lisas; tubérculos supranales presentes en los machos-----------------------strigatus

THAMNODYNASTES CHIMANTA Roze

1958 Thamnodynastes chimanta Roze, Acta Biol. Venezuélica, 2 (25): 305. Type-locality: Chimantá Tepui, Estado Bolívar, Venezuela.

Distribution: Known only from type locality.

THAMNODYNASTES PALLIDUS Linnaeus

1758 Coluber pallidus Linnaeus, Systema Naturae, Ed. 10: 221. Type-locality: "Indiis".
1824 Natrix punctatissima Wagler, in Spix, Sp. Nov. Serp. Bras.: 39, pl. 14, fig. 1. Type-locality: Bahia, Brazil.
1899 Thamnodynastes pallidus—Andersson, Bihang till K. Svenska Vet.-Akad. Handlingar, 24: 17.

Distribution: Guianas; Brazil; Peru; Venezuela.

THAMNODYNASTES RUTILUS Prado

1942 Dryophylax rutilus Prado, Ciência, Mexico City, 3: 204, figs. 1-2. Type-locality: Gália, São Paulo, Brazil.
1943 Dryophylax rutilus Prado, Mem. Inst. Butantan, 17: 2, figs. Type-locality: Gália, São Paulo, Brazil.
1947 Dryophylax rutilus—Prado, Mem. Inst. Butantan, 20(1948): 189.
1948 Thamnodynastes rutilus—Vanzolini, Rev. Brasil. Biol., 8: 382.

Distribution: Estado de São Paulo, Brazil.

THAMNODYNASTES STRIGATUS (Günther)

1858 Tomodon strigatus Günther, Cat. Sn. Brit. Mus.: 52. Type-locality: "India".
1863 M.[esotes] obtrusus Jan, Arch. Zool. Anat. Fis., 2: 306. Type-locality: La Plata, Argentina.
1953 Thamnodynastes strigatus—Hoge, Mem. Inst. Butantan, 24 (1952): 157, figs. 1-4, 6-13.

Distribution: Provincia Buenos Aires, Entre Rios, Corrientes, and Misiones, Argentina; Paraguay; southern and southeastern Brazil.

THAMNODYNASTES STRIGILIS (Thunberg)

1787 [Coluber] Strigilis Thunberg, Mus. Nat. Acad. Upsaliensis, Pt. 2: 22. Type-locality: None given.
1825 Coluber lineolatus Wied, Beitr. Naturg. Brasil, 1: 284. Type-locality: None given.
1828 Coluber nattereri Mikan, Delect. Faun. Flor. Braz.: fig. 1. Type-locality: "Lectus prope Sebastiano polim".
1860 T.[achymenis] hypoconia Cope, Proc. Acad. Nat. Sci. Phila., 1860: 247. Type-locality: Buenos Aires, Argentina.
1885 Thamnodynastes Nattereri var. laevis Boulenger, Ann. Mag. Nat. Hist., (5) 15: 195. Type-locality: Rio Grande do Sul, Brazil.
1896 Thamnodynastes strigilis—Lonnberg, Bihang till K. Svenska Vet.-Akad. Handlingar, 22 (4): 38.

Distribution: Colombia, Venezuela, Guyana, Brazil, to Uruguay, Paraguay and Argentina.

REPTILIA: SERPENTES: COLUBRIDAE ★ ★ ★ ★ THAMNOPHIS

Prepared by Douglas A. Rossman, Museum of Zoology, Louisiana State University, Baton Rouge, Louisiana

THAMNOPHIS Fitzinger

1843 *Thamnophis* Fitzinger, Systema Reptilium: 26. Type-species: *Coluber saurita* Linnaeus.
1853 *Eutainia* Baird and Girard, Cat. North Amer. Reptiles: 24. Type-species: None designated; first of 15 forms listed is *Coluber saurita* Linnaeus.
1859 *Eutaenia* Kennicott (substitute name for *Eutainia* Baird and Girard, preoccupied by *Eutaenia* Thompson, 1857), Proc. Acad. Nat. Sci. Phila., 1859: 98.
1861 *Prymnomiodon* Cope, Proc. Acad. Nat. Sci. Phila., 1860: 558. Type-species: *Prymnomiodon chalceus* Cope.
1875 *Chilopoma* Cope, in Yarrow, Wheeler's Rept. Explor. Surv. W. 100th Mer., 5: 543. Type-species: *Chilopoma rufopunctatum* Cope.
1883 *Atomarchus* Cope, Amer. Nat.: 1300. Type-species: *Atomarchus multimaculatus* Cope.
1885 *Stypocemus* Cope (substitute name for *Chilopoma* Cope, preoccupied by *Cheilopoma* Murray, 1867), Proc. Amer. Phil. Soc., 22: 387.

Distribution: Central Canada throughout North America to central Costa Rica.

Content: Twenty-two species, 19 of which are extralimital.

Key to the species

1. Vertical black markings border some supralabial sutures---------------------------------------2
   Supralabials without black markings----proximus

2. Belly with two rows of black spots, often interconnected; lateral stripe, when present, confined to row three on anterior part of body--------------------------------marcianus
   Belly unspotted; lateral stripe on rows two and three anteriorly--------------------cyrtopsis

Clave de especies

1. Marcas negras verticales bordean a algunas suturas labiales----------------------------2
   Supralabiales sin marcas negras--------proximus

2. Vientre con dos hileras de manchas negras, a menudo interconectadas; cinta lateral, cuando presente, confinada a la hilera tercera en parte anterior del cuerpo------------marcianus
   Vientre sin manchas; cinta lateral en hileras segunda y tercera anteriormente------cyrtopsis

THAMNOPHIS CYRTOPSIS (Kennicott)

1860 *E.*[utaenia] *cyrtopsis* Kennicott, Proc. Acad. Nat. Sci. Phila., 1860: 333. Type-locality: Rinconada, Coahuila, Mexico.
1861 *Thamnophis cyrtopsis*—Cope, Proc. Acad. Nat. Sci. Phila., 1861: 299.
1953 *Thamnophis cyrtopsis*—Milstead, Texas Jour. Sci., 5: 348.

Distribution: Southwestern United States throughout Mexico, exclusive of eastern lowlands, to western Honduras.

Content: Six subspecies, five of which are extralimital.

Thamnophis cyrtopsis fulvus (Bocourt)

1893 *Eutaenia cyrtopsis* var. *fulvus* Bocourt, Miss. Sci. Mex., Rept.: 777. Type-locality: Alta Verapaz, Guatemala.
1942 *Thamnophis sumichrasti cerebrosus* Smith, Zoologica, 27: 111. Type-locality: Escuintla, Guatemala.
1950 *Thamnophis sumichrasti salvini* Smith, Nixon and Smith, Linn. Soc. Jour. Zool., 41: 579. Type-locality: Río Chixoy, below town of Cubules (?Cubilguitz), Guatemala.
1965 *T.*[hamnophis] *c.*[yrtopsis] *fulvus*—Rossman, Copeia, 1965: 243.

Distribution: Upland areas, Chiapas, Mexico to western Honduras.

THAMNOPHIS MARCIANUS (Baird and Girard)

1853 *Eutainia Marciana* Baird and Girard, Cat. North Amer. Reptiles: 36. Type-locality: Red River, Arkansas; restricted to vicinity of Slough Creek, east of Hollister, Tillman County, Oklahoma, by Mittleman, Bull. Chicago Acad. Sci., 8, 1949, 243.
1907 *Thamnophis marciana*—Ruthven, Bull. Amer. Mus. Nat. Hist., 23: 589.
1949 *Thamnophis marcianus*—Mittleman, Bull. Chicago Acad. Sci., 8: 235.

Distribution: Southwestern United States and northern Mexico; Isthmus of Tehuantepec, Mexico, to northern Costa Rica.

Content: Three subspecies, one of which is extralimital, according to revision currently in press by author.

<table>
<tr><td>

Key to the subspecies

1. Vertebral stripe present, broad; black
   ventral spots small and separate----------
   ------------------------------praeocularis
   Vertebral stripe absent; black ventral
   spots large and often interconnected
   across venter--------------------bovallii

</td><td>

Clave de subespecies

1. Con cinta vertebral ancha; manchas ven-
   trales negras chicas y separadas----------
   ------------------------------praeocularis
   Sin cinta vertebral; manchas ventrales
   negras grandes y a menudo interconectadas
   a través del vientre-------------bovallii

</td></tr>
</table>

Thamnophis marcianus bovallii Dunn, new combination

　1940 Thamnophis bovallii Dunn, Herpetologica, 1: 191. Type-locality: Granada, Nicaragua.

　　Distribution: Lakes Managua and Nicaragua, Nicaragua, to northern Costa Rica.

Thamnophis marcianus praeocularis (Bocourt), new combination

　1892 Eutaenia praeocularis Bocourt, Le Naturaliste, (2) 14: 278. Type-locality: Belize,
　　　British Honduras.
　1937 Thamnophis arabdotus Andrews, Zool. Ser. Field Mus. Nat. Hist., 20: 357. Type-locality:
　　　Catmis, Quintana Roo, Mexico.
　1940 T.[hamnophis] praeocularis—Dunn, Herpetologica, 1: 191.
　1942 Thamnophis sumichrasti praeocularis—Smith, Zoologica, 27: 99.
　1945 Thamnophis eques praeocularis—Bogert and Oliver, Bull. Amer. Mus. Nat. Hist., 83: 385.

　　Distribution: Quintana Roo, Mexico, coastal British Honduras, and Lake Yojoa, Honduras.

THAMNOPHIS PROXIMUS (Say)

　1823 Coluber proximus Say, in James, Exped. Pittsburgh to Rocky Mts., 1: 339. Type-locality: Approxi-
　　　mately 3 mi east northeast of Fort Calhoun, Washington Co., Nebraska, according to Rossman,
　　　Bull. Florida St. Mus., 7: 109.
　1892 Thamnophis proxima—Garman, Bull. Essex Inst., 24: 105.
　1963 Thamnophis proximus—Rossman, Bull. Florida St. Mus., 7: 109.

　Distribution: Central United States through eastern Mexico to central Costa Rica.

　Content: Six subspecies, five of which are extralimital.

Thamnophis proximus rutiloris (Cope)

　1885 Eutaenia rutiloris Cope, Proc. Amer. Phil. Soc., 22: 388. Type-locality: Cozumel Island,
　　　Quintana Roo, Mexico.
　1938 Thamnophis sauritus rutiloris—Smith, Occ. Pap. Mus. Zool. Univ. Mich., 388: 5.
　1963 Thamnophis proximus rutiloris—Rossman, Bull. Florida St. Mus., 7: 138.

　　Distribution: Southern Tamaulipas, Mexico, to central Costa Rica, from sea level to 8000 ft;
　　occurs in Pacific lowlands only from vicinity of Acapulco, Guerrero, Mexico, south to
　　Isthmus of Tehuantepec; no records from highlands of Guatemala.

TOMODON Duméril and Bibron

    1853 _Tomodon_ Duméril and Bibron, Mém. Acad. Sci. Paris, 23: 495. Type-species: _Tomodon dorsatum_
        Duméril, Bibron and Duméril (name appears as nomen nudum, species described one year later in
        Erp. Gén.).

    Distribution: From central Brazil to Paraguay, Uruguay and north central Argentina.

    Content: Two species.

Key to the species	Clave de especies
1. Loreal present; two dorsal series of large, dark brown, black bordered, roundish spots---- --------------------------------------_ocellatus_ No loreal; small blackish spots present or not on back------------------------------_dorsatus_	1. Loreal presente; dos series de manchas dorsales pardo oscuras, grandes bordeadas de negro----- --------------------------------------_ocellatus_ Sin loreal; pequeños puntos negros presentes o no sobre el dorso--------------------_dorsatus_

TOMODON DORSATUS Duméril, Bibron and Duméril

    1854 _Tomodon dorsatum_ Duméril, Bibron and Duméril, Erp. Gén., 7: 934. Type-locality: Brazil?,
        America.
    1896 _Tomodon dorsatus_—Boulenger, Cat. Sn. Brit. Mus., 3: 121.

    Distribution: Central and southeastern Brazil, northern Argentina.

TOMODON OCELLATUS Duméril, Bibron and Duméril

    1854 _Tomodon ocellatum_ Duméril, Bibron and Duméril, Erp. Gén., 7: 938. Type-locality: Brazil.
    1896 _Tomodon ocellatus_—Boulenger, Cat. Sn. Brit. Mus., 3: 121.

    Distribution: Southern Brazil, Paraguay, Uruguay and Argentina.

TRACHYBOA Peters

1860 Trachyboa Peters, Monats. Akad. Wiss. Berlin, 1860: 200. Type-species: Trachyboa gularis
     Peters.

   Distribution: Panama; Pacific Colombia and Ecuador; possibly Brazil.

   Content: Two species.

                Key to the species   Clave de especies

1. Top of head without horns--------------gularis   1. Parte superior de la cabeza sin protu-
   Top of head, canthus rostralis, with horns-----   berancias----------------------------gularis
   --------------------------------boulengeri   Parte superior de la cabeza, canthus rostralis,
                                                           con protuberancias-----------------boulengeri

TRACHYBOA BOULENGERI Peracca

1910 Trachyboa boulengeri Peracca, Ann. Mus. Zool. Univ. Napoli, 3 (12): 1. Type-locality: unknown.

   Distribution: Rainforests of Pacific Ecuador and Colombia; Panama.

TRACHYBOA GULARIS Peters

1860 Trachyboa gularis Peters, Monats. Akad. Wiss. Berlin, 1860: 200. Type-locality: Guayaquil,
     Ecuador.
1905 Trachyboa gularis multimaculata Rosen, Ann. Mag. Nat. Hist. (7) 15: 169. Type-locality: Balao,
     Ecuador.

   Distribution: Dry parts of western coastal Ecuador (Brazil?).

TRETANORHINUS Duméril, Bibron and Duméril

1854 _Tretanorhinus_ Duméril, Bibron and Duméril, Erp. Gén., 7: 348. Type-species: _Tretanorhinus_
variabilis Duméril, Bibron and Duméril.

Distribution: Extreme southern Mexico to Colombia and Ecuador; Cuba, Isla Pinos and Caymans in
the Antilles.

Content: Four species, one extralimital (_variabilis_, which includes four subspecies, _wagleri_ (Jan),
insulaepinorum Barbour, _adnexus_ Bocourt and _variabilis_ Duméril, Bibron and Duméril, in the
Antilles).

<table>
<tr><td>

Key to the species

1. Three longitudinal stripes dorsally; ventrals
166 or more---------------------------------2
Two rows of alternating small dots dorsally
(very rarely a single row of large dots);
ventrals 151 or fewer--------------_nigroluteus_

2. Dorsal scales in 21 rows; three prefrontals;
subcaudals 74-81 in females, unknown in
males------------------------------_taeniatus_
Dorsal scales in 19 rows; one prefrontal
(rarely two); subcaudals 69-74 in females,
78-85 in males---------------------_mocquardi_

</td><td>

Clave de especies

1. Diseño dorsal de tres líneas longitudinales;
ventrales 166 o más--------------------------2
Diseño dorsal de dos filas de pequeños puntos
alternados (muy raro una única fila de puntos
grandes); ventrales 151 o menos----_nigroluteus_

2. Escamas en 21 filas; tres prefrontales; sub-
caudales en hembras 74-81, desconocido en
machos-----------------------------_taeniatus_
Escamas en 19 filas; una prefrontal (raramente
dos); subcaudales en hembras 69-74, en
machos 78-85-----------------------_mocquardi_

</td></tr>
</table>

TRETANORHINUS NIGROLUTEUS Cope

1861 _Tretanorhinus nigroluteus_ Cope, Proc. Acad. Nat. Sci. Phila., 1861: 298. Type-locality: Greytown, Nicaragua (in error, actually Aspinwall, Panama, according to USNM Catalogue).

Distribution: From Tabasco, Mexico, through Guatemala and Honduras to Panama and Costa Rica.

Content: Three subspecies.

<table>
<tr><td>

Key to the subspecies

1. First and second scale rows dark in color;
one loreal on each side-------------------2
First and second scale rows light in color;
generally two loreals on each side---------
--------------------------------_nigroluteus_

2. Three preoculars------------------_lateralis_
Two preoculars---------------------_mertensi_

</td><td>

Clave de subspecies

1. Primera y segunda fila de escamas de color
oscuro; sólo una loreal a cada lado-------2
Primera y segunda fila de escamas de color
claro; generalmente dos loreales a cada
lado-----------------------------_nigroluteus_

2. Tres preoculares------------------_lateralis_
Dos preoculares--------------------_mertensi_

</td></tr>
</table>

Tretanorhinus nigroluteus nigroluteus Cope

1865 _Helicops Agassizi_ Jan, Arch. Zool. Anat. Fisiol., 3: 248. Type-locality: San Juan del
Norte, Nicaragua.
1884 _Helicops bifrenatus_ Bocourt, Bull. Soc. Philom., (7) 8: 134. Type-locality: Colon
(Aspinweld), Panama.
1905 _Tretanorhinus intermedius_ Rosén, Ann. Mag. Nat. Hist., (7) 15: 171, pl. 12, fig. 2. Type-
locality: Central America.
1939 _Tretanorhinus nigroluteus nigroluteus_—Dunn, Copeia, 1939: 216.

Distribution: Low elevations of Caribbean slope from Panama and Costa Rica to extreme
eastern Guatemala.

Tretanorhinus nigroluteus lateralis Bocourt

1891 _Tretanorhinus lateralis_ Bocourt, Le Naturaliste, (2) 101: 122. Type-locality: Belize,
British Honduras.
1939 _Tretanorhinus nigroluteus lateralis_—Dunn, Copeia, 1939: 216.

Distribution: At present definitely known only from British Honduras; probably also elsewhere
on Yucatán Peninsula.

Tretanorhinus nigroluteus mertensi Smith and Gillespie

   1965 Tretanorhinus nigroluteus mertensi Smith and Gillespie, in Smith, Jour. Ohio Herp. Soc.,
       5: 1. Type-locality: north edge of Lake Catemaco, 5 km east of Catemaco, Veracruz,
       Mexico.

    Distribution: Southern Veracruz south and east through El Petén, Guatemala.

TRETANORHINUS MOCQUARDI Bocourt

   1891 Tretanorhinus Mocquardi Bocourt, Le Naturaliste, (2) 101: 122. Type-locality: "á Panamá";
       which is Panama City, according to Dunn, Copeia, 1939, 214.

    Distribution: Panama.

TRETANORHINUS TAENIATUS Boulenger

   1903 Tretanorhinus taeniatus Boulenger, Ann. Mag. Nat. Hist., (7) 12: 350. Type-locality: Río
       Sapayo, northwestern Ecuador, 450 ft.

    Distribution: Pacific lowlands in Colombia and Ecuador.

TRIMETOPON Cope

1885 _Trimetopon_ Cope, Proc. Amer. Phil. Soc., 22: 177. Type-species: _Ablabes gracilis_ Günther.

Distribution: Guatemala to Panama.

Content: Ten species.

Key to the species

1. Prefrontals fused------------------------------2
   Prefrontals separate, paired-----------------4

2. Dorsal scales in 15 rows----------------------3
   Dorsal scales in 17 rows-------------_pliolepis_

3. Two postoculars; ventrals fewer than 130-_simile_
   One postocular; ventrals more than 135--_gracile_

4. Dorsal scales in 17 rows----------------------5
   Dorsal scales in 15 rows--------------_barbouri_

5. Seven upper labials---------------------------6
   Eight upper labials---------------------------8

6. Two postoculars; fewer than 80 subcaudals-----7
   One postocular; more than 80 subcaudals-------
   ---_posadasi_

7. Fewer than 40 subcaudals----------------_viquezi_
   More than 45 subcaudals-----------------_slevini_

8. One postocular-------------------------------9
   Two postoculars--------------------_veraepacis_

9. More than 160 ventrals--------------_pilonaorum_
   Fewer than 160 ventrals------------_hannsteini_

Clave de especies

1. Prefrontales fusionados-----------------------2
   Prefrontales separados, en pares--------------4

2. Escamas dorsales en 15 hileras----------------3
   Escamas dorsales en 17 hileras-------_pliolepis_

3. Dos postoculares; menos de 130 ventrales-_simile_
   Un postocular; más de 135 ventrales-----_gracile_

4. Escamas dorsales en 17 hileras----------------5
   Escamas dorsales en 15 hileras---------_barbouri_

5. Siete labiales superiores---------------------6
   Ocho labiales superiores----------------------8

6. Dos postoculares; menos de 80 subcaudales-----7
   Un postocular; más de 80 subcaudales----------
   ---_posadasi_

7. Menos de 40 subcaudales-----------------_viquezi_
   Más de 45 subcaudales-------------------_slevini_

8. Un postocular--------------------------------9
   Dos postoculares-------------------_veraepacis_

9. Más de 160 ventrales----------------_pilonaorum_
   Menos de 160 ventrales-------------_hannsteini_

TRIMETOPON BARBOURI Dunn

1930 _Trimetopon barbouri_ Dunn, Occ. Pap. Boston Soc. Nat. Hist., 5: 331. Type-locality: Pedro Miguel, Canal Zone, Panama.

Distribution: Known from Ancon and Barro Colorado Island, Canal Zone, Panama, as well as from type locality.

TRIMETOPON GRACILE (Günther)

1872 _Ablabes gracilis_ Günther, Ann. Mag. Nat. Hist., (4) 9: 18, pl. 3, fig. D. Type-locality: Near Cartago, Costa Rica.
1885 _Trimetopon gracile_—Cope, Proc. Amer. Phil. Soc., 22: 177.

Distribution: Costa Rica.

TRIMETOPON HANNSTEINI Stuart

1949 _Trimetopon hannsteini_ Stuart, Proc. Biol. Soc. Washington, 62: 165. Type-locality: Finca La Paz, 18 km north of Coatepeque, Departamento San Marcos, Guatemala; 1450 m.

Distribution: Moderate elevations along Pacific slope of western Guatemala and Chiapas, Mexico.

TRIMETOPON PILONAORUM Stuart

1954 *Trimetopon pilonaorum* Stuart, Proc. Biol. Soc. Washington, 67: 176. Type-locality: Finca La
Gloria, about 12 km northeast of Chiquimulilla, Departamento Santa Rosa, Guatemala; about 950 m.

Distribution: Known only from type locality.

TRIMETOPON PLIOLEPIS Cope

1894 *Trimetopon pliolepis* Cope, Proc. Acad. Nat. Sci. Phila., 1894: 201. Type-locality: San José,
Costa Rica.

Distribution: Costa Rica.

TRIMETOPON POSADASI Slevin

1936 *Trimetopon posadasi* Slevin, Proc. Calif. Acad. Sci., 23: 79. Type-locality: Southern slope of
Volcán Zunil, Suchitepequez, Guatemala.

Distribution: Known only from immediate vicinity of type locality.

TRIMETOPON SIMILE Dunn

1930 *Trimetopon simile* Dunn, Occ. Pap. Boston Soc. Nat. Hist., 5: 331. Type-locality: Reventazón,
Costa Rica; said by Dunn to be same as La Junta; Taylor, Univ. Kansas Sci. Bull., 34, 1951, 79,
said it is Siquirres.

Distribution: Known only from type locality.

TRIMETOPON SLEVINI Dunn

1940 *Trimetopon slevini* Dunn, Proc. Acad. Nat. Sci. Phila., 92: 117. Type-locality: Near Boquete,
Provincia Chiriquí, Panama, 4000 ft.

Distribution: Known only from type locality.

TRIMETOPON VERAEPACIS (Stuart and Bailey)

1941 *Rhadinaea veraepacis* Stuart and Bailey, Occ. Pap. Mus. Zool., Univ. Mich., 442: 9. Type-locality:
Pine zone at Finca Chichén, Alta Verapaz, Guatemala, 5100 ft.
1949 *Trimetopon veraepacis*—Stuart, Proc. Biol. Soc. Washington, 62: 167.

Distribution: Known only from type locality.

TRIMETOPON VIQUEZI Dunn

1937 *Trimetopon viquezi* Dunn, Copeia, 1937: 215. Type-locality: Siquirres, Costa Rica.

Distribution: Known only from type locality.

TRIMORPHODON Cope

1861 _Trimorphodon_ Cope, Proc. Acad. Nat. Sci. Phila., 1861: 297. Type-species: <u>Lycodon</u> <u>lyrophanes</u>
         Cope.
1863 _Eteirodipsas_ Jan, Elenco Sist. Ofidi: 105. Type-species: Not indicated.
1901 _Hetaerodipsas_ Berg (emendation of <u>Eteirodipsas</u> Jan), Comun. Mus. Buenos Aires, 1: 290.

   Distribution: Southwestern United States through Central America to Costa Rica.

   Content: Eleven species, all but one of which are extralimital.

TRIMORPHODON <u>BISCUTATUS</u> (Duméril and Bibron)

1854 <u>Dipsas</u> <u>bi-scutata</u> Duméril and Bibron, Erp. Gén., 7: 1153. Type-locality: "Mexico".
1861 _Trimorphodon_ _biscutatus_—Cope, Proc. Acad. Nat. Sci. Phila., 1861: 297.

   Distribution: Pacific slope from Colima, Mexico, to Costa Rica.

   Content: Two subspecies, one of which (<u>biscutatus</u> Duméril and Bibron) is extralimital.

   Trimorphodon biscutatus quadruplex Smith

     1941 _Trimorphodon_ <u>biscutatus</u> <u>quadruplex</u> Smith, Proc. U.S. Nat. Mus., 91: 157. Type-locality:
             Esteli, Nicaragua.

       Distribution: Low and moderate elevations of Pacific slope, Guatemala to Costa Rica.

REPTILIA: SERPENTES: COLUBRIDAE   ★ ★ ★ ★   TRIPANURGOS

Prepared by Joseph R. Bailey, Duke University, Durham, North Carolina

TRIPANURGOS Fitzinger

     1843 Tripanurgos Fitzinger, Systema Reptilium: 27. Type-species: Given as Dipsas leucocephala
         Schlegel, which is same as Coluber leucocephalus Mikan.

    Distribution: As for single known species.

    Content: One species.

    Comment: Tropidodipsas leucomelas Werner, recently recognized as Tripanurgos leucomelas by Downs,
     Copeia, 1961, 386, is a member of the genus Oxyrhopus.

TRIPANURGOS COMPRESSUS (Daudin)

     1803 Coluber compressus Daudin, Hist. Nat. Rept., 6: 247. Type-locality: Surinam.
     1820 Coluber leucocephalus Mikan, Delect. Fauna Flora Brasil: fig. 2 on unnumbered pl. Type-locality:
         Corcovado Mountain, Rio de Janeiro, Brazil.
     1896 Trypanurgos compressus—Boulenger, Cat. Sn. Brit. Mus., 3: 58.

    Distribution: Discontinuous. Coastal strip of Brazil from Rio de Janeiro (city) to Sergipe.
     Mouth of Amazon and central Bolivia to Trinidad and Panama.

TROPIDODIPSAS Günther

1858 *Tropidodipsas* Günther, Cat. Sn. Brit. Mus.: 180. Type-species: *Tropidodipsas fasciata* Günther.
1863 *Galedon* Jan, Elenco Sist. Ofidi: 95. Type-species: *Galedon annularis* Jan.
1878 *Tropidogeophis* Müller, Verh. Naturforsch. Ges. Basel, 6: 411. Type-species: *Geophis annulatus* Peters.
1887 *Dipeltophis* Cope, Bull. U.S. Nat. Mus., 32: 91. Type-species: *Leptognathus albocinctus* Fischer.

Distribution: Mexico and Central America.

Content: About ten species, of which only three are found within limits of this work.

<table>
<tr><td colspan="2">Key to the species</td><td colspan="2">Clave de especies</td></tr>
<tr><td>1. Infralabials usually eight or more------------2
Infralabials normally seven------------*fasciata*</td><td></td><td>1. Normalmente ocho o más infralabiales---------2
Normalmente siete infralabiales-------*fasciata*</td><td></td></tr>
<tr><td>2. Dark annuli on body fewer than 25------*sartorii*
Dark annuli on body more than 25-------*fischeri*</td><td></td><td>2. Menos de 25 anillos oscuros en el cuerpo------
--*sartorii*
Más de 25 anillos oscuros en el cuerpo-*fischeri*</td><td></td></tr>
</table>

TROPIDODIPSAS FASCIATA Günther

1858 *Tropidodipsas fasciata* Günther, Cat. Sn. Brit. Mus.: 181. Type-locality: Mexico; restricted to Chichén Itzá, Yucatán, by Smith and Taylor, Univ. Kansas Sci. Bull., 33, 1950, 352.

Distribution: Guerrero on west and possibly Veracruz on east in Mexico to Alta Verapaz, Guatemala.

Content: Three subspecies, of which two (*fasciata* Günther and *guerreroensis* Taylor) are extralimital.

Tropidodipsas fasciata subannulata (Müller)

1887 *Leptognathus* (*Tropidodipsas*) *subannulatus* Müller, Ver. Nat. Ges. Basel, 8: 274, pl. 1, fig. 5. Type-locality: probably Mexico; restricted to Chichén Itzá, Yucatán, by Smith and Taylor, Univ. Kansas Sci. Bull., 33, 1950, 352; restriction rejected by Lynch and Smith, Trans. Kansas Acad. Sci., 69, 1966, 72.
1942 *Tropidodipsas kidderi* Stuart, Proc. Biol. Soc. Washington, 55: 177. Type-locality: Finca Samac, 6 km west of Cobán, Alta Verapaz, Guatemala, about 1500 m.
1956 *Tropidodipsas fasciata subannulata*—Álvarez del Toro and Smith, Herpetologica, 12: 14.
1966 *T.*[*ropidodipsas*] *fasciata subannulata*—Lynch and Smith, Trans. Kansas Acad. Sci., 69: 72.

Distribution: Upper elevations on Atlantic slope from southwestern Chiapas and southeastern Oaxaca, Mexico, to Alta Verapaz, Guatemala.

TROPIDODIPSAS FISCHERI Boulenger

1885 *Virginia fasciata* Fischer, Jahrb. Wiss. Anst. Hamburg, 2 (1884): 95. Type-locality: Guatemala.
1892 *Tropidoclonium annulatum* Bocourt (preoccupied in *Tropidodipsas* by *annulatus* Peters, 1870), Le Naturaliste, (2) 14: 132. Type-locality: Godinez, northeastern slope of Volcán Atitlan, Guatemala, 2151 m.
1894 *Tropidodipsas fischeri* Boulenger (substitute name for *Virginia fasciata* Fischer, preoccupied in *Tropidodipsas*), Cat. Sn. Brit. Mus., 2: 296.

Distribution: Intermediate elevations on plateau of Sierra de los Cuchumatanes, southwestern Guatemala, to Oaxaca, Mexico.

TROPIDODIPSAS SARTORII

1863 *Tropidodipsas sartorii* Cope, Proc. Acad. Nat. Sci. Phila., 1863: 100. Type-locality: Mirador, Veracruz, Mexico.

Distribution: San Luis Potosi and Chiapas, Mexico to Guatemala, on both slopes.

Content: Three subspecies, one of which (*macdougalli* Smith) is extralimital.

Key to the subspecies	Clave de subespecies
1. Light bands, including nuchal collar, yellow in life; bands very regular, all complete' on body and tail--------annulatus Light bands, red or orange, only nuchal collar yellow in life; bands variable, usually at least some incomplete on ventral surface----------------------sartorii	1. Bandas claras, incluyendo el collar nucal, amarillas en vida; bandas muy regulares, todas completas en cuerpo y cola-annulatus Bandas claras, rojas o naranjas, sólo el collar nucal amarillo en vida; bandas variables, generalmente al menos algunas incompletas en la superficie ventral------ -----------------------------------sartorii

Tropidodipsas sartorii sartorii Cope

1863 L.[eptognathus] Dumerili Jan, Elenco Sist. Ofidi: 101. Type-locality: Mexico.
1870 Galedon annularis Jan, Icon. Gén. Ophid., Livr. 36, pl. 5, fig. 1. Type-locality: Unknown.
1884 Leptognatus leucostomus Bocourt, Bull. Soc. Philom. Paris, (7) 8: 138. Type-locality: Yucatán.
1884 Leptognathus semicinctus Bocourt, Bull. Soc. Philom. Paris, (7) 8: 139. Type-locality: Alta Verapaz, Guatemala.
1887 Leptognathus (Tropidodipsas) cuculliceps Müller, Verh. Naturforsch. Ges. Basel, 8: 273, pl. 1, fig. 4. Type-locality: Verapaz, Guatemala.
1943 Tropidodipsas sartorii sartorii—Smith, Proc. U.S. Nat. Mus., 93: 494.

Distribution: Low and moderate elevations of Caribbean slope from San Luis Potosi, Mexico, south to Guatemala.

Tropidodipsas sartorii annulatus (Peters)

1870 Geophis annulatus Peters, Monats. Akad. Wiss. Berlin, 1870: 643, pl. 1, figs. 2-2c. Type-locality: "Probably South America"; in error.
1874 Leptognathus sexscutatus Bocourt, Bull. Soc. Philom. Paris, (7) 8: 137. Type-locality: Atitlan, Guatemala.
1887 Leptognathus (Tropidodipsas) Bernoullii Müller, Verh. Naturforsch. Ges. Basel, 8: 272, pl. 1, fig. 3. Type-locality: Chitalon, Guatemala.
1943 Tropidodipsas sartorii annulatus—Smith, Proc. U.S. Nat. Mus., 93: 495.

Distribution: Low and moderate elevations of Pacific slope of Chiapas, Mexico, and Guatemala.

<u>TROPIDOPHIS</u> Bibron

1840 <u>Tropidophis</u> Bibron, in de la Sagra, Hist. Fis. Pol. Nat. Cuba, Spanish Ed., 8: pl. 23, also vol.
    4, 1843: 125. Type-species: <u>Boa melanura</u> Schlegel.
1840 <u>Leionotus</u> Bibron, in de la Sagra, Hist. Fis. Pol. Nat. Cuba, Spanish Ed., 8: pl. 24, also vol.
    4, 1843: 125. Type-species: <u>Leionotus maculatus</u> Bibron.
1842 <u>Ungalia</u> Gray, Zool. Misc., 1842: 46. Type-species: <u>Boa melanura</u> Schlegel.
1843 <u>Erycopsis</u> Fitzinger, Systema Reptilium: 27. Type-species: <u>Boa melanura</u> Schlegel.
1856 <u>Nothophis</u> Hallowell, Proc. Acad. Nat. Sci. Phila., 1856: 156. Type-species: <u>Nothophis bicarinatus</u>
    Hallowell.
1868 <u>Ungualia</u> Cope (invalid emendation of <u>Ungalia</u> Gray), Proc. Acad. Nat. Sci. Phila., 1868: 128.

    Distribution: West Indies; Ecuador, Peru, and Brazil.

    Content: Fifteen species, all but three of which are extralimital, according to latest summary
    by Stimson, Das Tierreich, 89, 1969, 32.

Key to the species	Clave de especies

1. Dorsal scales smooth------------------------2
   Dorsal scales keeled--------------<u>taczanowskyi</u>
	1. Escamas dorsales lisas------------------------2
	   Escamas dorsales carenadas---------<u>taczanowskyi</u>

2. Scale rows at midbody 23; ventrals 200---------
   -----------------------------------<u>battersbyi</u>
   Scale rows at midbody 21; ventrals 178---------
   -----------------------------------<u>paucisquamis</u>
	2. Escamas al medio del cuerpo en 23 filas; ven-
	   trales 200--------------------------<u>battersbyi</u>
	   Escamas al medio del cuerpo en 21 filas; ven-
	   trales 178--------------------------<u>paucisquamis</u>

<u>TROPIDOPHIS</u> <u>BATTERSBYI</u> Laurent

    1949 <u>Tropidophis battersbyi</u> Laurent, Bull. Inst. Roy. Sci. Nat. Belg., 25(9): 6, figs. 10-12. Type-
        locality: Ecuador.

    Distribution: Known only from holotype, which has no definite locality data.

<u>TROPIDOPHIS</u> <u>PAUCISQUAMIS</u> (Müller)

    1901 <u>Ungalia paucisquamis</u> Müller, in Schenkel, Verh. Naturforsch. Ges. Basel, 13: 154. Type-locality:
        Tropical America.
    1901 <u>Ungalia brasiliensis</u> Andersson, Bihang Till K. Svenska Vet.-Akad. Handlingar, 27(4, No. 5): 4,
        pl. 1, fig. 1. Type-locality: Brazil.

    Distribution: Espirito Santo, Rio de Janeiro and São Paulo, Brazil, Northeastern Peru.

<u>TROPIDOPHIS</u> <u>TACZANOWSKYI</u> (Steindachner)

    1880 <u>Ungalia Taczanowskyi</u> Steindachner, Sitz. Math.-Naturwiss. Kl. Akad. Wiss. Wien, 80 (2): 522, 1
        pl. Type-locality: Tambillo, Peru.
    1928 <u>Tropidophis taczanowskyi</u>—Stull, Occ. Pap. Mus. Zool. Univ. Mich., 195: 21.

    Distribution: Peru and Ecuador; Brazil?

TYPHLOPHIS Fitzinger

> 1843 Typhlophis Fitzinger, Systema Reptilium: 24. Type-species: Typhlops squamosus Schlegel.
> 1844 Cephalolepis Duméril and Bibron, Erp. Gén., 6: 314. Type-species: Cephalolepis leucocephalus Duméril and Bibron.

> Distribution: As for single known species.

> Content: One species.

TYPHLOPHIS SQUAMOSUS (Schlegel)

> 1839 Typhlops squamosus Schlegel, Abbildungen . . . Amphibien, text: 36; Abbild.: pl. 32, figs. 9-12. Type-locality: Cayenne.
> 1844 Cephalolepis leucocephalus Duméril and Bibron, Erp. Gén., 6: 315. Type-locality: French Guiana.
> 1843 Typhlophis squamosus—Fitzinger, Systema Reptilium: 24.
> 1893 Typhlophis squamosus—Boulenger, Cat. Sn. Brit. Mus., 1: 57.

> Distribution: Trinidad; Atlantic coast of South America from Guianas to Grão Pará, Brazil.

TYPHLOPS Oppel

1811 Typhlops Oppel, Ordnungen, Familien und Gattungen der Reptilien: 54. Type-species: Anguis lumbricalis Linnaeus.
1815 Tiphlops Rafinesque (emendation of Typhlops Oppel), Analyse de la Nature: 78.
1830 Typhlina Wagler, Nat. Syst. Amphib.: 196. Type-species: Acontias lineatus Reinwardt = Typhlops lineatus Boie.
1843 Gerrhopilus Fitzinger, Systema Reptilium: 24. Type-species: Typhlops ater Schlegel.
1843 Aspidorhynchus Fitzinger, Systema Reptilium: 24. Type-species: Typhlops eschrichtii Schlegel = Acontias punctatus Leach.
1843 Pseudotyphlops Fitzinger, Systema Reptilium: 24. Type-species: Typhlops polygrammicus Schlegel.
1843 Rhamphotyphlops Fitzinger, Systema Reptilium: 24. Type-species: Typhlops multilineatus Schlegel.
1843 Rhinotyphlops Fitzinger, Systema Reptilium: 24. Type-species: Typhlops lalandii Schlegel.
1844 Pilidion Duméril and Bibron, Erp. Gén., 6: 257. Type-species: Pilidion lineatum Duméril and Bibron.
1844 Ophthalmidion Duméril and Bibron, Erp. Gén., 6: 262. Type-species: Ophthalmidion longissimum Duméril and Bibron.
1844 Cathetorhinus Duméril and Bibron, Erp. Gén., 6: 268. Type-species: Cathetorhinus melanocephalus Duméril and Bibron.
1844 Onychocephalus Duméril and Bibron, Erp. Gén., 6: 272. Type-species: Typhlops lalandii Schlegel.
1845 Anilios Gray, Cat. Liz. Brit. Mus.: 135. Type-species: Anilios leachii Gray = Anguis lumbricalis Linnaeus.
1845 Onychophis Gray, Cat. Liz. Brit. Mus.: 132. Type-species: Onychophis franklinii Gray = Typhlops lalandii Schlegel.
1845 Typhlinalis Gray (substitute name for Typhlina Wagler), Cat. Liz. Brit. Mus.: 134.
1845 Argyrophis Gray, Cat. Liz. Brit. Mus.: 136. Type-species: Argyrophis bicolor Gray = Typhlops nigroalbus Duméril and Bibron.
1845 Meditoria Gray, Cat. Liz. Brit. Mus.: 139. Type-species: Meditoria nasuta Gray = Anguis lumbricalis Linnaeus.
1846 Thyphlops Gistl (emendation of Typhlops Oppel), Naturgeschichte des Thierreichs: xi.
1861 Diaphorotyphlops Jan, Arch. Zool. Anat. Fis., 1: 185. Type-species: Diaphorolepis disparilis Jan.
1869 Letheobia Cope, Proc. Acad. Nat. Sci. Phila., 1868: 322. Type-species: Letheobia pallida Cope.
1881 Gryptotyphlops Peters, Sitz. Ges. Naturforsch. Freunde Berlin, 1881: 70. Type-species: Onychocephalus acutus Duméril and Bibron.

Distribution: World-wide, in tropical and subtropical regions.

Content: Probably somewhat more than 200 species, of which all but eight are extralimital.

Key to the species	Clave de especies

1. Preocular present; fewer than 26 scale rows---2
   No preocular; 26-28 scale rows------unilineatus
	1. Preocular presente; menos de 26 filas de escamas--2
	   Sin preocular; 26-28 filas de escamas--unilineatus

2. Scale rows 20----------------------------------3
   Scale rows 18---------------------------tenuis
	2. Con 20 filas de escamas----------------------3
	   Con 18 filas de escamas-----------------tenuis

3. Preocular in contact with upper labials two and three--------------------------------------4
   Preocular in contact with upper labial three only-----------------------------lumbricalis
	3. Preocular en contacto con segunda y tercera supralabial--------------------------------4
	   Preocular en contacto con sólo la tercera supralabial----------------------lumbricalis

4. Nasal suture complete, contacts rostral-------5
   Nasal suture incomplete, not in contact with rostral----------------------------reticulatus
	4. Sutura nasal completa que contacta con rostral--5
	   Sutura nasal incompleta que no contacta con rostral----------------------------reticulatus

5. More than 355 middorsal scales----------------6
   Fewer than 355 middorsal scales--------------7
	5. Más de 355 escamas mediodorsales--------------6
	   Menos de 355 escamas mediodorsales-----------7

6. Color with rows of brown dots on yellow background; third and fourth upper labials similar in size and shape, both higher than long; eye situated under ocular-preocular suture---------------------------------------trinitatus
   Color dull brown with irregular black spots; fourth labial large, much higher than long, extends up to posterior margin of ocular; eye not situated under ocular-preocular suture-------------------------------------costaricensis

7. Middorsal scales 347----------------stadelmani
   Middorsal scales 289-332---------------lehneri

6. Color de fondo amarillo con filas de puntos pardos; tercera y cuarta supralabial de similar forma y tamaño, ambas más altas que largas; ojo situado bajo la sutura óculo-preocular---------------------------trinitatus
   Color de fondo pardo apagado con manchas negras irregulares; cuarta labial grande, más alta que larga, que se extiende por encima del margen posterior de la ocular; ojo no situado bajo la sutura óculo-preocular---costaricensis

7. Con 347 escamas mediodorsales--------stadelmani
   Con 289-332 escamas mediodorsales-------lehneri

TYPHLOPS COSTARICENSIS Jiménez and Savage

1962 Typhlops costaricensis Jiménez and Savage, Rev. Biol. Trop., Costa Rica, 10: 199. Type-locality: Monteverde, Sierra de Tilarán, Provincia de Puntarenas, Costa Rica, 1500 m.

Distribution: Costa Rica.

TYPHLOPS LEHNERI Roux

1926 T.[yphlops] lehneri Roux, Rev. Suisse Zool., 33: 298. Type-locality: El Pozón, Estado Falcón, Venezuela.
1966 Typhlops lehneri—Roze, Los Ofidios de Venezuela: 35.

Distribution: Estado Falcón, Venezuela.

TYPHLOPS LUMBRICALIS (Linnaeus)

1766 Anguis lumbricalis Linnaeus, Systema Naturae, Ed. 12: 391. Type-locality: America.
1811 Typhl.[ops] lumbricalis—Oppel, Ordnungen, Familien, und Gattungen der Reptilien: 55.
1840 Typhlops Cubae Bibron, in de la Sagra, Historia . . . de Cuba, 4, Rept.: 122, pl. 22. Type-locality: Cuba.
1845 Anilios Leachii Gray, Cat. Liz. Brit. Mus.: 135. Type-locality: None given.
1904 Typhlops lumbricalis—Stejneger, Ann. Rept. U.S. Nat. Mus., 1902: 684, figs. 141-144.
1959 Typhlops silus Legler, Herpetologica, 15: 105, fig. 1. Type-locality: Banes, Provincia Oriente, Cuba.

Distribution: Cuba, Hispaniola, Bahamas; introduced into Guyana and Florida.

TYPHLOPS RETICULATUS (Linnaeus)

1766 Anguis reticulata Linnaeus, Systema Naturae, Ed. 12: 391. Type-locality: America.
1782 Anguis rostralis Weigel, Schrift. Berlin. Ges. Naturforsch. Freunde, 3: 193. Type-locality: Surinam.
1788 Anguis nasutus Gmelin, Systema Naturae, Ed. 13: 1120. Type-locality: Unknown.
1801 Anguis crocotatus Schneider, Hist. Amphib., 2: 340. Type-locality: None given.
1802 Anguis rostratus Daudin (in error for Anguis rostralis Weigel), Hist. Nat. Rept., 7: 316.
1844 Typhlops reticulatus—Duméril and Bibron, Erp. Gén., 6: 282, pl. 60.
1851 O.[phthalmidion] Crassum Duméril, Cat. Méth. Coll. Rept. Paris Mus.: 202. Type-locality: Unknown.
1864 Typhlops reticulatus Troscheli Jan, Icon. Gén. Ophidiens, Livr. 4: pl. 6, fig. c. Type-locality: None given.
1864 Typhlops reticulatus nigrolactea Jan, Icon. Gén. Ophidiens, Livr. 4: pl. 6, fig. d. Type-locality: None given.
1946 Typhlops reticulatus—Beebe, Zoologica, 31: 15, pl. 1, figs. 2-3.

Distribution: Tropical South America east of Andes.

TYPHLOPS STADELMANI Schmidt

    1936 Typhlops stadelmani Schmidt, Proc. Biol. Soc. Washington, 49: 48. Type-locality: Subirana
          Valley, Yoro, Honduras, 2800 ft.

    Distribution: Honduras.

TYPHLOPS TENUIS Salvin

    1860 Typhlops tenuis Salvin, Proc. Zool. Soc. London, 1860: 454. Type-locality: Cobán, Guatemala.
    1867 Typhlops basimaculatus Cope, Proc. Acad. Nat. Sci. Phila., 1866: 320. Type-locality: Córdoba
          and Orizaba, Veracruz, Mexico.
    1869 Typhlops perditus Peters, Monats. Akad. Wiss. Berlin, 1869: 435. Type-locality: Orizaba,
          Veracruz, Mexico.
    1885 Typhlops (praelongus n. sp.?) Müller, Verh. Naturforsch. Ges. Basel, 7: 674. Type-locality:
          Córdoba, Veracruz, Mexico.
    1893 Typhlops tenuis—Boulenger, Cat. Sn. Brit. Mus., 1: 28.

    Distribution: Moderate elevations in Alta Verapaz, Guatemala; Gulf area of Mexico.

TYPHLOPS TRINITATUS Richmond

    1965 Typhlops trinitatus Richmond, Proc. Biol. Soc. Washington, 78: 121, fig. 1. Type-locality: Arima
          Road, 3 mi above Simla, Trinidad.

    Distribution: Known only from Trinidad.

TYPHLOPS UNILINEATUS (Duméril and Bibron)

    1844 Onychocephalus unilineatus Duméril and Bibron, Erp. Gén., 6: 278: Type-locality: Cayenne.
    1863 T. yphlops (Onychocephalus) unilineatus—Jan, Elenco Sistema Ofidi: 13.
    1893 Typhlops unilineatus—Boulenger, Cat. Sn. Brit. Mus., 1: 15.

    Distribution: Surinam.

UMBRIVAGA Roze

    1964 *Umbrivaga* Roze, Senckenbergiana Biol., 45: 533. Type-species: *Umbrivaga mertensi* Roze.

      Distribution: As for single known species.

      Content: One species.

UMBRIVAGA MERTENSI Roze

    1964 *Umbrivaga mertensi* Roze, Senckenbergiana Biol., 45: 536. Type-locality: Parque Nacional Henri Pittier (Rancho Grande) Estado de Aragua, Venezuela.

      Distribution: Known only from type-locality.

UNGALIOPHIS Müller

   1882 Ungaliophis Müller, Verh. Naturforsch. Ges. Basel, 7: 142. Type-species: Ungaliophis
        continentalis Müller (an earlier description of this genus appears as an unknown genus of the
        Peropodes, i.e., boids, in Müller, loc. cit., 6, 1878, 652, pl. 1).
   1882 Peropodum Bocourt, Miss. Sci. Mex., Rept., 1882: 522. Type-species: Peropodum guatemalensis
        Bocourt (based on Müller's 1878 description, loc. cit.).

      Distribution: Mexico to Colombia.

      Content: Two species, according to most recent revision, by Bogert, Amer. Mus. Novitates, 2340,
         1968, 1-26, figs.

                    Key to the species   Clave de especies

   1. Scale rows at midbody fewer than 25---panamensis   1. Menos de 25 filas en el medio del cuerpo-------
      Scale rows at midbody 25----------continentalis   --------------------------------panamensis
                                                             Filas en el medio del cuerpo 25---continentalis

UNGALIOPHIS CONTINENTALIS Müller

   1882 Ungaliophis continentalis Müller, Verh. Naturforsch. Ges. Basel, 7: 142. (An earlier description
        appeared as "Nov. gen. Boid. Affin. Ungal[ia]. Spec. guatemalensis;" name was used by Müller,
        loc. cit., 6, 1878, 591; full description, Müller, loc. cit., 1878, 652, pl. 1). Type-locality:
        Retalhuléu, Guatemala.
   1882 Peropodum guatemalensis Bocourt, Miss. Sci. Mex., Rept., 1882: 523, pl. 31, figs. 5-5b (based on
        Müller's 1878 description, loc. cit.).
   1968 Ungaliophis continentalis—Bogert, Amer. Mus. Novitates, 2340: 14, figs. 2, 5, and 8.

      Distribution: Low elevations from eastern Chiapas, Mexico, to Guatemala and Honduras along Pacific
         slopes.

UNGALIOPHIS PANAMENSIS Schmidt

   1933 Ungaliophis panamensis Schmidt, Smithsonian Misc. Coll., 89 (1): 12. Type-locality: Cerro
        Brujo, Panama.
   1940 Ungaliophis danieli Prado, Mem. Inst. Butantan, 14: 35, 4 figs., 1 col. (p. 41). Type-locality:
        Andes, southeast of Antioquía, Colombia.
   1968 Ungaliophis panamensis—Bogert, Amer. Mus. Novitates, 2340: 14, figs. 1, 3-4, and 7.

      Distribution: Nicaragua, Panama, and Colombia.

UROMACERINA Amaral

   1929 Uromacerina Amaral, Mem. Inst. Butantan, 4: 18. Type-species: Uromacer ricardinii Peracca.

    Distribution: Estado de São Paulo, Brazil.

    Content: One species.

UROMACERINA RICARDINII (Peracca)

   1897 Uromacer Ricardinii Peracca, Boll. Mus. Zool. Anat. Comp. Torino, 12 (282): 1, fig. Type-locality:
      São Paulo, Brazil.
   1929 [Uromacerina] ricardinii—Amaral, Mem. Inst. Butantan, 4: 18

    Distribution: Estado de São Paulo, Brazil.

<u>XENOBOA</u> Hoge

    1953 <u>Xenoboa</u> Hoge, Mem. Inst. Butantan, 25 (1): 27. Type-species: <u>Xenoboa cropanii</u> Hoge.

    Distribution: Same as given below for single known species.

    Content: One species.

<u>XENOBOA CROPANII</u> Hoge

    1953 <u>Xenoboa cropanii</u> Hoge, Mem. Inst. Butantan, 25 (1): 27, figs. 1-5, col. pl. Type-locality:
        Miracato, State of São Paulo, Brazil.

    Distribution: Known only from type locality and Pedro de Toledo, Estado de São Paulo, Brazil.

XENODON Boie

1824 Ophis Wagler (preoccupied by Ophis Turton, 1807), in Spix, Sp. Nov. Serp. Bras.: 47. Type-species: Ophis Merremii Wagler.
1827 Xenodon Boie, in Schlegel, Isis von Oken, 20: 293. Type-species: Coluber severus Linnaeus.
1893 Acanthophallus Cope, Amer. Nat., 27: 482. Type-species: Xenodon colubrinus Günther.

Distribution: Mexico through Central America east of Andes in South America to Argentina (see comment).

Content: Seven species.

Comment: Eiselt, Ann. Naturhist. Mus. Wien, 66, 1963, 279, discussed the status of Procteria viridis Werner, 1924, and gave it the new name Xenodon werneri. The holotype was supposedly from Tsumeb, German Southwest Africa, but Eiselt questioned this, and indicated it was possibly from South America. It appears to be very similar to suspectus.

Key to the species

1. Maxillary teeth more than twelve, including those posterior to diastema------------------2
   Maxillary teeth 8-9, including those posterior to diastema---------------------------merremii

2. Dorsal scales in 19 rows----------------------3
   Dorsal scales in 21 rows----------------------6

3. Fewer than six labials in contact with first chinshield---------------------------------4
   Six labials in contact with first chinshield------------------------------------bertholdi

4. Anal plate entire----------------------------5
   Anal plate divided--------------------guentheri

5. Single black spot, bifurcated posteriorly on dorsum of head; tail 1/6 of total length-------------------------------rabdocephalus
   Dorsum of head with black spotting; tail 1/10 of total length---------------------suspectus

6. Caudals fewer than 42-----------------severus
   Caudals more than 42----------------neuwiedii

Clave de especies

1. Dientes maxilares más de doce, incluyendo los posteriores al diastema---------------------2
   Dientes maxilares 8-9, incluyendo los posteriores al diastema-------------------merremii

2. Con 19 hileras de escamas dorsales------------3
   Con 21 hileras de escamas dorsales------------6

3. Menos de seis labiales en contacto con el primer geneial---------------------------------4
   Seis labiales en contacto con el primer geneial------------------------------------bertholdi

4. Placa anal entera----------------------------5
   Placa anal dividida------------------guentheri

5. Sobre el casquete cefálico, una mancha negra bifurcada posteriormente; cola equivalente a 1/6 de la longitud total--------rabdocephalus
   Sobre el casquete cefálico manchas negras; cola equivalente a 1/10 de la longitud total------------------------------------suspectus

6. Caudales menos de 42-------------------severus
   Caudales más de 42--------------------neuwiedii

XENODON BERTHOLDI Jan

1863 X.[enodon] Bertholdi Jan, Arch. Zool. Anat. Fis., 2: 318. Type-locality: Mexico, probably in error.
1951 Xenodon bertholdi—Taylor, Univ. Kansas Sci. Bull., 34: 69.

Distribution: Costa Rica.

XENODON GUENTHERI Boulenger

1894 Xenodon guentheri Boulenger, Cat. Sn. Brit. Mus., 2: 147, pl. 7, fig. 1. Type-locality: Lagos, Santa Catarina, Brazil.

Distribution: Southern Brazil.

XENODON MERREMII (Wagler)

1824 Ophis Merremii Wagler, in Spix, Sp. Nov. Serp. Bras.: 47, pl. 17. Type-locality: Bahia, Brazil.
1826 X.[enodon] merremii—Fitzinger, Neue Classification der Reptilien: 57.
?1827 [Xenodon] ocellatus Boie, Isis von Oken, 20: 541. Type-locality: Brazil.
?1827 [Xenodon] aeneus Boie, Isis von Oken, 20: 541. Type-locality: Surinam.
1863 Xenodon irregularis Günther, Ann. Mag. Nat. Hist., (3) 12: 354, pl. 5, fig. D. Type-locality: Pará, Brazil.
1906 Trigonocephalus flavescens Bacqué, Rev. Mus. La Plata, 12: 114, fig. 1. Type-locality: Asunción, Paraguay.
1906 Trigonocephalus alternatus binocularius Bacqué, Rev. Mus. La Plata, 12: 115, fig. 2. Type-locality: Asunción, Paraguay.

Distribution: Guianas, Brazil, Bolivia, Paraguay, central and northern Argentina.

XENODON NEUWIEDII (Günther)

1863 Xenodon Neuwiedii Günther, Ann. Mag. Nat. Hist., (3) 12: 354, pl. 5, fig. C. Type-locality: Rio de Janeiro, Brazil.
1868 Xenodon neovidii Cope (emendation of neuwiedii Günther), Proc. Acad. Nat. Sci. Phila., 1868: 133.
1922 Xenodon hemileucurus Lutz and Mello, Folha Medica, 3 (1920): 98. Type-locality: S. Simão do Manhassú, Minas Gerais, Brazil.

Distribution: Central and southern Brazil, Paraguay, northern Argentina.

XENODON RABDOCEPHALUS (Wied)

1824 C.[oluber] rabdocephalus Wied, Isis von Oken, 6: 668. Type-locality: Brazil, stated further as Bahia, Brazil by Wied, Beiträge zur Naturgeschichte von Brasilien, 1, 1825, 356.
1826 X.[enodon] rabdocephalus—Fitzinger, Neue Classification der Reptilien: 57.

Distribution: Guerrero and Veracruz, Mexico through Central and South America to Bolivia.

Content: Two subspecies.

Key to the subspecies	Clave de subespecies
1. Ventrals 124-133------------------mexicanus	1. Ventrales 124-133----------------mexicanus
Ventrals 141-153-------------rabdocephalus	Ventrales 141-153------------rabdocephalus

Xenodon rabdocephalus rabdocephalus (Wied)

1837 X.[enodon] rhabdocephalus Schlegel (emendation of rabdocephalus Wied), Essai Physion. Serpens, 2: 87, pl. 3, figs. 6-7.
1858 Xenodon colubrinus Günther, Cat. Sn. Brit. Mus.: 55. Type-locality: Pará, Brazil.
1864 Xenodon angustirostris Peters, Monats. Akad. Wiss. Berlin, 1864: 390. Type-locality: Veragua, Panama.
1885 Xenodon bipraeoculis Cope, Proc. Amer. Phil. Soc., 23: 95. Type-locality: Río Mamoré, Bolivia.
1941 [Xenodon rabdocephalus rabdocephalus]—Schmidt (by inference), Zool. Ser. Field Mus. Nat. Hist., 22: 501.

Distribution: Nicaragua(?) through Central America to Colombia, Ecuador, Brazil and Bolivia.

Xenodon rabdocephalus mexicanus Smith

1940 Xenodon mexicanus Smith, Proc. Biol. Soc. Washington, 53: 57. Type-locality: Piedras Negras, Guatemala.
1941 Xenodon rabdocephalus mexicanus—Schmidt, Zool. Ser. Field Mus. Nat. Hist., 22: 501.

Distribution: Low and moderate elevations from Guerrero, Mexico , on Pacific and Veracruz, Mexico, on Caribbean south through Guatemala.

XENODON SEVERUS (Linnaeus)

1758 Coluber severus Linnaeus, Systema Naturae, Ed. 10: 219. Type-locality: "Asia"; restricted to South America by Günther, Ann. Mag. Nat. Hist., (3) 12, 1863, 353.
1802 Coluber breviceps Shaw, Gen. Zool., Amphib., 3 (2): 430. Type-locality: Ceylon and Brazil.
1820 [Coluber (Natrix)] versicolor Merrem, Tentamen Systematis Amphibiorum: 95. Type-locality: Brazil.
1824 C.[oluber] saurocephalus Wied, Isis von Oken, 6: 668. Type-locality: Brazil; stated more fully as Rio Ilhéus, Brazil, by Wied, Beiträge zur naturgeschichte von Brasilien, 1, 1825, 367.
1826 X.[enodon] severus—Fitzinger, Neue Classification der Reptilien: 57.

Distribution: Amazonian South America.

XENODON SUSPECTUS Cope

1868 Xenodon suspectus Cope, Proc. Acad. Nat. Sci. Phila., 1868: 133. Type-locality: Lago Jose Assu, Brazil.

Distribution: Eastern Peru.

<u>XENOPHOLIS</u> Peters

    1869 <u>Xenopholis</u> Peters, Monats. Akad. Wiss. Berlin, 1869: 440. Type-species: <u>Xenopholis Braconnieri</u>
        Peters.
    1874 <u>Gerrhosteus</u> Cope, Proc. Acad. Nat. Sci. Phila., 1874: 71. Type-species: <u>Gerrhosteus prosopis</u> Cope.
    1925 <u>Sympeltophis</u> Werner, Sitz. Math-Naturwiss. Kl. Akad. Wiss. Wien, Abt. 1, 134: 52, fig. 1.
        Type-species: <u>Sympeltophis ungalioides</u> Werner.

    Distribution: As for single known species.

    Content: One species.

<u>XENOPHOLIS</u> <u>SCALARIS</u> (Wucherer)

    1861 <u>Elapomorphus scalaris</u> Wucherer, Proc. Zool. Soc. London, 1861: 325. Type-locality: Cañavieras,
        Matta de São João, a few leagues south of Bahia, Brazil.
    1869 <u>Xenopholis Braconnieri</u> Peters, Monats. Akad. Wiss. Berlin, 1869: 441, pl., fig. 3.
        Type-locality: none given.
    1874 <u>Gerrhosteus prosopis</u> Cope, Proc. Acad. Nat. Sci. Phila., 1874: 71. Type-locality: Nauta, Peru.
    1925 <u>Sympeltophis ungalioides</u> Werner, Sitz. Math-Naturwiss. Kl. Akad. Wiss. Wien, Abt. 1, 134: 52,
        fig. 1. Type-locality: Central Brazil.

    Distribution: Amazonian Bolivia, Peru, Ecuador, and Brazil.

APOROPHIS CRUCIFER Ahl

1925 Aporophis crucifer Ahl, Zool. Anz., 63: 271. Type-locality: Either Buea, Cameroons or Paramaribo, Surinam.

Distribution: Unknown.

Comment: Werner, Zool. Jahrb., Abt. für Syst., 57, 1929, 114, assigned this to Lygophis, and stated that, although the locality for the type was uncertain, it was impossible for it to be Buea, Cameroons. He does not elaborate on this statement. The holotype will have to be re-examined for proper generic placement of the taxon.

ATRACTUS TRIHEDRURUS Amaral

1926 Atractus trihedrurus Amaral, Arch. Mus. Nac. Brazil, 26: 11, pl. 2, figs. 1-4. Type-locality: Southern Brazil.

Distribution: Known only from type specimen.

Comment: Savage, Misc. Publ. Mus. Zool. Univ. Mich., 112, 1960, 31, indicated that this was probably not an Atractus, but that its generic status must be regarded as uncertain until the holotype can be re-examined.

ATRACTUS VITTATUS Boulenger

1894 Atractus vittatus Boulenger, Cat. Sn. Brit. Mus., 2: 304, pl. 15, fig. 2. Type-locality: Caracas, Venezuela.

Distribution: Known only from type locality.

Comment: Savage, Misc. Publ. Mus. Zool. Univ. Mich., 112, 1960, 31, pointed out that the characters exhibited by the holotype and only known specimen did not permit its inclusion in Atractus, and suggested it might be a Geophis. Downs, Misc. Publ. Mus. Zool. Univ. Mich., 131, 1967, did not mention the species at all in his review and clearly did not consider it a valid taxon within the genus Geophis.

CALAMARIA FAVAE Filippi

1840 Calamaria favae Filippi, Catalogo Raggionato e Descrittivo...Serpenti del Museo dell' I. R. Universitá de Pavia, Bibliot. Ital., 99: 16. Type-locality: Unknown.
1854 Rabdosoma longicaudatum Duméril, Bibron and Duméril, Erp. Gén., 7: 106. Type-locality: Java.

Distribution: Unknown.

Comment: This taxon was called Atractus favae by Boulenger, Cat. Sn. Brit. Mus., 2, 1894, 313, and its distribution was given by Boulenger as "Brazil?" It is not mentioned by Inger and Marx in their recent revision of Calamaria, and it has not been included in any recent works on Javan species. Savage, Misc. Publ. Mus. Zool. Univ. Mich., 112, 1960, regarded it as a nomen dubium and did not include it in his list of species of the genus Atractus. Recent authors on Brazilian species have not mentioned it.

COCHLIOPHAGUS ISOLEPIS Müller

1924 Cochliophagus isolepis Müller, Mitt. Zool. Mus. Berlin, 11: 91. Type-locality: South America.

Distribution: Unknown.

Comment: This is clearly not a Dipsadine snake, although the genus Cochliphagus is a synonym of Sibynomorphus. We do not know where it properly belongs.

INCERTAE SEDIS

DIPSAS INFRENALIS Rosén

1905 Dipsas infrenalis Rosén, Ann. Mag. Nat. Hist., (7) 15: 180. Type-locality: None given.
1960 Dipsas infrenalis—Peters, Misc. Publ. Mus. Zool. Univ. Mich., 114: 214.

   Distribution: Unknown.

   Comment: Listed as incertae sedis by Peters, loc. cit.

DIPSAS SUBAEQUALIS Fischer

1880 Dipsas subaequalis Fischer, Arch. für Naturg., 46: 224, pl. 9, figs. 18-21. Type-locality:
     Unknown.

   Distribution: Unknown.

   Comment: Boulenger, Cat. Sn. Brit. Mus., 3, 1896, 88, suggested that this might be an Imantodes,
     but the coloration as described is so different from any other species in that genus that this
     seems a most improbable generic assignment.

DROMICUS AMAZONICUS Dunn

1922 Dromicus amazonicus Dunn, Proc. Biol. Soc. Washington, 35: 219. Type-locality: Santarem, Brazil.

   Distribution: Known only from type locality.

   Comment: The generic assignment of this species is very questionable. The holotype must be
     re-examined in the light of recent interpretations of generic lines.

ERYTHROLAMPRUS MENTALIS Werner

1909 Erythrolamprus mentalis Werner, Mitt. Naturhist. Mus. Hamburg, 26: 238. Type-locality:
     Guatemala.

   Distribution: Unknown. Stuart does not mention the species in his Guatemalan checklist (1963).

   Comment: This taxon has been placed in Coniophanes by various authors and in Rhadinaea by Bailey,
     Pap. Mich. Acad. Sci., Arts, Letters, 24, 1938 (1939), 5, but all such actions have been
     tentative, awaiting re-examination of the type. This specimen was destroyed during World War
     II, and the taxon may never be properly allocated.

HELICOPS LEPRIEURII MOESTA Jan

1865 [Helicops Leprieurii] var. moesta Jan, Arch. Zool. Anat. Fis., 3: 253. Type-locality: None
     Given.

   Distribution: Unknown.

   Comment: Boulenger, Cat. Sn. Brit. Mus., 1, 1893, 277, tentatively synonymized this variety with
     Helicops modestus, but this cannot be determined without question from Jan's description. The
     type,which has not yet been located, must be re-examined for proper allocation of the taxon.

HERPETODRYAS ANNECTENS Werner

1924 Herpetodryas annectens Werner, Sitz. Math.-Naturwiss. Kl. Akad. Wiss. Wien, Abt. 1, 133: 33.
     Type-locality: Presumed to be Brazil by Werner, since it was in bottle with two other snakes
     from that country.

   Distribution: Unknown.

   Comment: Amaral, Mem. Inst. Butantan, 4, 1929, 14, stated that this was not Brazilian, not neotrop-
     ical, and wrong in the generic assignment. Amaral did not attempt to assign it elsewhere.

LEPTOGNATHUS ANDREI Sauvage

  1884 Leptognathus Andrei Sauvage, Bull. Soc. Philom. Paris, (7) 8: 146. Type-locality: New Grenada.
  1960 Leptognathus andrei—Peters, Misc. Publ. Mus. Zool. Univ. Mich., 114: 212.

    Distribution: known only from locality given for holotype.

    Comment: Placed in incertae sedis in the Dipsadinae by Peters, loc. cit.

LEPTOGNATHUS BREVIS Duméril, Bibron and Duméril

  1854 Leptognathus brevis Duméril, Bibron and Duméril, Erp. Gén., 7: 476. Type-locality: Mexico.
  1960 Leptognathus brevis—Peters, Misc. Publ. Mus. Zool. Univ. Mich., 114: 212.

    Distribution: Unknown, except for vague type locality given by Duméril, Bibron and Duméril.

    Comment: This taxon may be synonymous with Sibon nebulata nebulata, according to Peters, Beitr. Neotrop. Fauna, 4, 1964, 49.

THANATOPHIS PATOQUILLA Posada Arango

  1889 Thanatophis patoquilla Posada Arango, Bull. Soc. Zool. France, 14: 343. Type-locality: Provincia de Medillin, Colombia.

    Distribution: Known only from type locality.

    Comment: This taxon is not mentioned in Boulenger, Cat. Sn. Brit. Mus., 3, 1896, or in Hoge, Mem. Inst. Butantan, 32, 1965 (1966), in their reviews of viperid snakes. We presume it belongs to Bothrops, but we are unsure of this. Blanchard, Bull. Soc. Zool. France, 1889, 347, suggested it may be a synonym of Bothrops nigroviridis (Peters).

UROTHECA WILLIAMSI Roze

  1958 Urotheca williamsi Roze, Breviora, Mus. Comp. Zool., 88: 1. Type-locality: El Junquito, Distrito Federal, Venezuela.

    Distribution: Central part of Cordillera de la Costa, Venezuela.

    Comment: Roze used Urotheca rather than Rhadinaea for this generic taxon, and presumably the species should be transferred to Rhadinaea here. Creation of this new taxonomic arrangement should await completion of review of Rhadinaea by C. W. Myers, and we do not make it here. It is not appropriate to Urotheca unless one considers it congeneric with Rhadinaea, which we do not do here.

ZAMENIS ARGENTINUS Bréthes

  1917 Zamenis argentinus Bréthes, Rev. Soc. Argentina Cien. Nat. Hist., 3: 93, fig. Type-locality: Argentina.

    Distribution: Uncertain.

    Comment: We have not seen this description, and the data presented are unverified. Werner, Sitz. Math.-Naturwiss. Kl. Akad. Wiss. Wien, Abt. 1, 133, 1924, 34, suggested that the taxon belonged in the genus Philodryas, but gives no reasons for this suggestion.

binotata
  Rhadinaea 180
bipraeocularis
  Liophis 143
  Oxyrhopus 233
bipraeoculis
  Xenodon 324
bipunctata
  Coronella 66
bipunctatus
  Coniophanes 66
  Coniophanes bipunctatus
    67
biscutata
  Dipsas 310
  Trimorphodon 310
biseriatus
  Atractus 27
bitaeniatus
  Zamenis 156
bitis
  Vipera 73
bitorquata
  Tachymenis 232
bivittatus
  Dendrophidion 79
  Leptophis 79
bizona
  Erythrolamprus 112
  Erythrolamprus aesculapii
    112
blombergi
  Boa annulata 72
  Corallus annulatus 72
blumii
  Calamaria 105
Boa 37
bocki
  Atractus 27
bocourti
  Atractus 27
  Elaps 203
  Leptophis 162
  Leptophis ahaetulla 162
  Micrurus 203
  Micrurus bocourti 203
  Thalerophis richardi 162
boddaerti
  Coluber 192
  Dryadophis 192
  Dryadophis boddaerti 193
  Mastigodryas 192
  Mastigodryas boddaerti
    193
boettgeri
  Atractus 27
  Dipsas 85
  Leptognathus 85
boliviana
  Leptognathus 85
  Tachymenis attenuata 290
bolivianus
  Bothrops neuwiedi 50
  Hydrops triangularis 130
  Leptophis ahaetulla 162
  Liophis 244
  Micrurus annellatus 203
  Philodryas 244
  Thalerophis richardi 162
bollei
  Elapomorphus 105

bondensis
  Helminthophis 182
borelli
  Apostolepis 23
  Philodryas 244
borrichiana
  Glauconia 168
borrichianus
  Leptotyphlops 168
boshelli
  Dendrophidion 79
Bothriechis 39
Bothriopsis 39
Bothrops 39
boulengeri
  Oxybelis 227
  Philodryas 243
  Trachyboa 305
boulengerii
  Atractus 28
boursieri
  Dromicus 186
  Lygophis 186
bovallii
  Rhinobothrium 269
  Rhinobothryum 269
  Thamnophis 303
  Thamnophis marcianus
    303
brachycephalus
  Colobognathus 119
  Geophis 119
Brachyrruton 62
brachystoma
  Teleuraspis castelnaui
    47
brachyurus
  Opheomorphus 150
braconnieri
  Xenopholis 326
brammianus
  Bothrops 46
brandon-jonesii
  Sordellina 282
brasiliensis
  Coluber 55
  Gomesophis 121
  Leptotyphlops 168
  Micrurus frontalis 209
  Tachymenis 121
  Ungalia 314
brasiliniana
  Vipera 55
brazili
  Bothrops 45
  Drymobius 100
  Drymoluber 100
  Liophis 177
  Rhachidelus 261
  Rhadinaea 177
breve
  Homalocranium 294
brevicauda
  Liophis 252
  Tantilla 294
breviceps
  Coluber 325
  Liophis 177
brevifacies
  Dipsas 86
  Tropidodipsas 86

brevifrenum
  Rabdosoma 29
brevifrons
  Coniophanes 66
brevior
  Leptophis 164
brevirostris
  Dromicus 264
  Dryophis 228
  Oxybelis 228
  Rhadinaea 264
brevis
  Leptognathus 328
  Tantilla 294
brevissimus
  Leptotyphlops 168
bronni
  Plastoseryx 184
browni
  Micrurus 204
  Micrurus browni 204
brunneus
  Dendrophidion 80
  Herpetodryas 80
bucephala
  Dipsas indica 87
  Coluber 87
buckleyi
  Elaps 211
Bungarus 82
burmeisteri
  Bothrops 43
  Dryophylax 242
  Philodryas 242

C

Cacocalyx 79
caerulea
  Anguis 19
caesius
  Opheomorphus doliatus
    147
Calamodon 56
Calamodontophis 56
calamus
  Elaps 213
californica
  Liophis poecilogyrus
    151
calligaster
  Contia 264
  Rhadinaea 264
Callirhinus 240
Callopistria 280
callostictus
  Hydrops 129
  Hydrops martii 129
Calonotus 262
Calophis 141
campicola
  Philodryas 241
canaima
  Liophis 177
cancellatus
  Geophis 119
canellei
  Helminthophis 182
canilatus
  Tachymenis 243

canina
  Boa 72
caninana
  Coluber (Natrix) 283
caninus
  Corallus 72
canula
  Tantilla 294
capistrata
  Tantilla 295
  Tantilla melanoceph-
    ala 295
capistratus
  Coluber 192
caracasensis
  Liotyphlops 182
carbonelli
  Philodryas 242
carinatus
  Chironius 59
  Coluber 59
carinicauda
  Micrurus 207
  Micrurus dumerilii 207
carinicaudus
  Coluber 123
  Helicops 123
  Helicops carinicaudus
    123
  Micrurus carinicaudus
    207
carpicinctus
  Scaphiodontophis 271
carri
  Sibon 274
  Tropidodipsas 274
carrioni
  Atractus 28
carvalhoi
  Micrurus lemniscatus
    212
cascavella
  Crotalus 75
  Crotalus (Crotalus)
    durissus 75
castelnaudi
  Bothrops 45
castelnaui
  Bothriechis 45
castelnautii
  Atropos 45
castelnavii
  Bothriopsis 45
catenata
  Tachymenis peruviana
    291
catenatus
  Scytale 136
catesbeji
  Coluber 86
catesbyi
  Dipsas 86
  Dryiophis 228
Cathetorhinus 316
Catodon 165
Catostoma 117
caucanus
  Sibynomorphus 89
Caudisona 74
cavalheiroi
  Dipsas albifrons 85

Part II   Lizards and Amphisbaenians

Addenda and Corrigenda to Part II Lizards and Amphisbaenia

P. E. Vanzolini

Ablepharus Fitzinger, 1823 = Cryptoblepharus Wiegmann, 1834, fide
        Fuhn, 1969, Rev. Roumaine Biol. 14:23-41. Distribution:
        may include Ecuador (Boulenger, 1887) and Chile (BMNH)

Abronia Gray, 1838.
        A. montecristoi Hidalgo, Occ. Pap. Mus. Nat. Hist. Univ.
            Kansas (105):6. Type-locality: El Salvador, Santa Ana,
            Hda. Montecristo, Metapan, 2250 m. Distribution: known
            only from type locality.
        A. salvadorensis Hidalgo, Ibid. (105):1. Type-locality: El
            Salvador, Morazan Canton Palo Blanco, 10 km NE Perquin,
            1900 m. Distribution: known only from type locality.

Alopoglossus Boulenger, 1885.
1973 A. atriventris Duellman, Herpetologica 29:228. Type-locality:
            Ecuador, Napo, Lago Agrio. Distribution: Amazonian basin
            of Ecuador and adjacent Colombia and Peru.
        A. copii Boulenger = Leposoma southi. fide Uzzell & Barry,
            Postilla 154.
        A. gracilis Werner, (Incertae sedis by Peters & Donoso-Barros)
            = Ecpleopus gaudichaudii Dumeril & Bibron, 1839, fide
            Uzzell, 1969, Postilla 135:1-23.
1984 A. lehmanni Ayala & Harris, Herpetologica 40:154.
            Type-locality: Colombia, Valle del Cauca, road from
            Buenaventura to San Isidro, km 22. Distribution: Pacific
            lowlands of Colombia (Ayala & Harris, 1984,
            Herpetologica 40:154-57).

Amapasaurus Cunha, 1970, Bol. Mus. Paraense Emilio Goeldi (Zool.)
            74:1-8. Type-species: A. tetradactylus Cunha, 1970, op.
            cit.
1970 A. tetradactylus Cunha, Ibid. 74:3. Type-locality: Brasil,
            Amapa, Igarape Camaipi, Alto Rio Maraca. Distribution:
            headwaters of Rio Maraca, Brasil.

Ameiva Meyer, 1795.
The key in Peters & Donoso-Barros is unreliable.
        A. ameiva (Linnaeus). The subspecies of A. ameiva are not
            biologically meaningful.
1977 A. anomala Echternacht, Copeia (1):1. Type-locality: Colombia,
            Cauca, Quebrada Guangui, 0.5 km above Rio Patia (Upper
            Rio Saija drainage), 100-200 m. Distribution: Pacific
            lowlands of Colombia.
        A. festiva niceforoi Dunn = A. niceforoi, fide Echternacht,
            1970, Breviora 354:1-9.
        A. major Dumeril & Bibron, 1839. Omitted by Peters &
            Donoso-Barros. See Presch, 1971, J. Herpetol. 5:183-85,
            Hoogmoed & Lescure, 1975, Zool. Med. 49(13):141-71.
        A. undulata thomasi Smith & Laufe = A. chaitzami, fide
            Echternacht, 1970, op. cit.

Cnemidophorus vittatus Boulenger = A. vittata, fide Vance, 1978, J. Herpetol. 12:98-100. Distribution: known only from type locality.

Amphisbaena Linnaeus, 1758
1977 A. medemi Gans & Mathers, Fieldiana Zool. 72:22.
     Type-locality: Colombia, Atlantico, Cienaga de
     Amajehuevo, Canal. Distribution: only type locality.
1979 A. minuta Hulse & McCoy, Ann. Carnegie Mus. 48:2.
     Type-locality: Argentina, Catamarca, 27 km S Andalgala,
     Distribution: Bolson de Pipinasco, Argentina.
1971 A. miringoera Vanzolini, Pap. Avul. Zool. 24:191.
     Type-locality: Brasil, Mato Grosso do Norte, Porto
     Velho, Rio Tapirapes. Distribution: only type locality.
1971 A. tragorrhectes Vanzolini, Ibid. 24:192. Type-locality:
     Brasil, Para, Oriximina. Distribution: type locality.

Anadia Gray, 1845. Includes Argalia Gray, 1846, fide Oftedal, 1974,
     Arq. Zool.(Sao Paulo) 25:203-65.
  A. angusticeps Parker = A. vittata Boulenger, 1913, fide
     Oftedal, 1974, op. cit.
  A. brevifrontalis (Boulenger), removed from Euspondylus by
     Oftedal, 1974, op. cit. = Ptychoglossus brevifrontalis,
     fide Dixon & Soini, 1975, Milwaukee Pub. Mus. Contrib.
     Biol. Geol. 4:51.
  A. duquei Lancini = A. marmorata Gray, 1846, fide Oftedal,
     1974. op. cit.
  A. marmorata (Gray) see Argalia.
  A. ocellata metallica (Cope) = A. ocellata, fide Oftedal,
     1974, op. cit.
1974 A. petersi Oftedal, Ibid 25:226. Type-locality: Ecuador, Loja,
     San Ramon, near Loja. Distribution: only type locality.

Anolis Daudin. 1802.
Anolis is a difficult group. Peters & Donoso-Barros provided a
character matrix; however, given the many changes that have and
will occur in anole taxonomy, identification should start with a
reading of Williams (1976, Pap. Avul. Zool. 29:259-68) and
segregation of taxa by geography. Well identified specimens for
comparison are essential.
1974 A. annectens Williams, Breviora 421:3. Type-locality:
     Venezuela, Zulia, Lago de Maracaibo. Distribution:
     questionably Lago de Maracaibo, Venezuela.
1985 A. antioquiae Williams, Breviora 482:3. Type-locality:
     Colombia, Antioquia, Quebrada Chaparral, 10 km E Andes
     (town), 2200-2300 m. Distribution: western Antioquia,
     Colombia.
  A. apollinaris Boulenger. Revalidated by Williams, 1970,
     Breviora 358:1-11.
  A. baleatus Cope.
1864 Eupristis baleatus Cope, Proc. Acad. Nat. Sci.
     Philadelphia 16:168. Type-locality: Santo Domingo.
     Anolis baleatus Schwartz, 1974, Bull. Mus. Comp. Zool.
     146:119. Distribution: Hispaniola; introduced into

Surinam (Hoogmoed, 1981, Amphibia-Reptilia 1:280).
1983 A. calimae Ayala, Harris & Williams, Breviora 475:2.
    Type-locality: Colombia, Valle del Cauca, San Antonio,
    Television Tower Mountain, 1800 m Distribution:
    westernmost Valle del Cauca, Colombia.
1974 A. caquetae Williams, Breviora 422:8. Type-locality: Colombia,
    Caqueta, Camp Soratama, Upper Apaporis. Distribution:
    Amazonian Colombia.
1971 A. carpenteri Echelle et al., Herpetologica 27:355.
    Type-locality: Costa Rica, Cartago, Rio Reventazon, 7 km
    ESE Turrialba. Distribution: Pacific lowlands of
    Nicaragua and Costa Rica.
A. chlorocyanus Dumeril & Bibron.
1837 Anolis chloro-cyanus D. & B., Erp. Gen. 4:117.
    Type-locality: Martinique et Saint Domingue.
1856 Anolis laeviceps Lichtenstein, Nomencl. Rept. Amphib.
    Mus. Berlin: 7. Type-locality: unknown. Distribution:
    Hispaniola; introduced into Surinam (Hoogmoed, 1981,
    Ibid. 1:279).
1970 A. chrysolepis brasiliensis Vanzolini & Williams, Arq. Zool.
    19:85. Type-locality: Brasil, Mato Grosso do Norte,
    Barra do Tapirapes. Distribution: northeastern Mato
    Grosso to northern Sao Paulo, Brasil; also northeastern
    Brasil (Williams & Vanzolini, 1980, Pap. Avul. Zool. 34.
A. chrysolepis planiceps Troschel, fide Vanzolini & Williams,
    1970, op. cit.
A. chrysolepis scypheus Cope, fide Vanzolini & Williams, 1970,
    Ibid. 19:1-298
A. crassulus Cope. Distribution: also Honduras (Meyer &
    Wilson, 1973, Contrib. Sci. (244):1-39.
A. crassulus haguei = A. haguei, fide Fitch et al., 1976,
    Univ. Kansas Sci. Bull. 51:117.
A. cupreus Hallowell. Content: five subspecies, fide Fitch et
    al., 1972, Occ. Pap. Mus. Kansas Univ. Kansas (8):1-20.
1984 A. cupreus dariense Fitch & Seigel, Milwaukee Pub. Mus.
    Contrib. Bio. Geol. 57:6. Type-locality: Nicaragua,
    Boaco, Puente Carlos Fonseca Amador. Distribution:
    Caribbean-montane Nicaragua.
A. cupreus hoffmanni Peters, fide Fitch et al., 1972, op. cit.
A. cupreus macrophallus Werner, fide Fitch et al., op. cit.
A. cupreus spilomelas Fitch et al., 1972, Ibid. (8):17. Type-
    locality: Costa Rica, Puntarenas, Quepos. Distribution:
    Quepos-Parrita area of Costa Rica.
A. cybotes cybotes Cope.
1863 Anolis cybotes Cope, Proc. Acad. Nat. Sci. Philadelphia
    14:177. Type-locality: Haiti, near Jeremie.
1863 A. riisei Reinhardt & Leutken, Vid. Med. Nat. For.
    Copenhagen [1862] :264. Type-locality: Haiti.
1864 A. citrinellus Cope, Proc. Acad Nat. Sci. Philadelphia
    16:170. Type-locality: Santo Domingo.
    Distribution: Hispaniola; introduced into Surinam
    (Hoogmoed, 1981, Ibid. 1:279).
1974 A. deltae Williams, Ibid. 422:11. Type-locality: Venezuela,
    Delta Amacuro, Mision Araquaimujo. Distribution: delta

of the Orinoco.

A. eewi Roze = A. chrysolepis planiceps Troschel, fide
   Vanzolini & Williams, 1970, op, cit.

1984 A. fitchi Williams & Duellman, Spec. Publ. Univ. Kansas Mus.
     Nat. Hist. (10):257. Type-locality: Ecuador, Napo, 16.5
     km N-NE of Santa Rosa. Distribution: Napo, Ecuador, and
     adjacent Putumayo, Colombia.

1971 A. fungosus Myers, Amer. Mus. Novitates (2471):13. Type-
     locality: Panama, Bocas del Toro, north slope Cerro
     Pando, Cordillera de Talamanca, 1450 m. Distribution:
     known only from type locality.

A. heteropholidotus Mertens = A. sminthus, fide Meyer &
   Wilson, 1971, Bull. So. California Acad. 70:106-14.

A. hoffmanni = A. cupreus hoffmanni, fide Fitch et al., 1972,
   op. cit.

1982 A. huilae Williams, Breviora 467:9. Type-locality: Colombia,
     Huila, Herberto Herrera´s coffee plantation, Palestina.
     Distribution: Huila and Tolima, Colombia.

A. humilis uniformis Cope = A. uniformis, fide Echelle et al.,
   1978, Herpetologica 34:205-207.

1975 A. ibague Williams, Breviora 433:1. Type-locality: Colombia,
     Tolima, Ibague. Distribution: only type locality.

A. incompertus Barbour = A. chrysolepis scypheus Cope, fide
   Vanzolini & Williams, 1970, Ibid. 19:1-298.

A. intermedius Peters = A. laeviventris, Meyer & Wilson, 1971,
   Ibid. 70:106-14.

1982 A. johnmeyeri Wilson & McCranie, Trans. Kansas Acad. Sci.
     85:133. Type-locality: Honduras, Cortes, El Cusuco, 5.6
     km WSW Buenos Aires, 1580 m. Distribution: Sierra de
     Omoa, Honduras (McCranie et al., 1984, J. Herpetol.
     18:337-38).

A. laeviventris (Wiegmann). Distribution: also Nicaragua
   (Fitch & Seigel, 1984, Ibid. 57:7).

A. limifrons rodriquezii Bocourt = A. rodriquezii, Fitch et
   al., 1976, Ibid. 51:119.

A. mariarum Barbour = A. antonii Boulenger, 1908, fide
   Williams, 1970, Breviora 358:1-11.

A. marmoratus speciosus Garman.

1888 Anolis speciosus Garman, Bull. Essex Inst. 19:45.
     Type-locality: Marie-Galante. Distribution: Guadeloupe
     and adjacent islets; introduced into French Guiana
     (Lescure, 1983, C. R. Soc. Biogeog. France 59:62).

1983 A. menta Ayala, Harris & Williams, Pap. Avul. Zool. 35:135.
     Type-locality: Colombia, Magdalena, Cuchilla
     Hierbabuena, 4 km SE San Pedro de la Sierra, Sierra
     Nevada de Santa Marta. Distribution: northern Sierra
     Nevada de Santa Marta, Colombia.

A. nannodes Cope = A. laeviventris, fide Meyer & Wilson, 1971,
   Ibid. 70:106-14.

A. nicefori Barbour = A. tropidogaster Hallowell, fide
   Williams, 1970, Ibid. 358:1-11

A. nitens bondi Fowler = A. chrysolepis planiceps Troschel,
   fide Vanzolini & Williams, 1970, op. cit.

1974 A. nigropunctatus Williams, Ibid. 422:2. Type-locality:

Colombia, Norte de Santander, El Diamante. Distribution: northeastern Colombia and western Venezuela.

A. onca (O´Shaughnessy). See Williams, 1974, Ibid. 421:1-21.

A. ortonii Cope. Distribution: also Atlantic forest, Brasil (Williams & Vanzolini, 1980, Ibid. 34:99-108).

A. oxylophus Cope. Revalidated by Fitch & Seigel, 1984, Ibid. 57:8.

1975 A. parilis Williams, Breviora 434:1. Type-locality: Ecuador, Pichincha, Rio Baba, 2.4 km S Santo Domingo de los Colorados. Distribution: only from type locality.

1971 A. procellaris Myers, Amer. Mus. Nov. (2470):2. Type-locality: Panama, Veraquas, nr. mouth Rio Concepcion. Distribution: known only from type locality.

1984 A. propinquus Williams, Breviora 477:1. Type-locality: Colombia, Valle del Cauca, Rio Calima, 1.5 km W Lago Calima. Distribution: known only from type locality.

A. punctatus Daudin. Distribution: forests of northern South American east of Andes and Atlantic forest of Brasil.

A. punctatus boulengeri O´Shaughnessy = A. punctatus Daudin, fide Williams & Vanzolini, 1980, Ibid. 34:99-108.

A. richardii Dumeril & Bibron.

1837 Anolis richardii D.& B., Erp. Gen. 4:141. Type-locality: Tortola. Distribution: Tobago, Grenada and Grenadines; introduced into Surinam (Hoogmoed, 1981, Ibid. 1:281).

1984 A. rivalis Williams, Breviora 478:7. Type-locality: Colombia, Antioquia, Belen, Rio Arquia. Distribution: Choco and western Antioquia, Colombia.

1982 A. santamartae Williams, Breviora 467:16. Type-locality: Colombia, Cesar, San Sebastian de Rabago, Sierra Nevada de Santa Marta. Distribution: only from type locality.

A. scypheus Cope = A. chrysolepis scypheus, fide Vanzolini & Williams, 1970, Ibid. 19:1-298.

A. steinbachi Griffin = A. meridionalis Boettger, 1885, fide Vanzolini & Williams, 1970, op. cit.

A. sulcifrons Cope, 1899. Revalidated by Myers, 1971, Amer. Mus. Nov. 2471:36. Distribution: east base of Cordillera de Bogota and edge of llanos east of Bogota, Colombia

A. uniformis Cope. Elevated by Meyer & Wilson, 1971, Ibid. 70.

1982 A. vaupesianus Williams, Breviora 467:2. Type-locality: Colombia, Comisaria de Vaupes, Timbo, on Rio Vaupes, E Mitu. Distribution: Amazonas and Vaupes, Colombia.

1976 A. villai Fitch & Henderson, Milwaukee Pub. Mus. Contrib. Biol. Geol. (9):1. Type-locality: Nicaragua, Great Corn Island. Distribution: Great Corn Island.

1971 A. vociferans Myers, Amer. Mus. Nov. (2471):10. Type-locality: Panama, Chiriqui, 4 km W Cerro Punta, 1829 m. Distribution: Pacific side Cordillera de Talamanca from Cerro de la Muerte to Volcan de Chiriqui.

A. woodi attenuatus Taylor = A. attenuatus, fide Fitch et al., 1976, Ibid. 51:114.

Anops Bell, 1833.

1972 Anops bilabialatus Stimson, Bull. British Mus. Nat. Hist. (Zool.) 24:205. Type-locality: Brasil, Mato Grosso do

Norte, 260 km N Xavantina. Distribution: type locality.

Anotosaura Amaral, 1933.
1974 A. brachylepis Dixon, Herpetologica 30:17. Type-locality:
      Brasil, Minas Gerais, Serra do Cipo. Distribution: known
      only from vicinity of type locality.
1974 A. collaris vanzolinia Dixon, Ibid. 30:16. Type-locality:
      "Argentina," misprint for Brasil, Pernambuco Agrestina.
      = A. vanzolinia, fide Vanzolini & Ramos, 1977, Pap.
      Avul. Zool. 31:19-47. Distribution: type locality.

Aperopristis Peracca. Type-species: A. paronae Peracca, 1897,
      revalidated by Cei, 1973, Physis(C) 32:447-58.
      A. catamarcensis Koslowsky, fide Laurent & Teran, 1981,
         Miscelanea (Fund. Miguel Lillo, Tucuman) 71:11.
         Distribution: northwestern Argentina.
      A. paronae Peracca, 1897.

Argalia Gray, 1846 = Anadia Gray, 1845, fide Oftedal, 1974, Ibid.
      25:203-65.

Arthrosaura Boulenger, 1885.
      A. amapaense Cunha = A. reticulata versteegii, fide Hoogmoed,
         1973, Liz. Amphisb. Surinam, W. Junk.
      A. versteegii Van Lidth = A. reticulata versteegii, fide
         Hoogmoed, 1973, op. cit.

Arthroseps Boulenger, 1898 = Ecpleopus Dumeril & Bibron, 1839, fide
      Uzzell, 1969, Postilla 135:1-23.
      A. fluminensis Amaral = Ecpleopus gaudichaudii D.& B., fide
         Uzzell, 1969, op. cit.
      A. werneri Boulenger = Ecpleopus gaudichaudii, D.& B., fide
         Uzzell, 1969, op. cit.

Aspidolaemus Peters, 1862. Type-species: Ecpleopus (Aspidolaemus)
      affinis Peters, 1862, revalidated by Uzzell (1969) =
      Pholidobolus Peters, 1862, fide Montanucci, 1973, Misc.
      Publ. Univ. Kansas Mus. Nat. Hist. 59:1-52.

Bachia Gray, 1845. Includes Ophiognomon, fide Dixon, 1973, Misc.
      Publ. Univ. Kansas Mus. Nat. Hist. 57:1-47.
      Ophiognomon abendrothii (Peters) = Bachia trisanale
         abendrothii, fide Dixon, 1973, op. cit.
      B. alleni trinitatis (Barbour) = B. heteropa trinitatis, fide
         Dixon, 1973, op. cit.
1977 B. guianensis Hoogmoed & Dixon, Zool. Med. 51:25.
         Type-locality: Venezuela, Bolivar, Guri. Distribution:
         known only from type locality.
1973 B. huallagana Dixon, Ibid. 57:25. Type-locality: Peru, San
         Martin, San Jose de Tocache (= Tocache Nuevo), Rio
         Huallaga. Distribution: Huanuco and San Martin, Peru.
      B. lineata Boulenger = B. heteropa lineata, fide Dixon, 1973,
         op. cit.
      B. lineata marcelae Donoso-Barros & Garrido = B. heteropa

6

　　　　　marcelae, fide Dixon, 1973, op. cit.
　　　B. monodactylus (Daudin) = B. cophias (Schneider), fide
　　　　　Hoogmoed, 1973, Biogeog. 4:1-419.
　　　B. parkeri Ruthven = B. cophias parkeri, fide Dixon, 1973,
　　　　　op. cit.
　　　B. schlegeli (Dumeril & Bibron) = B. flavescens schlegeli,
　　　　　fide Dixon, 1973, op. cit.
　　　Ophiognomon trisanale Cope = Bachia trisanale, fide Dixon,
　　　　　1973, op. cit.
　　　Ophiognomon vermiformis (Cope) = Bachia trisanale vermiformis,
　　　　　fide Dixon, 1973, op. cit.

Basiliscus Laurenti, 1768.
　　　B. plumifrons Cope. Distribution: also Honduras (Meyer &
　　　　　Wilson, 1973, Contrib. Sci. (244):21).

Bronia Gray, 1865.
1971 Bronia kraoh Vanzolini, Pap. Avul. Zool. 24:193. Type-
　　　　　locality: Brasil, Goias, Pedro Afonso. Distribution:
　　　　　known only from type locality.

Ceiolaemus Laurent, 1984, J. Herpetol. 18:370. Type-species:
　　　　　Leiosaurus marmoratus Burmeister. Distribution:
　　　　　provinces of La Rioja and Catamarca, Argentina. Content:
　　　　　two species.
　　　C. anomalus (Koslowsky).
　　　C. marmoratus (Burmeister).
　　　1981 Liolaemus pseudanomalus Cei, J. Herpetol. 15:253. Nomen
　　　　　novum for L. marmoratus Burmeister.

Celestus Gray, 1839. Content: seventeen species, five occur from
　　　　　Mexico to Nicaragua, fide Strahm & Schwartz, 1977,
　　　　　Biotropica 9:58-72.
　　　C. atitlanensis Smith = Diplogossus atitlanensis, fide Strahm
　　　　　& Schwartz, 1977, op. cit.
　　　C. cyanochloris Cope = Diploglossus cyanochloris, fide Strahm
　　　　　& Schwartz, 1977, op. cit.

Cnemidophorus Wagler, 1830.
1969 C. cozumelae maslini Fritts, Copeia (3):524. Type-locality:
　　　　　Mexico, Campeche, 16 mi SW Champoton. Distribution:
　　　　　coastal areas of Campeche, Mexico, to central El Peten,
　　　　　Guatemala.
　　　C. lemniscatus arubensis (Van Lidth) = C. arubenis, Schall,
　　　　　1973, J. Herpetol. 7:289-95.
　　　C. vittatus Boulenger, 1902 = Ameiva vittata, fide Vance,
　　　　　1978, J. Herpetol. 12:98-100.

Coleodactylus Parker, 1926.
1980 C. septentrionalis Vanzolini, Pap. Avul. Zool. 34:2.
　　　　　Type-locality: Brasil, Roraima, Ilha Maraca, Rio
　　　　　Uraricoera. Distribution: Roraima area, Brasil; Surinam.

Colobodactylus Amaral, 1933.

1977 C. dalcyanus Vanzolini & Ramos, Pap. Avul. Zool. 31:26.
        Type-locality: Brasil, Rio de Janeiro, Brejo da Lapa,
        Itatiaia. Distribution: Atlantic forest of Sao Paulo
        region, Brasil.

Colobosaura Boulenger, 1862. See Vanzolini & Ramos, 1977, Ibid.
        31:19-47.
    C. kraepelini (Werner) = incertae sedis, fide Vanzolini &
        Ramos, 1977, op. cit..
1977 C. landii Cunha, Bol. Mus. Paraense Emilio Goeldi, Zool. 86:3.
        Type-locality: Brasil, Para, Curupati. Distribution:
        eastern Para, Brasil.

Ctenoblepharis Tschudi, 1845. Includes Phrynosaura Werner, 1907,
        fide Donoso-Barros, 1972, Bol. Soc. Biol. Concepcion
        44:129-34; further modified by subsequent authors,
        considered monotypic by Laurent, 1984, J. Herpetol.
        18:357-73. Distribution: coastal desert of Peru.
    C. adspersa Tschudi.
    C. anomala (Koslowsky) = Liolaemus anomalus, fide Cei, 1979,
        J. Herpetol. 13:297-302 = Ceiolaemus anomalus, Laurent,
        1984, Ibid. 18:359.
1983 C. audituvelatus Nunez & Yanez, Copeia (2):454. Type-locality:
        Chile, Llano de Vilama, 10 km E San Pedro de Atacama.
        = Phrynosaura audituvelatus, fide Laurent, 1984, Ibid.
        18:371. Distribution: Llanos de Vilama y Paciencia,
        Antofagasta, Chile.
    C. jamesi Boulenger = Liolaemus jamesi fide Cei, 1979, Ibid.
        13:297-302.
    Phrynosaura marmorata (Burmeister) = Liolaemus marmoratus,
        fide Cei, 1980, J. Herpetol. 14:192-93 = Ctenoblepharis
        marmorata, fide Duellman, 1979, Mus. Nat. Hist. Univ.
        Kansas Monogr. 7:371-459 = Ceiolaemus marmoratus, fide
        Laurent, 1984, Ibid. 18:359.
    C. nigriceps Philippi = Liolaemus nigriceps, fide Laurent,
        1984, Ibid. 18:370.
    Phrynosaura reichei (Werner) = Ctenoblepharis reichei, fide
        Donoso-Barros, 1972, Ibid. 44:129-34 = Phrynosaura
        reichei, fide Laurent, 1984, Ibid. 18:371.
    C. schmidti Marx = Liolaemus schmidti, fide Cei, 1979, Ibid.
        13:297-302.
    C. stolzmanni (Steindachner) = Phrynosaura stolzmanni, fide
        Laurent, 1984, Ibid. 18:371.

Cupriguanus Gallardo, 1974 = Pristidactylus Fitzinger, 1843, fide
        Etheridge, in Paull, Williams & Hall, 1976, Breviora
        441:1-31.
1975 C. alvaroi Donoso-Barros, Bol. Soc. Biol. Concepcion [1974]
        48:221. Type-locality: Chile, Santiago, Cerro El Roble.
        Distribution: Nothofagus forest of central Chile.

Diploglossus Wiegmann, 1834. Content: twelve species, eight from
        Guatemala to Colombia and Ecuador, and disjunct
        populations in Brasil and Peru, fide Strahm & Schwartz,

8

```
              1977, Biotropica 9:58-72.
      D. fasciatus (Gray). Distribution: also Peru (MVZ).
1973 D. montisylvestris Myers, Amer. Mus. Nov. (2523):3. Type-
          locality: Panama, Darien, southeastern slope of Cerro
          Pirre, 1440 m. Distribution: Serrania de Pirre, Panama.


Ecpleopus Dumeril & Bibron, 1839. Includes Arthroseps Boulenger,
          1898, but not Aspidolaemus Peters, fide Uzzell, 1969,
          Postilla 135:1-23.
      E. affinis (Peters) = Pholidobolus affinis, fide Montanucci,
          1973, op. cit.
      E. gaudichaudii D.& B. See Uzzell, 1969, op. cit.


Enyalioides Boulenger, 1885.
1973 E. cofanorum Duellman, Herpetologica 29:230. Type-locality:
          Ecuador, Napo, Santa Cecilia. Distribution: Amazonian
          basin of Ecuador.


Enyalius Wagler, 1830.
      E. bibronii Boulenger = E. catenatus bibronii, fide Jackson,
          1978, Arq. Zool. 30:1-79.
1968 E. boulengeri Etheridge, Bull. British Mus. (Nat. Hist.)
          18:250. Type-locality: Brasil, Espirito Santo. = E.
          brasiliensis boulengeri, fide Jackson 1978, op. cit.
          Distribution: Espirito Santo and southeastern Minas
          Gerais, Brasil.
      E. pictus (Wied) = E. catenatus pictus, fide Jackson, 1978,
          op. cit.
1978 E. perditus Jackson, Ibid. 30:24. Type-locality: Brasil, Sao
          Paulo, Estacao Biologica de Boraceia. Distribution:
          Atlantic forest of southeastern Brasil.


Euspondylus Tschudi, 1845.
Generic concepts in the microteiids are very uncertain, and
Euspondylus at all times has been a catch-all genus. When
identifying an animal apparently belonging to it, also try other
related genera. Key in Uzzell, 1973, Postilla 159:1-67.
1968 E. ampuedae Lancini, Publ. Ocas. Mus. Cien. Nat. Caracas 12:4.
          Type-locality: Venezuela, Tachira, Villa Paez, 2000m =
          ?Prionodactylus vertebralis, fide Uzzell, 1973, op. cit.
          Distribution: known only from type locality.
      E. brevifrontalis Boulenger = Anadia brevifrontalis, fide
          Oftedal, 1974, Ibid. 25:203-65
      E. leucostictus (Boulenger) designated type-species of Riolama
          by Uzzell, 1973, op. cit.
      E. ocellifer (Werner) = Pholidobolus affinis, fide Montanucci,
          1973, Ibid. 59:1-52.
1968 E. phelpsi Lancini, Ibid. 12:2.  Type-locality: Venezuela,
          Bolivar, Cerro de Jaua, Alto Caura. Distribution: known
          only from type locality.
      E. spinalis Boulenger, 1911, not 1901.


Garbesaura Amaral, 1933 = Enyalius Wagler, fide Vanzolini, 1973,
          Pap. Avul. Zool. 27:173-75.
```

G. garbei Amaral = Enyalius leechii, fide Vanzolini, 1973,
op. cit.

Garthia Donoso-Barros & Vanzolini, 1965.
1970 G. gaudichaudii klugei Donoso-Barros, Bol. Mus. Nac. Hist.
Nat. Chile 31:83. Type-locality: Chile, Pichidangui,
Isla de Locos. Distribution: Pichidangui region, Chile.

Gonatodes Fitzinger, 1843.
1980 G. tapajonicus Rodrigues, Pap. Avul. Zool. 33:309.
Type-locality: Brasil, Para, Cachoeira do Limao, Rio
Tapajos. Distribution: known only from type locality.

Gymnodactylus Spix, 1825.
G. darwinii (Gray), fide Vanzolini, 1982, Pap. Avul. Zool.
34:406. Distribution: coastal forest of Brasil from
Pernambuco to Sao Paulo.
1982 G. guttulatus Vanzolini, Pap. Avul. Zool. 34:403.
Type-locality: Brasil, Minas Gerais, Guinda, 1320-60 m.
Distribution: southern end of Espinhaco Range, Brasil.

Hemidactylus Gray, 1825.
1978 H. agrius Vanzolini, Pap. Avul. Zool. 31:307. Type-locality:
Brasil, Piaui, Valenca. Distribution: northeast Brasil.
H. brookii leightoni Boulenger, 1911, revalidated by Kluge,
1969, Misc. Publ. Mus. Zool. Univ. Michigan 138:1-78.
Distribution: northwestern coast to central highlands of
Colombia
H. frenatus D.& B. Distribution: also Panama (USNM).
H. mabouia (Moreau de Jonnes). Distribution: in continental
So. America - Guyana, Surinam and French Guiana,
Amazonian Ecuador, Peru, Bolivia and Brasil, and Brasil
from northeast to southeast (Vanzolini, 1978, Ibid.
31:307-43).
1969 H. palaichthus Kluge, Ibid. 138:39. Type-locality: Guyana,
Kurupukari. Distribution: northern Brasil, Guyana,
central and northeastern Venezuela, Trinidad, and St.
Lucia.
H. peruvianus Wiegmann = H. garnotii, fide Kluge & Eckardt,
1969, Copeia (4):651-64. Comment: a senior synonym of
garnotii but K.& E. chose not to use it because of its
questionable type locality and nomenclatural stability.

Homonota Gray, 1845.
1978 H. andicola Cei, Publ. Ocas. Inst. Biol. Anim. Cuyo, Cien.
1:1. Type-locality: Argentina, Mendoza, 40 km N
Uspallata, 2300 m. Distribution: high valleys east of
Andes between Uspallata and Angualasto, Argentina.
1978 H. darwinii macrocephala Cei, Ibid. 4:1. Type-locality:
Argentina, Salta, El Quebrachal. Distribution: known
only from type locality.

Iguana Laurenti, 1768. Content: no subspecies, fide Lazell, 1973,
Bull. Mus. Comp. Zool. 145:1-28.

Iphisa Gray, 1851. Distribution: forests of Amazonian lowlands of
              Peru, Ecuador, Brasil, Bolivia, Colombia, and Guiana
              shield forest of Guyana, Surinam and French Guiana.
1974 Iphisa elegans soinii Dixon, Herpetologica 30:138.
              Type-locality: Peru, San Martin, Tocache Nuevo.
              Distribution: Bolivia and Peru.

Kentropyx Spix, 1825.
Key to all species in Gallagher & Dixon, 1980, Copeia (4):616-20.
(G.& D. place Lacerta vittata Schinz in synonymy of K. calcarata
and Monoplocus dorsalis Gunther in that of K. pelviceps; the two
synonyms are older than the current names and would replace them.
Neither name has a type specimen or a figure, hence replacement is
unjustified. I do not adopt these synonyms. P.E.V.)
              K. altamazonica Cope, fide Gallagher & Dixon, 1980, Ibid.:616.
              1876 Centropyx altamazonicus Cope.
              1929 Kentropyx williamsoni Ruthven.
                Distribution: Amazonia.
              K. borckiana Peters, revalidated by Hoogmoed, 1973, Liz.
                Amphisb. Surinam, W. Junk.
              K. calcarata Spix, fide Gallagher & Dixon, 1980, Ibid. :616.
              1825 Kentropyx calcarata Spix.
              1831 Teius (Centropyx) intermedius Gray.
                Distribution: Amazonia, Guianas, and eastern Brasil.
              K. pelviceps Cope, 1868. Distribution: western Amazonia.
1980 Kentropyx vanzoi Gallagher & Dixon, Ibid. :617. Type-locality:
              base camp Royal Society of London expedition to Mato
              Grosso. Distribution: central Brasil.
              K. viridistriga Boulenger, fide Gallagher & Dixon,1980,op.cit.
              1894 Centropyx viridistriga Boulenger.
              1962 Kentropyx lagartija Gallardo.
                Distribution: Mato Grosso in Brasil, Paraguay and Argentina
                as far south as Tucuman.

Leiolopisma Dumeril & Bibron.
Neotropical species now assigned to Sphenomorphus (assata, cherriei
& incerta) and Scincella, fide Greer, 1974, Australian J. Zool.,
Suppl. Ser. (31):1-67.

Leiosaurus Dumeril & Bibron, 1837.
              L. bardensis Gallardo = Cupriguanus bardensis, fide Cei &
                Roig, 1973, Deserta 4:69-91; = Pristidactylus fasciatus,
                fide Etheridge & Williams 1985, Breviora 483:1-18.
              L. fasciatus D´Orbigny & Bibron = Cupriguanus fasciatus, fide
                Barrio, 1969, Physis 29:268-270; = Pristidactylus
                fasciatus, fide Etheridge & Williams 1985, op. cit.
              L. paronae (Peracca) = Aperopristis paronae, fide Cei, 1973,
                Physis 32:447-58.

Lepidoblepharis Peracca, 1897.
The key in Peters & Donoso-Barros contains disabling errors.
1983 L. duolepis Ayala & Castro, Caldasia, 13:749. Type-locality:
              Colombia, Valle, Rio Pance, 3 km above Parque

11

Recreacional Departamental. Distribution: Valle del
Cauca and Antioquia, Colombia.
L. festae colombianus Mechler = L. colombianus, fide
Vanzolini, 1978, Pap. Avul. Zool. 31:203-11.
1985 L. grandis Miyata, Herpetologica 41:12. Type-locality:
Ecuador, Pichincha, 3.7 km E Dos Rios (village), 1190 m.
Distribution: Pacific slope of Pichincha, Ecuador.
1978 L. heyerorum Vanzolini, Ibid. 31:204. Type-locality: Brasil
Amazonas, Puruzinho, Rio Madeira. Distribution: middle
Madeira region, Brasil.
L. microlepis (Noble). Revalidated by Ayala & Castro, 1983,
Ibid. 13:744. Distribution: known only from type
locality.
1985 L. miyatai Lamar, Herpetologica 41:128. Type-locality:
Colombia, Magdalena, Ancon Guairara. Distribution: known
only from type locality.

Lepidodactylus Fitzinger, 1843. No changes.
L. lugubris (D.& B.). Distribution: also Nicaragua (Henderson
et al., 1976, Herpetol. Rev. 7:173)and Costa Rica (Mudde
& van Dijk, 1984, Lacerta 43:36-37).

Lepidophyma A. Dumeril, 1851.
1973 L. mayae Bezy, Contrib. Sci. Los Angeles Co. Mus. (239):1.
Type-locality: Guatemala, Alta Verapaz, nr. Chinaja, 140
m. Distribution: known only from type locality.

Leposoma Spix, 1825.
1982 L. hexalepis Ayala & Harris, Caldasia 13:468. Type-locality:
Colombia, Vichada, Puerto Carreno. Distribution:
Comisaria del Vichada, Colombia.
1971 L. ioanna Uzzell & Barry, Postilla 154:21. Type-locality:
Colombia, Valle del Cauca, 15 km W Rio Calima.
Distribution: Valle del Cauca, Colombia.

Liolaemus Wiegmann, 1834.
The key in Peters & Donoso-Barros is useless. The researcher should
prepare a matrix for geographic area of interest. The following
list contains all currently valid species and subspecies.
L. alticolor alticolor Barbour.
L. alticolor walkeri Shreve.
L. altissimus = L. belli altissimus Muller & Hellmich.
L. andinus Koslowsky, revalidated by Laurent, 1982, Neotropica
28:89. Distribution: Andes of Catamarca, Argentina.
L. annectens Boulenger, revalidated by Laurent, 1982, Bol.
Asoc. Herpetol. Argentina 1:16. Distribution: Andes of
southern Peru.
1971 L. archeforus Donoso-Barros & Cei, J. Herpetol. 5:93.
Type-locality: Argentina, Santa Cruz, Puesto Lebrun,
Meseta del Lago Buenos Aires, 1500 m. Distribution:
Buenos Aires lake region, Argentina.
1974 L. austromendocinus Cei, J. Herpetol. 8:224. Type-locality:
Argentina, Mendoza, 70 km S Nihuil Dam. Distribution:
southern Mendoza province, Argentina.

L. bellii (Gray), revalidated by Laurent, 1982, Ibid. 1:16; four subspecies recognized. Distrbution: Cordilleran region from 32 to 42 S in Chile and Argentina.

L. belli bellii (Gray).

1845 Leiolaemus bellii Gray.

1860 Proctotretus modestus Philippi.

1932 Liolaemus altissimus Muller & Hellmich.

L. bellii araucaniensis Muller & Hellmich.

L. bellii moradoensis Hellmich & Hellmich.

L. bellii neuquensis Muller & Hellmich.

L. bisignatus (Philippi), revalidated by Ortiz, 1981, An. Mus. Hist. Nat. Valparaiso 14:258. Distribution: provinces of Atacama and Coquimbo, Chile.

L. bibronii (Bell).

1984 L. bitaeniatus Laurent, Acta Zool. Lilloana 37:275. Type-locality: Argentina, Tucuman, La Angostura, Tafi del Valle. Distribution: northwestern Argentina from Jujuy and Salta to Tucuman.

L. buergeri Werner.

1979 L. capillitas Hulse, Ann. Carnegie Mus. 48:204. Type-locality: Argentina, Catamarca, 5 km S Minas Capillitas, 3900 m. Distribution: known only from type locality.

1971 L. ceii Donoso-Barros, Herpetologica 27:49 Type-locality: Argentina, Neuquen, Lonco Luan Plateau, 1550 m. Distribution: known only from type locality.

L. chacoensis Shreve.

L. chiliensis (Lesson).

1983 L. coeruleus Cei & Ortiz, Bol. Soc. Biol. Concepcion, Chile 54:36. Type-locality: Argentina, Neuquen, Zapala, 10 km W Primeros Pinos, 1700m. Distribution: known only from vicinity of type locality.

L. constanzae Donoso-Barros.

L. copiapensis Muller & Hellmich, revalidated by Ortiz, 1981, An. Mus. Hist. Nat. Valpariaiso 14:258. Distribution: vicinity of Copiapo, Argentina.

1973 Pelusaurus cranwelli Donoso-Barros = L. cranwelli Laurent, 1984, J. Herpetol. 18:370.

L. curicensis Muller & Hellmich, fide Ortiz, 1981, An. Mus. Hist. Nat. Valparaiso 14:258. Distribution: Cordillera de Curico, Chile.

1985 L. curis Nunez & Labra, Copeia (3):557. Type-locality: Chile, Termas de El Flaco on S shore of Tinguiririca River. Distribution: known only from type locality.

1980 L. fitzingeri cuyanus Cei & Scolaro, J. Herpetol. 14:38. Type-locality: Argentina, San Juan, 10 km E Caucete, 400 m. = L. cuyanus fide Cei & Scolaro, 1983, Bol. Asoc. Herpetol. Argentina 1:16. Distribution: provinces of La Rioja, San Juan, and Mendoza, Argentina.

L. cyanogaster cyanogaster (Dumeril & Bibron).

L. cyanogaster brattstroemi Donoso-Barros.

L. darwinii (Bell).

1974 Ctenoblepharis donosobarrosi Cei, Ibid. 8:72. Type-locality: Argentina, Mendoza, Matancilla = Liolaemus donosobarrosi fide Cei, 1979, Ibid. 13:297-302. Distribution: known

13

only from type locality.

1975 <u>L</u>. <u>donosoi</u> Ortiz, An. Mus. Nac. Hist. Nat. (Santiago) 8:62.
Type-locality: Chile, Antofagasta, Agua Verde, Quebrada
de Taltal.

<u>L</u>. <u>dorbignyi</u> Koslowsky.

1978 <u>L</u>. <u>duellmani</u> Cei, Occ. Pap. Univ. Kansas Mus. Nat. Hist. 76:1.
Type-locality: Argentina, Mendoza, Paso El Choique, 50
km S El Manzano, 2260 m. Distribution: known only from
type locality.

<u>L</u>. <u>elegans</u> Tschudi.

1985 <u>L</u>. <u>eleodori</u> Cei, Etheridge & Videla, Deserta [1983] 7:317.
Type-locality: Argentina, San Juan, Estepa de Llano de
Los Hoyos. Distribution: vicinity of type locality.

<u>L</u>. <u>elongatus</u> <u>elongatus</u> Koslowsky.

1971 <u>L</u>. <u>elongatus</u> <u>petrophilus</u> Donoso-Barros & Cei, Ibid. 5:94.
Type-locality: Argentina, Rio Negro, Meseta de
Somuncura, entre Laguna Raimunda y Laguna Clara, 1400 m
(= Lagunas Chara and Raimundo). Distribution: Somuncura
Plateau, Argentina.

1970 <u>L</u>. <u>emmae</u> Donoso-Barros, Bol. Soc. Biol. Concepcion 42:23.
Type-locality: Argentina, Cordoba, Salares de Totoralejo
= <u>Liolaemus</u> <u>chacoensis</u>, fide Cei, 1980, J. Herpetol.
14:192-93.

1984 <u>L</u>. <u>exploratorum</u> Cei & Williams, Rev. Mus. La Plata (N.S.)
13:187. Type-locality: Argentina, Santa Cruz, Lago
Buenos Aires. Distribution: known from type locality.

1983 <u>L</u>. <u>fabiani</u> Yanez & Nunez, Copeia (3):788. Type-locality:
Chile, 10 km E Sendero de Atacama in Llano de Vilama.
Distribution: known only from type locality.

1980 <u>L</u>. <u>famatinae</u> Cei, J. Herpetol. 14:60. Type-locality:
Argentina, La Rioja, 2 km E Cueva de Perez, 1400 m.
Distribution: Sierra de Famatina, Argentina.

<u>L</u>. <u>fitzgeraldi</u> Boulenger.

<u>L</u>. <u>fitzingeri</u> <u>fitzingeri</u> (Dumeril & Bibron).

1975 <u>L</u>. <u>fitzingeri</u> <u>canqueli</u> Cei, J. Herpetol. 9:290.
Type-locality: Argentina, Chubut, Callejas, Meseta
Canquel. Distribution: Canquel Plateau, Argentina.

<u>L</u>. <u>fitzingeri</u> <u>melanops</u> Burmeister, Type-locality: Argentina,
Chubut, Quele-cura; revalidated by Cei, 1973, Ibid.
32:447-58.

1982 <u>L</u>. <u>forsteri</u> Laurent, Spixiana 5:139. Type-locality: Bolivia,
Chacaltaya, nr. La Paz, 4700 m. Distribution: known only
from type locality.

<u>L</u>. <u>fuscus</u> Boulenger.

<u>L</u>. <u>gracilis</u> (Bell).

<u>L</u>. <u>gravenhorstii</u> (Gray).

1984 <u>L</u>. <u>griseus</u> Laurent, Acta Zool. Lilloana 37:278. Type-locality:
Argentina, Tucuman, nr. northern ridge of Cerro Isabel,
4600 m. Distribution: Cumbres Calchaquies, Argentina.

1975 <u>L</u>. <u>hellmichi</u> Donoso-Barros, Bol. Soc. Biol. Concepcion [1974]
48:224. Type-locality: Chile, Antofagasta, Cerro
Moreno. Distribution: only type locality.

<u>Ctenoblepharis</u> <u>jamesi</u> Boulenger = <u>Lioaemus</u> <u>jamesi</u> fide Cei,
1979, Ibid. 13:297-302.

14

<u>L</u>. <u>kingii</u> <u>kingii</u> (Bell).

1981 <u>L</u>. <u>kingii</u> <u>somuncurae</u> Cei & Scolaro, J. Herpetol. 15:207.
Type-locality: Argentina, Rio Negro, Meseta de Somuncura
nr. Lago Raimundo, 1400 m. Distribution: Meseta de
Somuncura, Argentina.

<u>L</u>. <u>kriegi</u> Muller & Hellmich.

<u>L</u>. <u>kuhlmanni</u> Muller & Hellmich, fide Ortiz, 1981, An. Mus.
Hist. Nat. Valparaiso 14:258. Distribution: provinces of
Coquimbo, Aconcagua, Valparaiso and Santiago, Chile.

<u>L</u>. <u>lemniscatus</u> Gravenhorst.

<u>L</u>. <u>lentus</u> Gallardo = <u>L</u>. <u>anomalus</u> Koslowsky, fide Cei, 1979,
Ibid. 13:297-302.

<u>L</u>. <u>leopardinus</u> <u>leopardinus</u> Muller & Hellmich.

<u>L</u>. <u>leopardinus</u> <u>ramonensis</u> Muller & Hellmich.

<u>L</u>. <u>leopardinus</u> <u>valdesianus</u> Hellmich.

<u>L</u>. <u>lineomaculatus</u> Boulenger.

<u>L</u>. <u>lorenzmuelleri</u> Hellmich.

<u>L</u>. <u>magellanicus</u> (Hombron & Jacquinot).

<u>L</u>. <u>melanops</u> Burmeister, revalidated by Cei & Scolaro, 1983,
Bol. Asoc. Herp. Argentina 1:15, with three subspecies.

<u>L</u>. <u>m</u>. <u>melanops</u> Burmeister.

1938 <u>L</u>. <u>goetschi</u> Muller & Hellmich.
Distribution: btw. Rios Chubut and Colorado, Argentina.

<u>L</u>. <u>m</u>. <u>canqueli</u> Cei, fide Cei & Scolaro, 1983, op. cit.

1975 <u>L</u>. <u>fitzingeri</u> <u>canqueli</u> Cei, J. Herpetol. 9:220.
Type-locality: Argentina, Chubut, Callejas, 900 m.
Distribution: Meseta de Canquel, Argentina.

<u>L</u>. <u>m</u>. <u>xanthoviridis</u> Cei & Scolaro, fide Cei & Scolaro, 1983,
op. cit. Distribution: S of Rio Chubut, Argentina.

1980 <u>L</u>. <u>fitzingeri</u> <u>xanthoviridis</u> Cei & Scolaro, J. Herpetol.
14:39. Type-locality: Argentina, Chubut, 18 km MW Dos
Pozos.

<u>L</u>. <u>mocquardi</u> Pellegrin.

<u>L</u>. <u>montanus</u> Koslowsky, fide Laurent, 1982, Neotropica 28:91.
Distribution: known only from type locality.

<u>L</u>. <u>monticola</u> <u>monticola</u> Muller & Hellmich.

<u>L</u>. <u>monticola</u> <u>chillanensis</u> Muller & Hellmich.

<u>L</u>. <u>monticola</u> <u>villaricensis</u> Muller & Hellmich.

<u>L</u>. <u>multicolor</u> Koslowsky, fide Laurent, 1982. op. cit.
Distribution: Laguna de Guatayo area, Jujuy, Argentina.

<u>L</u>. <u>multiformis</u> (Cope).

<u>L</u>. <u>multimaculatus</u> <u>multimaculatus</u> D. & B., fide Cei, 1979,
Ibid. 13:300. Distribution: coast of Buenos Aires.

1979 <u>L</u>. <u>multimaculatus</u> <u>riojanus</u> Cei, Ibid. 13:299. Type-locality:
Argentina, La Rioja, Baldecitos. Distribution: La Rioja
and San Juan provinces, western Argentina.

<u>L</u>. <u>nigriceps</u> (Philippi), fide Laurent, 1984, J. Herpetol.
18:370. Distribution: high cordillera of Atacama, Chile.

<u>L</u>. <u>nigromaculatus</u> (Wiegmann).

<u>L</u>. <u>nigroviridis</u> <u>nigroviridis</u> Muller & Hellmich.

<u>L</u>. <u>nigroviridis</u> <u>minor</u> Muller & Hellmich.

<u>L</u>. <u>nigroviridis</u> <u>nigroroseus</u> Donoso-Barros.

<u>L</u>. <u>nitidus</u> (Wiegmann).

<u>L</u>. <u>ornatus</u> Koslowsky.

1983 L. <u>ortizi</u> Laurent, Spixiana 5:142. Type-locality: Peru, Cuzco.
Distribution: known only from type locality (imprecise).
L. <u>pantherinus</u> Pellegrin.
L. <u>paulinae</u> Donoso-Barros.
L. <u>pictus pictus</u> (Dumeril & Bibron).
L. <u>pictus argentinus</u> Muller & Hellmich.
L. <u>pictus chiloeensis</u> Muller & Hellmich.
L. <u>pictus major</u> Boulenger.
1977 L. <u>pictus talcanensis</u> Urbina & Zuniga, An. Mus. Hist. Nat.
Valparaiso 10:. Type-locality: Chile, Chiloe, Isla
Talcan, Sector Tendedor.
L. <u>platei</u> Werner.
L. <u>pulcher</u> Pellegrin, fide Laurent, 1983, Bol. Asoc. Herpetol.
Argent. 1:16. Distribution: Peruvian-Bolivian altiplano.
1974 <u>Ctenoblepharis</u> <u>rabinoi</u> Cei, J. Herpetol. 8:73. Type-locality:
Argentina, Mendoza, Nihuil Dam, 1800 m = <u>Liolaemus</u>
<u>rabinoi</u>, fide Cei, 1978, Publ. Ocas. Inst. Biol. Anim,
Univ. Nac. Cuyo. 7:1-4. Distribution: type locality.
L. <u>robertmertensi</u> Hellmich.
L. <u>rothi</u> Koslowsky.
L. <u>ruibali</u> Donoso-Barros.
1971 L. <u>ruizleali</u> Donoso-Barros & Cei, Ibid. 5:93. Type-locality:
Argentina, Rio Negro, Cerro Corona, Meseta de Somuncura,
1600 m. Distribution: known only from type locality.
1982 L. <u>sanjuanensis</u> Cei, J. Herpetol. 16:179. Type-locality:
Argentina, San Juan, nr. Mogote, Corralitos, Sierra Pie
de Palo, 3200 m. Distribution: only from type locality.
1973 L. <u>sarmientoi</u> Donoso-Barros, Neotropica 19:163. Type-locality:
Chile, Magallanes, Monte Aymondi. = L. <u>archeforus</u>
<u>sarmientoi</u>. Distribution: known only from type locality.
1982 L. <u>scapularis</u> Laurent, Spixiana 5:144. Type-locality:
Argentina, Catamarca, Nacimiento. Distribution:
Catamarca and Tucuman, Argentina.
<u>Ctenoblepharis schmidti</u> Marx = <u>Liolaemus</u> <u>schmidti</u>, fide Cei,
1979, Ibid. 13:297-302.
L. <u>schroederi</u> Muller & Hellmich.
L. <u>signifer</u> (Dumeril & Bibron).
L. <u>simonsii</u> Boulenger, fide Laurent, 1983, Ibid. 1:16.
Distribution: Andes of southern Bolivia & northern
Argentina.
L. <u>tacnae</u> (Shreve), fide Duellman, 1979.
L. <u>tenuis tenuis</u> (Dumeril & Bibron).
L. <u>tenuis punctatissimus</u> Muller & Hellmich.
1982 L. <u>uspallatensis</u> Macola & Castro, Publ. Ocas. Inst. Biol.
Anim. Univ. Cuyo, Ser. Cien. 15:1. Type-locality:
Argentina, Mendoza, Uspallata. Distribution: vicinity of
type locality.
1984 L. <u>variegatus</u> Laurent, Acta Zool. Lilloana 37:273.
Type-locality: Bolivia, Cochabamba, Tiraque, 3100 m.
Distribution: Andes of Cochabamba.
L. <u>walkeri</u> Shreve, fide Laurent, 1983, Ibid. 1:16.
L. <u>zapallarensis</u> Muller & Hellmich, fide Ortiz, 1981, An. Mus.
Hist. Nat. Valparaiso 14:258, with three subspecies.
L. <u>z. zapallarensis</u> M. & H. Distribution: coast of Chile,

provinces of Coquimbo and Aconcagua.

L. z. **ater** M. & H. Distribution: islands in bay of Coquimbo.

L. z. **sieversi** Donoso-Barros. Distribution: type locality.

Lygodactylus Gray, 1864
    1880 **Scalabotes** Peters.
    1883 **Microscalabotes** Boulenger.
    1977 **Vanzoia** Smith, Martin & Swain, Pap. Avul. Zool. 30:196.
        Type-species: **Vanzoia klugei** S.,M.&S. = **Lygodactylus**
        Bons & Pasteur, 1977, C.R. Acad. Sci., Paris 284:2547.
        Distribution: Africa, Madagascar, northeastern Brasil, Mato
        Grosso do Sul, Paraguay and southern Bolivia.
    1977 **Vanzoia klugei** Smith, Martin & Swain, Ibid. 30:196.
        Type-locality: Brasil, Pernambuco, Carnaubeira. =
        Lygodactylus klugei, fide Bons & Pasteur, 1977, op. cit.
        Distribution: northeastern Brasil.
    1977 **V. wetzeli** Smith, Martin & Swain, Ibid. 30:198. Type-locality:
        Brasil, Mato Grosso do Sul, Urucum. = **Lygodactylus
        wetzeli**, Bons & Pasteur, 1977, op. cit. Distribution:
        Mato Grosso do Sul and adjacent Paraguay and Bolivia.

Mabuya Fitzinger, 1843
    1981 **M. arajara** Reboucas-Spieker, Pap. Avul. Zool. 34:121.
        Type-locality: Brasil, Ceara, Arajara. Distribution:
        northeastern Brasil.
    M. brachypoda Taylor = **M. unimarginata**, fide Savage, 1973,
        Herpetofauna Costa Rica.
    1974 **M. caissara** Reboucas-Spieker, Pap. Avul. Zool. 28:228.
        Type-locality: Brasil, Sao Paulo, Praia de Massaguassu,
        Caraguatatuba. Distribution: coast of Sao Paulo north of
        Santos and island of Sao Sebastiao.
    1973 **M. croizati** Horton, J. Herpetol. 7:75. Type-locality:
        Venezuela, Sucre, Mt. Turumiquire. Distribution: Mt.
        Turumiquire and Elvecia, Venezuela.
    1981 **M. ficta** Reboucas-Spieker, Ibid. 34:161. Type-locality:
        Brasil, Amazonas, Pauini. Distribution: Amazonia.
    M. mabouya mabouya (Lacepede) of Amazonia = **M. bistriata**, fide
        Reboucas-Speiker, 1981, Pap. Avul. Zool. 34:121-23.
    M. m. alliacea Cope = **M. unimarginata** fide Savage, 1973, Ibid.

Macropholidus Noble, 1921.
    M. annectens Parker = **Pholidobolus annectens**, fide Montanucci,
        1973, Ibid. 59:1-52.

Morunasaurus Dunn, 1932.
    M. annularis (O'Shaughnessy). Distribution: also Colombia
        (Corredor et al., 1985, J. Herpetol. 19:162-64) and Peru
        (MVZ & USNM).
    M. groi Dunn. Distribution: Andean foot hills in western
        Antioquia (Corredor et al., 1985, op. cit.)

Neusticurus Dumeril & Bibron, 1839.
    1981 **N. medemi** Dixon & Lamar, J. Herpetol. 15:309. Type-locality:
        Colombia, Vaupes, Cano Monserero, tributary of Cano Ti.

Distribution: Comisaria de Vaupes, Colombia.

Nothobachia Rodrigues, 1984, Pap. Avul. Zool. 35:361. Type-species:
    N. ablephara Rodrigues, 1984. Content: monotypic.
1984 N. ablephara Rodrigues, Ibid. 35:361. Type-locality: Brasil,
    Piaui, Sao Raimundo Nonato; corrected to Sal, Piaui
    (Rodrigues, 1985, Pap. Avul. Zool. 36:169-70).
    Distribution: northeastern Brasil.

Ophiognomon Cope, 1868 = Bachia, fide Dixon, 1973, Misc. Publ.
    Univ. Kansas Mus. Nat. Hist. 57:1-47.

Ophryoessoides A. Dumeril, 1851
    O. aculeatus (O'Shaughnessy). Distribution: Amazonian lowlands
        of Ecuador, Peru and Bolivia (USNM).
    O. arenarius (Tschudi) = Tropidurus arenarius, fide Fritts,
        1974, Mem. San Diego Soc. Nat. Hist. 7:1-89.
    O. festae (Peracca) = Stenocercus festae, fide Fritts, 1974,
        op. cit.
    O. formosus (Boulenger) = Stenocercus formosus, fide Fritts,
        1974, op. cit.
    O. guentheri (Boulenger) = Stenocercus guentheri, fide Fritts,
        1974, op. cit.
    O. haenschi (Werner) = Stenocercus haenschi, fide Fritts,
        1974, op. cit.
    O. ornatus (Gray) = Stenocercus ornatus, fide Fritts, 1974,
        op. cit.
    O. rhodomelas (Boulenger) = Steocercus rhodomelas, fide
        Fritts, 1974, op. cit.
    O. trachycephalus (A. Dumeril) = Stenocercus trachycephalus,
        fide Fritts, 1974, op. cit.

Pelusaurus Donoso-Barros, 1973, Neotropica 19:132. Type-species: P.
    cranwelli Donoso-Barros, 1973. = Liolaemus, fide
    Laurent, 1984, Ibid. 18:370.
1973 P. cranwelli Donoso-Barros, Ibid. 19:133. Type-locality:
    Bolivia, Santa Cruz, Nueva Moka. Distribution: known
    only from type locality.

Phenacosaurus Barbour, 1920.
1969 P. orcesi Lazell, Breviora 325:14. Type-locality: Ecuador,
    Napo, Mt. Sumaco. Distribution: Napo province, Ecuador.
    P. richteri Dunn = P. heterodermus (A. Dumeril, 1851), fide
        Lazell, 1969, Ibid. 325:1-24.

Pholidobolus Peters, 1862.
Montanucci, 1973, Misc. Publ. Univ. Kansas Mus. Nat. Hist. 59:1-5,
revised this genus and provided key, species descriptions and
distributions.
    P. affinis (Peters).
    P. annectens (Parker).
1973 P. macbrydei Montanucci, Ibid. 59:35. Type-locality: Ecuador,
    Canar, 9.1 km N 2.3 km W Biblian, near Hda. Oeste, 3070
    m. Distribution: crests and slopes of Eastern and

Western Cordilleras, Ecuador.
P. montium (Peters).
1973 P. prefrontalis Montanucci, Ibid. 59:32. Type-locality:
Ecuador, Chimborazo, 4.9 km S Tixan. Distribution:
Pacific slope of Western Cordillera from Guaranda to
Canar, Ecuador.

Phrynosaura Werner, 1907 = Ctenoblepharis Tschudi, 1845, fide
Donoso-Barros, 1972, Bol. Soc. Biol. Concepcion
44:129-134. Revalidated by Laurent, 1984, J. Herpetol.
18:370. Content: one species. Distribution: northernmost
Chile and Andes of Bolivia and Peru.
P. marmorata = Ceiolaemus marmoratus, fide Laurent, 1984,
Ibid. 18:359.
P. reichi Werner = Ceiolaemus reichei, Laurent, 1984, op. cit.
P. stolzmanni (Steindachner), fide Laurent, 1984, Ibid.
18:371. Distribution: Andes of Peru, Bolivia and Chile.
P. werneri Muller = Liolaemus anomalus, fide Cei, 1979, J.
Herpetol. 13:297-302.

Phyllodactylus Gray, 1828.
See Dixon & Huey, 1970, Los Angeles Co. Mus. Contrib. Sci.
192:1-78, for key to mainland South American species, descriptions
and maps for each species.
1970 P. angustidigitus Dixon & Huey, Ibid. 192:16. Type-locality:
Peru, Ica, Pisco. Distribution: beaches of Paracas
Peninsula and associated islands, Peru.
1970 P. clinatus Dixon & Huey, Ibid. 192:27. Type-locality: Peru,
Piura, Punto Aguija, 37 km SW Sechura. Distribution:
Cerro Illescas area, Peru.
1970 P. interandinus Dixon & Huey, Ibid. 192:34. Type-locality:
Peru, Cajamarca, Bellavista. Distribution: Chinchipe,
Maranon and Utcubamba river valleys, Peru.
1970 P. johnwrighti Dixon & Huey, Ibid. 192:56. Type-locality:
Peru, Cajamarca, Hacienda Molino Viejo. Distribution:
arid slopes of Rio Huancabamba, Peru.
1970 P. kofordi Dixon & Huey, Ibid. 192:39. Type-locality: Peru,
Lambayeque, Cerro de la Vieja, Motupe. Distribution:
periphery of Sechura Desert, western foothills of Andes
and coastal Peru.
1970 P. pumilus Dixon & Huey, Ibid. 192:60. Type-locality: Ecuador,
Manabi, Manta. Distribution: Cordillera de Balzar,
Ecuador.
1970 P. sentosus Dixon & Huey, Ibid. 192:48. Type-locality: Peru,
Lima. Distribution: Lima and vicinity, Peru.

Phymaturus Gravenhorst, 1838.
1980 P. mallimacci Cei, J. Herpetol. 14:58. Type-locality:
Argentina, La Rioja, 2 km E Cueva de Perez, 4200 m.
Distribution: Sierra de Famatina, Argentina.
P. patagonicus Koslowsky, elevated by Cei, 1971, Acta Zool.
Lilloana 28:37-46.
1973 P. patagonicus indistinctus Cei & Castro, J. Herpetol. 7:241.
Type-locality: Argentina, Chubut, Las Pulgas, 50 km from

Musters Lake, 800m. Distribution: known only from type
locality.

1975 P. patagonicus nevadoi Cei & Reig, J. Herpetol. 9:256.
Type-locality: Argentina, Mendoza, Agua de la India
Muerta, Nevado Mts. 1750 m.

1973 P. patagonicus payuniae Cei & Castro, Ibid. 7:244.
Type-locality: Argentina, Mendoza, Payun Plateau, 5 km
from Payun Volcan. Distribution: Payun Plateau,
Argentina.

1973 P. patagonicus somuncurensis Cei & Castro, Ibid. 7:242.
Type-locality: Argentina, Rio Negro, Somuncura Plateau,
Raimundo Lagoon, 1400 (= Laguna Raimundo). Distribution:
Somuncura Plateau, Argentina.

1973 P. patagonicus zapalensis Cei & Castro, Ibid. 7:243.
Type-locality: Argentina, Neuquen, Teru Lagoon, 40 km W
Zapala, 1200 m. Distribution: highlands west of Zapala.

1985 P. punae Cei, Etheridge & Videla, Deserta 7:320. Type-
locality: Argentina, San Juan, Llano de los Hoyos, Res.
Prov. de San Guillermo. Distribution: type locality.

Platynotus Wagler, 1831. Type-species: Agama semitaeniata Spix,
1824. Revalidated by Schmidt & Inger, 1951, and by
Vanzolini, Ramos-Costa & Vitt, 1980, Rept. Caatingas,
Acad. Bras. Cien. See Tapinurus.

Polychroides Noble, 1924 = Polychrus Cuvier, 1817, fide Etheridge,
1965, Herpetologica 21:161-68.
    P. peruvianus Noble = Polychrus peruvianus, fide Etheridge,
    1965, op. cit.

Polychrus Cuvier, 1817. Includes Polychroides Noble, 1924, fide
Etheridge, 1965, op. cit.
    P. marmoratus (Linnaeus). Distribution: Atlantic coastal
    forest to Brasil and northern South American hylaea to
    Caribbean coast (Vanzolini, 1983, Adv. Herpetol. Evol.
    Biol.)
    P. peruvianus Noble see Etheridge 1965, op. cit. and Gorman,
    Huey & Williams, 1969, Breviora 316:1-7.

Prionodactylus O´Shaughnessy, 1881.
A key, descriptions and maps of the species are in Uzzell, 1973,
Postilla 159:1-67.
1973 P. dicrus Uzzell, Ibid. 159:19. Type-locality: Ecuador,
Tungurahua, Mapoto, 1300 m. Distribution: eastern Andean
slopes of central Ecaudor.

Pristidactylus Fitzinger, 1843, substitutes for Cupriguanus
Gallardo, 1964, fide Etheridge & Williams, 1985,
Breviora 483:1-18, includes key to species.
    P. achalensis (Gallardo).
    P. alvaroi (Donoso-Barros).
    P. casuhatiensis (Gallardo).
    P. fasciatus (d´Orbigny).
    P. scapulatus (Burmeister).

P. torquatus (Philippi, 1861).
P. valeriae (Donoso-Barros, 1966).

Proctoporus Tschudi, 1845.
Key to Bolivian and Peruvian species in Uzzell, 1970, Postilla 142.
1919 P. bogotensis Boulenger, Proc. Zool. Soc. London :80.
        Type-locality: Colombia, Bogota. Distribution: only type
        locality. (Omitted by Peters & Donoso-Barros)

Pseudogonatodes Ruthven, 1915.
Key to species in Huey & Dixon, 1970, Copeia, (3):538-42.
        P. amazonicus Vanzolini = P. guianensis, fide Huey & Dixon,
            1970, op. cit.
        P. furvus Ruthven. Distribution: Santa Marta, not
            Villavicencio region of Colombia.
1970 P. peruvianus Huey & Dixon, Ibid. (3):539. Type-locality:
        Peru, Amazonas, Tingo, Rio Utcubamba. Distribution: Rio
        Utcubamba valley, Peru.

Ptychoglossus Boulenger, 1980.
        P. brevifrontalis Boulenger. New synonymy, fide Dixon & Soini,
            1975, Milwaukee Pub. Mus. Contrib. Biol. Geol. 4:51.
        1912 Ptychoglossus brevifrontalis Boulenger.
        1929 Anadia nicefori Loveridge.
        Distribution: western Amazonia.

Riolama Uzzell, 1973, Postilla 159:52. Type-species:
        Prionodactylus leucostictus Boulenger.

Sphaerodactylus Wagler, 1830.
A key for Middle and South America is in Harris & Kluge, 1984, Occ.
Pap. Mus. Zool. Univ. Michigan 706:1-59.
        S. argus Gosse. Distribution: West Indies; introduced into
            Panama, fide Harris & Kluge, op. cit.
        S. continentalis Werner = S. millepunctatus, fide Harris &
            Kluge, op. cit.
        S. dunni Schmidt. Distribution: northern Honduras, fide Harris
            & Kluge, op. cit.
        S. glaucus Cope. Distribution: southern Mexico to extreme
            northwestern Honduras, fide Harris & Kluge, op. cit.
1984 S. graptolaemus Harris & Kluge, Ibid. 706:4. Type-locality:
        Isla del Cano, Puntarenas, Costa Rica. Distribution:
        southern Costa Rica to Pacific western Panama.
1982 S. heliconiae Harris, Occ. Pap. Mus. Zool. Univ. Michigan
        (704):3. Type-locality: Colombia, Magdalena, 3 km E
        Candelaria. Distribution: lowlands immediately west of
        Santa Marta mountains, northern Colombia, fide Harris &
        Kluge, op. cit.
        S. homolepis Cope. Distribution: Caribbean versant of
            southern Nicaragua to western Panama, fide Harris &
            Kluge, op. cit.
        S. lineolatus (Lichtenstein). Distribution: Pacific western
            Panama to northwestern Colombia, fide Harris & Kluge,
            op. cit.

21

S. mertensi Wermuth = S. homolepis, fide Harris & Kluge, op.
     cit.
S. millepunctatus (Hallowell). Distribution: Isthmus of
     Tehuantepec to Costa Rica, and Cozumel, and Roatan,
     Guanaja and Maiz Grande islands, fide Harris & Kluge,
     op. cit.
S. molei Boettger. Distribution: Venezuela, Trinidad, Tobago
     and Guyana, fide Harris & Kluge, op. cit.
S. notatus (Baird). Distribution: southern Florida, Bahamas,
     Cuba, Swan Islands and introduced into Colombia, fide
     Harris, 1982, Ibid. (704):22.
S. rosaurae Parker. Distribution: Islas de la Bahia,
     Honduras.
S. scapularis Boulenger. Distribution: northwestern Ecuador
     to southwestern Colombia, fide Harris & Kluge, op. cit.

Stenocercus Dumeril & Bibron, 1837.
Key, species descriptions, and distributions are presented in
Fritts, 1974, Mem. San Diego Soc. Nat. Hist. 7:1-89.
1972 S. apurimacus Fritts, Occ. Pap. Mus. Nat. Hist. Univ. Kansas
          10:2. Type-locality: Peru, Apurimac, Puente Pachachaca,
          15 km west of Abancay, 1800 m. Distribution: upper
          valleys of Rio Apurimac, Peru.
1982 S. bolivarensis Castro & Ayala, Caldasia 13:474.
          Type-locality: Colombia, Cauca, Municipio de Bolivar.
          Distribution: known only from type locality.
1972 S. empetrus Fritts, Ibid. 10:7. Type-locality: Peru, Libertad,
          Huamachuco, 3350 m. Distribution: upper valleys of Rios
          Crisneja and Maranon, Peru.
S. festae (Peracca). Fritts, 1974, op. cit..
S. formosus (Tschudi). Fritts, 1974, op. cit.
S. guentheri (Boulenger). Fritts, 1974, op. cit.
S. haenschi (Werner, 1901). Fritts, 1974, op. cit.
1972 S. ivitus Fritts, Ibid. 10:10. Type-locality: Peru, Piura,
          Cordillera de Huancabamba, between Canchaque and
          Huancabamba, 3100 m. Distribution: type locality.
1983 S. lache Corredor, Lozania 37:2. Type-locality: Colombia,
          Boyaca, btw. La Esperanza & Pulpito del Diablo, by
          Quebrada Pantanogrande (afl. Rio Nevado), 3700-4000 m.
          Distribution: known only from type locality.
S. moestus = S. modestus (Tschudi, 1845), fide Laurent, 1984,
     J. Herpetol. 18:367.
1924 S. nigromaculatus Noble. Occ. Pap. Boston Soc. Nat. Hist.
          5:112. Type-locality: Peru, Piura, Huancabamba.
          Distribution: valley of Rio Huancabamba, Peru.
1972 S. nubicola Fritts, Ibid. 10:11. Type-locality: Peru, Piura,
          Cordillera de Huancabamba, between Canchaque and
          Huancabamba, 3100 m. Distribution: type locality.
1972 S. ochoai Fritts, Ibid. 10:13. Type-locality: Peru, Cusco, 10
          km northwest of Ollantaytambo, 270(m. Distribution:
          upper valleys of Rios Apurimac and Urubamba, Peru.
1972 S. orientalis Fritts, Ibid. 10:14. Type-locality: Peru,
          Amazonas Chachapoyas, 2340 m. Distribution: known only
          from type locality.

<u>S</u>. <u>ornatus</u> (Gray). Fritts, 1974, op. cit.
1972 <u>S</u>. <u>praeornatus</u> Fritts, Ibid. 10:16. Type-locality: Peru,
        Junin, Comas, 3320 m. Distribution: high elevations of
        Amazonian drainage in northern and central Peru.
    <u>S</u>. <u>rhodomelas</u> (Boulenger). Fritts, 1974, op. cit.
    <u>S</u>. <u>trachycephalus</u> (A. Dumeril). Fritts, 1974, op. cit.

<u>Strobilurus</u> Wiegmann, 1834.
Reviewed by Jackson, 1978, Arq. Zool. (Sao Paulo) 30:1-79 but no
changes.

<u>Tapinurus</u> Amaral, 1933. Replacement name for <u>Platynotus</u>, fide
        Rodrigues, 1984, Pap. Avul. Zool. 35:367. Distribution:
        northeastern Brasil.
1984 <u>T</u>. <u>pinima</u> Rodrigues, Ibid. 35:368. Type-locality: Brasil,
        Bahia, Santo Inacio. Distribution: type locality.
    <u>T</u>. <u>semitaeniatus</u> (Spix).

<u>Tarentola</u> Gray.
    <u>T</u>. <u>mauritanica</u> (Linnaeus). Distribution: Circum-Mediterranean
        region, Sahara, coastal West Africa, Madeira and
        Canaries; introduced into Uruguay, fide Achaval &
        Gudynas, 1983, Bol. Soc. Zool. Uruguay 1:7.

<u>Teius</u> Merrem. 1820.
    <u>T</u>. <u>teyou cyanogaster</u> Muller = <u>T</u>. <u>cyanogaster</u>, fide Blair,
        Hulse & Mares, 1976, J. Biogeog. 3:1-18.

<u>Teuchocercus</u> Fritts & Smith, 1969, Trans. Kansas Acad. Sci. 72:14.
        Type-species: <u>Teuchocercus keyi</u> F.&S. Content: monotypic
1969 <u>T</u>. <u>keyi</u> Fritts & Smith, Ibid. 72:15. Type-locality: Ecuador,
        Pichincha, 4 km E Rio Baba bridge, 600 m. Distribution:
        type locality and Esmeraldas Province (USNM).

<u>Tretioscincus</u> Cope, 1862.   No changes.
    <u>T</u>. <u>agilis</u> (Ruthven). Distribution: Amazonian Brasil, French
        Guiana, Surinam, Venezuela (Paolillo, 1985, Herpetol.
        Rev. 16:31-32).

<u>Tropidodactylus</u> Boulenger, 1885 = <u>Anolis</u> Daudin, 1802, fide
        Williams, 1974, Breviora 421:1-21.
    <u>T</u>. <u>onca</u> (O´Shaughnessy) = <u>Anolis</u> <u>onca</u>, fide Williams, 1974,
        op. cit

<u>Tropidurus</u> Wied, 1824.
1984 <u>T</u>. <u>amathites</u> Rodrigues, Pap. Avul. Zool. 35:169. Type-
        locality: Brasil, Bahia, Santo Inacio. Distribution:
        known oonly from type locality.
    <u>T</u>. <u>arenarius</u> (Tschudi), fide Fritts, 1974, Ibid. 7:1-89.
    <u>T</u>. <u>atacamensis</u> Donoso-Barros. Revalidated by Ortiz, 1980,
        Primera Reunion Iberoamericana, Zool. Vert. 1977:357.
        Distribution: coastal Chile, btw. Rios Loa y Huasco.
1982 <u>T</u>. <u>etheridgei</u> Cei, Occ. Pap. Mus. Nat. Hist. 97:2.
        Type-locality: Argentina, Cordoba, Mina Claveros, 1200

m. Distribution: lower Andean slopes of Bolivia and
Argentina, eastward into Mato Grosso, Brasil, and
Argentinian Chaco.

1983 T. catalanensis Gudynas & Skuk, C.E.D. Orione Biol. (10):1-10.
Distribution: northern Uruguay.

T. heterolepis Weigmann. Revalidated by Ortiz, 1980, Ibid.
1977:371. Distribution: coast from Tacna, Peru, to
Arica, Chile.

T. hispidus (Spix) = T. torquatus hispidus, fide Hoogmoed,
1973, Liz. Amphisb. Surinam.

T. hygomi Reinhardt & Luetken. Revalidated by Vanzolini &
Gomes, 1979, Pap. Avul. Zool. 32:243-60.

T. melanopleurus Boulenger. Content: Two subspecies, fide
Laurent, 1982, Act. 8th Cong. Latinoam. Zool. 621-23.

T. m. melanopleurus Boulenger. Distribution: La Paz, Bolivia.

T. m. pictus Muller. Distribution: southernmost Bolivia and
adjacent Argentina.

1981 T. nanuzae Rodrigues, Pap. Avul. Zool. 34:145. Type-locality:
Brasil, Minas Gerais, Serra do Cipo, route MG2 km 109.
Distribution: western slopes Serra do Cipo, Brasil.

T. occipitalis koepckeorum Mertens = T. koepckeorum, fide
Dixon & Wright, 1975, Nat. Hist. Mus. Los Angeles Co.
Contrib. Sci 27:1-39.

T. occipitalis stolzmanni Steindachner = T. stolzmanni, fide
Dixon & Wright, 1975, op. cit.

T. peruvianus marianus Donoso-Barros = T. atacamensis, fide
Ortiz, 1980, Ibid. 1977:357.

T. peruvianus tigris (Tschudi) = T. tigris, fide Dixon &
Wright. 1975. Ibid. 27:1-39.

T. quadrivittatus (Tschudi). Revalidated by Ortiz, 1981, Ibid.
1977:362. Distribution: coastal Peru & Chile to Rio Loa

T. semitaeniatus (Spix) = Platynotus semitaeniatus, fide
Vanzolini, Ramos-Costa & Vitt, 1980, Rept. Caatingas,
Acad. Bras. Cien. = Tapinurus semitaeniatus, fide
Rodrigues, 1984, Ibid. 35:367.

1975 T. thoracicus icae Dixon & Wright, Ibid. 27:22.
Type-locality: Peru, Ica, 12 km NW (by road) of Ica.
Distribution: vicinity of Ica, Peru.

1975 T. thoracicus talarae Dixon & Wright, Ibid. 27:23.
Type-locality: Peru, Piura, 2 km N Talara. Distribution:
vicinity of Talara, Peru.

1981 T. yanezi Ortiz, Ibid. 1977:373. Type-locality: Chile,
Tarapaca, Poconchile, 515 m, Valle de Lluta.
Distribution: known only from type locality.

Tupinambis Daudin, 1803. See Presch, 1973, Ibid. (4):740-46 and
Vanzolini, Ramos-Costa & Vitt, 1980, Rept. Caatingas.

T. duseni Lonnberg & Andersson = T. rufescens, fide Presch,
op. cit.

T. nigropunctatus Spix = T. teguixin, fide Presch, op. cit.

T. teguixin sebastiani Muller = T. rufescens, fide Presch, op.
cit.

Uracentron Kaup, 1826.

U. <u>guentheri</u> (Boulenger) = <u>U</u>. <u>azureum</u> <u>guentheri</u>, fide Greene, 1977, Herpetologica 33:256-60.

U. <u>werneri</u> Mertens = <u>U</u>. <u>azureum</u> <u>werneri</u>, fide Greene, 1977, op. cit.

<u>Urostrophus</u> Dumeril & Bibron, 1837.
U. <u>torquatus</u> (Philppi) = <u>Pristidactylus torquatus</u>, fide Etheridge, in Paull, Williams & Hall, 1976, Ibid. 441:1-31.

U. <u>valeriae</u> Donoso-Barros = <u>Pristidactylus valeriae</u>, fide Etheridge, in Paull, Williams & Hall, 1976, op. cit.

<u>Vanzoia</u> Smith, Martin & Swain, 1977, Pap. Avul. Zool. 30:195. Type-species: <u>V</u>. <u>klugei</u> Smith, Martin & Swain, 1977. = <u>Lygodactylus</u>, fide Bons & Pasteur, 1977, Ibid. 284:2547.

1977 <u>V</u>. <u>klugei</u> Smith, Martin & Swain = <u>L</u>. <u>klugei</u>, fide Bons & Pasteur, 1977, op. cit.

1977 <u>V</u>. <u>wetzeli</u> Smith, Martin & Swain = <u>L</u>. <u>wetzeli</u>, fide Bons & Pasteur, 1977, op. cit.

<u>Vilcunia</u> Donoso-Barros & Cei, 1971, J. Herpetol.5:90. Type-species: <u>V</u>. <u>silvanae</u> Donoso-Barros & Cei, 1971, op. cit.

1982 <u>V</u>. <u>periglacialis</u> Cei & Scolaro, J. Herpetol. 16:357. Type-locality: Argentina, Santa Cruz, 6 km E Lago Belgrano, 1000 m. Distribution: from Lago Belgrano area to mesetas Pampas del Aquila & Asador, Santa Cruz, Argentina.

1971 <u>V</u>. <u>silvanae</u> Donoso-Barros & Cei, Ibid. 5:91. Type-locality: Argentina, Santa Cruz, Puesto Lebrun, Meseta del Lago Buenos Aires, 1600 m. Distribution: Buenos Aires lake area, Argentina.

Incertae Sedis
1982 <u>Liolaemus insolitus</u> Cei & Pefaur, Act. 8th Cong. Latinoam. Zool. 2:373. Type-locality: Peru, Arequipa, Mollendo, Inclan Alto. Distribution: western slopes Andes, S. Peru.

This catalogue represents an attempt to make it possible for participants in the International Biological Program working in Latin America to identify the lizards encountered in the field. It was originally planned to include information on the ecology and ethology of the reptilian species, to permit field investigators to distinguish the unusual ecological event from the commonplace occurrence, but time has not permitted the inclusion of that degree of detail. We have instead focussed our attentions on the construction of a workable field manual with keys designed to help identification without laboratory facilities. We have not been entirely successful, because a few taxa cannot be separated without the use of a dissecting microscope or the checking of internal characteristics, but for the most part the keys can be used with little more than a hand lens for specimen examination.

The limits we have established for the area covered by this work are from the border between Mexico and Guatemala south throughout continental South America and all off-shore islands within the continental shelf. The Galapagos and the islands of the Caribbean are not included.

The synonymies presented for the taxa are very abbreviated. Within each genus we include only those generic synonyms whose type species are considered to belong to the genus under discussion. Only the original description for each genus is included, with no attempt made to document changes in the "generic concept". The type species, when given, has always been previously designated as such, unless we clearly indicate that we are taking such an action at this time. We apologize for our failure to indicate the method of type designation, but time did not permit us to undertake this difficult task. For each species we have included the original citation to it, its first assignment to its current generic position if other than as originally assigned, all "absolute" synonyms (i.e., those in which the holotype, lectotype, or neotype belongs to the species in which the synonym occurs), and, whenever possible, a citation to a recent work which includes a modern description and/or a figure, to aid the user in identification. No other generic shifts, no misidentifications, and no "in part" references are included. The author's name is not separated in any way from the binomial in the citations to original descriptions. In all other citations, the author's name is separated from the binomial by a dash. Each citation includes the actual date of publication; the name exactly as it was spelled by the original author, including capitalization of specific names; the author; the journal; the volume or the number, which stands alone if possible but which is qualified by material in parentheses if necessary; the page on which the taxon is first named; illustrations; and finally the type locality, with summaries of any restrictions or later clarifications of it.

Este catálogo representa un intento de posibilitar la identificación de lagartijas encontradas en el campo a los participantes del International Biological Program que trabajan en Sudamérica. Originariamente se había planeado la inclusión de información ecológica y etológica de las especies de reptiles, para permitir al investigador de campaña la distinción entre acontecimientos ecológicos desusados y los que son lugar común, pero la falta de tiempo impidió la inclusión de tal grado de detalles. En cambio hemos concentrado nuestra atención en la elaboración de un manual de campaña funcional con claves diseñadas para ayudar a la identificación sin las facilidades de un laboratorio. No hemos tenido éxito en todo porque unos pocos taxones no pueden ser separados sin usar el microscopio de disección o sin examinar las características internas, pero en su mayoría las claves se pueden usar con poco más que un lente de aumento con que examinar el ejemplar.

Los límites que hemos establecido para el área cubierta por este trabajo son desde la frontera entre Méjico y Guatemala hasta el extremo sur de Sudamérica continental y todas las islas costeras dentro de la plataforma continental. Las islas Galápagos y del Caribe no han sido incluidas.

Los sinónimos de los taxones presentados están muy abreviados. En cada género se incluyen solamente aquellos sinónimos genéricos cuya especie tipo es considerada como perteneciente al género en discusión. Se incluye solamente la descripción original de cada género, no hemos intentado documentar cambios en el "concepto genérico". Siempre que damos la especie tipo es porque ha sido designada como tal previamente, a menos que indiquemos claramente que hemos tomado aquí tal medida. Lamentamos no poder indicar el método de designación de tipos, pero la falta de tiempo no nos permite emprender tal difícil tarea. En cada especie hemos incluido su cita original, su primera asignación a la posición genérica corriente si es que se le ha asignado otra distinta que la original, todos los sinónimos "absolutos" (ej.: aquéllos en que el holotipo o neotipo pertenece a la especie en que ocurre el sinónimo) y, cuando posible, una cita de un trabajo reciente que incluye una descripción moderna y/o una figura, para ayudar al usuario en la identificación. No se incluye ninguna otra transferencia genérica, identificación falsa o referencia "parcial". El nombre del autor no ha sido separado de ningún modo del binomio en las citas de las descripciones originales. En todas las otras citas el nombre del autor está separado del binomio por un guión. Cada cita incluye la fecha efectiva de la publicación; el nombre con la misma ortografía que usó autor, incluyendo nombres específicos con mayúscula; el autor; la revista; el volumen o el número, por sí solos si es posible o con material aclaratorio entre paréntesis si es necesario; la página en que se nombra al taxón por primera vez; ilustraciones y, finalmente la localidad tipo con resúmenes de cualquier restricción o aclaración posterior.

INTRODUCTION

We have attempted to avoid any non-documented taxonomic changes in this catalogue, although it has proven necessary to make a few modifications in some taxa. When we have made such changes, we indicate it by the words "new combination" after the species heading, and we have given our reasons for so doing in the "Comments". In those genera prepared by cooperating herpetologists, however, we have not prevented the presentation of his concepts of the alignment of species within the genus, even though documentation has not been published elsewhere. In every instance we have ascertained that prompt publication of documentation is anticipated before including the changes, but we cannot guarantee that it will be done. In all cases where material has been furnished by a cooperator, his name and address will be found at the beginning of the generic discussion, and he should be given full credit in any citations of that material.

The date of publication is always the actual date, insofar as we could determine it, and it does not always agree with the date given in the publication itself. When there is a difference, the latter date is given in parentheses after the volume number. The only exception to this is volume 4 of the Memorias do Instituto Butantan. We learned too late to modify all of the many citations to this volume that it actually appeared in 1930, not 1929, as stated on the cover. All other volumes in the Memorias are cited here by actual year of publication, which is usually one or two years later than indicated on the publication.

The distribution given for each taxon is based on information in the literature, with additions and extensions from specimens we have been able to find in various collections. Some of our changes in known distribution have been documented, but we have made no attempt to do so for every modification we have included.

The names of all political and geographic units within any country have been given as spelled by that country, but country names have been given in English usage, so that "Brasil" is "Brazil" and "Panamá" is "Panama". Where names but not boundaries have been changed, we use the modern name, even in the citation of type localities. Thus, all localities in "British Guiana" are here given as "Guyana". We have corrected errors in orthography throughout, if we could successfully document the error. Our primary source has been the series of gazetteers prepared by the United States Board on Geographic Names, although many additional sources have been checked.

Most of the keys presented here are the standard dichotomous type, although occasionally we have found it useful to include "trichotomies" and the user should watch for this possibility. In such instances, of course, a choice is made from three possibilities rather than two. In the case of very large genera, however, we have intro-

Hemos tratado de evitar en este catálogo todos los cambios taxonómicos que no estuvieran documentados, si bien fue necesario hacer unas pocas modificaciones en algunos taxones. Cuando se han hecho tales cambios lo indicamos con las palabras "new combination" después del título de la especie y explicamos nuestra razones para el cambio en "Comments". Sin embargo en aquellos géneros preparados por nuestros colaboradores herpetólogos no hemos impedido la presentación de sus conceptos en el ordenamiento de las especies dentro del género, aun cuando no hubiera documentación previamente publicada. En cada caso hemos solicitado la pronta publicación de documentación antes de introducir tales cambios, pero no podemos garantizar que así se haga. En todos los casos en que un colaborador ha proporcionado material hemos puesto su nombre y dirección al comienzo de la discusión del género y a él le corresponde todo el crédito cuando dicho material sea citado.

La fecha de publicación es siempre la fecha real en la medida en que se pueda determinar ésta y no siempre coincide con la fecha dada por la publicación misma. En tales casos esta última aparece entre paréntesis después del número del volumen. Una excepción es el volumen 4 de las Memorias do Instituto Butántan. Cuando era demasiado tarde para modificar las numerosas citas de este volumen descubrimos que en realidad había aparecido en 1930, no en 1929. Los demás volúmenes de las Memorias son citados aquí con el año efectivo de de la publicación, que es usualmente uno o dos años más tarde del indicado en la portada.

La distribución dada en cada taxón se basa en información sacada de la literatura con adiciones y agregados basados en ejemplares que hemos encontrado en varias colecciones. Algunos de nuestros cambios en la distribución conocida han sido documentados, pero no hemos intentado documentar todas las modificaciones incluídas por nosotros.

Se dan los nombres de todas las unidades políticas y geográficas dentro de cada país de acuerdo a la ortografía de ese país, pero los nombres de los países se han escrito según la ortografía inglesa, así "Brasil" es "Brazil" y "Panamá" es "Panama". Donde los nombres han cambiado, pero no las fronteras, usamos el nombre moderno, aún al citar localidades tipo. Así aquí nos referimos a todos las localidades en "British Guiana" como "Guyana". Hemos corregido todos los errores ortográficos que pudieran ser documentados debidamente. Nuestra principal fuente de información ha sido la serie de gacetas preparadas por Board on Geographic Names del gobierno de los Estados Unidos, aunque también hemos consultado muchas otras fuentes.

La mayoría de las claves aquí presentadas son del tipo dicotómico común, aunque ocasionalmente ha sido conveniente incluir "tricotomías", y el usuario debe estar al tanto de esta posibilidad. En tales ocasiones, naturalmente, hay que elegir entre tres posibilidades en vez de dos. No obstante en el caso de géneros muy grandes se ha

duced a different concept. Any attempt at writing keys for poorly known, large genera is likely to be futile, and we have avoided this by presenting as much data as possible in the form of a matrix. This permits "random entry" identification, for the user can select any character in the matrix he wishes to check, and eliminate all taxa that do not possess that character, finally arriving at a considerably reduced number of taxa (hopefully, only one) after checking a series of characters. This concept has formed the basis of computer identification, since the machine can do such sorting more rapidly and efficiently than the human, and the random entry matrices presented here are organized in such a way that they can be incorporated in the computer programs now available for such machine sorting. It is our assumption that this method of identification will be used more and more in the future, and we hope that presenting these matrices will encourage others to begin to organize their data similarly, thus anticipating the day when computer keys are available to all users.

A work of this magnitude becomes very dependent upon the cooperation and collaboration of many people. We wish to express our gratitude to all those who have helped us in any way. The following list indicates the number of individuals who have contributed to this work. While we have tried to make the list inclusive, the omission of anyone who has aided us should be regarded solely as the consequence of the faulty nature of our memories rather than failure to appreciate the help.

introducido un concepto diferente. Probablemente resultaría inútil intentar escribir una clave de un género grande, poco conocido, hemos evitado esto al presentar la mayor cantidad de datos posibles en forma de una matriz. Esto permite la identificación de "entradas al azar," por que el usuario puedo seleccionar dentro de la matriz cualquier carácter que desee poner a prueba y eliminar todos los taxones que no posean tal carácter, llegando finalmente a un número sumamente reducido de taxones (es de esperar que sea uno solo) después de revisar una serie de caracteres. Este concepto constituye la base de la identificación por computadora, ya que esta máquina puede selecccionar más rápida y eficazmente que el ser humano y las matrices de entradas al azar presentadas aquí están organizadas en tal forma que se las puede incorporar en los programas para computadoras ahora disponibles para tal selección automática. Suponemos que este método de identificación se usará cada vez más en el futuro y esperamos que la presentación de estas matrices alentará a otros a empezar a organizar sus datos en forma similar, previendo así el día en que haya claves para computadoras disponibles para todos los usuarios.

Un trabajo de esta magnitud depende en alto grado de la cooperación de mucha gente. La siguiente lista indica el número de personas que han contribuido a esta obra. Aunque hemos tratado de incluir a todos en esta lista, la omisión de alguno de los que nos ayudaron debe ser considerada solamente como consecuencia de la naturaleza defectuosa de nuestra memoria, pero no como una inhabilidad de apreciar la ayuda recibida.

(In alphabetical order): Fernando Achaval, Avelino Barrio, Charles Bogert, Werner Bokermann, Simon Campden-Main, Nelly Carrillo de Espinoza, Antenor de Carvalho, Ronald Crombie, Carlos Diefenbach, James Dixon, Arthur Echternacht, Richard Etheridge, Marcos Freiberg, Jose Gallardo, Carl Gans, Robert Inger, George Jacobs, Miguel Klappenbach, Arnold Kluge, Abdem Lancini, Clarence McCoy, James McKenney, Nicéforo María, Marta Miranda, Olaf Oftedal, Gustavo Orcés-V., Neil Richmond, Carlos Rivero-Blanco, Richard Sage, Jay Savage, Wade Sherbrooke, Hobart Smith, Robert Tuck, Thomas Uzzell, Paulo Vanzolini, Ernest Williams, George Zug.

In addition to the above, we wish also to acknowledge several specific contributions to the work involved in the production of this volume. By far the bulk of the typing work was done by Jean Middleton, and the overall appearance of the text owes a great deal to her attention to detail, layout, arrangement, and so on. She functioned as a general manager of the entire project, and we cannot overestimate the magnitude of her contribution. Beatriz Moisset Peters spent many hours translating and correcting the spanish versions of the text after one of us (Donoso) returned to South America, and she also has contributed greatly to our overall accuracy. Additional typing assistance came from Mrs. Richard Banks and Dolores Icarangal. The figures in the text unless otherwise indicated were drawn by Thomas Yuskiw, with the exception of those illustrating the genus Liolaemus, which were done by Roberto Donoso.

We wish finally to record our debt to Braulio Orejas Miranda, who worked with us on this catalogue. He perhaps should have been recorded as an author rather than as a collaborator, since all three of us have worked closely together on the entire project.

Además de los mencionados, deseamos espresar nuestro reconocimiento por varias contribuciones específicas referentes a la producción de este volumen. Jean Middleton mecanografió la mayor parte de este trabajo y la apariencia general del texto ganó mucho gracias a su interés en los detalles. Ella operó como administradora general de todo el proyecto y no es posible sobreestimar el valor de su contribución. Beatriz Moisset Peters dedicó muchas horas a la traducción y corrección de la versión en español después uno de nosotros (Donoso) regresara a Sudamérica. También contribuyó en gran medida a la exactitud del trabajo. Las señoras Richard Banks y Dolores Icarangal mecanografiaron el resto del trabajo. Las figuras del texto fueron hechas por Thomas Yuskiw a menos que se especifique otra cosa, excepto las que ilustran el género Liolaemus que fueron hechas por Roberto Donoso.

Finalmente deseamos expresar nuestra deuda para con Braulio Orejas Miranda, que trabajó con nosotros en este catálogo. Talvez se lo debería incluir como uno de los autores en vez de colaborador, ya que los tres trabajamos en estrecho contacto a través de todo el proyecto.

INTRODUCTION

We are concerned that the users of this catalogue may regard everything presented as of equal value and significance, since there are considerable differences in the comparative reliability of the information given from one genus to another. In order to forestall assumptions of equivalent reliability, we have devised a code to indicate an evaluation of the information presented for each genus. The user will note one to four stars in the heading line for every genus. These stars have the following significance:

One Star: Low reliability. Keys and synonymies prepared by us from existing literature; difficulties encountered by us because of insufficient descriptions, non-availability of critical specimens, or other reasons; manuscript not checked by outside reviewer, since no one is currently engaged in revisionary study of the genus, to our knowledge. In the case of monotypic genera, one star means we have reasons to doubt its validity as a distinct genus.

Two Stars: Moderate reliability. Keys and synonymies prepared almost entirely by us, but usually checked against specimens and adequate information in the literature; manuscript often reviewed externally, although not necessarily by specialist actively studying genus. Further study needed to give better understanding of genus.

Three stars. Good reliability. Keys and synonymies prepared either by us in consultation with a specialist or by the expert himself, or modified from monographs, checklists, or regional studies. Added work is usually in progress on the genus by the specialist, and we anticipate early publication by him to improve our understanding even more.

Four Stars. High reliability. Manuscript either prepared externally, in which case the author is acknowledged in the heading material; or taken by us from a very recent generic monograph summarizing the literature and including all available specimens for study.

We have submitted this "reliability" list to all external authors and asked for their opinion before assigning the code, so it can be considered an indication of the author's personal evaluation, rather than ours.

Nos preocupa la posibilidad de que los usuarios de este catálogo vayan a dar igual valor o significado a las distintas partes del mismo, ya que la seguridad de la información suministrada varía considerablemente de unos géneros a otros. Para evitar que se llegue a la conclusión de que toda la información es igualmente digna de confianza hemos ideado un código que valore la calidad de la información presentada en cada género. El usuario verá de una a cuatro estrellas en el encabezamiento de cada género. Estas tienen el siguiente significado:

Una Estrella: Poca confianza. Claves y sinónimos preparados exclusivamente por nosotros a partir de la literatura existente; dificultades halladas por nosotros a causa de descripciones insuficientes, especímenes críticos no disponibles u otras razones; el manuscrito no ha sido revisado por nadie de afuera ya que no sabemos de nadie que esté ocupado en hacer un estudio de revisión del género en el momento actual. En el caso de géneros monotípicos una estrella significa que tenemos motivos para dudar de su validez como género aparte.

Dos Estrellas: Moderada confianza. Claves y sinónimos preparados casi totalmente por nosotros, pero usualmente confrontados con especímenes e información adecuada en la literatura; manuscrito a menudo revisado por alguien de afuera, aunque no necesariamente por un especialista en ese género. Se necesita más estudio para comprender mejor ese género.

Tres Estrellas: Bastante confianza. Claves y sinónimos preparados por nosotros en consulta con un especialista o por el experto mismo o modificados de monografías, listas de especies o estudios regionales. Usualmente hay trabajo adicional en marcha del especialista en el género, y anticipamos su pronta publicación para mejorar aun más nuestra comprensión del mismo.

Cuatro Estrellas. Mucha confianza. Manuscrito o bien preparado afuera en cuyo caso se nombra al autor en el encabezamiento o preparado por nosotros a partir de una monografía muy reciente que resume la literatura e incluye todos los especímenes disponibles para estudio.

Hemos presentado esta lista de "dignidad de confianza" a todos los autores de afuera y pedido su opinión antes de asignar el código, así que se la puede considerar como indicación de una valoración del autor antes que nuestra.

The work on this catalogue was supported by a Smithsonian Research Award to the senior author. The catalogue is listed as project no. 2 in the U.S.A. section of Section CT (Conservation Terrestrial) of the International Biological Program.

El trabajo del catálogo fue sufragado por Smithsonian Research Award al autor principal. El catálogo figura como proyecto no. 2 en la parte de los Estados Unidos de la Sección CT (Conservación Terrestre) del Programa Biológico Internacional.

KEY TO THE GENERA OF LIZARDS AND AMPHISBAENIANS[1]

1. At least one pair of limbs present, although
   may be very reduced--------------------------2
   No trace of limbs externally------------------9

2. Venter covered either with large, squarish,
   juxtaposed, plate-like scales or with large,
   smooth, imbricate, cycloid scales------------3
   Venter covered either with numerous small,
   rounded or pointed, imbricate or subimbricate
   scales, either smooth or keeled, or with very
   small, granular scales-----------------------8

3. Large number of scales on dorsum of head, most
   either knobby or granular in appearance-------
   ---4
   Scales on dorsum of head large and plate-like,
   few in number--------------------------------5

4. Third and fourth digits on hind limb equal or
   subequal in length; no enlarged supraocular
   scales----------------------------------Heloderma
   Fourth digit of hind limb considerably longer
   than third; several enlarged, plate-like
   supraocular scales-----------------Xenosaurus

5. Fewer than two pairs of scales between rostral
   and first median unpaired scale on head (Figs.
   2, 3)--6
   Two or more pairs of scales following rostral
   before first median unpaired scale on head
   (Fig. 1)------------------------------------14

6. Scales of dorsum differing from those
   of venter; femoral pores often present-------7
   Scales of dorsum same as those of venter,
   cycloid; no femoral pores-------------------19

7. Eyelid movable or absent--------------------22
   Eyelid fixed, not movable----------Lepidophyma

8. Upper surface of head covered with scales of
   variable size, often plate-like, but never
   granular------------------------------------68
   Upper surface of head covered with minute,
   granular scales-----------------------------103

9. Snout shovel-shaped, with horizontal edge----10
   Head rounded, pointed or vertically keeled---11

1. Por lo menos con un par de extremidades, aunque
   pueden estar muy reducidas-------------------2
   Sin trazas de extremidades externamente-------9

2. Vientre cubierto de escamas grandes, cuadradas,
   yuxtapuestas, laminares o bien de escamas
   cicloides, grandes, lisas, imbricadas---------
   ---3
   Vientre cubierto de numerosas escamas chicas,
   redondeadas o puntudas, imbricadas o subimbricadas, lisas o quilladas, o bien de escamas
   muy chicas granulares------------------------8

3. Gran número de escamas en dorso de la cabeza,
   la mayoría de aspecto granular o nudoso-------
   ---4
   Escamas del dorso de la cabeza grandes y laminares, en número reducido--------------------5

4. Longitud de tercer y cuarto dedos de extremidad
   posterior igual o casi igual; sin escamas
   supraoculares dilatadas------------Heloderma
   Cuarto dedo de extremidad posterior considerablemente más largo que el tercero; varias
   escamas supraoculares dilatadas, laminares----
   -----------------------------------Xenosaurus

5. Menos de dos pares de escamas entre rostral y
   primera escama media impar de la cabeza (Figs.
   2,3) ---------------------------------------6
   Dos o más pares de escamas siguen a la rostral
   antes de la primera escama media impar de la
   cabeza (Fig. 1)-----------------------------14

Fig. 1. Diploglossus, with two pairs
of scales between rostral and first
unpaired plate (from Bocourt, 1879).

6. Escamas del dorso diferentes de las
   ventrales; a menudo con poros femorales------7
   Escamas del dorso igual que las del vientre,
   cicloideas; sin poros femorales------------19

7. Párpado movible o ausente-------------------22
   Párpado fijo, no movible-----------Lepidophyma

8. Superficie superior de la cabeza cubierta de
   escamas de distinto tamaños, a menudo laminares pero nunca granulares----------------68
   Superficie superior de la cabeza cubierta de
   escamas granulares, diminutas-------------103

9. Hocico en forma de pala con borde horizontal-10
   Cabeza redondeada, puntuda o quillada
   verticalmente-------------------------------11

---

[1]The genus Garbesaura Amaral is not included in
this key.

[1]No se incluye el género Garbesaura Amaral en esta
clave.

10.Rostral folded around center of horizontal
   edge; three pairs of regular, paired shields,
   but no azygous ones, behind rostral along midline of head; tail very short and blunt but
   with well-marked narrow autotomy constriction-
   ---------------------------------------Aulura
   Rostral excluded from center of horizontal
   edge; one or more azygous shields along midline on dorsal surface of head; tail lacking
   autotomy constriction-------------Leposternon

11.Head keel-shaped; rostral enlarged, extending
   posteriorly, separating nasals, prefrontals,
   and sometimes frontals; keel occasionally
   keratinized; tail tip may bear vertical ridge;
   tail lacks autotomy plane--------------------12
   Head not keel-shaped; rostral not separating
   frontals and prefrontals---------------------13

12.Frontals in broad contact on midline; rostral
   process rarely keratinized; mental in contact
   with first and second infralabials; two precloacal pores on each side separated by median
   hiatus; tail tip with doubled vertical ridge--
   --------------------------------------Mesobaena
   Frontals and prefrontals separated by rostral;
   rostral process heavily keratinized in adults;
   mental in contact with first infralabials
   only; four precloacal pores in single row,
   their presence and size reflecting sexual
   dimorphism; tail tip elliptical---------------
   --Anops

13.Rostral in broad contact with prefrontals,
   restricting small nasals to sides of vertically
   compressed head; two pairs of precloacal pores
   separated by median hiatus-------------Bronia
   Rostral without or with only narrow median contact with prefrontals, unless they have fused
   with nasals; variable number of precloacal
   pores in single row of precloacal segments
   without median hiatus-------------Amphisbaena

14.All four limbs present----------------------15
   With hind limbs only, very reduced and flap-
   like----------------------------------Ophiodes

15.Body covered with plate-like scales-----------
   --16
   Body covered with finely striated cycloid
   scales of more or less uniform size---------18

16.Lateral fold weakly developed----------------17
   Lateral fold strongly developed---------------
   ----------------------------------Gerrhonotus

17.More than six scales in a single row across
   nape of neck----------------------Coloptychon
   Six or fewer scales in a single row across nape
   ------------------------------------Abronia

18.Claw retractile into terminal sheath----------
   ------------------------------------Diploglossus
   Claw not retractile into terminal sheath------
   ------------------------------------Celestus

10.Rostral plegada alrededor del centro del borde
   horizontal; le siguen tres pares de escudos
   regulares, apareados, pero ningún azygos a lo
   largo de la línea media de la cabeza; cola muy
   corta y roma con constricción autotómica angosta bien marcada-----------------------Aulura
   Rostral excluído del centro del borde horizontal; uno o más escudos azygos a lo largo de la
   línea media en superficie dorsal de la cabeza;
   cola sin constricción autotómica--------------
   ---------------------------------Leposternon

11.Cabeza en forma de quilla; rostral dilatado se
   extiende hacia posterior, separando las nasales, prefrontales y, a veces las frontales;
   quilla a veces queratinizada; ápice de la
   cola sin plano autotómico--------------------12
   Cabeza no en forma de quilla; rostral no separa
   a los frontales y prefrontales-------------13

12.Frontales en contacto amplio en la línea media;
   proceso rostral raramente queratinizado;
   mental en contacto con primera y segunda
   infralabiales; dos poros precloacales a cada
   lado separados por un hiato medio; punta de la
   cola con dos crestas verticales--------------
   ----------------------------------Mesobaena
   Frontales y prefrontales separados por rostral;
   proceso rostral densamente queratinizado en
   adultos; mental en contacto con primeras
   infralabiales solamente; cuatro poros precloacales en una sola hilera, su presencia y
   tamaño reflejan dimorfismo sexual; punta de la
   cola elíptica----------------------------Anops

13.Rostral en amplio contacto con prefrontales,
   restringiendo los pequeños nasales a los lados
   de la cabeza comprimida verticalmente; dos
   pares de poros precloacales separados por
   hiato medio----------------------------Bronia
   Rostral no contacta o sólo contacta ligeramente
   con los prefrontales en línea media a menos
   que éstos estén fusionados con los nasales;
   número variable de poros precloacales en una
   sola hilera de segmentos precloacales sin
   hiato medio----------------------Amphisbaena

14.Con cuatro extremidades----------------------15
   Sólo con extremidades posteriores, muy reducidas y como colgajo--------------------Ophiodes

15.Cuerpo cubierto de escamas laminares----------
   --16
   Cuerpo cubierto de escamas cicloides, finamente
   estriadas de tamaño más o menos uniforme----18

16.Pliegue lateral ligeramente desarrollado-------
   --17
   Pliegue lateral muy desarrollado---- Gerrhonotus

17.Más de seis escamas en cada hilera a través de
   la nuca----------------------------Coloptychon
   Seis o menos escamas en cada hilera a través de
   la nuca-------------------------------Abronia

18.Uña retráctil en vaina terminal----------------
   ------------------------------------Diploglossus
   Uña no retráctil en vaina terminal------------
   ------------------------------------Celestus

19. Pair of scales on dorsum of head between ros-
    tral and first unpaired median scale (Fig.
    2)--- 20
    Rostral in contact with unpaired median scale
    (Fig. 3)----------------------------------- 21

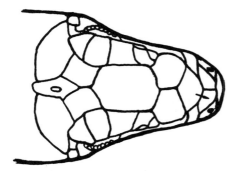

Fig. 2. <u>Eumeces</u>, with one pair
of scales between rostral and
first unpaired plate.

20. Temporal area between eye and ear opening
    covered with enlarged, well-differentiated
    scales---------------------------------<u>Eumeces</u>
    Temporal area covered with scales similar in
    appearance to body scales--------------<u>Mabuya</u>

21. Eyelid fixed, transparent, covering eye--------
    -------------------------------------<u>Ablepharus</u>
    Eyelid movable, not fixed in place over eye----
    ------------------------------------<u>Leiolopisma</u>

22. Anterior nasal scales in contact between ros-
    tral and frontonasal----------------------- 23
    Anterior nasal scales separated by rostral and
    frontonasal--------------------------------- 33

23. Limbs present, normal---------------------- 24
    Limbs rudimentary, peg-like-------------------
    --------------------------------<u>Ophiognomon</u>

24. Five toes on hind foot-------------------- 25
    Four toes on hind foot-----------------<u>Teius</u>

25. No keeled tubercles on dorsum------------- 26
    Dorsum with scattered keeled tubercles---------
    ------------------------------------<u>Dracaena</u>

26. No double row of tubercles on dorsum of tail---
    --- 27
    With double row of tubercles on dorsum of tail-
    -------------------------------<u>Crocodilurus</u>

27. Ventral scales smooth--------------------- 29
    Ventral scales keeled--------------------- 28

28. Femoral pores present---------------<u>Kentropyx</u>
    Femoral pores absent---------------<u>Monoplocus</u>[1]

---

[1] This monotypic genus (<u>Monoplocus</u> <u>dorsalis</u>) is of
dubious validity. It has never been taken since
Günther described it (Proc. Zool. Soc. London,
1859, 404).

19. Pares de escamas en dorso de la cabeza entre
    rostral y primera escama media impar (Fig. 2)
    --- 20
    Rostral en contacto con escama impar media
    (Fig. 3)----------------------------------- 21

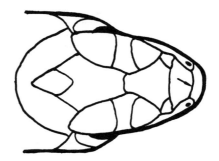

Fig. 3. <u>Leiolopisma</u>, with rostral and first unpaired plate
in contact.

20. Zona temporal entre ojo y orificio ótico cu-
    bierto de escamas dilatadas, bien diferencia-
    das------------------------------------<u>Eumeces</u>
    Zona temporal cubierta de escamas similares a
    las de cuerpo--------------------------<u>Mabuya</u>

21. Párpado fijo, transparente, cubriendo el ojo---
    -------------------------------------<u>Ablepharus</u>
    Párpado movible, no fijo sobre el ojo----------
    ------------------------------------<u>Leiolopisma</u>

22. Escamas nasales anteriores en contacto entre
    rostral y frontonasal---------------------- 23
    Escamas nasales anteriores separadas por ros-
    tral y frontonasal------------------------- 33

23. Extremidades presentes, normales------------- 24
    Extremidades rudimentarias, con forma de
    clavijas--------------------------<u>Ophiognomon</u>

24. Cinco dedos en extremidad posterior-----------
    --- 25
    Cuatro dedos en extremidad posterior------<u>Teius</u>

25. Sin tubérculos quillados en el dorso--------- 26

    Dorso con tubérculos quillados dispersos-------
    ------------------------------------<u>Dracaena</u>

26. Sin doble hilera de tubérculos en el dorso de
    la cola------------------------------------ 27
    Con doble hilera de tubérculos en el dorso de
    la cola--------------------------<u>Crocodilurus</u>

27. Escamas ventrales lisas------------------- 29
    Escamas ventrales quilladas--------------- 28

28. Con poros femorales------------------<u>Kentropyx</u>
    Sin poros femorales------------------<u>Monoplocus</u>[1]

---

[1] Este género monotípico (<u>Monoplocus</u> <u>dorsalis</u>) es
bastante discutido y desde la descripción de
Günther, Proc. Zool. Soc. London, 1859, 404, no
existen observaciones directas.

29. Femoral pores present------------------------30
    Femoral pores absent----------------Callopistes

30. Preanal pores absent------------------------31
    Preanal pores present---------------Tupinambis

31. Posterior teeth compressed longitudinally, bi-
    or tricuspid------------------------------32
    Posterior teeth compressed transversely,
    bicuspid-------------------------------Dicrodon

32. Tongue with posterior fold and entire glottal
    part---------------------------------Ameiva
    Tongue lacks posterior fold, with divided
    glottal part--------------------Cnemidophorus

33. Ear opening absent---------------------------34
    Ear opening present---------------------------36

34. Extremities normal----------------------------35
    Extremities rudimentary-----------------Bachia

35. Gular fold or collar present--------------------
    --------------------------------Anotosaurus
    Gular fold or collar absent-------------------
    -------------------------------Heterodactylus

36. Eyelids absent-------------------------------37
    Eyelids present-------------------------------38

37. Prefrontals present; frontoparietals absent
    (Fig. 4)--------------------Gymnophthalmus
    Prefrontals absent; frontoparietals present
    (Fig. 5)----------------------Micrablepharus

29. Con poros femorales-------------------------30
    Sin poros femorales-----------------Callopistes

30. Sin poros preanales-------------------------31
    Con poros preanales-----------------Tupinambis

31. Dientes posteriores comprimidos longitudinal-
    mente, bi o tricúspides--------------------32
    Dientes posteriores comprimidos transversal-
    mente, bicúspides---------------------Dicrodon

32. Lengua con pliegue posterior y parte glotal
    entera---------------------------------Ameiva
    Lengua sin pliegue posterior y parte glotal
    dividida-----------------------Cnemidophorus

33. Sin orificio ótico---------------------------34
    Con orificio ótico---------------------------36

34. Extremidades normales------------------------35
    Extremidades rudimentarias--------------Bachia

35. Con pliegue gular o collar----------------------
    --------------------------------Anotosaurus
    Sin pliegue gular o collar--------------------
    -------------------------------Heterodactylus

36. Sin párpados--------------------------------37
    Con párpados--------------------------------38

37. Prefrontales presentes; frontoparietales
    ausentes (Fig. 4)--------------Gymnophthalmus
    Prefrontales ausentes; frontoparietales
    presentes (Fig. 5)-------------Micrablepharus

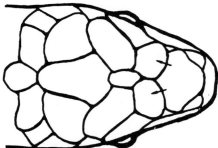

Fig. 4. Gymnophthalmus,
with prefrontals.

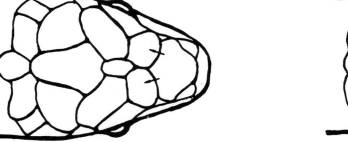

Fig. 5. Micrablepharus, with
frontoparietals.

38. Lower eyelid pigmented, lacks transparent disk-
    ---39
    Lower eyelid with transparent disk-----------45
    ----

39. Ventral scales larger than dorsals-------------
    ---40
    Ventral scales notably smaller than dorsals----
    -----------------------------------Argalia

40. Prefrontals present (Fig. 6)------------------41
    Prefrontals absent or barely outlined (Fig. 7)-
    --------------------------------Pholidobolus

38. Párpado inferior pigmentado, sin disco trans-
    parente-----------------------------------39
    Párpado inferior con disco transparente------45
    ----

39. Escamas ventrales más grandes que las dorsales-
    ---40
    Escamas ventrales mucho más chicas que las dor-
    sales------------------------------Argalia

40. Con prefrontales (Fig. 6)--------------------41
    Prefrontales **ausente** o ligeramente delineado
    (Fig. 7)-------------------------Pholidobolus

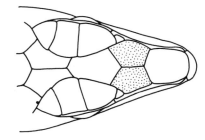

Fig. 6. Prefrontals present, shaded.
(Neusticurus, from Peters, 1967)

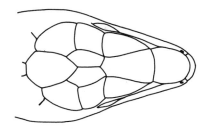

Fig. 7. Prefrontals absent.
(Pholidobolus, from Peters, 1967)

41.Five toes on hind foot-----------------------42
   Four toes on hind foot--------------------Teius

42.Postparietal and occipitals present (Fig. 8)-43
   Postparietal and occipitals absent (Fig. 9)----
   ------------------------------------Arthrosaura

41. Cinco dedos en extremidad posterior---------42
    Cuatro dedos en extremidad posterior-----Teius

42.Con postparietal y occipitales (Fig. 8)------43
   Sin postparietal ni occipitales (Fig. 9)---------
   ------------------------------------Arthrosaura

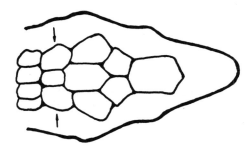

Fig. 8. Prionodactylus, with postparietals and occipitals.

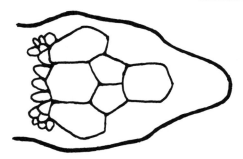

Fig. 9. Arthrosaura.

43. Dorsal scales keeled or striated, never smooth,
    much smaller than ventrals------------------44
    Dorsal scales smooth, only slightly smaller
    than ventrals--------------------------Anadia

44. Femoral pores present; dorsal scales imbricate,
    hexagonal-----------------------Prionodactylus
    Femoral pores absent; dorsal scales squarish,
    juxtaposed-------------------------Ecpleopus

45. Innermost digit rudimentary------------------46
    Innermost digit normal----------------------49

46. Dorsal scales normal, not greatly enlarged-----
    --47
    Dorsal scales greatly expanded, only two rows
    present on back-------------------------Iphisa

47. Ventrals scales in other than four longitudinal
    rows-----------------------------Tretioscincus
    Ventral scales in four longitudinal rows-------
    --48

48.Prefrontals present (Fig. 6)--------Colobosaura
   Prefrontals absent (Fig. 7)------Colobodactylus

43. Escamas dorsales quilladas o estriadas, nunca
    lisas, mucho más chicas que las ventrales---
    --44
    Escamas dorsales lisas, sólo ligeramente más
    chicas que las ventrales----------------Anadia

44. Con poros femorales; escamas dorsales imbrica-
    das, hexagonales----------------Prionodactylus
    Sin poros femorales; escamas dorsales cuadradas,
    yuxtapuestas-------------------------Ecpleopus

45. Dedo interno rudimentario--------------------46
    Dedo interno normal-------------------------49

46. Escamas dorsales normales, no muy dilatadas----
    --47
    Escamas dorsales muy dilatadas, sólo dos hile-
    ras en la espalda----------------------Iphisa

47. Hileras longitudinales de escamas ventrales en
    número distinto a cuatro---------Tretioscincus
    Cuatro hileras longitudinales de escamas ven-
    trales--------------------------------------48

48.Prefrontales presentes (Fig. 6)-----Colobosaura
   Prefrontales ausentes (Fig. 7)---Colobodactylus

49.Granular scales present dorsally------------50
   No granular scales dorsally------------------52

50.Dorsum with alternating granular scales, normal
   scales, and raised, keeled tubercles----------
   --51
   Dorsum uniformly covered by granular scales----
   ------------------------------------Neusticurus

51.Enlarged scales present between first digit and
   wrist-------------------------------Neusticurus
   Enlarged scales abse.t between first digit and
   wrist-------------------------------Echinosaura

52.Prefrontal absent (Fig. 7)-----------------53
   Prefrontal present-------------------------56

53.No enlarged middorsal scales-----------------54
   Two rows of enlarged middorsal scales, from
   occipital to tail---------------Macropholidus

54.No granular scales on sides------------------55
   Rows of granular scales between dorsal and ventral scales------------------------Proctoporus

55.Dorsal scales hexagonal, narrow, strongly
   keeled-------------------------------Stenolepis
   Dorsal scales squarish, as long as wide, weakly
   keeled------------------------------Ptychoglossus

56.Occipital and postparietals absent (Fig. 9)---
   ---57
   Occipital and postparietals present (Fig. 8)--
   ---61

57.Loreal separated from upper labials by fren-
   orbital------------------------------------58
   Loreal in contact with upper labials---------59

58.Second pair of postmentals partly separated
   along midventral line--------------Arthrosaura
   Second pair of postmentals in complete contact
   along midventral line------------Alopoglossus

59.Anterior limb with keeled scales--------------
   -------------------------------------Leposoma
   Anterior limb with smooth scales-------------60

60.Ventrals rounded and overlapping posteriorly---
   --------------------------------------Arthrosaura
   Ventrals squared off and juxtaposed-----------
   ------------------------------------Ptychoglossus

61.Lateral scales subequal---------------------62
   Lateral scales distinctly reduced in size------
   ---64

62.Dorsal scales keeled------------------------63
   Dorsal scales smooth--------------------Anadia

63.Four supraoculars------------------Arthroseps
   Three supraoculars---------------Pantodactylus

49.Con escamas granulares a dorsal--------------50
   Sin escamas granulares a dorsal--------------52

50.Dorso con escamas granulares que alternan con
   escamas normales y tubérculos quillados, ele-
   vados---------------------------------------51
   Dorso cubierto uniformemente de escamas granu-
   lares-------------------------------Neusticurus

51.Con escamas dilatadas entre primer dedo y
   muñeca------------------------------Neusticurus
   Sin escamas dilatadas entre primer dedo y
   muñeca------------------------------Echinosaura

52.Sin prefrontal (Fig. 7)--------------------53
   Con prefrontal-----------------------------56

53.Sin escamas dorsales medias dilatadas----------
   ---54
   Con dos hileras de escamas dorsales medias
   dilatadas, desde el occipital a la cola-------
   --------------------------------Macropholidus

54.Sin escamas granulares a los lados-----------55
   Con hileras de escamas granulares entre las
   escamas dorsales y ventrales-------Proctoporus

55.Escamas dorsales hexagonales, angostas, fuertemente quilladas---------------------Stenolepis
   Escamas dorsales cuadradas, de igual largo que
   ancho, débilmente quilladas------Ptychoglossus

56.Sin occipital ni postparietales (Fig. 9)----57
   Con occipital y postparietales (Fig. 8)-----61

57.Loreal separado de labiales superiores por
   frenorbital--------------------------------58
   Loreal en contacto con labiales superiores---59

58.Segundo par de postmentales separados parcial-
   mente a lo largo de la línea media ventral----
   ----------------------------------Arthrosaura
   Segundo par de postmentales completamente en
   contacto a lo largo de la línea media ventral-
   ----------------------------------Alopoglossus

59.Extremidad anterior con escamas quilladas------
   -------------------------------------Leposoma
   Extremidad anterior con escamas lisas--------60

60.Ventrales redondeadas y superpuestas a poste-
   rior--------------------------------Arthrosaura
   Ventrales cuadradas y yuxtapuestas-----------
   ----------------------------------Ptychoglossus

61.Escamas laterales casi iguales---------------62
   Escamas laterales de tamaño notoriamente redu-
   cido---------------------------------------64

62.Escamas dorsales quilladas------------------63
   Escamas dorsales lisas------------------Anadia

63.Cuatro supraoculares----------------Arthroseps
   Tres supraoculares---------------Pantodactylus

64.Lateral scales on neck not granular----------65
   Lateral scales on neck granular--------------66

65.Large, nearly circular, undivided transparent
   disk in lower eyelid; body scales smooth------
   ------------------------------------Opipeuter
   Transparent disk in lower eyelid made up of
   several scales; body scales smooth or keeled--
   --------------------------------Euspondylus

66.Dorsal scales not rectangular nor in longitudinal series------------------------------------67
   Dorsal scales rectangular, arranged in longitudinal series-----------------------Cercosaura

67.Palmar plates between thumb and wrist absent---
   -----------------------------------Placosoma
   Palmar plates between thumb and wrist present--
   ------------------------------Prionodactylus

68.Digits flat; subdigital lamellae smooth,
   usually also widened; adult males with extensile gular fan-------------------------------69
   Digits compressed or cylindrical; subdigital
   lamellae keeled or smooth; if smooth, adult
   males lack extensile gular fan--------------70

69.Temporal region of head swollen; tail
   compressed and prehensile; parietal bone
   expanded along temporal and occipital borders;
   sternal-xiphisternal ribs four----------------
   ----------------------------Phenacosaurus
   Temporal region of head normal; tail usually
   not compressed or prehensile; parietal bone
   not expanded; sternal-xiphisternal ribs five--
   --Anolis

70.Head strongly produced posteriorly, either as
   vertical fin or as horizontal shelf, may be
   inconspicuous in females and juveniles------
   ---71
   Head not expanded and drawn out posteriorly to
   form fin or shelf---------------------------73

71.Infradigital lamellae with several sharp keels;
   vertical fin on head------------------------72
   Infradigital lamellae with single tubercular
   keel; horizontal shelf on head---------------
   ----------------------------------Laemanctus

72.Toes of hind foot with fringe of flat scales
   forming serrate margin--------------Basiliscus
   Toes on hind foot without serrate margin------
   ----------------------------------Corytophanes

73.No large, flat, round scale below ear----------
   ---74
   Large, flat, round scale below ear opening-----
   --Iguana

74.Interparietal scale conspicuously enlarged, at
   least one fifth as wide as head, and at least
   several times larger than any scale adjacent
   to it (Fig. 10)-----------------------------75
   Interparietal scale present or absent; if present, less than one-fifth as wide as head, and
   not several times larger than any adjacent
   scale (Fig. 11)-----------------------------80

64.Escamas laterales del cuello no granulares---65
   Escamas laterales del cuello granulares------66

65.Con disco transparente indiviso, grande, casi
   circular en párpado inferior; escamas del
   cuerpo lisas-------------------------Opipeuter
   Disco transparente del párpado inferior formado
   por varias escamas; escamas del cuerpo lisas
   o quilladas------------------------Euspondylus

66.Escamas dorsales no rectangulares ni en series
   longitudinales-------------------------------67
   Escamas dorsales rectangulares, dispuestas en
   series longitudinales--------------Cercosaura

67.Sin láminas palmares entre pulgar y muñeca-----
   ------------------------------------Placosoma
   Con láminas palmares entre pulgar y muñeca-----
   ---------------------------------Prionodactylus

68.Dedos chatos; lamelas subdigitales lisas, generalmente también ensanchadas; machos adultos
   con abanico gular extensible-----------------69
   Dedos comprimidos o cilíndricos; lamelas subdigitales quilladas o lisas, si son lisas, entonces machos adultos sin abanico gular
   extensible-----------------------------------70

69.Región temporal de la cabeza hinchada; cola
   comprimida y prénsil, hueso parietal expandido
   a lo largo de los bordes temporal y occipital;
   costillas esternales-xifiesternales cuatro----
   ----------------------------Phenacosaurus
   Región temporal de la cabeza normal; cola
   usualmente no comprimida ni prénsil; hueso
   parietal no expandido; costillas esternales-
   xifiesternales cinco-------------------Anolis

70.Cabeza fuertemente prolongada hacia posterior,
   o bien como aleta vertical o bien como repisa
   horizontal, puede ser inconspicua en hembras y
   juveniles-----------------------------------71
   Cabeza no prolongada hacia posterior, sin aleta
   ni repisa-----------------------------------73

71.Lamelas infradigitales con varias quillas agudas; aleta vertical en la cabeza-----------72
   Lamelas infradigitales con una sola quilla tubercular; repisa horizontal en la cabeza------
   -----------------------------------Laemanctus

72.Dedos de extremidad posterior con fleco de es-
   camas chatas que forman un borde serrado------
   -----------------------------------Basiliscus
   Dedos de extremidad posterior sin borde serrado
   -----------------------------------Corytophanes

73.Sin escama redonda, grande, chata debajo del
   oído--74
   Con una escama redonda, grande, chata debajo
   del orificio ótico---------------------Iguana

74.Escama interparietal visiblemente agrandada,
   por lo menos un quinto de la anchura de la
   cabeza y varias veces más grande que cualquier
   escama adyacente (Fig. 10)-----------------75
   Escama interparietal presente o ausente, si
   presente menos de un quinto de la anchura de
   la cabeza y no varias veces más grande que
   cualquier escama adyacente (Fig. 11)--------80

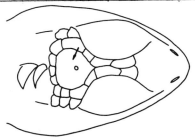

Fig. 10. _Tropidurus_, enlarged interparietal

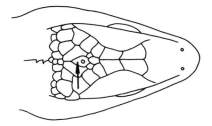

Fig. 11. _Ophryoessoides_, small interparietal

75. Tail length from slightly longer than to considerably shorter than snout-vent length; caudal scales form whorls of stout spines---76
Tail length much greater than snout-vent length; caudal scales may be mucronate but not spinose-------------------------------------77

76. Tail about one-half snout-vent length, non-autotomic, with equal whorls of spines-------------------------------------_Uracentron_
Tail about equal to snout-vent length, autotomic, with caudal scales in unequal whorls----------------------------------_Strobilurus_

77. Orbit bordered below by a single, wide, elongate subocular extending to anterior corner of orbit, may be preceded by preocular of equal width-----------------------------78
Orbit bordered below by an arc of five to seven subequal scales; no preocular---------------79

78. Femoral pores present---------------_Sceloporus_
Femoral pores absent----------------_Tropidurus_

79. Upper head scales small, subequal, pyramidal; supraoculars small, supraorbital semicircles not distinct; interparietal scale about as wide as distance between orbits---------------------------------_Uraniscodon_
Upper head scales of various sizes, flat or convex, or a few may be conical; supraoculars enlarged, supraorbital semicircles distinct; interparietal scale much wider than distance between orbits--------------------------_Plica_

80. Subdigital lamellae smooth-------------------81
Subdigital lamellae keeled-------------------87

81. Ventral scales keeled----------------------82
Ventral scales smooth----------------------84

82. No median vertebral scale row---------------83
Median vertebral row of enlarged scales--------------------------------_Enyalius_

83. Lateral scales of body homogeneous----------------------------------_Aptycholaemus_
Lateral scales of body heterogeneous, including small, smooth, juxtaposed scales with patches of much larger scales---------------_Anisolepis_

75. Cola desde ligeramente más larga a mucho más corta que la longitud hocico-ano; escamas caudales forman anillos de espinas fuertes---76
Longitud de la cola mucho mayor que longitud hocico-ano; escamas caudales pueden ser mucronadas pero no espinosas--------------------77

76. Cola aproximadamente la mitad de longitud hocico-ano, no autotómica, con anillos iguales de espinas------------------------_Uracentron_
Longitud de la cola aproximadamente igual a la hocico-ano, cola autotómica, con espinas caudales en anillos desiguales---_Strobilurus_

77. Orbita bordeada por debajo por una sola subocular ancha, alargada que se extiende hasta el ángulo anterior de la órbita, puede estar precedida por un preocular de igual anchura---78
Orbita bordeada por debajo por un arco de cinco a siete escamas casi iguales; sin preocular-79

78. Con poros femorales------------------_Sceloporus_
Sin poros femorales------------------_Tropidurus_

79. Escamas del dorso de la cabeza chicas, casi iguales, piramidales; supraoculares chicas, semicírculos supraorbitales no distintos; escama interparietal aproximadamente tan ancha como distancia entre órbitas--_Uraniscodon_
Escamas del dorso de la cabeza de varios tamaños, planas o convexas o unas pocas pueden ser cónicas; supraoculares dilatadas, semicírculos supraorbitales distintos; escama interparietal más ancha que la distancia entre las órbitas--------------------------------------_Plica_

80. Lamelas subdigitales lisas--------------------81
Lamelas subdigitales quilladas---------------87

81. Escamas ventrales quilladas------------------82
Escamas ventrales lisas--------------------84

82. Sin línea media vertebral de escamas--------83
Con línea media vertebral de escamas dilatadas-------------------------------------_Enyalius_

83. Escamas laterales del cuerpo homogéneas-------------------------------------_Aptycholaemus_
Escamas laterales del cuerpo heterogéneas, con escamas pequeñas, lisas, yuxtapuestas que alternan con grupos de escamas mucho más grandes-------------------------------_Anisolepis_

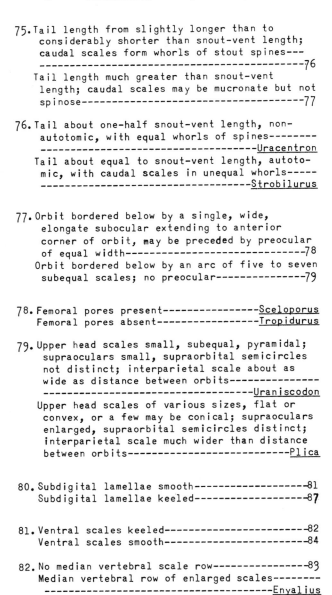

84. Dorsal scales granular or nearly so; more than 100 scales around midbody; distal subdigital lamellae with median groove----------------85
Dorsal scales flat, pavimentous, fewer than 100 scales around midbody; distal subdigital lamellae not grooved medially--Urostrophus

85. Caudal scales keeled distally; supraorbital semicircles usually in contact between orbits---86
All caudal scales smooth; supraorbital semicircles not in contact between orbits---Diplolaemus

86. Elongate subocular scale usually present; inconspicuous vertebral scale row present; usually with immaculate venter--Cupriguanus
Subocular scales usually subequal; no trace of vertebral scale row; venter with broken, brownish stripes--------------------Leiosaurus

87. Dorsal head scales not conspicuously multicarinate; ear opening many times larger than external nasal opening; males usually without extensile gular fan------------------------88
Most of dorsal head scales conspicuously multicarinate; ear opening about twice as large as external narial opening; male with large, extensile gular fan------------Tropidodactylus

88. Anterior superciliaries elongate and diagonally overlapping; usually with elongate subocular scale; no femoral pores; preanal pores present or absent; with large sternal fontanelle--89
Anterior superciliaries not conspicuous and overlapping; suboculars usually subequal; femoral pores present or absent; preanal pores absent; sternal fontanelle small or absent--95

89. Interparietal scale usually conspicuous, usually about one eighth as wide as head and accompanied by pair of enlarged parietal scales; males usually with preanal pores; no trace of vertebral scale row-----------------------90
Interparietal scale usually inconspicuous or absent; if present, less than one tenth width of head; vertebral scale row present or absent; no preanal pores in males----------93

90. Scales of body small to large, but not more than 180 around midbody--------------------91
Scales of body small, almost granular, 180 or more scales around midbody--Phymaturus

91. Palatine teeth absent; dorsal scales keeled-------------------------------------Liolaemus
Palatine teeth present; dorsal scales smooth-92

84. Escamas dorsales granulares o casi granulares; más de 100 escamas alrededor del medio cuerpo; lamelas subdigitales distales con surco medio--85
Escamas dorsales planas, pavimentosas, menos de 100 escamas alrededor del medio cuerpo; lamelas subdigitales distales sin surco medio--Urostrophus

85. Escamas caudales quilladas distalmente; semicírculos supraorbitales usualmente en contacto entre las órbitas------------------------86
Todas las escamas caudales lisas; semicírculos supraorbitales no en contacto entre las órbitas--------------------------Diplolaemus

86. Escama subocular alargada usualmente presente; con hilera vertebral de escamas inconspícua; usualmente con vientre inmaculado--Cupriguanus
Escamas suboculares usualmente casi iguales; sin trazas de hilera vertebral de escamas; vientre con cintas parduzcas fragmentarias--------------------------------------Leiosaurus

87. Escamas del dorso de la cabeza no conspicuamente multicarenadas; orificio ótico varias veces mayor que el orificio nasal externo; machos usualmente sin abanico gular extensible-------------------------------------88
La mayoría de las escamas del dorso de la cabeza conspicuamente multicarenadas; orificio ótico aproximadamente el doble de tamaño que orificio nasal externo; macho con abanico gular extensible grande--------Tropidodactylus

88. Superciliares anteriores alargadas y superpuestas diagonalmente; usualmente con escama subocular alargada; sin poros femorales; con o sin poros preanales; con fontanela esternal grande------------------------------------89
Superciliares anteriores no conspicuas ni superpuestas; suboculares generalmente casi iguales; con o sin poros femorales; sin poros preanales; fontanela esternal chica o ausente-------------------------------------95

89. Escama interparietal usualmente conspicua, usualmente aproximadamente un octavo del ancho de la cabeza y acompañada por par de escamas parietales dilatadas; machos usualmente con poros preanales; sin trazas de hilera vertebral de escamas----------------------------90
Escama interparietal usualmente inconspicua o ausente, si presente, menos de un décimo del ancho de la cabeza; con o sin hilera vertebral de escamas; machos sin poros preanales------93

90. Escamas del cuerpo chicas a grandes, pero no más de 180 alrededor del medio cuerpo--91
Escamas del cuerpo chicas, casi granulares, 180 o más escamas alrededor del medio cuerpo--Phymaturus

91. Sin dientes palatinos; escamas dorsales quilladas--------------------------Liolaemus
Con dientes palatinos; escamas dorsales lisas--92

92. Dorsal scales imbricate and overlapping--------
------------------------------------Phrynosaura
    Dorsal scales juxtaposed----------------------
    ------------------------------Ctenoblepharis

93. Scales along anterior margin of vent not form-
    ing denticulate border--------------------94
    Scales along anterior margin of vent enlarged,
    forming strongly denticulate border-----------
    ------------------------------Proctotretus

94. Proximal caudal scales much larger than ventral
    scales, forming whorls of spines; and/or
    vertebral scale row absent; and/or skin on
    sides of neck strongly folded, with scales
    that are granular or nearly so----------------
    ------------------------------Stenocercus
    Proximal caudal scales not much larger than
    ventrals and not spinose; conspicuous verte-
    bral scale row present; skin on sides of neck
    weakly to not at all folded; lateral nuchal
    scales subimbricate to imbricate and usually
    keeled--------------------------Ophryoessoides

95. Tail long or short, but if less than one and
    one half snout-vent length, it is spiny-----
    .--------------------------------------96
    Tail less than one and one half times snout-
    vent length, not at all spiny----------------
    ------------------------------Leiosaurus

96, Tail short or long, if longer than twice snout-
    vent length vertebral scale row is present----
    --97
    Tail at least twice as long as snout-vent
    length, no vertebral scale row---------------
    ------------------------------Polychrus

97. Vertebral scale row present, forming distinct
    denticulation----------------------------98
    Vertebral row present or absent, if present
    very inconspicuous and not at all denticulate-
    --------------------------------------102

98. Tail with enlarged, heavy spines-------------99
    Tail without heavy spines-------------------100

99. With group of enlarged, spinose, protuberant
    scales on lower leg--------------Enyaliosaurus
    No conspicuously enlarged scales on lower leg--
    ------------------------------Ctenosaura

100. Pterygoid teeth present--------------------101
     No pterygoid teeth-----------------Polychroides

101. Femoral pores usually present in males; no
     marked sexual dichromatism, i.e., no wide,
     light paravertebral stripes in female; tail
     spiny or not; scales heterogeneous or not-----
     ------------------------------Enyalioides
     Femoral pores absent in males; usually with
     marked sexual dichromatism; females often with
     wide, light, paravertebral stripes; tail not
     spiny; scales homogeneous-------------Enyalius

92. Escamas dorsales imbricadas y tejadas----------
-----------------------------------Phrynosaura
    Escamas dorsales yuxtapuestas-----------------
    ------------------------------Ctenoblepharis

93. Escamas del borde anterior del ano no forman
    borde denticulado--------------------------94
    Escamas del borde anterior del ano dilatadas,
    forman borde fuertemente denticulado----------
    ------------------------------Proctotretus

94. Escamas caudales proximales mucho más grandes
    que ventrales, formando remolinos de espinas;
    y/o sin hilera vertebral de escamas; y/o piel
    de los lados del cuello fuertemente plegada
    con escamas granulares o casi granulares------
    ------------------------------Stenocercus
    Escamas caudales proximales no mucho mayores
    que ventrales y no espinosas; con hilera ver-
    tebral de escamas conspicua; piel de los lados
    del cuello débilmente plegada o sin pliegue;
    escamas nucales laterales subimbricadas a
    imbricadas y usualmente quilladas-------------
    ------------------------------Ophryoessoides

95. Cola larga o corta, pero si menos que una y
    media veces la longitud hocico-ano entonces
    espinosa----------------------------------96
    Cola menos de una y media veces la longitud
    hocico-ano, sin espinas------------Leiosaurus

96. Cola corta o larga, si más del doble de la
    longitud hocico-ano entonces con hilera verte-
    bral de escamas---------------------------97
    Cola al menos el doble que la longitud hocico-
    ano, sin hilera vertebral de escamas----------
    ------------------------------Polychrus

97. Con hilera vertebral de escamas, que forma den-
    ticulación distinta-----------------------98
    Con o sin hilera vertebral de escamas, si pre-
    sente muy inconspicua y sin denticulación-----
    --102

98. Cola con espinas grandes, fuertes------------99
    Cola sin espinas grandes--------------------100

99. Con grupo de escamas dilatadas, espinosas, pro-
    tuberantes en tibio-fíbula--------------------
    ------------------------------Enyaliosaurus
    Sin escamas notoriamente dilatadas en tibio-
    fíbula------------------------------Ctenosaura

100. Con dientes pterigoideos--------------------101
     Sin dientes pterigoideos-----------Polychroides

101. Machos generalmente con poros femorales; sin
     dicromatismo sexual marcado, ej.: sin cintas
     paravertebrales claras, anchas en hembras; co-
     la espinosa o no; escamas heterogéneas o no---
     ------------------------------Enyalioides
     Machos sin poros femorales; usualmente con
     dicromatismo sexual marcado; hembras a menudo
     con cintas paravertebrales claras, anchas; co-
     la no espinosa; escamas homogéneas-----------
     ------------------------------Enyalius

102.Tail shorter, distinctly flattened, with whorls of spines; tail not autotomic---------------- -----------------------------------Hoplocercus
Tail longer, rounded, also spiny; tail autoto- mic----------------------------Morunasaurus

103.Eyelids rudimentary------------------------104
Both dorsal and ventral eyelids well developed- -----------------------------------Coleonyx

104.Digits not dilated, slender throughout their length-------------------------------------105
Digits dilated, at least partially----------110

105.Digits straight----------------------------106
Digits not straight, distal phalanges angulate- ---107

106.Claw retractile into sheath-------------Garthia
Claw not retractile into sheath---------------- ---------------------------------------Homonota

107.Claw between two scales, a small superior and large inferior------------------------------108
Claw between five or more scales-------------109

108.Dorsal scales homogeneous--------------Gonatodes
Dorsal scales heterogeneous------------------- ----------------------------------Gymnodactylus

109.Supralateral scales of claw sheath in contact throughout their length (Fig. 12)------------- ----------------------------Pseudogonatodes
Supralateral scales of claw sheath separated by single scale (Fig. 13)--------Lepidoblepharis

110.Dilation of digit either restricted to basal phalanges, or extends throughout entire digit- ---111
Dilation of digit restricted to most distal part---117

111.Claw in contact with or only slightly beyond dilation of basal phalanx--------------------- -----------------------------Thecadactylus
Claw much beyond dilated part of basal phalanx- ---112

112.Distal infradigital lamellae single---------113
Distal infradigital lamellae double---------115

113.Pollex well developed----------------------114
Pollex extremely reduced or absent------------ ---Bogertia

114.Claw of fifth finger retractile laterally------ ------------------------------------Aristelliger
Claw of fifth finger not retractile laterally-- -----------------------------------Phyllopezus

115.Pollex without claw, or, if present, extremely minute---------------------------------------116
Pollex with claw-------------------Hemidactylus

116.Enlarged tubercles present on dorsum of body--- --Briba
No enlarged tubercles on body------------------ ---------------------------------Lepidodactylus

102.Cola corta, distintamente aplanada, con anillos de espinas; cola no autotómica--------------- -----------------------------------Hoplocercus
Cola larga, redondeada, también espinosa; cola autotómica----------------------Morunasaurus

103.Párpados rudimentarios----------------------104
Párpados dorsal y ventral bien desarrollados--- -----------------------------------Coleonyx

104.Dedos no dilatados, delgados a todo lo largo--- ---105
Dedos dilatados, al menos parcialmente------110

105.Dedos rectos-------------------------------106
Dedos no rectos, falanges distales en ángulo--- ---107

106.Uña retráctil en vaina------------------Garthia
Uña no retráctil en vaina-------------Homonota

107.Uña entre dos escamas, una superior chica y una inferior grande----------------------------108
Uña entre cinco o más escamas--------------109

108.Escamas dorsales homogéneas-----------Gonatodes
Escamas dorsales heterogéneas----------------- ----------------------------------Gymnodactylus

109.Escamas supralaterales de la vaina de la uña en contacto a todo lo largo (Fig. 12)------------ ----------------------------Pseudogonatodes
Escamas supralaterales de la vaina de la uña separadas por una sola escama (Fig. 13)------- ---------------------------------Lepidoblepharis

110.Dilatación del dedo restringida a falanges ba- sales o extendida a todo lo largo----------111
Dilatación del dedo limitada a parte distal---- ---117

111.Uña en contacto con o ligeramente más allá de dilatación de falange basal------------------- --------------------------Thecadactylus
Uña mucho más allá de parte dilatada de falange basal--112

112.Lamela infradigital distal única------------113
Lamela infradigital distal doble------------115

113.Pollex bien desarrollado--------------------114
Pollex muy reducido o ausente----------------- ---Bogertia

114.Uña del quinto dedo retráctil lateralmente----- ------------------------------------Aristelliger
Uña del quinto dedo no retráctil lateralmente-- -----------------------------------Phyllopezus

115.Pollex sin uña, o si presente, extremadamente diminuta-------------------------------------116
Pollex con uña--------------------Hemidactylus

116.Con tubérculos dilatados en dorso del cuerpo--- --Briba
Sin tubérculos dilatados en cuerpo------------- ---------------------------------Lepidodactylus

117.Pollex not reduced in size--------------------118
    Pollex extremely reduced-----------Lygodactylus

118.Distal phalanges asymmetrical (Fig. 14)-----119
    Distal phalanges symmetrically dilated, with
    two ventral terminal plates--------------------
    ------------------------------------Phyllodactylus

119.Supraciliary spine present, terminal phalanges
    distinctly asymmetrical-----------------------
    ------------------------------Sphaerodactylus
    No supraciliary spine; terminal phalanges only
    slightly asymmetrical-----------Coleodactylus

117.Pollex de tamaño no reducido-----------------118
    Pollex extremadamente reducido-----------------
    -----------------------------------Lygodactylus

118.Falanges distales asimétricas (Fig. 14)-----119

    Falanges distales simétricamente dilatadas, con
    dos láminas terminales ventrales--------------
    ------------------------------Phyllodactylus

119.Con espina supraciliar; falanges terminales
    distintamente asimétricas--------------------
    ------------------------------Sphaerodactylus
    Sin espina supraciliar; falanges terminales
    sólo ligeramente asimétricas-------------------
    ------------------------------Coleodactylus

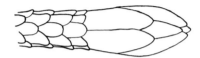
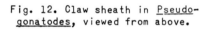
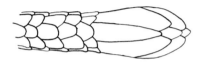

Fig. 12. Claw sheath in Pseudo-gonatodes, viewed from above.

Fig. 13. Claw sheath in Lepido-blepharis, viewed from above.

Fig. 14. Sphaerodactylus, showing asymmetry in distal phalanx.

ABLEPHARUS Fitzinger

1823 Ablepharus Fitzinger, in Lichtenstein, Verzeichniss der Doubletten des Zoologischen Museums der Königl. Universität zu Berlin: 103. Type-species: Ablepharus pannonicus Fitzinger.
1834 Cryptoblepharum Wiegmann, Herpetologia Mexicana: 12. Type-species: Ablepharus poecilopleuro Wiegmann (a nomen nudum).
1839 Petia Gray (substitute name for Cryptoblepharum), Ann. Mag. Nat. Hist., (1) 2: 335.
1843 Microblepharis Fitzinger, Systema Reptilium: 23. Type-species: Ablepharus Menestriesii Duméril and Bibron.
1845 Morethia Gray, Cat. Liz. Brit. Mus.: 65. Type-species: Morethia anomalus Gray.
1845 Menetia Gray, Cat. Liz. Brit. Mus.: 65. Type-species: Menetia Greyii Gray.
1872 Blepharosteres Stoliczka, Proc. Asiatic Soc. Bengal, 1872: 74. Type-species: Blepharosteres Grayanus Stoliczka.

Distribution: Australia, Europe, eastern Asia, Africa, Polynesian Islands, and coastal islands of Peru and Ecuador.

Content: About 50 species, of which only one occurs within limits of this work.

ABLEPHARUS BOUTONII (Desjardin)

1831 Scincus Boutonii Desjardin, Ann. Sci. Nat. Paris, 22: 298. Type-locality: Mauritius Island.
1868 Ablepharus Boutonii—Strauch, Mél. Biol. Acad. Imp. Sci. Saint-Pétersbourg, 6: 566.

Distribution: Africa, Australia, southern Asia, Polynesia and islands of Pacific coast of Peru.

Content: About 30 subspecies, only one of which is found within limits set for this work.

Ablepharus boutonii poecilopleurus Wiegmann

1836 Ablepharus poecilopleurus Wiegmann, Nova Acta Acad. Leop.-Carol.Caes., 17: 202, pl. 18, fig. 1. Type-locality: Pisacoma Island, Peru.
1887 Ablepharus boutoni poecilopleurus—Boulenger, Cat. Liz. Brit. Mus., 3: 347.
1928 Cryptoblepharus boutonii novocaledonicus Mertens, Zool. Anz., 78: 88. Type-locality: Hienghiène Island, New Caledonia Islands.
1928 Cryptoblepharus boutonii novohebridicus Mertens, Zool. Anz., 78: 89. Type-locality: Malo Island, New Hebrides Islands.

Distribution: Widely distributed on Pacific and Polynesian Islands. The type-locality, Pisacoma Island, coastal Peru, needs to be confirmed to prove existence in South America. No continental localities have been verified.

ABRONIA Gray

1838 <u>Abronia</u> Gray, Ann. Mag. Nat. Hist., (1) 1: 389. Type-species: <u>Gerrhonotus Deppii</u> Wiegmann.
1843 <u>Aspidosoma</u> Fitzinger, Systema Reptilium: 21. Type-species: <u>Gerrhonotus taeniatus</u> Wiegmann.
1843 <u>Leiogerrhon</u> Fitzinger, Systema Reptilium: 21. Type-species: <u>Gerrhonotus Deppii</u> Wiegmann.
1846 <u>Liogerrhon</u> Agassiz (corrected spelling of <u>Leiogerrhon</u> Fitzinger), Nomenclatoris Zoologici Index Universalis: 203 and 212.

Distribution: Guatemala and Mexico.

Content: Eleven species, nine of which are extralimital.

Key to the species

1. Postmentals paired----------------------aurita   1. Un par de posmentales-------------------aurita
   Postmental unpaired---------------vasconcelosii   Posmental impar------------------vasconcelosii

ABRONIA AURITA (Cope)

1869 <u>Gerrhonotus auritus</u> Cope, Proc. Acad. Nat. Sci. Phila., 1868: 306. Type-locality: Forest of Verapaz, Guatemala.
1885 <u>Barissia fimbriata</u> Cope, Proc. Amer. Phil. Soc., 22: 771. Type-locality: Pine Forest of Alta Verapaz, Guatemala.
1949 <u>Abronia aurita</u>—Tihen, Amer. Midl. Nat., 41: 591.

Distribution: Alta Verapaz, Guatemala.

ABRONIA VASCONCELOSII (Bocourt)

1871 <u>Gerrhonotus Vasconcelosii</u> Bocourt, Bull. Nouv. Arch. Mus. Hist. Nat. Paris, 7 (4): 107. Type-locality: Arqueta, Guatemala, above 2000 m.
1949 <u>Abronia vasconcelosii</u>—Tihen, Amer. Midl. Nat., 41: 591.

Distribution: Known only from type locality.

ALOPOGLOSSUS Boulenger

  1885 _Alopoglossus_ Boulenger, Cat. Liz. Brit. Mus., 2: 383. Type-species: _Alopoglossus copii_
     Boulenger.

    Distribution: Ecuador, Peru, Brazil, Guianas.

    Content: Five species, according to most recent revision, by Ruibal, Bull. Mus. Comp. Zool., 106,
     1952.

Key to the species

1. Gulars not arranged in two longitudinal rows;
   four preanal scales------------------------2
  Gulars transversely enlarged and arranged in
  two longitudinal rows; three preanal scales---
  --------------------------------------_festae_

2. Scales on sides of neck large and conical;
   scales on posterior half of dorsum in longitudinal rows---------------------------_copii_
  Not as above-------------------------------3

3. Scales on sides of neck keeled, imbricate, not
   granular-----------------------------------4
  Scales on sides of neck small, almost granular-
  ---------------------------------_buckleyi_

4. Gulars keeled or smooth, pointed, not truncate;
   ventrals spotless--------------_carinicaudatus_
  Gulars smooth with a convex posterior border;
  ventrals with basal and lateral margins pig-
  mented--------------------------------_andeanus_

Clave de especies

1. Gulares no dispuestas en dos hileras longitudinales; cuatro preanales------------------2
  Gulares ensanchadas transversalmente y dispuestas en dos hileras longitudinales; tres
  preanales----------------------------_festae_

2. Escamas de los lados del cuello grandes y
   cónicas; escamas de la mitad posterior del
   dorso en hileras longitudinales---------_copii_
  No como el anterior------------------------3

3. Escamas de los lados del cuello quilladas,
   imbricadas, no granulares-------------------4
  Escamas de los lados del cuello pequeñas, casi
  granulares--------------------------_buckleyi_

4. Gulares quilladas o lisas, puntiagudas, no
   truncadas; ventrales sin manchas-------------
  -------------------------------_carinicaudatus_
  Gulares lisas con un borde posterior convexo;
  ventrales con los márgenes basales y laterales
  pigmentados--------------------------_andeanus_

ALOPOGLOSSUS ANDEANUS Ruibal

  1952 _Alopoglossus andeanus_ Ruibal, Bull. Mus. Comp. Zool., 106: 510. Type-locality: La Pampa, Depto.
    Puno, Peru, 760 m.

    Distribution: Known only from type locality.

ALOPOGLOSSUS BUCKLEYI (O'Shaughnessy)

  1881 _Leposoma buckleyi_ O'Shaughnessy, Proc. Zool. Soc. London, 1881: 233, pl. 22, fig. 2, 2a, 2b.
    Type-locality: Canelos, Ecuador.
  1885 _Alopoglossus buckleyi_—Boulenger, Cat. Liz. Brit. Mus., 2: 385.
  1952 _Alopoglossus buckleyi_—Ruibal, Bull. Mus. Comp. Zool., 106: 506.

    Distribution: Amazonas, Brazil; Amazonian Ecuador, Colombia, and Peru (an unverified and very
    doubtful record from Babahoyo, on Pacific side of Ecuador, is given by Werner, Mitt. Naturhist.
    Mus. Hamburg, 27, 1910, 30).

ALOPOGLOSSUS CARINICAUDATUS (Cope)

  1876 _Lepidosoma carinicaudatum_ Cope, Jour. Acad. Nat. Sci. Phila., (2) 8: 160. Type-locality: Valley
    of Río Marañón, Peru.
  1885 _Alopoglossus carinicaudatus_—Boulenger, Cat. Liz. Brit. Mus., 2: 384.
  1924 _Alopoglossus amazonius_ Ruthven, Occ. Pap. Mus. Zool. Univ. Mich., 153: 1. Type-locality:
    Villa Murtinho, Mato Grosso, Brazil.
  1946 _Alopoglossus copii surinamensis_ Brongersma, Zool. Meded. Leyden, 26: 231, fig. 1. Type-locality:
    Forest on the Lucie River, Surinam.
  1952 _Alopoglossus carinicaudatus_—Ruibal, Bull. Mus. Comp. Zool., 106: 508.

    Distribution: Periphery of Amazon Basin in Surinam, Guyana, Brazil, Ecuador and Peru.

ALOPOGLOSSUS

ALOPOGLOSSUS COPII Boulenger

    1885 Alopoglossus copii Boulenger, Cat. Liz. Brit. Mus., 2: 383. Type-locality: Canelos and
        Pallatanga, Ecuador.
    1952 Alopoglossus copii—Ruibal, Bull. Mus. Comp. Zool., 106: 505.

   Distribution: Amazonian slopes of Ecuador.

ALOPOGLOSSUS FESTAE Peracca

    1904 Alopoglossus festae Peracca, Boll. Mus. Zool. Comp. Anat. Univ. Torino, 19 (465): 7. Type-locality:
        Vinces, Ecuador.
    1952 Alopoglossus festae—Ruibal, Bull. Mus. Comp. Zool., 106: 502.

   Distribution: Pacific slope of Ecuador.

AMEIVA Meyer

1795 Ameiua[1] Meyer, Synopsis Reptilium: 27. Type-species: Ameiua americana Meyer.
1800 Ameiva Bechstein (emendation of Ameiua Meyer), in Lacépède, Naturgeschichte der Amphibien, 2: 44.
1828 Cnemidotus Wagler, Isis von Oken, 21: 860. Type-species: Lacerta ameiva Linnaeus.
1833 Pachylobronchus Wagler, Isis von Oken, 26: 891. Type-species: Lacerta ameiva Linnaeus.
1840 Amieva Gray, Ann. Mag. Nat. Hist., (1) 5: 114. Type-species: Amieva trilineata Gray.
1843 Pholidoscelis Fitzinger, Systema Reptilium: 20. Type-species: Ameiva major Duméril and Bibron.
1869 Holcosus Cope, Proc. Acad. Nat. Sci. Phila., 1868: 306. Type-species: Holcosus bridgesii Cope.
1876 Amiva Cope (in error for Ameiva), Jour. Acad. Nat. Sci. Phila., (2) 8 (1875): 117.
1892 Tiaporus Cope, Proc. Amer. Phil. Soc., 30: 132. Type-species: Tiaporus fuliginosus Cope.
1900 Tejaporus Cope (emendation of Tiaporus), Ann. Rept. U.S. Nat. Mus., 1898: 560.

Distribution: Mexico, Central and South America.

Content: About 15 species, eleven of which are found within limits set for this work.

Key to the species

1. Head plates smooth----------------------------2
   Head plates rugose----------------septemlineata

2. Frontal plate divided------------------------3
   Frontal plate entire------------------------5

3. Frontal plate divided into several smaller
   scales---------------------------------------4
   Frontal plate divided in two equal scales------
   -----------------------------------bifrontata

4. Mesoptychium with enlarged scales--------orcesi
   Mesoptychium with subequal scales-----bridgesii

5. Frontoparietal and parietal plates in contact
   with interparietal--------------------------6
   Frontoparietal and parietal plates separated
   from interparietal by one or two rows of small
   scales---------------------------leptophrys

6. Gular region without enlarged scales----------7
   Gular region with median scales distinctly
   enlarged------------------------------------8

7. Twelve rows of ventral plates-----------ameiva
   Eight rows of ventral plates--------edracantha

8. Enlarged gular scales surrounded by smaller
   scales---------------------------------------9
   Enlarged gular scales surrounded by scales
   gradually decreasing in size--------------11

9. Enlarged gular scales not arranged in single
   longitudinal row; one interparietal---------10
   Enlarged gular scales arranged in single longitudinal row; two interparietals------chaitzami

10.Enlarged gular scales larger than mental-------
   ---------------------------------------festiva
   Enlarged gular scales much smaller than mental-
   --------------------------------------undulata

Clave de especies

1. Placas cefálicas lisas------------------------2
   Placas cefálicas rugosas----------septemlineata

2. Placa frontal dividida----------------------3
   Placa frontal entera------------------------5

3. Placa frontal dividida en varias escamas------4
   Placa frontal dividida en dos--------bifrontata

4. Mesoptychium con escamas ensanchadas-----orcesi
   Mesoptychium con escamas subiguales---bridgesii

5. Frontoparietales y parietales en contacto con
   el interparietal---------------------------6
   Frontoparietales y parietales separados del
   interparietal por una o dos hileras de
   escamitas---------------------------leptophrys

6. Región gular con escamas centrales no distintamente ensanchadas---------------------------7
   Región gular con escamas centrales nítidamente
   ensanchadas---------------------------------8

7. Doce hileras de escamas ventrales--------ameiva
   Ocho hileras de escamas ventrales----edracantha

8. Escamas gulares ensanchadas rodeadas por
   escamas menores-----------------------------9
   Escamas gulares ensanchadas rodeadas por
   escamas gradualmente menores----------------11

9. Escamas gulares ensanchadas no dispuestas en
   una hilera longitudinal; un interparietal---10
   Escamas gulares ensanchadas dispuestas en una
   hilera longitudinal; dos interparietales------
   -----------------------------------chaitzami

10.Escamas gulares ensanchadas de mayor extensión
   que el sinfisial----------------------festiva
   Escamas gulares ensanchadas mucho menores que
   el sinfisial--------------------------undulata

---

[1]Meyer actually named this genus Ameiua, not Ameiva. It is clear from the remainder of his text that the "V" is actually a capital "U", in Latin characters. While Ameiua has obvious priority, it is not used in this check list, which is only a summary of current usage.

11. Dorsal pattern of pair of dorsal yellow lines
separated by broad darker stripes and pair of
lateral yellow lines bordering broad dorsolateral blackish-brown stripe----quadrilineata
Dorsal pattern not as above-----------undulata

11. Diseño dorsal con un par de líneas amarillas,
separadas por anchas bandas oscuras y un par
de líneas amarillas bordeando una ancha banda
pardo negruzca dorsolateral------quadrilineata
Diseño dorsal no como el anterior------undulata

AMEIVA AMEIVA (Linnaeus)

1758 Lacerta Ameiva Linnaeus, Systema Naturae, Ed. 10: 202. Type-locality: Brazil.
1893 Ameiva ameiva—Cockerell, Jour. Inst. Jamaica, 1: 310.
1910 Cnemidophorus roeschmanni Werner, Mitt. Naturhist. Mus. Hamburg, 27: 28. Type-locality:
Provincia Beni, Bolivia (it is uncertain with which subspecies this taxon is synonymous. Burt,
Bull. U.S. Nat. Mus., 154, 1931, 21, indicated it as a synonym of Ameiva ameiva ameiva,
which does not occur in Bolivia, and no more recent author has re-evaluated its status).

Distribution: Panama, tropical South America, Trinidad, Tobago and Margarita Islands.

Content: Ten subspecies, of which one (aquilina Garman) is extralimital.

Key to the subspecies

1. Gular region suffused with black----------2
   Gular region not suffused with black------3

2. Dorsum brown with transverse rows of ocelli
   on sides, do not reach paravertebral
   region----------------------melanocephala
   Dorsum green with transverse rows of ocelli
   on sides and paravertebral region; vertebral region mottled with small black spots
   --------------------------------tobagana

3. Pale vertebral stripe present-------------4
   Pale vertebral stripe absent--------------5

4. Vertebral stripe not in contact with transverse rows of ocelli-----------praesignis
   Vertebral stripe in contact with transverse rows of ocelli--------------ornata

5. Transverse rows of ocelli discontinuous, do
   not cross vertebral region--------------6
   Transverse rows of ocelli continuous,
   crossing vertebral region-----------vogli

6. Ocelli regularly arranged-----------------7
   Ocelli irregularly arranged--------fischeri

7. Head with dark markings; sides dark,
   sharply distinct from dorsal color-------8
   Head without dark markings; small, scattered dark spotting on neck; sides
   slightly darkened--------------------laeta

8. Dorsal pattern confluent, forming irregular, reticulate markings on head, neck,
   and anterior third of body----------ameiva
   Dorsal pattern not reticulate, spots
   isolated from one another----------petersi

Clave de subespecies

1. Región gular con sufusión melánica--------2
   Región gular sin sufusión melánica--------3

2. Dorso pardo con hileras transversales de
   ocelos que no llegan a la región para-
   vertebral--------------------melanocephala
   Dorso verdoso con hileras transversales de
   ocelos que llegan a la región paravertebral; región vertebral ocupada por innu-
   merables manchitas----------------tobagana

3. Con una banda clara vertebral-------------4
   Sin banda vertebral-----------------------5

4. Banda clara vertebral no conectada con
   bandas transversales de ocelos--praesignis
   Banda clara vertebral conectada con bandas
   transversales de ocelos-------------ornata

5. Bandas de ocelos no continuas en la región
   vertebral--------------------------------6
   Bandas transversales de ocelos continuas,
   ininterrumpidas en la región vertebral----
   ------------------------------------vogli

6. Ocelos dispuestos regularmente------------7
   Ocelos dispuestos irregularmente--fischeri

7. Cabeza con diseños oscuros, flancos oscuros
   y nítidamente distintos del color dorsal-8
   Cabeza sin diseños oscuros, escasas manchitas oscuras sobre la nuca con flancos
   muy poco oscuros--------------------laeta

8. Los diseños confluyen formando trazos
   irregulares, que forman un retículos sobre
   la cabeza, cuello y tercio anterior del
   dorso--------------------------------ameiva
   Diseños no confluyen formando un retículo,
   y se mantienen como manchitas aisladas----
   ------------------------------------petersi

Ameiva ameiva ameiva (Linnaeus)

1768 <u>Seps surinamensis</u> Laurenti, Synopsin Reptilium: 59. Type-locality: None given.
1768 <u>Seps zeylanicus</u> Laurenti, Synopsin Reptilium: 59. Type-locality: None given.
1795 <u>Ameiua americana</u> Meyer (replacement name for <u>Lacerta ameiva</u> Gmelin), Synopsis Reptilium: 28.
1802 <u>Lacerta graphica</u> Daudin, Hist. Nat. Rept., 3: 112. Type-locality: America (after Seba).
1823 <u>Ameiva vulgaris</u> Lichtenstein (replacement name for <u>Lacerta ameiva</u> Linnaeus), Verzeichniss der Doubletten des Zoologischen Museums der Königl. Universität zu Berlin: 91.
1825 <u>Tejus Lateristriga</u> Spix, Sp. Nov. Lac. Bras.: 22, pl. 24, fig. 1. Type-locality: Brazil.
1825 <u>Tejus tritaeniatus</u> Spix, Sp. Nov. Lac. Bras.: 22, pl. 24, fig. 2. Type-locality: Estado da Bahia, Brazil.
1838 <u>Ameiva maculata</u> Gray, Ann. Mag. Nat. Hist., (1) 1: 277. Type-locality: Brazil.
1845 <u>Ameiva guttata</u> Gray, Cat. Liz. Brit. Mus.: 18. Type-locality: Demerara; Pernambuco; and Brazil.
1862 L.[acerta] <u>tristriata</u> Cope (in error for <u>Tejus tritaeniatus</u> Spix), Proc. Acad. Nat. Sci. Phila., 1862: 68.
1915 <u>Ameiva ameiva ameiva</u>—Barbour and Noble, Bull. Mus. Comp. Zool., 59: 462.
1915 <u>Ameiva ameiva bilineata</u> Barbour and Noble, Bull. Mus. Comp. Zool., 59: 464. Type-locality: Dunoon, Demarara River, Guyana.

Distribution: Southern Venezuela, Guyana, Surinam, French Guiana, northeastern Brazil.

Ameiva ameiva fischeri nomen novum

1879 <u>Cnemidophorus maculatus</u> Fischer, Verh. Naturwiss. Ver. Hamburg, 67: 95, pl. 4, figs. 1-6. Type-locality: Sabana Larga, Colombia.
1915 <u>Ameiva ameiva maculata</u> Barbour and Noble, Bull. Mus. Comp. Zool., 59: 467.

Distribution: Sabana Larga and Sierra de Santa Marta, Colombia.

Comment: This new name is necessary because of the prior name <u>Ameiva maculata</u> Gray, 1838. No previous author has replaced <u>maculatus</u> Fischer, 1879.

Ameiva ameiva laeta Cope

1862 A.[meiva] <u>laeta</u> Cope. Proc. Acad. Nat. Sci. Phila., 1862: 65. Type-locality: Near Rio de Janeiro, Brazil.
1915 <u>Ameiva ameiva laeta</u> Barbour and Noble, Bull. Mus. Comp. Zool., 59: 467.

Distribution: Rio de Janeiro, Minas Gerais and Goiás, Brazil.

Ameiva ameiva melanocephala Barbour and Noble

1915 <u>Ameiva ameiva melanocephala</u> Barbour and Noble, Bull. Mus. Comp. Zool., 59: 465. Type-locality: Cumanocoa, Venezuela.

Distribution: Eastern Venezuela, La Guayra Range in central Venezuela; Isla Margarita.

Ameiva ameiva ornata Müller and Hellmich

1940 <u>Ameiva ameiva ornata</u> Müller and Hellmich, Zool. Anz., 132: 179, figs. 1-2. Type-locality: La Puerta, Fusagasugá, Colombia, 1200 m.

Distribution: Llanos of Fusagasugá, Colombia.

Ameiva ameiva petersii Cope

1868 <u>Ameiva petersii</u> Cope, Proc. Acad. Nat. Sci. Phila., 1868: 99. Type-locality: Napo or Marañón, Ecuador.
1871 <u>Ameiva pleurotaenia</u> Peters, Monats. Akad. Wiss. Berlin, 1871: 652. Type-locality: Pebas and Pozuzu, Peru.
1915 <u>Ameiva ameiva petersi</u>—Barbour and Noble, Bull. Mus. Comp. Zool., 59: 466.

Distribution: Upper Amazonian Basin.

Ameiva ameiva praesignis (Baird and Girard)

    1852 Cnemidophorus praesignis Baird and Girard, Proc. Acad. Nat. Sci. Phila., 1852: 129. Type-
           locality: Chagres, Panama.
    1915 Ameiva ameiva praesignis—Barbour and Noble, Bull. Mus. Comp. Zool., 59: 468.

      Distribution: Lowlands of Colombia, Panama, and central llanos of western Venezuela.

Ameiva ameiva tobagana Cope

    1879 Amiva surinamensis tobaganus Cope, Proc. Amer. Phil. Soc., 18: 276. Type-locality:
           Tobago Island.
    1887 Ameiva surinamensis var. atrigularis Garman, Bull. Essex Inst., 19: 2. Type-locality:
           Trinidad.
    1962 Ameiva ameiva tobagana—Underwood, Caribb. Affairs, New Ser., 1: 90.

      Distribution: Trinidad and Tobago.

Ameiva ameiva vogli Müller

    1929 Ameiva ameiva vogli Müller, Zool. Anz., 83: 100, figs. 1-6. Type-locality: Barinas,
           Zamora, Venezuela.

      Distribution: Llanos de Barinas and Apure, Venezuela.

AMEIVA BIFRONTATA Cope

    1862 A.[meiva] bifrontata Cope, Proc. Acad. Nat. Sci. Phila., 1862: 67. Type-locality: St. Thomas,
      West Indies; and New Grenada = Colombia (Barbour and Noble, Bull. Mus. Comp. Zool., 59, 1915,
      471, express doubt that this species ever occurred on St. Thomas, and indicate they think all
      type specimens probably came from Venezuela).

    Distribution: Northern Peru, Colombia, and Venezuela; Testigos Island, Dutch Leeward Islands and
    Margarita Island.

    Content: Four subspecies.

Key to the subspecies	Clave de subespecies
1. Scales of outer row of ventrals small, not equal in length to neighboring ventral, usually separated by granules from next posterior ventral-----------------------2 Scales of outer row of ventrals large, equal in length to neighboring ventral, usually in contact with next posterior ventral--------------------------concolor	1. Escamas de la hilera ventral más externa chicas, no iguales en longitud a las ventrales vecinas, generalmente separadas por gránulos de la ventral siguiente posterior ---2 Escamas de la hilera ventral más externa, grandes, iguales en longitud a las ventrales vecinas, generalmente en contacto con la ventral siguiente posterior--concolor
2. Postbrachial scales dilated---------------3 Postbrachial scales all about same size as other scales on arm--------------insulana	2. Escamas postbraquiales ensanchadas--------3 Todas las escamas postbraquiales aproximadamente del mismo tamaño que las otras escamas del brazo----------------insulana
3. Supraocular granules extend beyond anterior border of third supraocular and occasionally surround it---------------bifrontata Supraocular granules may extend to but not beyond anterior border of third supraocular and never surround it--------divisa	3. Gránulos supraoculares se extienden más allá del margen anterior de la tercera supraocular, a veces delante rodeándola---------------------------------------bifrontata Gránulos supraoculares se extienden hasta, pero nunca más allá del margen de la tercera supraocular y nunca la rodean--divisa

Ameiva bifrontata bifrontata Cope

1924 [Ameiva bifrontata] bifrontata Ruthven, Occ. Pap. Mus. Zool. Univ. Mich., 155: 6.

Distribution: Northeastern South America, Dutch Leeward Islands, Margarita Island, Aruba Island.

Ameiva bifrontata concolor Ruthven

1924 Ameiva bifrontata concolor Ruthven, Occ. Pap. Mus. Zool. Univ. Mich., 155: 3. Type-locality: Paipoy, Río Crisnejas, Peru, 3500 ft.

Distribution: Canyons of Ríos Crisnejas and Marañón, Peru.

Ameiva bifrontata divisa (Fischer)

1879 Cnemidophorus divisus Fischer, Verh. Naturwiss. Ver. Hamburg, 67: 99, pl. 5, figs. 1-6. Type-locality: Barranquilla, Colombia.
1924 [Ameiva bifrontata] divisa Ruthven, Occ. Pap. Mus. Zool. Univ. Mich., 155: 6.

Distribution: Northwestern South America.

Ameiva bifrontata insulana Ruthven

1924 Ameiva insulana Ruthven, Occ. Pap. Mus. Zool. Univ. Mich., 149: 1. Type-locality: Testigos Island, Venezuela.
1924 [Ameiva bifrontata] insulana Ruthven, Occ. Pap. Mus. Zool. Univ. Mich., 155: 2.

Distribution: Testigos Island, Venezuela.

AMEIVA BRIDGESII (Cope)

1869 Holcosus bridgesii Cope, Proc. Acad. Nat. Sci. Phila., 1868: 306. Type-locality: Questionably Ecuador.
1915 Ameiva bridgesii—Barbour and Noble, Bull. Mus. Comp. Zool., 59: 478.
1964 Ameiva bridgesii—Peters, Bull. S. Calif. Acad. Sci., 63: 117, figs. 1b, 2b.

Distribution: Northwestern coastal areas of Ecuador, Chocó of Colombia, Gorgona Island.

AMEIVA CHAITZAMI Stuart

1942 Ameiva chaitzami Stuart, Proc. Biol. Soc. Washington, 55: 143. Type-locality: Along Cahabón-Lanquín trail about 2 km north of Finca Canihor, about 38 km east northeast of Cobán, Alta Verapaz, Guatemala.

Distribution: Known only from vicinity of type locality.

AMEIVA EDRACANTHA Bocourt

1874 Ameiva edracantha Bocourt, Ann. Sci. Nat. Zool. Paris, (5) 19 (4): 3. Type-locality: Mexico.
1876 Cnemidophorus armatulus Cope, Jour. Acad. Nat. Sci. Phila., (2) 8 (1875): 165. Type-locality: Valley of Jequetepeque, Peru.

Distribution: Coastal area of Ecuador and Peru.

AMEIVA FESTIVA (Lichtenstein)

1856 Cnemidophorus festivus Lichtenstein, Nomenclator Reptilium et Amphibiorum Musei Zoologici Berolinensis: 13. Type-locality: Veragoa, Panama.
1874 Ameiva festivus—Bocourt, Miss. Sci. Mex., Rept.: 260, pl. 20, fig. 2; pl. 20A, fig. 10, pl. 20D, fig. 6.

Distribution: Colombia through Central America to Isthmus of Tehuantepec, Mexico.
Content: Four subspecies.

Key to the subspecies	Clave de subespecies
1. Vertebral stripe with parallel borders----2 Vertebral stripe with zig-zag borders------ ------------------------------occidentalis	1. Cinta vertebral con bordes paralelos------2 Cinta vertebral con bordes en zig-zag------ ------------------------------occidentalis
2. Vertebral stripe 8-10 granules wide; half of parietals included in vertebral stripe- -------------------------------------3 Vertebral stripe 30-40 granules wide; entire parietals included in vertebral stripe-------------------------niceforoi	2. Cinta vertebral estrecha, 8-10 gránulos de ancho; mitad de los parietales incluida en la cinta vertebral----------------------3 Cinta vertebral ancha, 30-40 gránulos de ancho; parietales incluidos en la cinta vertebral----------------------niceforoi
3. Posteriormost sublabial one large shield--- ------------------------------------festiva Posteriormost sublabial divided into three smaller scales forming rough triangle (fig. 1)------------------------edwardsii	3. Último sublabial grande-------------festiva Último sublabial dividido en tres pequeñas escamas que forman un triángulo imperfecto (fig. 1)------------------------edwardsii

Fig. 1. On left, f. festiva, on right, f. edwardsii (from Stuart, 1943).

Ameiva festiva festiva (Lichtenstein)

1862 A.[meiva] eutropia Cope, Proc. Acad. Nat. Sci. Phila., 1862: 62. Type-locality: Truando River, northwestern Colombia.
1929 Ameiva festiva [festiva]—Barbour and Loveridge, Bull. Mus. Comp. Zool., 69: 141.
1956 Ameiva festiva festiva—Taylor, Univ. Kansas Sci. Bull., 38: 260, fig. 65.

Distribution: Northern Colombia to Panama.

Ameiva festiva edwardsii Bocourt

1873 Ameiva Edwardsii Bocourt, Ann. Sci. Nat. Zool. Paris, (5) 17 (art. 17): 1. Type-locality: Isabel and Santa Maria de Panzos, Guatemala.
1943 Ameiva festiva edwardsii—Stuart, Occ. Pap. Mus. Zool. Univ. Mich., 471: 21, fig. 7.

Distribution: Low and moderate elevations on Caribbean slope from Isthmus of Tehuantepec, Mexico, southeast to northern Honduras and Nicaragua, exclusive of outer end of Yucatán Peninsula.

Ameiva festiva niceforoi Dunn

1943 Ameiva festiva niceforoi Dunn, Notulae Naturae, Acad. Nat. Sci. Phila., 126: 1. Type-locality: Sasaima, 75 km northwest of Bogotá, Colombia, 1200 m.

Distribution: Western slope of eastern Andes in Colombia, 800-1800 m.

Ameiva festiva occidentalis Taylor

1956 Ameiva festiva occidentalis Taylor, Univ. Kansas Sci. Bull., 38: 264, fig. 66. Type-locality: 5 mi east of San Isidro del General, Provincia San José, Costa Rica.

Distribution: Provincias Puntarenas and San José, Costa Rica.

AMEIVA LEPTOPHRYS Cope

1893 Amiva leptophrys Cope, Proc. Amer. Phil. Soc., 31: 341. Type-locality: Buenos Aires, Costa Rica.
1915 Ameiva ruthveni Barbour and Noble, Bull. Mus. Comp. Zool., 59: 471. Type-locality: Near Panama City, Panama.

Distribution: Panama to Costa Rica.

AMEIVA ORCESI Peters

1964 Ameiva orcesi Peters, Bull. S. Calif. Acad. Sci., 63: 123. Type-locality: 1/2 km northeast of Abdon Calderon, Provincia Azuay, Ecuador, 1600 m.

Distribution: Valley of Río Jubones, Provincia Azuay, Ecuador, 1250-1700 m.

AMEIVA QUADRILINEATA (Hallowell)

1861 Cnemidophorus quadrilineatus Hallowell, Proc. Acad. Nat. Sci. Phila., 1860: 483. Type-locality: Nicaragua; restricted to Greytown, Nicaragua by Taylor, Univ. Kansas Sci. Bull., 38, 1956, 271.
1862 A.[meiva] quadrilineata—Cope, Proc. Acad. Nat. Sci. Phila., 1862: 62.
1876 Amiva gabbiana Cope, Jour. Acad. Nat. Sci. Phila., (2) 8 (1875): 117. Type-locality: Old Harbor, Puerto Viejo, Limon, Costa Rica.

Distribution: Panama to Nicaragua.

AMEIVA SEPTEMLINEATA Duméril

1851 A.[meiva] Septemlineata Duméril, Cat. Méth. Coll. Rept. Mus. Paris: 114. Type-locality: South America.
1859 Ameiva sex-scutata Günther, Proc. Zool. Soc. London, 1859: 402. Type-locality: Andes of western Ecuador.

Distribution: Moister areas of Ecuador lowlands, from Guayaquil north.

AMEIVA UNDULATA (Wiegmann)

1834 Cn.[emidophorus] undulatus Wiegmann, Herpetologia Mexicana: 27. Type-locality: Mexico.
1845 Ameiva undulatus—Gray, Cat. Liz. Brit. Mus.: 20.

Distribution: Costa Rica to southern Mexico.

Content: Twelve subspecies, six of which (amphigramma Smith and Laufe, dextra Smith and Laufe, podarga Smith and Laufe, sinistra Smith and Laufe, stuarti Smith, and undulata Wiegmann) are extralimital.

Key to the subspecies

1. Median gulars abruptly enlarged-----------2
   Median gulars enlarged but grading gradually into smaller surrounding throat scales----------------------------------4

2. One row of granules between third supraocular and superciliaries; third supraocular in contact with frontoparietals---3
   Two rows of granules between third supraocular and superciliaries; third supraocular separated from frontoparietals by granules----------------------------parva

3. Upper lateral light spots merged with dorso-lateral light line to form continuous light band--------------------thomasi
   Coloration not as above------------pulchra

Clave de subespecies

1. Gulares medianas abruptamente agrandadas--2
   Gulares medianas agrandadas gradualmente entre pequeñas escamas de la garganta----4

2. Una hilera de gránulos entre el tercer supraocular y los superciliares; tercer supraocular contacta con los frontoparietales-----------------------------------3
   Dos hileras de gránulos entre el tercer supraocular y los superciliares; tercer supraocular separado de los frontoparietales por gránulos------------------parva

3. Manchas claras súpero-laterales emergen con línea clara lateral y forman una banda clara contínua--------------------thomasi
   Coloración no como la anterior------pulchra

4. Middorsal region with few small blotches or none, never reticulate------------------5
Middorsal region heavily reticulate or blotched---------------------------miadis

5. Twelve or more light vertical stripes or lines between axilla and groin-----gaigeae
Fewer than twelve light vertical stripes or lines between axilla and groin----hartwegi

4. Región vertebral con pocas o ninguna manchas pequenas, nunca reticuladas---------5
Región vertebral densamente reticulada o manchada---------------------------miadis

5. Doce o más cintas claras laterales entre la axila e ingle----------------------gaigeae
Menos de doce cintas claras laterales entre la axila e ingle------------------hartwegi

Ameiva undulata gaigeae Smith and Laufe

1946 Ameiva undulata gaigeae Smith and Laufe, Univ. Kansas Sci. Bull., 31: 37, fig. 10, pl. 20. Type-locality: Progreso, Yucatán, Mexico.

Distribution: Lowlands of Yucatán Peninsula south to northern El Petén, Guatemala.

Ameiva undulata hartwegi Smith

1940 Ameiva undulata hartwegi Smith, Proc. Biol. Soc. Washington, 53: 55. Type-locality: Chiapas, Mexico, across Río Usumacinta from Piedras Negras, Guatemala.

Distribution: Low and moderate elevations of Caribbean slope from extreme southeastern Mexico through northern Guatemala to northern Honduras.

Ameiva undulata miadis Barbour and Loveridge, new combination

1929 Ameiva festiva miadis Barbour and Loveridge, Bull. Mus. Comp. Zool., 69: 141. Type-locality: Great Corn Island.

Distribution: Known only from Great Corn Island, forty miles off Nicaraguan coast.

Comment: The placement of this taxon as a subspecies of Ameiva undulata rather than of Ameiva festiva is at the suggestion of Arthur Echternacht, who will publish documentation of the change very shortly.

Ameiva undulata parva Barbour and Noble

1915 Ameiva undulata parva Barbour and Noble, Bull. Mus. Comp. Zool., 59: 476. Type-locality: Guatemala; restricted by Smith and Laufe, Univ. Kansas Sci. Bull., 31, 1946, 51, to Mazatenango, Guatemala.

Distribution: Low and moderate elevations of Pacific slope from Isthmus of Tehuantepec, Mexico, to Costa Rica.

Ameiva undulata pulchra Hallowell

1861 Ameiva pulchra Hallowell, Proc. Acad. Nat. Sci. Phila., 1860: 483. Type-locality: Nicaragua.
1942 Ameiva undulata pulchra—Stuart, Proc. Biol. Soc. Washington, 55: 146.

Distribution: Caribbean Honduras to Costa Rica.

Ameiva undulata thomasi Smith and Laufe

1946 Ameiva undulata thomasi Smith and Laufe, Univ. Kansas Sci. Bull., 31: 47, pl. 1A. Type-locality: La Libertad, Chiapas, Mexico, near Río Cuilco where it crosses Guatemalan border.

Distribution: Moderate elevations of upper valley of Río Grijalva, Chiapas, Mexico, and its headwater valleys in Guatemala.

INCERTAE SEDIS

1802 _Lacerta_ _litterata_ Daudin, Hist. Nat. Rept., 3: 106. Type-locality: Germany.

    Comment: This and the following species (_gutturosa_) were included as synonyms of _Ameiva_ _surinamensis_ by Boulenger, Cat. Liz. Brit. Mus., 2, 1885, 352. Barbour and Noble did not mention either in their review of the genus _Ameiva_, where the species including _surinamensis_ (_A_. _ameiva_) was divided into many subspecies. We do not know where they should be assigned.

1802 _Lacerta_ _gutturosa_ Daudin, Hist. Nat. Rept., 3: 119. Type-locality: Santiago, Chile.

Prepared by Carl Gans and Carlos O. Diefenbach, State University of New York, Buffalo, New York

AMPHISBAENA Linnaeus

1758 Amphisbaena Linnaeus, Systema Naturae, Ed. 10: 229. Type-species: Amphisbaena fuliginosa Linnaeus.
1843 Glyptoderma Fitzinger, Systema Reptilium: 22. Type-species: Amphisbaena vermicularis Wagler.
1843 Typhloblanus Fitzinger, Systema Reptilium: 22. Type-species: Amphisbaena caeca Cuvier.
1844 Sarea Gray, Cat. Tort., Croc., Amphis. Brit. Mus.: 71. Type-species: Amphisbaena ridleyi Boulenger, as stated by Gans and Alexander, Bull. Mus. Comp. Zool., 128, 1962, 82, because of a mistaken identification by Gray.
1861 Diphalus Cope, Proc. Acad. Nat. Sci. Phila., 1861: 75. Type-species: Diphalus fenestratus Cope.
1885 Aporarchus Cope, Proc. Amer. Phil. Soc., 22 (1884): 189. Type-species: Aporarchus prunicolor Cope.

Distribution: Continental South America; Panama; many Caribbean Islands; one species from southern Africa doubtfully included by Gans, 1967.

Content: Forty-five species, of which 35 are found within the limits of this work, following Gans, Bull. Amer. Mus. Nat. Hist., 135, 1967, 68-76.

Key to the species[1]

1. Without major fusions of head shields; pre-frontals, frontals, supralabials and oculars always separate--------------------------------2
   Fusion of head shields frequent and character-istic-------------------------------stejnegeri

2. Very large and thick, adults 40-50 cm long, 1.5 cm in diameter; more than 42 segments per mid-body annulus; lacking caudal autotomy--------3
   Small to medium sized, adults less than 35 cm long, less than 1 cm in diameter; fewer than 48 segments per midbody annulus; lacking caudal autotomy----------------------------4
   Small to large, generally more slender; fewer than 85 segments per midbody annulus; caudal autotomy annulus present---------------------8

3. More than 65 segments per midbody annulus; head bluntly rounded; with prominent temporal bulges in adults; tail of same diameter as trunk; terminal caudal annuli weakly delimited; 4-10 precloacal pores----------alba
   Fewer than 65 segments per midbody annulus; head elongate, acutely pointed, with spatulate rostral tip; temporal bulges not prominent; tail of smaller diameter than trunk, reducing toward tip; terminal caudal annuli clearly marked; precloacal pores 3-6, usually 4-------
   --------------------------------angustifrons

4. More than 238 body annuli---------------------5
   Fewer than 232 body annuli---------------------6

5. More than 40 segments per midbody annulus------
   ---------------------------------occidentalis
   Fewer than 41 segments per midbody annulus-----
   ---------------------------------steindachneri

Clave de especies[1]

1. Sin mayor fusión de escudos cefálicos; pre-frontales, frontales, supralabiales y oculares siempre separados----------------------------2
   Fusión de escudos cefálicos frecuente y carac-terística----------------------------stejnegeri

2. Adultos muy grandes y gruesos, 40-50 cm de longitud, 1.5 cm de diámetro; más de 42 seg-mentos por anillo del medio cuerpo; sin auto-tomía caudal----------------------------------3
   Tamaño pequeño a mediano, adultos menos de 35 cm de longitud, menos de 1 cm de diámetro; menos de 48 segmentos por anillo del medio cuerpo; sin autotomía caudal----------------4
   Pequeños a grandes, generalmente más delgados; menos de 85 segmentos por anillo del medio cuerpo; con anillo autotómico caudal---------8

3. Más de 65 segmentos por anillo del medio cuer-po; cabeza roma redondeada; con grandes pro-tuberancias temporales en adultos; cola del mismo diámetro que el tronco; anillos caudales terminales débilmente delimitados; 4-10 poros precloacales----------------------------alba
   Menos de 65 segmentos por anillo del medio cuerpo; cabeza alargada, muy puntuda, con ápice rostral espatulado; protuberancias tem-porales no prominentes; cola de menor diámetro que el tronco, afinándose hacia la punta; ani-llos caudales terminales bien marcados; poros precloacales 3-6, usualmente 4----angustifrons

4. Más de 238 anillos del cuerpo-----------------5
   Menos de 232 anillos del cuerpo---------------6

5. Más de 40 segmentos por anillo del medio cuerpo
   ---------------------------------occidentalis
   Menos de 41 segmentos por anillo del medio cuerpo--------------------------steindachneri

---

[1]This key omits the forms Amphisbaena gracilis, A. plumbea, and A. polygrammica as being insufficiently characterized.

[1]En esta clave se omiten las formas Amphisbaena gracilis, A. plumbea y A. polygrammica por no estar suficientemente caracterizadas.

6. Tail cylindrical; without conspicuous nuchal constriction; 185 or more body annuli; snout broad--7
   Tail sharply conical, tip only one-half diameter of base; distinct nuchal constriction; fewer than 193 body annuli; snout pointed-------------------------------ridleyi

7. Tail with marked vertical keel distally; 26-31 segments per midbody annulus----------bahiana
   Tail with round end; 29-42 segments per midbody annulus--------------------------------dubia

8. Two supralabials; fewer than three infralabials ---9
   More than two supralabials; more than two infralabials-----------------------------10

9. Body annuli 204-211; 22-26 segments per midbody annulus; postocular larger than prefrontals; two infralabials----------------------slevini
   Body annuli 225-228; 28-30 segments per midbody annulus; postocular smaller than parietals; one and one-half infralabials-------vanzolinii

10. Without postmalar row-----------------------11
    Postmalar row present-----------------------17

11. Two precloacal pores-----------------------12
    Four or more precloacal pores---------------15

12. Fewer than 182 body annuli--------------------13
    More than 202 body annuli--------------------14

13. Fewer than 162 body annuli; 24-28 segments per midbody annulus----------------------neglecta
    Body annuli 179-181; 20-24 segments per midbody annulus---------------------------silvestrii

14. Body annuli 203-220; precloacal pores large and oval; nasals as large as or larger than prefrontals; parietals as large as or larger than frontals; tip of tail round----------mitchelli
    Body annuli 240-265; precloacal pores round or faintly oval; nasals smaller than prefrontals; parietals never larger than frontals; tip of tail with vertical keel----------------roberti

15. Postmental shield faintly longer, same size as, or smaller than mental----------------------16
    Postmental shield markedly longer and of larger area than mental--------------------carvalhoi

16. Fewer than 219 body annuli; 16-19 caudal annuli; 28-36 segments per midbody annulus; no distinct neck constriction; tail with same pigmentation pattern as body--------pericensis
    Body annuli 222-226; 19-24 caudal annuli; 26 segments per midbody annulus; very distinct neck constriction; tail more darkly pigmented than body--------------------------nigricauda

6. Cola cilíndrica; sin constricción nucal conspicua; 185 o más anillos del cuerpo; hocico ancho---------------------------------------7
   Cola cónica, diámetro de la punta sólo la mitad del de la base; constricción nucal clara, menos de 193 anillos del cuerpo, hocico puntudo--ridleyi

7. Cola con quilla vertical marcada distalmente, 26-31 segmentos por anillo del medio cuerpo--bahiana
   Cola con punta redondeada; 29-42 segmentos por anillo del medio cuerpo------------------dubia

8. Dos supralabiales; menos de tres infralabiales--9
   Más de dos supralabiales, más de dos infralabiales-----------------------------------10

9. Anillos del cuerpo 204-211; 22-26 segmentos por anillo del medio cuerpo; postocular mayor que prefrontales, dos infralabiales--------slevini
   Anillos del cuerpo 225-228; 28-30 segmentos por anillo del medio cuerpo; postocular menor que parietales; un infralabial y medio-vanzolinii

10. Sin hilera postmalar-----------------------11
    Con hilera postmalar-----------------------17

11. Dos poros precloacales-----------------------12
    Cuatro o más poros precloacales--------------15

12. Menos de 182 anillos del cuerpo--------------13
    Más de 202 anillos del cuerpo----------------14

13. Menos de 162 anillos del cuerpo; 24-28 segmentos por anillo del medio cuerpo-------neglecta
    Anillos del medio cuerpo 179-181; 20-24 segmentos por anillo del medio cuerpo-----silvestrii

14. Anillos del cuerpo 203-220; poros precloacales grandes y ovales; nasales tan grandes como o mayores que prefrontales; parietales tan grandes como o mayores que frontales; cola de punta redondeada---------------------mitchelli
    Anillos del cuerpo 240-265; poros precloacales redondos o ligeramente ovales; nasales más chicos que prefrontales; parietales nunca mayores que frontales; punta de la cola con quilla vertical-----------------------roberti

15. Escudo postmental ligeramente más largo que el mental, superficie del mismo tamaño o menor que la de éste-------------------------------16
    Escudo postmental mucho más largo y de mayor superficie que el mental-------------carvalhoi

16. Menos de 219 anillos del cuerpo; 16-19 anillos caudales; 28-36 segmentos por anillo del medio cuerpo; sin constricción del cuello clara; cola con el mismo diseño de pigmentación que el cuerpo--------------------------pericensis
    Anillos del cuerpo 222-226; 19-24 anillos caudales; 26 segmentos por anillo del medio cuerpo; constricción del cuello bien neta; cola con pigmentación más oscura que el cuerpo-----------------------------------nigricauda

17. Fewer than 56 segments per midbody annulus---18
More than 54 segments per midbody annulus------
---camura

18. More than four precloacal pores--------------19
Fewer than five precloacal pores-------------22

19. Fewer than eleven precloacal pores; head with
same pattern of pigmentation as body--------20
More than ten precloacal pores; head and body
to sixth annulus lacking pigment--leucocephala

20. Nasals smaller than prefrontals; without conspicuous checkered pattern; third supralabial
not divided; suture between mental and first
infralabial distinct-----------------------21
Nasals larger than prefrontals; conspicuous
checkered pattern of coloration; third supralabial often divided; mental and first infralabial sometimes fused--------------fuliginosa

21. Parietals of same size as or larger than frontals; no preocular shields; pigmentation on
anterior part of body segments only; tail
distinctly segmented to tip-----------mertensi
Parietals never larger than frontals; preocular
shields split off second supralabial often
present; temporal bulges; tail relatively
blunt, without distinct segmentation to tip;
uniform brown with ventral fading------pretrei

22. Fewer than 261 body annuli--------------------23
More than 260 body annuli----------occidentalis

23. Medium to large, with three or fewer supralabials, or small to medium size animals, with
fewer than 219 body annuli and three or four
supralabials-------------------------------24
Medium to large, with more than 211 body annuli
and four supralabials------------vermicularis

24. Contact between mental and postmental forms
line; rarely with point contact between first
parietals----------------------------------25
Triangular mental and lozenge shaped postmental
meet in point contact; also point contact
between first parietals; head elongate and
flattened-----------------------------heathi

25. Body generally not uniformly colored, often
lighter ventrally; caudal tip not white-----26
Uniform dark brown color throughout most of
body; tip of tail white----------------slateri

26. Postmental shield of same size as or smaller
than mental-------------------------------27
Postmental shield markedly larger in both
length and area than mental---------spurrelli

17. Menos de 56 segmentos por anillo del medio
cuerpo-------------------------------------18
Más de 54 segmentos por anillo del medio
cuerpo---------------------------------camura

18. Más de cuatro poros precloacales-------------19
Menos de cinco poros precloacales------------22

19. Menos de once poros precloacales; cabeza con el
mismo diseño de pigmentación que el cuerpo--20
Más de diez poros precloacales; cabeza y cuerpo
hasta el sexto anillo sin pigmento----------
-----------------------------------leucocephala

20. Nasales menores que prefrontales; sin diseño
cuadriculado conspícuo; tercer supralabial no
dividido; sutura entre mental y primer infralabial distinta----------------------------21
Nasales mayores que prefrontales; coloración en
diseño cuadriculado conspícuo; tercer supralabial a menudo dividido; mental y primer
infralabial a veces fusionados------fuliginosa

21. Parietales iguales o mayores que frontales; sin
escudos preoculares; pigmentación sólo en la
parte anterior de segmentos del cuerpo; cola
con segmentación distinta hasta la punta------
-----------------------------------mertensi
Parietales nunca mayores que los frontales;
a menudo con escudos preoculares separados del
segundo supralabial; protuberancias temporales; cola relativamente roma, sin segmentación distinta hasta la punta; pardo uniforme,
más pálido a ventral-------------------pretrei

22. Menos de 261 anillos del cuerpo--------------23
Más de 260 anillos del cuerpo------occidentalis

23. Animales medianos a grandes con tres o menos
supralabiales, o animales medianos a chicos
con menos de 219 anillos del cuerpo y tres o
cuatro supralabiales-----------------------24
Animales medianos a grandes con más de 211 anillos del cuerpo y cuatro supralabiales--------
-----------------------------------vermicularis

24. Contacto entre mental y postmental a lo largo
de una línea; raramente con un punto de contacto entre primeros parietales-------------25
Mental triangular y postmental en forma de
losanje tienen un punto de contacto; los primeros parietales también tienen un punto de
contacto; cabeza alargada y aplanada----heathi

25. Color del cuerpo generalmente no uniforme, a
menudo más claro a ventral; punta de la cola no
blanca-------------------------------------26
Color pardo uniforme a lo largo de casi todo el
cuerpo; punta de la cola blanca--------slateri

26. Escudo postmental igual o menor que mental---27
Escudo postmental mucho mayor en longitud y
superficie que mental---------------spurrelli

27.Segments of body without tuberculation, or if tuberculation present, only posterior to caudal autotomy constriction; generally three supralabials----------------------------28
Segments of body and tail with squarish tuberculation; four supralabials; medium size; 205-209 body annuli------------------------*rozei*

28.Four, very rarely two precloacal pores; fewer than 219 body annuli------------------------29
Two precloacal pores; more than 216 body annuli -----------------------------------*leeseri*

29.Two rows of postgenials; generally more than seven postmalars; autotomy constriction generally beyond fifth caudal annulus-------30
Generally one row of postgenials, or, if two, second with very tiny segments; 6-8 postmalars; autotomy constriction at fourth to sixth caudal annuli; 177-191 body annuli-*hogei*

30.Second supralabial generally larger than first and third; fewer than 208 body annuli-------31
Second supralabial generally smallest of supralabials; more than 196 body annuli------*munoai*

31.Generally more than 24 segments in caudal annulus just anterior to autotomy constriction ----------------------------------*darwinii*
Generally 23 or fewer segments in caudal annulus just anterior to autotomy constriction---- ----------------------------------*prunicolor*

27.Segmentos del cuerpo sin tubérculos o con tubérculos sólo a posterior de constricción autotómica caudal; generalmente tres supralabiales--------------------------------28
Segmentos del cuerpo y cola con tubérculos cuadrados; cuatro supralabiales; tamaño mediano; 205-209 anillos del cuerpo---------------*rozei*

28.Cuatro, raramente dos, poros precloacales; menos de 219 anillos del cuerpo-------------29
Dos poros precloacales; más de 216 anillos del cuerpo----------------------------------*leeseri*

29.Dos hileras de postgeniales; generalmente más de siete postmalares; constricción autotómica generalmente más allá del quinto anillo caudal ---30
Generalmente una hilera de postgeniales, o si hay dos, la segunda con segmentos muy chicos; 6-8 postmalares; constricción autotómica en anillos caudales cuarto a sexto; 177-191 anillos del cuerpo-------------------------*hogei*

30.Segundo supralabial generalmente mayor que primero y tercero; menos de 208 anillos del cuerpo----------------------------------31
Segundo supralabiales generalmente el menor de los supralabiales; más de 196 anillos del cuerpo----------------------------------*munoai*

31.Generalmente más de 24 segmentos en anillo caudal inmediato anterior a constricción autotómica----------------------------------*darwinii*
Generalmente 23 o menos segmentos en anillo caudal inmediato anterior a constricción autotómica--------------------------*prunicolor*

AMPHISBAENA ALBA Linnaeus

1758 *Amphisbaena alba* Linnaeus, Systema Naturae, Ed. 10: 229. Type-locality: America.
1791 *Amphisbaena rosea* Shaw and Nodder, Naturalist's Miscellany, 3: pl. 86 plus text. Type-locality: America.
1822 *Amphisbaena pachyura* Wolf, Abbildungen und Beschreibungen merkwürdiger naturwissenschaftlicher Gegenstände, 2: 61. Type-locality: None designated.
1825 *Amphisbaena flavescens* Wied, Abbildungen zur Naturgeschichte Brasilens: pl. 9. Type-locality: "Bahía Belmonte, . . . grossen Waldungen am Flusse Mucurí" Brazil; restricted to mouth of Rio Mucurí by Gans, Amer. Mus. Novitates, 2105, 1962, 7.
1885 *Amphisbaena beniënsis* Cope, Proc. Amer. Phil. Soc., 22 (1884): 184. Type-locality: Upper Río Beni, Bolivia.
1885 *Amphisbaena alba* var. *radiata* Cope, Proc. Amer. Phil. Soc., 22 (1884): 194, fig. 7. Type-locality: Unknown.
1885 *Amphisbaena alba* var. *dissecta* Cope, Proc. Amer. Phil. Soc., 22 (1884): 194, fig. 8. Type-locality: Venezuela.
1955 *Amphisbaena alba*—Vanzolini, Arq. Mus. Nac. Brazil, 42: 683.
1962 *Amphisbaena alba*—Gans, Amer. Mus. Novitates, 2105: 1, figs. 1-7.

Distribution: Forested lowlands of South America, from Panama (?) through Venezuela and Guianas; Colombia, Peru and Bolivia east of Andes; Brazil and northern Paraguay; Trinidad.

AMPHISBAENA ANGUSTIFRONS Cope

1861 *Amphisbaena angustifrons* Cope, Proc. Acad. Nat. Sci. Phila., 1861: 76. Type-locality: Buenos Aires, Argentina.
1928 *Amphisbaena knighti* Parker, Ann. Mag. Nat. Hist., (10) 2: 383. Type-locality: Bonifacio, Argentina, about 36°49'S and 62°18'W.
1965 *Amphisbena angustifrons*—Gans, Amer. Mus. Novitates, 2225: 1, figs. 5-10.

Distribution: Central and northern Argentina to Bolivia.

AMPHISBAENA

AMPHISBAENA BAHIANA Vanzolini

  1964 Amphisbaena bahiana Vanzolini, Pilot Register of Zoology, Ithaca, New York, Card 8: 1. Type-
      locality: Villa Nova (= Senhor do Bonfim), Bahía, Brazil.
  1964 Amphisbaena bahiana—Gans, Senckenbergiana, 45: 412, figs. 18-20.

  Distribution: Bahía, Brazil.

AMPHISBAENA CAMURA Cope

  1862 Amphisbaena camura Cope, Proc. Acad. Nat. Sci. Phila., 1862: 350. Type-locality: Paraguay.
  1910 Amphisbaena boliviana Werner, Mitt. Naturhist. Mus. Hamburg, 27 (2): 35. Type-locality:
      Headwaters of Río Amazon, Provincia Beni, Bolivia.
  1929 Amphisbaena camura bolivica Mertens, Zool. Anz., 86: 60. Type-locality: Villa Montes, Río
      Pilcomayo, Bolivia.
  1965 Amphisbaena camura—Gans, Amer. Mus. Novitates, 2225: 22, figs. 11-16.

  Distribution: Central and northern Argentina, Paraguay, Amazonian Bolivia, Mato Grosso of Brazil.

AMPHISBAENA CARVALHOI Gans

  1965 Amphisbaena carvalhoi Gans, Proc. Calif. Acad. Sci., (4) 31: 625, figs. 8-12. Type-locality:
      Poção, Serra de Acahy, Municipio de Pesqueira, Pernambuco, Brazil, 1035 m.

  Distribution: Known only from type locality.

AMPHISBAENA DARWINII Duméril and Bibron

  1839 Amphisbaena Darwinii Duméril and Bibron, Erp. Gén., 5: 490. Type-locality: Montevideo, Uruguay.
  1966 Amphisbaena darwini —Gans, Bull. Amer. Mus. Nat. Hist., 134: 234.

  Distribution: São Paulo and Rio Grande do Sul, Brazil; southern Bolivia; Paraguay, Uruguay and
  northern Argentina.

  Content: Three subspecies.

Key to the subspecies	Clave de subespecies
1. Segments of annuli on tail not swollen, raised, or forming tubercles------------2 Segments of annuli on posterior end of tail modified into rounded tubercles; those on distalmost annuli with secondary, caudally directed, projecting points-------trachura	1. Segmentos de anillos en la cola no hincha-dos, elevados ni formando tubérculos-----2 Segmentos de anillos del extremo posterior de la cola formando tubérculos redondeados los de los anillos más distales con puntas salientes dirigidas hacia caudal--trachura
2. Tail generally not swollen beyond autotomy point; ventral surface of tail light, with no or only slightly emphasized darker pig-ment on autotomy segment---------darwinii Tail noticeably swollen beyond autotomy point; ventral surface of tail pigmented, with autotomy annulus marked with darker pigment----------------------heterozonata	2. Cola generalmente no hinchada más allá del punto de autotomía; superficie ventral de la cola clara, sin pigmento más oscuro en el segmento de autotomía o sólo ligera-mente pigmentado------------------darwinii Cola notablemente hinchada más allá del punto de autotomía; superficie ventral de la cola pigmentada, con anillo de autoto-mía marcado por pigmento oscuro---------- -----------------------------heterozonata

Amphisbaena darwinii darwinii Duméril and Bibron

  1966 Amphisbaena darwini darwini—Gans, Bull. Amer. Mus. Nat. Hist., 134: 234, pl. 37, fig. 1;
      pl. 38, figs. 1-2; pl. 39, fig. 6; pl. 40, figs. 1-2; figs. 29-30

  Distribution: Southern and central Uruguay.

<u>Amphisbaena</u> <u>darwinii</u> <u>heterozonata</u> Burmeister

    1861 A.⌈mphisbaena⌉ heterozonata Burmeister, Reise durch die La Plata-Staaten, 2: 527. Type-
        locality: Mendoza and Tucumán, Argentina; restricted to Mendoza, Argentina, by Müller,
        Zeits. für Naturwiss., 94, 1941, 195; corrected to Tucumán, Argentina, by Gans, Bull.
        Amer. Mus. Nat. Hist., 134, 1966, 231.
    1966 <u>Amphisbaena</u> <u>darwini</u> <u>heterozonata</u>—Gans, Bull. Amer. Mus. Nat. Hist., 134: 239, pl. 37,
        fig. 4; pl. 39, figs. 1-4; pl. 40, fig. 8; figs. 33-34.

    Distribution: Argentina north of Buenos Aires to southern Bolivia and central Paraguay.

<u>Amphisbaena</u> <u>darwinii</u> <u>trachura</u> Cope

    1878 <u>Amphisbaena</u> <u>mildei</u> Peters, Monats. Akad. Wiss. Berlin, 1878: 779, fig. 3. Type-locality:
        Porto Alegre, Rio Grande do Sul, Brazil.
    1885 <u>Amphisbaena</u> <u>trachura</u> Cope, Proc. Amer. Phil. Soc., 22 (1884): 189. Type-locality: San
        Joao do Monte Negro, which is Montenegro, Rio Grando do Sul, Brazil.
    1966 <u>Amphisbaena</u> <u>darwini</u> <u>trachura</u>—Gans, Bull. Amer. Mus. Nat. Hist., 134: 237, pl. 37, fig.
        3; pl. 38, figs. 3-6; pl. 39, fig. 5; pl. 40, figs. 3-7; figs. 31-32.

    Distribution: São Paulo and Rio Grande do Sul, Brazil, into northern Uruguay and extreme
    northeastern Argentina.

    Comment: A petition has been submitted to the International Committee on Zoological
    Nomenclature to set aside <u>mildei</u> Peters in favor of <u>trachura</u> Cope.

<u>AMPHISBAENA</u> <u>DUBIA</u> Müller

    1924 <u>Amphisbaena</u> <u>dubia</u> Müller, Mitt. Zool. Mus. Berlin, 11: 86. Type-locality: Piracicaba, Estado
        de São Paulo, Brazil.
    1964 <u>Amphisbaena</u> <u>dubia</u>—Gans, Breviora, 205: 2, figs. 1-7.

    Distribution: São Paulo, Paraná, and Santa Catarina, Brazil.

    Comment: This taxon is not preoccupied by <u>Amphisbaena</u> <u>dubia</u> Rathke, 1863, according to Gans, Bull.
    Zool. Nomen., 18, 1961, 220, and Opinion 664, Bull. Zool. Nomen., 20, 1963, 197.

<u>AMPHISBAENA</u> <u>FULIGINOSA</u> Linnaeus

    1758 <u>Amphisbaena</u> <u>fuliginosa</u> Linnaeus, Systema Naturae, Ed. 10: 229. Type-locality: America; believed
        to be Guianas by Vanzolini, Bull. Mus. Comp. Zool., 106, 1951, 58.

    Distribution: Amazonian Peru, Ecuador, Colombia and Brazil; northern South America; Pacific Ecuador
    and Colombia; Panama.

    Content: Five subspecies.

Key to the subspecies[1]	Clave de subespecies[1]
1. Abdomen always less densely pigmented than dorsum, may be immaculate----------------2 Abdomen and dorsum about equally densely pigmented------------------------------4	1. Abdomen siempre menos densamente pigmentado que el dorso, puede ser inmaculado-------2 Abdomen y dorso con pigmentación aproxima-damente igual---------------------------4
2. Dorsal spots rather crowded, with distinct margins, tending toward checkered pattern---3 Dorsal spots widely scattered, may be absent or show tendency to form narrow crossbands----------------------<u>bassleri</u>	2. Manchas dorsales bastante amontonadas, con márgenes netos, con tendencia a un diseño cuadriculado----------------------------3 Manchas dorsales ampliamente dispersas, pueden faltar o mostrar tendencia a formar bandas transversales angostas-----<u>bassleri</u>

[1]Key adapted from Vanzolini, Bull. Mus. Comp. Zool., 106, 1951.

3. Head immaculate or spotted; abdomen showing
   much less black than dorsum but still with
   many spots----------------------fuliginosa
   Head almost always immaculate; abdomen
   scarcely spotted----------------amazonica

4. Head as heavily pigmented as body-----varia
   Head immaculate or with very little spot-
   ting-----------------------------wiedi

3. Cabeza inmaculada o manchada; abdomen pre-
   senta mucho menos negro que el dorso pero
   aun con muchas manchas----------fuliginosa
   Cabeza casi siempre inmaculada; abdomen
   escasamente manchado------------amazonica

4. Cabeza tan densamente pigmentada como el
   cuerpo--------------------------------varia
   Cabeza inmaculada o escasamente manchada---
   --------------------------------------wiedi

Amphisbaena fuliginosa fuliginosa Linnaeus

1768 Amphisbaena vulgaris Laurenti, Synopsin Reptilium: 66. Type-locality: None given.
1768 Amphisbaena magnifica Laurenti, Synopsin Reptilium: 66. Type-locality: America.
1768 Amphisbaena flava Laurenti, Synopsin Reptilium: 67. Type-locality: America.
1844 Amphisbaena Americana Gray, Cat. Tort., Croc., and Amphis. Brit. Mus.: 70. Type-
     locality: South America, Demerara, and Berbice; restricted to Berbice, Guyana, through
     lectotype designation by Gans, Bull. Amer. Mus. Nat. Hist., 135, 1967, 70.
1951 Amphisbaena fuliginosa fuliginosa—Vanzolini, Bull. Mus. Comp. Zool., 106: 60.

   Distribution: Trinidad to French Guiana, eastern Venezuela.

Amphisbaena fuliginosa amazonica Vanzolini

1863 Amphisbaena dubia Rathke, Abh. Bayerischen Akad. Wiss. Math. Phys. Cl., 9: 128. Type-
     locality: None.
1951 Amphisbaena fuliginosa amazonica Vanzolini, Bull. Mus. Comp. Zool., 106: 62. Type-
     locality: Manaus, Amazonas, Brazil.

   Distribution: Amazon Valley from Manaus, Brazil, to Leticia, Colombia and southern
   Venezuela.

   Comment: The name Amphisbaena dubia Rathke, 1863, was suppressed in Opinion 664, Bull. Zool.
   Nomen., 20, 1963, 197.

Amphisbaena fuliginosa bassleri Vanzolini

1951 Amphisbaena fuliginosa bassleri Vanzolini, Bull. Mus. Comp. Zool., 106: 61. Type-
     locality: Roaboya, Loreto, Peru.
1963 A.[mphisbaena] f.[uliginosa] bassleri—Rhodes, Herpetologica, 19: 175.

   Distribution: Amazonian basin of Peru, Ecuador and northern Bolivia; Chaco of Argentina.

Amphisbaena fuliginosa varia Laurenti

1768 Amphisbaena varia Laurenti, Synopsin Reptilium: 66. Type-locality: America; restricted
     through neotype designation to Barro Colorado Island, Canal Zone, Panama, by Vanzolini,
     Bull. Mus. Comp. Zool., 106, 1951, 61.
1951 Amphisbaena fuliginosa varia—Vanzolini, Bull. Mus. Comp. Zool., 106: 61.

   Distribution: Panama to near Villavicencio, Colombia, and to near Trinidad, Venezuela;
   Pacific slope of Ecuador and Colombia.

Amphisbaena fuliginosa wiedi Vanzolini

1951 Amphisbaena fuliginosa wiedi Vanzolini, Bull. Mus. Comp. Zool., 106: 62. Type-locality:
     Santa Maria, Bahia, Brazil.

   Distribution: Known from type locality and lower Rio Amazonas, Brazil.

AMPHISBAENA GRACILIS Strauch

   1881 Amphisbaena gracilis Strauch, Bull. Acad. Imp. Sci. St. Pétersbourg, 28: col. 70. Type-locality: Unknown, but apparently America.

    Distribution: Known only from type material.

    Comment: The status of this form is in considerable doubt, according to Gans, Bull. Amer. Mus. Nat. Hist., 135, 1967, 71.

AMPHISBAENA HEATHI Schmidt

   1936 Amphisbaena heathi Schmidt, Herpetologica, 1: 29, pl. 3, fig. 1. Type-locality: Baixa Verde, Rio Grande do Norte, Brazil.
   1965 Amphisbaena heathi—Gans, Proc. Calif. Acad. Sci., (4) 31: 615, figs. 2-6.

    Distribution: Estado do Rio Grande do Norte, Brazil.

AMPHISBAENA HOGEI Vanzolini

   1950 Amphisbaena darwini hogei Vanzolini, Pap. Avul. Depto. Zool., São Paulo, 9: 70. Type-locality: Ilha dos Alcatrazes, São Paulo, Brazil.
   1966 Amphisbaena hogei—Gans, Bull. Amer. Mus. Nat. Hist., 134: 250, pl. 43, figs. 4-6; pl. 44, figs. 4-6; figs. 42-43.

    Distribution: Eastern São Paulo to Santa Catarina, Ilha dos Alcatrazes, Ilha Queimada Grande, Brazil.

AMPHISBAENA LEESERI Gans

   1964 Amphisbaena leeseri Gans, Copeia, 1964: 554, figs. 3-9. Type-locality: Urucum, Mato Grosso, Brazil.

    Distribution: Southwestern Mato Grosso, Brazil to Río Apa, northern Paraguay.

AMPHISBAENA LEUCOCEPHALA Peters

   1878 Amphisbaena leucocephala Peters, Monats. Akad. Wiss. Berlin, 1878: 778, fig. 1. Type-locality: Bahía, Brazil.
   1965 Amphisbaena leucocephala—Gans, Amer. Midl. Nat., 74: 402, figs. 12-14.

    Distribution: Bahía, Brazil.

AMPHISBAENA MERTENSII Strauch

   1881 Amphisbaena mertensii Strauch, Bull. Acad. Imp. Sci. St. Pétersbourg, 28: col. 66. Type-locality: "Wahrscheinlich an irgend einem Kustenpunkte Sud Amerikas"; restricted to State of São Paulo, Brazil, by Gans, Copeia, 1966, 535.
   1894 Amphisbaena Bohlsii Boulenger, Ann. Mag. Nat. Hist., (6) 13: 344. Type-locality: Near Asuncion, Paraguay.
   1898 Amphisbaena mattogrossensis Peracca, Boll. Mus. Zool. Comp. Anat. Univ. Torino, 13 (326): 1. Type-locality: Colonia Teresa Cristina, Mato Grosso, Brazil.
   1911 Amphisbaena carruccii Masi, Boll. Soc. Zool. Italiana, (2) 12: 230. Type-locality: Cerro S. Ana, Territorio de Misiones, Argentina.
   1911 Amphisbaena boulengeri Masi, Boll. Soc. Zool. Italiana, (2) 12: 232. Type-locality: Cerro S. Ana, Territorio de Misiones, Argentina.
   1933 Amphisbaena albissima Amaral, Mem. Inst. Butantan, 7 (1932): 55, figs. 4-6. Type-locality: Piracicaba, São Paulo, Brazil.
   1966 Amphisbaena mertensi—Gans, Copeia, 1966: 534, figs. 1-10.

    Distribution: Southeastern Brazil to Misiones, northern Argentina and eastern Paraguay.

AMPHISBAENA MITCHELLI Procter

1923 Amphisbaena mitchelli Procter, Proc. Zool. Soc. London, 1923: 1065, figs. 2a-d. Type-locality: Ilha do Marajó, mouth of Amazon, Brazil.
1963 Amphisbaena mitchelli—Gans, Amer. Mus. Novitates, 2127: 3, figs. 2-7.

Distribution: Ilha do Marajó and Belém, Pará, Brazil.

AMPHISBAENA MUNOAI Klappenbach

1960 Amphisbaena muñoai Klappenbach, Comun. Zool. Mus. Hist. Nat. Montevideo, 4 (84): 3, pl. 1, figs. 1-3, and pl. 3, figs. 4-7. Type-locality: Cerro de Animas, Departamento de Maldonado, Uruguay.
1966 Amphisbaena munoai—Gans, Bull. Amer. Mus. Nat. Hist., 134: 243, pl. 41, figs. 1-7; pl. 42, fig. 7; figs. 35-37.

Distribution: Elevated areas of southern and eastern Uruguay, north into Rio Grande do Sul, Brazil.

AMPHISBAENA NEGLECTA Dunn and Piatt

1936 Amphisbaena neglecta Dunn and Piatt, Proc. Acad. Nat. Sci. Phila., 88: 527. Type-locality: Chapada, Mato Grosso, Brazil.
1962 Amphisbaena neglecta—Gans, Copeia, 1962: 169, fig. 8.

Distribution: East central Mato Grosso into central Goiás, Brazil.

AMPHISBAENA NIGRICAUDA Gans

1966 Amphisbaena nigricauda Gans, Bull. Amer. Mus. Nat. Hist., 134: 252, pl. 45, figs. 1-7; figs. 44-45. Type-locality: Refugio Sooretama, Linhares, Espirito Santo, Brazil.

Distribution: Known only from type locality.

AMPHISBAENA OCCIDENTALIS Cope

1876 Amphisbaena occidentalis Cope, Jour. Acad. Nat. Sci. Phila., (2) 8 (1875): 176. Type-locality: Valley of Jequetepeque, north coast of Peru.

Distribution: Pacific slope of Peru.

Content: Two subspecies.

Key to the subspecies	Clave de subespecies
1. No autotomy constriction; 18-21 caudal annuli; three postgenials in first row; little if any elongation of dorsal segments of trunk annuli 7-12----occidentalis Autotomy constriction present; 22-26 caudal annuli; 4-5 postgenials in first row; marked elongation of dorsal segments of trunk annuli 7-12---------------townsendi	1. Sin constricción autotómica; 18-21 anillos caudales; tres postgeniales en la primera hilera; poco o ningún alargamiento de los segmentos dorsales de los anillos del tronco 7-12-------------------occidentalis Con constricción autotómica; 22-26 anillos caudales; 4-5 postgeniales en la primera hilera; alargamiento marcado de los segmentos dorsales de los anillos del tronco 7-12---------------------------townsendi

Amphisbaena occidentalis occidentalis Cope

1961 Amphisbaena occidentalis occidentalis—Gans, Postilla, Yale Univ., 56: 7, figs. 4, 6, 8-9.

Distribution: Chimbote to Chiclay, coastal plain of Peru.

Amphisbaena occidentalis townsendi Stejneger

    1911 Amphisbaena townsendi Stejneger, Proc. U.S. Nat. Mus., 41: 283. Type-locality: Piura, Peru.
    1961 Amphisbaena occidentalis townsendi—Gans, Postilla, Yale Univ., 56: 8, figs. 5, 7, 10-13.

      Distribution: Piura to Lobitos, coastal plain of Peru.

AMPHISBAENA PERICENSIS Noble

    1921 Amphisbaena pericensis Noble, Ann. New York Acad. Sci., 29: 141. Type-locality: Perico, Peru.
    1963 Amphisbaena pericensis—Gans, Breviora, 189: 3, figs. 1-8.

      Distribution: Arid inland valleys of Río Chinchipe and Río Marañón, from Perico to Bellavista, Peru.

AMPHISBAENA PLUMBEA Gray

    1872 Amphisbaena plumbea Gray, Cat. Shield Rept. Brit. Mus., 2: 36. Type-locality: Mendoza, Argentina.
    1928 Amphisbaena plumbea—Parker, Ann. Mag. Nat. Hist., (10) 2: 383.

      Distribution: West central Argentina.

AMPHISBAENA POLYGRAMMICA Werner

    1900 Amphisbaena polygrammica Werner, Abh. Ber. Zool. Anthrop. Mus. Dresden, 9 (2): 5. Type-locality: Chanchamayo, Peru.

      Distribution: Known only from type locality.

AMPHISBAENA PRETREI Duméril and Bibron

    1839 Amphisbaena Pretrei Duméril and Bibron, Erp. Gén., 5: 486. Type-locality: Brazil.
    1865 Amphisbaena petraei Gray (in error), Proc. Zool. Soc. London, 1865: 447.
    1878 Amphisbaena subocularis Peters, Monats. Akad. Wiss. Berlin, 1878: 779, fig. 2. Type-locality: Pernambuco, Brazil.
    1885 Amphisbaena pretrii Boulenger (emendation of pretrei Duméril and Bibron), Cat. Liz. Brit. Mus., 2: 440.
    1933 Amphisbaena brachyura Amaral, Mem. Inst. Butantan, 7 (1932): 55, figs. 1-3. Type-locality: Maceió, Alagoas, Brazil.
    1938 Amphisbaena petrei Amaral (in error), Mem. Inst. Butantan, 11 (1937): 197.
    1965 Amphisbaena pretrei—Gans, Amer. Midl. Nat., 74: 391, figs. 4-11.

      Distribution: Rio Grande do Norte to Minas Gerais, Brazil.

AMPHISBAENA PRUNICOLOR (Cope)

    1885 Aporarchus prunicolor Cope, Proc. Amer. Phil. Soc., 22 (1884): 189. Type-locality: São Joao do Monte Negro, Rio Grande do Sul, Brazil.
    1966 Amphisbaena prunicolor—Gans, Bull. Amer. Mus. Nat. Hist., 134: 246.

      Distribution: Northern Argentina, southeastern Brazil, Paraguay.

      Content: Two subspecies.

AMPHISBAENA

Key to the subspecies

1. Relatively short head; 24-35 segments per midbody annulus; with intercalated dorsal half annulus on neck; pigmentation dropping out at ventral surface generally in checkered pattern---------------prunicolor
Relatively elongate head; 27-30 segments per midbody annulus; without intercalated half annulus in nuchal region; light brown with ventral fading----albocingulata

Clave de subespecies

1. Cabeza relativamente corta; 24-35 segmentos por anillo del medio cuerpo; con medio anillo dorsal intercalado en el cuello; pigmentación generalmente en diseño cuadriculado desaparece a ventral---prunicolor
Cabeza relativamente alargada; 27-30 segmentos por anillo del medio cuerpo; sin medio anillo intercalado en región nucal; pardo claro que no palidece a ventral---------------------------------albocingulata

Amphisbaena prunicolor prunicolor (Cope)

1966 Amphisbaena prunicolor prunicolor—Gans, Bull. Amer. Mus. Nat. Hist., 134: 246, pl. 42, figs. 1-3; figs. 38-39.

Distribution: Misiones, Argentina, and Rio Grande do Sul, Brazil; possibly north into Espirito Santo, Brazil.

Amphisbaena prunicolor albocingulata Boettger

1885 Amphisbaena albocingulata Boettger, Zeits. für Naturwiss., 58: 219. Type-locality: Paraguay.
1966 Amphisbaena prunicolor albocingulata—Gans, Bull. Amer. Mus. Nat. Hist., 134: 248, pl. 43, figs. 1-3; pl. 44, figs. 1-3; figs. 40-41.

Distribution: Paraguay, perhaps north into Mato Grosso and Goiás, Brazil.

AMPHISBAENA RIDLEYI Boulenger

1890 Amphisbaena Ridleyi Boulenger, Jour. Linnean Soc., London, 20: 481. Type-locality: Porto Bello, West Indies, and Fernando do Noronha, Brazil; restricted to Fernando do Noronha, Brazil by Gans, Copeia, 1963, 103.
1963 Amphisbaena ridleyi—Gans, Copeia, 1963: 102, figs. 1-6.

Distribution: Ilha de Fernando do Noronha, Brazil.

AMPHISBAENA ROBERTI Gans

1964 Amphisbaena roberti Gans, Senckenbergiana, 45: 402, figs. 11-17. Type-locality: Ypiranga, São Paulo, São Paulo, Brazil.

Distribution: Coastal São Paulo inland to southwestern Minas Gerais and southern Goiás, Brazil.

AMPHISBAENA ROZEI Lancini

1963 Amphisbaena rozei Lancini, Publ. Ocas. Mus. Cien. Nat. Caracas, Zool., 6 (3): 1, figs. 1-4. Type-locality: Cabeceras del caño Majagua, Río Chajurá, tributary of Río Erebato, Estado Bolívar, Venezuela.

Distribution: Known only from type locality.

AMPHISBAENA SILVESTRII Boulenger

1902 Amphisbaena Silvestrii Boulenger, Ann. Mag. Nat. Hist., (7) 9: 287. Type-locality: Cuyaba, Mato Grosso, Brazil.
1962 Amphisbaena silvestrii—Gans, Copeia, 1962: 167, figs. 3, 5, 7.
1964 Amphisbaena silvestrii—Gans, Copeia, 1964: 554.

Distribution: Rio Tocantins, Mato Grosso, Brazil west to Bolivia.

AMPHISBAENA SLATERI Boulenger

  1907 Amphisbaena Slateri Boulenger, Ann. Mag. Nat. Hist., (7) 19: 487. Type-locality: Río San Gaban
        Valley, Provincia Carabaya, Peru, 2000-3000 ft.

   Distribution: Known only from type and from two Bolivian specimens that possibly represent a
   distinct southern race, according to Gans, Bull. Amer. Mus. Nat. Hist., 135, 1967, 74.

AMPHISBAENA SLEVINI Schmidt

  1936 Amphisbaena slevini Schmidt, Herpetologica, 1: 31, pl. 3, fig. 3. Type-locality: Manaus,
        Amazonas, Brazil.
  1963 Amphisbaena slevini—Gans, Amer. Mus. Novitates, 2127: 14, figs. 10-14.

   Distribution: Known from vicinity of type locality only.

AMPHISBAENA SPURRELLI Boulenger

  1915 Amphisbaena spurrelli Boulenger, Proc. Zool. Soc. London, 1915: 659, fig. 1. Type-locality:
        Andagoya, at junction of Ríos Condoto and San Juan, Colombia.
  1962 Amphisbaena spurrelli—Gans, Breviora, Mus. Comp. Zool., 171: 2, figs. 1-8.

   Distribution: Venezuela and northern Colombia to Panama.

AMPHISBAENA STEINDACHNERI Strauch

  1881 Amphisbaena steindachneri Strauch, Bull. Acad. Imp. Sci. St. Pétersbourg, 28: col. 81. Type-
        locality: Caiçara, Mato Grosso, Brazil.

   Distribution: Southwestern Brazil, and Chaco of Bolivia; possibly Argentina.

   Content: Two subspecies.

               Key to the subspecies[1]   Clave de subespecies[1]

  1. Ventral segments to one body annulus 16;   1. Segmentos ventrales de cada anillo del
     250-266 body annuli----------steindachneri   cuerpo 16; 250-266 anillos del cuerpo-----
     Ventral segments to one body annulus more   ----------------------------steindachneri
     than 16; 239-245 body annuli------borellii   Segmentos ventrales de cada anillo del
                                                         cuerpo más de 16; 239-245 anillos del
                                                         cuerpo----------------------------borellii

   Amphisbaena steindachneri steindachneri Strauch

     1930 Amphisbaena steindachneri [steindachneri]—Mertens, Folia Zool. Hydrobiol., Riga, 1: 164.
     1964 Amphisbaena steindachneri steindachneri—Gans, Senckenbergiana, 45: 391, figs. 2-7.

       Distribution: Southwestern Brazil.

   Amphisbaena steindachneri borellii Peracca

     1897 Amphisbaena Borellii Peracca, Boll. Mus. Zool. Comp. Anat. Univ. Torino, 12 (274): 8,
           figs. Type-locality: Caiza, Chaco of Bolivia.
     1964 Amphisbaena steindachneri borellii—Gans, Senckenbergiana, 45: 397, figs. 5-9.

       Distribution: Known only from types and one specimen with no data in Museo Argentino de
       Ciencias Naturales "Bernardino Rivadavia".

[1]Taken from Gans, Senckenbergiana, 45, 1964, 391.

AMPHISBAENA

AMPHISBAENA STEJNEGERI Ruthven

 1922 *Amphisbaena stejnegeri* Ruthven, Occ. Pap. Mus. Zool. Univ. Mich., 122: 1. Type-locality: Sand
        reef at Vreeden Rust, Demerara River, Guyana.
 1963 *Amphisbaena stejnegeri*—Gans, Amer. Mus. Novitates, 2128: 3, figs. 2-9.

   Distribution: Coastal Guyana.

AMPHISBAENA VANZOLINII Gans

 1963 *Amphisbaena vanzolinii* Gans, Amer. Mus. Novitates, 2138: 13, figs. 10-14. Type-locality:
        Marudi, on tributary of Kuyuwini River, at 2°5'N and 50°E, Guyana.

   Distribution: Guyana on Kuyuwini and New Rivers.

AMPHISBAENA VERMICULARIS Wagler

 1824 *Amphisbaena vermicularis* Wagler, in Spix, Sp. Nov. Serp. Bras.: 73. Type-locality: Bahía, Bahía,
        Brazil.
 1935 *Amphisbaena vermicularis centralis* Amaral, Mem. Inst. Butantan, 9: 255, fig. 9. Type-locality:
        Canna Brava, Goiás, Brazil.
 1936 *Amphisbaena spixi* Schmidt, Herpetologica, 1: 30, pl. 30, fig. 2. Type-locality: Ceará Mirim,
        Rio Grande do Norte, Brazil.
 1966 *Amphisbaena vermicularis*—Gans and Amdur, Proc. California Acad. Sci., (4) 33: 71, figs. 1-9.

   Distribution: Brazil, south of Amazon to Minas Gerais and inland across Goiás and Mato Grosso,
     Brazil; Bolivia.

ANADIA Gray

1845 _Anadia_ Gray, Cat. Liz. Brit. Mus.: 58. Type-species: _Anadia ocellata_ Gray.
1862 _Xestosaurus_ Peters, Abh. Akad. Wiss. Berlin, 1862: 216. Type-species: _Anadia_ (_Xestosaurus_) _Bogotensis_ Peters.
1876 _Chalcidolepis_ Cope, Jour. Acad. Nat. Sci. Phila., (2) 8 (1875): 116. Type-species: _Chalcidolepis metallicus_ Cope.

Distribution: Ecuador, Colombia, Venezuela, Panama, Costa Rica, Gorgona Id.

Content: Eleven species.

Key to the species

1. Dorsal scales squared and juxtaposed----------2
   Dorsal scales rounded and imbricate--_bogotensis_

2. More than 40 scales around middle of body-----3
   Fewer than 36 scales around middle of body-----5

3. Three supraoculars----------------------------4
   Four supraoculars----------------------_steyeri_

4. More than 40 rows of scales between occipital
   and base of tail---------------------_pulchella_
   Fewer than 35 rows of scales between occipital
   and base of tail--------------------_rhombifera_

5. Fewer than 30 scales around middle of body-----6
   More than 30 scales around middle of body-----7

6. Six supralabials------------------------_blakei_
   Seven supralabials--------------------_metallica_

7. More than 50 rows of scales between occipital
   and base of tail----------------------------8
   Fewer than 40 rows of scales between occipital
   and base of tail---------------------------10

8. Without lateral ocelli on body----------------9
   With lateral ocelli on body------------_ocellata_

9. Three pairs of postmentals in contact on mid-
   line----------------------------------_vittata_
   Two pairs of postmentals in contact on mid-
   line-------------------------------_angusticeps_

10. Number of scales between collar and post-
    mentals 16----------------------------_duquei_
    Number of scales between collar and post-
    mentals 12-14----------------------_bitaeniata_

Clave de especies

1. Escamas dorsales cuadradas y yuxtapuestas-----2
   Escamas dorsales redondeadas imbricadas--------
   ------------------------------------_bogotensis_

2. Más de 40 escamas al medio del cuerpo---------3
   Menos de 36 escamas al medio del cuerpo-------5

3. Tres supraoculares----------------------------4
   Cuatro supraoculares--------------------_steyeri_

4. Más de 40 hileras de escamas entre occipital y
   raíz de la cola----------------------_pulchella_
   Menos de 35 hileras de escamas entre occipital
   y raíz de la cola-------------------_rhombifera_

5. Menos de 30 escamas al medio del cuerpo-------6
   Más de 30 escamas al medio del cuerpo---------7

6. Seis supralabiales----------------------_blakei_
   Siete supralabiales-------------------_metallica_

7. Más de 50 hileras de escamas entre occipital y
   raíz caudal---------------------------------8
   Menos de 40 hileras de escamas entre occipital
   y raíz caudal-------------------------------10

8. Sin series de ocelos a los lados cuerpo-------9
   Series de ocelos a los lados del cuerpo-------
   ------------------------------------_ocellata_

9. Tres pares de posmentales en contacto en la
   línea media--------------------------_vittata_
   Dos pares de posmentales en contacto en la
   la línea media--------------------_angusticeps_

10. Diesiseis escamas entre collar y posmen-
    tales---------------------------------_duquei_
    Doce a catorce escamas entre collar y pos-
    mentales--------------------------_bitaeniata_

ANADIA ANGUSTICEPS Parker

1926 _Anadia angusticeps_ Parker, Ann. Mag. Nat. Hist., (9) 17: 550, 3 figs. Type-locality: Gorgona Island, Colombia.

Distribution: Known only from type locality.

ANADIA BITAENIATA Boulenger

1903 _Anadia bitaeniata_ Boulenger, Ann. Mag. Nat. Hist., (7) 12: 431. Escorial and Culata, Estado de Merida, Venezuela, 3300 m.
1944 _Anadia pamplonensis_ Dunn, Caldasia, 3 (11): 64. Type-locality: Pamplona, Colombia, 2340 m.

Distribution: Andean Venezuela and Colombia.

ANADIA BLAKEI Schmidt

1932 Anadia blakei Schmidt, Zool. Ser. Field Mus. Nat. Hist., 18: 161. Type-locality: Turumiquire
    mountains, Estado Sucre, Venezuela, 1600m.

Distribution: Known only from type-locality.

ANADIA BOGOTENSIS (Peters)

1862 Ecpleopus (Xestosaurus) Bogotensis Peters, Abh. Akad. Wiss. Berlin: 217, pl. 3, fig. 3, 3a-f.
    Type-locality: Santa Fe de Bogotá, Colombia.
1885 Anadia bogotensis—Boulenger, Cat. Liz. Brit. Mus., 2: 40.

Distribution: Bogotá area, Colombia; recorded in Venezuela by Donoso, Carib. Jour. Sci., 8, 1968
    (1969), 116.

ANADIA DUQUEI Lancini

1963 Anadia duquei Lancini, Publ. Oc. Mus. Cien. Nat. Caracas, Zool., 4: 1. Type-locality: Quebrada
    el Cedro, Catuche, Cerro El Avila, Distrito Federal, Venezuela.

Distribution: Known only from type locality.

ANADIA METALLICA (Cope)

1876 Chalcidolepis metallicus Cope, Jour. Acad. Nat. Sci. Phila., (2) 8 (1875): 116, pl. Type-
    locality: Aguacate mountains, Costa Rica.
1902 Anadia metallica—Günther, Biol. Centr. Amer., Rept.: 30.

Distribution: Mountains of Costa Rica.

Content: Three subspecies.

Key to the subspecies	Clave de subespecies
1. Less than 60 scale rows between occipital and posterior border of hind leg---------2 More than 60 scale rows in the same distance-----------------------------arborea	1. Menos de 60 hileras de escamas entre occipital y borde posterior del muslo--------2 Mas de 60 hileras de escamas en la misma distancia--------------------------arborea
2. Less than 24 scales around middle of body----------------------------------metallica More than 27 scales around middle of body---------------------------------attenuata	2. Menos de 24 escamas al medio del cuerpo--------------------------------------metallica Más de 27 escamas al medio del cuerpo---------------------------------attenuata

Anadia metallica metallica (Cope)

  1955 Anadia metallica metallica—Taylor, Univ. Kansas Sci. Bull., 37: 535.

  Distribution: Aguacate mountains, Costa Rica.

Anadia metallica arborea Taylor

  1955 Anadia metallica arborea Taylor, Univ. Kansas Sci. Bull., 37: 542, fig. 13. Type-
      locality: Las Flores, Tenorino, Las Cañas, Guanacaste Province, Costa Rica.

  Distribution: Known only from type locality.

Anadia metallica attenuata Taylor

  1955 Anadia metallica attenuata Taylor, Univ. Kansas Sci. Bull., 37: 537, fig. 12. Type-
      locality: Pacuare, Río Pacuare, on road between Turrialba and Moravia de Chirripó,
      Cartago Province, Costa Rica.

  Distribution: Province of Cartago, Costa Rica.

ANADIA OCELLATA Gray

1845 Anadia ocellata Gray, Cat. Liz. Brit. Mus.: 58. Type-locality: Tropical America.

Distribution: Known only from Jerico, Colombia, and Loja, Ecuador.

ANADIA PULCHELLA Ruthven

1926 Anadia pulchella Ruthven, Occ. Pap. Mus. Zool. Univ. Mich., 177: 1. Type-locality: La Cumbre, Hacienda Vista Nieve, Santa Marta Mountains, Colombia, 2100m.

Distribution: Known only from type locality.

ANADIA RHOMBIFERA (Günther)

1859 Cercosaurus rhombifer Günther, Proc. Zool. Soc. London, 1859: 405, pl. 20, fig. A. Type-locality: Western Ecuador.
1885 Anadia rhombifera—Boulenger, Cat. Liz. Brit. Mus., 2: 399.

Distribution: Pacific slope of Ecuador.

ANADIA STEYERI Nieden

1914 Anadia steyeri Nieden, Sitz. Ges. Naturf. Fr. Berlin, 7: 365. Type-locality: Puerto Cabello, Estado Aragua, Venezuela.

Distribution: Coastal range of central Venezuela.

ANADIA VITTATA Boulenger

1913 Anadia vittata Boulenger, Proc. Zool. Soc. London, 1913: 1033, pl. 57, fig. 2, 2a-d. Type-locality: Peña Lisa, Condoto, Chocó, Colombia, 300 ft.

Distribution: Known only from type locality.

ANISOLEPIS Boulenger

>1885 Anisolepis Boulenger, Ann. Mag. Nat. Hist., (5) 16: 85. Type-species: Anisolepis Iheringii Boulenger.

>Distribution: Paraná, Santa Catarina, and Rio Grande do Sul, Brazil; east central Argentina; Uruguay.

>Content: Two species.

Key to the species	Clave de especies
1. Hind limb reaching ear when brought forward; 20-22 longitudinal series of ventrals; no enlarged scales on flanks--------------grilli Hind limb does not reach ear when brought forward; 16-17 longitudinal series of ventrals; flanks with enlarged scales------------------------------------undulatus	1. Extremidad posterior llega al oido cuando extendida hacia adelante; 20-22 series longitudinales de ventrales; sin escamas ensanchadas en los flancos------------------------grilli Extremidad posterior no llega al oido cuando extendida hacia adelante; 16-17 series longitudinales de ventrales; flancos con escamas ensanchadas------------------------undulatus

ANISOLEPIS GRILLI Boulenger

>1891 Anisolepis grilli Boulenger, Ann. Mus. Civ. Stor. Nat. Cenova, (2) 10: 909. Type-locality: Palmeira, Paraná, Brazil.
>1896 Anisolepis lionotus Werner, Verh. Zool.-Bot. Ges. Wien, 46: 470. Type-locality: Blumenau, Santa Catarina, Brazil.

>Distribution: Rio de Janeiro, São Paulo, Paraná, Rio Grande do Sul, and Santa Catarina, Brazil.

>Comment: Anisolepis grilli and Anisolepis lionotus are here considered synonyms on the authority of Paulo Vanzolini, who has examined a large series of specimens.

ANISOLEPIS UNDULATUS (Wiegmann)

>1834 L.[aemanctus] undulatus Wiegmann, Herpetologia Mexicana: 46. Type-locality: Brazil.
>1834 L.[aemanctus] obtusirostris Wiegmann, Herpetologia Mexicana: 46. Type-locality: Brazil.
>1834 L.[aemanctus] Fitzingeri Wiegmann, Herpetologia Mexicana: 46. Type-locality: Brazil.
>1885 Anisolepis Iheringii Boulenger, Ann. Mag. Nat. Hist., (5) 16: 86. Type-locality: São Lourenço, Lagoa dos Patos, Rio Grande do Sul, Brazil.
>1891 Anisolepis undulatus—Boulenger, Ann. Mus. Civ. Stor. Nat. Genova, (2) 10: 909.
>1895 Anisolepis Bruchi Koslowsky, Rev. Mus. La Plata, 6: 417, pl. 1. Type-locality: Punta Lara, cerca de La Plata, Provincia de Buenos Aires, Argentina.

>Distribution: Southern Brazil, eastern central Argentina, Uruguay.

ANOLIS Daudin

1802 Anolis Daudin, Hist. Nat. Rept., 4: 50. Type-species: Anolis bullaris Latreille.
1817 Anolius Cuvier (emendation of Anolis Daudin), Le Règne Animal, 2: 41.
1826 Xiphosurus Fitzinger, Neue Classification der Reptilien: 17. Type-species: Anolis cuvieri Merrem.
1830 Dactyloa Wagler, Nat. Syst. Amph.: 148. Type-species: Anolis punctatus Daudin.
1830 Draconura Wagler, Nat. Syst. Amph.: 149. Type-species: Draconura nitens Wagler.
1830 Norops Wagler, Nat. Syst. Amph.: 149. Type-species: Anolis auratus Daudin.
1833 Phalangoptyon Wagler, Isis von Oken, 26: 896. Type-species: Anolis bimaculatus Daudin.
1836 Acantholis Cocteau, Comp. Rend. Acad. Sci. Paris, 3: 226. Type-species: None given; later designated as Acantholis Loysiana Cocteau.
1843 Ctenonotus Fitzinger, Systema Reptilium: 64. Type-species: Lacerta bimaculata Sparmann.
1843 Semiurus Fitzinger, Systema Reptilium: 64. Type-species: Anolis cuvieri Merrem.
1843 Eupristes Fitzinger, Systema Reptilium: 64. Type-species: Anolis equestris Merrem.
1843 Microctenus Fitzinger, Systema Reptilium: 64. Type-species: Anolis Edwardsii Merrem.
1843 Ptychonotus Fitzinger, Systema Reptilium: 65. Type-species: Anolis alligator Duméril and Bibron.
1843 Istiocercus Fitzinger, Systema Reptilium: 65. Type-species: Anolis cristatellus Duméril and Bibron.
1843 Eunotus Fitzinger, Systema Reptilium: 65. Type-species: Anolis gracilis Wied.
1843 Deiroptyx Fitzinger, Systema Reptilium: 66. Type-species: Anolis vermiculatus Duméril and Bibron.
1843 Trachycoelia Fitzinger, Systema Reptilium: 66. Type-species: Anolis lineatus Daudin.
1843 Ctenodeira Fitzinger, Systema Reptilium: 66. Type-species: Anolis Richardii Duméril and Bibron.
1843 Tropidopilus Fitzinger, Systema Reptilium: 66. Type-species: Anolis fuscoauratus D'Orbigny.
1843 Xiphocercus Fitzinger, Systema Reptilium: 67. Type-species: Anolis Valenciennii Duméril and Bibron.
1843 Eudactylus Fitzinger, Systema Reptilium: 67. Type-species: Anolis Goudotii Duméril and Bibron.
1843 Heterolepis Fitzinger, Systema Reptilium: 67. Type-species: Anolis pulchellus Duméril and Bibron.
1843 Trachypilus Fitzinger, Systema Reptilium: 67. Type-species: Anolis sagrei Duméril and Bibron.
1843 Pristicercus Fitzinger, Systema Reptilium: 67. Type-species: Dactyloa biporcatus Wiegmann.
1843 Ctenocercus Fitzinger, Systema Reptilium: 68. Type-species: Iguana bullaris Latreille.
1843 Gastrotropis Fitzinger, Systema Reptilium: 68. Type-species: Dactyloa nebulosa Wiegmann.
1843 Heteroderma Fitzinger, Systema Reptilium: 68. Type-species: Acantholis Loysiana Cocteau.
1843 Dracontopsis Fitzinger, Systema Reptilium: 69. Type-species: Draconura Nitzschii Wiegmann.
1845 Rhinosaurus Gray, Cat. Liz. Brit. Mus.: 199. Type-species: Anolis nasicus Duméril and Bibron.
1850 Placopsis Gosse, Ann. Mag. Nat. Hist., (2) 6: 346. Type-species: Placopsis ocellata Gosse.
1862 Coccoëssus Cope, Proc. Acad. Nat. Sci. Phila., 1862: 178. Type-species: Anolis (Coccoëssus) pentaprion Cope.
1876 Scytomycterus Cope, Jour. Acad. Nat. Sci. Phila., (2) 8 (1875): 165. Type-species: Scytomycterus laevis Cope.
1923 Diaphoranolis Barbour, Occ. Pap. Mus. Zool. Univ. Mich., 129: 7. Type-species: Diaphoranolis brooksi Barbour.
1934 Audantia Cochran, Occ. Pap. Boston Soc. Nat. Hist., 8: 171. Type-species: Audantia armouri Cochran.
1939 Mariguana Dunn, Notulae Naturae, 4: 1. Type-species: Anolis agassizi Stejneger.

Distribution: From southern United States to Bolivia and Paraguay including Caribbean Islands.

Content: Approximately 200 species, of which 116 are found within limits of this work.

Comment: Anolis godeti Roux, 1907, was thought to be South American by Burt and Burt, Trans. St. Louis Acad. Sci., 28, 1929, 16, but they also thought the type locality was unknown, although Roux gives it as "Antillen (kein näherer Fundort)".

0=Unknown 3=False
1=True 4=Inapplic.
2=Variable

	PROJECTING SNOUT	COMPRESSED, CRESTED TAIL	DORSALS < VENTRALS	VENTRALS SMOOTH	DORSALS < LATERALS	LARGE HEAD SCALES	HEAD SCALES SMOOTH	SUPRAOCULARS KEELED	OCCIPITAL < EAR	HEAD LENGTH < TIBIA L.	WITH OCCIPITAL CRESTS	WITH FRONTAL CRESTS	SUPRAOCS. TOUCH SEMICIRC.	POINT REACHED BY HIND LIMB[1]	DORSAL SCALES[1]	ROWS OF SCALES SEPARATING SUPRAORBITAL SEMICIRCLES	ROWS OF SCALES SEPARATING SEMICIRCLES AND OCCIPITAL	NUMBER ROWS OF LOREALS	NUMBER OF LABIALS TO CENTER OF EYE
														ACTUAL COUNTS					
ACHILLES	3	2	1	1	3	0	3	1	3	3	0	0	1	1	2	1	2	6	6-7
AENEUS	3	1	1	1	3	0	1	1	3	0	0	1	0	2	2	0	0	4-5	6-7
AEQUATORIALIS	3	3	3	3	3	3	1	1	0	1	0	0	4	4	1	X	X	X	X
AGASSIZI	3	3	1	3	3	0	3	1	1	3	1	1	3	3	2	1	1	4	X
ALLISONI	3	3	1	3	3	3	3	0	3	0	0	1	3	0	2	1	X	4	8
ALTAE	3	3	1	3	3	0	3	1	3	0	3	1	3	0	1	2	2	6	X
ANDIANUS	3	3	1	1	3	3	3	1	1	3	0	3	4	2	1	5	X	6	7
ANTONII	3	3	1	3	3	1	3	1	3	3	3	1	1	2	1	1-3	2-3	5-8	6-9
APOLLINARIS	3	3	1	3	3	3	3	1	1	3	3	3	3	3	1	2-3	X	5	7
AQUATICUS	3	1	1	3	3	3	3	1	1	2	0	1	3	4	2	3-4	6	9-11	8
AURATUS	3	3	2	3	3	3	1	3	3	3	3	3	1	2	3	0-1	1-2	6-7	5
BINOTATUS	3	3	1	3	3	3	3	1	3	3	3	1	2	0	3	1	2-3	X	X
BIPORCATUS	3	2	1	3	2	3	2	2	3	2	2	2	3	1-3	1	1-2	2-6	5-8	6-11
BISCUTIGER	3	3	1	1	3	0	2	3	3	3	3	3	4	3	1	1	3	7	6
BITECTUS	3	3	1	3	3	3	3	1	3	3	3	3	3	3	3	2-3	3-4	7	8
BOCOURTII	3	3	1	1	3	0	1	3	3	0	0	3	3	3	1	2-3	X	X	X
BOETTGERI	3	3	1	1	3	0	3	1	3	3	0	3	2	2	1	0	0	5-6	6-8
BOMBICEPS	3	3	1	3	3	0	1	2	3	0	3	1	0	3	1	2	X	6	X
BONAIRENSIS	3	1	1	1	3	0	1	3	3	3	3	3	0	0	1	0-1	0-1	3	X
BOUVIERII	3	1	1	1	3	3	1	3	0	3	3	3	3	0	1	0	1	6	X
CAPITO	3	3	1	3	3	3	3	1	1	1	3	3	2	3	1	2-4	2-3	6-8	9-10
CHLORIS	3	3	1	3	3	3	1	2	0	3	3	3	4	2	1	2	X	5	6
CHOCORUM	3	3	1	1	3	3	1	3	2	0	3	1	3	0	1	1-3	2-4	6-9	8-10
CHRYSOLEPIS	3	3	1	3	3	3	3	1	2	1	3	2	4	2-4	1	1-4	2-4	5-10	7-11
COBANENSIS	3	1	1	3	3	3	3	1	1	3	3	3	3	0	2	3	X	7	7
CONCOLOR	3	3	0	3	3	0	3	1	0	0	0	1	4	3	2	0-1	0	5-6	X
CRASSULUS	3	3	1	3	3	3	2	2	2	3	3	3	3	2	3	0-2	2-3	4-5	6-7
CUPREUS	3	3	1	3	3	3	3	1	3	3	3	2	1	3	3	1-2	2-3	6-7	6-7
CURTUS	3	3	1	3	3	3	3	1	1	0	3	3	3	3-4	1	5-7	5-6	7-8	7-9

[1]Significance of values:

Hind limb reaches between:
1. Shoulder and ear opening
2. Ear opening and eye
3. Eye and nasal aperture
4. Nasal aperture, tip of snout, and beyond

Dorsal scales:
0. Condition unknown
1. All granular or homogeneous
2. With two to six enlarged middorsal rows
3. With more than six enlarged middorsal rows

[1]Significado de valores:

Extremidad posterior llega entre:
1. Hombro y oído
2. Oído y ojo
3. Ojo y abertura nasal
4. Abertura nasal, hocico y más allá

Escamas dorsales:
0. Desconocido
1. Todas granulares u homogéneas
2. Con dos a seis hileras no granulares
3. Con más de seis hileras no granulares

	PROJECTING SNOUT	COMPRESSED, CRESTED TAIL	DORSALS < VENTRALS	VENTRALS SMOOTH	DORSALS < LATERALS	LARGE HEAD SCALES	HEAD SCALES SMOOTH	SUPRAOCULARS KEELED	OCCIPITAL < EAR	HEAD LENGTH < TIBIA L.	WITH OCCIPITAL CRESTS	WITH FRONTAL CRESTS	SUPRAOCS. TOUCH SEMICIRC.	POINT REACHED BY HIND LIMB	DORSAL SCALES[1]	ROWS OF SCALES SEPARATING SUPRAORBITAL SEMICIRCLES	ROWS OF SCALES SEPARATING SEMICIRCLES AND OCCIPITAL	NUMBER ROWS OF LOREALS	NUMBER OF LABIALS TO CENTER OF EYE
DAMULUS	3	1	1	1	3	3	3	1	0	0	0	1	3	3	1	1	X	5	X
DISSIMILIS	3	1	1	1	3	2	3	3	3	3	3	3	1	0	1	0	1	5	11
DOLLFUSIANUS	3	3	1	3	3	3	3	1	3	3	3	1	1	0	2	1	1	6	X
EEWI	3	3	1	3	3	0	3	1	3	0	0	0	3	0	3	1-2	X	6	10-11
EULAEMUS	3	3	1	1	3	3	3	1	1	3	0	1	4	4	1	2	5-6	8-9	7
FASCIATUS	3	3	1	1	3	3	1	1	1	3	3	3	4	2	1	1-2	X	5	7
FESTAE	3	3	1	1	3	3	1	3	3	3	3	3	3	1	2	1	3	6	8-9
FRASERI	3	2	1	2	3	3	3	3	0	3	3	3	4	1	1	X	X	6-7	8-9
FRENATUS	3	3	3	1	1	3	3	1	1	3	0	3	3	0	1	2-4	0	6	X
FUSCOAURATUS	3	3	1	3	3	3	3	1	3	3	3	1	3	2	1	1-3	2-3	5-6	6-8
GARBEI	3	3	3	3	3	3	3	1	3	1	3	0	0	4	1	2	2	5	8
GEMMOSUS	3	3	1	1	3	3	3	1	1	3	1	2	4	3	1	1-5	X	5-6	6-8
GIBBICEPS	3	3	1	1	3	0	3	1	0	0	0	1	3	0	1	3	X	8	X
GODMANI	3	3	1	3	3	3	3	1	3	3	0	1	0	4	1	2-4	3-5	6-8	6
GORGONAE	3	2	1	1	3	3	3	1	1	3	0	3	4	3	1	X	X	5	6
GRACILIPES	3	3	1	3	3	3	3	1	3	1	3	1	3	3-4	1	0-1	1-2	7-8	9-12
GRANULICEPS	3	3	1	3	3	3	3	3	1	3	3	3	3	3-4	1	3-5	4-5	7-8	8-9
HETEROPHOLIDOTUS	3	2	1	1	3	1	2	0	3	3	3	1	3	0	2	1	2	4	X
HOFFMANNI	3	3	1	3	3	3	3	1	3	3	3	3	1	X	1	1-2	3-4	6	X
HUMILIS	3	3	3	3	3	3	3	1	1	3	3	1	2	3	3	2-3	3-4	7-8	7-9
IMPETIGOSUS	3	3	1	1	3	1	1	3	3	3	1	3	3	1	1	0	2	2	7
INCOMPERTUS	3	3	1	3	3	0	3	1	3	0	3	3	4	X	3	3-4	5	X	9-10
INSIGNIS	3	3	1	1	3	3	1	3	1	3	0	3	4	1	1	0	X	5	7
INTERMEDIUS	3	3	1	3	3	1	2	2	3	3	3	3	1	1	1	0	1-2	3-4	6-7
JACARE	3	3	1	1	3	0	2	1	3	0	3	1	4	1-2	1	1-2	1-2	4-5	7-8
KEMPTONI	3	2	1	2	3	0	0	0	3	3	3	1	0	1	1	1-2	2	X	X
LAEVIS	1	0	3	1	3	1	1	3	0	3	0	3	0	1	0	0	0	2	X
LAEVIVENTRIS	3	3	1	3	3	3	1	3	3	3	3	3	3	0	2	1	3	0	0
LATIFRONS	3	3	3	1	3	3	1	3	0	0	0	0	4	0	1	0	0	X	X
LEMNISCATUS	3	2	1	1	3	3	3	1	3	3	0	1	3	3	3	1-2	2-3	6	8-10
LEMURINUS	3	3	1	3	3	0	3	1	3	3	0	0	3	2-3	2	0-1	2-4	6-7	6
LEPTOSCELIS	3	3	1	3	3	3	3	1	1	1	3	3	1	4	2	2-3	2-3	6-7	7-8
LIMIFRONS	3	3	1	2	3	3	2	1	2	2	0	1	3	3-4	1	1-3	2-5	5-7	X
LINDENI	3	1	1	1	3	0	1	1	3	3	3	3	0	2	1	0	1	5	X
LINEATUS	3	1	1	3	3	0	1	3	1	3	0	1	3	3	1	0	2	3-4	7
LIONOTUS	3	3	3	1	3	3	1	2	3	0	0	1	3	4	3	1-3	3	8-9	X
LONGICAUDA	3	3	1	3	3	0	3	1	0	0	0	1	0	0	2	X	X	6	X
LOVERIDGEI	3	1	1	3	3	0	3	1	0	1	3	3	0	3	1	4	7	12	12
MACROLEPIS	3	3	3	3	3	2	3	1	3	3	3	1	0	2	3	1	0	6	7
MACULIVENTRIS	3	3	1	1	3	3	3	1	0	3	3	1	4	2	1	3-4	X	8	8
MARIARUM	3	3	1	3	3	3	3	1	3	0	0	3	3	0	1	2	4-5	X	X
MERIDIONALIS	3	3	1	3	3	3	3	1	3	3	3	3	3	1-2	2	0-1	1-2	4-5	4-7
MICROTUS	3	2	2	1	3	1	1	3	2	3	1	2	3	1-2	1	2	3	3-5	7-8

0=Unknown 3=False
1=True 4=Inapplic.
2=Variable

ACTUAL COUNTS

ANOLIS

Legend: 0=Unknown 1=True 2=Variable 3=False 4=Inapplic.

	PROJECTING SNOUT	COMPRESSED, CRESTED TAIL	DORSALS ∨ VENTRALS	VENTRALS SMOOTH	DORSALS ∨ LATERALS	LARGE HEAD SCALES	HEAD SCALES SMOOTH	SUPRAOCULARS KEELED	OCCIPITAL ∨ EAR	HEAD LENGTH ∨ TIBIA L.	WITH OCCIPITAL CRESTS	WITH FRONTAL CRESTS	SUPRAOCS. TOUCH SEMICIRC.	POINT REACHED BY HIND LIMB[1]	DORSAL SCALES[1]	ROWS OF SCALES SEPARATING SUPRAORBITAL SEMICIRCLES	ROWS OF SCALES SEPARATING SEMICIRCLES AND OCCIPITAL	NUMBER ROWS OF LOREALS	NUMBER OF LABIALS TO CENTER OF EYE
																ACTUAL COUNTS			
MIRUS	3	3	1	3	3	3	2	0	1	0	1	1	1	0	2	4	4	7	10
NANNODES	3	3	1	3	3	3	2	0	3	3	3	3	3	0	2	0-1	X	5	7
NASOFRONTALIS	3	3	1	1	3	0	1	3	3	3	0	0	3	1	2	0	0	2-3	6
NICEFORI	3	3	1	3	3	0	3	1	3	0	3	1	4	X	3	3-4	5	X	9-10
NIGROLINEATUS	3	2	1	1	3	3	2	3	3	0	3	1	3	0	2	1-2	3-4	6	8-11
NITENS	3	3	1	3	3	3	2	1	3	2	3	3	1	4	2	0-1	2	X	X
NOTOPHOLIS	3	3	3	3	3	0	3	1	0	3	3	1	0	4	3	0-2	2-3	6-7	7-9
ORTONI	3	1	1	1	3	3	1	3	3	3	0	3	3	2	1	0-1	1-2	4-5	6-8
PACHYPUS	3	3	1	1	3	1	3	1	1	1	3	3	3	4	2	5	4	8	X
PALMERI	3	3	1	3	3	3	1	1	0	3	3	0		2	1	3-4	5-6	5	5
PENTAPRION	3	1	1	3	3	3	3	2	3	0	3	4		1	1	1	2	3-4	8
PERACCAE	3	3	1	3	3	3	1	2	3	3	1	1		2	1	1-2	3-4	5-6	6-7
PETERSII	3	3	1	3	3	3	1	1	3	3	3	3		2	1	1-2	X	6-7	9-11
PHYLLORHINUS	1	3	1	1	3	1	3	3	3	3	3	3		1	1	1-2	1-2	4-5	6-7
POECILOPUS	3	3	3	3	3	3	1	1	0	3	1	4		4	3	X	X	9-10	X
POLYLEPIS	3	1	1	1	3	1	3	1	1	3	0	1	3	4	2	3-4	3-5	6-9	7
PRINCEPS	3	3	1	2	3	3	3	1	0	3	0	3	4	3	1	4-5	X	9-11	10-12
PROBOSCIS	1	1	1	1	3	3	1	3	1	0	3	2	1	0	1	1-2	2	4-5	9-11
PSEUDOTIGRINUS	3	0	0	1	3	1	1	3	3	1	3	3	0	1	1	0	0	X	8
PUNCTATUS	2	3	1	2	3	2	1	2	2	3	3	2	3	X	1	0-2	1-4	4-7	6-10
PURPURESCENS	3	3	1	1	3	3	3	1	1	2	1	1	3	3	1	2-4	4-5	7-8	X
RADULINUS	3	2	0	3	3	3	3	0	0	0	3	1	4	3	2	3-4	X	6-7	X
RHOMBIFER	3	3	1	3	3	3	3	1	3	0	3	1	3	3	1	1-2	3-4	7	6
ROQUET	3	3	1	2	3	0	1	3	3	3	3	3	3	2	1	0	0	4-5	5-6
SAGREI	3	1	1	3	3	3	3	1	1	3	0	1	2	2	1	0-1	2-3	4-5	5-6
SALVINI	3	2	1	3	3	0	1	3	0	3	0	3	0	1	1	1	X	4	7
SCAPULARIS	3	2	1	1	3	0	3	1	3	3	3	1	0	2	2	2	3	6	7
SCYPHEUS	3	3	1	3	3	3	3	1	1	1	1	1	4	4	1	3	3-4	8-10	8-10
SERICEUS	3	3	1	3	3	3	3	1	2	3	3	1	3	1-2	3	0-3	1-5	4-6	6-8
SMINTHUS	3	3	1	3	3	0	3	1	2	0	3	1	1	0	3	0-1	3-4	5	X
SOLITARIUS	3	3	1	1	3	1	1	3	3	3	3	1	0	1	1	0-2	X	4	7-8
SQUAMULATUS	3	3	1	2	3	3	3	1	1	0	1	3	4	3	1	4-6	6	9	X
STEINBACHI	3	3	1	3	3	3	3	1	3	3	2	1	3	2	1	1-2	2	6	7
TIGRINUS	3	3	1	1	3	1	1	3	3	0	3	3	1	1	1	0	0	2	X
TOWNSENDI	3	3	1	3	3	3	3	1	3	3	3	3	1	3	2	2-3	2-3	5-6	8
TRACHYDERMA	3	3	1	3	3	0	3	1	1	0	3	3	0	2	2	X	2	6	X
TRANSVERSALIS	3	1	1	1	3	1	1	3	2	3	0	3	3	2	1	0-1	0-3	4-5	6-9
TRINITATIS	3	1	1	1	3	0	2	2	3	3	1	1	2	2	3	0	0	4-6	6-8
TROPIDOGASTER	3	3	1	3	3	3	3	1	2	2	3	1	2	3	1	1-3	2-4	6-8	6-7
TROPIDOLEPIS	3	3	1	3	3	3	3	1	1	3	0	3	0	4	1	3-5	3-5	7-9	7-8
TROPIDONOTUS	3	3	3	3	3	3	3	3	1	1	3	1	1	4	3	2	2-3	6-7	6-7
VENTRIMACULATUS	3	3	1	1	3	3	3	1	1	1	0	3	4	4	1	4	X	8	7
WILLIAMSII	3	3	1	3	3	3	1	3	3	3	3	3	3	X	3	1	2	X	X
WOODI	3	1	1	3	3	0	3	1	1	0	3	1	1	3	3	2-3	4	7-8	9

ANOLIS ACHILLES Taylor

  1956 Anolis achilles Taylor, Univ. Kansas Sci. Bull., 38: 153, fig. 43. Type-locality: La Palma, Provincia San José, Costa Rica.

    Distribution: Known only from type locality.

ANOLIS AENEUS Gray

  1840 Anolis aeneus Gray, Ann. Mag. Nat. Hist., (1) 5: 114. Type-locality: Unknown.
  1887 Anolis gentilis Garman, Bull. Essex Inst., 19: 10. Type-locality: Petit Martinique.

    Distribution: Petit Martinique, Grenadines, Trinidad and Guyana.

ANOLIS AEQUATORIALIS Werner

  1894 Anolis aequatorialis Werner, Zool. Anz., 17: 157. Type-locality: Ecuador.

    Distribution: Middle altitudes of western slopes in Ecuador.

ANOLIS AGASSIZI Stejneger

  1900 Anolis agassizi Stejneger, Bull. Mus. Comp. Zool., 36: 161, col. pl. Type-locality: Malpelo Island, Colombia.

    Distribution: Known only from type locality.

ANOLIS ALLISONI Barbour

  1928 Anolis allisoni Barbour, Proc. New England Zool. Club, 10: 58. Type-locality: Coxen Hole, Ruatan, Bay Islands, Honduras.
  1961 Anolis allisoni—Ruibal and Williams, Bull. Mus. Comp. Zool., 125: 183, figs. 2, 4-5, 10.
  1962 Anolis allisoni—Neill and Allen, Herpetologica, 18: 80, fig. 1.

    Distribution: Cuba; Bay Islands, Honduras; British Honduras.

ANOL'IS ALTAE Dunn

  1930 Anolis altae Dunn, Proc. New England Zool. Club, 12: 22. Type-locality: Finca Acosta, Volcán Barba, Costa Rica, 7000 ft.

    Distribution: Known only from type locality.

ANOLIS ANDIANUS Boulenger

  1885 Anolis andianus Boulenger, Cat. Liz. Brit. Mus., 2: 60. Type-locality: Milligalli, Ecuador, 2060 m.

    Distribution: Known only from type locality.

ANOLIS ANTONII Boulenger

  1908 Anolis antonii Boulenger, Ann. Mag. Nat. Hist., (8) 2: 517, fig. 2. Type-locality: San Antonio, Colombia.
  1916 Anolis tolimensis Werner, Zool. Anz., 47: 303. Type-locality: Cañon del Tolima, Colombia.

    Distribution: Interandean highlands of northern Colombia.

ANOLIS APOLLINARIS Boulenger

 1919 Anolis apollinaris Boulenger, Proc. Zool. Soc. London, 1919: 79, figs. 4a-4b. Type-locality:
      Bogotá, Colombia.

   Distribution: Known from vicinity of type locality.

ANOLIS AQUATICUS Taylor

 1956 Anolis aquaticus Taylor, Univ. Kansas Sci. Bull., 38: 141, fig. 39. Type-locality: Palmar,
      Provincia Puntarenas, Costa Rica.

   Distribution: Provincia Puntarenas, Costa Rica.

ANOLIS AURATUS Daudin

 1802 Anolis auratus Daudin, Hist. Nat. Rept., 4: 89. Type-locality: Unknown.
 1834 Dra.[conura] Nitzschii Wiegmann, Herpetologia Mexicana: 16. Type-locality: Unknown.
 1840 Draconura 12-striata Berthold, Abh. Ges. Wiss. Göttingen, 1: 62, pl. 2, fig. 7. Type-locality:
      Surinam.
 1843 Draconura Bertholdi Fitzinger (replacement name for Draconura 12-striata Berthold), Systema
      Reptilium: 70.
 1856 Norops macrodactylus Hallowell, Proc. Acad. Nat. Sci. Phila., 1856: 222. Type-locality: New
      Grenada.
 1885 Norops auratus—Boulenger, Cat. Liz. Brit. Mus., 2: 95.
 1896 Anolis Rosenbergii Boulenger, Ann. Mag. Nat. Hist., 6 (17): 16. Type-locality: Buenaventura,
      Colombia.

   Distribution: Panama, Colombia, Ecuador, Venezuela, French Guiana.

ANOLIS BINOTATUS Peters

 1863 Anolis binotatus Peters, Monats. Akad. Wiss. Berlin, 1863: 140. Type-locality: Guayaquil,
      Ecuador.
 1873 Anolis binotatus—Bocourt, Miss. Sci. Mex., Rept.: 92, pl. 16, figs. 22-23.

   Distribution: Pacific Ecuador and Colombia; southern Central America; Gorgona Island, Colombia.

ANOLIS BIPORCATUS (Wiegmann)

 1834 D.[actyloa] biporcata Wiegmann, Herpetologia Mexicana: 47. Type-locality: Mexico.
 1873 Anolis biporcatus—Bocourt, Miss. Sci. Mex., Rept.: 98, pl. 15, figs. 8-8a.
 1885 Anolis biporcatus—Boulenger, Cat. Liz. Brit. Mus., 2: 88.

   Distribution: Mexico through central America to Ecuador.

   Content: Two subspecies.

              Key to the subspecies   Clave de subespecies

 1. Ear opening nearly twice size of nostril;   1. Tamaño del oído el doble del nostril; esca-
    scales surrounding interparietal smaller   mas que rodean el interparietal más peque-
    than or only equal to middorsal scales;   ñas o sólamente iguales a las escamas
    dewlap black-edged------------parvauritus   mediodorsales saco gular bordeado de negro
    Ear opening four or more times larger than   -----------------------------parvauritus
    nostril; scales surrounding interparietal   Tamaño del oído cuatro o más veces el tama-
    larger than middorsal scales; dewlap not   ño del nostril; escamas que rodean el
    black-edged--------------------biporcatus   interparietal mayores que las escamas me-
                                                        diodorsales; saco gular no bordeado de
                                                        negro--------------------------biporcatus

Anolis biporcatus biporcatus (Wiegmann)

1873 Anolis Copei Bocourt, Miss. Sci. Mex., Rept.: 77, pl. 15, fig. 10-10a. Type-locality: Santa Rosa de Pansos, Guatemala.
1874 Anolis obtusirostris Peters, Monats. Akad. Wiss. Berlin, 1874: 407. Type-locality: Chiriquí, Panama.
1893 Anolis brevipes Boettger, Kat. Rept. Senckenberg. Mus., 1: 57. Type-locality: Cairo Plantation, near Limón, San José, Costa Rica.
1916 Anolis solifer Ruthven, Occ. Pap. Mus. Zool. Univ. Mich., 32: 4, pl. 2. Type-locality: La Concepción, Santa Marta Mountains, Colombia.
1966 Anolis biporcatus biporcatus Williams, Breviora, Mus. Comp. Zool., 239: 9, fig. 4.

Distribution: Mexico to northern Colombia.

Anolis biporcatus parvauritus Williams

1966 Anolis biporcatus parvauritus Williams, Breviora, Mus. Comp. Zool., 239: 7, figs. 2-4. Type-locality: Northern Gorgona Island, Cauca, Colombia.

Distribution: Pacific Ecuador and Colombia; Gorgona Island.

ANOLIS BISCUTIGER Taylor

1956 Anolis biscutiger Taylor, Univ. Kansas Sci. Bull., 38: 81, fig. 19. Type-locality: Golfito, Provincia Puntarenas, Costa Rica.

Distribution: Provincia Puntarenas, Costa Rica.

ANOLIS BITECTUS Cope

1864 Anolis bitectus Cope, Proc. Acad. Nat. Sci. Phila., 1864: 171. Type-locality: West Ecuador.
1885 Anolis bitectus—Boulenger, Cat. Liz. Brit. Mus., 2: 71, pl. 5, fig. 2.

Distribution: Pacific lowlands of Ecuador.

ANOLIS BOCOURTII Cope

1876 Anolis bocourtii Cope, Jour. Acad. Nat. Sci. Phila., (2) 8 (1875): 167. Type-locality: Nauta, Peru.
1885 Anolis bocourtii—Boulenger, Cat. Liz. Brit. Mus., 2: 50.

Distribution: Known only from type locality.

ANOLIS BOETTGERI Boulenger

1911 Anolis boettgeri Boulenger, Ann. Mag. Nat. Hist., (8) 7: 19. Type-locality: Huancabamba, Peru, 1000 m; actually Oxapampa, Peru, according to Barbour, Bull. Mus. Comp. Zool., 77, 1934, 125.

Distribution: Known only from type locality.

ANOLIS BOMBICEPS Cope

1876 Anolis bombiceps Cope, Jour. Acad. Nat. Sci. Phila., (2) 8 (1875): 168. Type-locality: Nauta, Peru.
1885 Anolis bombiceps—Boulenger, Cat. Liz. Brit. Mus., 2: 94.

Distribution: Amazonian Peru and Ecuador; Estado Amazonas, Brazil.

ANOLIS BONAIRENSIS Ruthven

1923 *Anolis bonairensis* Ruthven, Occ. Pap. Mus. Zool. Univ. Mich., 143: 4. Type-locality: Seroe Grandi, 4 1/2 km northeast of Kralendijk, Bonaire, Dutch Leeward Islands.

Distribution: Bonaire, Klein Bonaire, Aves Islands.

Content: Two subspecies.

<table>
<tr><th>Key to the subspecies</th><th>Clave de subespecies</th></tr>
<tr>
<td>1. Usually vermiculated with black, occasionally with black crossbars; distance from snout tip to anterior border of ear 1.15 length of tibia; occipital scale in contact with supraorbital semicircles; two pairs of scales between supraorbital semicircles--------------------bonairensis
With black crossbars, rarely vermiculated with black; distance from snout tip to anterior border of ear 1.25 length of tibia; occipital scale separated from supraorbital semicircles by one or two pairs of scales; one pair of scales between supraorbital semicircles----------
----------------------------blanquillanus</td>
<td>1. Usualmente vermiculado de negro, ocasionalmente con barras negras transversas; distancia de la punta del hocio al borde anterior del oído 1.15 de longitud de tibia; escama occipital en contacto con los semicírculos supraorbitales; dos pares de escamas entre los semicírculos supraorbitales----------------------bonairensis
Con barras negras transversas, raramente vermiculado con negro; distancia del hocico al borde anterior del oído 1.25 de longitud de la tibia; escama occipital separada por uno o dos pares de escamas; un par de escamas entre los semicírculos supraorbitales---------------blanquillanus</td>
</tr>
</table>

Anolis bonairensis bonairensis Ruthven

1940 *Anolis bonairensis bonairensis*—Hummelinck, Studies of the Fauna of Curaçao, Aruba, Bonaire and the Venezuelan Islands, 1: 78.

Distribution: Bonaire and Klein Bonaire Islands.

Anolis bonairensis blanquillanus Hummelinck

1940 *Anolis bonairensis blanquillanus* Hummelinck, Studies of the Fauna of Curaçao, Aruba, Bonaire and the Venezuelan Islands, 1: 79. Type-locality: El Jaque, Isla Blanquilla, Venezuela.

Distribution: Blanquilla and Los Hermanos Islands, Venezuela.

ANOLIS BOUVIERII Bocourt

1873 *Anolis Bouvierii* Bocourt, Miss. Sci. Mex., Rept.: 58, pl. 14, fig. 8-8a. Type-locality: Escuintla, Guatemala.
1955 *Anolis bouvierii*—Stuart, Misc. Publ. Mus. Zool. Univ. Mich., 91: 29.

Distribution: Known only from type locality.

ANOLIS CAPITO Peters

1863 *Anolis (Draconura) capito* Peters, Monats. Akad. Wiss. Berlin, 1863: 142. Type-locality: Costa Rica; restricted to Palmar, Costa Rica, by Smith and Taylor, Univ. Kansas Sci. Bull., 33, 1950, 316; see comment by Dunn and Stuart, Copeia, 1951, 57.
1864 *Anolis carneus* Cope, Proc. Acad. Nat. Sci. Phila., 1864: 171. Type-locality: Lower Verapaz Forest, Guatemala; see comment by Dunn and Stuart, Copeia, 1951, 59.
1873 *Anolis (Draconura) capito*—Bocourt, Miss. Sci. Mex., Rept.: 101, pl. 16, fig. 27-27a (type).
1893 *Anolis longipes* Cope, Proc. Amer. Phil. Soc., 31: 343. Type-locality: Palmar and Boruca, Costa Rica.
1956 *Anolis capito*—Taylor, Univ. Kansas Sci. Bull., 38: 126, figs. 34-36.

Distribution: Low and moderate elevations of Caribbean slope from Tabasco, Mexico, to Panama (possibly on both slopes in south).

ANOLIS CHLORIS Boulenger

   1898 Anolis chloris Boulenger, Proc. Zool. Soc. London, 1898: 110, pl. 10, fig. 3. Type-locality: Paramba, Ecuador.

    Distribution: Pacific lowlands of Ecuador and Colombia; Darién, Panama.

ANOLIS CHOCORUM Williams and Duellman

   1967 Anolis chocorum Williams and Duellman, Breviora, Mus. Comp. Zool., 256: 2, figs. 1-2, 4-6. Type-locality: Río Tuira at Quebrada La Plata, Darién, Panama, 100 m.

    Distribution: Darién, Panama, and Chocó, Colombia.

ANOLIS CHRYSOLEPIS Duméril and Bibron

   1837 Anolis chrysolepis Duméril and Bibron, Erp. Gén., 4: 94. Type-locality: French Guiana and Surinam.
   1848 Anolis planiceps Troschel, in Schomburgk, Reisen in Britisch-Guiana, 3: 649. Type-locality: British Guiana.
   1875 Anolis nummifer O'Shaughnessy, Ann. Mag. Nat. Hist., (4) 15: 278. Type-locality: Demerara Falls, Guyana.
   1875 Anolis turmalis O'Shaughnessy, Ann. Mag. Nat. Hist., (4) 15: 278. Type-locality: Grenada.
   1875 Anolis lentiginosus O'Shaughnessy, Ann. Mag. Nat. Hist., (4) 15: 279. Type-locality: Surinam.
   1885 Anolis chrysolepis—Boulenger, Cat. Liz. Brit. Mus., 2: 89.
   1907 Anolis longicrus Roux, Zool. Anz., 31: 763. Type-locality: Surinam.

    Distribution: Surinam; French Guiana; Pará and Amapa, Brazil.

ANOLIS COBANENSIS Stuart

   1942 Anolis cobanensis Stuart, Occ. Pap. Mus. Zool. Univ. Mich., 464: 6. Type-locality: Three km south of Finca Samac, Alta Verapaz, Guatemala, 1350 m.

    Distribution: Moderate and intermediate elevations in mountains of Alta Verapaz, Guatemala to Chiapas, Mexico.

ANOLIS CONCOLOR Cope

   1862 Anolis (Gastrotropis) concolor Cope, Proc. Acad. Nat. Sci. Phila., 1862: 180. Type-locality: Nicaragua.
   1885 Anolis concolor—Boulenger, Cat. Liz. Brit. Mus., 2: 74.

    Distribution: Known only from Providencia and San Andres Islands, Colombia; probably does not occur in Nicaragua.

ANOLIS CRASSULUS Cope

   1864 Anolis crassulus Cope, Proc. Acad. Nat. Sci. Phila., 1864: 173. Type-locality: Coban, Verapaz, Guatemala.
   1873 Anolis crassulus—Bocourt, Miss. Sci. Mex., Rept.: 82, pl. 16, fig. 17.

    Distribution: Plateau of Guatemala and Alta Verapaz, Guatemala; Chiapas, Mexico.

    Content: Two subspecies.

Key to the subspecies	Clave de subespecies
1. Dorsal scales generally fewer than 48 between axilla and groin--------crassulus Dorsal scales generally more than 50 between axilla and groin-----------haguei	1. Escamas dorsales menos de 48 entre axila e ingle------------------------crassulus Escamas dorsales más de 50 entre axila e ingle-------------------------------haguei

Anolis crassulus crassulus Cope

1948 [Anolis crassulus crassulus]—Stuart (by inference), Misc. Publ. Mus. Zool. Univ. Mich., 69: 47.

Distribution: Intermediate elevations on Plateau of Guatemala exclusive of Alta Verapaz; Chiapas, Mexico.

Anolis crassulus haguei Stuart

1942 Anolis haguei Stuart, Occ. Pap. Mus. Zool. Univ. Mich., 464: 3. Type-locality: Two km south of Finca Chichén, Alta Verapaz, Guatemala, 1750 m.
1948 Anolis crassulus haguei—Stuart, Misc. Publ. Mus. Zool. Univ. Mich., 69: 47.

Distribution: Known only from type locality.

ANOLIS CUPREUS Hallowell

1860 Anolis cupreus Hallowell, Proc. Acad. Nat. Sci. Phila., 1860: 481. Type-locality: None given; given as Nicaragua by Cochran, Bull. U.S. Nat. Mus., 220, 1961, 86.
1917 Anolis macrophallus Werner, Mitt. Zool. Mus. Hamburg, 34: 31. Type-locality: San José, Guatemala.
1956 Anolis cupreus—Taylor, Univ. Kansas Sci. Bull., 38: 110, fig. 29.

Distribution: Low and moderate elevations along Pacific slope from eastern Guatemala through Costa Rica.

ANOLIS CURTUS Boulenger

1898 Anolis curtus Boulenger, Proc. Zool. Soc. London, 1898: 919, pl. 55, figs. 2-2a. Type-locality: La Estrella, Provincia Cartago, Costa Rica.
1956 Anolis curtus—Taylor, Univ. Kansas Sci. Bull., 38: 151, fig. 42.

Distribution: Costa Rica.

ANOLIS DAMULUS Cope

1864 Anolis damulus Cope, Proc. Acad. Nat. Sci. Phila., 1864: 169. Type-locality: Unknown.
1885 Anolis damulus—Boulenger, Cat. Liz. Brit. Mus., 2: 47, pl. 2, figs. 2-2a.

Distribution: Unknown.

ANOLIS DISSIMILIS Williams

1965 Anolis dissimilis Williams, Breviora, Mus. Comp. Zool., 233: 2, fig. 1. Type-locality: Itahuania, Upper Río Madre de Dios, Peru.

Distribution: Known only from type locality.

ANOLIS DOLLFUSIANUS Bocourt

1873 Anolis Dollfusianus Bocourt, Miss. Sci. Mex., Rept.: 84, pl. 16, fig. 19-19a. Type-locality: San Agustin, on slopes of Volcán Atitlan, Guatemala, 1200 m.

Distribution: Moderate elevations along Pacific slope from eastern Chiapas, Mexico, to western Guatemala.

ANOLIS EEWI Roze

1958 Anolis eewi Roze, Acta Biol. Venezuelica, 2 (25): 311. Type-locality: Cumbe de Torono Tepui, Chimantá Tepui, Estado Bolívar, Venezuela, 2100 m.

Distribution: Known only from type locality.

ANOLIS EULAEMUS Boulenger

1908 Anolis eulaemus Boulenger, Ann. Mag. Nat. Hist., (8) 2: 516, fig. 1. Type-locality: Las Pavas, Colombia.

Distribution: Southwestern Colombia and northwestern Ecuador.

ANOLIS FASCIATUS Boulenger

1885 Anolis fasciatus Boulenger, Cat. Liz. Brit. Mus., 2: 59, pl. 3, fig. 1. Type-locality: Guayaquil, Ecuador.
1898 Anolis elegans Boulenger, Proc. Zool. Soc. London, 1898: 109, pl. 10, fig. 2. Type-locality: Chimbo, Ecuador.

Distribution: Pacific lowlands of Ecuador.

ANOLIS FESTAE Peracca

1904 Anolis Festae Peracca, Boll. Mus. Zool. Comp. Anat. Univ. Torino, 19 (465): 4. Type-locality: Balzar, Ecuador.

Distribution: Lowlands of western Ecuador.

ANOLIS FRASERI Günther

1859 Anolis fraseri Günther, Proc. Zool. Soc. London, 1859: 407. Type-locality: Andes of western Ecuador.
1873 Anolis Fraseri—Bocourt, Miss. Sci. Mex., Rept.: pl. 15, fig. 12-12a (type).
1880 Anolis de Villei Boulenger, Bull. Soc. Zool. France, 1880: 42. Type-locality: Andes of Ecuador.
1885 Anolis fraseri—Boulenger, Cat. Liz. Brit. Mus., 2: 65, pl. 4.
1966 Anolis fraseri—Williams, Breviora, Mus. Comp. Zool., 239: 3, fig. 1.

Distribution: Higher western slopes of Andes in Ecuador and Colombia.

ANOLIS FRENATUS Cope

1899 Anolis frenatus Cope, Sci. Bull. Philadelphia Mus., 1: 6, pl. 2, fig. 2. Type-locality: Unknown; Barranquilla, Colombia is suggested by Barbour, Bull. Mus. Comp. Zool., 71, 1934, 151.
1937 Anolis frenatus—Dunn, Proc. New England Zool. Club, 16: 9.

Distribution: Costa Rica and Panama; Caribbean Colombia and Venezuela.

ANOLIS FUSCOAURATUS D'Orbigny

1837 Anolis fusco-auratus D'Orbigny, in Duméril and Bibron, Erp. Gén., 4: 110. Type-locality: Chile (in error); corrected by D'Orbigny, 1847, to Río Mamoré, between Loreto and "le confluent du Río Sara", Bolivia; and to Provincia Moxas, Bolivia, by Bocourt, Miss. Sci. Mex., Rept., 1873, pl. 14, fig. 16.

Distribution: Bolivia and Peru to Venezuela, Colombia, Guianas and Atlantic forests of Brazil.

Content: Two subspecies.

Key to the subspecies	Clave de subespecies
1. Supraorbital semicircles separated by single row of scales--------------kugleri Supraorbital semicircles separated by two or more rows of scales--------fuscoauratus	1. Semicírculos supraorbitales separados por una fila de escamas---------------kugleri Semicírculos supraorbitales separados por dos o más filas de escamas----fuscoauratus

Anolis <u>fuscoauratus fuscoauratus</u> D'Orbigny

    1863 <u>Anolis viridiaeneus</u> Peters, Monats. Akad. Wiss. Berlin, 1863: 147. Type-locality: Quito, Ecuador.
    1887 <u>Anolis Brumetii</u> Thominot, Bull. Soc. Philom. Paris, (7) 11: 184. Type-locality: Brazil.
    1947 [<u>Anolis</u>] <u>fuscoauratus</u> [<u>fuscoauratus</u>]—Shreve, Bull. Mus. Comp. Zool., 99: 523.

    Distribution: Amazonian slopes of Andes in Ecuador, Bolivia, Peru and Brazil.

Anolis <u>fuscoauratus kugleri</u> Roux

    1929 <u>Anolis kugleri</u> Roux, Verh. Naturforsch. Ges. Basel, 40 (2): 29. Type-locality: El Mene, Acosta District, Estado Falcón, Venezuela.
    1947 <u>Anolis fuscoauratus kugleri</u>—Shreve, Bull. Mus. Comp. Zool., 99: 523.

    Distribution: Venezuela.

ANOLIS <u>GARBEI</u> Amaral

    1933 <u>Anolis garbei</u> Amaral, Mem. Inst. Butantan, 7 (1932): 62, fig. 17-18. Type-locality: Monte Christo, Rio Tapajóz, Pará, Brazil.

    Distribution: Known only from type locality.

ANOLIS <u>GEMMOSUS</u> O'Shaughnessy

    1875 <u>Anolis gemmosus</u> O'Shaughnessy, Ann. Mag. Nat. Hist., (4) 15: 280. Type-locality: Unknown.
    1885 <u>Anolis gemmosus</u>—Boulenger, Cat. Liz. Brit. Mus., 2: 60, pl. 3, fig. 2.

    Distribution: Pacific lowlands of Ecuador.

ANOLIS <u>GIBBICEPS</u> Cope

    1864 <u>Anolis gibbiceps</u> Cope, Proc. Acad. Nat. Sci. Phila., 1864: 174. Type-locality: Caracas, Venezuela.

    Distribution: Guyana; northern Venezuela.

ANOLIS <u>GODMANI</u> Boulenger

    1885 <u>Anolis godmani</u> Boulenger, Cat. Liz. Brit. Mus., 2: 85. Type-locality: Guatemala and Irazú, Costa Rica; restricted to Volcan Irazú, Costa Rica by Taylor, Univ. Kansas Sci. Bull., 38, 1956, 156.

    Distribution: Mountains of Costa Rica above 600 m.

ANOLIS <u>GORGONAE</u> Barbour

    1905 <u>Anolis gorgonae</u> Barbour, Bull. Mus. Comp. Zool., 46: 99. Type-locality: Gorgona Island, Colombia.

    Distribution: Known only from type locality.

ANOLIS <u>GRACILIPES</u> Boulenger

    1898 <u>Anolis gracilipes</u> Boulenger, Proc. Zool. Soc. London, 1898: 112, pl. 11, fig. 3. Type-locality: Paramba, Ecuador.

    Distribution: Known only from type locality.

ANOLIS GRANULICEPS Boulenger

1898 Anolis granuliceps Boulenger, Proc. Zool. Soc. London, 1898: 111, pl. 11, fig. 2. Type-locality: Paramba, Ecuador.
1913 Anolis breviceps Boulenger, Proc. Zool. Soc. London, 1913: 1031, pl. 107, fig. 1. Type-locality: Peñalisa,Condoto, Chocó, Colombia, 300 ft.
1959 Anolis granuliceps—Peters, Ciencia y Naturaleza, Quito, 2: 118.

   Distribution: Pacific lowlands of Colombia and Ecuador.

ANOLIS HETEROPHOLIDOTUS Mertens

1952 Anolis heteropholidotus Mertens, Zool. Anz., 148: 89. Type-locality: Hacienda Los Planes, Miramundo, Departamento Santa Ana, El Salvador, 2000 m.

   Distribution: Mountainous areas of El Salvador.

ANOLIS HOFFMANNI Peters

1863 Anolis Hoffmanni Peters, Monats. Akad. Wiss. Berlin, 1863: 142. Type-locality: Costa Rica.
1873 Anolis hoffmanni—Bocourt, Miss. Sci. Mex., Rept.: 86, pl. 15, figs. 15-16 (fig. 15 is holotype).
1966 Anolis hoffmanni—Williams and Smith, Carib. Jour. Sci., 6: 163.

   Distribution: Provincias Guanacaste, Puntarenas, and San José, Costa Rica.

ANOLIS HUMILIS Peters

1863 Anolis humilis Peters, Monats. Akad. Wiss. Berlin, 1863: 138. Type-locality: Veragua, Panama.
1873 Anolis humilis—Bocourt, Miss. Sci. Mex., Rept.: 105, pl. 16, fig. 31 (type).

   Distribution: Lowlands of Chiapas, Mexico through Panama.

   Content: Three subspecies.

             Key to the subspecies

1. Eight to ten enlarged dorsal scale rows, two median rows not larger than adjoining rows; no nuchal crest; axillary pouch small, not pigmented, without scales-----2
   Twelve to fourteen enlarged dorsal scale rows two median rows larger than adjoining rows; low nuchal crest and often trace of dorsal crest in males; axillary pouch large, pigmented, with scales--marsupialis

2. Dewlap with purple spot in basal part; all scales in enlarged rows of same size; semicircular scales undifferentiated from scales adjoining them------------uniformis
   Dewlap without purple spot in basal part; two median scale rows smaller than adjoining rows; semicircular scales differentiated from scales adjoining them-----humilis

             Clave de subespecies

1. Ocho a diez hileras dorsales de escamas ensanchadas; las dos medianas mayores que las adyacentes; no hay cresta nucal; saco axilar pequeño, no escamoso ni pigmentado--2
   Doce a catorce hileras dorsales de escamas ensanchadas, las dos filas medianas mayores que las filas vecinas; una cresta nucal baja y con frecuencia trazos de cresta dorsal en los machos; saco axilar grande, escamoso y pigmentado----------marsupialis

2. Saco gular con una mancha púrpura en la base; escamas ensanchadas del mismo tamaño; escamas de los semicírculos supraorbitales casi indiferenciadas de las escamas adyacentes----------------------uniformis
   Saco gular sin mancha púrpura en su parte basal; escamas ensanchadas con las dos hileras medianas más pequeñas que las adyacentes; escamas de los semicírculos diferenciados de las vecinas-------humilis

Anolis humilis humilis Peters

1885 Anolis quaggulus Cope, Proc. Amer. Phil. Soc., 22: 391. Type-locality: Río San Juan, Nicaragua.
1948 [Anolis humilis humilis]—Stuart (by inference), Misc. Publ. Mus. Zool. Univ. Mich., 69: 48.

   Distribution: Panama and Costa Rica, excluding Provincias Puntarenas and Cartago, Costa Rica.

Anolis humilis marsupialis Taylor

    1956 Anolis humilis marsupialis Taylor, Univ. Kansas Sci. Bull., 38: 97, fig. 23. Type-
        locality: 75 km west southwest of San Isidro de General, probably in Provincia
        Puntarenas, Costa Rica.

      Distribution: Pacific lowlands of Provincias Cartago and Puntarenas, Costa Rica.

Anolis humilis uniformis Cope

    1885 Anolis uniformis Cope, Proc. Amer. Phil. Soc., 22: 392. Type-locality: Guatemala and
        Yucatán; restricted to two mi north of Santa Teresa, El Péten, Guatemala, by Smith and
        Taylor; see comments by Dunn and Stuart, Copeia, 1957, 60.
    1935 Anolis ruthveni Stuart, Occ. Pap. Mus. Zool. Univ. Mich., 310: 1. Type-locality: Two mi
        north of Santa Teresa, El Péten, Guatemala.
    1948 Anolis humilis uniformis—Stuart, Misc. Publ. Mus. Zool. Univ. Mich., 69: 48.

      Distribution: Lowlands of Chiapas and Yucatán Peninsula, Mexico to Provincia Guanacaste,
      Costa Rica.

ANOLIS IMPETIGOSUS Cope

    1864 Anolis impetigosus Cope, Proc. Acad. Nat. Sci. Phila., 1864: 174. Type-locality: Unknown.
    1885 Anolis impetigosus—Boulenger, Cat. Liz. Brit. Mus., 2: 55, pl. 2, fig. 3.

      Distribution: Probably somewhere in South America.

ANOLIS INCOMPERTUS Barbour

    1932 Anolis incompertus incompertus Barbour, Proc. New England Zool. Club, 12: 99. Type-locality:
        Villavicencio, San Martín, Colombia.
    1944 [Anolis] incompertus—Dunn, Rev. Acad. Soc. Cienc. Exactas, Fis. Nat., 6: 74.

      Distribution: Region of type locality.

ANOLIS INSIGNIS Cope

    1871 Anolis insignis Cope, Proc. Acad. Nat. Sci. Phila., 1871: 213, pl. 24, fig. 2. Type-locality:
        San José, Costa Rica.
    1876 Anolis insignis—Cope, Jour. Acad. Nat. Sci. Phila., (2) 8 (1875): 120, pl. 24, fig. 1.

      Distribution: Panama to Costa Rica, in mountainous areas.

ANOLIS INTERMEDIUS Peters

    1863 Anolis intermedius Peters, Monats. Akad. Wiss. Berlin, 1863: 143. Type-locality: Veragua,
        Panama.
    1873 Anolis intermedius—Bocourt, Miss. Sci. Mex., Rept.: 69, pl. 15, fig. 4 (type).
    1875 Anolis tessellatus O'Shaughnessy, Ann. Mag. Nat. Hist., (4) 15: 279. Type-locality: Costa Rica.
    1956 Anolis intermedius—Taylor, Univ. Kansas Sci. Bull., 38: 106, figs. 27-28.

      Distribution: Panama to Costa Rica and Nicaragua.

ANOLIS JACARE Boulenger

    1903 Anolis jacare Boulenger, Ann. Mag. Nat. Hist., (7) 11: 482. Type-locality: Mérida, Venezuela,
        1600 m.

      Distribution: Venezuela, eastern Colombia.

ANOLIS KEMPTONI Dunn

1940 Anolis kemptoni Dunn, Proc. Acad. Nat. Sci. Phila., 92: 111. Type-locality: Finca Lérida,
Chiriquí, Panama, 5300 ft.

Distribution: Known only from type locality.

ANOLIS LAEVIS (Cope)

1876 Scytomycterus laevis Cope, Jour. Acad. Nat. Sci. Phila., (2) 8 (1875): 165. Type-locality:
Between Moyabamba and Puerto Balso, Río Huallaga, eastern Peru.
1885 Anolis laevis—Boulenger, Cat. Liz. Brit. Mus., 2: 56.

Distribution: Known only from type locality.

ANOLIS LAEVIVENTRIS (Wiegmann)

1834 D.[actyloa] (A.[nolis]) laeviventris Wiegmann, Herpetologia Mexicana: 47. Type-locality: Mexico;
restricted to Jalapa, Veracruz, by Smith and Taylor, Bull. U.S. Nat. Mus., 199, 1950, 63.
1843 Dactyloa wiegmanni Fitzinger, Systema Reptilium: 67. Type-locality: Mexico.
1873 Anolis laeviventris—Bocourt, Miss. Sci. Mex., Rept.: 87, pl. 16, figs. 18-18a (type).

Distribution: Moderate and intermediate elevations from central Veracruz, Mexico, through uplands of
Chiapas, Mexico, into northwestern Guatemala.

ANOLIS LATIFRONS Berthold

1846 Anolis latifrons Berthold, Nachr. Univ. Königl. Ges. Wiss. Göttingen, 8-10: 11. Type-locality:
Popayan, Colombia.
1885 Anolis latifrons—Boulenger, Cat. Liz. Brit. Mus., 2: 62.

Distribution: Northwestern Ecuador through Chocó of Colombia to southern Central America.

ANOLIS LEMNISCATUS Boulenger

1898 Anolis lemniscatus Boulenger, Proc. Zool. Soc. London, 1898: 113, pl. 10, fig. 4. Type-locality:
Chimbo, Ecuador.

Distribution: Western Ecuador.

ANOLIS LEMURINUS Cope

1861 Anolis (Gastrotropis) lemurinus Cope, Proc. Acad. Nat. Sci. Phila., 1861: 213. Type-locality:
Veragua, Panama.

Distribution: From central Veracruz, Mexico to northwestern South America.

Content: Two subspecies.

Key to the subspecies	Clave de subespecies
1. Supraorbital semicircles in contact-------- ------------------------------lemurinus Supraorbital semicircles separated--------- -------------------------------bourgeaei	1. Semicírculos supraorbitales en contacto---- ---------------------------------lemurinus Semicírculos supraorbitales separados------ ---------------------------------bourgeaei

Anolis lemurinus lemurinus Cope

    1862 Anolis (Dracontura) vittigerus Cope, Proc. Acad. Nat. Sci. Phila., 1862: 179. Type-locality: Truando region, Colombia.
    1873 Anolis palpebrosus Peters, Monats. Akad. Wiss. Berlin, 1873: 740. Type-locality: Chiriquí, Panama.
    1887 Anolis frontatus Thominot, Bull. Soc. Philom. Paris, (7) 11: 185. Type-locality: Darién, Panama.
    1948 [Anolis lemurinus lemurinus]—Stuart (by inference), Misc. Publ. Mus. Zool. Univ. Mich., 69: 49.
    1956 Anolis lemurinus lemurinus—Taylor, Univ. Kansas Sci. Bull., 38: 100, figs. 24-26.

    Distribution: Low and moderate elevations on Caribbean slope from Costa Rica to Panama and on Pacific slope from Chiapas, Mexico to El Salvador.

Anolis lemurinus bourgeaei Bocourt

    1873 Anolis Bourgeaei Bocourt, Miss. Sci. Mex., Rept.: 76, pl. 15, fig. 9. Type-locality: Orizaba and Huatusco, Mexico.
    1932 Anolis ustus verae-pacis Barbour, Proc. New England Zool. Club, 12: 98. Type-locality: Hacienda Chimoxan, Alta Verapaz, Guatemala, 1500 ft.
    1948 Anolis lemurinus bourgeaei—Stuart, Misc. Publ. Mus. Zool. Univ. Mich., 69: 49.

    Distribution: Low and moderate elevations of Caribbean slope from central Veracruz, Mexico to northern Honduras.

ANOLIS LEPTOSCELIS Boulenger

    1885 Anolis leptoscelis Boulenger, Cat. Liz. Brit. Mus., 2: 92, pl. 5, fig. 3. Type-locality: Pebas and Yurimaguas, Río Huallaga, northeastern Peru.
    1885 Anolis macropus Cope, Proc. Amer. Phil. Soc., 23: 101. Type-locality: Pebas, Upper Amazon, Peru.

    Distribution: Amazonian slopes of Peru and Ecuador.

ANOLIS LIMIFRONS Cope

    1862 Anolis (Dracontura) limifrons Cope, Proc. Acad. Nat. Sci. Phila., 1862: 178. Type-locality: Veragua; = Cucuyos, Veragua Province, Panama, according to Barbour, Bull. Mus. Comp. Zool., 77, 1934, 139.

    Distribution: Panama through central America on Caribbean slope to Isthmus of Tehuantepec, Mexico.

    Content: Three subspecies, one of which (microlepis Alvarez del Toro and Smith) is extralimital.

Key to the subspecies	Clave de subespecies
1. Head longer than tibia; head scales smooth or weakly keeled; slender form---rodriguezii Head same length as tibia; head scales distinctly keeled; not slender---limifrons	1. Cabeza más larga que la tibia; escudos cefálicos lisos o debilmente quillados; aspecto delgado----------------rodriguezii Cabeza del mismo tamaño que la tibia; escamas de la cabeza distintamente quilladas; especto no delgado---------------limifrons

Anolis limifrons limifrons Cope

    1871 Anolis trochilus Cope, Proc. Acad. Nat. Sci. Phila., 1871: 215. Type-locality: San José, Costa Rica.
    1873 Anolis pulchripes Peters, Monats. Akad. Wiss. Berlin, 1873: 739. Type-locality: Chiriquí, Panama.
    1874 Anolis bransfordii Cope, Proc. Acad. Nat. Sci. Phila., 1874: 67. Type-locality: Nicaragua.
    1882 Anolis Rivieri Thominot, Bull. Soc. Philom, Paris, (7) 6: 251. Type-locality: Panama.
    1948 [Anolis limifrons limifrons]—Stuart (by inference), Misc. Publ. Mus. Zool. Univ. Mich., 69: 49.

    Distribution: Caribbean slope, Panama to Nicaragua.

Anolis limifrons rodriguezii Bocourt

1873 Anolis Rodriguezii Bocourt, Miss. Sci. Mex., Rept.: 62, pl. 13, fig. 1-1a. Type-locality: Panzos, Guatemala.
?1873 Anolis rubiginosus Bocourt, Ann. Sci. Nat. Zool. Paris, (5) 17, art. 2: 1. Type-locality: Oaxaca, Mexico.
1885 Anolis aureolus Cope, Proc. Amer. Phil. Soc., 22: 390. Type-locality: Yucatán and Guatemala; restricted to Chichen Itzá, Yucatán, by Smith and Taylor, Bull. U.S. Nat. Mus., 199, 1950, 64.
1891 Anolis acutirostris Ives, Proc. Acad. Nat. Sci. Phila., 1891: 459. Type-locality: Citilpech, Yucatán, Mexico.
1948 Anolis limifrons rodriguezii—Stuart, Misc. Publ. Mus. Zool. Univ. Mich., 69: 49.

Distribution: Low elevations of Caribbean slope from Isthmus of Tehuantepec, Mexico to Honduras.

Comment: Stuart, Misc. Publ. Mus. Zool. Univ. Mich., 91, 1955, 19, suggested that Anolis guntheri Bocourt may also be synonymous with this taxon.

ANOLIS LINDENI Ruthven

1912 Anolis lindeni Ruthven, Proc. Biol. Soc. Washington, 25: 163. Type-locality: Santarem, Brazil; May be erroneous, E.E. Williams, in litt.

Distribution: Known only from type specimen.

ANOLIS LINEATUS Daudin

1804 Anolis lineatus Daudin, Hist. Nat. Rept., 4: 66, pl. 58, fig. 1. Type-locality: South America.
1885 Anolis lineatus—Boulenger, Cat. Liz. Brit. Mus., 2: 38.
1966 Anolis lineatus—Rand and Rand, Studies on the Fauna of Curaçao and other Caribbean Islands, 24: 112.

Distribution: Curaçao Island.

ANOLIS LIONOTUS Cope

1861 Anolis (Dracontura) lionotus Cope, Proc. Acad. Nat. Sci. Phila., 1861: 210. Type-locality: Cucuyas de Veragua, Panama.
1876 Anolis oxylophus Cope, Jour. Acad. Nat. Sci. Phila., (2) 8 (1875): 123, pl. 24, fig. 4. Type-locality: None given, probably type was from southeastern Costa Rica.
1894 Anolis rixi Boulenger, Proc. Zool. Soc. London, 1894: 727, pl. 48, fig. 1. Type-locality: Chontales, Nicaragua.
1956 Anolis lionotus—Taylor, Univ. Kansas Sci. Bull., 38: 137, fig. 38.

Distribution: Panama to Nicaragua.

ANOLIS LONGICAUDA Hallowell

1860 Anolis longicauda Hallowell, Proc. Acad. Nat. Sci. Phila., 1860: 481. Type-locality: Nicaragua.

Distribution: Known only from type specimen.

ANOLIS LOVERIDGEI Schmidt

1936 Anolis loveridgei Schmidt, Proc. Biol. Soc. Washington, 49: 47. Type-locality: Portillo Grande, Yoro, Honduras, 4100 ft.

Distribution: Known only from type locality.

ANOLIS MACROLEPIS Boulenger

1911 Anolis macrolepis Boulenger, Ann. Mag. Nat. Hist., (8) 7: 21. Type-locality: Novita, Río Tamaná and Condoto, Chocó, Colombia, 150-200 ft.

Distribution: Known only from type localities.

ANOLIS MACULIVENTRIS Boulenger

1898 Anolis maculiventris Boulenger, Proc. Zool. Soc. London, 1898: 111, pl. 11, fig. 1. Type-
   locality: Paramba, Ecuador.

   Distribution: Lowlands of northwestern Ecuador.

ANOLIS MARIARUM Barbour

1932 Anolis mariarum Barbour, Proc. New England Zool. Club, 12: 100. Type-locality: Sampedro, 45 km
   north of Medellín, Departamento Antioquia, Colombia.

   Distribution: Known only from type locality.

ANOLIS MERIDIONALIS Boettger

1885 Anolis (Draconura) chrysolepis—Boettger, Zeits. für Naturwiss., 58: 215.
1885 Anolis meridionalis Boettger, Zeits. für Naturwiss., 58: 437. Type-locality: Paraguay.
1895 Anolis holotropis Boulenger, Ann. Mag. Nat. Hist., (6) 15: 522. Type-locality: Mato Grosso,
   Brazil.
1903 Norops sladeniae Boulenger, Proc. Zool. Soc. London, 1903: 69, fig. 2. Type-locality: Chapadá,
   Mato Grosso, Brazil.
1933 Norops marmorata Amaral, Mem. Inst. Butantan, 7 (1932): 63, figs. 19-20. Type-locality: Jaguará,
   Rio Grande, Minas Gerais, Brazil.

   Distribution: Mato Grosso, Brazil and Paraguay.

ANOLIS MICROTUS Cope

1871 Anolis microtus Cope, Proc. Acad. Nat. Sci. Phila., 1871: 214, pl. 24, fig. 2. Type-locality:
   San José, Costa Rica.
1876 Anolis microtus—Cope, Jour. Acad. Nat. Sci. Phila., (2) 8 (1875): 119, pl. 24, fig. 2.
1923 Diaphoranolis brooksi Barbour, Occ. Pap. Mus. Zool. Univ. Mich., 129: 7. Type-locality: Sapo
   Mountain, eastern Panama, 2500 ft.

   Distribution:

ANOLIS MIRUS Williams

1963 Anolis mirus Williams, Bull. Mus. Comp. Zool., 129: 467, figs. 1-2. Type-locality: Río San Juan,
   southwestern Colombia.

   Distribution: Known only from type locality.

ANOLIS NANNODES Cope

1864 Anolis nannodes Cope, Proc. Acad. Nat. Sci. Phila., 1864: 173. Type-locality: Cobán, Alta
   Verapaz, Guatemala; Arriba, Costa Rica and Jalapa, Mexico; restricted to Cobán, Alta Verapaz,
   Guatemala, by Stuart, Misc. Publ. Mus. Zool. Univ. Mich., 69, 1948, 50; restricted to Arriba,
   Costa Rica, by Smith and Taylor, Univ. Kansas Sci. Bull., 33, 1950, 316; discussed by Smith and
   Taylor, Bull. U.S. Nat. Mus., 199, 1950, 63, and by Dunn and Stuart, Copeia, 1951, 57.
1873 Anolis nannodes—Bocourt, Miss. Sci. Mex., Rept.: 71, pl. 15, fig. 4 (type).
1942 Anolis cortezi Stuart, Occ. Pap. Mus. Zool. Univ. Mich., 464: 8. Type-locality: Finca Los Alpes,
   35 km east and slightly south of Cobán, Alta Verapaz, Guatemala.
1950 Anolis stuarti Smith, in Smith and Taylor, Bull. U.S. Nat. Mus., 199: 63. Type-locality: Cobán,
   Guatemala.

   Distribution: Moderate and intermediate elevations on Caribbean slope of Alta Verapaz, Guatemala,
   and also possibly Chiapas, Mexico.

ANOLIS <u>NASOFRONTALIS</u> Amaral

1933 <u>Anolis nasofrontalis</u> Amaral, Mem. Inst. Butantan, 7 (1932): 58, figs. 11-12. Type-locality:
   Estado do Espirito Santo, Brazil.
1945 <u>Anolis nasofrontalis</u>—Myers and Carvalho, Bol. Mus. Nac. Brazil, 43: 9.

   Distribution: Estado do Espirito Santo, Brazil.

ANOLIS <u>NICEFORI</u> Barbour

1932 <u>Anolis incompertus nicefori</u> Barbour, Proc. New England Zool. Club, 12: 100. Type-locality: Humbo,
   170 km north of Bogotá, Departamento de Boyacá, Colombia, 824 m.
1944 <u>Anolis nicefori</u>—Dunn, Rev. Acad. Col. Exactas, Fis. Nat., 6: 15.

   Distribution: Interandean highlands of Colombia.

ANOLIS <u>NIGROLINEATUS</u> Williams

1965 <u>Anolis nigrolineatus</u> Williams, Breviora, Mus. Comp. Zool., 233: 4, fig. 2. Type-locality:
   Machala, Provincia El Oro, Ecuador.

   Distribution: Machala and Guayaquil, Ecuador.

ANOLIS <u>NITENS</u> (Wagler)

1830 <u>Draconura nitens</u> Wagler, Nat. Syst. Amph.: 149. Type-locality: America.
1863 <u>Anolis</u> (<u>Draconura</u>) <u>nitens</u>—Peters, Monats. Akad. Wiss. Berlin, 1863: 142.

   Distribution: Northeastern South America.

   Content: Two subspecies.

Key to the subspecies

1. Upper head scales smooth; head not shorter
   than tibia; four series of enlarged dorsal
   scales; adpressed hind limb does not reach
   tip of snout-------------------------bondi
   Upper head scales keeled; head shorter than
   tibia; two series of enlarged dorsal
   scales; adpressed hind limb reaches tip of
   snout-------------------------------nitens

Clave de subespecies

1. Escamas supracefálicas lisas; cabeza no más
   corta que la tibia; cuatro series de escamas agrandadas dorsales; extremidad posterior hacia adelante no alcanza la punta del
   hocico-------------------------------bondi
   Escamas supracefálicas quilladas; cabeza
   más corta que la tibia; dos series de escamas dorsales agrandadas; extremidad
   posterior hacia adelante alcanza la punta
   del hocico---------------------------nitens

<u>Anolis nitens nitens</u> (Wagler)

1837 <u>Anolis refulgens</u> Duméril and Bibron, Erp. Gén., 4: 91. Type-locality: Surinam.
1913 <u>Anolis nitens</u> [<u>nitens</u>]—Fowler (by inference), Proc. Acad. Nat. Sci. Phila., 1913: 171.

   Distribution: Surinam, Guyana, and Venezuela.

<u>Anolis nitens bondi</u> Fowler

1913 <u>Anolis nitens bondi</u> Fowler, Proc. Acad. Nat. Sci. Phila., 1913: 171, pl. 10. Type-
   locality: Cariquito, Venezuela.

   Distribution: Eastern Venezuela.

ANOLIS

ANOLIS NOTOPHOLIS Boulenger

1896 Anolis notopholis Boulenger, Ann. Mag. Nat. Hist., (6) 17: 17. Type-locality: Buenaventura, Colombia.

Distribution: Coastal area near Buenaventura, Colombia.

ANOLIS ORTONII Cope

1868 Anolis ortonii Cope, Proc. Acad. Nat. Sci. Phila., 1868: 97. Type-locality: Río Napo or Upper Río Marañón, Ecuador or Peru.
1870 Anolis cynocephalus Bocourt, Nouv. Arch. Mus. Paris, Bull., 6: 13. Type-locality: French Guiana.
1873 Anolis cynocephalus—Bocourt, Miss. Sci. Mex., Rept.: pl. 14, figs. 7-7a (holotype).

Distribution: Amazonian Basin.

ANOLIS PACHYPUS Cope

1876 Anolis pachypus Cope, Jour. Acad. Nat. Sci. Phila., (2) 8 (1875): 122, pl. 24, fig. 3. Type-locality: Slopes of Pico Blanco, Costa Rica.
1956 Anolis pachypus—Taylor, Univ. Kansas Sci. Bull., 38: 145.

Distribution: Costa Rica; Volcán Chiriqui, Panama.

ANOLIS PALMERI Boulenger

1908 Anolis palmeri Boulenger, Ann. Mag. Nat. Hist., (8) 1: 112. Type-locality: Los Mangos, southwestern Colombia.

Distribution: Known only from type locality.

ANOLIS PENTAPRION Cope

1862 Anolis (Coccoëssus) pentaprion Cope, Proc. Acad. Nat. Sci. Phila., 1862: 178. Type-locality: Río Truando, Colombia.

Distribution: Low elevations on Caribbean slope from Colombia to Chiapas, Mexico.

Content: Two subspecies.

Key to the subspecies

1. Upper head scales smooth; ear opening very small and rounded; 18 lamellae under phalanges 2 and 3 of fourth toe; light grey above with white spots-------------beckeri
Upper head scales rugose; ear opening moderate and sub-oval; 22 lamellae under phalanges 2 and 3 of fourth toe; reddish-brown above marbled with blackish---------
--------------------------------pentaprion

Clave de subespecies

1. Escamas supracefálicas lisas; abertura auditiva muy pequeña; 18 lamelas bajo la falanges 2-3 del cuarto ortejo; gris pálido encima con manchas blancas---------beckeri
Escamas supracefálicas rugosas; abertura auditiva moderada sub oval; 22 lamelas bajo las falanges 2-3 del cuarto ortejo; rojizo café con marmoraciones negruzcas---
--------------------------------pentaprion

Anolis pentaprion pentaprion Cope

1899 Anolis sulcifrons Cope, Sci. Bull. Philadelphia Mus., 1: 6, pl. 2, fig. 1. Type-locality: Uncertain, perhaps from Bogotá, Colombia; restricted to Barranquilla, Colombia, by Smith and Taylor, Univ. Kansas Sci. Bull., 33, 1950, 363; restriction rejected by Dunn and Stuart, Copeia, 1951, 56.
1890 Anolis panamensis Boulenger, Proc. Zool. Soc. London, 1890: 81, pl. 8, figs. 3-3a. Type-locality: Panama; see Dunn and Stuart, Copeia, 1951, 56, for discussion of type locality.
1958 Anolis pentaprion [pentaprion]—Stuart, Cont. Lab. Vert. Biol. Univ. Mich., 75: 21.

Distribution: Lowlands of Colombia to Nicaragua; reported at 6000 ft on Volcán Chiriqui, Panama, by Walters, Copeia, 1953, 126.

Anolis pentaprion beckeri Boulenger

1881 Anolis beckeri Boulenger, Proc. Zool. Soc. London, 1881: 921. Type-locality: Yucatán, Mexico.
1958 Anolis pentaprion beckeri—Stuart, Cont. Lab. Vert. Biol. Univ. Mich., 75: 21.

Distribution: Low elevations on Caribbean slope from Chiapas, Mexico to Honduras, including Yucatán Peninsula and British Honduras.

ANOLIS PERACCAE Boulenger

1898 Anolis peraccae Boulenger, Proc. Zool. Soc. London, 1898: 108, pl. 10, fig. 1-1a. Type-locality: Chimbo, Ecuador.
1901 Anolis irregularis Werner, Verh. Zool.-Bot. Ges. Wien., 51: 594. Type-locality: Ecuador.

Distribution: Northwestern Ecuador.

ANOLIS PETERSII Bocourt

1873 Anolis Petersii Bocourt, Miss. Sci. Mex., Rept.: 79, pl. 13, fig. 2; pl. 15, figs. 11-11a. Type-locality: Alta Verapaz, Guatemala.
1896 Anolis petersii bivittata Werner, Verh. Zool.-Bot. Ges. Wien, 46: 351. Type-locality: Guatemala; restricted to Cobán, Guatemala, by Smith and Taylor, Univ. Kansas Sci. Bull., 33, 1950, 317; see comments by Dunn and Stuart, Copeia, 1951, 59.

Distribution: Moderate elevations on Caribbean slope from San Luis Potosi, Mexico and on Pacific slope from Isthmus of Tehuantepec, Mexico, south to Honduras.

ANOLIS PHYLLORHINUS Myers and Carvalho

1945 Anolis phyllorhinus Myers and Carvalho, Bol. Mus. Nac. Brazil, Zool., 43: 2, figs. 1-5. Type-locality: Borba, Rio Madeira, Estado do Amazonas, Brazil.

Distribution: Known only from type locality.

ANOLIS POECILOPUS Cope

1862 Anolis (Dracontura) poecilopus Cope, Proc. Acad. Nat. Sci. Phila., 1862: 179. Type-locality: Near Cartagena and on Río Truando, Colombia.
1885 Anolis poecilopus—Boulenger, Cat. Liz. Brit. Mus., 2: 84.

Distribution: Known only from type material.

ANOLIS POLYLEPIS Peters

1873 Anolis polylepis Peters, Monats. Akad. Wiss. Berlin, 1873: 738. Type-locality: Chiriquí, Panama.
1956 Anolis polylepis—Taylor, Univ. Kansas Sci. Bull., 38: 87, fig. 21.

Distribution: Panama to southwestern Costa Rica.

ANOLIS PRINCEPS

1902 Anolis princeps Boulenger, Ann. Mag. Nat. Hist., (7) 9: 54. Type-locality: Río Lita, Paramba, San Javier and Salidero, Ecuador.

Distribution: Lowlands of northwestern Ecuador.

ANOLIS PROBOSCIS Peters and Orcés

1956 Anolis proboscis Peters and Orcés, Breviora, Mus. Comp. Zool., 62: 2, fig. Type-locality: Cunuco, 5 km northwest of Mindo, Provincia Pichincha, Ecuador, 1200 m.

Distribution: Middle altitudes of western slopes in Provincia Pichincha, Ecuador.

64

ANOLIS
___

ANOLIS PSEUDOTIGRINUS Amaral

1933 Anolis pseudotigrinus Amaral, Mem. Inst. Butantan, 7 (1932): 60, figs. 13-14. Type-locality: Region of Rio Doce, Espirito Santo, Brazil.

Distribution: Known only from type locality.

ANOLIS PUNCTATUS Daudin

1802 Anolis punctatus Daudin, Hist. Nat. Rept., 4: 84, pl. 48, fig. 2. Type-locality: South America.

Distribution: Amazonian valley.

Content: Two subspecies.

Key to the subspecies

1. Ventral scales smooth------------punctatus
   Ventral scales keeled------------boulengeri

Clave de subespecies

1. Escamas ventrales lisas-----------punctatus
   Escamas ventrales quilladas------boulengeri

Anolis punctatus punctatus Daudin

1821 Anolis gracilis Wied, Reise nach Brasilien, 2: 131. Type-locality: San Pedro d'Alcantara, virgin forest, Brazil.
1821 Anolis viridis Wied, Reise nach Brasilien, 2: 132. Type-locality: Morro d'Arara, in virgin forest of Mucurí, Brazil.
1823 Anolis viridissimus Raddi, Mem. Math. Fis. Soc. Ital. Sci., 19: 60. Type-locality: Rio de Janeiro, Brazil.
1823 Anolis bullaris Raddi, Mem. Math. Fis. Soc. Ital. Sci., 19: 61. Type-locality: Rio de Janeiro, Brazil.
1823 Anolis violaceus Spix, Sp. Nov. Lac. Bras.: 15, pl. 17, fig. 2. Type-locality: Pará, Brazil.
1837 Anolis nasicus Duméril and Bibron, Erp. Gén., 4: 115. Type-locality: Rio de Janeiro, Brazil.
1925 Anolis catenifer Ahl, Zool. Anz., 62: 85. Type-locality: Brazil.
1933 Anolis transfasciatus Amaral, Mem. Inst. Butantan, 7 (1932): 60, figs. 15-16. Type-locality: Estado do Espirito Santo, Brazil.
1945 Anolis transfasciatus—Myers and Carvalho, Bol. Mus. Nac. Brasil, 43: 10, figs. 6-9.
1967 [Anolis punctatus punctatus]—Peters (by inference), Proc. U.S. Nat. Mus., 119: 18.

Distribution: Amazon region, Brazil, northeastern and eastern Venezuela.

Anolis punctatus boulengeri O'Shaughnessy

1881 Anolis boulengeri O'Shaughnessy, Proc. Zool. Soc. London, 1881: 242, pl. 24, fig. 1. Type-locality: Canelos, Ecuador.
1967 Anolis punctatus boulengeri—Peters, Proc. U.S. Nat. Mus., 119: 18.

Distribution: Amazonian Peru, Ecuador and Colombia; western Amazonas, Brazil.

ANOLIS PURPURESCENS Cope

1899 Anolis purpurescens Cope, Sci. Bull. Philadelphia Mus., 1: 7. Type-locality: Río Truando, Colombia.
1956 Anolis purpurescens—Taylor, Univ. Kansas Sci. Bull., 38: 75, fig. 18.

Distribution: Colombia to Costa Rica.

ANOLIS RADULINUS Cope

1862 Anolis (Gastrotropis) radulinus Cope, Proc. Acad. Nat. Sci. Phila., 1862: 180. Type-locality: Truando region, Colombia.
1885 Anolis radulinus—Boulenger, Cat. Liz. Brit. Mus., 2: 86.

Distribution: Known only from type material.

ANOLIS RHOMBIFER Boulenger

1894 Anolis rhombifer Boulenger, Proc. Zool. Soc. London, 1894: 728, pl. 48, fig. 2. Type-locality: Chontales, Nicaragua.

Distribution: Known only from type locality.

ANOLIS ROQUET (Bonnaterre)

1789 Lacerta roquet Bonnaterre, Tab. Encycl. Meth. Erpét.: 54, pl. 9, fig. 5. Type-locality: Martinique.
1923 Anolis roquet—Ruthven, Occ. Pap. Mus. Zool. Univ. Mich., 143: 6.

Distribution: Martinique, Grenada, Barbados, St. Lucia, Trinidad and Guyana.

Content: Two subspecies, of which one (roquet Lacépède) is extralimital.

Anolis roquet extremus Garman

1887 Anolis extremus Garman, Bull. Essex Inst., 19: 11. Type-locality: Barbados.
1964 Anolis roquet extremus—Underwood, Reptiles of the Eastern Caribbean, 1st Suppl.: i.

Distribution: Barbados, South Lucia and Georgetown, according to Underwood, loc. cit. A thriving population has been imported into Caracas, Venezuela.

ANOLIS SAGREI Duméril and Bibron

1837 Anolis Sagrei Duméril and Bibron, Erp. Gén., 4: 149. Type-locality: Cuba.
1873 Anolis Sagraei—Bocourt (emendation of sagrei Duméril and Bibron), Miss. Sci. Mex., Rept.: 80, pl. 15, fig. 14 (type).
1885 Anolis sagrae—Boulenger (emendation of sagrei Duméril and Bibron), Cat. Liz. Brit. Mus., 2: 40.

Distribution: Guatemala, Mexico, Cuba, Jamaica, Bahamas and southern Florida.

Content: Five subspecies, of which four (luteosignifer Garman, ordinatus Cope, sagrei Duméril and Bibron and stejnegeri Barbour) are extralimital.

Comment: Some authors regard the populations of this species living on the mainland as belonging to the nominate subspecies (Stuart, Duellman, Fugler), while others recognize a distinct mainland subspecies (Smith, Burger, Neill, Allen). We do not know who is correct, and we list the distinct subspecies here simply because it exists in the literature.

Anolis sagrei mayensis Smith and Burger

1950 Anolis sagrei mayensis Smith and Burger, Anal. Inst. Biol. Mexico, 20 (1949): 407. Type-locality: Panlao Island, in mouth of Río Mamantel, Laguna de Términos, Campeche, Mexico.
1965 Anolis sagrei mayensis—Neill, Bull. Florida St. Mus., 9: 91.

Distribution: Campeche, Mexico; British Honduras and Caribbean coast of Guatemala.

ANOLIS SALVINI Boulenger

1885 Anolis salvini Boulenger, Cat. Liz. Brit. Mus., 2: 75. Type-locality: Guatemala.

Distribution: Known only from type locality.

ANOLIS SCAPULARIS Boulenger

1908 Anolis scapularis Boulenger, Ann. Mag. Nat. Hist., (8) 1: 113. Type-locality: Provincia del Sara, eastern Bolivia, 600 m.

Distribution: Amazonian Bolivia and Peru.

ANOLIS SCYPHEUS Cope

1864 Anolis scypheus Cope, Proc. Acad. Nat. Sci. Phila., 1864: 172. Type-locality: None given;
        Caracas, Venezuela, according to Boulenger, below.
1885 Anolis scypheus—Boulenger, Cat. Liz. Brit. Mus., 2: 90.

   Distribution: Venezuela; Amazonian Colombia, Ecuador and Peru.

ANOLIS SERICEUS Hallowell

1856 Anolis sericeus Hallowell, Proc. Acad. Nat. Sci. Phila., 1856: 227. Type-locality: El Euceros
        de Jalapa, Veracruz, Mexico.
1859 Anolis sallaei Günther, Proc. Zool. Soc. London, 1859: 421. Type-locality: Central America;
        stated as Mexico by Boulenger, Cat. Liz. Brit. Mus., 1894, 80.
1864 Anolis heliactin Cope, Proc. Acad. Nat. Sci. Phila., 1864: 172. Type-locality: Mexico.
1873 Anolis Jacobi Bocourt, Miss. Sci. Mex., Rept.: 73, pl. 13, fig. 8 (specific name spelled Jabobi
        on p. 73, and Jacobis on p. 74, but intent is clear). Type-locality: Veracruz; restricted to
        Veracruz, Veracruz by Smith and Taylor, Bull. U.S. Nat. Mus., 199, 1950, 68.
1940 Anolis ustus wellbornae Ahl, Sitz. Ges. Naturforsch. Freunde Berlin, 1940: 246. Type-locality:
        El Salvador.

   Distribution: Low elevations in Mexico, from Tamaulipas on east and Isthmus of Tehuantepec on west,
   south to Nicaragua.

   Content: Two subspecies.

   Comment: When Duellman, Univ. Kansas Publ. Mus. Nat. Hist., 15, 1965, 596, put Anolis ustus in this
   species, he did not discuss the synonyms listed above. We therefore make no attempt to list them
   with the subspecies synonymies.

          Key to the subspecies   Clave de subespecies

1. Usually fewer than 56 dorsal scales counted   1. Usualmente menos de 56 escamas dorsales
   from axilla to groin; supraorbital semi-   desde la axila hasta la ingle; semicírcu-
   circles separated by two or three rows of   los supraorbitales separados por dos o
   scales----------------------------sericeus   tres hileras de escamas-----------sericeus
   Usually more than 57 dorsal scales; supra-   Usualmente más de 57 escamas dorsales,
   orbital semicircles in contact or separa-   semicírculos supraorbitales en contacto
   ted by one row of scales------------ustus   o separados por una hilera de escamas-----
                                                     ------------------------------------ustus

Anolis sericeus sericeus Hallowell

   1965 Anolis sericeus [sericeus]—Duellman, Univ. Kansas Publ. Mus. Nat. Hist., 15: 596.

      Distribution: Low elevations in Mexico, from Tamaulipas and Isthmus of Tehuantepec, to
      Nicaragua, excluding Yucatán Peninsula and British Honduras.

Anolis sericeus ustus Cope

   1864 Anolis ustus Cope, Proc. Acad. Nat. Sci. Phila., 1864: 172. Type-locality: Belize,
        British Honduras.
   1965 Anolis sericeus ustus—Duellman, Univ. Kansas Publ. Mus. Nat. Hist., 15: 596.

      Distribution: Yucatán Peninsula, Mexico; British Honduras.

ANOLIS SMINTHUS Dunn and Emlen

1932 Anolis sminthus Dunn and Emlen, Proc. Acad. Nat. Sci. Phila., 84: 26. Type-locality: San
        Juancito, Honduras, 6900 ft.

   Distribution: Known only from vicinity of type locality, 6400-7000 ft.

ANOLIS SOLITARIUS Ruthven

    1916 Anolis solitarius Ruthven, Occ. Pap. Mus. Zool. Univ. Mich., 32: 2, pl. 1. Type-locality: San Lorenzo, Santa Marta Mountains, Colombia, 5000 ft.

    Distribution: Santa Marta Mountains, Colombia.

ANOLIS SQUAMULATUS Peters

    1863 Anolis squamulatus Peters, Monats. Akad. Wiss. Berlin, 1863: 145. Type-locality: Puerto Cabello, Venezuela.
    1873 Anolis squamulatus—Bocourt, Miss. Sci. Mex., Rept.: pl. 14, fig. 21.
    1937 Anolis squamatulus—Dunn (in error for squamulatus Peters), Proc. New England Zool. Club, 16: 7.

    Distribution: Northern Venezuela, Panama.

ANOLIS STEINBACHI Griffin

    1917 Anolis steinbachi Griffin, Ann. Carnegie Mus., 11: 308, pl. 33, figs. 1-4. Type-locality: Provincia del Sara, Bolivia, 350 m.

    Distribution: Known only from type locality.

ANOLIS TIGRINUS Peters

    1863 Anolis tigrinus Peters, Monats. Akad. Wiss. Berlin, 1863: 143. Type-locality: Chile (in error).
    1874 Anolis tigrinus—Bocourt, Miss. Sci. Mex., Rept.: pl. 14, fig. 2.
    1885 Anolis tigrinus—Boulenger, Cat. Liz. Brit. Mus., 2: 55.

    Distribution: Recorded from Rancho Grande, Venezuela, by Test, Sexton, and Heatwole, Misc. Publ. Mus. Zool. Univ. Mich., 128, 1966, 13.

ANOLIS TOWNSENDI Stejneger

    1900 Anolis townsendi Stejneger, Bull. Mus. Comp. Zool., 36: 163. Type-locality: Cocos Island, Costa Rica.
    1956 Anolis townsendi—Taylor, Univ. Kansas Sci. Bull., 38: 123, fig. 33.

    Distribution: Cocos Island, Costa Rica.

ANOLIS TRACHYDERMA Cope

    1876 Anolis trachyderma Cope, Jour. Acad. Nat. Sci. Phila., (2) 8 (1875): 168. Type-locality: Nauta, Peru.
    1885 Anolis trachyderma—Boulenger, Cat. Liz. Brit. Mus., 2: 87.

    Distribution: Known only from type locality.

ANOLIS TRANSVERSALIS Duméril

    1851 Anolis Transversalis Duméril, Cat. Méth. Coll. Rept. Mus. Paris: 57. Type-locality: South America; actually Sarayacú, Peru, fide Williams and Vanzolini, Pap. Avuls. Depto. Zool. São Paulo, 19, 1966, 197.
    1873 Anolis transversalis—Bocourt, Miss. Sci. Mex., Rept.: pl. 14, fig. 3 (holotype).
    1880 Anolis buckleyi O'Shaughnessy, Proc. Zool. Soc. London, 1880: 492, pl. 49. Type-locality: Pallatanga, Ecuador.
    1966 Anolis transversalis—Williams and Vanzolini, Pap. Avuls. Depto. Zool. São Paulo, 19: 197.

    Distribution: Amazonian Venezuela, Ecuador, Peru and Colombia; Estado Amazonas, Brazil.

ANOLIS

ANOLIS TRINITATIS Reinhardt and Lütken

1863 Anolis Trinitatis Reinhardt and Lütken, Vidensk. Medd. Naturhist. Foren. Kjöbenhavn, 1862: 269. Type-locality: Trinidad.

Distribution: Trinidad, St. Vincent, St. Lucia.

Content: Three subspecies, of which two (vincentii Garman and procuratoris Underwood) are extralimital.

Anolis trinitatis trinitatis Reinhardt and Lutken

1959 Anolis trinitatis trinitatis—Underwood, Bull. Mus. Comp. Zool., 12: 212.

Distribution: Trinidad and St. Vincent Islands.

ANOLIS TROPIDOGASTER Hallowell

1857 Anolis (Draconura) tropidogaster Hallowell, Proc. Acad. Nat. Sci. Phila., 1857: 224. Type-locality: Colombia.
1869 Anolis stigmosus Bocourt, Bull. Nouv. Arch. Mus. Paris, 5: 43. Type-locality: Río Magdalena, Colombia.
1916 Anolis gaigei Ruthven, Occ. Pap. Mus. Zool. Mich., 32: 6, pl. 3. Type-locality: San Lorenzo, Santa Marta Mountains, Colombia.
1932 Anolis albi Barbour, Proc. New England Zool. Club, 12: 101. Type-locality: Andagoya, Departamento Chocó, Colombia.

Distribution: Western slopes of Colombia and Ecuador to Panama, Santa Marta area, Colombia and western Venezuela.

ANOLIS TROPIDOLEPIS Boulenger

1885 Anolis tropidolepis Boulenger, Cat. Liz. Brit. Mus., 2: 53. Type-locality: Irazu, Costa Rica.
1956 Anolis tropidolepis—Taylor, Univ. Kansas Sci. Bull., 38: 146, figs. 40-41.

Distribution: Provincias Cartago, San José and Heredia, Costa Rica, between 1600 and 2600 m.

ANOLIS TROPIDONOTUS Peters

1863 Anolis tropidonotus Peters, Monats. Akad. Wiss. Berlin, 1863: 135. Type-locality: Given as Huanusco, Veracruz, Mexico; Smith and Taylor, Bull. U.S. Nat. Mus., 199, 1950, 60, suggested this is in error for Huatusco, Veracruz.
1873 Anolis tropidonotus—Bocourt, Miss. Sci. Mex., Rept.: 103, pl. 16, fig. 30 (type).

Distribution: Lowlands of Pacific slope of Oaxaca and Caribbean slope of Veracruz, Mexico to Honduras and Nicaragua.

Content: Two subspecies, one of which (spilorhipis Álvarez del Toro and Smith) is extralimital.

Anolis tropidonotus tropidonotus Peters

1873 Anolis metallicus Bocourt, Ann. Sci. Nat. Zool. Paris, (5) 17, art. 2: 1. Type-locality: Mexico.
1906 Norops yucatanicus Barbour and Cole, Bull. Mus. Comp. Zool., 50: 149. Type-locality: Chichen Itzá, Yucatán, Mexico.
1956 A.[nolis] t.[ropidonotus] tropidonotus—Álvarez del Toro and Smith, Herpetologica, 12: 9.

Distribution: Lowlands of Caribbean slope from Veracruz, Mexico to Honduras and Nicaragua.

ANOLIS VENTRIMACULATUS Boulenger

1911 Anolis ventrimaculatus Boulenger, Ann. Mag. Nat. Hist., (8) 7: 20. Type-locality: Río San Juan, Chocó, Colombia.

Distribution: Known only from type locality.

ANOLIS WILLIAMSII Bocourt

1870 Anolis Williamsii Bocourt, Nouv. Arch. Mus. Paris, Bull., 6: 16. Type-locality: Bahia, Brazil.
1873 Anolis Williamsii—Bocourt, Miss. Sci. Mex., Rept.: pl. 13, fig. 9.

Distribution: Known only from type locality.

ANOLIS WOODI Dunn

1940 Anolis woodi Dunn, Proc. Acad. Nat. Sci. Phila., 92: 110. Type-locality: El Volcán, Chiriquí, Panama.

Distribution: Mountain areas from Panama to Costa Rica.

Content: Two subspecies.

Key to the subspecies	Clave de subespecies
1. Dewlap dark olive to blackish with magenta scales; 140 scales around middle of body; scales bordering occipital not enlarged------------------------------------attenuatus Dewlap pinkish orange on edge with whitish scales; 125 scales around middle of body; scales bordering occipital enlarged------------------------------------woodi	1. Saco gular oliva oscuro a negruzco con escamas magenta; 140 escamas al medio del cuerpo; escamas que bordean el occipital no agrandadas----------------------attenuatus Saco gular rosado naranja en el borde con escamas blancas; 125 escamas al medio del cuerpo; escamas que bordean el occipital bastante agrandadas------------------woodi

Anolis woodi woodi Dunn

1956 Anolis woodi woodi—Taylor, Univ. Kansas Sci. Bull., 38: 115, fig. 31.

Distribution: Chiriquí, Panama, to Puntarenas Province, Costa Rica on Pacific slope.

Anolis woodi attenuatus Taylor

1956 Anolis woodi attenuatus Taylor, Univ. Kansas Sci. Bull., 38: 118, fig. 32. Type-locality: Isla Bonita, southeastern slope of Volcán Póas, Costa Rica, 5500 ft.

Distribution: Known only from type locality.

ANOPS Bell

   1833 Anops Bell, Proc. Zool. Soc. London, 1833: 99. Type-species: Anops Kingii Bell.
   1867 Anopus Steindachner (in error for Anops Bell), Reise der Österreichischen Fregatten Novara,
        Zool., Rept.: 55.
   1916 Anopsibaena Stejneger (replacement name for Anops Bell), Proc. Biol. Soc. Washington, 29: 85.
        (Stejneger believed Anops Bell to be preoccupied by Anops Oken, Lehrb. Naturgesch., 3 (1),
        1815, 358, a name later shown to be unavailable.)

   Distribution: As for single species.

   Content: One species.

ANOPS KINGII Bell

   1833 Anops Kingii Bell, Proc. Zool. Soc. London, 1833: 99. Type-locality: "In America Australi".
   1964 Anops kingii—Gans and Rhodes, Amer. Mus. Novitates, 2186: 3.

   Distribution: Rio Grande do Sul, Brazil to Uruguay; inland to Córdoba and south to Río Negro, in
     Argentina.

ANOTOSAURA Amaral

1933 <u>Anotosaura</u> Amaral, Mem. Inst. Butantan, 7 (1932): 68. Type-species: <u>Anotosaura</u> <u>collaris</u> Amaral.

Distribution: As for single species.

Content: One species.

ANOTOSAURA COLLARIS Amaral

1933 <u>Anotosaura</u> <u>collaris</u> Amaral, Mem. Inst. Butantan, 7 (1932): 69, figs. 36-40. Type-locality:
Villa Nova (=Senhor do Bonfim), Bahia, Brazil.

Distribution: Bahia and Pernambuco, Brazil.

APTYCHOLAEMUS Boulenger

   1891 Aptycholaemus Boulenger, Ann. Mag. Nat. Hist., (6) 8: 85. Type-species: Aptycholaemus
        longicauda Boulenger.

   Distribution: As for single species.

   Content: One species.

APTYCHOLAEMUS LONGICAUDA Boulenger

   1891 Aptycholaemus longicauda Boulenger, Ann. Mag. Nat. Hist., (6) 8: 85. Type-locality: Riacho
        del Oro, Argentina.
   1895 Anisolepis argentinus Koslowsky, Rev. Mus. La Plata, 6: 419, pl. 2. Type-locality: Buenos Aires,
        Argentina (probably Province, not city, according to José Gallardo).

   Distribution: From Buenos Aires to Misiones, Argentina.

ARGALIA Gray

1846 Argalia Gray, Ann. Mag. Nat. Hist., (1) 18: 67. Type-species: Argalia marmorata Gray.

Distribution: As for only known species.

Content: One species.

ARGALIA MARMORATA Gray

1846 Argalia marmorata Gray, Ann. Mag. Nat. Hist., (1) 18: 67. Type-locality: Colombia.
1847 Argalia olivacea Gray, Proc. Zool. Soc. London, 1847: 97. Type-locality: Near Colonia de Tovar, Venezuela, 8000 ft.
1856 Gerrhonotus poecilochilus Lichtenstein, Nomenclator Reptilium et Amphibiorum Musei Zoologici Berolinensis: 16. Type-locality: Veragua, Puerto Cabello, Panama.

Distribution: Central Venezuela, northern Colombia, and probably southern Panama.

ARISTELLIGER Cope

1862 Aristelliger Cope, Proc. Acad. Nat. Sci. Phila., 1861: 496. Type-species: Aristelliger lar
       Cope.
1870 Idiodactylus Bocourt, Miss. Sci. Mex., Rept.: 41. Type-species: Idiodactylus georgeensis
       Bocourt.
1932 Aristelligella Noble and Klinger, Amer. Mus. Novitates, 549: 4. Type-species: Aristelligella
       barbouri Noble and Klinger.

   Distribution: West Indies and Peninsula of Yucatán, Mexico; British Honduras.

   Content: Four species, of which three (cochranae Grant, lar Cope, and praesignis Hallowell) are
      extralimital.

ARISTELLIGER GEORGEENSIS (Bocourt)

1870 Idiodactylus georgeensis Bocourt, Miss. Sci. Mex., Rept.: 41, pl. 10, figs. 1-1d. Type-locality:
       St. George Island, off Belize, British Honduras.
1885 Aristelliger irregularis Cope, Proc. Amer. Phil. Soc., 22: 387. Type-locality: Cozumel Island,
       Yucatán.
1950 Aristelliger georgeensis—Smith and Taylor, Bull. U.S. Nat. Mus., 199: 51.

   Distribution: Quintana Roo and Cozumel Island, Mexico, to British Honduras and neighboring islands.

ARTHROSAURA Boulenger

    1885 Arthrosaura Boulenger, Cat. Liz. Brit. Mus., 2: 389. Type-species: Cercosaura (Pantodactylus) reticulata O'Shaughnessy.

        Distribution: Brazil, Venezuela, Guyana, Surinam, French Guiana, eastern Ecuador.

        Content: Four species, according to most recent revision by Cunha, Atas Simp. Biota Amaz., 5, 1967, 141-170.

Key to the species	Clave de especies

1. Three supraoculars----------------------------2
   Four supraoculars----------------------kockii
	1. Tres supraoculares---------------------------2
	   Cuatro supraoculares--------------------kockii

2. Fewer than five preanal plates----------------3
   Six preanal plates------------------reticulata
	2. Menos que cinco placas preanales--------------3
	   Seis placas preanales---------------reticulata

3. Three preanals----------------------versteegii
   Four preanals-------------------------amapaense
	3. Tres placas preanales----------------versteegii
	   Cuatro placas preanales--------------amapaense

ARTHROSAURA AMAPAENSE Cunha

    1967 Arthrosaura amapaense Cunha, Atas Simp. Biota Amaz., 5: 151, fig. 1. Type-locality: Alta Rio Maracá, Território do Amapá, Brazil.

        Distribution: Known only from type locality.

ARTHROSAURA KOCKII (Van Lidth)

    1904 Prionodactylus Kockii Van Lidth, Notes Leyden Mus., 25: 91, pl. 7, figs. 3-4. Type-locality: Surinam; type received from Coppename Expedition.
    1923 Arthrosaura dorsistriata Müller, Zool. Anz., 57: 147. Type-locality: Peixeboi (Bragançabahn), Pará, Brazil.
    1928 Arthrosaura kocki—Brongersma, Zool. Anz., 78: 333.
    1967 Arthrosaura kockii—Cunha, Atas Simp. Biota Amaz., 5: 155, fig. 1.

        Distribution: Surinam to eastern Brazil.

ARTHROSAURA RETICULATA (O'Shaughnessy)

    1881 Cercosaura (Pantodactylus) reticulata O'Shaughnessy, Proc. Zool. Soc. London, 1881: 230, pl. 22, fig. 1. Type-locality: Canelos, Ecuador.
    1885 Arthrosaura reticulata—Boulenger, Cat. Liz. Brit. Mus., 2: 389.
    1931 Pantodactylus tyleri Burt and Burt, Bull. Amer. Mus. Nat. Hist., 61: 362, figs. 14-15. Type-locality: Summit of Mount Duida, Venezuela.
    1967 Arthrosaura reticulata—Cunha, Atas Simp. Biota Amaz., 5: 153, fig. 1.

        Distribution: Eastern Ecuador, western Amazonian Brazil, southern Venezuela.

ARTHROSAURA VERSTEEGII Van Lidth

    1904 Arthrosaura Versteegii Van Lidth, Notes Leyden Mus., 25: 89. Type-locality: Cottica Mountains, Surinam.
    1967 Arthrosaura versteegii—Cunha, Atas Simp. Biota Amaz., 5: 150, fig. 1.

        Distribution: Brazil, Surinam, Guyana, French Guiana.

ARTHROSEPS Boulenger

  1898 Arthroseps Boulenger, Proc. Zool. Soc. London, 1898: 920. Type-species: Arthroseps werneri Boulenger.

   Distribution: Brazil.

   Content: Two species.

Key to the species	Clave de especies
1. Prefrontal scales smaller than frontonasal; scales on caudal border of anus and proximal areas of thighs granular--------------werneri Prefrontal scales longer than frontonasal; scales on caudal border of anus and proximal areas of thighs not granular-------fluminensis	1. Escudos prefrontales notablemente menores que el frontonasal; borde caudal del ano y porcion proximal de los muslos granulosa-------werneri Escudos prefrontales mas largos que el fronto-nasal; borde caudal del ano y porcion proximal de los muslos no granulosa---------fluminensis

ARTHROSEPS FLUMINENSIS Amaral

  1933 Arthroseps fluminensis Amaral, Mem. Inst. Butantan, 7 (1932): 67, figs. 26-30. Type-locality: Serra de Macaé, Rio de Janeiro, Brazil.

   Distribution: Rio de Janeiro, Minas Gerais and Distrito Federal, Brazil.

ARTHROSEPS WERNERI Boulenger

  1898 Arthroseps werneri Boulenger, Proc. Zool. Soc. London, 1898: 921, pl. 55, fig. 3. Type-locality: Blumenau, Santa Catarina, Brazil.

   Distribution: São Paulo and Santa Catarina, Brazil.

AULURA Barbour

    1914 _Aulura_ Barbour, Proc. New England Zool. Club, 4: 96. Type-species: _Aulura anomala_ Barbour.

      Distribution: As for single known species.

      Content: One species.

AULURA ANOMALA Barbour

    1914 _Aulura anomala_ Barbour, Proc. New England Zool. Club, 4: 96. Type-locality: "Brazil".
    1948 _Aulura anomala_—Vanzolini, Bol. Mus. Paraense Emílio Goeldi, 10: 276, figs.

      Distribution: Estado do Pará and Estado de Maranhão, Brazil.

BACHIA Gray

1790 Chalcides Bonaterre (preoccupied by Chalcides Laurenti, 1768), Tabl. Encyclo. Meth., Erp.: 66.
   Type-species: Chalcides flavescens Bonnaterre.
1820 Chalcis Merrem (preoccupied by Chalcis Fabricius, 1787) Tent. Syst. Amph.: 75. Type-species:
   Chalcides tridactylus Daudin.
1820 Colobus Merrem (preoccupied by Colobus Illiger, 1811), Tent. Syst. Amph.: 76. Type-species:
   Seps monodactylus Daudin.
1826 Brachypus Fitzinger (preoccupied by Brachypus Swainson, 1824), Neue Classification der Reptilien:
   20: Type-species: Brachypus Cuvieri Fitzinger.
1843 Cophias Fitzinger (preoccupied by Cophias Merrem, 1820), Neue Classification der Reptilien: 20.
   Type-species: Chalcides d'Orbignyi Duméril and Bibron.
1844 Microdactylus (Tschudi MS) Agassiz (not of Fitzinger, 1843, preoccupied by Microdactylus Geoffroy,
   1809), Nomina Systematica Genera Reptilium: 28.
1845 Bachia Gray, Cat. Liz. Brit. Mus.: 58. Type-species: Chalcides Dorbignyi Duméril and Bibron.
1883 Herpetochalcis Boettger, Ber. Offenbach. Ver. Naturk., 1883: 150. Type-species: Chalcides
   heteropus Lichtenstein.
1885 Scolecosaurus Boulenger, Cat. Liz. Brit. Mus., 2: 416. Type-species: Brachypus cuvieri
   Fitzinger.
1896 Sesquipes Cope, Proc. Acad. Nat. Sci. Phila., 1896: 466. Type-species: Chalcides heteropus
   Lichtenstein.
1896 Heteroclonium Cope, Proc. Acad. Nat. Sci. Phila., 1896: 466. Type-species: Heteroclonium
   bicolor Cope.
1900 Anisoclonium Cope, Ann. Rep. U.S. Nat. Mus., 1898: 561. Type-species: None designated.
1935 Apatelus Amaral (preoccupied by Apatelus Mulsant and Rey, 1860), Mem. Inst. Butantan, 9: 249.
   Type-species: Apatelus bresslaui Amaral.

   Distribution: Northern South America east of Andes to southern Brazil and eastern Bolivia; Trinidad;
   Grenada, Grenadines.

   Content: Eighteen species.

Key to the species

1. Digits present on some or all feet------------2
   No digits on any foot-----------------bresslaui

2. Forefoot with more than two digits------------3
   Forefoot with two digits--------------barbouri

3. Prefrontal present-----------------------------4
   Prefrontal absent-----------------------------8

4. Three digits on hind foot---------------------5
   Four digits on hind foot----------------------6

5. Claws present--------------------------------17
   Claws absent--------------------------heteropa

6. Three supraoculars---------------------------7
   Two supraoculars-------------------scolecoides

7. Ventral scales squarish and juxtaposed-------18
   Ventral scales hexagonal and imbricate--------
   --panoplia

8. Interparietal present------------------------9
   Interparietal absent-------------------------13

9. Hind foot with fewer than three digits-------10
   Hind foot with three digits---------flavescens

Clave de especies

1. No todas las extremidades carecen de dedos----2
   Todas las extremidades carecen de dedos--------
   --bresslaui

2. Extremidades anteriores con más de dos dedos--3
   Extremidades anteriores con dos dedos--barbouri

3. Prefrontal presente----------------------------4
   Prefrontal ausente----------------------------8

4. Con tres dedos en las extremidades posteriores-
   --5
   Con cuatro dedos en las extremidades
   posteriores----------------------------------6

5. Uñas presentes-------------------------------17
   Uñas ausentes-------------------------heteropa

6. Tres supraoculares----------------------------7
   Dos supraoculares------------------scolecoides

7. Escamas ventrales cuadrangulares y yuxtapuestas
   --18
   Escamas ventrales hexagonales e imbricadas-----
   --panoplia

8. Interparietal presente------------------------9
   Interparietal ausente------------------------13

9. Extremidades posteriores con menos de tres
   dedos--10
   Extremidades posteriores con tres dedos--------
   --flavescens

10.Supraoculars absent------------------------11
   Supraoculars present-----------------------12

11.Forefoot with four digits---------------bicolor
   Forefoot with three digits-----------intermedia

12.Forefoot with four digits---------------lineata
   Forefoot with three digits-----------schlegelii

13.Supraoculars present-----------------------14
   Supraoculars absent------------------------15

14.One supraocular--------------------monodactylus
   Two supraoculars-----------------------parkeri

15.First and second pair of postmentals in contact
   on midline; second pair does not reach lip--16
   First pair of postmentals in contact on midline; second pair reaches lip------------talpa

16.Fourth supralabial in contact with parietal on
   each side-----------------------------peruana
   Fifth supralabial in contact with parietal on
   each side----------------------------dorbignyi

17.Two light lateral stripes-----------pallidiceps
   No light lateral stripes-----------------blairi

18.Prefrontals in contact on midline-------cuvieri
   Prefrontals separated by contact between internasal and frontal----------------------alleni

10.Supraoculares ausentes----------------------11
   Supraoculares presentes---------------------12

11.Extremidades anteriores con cuatro dedos-------
   -------------------------------------bicolor
   Extremidades anteriores con tres dedos---------
   -----------------------------------intermedia

12.Con cuatro dedos en la extremidades anteriores-
   --lineata
   Con tres dedos en las extremidades anteriores--
   ---------------------------------------schlegelii

13.Supraoculares presentes---------------------14
   Supraoculares ausentes----------------------15

14.Una supraocular--------------------monodactylus
   Dos supraoculares----------------------parkeri

15.Dos pares de posmentales medialmente en contacto, el segundo par de posmentales no llega
   al borde oral------------------------------16
   Primer par de posmentales medialmente en contacto, el segundo par de posmentales llega al
   borde oral----------------------------talpa

16.Cuarto supralabial en contacto con el parietal
   en cada lado-------------------------peruana
   Quinto supralabial en contacto con el parietal
   en cada lado-----------------------dorbignyi

17.Con dos cintas laterales claras-----pallidiceps
   Sin cintas laterales claras-------------blairi

18.Prefrontales medialmente en contacto----cuvieri
   Prefrontales separada por un contacto entre
   internasal y frontal-------------------alleni

BACHIA ALLENI (Barbour)

1914 Scolecosa[u]rus alleni Barbour, Mem. Mus. Comp. Zool., 44: 315. Type-locality: St. George's,
     Grenada.
1961 [Bachia] alleni—Vanzolini, Pap. Avul. Depto. Zool. São Paulo, 14: 204.

   Distribution: Trinidad and adjacent mainland in Venezuela; Grenadines, Grenada, and Tobago.

   Content: Two subspecies, one of which (alleni Barbour) is extralimital.

   Bachia alleni trinitatis (Barbour)

   1914 Scolecosaurus trinitatis Barbour, Mem. Mus. Comp. Zool., 44: 316. Type-locality: Caparo,
        Trinidad.
   1961 Scolecosaurus trinitatis—Vanzolini, Pap. Avul. Depto. Zool. São Paulo, 14: 183, figs.
        1-5.
   1965 Bachia alleni trinitatis—Thomas, Proc. Biol. Soc. Washington, 78: 152.

      Distribution: Trinidad and adjacent mainland in Venezuela.

BACHIA BARBOURI Burt and Burt

   1931 Bachia barbouri Burt and Burt, Bull. Amer. Mus. Nat. Hist., 61: 318, figs. 5-8. Type-locality:
        Perico, Cajamarca, Peru.

      Distribution: Northwestern Peru.

BACHIA BICOLOR (Cope)

1896 Heteroclonium bicolor Cope, Proc. Acad. Nat. Sci. Phila., 1896: 466. Type-locality: Bogotá, Colombia.
1922 Bachia bicolor—Ruthven, Misc. Publ. Mus. Zool. Univ. Mich., 8: 63.

    Distribution: Sierra de Perija, Venezuela; eastern Colombia.

BACHIA BLAIRI (Dunn), new combination

1940 Scolecosaurus blairi Dunn, Proc. Acad. Nat. Sci. Phila., 92: 115. Type-locality: Puerto Armuelles, Chiriquí, Panama.

    Distribution: Known only from type locality.

BACHIA BRESSLAUI (Amaral)

1935 Apatelus bresslaui Amaral, Mem. Inst. Butantan, 9: 250, figs. 1-3. Type-locality: Estado de São Paulo, Brazil.
1961 Bachia bresslaui—Vanzolini, Pap. Avul. Depto. Zool. São Paulo, 14: 200.

    Distribution: Originally thought to be Estado de São Paulo, Brazil, but Vanzolini, Pap. Avul. Depto. Zool. São Paulo, 19, 1966, 189, described a specimen from Mato Grosso and expressed doubt about the validity of type locality.

BACHIA CUVIERI (Fitzinger)

1826 Brachypus cuvieri Fitzinger, Neue Classification der Reptilien: 50. Type-locality: Unknown.
1885 Scolecosaurus cuvieri—Boulenger, Cat. Liz. Brit. Mus., 2: 416.
1961 [Bachia] cuvieri—Vanzolini, Pap. Avul. Depto. Zool. São Paulo, 14: 204.

    Distribution: Possibly Brazil; still not known from any specific locality. Barbour, Copeia, 1933, 76, assigned to this species a specimen that may have come from Brazil.

BACHIA DORBIGNYI (Duméril and Bibron)

1839 Chalcides Dorbignyi Duméril and Bibron, Erp. Gén., 5: 462. Type-locality: Santa Cruz, "Chile"; corrected by Vanzolini, Pap. Avul. Depto. Zool. São Paulo, 14, 1961, 198, to Santa Cruz de la Sierra, Bolivia.
1917 Bachia dorbignyi—Griffin, Ann. Carnegie Mus., 11: 312.
1961 Bachia dorbignyi—Vanzolini, Pap. Avul. Depto. Zool. São Paulo, 14: 198, figs. 4-7.

    Distribution: Eastern Bolivia; Mato Grosso, Brazil.

BACHIA FLAVESCENS (Bonnaterre)

1789 Chalcides flavescens Bonnaterre, Tabl. Encyclo. Meth., Erp.: 67, pl. 12, fig. 4. Type-locality: Unknown.
1801 Chamaesaura Cophias Schneider, Historiae Amphibiorum, 2: 209. Type-locality: None given.
1802 Chalcides tridactylus Daudin, Hist. Nat. Rept., 4: 367, pl. 58, fig. 3. Type-locality: Unknown.
1922 B.[achia] flavescens—Ruthven, Misc. Publ. Mus. Zool. Univ. Mich., 8: 63.

    Distribution: Northeastern South America to eastern Colombia.

    Comment: The trivial names flavescens, cophias, and tridactylus were all based on the figure on plate 32, of Lacépède, Hist. Nat. Quad. Ovip., 1789, with two of the authors reproducing the figure, and the third citing it in his text. All have the same "Iconotype", and are strict synonyms.

BACHIA HETEROPA (Lichtenstein)

1856 Chalcides heteropus Lichtenstein, Nomenclator Musei Zoologici Berolinensis: 17. Type-locality: La Guaira, Venezuela.
1925 B.[achia] heteropus—Ruthven, Proc. Boston Soc. Nat. Hist., 38: 105.

    Distribution: Venezuela.

<u>BACHIA</u> <u>INTERMEDIA</u> Noble

1921 <u>Bachia</u> <u>intermedia</u> Noble, Ann. New York Acad. Sci., 29: 142. Type-locality: Perico, Departamento Cajamarca, Peru.

Distribution: Northwestern Peru.

<u>BACHIA</u> <u>LINEATA</u> Boulenger

1903 <u>Bachia</u> <u>lineata</u> Boulenger, Ann. Mag. Nat. Hist., (7) 12: 432. Type-locality: Duaca, Estado Falcón, Venezuela.

Distribution: Venezuela.

Content: Two subspecies.

Key to the subspecies	Clave de subespecies
1. More than 44 scales between occiput and thigh; seven longitudinal rows of scales in front of enlarged pectorals-----<u>lineata</u> Fewer than 42 scales between occiput and thigh; five longitudinal rows of scales in front of enlarged pectorals----<u>marcelae</u>	1. Más de 44 filas de escamas entre occipucio y muslos; siete filas longitudinales de escamas frente a las pectorales agrandadas ----------------------------------<u>lineata</u> Menos de 44 filas de escamas entre occipucio y muslos; cinco filas longitudinales de escamas frente a las pectorales agrandadas----------------------<u>marcelae</u>

<u>Bachia</u> <u>lineata</u> <u>lineata</u> Boulenger

1929 <u>Bachia</u> <u>anomala</u> Roux, Verh. Naturforsch. Ges. Basel, 40 (2): 31. Type-locality: El Mene, Distrito Acosta, Provincia Falcón, Venezuela.
1969 <u>Bachia</u> <u>lineata</u> <u>lineata</u>—Donoso-Barros, Carib. Jour. Sci., 8 (1968): 117.

Distribution: Distrito Federal; Estados Yaracuy, Falcón, and Sucre, Venezuela.

<u>Bachia</u> <u>lineata</u> <u>marcelae</u> Donoso-Barros and Garrido

1964 <u>Bachia</u> <u>marcelae</u> Donoso-Barros and Garrido, Publ. Ocas. Mus. Cien. Nat. Caracas, Zool., 8: 3, figs. 1-8. Type-locality: Bosque La Luz, Barinas, Venezuela.
1969 <u>Bachia</u> <u>lineata</u> <u>marcelae</u>—Donoso-Barros, Carib. Jour. Sci., 8 (1968): 118.

Distribution: In isolated patches of tropical forest within llanos of southern part of Estado Barinas, Venezuela.

<u>BACHIA</u> <u>MONODACTYLUS</u> (Daudin)

1802 <u>Chalcides</u> <u>monodactylus</u> Daudin, Hist. Nat. Rept., 4: 370. Type-locality: None given.
1820 <u>Colobus</u> <u>Daudini</u> Merrem (replacement name for <u>Chalcides</u> <u>monodactylus</u> Daudin), Tent. Syst. Amphib.: 76.
1872 <u>Chalcides</u> <u>trilineatus</u> Peters, Monats. Akad. Wiss. Berlin, 1872: 775. Type-locality: South America.

Distribution: Guyana; Amazonian Basin of Brazil.

Comment: This synonymy and the use of this name follows Vanzolini, Pap. Avul. Depto. Zool. São Paulo, 14, 1961, 195, who used <u>Bachia</u> <u>cophias</u> Schneider for the taxon (see comment under <u>Bachia</u> <u>flavescens</u>). Since <u>cophias</u> is not available, the next most senior synonym is <u>monodactylus</u> Daudin, according to Vanzolini, and this name is used without evaluation by us as to its appropriateness.

<u>BACHIA</u> <u>PALLIDICEPS</u> (Cope)

1862 <u>Brachypus</u> <u>pallidiceps</u> Cope, Proc. Acad. Nat. Sci. Phila., 1862: 356. Type-locality: Río Truando region, Colombia.
1961 [<u>Bachia</u>] <u>pallidiceps</u>—Vanzolini, Pap. Avul. Depto. Zool. São Paulo, 14: 204.

Distribution: Lowlands of northwestern Colombia; Darién, Panama.

BACHIA

BACHIA PANOPLIA Thomas

   1965 Bachia panoplia Thomas, Herpetologica, 21: 18. Type-locality: Manaus, Amazonas, Brazil.

   Distribution: Known only from type locality.

BACHIA PARKERI Ruthven

   1925 Bachia parkeri Ruthven, Proc. Boston Soc. Nat. Hist., 38: 103, figs. 4-6. Type-locality: Chenapowu River, on the Upper Potaro River, Guyana.

   Distribution: Northeastern South America to eastern Colombia.

BACHIA PERUANA (Werner)

   1900 Cophias peruanus Werner, Abh. Ber. Zool. Anthr.-Ethn. Mus. Dresden, 9 (2): 5, 3 figs. Type-locality: Chanchamayo, Peru.
   1925 B.[achia] peruana Ruthven, Proc. Boston Soc. Nat. Hist., 38: 105.

   Distribution: Eastern Peru.

BACHIA SCHLEGELI (Duméril and Bibron)

   1839 Chalcides Schlegeli Duméril and Bibron, Erp. Gén., 5: 457. Type-locality: East Indies.
   1887 Cophias boettgeri Boulenger, Cat. Liz. Brit. Mus., 3: 508. Type-locality: Central America?
   1946 Bachia schlegeli—Brongersma, Zool. Meded., 26: 237, figs. 1a-e.

   Distribution: Guyana.

BACHIA SCOLECOIDES Vanzolini

   1961 Bachia scolecoides Vanzolini, Pap. Avul. Depto. Zool. São Paulo, 14: 202. Type-locality: Rio Teles Pires, Mato Grosso, Brazil.

   Distribution: Known only from type locality.

BACHIA TALPA Ruthven

   1925 Bachia talpa Ruthven, Proc. Boston Soc. Nat. Hist., 38: 101, figs. 1-3. Type-locality: Valle Dupar, Sierra de Santa Marta, Colombia.

   Distribution: Sierra de Santa Marta and Caquetá, Colombia.

BASILISCUS Laurenti

1768 Basiliscus Laurenti, Synopsin Reptilium: 50. Type-species: Basiliscus americanus Laurenti.
1828 Corythaeolus Kaup, Isis von Oken, 21: 1147. Type-species: Basiliscus vittatus Wiegmann.
1830 Oedicoryphus Wagler, Nat. Syst. Amph.: 148. Type-species: Basiliscus vittatus Wiegmann.
1845 Thysanodactylus Gray, Cat. Liz. Brit. Mus.: 193. Type-species: Ophryoessa bilineata Gray.
1852 Lophosaura Gray, Ann. Mag. Nat. Hist., (2) 10: 438. Type-species: Lophosaura Goodridgii Gray.
1852 Ptenosaura Gray, Ann. Mag. Nat. Hist., (2) 10: 438. Type-species: Ptenosaura Seemanni Gray.
1852 Cristasaura Gray, Ann. Mag. Nat. Hist., (2) 10: 439. Type-species: Cristasaura mitrella Gray.
1854 Craneosaura Gray, in Richardson, Zoology of Voyage of H.M.S. Herald, 1845-51: 148. Type-species: Ptenosaura Seemanni Gray.
1860 Daconura Hallowell, Proc. Acad. Nat. Sci. Phila., 1860: 482. Type-species: Daconura bivittata Hallowell.
1862 Paraloma Cope, Proc. Acad. Nat. Sci. Phila., 1862: 181. Type-species: Daconura bivittata Hallowell.
1893 Dactylocalotes Werner, Zool. Anz., 16: 361. Type-species: Dactylocalotes elisa Werner.

Distribution: Jalisco in western Mexico and Tamaulipas in eastern Mexico through Central America to Pacific Ecuador, and to Venezuela and perhaps Peru east of Andes.

Content: Four species.

Key to the species

1. Abdominal scales smooth----------------------2
   Abdominal scales keeled----------------vittatus

2. Vertebral region with irregularly distributed scales showing no evidence of regular spacing-
   --3
   Vertebral region with very large, raised, regularly spaced scales, separated by several very small scales-----------------------galeritus

3. Color primarily green, also including some blue
   -----------------------------------plumifrons
   Color primarily brown, no green or blue--------
   --------------------------------------basiliscus

Clave de especies

1. Escamas abdominales lisas---------------------2
   Escamas abdominales carenadas----------vittatus

2. Región vertebral con escamas distribuidas irregularmente sin trazas de espaciamiento regular---------------------------------------3
   Región vertebral con escamas muy grandes, levantadas, espaciadas regularmente, separadas por varias escamas muy pequeñas------galeritus

3. Color principalmente verde que también incluye algo de azul-----------------------plumifrons
   Color principalmente pardo, sin verde o azul---
   --------------------------------------basiliscus

BASILISCUS BASILISCUS (Linnaeus)

1758 Lacerta basiliscus Linnaeus, Systema Naturae, Ed. 10: 206. Type-locality: "America australi."
1830 [Basiliscus] basiliscus—Wagler, Nat. Syst. Amphib.: 148.

Distribution: Northwestern Ecuador, Pacific slopes of Colombia; Venezuela; southern Central America.

Content: Two subspecies.

Key to the subspecies

1. Head crest single, not erect but pendent on side of neck, ribbon-like, narrowing rapidly from base to form narrow lobe-----
   --------------------------------barbouri
   Head crest with dorsal rounded, erect lobe and second projection on posterior margin, not pendent, not narrowed-------basiliscus

Clave de subespecies

1. Cresta cefálica única, no erguida sino colgante a los lados del cuello, acintada, enangostándose rápidamente desde la base hasta formar un lóbulo angosto----barbouri
   Cresta cefálica con lóbulo dorsal redondeado, erguido y segunda proyección en margen posterior, no pendiente, no enangostada-----------------------basiliscus

Basiliscus basiliscus basiliscus (Linnaeus)

1768 Basiliscus americanus Laurenti, Synopsin Reptilium: 50. Type-locality: South America.
1802 Basiliscus mitratus Daudin (substitute name for basiliscus Linnaeus), Hist. Nat. Rept.,
    3: 310, pl. 42.
1839 Ophryoessa bilineata Gray, Zoology Beechey's Voyage, Reptiles: 94. Type-locality:
    Fernando de Noronha; questioned by Boulenger, Cat. Liz. Brit. Mus., 2, 1885, 108.
1852 Lophosaura Goodridgii Gray, Ann. Mag. Nat. Hist., (2) 10: 438. Type-locality: "Quibo".
1876 Basiliscus guttulatus Cope, Jour. Acad. Nat. Sci. Phila., (2) 8 (1875): 156. Type-
    locality: Camp at Buhio Soldado, Panama.
1962 B[asiliscus] basiliscus [basiliscus]—Maturana, Bull. Mus. Comp. Zool., 128: 26.

    Distribution: Southern Central America to northwestern Colombia and Ecuador.

Basiliscus basiliscus barbouri Ruthven

1914 Basiliscus barbouri Ruthven, Proc. Biol. Soc. Washington, 27: 9, pl. 1, figs. 1-2. Type-
    locality: Gaira River at Minca, San Lorenzo, Santa Marta Mountains, Colombia, 2200 ft.
1962 Basiliscus basiliscus barbouri—Maturana, Bull. Mus. Comp. Zool., 128: 26.

    Distribution: Western Venezuela and Santa Marta, Colombia.

BASILISCUS GALERITUS Duméril

1851 Basiliscus Galeritus Duméril, Cat. Méth. Coll. Rept. Mus. Paris: 61. Type-locality:
    "N.-Grenade", which is Colombia.
1852 Ptenosaura Seemanni Gray, Ann. Mag. Nat. Hist., (2) 10: 438. Type-locality: "Quibo", on west
    coast of America.

  Distribution: Pacific slopes of Colombia and Ecuador to Panama and Costa Rica.

BASILISCUS PLUMIFRONS Cope

1876 Basiliscus plumifrons Cope, Jour. Acad. Nat. Sci. Phila., (2) 8 (1875): 125, pl. 25, figs. 1-1a.
    Type-locality: Sipurio, Costa Rica.

  Distribution: Panama, Costa Rica, and Nicaragua.

BASILISCUS VITTATUS Wiegmann

1828 Basiliscus vittatus Wiegmann, Isis von Oken, 21: 373. Type-locality: Mexico, restricted by
    Smith and Taylor, Bull. U.S. Nat. Mus., 199, 1950, 72, to Veracruz, Veracruz.
1852 Cristasaura mitrella Gray, Ann. Mag. Nat. Hist., (2) 10: 439. Type-locality: Honduras.
1860 Daconura bivittata Hallowell, Proc. Acad. Nat. Sci. Phila., 1860: 482. Type-locality: Nicaragua;
    restricted to Greytown, Nicaragua, by Smith and Taylor, Univ. Kansas Sci. Bull., 33, 1950, 320.
1862 Basiliscus (Cristasaura) nuchalis Cope, Proc. Acad. Nat. Sci. Phila., 1862: 181. Type-locality:
    Near Greytown, Nicaragua.
1893 Dactylocalotes elisa Werner, Zool. Anz., 16: 361. Type-locality: Sumatra.

  Distribution: Jalisco and Tamaulipas, Mexico through Central America on both coasts as far as
  Colombia. Recorded from Ecuador by Boulenger, Cat. Liz. Brit. Mus., 2, 1885, 110.

BOGERTIA Loveridge

    1941 Bogertia Loveridge, Proc. Biol. Soc. Washington, 54: 195. Type-species: Bogertia lutzae
        Loveridge.

    Distribution: As for single known species.

    Content: One species.

BOGERTIA LUTZAE Loveridge

    1941 Bogertia lutzae Loveridge, Proc. Biol. Soc. Washington, 54: 196. Type-locality: Near Pituba,
        São Salvador, Bahia, Brazil.
    1968 Bogertia lutzae—Vanzolini, Arq. Zool. São Paulo, 17: 55.

    Distribution: Bahia and Pernambuco, Brazil.

BRIBA Amaral

   1935 Briba Amaral, Mem. Inst. Butantan, 9: 253.   Type-species: Briba brasiliana Amaral.

   Distribution: As for single known species.

   Content: One species.

BRIBA BRASILIANA Amaral

   1935 Briba brasiliana Amaral, Mem. Inst. Butantan, 9: 253.   Type-locality: Rio Pandeiros, Minas
        Gerais, Brazil.
   1968 Briba brasiliana—Vanzolini, Arq. Zool. São Paulo, 17: 56.

   Distribution: Estado de Minas Gerais and Estado da Bahia, Brazil.

BRONIA Gray

    1865 Bronia Gray, Proc. Zool. Soc. London, 1865: 448. Type-species: Bronia brasiliana Gray.

    Distribution: As for single known species.

    Content: One species.

BRONIA BRASILIANA Gray

    1865 Bronia brasiliana Gray, Proc. Zool. Soc. London, 1865: 448. Type-locality: Santarem, Rio Amazonas, Brazil.

    Distribution: Lower Amazon, Santarem to Belem, Brazil.

CALLOPISTES Gravenhorst

1838 Callopistes Gravenhorst, Nova Acta Acad. Caes. Leop. Carol., 18: 743. Type-species: Callopistes
maculatus Gravenhorst.
1839 Aporomera Duméril and Bibron, Erp. Gén., 5: 69. Type-species: Aporomera ornata Duméril and
Bibron.
1877 Tejovaranus Steindachner, Denkschr. Math.-Naturwiss. Cl. Akad. Wiss. Wien, 38: 93. Type-species:
Tejovaranus Branickii Steindachner.

Distribution: Ecuador, Peru and Chile.

Content: Two species.

Key to the species

1. Azygous frontal present; frontoparietal and
interparietal conspicuous, clearly differen-
tiated--------------------------------maculatus
Azygous frontal absent; frontoparietal and
interparietal replaced by small scales--------
--------------------------------flavipunctatus

Clave de especies

1. Azygos frontal característico; con frontoparietal e interparietal diferenciados--------
---maculatus
No hay azygos frontal; frontoparietal e interparietal indiferenciados y reemplazados por
escamas pequeñas----------------flavipunctatus

CALLOPISTES FLAVIPUNCTATUS (Duméril and Bibron)

1839 Aporomera flavipunctata Duméril and Bibron, Erp. Gén., 5: 72, pl. 51. Type-locality: Tropical
South America.
1877 Tejovaranus Branickii Steindachner, Denkschr. Math.-Naturwiss. Cl. Akad. Wiss. Wien, 38: 93, pl.
1, figs. a-d. Type-locality: Tumbez, Peru.
1845 Callopistes flavipunctatus—Gray, Cat. Liz. Brit. Mus.: 17.

Distribution: Interandean valleys of Peru and southern Ecuador.

CALLOPISTES MACULATUS Gravenhorst

1838 Callopistes maculatus Gravenhorst, Nova Acta Acad. Caes. Leop. Carol., 18: 744, pl. 55, fig. 1.
Type-locality: At foot of Cordillera, Chile.

Distribution: Southern Antofagasta to Maule Province, Chile.

Content: Three subspecies.

Key to the subspecies

1. Rows of ocelli present only on posterior
half of dorsum--------------------------2
Four rows of ocelli from neck to base of
tail-------------------------------maculatus

2. Ground color milky brown with lineate and
irregular dorsal pattern-------atacamensis
Ground color not milky brown, with dorsal
pattern of small paravertebral black spots
lacking white borders---------------manni

Clave de subespecies

1. Hileras de manchas dorsales extendidad
desde la mitad del dorso a la cola-------2
Cuatro hileras de manchas oceladas desde el
cuello a la cola-----------------maculatus

2. Color castaño lechoso con dibujos lineales
e irregulares en la mitad del dorso-------
--------------------------------atacamensis
Líneas de manchas paravertebrales pequeñas
no circundadas de blanco------------manni

Callopistes maculatus maculatus Gravenhorst

1839 Aporomera ornata Duméril and Bibron, Erp. Gén., 5: 76. Type-locality: Chile.
1847 Ameiva oculata D'Orbigny and Bibron, Voyage dans l'Amerique Meridionale, Rept.: 9, pl. 5,
figs. 6-10. Type-locality: Valparaiso, Chile.
1848 Aporomera ocellata Guichenot, in Gay, Hist. Fis. Pol. Chile, Zool., 2: 61, pl. 3, fig. 2.
Type-locality: Santiago, Chile.
1960 Callopistes maculatus maculatus—Donoso-Barros, Rev. Chilena Hist. Nat., 55: 43, pl. 1.

Distribution: Cauquenes to Copiapo, Chile.

Callopistes maculatus atacamensis Donoso-Barros

  1960 Callopistes maculatus atacamensis Donoso-Barros, Rev. Chilena Hist. Nat., 55: 49, pl. 2.
       Type-locality: Rocky coast of Caldera, Chile.

   Distribution: Coastal area near beach, Copiapo Province, Chile.

Callopistes maculatus manni Donoso-Barros

  1960 Callopistes maculatus manni Donoso-Barros, Rev. Chilena Hist. Nat., 55: 47, pl. 2. Type-
       locality: Quebradas de Paposo, southern Antofagasta, Chile.

   Distribution: Southern Antofagasta, Chile.

CELESTUS Gray

1839 Celestus Gray, Ann. Mag. Nat. Hist., (1) 2: 288. Type-species: Celestus striatus Gray.
1839 Microlepis Gray, Ann. Mag. Nat. Hist., (1) 2: 334. Type-species: Microlepis undulata Gray.
1845 Oneyda Gray, Cat. Liz. Brit. Mus.: 118. Type-species: Diploglossus Owenii Duméril and Bibron.
1861 Siderolamprus Cope, Proc. Acad. Nat. Sci. Phila., 1860: 368. Type-species: Siderolamprus
        enneagrammus Cope.
1862 Panolopus Cope, Proc. Acad. Nat. Sci. Phila., 1861: 494. Type-species: Panolopus costatus Cope.

Distribution: Mexico to Costa Rica; Antilles.

Content: Twenty species, only four of which occur within the limits set for this work.

Key to the species   Clave de especies

1. No lateral prefrontals, single median   1. Sin prefrontales laterales, prefrontal mediana
   prefrontal in contact with supraocular scales   única en contacto con escamas supraoculares y
   and frontal--------------------------------2   frontal-------------------------------------2
   Three prefrontal scales, including median and   Tres escamas prefrontales, una mediana y dos
   two lateral prefrontals, all in contact with   laterales, todas en contacto con frontal;
   frontal; green above, lighter on sides-------   verde arriba más claro a los lados-----------
   -----------------------------------montanus   -----------------------------------montanus

2. Prefrontal and frontonasal not fused; caudal   2. Prefrontal y frontonasal no fusionado; escamas
   scales not keeled--------------------------3   caudales no quilladas------------------------3
   Prefrontal and frontonasal fused; caudal   Prefrontal y frontonasal fusionado; escamas
   scales strongly keeled----------cyanochloris   caudales fuertemente quilladas----cyanochloris

3. Median prefrontal wider than long and in con-   3. Prefrontal mediano contacta con dos supra-
   tact with two supraoculars; no lateral pre-   oculares, más ancho que largo; no hay prefrontals; two dorsolateral light stripes------   frontales laterales; dos cintas claras dorso-
   -------------------------------atitlanensis   laterales-----------------------atitlanensis
   Median prefrontal as long as wide and in con-   Prefrontal mediano contacta sólo con el supra-
   tact only with anterior supraocular; lateral   ocular anterior, tan largo como ancho; pre-
   prefrontals usually present; dorsolateral   frontales laterales usualmente presentes;
   light stripe absent-----------------rozellae   cintas claras dorsolaterales ausentes-rozellae

CELESTUS ATITLANENSIS Smith

1950 Celestus atitlanensis Smith, in Smith and Taylor, Bull. U.S. Nat. Mus., 199: 195. Type-locality:
        Atitlán, Guatemala.

Distribution: Known only from type locality.

CELESTUS CYANOCHLORIS Cope

1894 Celestus cyanochloris Cope, Proc. Acad. Nat. Sci. Phila., 1894: 200. Type-locality: Volcán
        Irazú, Costa Rica.
1956 Celestus chrysochlorus Taylor (lapsus for cyanochloris), Univ. Kansas Sci. Bull., 38: 205.

Distribution: Mountains of Heredia Province, central Costa Rica.

CELESTUS MONTANUS Schmidt

1933 Celestus montanus Schmidt, Zool. Ser. Field Mus. Nat. Hist., 20: 21. Type-locality: Sierra de
        Merendon, west of San Pedro, Honduras, 4500 ft.

Distribution: Known only from type locality.

CELESTUS ROZELLAE Smith

1942 Celestus rozellae Smith, Proc. U.S. Nat. Mus., 92: 372. Type-locality: Palenque, Chiapas,
        Mexico.

Distribution: Isthmus of Tehuantepec, Mexico to El Petén, Guatemala, and British Honduras.

CERCOSAURA Wagler

1830 _Cercosaura_ Wagler, Nat. Syst. Amph.: 158. Type-species: _Cercosaura ocellata_ Wagler.
1845 _Emminia_ Gray, Cat. Liz. Brit. Mus.: 24. Type-species: _Emminia olivacea_ Gray.

Distribution: As for single species.

Content: One species, according to most recent revision, by Ruibal, Bull. Mus. Comp. Zool., 106, 1952.

CERCOSAURA OCELLATA Wagler

1830 _Cercosaura ocellata_ Wagler, Nat. Syst. Amph.: 158. Type-locality: "Asia?"

Distribution: Tropical South America.

Content: Three subspecies.

Key to the subspecies	Clave de subespecies

1. Loreal large, undivided------------------2
   Loreal horizontally divided--------_bassleri_
	1. Loreal grande, no dividido----------------2
	   Loreal horizontalmente dividido-----_bassleri_

2. Midbody scale count 25-31----------_ocellata_
   Midbody scale count 22-24----------_petersi_
	2. Escamas al medio del cuerpo 25-31--_ocellata_
	   Escamas al medio del cuerpo 22-24---_petersi_

Cercosaura ocellata ocellata Wagler

1845 _Emminia olivacea_ Gray, Cat. Liz. Brit. Mus.: 24. Type-locality: Pernambuco, Brazil.
1862 _Cercosaura humilis_ Peters, Abh. Akad. Wiss. Berlin, 1862: 180. Type-locality: Brazil.
1952 _Cercosaura ocellata ocellata_—Ruibal, Bull. Mus. Comp. Zool., 106: 494.

Distribution: Pará and Bahia, northern Brazil; Guyana.

Cercosaura ocellata bassleri Ruibal

1952 _Cercosaura ocellata bassleri_ Ruibal, Bull. Mus. Comp. Zool., 106: 499. Type-locality: Río Perené, Perené, Peru.

Distribution: Amazonian drainage of Peru; Amazonas, Brazil.

Cercosaura ocellata petersi Ruibal

1952 _Cercosaura ocellata petersi_ Ruibal, Bull. Mus. Comp. Zool., 106: 497. Type-locality: Santa Maria, Estado do Rio Grande do Sul, Brazil.

Distribution: Estado do Rio Grande do Sul and Estado de São Paulo, Brazil; Provincia Sara, Bolivia.

CNEMIDOPHORUS Wagler

1830 <u>Cnemidophorus</u> Wagler, Nat. Syst. Amph.: 154. Type-species: <u>Seps</u> <u>murinus</u> Laurenti.
1843 <u>Aspidoscelis</u> Fitzinger, Systema Reptilium: 20. Type-species: <u>Lacerta</u> <u>sexlineata</u> Linnaeus.
1869 <u>Verticaria</u> Cope, Proc. Amer. Phil. Soc., 11: 158. Type-species: <u>Cnemidophorus hyperythrus</u> Cope.

Distribution: From Wisconsin in United States to Bahía Blanca in Argentina; absent on Pacific coast of South America.

Content: 36 species, of which 26 are extralimital.

Key to the species

1. Fewer than nine rows of longitudinal ventral plates--2
   More than nine rows of longitudinal ventral plates--6

2. Frontonasal entire----------------------------3
   Frontonasal divided-------------------<u>motaguae</u>

3. With one interparietal and two parietals------4
   With one interparietal and four parietals-----5

4. Three supraoculars---------------------------9
   Four supraoculars-----------------<u>angusticeps</u>

5. Nostril within nasal suture---------<u>lemniscatus</u>
   Nostril anterior to nasal suture------<u>ocellifer</u>

6. Enlarged plates on forelimb-------------------7
   No enlarged plates on forelimb----------<u>murinus</u>

7. With more than two supraoculars--------------8
   With two supraoculars-----------------<u>vittatus</u>

8. Supraoculars completely separated from other dorsal head scales by circle of granular scales---------------------------<u>longicaudus</u>
   Supraoculars not completely isolated by granular scales, latter only present posteriorly and on external border-------<u>lacertoides</u>

9. Frontoparietals separated from parietals by one or more accessory scales-------------<u>cozumela</u>
   Frontoparietals in contact with parietals--<u>deppii</u>

Clave de especies

1. Menos de nueve hileras longitudinales de placas ventrales-----------------------------------2
   Más de nueve hileras longitudinales de placas ventrales-----------------------------------6

2. Frontonasal entero---------------------------3
   Frontonasal dividido-----------------<u>motaguae</u>

3. Parietales e interparietales suman tres escudos---------------------------------------4
   Parietales e interparietales suman cinco escudos---------------------------------------5

4. Supraoculares tres---------------------------9
   Supraoculares cuatro---------------<u>angusticeps</u>

5. Abertura nasal situada entre la sutura---<u>lemniscatus</u>
   Abertura nasal situada anteriormente a la sutura-------------------------------<u>ocellifer</u>

6. Placas braquiales agrandadas------------------7
   Placas braquiales no agrandadas---------<u>murinus</u>

7. Con más de dos supraoculares------------------8
   Con dos supraoculares-----------------<u>vittatus</u>

8. Supraoculares rodeados completamente por una hilera de gránulos----------------<u>longicaudus</u>
   Supraoculares con una hilera de gránulos sólo en la porción posterior y en el borde externo----------------------------------<u>lacertoides</u>

9. Frontoparietales separados de los parietales por uno o más escudos accesorios-----<u>cozumela</u>
   Frontoparietales en contacto con los parietales-------------------------------------<u>deppii</u>

CNEMIDOPHORUS ANGUSTICEPS Cope

1877 <u>Cnemidophorus angusticeps</u> Cope, Proc. Amer. Phil. Soc., 17: 95. Type-locality: Yucatán.

Distribution: Lowlands of Yucatán Peninsula south to central El Petén, Guatemala and British Honduras.

Content: Two subspecies, one (<u>angusticeps</u> Cope) extralimital.

Cnemidophorus angusticeps petenensis Beargie and McCoy

1964 <u>Cnemidophorus angusticeps petenensis</u> Beargie and McCoy, Copeia, 1964: 565, fig. 3a-b. Type-locality: La Libertad, El Petén, Guatemala.

Distribution: El Petén, Guatemala and Belize district of British Honduras.

CNEMIDOPHORUS COZUMELA Gadow

1906 Cnemidophorus deppei var. cozumela Gadow, Proc. Zool. Soc. London, 1906: 316. Type-locality: Cozumel Island, Yucatán, Mexico.
1962 Cnemidophorus cozumelus—McCoy and Maslin, Copeia, 1962: 620.

Distribution: Caribbean lowlands from Veracruz to Guatemala.

Content: Two subspecies, one (rodecki McCoy and Maslin, from Mujeres Island) extralimital, according to the most recent revision by McCoy and Maslin, Copeia, 1962, 620.

Cnemidophorus cozumela cozumela Gadow

1962 Cnemidophorus cozumelus cozumelus—McCoy and Maslin, Copeia, 1962: 621.

Distribution: Yucatán and Quintana Roo, including offshore islands, to El Petén, Guatemala.

CNEMIDOPHORUS DEPPII Wiegmann

1830 Cnemidophorus Deppii Wiegmann, Herpetologia Mexicana: 28. Type-locality: Mexico.

Distribution: Northern Veracruz and Michoacán south to Costa Rica, including Isla de Cozumel and Isla Mujeres, Yucatán.

Content: Two subspecies, one (infernalis Duellmen and Wellman) extralimital.

Cnemidophorus deppii deppii Wiegmann

1860 Cnemidophorus decemlineatus Hallowell, Proc. Acad. Nat. Sci. Phila., 1860: 482. Type-locality: Nicaragua.
1877 Cnemidophorus lativittis Cope, Proc. Amer. Phil. Soc., 17: 94. Type-locality: Juchitán, Tehuantepec, Mexico.
1894 Cnemidophorus alfaronis Cope, Proc. Acad. Nat. Sci. Phila., 1894: 199. Type-locality: San Mateo, Costa Rica.
1931 Cnemidophorus deppii deppii—Burt, Bull. U.S. Nat. Mus., 154: 56.
1939 Cnemidophorus deppei oligoporus Smith, Zool. Ser. Field Mus. Nat. Hist., 24: 26. Type-locality: Pérez, Veracruz, Mexico.
1960 Cnemidophorus deppei deppei—Duellman and Wellman, Misc. Publ. Mus. Zool. Univ. Mich., 111: 24, figs. 11a-c, pl. 1, top fig.

Distribution: On Pacific slope from Michoacán, Mexico, to Costa Rica; Atlantic slope in Veracruz, Mexico and Honduras.

CNEMIDOPHORUS LACERTOIDES Duméril and Bibron

1839 Cnemidophorus lacertoides Duméril and Bibron, Erp. Gén., 5: 134. Type-locality: Montevideo, Uruguay.
1845 Cnemidophorus lacertinoides Gray (in error for lacertoides), Cat. Liz. Brit. Mus.: 22. Type-locality: Montevideo, Uruguay (although Gray wrote "Chile", it is in error for Uruguay).
1869 Cnemidophorus grandensis Cope, Proc. Amer. Phil. Soc., 11: 158. Type-locality: Rio Grande, Brazil.
1897 Cnemidophorus leachi Peracca, Boll. Mus. Zool. Comp. Anat. Torino, 12 (274): 6. Type-locality: San Lorenzo, Jujuy, Argentina.
1966 Cnemidophorus lacertoides—Gallardo, Neotropica, 12: 24.

Distribution: Uruguay; from southern Buenos Aires Province through northern Argentina to southern Brazil.

CNEMIDOPHORUS LEMNISCATUS (Linnaeus)

1758 Lacerta Lemniscata Linnaeus, Systema Naturae, Ed. 10: 209. Type-locality: Guinea; probably in error for Guiana.
1839 Cnemidophorus lemniscatus—Duméril and Bibron, Erp. Gén., 5: 123.

Distribution: Central America from Guatemala to northern South America east of Andes, including many offshore islands.

Content: Three subspecies.

CNEMIDOPHORUS

Key to the subspecies	Clave de subespecies

1. Some colors other than black on body------2
   Body uniformly black-------------nigricolor
	1. No hay melanismo--------------------------2
	   Con melanismo generalizado-------nigricolor

2. Sides with large rounded spots; femoral
   pores 27-33----------------------arubensis
   Sides unspotted or with very few small
   spots; femoral pores 15-29-----lemniscatus
	2. Lados con manchas grandes, poros femorales
	   27-33----------------------------arubensis
	   Lados con manchas pequeñas o ausentes;
	   poros femorales 15-29----------lemniscatus

Cnemidophorus lemniscatus lemniscatus (Linnaeus)

1768 Seps caeruleus Laurenti, Synopsin Reptilium: 63. Type-locality: America.
1789 Lacerta caerulescens Bonaterre, Tabl. Ency. Meth. Quad. Ovip.: 46. Type-locality:
      Unknown.
1802 Lacerta coeruleo-cephala Sonnini and Latreille, Hist. Nat. Rept., 1: 242, pl. 221, fig. 3.
      Type-locality: Brazil.
1820 Teius cyaneus Merrem, Tentamen Systematis Amphibiorum: 61. Type-locality: Tropical South
      America.
?1825 T.[eius] cyanomelas Wied, Beiträge zur Naturgeschichte von Brazilien, 1: 180. Type-
      locality: Mucurí, Brazil.
1838 Ameiva lineata Gray, Ann. Mag. Nat. Hist., 1: 278. Type-locality: Unknown.
1845 Cnemidophorus scutata Gray, Cat. Liz. Brit. Mus.: 21. Type-locality: Unknown.
1885 Cnemidophorus espeuti Boulenger, Cat. Liz. Brit. Mus., 2: 362, pl. 19. Type-locality:
      Old Providence Island, Colombia.
1915 Cnemidophorus lemniscatus gaigei Ruthven, Occ. Pap. Mus. Zool. Univ. Mich., 16: 1. Type-
      locality: Sierra Nevada de Santa Marta, Colombia.
1919 Cnemidophorus lemniscatus lemniscatus—Beebe, Zoologica, 2: 212.
1928 Cnemidophorus lemniscatus ruatanus Barbour, Proc. New England Zool. Club, 10: 60. Type-
      locality: Coxen Hole, Ruatán, Bay Islands of Honduras.
1931 Cnemidophorus lemniscatus lemniscatus—Burt, Bull. U.S. Nat. Mus., 154: 30.

   Distribution: Lowlands of tropical South America and Central America; and on following
   Caribbean Islands: Trinidad, Tobago, Pato, Margarita, Coche, Cubagua, Old Providence,
   St. Thomas, Swan, and Milford.

Cnemidophorus lemniscatus arubensis (Van Lidth)

1887 Cnemidophorus arubensis Van Lidth, Notes Leyden Mus., 9: 132. Type-locality: Aruba,
      Dutch West Indies.
1940 Cnemidophorus lemniscatus arubensis—Hummelinck, Studies Fauna Curaçao, Aruba, Bonaire,
      Venez. Islands, 1: 85, pl. 13.

   Distribution: Aruba Island.

Cnemidophorus lemniscatus nigricolor (Peters)

1873 Cnemidophorus nigricolor Peters, Sitz. Ges. Naturforsch. Freunde Berlin, 1873: 76. Type-
      locality: Los Roques Island, Venezuela.
1931 Cnemidophorus lemniscatus nigricolor—Burt, Bull. U. S. Nat. Mus., 154: 40.

   Distribution: Restricted to Los Roques Archipielago; Aves, Orchila and Blanquilla Islands.

CNEMIDOPHORUS LONGICAUDUS (Bell)

1843 Ameiva longicauda Bell, Zool. Voyage Beagle, Rept.: 28, pl. 15, fig. 1. Type-locality: Bahía
      Blanca, Argentina.
1845 Cnemidophorus longicaudus—Gray, Cat. Liz. Brit. Mus.: 21.
1869 Cnemidophorus multilineatus Philippi, Arch. für Naturg., 35: 41. Type-locality: Mendoza,
      Argentina.
1966 Cnemidophorus longicauda—Gallardo, Neotropica, 12: 24, fig. 2.

   Distribution: Northern Argentina.

CNEMIDOPHORUS MOTAGUAE Sackett

1941 Cnemidophorus motaguae Sackett, Notulae Naturae, 77: 1, figs. 1-3. Type-locality: Motagua
     River, Zacapa, Guatemala.

   Distribution: Oaxaca, Mexico to Guatemala, Salvador, and Honduras.

CNEMIDOPHORUS MURINUS (Laurenti)

1768 Seps murinus Laurenti, Synopsin Reptilium: 63. Type-locality: Java; based on figure in Seba,
     vol. 2, pl. 105, fig. 2.
1830 Cnemidophorus murinus—Wagler, Nat. Syst. Amph.: 154.

   Distribution: Curaçao and Bonaire Islands.

   Content: Two subspecies.

             Key to the subspecies   Clave de subespecies

1. Femoral pores fewer than 34----------murinus   1. Poros femorales menos de 34---------murinus
   Femoral pores more than 35---------ruthveni   Poros femorales más de 35----------ruthveni

Cnemidophorus murinus murinus (Laurenti)

1899 Cnemidophorus minimus Cope (incorrect spelling for murinus), Sci. Bull. Phila. Mus., 1: 9.
1940 Cnemidophorus murinus murinus—Hummelinck, Studies Fauna Curaçao, Aruba, Bonaire, Venez.
     Islands, 1: 85.

   Distribution: Found only on Curaçao and Klein Curaçao Islands.

Cnemidophorus murinus ruthveni Burt

1935 Cnemidophorus murinus ruthveni Burt, Occ. Pap. Mus. Zool. Univ. Mich., 324: 1. Type-
     locality: Seroe Grandi, Bonaire Island.

   Distribution: Bonaire and Klein Bonaire Islands.

CNEMIDOPHORUS OCELLIFER (Spix)

1825 Teius ocellifer Spix, Spec. Nov. Lacert. Bras.: 23, pl. 25. Type-locality: Bahia, Brazil.
1862 Cnemidophorus Hygomi Reinhardt and Lütken, Vidensk. Medd. Naturhist. Foren. Kjöbenhavn, 3 (1861):
     231. Type-locality: Marium, Brazil.
1877 Cnemidophorus ocellifer—Peters, Monats. Akad. Wiss. Berlin, 1877: 414.
1960 Cnemidophorus ocellifer—Hellmich, Abh. Bayerischen Akad. Wiss. Math.-Naturwiss. Kl., new ser.,
     101: 72.
   Distribution: Brazil, Bolivia and Paraguay.

CNEMIDOPHORUS VITTATUS Boulenger

1902 Cnemidophorus vittatus Boulenger, Ann. Mag. Nat. Hist., (7) 10: 400. Type-locality: Paratani,
     Bolivia, 2500 m.

   Distribution: Known only from type locality.

COLEODACTYLUS Parker

    1926 Coleodactylus Parker, Ann. Mag. Nat. Hist., (9) 17: 298. Type-species: Sphaerodactylus meridi-
        onalis Boulenger.

    Distribution: Brazil and Guyana.

    Content: Four species.

Key to the species

1. Dorsal scales smooth-------------------------2
   Dorsal scales keeled-----------------amazonicus

2. More than 40 ventral scales------------------3
   Fewer than 40 ventral scales---------guimaraesi

3. Snout rounded; sheath of claw formed dorsally
   by a single scale------------------brachystoma
   Snout pointed; sheath of claw formed dorsally
   by three scales-------------------meridionalis

Clave de especies

1. Escamas dorsales lisas------------------------2
   Escamas dorsales quilladas----------amazonicus

2. Número de escamas ventrales mayor que 40-------
   --3
   Número de escamas ventrales no mayor de 40-----
   ------------------------------------guimaraesi

3. Hocico romboidal; vaina de la uña formada dorsalmente por una escama------------brachystoma
   Hocico puntiagudo; vaina de la uña formada dorsalmente por tres escamas---------meridionalis

COLEODACTYLUS AMAZONICUS (Andersson)

    1918 Sphaerodactylus amazonicus Andersson, Ark. för Zool., 11 (16): 1. Type-locality: Lago
        Poraquêcuare, Manaus, Amazonas, Brazil.
    1928 Coleodactylus zernyi Wettstein, Zool. Anz., 76: 110, fig. 1. Type-locality: Taperinha,
        Santarem, Pará, Brazil.
    1957 Coleodactylus amazonicus—Vanzolini, Pap. Avul. Depto. Zool. São Paulo, 13: 6, fig. 2.

    Distribution: Amazon Basin in Brazil; French Guiana, Guyana; Territorio Amazonas, Venezuela.

COLEODACTYLUS BRACHYSTOMA (Amaral)

    1935 Homonota brachystoma Amaral, Mem. Inst. Butantan, 9: 254, fig. 8. Type-locality: Cana Brava,
        Goiás, Brazil.
    1939 Sphaerodactylus pfrimeri Miranda-Ribeiro, O Campo, 1937, 10: 46. Type-locality: Rio Las Palmas,
        Goiás, Brazil.
    1957 Coleodactylus brachystoma—Vanzolini, Pap. Avul. Depto. Zool. São Paulo, 13: 4, fig. 4.

    Distribution: Estado de Goiás, Brazil.

COLEODACTYLUS GUIMARAESI Vanzolini

    1957 Coleodactylus guimarãesi Vanzolini, Pap. Avul. Depto. Zool. São Paulo, 13: 8. Type-locality:
        Pôrto Velho, Territorio de Rondônia, Brazil.

    Distribution: Known only from type locality.

COLEODACTYLUS MERIDIONALIS (Boulenger)

    1888 Sphaerodactylus meridionalis Boulenger, Ann. Mag. Nat. Hist., (6) 2: 40. Type-locality:
        Igaraçu, Pernambuco, Brazil.
    1926 Coleodactylus meridionalis—Parker, Ann. Mag. Nat. Hist., (9) 17: 300.
    1957 Coleodactylus meridionalis—Vanzolini, Pap. Avul. Depto. Zool. São Paulo, 13: 2, fig. 1.

    Distribution: Guyana, southern Venezuela, and northern Brazil.

COLEONYX Gray

1845 Coleonyx Gray, Ann. Mag. Nat. Hist., (1) 16: 162. Type-species: Coleonyx elegans Gray.
1863 Brachydactylus Peters (preoccupied by Brachydactylus Smith, 1835), Monats. Akad. Wiss. Berlin,
    1863: 41. Type-species: Brachydactylus mitratus Peters.

Distribution: Southwestern North America and Central America.

Content: Twelve species and subspecies, all but two of which are extralimital.

Key to the species

1. Claws on digits completely hidden by terminal sheath--------------------------elegans
   Claws on digits extended beyond terminal
   sheath, clearly visible--------------mitratus

Clave de especies

1. Uña de los digitos completamente oculatas en
   vainas terminales---------------------elegans
   Uña de los digitos extendidas desde la vaina
   y claramente visibles----------------mitratus

COLEONYX ELEGANS Gray

1845 Coleonyx elegans Gray, Ann. Mag. Nat. Hist., (1) 16: 163. Type-locality: Belize, British
    Honduras.

Distribution: Mexico to Honduras and Guatemala.

Content: Two subspecies, one (nemoralis Klauber) extralimital.

Coleonyx elegans elegans Gray

1851 G[ymnodactylus] scapularis A. Duméril, in Duméril, Bibron, and Duméril, Cat. Method. Coll.
    Rept. Mus. Hist. Nat. Paris: 45. Type-locality: Petén, Guatemala; restricted by Smith
    and Taylor, Univ. Kansas Sci. Bull., 33, 1950, 318, to La Libertad, Guatemala.
1856 Gymnodactylus coleonyx A. Duméril (substitute name for Coleonyx elegans Gray), Arch. Mus.
    Hist. Nat., Paris, 8: 483.
1945 Coleonyx elegans elegans—Klauber, Trans. San Diego Soc. Nat. Hist., 10: 191.

Distribution: From southern Mexico (central Veracruz, Oaxaca, Tabasco, Yucatán, Chiapas,
    Quintana Roo), southward to Honduras and northern Guatemala.

COLEONYX MITRATUS (Peters)

1863 Brachydactylus mitratus Peters, Monats. Akad. Wiss. Berlin, 1863: 42. Type-locality: Costa
    Rica.
1885 Eublepharis dovii Boulenger, Cat. Liz. Brit. Mus., 1: 233. Type-locality: Panama.
1928 Coleonyx mitratus—Schmidt, Zool. Ser. Field Mus. Nat. Hist., 12: 194.
1956 Coleonyx mitratus—Taylor, Univ. Kansas Sci. Bull., 38: 16, fig. 1.

Distribution: El Salvador, Honduras, Nicaragua, Costa Rica and Panama.

COLOBODACTYLUS Amaral

    1933 Colobodactylus Amaral, Mem. Inst. Butantan, 7 (1932): 70. Type-species: Colobodactylus taunayi
        Amaral.

     Distribution: As for single known species.

     Content: One species.

COLOBODACTYLUS TAUNAYI Amaral

    1933 Colobodactylus taunayi Amaral, Mem. Inst. Butantan, 7 (1932): 70, figs. 41-45. Type-locality:
        Iguape, Estado de São Paulo, Brazil.

     Distribution: Estado de São Paulo, Estado de Santa Catarina, and Queimada Grande Island, Brazil.

COLOBOSAURA Boulenger

1862 Perodactylus Reinhardt and Lütken (preoccupied by Perodactylus Fitzinger, 1843), Vidensk. Medd. Naturhist. Foren. Kjöbenhavn, 3 (1861): 218. Type-species: Perodactylus modestus Reinhardt and Lütken.
1887 Colobosaura Boulenger, Cat. Liz. Brit. Mus., 3: 508. Type-species: Perodactylus modestus Reinhardt and Lütken.

Distribution: Brazil and Paraguay.

Content: Three species.

Key to the species	Clave de especies

1. Two pairs of enlarged postmental scales▬▬▬▬2
   Three pairs of enlarged postmental
   scales▬▬▬▬▬▬▬▬▬▬▬▬▬▬▬▬▬▬▬mentalis
	1. Dos pares de escudos posmentales agrandados▬▬▬2
	   Tres pares de escudos posmentales agrandados▬▬
	   ▬▬▬▬▬▬▬▬▬▬▬▬▬▬▬▬▬▬▬▬▬mentalis

2. Interparietal as broad as parietals▬▬kraepelini
   Interparietal narrower than parietals▬▬▬modesta
	2. Interparietal tan ancho como los parietales▬▬▬▬
	   ▬▬▬▬▬▬▬▬▬▬▬▬▬▬▬▬▬▬▬▬kraepelini
	   Interparietal estrechado, mas angosto que
	   parietales▬▬▬▬▬▬▬▬▬▬▬▬▬▬▬▬modesta

COLOBOSAURA KRAEPELINI (Werner)

1910 Perodactylus Kraepelini Werner, Mitt. Naturhist. Mus. Hamburg, 27 (2): 32. Type-locality: Puerto Max, Paraguay.
1933 Colobosaura kraepelini—Amaral, Mem. Inst. Butantan, 7 (1932): 71.

Distribution: Known only from type locality.

COLOBOSAURA MENTALIS Amaral

1933 Colobosaura mentalis Amaral, Mem. Inst. Butantan, 7 (1932): 72, figs. 46-50. Type-locality: Villa Nova (= Senhor do Bonfim), Bahía, Brazil.

Distribution: Known only from type locality.

COLOBOSAURA MODESTA (Reinhardt and Lütken)

1862 Perodactylus modestus Reinhardt and Lütken, Vidensk. Medd. Naturhist. Foren. Kjöbenhavn, 3 (1861): 218, pl. 15, figs. 7, 7a-e. Type-locality: Morro da Garcza, north of Curvelo, Minas Gerais, Brazil.
1887 Colobosaura modesta—Boulenger, Cat. Liz. Brit. Mus., 3: 508.

Distribution: Minas Gerais and Bahía, Brazil.

COLOPTYCHON Tihen

 1949 Coloptychon Tihen, Amer. Midl. Nat., 41: 584. Type-species: Gerrhonotus rhombifer Peters.

  Distribution: As for single known species.

  Content: One species.

COLOPTYCHON RHOMBIFER (Peters)

 1877 Gerrhonotus rhombifer Peters, Monats. Akad. Wiss. Berlin, 1877: 298. Type-locality: Chiriqui, Panama.
 1949 Coloptychon rhombifer—Tihen, Amer. Midl. Nat., 41: 585, figs. 2-3.

  Distribution: Known only from type locality.

REPTILIA: SAURIA: IGUANIDAE   CORYTOPHANES

Prepared by Clarence J. McCoy, Carnegie Museum, Pittsburgh, Pennsylvania

CORYTOPHANES Boie

1827 Corytophanes Boie, in Schlegel, Isis von Oken, 20: 290. Type-species: Agama cristata Merrem.
1830 Corythophanes Wagler (emendation of Corytophanes Boie), Syst. Amph.: 151.
1831 Chamaeleopsis Wiegmann, in Gray, Synopsis Species Class Reptilia, in Griffith, Cuvier's Animal Kingdom, 9: 45. Type-species: Chamaeleopsis Hernandesii Wiegmann.

Distribution: Central Veracruz and San Luis Potosí, Mexico, to northwestern Colombia.

Content: Three species.

Key to the species	Clave de especies
1. Occipital crest continuous with body crest----2 Occipital crest not continuous with body crest, interrupted on neck---------------hernandesii	1. Cresta occipital continua con cresta del cuerpo ---2 Cresta occipital descontinua con cresta del cuerpo, interrumpida en el cuello--hernandesii
2. Occipital crest not projecting beyond end of casque; upper head scales keeled or rugose--percarinatus Occipital crest projecting beyond end of casque; upper head scales smooth-----cristatus	2. Cresta occipital sin prolongación nucal; escamas dorsales de la cabeza quilladas--percarinatus Cresta occipital prolongada en la nuca; escamas dorsales de la cabeza lisas----------cristatus

CORYTOPHANES CRISTATUS (Merrem)

1821 Agama cristata Merrem, Tentamen Systematis Amphibiorum: 50. Type-locality: Ceylon; restricted to Orizaba, Veracruz, Mexico by Smith and Taylor, Bull. U.S. Nat. Mus., 199, 1950, 69.
1827 [Corytophanes] cristatus—Boie (by inference), in Schlegel, Isis von Oken, 20: 290.
1956 Corythophanes cristatus—Taylor, Univ. Kansas Sci. Bull., 38: 161, fig. 45.

Distribution: Lowlands and foothills from central Veracruz, Mexico, to Chocó and Magdalena Valley of northwestern Colombia.

CORYTOPHANES HERNANDESII (Wiegmann)

1831 Chamaeleopsis Hernandesii Wiegmann, in Gray, Synopsis Species Class Reptilia, in Griffith, Cuvier's Animal Kingdom, 9: 45. Type-locality: Mexico; restricted to Jalapa, Veracruz, Mexico, by Smith and Taylor, Bull. U.S. Nat. Mus., 199, 1950, 69.
1837 Corythophanes chamaeleopsis Duméril and Bibron (substitute name for Chamaeleopsis Hernandesii Wiegmann), Erp. Gén., 4: 175.
1856 Corythophanes Hernandezii—Lichtenstein, Nomenclator Reptilium et Amphibiorum Musei Zoologici Berolinensis: 8.
1874 Corythophanes mexicanus Bocourt (substitute name for Chamaeleopsis Hernandesii Wiegmann), Miss. Sci. Mex., Rept.: 122, pl. 17, fig. 1.
1960 Corythophanes hernandezii—Alvarez del Toro, Reptiles de Chiapas: 84, two figs.

Distribution: Atlantic foothills and lowlands from central Veracruz, Mexico, southward through Guatemala.

CORYTOPHANES PERCARINATUS Duméril

1856 Corytophanes percarinatus Duméril, Arch. Mus. Hist. Nat. Paris, 8: 518, pl. 20, fig. 3-3a. Type-locality: Ascuintla in Central America, 30 leagues from Guatemala; = Escuintla, Guatemala, according to Stuart, Misc. Publ. Mus. Zool. Univ. Mich., 122, 1963, 67.
1962 Corytophanes percarinatus—Mertens, Abh. Senck. Naturforsch. Ges., 487: 46, pl. 12, fig. 71.

Distribution: Foothills from the Isthmus of Tehuantepec, Mexico, to El Salvador. Boulenger's record from "Ecuador (?)" (Catalogue of Lizards, 2, 1885, 103) requires verification.

CROCODILURUS Spix

　　1825 Crocodilurus Spix, Spec. Nov. Lacert. Bras.: 19. Type-species: Crocodilurus amazonicus Spix.

　　　Distribution: Guyana, Surinam, French Guiana and Amazonian Basin of Brazil.

　　　Content: One species.

CROCODILURUS LACERTINUS (Daudin)

　　1802 Tupinambis lacertinus Daudin, Hist. Nat. Rept., 3: 85. Type-locality: Islands adjacent to
　　　　tropical South America.
　　1825 Crocodilurus amazonicus Spix, Spec. Nov. Lacert. Bras.: 19, pl. 21. Type-locality: Rio Solimões,
　　　　near São Paulo de Olivença, Brazil.
　　1825 Crocodilurus ocellatus Spix, Spec. Nov. Lacert. Bras.: 20, pl. 22, fig. 1. Type-locality:
　　　　Rio Solimões, Brazil.
　　1839 Crocodilurus Lacertinus—Duméril and Bibron, Erp. Gén., 5: 46.

　　　Distribution: Guianas; Amazonian Basin of Brazil.

CTENOBLEPHARIS Tschudi

1845 Ctenoblepharys Tschudi, Arch. für Naturg., 11: 158. Type-species: Ctenoblepharys adspersa Tschudi.
1885 Ctenoblepharis—Boulenger (valid emendation of Ctenoblepharys Tschudi), Cat. Liz. Brit. Mus., 2: 136.
1860 Helocephalus Philippi, Reise durch die Wüste Atacama: 167. Type-species: Helocephalus nigriceps Philippi.

  Distribution: Peru, Chile, Bolivia and Argentina.

  Content: Six species.

Key to the species

1. Dorsal scales larger than ventrals; more than 55 scales around middle of body--------------2
   Dorsal scales smaller than ventrals; fewer than 55 scales around middle of body--------------3

2. Tympanic scale absent; dorsal scales smooth, not depressed; vertebral scales weakly keeled; scales on legs keeled------------------jamesi
   Tympanic scale present; dorsal scales smooth, depressed centrally; vertebral scales not keeled; scales on legs smooth-------stolzmanni

3. Head scales differentiated--------------------4
   Head scales undifferentiated; only inter-parietal is recognizable-------------adspersus

4. Head not black; fewer than 90 scales around middle of body-----------------------------5
   Head black; more than 90 scales around middle of body----------------------------nigriceps

5. Scales on legs smooth; no patch of enlarged scales on posterior part of thigh-----schmidti
   Scales on legs keeled; with patch of enlarged scales on posterior part of thigh-----anomalus

Clave de especies

1. Escamas dorsales mayores que los ventrales; más de 55 escamas al medio del cuerpo------------2
   Escamas dorsales menores que ventrales; menos de 55 escamas al medio del cuerpo------------3

2. Escama timpánica ausente; escamas dorsales lisas, no deprimidas; escamas vertebrales débilmente quilladas; escamas de miembros quilladas--------------------------------jamesi
   Escama timpánica presente; escamas dorsales lisas, deprimidas centralmente, escamas vertebrales no quilladas; escamas de miembros lisas --------------------------------stolzmanni

3. Escamas céfalicas diferenciadas---------------4
   Escamas céfalicas indiferenciadas; sólo se reconoce la interparietal-----------adspersus

4. Sin cabeza negra; menos de 90 escamas al medio del cuerpo-------------------------------------5
   Cabeza negra; más de 90 escamas al medio del cuerpo--------------------------------nigriceps

5. Escamas de extremidades lisas; sin parche de escamas agrandadas en el borde posterior del muslo-------------------------------------schmidti
   Escamas de extremidades quilladas; con parche de escamas agrandadas en el borde posterior del muslo-------------------------------anomalus

CTENOBLEPHARIS ADSPERSUS Tschudi

1845 Ctenoblepharys adspersa Tschudi, Arch. für Naturg., 11: 158. Type-locality: Hacienda Acaray, near Huacho, Peru.
1885 Ctenoblepharis adspersus—Boulenger, Cat. Liz. Brit. Mus., 2: 136.

  Distribution: Coastal desert of Peru from Huacho south.

CTENOBLEPHARIS ANOMALUS (Koslowsky), new combination

1896 Liolaemus anomalus Koslowsky, Rev. Mus. La Plata, 7: 452, pl. 11. Type-locality: Rioja, Argentina.

  Distribution: Provincia de la Rioja, Argentina.

  Comment: The justification for putting this species in this genus has not yet been published, but is in a manuscript prepared by one of us (Donoso).

CTENOBLEPHARIS JAMESI Boulenger

1891 Ctenoblepharis jamesi Boulenger, Proc. Zool. Soc. London, 1891: 3, pl. Type-locality: Andes of Tarapaca, Chile, 3300-4000 m.
1958 Ctenoblepharis jamesi—Donoso-Barros, Invest. Zool. Chilenas, 4: 254, fig. 1a-c.
1966 Ctenoblepharis jamesi—Donoso-Barros, Reptiles de Chile: 337, col. pl. 24.

  Distribution: Andes of Tarapaca above 3000 m, Chile.

CTENOBLEPHARIS

CTENOBLEPHARIS NIGRICEPS (Philippi)

    1860 Helocephalus nigriceps Philippi, Reise durch die Wüste Atacama: 167, pl., fig. 7. Type-locality: Pajonal, Atacama, Chile.
    1966 Ctenoblepharis nigriceps—Donoso-Barros, Reptiles de Chile: 335, pl. 25.

    Distribution: High cordillera of Atacama, Chile.

CTENOBLEPHARIS SCHMIDTI Marx

    1960 Ctenoblepharis schmidti Marx, Fieldiana: Zool., 39: 407. Type-locality: Forty mi east of San Pedro de Atacama, Antofagasta, Chile.

    Distribution: Andes of Antofagasta, between Chile and Bolivia.

CTENOBLEPHARIS STOLZMANNI Steindachner

    1891 Ctenoblepharis Stolzmanni Steindachner, Sitz. Math.-Naturwiss. Kl. Akad. Wiss. Wien, 50, abt. 1: 295. Type-locality: Highlands of Peru.
    1966 Ctenoblepharis stolzmani—Donoso-Barros (emendation of stolzmanni), Reptiles de Chile: 341, col. pl. 25.

    Distribution: Andes of Peru and Chile; possibly Bolivia.

CTENOSAURA Wiegmann

1828 Ctenosaura Wiegmann, Isis von Oken, 21: 371. Type-species: Ctenosaura cycluroides Wiegmann.

Distribution: Baja California, Mexico, through Central America, including many coastal islands; San Andres and Old Providence Island.

Content: Five species, only two of which occur within limits of this work.

Key to the species

1. Median row of dorsal scales distinctly enlarged into spiny crest, which occurs from nape to end of tail without interruption at sacrum---similis
Median row of dorsal scales low and interrupted at the sacrum--------------------------bakeri

Clave de especies

1. Hilera medio dorsal de escamas agrandadas y extendidas desde la nuca al término de la cola, sin interrupción en el sacro-----similis
Hilera medio dorsal de escamas bajas y no extendidas continuamente desde la nuca al término de la cola, interrupción sacral presente---------------------------------bakeri

CTENOSAURA BAKERI Stejneger

1901 Ctenosaura bakeri Stejneger, Proc. U.S. Nat. Mus., 23: 467. Type-locality: Utilla Island, Honduras.

Distribution: Utilla, Bonacca and Roatan Islands, Honduras.

CTENOSAURA SIMILIS (Gray)

1831 Iguana (Ctenosaura) Similis Gray, Synopsis Species Class Reptilia, in Griffith, Cuvier's Animal Kingdom, 9: 38. Type-locality: none given; restricted to Tela, Honduras, by Bailey, Proc. U. S. Nat. Mus., 73 (12), 1929, 32.
1929 Ctenosaura similis—Bailey, Proc. U. S. Nat. Mus., 73 (12): 32.

Distribution: Lowlands of southern Mexico to sandy beaches of Panama; Old Providence and San Andres Islands.

Content: Two subspecies, one of which (multipunctata Barbour and Shreve) is extralimital.

Ctenosaura similis similis (Gray)

1874 Ctenosaura completa Bocourt, Miss. Sci. Mex., Reptl.: 145. Type-locality: Guatemala and La Union, Salvador; restricted by Smith and Taylor, Bull. U. S. Nat. Mus., 199, 1950, 73.
1934 Ctenosaura similis similis—Barbour and Shreve, Occ. Pap. Boston Soc. Nat. Hist., 8: 197.

Distribution: Low and moderate elevations from Isthmus of Tehuantepec, Mexico, south to Panama.

CUPRIGUANUS Gallardo

  1964 Cupriguanus Gallardo, Neotropica, 10: 127. Type-species: Cupriguanus achalensis Gallardo.

   Distribution: Central and north central Argentina.

   Content: Four species.

Key to the species[1]

1. Six scales in contact with rostral; two scales
   between nasal and rostral--------------------2
   Three to five scales in contact with rostral;
   three scales between nasal and rostral-------3

2. Tail less than 3/4 length of body-casuhatiensis
   Tail more than 3/4 length of body, often
   equally as long--------------------scapulatus

3. Scales of loreal region granular; venter light;
   dorsal bars distinct; fourth toe on forefoot
   equal in length to third-------------araucanus
   Scales of loreal region enlarged; venter green;
   dorsal bars indistinct; fourth toe longer than
   third----------------------------achalensis

Clave de especies[1]

1. Seis escamas en contacto con la rostral; dos
   escamas entre la narina y la rostral---------2
   Tres a cinco escamas en contacto con la
   rostral; tres escamas entre la narina y la
   rostral--------------------------------------3

2. Cola menos que 3/4 longitud del cuerpo---------
   ---------------------------------casuhatiensis
   Cola más que 3/4 longitud del cuerpo; a veces
   cola y cuerpo de igual longitud-----scapulatus

3. Escamas de la región loreal granulares;
   ventralmente claro; barras dorsales generalmente bien visibles; el cuarto dedo de la mano
   y el tercero son de igual longitud---araucanus
   Escamas de la región loreal mayores (medianas);
   ventralmente verde; barras dorsales oscuras
   borrosas; el cuarto dedo de la mano algo más
   largo que el tercero---------------achalensis

CUPRIGUANUS ACHALENSIS Gallardo

  1964 Cupriguanus achalensis Gallardo, Neotropica, 10: 132, fig. 4. Type-locality: Posta de la Pampa
     de Achala, Provincia de Córdoba, Argentina.

   Distribution: Provincia de Córdoba, Argentina.

CUPRIGUANUS ARAUCANUS Gallardo

  1964 Cupriguanus araucanus Gallardo, Neotropica, 10: 129, figs. 2-3. Type-locality: Laguna Blanca,
     Neuquén, Argentina.

   Distribution: Provincia Neuquén, Argentina.

CUPRIGUANUS CASUHATIENSIS Gallardo

  1968 Cupriguanus casuhatiensis Gallardo, Neotropica, 14: 2, fig. Type-locality: Sierra de la
     Ventana, Provincia de Buenos Aires, Argentina.

   Distribution: Known from type locality and Cerro Tres Picos, Argentina.

CUPRIGUANUS SCAPULATUS (Burmeister)

  1861 L.[eiosaurus] scapulatus Burmeister, Reise Durch Die La Plata Staaten, 2: 523. Type-locality:
     Near Uspallata, Sierra de Uspallata, Mendoza, Argentina, 5000 ft.
  1861 L.[eiosaurus] multipunctatus Burmeister, Reise Durch Die La Plata Staaten, 2: 524. Type-
     locality: Near Paramillo, Sierra de Uspallata, Mendoza, Argentina, more than 8000 ft.
  1964 Cupriguanus scapulatus—Gallardo, Neotropica, 10: 128.

   Distribution: Sierra de Uspallata, Provincia Mendoza, Argentina.

---

[1]This key, which was drawn up from the original
descriptions, does not work well even with types.
Jose Gallardo is preparing a more adequate key.

[1]Esta clave, que fue hecha en base a descripciones
originales, no da buenos resultados ni con tipos.
Jose Gallardo esta preparando una clave mas
adecuada.

DICRODON Duméril and Bibron

> 1839 Dicrodon Duméril and Bibron, Erp. Gén., 5: 137. Type-species: Dicrodon guttulatum Duméril and Bibron.

Distribution: Coastal areas of Peru and Ecuador.

Content: Three species, according to most recent review by Schmidt, Fieldiana: Zool., 39, 1957.

<table>
<tr><td>Key to the species</td><td>Clave de especies</td></tr>
</table>

1. Posterior dorsal scales granular, small and juxtaposed------------------------------2 Posterior dorsal scales enlarged, keeled and imbricate--------------------------heterolepis	1. Escamas dorsales posteriores granulares, pequeñas yuxtapuestas----------------------2 Escamas dorsales posteriores agrandadas, quilladas e imbricadas-------------heterolepis
2. Supraoculars completely surrounded by granular scales------------------------------holmbergi Supraoculars not completely surrounded by granular scales--------------------guttulatum	2. Escudos supraoculares circundados completa-mente por escuditos granulares-------holmbergi Escudos supraoculares no circundados completa-mente por escuditos granulares------guttulatum

DICRODON GUTTULATUM Duméril and Bibron

> 1839 Dicrodon guttulatum Duméril and Bibron, Erp. Gén., 5: 138. Type-locality: Peru.
> 1892 Cnemidophorus lentiginosus Garman, Bull. Essex Inst., 24: 92. Type-locality: San Francisco de Posorja, Ecuador.
> 1899 Ameiva leucostigma Boulenger, Proc. Zool. Soc. London, 1899: 517, pl. 28. Type-locality: Near Guayaquil, Ecuador.
> 1924 Dicrodon barbouri Noble, Occ. Pap. Boston Soc. Nat. Hist., 5: 108. Type-locality: Valley of Río Chira, Piura, Peru.

Distribution: Dry coastal areas of Ecuador and northern Peru.

DICRODON HETEROLEPIS (Tschudi)

> 1845 Cnemidophorus (Aspidoscelis) heterolepis Tschudi, Arch. für Naturg., 11: 160. Type-locality: Warm forests on eastern slopes of Andes in Peru.
> 1876 Dicrodon calliscelis Cope, Jour. Acad. Nat. Sci. Phila., (2) 8 (1875): 163. Type-locality: Pacasmayo, Pacific coast of Peru.
> 1891 Cnemidophorus centropyx Steindachner, Ann. K.K. Naturhist. Hofmus. Wien, 6: 374, pl. 12, figs. 1-3. Type-locality: Eastern slope of Andes, Peru.
> 1891 Cnemidophorus peruanus Steindachner, Ann. K.K. Naturhist. Hofmus. Wien, 6: 375. Type-locality: Peru.
> 1891 Cnemidophorus tumbezanus Steindachner, Ann. K.K. Naturhist. Hofmus. Wien, 6: 375. Type-locality: Tumbez, Peru.
> 1933 Dicrodon heterolepis—Burt and Burt, Trans. Acad. Sci. St. Louis, 28: 60.

Distribution: Coastal areas of southern Peru, according to Schmidt, Fieldiana: Zool., 39, 1957, 66.

DICRODON HOLMBERGI Schmidt

> 1957 Dicrodon holmbergi Schmidt, Fieldiana: Zool., 39: 66, figs. 10-11. Type-locality: Chao Valley, Libertad, Peru.

Distribution: Chao Valley and adjacent areas, Peru.

DIPLOGLOSSUS Wiegmann

1834 Diploglossus Wiegmann, Herpetologia Mexicana: 36. Type-species: Tiliqua fasciatus Gray.
1845 Camilia Gray, Cat. Liz. Brit. Mus.: 118. Type-species: Tiliqua jamaicensis Gray.

Distribution: Costa Rica and Panama; Pacific slopes of Colombia and Ecuador; northeastern Brazil; Amazonian Bolivia.

Content: Six species.

Key to the species

1. Frontal in contact anteriorly with one scale--2
   Frontal in contact anteriorly with two or
   more scales---------------------------------4

2. Dorsal scales smooth-------------------------3
   Dorsal scales keeled-----------------monotropis

3. Fewer than 50 scales around middle of body;
   dorsum with wide transverse bands----fasciatus
   More than 50 scales around middle of body;
   dorsum with many light spots----millepunctatus

4. Two subequal loreals; prefrontal separated from
   loreals; 37-42 scales around middle of body---
   -----------------------------------bilobatus
   One loreal larger than other; prefrontal in
   contact with first loreal; 33-37 scales around
   middle of body-----------------------lessonae

Clave de especies

1. Frontal contacta anteriormente con un sólo
   escudo--2
   Frontal contacto anteriormente con dos o más
   escudos---------------------------------------4

2. Escamas dorsales lisas-----------------------3
   Escamas dorsales quilladas----------monotropis

3. Menos de 50 escamas al medio del cuerpo;
   diseño dorsal formado por fajas transversales
   anchas-------------------------------fasciatus
   Más de 50 escamas al medio del cuerpo; diseño
   dorsal multimaculado de claro--millepunctatus

4. Dos loreales subiguales; prefrontal separado
   del loreales; 37-42 escamas al medio del
   cuerpo-------------------------------bilobatus
   Dos loreales desiguales; prefrontal contacta
   con primer loreal; 33-37 escamas al medio
   del cuerpo----------------------------lessonae

DIPLOGLOSSUS BILOBATUS (O'Shaughnessy)

1847 Celestus bilobatus O'Shaughnessy, Ann. Mag. Nat. Hist., (4) 14: 257. Type-locality: Costa Rica.
1885 Diploglossus bilobatus—Boulenger, Cat. Liz. Brit. Mus., 2: 286.
1956 Diploglossus bilobatus—Taylor, Univ. Kansas Sci. Bull., 38: 200, fig. 53.

Distribution: Caribbean and Pacific slopes of Costa Rica.

DIPLOGLOSSUS FASCIATUS (Gray)

1831 Tiliqua Fasciatus Gray, Synopsis Species Class Reptilia, in Griffith, Cuvier's Animal Kingdom,
   9: 71. Type-locality: none given.
1834 [Diploglossus] fasciatus—Wiegmann, Herpetologia Mexicana: 36.
1839 Diploglossus Houttuynii Cocteau, in Duméril and Bibron, Erp. Gén., 5: 597. Type-locality: Brazil.
1909 Diploglossus resplendens Barbour, Proc. New England Zool. Club, 4: 50, pl. 4, 2 figs.
   Type-locality: Junction of Río Kaka and Río Beni, eastern Bolivia.

Distribution: Discontinuous; southeastern coastal Brazil; also Territorio do Acre, Brazil and northeastern Bolivia.

Comment: The synonymy of resplendens Barbour with fasciatus Gray is made on the authority of Paulo Vanzolini, who has good material of the species available, and who has also examined the holotype of resplendens.

DIPLOGLOSSUS LESSONAE Peracca

1890 Diploglossus Lessonae Peracca, Bol. Mus. Zool. Anat. Comp. Torino, 5 (77): 1. Type-locality: Brazil.
1924 Diploglossus tenuifasciatus Parker, Ann. Mag. Nat. Hist., (9) 13: 586, fig. Type-locality: Natal, Rio Grande do Norte, Brazil.
1958 Diploglossus lessonae—Vanzolini, Pap. Avul. Dept. Zool. Sao Paulo, 13: 179.

Distribution: Rio Grande do Norte to Pernambuco in northeastern Brazil.

DIPLOGLOSSUS MILLEPUNCTATUS O'Shaughnessy

1874 Diploglossus millepunctatus O'Shaughnessy, Ann. Mag. Nat. Hist., (4) 13: 301. Type-locality:
    Northwest coast of America.
1928 Celestus hancocki Slevin, Proc. Calif. Acad. Sci., 16: 682. Type-locality: Malpelo Island,
    Colombia.

   Distribution: Endemic to Malpelo Island, Pacific coast of Colombia.

DIPLOGLOSSUS MONOTROPIS (Kuhl)

1820 Scincus monotropis Kuhl, Beiträge zur Zoologie und vergleichende Anatomie: 128. Type-locality:
    unknown, according to Kuhl.
1834 [Diploglossus] Monotropis—Wiegmann, Herpetologia Mexicana: 36.
1839 Tiliqua Jamaicensis Gray, Ann. Mag. Nat. Hist., (1) 2: 293. Type-locality: Jamaica (in error).

   Distribution: Costa Rica and Panama; Colombia and Ecuador.

DIPLOLAEMUS Bell

> 1843 *Diplolaemus* Bell, Zool. Voyage Beagle, Rept.: 19, pl. 10. Type-species: *Diplolaemus darwinii* Bell.
>
> Distribution: Patagonia, 38° S. to straits of Magellan, Argentina.
>
> Content: Three species.

Key to the species	Clave de especies
1. Pattern formed by brown crossbands containing dark brown spots----------------------------2 Pattern formed by isolated brown spots---**leopardinus**	1. Diseño dorsal con bandas pardas transversales con manchitas negras-------------------------2 Diseño dorsal con manchas pardas aisladas--**leopardinus**
2. Head scales convex; dorsal bands butterfly-shaped, interrupted across vertebral line--**darwinii** Head scales **flat**; dorsal bands not butterfly-shaped, frequently continuous across vertebral line---------------------------------**bibronii**	2. Escamas cefálicas convexas; bandas dorsales en ala de mariposa, interrumpidas en la línea mediovertebral----------------------**darwinii** Escamas cefálicas planas; bandas dorsales sin forma de mariposa, frecuentemente contínuas en la línea mediovertebral--------------**bibronii**

DIPLOLAEMUS BIBRONII Bell

> 1843 *Diplolaemus Bibronii* Bell, Zool. Voyage Beagle, Rept.: 21, pl. 11. Type-locality: Puerto Deseado, Argentina.
>
> Distribution: Patagonia, from Santa Cruz to Aysén and Magallanes, Argentina.

DIPLOLAEMUS DARWINII Bell

> 1843 *Diplolaemus Darwinii* Bell, Zool. Voyage Beagle, Rept.: 20, pl. 10. Type-locality: Puerto Deseado, Argentina.
>
> Distribution: Patagonia, from Puerto Deseado to straits of Magellan, Argentina.

DIPLOLAEMUS LEOPARDINUS (Werner)

> 1898 *Liosaurus leopardinus* Werner, Zool. Jahrb. Abt. Syst. Oekol. Geogr. Tiere, 1 (suppl. 4): 249, pl. 13, figs. 1-1b. Type-locality: Santiago, Chile (in error, according to Donoso-Barros, below).
> 1965 *Diplolaemus leopardinus*—Donoso-Barros, An. Segundo Cong. Latino-Amer. Zool., São Paulo, 2: 223, fig. 3.
>
> Distribution: Patagonia, in region of Lonquimay valley in Chile and Neuquén, Argentina.

DRACAENA Daudin

1802 Dracaena Daudin, Hist. Nat. Rept., 2: 421. Type-species: Dracaena guianensis Daudin.
1825 Ada Gray, Ann. Philos., 10 (7): 20. Type-species: Teius crocodilinus Merrem.
1830 Thorictis Wagler, Nat. Syst. Amph.: 153. Type-species: Dracaena guianensis Daudin.

Distribution: Amazonian drainage; Mato Grosso and Paraguay.

Content: Two species, according to most recent revision by Vanzolini and Valencia, Arq. Zool. Dept. Zool. Sao Paulo, 13, 1965 (1966), 7-35.

Key to the species

1. Single unpaired scale lying posterior to mid-dorsal suture between nasals-----paraguayensis
   Pair of scales on dorsum of snout immediately behind middorsal suture between nasals--------
   -------------------------------------guianensis

Clave de especies

1. Una escama posterior a sutura entre nasales----
   ---------------------------------------paraguayensis
   Un par de escamas posterior a sutura entre nasales---------------------------guianensis

DRACAENA GUIANENSIS Daudin

1788 Lacerta Dracoena—Lacépède (not of Linnaeus, 1758) Hist. Nat. Quad. Ovip., 1: 622.
1802 Dracaena guianensis Daudin, Hist. Nat. Rept., 2: 421, pl. 28. Type-locality: Cayenne (using same specimen seen by Lacépède, 1788).
1820 Teius crocodilinus Merrem, Tent. Syst. Amph.: 62. Type-locality: "America meridionali".
1966 Dracaena guianensis—Vanzolini and Valencia, Arq. Zool. Depto. Zool. São Paulo, 13 (1965): 15, figs.

Distribution: Northeastern South America in Amazonian Basin.

DRACAENA PARAGUAYENSIS Amaral

1950 Dracaena paraguayensis Amaral, Copeia: 283. Type-locality: São Lourenço, Mato Grosso, Brazil.
1966 Dracaena paraguayensis—Vanzolini and Valencia, Arq. Zool. Depto. Zool. São Paulo, 13 (1965): 11, figs.

Distribution: Mato Grosso, Brazil and Paraguay.

ECHINOSAURA

1890 Echinosaura Boulenger, Proc. Zool. Soc. London, 1890: 82. Type-species: Echinosaura horrida Boulenger.

Distribution: As for only known species.

Content: One species, according to most recent review by Uzzell, Copeia, 1965.

ECHINOSAURA HORRIDA Boulenger

1890 Echinosaura horrida Boulenger, Proc. Zool. Soc. London, 1890: 83, pl. 10, fig. 1-1c. Type-locality: Ecuador.

Distribution: Pacific Ecuador to Panama.

Content: Three subspecies, according to Uzzell, 1965.

Key to the subspecies

1. Frontonasal single; frontal undivided, short, scarcely longer than wide; dorsum with two juxtaposed longitudinal rows of tubercles------------------------horrida
Frontonasal divided; frontal undivided and much longer than wide, or transversely divided, two parts together much longer than wide; dorsum with longitudinal, usually sinuous or angled, occasionally straight, rows of tubercles, these separated by five to ten small scales---------2

2. Frontal transversely divided, length of two parts much greater than greatest width; infralabials more than 4-5------panamensis
Frontal undivided, long; infralabials fewer than 4-5-------------------------palmeri

Clave de subespecies

1. Frontonasal único; frontal no dividido, corto, ligeramente más largo que ancho; dorso con dos hileras longitudinales de tubérculos yuxtapuestos------------horrida
Frontonasal dividido; frontal dividido o no, y mucho más largo que ancho, cuando esta dividido las dos partes juntas son más largas que anchas; dorso con hileras de pequeñas tubérculos separados entre si por cinco a diez escamitas-----·----------2

2. Frontal transversalmente dividido, la longitud de los dos partes mucho mayor que el ancho más grande; infralabiales más de 4-5----------------------------panamensis
Frontal no dividido, largo; infralabiales menos de 4-5-----------------------palmeri

Echinosaura horrida horrida Boulenger

1965 Echinosaura horrida horrida—Uzzell, Copeia, 1965: 83.

Distribution: Northwestern lowlands of Ecuador; Gorgona Island, Colombia.

Echinosaura horrida palmeri Boulenger

1911 Echinosaura palmeri Boulenger, Ann. Mag. Nat. Hist., 8 (7): 23. Type-locality: Noananoá, Río San Juan, Chocó, Colombia.
1944 Echinosaura centralis Dunn, Caldasia, 2: 397. Type-locality: Muzo (Humbo), Colombia.
1965 Echinosaura horrida palmeri—Uzzell, Copeia, 1965: 85.

Distribution: Darién, Panama, to Colombia.

Echinosaura horrida panamensis Barbour

1924 Echinosaura panamensis Barbour, Proc. New England Zool. Club, 9: 8. Type-locality: La Loma, Bocas del Toro Province, Panama.
1965 Echinosaura horrida panamensis—Uzzell, Copeia, 1965: 85.

Distribution: Chiriqui, Bocas del Toro and Cocle, Panama.

ECPLEOPUS Duméril and Bibron

    1839 Ecpleopus Duméril and Bibron, Erp. Gén., 5: 434. Type-species: Ecpleopus Gaudichaudii Duméril
        and Bibron.
    1862 Aspidolaemus Peters, Abh. Akad. Wiss. Berlin, 1862: 199. Type-species: Ecpleopus (Aspidolaemus)
        affinis Peters.

   Distribution: Brazil and Ecuador.

   Content: Two species.

<table>
<tr><td>Key to the species</td><td>Clave de especies</td></tr>
<tr><td>

1. Loreal absent, anterior supraciliary reaches
frontonasal; number of scales from occiput to
sacrum 33-----------------------gaudichaudii
Loreal present, anterior supraciliary does not
reach frontonasal; number of scales from occi-
put to sacrum 46-48--------------------affinis

</td><td>

1. Loreal ausente; supraciliar anterior alcanza
el frontonasal; número de escamas entre
occipucio y sacro 33------------gaudichaudii
Loreal presente; supraciliar anterior no
alcanza el frontonasal; número de escamas
entre occipucio y sacro 46-48---------affinis

</td></tr>
</table>

ECPLEOPUS AFFINIS Peters

    1862 Ecpleopus (Aspidolaemus) affinis Peters, Abh. Akad. Wiss. Berlin, 1862: 199, pl. 3, fig. 1, 1a-f.
        Type-locality: Unknown.
    1885 Ecpleopus affinis—Boulenger, Cat. Liz. Brit. Mus., 2: 402.

   Distribution: Higher Pacific slopes and inter-Andean valleys, from Ambato south, in Ecuador.

ECPLEOPUS GAUDICHAUDII Duméril and Bibron

    1839 Ecpleopus Gaudichaudii Duméril and Bibron, Erp. Gén., 5: 436. Type-locality: Brazil.
    1885 Ecpleopus gaudichaudii—Boulenger, Cat. Liz. Brit. Mus., 2: 401.

   Distribution: Brazil.

ENYALIOIDES Boulenger

1885 *Enyalioides* Boulenger, Cat. Liz. Brit. Mus., 2: 112. Type-species: *Enyalius heterolepis* Bocourt.

Distribution: Southern Central America; northwestern South America.

Content: Seven species.

<table>
<tr><td>Key to the species</td><td>Clave de especies</td></tr>
<tr><td>

1. Spines of nuchal crest not isolated from spines on dorsal crest------------------------------2
   Spines of nuchal crest prominent and completely isolated from spines on dorsal crest-------------------------------------palpebralis

2. One or two femoral pores on each side---------3
   Three or four femoral pores on each side------5

3. Ventrals keeled-------------------------------4
   Ventrals smooth or indistinctly keeled------------------------------------praestabilis

4. Dorsal granules very fine, more than sixteen between lateral denticulation and dorsal crest-------------------------------microlepis
   Dorsal granules larger, fewer than sixteen between lateral denticulation and dorsal crest----------------------------oshaughnessyi

5. Dorsal scales heterogeneous in size-----------6
   Dorsal scales homogeneous--------------laticeps

6. Larger scales forming two irregular longitudinal series on each side of back and irregular vertical series on flanks----------heterolepis
   A single series of enlarged scales on each side of dorsum--------------------------microlepis

</td><td>

1. Espinas de la cresta nucal no aisladas de espinas de la cresta dorsal-------------------2
   Espinas de la cresta nucal prominentes y completamente aisladas de espinas de la cresta dorsal-----------------------------palpebralis

2. Uno o dos poros femorales a cada lado---------3
   Tres o cuatro poros femorales a cada lado-----5

3. Ventrales quilladas---------------------------4
   Ventrales lisas o indistintamente quilladas--------------------------------------praestabilis

4. Gránulos dorsales muy finos, más de dieciseis entre denticulación lateral y cresta dorsal--microlepis
   Gránulos dorsales grandes, menos de dieciseis entre denticulación lateral y cresta dorsal-------------------------------oshaughnessyi

5. Escamas dorsales de tamaño heterogéneo--------6
   Escamas dorsales homogéneas------------laticeps

6. Escamas ensanchadas formando dos series longitudinales irregulares a cada lado del dorso y series verticales irregulares en los flancos---------------------------------------heterolepis
   Una sola serie de escamas ensanchadas a cada lado del dorso----------------------microlepis

</td></tr>
</table>

ENYALIOIDES HETEROLEPIS (Bocourt)

1874 *Enyalus heterolepis* Bocourt, Ann. Sci. Nat. Paris, (5) 19 (4): 1. Type-locality: Veragua, Panama.
1885 *Enyalioides heterolepis*—Boulenger, Cat. Liz. Brit. Mus., 2: 114.
1905 *Enyalioides insulae* Barbour, Bull. Mus. Comp. Zool., 46: 100. Type-locality: Isla de Gorgona, Colombia.
1911 *Enyalioides Mocquardi* Despax, Bull. Mus. Nat. Hist. Paris, 17: 10. Type-locality: "Ecuador".

Distribution: Northwestern Ecuador to Panama.

ENYALIOIDES LATICEPS (Guichenot)

1855 *Enyalus laticeps* Guichenot, in Castelnau, Exp. Amér. Sud, Reptiles: 20, pl. 5, figs. A and B. Type-locality: Fonteboa, Upper Amazon, Brazil.
1885 *Enyalioides laticeps*—Boulenger, Cat. Liz. Brit. Mus., 2: 113.

Distribution: Upper Amazonian Brazil, Colombia, and Ecuador.

Content: Two subspecies.

Key to the subspecies

1. Ventral scales smooth or indistinctly
   keeled--------------------------laticeps
   Ventral scales usually strongly keeled-----
   ---------------------------------festae

Clave de subespecies

1. Escamas ventrales lisas o indistintamente
   quilladas-------------------------laticeps
   Escamas ventrales usualmente fuertemente
   quilladas-------------------------festae

Enyalioides laticeps laticeps (Guichenot)

1855 Enyalus planiceps Guichenot, in Castelnau, Exp. Amér. Sud, Reptiles: 21, pl. 6, figs. A-B.
      Type-locality: Fonteboa, Upper Amazon, Brazil.
1876 Enyalius coerulescens Cope, Jour. Acad. Nat. Sci. Phila., (2) 8 (1875): 169. Type-
      locality: None given; Gansaand Vanzolini, Ann. Carnegie Mus., 33, 1953, 125, pointed out
      that the type came from the Amazon from Santarem to Peru.
1885 Enyalioides caerulescens Boulenger (invalid emendation of coerulescens Cope), Cat. Liz.
      Brit. Mus., 2: 112.
1930 Enyalioides laticeps laticeps—Burt and Burt, Proc. U. S. Nat. Mus., 78 (6): 9.

   Distribution: Upper Amazonian Brazil and Amazonian Ecuador.

Enyalioides laticeps festae Peracca

1897 Enyalioides Festae Peracca, Bol. Mus. Zool. Comp. Anat. Univ. Torino, 12 (300): 3.
      Type-locality: Valley of Río Santiago, Ecuador.
1931 Enyalioides laticeps festae—Burt and Burt, Bull. Amer. Mus. Nat. Hist., 61: 266.

   Distribution: Amazonian Colombia and Ecuador.

ENYALIOIDES MICROLEPIS (O'Shaughnessy)

1881 Enyalius microlepis O'Shaughnessy, Proc. Zool. Soc. London, 1881: 238, pl. 24, fig. 2. Type-
      locality: Sarayacu, Ecuador.
1885 Enyalioides microlepis—Boulenger, Cat. Liz. Brit. Mus., 2: 115.

   Distribution: Pacific lowlands of Ecuador.

ENYALIOIDES OSHAUGHNESSYI (Boulenger)

1881 Enyalius oshaughnessyi Boulenger, Proc. Zool. Soc. London, 1881: 246, pl. 26, figs. 1-1a. Type-
      locality: Ecuador.
1885 Enyalioides oshaughnessyi—Boulenger, Cat. Liz. Brit. Mus., 2: 115.

   Distribution: Amazonian Ecuador and Colombia.

ENYALIOIDES PALPEBRALIS (Boulenger)

1883 Enyalius palpebralis Boulenger, Proc. Zool. Soc. London, 1883: 46, pl. 10. Type-locality:
      Cashiboya, eastern Peru.
1885 Enyalioides palpebralis—Boulenger, Cat. Liz. Brit. Mus., 2: 116.

   Distribution: Eastern Peru; Territorio do Acre, Brazil.

ENYALIOIDES PRAESTABILIS (O'Shaughnessy)

1881 Enyalius praestabilis O'Shaughnessy, Proc. Zool. Soc. London, 1881: 240, pl. 25, fig. 1. Type-
      locality: Pallatanga and Canelos, Ecuador.
1885 Enyalioides praestabilis—Boulenger, Cat. Liz. Brit. Mus., 2: 113.

   Distribution: Amazonian Ecuador.

ENYALIOSAURUS Gray

 1845 Enyaliosaurus Gray, Cat. Liz. Brit. Mus.: 192. Type-species: Cyclura quinquecarinata Gray.
 1866 Cachryx Cope, Proc. Acad. Nat. Sci. Phila., 1866: 124. Type-species: Cachryx defensor Cope.

  Distribution: Mexico and Guatemala.

  Content: Four species, of which two (defensor Cope and clarki Bailey) are
    extralimital.

Key to the species	Clave de especies
1. Dewlap present; keeled scales on dorsal surface of upper arm; central row of caudal spines smaller than lateral spines----------palearis Dewlap absent; smooth scales on dorsal surface of upper arm; central row of caudal spines equal in size to lateral spines--------------- ----------------------------quinquecarinatus	1. Con papada; escamas quilladas en la superficie dorsal del brazo; espinas caudales de hilera central menores que espinas laterales-palearis Sin papada; escamas lisas en la superficie dorsal de brazo; espinas caudales de hilera central de igual tamaño que espinas laterales- ----------------------------quinquecarinatus

ENYALIOSAURUS PALEARIS (Stejneger)

 1899 Ctenosaura palearis Stejneger, Proc. U.S. Nat. Mus., 21: 381. Type-locality: Gualan, Guatemala.
 1950 [Enyaliosaurus] palearis—Smith and Taylor, Bull. U.S. Nat. Mus., 199: 76.

  Distribution: Low elevations of valley of Río Motagua, Guatemala; Aguan Valley of Honduras.

ENYALIOSAURUS QUINQUECARINATUS (Gray)

 1842 Cyclura quinquecarinata Gray, Zoological Miscellany: 59. Type-locality: None given; restricted
        to Tehuantepec, Oaxaca, by Bailey, Proc. U.S Nat. Mus., 73, 1928, 43.
 1845 Enyaliosaurus quinquecarinata—Gray, Cat. Liz. Brit. Mus.: 192.

  Distribution: Lowlands of southern Oaxaca; Matagalpa region of Nicaragua; Honduras.

REPTILIA: SAURIA: IGUANIDAE   ★ ★ ★ ★   ENYALIUS

Prepared by Richard Etheridge, San Diego State College, San Diego, California

ENYALIUS Wagler

1830 _Enyalius_ Wagler, Nat. Syst. Amphib.: 150. Type-species: _Agama catenata_ Wied.
1837 _Enyalus_ Duméril and Bibron (in error for _Enyalius_ Wagler), Erp. Gén., 4: 231.
1843 _Dryophilus_ Fitzinger, Systema Reptilium: 16. Type-species: _Enyalius bilineatus_ Duméril and Bibron.

Distribution: Forested areas in eastern South America.

Content: Seven species.

Key to the species

1. All subdigital lamellae distinctly keeled; distal four or five lamellae without median groove, or groove obscured by keels----------2
All subdigital lamellae smooth, or some with one or two indistinct keels; distal four or five lamellae of each digit with median, longitudinal groove-------------------------3

2. Dorsal head scales, including those on snout, distinctly keeled; condition of vertebral crest unknown------------------------leechii
Scales on snout smooth, other dorsal head scales smooth or keeled; vertebral crest present--------------------------brasiliensis

3. Tail less than 2.5 times snout-vent length; no elongate subocular; no longitudinal stripes on belly--4
Tail more than 2.5 times snout-vent length; usually elongate subocular; belly with three longitudinal dark stripes-----------bilineatus

4. Ventral scales smooth------------------------5
Ventral scales keeled------------------------6

5. Tail more than twice as long as snout-vent length; not more than 60 scales in vertebral crest between occiput and anterior margin of thigh; both sexes marked with wide crossbands--pictus
Tail less than twice as long as snout-vent length; more than 60 scales in vertebral crest; females not with wide crossbands (males not known)---------------------------bibronii

6. Tail not autotomic, caudal scales not in regular segments; adpressed hind limb reaches about to middle of orbit-------------iheringii
Tail autotomic, caudal scales in regular segments with five or six dorsal and three ventral scales per segment; adpressed hind limb reaches beyond tip of snout-----catenatus

Clave de especies

1. Todas las lamelas subdigitales distintamente quilladas; las cuatro o cinco lamelas distales sin surco medio o con surco disimulado por las quillas------------------------------------2
Todas las lamelas subdigitales lisas o algunas de ellas con una o dos quillas indiferenciadas; las cuatro o cinco lamelas distales de cada dígito con un surco longitudinal medio-------3

2. Escamas dorsales de la cabeza, incluyendo las del hocico, distintamente quilladas; condición de la cresta vertebral desconocida-----leechii
Escamas del hocico lisas, las demás escamas dorsales de la cabeza lisas o quilladas; cresta vertebral presente---------brasiliensis

3. Longitud de la cola menos de 2.5 veces la del hocico-ano; sin subocular alargada; sin cintas longitudinales en el vientre----------------4
Longitud de la cola más de 2.5 veces la del hocico-ano; subocular generalmente alargada; vientre con tres cintas longitudinales oscuras ---------------------------------bilineatus

4. Escamas ventrales lisas----------------------5
Escamas ventrales quilladas------------------6

5. Longitud de la cola más del doble que la del hocico-ano; no más de 60 escamas en cresta vertebral entre el occipucio y el margen anterior del muslo; ambos sexos marcados con bandas transversales anchas----------------pictus
Longitud de la cola menos del doble que la del hocico-ano; más de 60 escamas en cresta vertebral; hembras sin bandas transversales anchas (machos desconocidos)-----------------bibronii

6. Cola no autotómica, escamas caudales no en segmentos regulares; miembro posterior extendido hacia adelante llega hasta la mitad de la órbita-------------------------------iheringii
Cola autotómica, escamas caudales en segmentos regulares con cinco o seis escamas dorsales y tres ventrales por segmento; extremidad posterior extendida hacia adelante llega más allá de la punta del hocico--------------catenatus

ENYALIUS BIBRONII Boulenger

1885 _Enyalius Bibronii_ Boulenger, Cat. Liz. Brit. Mus., 2: 119. Type-locality: Bahia, Brazil.

Distribution: Bahia, Linhares, and Espirito Santo, Brazil.

ENYALIUS BILINEATUS Duméril and Bibron

    1837 *Enyalus bilineatus* Duméril and Bibron, Erp. Gén., 4: 234. Type-locality: Brazil.

      Distribution: Minas Gerais and Espirito Santo, Brazil.

ENYALIUS BRASILIENSIS (Lesson), new combination

    1828 *Lophyrus brasiliensis* Lesson, Voyage Coquille, Rept.: 32, pl. 1, fig. 3. Type-locality: Santa Catarina, Brazil.

      Distribution: Southeastern Brazil and northeastern Uruguay.

ENYALIUS CATENATUS (Wied)

    1821 *Agama catenata* Wied, Reise nach Brasil, 2: 247. Type-locality: Cabeça do Boi, Bahia, Brazil.
    1825 *Lophyrus Rhombifer* Spix, Sp. Nov. Lac. Bras.: 9, pl. 11. Type-locality: Rio Solimoëns, Brazil.
    1825 *Lophyrus margaritaceus* Spix, Sp. Nov. Lac. Bras.: 10, pl. 12, fig. 1. Type-locality: Bahia and Rio Solimoëns, Brazil.
    1825 *Lophyrus albomaxillaris* Spix, Sp. Nov. Lac. Bras.: 11, pl. 13, fig. 2. Type-locality: Rio de Janeiro and Pará, Brazil.
    1830 [*Enyalius*] *catenatus*—Wagler, Nat. Syst. Amphib.: 150.
    ?1831 *Oph.*[*yessa*] (*Plica*) *Braziliensis* Gray (not of Lesson), Synopsis Species Class Reptilia, in Griffith, Cuvier's Animal Kingdom, 9: 40. Type-locality: Brazil.
    1898 *Enyalius catenatus paulista* Ihering, Proc. Acad. Nat. Sci. Phila., 49: 102. Type-locality: São Paulo, Brazil.

      Distribution: Eastern Brazil, from Pernambuco south to Santa Catarina.

ENYALIUS IHERINGII Boulenger

    1885 *Enyalius Iheringii* Boulenger, Ann. Mag. Nat. Hist., (5) 15: 192. Type-locality: Rio Grande do Sul, Brazil.
    1885 *Enyalius iheringii*—Boulenger, Cat. Liz. Brit. Mus., 2: 120, pl. 7.

      Distribution: Southeastern Brazil, from São Paulo south to Rio Grande do Sul.

ENYALIUS LEECHII (Boulenger), new combination

    1885 *Enyalioides leechii* Boulenger, Cat. Liz. Brit. Mus., 2: 473. Type-locality: Santarem, Brazil.

      Distribution: Known only from type locality.

ENYALIUS PICTUS (Wied), new combination

    1825 *Agama picta* Wied, Abbildungen zur Naturgeschichte Brasiliens: 125. Type-locality: Mucurí and Lago d'Arara, Bahia, Brazil.
    1926 *Enyalius zonatus* Wettstein, Anz. Acad. Wiss. Wien, 63: 1. Type-locality: Ecuador.

      Distribution: Known definitely only from near mouth of Rio Mucurí in extreme southeastern Bahia, Brazil.

EUMECES Wiegmann

1834 <u>Eumeces</u> Wiegmann, Herpetologia Mexicana: 36. Type-species: <u>Scincus pavimentatus</u> Geoffroy.
1839 <u>Plestiodon</u> Duméril and Bibron, Erp. Gén., 5: 697. Type-species: <u>Plestiodon Aldrovandii</u> Duméril and Bibron.
1843 <u>Pariocela</u> Fitzinger, Systema Reptilium: 22. Type-species: <u>Plestiodon laticeps</u> Duméril and Bibron.
1845 <u>Cyprius</u> Gray, Cat. Liz. Brit. Mus.: 91. Type-species: <u>Plestiodon auratus</u> Schneider.
1852 <u>Lamprosaurus</u> Hallowell, Proc. Acad. Nat. Sci. Phila., 1852: 206. Type-species: <u>Lamprosaurus guttulatus</u> Hallowell.
1854 <u>Eurylepis</u> Blyth, Journ. Asiatic Soc. Bengal, 23: 739. Type-species: <u>Eurylepis taeniolatus</u> Blyth.
1891 <u>Platypholis</u> Dugés, La Naturaleza (2) 1: 3, pl. 23. Type-species: <u>Eumeces Altamiranii</u> Dugés.

Distribution: Central and North America, Africa and Asia.

Comment: Several authors, including Cope, have used variant spellings of <u>Plestiodon</u> Duméril and Bibron, such as <u>Plistodon</u> and <u>Pleistodon</u>.

Content: Approximately 40 species, all but three of which are extralimital.

Key to the species

1. Middorsal scales much broader than those of paravertebral region-----------------------2
   Middorsal scales not conspicuously broader than paravertebral scales--------------<u>sumichrasti</u>

2. Scales around middle of body 21; limbs meet when adpressed; parietals not in contact; two rows of nuchal scales--------------<u>schwartzei</u>
   Scales around middle of body 17-19; limbs widely separated when adpressed; parietals in contact behind interparietal; four pairs of nuchal scales-------------------------<u>managuae</u>

Clave de especies

1. Escamas medio dorsales mucho más anchas que los paravertebrales-----------------------------2
   Escamas medio dorsales no conspicuamente más ensanchadas que los paravertebrales----------
   -------------------------------------<u>sumichrasti</u>

2. Escamas al medio del cuerpo 21; extremidades se encuentran cuando se oponen; parietales no contactan; dos filas de escamas nucales-------
   -------------------------------------<u>schwartzei</u>
   Escamas al medio del cuerpo 17-19; extremidades ampliamente separadas cuando se oponen; parietales en contacto detrás del interparietal; cuatro pares de escamas nucales-------<u>managuae</u>

EUMECES MANAGUAE Dunn

1933 <u>Eumeces managuae</u> Dunn, Proc. Biol. Soc. Washington, 46: 67. Type-locality: Aviation field, Managua, Nicaragua.
1956 <u>Eumeces managuae</u>—Taylor, Univ. Kansas Sci. Bull., 38: 292, fig. 73.

Distribution: Costa Rica to Nicaragua.

EUMECES SCHWARTZEI Fischer

1885 <u>Eumeces schwartzei</u> Fischer, Abh. Naturwiss. Ver. Hamburg, 8: 3, pl. 7, fig. 1. Type-locality: Small island in Laguna de Términos, Campeche, Mexico.
1935 <u>Eumeces schwartzei</u>—Taylor, Kansas Univ. Sci. Bull., 23: 94, fig. 5.

Distribution: Yucatán Peninsula and adjacent Tabasco, Mexico to central El Petén, Guatemala.

EUMECES SUMICHRASTI (Cope)

1867 <u>Plistodon sumichrasti</u> Cope, Proc. Acad. Nat. Sci. Phila., 1866: 321. Type-locality: Orizaba, Mexico.
1879 <u>Eumeces sumichrasti</u>—Bocourt, Miss. Sci. Mex., Rept.: 422.
1895 <u>Eumeces rovirosae</u> Dugès, La Naturaleza, (2) 2: 298, pl. 13. Type-locality: Mineral de Santa Fé, Chiapas, Mexico.
1932 <u>Eumeces schmidti</u> Dunn, Proc. Acad. Nat. Sci. Phila., 84: 30. Type-locality: Lancetilla, Honduras.
1935 <u>Eumeces sumichrasti</u>—Taylor, Kansas Univ. Sci. Bull., 23: 178, figs. 21-22.

Distribution: Central Veracruz to Guatemala and northern Honduras.

EUSPONDYLUS Tschudi

   1845 Euspondylus Tschudi, Arch. für Naturg., 11: 160. Type-species: Euspondylus maculatus Tschudi.

   Distribution: Venezuela to Peru.

   Content: Ten species.

   Comment: The arrangement of species seen here reflects the suggestions of Thomas Uzzell, who has
      reviewed this and related genera of microteiids for us.

Key to the species	Clave de especies
1. Either all dorsal scales smooth, or most smooth with some weakly keeled on posterior part of body--2 All dorsal scales keeled----------------------5	1. Todas las escamas dorsales lisas, o la mayoría lisas y algunas ligeramente quilladas en la parte posterior del cuerpo-------------------2 Todas las escamas dorsales quilladas----------5
2. Frontal not in contact with frontonasal (Fig. 1)--3 Frontal in contact with frontonasal (Fig. 2)--- ----------------------------------brevifrontalis	2. Frontal no contacta con el frontonasal (Fig. 1)--3 Frontal en contacto con el frontonasal (Fig. 2) --------------------------------brevifrontalis

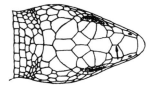

Fig. 1. E. maculatus, showing contact of prefrontals (from Peters, 1862).

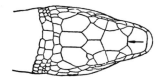

Fig. 2. E. stenolepis, showing contact of frontal and frontonasal (from Boulenger, 1908).

3. Infraorbitals smaller than upper labials------4 Infraorbitals subequal to or larger than upper labials-------------------------guentheri	3. Infraorbitales más pequeñas que las supra-labiales----------------------------------4 Infraorbitales iguales o mayores que las supralabiales------------------------guentheri
4. Transparent ocular disk divided; 40 scales around midbody-----------------------maculatus Transparent ocular disk not divided; fewer than 35 scales around midbody---------simonsii	4. Disco ocular transparente dividido; 40 escamas al medio del cuerpo-------------------maculatus Disco ocular transparente no dividido; menos de 35 escamas al medio del cuerpo--------simonsii
5. Frontal not in contact with frontonasal-------6 Frontal in contact with frontonasal--stenolepis	5. Frontal no contacta con el frontonasal--------6 Frontal en contacto con el frontonasal--------- -------------------------------------stenolepis
6. Fewer than 25 transverse rows of ventral plates, counted from edge of collar to preanal plates--------------------------------7 More than 25 transverse rows of ventrals------9	6. Menos de 25 hileras transversales de láminas ventrales, contando desde el borde del collar hasta las láminas preanales------------------7 Más de 25 hileras transversales de ventrales--9
7. Four supraoculars, first smallest of series---8 Three supraoculars, first as large as or larger than third, which it sometimes contacts------------------------------spinalis	7. Cuatro supraoculares, el primero es el menor de la serie----------------------------------8 Tres supraoculares, el primero igual o mayor que el tercero, con el que contacta a veces--- --spinalis
8. More than eight longitudinal rows of ventrals-- --rahmi Eight longitudinal rows of ventrals----------- ----------------------------------leucostictus	8. Más de ocho hileras longitudinales de ventrales-----------------------------------rahmi Ocho hileras longitudinales de ventrales------- ----------------------------------leucostictus
9. Thirteen gular scales from mental shield to edge of collar----------------------ocellifer Nineteen gular scales from mental shield to edge of collar-------------------acutirostris	9. Trece escamas gulares desde escudo mental a borde del collar---------------------ocellifer Diecinueve escamas gulares desde escudo mental a borde del collar----------------acutirostris

EUSPONDYLUS ACUTIROSTRIS (Peters)

1862 Ecpleopus (Euspondylus) acutirostris Peters, Abh. Akad. Wiss. Berlin, 1862: 209. Type-locality: Venezuela.
1885 Euspondylus acutirostris—Boulenger, Cat. Liz. Brit. Mus., 2: 407.

  Distribution: Rancho Grande Mountains, Estado Aragua, and Pico Naiguata, Distrito Federal, Venezuela.

EUSPONDYLUS BREVIFRONTALIS Boulenger

1903 Euspondylus brevifrontalis Boulenger, Ann. Mag. Nat. Hist., (7) 12: 431. Type-locality: Río Albarregas and Escorial, Estado Mérida, Venezuela.

  Distribution: Andes of Mérida, Venezuela, at altitudes above 3000 m.

EUSPONDYLUS GUENTHERI (O'Shaughnessy)

1881 Ecpleopus (Euspondylus) guentheri O'Shaughnessy, Proc. Zool. Soc. London, 1881: 235, pl. 23, fig. 1. Type-locality: Sarayacú, Ecuador.
1885 Euspondylus guentheri—Boulenger, Cat. Liz. Brit. Mus., 2: 407.

  Distribution: Amazonian Ecuador.

EUSPONDYLUS LEUCOSTICTUS (Boulenger)

1900 Prionodactylus leucostictus Boulenger, Trans. Linn. Soc. London, (2) 8: 54. Type-locality: Summit of Mount Roraima, Venezuela.
1933 Euspondylus leucostictus—Burt and Burt, Trans. St. Louis Acad. Sci., 28: 63.

  Distribution: Known only from type locality.

EUSPONDYLUS MACULATUS Tschudi

1845 Euspondylus maculatus Tschudi, Arch. für Naturg., 11: 161. Type-locality: Peru; further specified as vicinity of Moyobamba, Peru, by Tschudi, Fauna Peruana, Reptiles, 1846, 43.
1862 Ecpleopus (Euspondylus) maculatus—Peters, Abh. Akad. Wiss. Berlin, 1862: 206, pl. 2, figs. 4, 4a-e.
1897 Ecpleopus (Proctoporus) Fraseri O'Shaughnessy, Ann. Mag. Nat. Hist., (5) 4: 296. Type-locality: Guayaquil, Ecuador.

  Distribution: Coastal areas of northern Peru and southern Ecuador.

EUSPONDYLUS OCELLIFER (Werner)

1901 Prionodactylus ocellifer Werner, Verh. Zool.-Bot. Ges. Wien, 51: 596. Type-locality: Ecuador.
1933 Euspondylus ocellifer—Burt and Burt, Trans. St. Louis Acad. Sci., 28: 63.

  Distribution: Still known only from type specimen, which lacks specific locality data.

EUSPONDYLUS RAHMI (Grijs), new combination

1936 Prionodactylus rahmi Grijs, Zool. Anz., 116: 27. Type-locality: Andes of Cuzco, Peru.

  Distribution: Still known only from type specimen.

  Comment: This species is placed in this genus upon the recommendation of Thomas Uzzell, who is engaged in a revision of this and related genera of microteiids.

EUSPONDYLUS SIMONSII Boulenger

1901 Euspondylus Simonsii Boulenger, Ann. Mag. Nat. Hist., (7) 7: 549. Type-locality: Puntoyacu, Río Perené, Peru, 5000 ft.

  Distribution: Known only from type locality.

EUSPONDYLUS SPINALIS (Boulenger)

   1901 Prionodactylus spinalis Boulenger, Ann. Mag. Nat. Hist., (8) 7: 23. Type-locality: Huancabamba, Peru.

   1933 [Euspondylus] spinalis—Burt and Burt (by inference), Trans. St. Louis Acad. Sci., 28: 63.

    Distribution: Known only from type locality.

EUSPONDYLUS STENOLEPIS Boulenger

   1908 Euspondylus stenolepis Boulenger, Ann. Mag. Nat. Hist., (8) 2: 519, figs. 4a-d. Type-locality: San Antonio, Colombia.

    Distribution: Known only from type locality.

GARBESAURA Amaral

    1933 Garbesaura Amaral, Mem. Inst. Butantan, 7 (1932): 64. Type-species: Garbesaura garbei Amaral.

    Distribution: As for only known species.

    Content: One species.

GARBESAURA GARBEI Amaral

    1933 Garbesaura garbei Amaral, Mem. Inst. Butantan, 7 (1932): 64, fig. 1. Type-locality: Monte Christo, Tapajoz, Pará, Brazil.

    Distribution: Known only from type locality.

<u>GARTHIA</u> Donoso-Barros and Vanzolini

   1965 <u>Garthia</u> Donoso-Barros and Vanzolini, in Donoso-Barros, Publ. Oc. Mus. Nac. Hist. Nat. Chile, 7:
       1. Type-species: <u>Gymnodactylus gaudichaudii</u> Duméril and Bibron.

   Distribution: Chile.

   Content: Two species.

   Comment: Donoso-Barros, Reptiles of Chile, 1966, 122, included <u>Gymnodactylus dorbignii</u> Duméril and
     Bibron in this genus, but Kluge, Amer. Mus. Novitates, 2193, 1964, 33, considered it a species of
     <u>Homonota</u>, and it is included there tentatively at this time.

Key to the species	Clave de especies
1. Occipital region bounded by white ring from eye to eye; 14-16 lamellae under fourth toe------- ---------------------------------<u>penai</u> Occipital region without white line or boundary; fewer than 14 lamellae under fourth --------------------------------<u>gaudichaudii</u>	1. Con región occipital circundata de un franja anular blanca; 14-16 lamelas bajo el cuarto dedo------------------------------------<u>penai</u> Sin un franja blanca en el región occipital; menos de 14 lamelas bajo el cuarto dedo------- ----------------------------------<u>gaudichaudii</u>

<u>GARTHIA</u> <u>GAUDICHAUDII</u> (Duméril and Bibron)

   1836 <u>Gymnodactylus Gaudichaudii</u> Duméril and Bibron, Erp. Gén., 3: 413. Type-locality: Coquimbo
     (Provincia Coquimbo), Chile.
   1964 <u>Homonota gaudichaudii</u>—Kluge, Amer. Mus. Novitates, 2193: 31, fig. 9.
   1965 <u>Garthia gaudichaudii</u>—Donoso-Barros and Vanzolini, in Donoso-Barros, Pub. Oc. Mus. Nac. Hist. Nat.
     Chile, 7: 4.

   Distribution: West coast of Chile between 25°S and 30°S.

<u>GARTHIA</u> <u>PENAI</u> Donoso-Barros

   1966 <u>Garthia peñai</u> Donoso-Barros, Reptiles de Chile: 125, col. pl. 4. Type-locality: Los Molles,
     Combabarlá, Provincia de Coquimbo, Chile, 1500 m.

   Distribution: Precordilleran and cordilleran regions of Provincia de Coquimbo, Chile.

GERRHONOTUS Wiegmann

1828 Gerrhonotus Wiegmann, Isis von Oken, 21: 379. Type-species: Gerrhonotus tessellatus Wiegmann.
1830 Pterogastenes Peale and Green, Jour. Acad. Nat. Sci. Phila., 6: 234. Type-species: Pterogastenes ventralis Peale and Green.
1838 Elgaria Gray, Ann. Mag. Nat. Hist., (1) 1: 390. Type-species: Cordylus (Gerrhonotus) multicarinatus Blainville.
1838 Barisia Gray, Ann. Mag. Nat. Hist., (1) 1: 390. Type-species: Gerrhonotus imbricatus Wiegmann.
1843 Trachypeltis Fitzinger, Syst. Rept.: 21. Type-species: Gerrhonotus multicarinatus Blainville.
1843 Tropidogerrhon Fitzinger, Syst. Rept.: 21. Type-species: Gerrhonotus rudicollis Wiegmann.
1845 Pterogasterus Gray (emendation of Pterogastenes Peale and Green), Cat. Liz. Brit. Mus.: 53.
1846 Tropidogerrhum Agassiz (corrected spelling of Tropidogerrhon Fitzinger), Nomenclator Zoologica Index Universalis: 203.
1878 Mesaspis Cope, Proc. Amer. Phil. Soc., 17: 96. Type-species: Gerrhonotus moreletii Bocourt.

Distribution: Central Texas throughout Mexico and Central America to Panama.

Content: Twenty species, of which only two are found within limits of this work.

Comment: Gerrhonotus modestus (Cope) was supposedly from Guatemala, but it is known only from Mexico.

Key to the species	Clave de especies
1. Prefrontals usually absent; 18-20 longitudinal dorsal scale rows-----------moreletii Prefrontals usually present; 14-16 longitudinal dorsal scale rows-----------monticolus	1. Prefrontales usualmente ausente; 18-20 filas longitudinales de escamas dorsales---moreletii Prefrontales usualmente presentes; 14-16 filas longitudinales de escamas dorsales--monticolus

GERRHONOTUS MONTICOLUS Cope

1877 Gerrhonotus monticolus Cope, Proc. Amer. Phil. Soc., 17: 97. Type-locality: Pico Blanco, Costa Rica.
1907 Gerrhonotus alfaroi Stejneger, Proc. U. S. Nat. Mus., 32: 505. Type-locality: Santa María de Dota, Costa Rica, 2000 m.
1956 Barisia monticola—Taylor, Univ. Kansas Sci. Bull., 38: 208, figs. 54-55.

Distribution: Costa Rica to Chiriqui, Panama.

GERRHONOTUS MORELETII Bocourt

1871 Gerrhonotus moreletii Bocourt, Bull. Nouv. Arch. Mus. Hist. Nat. Paris, 7: 102. Type-locality: Petén and pine forests of Alta Verapaz, Guatemala.

Distribution: Guatemala to Mexico.

Content: Five subspecies, one (temporalis Hartweg and Tihen) extralimital.

Key to the subspecies	Clave de subspecies
1. Upper and lower postnasal in contact------2 Upper postnasal separated from lower by contact between loreal and nasal---rafaeli	1. Posnasales superiores e inferiores en contacto-------------------------------2 Posnasales superiores separados de los inferiores por contacto entre loreal y nasal-------------------------------rafaeli
2. Lowest primary temporal usually in contact with two lower secondaries; prefrontals usually present; posterior loreal normally in contact with supralabials-------------3 Lowest primary temporal usually contacts only lowest secondary temporal; prefrontals usually absent; posterior loreal usually not in contact with supralabials----------------------------salvadorensis	2. Temporal primaria más baja, frecuentemente en contacto con las dos más bajas secundarias; prefrontales usualmente presentes; loreal posterior normalmente en contacto con supralabiales------------------------3 Temporal primaria más baja, frecuentemente en contacto con sólo la más baja secundaria; prefrontales usualmente ausentes; loreal posterior normalmente no contacta con supralabiales------------salvadorensis

3. Anterior sublabial usually in contact with only third or a more posterior infralabial; ground color usually olive to blackish--------------------------moreletii
Anterior sublabial usually in contact with second infralabial; ground color frequently brownish--------------------------fulvus

3. Sublabial anterior frecuentemente en contacto con solo la tercera a otra más posterior infralabial; color frecuentemente oliva o negruzco------------------moreletii
Sublabial anterior frequentemente en contacto con la segunda infralabial; color generalmente pardo------------------fulvus

Gerrhonotus moreletii moreletii Bocourt

    1932 [Gerrhonotus moreletii moreletii]—Dunn and Emlen, Proc. Acad. Nat. Sci. Phila., 84: 28.

    Distribution: Mountains of Alta Verapaz, Guatemala.

Gerrhonotus moreletii fulvus Bocourt

    1871 Gerrhonotus fulvus Bocourt, Bull. Nouv. Arch. Mus. Hist. Nat. Paris, 7: 104. Type-locality: Pine forest of Totonicapán on western slopes of Cordillera, Guatemala.
    1943 Gerrhonotus moreleti fulvus—Stuart, Occ. Pap. Mus. Zool. Univ. Mich., 471: 20.

    Distribution: Intermediate and higher elevations on Plateau of Guatemala, except mountains of Alta Verapaz.

Gerrhonotus moreletii rafaeli Hartweg and Tihen

    1946 Gerrhonotus moreletii rafaeli Hartweg and Tihen, Occ. Pap. Mus. Zool. Univ. Mich., 497: 8. Type-locality: Sixteen km south of Siltepec, Chiapas, Mexico.

    Distribution: Intermediate and higher elevations of Sierra Madre of Chiapas, Mexico, into extreme southwestern Guatemala.

Gerrhonotus moreletii salvadorensis Schmidt

    1928 Gerrhonotus salvadorensis Schmidt, Zool. Ser. Field Mus. Nat. Hist., 12: 196, fig. 1. Type-locality: Los Esesmiles, Chalatenango, Salvador.
    1932 Gerrhonotus moreletii salvadorensis—Dunn and Emlen, Proc. Acad. Nat. Sci. Phila., 84: 28.

    Distribution: Honduras and Salvador south to Matagalpa, Nicaragua.

GONATODES Fitzinger

1843 Gonatodes Fitzinger, Systema Reptilium: 91. Type-species: Gymnodactylus albogularis Duméril and Bibron.

Distribution: Central America; northern South America; West Indies.

Content: Wermuth, Das Tierreich, 80, 1965, 42-45, listed 18 species in this genus. Five of these (beebei Noble, boonii Van Lidth, collaris Garman, gaudichaudii Duméril and Bibron, and oxycephalus Werner) have either been synonymized with other Gonatodes or removed to other genera. Four additional valid species have been added in recent literature. The status of australis Gray remains highly questionable, leaving 17 currently recognized species.

Key to the species	Clave de especies

1. Pupil round-----------------------------------2
   Pupil vertical----------------------antillensis

2. Without dorsolateral light bands-------------3
   Body with two dorsolateral light bands running
   from eye to base of tail (Fig. 1); supraciliary spine in male--------------------hasemani

3. Some dorsal pattern present-------------------4
   Without pattern dorsally; no ventral markings;
   dorsal color reddish brown-----------annularis

4. Ground color not dark green, body without irregularly spaced small light spots-----------5
   Ground color dark green with many small light
   spots (Fig. 2)----------------------annularis

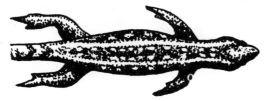

Fig. 1. Gonatodes hasemani

5. No vertebral stripe--------------------------6
   Vertebral stripe present, may be somewhat
   inconspicuous-------------------------------7

6. No supraciliary spine; enlarged scales on lower
   surface of tail in continuous series; fewer
   than eight supralabials--------------------10
   Supraciliary spine present; enlarged scales on
   lower surface of tail isolated, separated by
   whorls of tiny scales; 8 supralabials; pattern
   as in Fig. 3--------------------------annularis

---

1. Pupila redonda-------------------------------2
   Pupila vertical---------------------antillensis

2. Sin cintas latero-dorsales claras------------3
   Con dos cintas latero-dorsales, claras y estre-
   chas, desde el ojo a la base de la cola (Fig.
   1); una espina supraciliar en el macho------
   --------------------------------------hasemani

3. Con diseño dorsal, no uniformemente coloreado--4
   Sin diseño dorsal, uniformemente coloreado de
   pardo rojizo-------------------------annularis

4. Color general no verde oscuro, y sin manchitas
   irregularmente dispuestas------------------5
   Color general verde oscuro maculado por multi-
   ples manchitas claras (Fig. 2)------annularis

Fig. 2. Gonatodes annularis (boonii pattern type)

5. Sin cinta vertebral--------------------------6
   Con cinta vertebral conspícua o no-----------7

6. No hay espina supraciliar proyectada; escamas
   subcaudales ensanchadas, dispuestas en una
   línea contínua; menos de ocho supralabiales-10
   Una espina proyectada en la región supraciliar;
   escamas ensanchadas en la cara inferior de la
   cola aisladas y separadas por anillos de pequeñas escamas; 8 supralabiales; diseño dorsal
   como Fig. 3 --------------------------annularis

Fig. 3. Gonatodes annularis (annularis
         pattern type)

7. Fewer than 21 lamellae under fourth toe; head slender with pointed snout------------------8
   Vertebral stripe bordered by ground color; more than 22 lamellae on ventral surface of fourth toe on hind foot; head broad, with rounded snout; vertebral stripe in females narrower than in males, black dorsolateral spots (Fig. 4)-----------------------------------petersi

8. Gular region not black with spotting; in females vertebral line begins on occipital region--9
   Gular region black with white spotting in males (Fig. 5); in females vertebral line begins at eye level and has three expansions along its length (Fig. 6)----------------atricucullaris

7. Menos de 21 lamelas bajo el cuarto ortejo; cabeza delgada con hocico agudo--------------8
   Más de 22 lamelas bajo el cuarto ortejo; cabeza ancha con hocico redondeado; faja vertebral limitada por el color general, en machos; cinta vertebral de la hembra estrechada, con manchas dorso-laterales oscuras (Fig. 4)--------
   ----------------------------------petersi

8. Región gular no negra con manchas blancas en machos; la línea vertebral de la hembra comienza en la región occipital--------------9
   Región gular negra manchada de blanco en el macho (Fig. 5); la línea vertebral comienza a nivel de los ojos en la hembra (Fig. 6)----
   -----------------------------atricucullaris

Fig. 4. Gonatodes petersi

Fig. 5. Gonatodes atricucullaris, venter of male.

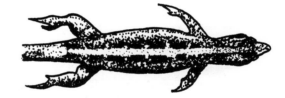

Fig. 6. Gonatodes atricucullaris, dorsum of female.

9. Vertebral stripe bordered with black, continuous in males (Fig. 7), but a series of spots in females (Fig. 8)-------------------vittatus
   Vertebral stripe obsolete or without black border in males (Fig. 9), males light greyish above with diffuse lateral spots; sides of ventral surface with black suffusion (Fig. 10); female identical with that of vittatus---
   -------------------------------------bodinii

9. Faja vertebral bordeada de negro, contínuo en machos (Fig. 7), y manchada en las hembras (Fig. 8)----------------------------vittatus
   Faja vertebral obsoleta, sin bordeado negro, en machos (Fig. 9); grisáceo claro encima con manchas difusas laterales; lados del vientre con dos sufusiones oscuras (Fig. 10); hembra igual que en vittatus-----------------bodinii

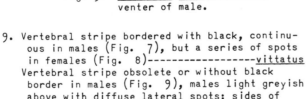

Fig. 7. Gonatodes vittatus, male

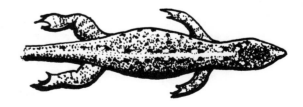

Fig. 8. Gonatodes vittatus, female

Fig. 9. Gonatodes bodinii, dorsum of male

Fig. 9. Gonatodes bodinii, dorsum of male

Fig. 10. Gonatodes bodinii, venter of male

10.Head with variegated pattern-----------------11
   Head without any variegation-----------------18

10.Sobre la cabeza un conjunto de fajas---------11
   Cabeza sin un conjunto de fajas--------------18

11.Dorsum without ocelli-----------------------12
   One or two pairs of blue ocelli bordered in
   black on either side of dorsum behind shoulder
   (Fig. 11)----------------------------ocellatus

11.Sin ocelos a los lados del dorso-------------12
   Uno o dos pares de ocelos celestes bordeados de
   negro, en el dorso a cada lado por detrás de
   las hombros (Fig. 11)----------------ocellatus

12.Extremities of digits not strongly compressed--
   --13
   Extremities of digits strongly compressed----16

12.Extremos de los dígitos no fuertemente compri-
   midos--13
   Extremos de los dígitos fuertemente comprimidos
   --16

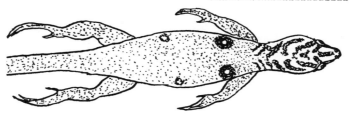

Fig. 11. Gonatodes ocellatus

13.Rostral, symphysial, and first three supralabials smooth-------------------------------14
   Rostral, symphysial, and first three supralabials with granular surface, pattern as in
   Fig. 13---------------------------------seigliei

13.Rostral, sinfisial y labial lisos------------14
   El rostral, sinfisial y los tres primeros
   supralabiales con superficie granular en los
   dos sexos, diseño como en Fig. 13-----seigliei

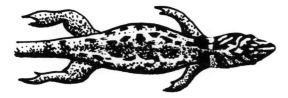

Fig. 12. Gonatodes caudiscutatus

Fig. 13. Gonatodes seigliei

14.Spots on dorsum not confluent in males; females
   not as below--------------------------------15
   Spots on dorsum confluent along median line in
   males (Fig. 14); scattered brownish dorsal
   spots throughout dorsum and tail in females
   (Fig. 15)----------------------------ceciliae

14.Manchas dorsales no confluentes en los machos;
   hembras no como el siguiente----------------15
   Dorso con manchas pardas confluentes en la
   línea media (Fig. 14); hembra pardo pálido con
   dos hileras de manchas sobre la espalda (Fig.
   15)----------------------------------ceciliae

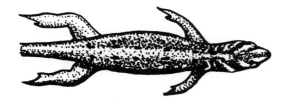

Fig. 14. Gonatodes ceciliae, male

Fig. 15. Gonatodes ceciliae, female

15.Ventral scales larger than two dorsal granules-
   --17
   Ventral scales and dorsal granules approximately same size------------------------------varius

15.Escamas ventrales mayores que dos gránulos
   dorsales--------------------------------------17
   Escamas ventrales y gránulos dorsales casi del
   mismo tamaño------------------------------varius

16.Back with two rows of narrow, grayish,
   transverse bars, each alternating with,
   or almost meeting, opposite series on
   vertebral line--------------------falconensis
   Dorsum not as above, pattern as in fig. 12-----
   ------------------------------------caudiscutatus

16.Dorso con dos hileras de barras transversas
   angostas grisáceas, cada una alternando o casí
   enfrentando a la opuesta en la línea vertebral
   ------------------------------------falconensis
   Dorso no como el anterior, diseño dorsal como
   en fig. 12----------------------------caudiscutatus

17. With light collar bordered by dark brown (Fig. 16)------------------------------concinnatus
Without light collar (Fig. 17)-----------taniae

17. Con un collar claro bordeado del pardo oscuro (Fig. 16)--------------------------concinnatus
Sin collar claro (Fig. 17)--------------taniae

18. Infradigital lamellae not flattened, not wider than rest of digit-----------------albogularis
Infradigital lamellae flattened and distinctly wider than the rest of the digit in both sexes (see also Figs. 18, 19)--------------humeralis

18. Lamelas infradigitales no aplanadas ni más anchas que el dígito---------------albogularis
Lamelas infradigitales aplanadas y claramente más anchas que el dígito (también ver Figs. 18, 19)-------------------------------humeralis

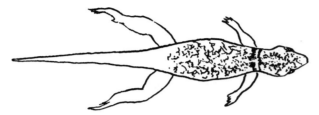

Fig. 16. Gonatodes concinnatus

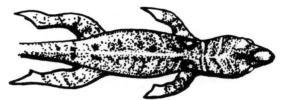

Fig. 17. Gonatodes taniae

Fig. 18. Gonatodes humeralis, dorsum

Fig. 19. Gonatodes humeralis, venter

GONATODES ALBOGULARIS (Duméril and Bibron)

1836 Gymnodactylus albogularis Duméril and Bibron, Erp. Gén., 3: 415. Type-locality: Martinique.
1843 Gonatodes albigularis Fitzinger (substitute name for Gymnodactylus albogularis Duméril and Bibron, 1836), Systema Reptilium: 92.
1867 Gymnodactylus maculatus Steindachner (not Gymnodactylus maculatus Beddome; not Gymnodactylus kotschyi maculatus Bedriaga), Reise der Österreichen Fregatte Novara, Zool., Rept.: 16, pl. 1, figs. 4-4a. Type-locality: Apparently West Indies.
1885 Gonatodes albogularis—Boulenger, Cat. Liz. Brit. Mus., 1: 59.

Distribution: Central America; northern half of South America; Antilles.

Content: Three subspecies, one of which (notatus Reinhardt and Lütken) is extralimital.

Key to the subspecies

1. In males, dark dorsum; dark, vinaceous spot from lips to side of neck, sometimes reaching shoulder, sometimes interrupted; throat white, color extending on chest, diluted; escutcheon, ventral surfaces of thighs and base of tail almost white; irregular light smear connecting thoracic and longer ventral light areas, more or less narrowed or even interrupted by dark color of sides of belly--------albogularis
Head sometimes lighter than dark dorsum, pinkish, resulting in "hooded" aspect; venter tan or somewhat darker; throat dirty pink, with more or less distinct gray chevrons; escutcheon and thighs slightly lighter than rest of venter------ -------------------------------------fuscus

Clave de subespecies

1. Dorso oscuro en machos; mancha color vino desde los labios hasta los lados de la nuca, a veces llegando hasta el hombro y a veces interrumpida; garganta blanca, esté color se extiende hasta la mejilla algo diluído; escutcheon superficie ventral de los muslos y base de la cola, casi blancas; el color claro del vientre y del tórax conectado entre sí, más o menos angostamente o aún interrumpido por color oscuro de los lados del vientre---------- -------------------------------albogularis
Cabeza a veces más clara que el dorso, rosada, dando aspecto de capucha; vientre gris plomizo de oscuro; garganta rosa sucio con manchas paralelas en forma de V más o menos distintas, escutcheon y muslos algo más claros que el resto del vientre-- -------------------------------------fuscus

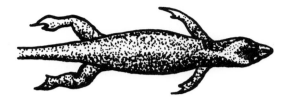

Fig. 20. Gonatodes a. albogularis, dorsum

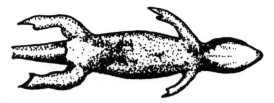

Fig. 21. Gonatodes a. albogularis, venter

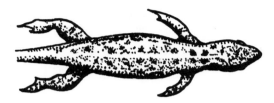

Fig. 22. Gonatodes a. fuscus

Gonatodes albogularis albogularis (Duméril and Bibron)

   1962 Gonatodes albogularis albogularis—Vanzolini and Williams, Bull. Mus. Comp. Zool., 127:
       490.
   1968 Gonatodes albogularis albogularis—Rivero Blanco, Mem. Soc. Cien. Nat. La Salle Caracas,
       27 (1967): 108, figs. 2B, 3B.

     Distribution: Lesser Antilles, Curaçao, northern Colombia and western Venezuela.

Gonatodes albogularis fuscus (Hallowell)

   1855 Stenodactylus fuscus Hallowell, Jour. Acad. Nat. Sci. Phila., (2) 3: 33. Type-locality:
       Nicaragua; restricted by Smith and Taylor, Univ. Kansas Sci. Bull., 33, 1950, 320, to
       Rama, Nicaragua.
   1875 Goniodactylus Braconnieri O'Shaughnessy, Ann. Mag. Nat. Hist., (4) 16: 265. Type-
       locality: Barranquilla, New Grenada, Chile; Boulenger, Cat. Liz. Brit. Mus., 1, 1885,
       60, lists types as only from Barranquilla, Colombia.
   1885 Gonatodes albogularis var. fuscus—Boulenger, Cat. Liz. Brit. Mus., 1: 59.
   1962 Gonatodes albogularis fuscus—Vanzolini and Williams, Bull. Mus. Comp. Zool., 127: 491.

     Distribution: Cuba; El Salvador to western Colombia; introduced into southeastern United
     States.

GONATODES ANNULARIS Boulenger

   1887 Gonatodes annularis Boulenger, Proc. Zool. Soc. London, 1887: 154, two figs. Type-locality:
       Maccasseema, Pomeroon River, Guyana.
   1904 Gonatodes Boonii Van Lidth, Notes Leyden Mus., 25: 87, pl. 7, figs. 1-2. Type-locality: Region
       of Coppename, Surinam.
   1923 Gonatodes beebei Noble, Zoologica, 3: 301. Type-locality: Kartabo, Guyana.
   1968 Gonatodes annularis—Rivero Blanco, Mem. Soc. Cien. Nat. La Salle Caracas, 27 (1967): 107, figs.
       1c-e.

     Distribution: Antilles; Central America; northern South America.

GONATODES ANTILLENSIS (Van Lidth)

   1887 Gymnodactylus antillensis Van Lidth, Notes Leyden Mus., 9: 129, pl. 2, fig. 1. Type-locality:
       Curaçao and Aruba, Dutch West Indies.
   1964 Gonatodes antillensis—Rivero Blanco, Acta Biol. Venezuelica, 4: 170.

     Distribution: Northern Venezuela and following Caribbean Islands: Curaçao, Klein-Curaçao,
     Bonaire, Klein-Bonaire, Las Aves, Aruba, and Orchila.

GONATODES

GONATODES ATRICUCULLARIS Noble

1921 Gonatodes atricucullaris Noble, Ann. New York Acad. Sci., 29: 135. Type-locality: Bellavista, Peru.

Distribution: Departamento Cajamarca, Peru.

GONATODES BODINII Rivero Blanco

1964 Gonatodes Bodinii Rivero Blanco, Acta Biol. Venezuelica, 4: 170, figs. 1-4, 10. Type-locality: Monje Grande del Sur, Archipiélago de Los Monjes, Dependencia Federal, Venezuela.

Distribution: Archipiélago de Los Monjes, Venezuela.

GONATODES CAUDISCUTATUS (Günther)

1859 Gymnodactylus caudiscutatus Günther, Proc. Zool. Soc. London, 1859: 410. Type-locality: Western Andes of Ecuador.
1885 Gonatodes caudiscutatus—Boulenger, Cat. Liz. Brit. Mus., 1: 61, pl. 5, fig. 2.
1892 Gonatodes collaris Garman, Bull. Essex Inst., 24: 83. Type-locality: Wreck Bay, Chatham Island, Galapagos Islands.
1955 Gonatodes caudiscutatus—Vanzolini, Pap. Avul. Depto. Zool. São Paulo, 12: 125.

Distribution: Caribbean coast of South America; Pacific Colombia and Ecuador.

GONATODES CECILIAE Donoso-Barros

1966 Gonatodes ceciliae Donoso-Barros, Publ. Ocas. Mus. Hist. Nat. Santiago, 11: 5, fig. Type-locality: Cerro Azul, Cerca de Macuro, Península de Paria, Estado Sucré, Venezuela.

Distribution: Cloud forest of Paria Mountains, Venezuela.

GONATODES CONCINNATUS (O'Shaughnessy)

1881 Goniodactylus concinnatus O'Shaughnessy, Proc. Zool. Soc. London, 1881: 237, pl. 23, fig. 2. Type-locality: Canelos, Ecuador.
1881 Goniodactylus buckleyi O'Shaughnessy, Proc. Zool. Soc. London, 1881: 238, pl. 23, fig. 3. Type-locality: Pallatanga and Canelos, Ecuador; Rivero Blanco, Mem. Soc. Cien. Nat. La Salle Caracas, 27, 1967 (1968), 105, discussed the probable erroneous nature of Pallatanga as a type locality.
1885 Gonatodes concinnatus—Boulenger, Cat. Liz. Brit. Mus., 1: 61.
1955 Gonatodes concinnatus—Vanzolini, Pap. Avul. Depto. Zool. São Paulo, 12: 125, pl. 1, fig. 3; pl. 3, figs. 1-3.
1967 Gonatodes ligiae Donoso-Barros, Not. Mens. Mus. Nac. Hist. Nat. Chile, 11 (129): Fourth unnumbered page. Type-locality: Bosque de la Carabela, Cerca de Baranitas, Venezuela.
1968 Gonatodes concinnatus—Rivero Blanco, Mem. Soc. Cien. Nat. La Salle Caracas, 27 (1967): 104, figs. 1a-b.

Distribution: Lower Amazonian slopes of Colombia and Ecuador; northern Venezuela; Amazonas, Brazil.

GONATODES FALCONENSIS Shreve

1947 Gonatodes caudiscutatus falconensis Shreve, Bull. Mus. Comp. Zool., 99: 520. Type-locality: Pauji, Distrito Acosta, Estado Falcón, Venezuela.
1968 Gonatodes falconensis—Vanzolini, Arq. Zool. São Paulo, 17: 18.
1968 Gonatodes falconensis—Rivero Blanco, Mem. Soc. Cien. Nat. La Salle Caracas, 27 (1967): 114.

Distribution: Estado Falcón, Venezuela.

GONATODES HASEMANI Griffin

1917 Gonatodes hasemani Griffin, Ann. Carnegie Mus., 11: 304, pl. 32. Type-locality: Villa Bella, Río Beni, Bolivia.
1933 Gonatodes spinulosus Amaral, Mem. Inst. Butantan, 7 (1932): 56, figs. 7-8. Type-locality: Rio Juruá region, Amazonas, Brazil.
1953 Gonatodes hasemanni—Vanzolini (in error for hasemani Griffin), Rev. Brasil. Biol., 13: 73.

Distribution: Bolivia and Brazil.

GONATODES HUMERALIS (Guichenot)

1855 Gymnodactylus humeralis Guichenot, in Castelnau, Expéd. Amér. Sud, Zool., Rept.: 13, pl. 3, figs. 1, 1a-b. Type-locality: Río Ucayali, Mission de Sarayacu, Peru.
1863 Gonatodes ferrigineus Cope, Proc. Acad. Nat. Sci. Phila., 1863: 102. Type-locality: Trinidad.
1871 Gymnodactylus incertus Peters, Monats. Akad. Wiss. Berlin, 1871: 397. Type-locality: Pebas, Peru.
1875 Goniodactylus sulcatus O'Shaughnessy, Ann. Mag. Nat. Hist., (4) 16: 265. Type-locality: Cuba.
1885 Gonatodes humeralis—Boulenger, Cat. Liz. Brit. Mus., 1: 62, pl. 5, fig. 3.

Distribution: Trinidad, Tobago, northeastern Venezuela, Colombia and Guianas to Mato Grosso, Brazil and Bolivia.

GONATODES OCELLATUS (Gray)

1831 Cyrtodactylus Ocellatus Gray, Synopsis Species Class Reptilia, in Griffith, Cuvier's Animal Kingdom, 9: 51. Type-locality: None given; stated as Tobago Island by Boulenger, Cat. Liz. Brit. Mus., 1, 1885, 61.
1885 Gonatodes ocellatus—Boulenger, Cat. Liz. Brit. Mus., 1: 60, pl. 5, fig. 1.

Distribution: Tobago and Trinidad as well as neighboring mainland of Venezuela.

GONATODES PETERSI Donoso-Barros

1967 Gonatodes petersi Donoso-Barros, Not. Mens. Mus. Nac. Hist. Nat. Chile, 11 (129): Fourth unnumbered page. Type-locality: Sierra de Perijá, Estado Zulia, Venezuela.

Distribution: Known only from type locality.

GONATODES SEIGLIEI Donoso-Barros

1966 Gonatodes seigliei Donoso-Barros, Publ. Ocas. Mus. Nat. Hist., 11: 11, fig. Type-locality: Bosque de Miraflores, Puertas del Guarapiche, a los límites del Estados Sucré y Monagas, Venezuela.

Distribution: Region of type locality.

GONATODES TANIAE Roze

1963 Gonatodes taniae Roze, Publ. Oc. Mus. Cienc. Nat. Caracas, Zool., 5: 1, fig. 1. Type-locality: Parque Nacional Henri Pittier de Rancho Grande, Estado Aragua, Venezuela, 950 m.

Distribution: Estado Aragua, Venezuela.

GONATODES VARIUS (Duméril)

1856 Gymnodactylus varius Duméril, Arch. Mus. Hist. Nat. Paris, 8: 475. Type-locality: Cayenne.
1955 Gonatodes varius—Vanzolini, Pap. Avul. Depto. Zool. São Paulo, 12: 119, pl. 1, fig. 1; pl. 2, figs. 1-4.

Distribution: Guianas.

GONATODES VITTATUS (Lichtenstein)

1856 Gymnodactylus vittatus Lichtenstein, Nomenclator Musei Zoologici Berolinensis: 6. Type-locality: La Guayra, Puerto Cabello and Caracas, Venezuela.
1885 Gonatodes vittatus—Boulenger, Cat. Liz. Brit. Mus., 1: 60.

Distribution: Colombia, Venezuela and offshore islands.

Content: Two subspecies.

Key to the subspecies	Clave de subespecies
1. Males without vertebral white line, or, if present, poorly defined and narrow; 12-17 lamellae under fourth toe of forefoot; large mouth; females very difficult to distinguish, 17-21 lamellae under fourth toe of hind foot-----------------roquensis Males with distinct, wide, white vertebral line; 15-18 lamellae under fourth toe; small mouth; females with 16-20 lamellae under fourth toe-----------------vittatus	1. Los machos sin línea dorsal blanca, o, si está presente, mal definida y estrecha; 12-17 láminas debajo del cuarto dedo de la pata anterior; la boca más grande; las hembros se distinguen difícilmente; 17-21 láminas debajo del cuarto dedo de la pata posterior------------------------roquensis Los machos con una línea dorsal bien definida, ancha, blanca; 15-18 láminas debajo del cuarto dedo; la boca chica; las hembras con 16-20 láminas debajo del cuarto dedo------- ------------------------------------vittatus

Gonatodes vittatus vittatus (Lichtenstein)

1864 Gonatodes gillii Cope, Proc. Acad. Nat. Sci. Phila., 1863: 102. Type-locality: Trinidad.
1956 G. onatodes vittatus vittatus—Roze, in Sociedad de Ciencias Naturales La Salle, Caracas, El Archipiélago de Los Roques y La Orchila: 81, fig.

Distribution: Colombia, Venezuela, Aruba, Curaçao?, Margarita, Coche, Cubagua, Los Frailes, Los Testigos, Tobago and Trinidad.

Gonatodes vittatus roquensis Roze

1956 Gonatodes vittatus roquensis Roze, in Sociedad de Ciencias Naturales La Salle, Caracas, El Archipiélago de Los Roques y La Orchila: 81, fig. Type-locality: El Gran Roque, Archipiélago de Los Roques, Venezuela.

Distribution: Los Roques Islands, Venezuela.

GYMNODACTYLUS Spix

1825 Gymnodactylus Spix, Sp. Nov. Lac. Bras.: 17. Type-species: Gymnodactylus geckoides Spix.
1827 Cyrtodactylus Gray, Phil. Mag., (2) 2: 56. Type-species: Cyrtodactylus pulchella Gray.
1843 Anomalurus Fitzinger (preoccupied by Anomalurus Waterhouse, 1843), Systema Reptilium: 90. Type-species: Phyllurus miliusii (= milii) Duméril and Bibron.
1843 Dasyderma Fitzinger, Systema Reptilium: 92. Type-species: Gonyodactylus spinulosus Fitzinger.
1843 Cyrtopodion Fitzinger, Systema Reptilium: 93. Type-species: Stenodactylus scaber Heyden.
1860 Puellula Blyth, Jour. Asiatic Soc. Bengal, 29: 109. Type-species: Puellula rubida Blyth.
1867 Geckoella Gray, Proc. Zool. Soc. London, 1867: 98. Type-species: Geckoella punctata Gray = Gymnodactylus triedrus Günther.
1868 Dinosaura Gistl, Blicke in das Leben der Natur: 145. Type-species: Stenodactylus scaber Heyden.
1965 Underwoodisaurus Wermuth, Das Tierreich, 80: ix. Type-species: Gymnodactylus milii (Bory).

   Distribution: Worldwide in warmer climates.

   Content: About 70 species, only one of which occurs within limits of this work.

GYMNODACTYLUS GECKOIDES Spix

1825 Gymnodactylus geckoides Spix, Sp. Nov. Lac. Bras.: 17, pl. 18, fig. 1. Type-locality: Bahia, Brazil.
1953 Gymnodactylus geckoides—Vanzolini, Pap. Avul. Depto. Zool. São Paulo, 11: 225.

   Distribution: Brazil.

   Content: Three subspecies.

             Key to the subspecies   Clave de subespecies

1. With fewer than 60 tubercles along para-   1. Menos de 60 tubérculos en la hilera paramedian line-------------------------------2   mediana------------------------------------2
   With more than 64 tubercles along para-   Más de 64 tubérculos en la hilera paramedian line-----------------------darwinii   mediana--------------------------darwinii

2. With 17-20 rows of ventrals; 37-45 tuber-   2. Diseño dorsal uniforme o marmorado; 37-45
   cles along paramedian line; dorsal pattern   tubérculos en la hilera paramediana; 17-20
   uniform or spotted; 17-20 lamellae under   hileras de ventrales; 17-20 lamelas bajo
   fourth toe----------------------geckoides   el cuarto dedo-------------------geckoides
   With 19-24 rows of ventrals; 32-43 tuber-   Diseño dorsal raramente uniforme, marmorado
   cles along paramedian line; dorsal pattern   o con ocelos; 32-43 tubérculos en la
   rarely uniform, may be spotted or with   hilera paramediana; 19-24 hileras de
   ocelli; 13-19 lamellae under fourth toe---   ventrales; 13-19 lamelas bajo el cuarto
   ------------------------------------amarali   dedo---------------------------------amarali

Gymnodactylus geckoides geckoides Spix

1831 Cyrtodactylus Spixii Gray (substitute name for Gymnodactylus geckoides Spix), Synopsis Species Class Reptilia, in Griffith, Cuvier's Animal Kingdom, 9: 52.
1833 Gecko gymnodactylus Schinz (substitute name for Gymnodactylus geckoides Spix), Naturgeschichte und Abbildungen der Reptilien: 75, pl. 16.
1843 Gonyodactylus (Dasyderma) spinulosus Fitzinger (substitute name for Gymnodactylus geckoides Spix), Systema Reptilium: 92.
1933 Gymnodactylus conspicuus Amaral, Mem. Inst. Butantan, 7 (1932): 57, figs. 9, 10. Type-locality: Villa Nova (= Senhor do Bonfim), Bahia, Brazil.
1953 Gymnodactylus geckoides geckoides—Vanzolini, Pap. Avul. Depto. Zool. São Paulo, 11: 252, pl. 1, figs. 1-5.

   Distribution: Salvador, Bahia, to northern Paraiba, Brazil.

Gymnodactylus geckoides amarali Barbour

1925 Gymnodactylus amarali Barbour, Proc. Biol. Soc. Washington, 38: 101. Type-locality: Engenheiro Dodt, Santa Philomena, upper Rio Parnahyba, Brazil.
1953 Gymnodactylus geckoides amarali—Vanzolini, Pap. Avul. Depto. Zool. São Paulo, 11: 255, pl. 2, figs. 2-3.

   Distribution: Rio Parnahyba to Rio das Mortes, south to southern Goiás, east to southern Bahia, Brazil.

Gymnodactylus geckoides darwinii (Gray)

1845 Cubinia Darwinii Gray, Cat. Liz. Brit. Mus.: 274. Type-locality: Bahia and Rio de
      Janeiro, Brazil.
1867 Gymnodactylus Girardi Steindachner, Reise der Österreichischen Fregatte Novara, Zool.,
      Rept.: 15, pl. 2, figs. 3-3a. Type-locality: Unknown.
1950 Gonatodes helgae Amaral, Copeia, 1950: 281. Type-locality: Ilha de São Sebastião,
      Estado de São Paulo, Brazil.
1953 Gymnodactylus geckoides darwini—Vanzolini, Pap. Avul. Depto. Zool. São Paulo, 11: 256,
      pl. 2, fig. 1.

   Distribution: Espirito Santo to São Paulo, Brazil.

GYMNOPHTHALMUS Merrem

1820 Gymnophthalmus Merrem, Tentamen Systematis Amphibiorum: 74. Type-species. Lacerta quadrilineata Linnaeus.
1861 Blepharactisis Hallowell, Proc. Acad. Nat. Sci. Phila., 1860: 484. Type-species: Blepharactisis speciosa Hallowell.
1876 Epaphelus Cope, Jour. Acad. Nat. Sci. Phila., (2) 8 (1875): 115. Type-species: Epaphelus sumichrastii Cope.

Distribution: Central America, South America from Argentina north, Leeward Islands, Margarita Island, Trinidad and adjacent islands.

Content: Six species, one (pleii Bocourt) extralimital.

Key to the species

1. Frontal not in contact with internasal-------2
   Frontal in contact with internasal--rubricauda

2. One supraocular------------------------------3
   Two supraoculars---------------multiscutatus

3. Without white dorsolateral stripes on body----
   --4
   With white dorsolateral stripes on body-------
   --------------------------------------lineatus

4. Tail orange-red; males with femoral pores;
   ventrals scales between triangular chest
   scale and anal plate average 27 in males,
   32 in females---------------------speciosus
   Tail not orange-red; males lack femoral pores;
   ventral scales average 24---------underwoodi

Clave de especies

1. Frontal no contacta con internasal-----------2
   Frontal contacten con internasal----rubricauda

2. Un supraocular-------------------------------3
   Dos supraoculares---------------multiscutatus

3. Sin cinta dorsolateral blanca a los lados del
   cuerpo---------------------------------------4
   Con cinta dorsolateral blanca a los lados del
   cuerpo-------------------------------lineatus

4. Cola rojo-naranja; machos con poros femorales;
   escamas ventrales entre escama triangular del
   pecho y lámina anal promedian 27 en machos,
   32 en hembras---------------------speciosus
   Cola no rojo-naranja; machos sin poros
   femorales; escamas ventrales promedian 24----
   ------------------------------------underwoodi

GYMNOPHTHALMUS LINEATUS (Linnaeus)

1758 Lacerta lineata Linnaeus, Systema Naturae, Ed. 10: 209. Type-locality: Ceylon.
1766 Lacerta quadrilineata Linnaeus, Systema, Ed. 12: 371. Type-locality: North America?
1863 Gymnophthalmus nitidus Reinhardt and Lütken, Vidensk. Medd. Naturhist. Foren. Kjöbenhavn, 4 (1862): 226. Type-locality: Danish West Indies.
1885 [Gymnophthalmus] merremii Boulenger (name attributed to Cocteau, but apparently coined by Boulenger, with this as first publication), Cat. Liz. Brit. Mus., 2: 427.
1900 Gymnophthalmus lineatus—Andersson, Bihang. K. Svenska Vet.-Akad. Handlingar, 26 (4, No.1): 16.

Distribution: Dutch Leeward Islands; Surinam.

GYMNOPHTHALMUS MULTISCUTATUS Amaral

1933 Gymnophthalmus multiscutatus Amaral, Mem. Inst. Butantan, 7 (1932): 73, figs. 51-55. Type-locality: Villa Nova (≠ Senhor do Bonfim), Bahia, Brazil.

Distribution: Bahia, Ceará and Pernambuco, Brazil.

GYMNOPHTHALMUS RUBRICAUDA Boulenger

1902 Gymnophthalmus rubricauda Boulenger, Ann. Mag. Nat. Hist., (7) 9: 337. Type-locality: Cruz del Eje, Argentina.
1951 Gymnophthalmus rubricauda—Gallardo, Comun. Inst. Nac. Invest. Cien. Nat., Buenos Aires, Cienc. Zool., 2: 1, fig. 1.

Distibution: Beni, Bolivia to northern Argentina.

GYMNOPHTHALMUS SPECIOSUS (Hallowell)

1861 Blepharictisis speciosa Hallowell, Proc. Acad. Nat. Sci. Phila., 1860: 484. Type-locality: Nicaragua.
1939 Gymnophthalmus speciosus—Stuart, Occ. Pap. Mus. Zool. Univ. Mich., 409: 4, pl. 1, figs. 3-4.

Distribution: Central America and northern South America.

Content: Three subspecies.

Key to the subspecies	Clave de subespecies
1. Prefrontals in contact with loreal--------2 Prefrontals separated from loreal-----birdi	1. Prefrontales contactan con la loreal-----2 Prefrontales separados de la loreal--birdi
2. Five supralabials to posterior margin of eye----------------------------speciosus Four supralabials to posterior margin of eye--------------------------sumichrastii	2. Cinco supralabiales hasta el margen posterior del ojo--------------------speciosus Cuatro supralabiales hasta el margen posterior del ojo----------------sumichrastii

Gymnophthalmus speciosus speciosus (Hallowell)

1871 Iretioscincus laevicaudus Cope, Proc. Amer. Phil. Soc., 11 (1870): 557. Type-locality: Departamento Occidental, Nicaragua (three cotypes in Museum of Comparative Zoology are labeled as coming from Poluon, Nicaragua).
1952 Gymnophthalmus speciosus speciosus Mertens, Abh. Senckenberg. Naturforsch. Ges., 487: 56, pl. 13, fig. 77.

Distribution: Honduras and Nicaragua to northern South America; Margarita Island.

Gymnophthalmus speciosus birdi Stuart

1939 Gymnophthalmus birdi Stuart, Occ. Pap. Mus. Zool. Univ. Mich., 409: 1, pl. 1, figs. 1-2. Type-locality: Desert flats of Salamá Basin, San Gerónimo, Baja Verapaz, Guatemala.
1952 Gymnophthalmus speciosus birdi—Mertens, Abh. Senckenberg. Naturforsch. Ges., 487: 56.

Distribution: Dry basins and valleys of central Guatemala across southeastern highlands of Guatemala and El Salvador.

Gymnophthalmus speciosus sumichrastii (Cope)

1876 Epaphelus sumichrastii Cope, Jour. Acad. Nat. Sci. Phila., (2) 8 (1875): 115. Type-locality: Estado Tehuantepec, Mexico.
1963 Gymnophthalmus speciosus sumichrasti—Stuart, Misc. Publ. Mus. Zool. Univ. Mich., 122: 80.

Distribution: Pacific slope from Isthmus of Tehuantepec, Mexico to western Guatemala.

GYMNOPHTHALMUS UNDERWOODI Grant

1958 Gymnophthalmus underwoodi Grant, Herpetologica, 14: 228. Type-locality: Barbados.

Distribution: Barbados, Trinidad and Tobago.

REPTILIA: SAURIA: HELODERMATIDAE ★ ★ ★ HELODERMA

HELODERMA Wiegmann

   1829 Trachyderma Wiegmann (preoccupied by Trachyderma Latreille,1829, Insecta), Isis von Oken, 22: 421. Type-species: Trachyderma horridum Wiegmann.
   1829 Heloderma Wiegmann (substitute name for Trachyderma Wiegmann), Isis von Oken, 22: 627.
   1831 Holoderma Gray (in error for Heloderma Wiegmann), Synopsis Species Class Reptilia, in Griffith, Cuvier's Animal Kingdom, 9: 28.

   Distribution: Guatemala through Mexico to Arizona.

   Content: Two species, one (suspectum Cope) extralimital.

HELODERMA HORRIDUM (Wiegmann)

   1829 Trachyderma horridum Wiegmann, Isis von Oken, 22: 421. Type-locality: Mexico.
   1829 Heloderma Horridum Wiegmann, Isis von Oken, 22: 627.

   Distribution: Pacific Slope from Sonora, Mexico, to Northern Guatemala.

   Content: Three subspecies, two (horridum Wiegmann and exasperatum Bogert and Martin del Campo) extralimital.

   Heloderma horridum alvarezi Bogert and Martin del Campo

      1956 Heloderma horridum alvarezi Bogert and Martin del Campo, Bull. Amer. Mus. Nat. Hist., 109: 32, figs. 7, 11, 15; pl. 3, figs. 1-3; pl. 13, fig. 5. Type-locality: Tuxtla Gutiérrez, Chiapas, Mexico.

      Distribution: Valley of Río Grijalva, Chiapas to Río Lagartero Depression, southwestern Guatemala.

HEMIDACTYLUS Gray

1817 Hemidact[ylus] Oken, Isis von Oken, 1817: 1183. Type-species: Gecko tuberculosus Daudin.
1825 Hemidactylus Gray, Ann. Phil., New Ser., 10: 199. Type-species: Gecko tuberculosus Daudin.
1842 Boltalia Gray, Zoological Miscellany, 1842: 58. Type-species: Boltalia sublevis Gray.
1843 Hoplopodion Fitzinger, Systema Reptilium: 103. Type-species: Hemidactylus Coctaei Duméril and Bibron.
1843 Microdactylus Fitzinger (preoccupied by Microdactylus Geoffroy, 1809), Systema Reptilium: 104. Type-species: Hemidactylus peruvianus Wiegmann.
1843 Onychopus Fitzinger, Systema Reptilium: 104. Type-species: Hemidactylus Garnotii Duméril and Bibron.
1843 Tachybates Fitzinger, Systema Reptilium: 105. Type-species: Given as Hemidactylus Mabouia Cuvier, which = Gecko mabouia Moreau de Jonnès.
1843 Pnoepus Fitzinger, Systema Reptilium: 106. Type-species: Hemidactylus javanicus Cuvier.
1845 Doryura Gray, Cat. Liz. Brit. Mus.: 156. Type-species: Doryura Bowringii Gray.
1845 Velernesia Gray, Cat. Liz. Brit. Mus.: 156. Type-species: Velernesia Richardsonii Gray.
1845 Leiurus Gray (preoccupied by Leiurus Hemprich and Ehrenberg, 1829 and Leiurus Swainson, 1839), Cat. Liz. Brit. Mus.: 157. Type-species: Leiurus ornatus Gray = Hemidactylus fasciatus fasciatus Gray.
1845 Nubilia Gray, Cat. Liz. Brit. Mus.: 273. Type-species: Nubilia Argentii Gray = Hemidactylus depressus Gray.
1861 Eurhous Fitzinger, Sitz. Math.-Naturwiss. Kl. Akad. Wiss. Wien, 42 (1860): 400. Type-species: Hemidactylus leschenaultii Duméril and Bibron.
1862 Liurus Cope (substitute name for Leiurus Gray, 1945; preoccupied by Liurus Ehrenberg, 1831), in Slack, Handbook Mus. Acad. Nat. Sci. Phila.: 32.
1870 Emydactylus Bocourt, Bull. Arch. Mus. Hist. Nat. Paris, (2) 6: 17. Type-species: Emydactylus bouvieri Bocourt.
1894 Bunocnemis Günther, Proc. Zool. Soc. London, 1894: 85. Type-species: Bunocnemis modestus Günther.
1934 Lophopholis Smith and Deraniyagala, Ceylon Jour. Sci. (B) 18: 230. Type-species: Teratolepis scabriceps Annandale.
1940 Aliurus Dunn and Dunn (substitute name for Liurus Cope, 1862), Copeia, 1940: 71.

Distribution: Africa, south Asia, Oceania, southern United States to Brazil and to Pacific coast of Peru.

Content: About seventy species, of which all but five are extralimital.

Key to the species	Clave de especies
1. Scalation of body composed of granules interspersed with tubercles; toes strongly dilated------------------------------------2 Scalation of body composed of uniform granules; toes weakly dilated----------------peruvianus	1. Cuerpo cubierto por gránulos y tubérculos; dedos fuertemente dilatados------------------2 Cuerpo cubierto por gránulos iguales; dedos ligeramente dilatados--------------peruvianus
2. Tubercles on body reduced, separated by granules; fewer than 15 transverse rows of tubercles-----------------------------------3 Tubercles on body raised, pointed and touching or closely approximated; more than 15 transverse rows of tubercles---------------------4	2. Tubérculos separados; ligeramente deprimidos; hilera transversal formada por menos de 15 tubérculos----------------------------------3 Tubérculos aproximados, grandes, quillados; línea transversal de tubérculos dorsales mayor que 15--4
3. Sides of head without tubercles; transverse row of tubercles on middle of body with fewer than eight tubercles---------------------frenatus Sides of head with tubercles; transverse row of tubercles on middle of body with more than eight tubercles-----------------------mabouia	3. Lados de la cabeza sin tubérculos; fila transversal de tubérculos con menos de ocho tubérculos---------------------------frenatus Lados de la cabeza con tubérculos; fila transversal de tubérculos con más de ocho tubérculos------------------------------------mabouia
4. Eight to ten tubercles on base of tail; each dorsal tubercle encircled by ten smaller granules------------------------------brookii Six tubercles on base of tail; each dorsal tubercle encircled by 15-20 smaller granules-------------------------------------turcicus	4. Ocho a diez tubérculos sobre la base de la cola; cada tubérculo dorsal rodeado de diez gránulos------------------------------brookii Seis tubérculos sobre la base de la cola; cada tubérculo dorsal rodeado por 15-20 gránulos-------------------------------turcicus

HEMIDACTYLUS BROOKII Gray

1845 Hemidactylus Brookii Gray, Cat. Liz. Brit. Mus.: 153. Type-locality: Borneo and Australia;
    Wermuth, Das Tierreich, 90, 1965, 71, indicated that Malcolm Smith, Fauna of British India,
    Sauria, 1935, 89, restricted the type-locality to Borneo, but Smith gives no indication of such
    intent, and we do not consider Smith's statement to be a valid restriction.
1911 Hemidactylus leightoni Boulenger, Ann. Mag. Nat. Hist., (8) 7: 19. Type-locality: Honda, Río
    Magdalena, Colombia, 300-400 ft.
1936 Hemidactylus neotropicalis Shreve, Occ. Pap. Boston Soc. Nat. Hist., 8: 270. Type-locality:
    Curumani, northeast of Salva, Departamento Magdalena, Colombia; corrected by Shreve,
    Herpetologica, 1, 1938, 124, to Puerto Wilches, Departamento Santander, Colombia.

    Distribution: Africa, India, Indo-Australian Archipelago, northern South America and Antillean
    Islands.

    Content: Five subspecies, four of which (brookii Gray, angulatus Hallowell, parvimaculatus
    Deraniyagala and subtriedroides Annandale) are extralimital. Hemidactylus leightoni Boulenger,
    from Colombia, was recently synonymized with brookii by Kluge, Bull. Amer. Mus. Nat. Hist., 135,
    1967, 49, but he did not indicate the subspecies to which it was assigned. Mechler, Rev. Suisse
    Zool., 75, 1968, did not accept Kluge's synonymy of leightoni and neotropicalis with brookii, but
    he did use haitianus for the Colombian form.

    Hemidactylus brookii haitianus Meerwarth

    1901 Hemidactylus brookii haitianus Meerwarth, Mitt. Naturwiss. Mus. Hamburg, 18: 17. Type-
        locality: Port-au-Prince, Haiti.

        Distribution: Caribbean coast of Colombia; Haiti, Cuba; Puerto Rico; Trinidad.

        Comment: See remarks under Hemidactylus brookii.

HEMIDACTYLUS FRENATUS Duméril and Bibron

1836 Hemidactylus frenatus Duméril and Bibron, Erp. Gén., 3: 366. Type-locality: Many localities
    given by Duméril and Bibron; restricted to Java by Loveridge, Bull. Mus. Comp. Zool., 98, 1947,
    127.
1843 Hemidactylus [Pnoepus] javanicus Fitzinger, Systema Reptilium: 106. Type-locality: Asia; India;
    Bengal; Ceylon; Java; Timor; Amboina; and Marianna Islands; restricted to Java by Loveridge,
    Bull. Mus. Comp. Zool., 98, 1947, 127.
1843 Hemidactylus [Pnoepus] Bojeri Fitzinger, Systema Reptilium: 106. Type-locality: Cape of Good
    Hope, Madagascar and Mauritius Island.
1845 Hemidactylus vittatus Gray, Cat. Liz. Brit. Mus.: 155. Type-locality: Borneo.
1853 Hemidactylus punctatus Jerdon, Jour. Asiatic Soc. Bengal, 22: 467. Type-locality: Tellicherry,
    Malabar.
1861 Hemidactylus inornatus Hallowell, Proc. Acad. Nat. Sci. Phila., 1860: 492. Type-locality: Loo
    Choo, Ryukyu Islands.
1861 Hemidactylus pumilus Hallowell, Proc. Acad. Nat. Sci. Phila., 1860: 502. Type-locality: Hong
    Kong.
1865 Gecko caracal Tytler, Jour. Asiatic Soc. Bengal, 33: 547. Type-locality: Rangoon, Burma;
    restricted, apparently unnecessarily, to Rangoon, Burma, by Loveridge, Bull. Mus. Comp. Zool.,
    98, 1947, 127.
1865 Gecko chaus Tytler, Jour. Asiatic Soc. Bengal, 33: 547. Type-locality: Moulmein and Rangoon,
    Burma; restricted to Rangoon, Burma, by Loveridge, Bull. Mus. Comp. Zool., 98, 1947, 128.
1869 Hemidactylus longiceps Cope, Proc. Acad. Nat. Sci. Phila., 1868: 320. Type-locality: Manila,
    Philippines.
1869 Hemidactylus hexaspis Cope, Proc. Acad. Nat. Sci. Phila., 1868: 320. Type-locality: Madagascar.
1878 Peripia papuensis Macleay, Proc. Linn. Soc. New South Wales, 2: 97. Type-locality: "Katow", =
    Katau, near Binaturi River, New Guinea.
1879 Hemidactylus tristis Sauvage, Bull. Soc. Philom. Paris, (7) 3: 49. Type-locality: New Guinea.
1915 Hemidactylus fragilis Calabresi, Monit. Zool. Ital., 26: 236, fig. 1a-b. Type-locality: Bur
    Meldàc, Italian Somaliland.

    Distribution: Widespread through much of Africa, Asia, Australia and Polynesia; Mexico and
    Guatemala.

HEMIDACTYLUS MABOUIA (Moreau de Jonnès)

1818 Gecko Mabouia Moreau de Jonnès, Bull. Soc. Philom. Paris, 1818: 138. Type-locality: Antilles; restricted by Smith and Taylor, Univ. Kansas Sci. Bull., 33, 1950, 364, to St. Vincent Island, Lesser Antilles.

1824 Gekko incanescens Wied, Isis von Oken, 14 (1): 662. Type-locality: Brazil; Wied, Beitr. Naturgesch. Brasil., 1, 1825, 103, said Rio de Janeiro, Cabo Frio, Campos de Goaytacases and Espirito Santo, Brazil.

1824 Gekko armatus Wied, Isis von Oken, 14 (1): 662. Type-locality: Brazil.

1825 Gecko aculeatus Spix, Spec. Nov. Lacert. Bras.: 16, pl. 18, fig. 3. Type-locality: Rio de Janeiro, Brazil.

1825 Gecko cruciger Spix, Spec. Nov. Lacert. Bras.: 16, pl. 13, fig. 3. Type-locality: Bahia, Brazil.

1829 G[ecko] mabuia Cuvier (substitute name for Gecko mabouia Moreau de Jonnès, 1818), Règne Animal, Ed. 2, 2: 54.

1843 Hemidactylus (Tachybates) mabuya Fitzinger (substitute name for Gecko mabouia Moreau de Jonnès, 1818), Systema Reptilium: 105.

1878 Hemidactylus frenatus var. calabaricus Boettger, Ber. Offenbacher Verein Naturk., 17/18: 1. Type-locality: Old Calabar, Guinea coast of West Africa (Nigeria).

1893 Hemidactylus benguellensis Bocage, Jour. Sci. Math. Phys. Nat. Acad. Lisbon, (2) 10: 115. Type-locality: Cahata, Benguela, Angola.

Distribution: South Africa north to Liberia and Abyssinia; Madagascar and neighboring islands; Veracruz, Mexico; Cuba, Hispaniola, Barbados and Martinique; Trinidad, Venezuela, Guyana, Amazonian Brazil and offshore islands, Ecuador, Peru, and Colombia.

HEMIDACTYLUS PERUVIANUS Wiegmann

1835 Hemidactylus peruvianus Wiegmann, Nova Acta Acad. Caes. Leop.-Carol., 17: 240. Type-locality: Tacna, Peru.

1885 Hemidactylus peruvianus—Boulenger, Cat. Liz. Brit. Mus., 1: 141.

Distribution: This species has never been found again, at the type-locality or elsewhere.

HEMIDACTYLUS TURCICUS (Linnaeus)

1758 Lacerta turcica Linnaeus, Systema Naturae, Ed. 10: 202. Type-locality: "Oriente"; Wermuth, Das Tierreich, 80, 1965, 86, said that K. P. Schmidt, Fieldiana, Zool., 34, 1953, 257, restricted the type-locality to Asiatic Turkey, but Schmidt does not clearly intend his reference to Turkey as a restriction, and we do not consider it to be such.

1876 Hemidactylus turcicus—Boettger, Ber. Offenbacher Verein Naturk., 15/16: 57.

Distribution: Mediterranean region; Red Sea coast east to India and south to Kenya; southern United States; Tamaulipas to Yucatán peninsula; Antilles; Chile.

Content: Three subspecies, two of which (macropholis Boulenger and spinalis Buchholz) are extralimital.

Hemidactylus turcicus turcicus (Linnaeus)

1810 Gecus Cyanodactylus Rafinesque, Caratteri di Alcuni Nuove Generi e Nuove Specie di Animali e Pianti Della Sicilia: 9. Type-locality: Sicily.

1826 Geko meridionalis Risso, Histoire Naturelle des Principales Productions de l'Europe Méridionale, 3: 87. Type-locality: Province of Alpes Maritimes, France; restricted to Nice by Mertens and Wermuth, die Amphibien und Reptilien Europas, 1960, 79.

1827 Hemidactylus granosus Heyden, Reptilien, in Rüppell, Atlas zu der Reise im Nördlichen Africa: 17, pl. 5, fig. 1. Type-locality: Egypt, Arabia, and Abyssinia; Mertens, Senckenbergiana, 3, 1922, 169, lists one of the syntypes in Senckenberg Museum as from "Arabia Petraea," and Wermuth, Das Tierreich, 80, 1965, 87, regards this as a restriction of type-locality to the Sinai Peninsula, but we do not regard this to be Merten's intent.

Hemidactylus turcicus turcicus (Linnaeus), continued

1827 Hemidactylus robustns Heyden (typographical error), Reptilien, in Rüppell, Atlas zu der
    Reise im Nördlichen Africa: 19. Type-locality: Abyssinia.
1829 G[ecko] verruculatus Cuvier, Règne Animal, Ed. 2, 2: 54. Type-locality: Provence,
    France; Sicily; Italy.
1831 Gecko Verrucosus Gray (error), Synopsis Species Class Reptilia, in Griffith, Cuvier's
    Animal Kingdom, 9: 50.
1884 Hemidactylus karachiensis Murray, Vertebrate Zoology of Sind: 361, pl. 9, fig. 2. Type-
    locality: Karachi, Sind, Pakistan.
1885 Hemidactylus sinaitus Boulenger, Cat. Liz. Brit. Mus., 1: 126. Type-locality: Mount
    Sinai, Palestine.
1906 Hemidactylus exsul Barbour and Cole, Bull. Mus. Comp. Zool., 50: 148. Type-locality:
    Progreso, Yucatán, Mexico.
1925 Hemidactylus turcicus turcicus—Mertens, Abh. Senckenbergischen Naturforsch. Ges., 39: 60.

    Distribution: India and northeastern Africa; Louisiana, Texas, and Florida; Cuba; Tamaulipas
    to Yucatán, Mexico; and one specimen (MCZ 56249) from Chile.

HETERODACTYLUS Spix

> 1825 <u>Heterodactylus</u> Spix, Spec. Nov. Lacert. Bras.,: 25. Type-species: <u>Heterodactylus</u> <u>imbricatus</u>
>   Spix.
> 1830 <u>Chirocolus</u> Wagler, Nat. Syst. Amph.: 157. Type-species: <u>Heterodactylus</u> <u>imbricatus</u> Spix.

> Distribution: Estados do Rio de Janeiro and Minas Gerais, Brazil.

> Content: Two species.

Key to the species	Clave de especies
1. Parietals separated by frontal and inter- parietal--------------------------------<u>lundii</u> Parietals in contact on median line---<u>imbricatus</u>	1. Parietales separados por el frontal y el interparietal--------------------------<u>lundii</u> Parietales contactan en la linea media--------- ----------------------------------<u>imbricatus</u>

HETERODACTYLUS IMBRICATUS Spix

> 1825 <u>Heterodactylus</u> <u>imbricatus</u> Spix, Spec. Nov. Lacert. Bras.: 25, pl. 27, fig. 1. Type-locality:
>   Estado do Rio de Janeiro, Brazil.

> Distribution: Valley of Paraiba River; Distrito Federal; Estado do Rio de Janeiro to central Minas
> Gerais, Brazil.

HETERODACTYLUS LUNDII Reinhardt and Lütken

> 1862 <u>Heterodactylus</u> <u>Lundii</u> Reinhardt and Lütken, Vidensk. Medd. Naturhist. Foren. Kjöbenhaven, 3
>   (1861): 214, pl. 6, figs. 10. Type-locality: Serra da Piedade, Minas Gerais, Brazil.

> Distribution: Known only from type locality.

HOMONOTA Gray

1845 Homonota Gray, Cat. Liz. Brit. Mus.: 171. Type-species: Gymnodactylus Guidichaudi Duméril and
Bibron (lapsus for Gymnodactylus gaudichaudii Duméril and Bibron) = Homonota darwinii
Boulenger.
1845 Cubina Gray, Cat. Liz. Brit. Mus.: 174. Type-species: Gymnodactylus fasciatus Duméril and
Bibron.
1845 Cubinia Gray (substitute name for Cubina Gray, 1845), Cat. Liz. Brit. Mus.: 274.
1954 Wallsaurus Underwood, Proc. Zool. Soc. London, 124: 475. Type-species: Gymnodactylus horridus
Burmeister.

Distribution: South America south of about 25°S, on both sides of Andes.

Content: Eight species, according to most recent revision, by Kluge, Amer. Mus. Novitates, 2193,
1964. Kluge also included Gymnodactylus gaudichaudi Duméril and Bibron, here considered a member
of the genus Garthia.

Key to the species	Clave de especies
1. Rostral crease not $\wedge$-shaped; subcaudals enlarged----------------------------------2 Rostral crease $\wedge$-shaped; subcaudals undifferentiated------------------------dorbignii	1. Surco rostral sin forma de $\wedge$; subcaudales agrandadas-----------------------------------2 Surco rostral en forma de $\wedge$; subcaudales indiferenciadas---------------------dorbignii
2. Dorsal body surfaces with regular longitudinal rows of keeled scales-----------3 Dorsal body surfaces without regular longitudinal rows of keeled scales-----------6	2. Superficie dorsal del cuerpo con filas longitudinales regulares de escamas quilladas---3 Superficie dorsal del cuerpo sin filas longitudinales regulares de escamas quilladas-----------------------------------6
3. Enlarged keeled scales of longitudinal rows not imbricate; general coloration brownish yellow-------------------------------------4 Enlarged keeled scales of longitudinal rows imbricate; general coloration grayish black-----------------------------------uruguayensis	3. Escamas quilladas agrandadas de filas longitudinales no imbricadas; coloración general pardo amarillento---------------------------4 Escamas quilladas agrandadas de filas longitudinales imbricadas; coloración general negro grisácea------------------------uruguayensis
4. External ear opening large, oval; keeled scales of longitudinal body rows strongly developed; fewer than 25 scales in primary paravertebral row between axilla and groin------------------5 External ear opening small, round; keeled scales of longitudinal body rows weakly developed; 25 or more scales in primary paravertebral row between axilla and groin--borelli	4. Abertura auditiva externa grande y oval; escamas quilladas de filas longitudinales sobre el cuerpo fuertemente desarrolladas; menos de 25 escamas en la fila paravertebral primaria, entre la axila y la ingle----------5 Abertura auditiva externa pequeña y circular; escamas quilladas de filas longitudinales sobre el cuerpo débilmente desarrolladas; 25 o más escamas en la fila paravertebral primaria entre la axila y la ingle-------------borelli
5. Fifteen or more enlarged interorbital scales; parts of margin of external ear opening not denticulate; anterior gular scales small, granular----------------------------fasciata Fewer than 15 enlarged interorbital scales; all margins of external ear opening denticulate; anterior gular scales large, platelike--horrida	5. Con 15 o más escamas interorbitales agrandadas; parte de los márgenes de la abertura auditiva externa sin denticulación; gulares anteriores pequeñas y granulares---------------------fasciata Menos de 15 escamas interorbitales agrandadas; denticulación en todos los márgenes de la abertura auditiva externa; gulares anteriores grandes y planas---------------------horrida
6. Subcaudals triangular or round, not greatly enlarged, lateral margins bordered by one large or two small scales, regularly alternating this sequence-------------------------7 Subcaudals rectangular, greatly enlarged, lateral margins in every case bordered by only one scale--------------------------------whitii	6. Subcaudales triangulares o circulares, no agrandadas considerablemente, márgenes laterales bordeados por la alternancia regular de una escama grande seguida de dos pequeñas----7 Subcaudales rectangulares, agrandadas considerablemente, márgenes laterales bordeadas en todos los casos por una sóla escama-----------whitii

7. Belly immaculate (devoid of all chromato-
phores)--__underwoodi__
Belly covered with sparsely scattered chromato-
phores--__darwinii__

7. Vientre inmaculado (ausente de cromatóforos)---
--__underwoodi__
Vientre cubierto con escasos y esparcidos
cromatóforos--__darwinii__

HOMONOTA BORELLII (Peracca)

1897 Gymnodactylus Borellii Peracca, Boll. Mus. Zool. Anat. Comp. Univ. Torino, 12 (274): 2. Type-
locality: Salta, Argentina.
1964 Homonota borelli—Kluge, Amer. Mus. Novitates, 2193: 10, fig. 3.

Distribution: Northern Argentina, Chaco region and Provincias de La Rioja, Buenos Aires, Salta and
Córdoba.

HOMONOTA DARWINII Boulenger

1845 Homonota Guidichaudi—Gray, Cat. Liz. Brit. Mus.: 171.
1885 Homonota darwinii Boulenger, Cat. Liz. Brit. Mus., 1: 21, pl. 3, fig. 7. Type-locality: Puerto
Deseado, Santa Cruz Provincia, Argentina.
1964 Homonota darwinii—Kluge, Amer. Mus. Novitates, 2193: 22, fig. 6.

Distribution: Uruguay and Argentina, 25°- 47°S.

HOMONOTA DORBIGNII (Duméril and Bibron)

1836 Gymnodactylus Dorbignii Duméril and Bibron, Erp. Gén., 3: 418. Type-locality: Provincia de la
Laguna and Valparaiso, Chile; corrected and restricted by Duméril, Cat. Méth. Coll. Rept., 1851,
44, to area along Río Grandé, at Pampa Ruiz (between Vallé Grandé and Pescado), Departamento
Chuquisaca, Bolivia; additional clarification in d'Orbigny, Voyage dans l'Amérique Méridionale,
Strasbourg, 5 (1), Reptiles, according to Kluge, Amer. Mus. Novitates, 2193, 1964, 35-36.
1964 Homonota dorbignii—Kluge, Amer. Mus. Novitates, 2193: 33, fig. 10.

Distribution: Central and northern Chile; south central Bolivia.

Comment: Donoso-Barros, Reptiles de Chile, 1966, 122, considers this species to belong in Garthia.

HOMONOTA FASCIATA (Duméril and Bibron)

1836 Gymnodactylus fasciatus Duméril and Bibron, Erp. Gén., 3: 420. Type-locality: "Martinique";
considered as unknown by Kluge, Amer. Mus. Novitates, 2193, 1964, 21.
1964 Homonota fasciata—Kluge, Amer. Mus. Novitates, 2193: 20.
1965 Gymnodactylus (Gymnodactylus) pasteuri Wermuth (replacement name for Gymnodactylus fasciatus
Duméril and Bibron), Das Tierreich, 80: 63.
1965 Homonota pasteuri Wermuth (replacement name for Gymnodactylus fasciatus Duméril and Bibron), Das
Tierreich, 80: 201.

Distribution: Unknown. Kluge, loc. cit., 21, rejects Martinique as a valid locality for the
species.

HOMONOTA HORRIDA (Burmeister)

1861 Gymnodactylus horridus Burmeister, Reise Durch die La Plata Staaten, 2: 522. Type-locality: Near
Mendoza, in a gorge near Challao, Provincia Mendoza, Argentina.
1895 Gymnodactylus mattogrossensis Berg, An. Mus. Buenos Aires, 4: 191. Type-locality: Mato Grosso,
Brazil.
1964 Homonota horrida—Kluge, Amer. Mus. Novitates, 2193: 16, fig. 5.

Distribution: Paraguay; southeastern Bolivia; Mato Grosso, Brazil, to Provincia Mendoza, western
Argentina.

HOMONOTA UNDERWOODI Kluge

1964 Homonota underwoodi Kluge, Amer. Mus. Novitates, 2193: 25, fig. 7. Type-locality: Agua de la
Pena, Hoyada de Ischigualasto, 82 km northwest of San Augustin de Valle Fertil, Provincia San
Juan, Argentina.

Distribution: Provincias San Juan and Mendoza, Argentina.

HOMONOTA URUGUAYENSIS (Vaz-Ferreira and Sierra de Soriano)

1961 Wallsaurus uruguayensis Vaz-Ferreira and Sierra de Soriano, Comun. Zool. Mus. Hist. Nat. Montevideo, 5 (91): 2, pl.1, figs. 1-2; pl. 2, figs. 1-3. Type-locality: Arroyo de la Invernada, Departamento de Artigas, Uruguay.
1964 Homonota uruguayensis—Kluge, Amer. Mus. Novitates, 2193: 13, fig. 4.

   Distribution: Departamentos de Artigas and Tacuarembó, Uruguay.

HOMONOTA WHITII Boulenger

1885 Homonota whitii Boulenger, Cat. Liz. Brit. Mus., 1: 22, pl. 3, fig. 6-6a. Type-locality: Cosquin, Provincia Córdoba, Argentina.
1964 Homonota whitii—Kluge, Amer. Mus. Novitates, 2193: 29, fig. 8.

   Distribution: Provincias de Catamarca, Córdoba, La Rioja, Mendoza, Salta and Tucumán; Argentina.

HOPLOCERCUS Fitzinger

1843 Hoplocercus Fitzinger, Syst. Rept.: 78. Type-species: Hoplocercus spinosus Fitzinger.
1854 Pachycercus Dugés and Braconnier, in A. Duméril, Rev. Mag. Zool., 9: 29. Type-species:
Pachycercus aculeatus Dugés and Braconnier.

Distribution: As for single known species.

Content: One species.

HOPLOCERCUS SPINOSUS Fitzinger

1843 Hoplocercus spinosus Fitzinger, Syst. Rept.: 78. Type-locality: America and Brazil.
1854 Pachycercus aculeatus Dugés and Braconnier, in A. Duméril, Rev. Mag. Zool., 9: 29, pl. 12, figs.
1-4. Type-locality: São Paulo, Brazil.

Distribution: Mato Grosso, Goiás, and southern Pará, Brazil; does not occur in São Paulo,
according to P. Vanzolini.

IGUANA Laurenti

1768 Iguana Laurenti, Synopsin Reptilium: 47. Type-species: Iguana tuberculata Laurenti.
1830 Hypsilophus Wagler, Nat. Syst. Amph.: 147. Type-species: Lacerta iguana Linnaeus.
1828 Prionodus Wagler, Isis von Oken, 21 (8/9): 860. Type-species: Lacerta iguana Linnaeus.

Distribution: Tropical America from Mexico to southern Brazil and Paraguay; coastal islands of Caribbean area; West Indies.

Content: Two species, one (delicatissima Laurenti) extralimital.

IGUANA IGUANA (Linnaeus)

1758 Lacerta iguana Linnaeus, Systema Naturae, Ed. 10: 206. Type-locality: "In Indiis".
1898 Iguana [iguana]—Van Denburgh, Proc. Acad. Nat. Sci. Phila., 1897: 461.

Distribution: From Mexico and adjacent Caribbean islands to southern Brazil and Paraguay.

Content: Two subspecies.

Key to the subspecies

1. With two or three soft tubercles on
     snout--------------------------rhinolopha
   No tubercles on snout----------------iguana

Clave de subespecies

1. Con dos o tres tubérculos blandos y cónicos
     en el hocico--------------------rhinolopha
   Sin tubérculos en el hocico----------iguana

Iguana iguana iguana (Linnaeus)

?1768 Iguana minima Laurenti, Synopsin Reptilium: 48. Type-locality: Unknown.
1768 Iguana tuberculata Laurenti, Synopsin Reptilium: 48. Type-locality: Unknown.
1802 Iguana caerulea Daudin, Hist. Nat. Rept., 3: 286. Type-locality: Surinam and Formosa.
1806 I[guana] vulgaris Link (replacement name for Lacerta iguana Linnaeus), Beschreibung der Naturalien-Sammlung der Universität zu Rostock, 2: 58.
1820 Iguana sapidissima Merrem, Tentamen Systematis Amphibiorum: 47. Type-locality: Tropical America.
1825 Iguana squamosa Spix, Spec. Nov. Lacert. Braz.: 5, pl. 5. Type-locality: Bahia and Pará, Brazil.
1825 Iguana viridis Spix, Spec. Nov. Lacert. Bras.: 6, pl. 6. Type-locality: Rio San Francisco, Itapicuru, Brazil.
1825 Iguana emarginata Spix, Spec. Nov. Lacert. Bras.: 7, pl. 8. Type-locality: Rio San Francisco, Brazil.
1825 Iguana lophyroides Spix, Spec. Nov. Lacert. Bras.: 8, pl. 9. Type-locality: Forest of Rio de Janeiro, and Bahia, Brazil.
1898 Iguana iguana [iguana]—Van Denbergh, Proc. Acad. Nat. Sci. Phila., 1897: 461.

Distribution: From southern Costa Rica and adjacent Caribbean islands to tropical South America.

Iguana iguana rhinolopha Wiegmann

1834 Iguana (Hypsilophus) rhinolophus Wiegmann, Herpetologia Mexicana: 44. Type-locality: Mexico; restricted to Córdoba, Veracruz, Mexico, by Smith and Taylor, Univ. Kansas Sci. Bull., 33, 1950, 347.
1898 Iguana iguana rhinolopha—Van Denburgh, Proc. Acad. Nat. Sci. Phila., 1897: 461.

Distribution: Sinaloa and Veracruz, Mexico to southern Costa Rica.

IPHISA Gray

    1851 _Iphisa_ Gray, Proc. Zool. Soc. London, 1851: 39. Type-species: _Iphisa elegans_ Gray.

    Distribution: As for single known species.

    Content: One species.

IPHISA ELEGANS Gray

    1851 _Iphisa elegans_ Gray, Proc. Zool. Soc. London, 1851: 39, pl. 6. fig. 3. Type-locality:
        Pará, Brazil.
    1885 _Iphisa elegans_—Boulenger, Cat. Liz. Brit. Mus., 2: 424.

    Distribution: Amazonian Brazil; Guianas; Amazonian lowlands of Colombia, Ecuador and Peru.

KENTROPYX Spix

1825 Kentropyx Spix, Spec. Nov. Lacert. Bras.: 21, pl. 22, fig. 2. Type-species: Kentropyx
    calcaratus Spix
1826 Pseudoameiva Fitzinger, Neue Classification Reptilien: 21. Type-species: Lacerta striata Daudin.
1830 Trachygaster Wagler, Nat. Syst. Amph.: 154. Type-species: Kentropyx calcaratus Spix.
1834 Centropyx Wiegmann (emendation of Kentropyx Spix), Herpetologia Mexicana: 9.
1845 Acanthopyga Gray, Cat. Liz. Brit. Mus.: 23. Type-species: Lacerta striata Daudin.

Distribution: South America east of Andes.

Content: Nine species.

Key to the species

1. Dorsal scales keeled--------------------------2
   Dorsal scales smooth------------altamazonicus

2. Head concave dorsally----------------------3
   Head flat dorsally----------------williamsoni

3. First pair of mental shields separated-------4
   First pair of mental shields in contact------5

4. Dorsal scales imbricate-----------viridistriga
   Dorsal scales juxtaposed-------------paulensis

5. Middorsal scales considerably larger than
   laterals-----------------------------------6
   Middorsal scales not appreciably larger than
   laterals-----------------------------------7

6. Number of femoral pores 11-15------intermedius
   Number of femoral pores 5-7----------striatus

7. Three supraocular scales, second never
   smallest------------------------------------8
   Four supraocular scales, second smallest------
   ------------------------------------lagartija

8. Femoral scales in contact with row of femoral
   pore scales same size as median gular scales-
   ------------------------------------calcaratus
   Femoral scales in contact with row of femoral
   pore scales larger than median gular scales--
   ------------------------------------pelviceps

Clave de especies

1. Escamas dorsales quilladas--------------------2
   Escamas dorsales lisas-----------altamazonicus

2. Cabeza dorsalmente cóncava--------------------3
   Cabeza dorsalmente plana-----------williamsoni

3. Primer par de escudos mentales separados------4
   Primer par de escudos mentales en contacto----5

4. Escamas dorsales imbricadas--------viridistriga
   Escamas dorsales yuxtapuestas--------paulensis

5. Escamas mediodorsales notablemente mayores que
   las laterales------------------------------6
   Escamas mediodorsales no apreciablemente
   mayores que las laterales--------------------7

6. Número de poros femorales 11-15-----intermedius
   Número de poros femorales 5-7----------striatus

7. Tres supraoculares, la segunda nunca más
   pequeña-------------------------------------8
   Cuatro supraoculares, con la segunda más
   pequeña------------------------------lagartija

8. Escamas femorales que tocan la hilera de poros
   femorales apenas tan grandes como las gulares
   medianas------------------------------calcaratus
   Las mismas escamas mayores que las gulares
   medianas------------------------------pelviceps

KENTROPYX ALTAMAZONICUS Cope

1876 Centropyx altamazonicus Cope, Jour. Acad. Nat. Sci. Phila., (2) 8 (1875): 162. Type-locality:
    Moyabamba, Peru.

Distribution: Amazonian Ecuador and Peru.

KENTROPYX CALCARATUS Spix

1825 Kentropyx calcaratus Spix, Spec. Nov. Lacert. Bras., 21: pl. 22, fig. 2. Type-locality: Rio
    Itapicurú, Maranhão, Brazil.

Distribution: Northern part of Amazonian Basin of South America.

Comment: Boulenger, Cat. Liz. Brit. Mus., 2, 1885, 391, included a "Centropyx vittatus Wiegmann"
    in the synonymy of this species, but in the original publication, Wiegmann (Herpetologia Mexicana,
    1834, 26) simply stated that specimens of K. calcaratus Spix had been called "Centropygem
    vittatum", (without italics) on the museum shelves. This appear to be a nomen nudum, and is not
    admissible as an available name.

Stejneger, in a handwritten note in an interleaved copy of Boulenger, Cat. Sn. Brit. Mus., 2, 1885, has noted that Boulenger did not include Lacerta vittata Schinz, in Cuvier, Das Thierr., 2, 1822, 45, from Brazil, as a species of Kentropyx. It is unclear to us what its relationship is, although Stejneger placed it opposite calcaratus Spix, suggesting a possible synonymy.

KENTROPYX INTERMEDIUS (Gray)

1831 Teius (C.[entropyx]) Intermedius Gray, Synopsis Species Class Reptilia, in Griffith, Cuvier's Animal Kingdom, 9: 31. Type-locality: Surinam.
1869 Centropyx Borckiana Peters, Monats. Akad. Wiss. Berlin, 1869: 64. Type-locality: Guiana.
1887 Centropyx Copii Garman, Bull. Essex Inst., 19: 2. Type-locality: Barbados.
1926 Gastropholis mertensi De Grijs, Mitt. Zool. Staatinst. Hamburg, 42: 37. Type-locality: Wari, Niger-Delta, Africa, in error.

Distribution: Northeastern South America.

KENTROPYX LAGARTIJA Gallardo

1962 Kentropyx lagartija Gallardo, Acta Zool. Lilloana, 18: 246, figs. 1-2. Type-locality: Río Sali, Tucumán, Argentina.

Distribution: Known only from type-locality.

KENTROPYX PAULENSIS Boettger

1893 Centropyx paulensis Boettger, Katalog der Reptilien-Sammlung im Mus. Senckenbergschen Naturforsch. Ges., 1: 73. Type-locality: São Paulo, Brazil.

Distribution: Southern Brazil.

KENTROPYX PELVICEPS Cope

1868 Centropyx pelviceps Cope, Proc. Acad. Nat. Sci. Phila., 1868: 98. Type-locality: Napo or Upper Amazon of Ecuador.

Distribution: Amazonian lowlands of Ecuador.

KENTROPYX STRIATUS (Daudin)

1802 Lacerta striata Daudin, Hist. Nat. Rept., 3: 247. Type-locality: Surinam.
1862 Centropyx decodon Cope, Proc. Acad. Nat. Sci. Phila., 1861: 495. Type-locality: Surinam.
1869 Centropyx Renggerii Peters, Monats. Akad. Wiss. Berlin, 1869: 63. Type-locality: Paraguay.

Distribution: Northern South America.

KENTROPYX VIRIDISTRIGA Boulenger

1894 Centropyx viridistriga Boulenger, Ann. Mag. Nat. Hist., (6) 13: 343. Type-locality: near Asunción, Paraguay.
1960 Kentropyx viridistriga—Hellmich, Abh. Bayerischen Akad. Wiss. Math.-Naturwiss. Kl., new ser., 101: 62.

Distribution: Paraguay; Chaco, Argentina; Mato Grosso, Brazil.

KENTROPYX WILLIAMSONI Ruthven

1929 Kentropyx williamsoni Ruthven, Occ. Pap. Mus. Zool. Univ. Mich., 206: 1. Type-locality: Manaus, Brazil.

Distribution: Known only from type locality.

REPTILIA: SAURIA: IGUANIDAE ★ ★ ★ ★ LAEMANCTUS

Prepared by Clarence J. McCoy, Jr., Carnegie Museum, Pittsburgh, Pennsylvania

LAEMANCTUS Wiegmann

1834 Laemanctus Wiegmann, Herpetologia Mexicana: 45. Type-species: Laemanctus longipes Wiegmann.

Distribution: Atlantic lowlands from Tamaulipas, Mexico to northwestern Honduras, below 650 meters.

Content: Two species, according to the most recent revision by McCoy, Copeia, 1968, 665, one of which (serratus Cope) is extralimital.

LAEMANCTUS LONGIPES Wiegmann

1834 Laemanctus longipes Wiegmann; Herpetologia Mexicana: 46, pl. 4. Type-locality: Jalapa, Mexico.

Distribution: Central Veracruz, Mexico to northwestern Honduras and possibly Nicaragua.

Content: Three subspecies are recognized by McCoy, Copeia, 1968, 666 et seq., one of which (longipes Wiegmann) is extralimital.

Key to the subspecies	Clave de subespecies
1. Scales around midbody 34-49 (average 44); gular fold continuous across throat--deborrei Scales around midbody 30-32 (average 31); gular fold interrupted or absent--waltersi	1. Escamas en el medio cuerpo 34-49 (promedio 44); pliegue gular contínuo a través de la garganta-------------------------deborrei Escamas en el medio cuerpo 30-32 (promedio 31); pliegue gular interrumpido o ausente----------------------------------waltersi

Laemanctus longipes deborrei Boulenger

1877 Laemanctus de Borrei Boulenger, Bull. Soc. Zool. France, 2: 464, pl. 7. Type-locality: Tabasco, Mexico.
1968 Laemanctus longipes deborrei—McCoy, Copeia, 1968: 668.

Distribution: Isthmus of Tehuantepec, Mexico, to northwestern Honduras, and coastal areas northward to central Veracruz, Mexico. A record from Nicaragua requires verification.

Laemanctus longipes waltersi Schmidt

1933 Laemanctus waltersi Schmidt, Zool. Ser. Field Mus. Nat. Hist., 20: 20. Type-locality: Lake Ticamaya, Honduras.
1968 Laemanctus longipes waltersi—McCoy, Copeia, 1968: 670.

Distribution: Caribbean slopes of northwestern Honduras.

LEIOLOPISMA Duméril and Bibron

1839 Leiolopisma Duméril and Bibron, Erp. Gén., 5: 742. Type-species: Scincus Telfairi Desjardins.
1843 Eulepis Fitzinger, Systema Reptilium: 22. Type-species: Lygosoma Duperreyi Duméril and Bibron.
1843 Leiolepisma Fitzinger (emendation of Leiolopisma), Systema Reptilium: 22.
1843 Lampropholis Fitzinger, Systema Reptilium: 22. Type-species: Lygosoma Guichenoti Duméril and Bibron.
1845 Lipinia Gray, Cat. Liz. Brit. Mus.: 84. Type-species: Lipinia pulchella Gray.
1845 Carlia Gray, Cat. Liz. Brit. Mus.: 271. Type-species: Lygosoma melanopogon Duméril and Bibron.
1857 Cyclodina Girard, Proc. Acad. Nat. Sci. Phila., 1857: 195. Type-species: Cyclodina aenea Girard.
1857 Hombronia Girard, Proc. Acad. Nat. Sci. Phila., 1857: 196. Type-species: Hombronia fasciolaris Girard.
1857 Lygosomella Girard, Proc. Acad. Nat. Sci. Phila., 1857: 196. Type-species: Lygosomella aestuosa Girard.
1857 Oligosoma Girard, Proc. Acad. Nat. Sci. Phila., 1857: 196. Type-species: Mocoa zeylandica Gray.
1873 Lioscincus Bocage, Jour. Acad. Sci. Math. Phys. Nat. Lisbon, 4: 228. Type-species: Lioscincus Steindachnerii Bocage.
1873 Tropidoscincus Bocage, Jour. Acad. Sci. Math. Phys. Nat. Lisbon, 4: 230. Type-species: Tropidoscincus Aubrianus Bocage.
1879 Sauroscincus Peters, Sitz. Ges. Naturforsch. Freunde Berlin, 1879: 149. Type-species: Sauroscincus braconnieri Peters.
1884 Myophila DeVis, Proc. Roy. Soc. Queensland, 1: 77. Type-species: Myophila vivax DeVis.
1884 Lygisaurus DeVis, Proc. Roy. Soc. Queensland, 1: 77. Type-species: Lygisaurus foliorum DeVis.
1950 Scincella Mittleman, Herpetologica, 6: 19. Type-species: Scincus lateralis Say.

Distribution: North and Central America, South Asia, Australia, Pacific Islands.

Content: About 105 species, only three of which occur within limits of this work. Synonymy of genus follows Romer, Osteology of the Reptiles, 1952, 549.

Key to the species

1. Addressed limbs do not overlap in adults-----2
   Addressed limbs strongly overlapping in
   adults--------------------------------cherriei

2. More than 65 dorsal scales between parietals
   and level of anus; 28 or more scales around
   middle of body----------------------assatum
   Fewer than 65 dorsal scales between parietals
   and level of anus; 28 or fewer (usually 26)
   scales around middle of body---------incertum

Clave de especies

1. Extremidad anterior y posterior opuestas entre
   sí no se juntan en adultos------------------2
   Extremidad anterior y posterior opuestas entre
   sí, se cruzan en adultos-------------cherriei

2. Escamas dorsales entre parietales y nivel anal
   más de 65; 28 o más escamas al medio del
   cuerpo------------------------------assatum
   Escamas dorsales entre parietales y nivel anal
   menos de 65; 28 o menos escamas (generalmente
   26) alrededor del medio del cuerpo----incertum

LEIOLOPISMA ASSATUM (Cope)

1864 Lampropholis assatus Cope, Proc. Acad. Nat. Sci. Phila., 1864: 179. Type-locality: Volcán Izalco, El Salvador.
1937 Leiolopisma assatum—Oliver, Occ. Pap. Mus. Zool. Univ. Mich., 360: 12.

Distribution: Colima, Mexico to El Salvador.

Content: Two subspecies, one (taylori Oliver) extralimital.

Leiolopisma assatum assatum Cope

1937 Leiolopisma assatum assatum Oliver, Occ. Pap. Mus. Zool. Univ. Mich., 360: 15.

Distribution: Eastern Chiapas, Mexico, to El Salvador.

LEIOLOPISMA CHERRIEI (Cope)

1893 Mocoa cherriei Cope, Proc. Amer. Phil. Soc., 31: 340. Type-locality: El Palmar, Costa Rica.

Distribution: Tabasco, Mexico to Panama.

Content: Four subspecies, one of which (stuarti Smith) is extralimital.

<table>
<tr><td>Key to the subspecies</td><td>Clave de subespecies</td></tr>
<tr><td>

1. More than 27 scales around midbody; more than 60 scales between parietals and level of anus---------------------------2
Less than 29 scales around midbody; less than 60 scales between parietals and level of anus---------------------ixbaac

2. Primary temporal normally single, if not, lower scale much larger than upper and touches upper secondary temporal; upper secondary temporal larger--------cherriei
Two primary temporals, upper equal to or slightly smaller than lower, only upper touching upper secondary temporal; upper secondary temporal smaller--------------------------------------lampropholis

</td><td>

1. Más de 27 escamas alrededor del medio del cuerpo; más de 60 escamas entre los parietales y el nivel anal--------------------2
Menos de 29 escamas alrededor del medio del cuerpo; menos de 60 escamas entre los parietales y el nivel anal----------ixbaac

2. Temporal primaria frecuentemente única, si no la escama inferior es mucho más grande que la superior y toca la temporal secundaria superior; temporal secundaria superior mucho más grande---------cherriei
Dos temporales primarias, la superior igual o ligeramente menor que la inferior, la única superior toca la temporal secundaria superior; temporal secundaria superior menor------------------------lampropholis

</td></tr>
</table>

Leiolopisma cherriei cherriei (Cope)

1903 Lygosoma assatum var. brevis Werner, Abh. K. Bayer Akad. Wiss. München, 22: 345. Type-locality: Cobán, Guatemala.
1946 Leiolopisma cherriei cherriei—Smith, Herpetologica, 3: 111.

Distribution: Tabasco, Mexico, to southwestern Costa Rica.

Leiolopisma cherriei ixbaac (Stuart)

1940 Lygosoma assatum ixbaac Stuart, Occ. Pap. Mus. Zool. Univ. Mich., 421: 8. Type-locality: Chichen Itza, Yucatán, Mexico.
1946 Leiolopisma cherriei ixbaac—Smith, Herpetologica, 3: 111.

Distribution: Lowlands of Yucatán Peninsula south to central El Petén, Guatemala.

Leiolopisma cherriei lampropholis Taylor

1956 Leiolopisma cherriei lampropholis Taylor, Univ. Kansas Sci. Bull., 38: 287, figs. 71-72. Type-locality: Bataan, Limón, Costa Rica.

Distribution: Northern and eastern Costa Rica.

LEIOLOPISMA INCERTUM (Stuart)

1940 Lygosoma incertum Stuart, Occ. Pap. Mus. Zool. Univ. Mich., 421: 10. Type-locality: Volcán Tajumulco, Guatemala.
1946 Leiolopisma incertum—Smith, Herpetologica, 3: 111.

Distribution: Moderate elevations on Pacific slopes of southwestern Guatemala, as well as Alta Verapaz, Guatemala.

LEIOSAURUS Duméril and Bibron

1837 Leiosaurus Duméril and Bibron, Erp. Gén., 4: 241. Type-species: Leiosaurus Bellii Duméril and Bibron.
1847 Liosaurus Agassiz (substitute name for Leiosaurus Duméril and Bibron), Nomenclator Zoologici Index Universalis: 212.
1897 Aperopristis Peracca, Bol. Mus. Zool. Anat. Comp. Univ. Torino, 12 (299): 1. Type-species: Aperopristis Paronae Peracca.

Distribution: Argentina and presumably adjacent Brazil.

Content: In most recent revision by Gallardo, Physis, 22, 1961, 113-118, five species were included. Two of these have been transferred elsewhere, but two others have since been added, leaving total at five.

Key to the species

1. Infradigital lamellae smooth or indistinctly keeled-------------------------------------2
   Infradigital lamellae keeled------------------3

2. Venter with broken brown longitudinal lines; no black antehumeral collar----------------bellii
   Venter light, without brown longitudinal lines; black antehumeral collar present-----bardensis

3. Dorsal scales homogeneous; ventrals smooth; no dorsal or nuchal crests----------------------4
   Dorsal scales heterogeneous, with tubercular scales sometimes arranged in rows; ventrals keeled; weak nuchal and dorsal crests of pointed scales--------------------------paronae

4. Dorsal pattern of arrowhead-shaped dark spots-- --------------------------------catamarcensis
   Dorsal pattern of broad, transverse dark bands- ------------------------------------fasciatus

Clave de especies

1. Lamelas infradigitales lisas o indistintamente quilladas------------------------------------2
   Lamelas infradigitales quilladas--------------3

2. Vientre con líneas pardas quebradas; no hay collar negro prehumeral-----------------bellii
   Vientre claro, sin líneas longitudinales pardas; collar negro prehumeral presente------ -------------------------------------bardensis

3. Dorsales homogéneas; ventrales lisas; no hay cresta dorsal ni nucal----------------------4
   Escamas dorsales heterogéneas con escamas tuberculadas a veces ordenadas en hileras; ventrales quilladas; con débiles crestas nucal y dorsal de escamas puntiagudas--------paronae

4. Diseño dorsal de manchas oscuras con forma de punta de flecha------------------catamarcensis
   Diseño dorsal de bandas transversales, anchas y oscuras-----------------------------------fasciatus

LEIOSAURUS BARDENSIS Gallardo

1968 Leiosaurus bardensis Gallardo, Neotropica, 14: 5, fig. Type-locality: Altos de Cochicó, Cochicó, Puelén, La Pampa, Argentina.

Distribution: Provincias de La Pampa and San Juan, Argentina.

LEIOSAURUS BELLII Duméril and Bibron

1837 Leiosaurus Bellii Duméril and Bibron, Erp. Gén., 4: 242. Type-locality: Mexico, in error.
1961 Leiosaurus bellii—Gallardo, Physis, 22: 114.

Distribution: Santa Cruz, Chubut, Río Negro, Mendoza and Neuquén, Argentina.

LEIOSAURUS CATAMARCENSIS (Koslowsky)

1898 Liosaurus catamarcensis Koslowsky, Rev. Mus. La Plata, 8: 169, pl. 1. Type-locality: Provincia de Catamarca, Argentina.
1961 Leiosaurus catamarcensis—Gallardo, Physis, 22: 114.

Distribution: Western parts of Provincias Mendoza, San Juan, La Rioja and Catamarca, Argentina.

LEIOSAURUS FASCIATUS D'Orbigny and Bibron

1847 Leiosaurus fasciatus D'Orbigny and Bibron, Voyage dans L'Amerique Meridionale, 5 (1): 8, pl. 3, figs. 5-7. Type-locality: Río Negro, Patagonia, Argentina.

Distribution: Patagonia, Argentina.

LEIOSAURUS PARONAE (Peracca)

1897 Aperopristis Paronae Peracca, Bol. Mus. Zool. Anat. Comp. Univ. Torino, 12 (299): 1, pl. Type-
        locality: Brazil.
1961 Leiosaurus paronae—Gallardo, Physis, 22: 115.

   Distribution: Brazil (probably southern); central parts of northern half of Argentina.

LEPIDOBLEPHARIS Peracca

1897 <u>Lepidoblepharis</u> Peracca, Boll. Mus. Zool. Anat. Comp. Univ. Torino, 12 (300): 1. Type-species: <u>Lepidoblepharis</u> <u>festae</u> Peracca.
1916 <u>Lathrogecko</u> Ruthven, Occ. Pap. Mus. Zool. Univ. Mich., 21: 1. Type-species: <u>Lepidoblepharis</u> <u>sanctae-martae</u> Ruthven.

Distribution: Central America, northern South America.

Content: Eight species.

Key to the species

1. Dorsal scales juxtaposed----------------------2
   Dorsal scales imbricate-----------<u>sanctaemartae</u>

2. Dorsal scales uniform in size-----------------3
   Dorsal scales heterogeneous, granules mixed
   with enlarged scales------------------<u>ruthveni</u>

3. Dorsal scales without keels------------------4
   Dorsal scales strongly keeled or tubercular----
   ----------------------------------<u>xanthostigma</u>

4. Scales on the snout larger than those on rest
   of head------------------------------------5
   Scales on the snout not larger than those on
   rest of head-------------------------------7

5. Scales bordering postmentals same size as the
   other gular scales--------------------------6
   Scales bordering postmentals larger than remaining gulars----------------------<u>buchwaldi</u>

6. No grooves in mental----------------<u>oxycephalus</u>
   Two grooves in posterior half of mental--------
   -----------------------------------<u>intermedius</u>

7. Granules on snout larger than dorsal granules;
   postmentals enlarged-------------------<u>festae</u>
   Granules on snout smaller than dorsal granules;
   postmentals not enlarged-------------<u>peraccae</u>

Clave de especies

1. Escamas dorsales yuxtapuestas-----------------2
   Escamas dorsales imbricadas-------<u>sanctaemartae</u>

2. Escamas dorsales de tamaño uniforme-----------3
   Escamas dorsales heterogéneas, gránulos con
   escamas grandes-----------------------<u>ruthveni</u>

3. Escamas dorsales no quilladas-----------------4
   Escamas dorsales fuertemente quilladas o tu-
   berculares-------------------------<u>xanthostigma</u>

4. Escamas del hocico mayores que las del resto de
   la cabeza----------------------------------5
   Escamas del hocico no mayores que las del resto
   de la cabeza-------------------------------7

5. Escamas inmediatas a las posmentales no mayores
   que las gulares anteriores------------------6
   Escamas inmediatas a las posmentales mayores
   que las restantes gulares-----------<u>buchwaldi</u>

6. Mental sin ranuras-----------------<u>oxycephalus</u>
   Dos ranuras en la parte posterior del mental---
   -----------------------------------<u>intermedius</u>

7. Gránulos del hocico mayores que los dorsales;
   posmentales agrandados-----------------<u>festae</u>
   Gránulos del hocico menores que los dorsales;
   posmentales no agrandados------------<u>peraccae</u>

LEPIDOBLEPHARIS <u>BUCHWALDI</u> Werner

1910 <u>Lepidoblepharis</u> <u>buchwaldi</u> Werner, Mitt. Nat. Mus. Hamburg, 27: 8. Type-locality: Hacienda Clementina, Babahoyo, Ecuador.

Distribution: Known only from type locality.

LEPIDOBLEPHARIS <u>FESTAE</u> Peracca

1897 <u>Lepidoblepharis</u> <u>festae</u> Peracca, Boll. Mus. Zool. Anat. Comp. Univ. Torino, 12 (300): 2, fig. Type-locality: San José de Cuchipamba, Ecuador.

Distribution: Amazonian slopes of Colombia, Ecuador and Peru; Amapá, Amazonas, and Pará, Brazil.

Content: Two subspecies.

<table>
<tr><td>Key to the subspecies</td><td>Clave de subespecies</td></tr>
</table>

Key to the subspecies

1. Mental bordered by scales identical in size with gular scales; 14-16 transverse rows of ventrals; 14-15 infradigital lamellae under fourth toe on hind foot-------festae
Mental bordered by row of scales much larger than gular scales; 20-22 transverse rows of ventrals; 11-12 infradigital lamellae under fourth toe------colombianus

Clave de subespecies

1. Escamas que forman el borde posterior del mental son del mismo tamaño que las gulares; 14-16 hileras transversales de ventrales; 14-15 lamelas bajo del cuarto dedo de la extremidad posterior-----festae
Escamas que forman el borde posterior del mental son más grandes que las gulares; 20-22 hileras transversales de ventrales; 11-12 lamelas bajo del cuarto dedo--------
------------------------------colombianus

Lepidoblepharis festae festae Peracca

1968 L[epidoblepharis] f[estae] festae—Mechler, Rev. Suisse Zool., 75: 339, figs. 10-12.

Distribution: Amazonian slopes of Ecuador and Peru; Amapá, Amazonas, and Pará, Brazil.

Lepidoblepharis festae colombianus Mechler

1968 Lepidoblepharis festae colombianus Mechler, Rev. Suisse Zool., 75: 339, figs. 13-18. Type-locality: Cafetal Argalia, Departamento Cundinamarca, Colombia, 1600 m.

Distribution: Known only from type locality.

LEPIDOBLEPHARIS INTERMEDIUS Boulenger

1914 Lepidoblepharis intermedius Boulenger, Proc. Zool. Soc. London, 1914: 814, pl. 1, fig. 2. Type-locality: Peña Lisa, Condoto, Colombia.
1968 Lepidoblepharis intermedius—Mechler, Rev. Suisse Zool., 75: 341, figs. 19-23.

Distribution: Pacific lowlands of Colombia and northwestern Ecuador.

LEPIDOBLEPHARIS OXYCEPHALUS (Werner)

1894 Gonatodes oxycephalus Werner, Zool. Anz., 17: 413. Type-locality: "Ecuador".
1953 Lepidoblepharis oxycephalus—Vanzolini, Rev. Brasil. Biol., 13: 74.

Distribution: Unknown; still not verified from Ecuador.

LEPIDOBLEPHARIS PERACCAE Boulenger

1908 Lepidoblepharis peraccae Boulenger, Ann. Mag. Nat. Hist., (8) 1: 111. Type-locality: Los Mangos, Colombia, 300 m.

Distribution: Southwestern Colombia.

LEPIDOBLEPHARIS RUTHVENI Parker

1926 Lepidoblepharis ruthveni Parker, Ann. Mag. Nat. Hist., (9) 17: 295. Type-locality: Chimbo, Ecuador.

Distribution: Pacific slope of Ecuador.

LEPIDOBLEPHARIS SANCTAEMARTAE (Ruthven)

1916 Lathrogecko sanctae-martae Ruthven, Occ. Pap. Mus. Zool. Univ. Mich., 21: 2. Type-locality: Fundación, Colombia.
1926 Lepidoblepharis sanctae-martae—Parker, Ann. Mag. Nat. Hist., (9) 17: 294.

Distribution: Panama and Colombia.

Content: Two subspecies.

Key to the subspecies   Clave de subespecies

1. Mental bordered posteriorly by four or five   1. Mental bordeado posteriormente por cuatro o
   scales slightly larger than the throat   cinco escamas un poco mayores que las
   granules----------------------------fugax   escamas de la garganta--------------fugax
   Mental bordered posteriorly by three scales   Mental bordeado posteriormente por tres
   much larger than the throat granules------   escamas, mucho mayores que las escamas de
   ----------------------------sanctaemartae   la garganta------------------sanctaemartae

Lepidoblepharis sanctaemartae sanctaemartae (Ruthven)

   1928 Lepidoblepharis [sanctae-martae] sanctae-martae—Ruthven, Occ. Pap. Mus. Zool. Univ.
        Mich., 191: 2.
   1968 Lepidoblepharis sanctaemartae sanctaemartae—Mechler, Rev. Suisse Zool., 75: 346, figs.
        24-28.

   Distribution: Santa Marta Mountains, Colombia.

Lepidoblepharis sanctaemartae fugax Ruthven

   1928 Lepidoblepharis sanctae-martae fugax Ruthven, Occ. Pap. Mus. Zool. Univ. Mich., 191: 2.
        Type-locality: Barro Colorado Island, Gatun Lake, Panama.

   Distribution: Eastern Panama from Canal Zone to Sapo Mountains.

LEPIDOBLEPHARIS XANTHOSTIGMA (Noble)

   1916 Lathrogecko xanthostigma Noble, Proc. Biol. Soc. Washington, 29: 87. Type-locality: Zent, near
        Puerto Limón, Costa Rica.
   1923 Lathrogecko microlepis Noble, Amer. Mus. Novitates, 88: 2. Type-locality: Río Quesado, region
        of Río Atrato, Colombia.
   1928 Lepidoblepharis xanthostigma—Ruthven, Occ. Pap. Mus. Zool. Univ. Mich., 191: 2.
   1956 Lepidoblepharis xanthostigma—Taylor, Univ. Kansas Sci. Bull., 38: 20, figs. 2-3.

   Distribution: Costa Rica to Colombia.

   Comment: Vanzolini, Arq. Zool. São Paulo, 17, 1968, 30, recognized L. microlepis Noble as a
        valid species, but does not discuss or include L. xanthostigma in his review of the South
        American species. It is not clear to us whether he rejects previous synonymy of the two
        species or not.

LEPIDODACTYLUS Fitzinger

1843 <u>Lepidodactylus</u> Fitzinger, Systema Reptilium: 98. Type-species: <u>Platydactylus</u> <u>Lugubris</u> Duméril
and Bibron.
1845 <u>Amydosaurus</u> Gray, Cat. Liz. Brit. Mus.: 162. Type-species: <u>Platydactylus lugubris</u> Duméril and
Bibron.

Distribution: East Indies; South Asia; Philippines; Polynesia; Australia and New Zealand, acciden-
tally transported to Central and South America.

Content: Twelve species, according to Kluge, Philippine Jour. Sci., 95, 1966 (1968), 336, only one
of which occurs within limits of this work.

LEPIDODACTYLUS LUGUBRIS (Duméril and Bibron)

1836 <u>Platydactylus</u> <u>Lugubris</u> Duméril and Bibron, Erp. Gén., 3: 304. Type-locality: Otaїti, which is
same as Tahiti.
1858 <u>Peropus</u> <u>neglectus</u> Girard, Proc. Acad. Nat. Sci. Phila., 1857: 197. Type-locality: Rio de
Janeiro, Brazil.
1859 <u>Hemidactylus</u> <u>Meijeri</u> Bleeker, Natuurk. Tijds. Nederl.-Indiё,(4) 16: 47. Type-locality: Bintang,
Rhio Archipelago.
1864 <u>Peripia</u> <u>cantoris</u> Günther, Reptiles of British India: 110. Type-locality: Penang.
1867 <u>Gecko</u> <u>labialis</u> Peters, Monats. Akad. Wiss. Berlin, 1867: 14. Type-locality: Mindanao,
Philippines.
1867 <u>Gecko</u> <u>moestus</u> Peters, Monats. Akad. Wiss. Berlin, 1867: 13. Type-locality: Pelew Island.
1869 <u>Peropus</u> <u>roseus</u> Cope, Proc. Acad. Nat. Sci. Phila., 1868: 319. Type-locality: Not given.
1869 <u>Gymnodactylus</u> <u>Caudeloti</u> Bavay, Mém. Soc. Linn. Normandie, 5: 13. Type-locality: New Caledonia.
1874 <u>Peripia</u> <u>mysorensis</u> Meyer, Monats. Akad. Wiss. Berlin, 1874: 129. Type-locality: Mysore Island,
Schouten Islands, near New Guinea.
1878 <u>Peripia</u> <u>ornata</u> MacLeay, Proc. Linn. Soc. New South Wales, 2: 98. Type-locality: Port Moresby,
New Guinea.
1885 <u>Lepidodactylus</u> <u>lugubris</u>—Boulenger, Cat. Liz. Brit. Mus., 1: 165.
1918 <u>Lepidodactylus</u> <u>divergens</u> Taylor, Philippine Jour. Sci., (D) 13: 242, pl. 1, figs. 1-3. Type-
locality: Great Govenen Island, Sulu Archipelago.
1929 <u>Lepidodactylus</u> <u>lombocensis</u> Mertens, Senckenbergiana, 11: 239, fig. 1. Type-locality: Ekas,
Lombok Island.
1964 <u>Lepidodactylus</u> <u>intermedius</u> Darevsky, Zool. Anz., 173: 169, figs. 1-2. Type-locality: Komodo
Island.

Distribution: Ceylon; Nicobars; Andamans; Burma, Malay Archipelago, Indo-Australian Archipelago;
Oceania. Apparently introduced in Colombia, Ecuador, and Panama; also recorded from Rio de
Janeiro, Brazil.

Comment: This synonymy follows Kluge, Philippine Jour. Sci., 96, 1966 (1968), 338.

LEPIDOPHYMA Duméril

    1851 Lepidophyma Duméril, Cat. Méth. Coll. Rept. Mus. Paris: 137. Type-species: Lepidophyma
        flavimaculatus Duméril.
    1863 Poriodogaster Smith, in Gray, Proc. Zool. Soc. London, 1863: 154. Type-species: Poriodogaster
        grayii Smith.
    1878 Akleistops Müller, Verh. Naturforsch. Ges. Basel, 6: 390. Type-species: Akleistops
        guatemalensis Müller.
    1939 Gaigeia Smith, Zool. Ser. Field Mus. Nat. Hist., 24: 24. Type-species: Lepidophyma gaigeae
        Mosauer.

    Distribution: Mexico to Panama.

    Content: Seven species, six of which (gaigeae Mosauer, dontomasi Smith, sylvaticum Taylor, radula
    Smith, micropholis Walker and pajapanensis Werler) are extralimital, according to last summary by
    Savage, Contr. Sci. Los Angeles Co. Mus., 71, 1963.

LEPIDOPHYMA FLAVIMACULATUM Duméril

    1851 Lepidophyma flavimaculatus Duméril, Cat. Méth. Coll. Rept. Mus. Paris: 137. Type-locality: El
        Petén, Guatemala.

    Distribution: Tamaulipas and Veracruz, Mexico, to Panama.

    Content: Eight subspecies, three of which (tehuanae Smith, tenebrarum Walker, tuxtlae Werler and
    Shannon) are extralimital, and two of which are of doubtful status (see remarks under
    ophiophthalmum Taylor).

          Key to the subspecies

1. More than 12 femoral pores on each leg---2
   Fewer than 12 femoral pores on each leg----
   ------------------------------------smithii

2. Throat region behind chinshields marked
   with dark brown or black reticulations
   enclosing rounded cream spots-----------3
   Throat region behind chinshields lacking
   definite reticulations, area usually
   light with nearly uniform distribution
   of pigment-----------------------------4

3. Dorsal surface of head brown with marks
   tending to form radiating symmetrical
   pattern; belly cream anteriorly and black
   posteriorly-------------------reticulatum
   Dorsal surface of head yellowish brown
   with isolated small spots, belly yellow-
   ish----------------------flavimaculatum

4. Femoral pores 13-15; one pair of postparietals which may be partly sutured;
   first loreal higher than posterior nasal-
   --------------------------------obscurum
   Femoral pores 16-18; no trace of postparietals or partial sutures; first
   loreal lower than posterior nasal--------
   -------------------------ophiophthalmum

          Clave de subespecies

1. Más de 12 poros femorales en cada muslo---2
   Menos de 12 poros femorales en cada muslo--
   ------------------------------------smithii

2. Región del cuello detrás de los escudos
   mentonianos con reticulaciones negras o
   café encerrando manchas cremosas redondas-
   --3
   Región del cuello detrás de los escudos
   mentonianos sin reticulaciones, el área es
   clara con distribución igual de pigmento-4

3. Dorsocefálico pardo con marcas que tienden
   a formar una radiación simétrica; vientre
   cremoso anteriormente y negro posterior-
   mente-------------------------reticulatum
   Dorsocefálico amarillo pardo con manchas
   aisladas; vientre amarillento------------
   --------------------------flavimaculatum

4. Poros femorales 13-15; un par de postparietales que puede estar parcialmente
   suturado; primer loreal más alto que el
   nasal posterior------------------obscurum
   Poros femorales 16-18; no hay trazos de
   postparietales ni de suturas parciales;
   primer loreal más bajo que el nasal
   posterior-------------------ophiophthalmum

Lepidophyma flavimaculatum flavimaculatum Duméril

    1863 Poriodogaster Grayii Smith, in Gray, Proc. Zool. Soc. London, 1863: 154, pl. 21. Type-
        locality: Unknown.
    1878 Lepidophyma flavimaculatum—Bocourt, Miss. Sci. Mex., Rept., 5: 306, pl. 20, figs.
        2a-2g.
    1963 Lepidophyma flavimaculatum flavimaculatum—Savage, Contr. Sci. Los Angeles Co. Mus., 71:
        35.

        Distribution: Southern Mexico to Guatemala.

Lepidophyma flavimaculatum obscurum Barbour

   1924 Lepidophyma flavimaculatum obscurum Barbour, Proc. New England Zool. Club, 9: 10. Type-
          locality: Río Chilibrillo, Panama.
   1955 Lepidophyma anomalum Taylor, Univ. Kansas Sci. Bull., 37: 554, fig. 14. Type-locality:
          Los Diamantes, Guápiles, Limón Province, Costa Rica.
   1963 Lepidophyma flavimaculatum obscurum——Savage, Contr. Sci. Los Angeles Co. Mus., 71: 35.

      Distribution: Costa Rica and Panama.

?Lepidophyma flavimaculatum ophiophthalmum Taylor

   1955 Lepidophyma ophiophthalmum Taylor, Univ. Kansas Sci. Bull., 37: 558, fig. 15. Type-
          locality: Five km north-northeast of Tilarán, Guanacaste Province, Costa Rica.
   ?1965 Lepidophyma flavimaculatum ophiophthalmum——Wermuth, Das Tierreich, 80: 196.

      Distribution: Known only from type locality.

      Comment: Savage, Contr. Sci. Los Angeles Co. Mus., 71, 1963, 32, indicated that this taxon and
         reticulatum Taylor were "members of the flavimaculatum group", but he omitted both names
         from his summary classification on p. 35. Wermuth, Das Tierreich, 80, 1965, 196, indicated
         both taxa as subspecies of flavimaculatum, but with a question mark to indicate doubt as
         to the legitimacy of his action. Savage's intent is not clear, and we are most dubious
         as to the proper placement of the two taxa, but we follow Wermuth and retain the query.

?Lepidophyma flavimaculatum reticulatum Taylor

   1955 Lepidophyma reticulatum Taylor, Univ. Kansas Sci. Bull., 37: 551, fig. 14. Type-locality:
          Agua Buena, Puntarenas Province, Costa Rica.
   ?1965 Lepidophyma flavimaculatum reticulatum——Wermuth, Das Tierreich, 80: 196.

      Distribution: Known only from type locality.

      Comment: See comment under ophiophthalmum Taylor.

Lepidophyma flavimaculatum smithii Bocourt

   1876 Lepidophyma Smithii Bocourt, Jour. Zool. Paris, 5: 402. Type-locality: Tehuantepec and
          western Guatemala; restricted to Mazatenango, Suchitepequez, Guatemala, by Smith and Taylor,
          Bull. U.S. Nat. Mus., 199, 1950, 152.
   1878 Akleistops guatemalensis Müller, Verh. Naturforsch. Ges. Basel, 6: 390, pls. 1-2. Type-
          locality: Mazatenango, Guatemala.
   1955 Lepidophyma maculatum Taylor (in error for flavimaculatum), Univ. Kansas Sci. Bull., 37:
          549.
   1963 Lepidophyma flavimaculatum smithii——Stuart, Misc. Publ. Mus. Zool. Univ. Mich., 122: 58.

      Distribution: Low elevations of Pacific slope from eastern Chiapas, Mexico, to El Salvador.

LEPOSOMA Spix

1825 Leposoma Spix, Spec. Nov. Lacert. Bras.: 24, pl. 27, fig. 2. Type-species: Leposoma scincoides Spix.
1830 Lepidosoma Wagler, Nat. Syst. Amph.: 157. Type-species: Leposoma scincoides Spix.
1845 Lepisoma Gray, Cat. Liz. Brit. Mus.: 60. Type-species: Leposoma scincoides Spix.
1868 Loxopholis Cope, Proc. Acad. Nat. Sci. Phila., 1868: 305. Type-species: Loxopholis rugiceps Cope.
1885 Mionyx Cope, Proc. Amer. Phil. Soc., 23: 96. Type-species: Mionyx parietale Cope.
1923 Hylosaurus Müller, Zool. Anz., 57: 145. Type-species: Hylosaurus percarinatus Müller.

Distribution: Costa Rica to southern Brazil.

Content: Seven species, according to most recent revision, by Ruibal, Bull. Mus. Comp. Zool., 106, 1962.

Key to the species

1. Frontonasal longitudinally divided------------2
   Frontonasal single--------------------------4

2. Pregulars convex, posteriorly pointed; ventrals not in longitudinal rows---------------------3
   Pregulars flat and quadrangular, ventrals in longitudinal rows----------------------southi

3. Interparietal neither longer nor broader than parietals; third pair of postmentals in contact with lower labials-------------scincoides
   Interparietal longer and broader than parietals; third pair of postmentals separated from lower labials--------------------annectans

4. Scales on side of neck not shaped like dorsals; 32-39 scales from parietals to posterior margin of hind limbs-----------------------5
   Scales on side of neck keeled, imbricate and shaped like dorsals; 27-31 scales from parietals to posterior margin of hind limbs------ -------------------------------------rugiceps

5. Five preanal scales, median preanal much smaller than other preanal scales; female body color not uniform----------------------6
   Five preanal scales, median preanal large, elongate; female with uniform body color------ --------------------------------guianense

6. Irregular dorsolateral dark stripe one or two scales wide, extending onto tail where it is bordered below by white stripe originating at insertion of hind limb; 36-39 scales from parietals to posterior margin of hind limbs--- --------------------------------percarinatum
   A dark lateral band 4-5 scales wide; no white stripe on tail; 32-36 scales from parietals to posterior margin of hind limbs----parietale

Clave de especies

1. Frontonasal longitudinalmente dividido--------2
   Frontonasal único---------------------------4

2. Pregulares convexas, posteriormente puntiagudas, ventrales no en hileras longitudinales- ---3
   Pregulares planas y cuadrangulares; ventrales en hileras longitudinales---------------southi

3. Interparietal ni más largo ni ancho que los parietales; tercer par de posmentales en contacto con los infralabiales---------scincoides
   Interparietal más largo y ancho que los parietales; tercer par de posmentales separado de los infralabiales por una escamita---annectans

4. Escamas a los lados del cuello de contorno diferente a las dorsales; 32-39 escamas de los parietales al margen posterior de los muslos-- ---5
   Escamas de los lados del cuello quilladas, imbricadas y de contorno como las dorsales; 27-31 escamas desde los parietales al margen posterior de los muslos---------------rugiceps

5. Escamas preanales cinco, preanal mediana mucho más pequeña que las otras escamas preanales; hembra sin color uniforme--------------------6
   Escamas preanales cinco, preanal mediana grande elongada; hembra de color uniforme---guianense

6. Una cinta oscura lateral e irregular de una a dos escamas de ancho extendida en la cola donde está bordeada debajo por una cinta blanca originada en la inserción de la extremidad posterior; 36-39 escamas de las parietals al margen posterior de las extremidades posteriores----------------------percarinatum
   Una banda lateral oscura de cuatro a cinco escamas de ancho; no cinta blanca sobre la cola; 32-36 escamas de los parietales al margen posterior de las extremidades posteriores--------------------------------parietale

LEPOSOMA ANNECTANS Ruibal

1952 Leposoma annectans Ruibal, Bull. Mus. Comp. Zool., 106: 486. Type-locality: Bahia, Estado da Bahia, Brazil.

Distribution: Estado da Bahia, Brazil.

LEPOSOMA GUIANENSE Ruibal

1952 Leposoma guianense Ruibal, Bull. Mus. Comp. Zool., 106: 489, figs. 1-2. Type-locality: Dunoon, Demerara River, Guyana.

Distribution: Guyana and French Guiana.

LEPOSOMA PARIETALE (Cope)

1885 Mionyx parietalis Cope, Proc. Amer. Phil. Soc., 23: 96. Type-locality: Pebas, Peru.
1952 Leposoma parietale—Ruibal, Bull. Mus. Comp. Zool., 106: 492.

Distribution: Amazonian region of Colombia, Ecuador and Peru.

LEPOSOMA PERCARINATUM (Müller)

1923 Hylosaurus percarinatus Müller, Zool. Anz., 57: 146. Type-locality: Peixeboi, Estado do Pará, Brazil.
1923 Leposoma taeniata Noble, Zoologica, 3: 303. Type-locality: Kartabo, British Guiana.
1925 Hylosaurus muelleri Mertens, Senckenbergiana, 7: 76. Type-locality: Inirida River, southern Venezuela.
1931 Leposoma percarinatum—Burt and Burt, Bull. Amer. Mus. Nat. Hist., 61: 349.
1952 Leposoma percarinatum—Ruibal, Bull. Mus. Comp. Zool., 106: 490.

Distribution: Northeastern South America, in Guyana, Venezuela and Brazil.

LEPOSOMA RUGICEPS (Cope)

1869 Loxopholis rugiceps Cope, Proc. Acad. Nat. Sci. Phila., 1868: 305. Type-locality: Río Magdalena, Colombia.
1880 Leposoma dispar Peters, Monats. Akad. Wiss. Berlin, 1880: 217, pl. 309, fig. 2-2c. Type-locality: Cáceres, Cauca, Colombia.
1952 Leposoma rugiceps—Ruibal, Bull. Mus. Comp. Zool., 106: 487.

Distribution: Colombia north and east of Andes; Panama.

LEPOSOMA SCINCOIDES Spix

1825 Leposoma scincoides Spix, Spec. Nov. Lacert. Bras.: 24, pl. 27, fig. 2. Type-locality: Banks of Rio Amazon, Brazil.
1962 Leposoma scincoides—Ruibal, Bull. Mus. Comp. Zool., 106: 485.

Distribution: Northern and central Brazil.

LEPOSOMA SOUTHI Ruthven and Gaige

1924 Leposoma southi Ruthven and Gaige, Occ. Pap. Mus. Zool. Univ. Mich., 147: 1. Type-locality: Progreso, Chiriquí Province, Panama.

Distribution: Panama to Costa Rica.

Content: Two subspecies.

Key to the subspecies	Clave de subespecies
1. Seven dorsal scale rows; gular scales smaller and more numerous; third chin shield single; 26 scales around middle of body; femoral pores 7-7----------southi Five dorsal scale rows; gular scales larger and fewer in number (2-4 rows); third chin shield replaced by two scales; scales around middle of body fewer than 26; femoral pores 4-4--------------orientalis	1. Siete filas de escamas dorsales; escamas gulares pequeñas y numerosas; tercer escudo mental único; 26 escamas al medio del cuerpo; poros femorales 7-7-----southi Cinco filas de escamas dorsales; escamas gulares mayores en número bajo (2-4 filas); tercer escudo mental reemplazado por dos escamas; escamas al medio del cuerpo menos de 26; poros femorales 4-4------orientalis

<u>Leposoma</u> <u>southi</u> <u>southi</u> Ruthven and Gaige

    1949 <u>Leposoma</u> <u>bisecta</u> Taylor, Univ. Kansas Sci. Bull., 33: 275. Type-locality: El Genéral, Pacific slope, Costa Rica.
    1955 <u>Leposoma</u> <u>southi</u> <u>southi</u>—Taylor, Univ. Kansas Sci. Bull., 37: 546.

    Distribution: Panama to Costa Rica.

<u>Leposoma</u> <u>southi</u> <u>orientalis</u> Taylor

    1955 <u>Leposoma</u> <u>southi</u> <u>orientalis</u> Taylor, Univ. Kansas Sci. Bull., 37: 546. Type-locality: Volio, Limón Province, Costa Rica.

    Distribution: Known from type locality; Taylor, Univ. Kansas Sci. Bull., 38, 1956, 238, indicates that specimens from Suretka, Costa Rica, also belong to this subspecies.

REPTILIA: AMPHISBAENIA: AMPHISBAENIDAE ★ ★ ★ LEPOSTERNON

Prepared by Carl Gans, State University of New York, Buffalo, New York

LEPOSTERNON Wagler

1824 Leposternon Wagler, in Spix, Sp. Nov. Serp. Bras.: 70. Type-species: Leposternon microcephalus Wagler.
1825 Leptostermon Gray (emendation of Leposternon Wagler), Thomson's Ann. Phil., (2) 10: 204.
1830 Lepidosternon Wagler (emendation of Leposternon Wagler), Nat. Syst. Amph.: 197.
1832 Cephalopeltis Müller, Zeits. für Physiol., 4 (2), art. 19: 256. Type-species: Cephalopeltis cuvierii Müller.
1847 Leposternum Agassiz (emendation of Leposternon Wagler), Nomenclator Zoologici Index Universalis: 205.
1865 Sphenocephalus Gray (preoccupied by Sphenocephalus Fitzinger, 1843), Proc. Zool. Soc. London, 1865: 452. Type-species: Lepidosternon Grayii Gray.

Distribution: Southern Brazil, Paraguay, and northern Argentina.

Content: Six species.

Comment: Detailed information on the new synonymies to be found in this account will be published elsewhere by the author of this section. The key below was prepared with the aid of Carlos G. Diefenbach.

Key to the species	Clave de especies
1. Only two rows of enlarged scales on dorsum of head, rostronasal, followed by azygous shield, which may or may not be followed by fringe of much smaller segments in the occipital region; suture pattern simple; pectoral region covered with large, geometrically regular shields------------------------------2 Three or more rows of enlarged shields on dorsum of head, suture pattern often complex; pectoral region divided or not--------------3	1. Sólo dos hileras de escamas ensanchadas en parte dorsal de la cabeza, la rostronasal, seguida de escudo azygos puede estar seguida o no por un fleco de segmentos mucho más pequeños en la región occipital; diseño de suturas simple; región pectoral cubierta de escudos grandes geométricamente regulares------2 Tres o más hileras de escudos ensanchados en dorso de la cabeza, diseño de suturas a menudo complejo; región pectoral dividida o no------3
2. Rostronasal followed by enormous azygous shield which covers nearly entire dorsal surface of head, narrowly fringed posteriorly by single row of much smaller segments; head shield strongly keratinized; both mental and postmental present; 253-305 postpectoral annuli----------------------------------scutigerum Rostronasal followed by large azygous shield, flanked by triangular prefrontals and small temporals; headshields not significantly keratinized; single mental-postmental segment; 378 postpectoral annuli----------------octostegum	2. Rostronasal seguido de un escudo azygos enorme que cubre casi toda la superficie dorsal de la cabeza, bordeada angostamente a posterior por una sola hilera de segmentos mucho más chicos; escudo de la cabeza densamente queratinizado; mental y postmental presentes; 253-305 anillos postpectorales--------------------scutigerum Rostronasal seguido de escudo azygos grande, flanqueado de prefrontales triangulares y temporales chicos; escudo cefálico no muy queratinizado; segmento mental-postmental único; 378 anillos postpectorales----------octostegum
3. First supralabial small, followed by large second and small third supralabial-----------4 First supralabial large, followed by smaller second supralabial-------------------------5	3. Primer supralabial chico, seguido de segundo grande y tercero chico-----------------------4 Primer supralabial grande seguido de segundo más chico--------------------------------------5
4. Azygous shield in contact with rostronasal; frontals and median temporals much larger than azygous, longer than wide and arranged linearly; infraocular absent; first infralabial small, followed by large second infralabial, arrangement of large pectoral shields reminiscent of hourglass; number of dorsal postpectoral annuli generally equal to or rarely up to 10 more than ventral number, adult snout vent length 205-432 mm--------------polystegum (Second half of dichotomy on following page)	4. Escudo azygos en contacto con rostronasal; frontales y temporales medios mucho mayores que azygos, más largos que anchos y dispuestos linealmente; infraocular ausente; primer infralabial chico seguido de segundo infralabial grande; disposición de escudos pectorales grandes parecida a reloj de arena; número de anillos postpectorales dorsales generalmente igual o, raramente hasta 10 más que el número de ventrales; longitud del adulto del hocico al ano 205-432 mm------------------polystegum (Segunda mitad de la dicotomía en la página siguiente)

4. (Cont.) Azygous shield separated from rostronasal by wide suture between prefrontals;
frontals about as wide as long, not signifi-
cantly larger than azygous shield, temporals
much smaller, infraocular generally present;
first infralabial large; pectoral segments
only slightly enlarged and rounded, sometimes
with irregular longitudinal fusions; number of
dorsal postpectoral annuli always 5-25 higher
than ventral number; adult snout-vent length
285-600 mm----------------------<u>infraorbitale</u>

5. Azygous always distinct; pectoral region
covered by three or four pairs of elongate,
regular shields which may fuse except for midline suture; number of dorsal and ventral
postpectoral annuli about equal; 242-265
postpectoral annuli-----------------<u>wuchereri</u>
Azygous often irregularly fused with adjacent
head shields; one median pair of elongate
pectoral shields, with other modified, possibly enlarged shields radiating from these
anteriorly; 5-25 more dorsal than ventral
postpectoral annuli, with increase greater
in second, third and fourth fifths of trunk;
177-242 postpectoral annuli------<u>microcephalum</u>

4. Escudo azygos separado del rostronasal por sutura ancha entre prefrontales; frontales
aproximadamente tan anchos como largos, no notoriamente mayores que escudo azygos, temporales mucho menores; infraocular generalmente
presente; primer infralabial grande; segmentos
pectorales sólo ligeramente ensanchados y re-
dondeados, a veces con fusiones longitudinales
irregulares; número de anillos postpectorales
dorsales siempre 5-25 más que el número de
ventrales; longitud hocico-ano de adultos 285-
600 mm--------------------------<u>infraorbitale</u>

5. Azygos siempre distinto; región pectoral cubierta de tres a cuatro pares de escudos regulares, alargados que pueden estar fusionados
excepto en la línea media; número de anillos
postpectorales dorsales y ventrales aproximadamente igual; 242-265 anillos postpectorales-
-------------------------------------<u>wuchereri</u>
Azygos a menudo fusionado irregularmente con
escudos cefálicos adyacentes; un par mediano
de escudos pectorales alargados, con otros
escudos modificados, posiblemente ensanchados
que irradian de éstos hacia anterior; 5-25 más
anillos postpectorales dorsales que ventrales,
con mayor incremento en segundo, tercer y
cuarto quintos del tronco; 177-242 anillos
postpectorales--------------------<u>microcephalum</u>

<u>LEPOSTERNON INFRAORBITALE</u> (Berthold)

  1859 <u>Lepidosternon infraorbitale</u> Berthold, Nach. Ges. Wiss. Göttingen, 17: 179. Type-locality:
      Bahia, Brazil.
  1881 <u>Lepidosternum rostratum</u> Strauch, Bull. Acad. Imp. Sci. St. Pétersbourg, 28: col. 99. Type-
      locality: Bahia, Brazil.
  1967 <u>Leposternon infraorbitale</u>—Gans, Bull. Amer. Mus. Nat. Hist., 135: 82.

    Distribution: Mato Grosso, Goiás, Pernambuco, Bahia, Espirito Santo, Minas Gerais, and Rio de
    Janeiro, Brazil.

<u>LEPOSTERNON MICROCEPHALUM</u> Wagler

  1824 <u>Leposternon microcephalus</u> Wagler, in Spix, Sp. Nov. Serp. Bras., 70. Type-locality: Vicinity of
      Mandiocca village, near Orgãos mountain, Rio de Janeiro, Brazil.
  1825 <u>A.</u>[<u>mphisbaena</u>] <u>punctata</u> Wied (substitute name for <u>Leposternon microcephalus</u> Wagler), Beiträge zur
      Naturgeschichte von Brasilien, 1: 500.
  1826 <u>Leposternon microcephalum</u> Fitzinger, Neue Classification der Reptilien: 53.
  1834 <u>Lepidosternon Maximiliani</u> Wiegmann (substitute name for <u>Amphisbaena punctata</u> Wied), Herpetologia
      Mexicana: 21.
  1848 <u>Lepidosternon macrocephalum</u> Smith (<u>lapsus</u> for <u>Leposternon microcephalum</u> Wagler, according to Gans,
      1966), Illustrations of the Zoology of South Africa, 1834-1849, pl. 67.
  1839 <u>Lepidosternon phocaena</u> Duméril and Bibron, Erp. Gén., 5: 507. Type-locality: Buenos Aires,
      Argentina.
  1881 <u>Lepidosternon güntheri</u> Strauch, Bull. Acad. Imp. Sci. St. Pétersbourg, 28: col. 110. Type-
      locality: Unknown, but apparently Brazil, according to Strauch.
  1881 <u>Lepidosternon crassum</u> Strauch, Bull. Acad. Imp. Sci. St. Pétersbourg, 28: col. 106. Type-
      locality: Brazil.
  1881 <u>Lepidosternon petersi</u> Strauch, Bull. Acad. Imp. Sci. St. Pétersbourg, 28: col. 103. Type-
      locality: Brazil.
  1885 <u>Lepidosternum Boulengeri</u> Boettger, Zeits. für Naturwiss., 58: 220. Type-locality: Paraguay.
  1885 <u>Lepidosternum Strauchi</u> Boettger, Zeits. für Naturwiss., 58: 221. Type-locality: Paraguay.
  1885 <u>Lepidosternum affine</u> Boettger, Zeits. für Naturwiss., 58: 223. Type-locality: Paraguay.
  1885 <u>Lepidosternum onychocephalum</u> Boettger, Zeits. für Naturwiss., 58: 224. Type-locality: Paraguay.
  1885 <u>Lepidosternon boettgeri</u> Boulenger, Cat. Liz. Brit. Mus., 2: 466, pl. 24, figs. 5a-5d. Type-
      locality: Corrientes, Argentina.
  1894 <u>Lepidosternum latifrontale</u> Boulenger, Ann. Mag. Nat. Hist., (6) 13: 345. Type-locality: Near
      Asuncion, Paraguay.

LEPOSTERNON MICROCEPHALUM Wagler, continued

    1895 Lepidosternum Borellii Peracca, Boll. Mus. Zool. Comp. Anat. Univ. Torino, 10 (195): 10, fig.
        Type-locality: Resistencia, Chaco of Argentina.
    1895 Lepidosternum Camerani Peracca, Boll. Mus. Zool. Comp. Anat. Univ. Torino, 10 (195): 12, fig.
        Type-locality: Luque, Paraguay.
    1904 Lepidosternon laticeps Peracca, Boll. Mus. Zool. Comp. Anat. Univ. Torino, 19 (460): 3, 3 figs.
        Type-locality: Urucum, Mato Grosso, Brazil.
    1904 Lepidosternon Carcani Peracca, Boll. Mus. Zool. Comp. Anat. Univ. Torino, 19 (460): 5, fig.
        Type-locality: Urucum, Mato Grosso, Brazil.
    1910 Lepidosternon pfefferi Werner, Mitt. Naturhist. Mus. Hamburg, 27 (2): 35. Type-locality:
        Paraguay.
    1960 Leposternon microcephalum—Hellmich, Abh. Bayerischen Akad. Wiss., Math. Nat. Kl., new series,
        101: 104.

        Distribution: Amazonian Brazil and Bolivia, Paraguay, Uruguay, northern Argentina.

LEPOSTERNON OCTOSTEGUM (Duméril)

    1851 L.[epidosternon] octostegum Duméril, Cat. Méth. Coll. Rept. Mus. Hist. Nat. Paris: 150. Type-
        locality: Brazil.
    1967 Leposternon octostegum—Gans, Bull. Amer. Mus. Nat. Hist., 135: 82.

        Distribution: Known only from type and a specimen from Bahia, Brazil, recorded by Strauch, 1881.

LEPOSTERNON POLYSTEGUM (Duméril)

    1851 L.[epidosternon] Polystegum Duméril, Cat. Méth. Coll. Rept. Mus. Hist. Nat. Paris: 149. Type-
        locality: Bahia, Brazil.
    1865 Lepidosternon grayii Gray, Proc. Zool. Soc. London, 1865: 452. Type-locality: "South America?"
    1936 Leposternon polystegum—Schmidt, Herpetologica, 1: 31.
    1936 Leposternon polystegoides Schmidt, Herpetologica, 1: 31, pl. 3, fig. 4. Type-locality: Lago
        Papary, Rio Grande do Norte, Brazil.

        Distribution: Pará, Rio Grande do Norte, Pernambuco, and Bahia, Brazil.

LEPOSTERNON SCUTIGERUM (Hemprich)

    1829 Amphisbaena scutigera Hemprich, Verh. Ges. Naturforsch. Freunde Berlin, 1: 129. Type-locality:
        Brazil.
    1831 L.[epidosternon] Hemprichii Wiegmann and Ruthe (substitute name for Amphisbaena scutigera
        Hemprich), Handbuch der Zoologie: 186.
    1832 Cephalopeltis cuvieri Müller, Zeits. für Physiol., 4 (2), art. 19: 256. Type-locality: Brazil.
    1839 Lepidosternon scutigerum Duméril and Bibron, Erp. Gén., 5: 509.
    1967 Leposternon scutigerum—Gans, Bull. Amer. Mus. Nat. Hist., 135: 83.

        Distribution: Estado do Rio de Janeiro, Brazil.

LEPOSTERNON WUCHERERI (Peters)

    1879 Lepidosternon Wuchereri Peters, Monats. Akad. Wiss. Berlin, 1879: 276, pl., figs. 2-2c. Type-
        locality: Bahia, Brazil.
    1895 Lepidosternum sinuosum Peracca, Boll. Mus. Zool. Comp. Anat. Univ. Torino, 10 (200): 1, fig.
        Type-locality: Brazil.
    1938 Leposternon wuchereri—Amaral, Mem. Inst. Butantan, 11 (1937): 203.

        Distribution: Bahia, Espirito Santo and Rio de Janeiro, Brazil.

Prepared by Roberto Donoso-Barros, Universidad de Concepción, Concepción, Chile

LIOLAEMUS Wiegmann

1834 *Liolaemus* Wiegmann, Herpetologia Mexicana: 18. Type-species: *Calotes chiliensis* Lesson.
1843 *Ptychodeira* Fitzinger, Systema Reptilium: 17. Type-species: *Tropidurus nigromaculatus* Wiegmann.
1843 *Liodeira* Fitzinger, Systema Reptilium: 17. Type-species: *Proctotretus tenuis* Duméril and Bibron.
1845 *Sauridis* Tschudi, Arch. für Naturg., 2 (1): 156. Type-species: *Liolaemus (Sauridis) modestus* Tschudi.
1845 *Leiodera* Gray (emendation of *Liodeira* Fitzinger), Cat. Liz. Brit. Mus.: 211.
1848 *Chrysosaurus* Gay, Hist. Fis. Pol. Chile, Zool., 2: 47. Type-species: *Chrysosaurus morio* Gay.
1857 *Rhytidodeira* Girard, Proc. Acad. Nat. Sci. Phila., 1857: 198. Type-species: None specified.
1857 *Eulaemus* Girard, Proc. Acad. Nat. Sci. Phila., 1857: 198. Type-species: None specified.
1857 *Ortholaemus* Girard, Proc. Acad. Nat. Sci. Phila., 1857: 198. Type-species: None specified.

Distribution: South America between 25° and 55° south, in plateaus, mountains, and coast of transandine countries, including Peru, Bolivia and Chile, all of Patagonia, Argentina, Paraguay, coastal Uruguay and southern Brazil.

Content: Forty-seven species.

Key to the species

1. Black antehumeral spot present----------------2
   Without antehumeral spot---------------------3

2. One row of scales between labials and infra-
   orbital--------------------------------------55
   More than one row of scales between labials and
   infraorbital---------------------------------56

3. Two or more rows of scales between labials and
   infraorbital---------------------------------4
   Single row of scales between labials and
   infraorbital---------------------------------7

4. Dorsal pattern not as below-------------------5
   Dorsal pattern with numerous small black spots,
   some bordered with white (Fig. 1)------------
   -------------------------------*multimaculatus*

Fig. 1. *L. multimaculatus*

5. Ventral scales larger than dorsals; more than
   55 scales around middle of body; dorsal
   pattern with median dorsal band--------------6
   Ventral scales smaller than dorsals; 45-54
   scales around middle of body; dorsal pattern
   without median dorsal band (Fig. 2)-*wiegmannii*

Fig. 3. *L. occipitalis*

Clave de especies

1. Con una mancha negra antehumeral-------------2
   Sin mancha antehumeral-----------------------3

2. Una hilera de escamas entre labiales e infra-
   orbital--------------------------------------55
   Más de una hilera de escamas entre labiales e
   infraorbital---------------------------------56

3. Dos o más series de escamas entre labiales e
   infraorbital---------------------------------4
   Una serie simple de escamas entre labiales e
   infraorbital---------------------------------7

4. No como el siguiente-------------------------5
   Diseño dorsal caracterizado por manchitas ne-
   gras, algunas de ellas bordeadas de blanco
   (Fig. 1)---------------------*multimaculatus*

Fig. 2. *L. wiegmannii*

5. Ventrales mayores que las dorsales; más de 55
   escamas al medio del cuerpo; diseño dorsal con
   banda dorsal mediana-------------------------6
   Ventrales menores que las dorsales; 45-54 escamas al medio del cuerpo; diseño dorsal sin
   banda dorsal mediana (Fig. 2)-------*wiegmannii*

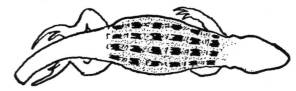

Fig. 4. *L. lutzae*

6. Scales between upper canthals 8-9; middorsal
   region light gray (Fig. 3); keels of dorsal
   scales blunt, somewhat irregular; throat with
   numerous distinct dark spots-------occipitalis
   Scales between upper canthals 4-5; middorsal
   region always dark brown (Fig. 4); keels of
   dorsal scales sharp and regular; throat
   immaculate-------------------------------lutzae

7. Fewer than 45 scales around middle of body----8
   More than 45 scales around middle of body----17

8. Sides of neck not folded---------------------9
   Sides of neck folded------------------------11

9. Fewer than 36 scales around middle of body;
   ground color not brown; longitudinal pale
   stripes absent or interrupted---------------10
   More than 36 scales around middle of body;
   ground color brown with two uninterrupted
   longitudinal pale stripes (Fig. 5)-----------
   --------------------------------gravenhorstii

6. Escamas entre los supracantales 8-9; región
   medio dorsal gris claro (Fig. 3); quillas de
   las escamas dorsales romas, algo irregulares; garganta con numerosas manchas oscuras-
   -------------------------------------occipitalis
   Escamas entre los supracantales 4-5; región
   medio dorsal siempre café oscura (Fig. 4);
   quillas de las escamas dorsales agudas y regulares; garganta inmaculada--------------lutzae

7. Menos de 45 escamas al medio del cuerpo-------8
   Más de 45 escamas al medio del cuerpo--------17

8. Lados del cuello lisos-----------------------9
   Lados del cuello plegados--------------------11

9. Menos de 36 escamas al medio del cuerpo; color
   general no pardo, cintas longitudinales
   ausentes o interrumpidas--------------------10
   Más de 36 escamas al medio del cuerpo; color
   general pardo con dos cintas longitudinales
   pálidas no interrumpidas (Fig. 5)------------
   --------------------------------gravenhorstii

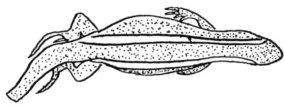

Fig. 5. L. gravenhorstii

Fig. 6. L. magellanicus

10. Tympanic scale absent; ground color green with
    broad, black-spotted middorsal band (Fig. 7);
    longitudinal stripes interrupted----chiliensis
    Tympanic scale present; ground color not green,
    lacking both median band and longitudinal
    stripes (Figs. 8-10)--------------------nitidus

10. Escama timpánica ausente; color general verde
    con una ancha banda medio dorsal manchada de
    negro (Fig. 7); cintas longitudinales
    interrumpidas----------------------chiliensis
    Escama timpánica presente, color general no
    verde, sin banda mediana ni cintas longitudi-
    nales (Figs. 8-10)----------------------nitidus

Fig. 7. L. chiliensis

Fig. 8. L. nitidus, juvenile

Fig. 9. L. nitidus, semiadult

Fig. 10. L. nitidus, adult

11. Lacks five dorsal pale stripes (Figs. 11, 12);
dorsal scales not mucronate; ground color not
pale grayish--------------------------------12
Five dorsal pale stripes with black squarish
spots on each side; dorsal scales mucronate;
ground color pale grayish (Fig. 6)----------
-------------------------------------magellanicus

12. Some dorsal pattern present; dorsal scales
strongly imbricate; azygous frontal present;
ventral scales smaller than dorsals---------13
Unicolor, no dorsal pattern; dorsal scales subimbricate; azygous frontal absent; ventral
scales same size as dorsals-----------modestus

13. With vertebral black line (Fig. 11)-----------14
No vertebral black line (Fig. 12)------------15

11. Sin cinco cintas dorsales claras; escamas dorsales no mucronadas; color general no pálido
grisáceo--------------------------------------12
Cinco cintas claras dorsales con manchas negras
cuadradas a cada lado; escamas dorsales mucronadas; color general pálido grisáceo (Fig.
6)------------------------------------magellanicus

12. Con diseño dorsal; escamas dorsales fuertemente
imbricadas; azygos frontal presente, escamas
ventrales menores que dorsales--------------13
Sin diseño dorsal; escamas dorsales subimbricadas; azygos frontal ausente; escamas ventrales
igual tamaño que dorsales------------modestus

13. Con una línea vertebral negra (Fig. 11)------14
Sin línea vertebral negra (Fig. 12)----------15

Fig. 11. L. gracilis

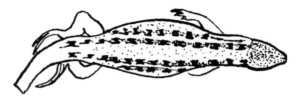

Fig. 12. L. lemniscatus

14. Temporal scales smooth; sides of neck without
longitudinal fold; dorsal light stripes wider
posteriorly-----------------------------alticolor
Temporal scales keeled; sides of neck with
longitudinal fold; dorsal light stripes not
wider posteriorly (Fig. 11)-----------gracilis

15. More than 35 scales around middle of body----16
Fewer than 35 scales around middle of body-----
----------------------------------robertmertensi

16. Scales on middle of back larger than those on
sides of belly; lower surface white-----------
-----------------------------------lemniscatus
Scales on middle of back not larger than those
on sides of belly; lower surface green or blue
----------------------------------cyanogaster

17. Dorsal pattern of spots not connected by
longitudinal stripes-----------------------18
Not as above------------------------------23

18. Dorsal spots and scales not as below---------19
Dorsal spots resemble Arabic letters (Fig. 14);
most dorsal scales smooth-------------signifer

14. Escamas temporales lisas; lados del cuello sin
pliegues longitudinales; cintas dorsales claras dilatadas posteriormente---------alticolor
Escamas temporales quilladas; lados del cuello
con un pliegue longitudinal; cintas dorsales
claras no dilatadas posteriormente (Fig. 11)--
---------------------------------------gracilis

15. Más de 35 escamas al medio del cuerpo---------16
Menos de 35 escamas al medio del cuerpo--------
----------------------------------robertmertensi

16. Escamas del medio de la espalda mayores que
aquéllas de los lados del vientre; superficie
inferior blanca-------------------lemniscatus
Escamas del medio de la espalda no mayores que
aquéllas de los lados del vientre; superficie
inferior verde o azul------------cyanogaster

17. Diseño dorsal formado por manchas no conectadas
con cintas longitudinales--------------------18
No como el anterior--------------------------23

18. Escamas dorsales y manchas no como el siguiente
---19
Las manchas dorsales parecen letras árabes
(Fig. 14); mayoría de las escamas dorsales son
lisas---------------------------------signifer

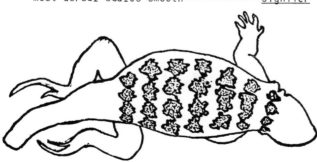

Fig. 13. L. rothi

Fig. 14. L. signifer

19.Dorsal spots not disposed in transverse rows---
---20
   Dorsal spots disposed in transverse rows (Fig.
   13)-----------------------------------rothi

20.Spots not ocellated; no vertebral dark line--21
   Dorsum patterned with ocelli; at least one
   short, dark paravertebral line-----leopardinus

21.Spots regularly disposed in dorsal longitudinal
   rows; fewer than 70 scales around middle of
   body---------------------------------------22
   Spots irregularly disposed (Fig. 15), except in
   juveniles (Fig. 16); more than 70 scales
   around middle of body-------------multiformis

19.Manchas dorsales no dispuestas en hileras
   transversales------------------------------20
   Manchas dorsales dispuestas en filas transversales (Fig. 13)-----------------------rothi

20.Manchas no oceladas; sin línea vertebral oscura-21
   Manchas oceladas como piel de leopardo; por lo
   menos una corta línea oscura paravertebral-----
   --------------------------------------leopardinus

21.Manchas regularmente dispuestas en hileras longitudinales dorsales; menos de 70 escamas al
   medio del cuerpo---------------------------22
   Manchas dispuestas irregularmente (Fig. 15),
   excepto en juveniles (Fig. 16); más de 70 escamas alrededor del medio del cuerpo----------
   ------------------------------------multiformis

Fig. 16. L. multiformis, juvenile

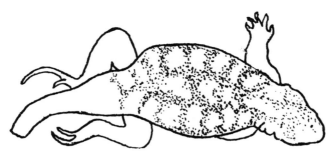

Fig. 15. L. multiformis, adult

Fig. 16. L. lineomaculatus

22.Without white vertebral line; ear opening with
   prominent scales----------------------------57
   With vertebral white line (Fig. 17); ear
   opening without prominent scales-------------
   -----------------------------------lineomaculatus

23.More than 75 scales around middle of body----24
   Fewer than 75 scales around middle of body---33

24.With patch of enlarged scales on posterior
   border of thigh-----------------------------25
   Without patch of enlarged scales on posterior
   border of thigh-----------------------------26

25.More than 80 scales around middle of body;
   frequently black gular spot present, sometimes
   ring-like, occasionally fused with ventral
   melanism; dorsal scales keeled; also see Fig.
   19----------------------------------fitzingerii
   Fewer than 80 scales around middle of body; no
   black gular spot or ventral melanism; dorsal
   scales weakly keeled or smooth; also see Fig.
   18-----------------------------------ornatus

22.Sin línea blanca vertebral; oído con escamas
   prominentes---------------------------------57
   Con una línea vertebral blanca (Fig. 17); oído
   sin escamas prominentes--------lineomaculatus

23.Más de 75 escamas al medio del cuerpo--------24
   Menos de 75 escamas al medio del cuerpo------33

24.Con un parche de escamas agrandadas en el borde
   posterior del muslo-------------------------25
   Sin parche de escamas agrandadas en el borde
   posterior del muslo-------------------------26

25.Más de 80 escamas al medio del cuerpo; frecuentemente una mancha negra gular a veces como
   anillo, ocasionalmente fusionada con el melanismo ventral; escamas dorsales quilladas;
   también ver Fig. 19----------------fitzingerii
   Menos de 80 escamas alrededor del medio del
   cuerpo; no hay mancha negra gular ni tampoco
   melanismo ventral; escamas dorsales muy débilmente quilladas; también ver Fig. 18---ornatus

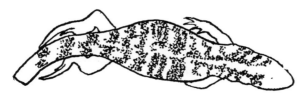

Fig. 18. L. ornatus

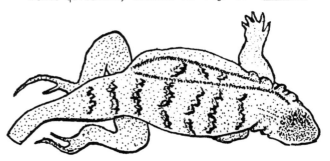

Fig. 19. L. fitzingerii

26.Without dorsal pattern----------------------27
   With distinct dorsal pattern-----------------28

27.Head black, contrasting with body color (Fig.
   20); belly reddish; 100 scales around midbody-
   --<u>kriegi</u>
   Head same color as body; belly not reddish;
   fewer than 100 scales around midbody----------
   ------------------------------------<u>multiformis</u>

28.Dorsal pattern characterized by median dorsal
   band limited by two light paravertebral
   stripes (Fig. 21)----------------------------29
   Dorsal pattern without median dorsal band (Fig.
   24)--32

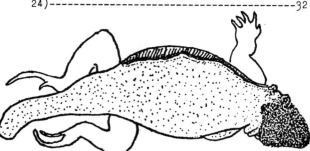

Fig. 20. L. <u>kriegi</u>

26.Sin diseño dorsal-----------------------------27
   Con diseño dorsal diferenciado---------------28

27.Cabeza negra contrasta con color corporal (Fig.
   20); vientre rojizo; 100 escamas al medio del
   cuerpo------------------------------------<u>kriegi</u>
   Cabeza igual color que cuerpo; vientre no
   rojizo; menos de 100 escamas al medio del
   cuerpo--------------------------------<u>multiformis</u>

28.Diseño dorsal caracterizado por una banda medio
   dorsal, limitada por dos cintas paravertebrales claras (Fig. 21)-------------------------29
   Diseño dorsal sin banda medio dorsal (Fig. 24)-
   ---32

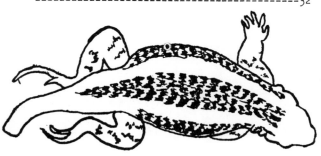

Fig. 21. L. <u>buergeri</u>

29.With festooned dorsal band, sometimes in zig-
   zag pattern----------------------------------30
   Dorsal band not festooned (Fig. 21)----<u>buergeri</u>

30.Dorsal band not connected with color on flanks-
   ---31
   Dorsal band with lateral projections, sometimes
   fused with dark color of flanks (Fig. 22)-----
   -------------------------------------<u>elongatus</u>

31.Dorsal band in zig-zag pattern; dorsally
   spotted with green, yellow or blue (Fig. 23)--
   ---------------------------------------<u>pictus</u>
   Dorsal band not zig-zag patterned; no colored
   spots---------------------------------<u>elongatus</u>

29.Banda dorsal festoneada, a veces en zig-zag----
   ---30
   Banda dorsal no festoneada (Fig. 21)---<u>buergeri</u>

30.Banda dorsal no conectada con el color de los
   flancos--------------------------------------31
   Banda dorsal con proyecciones laterales a veces
   fusionadas con el color oscuro de los flancos
   (Fig. 22)----------------------------<u>elongatus</u>

31.Banda dorsal en zig-zag; manchado dorsalmente
   de amarillo, verde o azul (Fig. 23)-----<u>pictus</u>
   Banda dorsal no en zig-zag; no hay manchitas de
   color----------------------------------<u>elongatus</u>

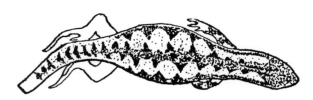

Fig. 23. L. <u>pictus</u>

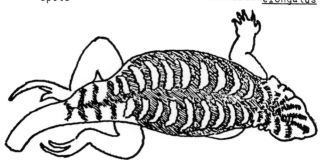

Fig. 22. L. <u>elongatus</u>

32.Flanks with black patch; dorsal scales keeled;
   limbs of normal length--------------<u>monticola</u>
   No black patch on flank; dorsal scales smooth;
   limbs very short----------------------<u>ruibali</u>

32.Flancos con bloques negros; escamas dorsales
   quilladas; extremidades de longitud normal----
   -------------------------------------<u>monticola</u>
   Flancos sin bloques negros; escamas dorsales
   lisas; extremidades muy cortas---------<u>ruibali</u>

33.Without distinct dorsal pattern--------------34
   With distinct pattern dorsally---------------35

34.Ground color brown with reddish flanks (Fig.
   25); fewer than 53 scales around midbody------
   --paulinae
   Ground color salt-and-pepper, without reddish
   flanks; more than 53 scales around midbody----
   ----------------------------------lorenzmuelleri

Fig. 24. L. ruibali

35.Dorsal pattern of two light paravertebral
   stripes with black margins; ground color olive
   brown or greenish---------------------------36
   Dorsal pattern and ground color not as above---
   --46

36.Light paravertebral stripes without rows of
   black spots--------------------------------37
   Light paravertebral stripes with rows of
   lateral black spots (Figs. 28, 29)----------39

37.Vertebral line absent------------------------38
   Vertebral line present (Fig. 26)-------bibronii

Fig. 26. L. bibronii

38.Cervical fold V-shaped; more than 50 scales
   around midbody; dorsal band with parallel
   borders-------------------------cyanogaster
   Cervical fold not V-shaped; fewer than 50
   scales around midbody; vertebral band with
   angulate borders (Fig. 27)----------schroederi

39.Without azygous frontal----------------------40
   With azygous frontal-------------------------41

40.More than 65 scales around midbody; head
   scales equal in size---------------boulengeri
   Fewer than 65 scales around midbody; head
   scales of different sizes-----------chacoensis

Fig. 28. L. boulengeri

33.Dorsalmente sin diseño diferenciado----------34
   Dorsalmente con diseño diferenciado----------35

34.Color general pardo con flancos rojizos (Fig.
   25); menos de 53 escamas alrededor del medio
   del cuerpo---------------------------paulinae
   Color general sal y pimienta sin flancos rojizos; más de 53 escamas al medio del cuerpo----
   ----------------------------------lorenzmuelleri

Fig. 25. L. paulinae

35.Diseño dorsal caracterizado por dos cintas
   claras paravertebrales con márgenes negros;
   color general pardo olivaceo o verdoso------36
   Diseño dorsal y color general no como el
   anterior------------------------------------46

36.Cintas paravertebrales claras sin hileras de
   manchas negras------------------------------37
   Cintas claras paravertebrales con hileras de
   manchas negras lateralmente (Figs. 28, 29)--39

37.Línea vertebral ausente----------------------38
   Línea vertebral presente (Fig. 26)-----bibronii

Fig. 27. L. schroederi

38.Pliegue cervical en V; más de 50 escamas al
   medio del cuerpo; banda dorsal con bordes
   paralelos-------------------------cyanogaster
   Pliegue cervical no en V; menos de 50 escamas
   alrededor del medio del cuerpo; banda vertebral con bordes angulados (Fig. 27)-schroederi

39.Sin azygos frontal--------------------------40
   Con azygos frontal--------------------------41

40.Más de 65 escamas al medio del cuerpo; escamas
   cefálicas del mismo tamaño---------boulengeri
   Menos de 65 escamas al medio del cuerpo; escamas de la cabeza de diferente tamaño---------
   -----------------------------------chacoensis

Fig. 29. L. chacoensis

41. Without broad pigmented vertebral band-------42
    With broad black vertebral band--------------53

42. Vertebral line present (Fig. 30)-------------43
    Vertebral line absent (Fig. 31)--------------44

43. Posterior border of thigh with protruding row
    of scales; belly white----------------bibronii
    No row of protruding scales on thigh; belly
    reddish--------------------------------fuscus

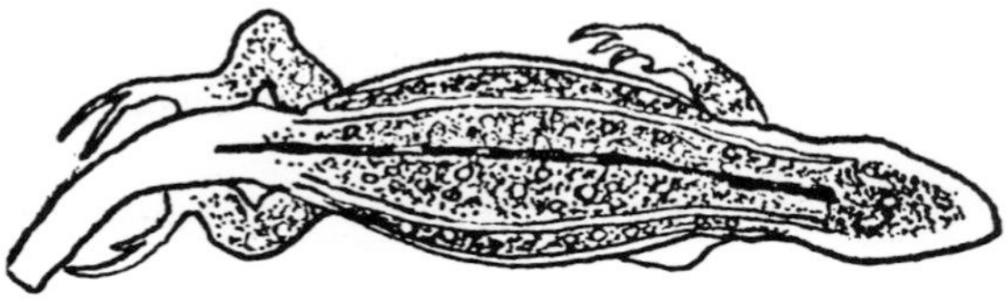

41. Sin banda vertebral ancha y pigmentada-------42
    Con una banda vertebral ancha pigmentada de
    negro--53

42. Línea vertebral presente (Fig. 30)----------43
    Línea vertebral ausente (Fig. 31)-----------44

43. Borde posterior de los muslos con una hilera de
    escamas sobresalientes; vientre blanco--------
    --bibronii
    Sin hilera de escamas sobresalientes en los
    muslos; vientre rojizo------------------fuscus

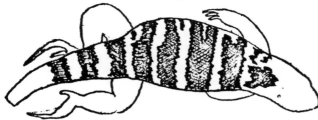

Fig. 30. L. fuscus

Fig. 31. L. darwinii

44. Not as below----------------------------------45
    Two rows of squarish spots on each side of
    paravertebral stripes; patch of enlarged
    scales on posterior femoral border (Fig. 31)--
    ------------------------------------darwinii

45. Dorsal band pale brown; light stripes contrast-
    ing with dark brown flanks (juvenile)---pictus
    Dorsal band brown, flanks not darker; lateral
    stripes inconspicuous (juvenile)------paulinae

46. Dorsal pattern formed by transverse bars fused
    in vertebral region (Fig. 32)---------------47
    Dorsal pattern formed by transverse bars that
    do not fuse in vertebral region------------48

47. Tail equal to head-body length; lateral scales
    on neck not granular; five supraoculars-kingii
    Tail longer than head-body length; lateral
    scales on neck granular; fewer than five
    supraoculars----------------------nigroviridis

48. Vertebral line present----------------------49
    Vertebral line absent (Fig. 34)------------50

44. No como el siguiente------------------------45
    Dos hileras de manchas cuadriláteras a cada
    lado de las cintas paravertebrales; parche de
    escamas agrandadas en el borde femoral poste-
    rior (Fig. 31)------------------------darwinii

45. Banda dorsal pálida, con las cintas claras muy
    contrastadas por los flancos oscuros (juvenil)
    ---------------------------------------pictus
    Banda dorsal parda, flancos no más oscuros;
    cintas laterales apenas visibles (juvenil)----
    --------------------------------------paulinae

46. Diseño dorsal formado por barras transversales
    fusionadas en la región vertebral (Fig. 32)-47
    Diseño dorsal formado por barras transversales
    no unidas en la región vertebral-----------48

47. Cola del mismo largo que cabeza-tronco; escamas
    laterales del cuello no granulares; cinco
    supraoculares--------------------------kingii
    Cola más larga que cabeza-tronco; escamas late-
    rales del cuello granulares; menos de cinco
    supraoculares--------------------nigroviridis

48. Línea vertebral presente--------------------49
    No hay línea vertebral (Fig. 34)-----------50

Fig. 32. L. kingii

Fig. 33. L. constanzae

49. Short vertebral line; ground color greenish
    black; transverse bars arranged in reticulum;
    belly white (subspecies nigroroseus is
    reddish)--------------------------nigroviridis
    Long vertebral line which reaches sacrum;
    ground color pale brown; transverse bars not
    reticulated (Fig. 33); belly reddish----------
    ------------------------------------constanzae

49. Línea vertebral corta; color general verde
    negruzco; barras transversales dispuestas como
    una red; vientre blanco (salvo en subespecies
    nigroroseus que es rojizo)--------nigroviridis
    Línea vertebral larga; color general pardo cla-
    ro; barras transversales no dispuestas como
    una red (Fig. 33); vientre rojizo---constanzae

50.Without patch of enlarged scales on posterior
   border of thigh----------------------------51
   With patch of enlarged scales on posterior
   border of thigh----------------------goetschi

51.Fewer than five supraoculars and eight supra-
   labials----------------------------------52
   Five supraoculars and eight supralabials; also
   see Fig. 35-------------------------dorbignyi

50.Sin parche de escamas ensanchadas------------51
   Con un parche de escamas ensanchadas en el
   border posterior de los muslos-------goetschi

51.Menos de cinco supraoculares y ocho suprala-
   biales------------------------------------52
   Cinco supraoculares y ocho supralabiales; también ver Fig. 35--------------------dorbignyi

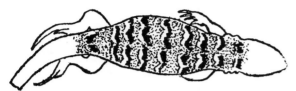

Fig. 34. L. goetschi

Fig. 35. L. dorbignyi

52.More than 65 scales around middle of body;
   ground color grayish or black with small
   green, yellow or blue spots; adpressed hind
   limb reaches area between eye and snout-tenuis
   Fewer than 65 scales around middle of body;
   ground color light brown with green or blue
   spots (Fig. 36); adpressed hind limb reaches
   area between ear opening and eye--------platei

53.Vertebral band with irregular black markings---
   ---54
   Vertebral band without irregular black markings
   --pictus

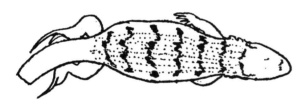

Fig. 36. L. platei

54.Dorsum with longitudinal line and lateral
   triangles usually in contact with it (Fig.
   37); vertebral band brown; 52 scales around
   middle of body---------------------fitzgeraldi
   If lateral pattern present, usually not in contact with longitudinal line; vertebral band
   greenish; fewer than 52 scales around middle
   of body----------------------------altissimus

55.Two rows of black spots on each side of lateral
   stripes; ground color brown; posterior border
   of thigh with patch of enlarged scales--------
   ---darwinii
   Without rows of black spots on each side of
   lateral stripes; ground color not brown; no
   patch of enlarged scales on thigh------------
   --------------------------------nigromaculatus

52.Más de 65 escamas al medio del cuerpo; color
   general gris o negro con manchitas verdes,
   amarillas o azules; extremidad hacia adelante
   alcanza delante del ojo------------------tenuis
   Menos de 65 escamas alrededor del medio del
   cuerpo; color general pardo claro con manchitas verdes o azules (Fig. 36); extremidad posterior hacia delante sobrepasa el oído--platei

53.Banda vertebral con dibujos e impresiones
   negras-----------------------------------54
   Banda vertebral sin dibujos e impresiones
   negras-----------------------------------pictus

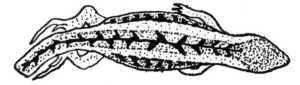

Fig. 37. L. fitzgeraldi

54.Dibujo de la banda vertebral formado por pequeños triángulos que contactan interiormente en
   una línea longitudinal (Fig. 37); banda vertebral parda; 52 escamas al medio del cuerpo--
   ------------------------------------fitzgeraldi
   Dibujo central no contacta con ninguna línea
   longitudinal; banda vertebral verdosa; menos
   de 52 escamas alrededor del medio del cuerpo--
   ------------------------------------altissimus

55.Dos hileras de manchas negras a cada lado de
   las cintas laterales; color general pardo;
   borde posterior de los muslos con una placa de
   escamas agrandadas--------------------darwinii
   Sin hileras de manchas negras a cada lado de
   las cintas laterales; color general no pardo;
   no hay parche de escamas agrandadas en los
   muslos------------------------nigromaculatus

56. Two rows of crescent-shaped spots on back; 45-
54 scales around midbody-----------wiegmannii
Back densely black-spotted; more than 60 scales
around midbody------------------multimaculatus

57. Ventral scales equal to or smaller than dorsals; no patch of enlarged scales on posterior
border of thigh; fewer than six supraoculars;
also see Fig. 38-------------------pantherinus
Ventral scales larger than dorsals; patch of
enlarged scales on posterior border of thigh;
more than six supraoculars; also see Fig. 39 --
------------------------------------mocquardi

56. Dos hileras de manchas semilunares al medio del
dorso; 45-54 escamas alrededor del cuerpo-----
------------------------------------wiegmannii
Espalda densamente manchada de negro; 60 escamas al medio del cuerpo---------multimaculatus

57. Escamas ventrales de mismo tamaño que las dorsales; no hay parches de escamas agrandadas en
el borde posterior de los muslos; menos de
seis supraoculares; también ver Fig. 38------
------------------------------------pantherinus
Escamas ventrales mayores que las dorsales; un
parche de escamas agrandadas en el borde posterior de los muslos; más de seis supraoculares; también ver Fig. 39-----------mocquardi

Fig. 38. L. pantherinus

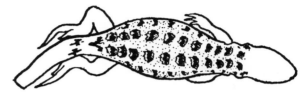

Fig. 39. L. mocquardi

LIOLAEMUS ALTICOLOR Barbour

1909 Liolaemus alticolor Barbour, Proc. New England Zool. Club, 4: 51, pl. 5. Type-locality:
Tihauanacu, Bolivia, 13,100 ft.

Distribution: Altiplano of Chile, Bolivia, Peru and northern Argentina.

Content: Two subspecies.

Key to the subspecies

1. More than 54 scales around middle of body;
pale stripes on back with black spots
laterally (Fig. 40)---------------walkeri
Fewer than 54 scales around middle of body;
pale stripes on back without black spots
(Fig. 41)------------------------alticolor

Clave de subespecies

1. Más de 54 escamas al medio del cuerpo; cintas pálidas de la espalda con manchas
negras lateralmente (Fig. 40)------walkeri
Menos de 54 escamas al medio del cuerpo;
cintas pálidas de la espalda sin manchas
negras (Fig. 41)------------------alticolor

Fig. 40. L. alticolor walkeri

Fig. 41. L. alticolor alticolor

Liolaemus alticolor alticolor Barbour

?1904 Liolaemus lativittatus Werner, Hamburger Magalhaenische Sammelreise, 1, Reptilien und
Batrachier: 8, figs. 3-4. Type-locality: Lo Chaparro, Valparaíso, Chile (in error).
1961 Liolaemus alticolor alticolor—Hellmich, Opuscula Zool., Zool. Staatsmus. München, 58: 2.
1966 Liolaemus alticolor alticolor Donoso-Barros, Reptiles de Chile: 198, fig. 33, col. pl. 17.

Distribution: High Andes of Tarapacá, Chile; Bolivia; southern Peru; northwestern Argentina.

Comment: If the taxon lativittatus Werner, 1904, is shown to be a valid synonym of this
subspecies it will take priority over alticolor Barbour, 1909.

Liolaemus alticolor walkeri Shreve

?1845 L.[iolaemus] elegans Tschudi, Arch. für Naturg., 11 (1): 157. Type-locality: Peru;
further specified as Chancay, Peru, by Tschudi, Fauna Peruana, 1846, 34.
1938 Liolaemus walkeri Shreve, Jour. Washington Acad. Sci., 28: 404. Type-locality:
Llocllapampa, Junín, Peru, about 10,000 ft.
1961 Liolaemus alticolor walkeri—Hellmich, Opuscula Zool., Zool. Staats Mus. München, 58: 5.
1966 Liolaemus alticolor walkeri—Donoso-Barros, Reptiles de Chile: 201, col. pl. 17.

Distribution: High Andean plateaus of Junín in Peru and Antofagasta in Chile.

Comment: If the taxon elegans Tschudi, 1845, is shown to be a valid synonym of this subspecies, it will take priority over walkeri Shreve, 1938.

LIOLAEMUS ALTISSIMUS Müller and Hellmich

1860 Proctotretus modestus Philippi (preoccupied by modestus Tschudi, 1845), Reise durch die Wueste
Atacama: 166. Type-locality: Provincia de Santiago, Chile.
1932 Liolaemus altissimus Müller and Hellmich, Zool. Anz., 98: 197. Type-locality: Fierro Carrera,
Río San Francisco, 2700 m, near Cerro Plomo, Provincia Santiago, Chile.

Distribution: Cordilleran regions from 32° to 42°, Chile and Argentina.

Content: Four subspecies.

Key to the subspecies	Clave de subespecies
1. Lateral stripes present (Fig. 42)---------2 Lateral stripes absent----------altissimus	1. Cintas laterales presentes(Fig. 42)-------2 Cintas laterales ausentes--------altissimus
2. Belly not black; fewer than 60 scales around midbody---------------------------3 Belly black (Fig. 43); more than 60 scales around midbody------------------neuquensis	2. Vientre no negro; menos de 60 escamas alrededor del medio del cuerpo-----------3 Vientre negro;(Fig. 43); más de 60 escamas al medio del cuerpo-------------neuquensis

Fig. 42. L. a. neuquensis, dorsum Fig. 43. L. a. neuquensis, venter Fig. 44. L. a. araucaniensis

3. Sides of body without black blotches; occipital band without red color---------4 Sides of body with black blotches (Fig. 44); occipital band reddish-olive-------- -----------------------------araucaniensis	3. Lados del cuerpo sin bloques negros; banda occipital sin color rojo-----------------4 Lados del cuerpo con bloques negros (Fig. 44); banda occipital roja oliva---------- -----------------------------araucaniensis
4. Occipital band with rhomboidal spots not connected with vertebral line (Fig. 45)--- -----------------------------moradoensis Occipital band with transverse lines connected with vertebral line (Fig. 46)----------------------------altissimus	4. Banda occipital con manchas romboidales no conectadas con línea vertebral (Fig. 45)-- -----------------------------moradoensis Banda occipital con líneas transversales conectadas con una línea vertebral (Fig. 46)----------------------------altissimus

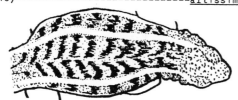

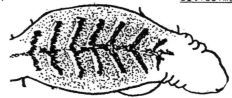

Fig. 45. L. a. moradoensis   Fig. 46. L. a. altissimus

Liolaemus altissimus altissimus Müller and Hellmich

    1932 Liolaemus altissimus altissimus Müller and Hellmich, Zool. Anz., 98: 197, figs. 1-2.
    1966 Liolaemus altissimus altissimus—Donoso-Barros, Reptiles de Chile: 299, col. pl. 18.

       Distribution: High cordilleras of Provincia Santiago, Chile.

Liolaemus altissimus araucaniensis Müller and Hellmich

    1932 Liolaemus altissimus araucaniensis Müller and Hellmich, Zool. Anz., 98: 205. Type-
         locality: Volcán Villarrica, Provincia Cautín, Chile, 1400 m.
    1966 Liolaemus altissimus araucaniensis—Donoso-Barros, Reptiles de Chile: 305.

       Distribution: Cordillera de Cautín, Chile.

Liolaemus altissimus moradoensis Hellmich

    1950 Liolaemus altissimus moradoënsis Hellmich, Veröff. Zool. Staatssamml. München, 1: 136, pl.
         11, figs. 22-23. Type-locality: Lo Valdés, Laguna de Morado, Volcán Morado, Provincia
         Santiago, Chile, 2400 m.
    1966 Liolaemus altissimus moradoensis—Donoso-Barros, Reptiles de Chile: 302, fig. 44, col. pl.
         19.

       Distribution: Volcán Morado, Provincia Santiago, Chile.

Liolaemus altissimus neuquensis Müller and Hellmich

    1939 Liolaemus altissimus neuquensis Müller and Hellmich, Zool. Anz., 125: 113, fig. 1. Type-
         locality: Volcán Copahué, Provincia de Neuquén, Argentina, about 1800 m.

       Distribution: High Cordilleras, Provincia de Neuquén, Argentina.

LIOLAEMUS BIBRONII (Bell)

   1843 Proctotretus Bibronii Bell, Zoology of the Voyage of H.M.S. Beagle, 5, Reptiles: 6, pl. 3, fig. 1.
      Type-locality: Puerto Deseado, Patagonia, Argentina.
   1845 Leiolaemus Bellii Gray, Cat. Liz. Brit. Mus.: 212. Type-locality: Chile.
   1885 Liolaemus bibronii—Boulenger, Cat. Liz. Brit. Mus., 2: 146.
   1966 Liolaemus bibroni—Donoso-Barros, Reptiles de Chile: 204, fig. 30, col. pl. 11.

    Distribution: Patagonian regions of Argentina and Chile, in Cordillera to Mendoza Province in Argen-
    tina.

LIOLAEMUS BOULENGERI Koslowsky

   1896 Liolaemus Boulengeri Koslowsky, Rev. Mus. La Plata, 7: 176, pl. 3. Type-locality: Near Las
      Cordilleras de los Andes, Territorio de Chubut, Argentina.
   1910 Liolaemus micropholis Werner, Zool. Jahrb., Abt. Syst. Geog. Biol. Tiere, 28: 268. Type-locality:
      Chile (in error).

    Distribution: Middle elevations; Provincias Mendoza to Chubut, Argentina.

LIOLAEMUS BUERGERI Werner

   1907 Liolaemus buergeri Werner, in Bürger, Anales Univ. Chile, 1907: 6, pl. 1, fig. 1. Type-locality:
      Planchón, Cordillera de Curicó, Provincia de Curicó, Chile.
   1966 Liolaemus buergeri—Donoso-Barros, Reptiles de Chile: 287, col. pl. 21.

    Distribution: High mountains of Provincias de Curicó and Talca, Chile; 35° to 42° in cordillera of
    Argentina.

LIOLAEMUS CHACOENSIS Shreve

1948 Liolaemus chacoensis Shreve, Copeia, 1948: 111. Type-locality: Fortín Guachalla, Río Pilcomayo, Chaco, Paraguay.
1960 Liolaemus chacoensis—Hellmich, Abh. Bayerische Akad. Wiss. New Ser., 101: 38.

Distribution: Known only from type locality.

LIOLAEMUS CHILIENSIS (Lesson)

1830 Calotes chiliensis Lesson, in Duperrey, Voyage sur la Coquille, 2 (1): 36, pl. 1, fig. 2. Type-locality: Talcahuano, Provincia de Concepción, Chile.
1835 Tropidurus olivaceus Wiegmann, Nova Acta Acad. Caes. Leop.-Carol., 17: 268c. Type-locality: Chile.
1843 Liolaemus chilensis—Fitzinger, Systema Reptilium: 75.
1966 Liolaemus chilensis—Donoso-Barros, Reptiles de Chile: 170, figs. 45, 60; col. pl. 8.

Distribution: Lowlands of Coquimbo to Cautín provinces, Chile; Neuquén, Argentina.

LIOLAEMUS CONSTANZAE Donoso-Barros

1961 Liolaemus constanzae Donoso-Barros, Copeia, 1961: 389, fig. 1b. Type-locality: Peine, Antofagasta, Chile, 3000 m.
1966 Liolaemus constanzae—Donoso-Barros, Reptiles de Chile: 239, col. pl. 17.

Distribution: San Pedro de Atacama Valley, Salar de Atacama, Peine, Antofagasta Province, Chile.

LIOLAEMUS CYANOGASTER (Duméril and Bibron)

1837 Proctotretus cyanogaster Duméril and Bibron, Erp. Gén., 4: 273. Type-locality: Chile.
1885 Liolaemus cyanogaster—Boulenger, Cat. Liz. Brit. Mus., 2: 145.

Distribution: Concepción to Chiloé Island, Chile; Parque Nacional Nahuel Huapí, Argentina.

Content: Two subspecies.

Key to the subspecies	Clave de subespecies
1. Scales around midbody 58-60; dorsal scales smooth or slightly keeled; also see Fig. 47--------------------------brattstroemi Fewer than 58 scales around midbody; dorsal scales strongly keeled; also see Fig. 48----------------------------------cyanogaster	1. Escamas al medio del cuerpo 58-60; escamas dorsales lisas o ligeramente quilladas; también ver Fig. 47----------brattstroemi Menos de 58 escamas al medio del cuerpo; escamas dorsales fuertemente quilladas; también ver Fig. 48-----------cyanogaster

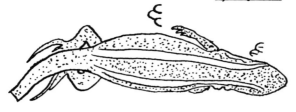

Fig. 47. L. cyanogaster brattstroemi, with outlines of body scales

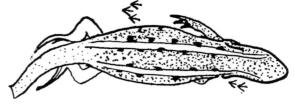

Fig. 48. L. cyanogaster cyanogaster, with outlines of body scales

Liolaemus cyanogaster cyanogaster (Duméril and Bibron)

1846 Proctotretus intermedius Duméril, Voyage autour du Monde sur la Frégate La Venus, Atlas (1846): pl. 2, figs. 1a-d; text (1855): 290.
1961 L.[iolaemus] c.[yanogaster] cyanogaster—Donoso-Barros, Copeia, 1961: 486.
1966 Liolaemus cyanogaster cyanogaster—Donoso-Barros, Reptiles de Chile: 184, figs. 30, 45, 60; col. pl. 10.

Distribution: Concepción to Puerto Montt, Chile, Nahuel Huapí, Argentina.

Liolaemus cyanogaster brattstroemi Donoso-Barros

   1961 Liolaemus cyanogaster brattstroemi Donoso-Barros, Copeia, 1961: 486, fig. 1. Type-
      locality: Forest near Lechagua, Chiloé Island, Chile.
   1966 Liolaemus cyanogaster brattstroemi—Donoso-Barros, Reptiles de Chile: 187, fig. 47.

   Distribution: Chiloé Island, Chile.

LIOLAEMUS DARWINII (Bell)

   1843 Proctotretus Darwinii Bell, Zoology of the Voyage of H.M.S. Beagle, 5, Reptiles: 14, pl. 7, figs.
      1-2. Type-locality: Bahía Blanca, northern Patagonia, Argentina.
   1885 Liolaemus darwinii—Boulenger, Cat. Liz. Brit. Mus., 2: 155.
   1966 Liolaemus darwini—Donoso-Barros, Reptiles de Chile: 281, figs. 31, 61; col. pl. 19.

   Distribution: Patagonia, Argentina; Lago Buenos Aires, Provincia de Aisén, Chile.

LIOLAEMUS DORBIGNYI Koslowsky

   1898 Liolaemus D'Orbignyi Koslowsky, Rev. Mus. La Plata, 8: 174, pl. 2. Type-locality: Provincia de
      Catamarca, Argentina.
   1966 Liolaemus d'orbignyi—Donoso-Barros, Reptiles de Chile: 285, figs. 44, 62.

   Distribution: Catamarca; Argentina; Patagonia to Laguna Amarga, Territorio de Magallanes, Chile.

LIOLAEMUS ELONGATUS Koslowsky

   1896 Liolaemus elongatus Koslowsky, Rev. Mus. La Plata, 7: 448, pl. 1. Type-locality: Near the
      Cordilleras, Territorio Chubut, Argentina.

   Distribution: Provincia de Mendoza to Chubut, Argentina.

LIOLAEMUS FITZGERALDI Boulenger

   1899 Liolaemus fitzgeraldi Boulenger, in Fitzgerald, The Highest Andes: 355, fig. 1. Type-locality:
      Puente del Inca, Argentina.
   1966 Liolaemus fitzgeraldi—Donoso-Barros, Reptiles de Chile: 307, col. pl. 20.

   Distribution: Both sides of Andes, near International Highway between Chile and Argentina.

LIOLAEMUS FITZINGERII (Duméril and Bibron)

   1837 Proctotretus Fitzingerii Duméril and Bibron, Erp. Gén., 4: 286. Type-locality: Chile.
   1858 Eulaemus affinis Girard, U.S. Expl. Exped., Herp.: 366. Type-locality: Puerto Deseado and Santa
      Cruz, Patagonia, Argentina.
   1888 Liolaemus melanops Burmeister, An. Mus. Nac. Buenos Aires, 3: 252. Type-locality: Quele-Cura,
      Chubut, Patagonia, Argentina.
   1966 Liolaemus fitzingeri—Donoso-Barros, Reptiles de Chile: 293, figs. 30, 53, 69, col. pl. 20.

   Distribution: Patagonia of Chile and Argentina.

LIOLAEMUS FUSCUS Boulenger

   1885 Liolaemus fuscus Boulenger, Cat. Liz. Brit. Mus., 2: 144, pl. 10, fig. 2. Type-locality:
      Valparaíso, Chile.
   1898 Liolaemus erythrogaster Werner, Zool. Jahrb., Suppl., 4: 250, pl. 13, fig. 3. Type-locality:
      Coquimbo, Chile.
   1966 Liolaemus fuscus—Donoso-Barros, Reptiles de Chile: 195, fig. 59, col. pl. 11.

   Distribution: Coquimbo to Ñuble, Chile; some Patagonian areas of Argentina.

LIOLAEMUS GOETSCHI Müller and Hellmich

1938 Liolaemus goetschi Müller and Hellmich, Zool. Anz., 123: 130, fig. 1. Type-locality: Road to Laguna Playa, near Fuerte General Roca, Argentina.

Distribution: Northern Patagonian region, Argentina.

LIOLAEMUS GRACILIS (Bell)

1843 Proctotretus gracilis Bell, Zoology of the Voyage of H.M.S. Beagle, 5, Reptiles: 4, pl. 1, fig. 2. Type-locality: Puerto Deseado, Argentina.
1885 Liolaemus gracilis—Boulenger, Cat. Liz. Brit. Mus., 2: 145.

Distribution: Patagonia, Argentina.

LIOLAEMUS GRAVENHORSTII (Gray)

1845 Leiodera Gravenhorstii Gray, Cat. Liz. Brit. Mus.: 211. Type-locality: Chile.
1855 Proctotretus stantoni Girard, Proc. Acad. Nat. Sci. Phila., 1854: 227. Type-locality: Santiago, Chile.
1966 Liolaemus gravenhorsti—Donoso-Barros, Reptiles de Chile: 180, fig. 60, col. pl. 8.

Distribution: Central Chile.

LIOLAEMUS KINGII (Bell)

1843 Proctotretus Kingii Bell, Zoology of the Voyage of H.M.S.Beagle, 5, Reptiles: 13, pl. 6, fig. 1. Type-locality: Puerto Deseado, Argentina.
1885 Liolaemus kingii—Boulenger, Cat. Liz. Brit. Mus., 2: 149.
1966 Liolaemus kingi—Donoso-Barros, Reptiles de Chile: 273, figs. 31, 64; col. pl. 19.

Distribution: Southern Patagonian region, Argentina and Chile.

LIOLAEMUS KRIEGI Müller and Hellmich

1939 Liolaemus kriegi Müller and Hellmich, Zool. Anz., 127: 44, fig. 1. Type-locality: Estancia El Cóndor, Bariloche, Argentina.
1966 Liolaemus kriegi—Donoso-Barros, Reptiles de Chile: 289, fig. 43, col. pl. 21.

Distribution: Southern Argentina; eastern slopes of Andes in Curicó, Chile.

LIOLAEMUS LEMNISCATUS Gravenhorst

1838 Liolaemus lemniscatus Gravenhorst, Nova Acta Acad. Caes. Leop.-Carol., 18: 731, pl. 54, fig. 12. Type-locality: Valparaíso, Chile.
1838 Liolaemus hieroglyphicus Gravenhorst, Nova Acta. Acad. Caes. Leop.-Carol., 18: 732. Type-locality: Cauquenes, Chile.
1847 Proctotretus mosaicus Hombron and Jacquinot, in Dumont-D'Urville, Voyage au Pole Sud et dans l'Oceanie sur . . . l'Astrolabe et la Zélée, Reptiles: pl. 2, fig. 1. Type-locality: Talcahuano, Chile.
1855 Proctotretus femoratus Girard, Proc. Acad. Nat. Sci. Phila., 1854: 227. Type-locality: Santiago, Chile.
1885 Liolaemus lemniscatus—Boulenger, Cat. Liz. Brit. Mus., 2: 143.
1966 Liolaemus lemniscatus—Donoso-Barros, Reptiles de Chile: 191, figs. 32, 59; col. pl. 10.

Distribution: Coquimbo to Cautín, Chile; Pino Hachado Valley, Patagonian Argentina.

LIOLAEMUS LEOPARDINUS Müller and Hellmich

1932 Liolaemus leopardinus Müller and Hellmich, Zool. Anz., 97: 309. Type-locality: Fierro Carrera, Valle del Río San Francisco, Cerro El Plomo, Cordillera de Santiago, Chile, 2700 m.

Distribution: High mountains in Cajón del Mapocho, Valle del Volcán and Cerro Ramón, Provincia Santiago, Chile.

Content: Three subspecies.

Key to the subspecies

1. Dorsal spots not arranged in transverse
   rows; fewer than 85 scales around midbody-
   ---2
   Dorsal spots arranged in transverse rows
   (Fig. 49); more than 85 scales around mid-
   body-------------------------------ramonensis

2. Dorsal spots not prominent, large and confluent on vertebral region (Fig. 50)------
   -----------------------------valdesianus
   Dorsal spots small, well marked, not confluent on vertebral region (Fig. 51)------
   --------------------------leopardinus

Clave de subespecies

1. Manchas dorsales no dispuestas en bandas
   transversales; menos de 85 escamas al
   medio del cuerpo-------------------------2
   Manchas dorsales dispuestes en fajas transversales (Fig. 49); más de 85 escamas al
   medio del cuerpo----------------ramonensis

2. Manchas dorsales débilmente estampadas y
   confluentes en la región vertebral (Fig.
   50)---------------------------valdesianus
   Manchas dorsales bien estampadas no confluentes en la región vertebral (Fig. 51)----
   ---------------------------leopardinus

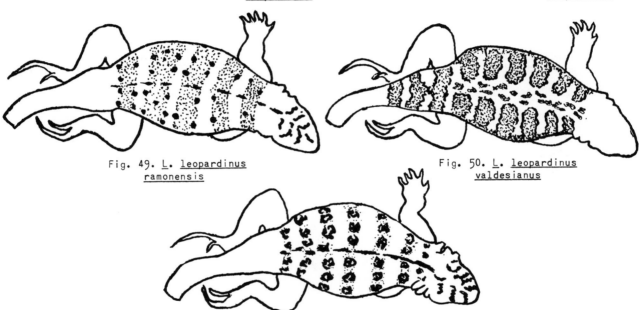

Fig. 49. L. leopardinus
ramonensis

Fig. 50. L. leopardinus
valdesianus

Fig. 51. L. leopardinus leopardinus

Liolaemus leopardinus leopardinus Müller and Hellmich

1932 Liolaemus leopardinus leopardinus Müller and Hellmich, Zool. Anz., 97: 309, fig. 1.
1966 Liolaemus leopardinus leopardinus—Donoso-Barros, Reptiles de Chile: 311, fig. 42, col.
   pl. 22.

Distribution: High mountains near Cajón del Mapocho, Provincia Santiago, Chile.

Liolaemus leopardinus ramonensis Müller and Hellmich

1932 Liolaemus leopardinus ramonensis Müller and Hellmich, Zool. Anz., 97: 314, fig. 2. Type-
   locality: Cerro de Ramón, Provincia Santiago, Chile, 2600 m.
1966 Liolaemus leopardinus ramonensis—Donoso-Barros, Reptiles de Chile: 311, fig. 42, col. pl.
   22.

Distribution: Cerro de Ramón, Chile.

Liolaemus leopardinus valdesianus Hellmich

1950 Liolaemus leopardinus valdesianus Hellmich, Veröff. Zool. Staatsamml. München, 1: 142,
   pl. 12, figs. 28-29. Type-locality: Baños Morales, Lo Valdes, Provincia Santiago,
   Chile.
1966 Liolaemus leopardinus valdesianus—Donoso-Barros, Reptiles de Chile: 313, fig. 42, col.
   pl. 23.

   Distribution: High mountains of Cajón del Río Maipo, Provincia Santiago, Chile.

LIOLAEMUS LINEOMACULATUS Boulenger

1885 Liolaemus lineomaculatus Boulenger, Cat. Liz. Brit. Mus., 2: 149. Type-locality: Patagonia.
1966 Liolaemus lineomaculatus—Donoso-Barros, Reptiles de Chile: 275, figs. 31, 69; col. pl. 19.

   Distribution: Southern Patagonia of Chile and Argentina.

LIOLAEMUS LORENZMUELLERI Hellmich

1950 Liolaemus lorenzmülleri Hellmich, Veröff. Zool. Staatsamml. München, 1: 144, pl. 12, figs. 26, 27.
   Type-locality: Nueva Elqui, Coquimbo, Chile, 2300 m.
1966 Liolaemus lorenzmülleri—Donoso-Barros, Reptiles de Chile: 297, fig. 43.

   Distribution: Region of type locality, 2300-3200 m.

LIOLAEMUS LUTZAE Mertens

1938 Liolaemus lutzae Mertens, Zool. Anz., 123: 221, fig. 1. Type-locality: Recreio dos Bandeirantes,
   Rio de Janeiro, Brazil.

   Distribution: Coastal areas of Rio de Janeiro and Guanabara, Brazil.

LIOLAEMUS MAGELLANICUS (Hombron and Jacquinot)

1847 Proctotretus magellanicus Hombron and Jacquinot, in Dumont-D'Urville, Voyage au Pole Sud et dans
   l'Oceanie sur . . . l'Astrolabe et la Zélée, Reptiles: pl. 2, fig. 2. Type-locality: Havre
   Pecquet, Estrecho de Magallanes, Chile.
1904 Liolaemus (Saccodeira) proximus Werner, Hamburger Magalhaenische Sammelreise, 1, Reptilien und
   Batrachier: 12, figs. 1-2. Type-locality: Ultima Esperanza, southwest Patagonia, Chile.
1909 Liolaemus hatcheri Stejneger, Rep. Princeton Univ. Exp. Patagonia, 3: 218. Type-locality: North
   of Río Santa Cruz, Territorio de Santa Cruz, Patagonia, Argentina.
1910 Saccodeira arenaria Werner, Mitt. Naturhist. Mus. Hamburg, 27: 26. Type-locality: Punta Arenas,
   Estrecho de Magallanes, Chile.
1966 Liolaemus magellanicus—Donoso-Barros, Reptiles de Chile: 277, fig. 64, col. pl. 19.

   Distribution: Tierra del Fuego and southern Patagonia of Chile and Argentina.

LIOLAEMUS MOCQUARDI Pellegrin

1909 Liolaemus Mocquardi Pellegrin, Bull. Mus. Hist. Nat. Paris, 1909: 326. Type-locality: Créqui
   and Sénéchal, higher plateau of Bolivia and Peru; Tiahuanacu, La Paz, Bolivia.
1966 Liolaemus mocquardi—Donoso-Barros, Reptiles de Chile: 325, fig. 51, col. pl. 20.

   Distribution: Altiplano of Peru, Bolivia and Chile.

LIOLAEMUS MODESTUS Tschudi

1845 L.[iolaemus (Sauridis)] modestus Tschudi, Arch. für Naturg., 2 (1): 157. Type-locality: Peru;
   further specified as Miraflores, Peru, by Tschudi, Fauna Peruana, Herp., 1846, 34.
1907 Liolaemus modestus—Roux, Rev. Suisse Zool., 15: 297.

   Distribution: Known only from type locality.

LIOLAEMUS MONTICOLA Müller and Hellmich

1932 Liolaemus monticola Müller and Hellmich, Zool. Anz., 99: 177. Type-locality: Valle del Río San Francisco, Santiago, Chile, 1700 m.

Distribution: Cordillera de la Costa in Central Chile; Andean Cordillera in Chillán and Cautín, Chile.

Content: Three subspecies.

Key to the subspecies	Clave de subespecies
1. More than 80 scales around midbody--------2 Fewer than 80 scales around midbody-------- -------------------------------monticola	1. Más de 80 escamas al medio del cuerpo-----2 Menos de 80 escamas al medio del cuerpo---- ---------------------------------monticola
2. Dorsum and pileus melanistic---chillanensis Dorsum and pileus not melanistic----------- ----------------------------villaricensis	2. Dorso y pileus melánicos-------chillanensis Dorso y pileus no melánicos---villaricensis

Liolaemus monticola monticola Müller and Hellmich

1932 Liolaemus monticola monticola Müller and Hellmich, Zool. Anz., 99: 177, fig. 1.
1966 Liolaemus monticola monticola—Donoso-Barros, Reptiles de Chile: 226, col. pl. 14.

Distribution: Cordillera de los Andes and Cordillera de la Costa, central Chile.

Liolaemus monticola chillanensis Müller and Hellmich

1932 Liolaemus monticola chillanensis Müller and Hellmich, Zool. Anz., 99: 183, fig. 2. Type-locality: Termas de Chillán, Nuble, Chile, 1700 m.
1966 Liolaemus monticola chillanensis—Donoso-Barros, Reptiles de Chile: 229, fig. 40, col. pl. 14.

Distribution: Provincia de Ñuble, Cordillera de los Andes, Chile.

Liolaemus monticola villaricensis Müller and Hellmich

1932 Liolaemus monticola villaricensis Müller and Hellmich, Zool. Anz., 99: 189, fig. 3. Type-locality: Volcán Villarrica, Chile, 1400 m.
1966 Liolaemus monticola villaricensis—Donoso-Barros, Reptiles de Chile: 231, fig. 40.

Distribution: Cordillera de Cautín, Chile.

LIOLAEMUS MULTIFORMIS (Cope)

1876 Proctotretus multiformis Cope, Jour. Acad. Nat. Sci. Phila., (2) 8 (1875): 173. Type-locality: Lago Titicaca, Peru.
1885 Liolaemus multiformis—Boulenger, Cat. Liz. Brit. Mus., 2: 153.

Distribution: High plateau of Andes between Peru, Bolivia, Chile and Argentina.

Content: Two subspecies.

Key to the subspecies	Clave de subespecies
1. Dorsal scales distinctly keeled, smaller than ventrals--------------------simonsii Dorsal scales smooth or indistinctly keeled, slightly smaller than ventrals---- -----------------------------multiformis	1. Escamas dorsales distintamente quilladas y menores que ventrales------------simonsii Escamas dorsales lisas o indistintamente quilladas, ligeramente menores que ventra- les--------------------------multiformis

Liolaemus multiformis multiformis (Cope)

1891 Liolaemus Lenzi Boettger, Zool. Anz., 14: 344. Type-locality: Lago Titicaca, Bolivia.
1895 Liolaemus andinus Koslowsky, Rev. Mus. La Plata, 6: 338, pl. 3. Type-locality: Andes of
Catamarca, Argentina.
1901 Liolaemus annectens Boulenger, Ann. Mag. Nat. Hist., (7) 7: 546. Type-locality: Caylloma
and Sumbay, Andes of Peru.
1902 Liolaemus tropidonotus Boulenger, Ann. Mag. Nat. Hist., (7) 10: 397. Type-locality:
Tirapata, north of Lago Titicaca, Peru, 13000 ft.
1909 Liolaemus variabilis Pellegrin, Bull. Mus. Hist. Nat. Paris, 1909: 327. Type-locality:
Although Pellegrin gave no locality for this as a species, the localities given for the
following three varieties were identical. These were: Tiahuanaco (= Tiahuanacu), La
Paz, Bolivia; Créqui and Sénéchal, noted as on the high plateaus of Peru and Bolivia on
p. 326. Guibé, Catalogue des Types de Lézards, Paris, 1954, 49, does not mention the
latter localities at all.
1909 [Liolaemus variabilis] var. Crequii Pellegrin, Bull. Mus. Hist. Nat. Paris, 1909: 327.
Type-locality: See variabilis, above.
1909 [Liolaemus variabilis] var. Neveui Pellegrin, Bull. Mus. Hist. Nat. Paris, 1909: 327.
Type-locality: See variabilis, above.
1909 [Liolaemus variabilis] var. Courtyi Pellegrin, Bull. Mus. Hist. Nat. Paris, 1909: 328.
Type-locality: See variabilis, above.
1909 Liolaemus bolivianus Pellegrin, Bull. Mus. Hist. Nat. Paris, 1909: 328. Type-locality:
Créqui and Maréchal, high plateaus of Peru and Bolivia.
1966 Liolaemus multiformis multiformis—Donoso-Barros, Reptiles de Chile: 317, figs. 49, 50,
73, col. pl. 24.

Distribution: Altiplano of Peru, Chile and Bolivia.

Liolaemus multiformis simonsii Boulenger

?1898 [Liolaemus signifer] var. montanus Koslowsky, Rev. Mus. La Plata, 8: 182, pl. 6, fig. 6.
Type-locality: Provincia de Catamarca, Argentina.
1902 Liolaemus Simonsii Boulenger, Ann. Mag. Nat. Hist., (7) 10: 398. Type-locality: Potosí,
Challapata, and Uyuni, Bolivia.
1924 Liolaemus annectens orientalis Müller, Mitt. Zool. Mus. Berlin, 11: 81. Type-locality:
Río Pilcomayo, between Tarija and San Francisco, Bolivia.
1933 Liolaemus multiformis simonsii—Burt and Burt, Trans. Acad. Sci. St. Louis, 28: 35.

Distribution: Southwestern Andes of Bolivia; northern Andes of Argentina.

LIOLAEMUS MULTIMACULATUS (Duméril and Bibron)

1837 Proctotretus multimaculatus Duméril and Bibron, Erp. Gén., 4: 290. Type-locality: Chile.
1857 Ortholaemus Beaglii Girard, Proc. Acad. Nat. Sci. Phila., 1857: 199. Type-locality: None
given; Bahía Blanca, Argentina, is original locality for specimens upon which Bell's plate
was based and for which Girard proposed this name, according to Boulenger, Cat. Liz. Brit.
Mus., 2, 1885, 158.
1885 Liolaemus multimaculatus—Boulenger, Cat. Liz. Brit. Mus., 2: 158.

Distribution: Known only from Argentinian Patagonia; records from Chile are erroneous.

LIOLAEMUS NIGROMACULATUS (Wiegmann)

1835 Tropidurus nigromaculatus Wiegmann, Nova Acta Acad. Caes. Leop.-Carol., 17: 229. Type-locality:
Chile; restricted to Huasco, Chile, by Müller and Hellmich, Zool. Anz., 101, 1933, 129.
1885 Liolaemus nigromaculatus—Boulenger, Cat. Liz. Brit. Mus., 2: 147.

Distribution: Atacama Province to Valparaíso Province, Chile.

Content: Eight subspecies.

Key to the subspecies	Clave de subespecies
1. Melanistic (Fig. 52)----------------------2	1. Lagartos melánicos (Fig. 52)--------------2
Not melanistic---------------------------3	Lagartos no melánicos--------------------3

2. Belly black----------------------------ater
   Belly not black--------------------sieversi

3. With dorsal pattern; ground color not pale
   grayish--------------------------------4
   Without dorsal pattern; ground color pale
   grayish (Figs. 53,54)-----------bisignatus

2. Vientre negro-------------------------ater
   Vientre no negro-------------------sieversi

3. Con diseño dorsal; color general no grisáceo pálido------------------------------4
   Sin diseño dorsal; color general gris (Figs.
   53,54) ------------------------bisignatus

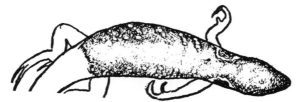

Fig. 52. L. nigromaculatus ater

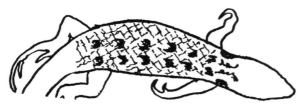

Fig. 53. L. nigromaculatus bisignatus

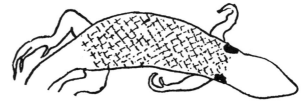

Fig. 54. L. nigromaculatus bisignatus

4. Scales on sides of neck enlarged and
   prominent; those on neck fold mucronate--5
   Scales on sides of neck not very enlarged
   or prominent; those on neck fold not
   mucronate------------------------------6

5. Sulphurous yellow bars across back (Fig.
   55); fewer than 55 scales around midbody--
   ----------------------------zapallarensis
   Two longitudinal pale dorsolateral stripes
   (Fig. 56); more than 55 scales around
   midbody--------------------------kuhlmanni

4. Escamas a los lados del cuello ensanchadas
   y sobresalientes; en el pliegue mucronadas
   ---5
   Escamas en los lados del cuello no ensanchadas ni sobresalientes; en el pliegue no
   mucronadas------------------------------6

5. Barras amarillento sulfúreas a través del
   dorso (Fig. 55); menos de 55 escamas al
   medio del cuerpo------------zapallarensis
   Dos cintas longitudinales claras a los lados del dorso (Fig. 56); más de 55 escamas
   al medio del cuerpo--------------kuhlmanni

Fig. 55. L. nigromaculatus zapallarensis

Fig. 56. L. nigromaculatus kuhlmanni

6. Not as below (Figs. 58,59)--------------7
   Scales on sides of neck larger than dorsal
   neck scales; dorsally brown with two middorsal dark lines (Fig. 57)-nigromaculatus

6. No como el siguiente (Figs. 58,59)--------7
   Escamas laterales de los lados de la nuca
   mayores que las dorsales de la nuca; dorsalmente pardo con dos líneas dorsales
   oscuras (Fig. 57)-----------nigromaculatus

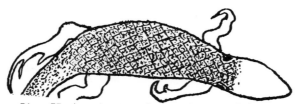

Fig. 57. L. nigromaculatus nigromaculatus

7. Temporal scales smooth; more than 49 scales
   around midbody----------------copiapensis
   Temporal scales weakly keeled; fewer than
   49 scales around midbody-------atacamensis

7. Escamas temporales lisas; más de 49 escamas
   al medio del cuerpo-----------copiapensis
   Escamas temporales débilmente quilladas;
   menos de 49 escamas al medio del cuerpo---
   ------------------------------atacamensis

Fig. 58. L. nigromaculatus atacamensis

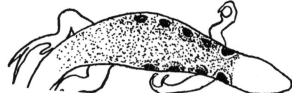

Fig. 59. L. nigromaculatus atacamensis

Liolaemus nigromaculatus nigromaculatus (Wiegmann)

   1835 Tropidurus oxycephalus Wiegmann, Nova Acta Acad. Caes. Leop.-Carol., 17: 232. Type-
        locality: Chile.
   1838 Liolaemus conspersus Gravenhorst, Nova Acta Acad. Caes. Leop.-Carol., 18: 737, pl. 54,
        fig. 14. Type-locality: Cauquenes, Chile.
   1845 Liolaemus inconspicuus Gray, Cat. Liz. Brit. Mus.: 213. Type-locality: Chile.
   1860 Proctotretus pallidus Philippi, Reise durch die Wueste Atacama: 166, pl. 6, fig. 3.
        Type-locality: Paposo, Chile.
   1933 Liolaemus nigromaculatus nigromaculatus—Müller and Hellmich, Zool. Anz., 101: 127.
   1966 Liolaemus nigromaculatus nigromaculatus—Donoso-Barros, Reptiles de Chile: 242, figs. 20,
        34.

      Distribution: Huasco Valley and adjacent areas, Chile.

Liolaemus nigromaculatus atacamensis Müller and Hellmich

   1933 Liolaemus nigromaculatus atacamensis Müller and Hellmich, Zool. Anz., 103: 129, figs. 1-2.
        Type-locality: Atacama, northeastern Copiapó, Chile.
   1966 Liolaemus nigromaculatus atacamensis—Donoso-Barros, Reptiles de Chile: 252, fig. 39,
        col. pl. 16.

      Distribution: Desert areas in Coquimbo and Atacama, Chile.

Liolaemus nigromaculatus ater Müller and Hellmich

   1933 Liolaemus nigromaculatus ater Müller and Hellmich, Zool. Anz., 101: 129. Type-locality:
        Isla de Pájaros, Puerto Coquimbo, Chile.
   1966 Liolaemus nigromaculatus ater—Donoso-Barros, Reptiles de Chile: 261.

      Distribution: Small islands in Bahía, Coquimbo, Chile.

Liolaemus nigromaculatus bisignatus (Philippi)

   1860 Proctotretus bisignatus Philippi, Reise durch die Wueste Atacama: 166, pl. 6, fig. 2.
        Type-locality: Unknown.
   1933 Liolaemus nigromaculatus bisignatus—Müller and Hellmich, Zool. Anz., 103: 132, fig. 3.
   1966 Liolaemus nigromaculatus bisignatus—Donoso-Barros, Reptiles de Chile: 250, fig. 39, col.
        pl. 16.

      Distribution: Coastal areas of Atacama, Chile.

Liolaemus nigromaculatus copiapensis Müller and Hellmich

   1933 Liolaemus nigromaculatus copiapensis Müller and Hellmich, Zool. Anz., 103: 135. Type-
        locality: Copiapó, Atacama, Chile.
   1966 Liolaemus nigromaculatus copiapoensis—Donoso-Barros (in error for copiapensis), Reptiles
        de Chile: 255.

      Distribution: Copiapó and adjacent areas, Chile.

Lioaemus nigromaculatus kuhlmanni Müller and Hellmich

   1933 Liolaemus nigromaculatus kuhlmanni Müller and Hellmich, Zool. Anz., 103: 139, fig. 5.
      Type-locality: Jalmel, Los Andes, Chile; corrected to Jahuel de los Andes, Chile by
      Donoso-Barros, Reptiles de Chile, 1966, 247.
   1966 Liolaemus nigromaculatus kuhlmani—Donoso-Barros (in error for kuhlmanni), Reptiles de
      Chile: 245, fig. 34, col. pls. 15, 17.

   Distribution: Coastal plateau from Valparaíso to Coquimbo, Chile.

Liolaemus nigromaculatus sieversi Donoso-Barros

   1954 Liolaemus nigromaculatus sieversi Donoso-Barros, Zooiatria, 3 (11): 4, fig. 2. Type-
      locality: Isla de los Locos, Bahía Pichidangui, Provincia de Coquimbo, Chile.
   1966 Liolaemus nigromaculatus sieversi—Donoso-Barros, Reptiles de Chile: 259, fig. 47, col.
      pl. 17.

   Distribution: Known only from type locality.

Liolaemus nigromaculatus zapallarensis Müller and Hellmich

   1933 Liolaemus nigromaculatus zapallarensis Müller and Hellmich, Zool. Anz., 103: 137, fig. 4.
      Type-locality: Zapallar, Chile.
   1966 Liolaemus nigromaculatus zapallarensis—Donoso-Barros, Reptiles de Chile: 247, figs. 39,
      47; col. pl. 15.

   Distribution: Coastal border from Aconcagua to Coquimbo, Chile.

LIOLAEMUS NIGROVIRIDIS Müller and Hellmich

   1932 Liolaemus nigroviridis Müller and Hellmich, Zool. Anz., 97: 318. Type-locality: Valle del Río
      San Francisco, Santiago, Chile, 2400 m.

   Distribution: Andes and Cordillera de la Costa, between southern Antofagasta and Santiago
   provinces, Chile.

   Content: Four subspecies.

Key to the subspecies	Clave de subespecies

1. More than 65 scales around midbody--------2
   Fewer than 65 scales around midbody-------3
	1. Más de 65 escamas al medio del cuerpo-----2
	   Menos de 65 escamas al medio del cuerpo---3

2. Neck same width as head; temporal scales
   smooth; four supraoculars; flanks reddish-
   -------------------------------nigroroseus
   Neck more slender than head; temporal
   scales keeled; fewer than four supraocu-
   lars; flanks greenish----------------minor
	2. Cuello del mismo ancho que cabeza; escamas
	   temporales lisas; cuatro supraoculares;
	   flancos rojizos----------------nigroroseus
	   Cuello más delgado que la cabeza; escamas
	   temporales quilladas; menos de cuatro
	   supraoculares; flancos del cuerpo verdosos
	   ------------------------------------minor

3. Dorsal black bars alternating with yellow-
   ish green areas--------------nigroviridis
   Dorsal black bars alternating with sky blue
   interspaces----------------------campanae
	3. Barras dorsales alternan con áreas verde
	   amarillentas------------------nigroviridis
	   Barras dorsales negras alternan con espa-
	   cios celestes--------------------campanae

Liolaemus nigroviridis nigroviridis Müller and Hellmich

   1932 Liolaemus nigroviridis nigroviridis Müller and Hellmich, Zool. Anz., 97: 318, fig. 3.
   1966 Liolaemus nigroviridis nigroviridis—Donoso-Barros, Reptiles de Chile: 261, fig. 41; col.
      pl. 14.

   Distribution: Cajón del Mapocho, Cordillera de los Andes, Santiago, Chile.

Liolaemus nigroviridis campanae Hellmich

1950 Liolaemus nigroviridis campanae Hellmich, Veröff. Zool. Staatsamml. Munchen, 1: 152, pl.
2, figs. 24-25. Type-locality: Cerro Campana, Valparaíso, Chile, 1800 m.
1966 Liolaemus nigroviridis campanae—Donoso-Barros, Reptiles de Chile: 267, fig. 41, col. pl.
14.

Distribution: Cerro El Roble and Cerro Campana, in Cordillera de la Costa, Chile.

Liolaemus nigroviridis minor Müller and Hellmich

1932 Liolaemus nigroviridis minor Müller and Hellmich, Zool. Anz., 97: 326, fig. 4a-b. Type-
locality: Valle del Volcán, Provincia de Santiago, Chile.
1966 Liolaemus nigroviridis minor—Donoso-Barros, Reptiles de Chile: 264, fig. 41, col. pl. 15.

Distribution: El Valle del Río Maipo, Provincia de Santiago, Chile, 1800-3000 m.

Liolaemus nigroviridis nigroroseus Donoso-Barros

1966 Liolaemus nigroviridis nigroroseus Donoso-Barros, Reptiles de Chile: 271, col. pl. 14.
Type-locality: San Pedro de Atacama, Cordillera de Puricó, Provincia de Antofagasta,
Chile.

Distribution: Cordilleras de Antofagasta and Atacama, Chile.

LIOLAEMUS NITIDUS (Wiegmann)

1835 Tropidurus nitidus Wiegmann, Nova Acta Acad. Caes. Leop.-Carol., 17: 234, pl. 17, fig. 2. Type-
locality: Chile.
1838 Liolaemus lineatus Gravenhorst, Nova Acta Acad. Caes. Leop.-Carol., 18: 723, pl. 54, figs. 1-7.
Type-locality: Valparaíso, Chile.
1838 Liolaemus unicolor Gravenhorst, Nova Acta Acad. Caes. Leop.-Carol., 18: 728. Type-locality:
Cauquenes, Chile.
1838 Liolaemus marmoratus Gravenhorst, Nova Acta Acad. Caes. Leop-Carol., 18: 729, pl. 54, fig. 11.
Type-locality: Cauquenes, Chile.
1885 Liolaemus nitidus—Boulenger, Cat. Liz. Brit. Mus., 2: 140.
1966 Liolaemus nitidus—Donoso-Barros, Reptiles de Chile: 173, figs. 32, 53, 60; col. pl. 9.

Distribution: Coquimbo to Maule, in coastal areas near Cordillera de la Costa, also found in
Andes and Cordillera de la Costa in central Chile.

LIOLAEMUS OCCIPITALIS Boulenger

1885 Liolaemus occipitalis Boulenger, Ann. Mag. Nat. Hist., (5) 15: 192. Type-locality: Rio Grande
do Sul, Brazil.
1925 Liolaemus glieschi Ahl, Zool. Anz., 62: 88. Type-locality: Torres, Estado do Rio Grande do Sul,
Brazil.

Distribution: Coastal area, Rio Grande do Sul, Brazil.

LIOLAEMUS ORNATUS Koslowsky

1898 Liolaemus ornatus Koslowsky, Rev. Mus. La Plata, 8: 178, pl. 5. Type-locality: Cordillera de
Jujuy, Argentina.
?1898 [Liolaemus signifer] var. multicolor Koslowsky, Rev. Mus. La Plata, 8: 182. Type-locality:
Provincia de Jujuy, Argentina.
1909 Liolaemus pulcher Pellegrin, Bull. Mus. Hist. Nat. Paris, 1909: 325. Type-locality: Créqui and
Sénéchal, high plateau of Peru and Bolivia; and Tiahuanacu, Bolivia.
1966 Liolaemus ornatus—Donoso-Barros, Reptiles de Chile: 323, figs. 44, 51-52; col. pl. 20.

Distribution: Altiplano of Chile, Argentina and Bolivia.

LIOLAEMUS PANTHERINUS Pellegrin

1909 Liolaemus pantherinus Pellegrin, Bull. Mus. Hist. Nat. Paris, 1909: 324. Type-locality: Créqui and Sénéchal, high plateau of Peru and Bolivia.
1966 Liolaemus pantherinus—Donoso-Barros, Reptiles de Chile: 327, fig. 52; col. pl. 21.

Distribution: Altiplano of Peru, Bolivia and Chile.

LIOLAEMUS PAULINAE Donoso-Barros

1961 Liolaemus paulinae Donoso-Barros, Copeia, 1961: 387, fig. 1c. Type-locality: Calama, Río Loa, Provincia de Antofagasta, Chile.
1966 Liolaemus paulinae—Donoso-Barros, Reptiles de Chile: 189, fig. 48; col. pl. 10.

Distribution: Vicinity of Calama, Antofagasta, Chile.

LIOLAEMUS PICTUS (Duméril and Bibron)

1837 Proctotretus pictus Duméril and Bibron, Erp. Gén., 4: 276. Type-locality: Chile.
1845 Leiolaemus pictus—Gray, Cat. Liz. Brit. Mus.: 213.

Distribution: Southern Chilean forests from Malleco to Chiloé and adjacent islands; Nahuel Huapí, Argentina.

Content: Four subspecies.

Key to the subspecies	Clave de subespecies
1. Fewer than 77 scales around midbody-------2 More than 77 scales around midbody--argentinus	1. Menos de 77 escamas al medio del cuerpo---2 Más de 77 escamas al medio del cuerpo--argentinus
2. Ground color not melanistic---------------3 Ground color melanistic--------------major	2. Color general no melánico-----------------3 Color general melánico----------------major
3. Lateral back bands greenish; fewer than 64 scales around midbody-----------chiloensis Lateral back bands yellowish-white; more than 64 scales around midbody-------pictus	3. Bandas laterales del dorso verdosas; menos de 64 escamas alrededor del medio del cuerpo-----------------------------chiloensis Bandas laterales blanco amarillentas; más de 64 escamas al medio del cuerpo---pictus

Liolaemus pictus pictus (Duméril and Bibron)

1848 Chrysosaurus morio Gay, Historia Física y Política de Chile, 2: 47. Type-locality: Valdivia, Chile.
1868 Proctotretus prasinus Cope, Proc. Acad. Nat. Sci. Phila., 1868: 120. Type-locality: Chile.
1930 Liolaemus pictus pictus—Burt and Burt, Proc. U.S. Nat. Mus., 78 (6): 17.
1966 Liolaemus pictus pictus—Donoso-Barros, Reptiles de Chile: 215, figs. 34, 68, col. pl. 11.

Distribution: Concepción to Puerto Montt, Chile.

Liolaemus pictus argentinus Müller and Hellmich

1939 Liolaemus pictus argentinus Müller and Hellmich, Zool. Anz., 128: 7, fig. 2. Type-locality: Estancia El Cóndor, Lago Nahuel Huapí, Argentina.
1966 Liolaemus pictus argentinus—Donoso-Barros, Reptiles de Chile: 224.

Distribution: Nahuel Huapí and adjacent areas, Argentina.

Liolaemus pictus chiloeensis Müller and Hellmich

  1939 Liolaemus pictus chiloëensis Müller and Hellmich, Zool. Anz., 128: 12. Type-locality:
       Ancud, Chiloé Island, Chile.
  1966 Liolaemus pictus chiloëensis—Donoso-Barros, Reptiles de Chile: 219, col. pl. 11.

     Distribution: Chiloé Island, Chile.

Liolaemus pictus major Boulenger

  1885 [Liolaemus pictus] var. major Boulenger, Cat. Liz. Brit. Mus., 2: 152. Type-locality:
       Chile.
  1931 Liolaemus pictus major—Burt and Burt, Bull. Amer. Mus. Nat. Hist., 61: 278.
  1966 Liolaemus pictus major—Donoso-Barros, Reptiles de Chile: 222.

     Distribution: Islands adjacent to Chiloé Island, Chile.

LIOLAEMUS PLATEI Werner

  1898 Liolaemus platei Werner, Zool. Jahrb., Suppl., 4: 255, pl. 13, fig. 2. Type-locality: Coquimbo,
       Chile.

   Distribution: Distribution discontinuous; Copiapó and Coquimbo; Curicó, Chile.

   Content: Two subspecies.

              Key to the subspecies   Clave de subespecies

  1. Fewer than 60 scales around midbody--platei   1. Menos de 60 escamas al medio cuerpo--platei
     More than 60 scales around midbody---------   Más de 60 escamas al medio cuerpo----------
     --------------------------------curicensis   --------------------------------curicensis

Liolaemus platei platei Werner

  1938 Liolaemus platei platei—Müller and Hellmich, Zool. Anz., 122: 231.
  1966 Liolaemus platei platei—Donoso-Barros, Reptiles de Chile: 234, fig. 46; col. pl. 15.

     Distribution: Coquimbo and Atacama, Chile.

Liolaemus platei curicensis Müller and Hellmich

  1938 Liolaemus platei curicensis Müller and Hellmich, Zool. Anz., 122: 231, fig. 2. Type-
       locality: Los Queñes, Curicó, Chile.
  1966 Liolaemus platei curicensis—Donoso-Barros, Reptiles de Chile: 237, fig. 46.

     Distribution: Known only from type locality.

LIOLAEMUS ROBERTMERTENSI Hellmich

  1964 Liolaemus robertmertensi Hellmich, Senckenbergiana Biol., 45: 505, fig. 1. Type-locality:
       Mountains in region of Belém, Provincia de Catamarca, Argentina.

   Distribution: Cordillera de Catamarca, Argentina.

LIOLAEMUS ROTHI Koslowsky

  1898 Liolaemus Rothi Koslowsky, Rev. Mus. La Plata, 8: 177, pl. 4. Type-locality: Territorio de
       Neuquén, Argentina.

   Distribution: Patagonia, Argentina.

LIOLAEMUS RUIBALI Donoso-Barros

1961 *Liolaemus ruibali* Donoso-Barros, Copeia, 1961: 390, fig. la. Type-locality: Between Villavicencio and Uspallata, Mendoza, Argentina, 3000 m.

Distribution: Known only from type locality.

LIOLAEMUS SCHROEDERI Müller and Hellmich

1938 *Liolaemus schröderi* Müller and Hellmich, Zool. Anz., 122: 225, fig. 1. Type-locality: Los Queñes, Curicó, Chile, 1600 m.
1966 *Liolaemus schröderi*—Donoso-Barros, Reptiles de Chile: 177, fig. 46; col. pl. 8.

Distribution: Coastal Cordillera and Andes between Talca and Santiago, central Chile.

LIOLAEMUS SIGNIFER (Duméril and Bibron)

1837 *Proctotretus Signifer* Duméril and Bibron, Erp. Gén., 4: 288. Type-locality: Chile.
1882 *Liolaemus signifer* var. *zonatus* Koslowsky, Rev. Mus. La Plata, 8: 181, pl. 6, fig. 3. Type-locality: Provincia de Catamarca, Argentina.
1966 *Liolaemus signifer*—Donoso-Barros, Reptiles de Chile: 329, col. pl. 21.

Distribution: Altiplano of Chile, Bolivia and Argentina.

LIOLAEMUS TENUIS (Duméril and Bibron)

1837 *Proctotretus tenuis* Duméril and Bibron, Erp. Gén., 4: 279. Type-locality: Chile.
1885 *Liolaemus tenuis*—Boulenger, Cat. Liz. Brit. Mus., 2: 152.

Distribution: Southern Coquimbo province to Puerto Montt, Chile.

Content: Two subspecies.

Key to the subspecies	Clave de subespecies

1. Dorsal spots not reduced (Fig. 60); females without lateral black blotches (Fig. 61)-- --------------------------------------tenuis Dorsal spotting reduced to tiny punctulations (Fig. 62); females with lateral black blotches (Fig. 63)----punctatissimus

1. Diseño dorsal formado por manchitas de regular tamaño (Fig. 60); hembras sin depósitos melánicos en los flancos (Fig. 61)-- --------------------------------------tenuis Diseño dorsal con manchitas puntiformes (Fig. 62); hembras con depósitos melánicos en los flancos (Fig. 63)----punctatissimus

Fig. 60. L. *tenuis tenuis*, male

Fig. 61. L. *tenuis tenuis*, female

Fig. 62. L. *tenuis punctatissimus*, male

Fig. 63. L. *tenuis punctatissimus*, female

Liolaemus tenuis tenuis (Duméril and Bibron)

1856 Tropidurus ptychopleurus Lichtenstein, Nomenclator Reptilium et Amphibiorum Musei
     Zoologici Berolinensis: 9. Type-locality: None given.
1932 [Liolaemus] tenuis tenuis—Goetsch and Hellmich, Zeits. für Induktive Abstammungs-und
     Vererbungslehre, 62: 70.
1966 Liolaemus tenuis tenuis—Donoso-Barros, Reptiles de Chile: 207, figs. 30, 70; col. pl. 12.

    Distribution: Southern Coquimbo to Puerto Montt, Chile.

Liolaemus tenuis punctatissimus Müller and Hellmich

?1856 Proctotretus niger Hallowell, Proc. Acad. Nat. Sci. Phila., 1856: 233. Type-locality:
      Isla Quinquina, Chile; in error for Isla Quiriguina, Chile.
1932 Liolaemus tenuis micropunctatus Goetsch and Hellmich (nomen nudum), Zeits. für Induktive
     Abstammungs-und Vererbungslehre, 62: 70.
1933 Liolaemus tenuis punctatissimus Müller and Hellmich, Zool. Anz., 104: 307, fig. 2. Type-
     locality: Parque Lota, Lota, Concepción, Chile.
1966 Liolaemus tenuis punctatissimus—Donoso-Barros, Reptiles de Chile: 212, figs. 43, 70; col.
     pl. 12.

    Distribution: Coastal border, Concepción to southern Chile.

LIOLAEMUS WIEGMANNII (Duméril and Bibron)

1837 Proctotretus Wiegmannii Duméril and Bibron, Erp. Gén., 4: 284. Type-locality: Chile.
1857 Ortholaemus Fitzroii Girard, Proc. Acad. Nat. Sci. Phila., 1857: 198. Type-locality: Maldonado,
     Bahía Blanca, and Río Negro, Argentina; taken from Girard, U.S. Exploring Expedition, Herp.,
     1858, 373.
1885 Liolaemus wiegmannii—Boulenger, Cat. Liz. Brit. Mus., 2: 156.

    Distribution: Region of southern Brazil, Uruguay and Argentina.

LYGODACTYLUS Gray

 1864 Lygodactylus Gray, Proc. Zool. Soc. London, 1864: 59. Type-species: Lygodactylus strigatus Gray
       (= Lygodactylus capensis Smith).
 1880 Scalabotes Peters, Monats. Akad. Wiss. Berlin, 1880: 795. Type-species: Scalabotes thomensis
       Peters.
 1883 Microscalabotes Boulenger, Ann. Mag. Nat. Hist., (5) 11: 174. Type-species: Microscalabotes
       Cowanii Boulenger.

 Distribution: Tropical Africa and Malagasy Republic; Brazil.

 Content: About 30 species, of which only one occurs within limits of this work.

 Comment: Vanzolini, Arq. Zool. São Paulo, 17, 1968, 63, includes this genus in the South American
     fauna on the basis of an unnamed species from Bahia and Mato Grosso, Brazil.

MABUYA Fitzinger

1826 Mabuya Fitzinger, Neue Classification der Reptilien: 23. Type-species: Mabuya dominicensis Fitzinger, = Mabuya mabouya (Lacépède).
1826 Spondylurus Fitzinger, Neue Classification der Reptilien: 23. Type-species: Scincus sloani Daudin.
1830 Euprepis Wagler, Nat. Syst. Amph.: 162. Type-species: Lacerta punctata Linnaeus.
1834 Euprepes Wiegmann (substitute name for Euprepis Wagler), Herpetologia Mexicana: 11.
1839 Mabouya Duméril and Bibron (substitute name for Mabuya Fitzinger), Erp. Gén., 5: 579 (first page on which emendation is used; repeated throughout Scincid synonymies).
1839 Herinia Gray, Ann. Mag. Nat. Hist., (1) 2: 332. Type-species: Herinia capensis Gray.
1843 Trachylepis Fitzinger, Systema Reptilium: 22. Type-species: Euprepes savignyi Duméril and Bibron.
1843 Eutropis Fitzinger, Systema Reptilium: 22. Type-species: Euprepes Sebae Duméril and Bibron.
1843 Oxytropis Fitzinger, Systema Reptilium: 22. Type-species: Euprepes Merremii Duméril and Bibron.
1845 Heremites Gray, Cat. Liz. Brit. Mus.: 113. Type-species: Scincus vittatus Oliver.
1845 Copeoglossum Tschudi, Arch. für Naturg., 11: 162. Type-species: Copeoglossum cinctum Tschudi.
1845 Xystrolepis Tschudi, Arch. für Naturg., 11: 162. Type-species: Trachylepis (Xystrolepis) punctata Tschudi.
1845 Chioninia Gray, Cat. Liz. Brit. Mus.: 116. Type-species: Euprepes Delalandii Duméril and Bibron.
1848 Elabites Gistl (substitute name for Euprepis Wagler), Naturgeschichte des Thierreichs: IX.
1862 Mabuia Cope (emendation of Mabuya Fitzinger), Proc. Acad. Nat. Sci. Phila., 1862: 185.
1925 Mabuiopsis Angel, Rept. et Batr., Voyage de Ch. Allaud et R. Jeannel en Afrique Orientale, 1911-1912, Vertebrata, 2: 21. Type-species: Mabuia Jeanneli Angel.

Distribution: Africa, Madagascar and southern Asia; Mexico through South America excluding only Chile; Antilles.

Content: About 85 species, only nine of which occur within limits of this work.

Key to the species

1. Auditory denticles absent; dorsal scales not keeled; stripes present or absent on body——2
   Auditory denticles present; dorsal scales keeled; all stripes absent------------maculata

2. One frontoparietal----------------------------3
   Two frontoparietals---------------------------4

3. Prefrontals separated------------------frenata
   Prefrontals in contact------------nigropalmata

4. Distance from snout to eye less than half of head length--------------------------------5
   Distance from snout to eye as long as, or longer than, half of head length------------- ---------------------------------macrorhyncha

5. Adpressed limbs not overlapping--------------6
   At least digits of adpressed limbs over-lapping---------------------------------------8

6. Dorsum with longitudinal stripes-------------7
   Dorsum without longitudinal stripes, present only on sides----------------------brachypoda

7. Dorsal scales grooved; six dark body stripes----------------------------------heathi
   Dorsal scales not grooved; nine or ten dark body stripes----------------------guaporicola

Clave de especies

1. Dentículos auditorios ausentes; escamas dorsales no quilladas; cintas longitudinales presentes o ausentes---------------------2
   Dentículos auditorios presente; escamas dorsales quilladas; cintas ausentes------maculata

2. Un frontoparietal-----------------------------3
   Dos frontoparietales---------------------------4

3. Prefrontales separados------------------frenata
   Prefrontales en contacto----------nigropalmata

4. Distancia ojo-hocico menos que la mitad del largo de la cabeza--------------------------5
   Distancia ojo-hocico de igual o mayor longitud que la mitad del largo de la cabeza---------- ----------------------------------macrorhyncha

5. Extremidades en oposición no se cruzan a los lados del cuerpo----------------------------6
   Extremidades en oposición, al menos los digitos se cruzan--------------------------8

6. Dorso con cintas longitudinales--------------7
   Dorso medianamente sin cintas longitudinales, sólo presentes en los lados--------brachypoda

7. Escamas dorsales surcadas; seis cintas oscuras corporales----------------------------heathi
   Escamas dorsales no surcadas; nueve a diez cintas oscuras corporales---------guaporicola

8. Frequently four supraoculars; vertebral dark
   stripe absent------------------------mabouya
   Frequently three supraoculars; vertebral dark
   stripe present------------------dorsovittata

8. Frecuentemente cuatro supraoculares; cinta
   vertebral oscura ausente--------------mabouya
   Frecuentemente tres supraoculares; cinta vertebral oscura presente--------------dorsovittata

MABUYA BRACHYPODA Taylor

1956 Mabuya brachypodus Taylor, Univ. Kansas Sci. Bull., 38: 308, fig. 76. Type-locality: Four km
     ESE of Los Angeles de Tilarán, Guanacaste, Cos'a Rica.
1958 Mabuya brachypoda—Webb, Univ. Kansas Sci. Bull., 38 (2): 1303.

   Distribution: Pacific slopes from Yucatán Peninsula, Mexico to Costa Rica.

MABUYA DORSIVITTATA Cope

1862 Mabuia dorsivittata Cope, Proc. Acad. Nat. Sci. Phila., 1862: 350. Type-locality: Paraguay.
1874 Euprepes (Mabuia) virgatus Peters, Monats. Akad. Wiss. Berlin, 1874: 621. Type-locality:
     Unknown, possibly from Australian Islands.
1884 Mabuya Jobertii Thominot, Bull. Soc. Philom. Paris, (7) 8: 148. Type-locality: Itatiaha, Brazil.
1885 Mabuia tetrataenia Boettger, Zeitsch. für Naturwiss., 58: 227. Type-locality: Paraguay.
1968 Mabuya dorsovittata—Gallardo, Rev. Mus. Argentino Cien. Nat., Zool., 9: 180, figs. 1-2.

   Distribution: Uruguay, Paraguay, northern Argentina and southern Brazil.

MABUYA FRENATA (Cope)

1862 Emoea frenata Cope, Proc. Acad. Nat. Sci. Phila., 1862: 187. Type-locality: Río Paraguay
     valley, Paraguay.
1879 Mabuya frenata—Bocourt, Miss. Sci. Mex., Rept.: 404.
1968 Mabouya frenata—Gallardo, Rev. Mus. Argentino Cien. Nat., Zool., 9: 187, fig. 3.

   Distribution: Bolivia, Brazil, Paraguay and Argentina.

   Content: Two subspecies.

                    Key to the subspecies

1. Usually with dark vertebral stripe;
   pronounced dark dorsal stripes; three
   supraoculars------------------cochabambae
   Usually without dark vertebral stripe; dark
   dorsal stripes faintly marked; usually
   four supraoculars------------------frenata

                    Clave de subespecies

1. Usualmente una cinta vertebral oscura;
   cintas dorsales marcadas; tres supra-
   oculares----------------------cochabambae
   Usualmente sin cinta vertebral oscura;
   cintas dorsales poco marcadas; usualmente
   cuatro supraoculares--------------frenata

Mabuya frenata frenata (Cope)

1870 Eumeces (Mabouya) Nattereri Steindachner, Sitz. Math.-Naturwiss. Kl. Akad. Wiss. Vienna,
     62: 339, pl. 3, fig. 4. Type-locality: Brazil.
1935 Mabouya frenata frenata—Dunn, Proc. Acad. Nat. Sci. Phila., 87: 551.

   Distribution: Amazonian Bolivia; Mato Grosso, Brazil; Paraguay; Misiones to Mendoza,
   Argentina.

Mabuya frenata cochabambae Dunn

1935 Mabuya frenata cochabambae Dunn, Proc. Acad. Nat. Sci. Phila., 87: 553. Type-locality:
     Pocona, Departamento Cochabamba, Bolivia.

   Distribution: Known from Cochabamba and Santa Cruz, Bolivia.

MABUYA GUAPORICOLA Dunn

1935 *Mabuya guaporicola* Dunn, Proc. Acad. Nat. Sci. Phila., 87: 549. Type-locality: Bastos Farm on Río Alegre, Headwaters of Río Guaporé, western Mato Grosso, Brazil.

  Distribution: Mato Grosso, Brazil and Santa Cruz, Bolivia.

MABUYA HEATHI Schmidt and Inger

1951 *Mabuya heathi* Schmidt and Inger, Fieldiana, Zool., 31: 455. Type-locality: Fortaleza, Ceara, Brazil.

  Distribution: Ceara, Parahyba, and Rio Grande do Norte, Brazil.

MABUYA MABOUYA (Lacépède)

1788 *Lacertus Mabouya* Lacépède, Synopsis Methodica Quadrupedum Oviparorum, in Hist. Nat. Quadrup. Ovipares, 1: unpaged; description in Hist. Nat. Quad. Ovip., 1: 376, pl. 24. Type-locality: America and Antilles; restricted to the Antilles by Latreille, 1802 (fide Dunn); further restricted to the Lesser Antilles by Dunn, Proc. Acad. Nat. Sci. Phila., 87, 1936, 544; still further restricted to St. Vincent Island by Smith and Taylor, Bull. U.S. Nat. Mus., 199, 1950, 156.
1826 *Mabuya* [*mabouya*]—Fitzinger, Neue Classification der Reptilien: 52.

  Distribution: Mexico to South America, Lesser Antilles, Trinidad and Tobago.

  Content: Three subspecies, one (*sloani* Daudin) extralimital.

Key to the subspecies	Clave de subespecies

1. Dorsolateral light stripe prominent, always present on sides between legs------------2
 	
   Dorsolateral light stripe vague, usually only on neck to arm insertion----*pergravis*
	1. Línea clara dorsolateral prominente, siempre presente en los lados, entre los miembros--------------------------------2
	   Línea clara dorsolateral poco conspícua, usualmente sólo presente entre nuca e inserción del miembro anterior---*pergravis*

2. Dorsolateral dark stripe one and one-half to two scale rows wide; fifth supralabial under eye------------------------*alliacea*
   Dorsolateral dark stripe two and one-half to three scale rows wide; usually sixth labial under eye, sometimes fifth on one side, sixth on other--------------*mabouya*
	2. Bandas oscuras dorsolaterales del ancho de una y media a dos filas de escamas; quinta supralabial bajo el ojo----------*alliacea*
	   Bandas dorsolaterales del ancho de dos y media a tres filas de escamas; usualmente sexta supralabial bajo el ojo; a veces quinta de un lado y sexta del otro-*mabouya*

Mabuya mabouya mabouya (Lacépède)

1820 *Scincus cepedii* Merrem, Tentamen Systematis Amphibiorum: 71. Type-locality: Unknown.
1823 *Scincus agilis* Raddi, Mem. Soc. Italiana Sci. Modena, 19: 62. Type-locality: Rio de Janeiro, Brazil.
1825 *Scincus bistriatus* Spix, Spec. Nov. Lacert. Bras.: 23, pl. 26, fig. 1. Type-locality: Pará, Brazil.
1825 *Scincus nigropunctatus* Spix, Spec. Nov. Lacert. Bras.: 24, pl. 26, fig. 2. Type-locality: Ecgá, Brazil.
1826 *Mabuya dominicensis* Fitzinger, Neue Classification der Reptilien: 52. Type-locality: Dominica Island, Lesser Antilles.
1831 *Scincus (Tiliqua) aenea* Gray, Synopsis Species Class Reptilia, in Griffith, Cuvier's Animal Kingdom, 9: 70. Type-locality: Brazil.
1838 *Tiliqua albolabris* Gray, Ann. Mag. Nat. Hist., (1) 2: 292. Type-locality: Unknown.
1839 [*Gongylus*] (*Eumeces*) *Spixii* Duméril and Bibron, Erp. Gén., 5: 642. Type-locality: Cayenne, French Guiana and Brazil.
1845 *Copeoglossum cinctum* Tschudi, Arch. für Naturg., 11: 162. Type-locality: Forested region of Peru.

Mabuya mabouya mabouya (Lacépède), continued

1845 Trachylepis (Xystrolepis) punctata Tschudi, Arch. für Naturg., 11: 162. Type-locality: Peru.
1857 Euprepis surinamensis Hallowell, Proc. Acad. Nat. Sci. Phila., 1856: 154. Type-locality: Surinam.
1862 Mabuia unimarginata Cope, Proc. Acad. Nat. Sci. Phila., 1862: 187. Type-locality: Panama.
1862 Mabuia lanceolata Cope, Proc. Acad. Nat. Sci. Phila., 1862: 187. Type-locality: Barbados.
1879 Mabuya metallica Bocourt, Miss. Sci. Mex., Rept.: 400, pl. 22B, fig. 1. Type-locality: Martinique.
1887 Mabuia luciae Garman, Bull. Essex Inst., 19: 51. Type-locality: Santa Lucia Island.
1887 Mabuia dominicana Garman, Bull. Essex Inst., 19: 51. Type-locality: Dominica Island, Lesser Antilles.
1935 Mabuya mabouya mabouya——Dunn, Proc. Acad. Nat. Sci. Phila., 87: 544.
1935 Mabuya deserticola Dunn, Proc. Acad. Nat. Sci. Phila., 87: 554. Type-locality: Mollendo, Peru.

Distribution: Panama; Pacific Colombia and Ecuador; entire Amazonian region; Caribbean Islands including Pato, Trinidad, Tobago, Barbados and Lesser Antilles.

Mabuya mabouya alliacea Cope

1875 Mabuia alliacea Cope, Jour. Acad. Nat. Sci. Phila., (2) 8 (1875): 115, pl. 28, fig. 1. Type-locality: Costa Rica.
1952 Mabuya mabouya alliacea——Burger, Copeia, 1952: 186.

Distribution: Veracruz and Sinaloa, Mexico to Costa Rica.

Mabuya mabouya pergravis Barbour

1921 Mabuya pergravis Barbour, Proc. New England Zool. Club, 7: 85. Type-locality: Colombia.
1950 Mabuya mabouya pergravis——Dunn and Saxe, Proc. Acad. Nat. Sci. Phila., 102: 154.

Distribution: Providence Island, Colombia, and presumably nearby mainland of Colombia.

MABUYA MACRORHYNCHA Hoge

1946 Mabuya macrorhyncha Hoge, Mem. Inst. Butantan, 19: 241, pls. 1-4. Type-locality: Ilha Queimada Grande, Brazil.

Distribution: Ilha Queimada Grande, Brazil.

MABUYA MACULATA (Gray)

1839 Tiliqua punctata Gray (preoccupied by Lacerta punctata Linnaeus = Mabuya punctata), Ann. Mag. Nat. Hist., (1) 2: 289. Type-locality: Fernando de Noronha, Brazil.
1839 Tiliqua maculata Gray, Ann. Mag. Nat. Hist., (1) 2: 289. Type-locality: Surinam (in error).
1874 Mabouya punctatissima O'Shaughnessy, Ann. Mag. Nat. Hist., (4) 13: 300. Type-locality: Cape of Good Hope?
1945 Mabuya atlantica Schmidt (replacement name for Mabuya punctata), Copeia, 1945: 45, fig. 1.
1946 Mabuya punctata——Travassos, Bol. Mus. Nac. Brasil, 60: 3, pls. 1-11.

Distribution: Ilha Fernando de Noronha, Brazil.

MABUYA NIGROPALMATA Andersson

1918 Mabuia nigropalmata Andersson, Ark. för Zool., 11 (16): 8. Type-locality: Rio Curucá, Brazil and San Fermin, Bolivia.

Distribution: Known from type localities; material from Monte Turumiquire, Venezuela, is included under this name by Dunn, Proc. Acad. Nat. Sci. Phila., 87, 1955, 554.

MACROPHOLIDUS Noble

1921 **Macropholidus** Noble, Ann. New York Acad. Sci., 29: 137. Type-species: **Macropholidus ruthveni** Noble.

Distribution: Ecuador and northern Peru.

Content: Two species.

Key to the species	Clave de especies
1. Dorsal scales smooth------------------**ruthveni**	1. Escamas dorsales lisas-----------------**ruthveni**
Dorsal scales striated and keeled-----**annectens**	Escamas dorsales estriadas o quilladas---------- -----------------------------------**annectens**

MACROPHOLIDUS ANNECTENS Parker

1930 **Macropholidus annectens** Parker, Ann. Mag. Nat. Hist., (10) 5: 569. Type-locality: Vicinity of Loja City, Ecuador.

Distribution: Upper drainage of Río Zamora, Ecuador.

MACROPHOLIDUS RUTHVENI Noble

1921 **Macropholidus ruthveni** Noble, Ann. New York Acad. Sci., 29: 138. Type-locality: Cordillera between Departments of Piura and Cajamarca, Peru.

Distribution: Known only from type locality.

MESOBAENA Mertens

  1925 Mesobaena Mertens, Senckenbergiana, 7: 170. Type-species: Mesobaena huebneri Mertens.

    Distribution: As for single known species.

    Content: One species.

MESOBAENA HUEBNERI Mertens

  1925 Mesobaena huebneri Mertens, Senckenbergiana, 7: 170, figs. 1-2. Type-locality: Inirida, south
        Venezuela; corrected to Colombia by Gans, Bull. Amer. Mus. Nat. Hist., 135, 1967, 84.

    Distribution: Amazonian Venezuela and Colombia.

MICRABLEPHARUS Boettger

    1885 Micrablepharus Boettger, Zeitsch. für Naturwiss., 58: 217. Type-species: Micrablepharus
        glaucurus Boettger.

    Distribution: Brazil and Paraguay.

    Content: Two species.

Key to the species	Clave de especies
1. Anterior supraciliary scale in contact with frontonasal; first finger absent---maximiliani Anterior supraciliary scale not in contact with frontonasal; first finger present--------dunni	1. Supraciliar anterior contacta con el fronto-nasal; dedo interno ausente--------maximiliani Supraciliar anterior no contacta con el fronto-nasal; dedo interno presente------------dunni

MICRABLEPHARUS MAXIMILIANI (Reinhardt and Lütken)

    1862 Gymnophthalmus Maximiliani Reinhardt and Lütken, Vidensk. Medd. Naturhist. Foren. Kjöbenhavn,
        3 (1861): 211, pl. 5, fig. 6. Type-locality: Brazil.
    1885 Micrablepharus glaucurus Boettger, Zeitsch. für Naturwiss., 58: 218. Type-locality: Paraguay.
    1885 Micrablepharus maximiliani—Boulenger, Cat. Liz. Brit. Mus., 2: 426.

    Distribution: Brazil and Paraguay.

MICRABLEPHARUS DUNNI Laurent

    1949 Micrablepharus dunni Laurent, Bull. Inst. Roy. Sci. Nat. Belgique, 25 (9): 3, figs. 4-6. Type-
        locality: "Santa Marta", with country unknown; Laurent suggested either Colombia or Brazil,
        but the name occurs commonly throughout South America.

    Distribution: Unknown.

<u>MORUNASAURUS</u> Dunn

> 1933 <u>Morunasaurus</u> Dunn, Occ. Pap. Boston Soc. Nat. Hist., 8: 75. Type-species: <u>Morunasaurus</u> <u>groi</u> Dunn.

> Distribution: Disjunct; known from Amazonian Ecuador and one locality in Panama.

> Content: Two species.

Key to the species

1. Dorsonuchal crest present; tail compressed; annuli of spines on tail separated by three scale rows dorsally and two ventrally---<u>annularis</u>
   Dorsonuchal crest absent; tail circular; annuli of spines on tail separated by four scale rows dorsally and three ventrally-------------<u>groi</u>

Clave de especies

1. Cresta dorsonucal presente; cola comprimida; anillos espinosos caudales separados por tres hileras dorsales y dos hileras ventrales de escamas------------------------------<u>annularis</u>
   Cresta dorsonucal ausente; cola circular; anillos espinosos separados por cuatro hileras dorsales y tres hileras ventrales de escamas---------------------------------------<u>groi</u>

<u>MORUNASAURUS</u> <u>ANNULARIS</u> (O'Shaughnessy)

> 1881 <u>Hoplocercus</u> <u>annularis</u> O'Shaughnessy, Proc. Zool. Soc. London, 1881: 244, pl. 25, fig. 2. Type-locality: Canelos, Ecuador.
> 1933 <u>Morunasaurus</u> <u>annularis</u>—Dunn, Occ. Pap. Boston Soc. Nat. Hist., 8: 76.

> Distribution: Amazonian Ecuador.

<u>MORUNASAURUS</u> <u>GROI</u> Dunn

> 1933 <u>Morunasaurus</u> <u>groi</u> Dunn, Occ. Pap. Boston Soc. Nat. Hist., 8: 76. Type-locality: Valle de San Antón, Panama.

> Distribution: Known only from type locality.

NEUSTICURUS Duméril and Bibron

1839 Neusticurus Duméril and Bibron, Erp. Gén., 5: 61. Type-species: Lacerta bicarinata Linnaeus.

Distribution: Mountain areas of Costa Rica to Amazonian region, east of Andes.

Content: Seven species, according to most recent revision, by Uzzell, Bull. Amer. Mus. Nat. Hist., 32, 1966, plus an eighth (racenisi) recently revived from synonymy.

Key to the species

1. Dorsum covered by regular scales, not granules---------------------------------------2
   Dorsum covered with fine, granular scales-------------------------------racenisi

2. Tympanum deeply recessed within an external auditory meatus (except in holotype of tatei); tail strongly compressed in adults, less so in juveniles------------------------3
   Tympanum not or but slightly recessed; tail slightly or moderately compressed------------4

3. Body with several longitudinal rows of tuberculate scales; temporal scales keeled, keels parallel and longitudinal; frontonasal-frontal area usually with regular scales; two scales along side of tail for each two median ventral caudal scales (Fig. 1)------------bicarinatus
   Body with at most one posterior dorsolateral series of enlarged scales; temporal scales conical; frontonasal-frontal area usually with irregular scales; three to five scales along side of tail for each two median ventral caudal scales (Fig. 2)-------------------tatei

Clave de especies

1. Dorso no cubierto con escamas finamente granulares----------------------------------2
   Dorso cubierto con escamas finamente granulares----------------------------racenisi

2. Tímpano profundamente deprimido dentro del meato auditivo (excepto en el holotipo de tatei); cola fuertemente comprimida en adultos; menos en juveniles------------------3
   Tímpano no deprimido o ligeramente; cola moderadamente comprimida----------------------4

3. Cuerpo con varias hileras longitudinales de tubérculos; escamas temporales quilladas, quillas longitudinales y paralelas; área frontonasal y frontal frecuentemente con escamas regulares; dos escamas a lo largo de los lados de la cola por cada dos escamas caudales medio ventrales (Fig. 1)--bicarinatus
   Cuerpo con la serie más posterior de escamas dorsolaterales ensanchadas; escamas temporales cónicas; área frontonasal y frontal frecuentemente con escamas irregulares; tres a cinco escamas a lo largo de los lados de la cola por cada dos escamas caudales medio ventrales (Fig. 2)---------------------tatei

Fig. 1. Lateral view of tail, showing two lateral scales for each two median ventral caudal scales.

Fig. 2. Lateral view of tail, showing three to five lateral scales for each two median ventral caudal scales.

4. Tympanum slightly recessed; body with irregular rows of dorsal tubercles; disc in lower eyelid divided into sections by vertical grooves; three to five scales along side of tail for each two median ventral caudal scales----rudis
   Tympanum slightly or not recessed; body with regular or irregular rows of tubercles, or no tubercles present; disc in lower eyelid divided or not; two or three scales along side of tail for each two median ventral caudal scales---------------------------------------5

4. Tímpano ligeramente hundido; cuerpo con hileras irregulares de tubérculos dorsales; disco del párpado inferior dividido por surcos verticales; tres a cinco escamas a los lados de la cola por cada dos escamas medioventrales---rudis
   Tímpano hundido (ligeramente o no); cuerpo con hileras regulares o irregulares de tubérculos o bien sin tubérculos; disco en el párpado inferior dividido o no; dos o tres escamas a lo largo de los lados de la cola por cada dos escamas caudales medioventrales--------------5

5. Tympanum not recessed; tubercles, if present, in regular or irregular rows; if tubercles present, lateral scales heterogeneous; tail 1.4 to 2.1 times body length------------------6
Tympanum slightly recessed; enlarged dorsal scales on body in four regular rows; lateral scales uniform, small; no tubercles on head or sides; tail short, 1.1 to 1.5 times body length; nostril surrounded by brown or black spot--------------------------------cochranae

6. Upper lateral nuchal scales conical, forming one or more longitudinal rows of tubercles; two to five posterior preanals---------------7
Upper lateral nuchal scales small, uniform, not forming longitudinal rows; two large posterior preanals; no conspicuous light areas on upper forelimbs---------------strangulatus

7. Frontonasal-frontal area with irregular scales; two series of supraoculars; three scales along side of tail for each two median ventral caudal scales; translucent disc in lower eyelid divided into sections by vertical grooves---------------------------------------apodemus
Frontonasal-frontal area with regular scales; one series of supraoculars; usually two scales along side of tail for each two median ventral caudal scales; translucent disc in lower eyelid rarely divided----------------ecpleopus

5. Tímpano no hundido; tubérculos si están presentes en hileras regulares o irregulares; si los tubérculos están presentes las escamas laterales son heterogéneas; cola 1,4 to 2,1 veces la longitud del cuerpo-----------------6
Tímpano ligeramente hundido; escamas dorsales ensanchadas en el cuerpo en cuatro hileras regulares; escamas laterales uniformes, pequeñas; no hay tubérculos a los lados de la cabeza; cola corta, 1,1 to 1,5 veces la longitud del cuerpo; orificio nasal rodeado de manchas negras o castañas------------cochranae

6. Escamas nucales supralaterales cónicas formando una o más hileras longitudinales de tubérculos; dos a cinco preanales posteriores-----7
Escamas nucales supralaterales pequeñas, uniformes no forman hileras longitudinales; dos preanales posteriores anchas; ausencia de áreas claras conspícuas en las extremidades anteriores-----------------------strangulatus

7. Area frontonasal y frontal con escamas irregulares; dos series de supraoculares; tres escamas a lo largo de los lados de la cola por cada dos escamas caudales medioventrales; disco transparente ocular dividido en secciones por surcos verticales-------apodemus
Area frontonasal y frontal con escamas regulares; una serie de supraoculares; usualmente dos escamas a lo largo de los lados de la cola por cada dos escamas caudales medioventrales; disco transparente ocular raramente dividido-----------------------ecpleopus

NEUSTICURUS APODEMUS Uzzell

1966 Neusticurus apodemus Uzzell, Bull. Amer. Mus. Nat. Hist., 132: 298, figs. 3-4. Type-locality: San Isidro del General, San José, Costa Rica, 865 m.

Distribution: Known only from type-locality.

NEUSTICURUS BICARINATUS (Linnaeus)

1758 Lacerta bicarinata Linnaeus, Systema Naturae, Ed. 10: 201. Type-locality: "Indiis."
1839 Neusticurus bicarinatus—Duméril and Bibron, Erp. Gén., 5: 64.
1966 Neusticurus bicarinatus—Uzzell, Bull. Amer. Mus. Nat. Hist., 132: 281.

Distribution: Guyana; eastern Venezuela; Estado do Pará and Estado de Rondônia, Brazil.

NEUSTICURUS COCHRANAE Burt and Burt

1931 Neusticurus ecpleopus cochranae Burt and Burt, Bull. Amer. Mus. Nat. Hist., 61: 350. Type-locality: San José de Sumaco, Ecuador.
1966 Neusticurus cochranae—Uzzell, Bull. Amer. Mus. Nat. Hist., 32: 307.

Distribution: Amazonian lowlands of northern Ecuador.

NEUSTICURUS ECPLEOPUS Cope

1876 <u>Neusticurus</u> <u>ecpleopus</u> Cope, Jour. Acad. Nat. Sci. Phila., (2) 8 (1875): 161. Type-locality: Peru; according to Uzzell, Bull. Amer. Mus. Nat. Hist., 132, 1966, 290, probably in drainage of Río Huallaga, between Rioja, Moyobamba, Balsaspuerto, and exit of Huallaga into Amazon Basin.
1930 <u>Neusticurus</u> <u>ocellatus</u> Sinitsin, Amer. Mus. Novitates, 408: 1. Type-locality: Rurrenabaque, Bolivia.
1935 <u>Neusticurus</u> <u>tuberculatus</u> Shreve, Occ. Pap. Boston Soc. Nat. Hist., 8: 209. Type-locality: Sarayacu, Ecuador.
1966 <u>Neusticurus</u> <u>ecpleopus</u>—Uzzell, Bull. Amer. Mus. Nat. Hist., 132: 290.

Distribution: Eastern slopes of Andes from southern Colombia to central Bolivia; Territorio do Acre and Estado do Amazonas, Brazil.

NEUSTICURUS RACENISI Roze

1958 <u>Neusticurus</u> <u>racenisi</u> Roze, Acta Biol. Venezuelica, 2: 252. Type-locality: Auyantepuí, Estado Bolivar, Venezuela.

Distribution: Known only from type locality.

NEUSTICURUS RUDIS Boulenger

1900 <u>Neusticurus</u> <u>rudis</u> Boulenger, Trans. Linnaean Soc. London, (2) 8: 53. Type-locality: Foot of Mount Roraima, Guyana, 1050 m.
1923 <u>Neusticurus</u> <u>surinamensis</u> Müller, Zool. Anz., 58: 295. Type-locality: Albina, near mouth of Maroni River, Surinam.
1927 <u>Neusticurus</u> <u>dejongi</u> Brongersma, Ann. Mag. Nat. Hist., (9) 20: 543. Type-locality: Surinam.
1966 <u>Neusticurus</u> <u>rudis</u>—Uzzell, Bull. Amer. Mus. Nat. Hist., 132: 286.

Distribution: Guyana, Surinam, and extreme eastern Venezuela.

NEUSTICURUS STRANGULATUS (Cope)

1868 <u>Euspondylus</u> <u>strangulatus</u> Cope, Proc. Acad. Nat. Sci. Phila., 1868: 99. Type-locality: Ecuador; according to Uzzell (below) probably either between Papallacta and Napo, or along Río Napo, before it joins Río Marañón, in Ecuador or Peru.
1966 <u>Neusticurus</u> <u>strangulatus</u>—Uzzell, Bull. Amer. Mus. Nat. Hist., 132: 302.

Distribution: Amazonian slopes of Andes, Ecuador and Peru.

Content: Two subspecies.

Key to the subspecies	Clave de subespecies

1. Tubercles absent---------------<u>strangulatus</u>
    Tubercles present----------------<u>trachodus</u>
	1. Tubérculos ausentes------------<u>strangulatus</u>
	    Tubérculos presentes-------------<u>trachodus</u>

<u>Neusticurus strangulatus strangulatus</u> (Cope)

1897 <u>Euspondilus</u> <u>Festae</u> Peracca, Boll. Mus. Zool. Comp. Anat. Univ. Torino, 12 (300): 10. Type-locality: Valley of Río Zamora and Río Santiago, Ecuador.
1966 <u>Neusticurus</u> <u>strangulatus</u> <u>strangulatus</u>—Uzzell, Bull. Amer. Mus. Nat. Hist., 132: 302.

Distribution: Amazonian slopes in Ecuador and northern Peru.

<u>Neusticurus strangulatus trachodus</u> Uzzell

1966 <u>Neusticurus</u> <u>strangulatus</u> <u>trachodus</u> Uzzell, Bull. Amer. Mus. Nat. Hist., 32: 305. Type-locality: Divisoria (=Cordillera Azul), Huánuco, Peru, 1300-1600 m.

Distribution: Departamento de Huánuco, in Andes of Central Peru, between 750 and 1600 m.

NEUSTICURUS TATEI (Burt and Burt)

1931 Arthrosaura tatei Burt and Burt, Bull. Amer. Mus. Nat. Hist., 61: 313. Type-locality: Vegas
        Falls, 15 mi north of Esmeraldas, Venezuela, 1400 m.
1966 Neusticurus tatei—Uzzell, Bull. Amer. Mus. Nat. Hist., 132: 283.

    Distribution: Highlands of Estado Bolívar and Territorio Federal de Amazonas, Venezuela, as well
        as neighboring Brazil, 400 to 1400 m.

OPHIODES Wagler

> 1828 <u>Ophiodes</u> Wagler, Isis von Oken, 21: 740. Type-species: <u>Pygopus striatus</u> Spix.
>
> Distribution: Brazil, Bolivia, Paraguay, Uruguay and Argentina.
>
> Content: Four species.

Key to the species

1. Supralabials with black bars------------------2
   Supralabials immaculate-------------<u>vertebralis</u>

2. Fewer than 21 dorsal scales in head length; fewer than 147 scales between nape and anus; nasal scale not smaller than second supralabial; nostril in posterior **border** of **nasal** scale; fewer than four postmentals in contact with infralabials-------------------------------3
   Head length includes 21 dorsal scales; 147 scales between nape and anus; nasal scale smaller than second supralabial; nostril in middle of nasal scale; four postmentals in contact with infralabials----------<u>intermedius</u>

3. Head length includes 14-15 dorsal scales; hind leg shorter than or equal to eye-snout distance; dorsal longitudinal lines distinct---------------------------------------<u>striatus</u>
   Head length includes 18 dorsal scales; hind leg longer than eye-snout distance; dorsal longitudinal lines indistinct--------------<u>yacupoi</u>

Clave de especies

1. Supralabiales con barritas negras--------------2
   Supralabiales inmaculados------------<u>vertebralis</u>

2. Longitud cefálica menos que 21 escamas dorsales; menos de 147 escamas entre nuca y ano; escama nasal no menor que segunda supralabial; narina en el borde posterior del nasal; menos de cuatro posmentales contactando con los infralabiales-----------------------------------3
   Longitud cefálica igual a 21 escamas dorsales; 147 escamas entre nuca y ano; nasal menor que segunda supralabial; narina al medio del nasal; cuatro posmentales contactan con los infralabiales---------------------------<u>intermedius</u>

3. Longitude cefálica igual a 14-15 escamas dorsales; extremidad posterior más corta o igual que la distancia ojo-hocico; líneas longitudinales dorsales distintas------<u>striatus</u>
   Longitud cefálica igual a 18 escamas dorsales; extremidad posterior más larga que la distancia ojo-hocico; líneas longitudinales dorsales indistintas----------------------<u>yacupoi</u>

OPHIODES <u>INTERMEDIUS</u> Boulenger

> 1894 <u>Ophiodes intermedius</u> Boulenger, Ann. Mag. Nat. Hist., (6) 13: 343. Type-locality: Near Asunción, Paraguay.
>
> 1966 <u>Ophiodes intermedius</u>—Gallardo, Rev. Mus. Argentino Cienc. Nat. "Bernardino Rivadavia", 9: 134, fig. 5.
>
> Distribution: Bolivia and Paraguay to Chubut, western Argentina.

OPHIODES <u>STRIATUS</u> (Spix)

> 1824 <u>Pygopus striatus</u> Spix, Spec. Nov. Lac. Bras.: 25, pl. 28, fig. 1. Type-locality: Rio de Janeiro, Brazil.
> 1824 <u>Pygopus cariococca</u> Spix, Spec. Nov. Lac. Bras.: 26, pl. 28, fig. 2. Type-locality: Cariococca, Corcovado Mountain, Rio de Janeiro, Brazil.
> 1828 <u>Ophiodes striatus</u>—Wagler, Isis von Oken, 21: 740.
> 1913 <u>Ophiodes grilli</u> Boulenger, Ann. Mus. Civ. Stor. Nat. Genova, (3) 6: 49. Type-locality: Curityba, Parana, Brazil.
>
> Distribution: Northern Argentina, Uruguay and Brazil.

OPHIODES <u>VERTEBRALIS</u> Bocourt

> 1881 <u>Ophiodes vertebralis</u> Bocourt, Miss. Sci. Mex., Rept.: 459, **pl.** 22, figs. 3-3e. Type locality: southern Brazil and Uruguay.
> 1966 <u>Ophiodes vertebralis</u>—Gallardo, Rev. Mus. Argentino Cienc. Nat. "Bernardino Rivadavia", 9: 128, fig. 3.
>
> Distribution: Argentina, Uruguay and southern Brazil.

OPHIODES YACUPOI Gallardo

   1966 Ophiodes yacupoi Gallardo, Rev. Mus. Argentino Cienc. Nat. "Bernardino Rivadavia", 9: 139, fig. 6.
       Type-locality: Yerbal San Martín, Puerto Libertad, Misiones, Argentina.

   Distribution: From Misiones, Argentina to Mato Grosso, Brazil.

OPHIOGNOMON Cope

1868 Ophiognomon Cope, Proc. Acad. Nat. Sci. Phila., 1868: 100. Type-species: Ophiognomon trisanale
Cope.
1871 Hapalolepis Peters, Monats. Akad. Wiss. Berlin, 1871: 399. Type-species: Chalcides (Hapalolepis)
Abendrothii Peters.
1874 Propus Cope (preoccupied by Propus Oken, 1816), Proc. Acad. Nat. Sci. Phila., 1874: 70.
Type-species: Propus vermiformis Cope.

Distribution: Western part of Amazonian basin in Ecuador and Peru.

Content: Three species.

Key to the species

1. Forelegs present--------------------------------2
Forelegs absent----------------------vermiformis

2. Fewer than 38 body annuli between axilla and
groin; hind leg same length as preanal
scale---------------------------------trisanale
More than 40 body annuli between axilla and
groin; hind leg reduced to minute tubercle----
----------------------------------abendrothii

1. Extremidad anterior presente------------------2
Extremidad anterior ausente---------vermiformis

2. Menos de 38 anillos corporales entre extremidad
anterior y posterior; extremidad posterior de
longitud igual al escudo preanal-----trisanale
Más de 40 anillos corporales entre extremidad
anterior y posterior; extremidad posterior reducida a un tubérculo-------------abendrothii

OPHIOGNOMON ABENDROTHII (Peters)

1871 Chalcides (Hapalolepis) Abendrothii Peters, Monats. Akad. Wiss. Berlin, 1871: 399. Type-
locality: Sarayacu, Peru.
1885 Ophiognomon abendrothii—Boulenger, Cat. Liz. Brit. Mus., 2: 421.
1961 Ophiognomon abendrothii—Vanzolini, Pap. Avul. Dept. Zool. São Paulo, 14: 249, figs.

Distribution: Amazonian lowlands of Ecuador and Peru.

OPHIOGNOMON TRISANALE Cope

1868 Ophiognomon trisanale Cope, Proc. Acad. Nat. Sci. Phila., 1868: 100. Type-locality: Napo or
Alto Marañon, Ecuador.
1961 Ophiognomon trisanale—Vanzolini, Pap. Avul. Dept. Zool. São Paulo, 14: 250.

Distribution: Amazonian Ecuador.

OPHIOGNOMON VERMIFORMIS (Cope)

1874 Propus vermiformis Cope, Proc. Acad. Nat. Sci. Phila., 1874: 70. Type-locality: Nauta,
Amazonian Peru.
1885 Ophiognomon vermiforme—Boulenger, Cat. Liz. Brit. Mus., 2: 421.

Distribution: Amazonian Peru.

Prepared by Richard Etheridge, San Diego State College, San Diego, California

OPHRYOESSOIDES Duméril

1845 *Eulophus* Tschudi (preoccupied by *Eulophus* Geoffrey, 1762), Arch. für Naturg., 11: 154. Type-species: *Steironotus (Eulophus) arenarius* Tschudi.
1851 *Ophryoessoides* Duméril, Cat. Méth. Coll. Rept. Mus. Paris: 66. Type-species: *Ophryoessoides tricristatus* Duméril.
1856 *Brachysaurus* Hallowell, Proc. Acad. Nat. Sci. Phila., 1856: 232. Type-species: *Brachysaurus erythrogaster* Hallowell.
1862 *Scartiscus* Cope, Proc. Acad. Nat. Sci. Phila., 1862: 182. Type-species: *Scartiscus caducus* Cope.

Distribution: Andes region of Colombia, Ecuador, Peru and Bolivia; also known from Brazil and Paraguay.

Content: Fourteen species.

Key to the species

1. Ventral scales sharply keeled, equal to or even more sharply keeled than dorsal scales-------2
Ventral scales smooth or weakly keeled; if keeled, much less strongly keeled than dorsal scales--------------------------------------5

2. No very large scales in occipital region; all head scales keeled--------------------------3
Two or three very large, smooth scales in occipital region posterior to orbits-aculeatus

3. Fewer than 55 paravertebral scales; fewer than 50 midbody scales--------------------------4
More than 55 paravertebral scales from occiput to anterior margin of thigh; more than 50 scales around midbody--------------scapularis

4. No projecting superciliaries; tail more than twice as long as head and body--------caducus
Superciliaries projecting at posterolateral corner of orbit; tail less than twice length of head and body------------------tricristatus

5. Supraoculars broadly dilated------------------6
Supraoculars not broadly dilated--------------7

6. Four broadly dilated supraoculars------formosus
Six broadly dilated supraoculars-------haenschi

7. Fewer than 80 paravertebral scales------------8
More than 80 paravertebral scales-----arenarius

8. No very large scales in occipital region, scales on top of head keeled----------------9
Two or three very large, smooth scales in occipital region--------------------iridescens

9. Ventrals weakly keeled----------------------10
Ventrals smooth----------------------------11

10. More than 40 scales around midbody-------------
------------------------------trachycephalus
Fewer than 40 scales around midbody-----------
--------------------------------erythrogaster

11. Fewer than 60 scales around middle of body--12
More than 60 scales around middle of body-----
--------------------------------------guentheri

Clave de especies

1. Escamas ventrales agudamente quilladas, iguales o más quilladas que las dorsales-------------2
Escamas ventrales lisas o débilmente quilladas, si son quilladas lo son mucho menos que las dorsales--------------------------------------5

2. Sin escamas grandes en la región occipital; todas las escamas de la cabeza son quilladas-3
Dos o tres escamas grandes lisas en la región occipital posterior a la órbita------aculeatus

3. Menos de 55 escamas paravertebrales; menos de 50 escamas alrededor del cuerpo--------------4
Más de 55 escamas paravertebrales desde el occipucio al margen anterior del muslo; más de 50 escamas alrededor del cuerpo-----scapularis

4. Superciliares no se proyectan; cola más del doble del largo de la cabeza y el cuerpo------
--caducus
Superciliares se proyectan al ángulo postero-lateral de la órbita; cola menos del doble del largo de la cabeza y el cuerpo----tricristatus

5. Supraoculares dilatadas anchamente------------6
Supraoculares no dilatadas--------------------7

6. Cuatro supraoculares dilatadas---------formosus
Seis supraoculares dilatadas----------haenschi

7. Menos de 80 escamas paravertebrales-----------8
Más de 80 escamas paravertebrales-----arenarius

8. Región occipital sin escamas grandes; escamas de la parte superior de la cabeza quilladas--9
Dos o tres escamas lisas muy grandes en la región occipital--------------------iridescens

9. Ventrales débilmente quilladas---------------10
Ventrales lisas----------------------------11

10. Más de 40 escamas alrededor del medio cuerpo---
--------------------------------trachycephalus
Menos de 40 escamas alrededor del medio cuerpo-
--------------------------------erythrogaster

11. Menos de 60 escamas alrededor del medio cuerpo
---12
Más de 60 escamas alrededor del medio cuerpo--
--------------------------------------guentheri

12. Sides of belly black; small postfemoral and
    postaxillary dermal pouches-----------------13
    Sides of belly red or pink; large postfemoral
    and postaxillary dermal pouches-----_rhodomelas_

13. More than 46 scales around body----------_festae_
    Fewer than 47 scales around body--------_ornatus_

12. Lados del abdomen negros; bolsas dermales post-
    femorales y postaxilares pequeñas-----------13
    Lados del abdomen rojos o rosados; bolsas der-
    males postfemorales y postaxilares grandes----
    -----------------------------------_rhodomelas_

13. Más de 46 escamas alrededor del medio cuerpo---
    ---_festae_
    Menos de 47 escamas alrededor del medio cuerpo-
    ---_ornatus_

OPHRYOESSOIDES ACULEATUS (O'Shaughnessy)

1879 _Leiocephalus aculeatus_ O'Shaughnessy, Ann. Mag. Nat. Hist., (5) 4: 303. Type-locality:
     Moyobamba, Peru.
1901 _Liocephalus angulifer_ Werner, Verh. Zool.-Bot. Ges. Wien, 51: 595. Type-locality: Ecuador.
1966 [_Ophryoessoides_] _aculeatus_—Etheridge, Copeia, 1966: 88.

   Distribution: Amazonian slopes of Ecuador and Peru.

OPHRYOESSOIDES ARENARIUS (Tschudi)

1845 _Steironotus_ (_Eulophus_) _arenarius_ Tschudi, Arch. für Naturg., 11: 154. Type-locality: Peru; given
     as Huacho, north of Lima, Peru, by Tschudi, Fauna Peruana, Herp., 1846, 26.
1901 _Liocephalus rhodogaster_ Boulenger, Ann. Mag. Nat. Hist.., (7) 7: 547. Type-locality: Merced,
     Río Perené, Peru, 3250 ft.
1901 _Liocephalus lineogularis_ Werner, Abh. Ber. K. Zool. Anthro.-Ethn. Mus. Dresden, 9 (2): 3. Type-
     locality: Chanchamayo, Peru.
1966 [_Ophryoessoides_] _arenarius_—Etheridge, Copeia, 1966: 88.

   Distribution: Peru.

OPHRYOESSOIDES CADUCUS (Cope)

1862 _Scartiscus caducus_ Cope, Proc. Acad. Nat. Sci. Phila., 1862: 182. Type-locality: Paraguay.
1890 _Liocephalus bolivianus_ Boulenger, Proc. Zool. Soc. London, 1890: 82, pl. 9. Type-locality:
     Bolivia.
1910 _Scartiscus liocephaloides_ Werner, Mitt. Naturhist. Mus. Hamburg, 27 (2): 23. Type-locality:
     Paraguay.
1966 [_Ophryoessoides_] _caducus_—Etheridge, Copeia, 1966: 88.

   Distribution: Bolivia, Paraguay, and Mato Grosso, Brazil.

OPHRYOESSOIDES ERYTHROGASTER Hallowell

1856 _Brachysaurus erythrogaster_ Hallowell, Proc. Acad. Nat. Sci. Phila., 1856: 232. Type-locality:
     New Grenada.
1966 [_Ophryoessoides_] _erythrogaster_—Etheridge, Copeia, 1966: 88.

   Distribution: Sierra do Santa Marta and northern Andean highlands of Colombia.

OPHRYOESSOIDES FESTAE (Peracca)

1897 _Leiocephalus Festae_ Peracca, Bol. Mus. Zool. Comp. Anat. Univ. Torino, 12 (300): 6, fig. Type-
     locality: Cuenca, Ecuador.
1966 [_Ophryoessoides_] _festae_—Etheridge, Copeia, 1966: 88.

   Distribution: Inter-Andean plateau in Cuenca valley, Ecuador.

OPHRYOESSOIDES FORMOSUS (Boulenger)

  1880 Liocephalus formosus Boulenger, Bull. Soc. Zool. France, 1880: 43. Type-locality: Andes of
      Ecuador.
  1966 [Ophryoessoides] formosus—Etheridge, Copeia, 1966: 88.

    Distribution: Still known only from type specimen.

OPHRYOESSOIDES GUENTHERI (Boulenger)

  1885 Liocephalus guentheri Boulenger, Cat. Liz. Brit. Mus., 2: 169, pl. 13. Type-locality: Guayaquil
      and Sarayacu, Ecuador, and a questioned specimen from Colombia.
  1966 [Ophryoessoides] guentheri—Etheridge, Copeia, 1966: 88.

    Distribution: Apparently confined to inter-Andean plateau in Ecuador.

OPHRYOESSOIDES HAENSCHI (Werner)

  1901 Liocephalus haenschi Werner, Verh. Zool.-Bot. Ges. Wien, 51: 595. Type-locality: Balzapamba,
      Ecuador.
  1933 Leiocephalus haenchi—Burt and Burt (in error for haenschi), Trans. Acad. Sci. St. Louis, 28: 27.
  1966 [Ophryoessoides] haenschi—Etheridge, Copeia, 1966: 88.

    Distribution: Known only from type locality.

OPHRYOESSOIDES IRIDESCENS (Günther)

  1859 Liocephalus iridescens Günther, Proc. Zool. Soc. London, 1859: 409, pl. 20, fig. B. Type-
      locality: Andes of Ecuador.
  1966 [Ophryoessoides] iridescens—Etheridge, Copeia, 1966: 88.

    Distribution: Guayaquil to El Oro Province, in drier coastal areas of Ecuador.

OPHRYOESSOIDES ORNATUS (Gray)

  1845 Leiocephalus ornatus Gray, Cat. Liz. Brit. Mus.: 219. Type-locality: Guayaquil, Ecuador.
  1966 [Ophryoessoides] ornatus—Etheridge, Copeia, 1966: 88.

    Distribution: West coast of Ecuador; northern coast of Peru.

OPHRYOESSOIDES RHODOMELAS (Boulenger)

  1899 Liocephalus rhodomelas Boulenger, Ann. Mag. Nat. Hist., (7) 4: 455. Type-locality: Oña, Ecuador,
      6500 ft.
  1966 [Ophryoessoides] rhodomelas—Etheridge, Copeia, 1966: 88.

    Distribution: Inter-Andean plateaus of southern Ecuador.

OPHRYOESSOIDES SCAPULARIS (Boulenger)

  1901 Liocephalus scapularis Boulenger, Ann. Mag. Nat. Hist., (7) 7: 548. Type-locality: Perené, Peru,
      2600 ft.
  1966 [Ophryoessoides] scapularis—Etheridge, Copeia, 1966: 89.

    Distribution: Amazonian slopes of Peru.

OPHRYOESSOIDES TRACHYCEPHALUS (Duméril)

  1851 [Holotropis] Trachycephalus Duméril, Cat. Méth. Coll. Rept. Mus. Paris: 70. Type-locality: Santa
      Fé de Bogotá, Colombia.
  1966 [Ophryoessoides] trachycephalus—Etheridge, Copeia, 1966: 89.

    Distribution: Highlands of eastern Andes of Colombia.

OPHRYOESSOIDES TRICRISTATUS Duméril

1851 Ophryoessoides Tricristatus Duméril, Cat. Méth. Coll. Rept. Mus. Paris: 66. Type-locality: Brazil.
1869 Ophryoessoides Dumerilii Steindachner, Reise der Österreichischen Fregatte Novara, Zool., Rept.: 33, pl. 2, fig. 5. Type-locality: Pará, Brazil.
1966 Ophryoessoides tricristatus—Etheridge, Copeia, 1966: 88.

Distribution: Western Brazil.

REPTILIA: SAURIA: TEIIDAE  OPIPEUTER

Prepared by Thomas Uzzell, Yale University, New Haven, Connecticut

<u>OPIPEUTER</u> Uzzell

> 1969 <u>Opipeuter</u> Uzzell, Postilla, 129: 3. Type-species: <u>Opipeuter</u> <u>xestus</u> Uzzell.
>
> Distribution: As for only known species.
>
> Content: One species.

<u>OPIPEUTER</u> <u>XESTUS</u> Uzzell

> 1969 <u>Opipeuter</u> <u>xestus</u> Uzzell, Postilla, 129: 4. Type-locality: Incachaca, Cochabamba, Bolivia 2200 m.
>
> Distribution: Eastern Andean slopes of central Bolivia, headwaters of Río Chapare between 1000 and 3000 m.

PANTODACTYLUS Duméril and Bibron

   1839 Pantodactylus Duméril and Bibron, Erp. Gén., 5: 428. Type-species: Pantodactylus d'Orbignyi
       Duméril and Bibron.

   Distribution: South America east of Andes and below 10° S.

   Content: Two species, according to most recent revision by Ruibal, Bull. Mus. Comp. Zool., 106,
      1952.

             Key to the species   Clave de especies

1. Males with fewer than 8/8 femoral pores; two   1. Machos con menos de 8/8 poros femorales; dos
   preanal scales--------------------schreibersi   escamas preanales------------------schreibersi
   Males with 8/8 femoral pores or more; three   Machos con 8/8 poros femorales o más; tres
   preanal scales-----------------quadrilineatus   escamas preanales--------------quadrilineatus

PANTODACTYLUS QUADRILINEATUS (Boettger)

   1876 Cercosaura (Pantodactylus) quadrilineatus Boettger, Ber. Senckenbergischen Naturforsch. Ges.,
       1876: 141. Type-locality: São Paulo, Brazil.
   1948 Pantodactylus femoralis Vanzolini, Pap. Avul. Depto. Zool., São Paulo, 8: 337, fig. Type-
       locality: Mariana, Estado de Minas Gerais, Brazil.
   1952 Pantodactylus quadrilineatus—Ruibal, Bull. Mus. Comp. Zool., 106: 513.

   Distribution: São Paulo, Minas Gerais, and Rio de Janeiro, Brazil.

PANTODACTYLUS SCHREIBERSII Wiegmann

   1834 Cercosaurus Schreibersii Wiegmann, Herpetologia Mexicana: 10. Type-locality: Brazil.
   1885 Pantodactylus schreibersii—Boulenger, Cat. Liz. Brit. Mus., 2: 358.

   Distribution: Argentina, Uruguay, Paraguay, Bolivia, southern Brazil, and southeastern Peru.

   Content: Three subspecies, according to revision by Ruibal, 1952.

             Key to the subspecies   Clave de subespecies

1. Lateral white stripe originating below eye,   1. Cinta lateral blanca, originada bajo el
   passing through lower half of ear and   ojo, que pasa por debajo del medio del
   above forelimb-----------------------2   oído y encima de la extremidad anterior--2
   No lateral white stripe; overall color gray   Sin cinta lateral; dorsal color gris o
   or black; usually with dorsolateral white   negruzco; usualmente con una cinta
   stripe----------------------schreibersii   blanca dorso lateral----------schreibersii

2. Some dorsal scales black-tipped and   2. Algunas manchas del punteado negro dorsal
   arranged to form irregular vertebral and   se disponen formando líneas longitudinales
   paravertebral longitudinal stripes;   irregulares que corren vertebral y para-
   females with 0/0 or 1/1 femoral pores-----   vertebralmente; hembras con 0/0 a 1/1
   ----------------------------albostrigatus   poros femorales--------------albostrigatus
   Color pattern not as above; females with   Diseño no como el anterior; hembras con 2/2
   2/2 or 3/3 femoral pores-----------parkeri   o 3/3 poros femorales-------------parkeri

   Pantodactylus schreibersii schreibersii (Wiegmann)

      1839 Pantodactylus d'Orbignyi Duméril and Bibron, Erp. Gén., 5: 431. Type-locality: Buenos
          Aires, Argentina.
      1863 Pantodactylus bivittatus Cope, Proc. Acad. Nat. Sci. Phila., 1863: 103. Type-locality:
          Paysandú, Uruguay.
      1894 Pantodactylus Borellii Peracca, Boll. Mus. Zool. Comp. Anat. Univ. Torino, 9 (176): 1.
          Type-locality: Colonia Apa, alto río Paraguay, Paraguay.
      1952 Pantodactylus schreibersii schreibersii—Ruibal, Bull. Mus. Comp. Zool., 106: 515.

      Distribution: Northern Argentina, Uruguay, Paraguay and southern Brazil.

Pantodactylus schreibersii albostrigatus (Griffin)

1917 Prionodactylus albostrigatus Griffin, Ann. Carnegie Mus., 11: 314, pl. 34. Type-locality: Sete Lagoas, Estado de Minas Gerais, Brazil.
1952 Prionodactylus schreibersii albostrigatus—Ruibal, Bull. Mus. Comp. Zool., 106: 517.

Distribution: Estado de Minas Gerais to Estado de Mato Grosso, Brazil.

Pantodactylus schreibersii parkeri Ruibal

1952 Pantodactylus schreibersii parkeri Ruibal, Bull. Mus. Comp. Zool., 106: 518. Type-locality: Buenavista, Departamento de Santa Cruz, Bolivia.

Distribution: Amazonian Bolivia, southeastern lowlands of Peru, and Mato Grosso, Brazil.

PHENACOSAURUS Barbour

1920 <u>Phenacosaurus</u> Barbour, Proc. New England Zool. Club, 7: 62. Type-species: <u>Anolis heterodermus</u> Duméril.

Distribution: Mountainous areas of Colombia.

Content: Three species.

Comment: A revision soon to be published by James Lazell will change this genus considerably.

Key to the species

1. Single row of scales in dorsal crest, best developed on nape of neck------------------2
Two rows of pointed scales in dorsal crest--------------------------------<u>heterodermus</u>

2. No granules in dorsal scalation, some scales larger than others but never as much as twice as large---------------------------<u>nicefori</u>
Large, flat scales in dorsal scalation completely separated from one another by much smaller scales, granules, and even naked skin --------------------------------------<u>richteri</u>

Clave de especies

1. Una sola hilera de escamas en la cresta dorsal, con máximo desarrollo en la nuca-------------2
Dos hileras de escamas puntudas en la cresta dorsal---------------------------<u>heterodermus</u>

2. Escamas dorsales sin gránulos, algunas escamas mayores que otras pero nunca el doble de tamaño---------------------------------<u>nicefori</u>
Escamas dorsales grandes planas completamente separadas entre sí por escamas mucho más chicas, gránulos y aun piel desnuda------------ --------------------------------------<u>richteri</u>

PHENACOSAURUS HETERODERMUS (Duméril)

1851 A.[<u>nolis</u>] <u>heterodermus</u> Duméril, Cat. Meth. Coll. Rept. Mus. Hist. Nat. Paris: 59. Type-locality: Colombia.
1920 [<u>Phenacosaurus</u>] <u>heterodermus</u>—Barbour, Proc. New England Zool. Club, 7: 62.
1949 <u>Phenacosaurus paramoensis</u> Hellmich, Deutsche Aquar.-Zeits., 2: 105, fig. Type-locality: Paramo de Sumapaz, Colombia, 3750 m.
1969 <u>Phenacosaurus heterodermus</u>—Marinkelle, Lacerta, 27: 37, figs.

Distribution: Cundinamarca and Boyaca, Colombia.

PHENACOSAURUS NICEFORI Dunn

1944 <u>Phenacosaurus nicefori</u> Dunn, Caldasia, 3 (11): 59, fig. Type-locality: Vicinity of Pamplona, Norte de Santander, Colombia, 2340 m.

Distribution: Norte de Santander, Colombia and Sierra de Perija, Venezuela.

PHENACOSAURUS RICHTERI Dunn

1944 <u>Phenacosaurus richteri</u> Dunn, Caldasia, 3 (11): 60, fig. Type-locality: Tabio, Cundinamarca, Colombia, 2645 m.

Distribution: Cundinamarca, Caldas, and possibly Antioquia, Colombia.

PHOLIDOBOLUS Peters

    1862 Pholidobolus Peters, Abh. Akad. Wiss. Berlin, 1862: 195. Type-species: Ecpleopus (Pholidobolus)
         montium Peters.

    Distribution: Interandean Peru and Ecuador.

    Content: Two species.

                    Key to the species   Clave de especies

    1. Prefrontal absent---------------------montium   1. Prefrontal ausente---------------------montium
       Prefrontal rudimentary----------------anomalus   Prefrontal rudimentario---------------anomalus

PHOLIDOBOLUS ANOMALUS Müller

    1923 Pholidobolus anomalus Müller, Zool. Anz., 57: 52. Type-locality: Cuzco, Peru.

    Distribution: Known only from type locality.

PHOLIDOBOLUS MONTIUM (Peters)

    1862 Ecpleopus (Pholidobolus) montium Peters, Abh. Akad. Wiss. Berlin,1862: 196, pl. 2, fig. 3.
         Type-locality: Quito, Ecuador.
    1885 Pholidobolus montium—Boulenger, Cat. Liz. Brit. Mus., 2: 403.

    Distribution: Interandean Ecuador.

PHRYNOSAURA Werner

1907 <u>Phrynosaura</u> Werner, in Bürger, An. Univ. Chile, 121: 151. Type-species: <u>Phrynosaura</u>
    <u>reichei</u> Werner.

Distribution: Northern Chile and western Argentina, possibly desert areas of southern Peru.

Content: Three species.

	Clave de especies

Key to the species

1. One row of scales between subocular and supra-
   labials--2
   Two rows of scales between subocular and supra-
   labials--------------------------------<u>werneri</u>

2. Ventral scales on tail keeled; eleven supra-
   labials-----------------------------<u>marmoratus</u>
   Ventral scales on tail smooth; six supra-
   labials--------------------------------<u>reichei</u>

Clave de especies

1. Una fila de escamas entre subocular y supra-
   labiales---------------------------------------2
   Dos filas de escamas entre subocular y supra-
   labiales-------------------------------<u>werneri</u>

2. Escamas ventrales de la cola quilladas; once
   supralabiales----------------------<u>marmoratus</u>
   Escamas ventrales de la cola lisas; seis
   supralabiales-------------------------<u>reichei</u>

PHRYNOSAURA <u>MARMORATA</u> (Burmeister)

1861 <u>Leiosaurus</u> <u>marmoratus</u> Burmeister, Reise durch die La Plata-Staaten, 2: 524. Type-locality:
    Quebrada de la Troya, north of Anillaco; also Alpaquinche and Anapa, west of Catamarca; all in
    Provincia Catamarca, Argentina.
1928 <u>Phrynosaura</u> <u>marmorata</u>—Müller, Zool. Anz., 77: 62.

Distribution: Desert and arid areas of Catamarca, Argentina.

PHRYNOSAURA <u>REICHEI</u> Werner

1907 <u>Phrynosaura</u> <u>reichei</u> Werner, in Bürger, An. Univ. Chile, 121: 151, pl. 1, figs. 2a-b. Type-
    locality: Iquique, Chile.

Distribution: Desert of Antofagasta and Tarapaca, Chile; probably deserts of southern Peru.

PHRYNOSAURA <u>WERNERI</u> Müller

1928 <u>Phrynosaura</u> <u>werneri</u> Müller, Zool. Anz., 77: 64. Type-locality: Unknown.
1966 <u>Liolaemus</u> <u>lentus</u> Gallardo, Neotropica, 12 (37): 17, fig. 1. Type-locality: Altos de Cochico,
    Puelen, La Pampa, Argentina.

Distribution: Salitral de Cochica, La Pampa, Argentina.

PHYLLODACTYLUS Gray

1828 <u>Phyllodactylus</u> Gray, Spicileg. Zool.: 3. Type-species: <u>Phyllodactylus</u> <u>pulcher</u> Gray.
1843 <u>Euleptes</u> Fitzinger, Systema Reptilium: 95. Type-species: <u>Euleptes</u> <u>wagleri</u> Fitzinger =
   <u>Phyllodactylus</u> <u>europaeus</u> Gené.
1843 <u>Discodactylus</u> Fitzinger (preoccupied by <u>Discodactylus</u> Wagler, 1833), Systema Reptilium: 95.
   Type-species: <u>Phyllodactylus</u> <u>tuberculosus</u> Wiegmann.
1845 <u>Gerrhopygus</u> Gray, Cat. Spec. Liz. Coll. Brit. Mus.: 150. Type-species: <u>Diplodactylus</u>
   <u>gerrhopygus</u> Wiegmann.
1879 <u>Paroedura</u> Günther, Ann. Mag. Nat. Hist., (5) 3: 217. Type-species: <u>Paroedura</u> <u>sancti</u> <u>johannis</u>
   (sic) Günther.

   Distribution: Southern Europe, southwestern Asia, Africa, Madagascar, Australia, Oceania and
      North, Central, and South America.

   Content: About 60 species, all but fourteen of which are extralimital. <u>Phyllodactylus</u>
      <u>albogutattus</u> Boulenger, as listed in Wermuth, Das Tierreich, 80, 1965, 133, is an erroneous
      reference to <u>Phyllobates</u> <u>alboguttatus</u> Boulenger, 1903, a frog species.

Key to the species

1. Preanal plate enlarged, clearly distinguishable; all dorsal scales equal in size, no
   tubercles on dorsum------------------------2
   Preanal scales same size as surrounding scales;
   dorsal scales alternate with tubercles-------3

2. A double row of lateral, enlarged tubercles on
   tail--------------------------------<u>heterurus</u>
   No tubercles on tail---------------<u>gerrhopygus</u>

3. Dorsal tubercles well-defined, trihedral and
   keeled-------------------------------------4
   Dorsal tubercles flat and smooth, but clearly
   differentiated from smaller scales----------13

4. Dorsal surface of tibia with enlarged tubercles
   --5
   Dorsal surface of tibia without enlarged
   tubercles-------------------------<u>lepidopygus</u>

5. More than ten rows of dorsal tubercles---------6
   Dorsal tubercles in ten parallel rows, clearly
   delimited, with area between them covered by
   small scales; ear opening bordered by denticulate scales----------------------------<u>reissii</u>

6. Individual dorsal tubercles not in contact with
   each other, area between them relatively large
   and occupied by small scales----------------7
   Individual tubercles large, in contact with
   each other; small area between angles of tubercles occupied by small scales-----<u>ventralis</u>

7. With 13-18 rows of dorsal tubercles-----------8
   With more than 18 rows of dorsal tubercles----9

8. With denticles bordering ear opening---------11
   No denticles bordering ear opening------------
   -------------------------------<u>tuberculosus</u>

9. Two postmentals; more than two rows of caudal
   tubercles----------------------------------10
   Three postmentals; two rows of tubercles
   on proximal quarter of tail------------<u>julieni</u>

Clave de especies

1. Con placa preanal bien desarrollada; escamas
   dorsales iguales, sin tubérculos dorsales----2
   Sin placa preanal; escamas dorsales alternan
   con tubérculos------------------------------3

2. Cola con una doble hilera de tubérculos laterales agrandados--------------------<u>heterurus</u>
   Cola sin tubérculos laterales-------<u>gerrhopygus</u>

3. Tubérculos muy definidos y diferentes de la
   lepidosis básica; trihedrales y carenados----4
   Tubérculos de diferente tamaño, aplanados lisos
   contrastando con escamas pequeñas-----------13

4. Superficie dorsal de la tibia con tubérculos
   agrandados----------------------------------5
   Superficie dorsal de la tibia sin tubérculos
   agrandados------------------------<u>lepidopygus</u>

5. Más de diez hileras de tubérculos dorsales----6
   Tubérculos dispuestos en diez hileras paralelas, claramente delimitadas, entre ellos
   quedan espacios cubiertos por escamas
   pequeñas; escamas denticulares en el oído-----
   ---------------------------------------<u>reissii</u>

6. Tubérculos dorsales no apegados entre sí, dejan
   espacios relativamente amplios ocupados por
   escamas pequeñas----------------------------7
   Tubérculos dorsales grandes, numerosos, apegados entre sí, dejando en los ángulos pequeños
   espacios ocupados por escamas pequeñas--------
   --------------------------------------<u>ventralis</u>

7. Con 13-18 hileras de tubérculos dorsales------8
   Con más de 18 hileras de tubérculos dorsales--9

8. Con dentículos auditivos--------------------11
   Sin dentículos auditivos----------<u>tuberculosus</u>

9. Dos posmentales; más de dos hileras de tubérculos caudales-------------------------------10
   Tres posmentales; dos hileras de tubérculos
   en el cuarto proximal de la cola-------<u>julieni</u>

10. Eight to ten rows of tubercles at base of tail; 28 rows of tubercles across dorsum of body--rutteni
    Six to eight rows of tubercles at base of tail; 18 rows of tubercles across dorsum-----martini

11. With 16-18 rows of dorsal tubercles----------12
    With 13-16 rows of dorsal tubercles------dixoni

12. With 48-60 transverse ventral scales from throat to anus; 39-47 tubercles in single paravertebral row from rear of head to base of tail-----------------------------------palmeus
    With 60-66 transverse ventral scales; 46-52 tubercles in single paravertebral row---insularis

13. Terminal lamellae of digits much enlarged, most of claw hidden when viewed from above; nostril not swollen------------------------inaequalis
    Terminal lamellae of digits very small, most of claw exposed when viewed from above; nostril greatly swollen-------------------microphyllus

10. Ocho a diez hileras de tubérculos en la base de la cola; 28 hileras de tubérculos a través del dorso-------------------------------------rutteni
    Seis a ocho hileras de tubérculos en la base de la cola; 18 hileras de tubérculos a través del dorso--------------------------------martini

11. Con 16-18 hileras de tubérculos dorsales-----12
    Con 13-16 hileras de tubérculos dorsales-dixoni

12. Con 48-60 escamas ventrales transversas desde garganta hasta ano; 39-47 tubérculos en cada hilera paravertebral desde posterior de la cabeza hasta base de la cola-----------palmeus
    Con 60-66 escamas ventrales transversales; 46-52 tubérculos en cada hilera paravertebral--insularis

13. Lamelas terminales de dedos muy agrandadas, la mayor parte de la uña oculta en vista dorsal; narina no hinchada--------------------inaequalis
    Lamelas terminales de dedos muy chicas, la mayor parte de la uña expuesta en vista dorsal; narina muy hinchada---------------microphyllus

PHYLLODACTYLUS DIXONI Rivero and Lancini

   1968 Phyllodactylus dixoni Rivero and Lancini, Mem. Soc. Cien. Nat. La Salle, Caracas, No. 78: 168, figs. 1-4. Type-locality: Mouth of Río Parguaza, tributary of Río Orinoco, Estado Bolívar, Venezuela.

   Distribution: Region of Río Orinoco, Estado Bolívar, south-central Venezuela.

PHYLLODACTYLUS GERRHOPYGUS (Wiegmann)

   1835 Diplodactylus gerrhopygus Wiegmann, Nova Acta Acad. Leop.-Carol., 17: 242. Type-locality: Tacna, Peru.
   1836 Phyllodactylus gymnopygus Duméril and Bibron, Erp. Gén., 3: 394. Type-locality: Chile.
   1885 Phyllodactylus gerrhopygus—Boulenger, Cat. Liz. Brit. Mus., 1: 95.

   Distribution: From Arequipa, southern Peru, to Tarapaca, northern Chile.

PHYLLODACTYLUS HETERURUS Werner

   1907 Phyllodactylus heterurus Werner, in Bürger, An. Univ. Santiago, Chile, 121 (2): 149, pl. 1, fig. 3a-b. Type-locality: Oasis de Pica, Tarapaca, Chile.

   Distribution: Known only from type locality.

PHYLLODACTYLUS INAEQUALIS Cope

   1876 Phyllodactylus inaequalis Cope, Jour. Acad. Nat. Sci. Phila., (2) 8 (1875): 174. Type-locality: Pacasmayo, Peru.

   Distribution: Extreme northwestern Peru and probably southwestern Ecuador.

PHYLLODACTYLUS INSULARIS Dixon

   1960 Phyllodactylus insularis Dixon, Herpetologica, 16: 9. Type-locality: Half Moon Cay, Roatan Islands, British Honduras.

   Distribution: Known only from type locality.

PHYLLODACTYLUS JULIENI Cope

1885 *Phyllodactylus julieni* Cope, Proc. Amer. Phil. Soc., 22: 180. Type-locality: Aruba
      Island.
1962 *Phyllodactylus julieni*—Dixon, Southwestern Naturalist, 7: 212.

   Distribution: Aruba Island, Dutch West Indies.

PHYLLODACTYLUS LEPIDOPYGUS (Tschudi)

1845 *Diplodactylus lepidopygus* Tschudi, Ark. für Naturg., 11: 159. Type-locality: Peru.
1845 *Discodactylus phacophorus* Tschudi, Ark. für Naturg., 11: 159. Type-locality: Peru.
1878 *Phyllodactylus nigrofasciatus* Cope, Proc. Amer. Phil. Soc., 17: 36. Type-locality:
      Chimbote Valley, Peru, 2000 ft.
1900 *Phyllodactylus variegatus* Werner, Abh. Ber. K. Zool. Anthro.-Ethno. Mus. Dresden, 9 (2): 2.
      Type-locality: Lima and Chanchamayo, Peru.
1907 *Phyllodactylus lepidopygus*—Roux, Rev. Suisse Zool., 15: 294.

   Distribution: Western coast of Peru.

PHYLLODACTYLUS MARTINI Van Lidth

1887 *Phyllodactylus martini* Van Lidth, Notes Leyden Mus., 9: 130, pl. 2, figs. 2-3. Type-locality:
      Curaçao.
1962 *Phyllodactyius* (sic) *martini*—Dixon, Southwestern Naturalist, 7: 214.

   Distribution: Dutch Leeward Islands.

PHYLLODACTYLUS MICROPHYLLUS Cope

1876 *Phyllodactylus microphyllus* Cope, Jour. Acad. Nat. Sci. Phila., (2) 8 (1875): 175. Type-locality:
      Valley of Río Tequetepeque, Peru.
1910 *Phyllodactylus lobensis* Werner, Mitt. Naturhist. Mus. Hamburg, 27: 6. Type-locality: Isla Lobos,
      Peru.

   Distribution: Extreme northwestern to central Peru.

PHYLLODACTYLUS PALMEUS Dixon

1968 *Phyllodactylus palmeus* Dixon, Proc. Biol. Soc. Washington, 81: 419, fig. 1. Type-locality:
      0.5 km north of Roatan, Isla de Roatan, Bay Islands, Honduras, 25 m.

   Distribution: Bay Islands, Honduras.

PHYLLODACTYLUS REISSII Peters

1862 *Phyllodactylus reissii* Peters, Monats. Akad. Wiss. Berlin, 1862: 626. Type-locality: Guayaquil,
      Ecuador.
1900 *Phyllodactylus baessleri* Werner, Abh. Ber. K. Zool. Anthro.-Ethno. Mus. Dresden, 9 (2): 2. Type-
      locality: Chanchamayo, Peru.
1910 *Phyllodactylus guayaquilensis* Werner, Mitt. Naturhist. Mus. Hamburg, 27: 4. Type-locality:
      Guayaquil, Ecuador.
1913 *Phyllodactylus abrupteseriatus* Werner, Mitt. Naturhist. Mus. Hamburg, 30: 4. Type-locality:
      "wahrscheinlich Brasilien".
1924 *Phyllodactylus magister* Noble, Occ. Pap. Boston Soc. Nat. Hist., 5: 110. Type-locality: Perico,
      Valley of Río Chinchipe, Peru.

   Distribution: Coastal Ecuador and Peru to 1250 m.

PHYLLODACTYLUS RUTTENI Hummelinck

> 1947 Phyllodactylus rutteni Hummelinck, Studies Fauna Curaçao, 1: 77. Type-locality: Isla
> Blanquilla, Venezuela.
> 1962 Phyllodactylus rutteni—Dixon, Southwestern Naturalist, 7: 217.

> Distribution: Islands on Venezuelan coast; La Tortuga, Los Hermanos, Blanquilla, Orchila,
> Archipielago de los Roques.

PHYLLODACTYLUS TUBERCULOSUS Wiegmann

> 1835 Phyllodactylus tuberculosus Wiegmann, Nova Acta Acad. Leop.-Carol., 17 (1): 241, pl. 18, figs.
> 2-2a. Type-locality: California; restricted by Dixon, Herpetologica, 16, 1960, 4, to the
> village of California, Nicaragua.
> 1960 Phyllodactylus tuberculosus—Dixon, Herpetologica, 16: 4.

> Distribution: West coast of Mexico through Central America to Costa Rica.

> Content: Four subspecies, one (saxatilis Dixon) extralimital.

Key to the subspecies	Clave de subespecies

1. Fewer than 21 interorbital scales---------2
  With 24 interorbital scales----------ingeri
	1. Con menos de 21 escamas interorbitales----2
	  Con 24 escamas interorbitales--------ingeri

2. Fewer than 28 scale rows across belly; 37
  or more paravertebral tubercles; venter
  bright ochre-----------------------magnus
  More than 30 scale rows across belly; fewer
  than 35 paravertebral tubercles; venter
  lemon yellow-----------------tuberculosus
	2. Con menos de 28 escamas a través de vien-
	  tre; 37 o más tubérculos paravertebrales;
	  vientre ocre brillante-------------magnus
	  Más de 30 escamas a través del vientre;
	  tubérculos dorsales menos de 35; vientre
	  amarillo limón---------------tuberculosus

Phyllodactylus tuberculosus tuberculosus (Wiegmann)

> 1952 Phyllodactylus eduardofischeri Mertens, Zool. Anz., 148: 88. Type-locality: Río Chilama,
> La Libertad, El Salvador.
> 1964 Phyllodactylus tuberculosus tuberculosus—Dixon, New Mexico St. Univ. Sci. Bull., 64 (1):
> 22, figs. 1-4.

> Distribution: Pacific coastal areas, Guatemala to Costa Rica.

Phyllodactylus tuberculosus ingeri Dixon

> 1964 Phyllodactylus tuberculosus ingeri Dixon, New Mexico St. Univ. Sci. Bull., 64 (1): 36.
> Type-locality: Stann Creek, British Honduras.

> Distribution: Coastal region of British Honduras.

Phyllodactylus tuberculosus magnus Taylor

> 1942 Phyllodactylus magnus Taylor, Univ. Kansas Sci. Bull., 28: 99, fig. 3. Type-locality:
> Tierra Colorado, Guerrero, Mexico.
> 1964 Phyllodactylus tuberculosus magnus—Dixon, New Mexico St. Univ. Sci. Bull., 64 (1): 27.

> Distribution: Michoacán, Mexico to Guatemala.

PHYLLODACTYLUS VENTRALIS O'Shaughnessy

> 1875 Phyllodactylus ventralis O'Shaughnessy, Ann. Mag. Nat. Hist., (4) 16: 263. Type-locality:
> "Jamaica"; suggested that it might be Colombia or Venezuela by Dixon, Southwestern Naturalist,
> 7, 1962, 222.
> 1935 Phyllodactylus mülleri Parker, Ann. Mag. Nat. Hist., (10) 15: 483. Type-locality: Patos Island,
> Venezuela.
> 1962 Phyllodactylus ventralis—Dixon, Southwestern Naturalist, 7: 220, fig. 2.

> Distribution: Northern Colombia and Venezuela, Margarita and Patos Islands.

<u>PHYLLOPEZUS</u> Peters

    1877 <u>Phyllopezus</u> Peters, Monats. Akad. Wiss. Berlin, 1877: 414, fig. 1. Type-species: <u>Phyllopezus</u>
        <u>goyazensis</u> Peters.

    Distribution: As for single known species.

    Content: One species.

<u>PHYLLOPEZUS POLLICARIS</u> (Spix)

    1825 <u>Thecadactylus</u> <u>pollicaris</u> Spix, Sp. Nov. Lac. Bras.: 17, pl. 18, fig. 2. Type-locality: Bahia,
        Brazil.
    1885 <u>Phyllopezus</u> <u>pollicaris</u>—Boulenger, Cat. Liz. Brit. Mus., 1: 145.

    Distribution: South America, south of equator and east of Andes.

    Content: Two subspecies.

Key to the subspecies	Clave de subespecies
1. Lamellae under fourth toe 9-13; ventrals counted along midline 28-32; tubercles present lateral to anus--------<u>pollicaris</u> Lamellae under fourth toe 8-11; ventrals 26-29; adanal tubercles not constant in adults------------------------<u>przewalskii</u>	1. Lamelas bajo el cuarto dedo 9-13; ventrales a lo largo de la línea media 28-32; tubérculos presentes lateralmente al ano------- -------------------------------<u>pollicaris</u> Lamelas bajo el cuarto dedo 8-11; ventrales 26-29; tubérculos laterales al ano no constantes en adultos----------<u>przewalskii</u>

<u>Phyllopezus pollicaris pollicaris</u> (Spix)

    1887 <u>Phyllopezus</u> <u>goyazensis</u> Peters, Monats. Akad. Wiss. Berlin, 1887: 415, fig. 1. Type-
        locality: Goiás, Brazil.
    1933 <u>Platydactylus</u> <u>Spixii</u> Schlegel, in Müller and Brongersma, Zool. Meded., 15: 161, fig. 1.
        Type-locality: Brazil.
    1937 <u>Phyllopezus</u> <u>pollicaris</u> <u>pollicaris</u>—Amaral, Mem. Inst. Butantan, 11: 171.
    1953 <u>Phyllopezus</u> <u>pollicaris</u> <u>pollicaris</u>—Vanzolini, Pap. Avul. Depto. Zool. São Paulo, 11: 354,
        pls. 1-2.

      Distribution: Bahia, Minas Gerais, Goiás, Maranhão, and Paraíba, Brazil.

<u>Phyllopezus pollicaris przewalskii</u> Koslowsky

    1895 <u>Phyllopezus</u> <u>przewalskii</u> Koslowsky, Rev. Mus. La Plata, 6: 371, pl. 1. Type-locality:
        Descalvado, Distrito Cáceres, Mato Grosso, Brazil.
    1953 <u>Phyllopezus</u> <u>pollicaris</u> <u>przewalskii</u>—Vanzolini, Pap. Avul. Depto. Zool. São Paulo, 11:
        357.

      Distribution: Provincia La Pampa, Argentina, through Paraguay and Bolivia to Mato Grosso,
      Brazil.

PHYMATURUS Gravenhorst

1838 <u>Phymaturus</u> Gravenhorst, Nova Acta Acad. Caes. Leop. Carol., 18: 740. Type-species: <u>Lacerta</u>
<u>palluma</u> Molina.
1843 <u>Centrura</u> Bell, Zool. Voy. Beagle, Rept., 5: 25. Type-species: <u>Centrura flagellifer</u> Bell.

Distribution: Both sides of Andean Cordillera from Coquimbo-Catamarca to Patagonia.

Content: One species.

PHYMATURUS <u>PALLUMA</u> (Molina)

1782 <u>Lacerta palluma</u> Molina, Saggio Stor. Nat. Chile: 345. Type-locality: Central Chile.
1838 <u>Phymaturus palluma</u>—Gravenhorst, Nova Acta Acad. Caes. Leop. Carol., 18: 750, pl. 55, fig. 2.
Type-locality: Higher Cordillera of Chile.

Distribution: Both sides of Andean Cordillera from Coquimbo-Catamarca to Patagonia.

Content: Two subspecies.

<table>
<tr><td>Key to the subspecies</td><td>Clave de subespecies</td></tr>
<tr><td>1. Median dorsal granules much larger than lateral granules; caudal scales strongly mucronate----------------------<u>palluma</u>
Median dorsal granules only slightly larger than lateral granules; caudal scales slightly mucronate------------<u>patagonicus</u></td><td>1. Gránulos medio dorsales mucho mayores que los laterales; caudales fuertemente mucronadas-----------------------<u>palluma</u>
Gránulos medio dorsales apenas mayores que los laterales; caudales ligeramente mucronadas--------------------<u>patagonicus</u></td></tr>
</table>

<u>Phymaturus palluma palluma</u> (Molina)

1843 <u>Centrura flagellifer</u> Bell, Zool. Voy. Beagle, Rept., 5: 25, pl. 14, fig. 2. Type-
locality: Chile.
1848 <u>Oplurus Bibronii</u> Guichenot, in Gay, Hist. Fis. Pol. Chile; Zool. 2: 53, Atlas pl. 14,
fig. 2. Type-locality: High Cordillera of Ovalle, Province of Coquimbo, Chile.
1931 <u>Phymaturus palluma palluma</u> Burt and Burt, Bull. Amer. Mus. Nat. Hist., 61: 281.

Distribution: Chilean and Argentinian Andes, from Coquimbo to region north of Río Negro.

<u>Phymaturus palluma patagonicus</u> Koslowsky

1896 <u>Phymaturus patagonicus</u> Koslowsky, Rev. Mus. La Plata, 8: 184, pl. 17. Type-locality:
Territorio del Chubut (Patagonia), Argentina.
1921 <u>Phymaturus spurcus</u> Barbour, Proc. Biol. Soc. Wash., 34: 139. Type-locality: Huanuluan,
Río Negro, Argentina.
1931 <u>Phymaturus palluma patagonicus</u>—Burt and Burt, Bull. Amer. Mus. Nat. Hist., 61: 281.

Distribution: Patagonian cordillera south of Río Negro, Argentina.

PLACOSOMA Tschudi

1847 Placosoma Tschudi, Arch. für Naturg., 13: 50. Type-species: Placosoma cordylinum Tschudi.
1870 Urosaura Peters, Monats. Akad. Wiss. Berlin, 1870: 641. Type-species: Cercosaura (Urosaura) glabella Peters.
1933 Elaphrosaura Amaral, Mem. Inst. Butantan, 7 (1932): 67. Type-species: Elaphrosaura spitzi Amaral.

Distribution: Estado de São Paulo to Estado do Rio de Janeiro, Brazil.

Content: Three species, two according to most recent revision by Uzzell, Occ. Pap. Mus. Zool. Univ. Mich., 606, 1959, with third added recently by Cunha.

Key to the species

1. More than 19 total femoral pores (except in females of cordylinum); dorsal pattern not as below--------------------------------2
Fewer than 18 femoral pores in total; dorsal part of head yellow extending on back as dorsal band; rest of body dark brown; two darker lateral bands and third band dorsoventrally-----------------------------------cipoense

2. Total femoral pores 27-32 on males, 0-6 on on females; 28-30 scales around middle of body; ventral scales with angular posterior borders; anterior margin of tympanum not depressed--------------------------cordylinum
Total femoral pores 19-22 in both sexes; 21-25 dorsal scales around middle of body; posterior border of ventral scales rounded; anterior margin of tympanum slightly depressed--------------------------glabellum

Clave de especies

1. Más de 19 poros femorales (excepto en las hembras de cordylinum); distribución del diseño y color dorsal no como el que sigue--2
Menos de 18 poros femorales totales; parte dorsal de la cabeza amarillenta se continúa sobre el dorso como faja clara mediana; resto pardo oscuro, más acentuado a los lados; dos fajas laterales oscuras y una tercera faja separando dorso de vientre------------cipoense

2. Poros femorales totales en el macho 27-32; 0-6 en las hembras; 28-30 escamas dorsales en el medio del cuerpo; escamas ventrales angulares en los bordes posteriores; margen anterior del tímpano no deprimido----------------cordylinum
Poros femorales totales 19-22 en el macho y hembra; 21-25 escamas dorsales en el medio del cuerpo; escamas ventrales redondeadas en los bordes; margen anterior del tímpano ligeramente deprimido----------------------glabellum

PLACOSOMA CIPOENSE Cunha

1966 Placosoma cipoense Cunha, Bol. Mus. Paraense Emilio Goeldi, Zool., 61: 2. Type-locality: Serra do Cipo (near Belo Horizonte), Minas Gerais, Brazil.

Distribution: Known only from type-locality.

PLACOSOMA CORDYLINUM Tschudi

1847 Placosoma cordylinum Tschudi, Arch. für Naturg., 13: 51. Type-locality: Northern Brazil.

Distribution: Rio de Janeiro, São Paulo, Minas Gerais, Mato Grosso, and Santa Catarina, Brazil.

Content: Two subspecies.

Key to the subspecies

1. Scales in two median dorsal rows broader than long; fewer than seven enlarged scales between granular areas in axillae; light line between eye and shoulder, separated from tympanum by at least one row of dark granules------------cordylinum
Scales in two median dorsal rows longer than broad; more than seven enlarged scales between granular areas in axillae; light line not separated from tympanum-------------------------------------champsonotus

Clave de subespecies

1. Escamas dorsales en dos hileras medianas más anchas que largas; seis o menos dorsales ensanchadas entre las áreas granulares de la inserción del brazo; una línea clara húmero ocular separada del tímpano a lo menos por una hilera de gránulos oscuros----------------cordylinum
Escamas dorsales en dos hileras medianas más largas que anchas; ocho o más dorsales ensanchadas entre las áreas granulares de la inserción del brazo; línea clara húmero ocular no separada del tímpano--champsonotus

Placosoma cordylinum cordylinum Tschudi

　　1944 Ecpleopus lutzae Loveridge, Proc. Biol. Soc. Washington, 57: 97. Type-locality:　Rio
　　　　Beija-Flor, Therezopolis, Rio de Janeiro, Brazil.
　　1959 Placosoma cordylinum cordylinum—Uzzell, Occ. Pap. Mus. Zool. Univ. Mich., 606: 3.

　　　Distribution:　Estado do Rio de Janeiro, Brazil.

Placosoma cordylinum champsonotus (Werner)

　　1910 Prionodactylus champsonotus Werner, Mitt. Naturhist. Mus. Hamburg, 27: 31.　Type-locality:
　　　　Itapocú, Jaraguá, Santa Catharina, Brazil.
　　1916 Euspondylus cupreus Andersson, Göteborgs Kungl. Vetens. Vitterhets. Handl., (4) 17 (5):
　　　　6.　Type-locality:　Brazil.
　　1933 Elaphrosaura spitzi Amaral, Mem. Inst. Butantan, 7 (1932): 68.　Type-locality:　Serra de
　　　　Cubatão, São Paulo, Brazil.
　　1959 Placosoma cordylinum champsonotus—Uzzell, Occ. Pap. Mus. Zool. Univ. Mich., 606: 9.

　　　Distribution:　Santa Catarina, São　Paulo, Minas Gerais and Mato Grosso, Brazil.

PLACOSOMA GLABELLUM (Peters)

　　1870 Cercosaura (Urosaura) glabella Peters, Monats. Akad. Wiss. Berlin, 1870: 641, pl. 1, fig. 1.
　　　　Type-locality:　Santa Catharina, Brazil.
　　1959 Placosoma glabellum—Uzzell, Occ. Pap. Mus. Zool. Univ. Mich., 606: 11.

　　　Distribution:　Coastal areas of São Paulo, Paraná, Espirito Santo, Rio de Janeiro and Santa
　　　Catarina, Brazil.

REPTILIA: SAURIA: IGUANIDAE ★ ★ ★ ★ PLICA

Prepared by Richard Etheridge, San Diego State College, San Diego, California

PLICA Gray

1831 _Plica_ Gray, Synopsis Species Class Reptilia, in Griffith, Cuvier's Animal Kingdom, 9: 40. Type-species: _Lacerta plica_ Linnaeus.
1831 _Hypsibatus_ Wagler (preoccupied by _Hypsibatus_ Nitzsch), Nat. Syst. Amphib.: 150. Type-species: _Lacerta umbra_ Linnaeus.
1835 _Hypsilophus_ Wiegmann (replacement name for _Hypsibatus_ Wagler), Arch. für Naturg., 1 (2): 289.
1837 _Uperanodon_ Duméril and Bibron, Erp. Gén., 4: 247. Type-species: _Lophyrus ochrocollaris_ Spix.
1843 _Ptychopleura_ Fitzinger, Systema Reptilium: 59. Type-species: _Lacerta plica_ Linnaeus.
1843 _Ptychosaurus_ Fitzinger, Systema Reptilium: 59. Type-species: _Hypsibates punctatus_ Duméril and Bibron.
1847 _Hyperanodon_ Agassiz (replacement name for _Uperanodon_ Duméril and Bibron), Nomenclator Zoologici Index Universalis: 190.

Distribution: Northern South America east of Andes.

Content: Two species.

Key to the species	Clave de especies
1. Sides of neck with groups of enlarged, spinose scales---------------------------------_plica_ No enlarged spinose scales on sides of neck--_umbra_	1. Grupos de escamas espinosas a los lados del cuello---------------------------------_plica_ Sin grupos de escamas espinosas a los lados del del cuello-----------------------------_umbra_

PLICA PLICA (Linnaeus)

1758 _Lacerta Plica_ Linnaeus, Systema Naturae, Ed. 10: 208. Type-locality: "Indiis".
1768 _Iguana chalcidica_ Laurenti, Synopsin Reptilium: 48. Type-locality: "Gallaecia".
1827 _Lophyrus (Ophryesa) Agamoides_ Gray, Phil. Mag., (2) 2: 208. Type-locality: None given.
1831 [_Plica_] _plica_—Gray, Synopsis Species Class Reptilia, in Griffith, Cuvier's Animal Kingdom, 9: 41.
1837 _Hypsibatus punctatus_ Duméril and Bibron, Erp. Gén., 4: 258. Type-locality: None given.

Distribution: Northern South America, east of Andes.

PLICA UMBRA (Linnaeus)

1758 _Lacerta Umbra_ Linnaeus, Systema Naturae, Ed. 10: 207. Type-locality: "Meridionalibus".
1881 _Plica umbra_—O'Shaughnessy, Proc. Zool. Soc. London, 1881: 245.

Distribution: Northern South America, east of Andes.

Content: Two subspecies.

Key to the subspecies	Clave de subespecies
1. Vertebral scale row continuous from occiput to tail, forming denticulate crest on neck; 34-46 vertebral scales from occiput to anterior margin of thigh; 50-66 paravertebral scales from occiput to anterior margin of thigh; 46-56 scales around body; dorsal head scales swollen, with blunt, irregular keels, a pair of pyramidal parietal scales; all scales more sharply keeled and more strongly mucronate---_umbra_ Vertebral scales usually not distinguishable from adjacent scales on posterior back, forming less distinct **crest**; 48-58 vertebral scales; 68-81 paravertebral scales; 54-65 scales around body; dorsal head scales smooth or nearly so, parietals flat or slightly convex, not pyramidal; all scales less sharply keeled and mucronate--------------------_ochrocollaris_	1. Fila de escamas vertebrales continua desde el occipucio a la cola, formando una cresta denticulada en el cuello, 34-46 escamas vertebrales desde el occipucio hasta el borde anterior del muslo; 50-66 escamas paravertebrales desde el occipucio al borde anterior del muslo; 46-56 escamas alrededor del cuerpo; escamas dorsales de la cabeza ensanchadas, con quillas irregulares, obtusas; un par de escamas parietales piramidales; todas las escamas más fuertemente quilladas y mucronadas----------------_umbra_ Escamas vertebrales generalmente no diferenciadas de las escamas adyacentes en la parte posterior de la espalda, que forman una cresta no tan distinta; 48-58 escamas vertebrales; 68-81 escamas paravertebrales; 54-65 escamas alrededor del cuerpo; escamas dorsales de la cabeza lisas o casi lisas, parietales planas o ligeramente convexas, no piramidales; todas las escamas no tan quilladas ni mucronadas-------_ochrocollaris_

Plica umbra umbra (Linnaeus), new combination

1899 Tropidurus unicarinatus Werner, Zool. Anz., 22: 480. Type-locality: Surinam.

Distribution: Eastern Amazonian region of South America; southern Venezuela, Guianas, and northeastern Brazil.

Plica umbra ochrocollaris (Spix), new combination

1825 Lophyrus ochrocollaris Spix, Sp. Nov. Lac. Bras.: 10, pl. 12, figs. 2. Type-locality: Amazon River.
1825 Lophyrus Panthera Spix, Sp. Nov. Lac. Bras.: 11, pl. 13, fig. 1. Type-locality: "In sylvis ad pagum Ecgá".
1876 Hyperanodon peltigerus Cope, Jour. Acad. Nat. Sci. Phila., (2) 8 (1875): 170. Type-locality: Middle and upper Amazon and western Peru.
1912 Tropidurus holotropis Boulenger, Ann. Mag. Nat. Hist., (8) 10: 420. Type-locality: Alpayacú, Río Pastaza, Ecuador, 3600 ft.
1918 Uraniscodon tuberculatum Andersson, Ark. fór Zool., 11 (16): 2, figs. 1-2. Type-locality: San Fermin, northwest Bolivia.

Distribution: Western Amazonian Basin of South America; southern Colombia, Peru, Ecuador, northern Bolivia, and western Brazil.

POLYCHROIDES Noble

> 1924 Polychroides Noble, Occ. Pap. Boston Soc. Nat. Hist., 5: 109. Type-species: Polychroides peruvianus Noble.

> Distribution: As for single known species.

> Content: One species.

POLYCHROIDES PERUVIANUS Noble

> 1924 Polychroides peruvianus Noble, Occ. Pap. Boston Soc. Nat. Hist., 5: 109. Type-locality: Near Querocotilla, Cajamarca, Peru.

> Distribution: Wooded valleys of Andes in northern Peru; known from Cajamarca and Piura Provinces.

POLYCHRUS Cuvier

1817 Polychrus Cuvier, Règne Animal, 2: 40. Type-species: Lacerta marmorata Linnaeus.
1827 Polycrus Gray (emendation of Polychrus Cuvier), Phil. Mag., 2: 57.
1827 Polychnus Berthold (in error for Polychrus Cuvier), in Latreille's Natürliche Familien des Thierreichs: 94.
1843 Ecphymatotes Ftizinger, Systema Reptilium: 62. Type-species: Polychrus acutirostris Spix.
1845 Sphaerops Gray, Cat. Liz. Brit. Mus.: 183. Type-species: Polychrus anomalus Wiegmann.
1870 Chaunolaemus Peters, Monats. Akad. Wiss. Berlin, 1869: 786. Type-species: Polychrus (Chaunolaemus) multicarinatus Peters.

Distribution: South America.

Content: Five species.

Key to the species

1. Scales of sides larger than middorsal scales, and separated by much smaller granules-------2
   Scales of flanks not larger than middorsals and in contact with each other, not separated by granules-----------------------------------3

2. Femoral pores fewer than 12, dorsals distinctly keeled-------------------------acutirostris
   Femoral pores more than 15, dorsals smooth or weakly keeled-----------------------femoralis

3. Low series of raised scales forming midventral crest from mental to gular appendage---------4
   No low series of raised scales on midventral line between chin and throat-------gutturosus

4. Pectoral and ventral scales keeled---marmoratus
   Pectoral and ventral scales smooth----liogaster

Clave de especies

1. Escamas de los lados mayores que escamas del medio dorso y separadas por gránulos mucho más chicos------------------------------------2
   Escamas de los flancos no mayores que las del medio dorso y en contacto, no separadas por gránulos------------------------------------3

2. Menos de 12 poros femorales, dorsales distinta- mente quilladas-------------------acutirostris
   Más de 15 poros femorales, dorsales lisas o ligeramente quilladas----------------femoralis

3. Serie baja de escamas levantadas que forman una cresta ventral media desde el mental al apéndice gular------------------------------4
   Serie de escamas levantadas en la línea media ventral entre mentón y garganta ausente------- -----------------------------------gutturosus

4. Escamas pectorales y ventrales quilladas------- -----------------------------------marmoratus
   Escamas pectorales y ventrales lisas--liogaster

POLYCHRUS ACUTIROSTRIS Spix

1825 Polychrus acutirostris Spix, Sp. Nov. Lac. Bras.: 15, pl. 14a. Type-locality: Bahia, Brazil.
1834 Polychrus anomalus Wiegmann, Herpetologia Mexicana: 16. Type-locality: Brazil.

Distribution: Southern Brazil, Uruguay, Paraguay, Argentina, and eastern Bolivia.

POLYCHRUS FEMORALIS Werner

1910 Polychrus femoralis Werner, Mitt. Naturhist. Mus. Hamburg, 27 (2): 21. Type-locality: Guayaquil, Ecuador.

Distribution: Lowlands in southwestern Ecuador.

POLYCHRUS GUTTUROSUS Berthold

1846 Polychrus gutturosus Berthold, Nachr. Univ. Königl. Gesell, Wiss. Gottingen, 8-10: 11. Type- locality: Popayán, Colombia.

Distribution: Pacific Ecuador north into Costa Rica and Nicaragua.

Content: Two subspecies.

Key to the subspecies

Clave de subespecies

1. Canthus rostralis somewhat rounded; scales on pectoral region smooth or very weakly keeled------------------------spurrellii
   Canthus rostralis distinctly angular; scales on pectoral region strongly keeled, may be bi- or tricarinate, usually unicarinate-----------------------gutturosus

1. Canto rostral algo redondeado; escamas de la región pectoral lisas o ligeramente quilladas----------------------spurrellii
   Canto rostral distintamente angular; escamas de la región pectoral fuertemente quilladas, pueden ser bi- o tricarenadas, generalmente unicarenadas-------gutturosus

Polychrus gutturosus gutturosus Berthold

1870 Polychrus (Chaunolaemus) multicarinatus Peters, Monats. Akad. Wiss. Berlin, 1869: 786. Type-locality: Costa Rica.
1935 Polychrus gutturosus gutturosus—Parker, Proc. Zool. Soc. London, 1935: 576.

Distribution: Higher western Andean slopes of Ecuador and Colombia north to Costa Rica and Nicaragua.

Polychrus gutturosus spurrellii Boulenger

1914 Polychrus spurrelli Boulenger, Proc. Zool. Soc. London, 1914: 814, pl. 1, fig. 2. Type-locality: Peña Lisa, Condoto, Colombia.
1935 Polychrus gutturosus spurrellii—Parker, Proc. Zool. Soc. London, 1935: 516.

Distribution: Lowland rain forests of northwestern Ecuador and Colombia.

POLYCHRUS LIOGASTER Boulenger

1908 Polychrus liogaster Boulenger, Ann. Mag. Nat. Hist., (8) 1: 113. Type-locality: Provincia Sara, Bolivia, 750 m, and Chanchamayo, eastern Peru.

Distribution: Lowlands of Amazonian Bolivia and Peru; Acré, Brazil.

POLYCHRUS MARMORATUS (Linnaeus)

1758 Lacerta marmorata Linnaeus, Systema Naturae, Ed. 10: 208. Type-locality: "Hispania".
1820 Polychrus marmoratus—Merrem, Tentamen Systematis Amphibiorum: 48.
1821 [Polychrus] strigiventris Wagler, Descriptiones et Icones Amphibiorum: pl. 12, and third page of unnumbered text. Type-locality: None given.
1822 Polych.[rus] virescens Schinz, in Cuvier's Das Thierreich, 2: 65. Type-locality: None given.
1833 Polychrus Neovidanus Wagler, Isis von Oken, 26: 897. Type-locality: None given.

Distribution: Amazonian basin of South America; Venezuela.

REPTILIA: SAURIA: TEIIDAE ★ ★ ★ ★ PRIONODACTYLUS

Prepared by Thomas Uzzell, Yale University, New Haven, Connecticut

PRIONODACTYLUS O'Shaughnessy ·

1881 _Prionodactylus_ O'Shaughnessy, Proc. Zool. Soc. London, 1881: 231. Type-species: _Cercosaura_ (_Prionodactylus_) _manicata_ O'Shaughnessy.

Distribution: Panama to Bolivia.

Content: Four species.

Key to the species	Clave de especies

1. Frontonasal single--------------------------2
  Frontonasal divided--------------------_argulus_
	1. Con una frontonasal--------------------------2
	  Con dos frontonasales------------------_argulus_

2. Loreal in contact with supralabials----------3
  Loreal separated from supralabials--_vertebralis_
	2. Loreal en contacto con supralabiales----------3
	  Loreal separada de supralabiales----_vertebralis_

3. With 32-35 scales around middle of body; 14-15 subdigital lamellae under fourth toe; subdigital lamellae denticulate, some lamellae bearing one, others, two denticles------_eigenmanni_
  With 35-52 scales around middle of body; 14-23 subdigital lamellae under fourth toe; subdigital lamellae, if denticulate, with single denticle per lamella-----------------_manicatus_
	3. Con 32-35 escamas alrededor del medio cuerpo; 14-15 lamelas subdigitales bajo el cuarto dedo; lamelas subdigitales denticuladas, algunas con uno y otras con dos dentículos---_eigenmanni_
	  Con 35-52 escamas alrededor del medio cuerpo; 14-23 lamelas subdigitales bajo el cuarto dedo; si las escamas subdigitales son denticuladas poseen un solo dentículo-----_manicatus_

PRIONODACTYLUS ARGULUS (Peters)

1862 _Cercosaura_ (_Pantodactylus_) _argulus_ Peters, Abh. Akad. Wiss. Berlin, 1862: 184. Type-locality: Santa Fé de Bogotá, Colombia.
1885 _Prionodactylus oshaughnessyi_ Boulenger, Cat. Liz. Brit. Mus., 2: 392, pl. 21, fig. 1. Type-locality: Canelos and Pallatanga, Ecuador.
1914 _Prionodactylus holmgreni_ Andersson, Ark. för Zool., 9 (3): 9, fig. 3. Type-locality: San Fermin, northwestern Bolivia.
1916 _Prionodactylus columbiensis_ Werner, Zool. Anz., 47: 306. Type-locality: Cañon del Tolima, Colombia.
1917 _P._[_rionodactylus_] _argulus_—Griffin, Ann. Carnegie Mus., 11: 428.

Distribution: Amazonian Colombia, Ecuador, and Bolivia.

PRIONODACTYLUS EIGENMANNI Griffin

1917 _Prionodactylus eigenmanni_ Griffin, Ann. Carnegie Mus., 11: 316. Type-locality: Provincia del Sara, Bolivia.

Distribution: Known only from type material.

PRIONODACTYLUS MANICATUS (O'Shaughnessy)

1881 _Cercosaura_ (_Prionodactylus_) _manicata_ O'Shaughnessy, Proc. Zool. Soc. London, 1881: 231, pl. 22, fig. 3. Type-locality: Canelos and Pallatanga, Ecuador.
1885 _Prionodactylus manicatus_—Boulenger, Cat. Liz. Brit. Mus., 2: 393.

Distribution: Amazonian Ecuador, Peru and Bolivia.

Content: Two subspecies.

Key to the subspecies	Clave de subespecies

1. Subdigital lamellae denticulate; eye disc divided into two scales---------_manicatus_
  Subdigital lamellae not denticulate; eye disc not divided into two or more scales-------------------------------_bolivianus_
	1. Lamelas subdigitales denticuladas; disco ocular dividido, formando dos escamas---------------------------------------_manicatus_
	  Lamelas subdigitales no denticuladas; disco ocular no dividido-------------_bolivianus_

Prionodactylus manicatus manicatus (O'Shaughnessy), new combination

    Distribution: Amazonian Ecuador.

Prionodactylus manicatus bolivianus Werner, new combination

  1899 Prionodactylus bolivianus Werner, Zool. Anz., 22: 481. Type-locality: Chaco, Bolivia.
  1907 Prionodactylus Ockendeni Boulenger, Ann. Mag. Nat. Hist., (7) 19: 486. Type-locality:
      Carabaya, eastern Peru, 6000 - 7000 ft.

    Distribution: Amazonian Peru and Bolivia.

PRIONODACTYLUS VERTEBRALIS (O'Shaughnessy)

  1879 Cercosaura (Pantodactylus) vertebralis O'Shaughnessy, Ann. Mag. Nat. Hist., (5) 4: 298. Type-
      locality: Intac, Ecuador.
  1885 Prionodactylus vertebralis—Boulenger, Cat. Liz. Brit. Mus., 2: 394, pl. 21, fig. 2.
  1908 Prionodactylus palmeri Boulenger, Ann. Mag. Nat. Hist., (8) 2: 518, figs. 3a-d. Type-locality:
      San Antonio, Colombia.
  1921 Prionodactylus marianus Ruthven, Occ. Pap. Mus. Zool. Univ. Mich., 103: 1. Type-locality: San
      Pedro, Antioquia, Colombia.

    Distribution: Darién, Panama; Pacific slopes of Ecuador and Colombia; also reported from Zamora,
    Ecuador.

PROCTOPORUS Tschudi

1845 <u>Proctoporus</u> Tschudi, Ark. für Naturg., 11: 161. Type-species: <u>Proctoporus pachyurus</u> Tschudi.
1858 <u>Riama</u> Gray, Proc. Zool. Soc. London, 1858: 445. Type-species: <u>Riama unicolor</u> Gray.
1862 <u>Oreosaurus</u> Peters, Abh. Akad. Wiss. Berlin, 1862: 201. Type-species: <u>Ecpleopus</u> (<u>Oreosaurus</u>)
    <u>striatus</u> Peters.
1879 <u>Emphrassotis</u> O'Shaughnessy, Ann. Mag. Nat. Hist., (5) 4: 295. Type-species: <u>Emphrassotis</u>
    <u>simoterus</u> O'Shaughnessy.

   Distribution: Tropical South America, including northern Bolivia, Peru, Ecuador, Colombia,
   Venezuela and Trinidad.

   Content: Fifteen species.

   Comment: The data presented below reflect the arrangement to be found in a manuscript submitted for
   publication in Postilla by Thomas Uzzell, and generously made available to us for inclusion here.

Key to the species

1. Supranasals, if present, not in contact on
   median dorsal line--------------------------2
   Supranasals in contact on median dorsal line---
   ------------------------------------guentheri

2. No area of granular scales between axilla and
   groin---------------------------------------3
   With a band of granules between axilla and
   groin---------------------------------------7

3. With light dorsolateral lines, at least on
   shoulder------------------------------------4
   Without light dorsolateral lines-------------6

4. Loreal present; venter spotted with black; no
   preanal pores in males----------------------5
   Loreal absent; venter immaculate; males with
   preanal pores------------------------shrevei

5. Dorsal scales smooth; no light lines across
   lip; approximately 34 scales around middle of
   body-----------------------------------laevis
   Dorsal scales keeled; light lines across lip
   extending from eye; about 46 scales around
   middle of body---------------------luctuosus

6. Fewer than nine longitudinal rows of ventrals;
   more than twelve femoral pores in females;
   more than 25 in males----------------achlyens
   Ten longitudinal rows of ventrals; total
   number of femoral pores in males fewer than
   twelve-----------------------------oculatus

7. Preanal pores present------------------------8
   Preanal pores absent-------------------------9

8. Three supraoculars, only two of which contact
   palpebrals; sexual dimorphism in number of
   preanal pores-------------------------unicolor
   Four supraoculars; second, third and fourth in
   contact with palpebrals; no sexual dimorphism
   in number of preanal pores----------meleagris

9. Fewer than 50 scales from occipital to base of
   tail--10
   More than 50 scales from occipital to base of
   tail-------------------------------pachyurus

Clave de especies

1. Supranasales, si existen, no contactan en la
   línea media---------------------------------2
   Supranasales contactan en la línea media
   dorsal--------------------------------guentheri

2. Sin banda granular contínua entre axila e
   ingle---------------------------------------3
   Con una banda granular contínua entre axila e
   ingle---------------------------------------7

3. Con líneas dorso laterales claras a lo menos en
   el hombro-----------------------------------4
   Sin líneas dorso laterales claras------------6

4. Loreal presente, vientre manchado de negro; sin
   poros preanales en los machos---------------5
   Loreal ausente, vientre inmaculado; poros en
   las escamas preanales de los machos----shrevei

5. Escamas dorsales lisas; labio sin líneas
   claras; aproximadamente 34 escamas al medio
   del cuerpo----------------------------laevis
   Escamas dorsales quilladas; labio con líneas
   claras extendidas desde el ojo; aproximadamente 46 escamas al medio del cuerpo-luctuosus

6. Ocho o menos hileras longitudinales de ventrales; más de doce poros femorales en las
   hembras y vienticinco en los machos---achlyens
   Diez hileras longitudinales de ventrales;
   número total de poros femorales en los machos
   once----------------------------------oculatus

7. Poros presentes en el area preanal----------8
   Poros ausente en el area preanal-------------9

8. Tres supraoculares, solamente dos de ellas en
   contacto con las palpebrales; dimorfismo
   sexual en número de poros preanales---unicolor
   Cuatro supraoculares; segunda, tercera y cuarta
   en contacto con las palpebrales; no hay dimorfismo sexual en el número de poros preanales--
   --------------------------------------meleagris

9. Menos de 50 escamas desde el occipital a la
   base de la cola-----------------------------10
   Más de 50 escamas del occipital a la base de la
   cola----------------------------------pachyurus

10. Superciliary series of scales complete (occasionally not true in striatus); fore and hind limbs overlap when stretched along body-----11
    Superciliary series of scales incomplete; second or second and third supraocular in contact with palpebrals; limbs do not overlap or do so very slightly, when stretched along body--------------------------------columbianus

11. Dorsals smooth------------------------------12
    Dorsals not smooth--------------------------14

12. Median occipital present--------------------13
    Median occipital absent; two large lateral occipitals--------------------------simoterus

13. Three subequal occipitals; venter spotted----------------------------------ventrimaculatus
    Three occipitals, median much smaller than others; venter uniform yellowish----bolivianus

14. Loreal present-----------------------------15
    Loreal absent------------------------------16

15. With 40 scales around midbody; three pairs of postmentals----------------------hypostictus
    With 30 scales around midbody; four pairs of postmentals------------------------guentheri

16. With four supraoculars----------------------17
    With three supraoculars--------------bolivianus

17. Dorsal pattern unicolor or with longitudinal brown stripes; striated scales--------striatus
    Dorsal pattern brown with darker sides; light line on sides of anterior part of body; row of seven or eight light ocelli on each side of body; keeled scales------------------guentheri

10. Series superciliares completas (ocasionalmente puede faltar en striatus); extremidades usualmente se entrecruzan------------------------11
    Series superciliares incompletas; segunda, o segunda y tercera supraocular en contacto con la palpebral; extremidades opuestas proyectadas entre sí no se tocan o a lo menos ligeramente------------------------columbianus

11. Dorsales lisas-------------------------------12
    Dorsales no lisas----------------------------14

12. Occipital mediano presente-------------------13
    Dos occipitales laterales grandes; no hay occipital mediano-------------------simoterus

13. Tres occipitales subiguales; vientre manchado--------------------------------ventrimaculatus
    Tres occipitales, el mediano mucho menor; vientre amarillento homogéneo-------bolivianus

14. Loreal presente-----------------------------15
    Loreal ausente------------------------------16

15. Con 40 escamas al medio cuerpo; tres pares de posmentales----------------------hypostictus
    Con 30 escamas al medio cuerpo, cuatro pares de posmentales-----------------------guentheri

16. Con cuatro supraoculares---------------------17
    Con tres supraoculares--------------bolivianus

17. Diseño dorsal formado por cintas longitudinales pardas, también puede ser uniforme; escamas estriadas----------------------------striatus
    Diseño dorsal castaño oscuro con los lados más oscuros; una línea clara a los lados del cuerpo al comienzo de la mitad anterior; series de siete u ocho ocelos negros con centros blancos a cada lado del cuerpo; escamas quilladas--------------------guentheri

PROCTOPORUS ACHLYENS Uzzell

1958 Proctoporus achlyens Uzzell, Occ. Pap. Mus. Zool. Univ. Mich., 597: 8. Type-locality: Maracay-Rancho Grande Road, Estado Aragua, Venezuela, 1150 m.

Distribution: Montane forest of Rancho Grande, Parque Nacional Henri Pittier, Estado Aragua, Venezuela.

PROCTOPORUS BOLIVIANUS Werner

1910 Proctoporus bolivianus Werner, Mitt. Naturhist. Mus. Hamburg, 27 (2): 30. Type-locality: Sorata, Bolivia.
1913 Oreosaurus lacertus Stejneger, Proc. U. S. Nat. Mus., 45: 546. Type-locality: Tincochchaca, Peru, 2300 m.; corrected to Tinccochaca by Cochran, Bull. U. S. Nat. Mus., 220, 1961, 127.
1914 Proctoporus longicaudatus Andersson, Ark. für Zool., 9 (3): 6, figs. 2a-d. Type-locality: Pelechuco, western Bolivia.
1920 Proctoporus obesus Barbour and Noble, Proc. U.S. Nat. Mus., 58: 616. Type-locality: Ñusta Hispana, Peru.

Distribution: Amazonian slopes of Andes in Bolivia and Peru.

Comment: The use of this taxon is based on Uzzell, Postilla, in press.

PROCTOPORUS COLUMBIANUS Andersson

   1914 Proctoporus columbianus Andersson, Ark. för Zool., 9 (3): 3, fig. 1a-d. Type-locality: Colombia.

     Distribution: Eastern slopes of Andes in Colombia and Ecuador.

PROCTOPORUS GUENTHERI (Boettger)

   1891 Oreosaurus Guentheri Boettger, Zool. Anz., 14: 345. Type-locality: Sorata, Bolivia.
   1902 Oreosaurus ocellifer Boulenger, Ann. Mag. Nat. Hist., (7) 10: 400. Type-locality: Marcapata
      Valley, Peru.
   1920 Oreosaurus anomalus Barbour and Noble, Proc. U. S. Nat. Mus., 58: 614. Type-locality:
      San Fernando, valley of Río San Miguel, Peru.

     Distribution: Amazonian slopes of Bolivia and Peru.

     Comment: This arrangement of synonyms follows Uzzell, Postilla, in press.

PROCTOPORUS HYPOSTICTUS Boulenger

   1902 Proctoporus hypostictus Boulenger, Ann. Mag. Nat. Hist., (7) 9: 55. Type-locality: Paramba,
      Ecuador, 1160 m.

     Distribution: Higher western slopes of Andes in Ecuador.

PROCTOPORUS LAEVIS (Boulenger)

   1908 Oreosaurus laevis Boulenger, Ann. Mag. Nat. Hist., (8) 2: 521, figs. 5a-d. Type-locality: San
      Antonio, Colombia.
   1933 Proctoporus laevis—Burt and Burt, Trans. Acad. Sci. St. Louis, 28: 73.

     Distribution: Southwestern Colombia.

PROCTOPORUS LUCTUOSUS (Peters)

   1862 Ecpleopus (Oreosaurus) luctuosus Peters, Abh. Akad. Wiss. Berlin, 1862: 203. Type-locality:
      Venezuela.
   1933 Proctoporus luctuosus—Burt and Burt, Trans. Acad. Sci. St. Louis, 28: 73.

     Distribution: Rancho Grande, Estado Aragua, Venezuela.

PROCTOPORUS MELEAGRIS Boulenger

   1885 Proctoporus meleagris Boulenger, Cat. Liz. Brit. Mus., 2: 415, pl. 22, fig. 2. Type-locality:
      Western Ecuador.

     Distribution: Higher western slopes of Andes in Ecuador, to 3000 m.

PROCTOPORUS OCULATUS (O'Shaughnessy)

   1879 Ecpleopus oculatus O'Shaughnessy, Ann. Mag. Nat. Hist., (5) 4: 297. Type-locality: Intac,
      Ecuador.
   1933 Proctoporus oculatus—Burt and Burt, Trans. Acad. Sci. St. Louis, 28: 73.

     Distribution: Higher western slopes of Andes in Ecuador.

PROCTOPORUS PACHYURUS Tschudi

   1845 Proctoporus pachyurus Tschudi, Ark. für Naturg., 11: 161. Type-locality: Valley of Río
      Chanchamayo, eastern slope of Andes, Peru.

     Distribution: Inter-Andean valleys in Chanchamayo region of Peru.

PROCTOPORUS SHREVEI Parker

    1935 Proctoporus (Oreosaurus) shrevei Parker, Tropical Agriculture, Trinidad, 12: 283. Type-locality: Heaths of Aripo Mountain Range, Trinidad.

    Distribution: Trinidad.

PROCTOPORUS SIMOTERUS (O'Shaughnessy)

    1879 Emphrassotis simoterus O'Shaughnessy, Ann. Mag. Nat. Hist., (5) 4: 296. Type-locality: Intac, Ecuador.
    1885 Proctoporus simoterus—Boulenger, Cat. Liz. Brit. Mus., 2: 414.

    Distribution: Western slopes of Andes in Ecuador.

PROCTOPORUS STRIATUS (Peters)

    1862 Ecpleopus (Oreosaurus) striatus Peters, Abh. Akad. Wiss. Berlin, 1862: 201, pl. 3, fig. 2. Type-locality: Santa Fe de Bogotá, Colombia.
    1885 Proctoporus striatus—Cope, Proc. Amer. Phil. Soc., 23: 98.

    Distribution: Upper eastern slopes of Andes in Colombia; questionable record from El Chiral, El Oro Province, Ecuador (see Peters, Proc. U.S. Nat. Mus., 3545, 1967, 33).

PROCTOPORUS UNICOLOR (Gray)

    1858 Riama unicolor Gray, Proc. Zool. Soc. London, 1858: 446, pl. 15, fig. 2. Type-locality: Ecuador.
    1878 Ecpleopus (Oreosaurus) Petersi Boettger, Ber. Offen. Ver. für Natur., 17-18: 9. Type-locality: Province of Pará, Brazil; considered to be erroneous by Burt and Burt, Trans. Acad. Sci. St. Louis, 28, 1933, 74.
    1885 Proctoporus unicolor—Boulenger, Cat. Liz. Brit. Mus., 2: 413.
    1889 Proctoporus lividus Thominot, Bull. Soc. Philom. Paris, (8) 1: 25. Type-locality: unknown.

    Distribution: Higher western slopes and inter-Andean valleys of northern Ecuador.

PROCTOPORUS VENTRIMACULATUS Boulenger

    1900 Proctoporus ventrimaculatus Boulenger, Ann. Mag. Nat. Hist., (7) 6: 185. Type-locality: Cajamarca, Peru, 3300 m.

    Distribution: Inter-Andean valleys of northern Peru.

PROCTOTRETUS Duméril and Bibron

  1837 Proctotretus Duméril and Bibron, Erp. Gén., 4: 266. Type-species: Proctotretus pectinatus
      Duméril and Bibron.
  1845 Ptygoderus Gray, Cat. Liz. Brit. Mus.: 216. Type-species: Proctotretus pectinatus Duméril and
      Bibron.
  1882 Tropidocephalus Müller, Verh. Naturf. Ges. Basel, 7: 162. Type-species: Tropidocephalus azureus
      Müller.

    Distribution: Southern South America east of Andes; Paraguay, Argentina, Uruguay, extreme southern
    Brazil.

    Content: Three species.

                Key to the species   Clave de especies

  1. Vertebral and dorsolateral crests distinct;   1. Crestas vertebral y dorsolateral distintas;
     triple row of semicircular spots; lateral   diseño con triple hilera de manchas semi-
     light stripes not broken; throat immaculate---   circulares; cintas laterales claras no que-
     --2   bradas; cuello inmaculado-------------------2
     Vertebral crest indistinct; dorsolateral crests   Cresta vertebral indistinta; crestas dorso-
     absent; double row of semicircular spots;   laterales faltan; diseño con doble fila de
     lateral light stripes broken; throat with   manchas semicirculares; cintas laterales
     brown markings-------------------doellojuradoi   claras quebradas; cuello con marcas pardas----
                                                        --------------------------------doellojuradoi

  2. Lamellae on fourth digit of forelimb 9-12;   2. Lamelas bajo el cuarto dedo de la extremidad
     postfemoral scales granular; ventral scales   anterior 9-12; escamas posfemorales granu-
     smooth----------------------------pectinatus   lares; escamas ventrales lisas------pectinatus
     Lamellae on fourth digit of forelimb 14-15;   Lamelas bajo el cuarto dedo de la extremidad
     postfemoral scales not granular; ventral   anterior 14-15; escamas posfemorales no granu-
     scales keeled------------------------azureus   lares; escamas ventrales quilladas-----azureus

PROCTOTRETUS AZUREUS (Müller)

  1882 Tropidocephalus azureus Muller, Verh. Naturf. Ges. Basel, 7: 162. Type-locality: Uruguay.
  1930 Proctotretus azureus—Burt and Burt, Proc. U.S. Nat. Mus., 78: 21.

    Distribution: Uruguay and extreme southern Brazil.

PROCTOTRETUS DOELLOJURADOI Freiberg

  1944 Proctotretus doellojuradoi Freiberg, Physis, 19: 473, figs. 1-4. Type-locality: La Rioja,
      Argentina.

    Distribution: Provincias de Córdoba, Cajamarca, La Rioja, San Luis and Santiago del Estero, Argentina.

PROCTOTRETUS PECTINATUS Duméril and Bibron

  1837 Proctotretus pectinatus Duméril and Bibron, Erp. Gén., 4: 292. Type-locality: Chile (in error).
  1857 Proctotretus splendidus Girard, Proc. Acad. Nat. Sci. Phila., 1857: 198. Type-locality: Río
      Negro, Patagonia, Argentina.

    Distribution: Río Negro to La Pampa and Buenos Aires, Argentina; Uruguay.

PSEUDOGONATODES Ruthven

1915 Pseudogonatodes Ruthven, Occ. Pap. Mus. Zool. Univ. Mich., 19: 1. Type-species: Pseudogonatodes furvus Ruthven.

Distribution: Northern South America.

Content: Five species (plus a sixth, described but not named by Mechler, Rev. Suisse Zool., 75, 1968, 352).

Key to the species	Clave de especies

1. Dorsal scales granular-----------------------2
   Dorsal scales imbricate---------------barbouri

2. Length of head[1] contained four and one half
   times in snout-vent distance; rostral bordered
   by three scales-------------------------------3
   Length of head contained five times in the
   snout-vent distance; rostral bordered by two
   scales-----------------------------guianensis

3. Posterior margin of first lower labial reaches
   anterior border of eye; fewer than 41 scales
   from level of arm insertion to vent; fewer than
   25 scales across belly at midbody------------4
   Posterior margin of first lower labial below
   loreal; more than 41 longitudinal rows of
   scales on belly; more than 26 rows across
   belly--------------------------------furvus

4. Posterior margin of mental transverse; 37-38
   longitudinal rows of ventrals--------lunulatus
   Posterior end of mental forms a "V" with
   open end towards rear; 40-41 longitudinal rows
   of ventrals------------------------amazonicus

1. Escamas dorsales granulares--------------------2
   Escamas dorsales imbricadas------------barbouri

2. Longitud de la cabeza[2] contenida cuatro veces y
   media en la distancia hocico-ano; rostral bordeado por tres escamas-----------------------3
   Longitud de la cabeza contenida cinco veces en
   la distancia hocico-ano; rostral bordeado por
   dos escamas------------------------guianensis

3. Margen posterior de la primera infralabial
   llega al borde anterior del ojo; menos de 41
   escamas desde la inserción braquial al ano;
   menos de 25 escamas a través del medio vien-
   tre---4
   Margen posterior de la primera infralabial
   llega a la loreal; más de 41 escamas ventrales, más de 26 escamas a través del medio
   vientre-------------------------------furvus

4. Margen mental posterior, transverso; 37-38
   hileras longitudinales de ventrales--lunulatus
   Margen mental posterior en forma de "V" abierto
   hacia atrás; 40-41 hileras longitudinales de
   ventrales--------------------------amazonicus

PSEUDOGONATODES AMAZONICUS Vanzolini

1967 Pseudogonatodes amazonicus Vanzolini, Pap. Avul. Depto. Zool. São Paulo, 21(1): 2, fig. 1-2. Type-locality: Igarapé Belém, Rio Solimões, Amazonas, Brazil.

Distribution: Known only from type locality.

PSEUDOGONATODES BARBOURI (Noble)

1921 Lepidoblepharis barbouri Noble, Ann. N.Y. Acad. Sci., 29: 133. Type-locality: Perico, Peru.
1926 Pseudogonatodes barbouri—Parker, Ann. Mag. Nat. Hist., (9) 17: 298.

Distribution: Arid valleys of Río Chinchipe and Río Marañón, Peru.

PSEUDOGONATODES FURVUS Ruthven

1915 Pseudogonatodes furvus Ruthven, Occ. Pap. Mus. Zool. Univ. Mich., 19: 2. Type-locality: San Lorenzo, Santa Marta Mountains, Colombia, 5000 ft.

Distribution: Villavicencio region of Colombia.

---

[1]Measured from tip of snout to anterior edge of ear.

[2]Medida desde la punta del hocico al borde anterior del oído.

PSEUDOGONATODES GUIANENSIS Parker

1935 Pseudogonatodes guianensis Parker, Proc. Zool. Soc. London, 1935: 514. Type-locality: Upper Cuyuni River, Guyana.

Distribution: Guyana.

PSEUDOGONATODES LUNULATUS (Roux)

1927 Lepidoblepharis lunulatus Roux, Verh. Naturf. Ges. Basel, 38: 252. Type-locality: El Mene, Falcón, Venezuela.
1949 Pseudogonatodes lunulatus—Shreve, Bull. Mus. Comp. Zool., Harvard, 99: 522.

Distribution: Known only from Estados de Falcón and Aragua, Venezuela.

PTYCHOGLOSSUS Boulenger

1890 Ptychoglossus Boulenger, Proc. Zool. Soc. London, 1890: 83. Type-species: Ptychoglossus
bilineatus Boulenger.
1896 Diastemalepis Peracca, Boll. Mus. Zool. Comp. Anat. Univ. Torino, 11 (235): 1. Type-species:
Diastemalepis festae Peracca.
1916 Gonioptychus Werner, Zool. Anz., 47: 304. Type-species: Gonioptychus bicolor Werner.

Distribution: Costa Rica to Ecuador and Venezuela.

Content: Seven species.

Key to the species

1. Prefrontals present---------------------------2
   Prefrontals absent---------------------bicolor

2. More than five longitudinal rows of ventral
   scales---------------------------------------3
   Four longitudinal rows of ventral scales-------
   --plicatus

3. Ten rows of longitudinal ventral scales-------4
   Six or eight rows of longitudinal ventral
   scales---------------------------------------5

4. Four supraoculars; prefrontals forming
   suture---------------------------------festae
   Three supraoculars; prefrontals not in
   contact------------------------------picticeps

5. Four supraoculars; prefrontals in contact-----6
   Three supraoculars; prefrontals not in
   contact------------------------------kugleri

6. Scales between occipital and sacrum 32;
   uniform brown-------------------------nicefori
   Scales between occipital and sacrum 24; two
   lateral light stripes-----------brevifrontalis

Clave de especies

1. Prefrontales presentes-----------------------2
   Prefrontales ausentes-------------------bicolor

2. Escamas ventrales en más de cinco hileras
   longitudinales-------------------------------3
   Escamas ventrales en cuatro hileras longitudi-
   nales----------------------------------plicatus

3. Ventrales en diez hileras longitudinales------4
   Ventrales en seis a ocho hileras longitudi-
   nales--5

4. Cuatro supraoculares; prefrontales forman
   sutura---------------------------------festae
   Tres supraoculares; prefrontales apenas se
   tocan--------------------------------picticeps

5. Cuatro supraoculares; prefrontales contactan
   entre si-------------------------------------6
   Tres supraoculares; prefrontales no con-
   tactan---------------------------------kugleri

6. Del occipital al sacro 32 escamas; castaño sin
   diseños-------------------------------nicefori
   Del occipital al sacro 24 escamas; dos cintas
   claras laterales----------------brevifrontalis

PTYCHOGLOSSUS BICOLOR (Werner)

1916 Gonioptychus bicolor Werner, Zool. Anz., 47: 305. Type-locality: Cañon del Tolima, Colombia.
1958 Ptychoglossus bicolor—Uzzell, Occ. Pap. Mus. Zool. Univ. Mich., 592: 1.

Distribution: Mountain area of Tolima, Colombia.

PTYCHOGLOSSUS BREVIFRONTALIS Boulenger

1912 Ptychoglossus brevifrontalis Boulenger, Ann. Mag. Nat. Hist., (8) 10: 421. Type-locality:
El Topo, Río Pastaza, Ecuador.

Distribution: Amazonian slopes of Ecuador.

PTYCHOGLOSSUS FESTAE (Peracca)

1896 Diastemalepis festae Peracca, Boll. Mus. Zool. Comp. Anat. Univ. Torino, 11 (235): 2.
Type-locality: Río Cianati, Darién, Panama.
1931 Ptychoglossus festae—Burt and Burt, Bull. Amer. Mus. Nat. Hist., 51: 373.

Distribution: Colombia and Panama.

PTYCHOGLOSSUS KUGLERI Roux

  1927 Ptychoglossus kugleri Roux, Verh. Naturforsch. Ges. Basel, 38: 256. Type-locality: El Mene, Estado Falcón, Venezuela.

  Distribution: Mountains of coastal Cordillera in Falcón and Aragua, Venezuela.

PTYCHOGLOSSUS NICEFORI (Loveridge)

  1929 Anadia nicefori Loveridge, Proc. Biol. Soc. Washington, 42: 99. Type-locality: Río Garagoa at Macanal, eastern Andes, Colombia.
  1944 Ptychoglossus nicefori—Dunn, Caldasia, 3 (11): 67.

  Distribution: Eastern slopes of Andes in Colombia.

PTYCHOGLOSSUS PICTICEPS

  1885 Leposoma picticeps Cope, Proc. Amer. Phil. Soc., 23: 99. Type-locality: Pebas, Peru.
  1890 Ptychoglossus bilineatus Boulenger, Proc. Zool. Soc. London, 1890: 84, pl. 10, fig. 2. Type-locality: Ecuador.
  1931 P[tychoglossus] picticeps—Burt and Burt, Bull. Amer. Mus. Nat. Hist., 61: 372.

  Distribution: Amazonian Ecuador and Peru.

PTYCHOGLOSSUS PLICATUS (Taylor)

  1949 Alopoglossus plicatus Taylor, Univ. Kansas Sci. Bull., 33: 272. Type-locality: Morehouse Finca, 5 mi southwest of Turrialba, Cartago, Costa Rica.
  1952 Ptychoglossus plicatus—Ruibal, Bull. Mus. Comp. Zool., 106: 479.

  Distribution: Known from type-locality and La Lola Provincia, Limón, Costa Rica.

SCELOPORUS Wiegmann

1828 Sceloporus Wiegmann, Isis von Oken, 21: 369. Type-species: Sceloporus torquatus Wiegmann.

Distribution: Throughout temperate North America, Mexico, and Central America to and including Panama.

Content: About 95 species, according to last major revision by Smith, Zool. Ser. Field Mus. Nat. Hist., 26, 1939, of which twelve are found within limits of this work. Sceloporus salvinii Günther, based in part on Guatemalan specimens, has been restricted to a Mexican population of Sceloporus malachiticus through lectotype designation by Smith, loc. cit., p. 40.

Key to the species

1. Postfemoral dermal pocket present-------------2
   No postfemoral dermal pocket------------------3

2. Dorsal scales (occiput to above posterior margins of thighs) usually fewer than 48----------
   -----------------------------------teapensis
   Dorsal scales usually more than 48------------
   -----------------------------------variabilis

3. Dorsal pattern gives impression of dorsolateral light stripe--------------------------------4
   Dorsal pattern extremely variable but never giving impression of dorsolateral light stripe
   ---7

4. Total femoral pores fewer than 25-------------5
   Femoral pores more than 25--------chrysostictus

5. Single canthal scale-------------------------6
   Two canthal scales--------------------siniferus

6. Total femoral pores more than 12------carinatus
   Femoral pores fewer than 12-----------squamosus

7. Dark collar on sides of neck and in some instances complete across shoulders and unbroken middorsally------------------------8
   No dark collar; conspicuous dark nape patch----
   ----------------------------------melanorhinus

8. Single canthal-------------------------------9
   Two canthals---------------------------------10

9. Supraorbitals in two rows----------malachiticus
   Supraorbitals in a single row--------acanthinus

10. More than 35 dorsal scales between interparietal and posterior level of thighs-----------11
    Fewer than 35 dorsal scales between interparietal and posterior level of thighs-----------12

11. Supraorbitals in a single row--------acanthinus
    Supraorbitals in two rows----------malachiticus

12. Parietals and frequently frontoparietals separated from posterior supraorbital by row of small scales-----------------------------13
    Parietals in contact with posterior supraorbitals----------------------------lundelli

13. Lower row of labiomentals extending forward to contact second postmental-------------prezygus
    Lower row of labiomentals extending forward only to third postmental--------------serrifer

Clave de especies

1. Bolsillo posfemoral presente------------------2
   Bolsillo posfemoral ausente--------------------3

2. Escamas dorsales (desde el occipucio hasta encima del margen posterior del fémur) usualmente menos de 48--------------------teapensis
   Escamas dorsales usualmente más de 48----------
   -----------------------------------variabilis

3. Diseño dorsal da la impresión de una línea dorsolateral clara---------------------------4
   Diseño dorsal extremadamente variable que nunca da la impresión de una línea dorsolateral clara---7

4. Poros femorales en total menos de 25----------5
   Poros femorales más de 25---------chrysostictus

5. Una sola cantal-----------------------------6
   Dos escamas cantales------------------siniferus

6. Poros femorales en total más de 12----carinatus
   Poros femorales menos de 12-----------squamosus

7. Con collar oscuro a los lados del cuello, en algunos casos completo a través de los hombros; no quebrado mediodorsalmente-----------8
   Sin collar oscuro; con conspícuo parche oscuro en la nuca-----------------------melanorhinus

8. Una sola cantal------------------------------9
   Dos cantales---------------------------------10

9. Supraorbitales en dos filas--------malachiticus
   Supraorbitales en una fila----------acanthinus

10. Más de 35 escamas dorsales entre la interparietal y el nivel posterior del fémur----------11
    Menos de 35 escamas dorsales entre la interparietal y nivel posterior del fémur--------12

11. Supraorbitales en una fila----------acanthinus
    Supraorbitales en dos filas--------malachiticus

12. Parietales y frecuentemente frontoparietales separadas del supraorbital posterior por una fila de pequeñas escamas--------------------13
    Parietales en contacto con supraorbitales posteriores---------------------------lundelli

13. Fila inferior de labiomentales extendiéndose hasta contactar con segunda posmental-prezygus
    Fila inferior de labiomentales extendiéndose sólo hasta tercera posmental----------serrifer

SCELOPORUS ACANTHINUS Bocourt

1873 Sceleporus acathhinus Bocourt (erroneous spelling), Ann. Sci. Nat. Zool. Paris, (5) 17, art. 6
bis: 24. Type-locality: San Agustin, Volcan Atitlán, Guatemala, 610 m.
1874 Sceloporus acanthinus—Bocourt (corrected spelling), Miss. Sci. Mex., Rept.: 180, pl. 18, figs.
10-10b, pl. 19, figs. 4-4a.

Distribution: Low and moderate elevations from eastern Chiapas, Mexico to Guatemala and El
Salvador.

Content: Two subspecies.

Key to the subspecies

1. Two canthal scales--------------acanthinus
   Single canthal scale----------------lunaei

Clave de subespecies

1. Dos escamas cantales-------------acanthinus
   Una sola escama cantal--------------lunaei

Sceloporus acanthinus acanthinus Bocourt

1918 Sceloporus guentheri Stejneger, Proc. Biol. Soc. Washington, 31: 92. Type-locality:
Mexico.
1930 Sceloporus acanthinurus Gadow (erroneous spelling of acanthinus), Jorullo: 66.
1939 Sceloporus acanthinus Smith, Zool. Ser. Field Mus. Nat. Hist., 26: 74, pls. 6-7.
1963 Sceloporus acanthinus acanthinus—Stuart, Misc. Publ. Mus. Zool. Univ. Mich., 122: 70.

Distribution: Low and moderate elevations of Pacific slope from eastern Chiapas, Mexico to
El Salvador.

Sceloporus acanthinus lunaei Bocourt

1873 Sceloporus lunaei Bocourt, Ann. Sci. Nat. Zool. Paris, (5) 17, art. 10: 1. Plateau of
Guatemala, 1500 m.
1939 Sceloporus lunaei—Smith, Zool. Ser. Field Mus. Nat. Hist., 26: 63, pl. 5.
1963 Sceloporus acanthinus lunaei—Stuart, Misc. Publ. Mus. Zool. Univ. Mich., 122: 70.

Distribution: Moderate elevations from central through eastern Guatemala, to El
Salvador.

SCELOPORUS CARINATUS Smith

1936 Sceloporus carinatus Smith, Proc. Biol. Soc. Washington, 49: 89, pl. 2, figs. 2-3. Type-locality:
Near Tuxtla Gutiérrez, Chiapas, Mexico.

Distribution: Headwaters of Río Grijalva, from Chiapas, Mexico to headwaters of Río Negro,
Guatemala.

SCELOPORUS CHRYSOSTICTUS Cope

1866 Sceloporus chrysostictus Cope, Proc. Acad. Nat. Sci. Phila., 1866: 125. Type-locality: Yucatán,
Mexico.
1939 Sceloporus chrysostictus—Smith, Zool. Ser. Field Mus. Nat. Hist., 26: 295, pl. 24.

Distribution: Yucatán Peninsula south to central El Petén, Guatemala and northern British Honduras.

SCELOPORUS LUNDELLI Smith

1939 Sceloporus lundelli Smith, Zool. Ser. Field Mus. Nat. Hist., 26: 66, pl. 4. Type-locality:
Cohune Ridge, 20 mi SE of Benque Viejo, British Honduras.

Distribution: Yucatán Peninsula to British Honduras and El Petén, Guatemala.

Content: Two subspecies, one of which (gaigeae Smith) is extralimital.

Sceloporus <u>lundelli</u> <u>lundelli</u> Smith

   1939 <u>Sceloporus</u> <u>lundelli</u> <u>lundelli</u> Smith, Zool. Ser. Field Mus. Nat. Hist., 26: 66, pl. 4.

      Distribution: Southern parts of Yucatán Peninsula to British Honduras and El Petén, Guatemala.

SCELOPORUS MALACHITICUS Cope

  1864 <u>Sceloporus</u> <u>malachiticus</u> Cope, Proc. Acad. Nat. Sci. Phila., 1864: 178. Type-locality: Near Arriba, Costa Rica.

    Distribution: Veracruz and Chiapas, Mexico, to Panama.

    Content: Five subspecies, of which two (<u>internasalis</u> Smith and Bumzahen and <u>salvini</u> Günther) are extralimital.

Key to the subspecies	Clave de subespecies

1. Dorsal scales usually more than 37--------2
   Dorsal scales usually less than 38---------
   -----------------------------<u>malachiticus</u>
	1. Normalmente más de 37 dorsales------------2
	   Normalmente menos de 38 dorsales-----------
	   -----------------------------<u>malachiticus</u>

2. Two canthal scales------------<u>taeniocnemis</u>
   Single canthal scale------------<u>smaragdinus</u>
	2. Dos escamas cantales-----------<u>taeniocnemis</u>
	   Una sola escama cantal----------<u>smaragdinus</u>

Sceloporus <u>malachiticus</u> <u>malachiticus</u> Cope

   1890 <u>Sceloporus</u> <u>irazuensis</u> Günther, Biol. Cent. Amer., Rept.: 67. Type-locality: Irazú, Costa Rica.
   1942 [<u>Sceloporus</u>] <u>malachiticus</u> <u>malachiticus</u>—Smith, Proc. U.S. Nat. Mus., 92: 356.

     Distribution: Guatemala to Panama.

Sceloporus <u>malachiticus</u> <u>smaragdinus</u> Bocourt

   1873 <u>Sceloporus</u> <u>smaragdinus</u> Bocourt, Ann. Sci. Nat. Paris, (5) 17, art. 10: 1. Type-locality: Solola, Totonicapan, and Quezaltenango, Guatemala, 2000 m.
   1927 <u>Sceloporus</u> <u>schmidti</u> Jones, Occ. Pap. Mus. Zool. Univ. Mich., 186: 4. Type-locality: Mountain camp west of San Pedro, Honduras, 4500 ft.
   1939 <u>Sceloporus</u> <u>formosus</u> <u>smaragdinus</u>—Smith, Zool. Ser. Field Mus. Nat. Hist., 26: 41.
   1942 <u>Sceloporus</u> <u>malachiticus</u> <u>smaragdinus</u>—Smith, Proc. U.S. Nat. Mus., 92: 356.

    Distribution: Intermediate and high elevations of plateaus of Guatemala, excluding Alta Verapaz and Caribbean slope of Sierra de los Cuchumatanes.

Sceloporus <u>malachiticus</u> <u>taeniocnemis</u> Cope

   1885 <u>Sceloporus</u> <u>taeniocnemis</u> Cope, Proc. Amer. Phil. Soc., 22: 399. Type-locality: Guatemala; restricted to Cobán, Guatemala, by Smith and Taylor, Bull. U.S. Nat Mus., 199, 1950, 108.
   1949 <u>Sceloporus</u> <u>malachiticus</u> <u>taeniocnemis</u>—Smith, Jour. Washington Acad. Sci., 39: 39.

    Distribution: Moderate and high elevations of Alta Verapaz and Caribbean slope of Sierra de los Cuchumatanes in Guatemala; Mesa Central and Sierra Madre in Chiapas, Mexico; encircling <u>Sceloporus</u> <u>malachiticus</u> <u>smaragdinus</u> on east, north, and northwest.

SCELOPORUS MELANORHINUS Bocourt

1876 _Sceloporus melanorhinus_ Bocourt, Ann. Sci. Nat. Zool., Paris, (6) 3, art. 12: 2. Type-locality: Isthmus of Tehuantepec, restricted to Cuidad de Tehuantepec, Mexico, by Smith and Taylor, Bull. U.S. Nat. Mus., 199, 1950, 112.

Distribution: Nayarit to Oaxaca, Mexico; apparently discontinuous in Chiapas; in Río Grijalva drainage of Guatemala.

Content: Three subspecies, two of which (_melanorhinus_ Bocourt and _calligaster_ Smith) are extra-limital.

Sceloporus melanorhinus _stuarti_ Smith

1948 _Sceloporus melanorhinus stuarti_ Smith, Nat. Hist. Misc., Chicago Acad. Sci., 20: 1. Type-locality: Finca Canibal, Huehuetenango, Guatemala, about 3000 ft.

Distribution: Moderate elevations of valley of Río Grijalva in Chiapas, Mexico, and head-water valleys in adjacent Guatemala.

SCELOPORUS PREZYGUS Smith

1942 _Sceloporus prezygus_ Smith, Proc. U.S. Nat. Mus., 92: 354. Type-locality: Conjab (between San Bartolomé and Comitán), Chiapas, Mexico; 5300 ft.

Distribution: Moderate and intermediate elevations on Mesa Central of Chiapas, Mexico, through drier parts of headwater valleys of Río Grijalva and upper Río Negro of Guatemala.

SCELOPORUS SERRIFER Cope

1866 _Sceloporus serrifer_ Cope, Proc. Acad. Nat. Sci. Phila., 1866: 124. Type-locality: Yucatán, Mexico; restricted by Smith and Taylor, Bull. U.S. Nat. Mus., 199, 1950, 124, to Mérida, Yucatán, Mexico.

Distribution: Tamaulipas, Mexico, to El Petén, Guatemala.

Content: Three subspecies, two (_plioporus_ Smith and _cariniceps_ Martin) extralimital.

Comment: Specimens from Guatemala called _Sceloporus serrifer plioporus_ Smith are all _Sceloporus prezygus_, according to Stuart, Misc. Publ. Mus. Zool. Univ. Mich., 122, 1963, 72.

Sceloporus serrifer serrifer Cope

1939 _Sceloporus serrifer serrifer_—Smith, Zool. Ser. Field Mus. Nat. Hist., 26: 212.

Distribution: Yucatán Peninsula south to central El Petén, Guatemala.

SCELOPORUS SINIFERUS Cope

1869 _Sceloporus siniferus_ Cope, Proc. Amer. Phil. Soc., 11: 159. Type-locality: Pacific side of the Isthmus of Tehuantepec, Mexico.
1939 _Sceloporus siniferus_—Smith, Zool. Ser. Field Mus. Nat. Hist., 26: 313, pl. 25.

Distribution: Guerrero to western Guatemala; highlands of Oaxaca, Mexico.

Content: Two subspecies, one (_cupreus_ Bocourt) extralimital.

Sceloporus siniferus siniferus Cope

1873 _Sceloporus humeralis_ Bocourt, Ann. Sci. Nat. Zool. Paris, (5) 17, art. 10: 2. Type-locality: Oaxaca, Mexico.
1950 _Sceloporus siniferus siniferus_—Smith and Taylor, Bull. U.S. Nat. Mus., 199: 134.

Distribution: Low and moderate elevations of Pacific slope; Guerrero, Mexico to Pacific coastal plain of western Guatemala.

SCELOPORUS SQUAMOSUS Bocourt

1874 Sceloporus squamosus Bocourt, Miss. Sci. Mex., Rept.: 212, pl. 18 bis, figs. 7-7c and pl. 19, fig. 3. Type-locality: Guatemala [? city]; Antigua, 1500 m; and embayment of Río Nagualate; Guatemala.

1874 Sceloporus fulvus Bocourt, Miss. Sci. Mex., Rept.: 214, pl. 18 bis, figs. 8-8c. Type-locality: La Union, Salvador.

1939 Sceloporus squamosus—Smith, Zool. Ser. Field Mus. Nat. Hist., 26: 319, pl. 24.

Distribution: Low and moderate elevations from eastern Chiapas, Mexico, along Pacific slope to Costa Rica; dry valleys on Caribbean slope of Guatemala and Honduras, also on southeastern highlands of Guatemala.

SCELOPORUS TEAPENSIS Günther

1890 Sceloporus teapensis Günther, Biol. Cent. Amer., Rept.: 75. Type-locality: Teapa, Tabasco, Mexico.

1939 Sceloporus teapensis—Smith, Zool. Ser. Field Mus. Nat. Hist., 26: 256, pl. 21.

Distribution: Low and moderate elevations along Caribbean slope; southern Veracruz, Mexico to eastern Guatemala, excluding outer end of Yucatán Peninsula.

SCELOPORUS VARIABILIS Wiegmann

1834 Sc[eloporus] variabilis Wiegmann, Herpetologia Mexicana: 51. Type-locality: Mexico; restricted to Veracruz, Mexico by Smith and Taylor, Bull. U.S. Nat. Mus., 199, 1950, 130.

Distribution: Mexico to Costa Rica.

Content: Four subspecies, two of which (marmoratus Hallowell and smithi Hartweg and Oliver) are extralimital.

Key to the subspecies	Clave de subespecies
1. Total femoral pores more than 20---variabilis Femoral pores fewer than 20--------olloporus	1. Poros femorales en total más de 20---variabilis Poros femorales menos de 20-------olloporus

Sceloporus variabilis variabilis

1934 Sceloporus variabilis variabilis—Smith, Proc. Biol. Soc. Washington, 47: 128.

Distribution: Low, moderate and intermediate elevations from Tamaulipas and Queretaro, Mexico, south on plateau and on Caribbean slope to Isthmus of Tehuantepec, thence through valley of Río Grijalva, Chiapas, Mexico, through headwater valleys of same river in Guatemala.

Sceloporus variabilis olloporus Smith

1937 Sceloporus variabilis olloporus Smith, Occ. Pap. Mus. Zool. Univ. Mich., 358: 11. Type-locality: San Juanillo, Costa Rica.

Distribution: Low and moderate elevations from dry basins of central Guatemala into northern and central Honduras and south along Pacific slope to Costa Rica.

SPHAERODACTYLUS Wagler

    1830 Sphaerodactylus Wagler, Nat. Syst. Amph.: 143. Type-species: Lacerta sputator Sparrman.
    1831 Sphaeriodactylus Gray (substitute name for Sphaerodactylus Wagler, 1830), Synopsis Species Class
        Reptilia, in Griffith, Cuvier's Animal Kingdom, 9: 52.

    Distribution: Antilles, Central America, northern South America; introduced in Florida and Florida
    keys.

    Content: 61 species, of which 50 are extralimital, according to Wermuth, Das Tierreich, 80, 1965.
    One species, fantasticus Duméril and Bibron, has been erroneously recorded from Venezuela.

Key to the species

1. Dorsal scales keeled------------------------2
   Dorsal scales smooth------------------------6

2. Dorsal scales flat, very small, weakly keeled;
   snout rounded; scales on ventral surface of
   tail widened-------------------------------3
   Dorsal scales may or may not be flat; snout
   pointed; scales on ventral surface of tail may
   or may not be widened----------------------4

3. Ventral scales weakly imbricate; juveniles with
   transverse bands on shoulder, dorsum, lumbar
   region and tail; ground color in adults pale
   brown with chestnut spotting-------lineolatus
   Ventral scales distinctly imbricate; black
   streaks on head (nasal-auricular and interocular-occipital); finely spotted with black
   dorsally-------------------------continentalis

4. Dorsal scales imbricate----------------------5
   Dorsal scales juxtaposed; dorsal pattern with
   two light bands length of body-----------molei

5. Middorsal scales smaller than other dorsals;
   head with irregular black and white stripes;
   dorsum without transverse light lines---------
   ---------------------------------------mertensi
   Middorsal scales same as other dorsals; head
   without irregular black and white stripes;
   dorsal pattern with transverse light lines----
   --dunni

6. Dorsal scales imbricate; snout rounded--------7
   Dorsal scales juxtaposed; snout pointed-------8

7. Subcaudal scales widened; dorsum finely
   spotted------------------------millepunctatus
   Subcaudal scales not widened; dorsum heavily
   spotted----------------------------pacificus

8. Dorsal scales granular, dorsal pattern generally spotted-----------------------------9
   Dorsal scales not granular but flat; dorsal
   pattern generally without spots------------10

9. Ocular spine present; dorsal granular scales
   tuberculate, trihedral, strongly differentia-
   ted-----------------------------------rosaurae
   Ocular spine absent; dorsal scales flat,
   neither tuberculate nor trihedral------------
   -----------------------------------scapularis

10. Snout pointed; subcaudal scales not widened----
    -----------------------------------homolepis
    Snout rounded; subcaudal scales widened-------
    -------------------------------------glaucus

Clave de especies

1. Escamas dorsales quilladas--------------------2
   Escamas dorsales lisas----------------------6

2. Escamas dorsales planas, muy pequeñas, debil-
   mente carenadas; hocico redondeado; escamas
   inferiores de la cola ensanchadas-----------3
   Escamas dorsales planas o no; hocico puntiagudo; escamas inferiores de la cola ensanchadas o no---------------------------------4

3. Escamas ventrales ligeramente imbricadas;
   bandas transversales en los juveniles en
   cuello, dorso, región lumbar y cola; adultos
   manchados de castaño oscuro sobre pardo
   claro----------------------------------lineolatus
   Escamas ventrales claramente imbricadas; sobre
   la cabeza líneas negras (nasal-auricular e
   interocular-occipital); manchados finamente
   de negro------------------------continentalis

4. Escamas dorsales imbricadas------------------5
   Escamas dorsales yuxtapuestas; dos bandas
   claras a lo largo del dorso-------------molei

5. Escamas dorsales medianas más pequeñas; cabeza
   con líneas negras y blancas irregulares; dorso
   sin líneas claras transversales-------mertensi
   Escamas dorsales del mismo tamaño que las otras
   escamas; cabeza sin líneas negras y blancas
   irregulares; diseño dorsal sin líneas claras
   transversales--------------------------dunni

6. Escamas dorsales imbricadas; hocico redon-
   deado---------------------------------------7
   Escamas dorsales yuxtapuestas; hocico agudo---8

7. Subcaudales ensanchadas, dorso finamente man-
   chado--------------------------millepunctatus
   Subcaudales no ensanchadas; dorso con manchas
   densas e irregulares----------------pacificus

8. Escamas dorsales granulares; diseño dorsal
   generalmente manchado----------------------9
   Escamas dorsales no granulares, planas; diseño
   generalmente no manchado-------------------10

9. Espina ocular presente; gránulos dorsales
   tuberculares, trihedrales, fuertemente
   diferenciados------------------------rosaurae
   Espina ocular ausente; gránulos dorsales no
   tuberculares ni trihedrales--------scapularis

10. Hocico agudo; escamas subcaudales no ensan-
    chadas-----------------------------homolepis
    Hocico redondeado; escamas subcaudales ensan-
    chadas-------------------------------glaucus

SPHAERODACTYLUS CONTINENTALIS Werner

1896 Sphaerodactylus argus var. continentalis Werner, Verh. Zool. Bot. Ges. Wien, 46: 345. Type-locality: "Honduras".
1962 Sphaerodactylus continentalis—Smith and Del Toro, Herpetologica, 18: 102.

Distribution: Mexico south to Costa Rica.

SPHAERODACTYLUS DUNNI Schmidt

1936 Sphaerodactylus dunni Schmidt, Proc. Biol. Soc. Wash., 49: 46. Type-locality: Río Naco, near Cofradia, Honduras.

Distribution: Known only from type locality.

SPHAERODACTYLUS GLAUCUS Cope

1865 Sphaerodactylus glaucus Cope, Proc. Acad. Nat. Sci. Phila., 1865: 192. Type-locality: near Mérida, Yucatán, Mexico.

Distribution: Mexico and Guatemala.

Content: Two subspecies, one (inornatus Peters) extralimital.

Sphaerodactylus glaucus glaucus Cope

1949 Sphaerodactylus glaucus glaucus—Smith, Jour. Wash. Acad. Sci., 39: 34.

Distribution: Caribbean slope from Veracruz, Mexico, including Yucatán, to eastern Guatemala.

SPHAERODACTYLUS HOMOLEPIS Cope

1886 Sphaerodactylus homolepis Cope, Proc. Amer. Philos. Soc., 23: 277. Type-locality: Nicaragua.
1916 Sphaerodactylus homolepis var. carinatus Andersson, Meddel. Göteborg. Mus. Zool., 9: 5. Type-locality: Costa Rica.

Distribution: Nicaragua and Costa Rica.

SPHAERODACTYLUS LINEOLATUS (Lichtenstein)

1856 Sphaeriodactylus lineolatus Lichtenstein, Nomencl. Rept. Amph. Mus. Zool. Berlin: 6. Type-locality: Veragua, Panama.
1862 S.[phaerodactylus] lineolatus—Cope, Proc. Acad. Nat. Sci. Phila., 1861: 497.
1862 Sphaerodactylus casicolus Cope, Proc. Acad. Nat. Sci. Phila., 1861: 499. Type-locality: Truando Region, Colombia.

Distribution: British Honduras south to Panama and northwestern Colombia; a doubtful record in Ecuador on basis of USNM 65451, from Macas.

SPHAERODACTYLUS MERTENSI Wermuth

1916 Sphaerodactylus lineolatus var. imbricatus Andersson (preoccupied by Sphaerodactylus imbricatus Fischer, 1881), Meddel. Göteborg. Mus. Zool., 9: 5. Type-locality: Costa Rica.
1956 Sphaerodactylus imbricatus—Taylor, Univ. Kansas Sci. Bull., 38: 45, figs. 10-11.
1965 Sphaerodactylus mertensi Wermuth (substitute name for imbricatus Andersson), Das Tierreich, 80: 170. Type-locality: Costa Rica.

Distribution: Costa Rica.

SPHAERODACTYLUS MILLEPUNCTATUS (Hallowell)

   1861 Sphaeriodactylus millepunctatus Hallowell, Proc. Acad. Nat. Sci. Phila., 1860: 480. Type-
       locality: Nicaragua.
   1862 Sphaerodactylus millepunctatus—Cope, Proc. Acad. Nat. Sci. Phila., 1861: 499.

    Distribution: Central America: Nicaragua and Costa Rica.

SPHAERODACTYLUS MOLEI Boettger

   1894 Sphaerodactylus molei Boettger, J. Field Natural. Club, Trinidad, 2: 80. Type-locality: Caparo,
       Trinidad.
   1900 Sphaerodactylus buergeri Werner, Verh. Zool. Bot. Ges. Wien, 50: 264. Type-locality: Port of
       Spain, Trinidad.
   1927 Sphaerodactylus venezuelanus Roux, Verh. Naturf. Ges. Basel, 38: 254. Type-locality: El Mene,
       Estado Falcón, Venezuela.

    Distribution: Northern Colombia, Venezuela, Guyana, Trinidad and Tobago.

SPHAERODACTYLUS PACIFICUS Stejneger

   1903 Sphaerodactylus pacificus Stejneger, Proc. Biol. Soc. Wash., 16: 3. Type-locality: Cocos
       Island, west coast of Costa Rica.

    Distribution: Cocos Island, on Pacific Coast of Costa Rica.

SPHAERODACTYLUS ROSAURAE Parker

   1940 Sphaerodactylus rosaurae Parker, Ann. Mag. Nat. Hist., (17) 5: 264. Type-locality: Helene
       Island, Bay Islands, Honduras.

    Distribution: Known only from the type locality.

SPHAERODACTYLUS SCAPULARIS Boulenger

   1902 Sphaerodactylus scapularis Boulenger, Ann. Mag. Nat. Hist., (7) 9: 54. Type-locality: San
       Javier, Esmeraldas Province, Ecuador.

    Distribution: Northwestern Ecuador and Colombia.

REPTILIA: SAURIA: IGUANIDAE   ★ ★ ★   STENOCERCUS

Prepared by Richard Etheridge, San Diego State College, San Diego, California

STENOCERCUS Duméril and Bibron

> 1837 _Stenocercus_ Duméril and Bibron, Erp. Gén., 4: 349. Type-species: _Stenocercus rosei-ventris_ Duméril and Bibron.
> 1837 _Trachycyclus_ Duméril and Bibron, Erp. Gén., 4: 355. Type-species: _Trachycyclus marmoratus_ Duméril and Bibron.
> 1843 _Steironotus_ (_Stenocercus_) Fitzinger, Systema Reptilium: 71. Type-species: _Stenocercus rosei-ventris_ Duméril and Bibron.
> 1843 _Heterotropis_ (_Trachycyclus_) Fitzinger, Systema Reptilium: 71. Type-species: _Trachycyclus marmoratus_ Duméril and Bibron.
> 1845 _Scelotrema_ Tschudi, Arch. für Naturg., 11 (1): 154. Type-species: _Scelotrema crassicaudatum_ Tschudi.
> 1859 _Microphractus_ Günther, Proc. Zool. Soc. London, 1859: 90. Type-species: _Microphractus humeralis_ Günther.

> Distribution: Andean South America.

> Content: Fourteen species.

Key to the species[1]

1. Caudal scales not much larger than ventral scales of body, their mucrons not forming stout, projecting spines; each autotomy segment of tail with three rows of scales (except _cupreus_ with two)--------------------------2
   Caudal scales much larger than ventral scales of body, their mucrons forming stout, projecting spines; each autotomy segment of tail with two rows of scales---------------------10

2. Vertebral scale row absent, or, if present, scales identical to adjacent scales----------3
   Vertebral scale row present, scales distinctly larger than adjacent scales, at least on neck and anterior part of body--------------------7

3. Lateral neck scales not much smaller than dorsal neck scales (except for granular pocket), and imbricate----------------------4
   Lateral neck scales abruptly smaller than dorsal neck scales, barely imbricate or granular--------------------------------6

4. Tail at least twice length of head and body; no postfemoral dermal pocket present; anal region of males not black--------------------------5
   Tail not more than twice length of head and body; postfemoral dermal pocket present; anal region of adult male black---------_melanopygus_

5. Tail longer, 2.8 to 3.0 times head and body length; midbody scales 30-39-----------_moestus_
   Tail shorter, 2.0 to 2.4 times longer than head and body; midbody scales 37-62----_ornatissimus_

Clave de especies[1]

1. Escamas caudales no mayores que las ventrales del cuerpo; sus mucrones no forman gruesas espinas proyectadas; cada segmento autotómico de la cola tiene tres filas de escamas (excepto _cupreus_ con dos)--------------------2
   Escamas caudales mayores que las ventrales del cuerpo, sus mucrones forman gruesas espinas proyectadas; cada segmento autotómico de la cola tiene dos filas de escamas-------------10

2. Fila vertebral de escamas ausente, o si está presente las escamas son idénticas a las de las filas adyacentes-------------------------3
   Fila vertebral de escamas presente, escamas distintamente mayores que las adyacentes, por lo menos en la nuca y anteriormente en el cuerpo------------------------------------7

3. Escamas laterales de la nuca no más pequeñas que las dorso nucales (excepto por el bolsillo granular), e imbricadas---------------------4
   Escamas laterales de la nuca abruptamente menores que las dorso nucales apenas imbricadas o granulares------------------------6

4. Cola por lo menos el doble que la longitud de la cabeza y el cuerpo; con bolsillo dérmico postfemoral; escamas de la región anal no negras------------------------------------5
   Cola no más que el doble de la longitud de la cabeza y el cuerpo; con bolsillo dérmico postfemoral; escamas de la región anal, en machos adultos, negras-------------------_melanopygus_

5. Cola larga, 2.8 a 3.0 veces el largo de la cabeza y el cuerpo; 30-39 filas de escamas en el medio del cuerpo--------------------_moestus_
   Cola corta, 2.0 a 2.4 veces el largo de la cabeza y el cuerpo; 37-62 filas de escamas en el medio cuerpo------------------_ornatissimus_

---

[1]Vertebral and paravertebral scales counted from occiput to anterior margin of thigh when hind leg is at right angles to body; midbody scales around the body at point half way between limb insertions.

[1]Escamas vertebrales y paravertebrales contadas desde el occipucio al margen anterior del muslo, con el miembro posterior en ángulo recto con el cuerpo; las escamas alrededor del cuerpo, son contadas en el punto medio entre las dos inserciones de los pares de miembros.

6. Scales of body and tail more sharply keeled; autotomy segments of tail distinct with two scale rows per segment; antehumeral folds more closely approximate midventrally, separated by about six pectoral scales--------------cupreus
Scales of body and tail less sharply keeled, less strongly mucronate; autotomy segments of tail barely apparent, with three rows per segment; antehumeral folds widely separated by about ten pectoral scales----------chrysopygus

7. More than 70 scales around middle of body-----8
Fewer than 70 scales around middle of body------------------------------------variabilis

8. Fewer than 115 paravertebral scales-----------9
More than 115 paravertebral scales----humeralis

9. Midbody scales 74-88; paravertebral scales 73-92--------------------------------------varius
Midbody scales 80-101; paravertebral scales 90-110--------------------------------boettgeri

10. Lateral nuchal scales elongate and distinctly imbricate-------------------------------------2
Lateral nuchal scales granular or subimbricate and convex--------------------------------11

11. Ventral scales smooth; scales on posterior surface of thighs granular or nearly so-----12
Ventral body scales weakly keeled, at least on throat and chest; scales on posterior surface of thigh small but distinctly imbricate-------------------------------------roseiventris

12. More than 60 scales around middle of body; postfemoral dermal pocket usually present---13
Fewer than 60 scales around body; no postfemoral dermal pocket--------------marmoratus

13. Lateral scales on posterior part of body larger, subimbricate; fewer than 105 scales around midbody-------------------------------------14
All scales on sides of body very small and granular; more than 105 scales around midbody-------------------------------crassicaudatus

14. Caudal whorls subequal----------------simonsii
Caudal whorls alternating large and small, latter 1/3 to 2/3 length of former----carrioni

6. Escamas del cuerpo y cola más fuertemente quilladas; segmentos autotómicos de la cola distintos con dos filas de escamas por segmento; pliegues antehumerales cercanos aproximadamente en el medioviente, separados por alrededor de seis escamas pectorales---cupreus
Escamas del cuerpo y la cola menos quilladas y mucronadas menos fuertemente; segmentos autotómicos de la cola poco aparentes con tres filas por segmento, pliegues antehumerales anchamente separados por diez escamas pectorales----------------------------chrysopygus

7. Más de 70 escamas alrededor del cuerpo--------8
Menos de 70 escamas alrededor del cuerpo------------------------------------variabilis

8. Menos de 115 escamas paravertebrales----------9
Más de 115 escamas paravertebrales----humeralis

9. Escamas al medio cuerpo 74-88; escamas paravertebrales 73-92----------------------varius
Escamas al medio cuerpo 80-101; escamas paravertebrales 90-110-----------------boettgeri

10. Escamas nucales laterales, alargadas y distintamente imbricadas--------------------------2
Escamas nucales laterales, granulares o subimbricadas y convexas----------------------11

11. Escamas ventrales lisas; escamas de superficie posterior del muslo granulares o casi granulares--------------------------------------12
Escamas ventrales del cuerpo débilmente quilladas, por lo menos en la garganta y mejilla; escamas de superficie posterior del muslo pequeñas pero distintamente imbricadas----------------------------------roseiventris

12. Más de 60 escamas alrededor del medio cuerpo; bolsillo dérmico postfemoral usualmente presente--------------------------------------13
Menos de 60 escamas alrededor del medio cuerpo; sin bolsillo postfemoral dérmico----marmoratus

13. Escamas laterales de la parte posterior del cuerpo grandes, subimbricadas; menos de 105 escamas alrededor del medio cuerpo----------14
Todas las escamas de los lados del cuerpo muy pequeñas y granulares; más de 105 escamas alrededor del medio cuerpo------crassicaudatus

14. Anillos de espinas subiguales----------simonsii
Anillos de espinas alternas de grandes y pequeñas, los últimos 1/3 a 2/3 el tamaño de los primeros--------------------------carrioni

STENOCERCUS BOETTGERI Boulenger
    humeralis group

1911 Stenocercus boettgeri Boulenger, Ann. Mag. Nat. Hist., (8) 7: 22. Type-locality: Huancabamba, Peru.
1941 Stenocercus juninensis Shreve, Proc. New England Zool. Club, 18: 75. Type-locality: Huasqui, near Tarma, Departmento de Junin, Peru.

Distribution: Highlands of southern Ecuador and northern and central Peru.

STENOCERCUS CARRIONI Parker
crassicaudatus group

1934 Stenocercus carrioni Parker, Ann. Mag. Nat. Hist., (10) 14: 268. Type-locality: Zamora, Ecuador, 3250 ft.

Distribution: Southern highlands of Ecuador.

STENOCERCUS CHRYSOPYGUS Boulenger
chrysopygus group

1900 Stenocercus chrysopygus Boulenger, Ann. Mag. Nat. Hist., (7) 6: 183. Type-locality: Carao, 8000 ft, Huaras, 10,000 ft, and Recuay, 11,000 ft, Peru.

Distribution: Cordillera Blanca of western Peru to about 3400 m.

STENOCERCUS CRASSICAUDATUS (Tschudi)
crassicaudatus group

1845 Sc.[elotrema] crassicaudatum Tschudi, Arch. für Naturg., 11 (1): 155. Type-locality: Peru; further specified by Tschudi, Fauna Peruana, Rept., 1846, 28, as Urubamba, Peru.
1885 Stenocercus torquatus Boulenger, Cat. Liz. Brit. Mus., 2: 133, pl. 8, fig. 1. Type-locality: Peru.
1900 Urocentrum meyeri Werner, Abh. Ber. K. Zool. Anthro.-Ethn. Mus. Dresden, 9: 4. Type-locality: Lima, Peru.
1907 Stenocercus crassicaudatus—Roux, Rev. Suisse Zool., 15: 299.
1913 Stenocercus ervingi Stejneger, Proc. U.S. Nat. Mus., 45: 545. Type-locality: Huadquinia, Peru, 5000 ft.

Distribution: Amazonian side of Andes in central and southern Peru to about 2000 m.

STENOCERCUS CUPREUS Boulenger
chrysopygus group

1885 Stenocercus cupreus Boulenger, Cat. Liz. Brit. Mus., 2: 135, pl. 9, fig. 1. Type-locality: Huánuco, Peru.

Distribution: Known only from state of Huánuco, in central Peru.

STENOCERCUS HUMERALIS (Günther)
humeralis group

1859 Microphractus humeralis Günther, Proc. Zool. Soc. London, 1859: 90. Type-locality: Andes of western Ecuador.
1885 Stenocercus humeralis—Boulenger, Cat. Liz. Brit. Mus., 2: 134, pl. 8, fig. 2.

Distribution: Inter-Andean plateau of Ecuador, from valley of Cuenca south.

STENOCERCUS MARMORATUS (Duméril and Bibron)
crassicaudatus group

1837 Trachycyclus marmoratus Duméril and Bibron, Erp. Gén., 4: 356. Type-locality: Rio-Grande, Brazil; according to Guibé, Cat. Types Lézards Paris Mus., 1954, 50.
1885 Stenocercus marmoratus—Boulenger, Cat. Liz. Brit. Mus., 2: 132.
1910 Stenocercus difficilis Werner, Mitt. Naturhist. Mus. Hamburg, 27 (2): 23. Type-locality: Cochabamba, Bolivia.

Distribution: Andes of central Bolivia to about 3500 m.

STENOCERCUS MELANOPYGUS Boulenger
    chrysopygus group

  1900 Stenocercus melanopygus Boulenger, Ann. Mag. Nat. Hist., (7) 6: 182. Type-locality: Baños, Cajamarca, Peru, 9000 ft.

   Distribution: Estado de Cajamarca in northern Peru.

STENOCERCUS MOESTUS Boulenger
    chrysopygus group

  1885 Stenocercus moestus Boulenger, Cat. Liz. Brit. Mus., 2: 136, pl. 9, fig. 2. Type-locality: Lima, Peru.

   Distribution: Valley of Río Rimac, from Callao on coast to Chosica at 2500 ft, western central Peru.

STENOCERCUS ORNATISSIMUS (Girard), new combination
    chrysopygus group

  1857 Saccodeira ornatissima Girard, Proc. Acad. Nat. Sci. Phila., 1857: 198. Type-locality: Obrajillo, and Yanga, Peru.

   Distribution: Pacific slopes of Andes and adjacent coastal lowlands of Peru.

STENOCERCUS ROSEIVENTRIS Duméril and Bibron
    crassicaudatus group

  1837 Stenocercus rosei-ventris Duméril and Bibron, Erp. Gén., 4: 350. Type-locality: Bolivia.
  1913 Stenocercus atrigularis Werner, Mitt. Naturhist. Mus. Hamburg, 30 (2): 11. Type-locality: Provincia Beni, Bolivia (southern drainage of Amazon).

   Distribution: Eastern slopes of Andes and adjacent lowlands of Peru, Bolivia; northern Argentina south to Estado de Salta; Acré, Brazil.

STENOCERCUS SIMONSII Boulenger
    crassicaudatus group

  1899 Stenocercus Simonsii Boulenger, Ann. Mag. Nat. Hist., (7) 4: 454. Type-locality: Oña, Ecuador, 6500 ft.

   Distribution: Highlands of Ecuador.

STENOCERCUS VARIABILIS Boulenger
    humeralis group

  1901 Stenocercus variabilis Boulenger, Ann. Mag. Nat. Hist., (7) 7: 546. Type-locality: Palca, Bolivia, 10,000 ft.

   Distribution: Uncertain, highlands of northwestern Bolivia and possibly southern and central Peru.

STENOCERCUS VARIUS Boulenger
    humeralis group

  1885 Stenocercus varius Boulenger, Cat. Liz. Brit. Mus., 2: 134, pl. 8, fig. 3. Type-locality: Unknown.

   Distribution: Known only from Chiriboga, Ecuador, at 5000 ft on western slopes.

STENOLEPIS Boulenger

1887 Stenolepis Boulenger, Proc. Zool. Soc. London, 1887: 640. Type-species: Stenolepis ridleyi Boulenger.

Distribution: As for only known species.

Content: One species.

STENOLEPIS RIDLEYI Boulenger

1887 Stenolepis ridleyi Boulenger, Proc. Zool. Soc. London, 1887: 640, figs. a-d. Type-locality: Iguarassu forest, Pernambuco, Brazil.

Distribution: Known only from type locality.

STROBILURUS Wiegmann

1834 Strobilurus Wiegmann, Herpetologia Mexicana: 18. Type-species: Strobilurus torquatus Wiegmann.

Distribution: As for single known species.

Content: One species, according to most recent revision by Etheridge, Bull. Brit. Mus. (Nat. Hist.)
Zool., 17; 1968, 60-62.

STROBILURUS TORQUATUS Wiegmann

1834 Strobilurus torquatus Wiegmann, Herpetologia Mexicana: 18. Type-locality: Brazil.
1855 Doryphorus spinosus Guichenot, Reptiles, in Castelnau, Animaux Nouveaux...de l'Amérique du Sud:
27, pl. 7, fig. 1, 1a. Type-locality: Bahia, Brasil.
1968 Strobilurus torquatus—Etheridge, Bull. Brit. Mus. (Nat. Hist.) Zool., 17: 61.

Distribution: Eastern Brazil.

TEIUS Merrem

1820 Teius Merrem, Tentamen Systematis Amphibiorum: 60. Type-species: Teius viridis Merrem.
1826 Tejus Fitzinger, Neue Classification der Reptilien: 21. Type-species: Lacerta Teyou Daudin.
1830 Acrantus Wagler, Nat. Syst. Amphib.: 154. Type-species: Lacerta Teyou Daudin.

Distribution: As for single known species.

Content: One species.

TEIUS TEYOU (Daudin)

1802 Lacerta Teyou Daudin, Hist. Nat. Rept., 3: 195. Type-locality: Paraguay.
1885 Teius teyou—Boulenger, Cat. Liz. Brit. Mus., 2: 379.

Distribution: Brazil, Bolivia, Paraguay and Uruguay to Provincia Río Negro, Argentina.

Content: Two subspecies.

Key to the subspecies	Clave de subespecies
1. Belly blue---------------------cyanogaster	1. Vientre azul--------------------cyanogaster
Belly not blue-----------------------teyou	Vientre no azul-----------------------teyou

Teius teyou teyou (Daudin)

1820 Teius viridis Merrem, Tentamen Systematis Amphibiorum: 60. Type-locality: South America.
1823 Am.[eiva] Teju Lichtenstein (emendation of teyou Daudin), Verzeichniss der Doubletten des
     Zoologischen Museums, Berlin: 91.
1847 Ameiva coelestis Bibron, in D'Orbigny, Voyage dans l'Amerique meridionale, Reptiles: 2, pl.
     5, figs. 1-5.
1928 Teius teyou teyou—Müller, Zool. Anz., 77: 69.
1960 Teius teyou teyou—Hellmich, Abh. Bayerische Akad. Wiss., Math.-Naturwiss. Kl., new ser.,
     101: 79.

  Distribution: Eastern Argentina, Paraguay and Uruguay to southern Brazil.

Teius teyou cyanogaster Müller

1928 Teius teyou cyanogaster Müller, Zool. Anz., 77: 69. Type-locality: San José de
     Chiquitos, Bolivia.
1960 Teius teyou cyanogaster—Hellmich, Abh. Bayerische Akad. Wiss., Math.-Naturwiss. Kl.,
     new ser., 101: 75, pl. 2, figs. 5-6.

  Distribution: Southeastern Bolivia and adjacent Brazil, northwestern Argentina and
  northern part of Paraguay.

REPTILIA: SAURIA: GEKKONIDAE THECADACTYLUS

THECADACTYLUS Oken

1820 Thecadactylus Goldfuss, Handbuch der Zoologie, 2: 157. Type-species: Gecko laevis
    Daudin.
1830 Thecodactylus Wagler (emendation of Thecadactylus Goldfuss), Nat. Syst. Amphib.: 142.

    Distribution: Mexico; Central and South America, West Indies.

    Content: One species.

THECADACTYLUS RAPICAUDUS (Houttuyn)

1782 Gekko Rapicauda Houttuyn, Verh. Zeeuw. Genootsch. Wet. Vlissingen, 9: 323, pl., fig. 1. Type-
    locality: West Indies; restricted to Chichén Itzá, Yucatán, Mexico, by Smith and Taylor, Bull.
    U.S. Nat. Mus.., 199, 1950, 49.
1793 Stellio perfoliatus Schneider (substitute name for Gekko rapicauda Houttuyn), Amphibiorum
    Physiologiae, 2: 26.
1802 Gecko laevis Daudin, Hist. Nat. Rept., 4: 112. Type-locality: South America.
1802 Gecko surinamensis Daudin, Hist. Nat. Rept., 4: 126. Type-locality: Surinam.
1836 Platydactylus Theconyx Duméril and Bibron (substitute name for Gekko rapicauda Houttuyn 1782),
    Erp. Gén., 3: 306, pl. 33, figs.2-2a.
1845 Thecadactylus rapicaudus—Gray, Cat. Liz. Brit. Mus.: 146.
?1856 Pachydactylus tristis Hallowell, Proc. Acad. Nat. Sci. Phila., 1854: 98. Type-locality: Liberia,
    west coast of Africa.

    Distribution: Lesser Antilles, Mexico, Central America, northwestern South America, to Guianas and
    Trinidad. Known from lowlands on both sides of the Andes in Ecuador.

TRETIOSCINCUS Cope

1862 Tretioscincus Cope, Proc. Acad. Nat. Sci. Phila., 1862: 184. Type-species: Tretioscincus
　　　castanicterus Cope.
1916 Calliscincopus Ruthven, Occ. Pap. Mus. Zool. Univ. Mich., 22: 1. Type-species: Calliscincopus
　　　agilis Ruthven.

　　Distribution: Northern South America; Colombia to Amazonian Brazil including Venezuela and Guianas;
　　　offshore islands along northern coast.

　　Content: Two species.

　　　　　　　Key to the species　　　　　　　　　　　　　　Clave de especies

1. Dorsal scales keeled----------------bifasciatus　　1. Escamas dorsales carenadas----------bifasciatus
　 Dorsal scales smooth---------------------agilis　　　 Escamas dorsales lisas-----------------agilis

TRETIOSCINCUS AGILIS (Ruthven)

1916 Calliscincopus agilis Ruthven, Occ. Pap. Mus. Zool. Univ. Mich., 22: 2. Type-locality: Sand
　　　ridges on Demerara River near Dunoon, Guyana.
1918 Tretioscincus romani Andersson, Ark. för Zool., 11 (16): 5. Type-locality: Bosque Municipal,
　　　Manáus, Amazonas, Brazil.
1923 Tretioscincus brasiliensis Müller, Zool. Anz., 57: 49. Type-locality: Lower Rio Tocantins,
　　　Pará, Brazil.
1969 Tretioscincus agilis—Vanzolini and Rebouças-Spieker, Pap. Avul. Depto. Zool. São Paulo, 22 (13):
　　　124, figs.

　　Distribution: Guyana, Amazonian Brazil.

TRETIOSCINCUS BIFASCIATUS (Duméril)

1851 Heteropus Bifasciatus Duméril, Cat. Méth. Coll. Rept. Mus. Paris: 182. Type-locality: Río
　　　Magdalena valley, Colombia.
1864 Tretioscincus bifasciatus—Cope, Proc. Acad. Nat. Sci. Phila., 1864: 229.

　　Distribution: Northern South America, Dutch Leeward Islands and Margarita Island, Venezuela.

　　　　　　　Key to the subspecies　　　　　　　　　　　　Clave de subespecies

1. Light lateral stripes with distinct black　　　　1. Cintas laterales claras con un borde negro
　 border---------------------------kugleri　　　　　　distinto---------------------------kugleri
　 Light lateral stripes lack distinct black　　　　　 Cintas laterales clara sin borde negro
　 border-----------------------bifasciatus　　　　　　distinto----------------------bifasciatus

　　Tretioscincus bifasciatus bifasciatus (Duméril)

　　　1862 Tretioscincus castanicterus Cope, Proc. Acad. Nat. Sci. Phila., 1862: 184. Type-
　　　　　locality: Colombia.
　　　1947 Tretioscincus bifasciatus [bifasciatus]—Shreve, Bull. Mus. Comp. Zool., 99: 527.

　　　　Distribution: Caribbean Colombia.

　　Tretioscincus bifasciatus kugleri Shreve

　　　1947 Tretioscincus bifasciatus kugleri Shreve, Bull. Mus. Comp. Zool., 99: 527. Type-locality:
　　　　　Paují, Acosta, Estado Falcón, Venezuela.

　　　　Distribution: Northern Venezuela, including Isla Margarita; Dutch Leeward Islands.

REPTILIA: SAURIA: IGUANIDAE TROPIDODACTYLUS

TROPIDODACTYLUS Boulenger

  1885 Tropidodactylus Boulenger, Cat. Liz. Brit. Mus., 2: 97. Type-species: Norops onca
      O'Shaughnessy.

    Distribution: As for single known species.

    Content: One species.

TROPIDODACTYLUS ONCA (O'Shaughnessy)

  1875 Norops onca O'Shaughnessy, Ann. Mag. Nat. Hist., (4) 15: 280. Type-locality: Venezuela, and
      Island of Dominica.
  1885 Tropidodactylus onca—Boulenger, Cat. Liz. Brit. Mus., 2: 97, pl. 6, fig. 2.

    Distribution: Northern Venezuela, Margarita Island.

Prepared by Richard Etheridge, San Diego State College, San Diego, California

TROPIDURUS Wied

1824 <u>Tropidurus</u> Wied, Abb. Nat. Brasil: 6. Type-species: <u>Stellio torquatus</u> Wied.
1831 <u>Platynotus</u> Wagler, Nat. Syst. Amphib.: 146. Type-species: <u>Agama semitaeniata</u> Spix.
1837 <u>Microlophus</u> Duméril and Bibron, Erp. Gén., 4: 334. Type-species: <u>Microlophus Lessonii</u> Duméril and Bibron.
1843 <u>Steirolepis</u> Fitzinger, Systema Reptilium: 72. Type-species: <u>Tropidurus microlophus</u> Wiegmann.
1845 <u>Taraguira</u> Gray, Cat. Liz. Brit. Mus.: 219. Type-species: None designated.
1847 <u>Stirolepis</u> Agassiz (replacement name for <u>Steirolepis</u> Fitzinger), Nomenclatoris Zoologici Index Universalis: 353.
1871 <u>Craniopeltis</u> Peters, Monats. Akad. Wiss. Berlin: 645. Type-species: <u>Tropidurus</u> (<u>Craniopeltis</u>) <u>bivittata</u> Peters.
1871 <u>Laemopristus</u> Peters, Monats. Akad. Wiss. Berlin: 645. Type-species: <u>Tropidurus</u> (<u>Laemopristus</u>) <u>occipitalis</u> Peters.
1874 <u>Aneuporus</u> Bocourt, Miss. Sci. Mex., Rept.: 215. Type-species: <u>Aneuporus occipitalis</u> Bocourt.
1933 <u>Tapinurus</u> Amaral, Mem. Inst. Butantan, 7: 65. Type-species: <u>Tapinurus scutipunctatus</u> Amaral.

Distribution: The Galápagos Islands and South America except for western Colombia, southern Chile and southern Argentina.

Content: About 20 species, all but twelve of which are extralimital, on the Galápagos.

Key to the species[1]

1. No trace of median, longitudinal, vertebral scale row------------------------------------2
   Scales along middle of back form longitudinal row, which may or may not form denticulate crest, and which may or may not be continuous from occiput to tail------------------------5

2. No isolated groups of spinose scales on sides of neck--------------------------------------3
   Isolated groups of enlarged, spinose scales on sides of neck------------------------<u>bogerti</u>

3. Fewer than 90 midbody scales------------------4
   More than 90 scales around middle of body----10

4. Supraoculars band-like; ventrals equal to or larger than dorsals; maximum adult size 70 mm-
   --------------------------------------<u>hygomi</u>
   Supraoculars not band-like; ventrals smaller than dorsals; maximum adult size at least 100 mm------------------------------------<u>hispidus</u>

5. No spinose scales on side of neck-------------6
   Patches or groups of spinose scales on neck----
   --------------------------------<u>spinulosus</u>

6. Dorsal scales of body small, smooth or faintly keeled; more than 115 midbody scales---------7
   Dorsal scales of body large, strongly keeled and imbricate; fewer than 115 midbody scales--
   --------------------------------<u>occipitalis</u>

Clave de especies[1]

1. Ausencia de hilera de escamas vertebral, longitudinal, media------------------------------2
   Escamas a lo largo de la mitad del dorso forman una hilera longitudinal, que puede o no formar una cresta denticulada, y que puede o no ser contínua del occipucio a la cola-------------5

2. Ausencia de grupos aislados de escamas espinosas a los lados del cuello-------------------3
   Grupos aislados de escamas espinosas, ensanchadas a los lados del cuello------------<u>bogerti</u>

3. Menos de 90 escamas alrededor del medio cuerpo-
   --4
   Más de 90 escamas alrededor del medio cuerpo-10

4. Supraoculares acintados; ventrales iguales o más grandes que los dorsales; tamaño máximo del adulto 70 mm----------------------<u>hygomi</u>
   Supraoculares no acintados; ventrales menores que los dorsales; tamaño máximo del adulto por lo menos 100 mm----------------------<u>hispidus</u>

5. Sin escamas espinosas a los lados del cuello--6
   Con grupos de escamas espinosas y ensanchadas a los lados del cuello----------------<u>spinulosus</u>

6. Escamas dorsales del cuerpo chicas, lisas o ligeramente quilladas; más de 115 escamas del medio cuerpo--------------------------------7
   Escamas dorsales del cuerpo grandes, fuertemente quilladas e imbricadas; menos de 115 escamas del medio cuerpo----------<u>occipitalis</u>

---

[1]Note: Vertebral and paravertebral scales are counted from occiput to pointeven with anterior margin of thigh when hind leg is at right angles to body; midbody scales are counted around body half way between limb insertions.
   Two species are omitted from the key—<u>theresioides</u> and <u>tarapacensis</u>.

[1]Nota: Las escamas vertebrales y paravertebrales se cuentan desde el occipucio hasta un punto parejo con el borde anterior del muslo cuando la pata posterior forma un ángulo recto con el cuerpo; las escamas del medio cuerpo se cuentan alrededor del cuerpo a mitad de camino entre las inserciones de los miembros.
   En la clave se omiten dos especies—<u>theresioides</u> y <u>tarapacensis</u>.

7. Lateral body scales very small, almost granular,
   grading abruptly into much larger ventrals---8
   Lateral body scales small but imbricate, grading gradually into somewhat larger ventrals---
   --------------------------------melanopleurus

8. Vertebral scale row conspicuous, uninterrupted
   from occiput to tail, forming a low, denticulate crest on neck, at least in adults; paravertebral scales fewer than 150--------------9
   Vertebral scale row inconspicuous, interrupted
   over shoulders, not at all arched or keeled on
   body; scales adjacent to vertebral row more
   than 170----------------------------theresiae

9. Frontal scales paired between orbits; interparietal width not greater than 1 1/2 times its
   length; fourth toe of adpressed hind limb
   reaches to front of eye------------peruvianus
   Frontal scales single, median between orbits;
   interparietal scale about wice as wide as
   long; fourth toe of adpressed hind limb
   reaches to tympanum----------------thoracicus

10.Dorsal scales smooth--------------semitaeniatus
   Dorsal scales keeled----------------torquatus

7. Escamas de los lados del cuerpo muy chicas,
   casi granulares, pasando abruptamente a escamas ventrales mucho más grandes--------------8
   Escamas laterales del cuerpo chicas pero imbricadas, pasando gradualmente a ventrales algo
   más grandes---------------------melanopleurus

8. Hilera vertebral de escamas conspícua, inin-
   terrumpida desde el occípucio a la cola, formando una cresta baja, denticulada, al menos
   en adultos; menos de 150 escamas paraverte-
   brales---------------------------------------9
   Hilera vertebral de escamas inconspícua, interrumpida sobre los hombros, escamas del cuerpo
   no quilladas o arqueadas; más de 170 escamas
   adyacentes a la hilera vertebral-----theresiae

9. Escamas frontales pares entre las órbitas;
   ancho del interparietal no mayor que 1 1/2
   veces su longitud; cuarto dedo de la extremidad posterior hacia adelante llega hasta el
   frente del ojo---------------------peruvianus
   Escamas frontales de a una, en el medio entre
   las órbitas; escama interparietal aproximadamente dos veces tan ancha como larga; cuarto
   dedo de la extremidad posterior extendida
   hacia adelante llega hasta el tímpano---------
   --------------------------------thoracicus

10.Escamas dorsales lisas-----------semitaeniatus
   Escamas dorsales quilladas-----------torquatus

TROPIDURUS BOGERTI Roze

   1958 Tropidurus bogerti Roze, Acta Biol. Venezuelica, 2: 247, figs. 1-4. Type-locality: Auyantepui,
        Estado Bolívar, Venezuela.

   Distribution: Known only from type locality.

TROPIDURUS HISPIDUS (Spix)

   1825 Agama hispida Spix, Sp. Nov. Lac. Bras.: 12, pl. 15, fig. 2. Type-locality: Rio de Janeiro and
        Bahia, Brazil.
   1825 Agama nigrocollaris Spix, Sp. Nov. Lac. Bras.: 13, pl. 16, fig. 2. Type-locality: Interior of
        Bahia, Brazil.
   1825 Agama cyclurus Spix, Sp. Nov. Lac. Bras.: 14, pl. 17, fig. 1. Type-locality: Bahia, Brazil.
   1845 Taraguira Smithii Gray, Cat. Liz. Brit. Mus.: 221. Type-locality: Pernambuco, Brazil.
   1859 Proctotretus Toelsneri Berthold, Nach. Ges. Wiss. Göttingen, 17: 179. Type-locality: Bahia,
        Brazil.
   1861 Trachycyclus superciliaris Günther, Proc. Zool. Soc. London, 1861: 16. Type-locality: Bahia,
        Brazil.
   1861 T.[ropidurus] macrolepis Reinhardt and Lütken, Vidensk. Medd. Naturhist. Foren. Kjöbenhavn, 1861:
        227, pl. 5, fig. 8. Type-locality: Cotinquiba and Maruim, Estado de Sergipe, Brazil.
   1885 Tropidurus hispidus—Boulenger, Cat. Liz. Brit. Mus., 2: 177.

   Distribution: Venezuela, Guianas, Brazil, Uruguay, Paraguay, and Bolivia.

TROPIDURUS HYGOMI Reinhardt and Lütken

   1861 Tropidurus hygomi Reinhardt and Lütken, Vidensk. Medd. Naturhist. Foren. Kjöbenhavn, 1861: 228,
        pl. 5, fig. 9. Type-locality: Cotinquiba and Maruim, Estado de Sergipe, Brazil.

   Distribution: Estado de Sergipe near coast, eastern Brazil.

TROPIDURUS MELANOPLEURUS Boulenger

1902 Tropidurus melanopleurus Boulenger, Ann. Mag. Nat. Hist., (7) 10: 399. Type-locality: Tamampoya, Bolivia, 1200 m.
1924 Tropidurus praeornatus Müller, Mitt. Zool. Mus. Berlin, 11 (1923): 83. Type-locality: Río Pilcomayo, between Tarija and San Francisco, Bolivia.
1924 Tropidurus pictus Müller, Mitt. Zool. Mus. Berlin, 11 (1923): 86. Type-locality: Río Pilcomayo, between Tarija and San Francisco, Bolivia.

Distribution: Eastern foothills of Andes, in southern Peru and Bolivia.

TROPIDURUS OCCIPITALIS Peters

1871 Tropidurus (Laemopristus) occipitalis Peters, Monats. Akad. Wiss. Berlin, 1871: 645. Type-locality: Peru.

Distribution: Coastal areas and western foothills of Andes in southwestern Ecuador and northern and central Peru.

Content: Three subspecies.

Key to the subspecies

1. Vertebral scales at least 35; paravertebral scales at least 50; midbody scales at least 60; throat of adult male with brown markings; dorsal neck and anterior body with narrow brown transverse marks-------2
Vertebral scales not more than 40, paravertebral scales not more than 55; midbody scales not more than 65; male throat gray with light bluish spots; dorsal neck and anterior body with wide dark brown transverse spots-------------------occipitalis

2. Fewer than 80 paravertebral scales; fewer than 80 midbody scales; adult male throat with bold, dark brown spots-----koepkeorum
More than 80 paravertebral scales; more than 80 midbody scales; adult male throat with light brown spots and dark brown transverse gular band-----------stolzmanni

Clave de subespecies

1. Escamas vertebrales por lo menos 35; escamas paravertebrales por lo menos 50; escamas del medio cuerpo por lo menos 60; garganta del macho adulto con marcas pardas; parte dorsal del cuello y cuerpo anterior con marcas transversales pardas angostas-2
Escamas vertebrales no más de 40, escamas paravertebrales no más de 55; escamas del medio cuerpo no más de 65; garganta del macho gris con manchas azuladas claras; parte dorsal del cuello y cuerpo anterior con manchas transversales pardas oscuras anchas------------------------occipitalis

2. Menos de 80 escamas paravertebrales; menos de 80 escamas del medio cuerpo; garganta del macho adulto con manchas pardas oscuras conspícuas-----------------koepkeorum
Más de 80 escamas paravertebrales; más de 80 escamas del medio cuerpo; garganta del macho adulto con manchas pardas claras y una banda gular transversal parda oscura-- --------------------------------stolzmanni

Tropidurus occipitalis occipitalis Peters

1874 Aneuporus occipitalis Bocourt (preoccupied by Tropidurus occipitalis Peters, 1871), Miss. Sci. Mex., Rept.: 215, pl. 18, fig. 1, la-b. Type-locality: Peru.
1885 Tropidurus bocourtii Boulenger (replacement name for Aneuporus occipitalis Bocourt, 1874), Cat. Liz. Brit. Mus., 2: 173.
1907 Tropidurus tschudii Roux, Rev. Suisse Zool., 15: 296. Type-locality: Peru.
1924 Tropidurus continentalis Müller, Mitt. Zool. Mus. Berlin, 11 (1923): 82. Type-locality: Machalilla, Ecuador.
1956 Tropidurus occipitalis occipitalis—Mertens, Senckenbergiana Biol., 37: 115, pl. 16, fig. 26-28; pl. 17, fig. 31.

Distribution: Coastal areas of southwestern Ecuador and northwestern and western central Peru.

Tropidurus occipitalis koepkeorum Mertens

> 1956 Tropidurus occipitalis koepkeorum Mertens, Senckenbergiana Biol., 37: 117, pl. 16, figs. 27-30; pl. 17, fig. 32. Type-locality: Pariakoto, Departamento Ancash, Peru, 1600 m.
>
> Distribution: Olmos to Pariakoto, northwestern Peru.

Tropidurus occipitalis stolzmanni Steindachner

> 1891 Tropidurus Stolzmanni Steindachner, Ann. Naturhist. Mus. Wien, 6: 376. Type-locality: Chota, Peru.
> 1956 Tropidurus occipitalis stolzmanni—Mertens, Senckenbergiana Biol., 37: 119, pl. 17, figs. 33-34.
>
> Distribution: Northwestern Peru and possibly southwestern Ecuador.

TROPIDURUS PERUVIANUS (Lesson)

> 1826 Stellio peruvianus Lesson, in Duperrey, Voy. "Coquille", Reptiles, 5: pl. 2, fig. 2; 2 (1) 1830: 40. Type-locality: Callao and Payta, Peru.
> 1885 Tropidurus peruvianus—Boulenger, Cat. Liz. Brit. Mus., 2: 174.
>
> Distribution: South America west of Andes from southern Ecuador to northern Chile.
>
> Content: Nine subspecies.

Key to the subspecies

1. Snout rounded-----------------------------2
   Snout acutely pointed----------atacamensis

2. With irregular dorsal spotting------------3
   With four black bands dorsally-------------
   --------------------------quadrivittatus

3. Adpressed hind limb reaches beyond ear----4
   Adpressed hind limb reaches shoulder-------
   --------------------------------araucanus

4. Gular and pectoral regions lack transverse
   stripes-----------------------------------5
   Gular and pectoral regions with transverse
   stripes-----------------------------------7

5. Pectoral region not black; body not
   melanistic--------------------------------6
   Pectoral region black; body melanistic-----
   ----------------------------salinicola

6. With low dorsal crest-----------heterolepis
   Lacking dorsal crest--------------marianus

7. Gular stripes continuous------------------8
   Gular stripes formed by row of small, light
   bordered spots---------------------tigris

8. Gular stripes bordered by small, multicolored spots; lacking spot in groin------
   --------------------------------maminensis
   Gular stripes not bordered by multicolored
   spots; with spot in groin-------peruvianus

Clave de subespecies

1. Hocico de extremo redondeado--------------2
   Hocico de extremo aguzado-------atacamensis

2. Con manchas dorsales irregulares----------3
   Con cuatro bandas negras dorsales----------
   --------------------------quadrivittatus

3. Extremidad posterior hacia delante sobrepasa el oído------------------------------4
   Extremidad posterior hacia delante alcanza
   el hombro----------------------araucanus

4. Región gular y pectoral sin cintas trans-
   versales----------------------------------5
   Región gular y pectoral con cintas trans-
   versales----------------------------------7

5. Región pectoral no negra; cuerpo no
   melánico----------------------------------6
   Región pectoral negra; cuerpo melánico-----
   ----------------------------salinicola

6. Con cresta dorsal baja----------heterolepis
   Sin cresta dorsal------------------marianus

7. Cintas gulares continuas------------------8
   Cintas gulares formadas por hileras de
   pequeñas manchas bordeadas de claro-tigris

8. Cintas gulares bordeadas por manchitas
   multicolores; sin mancha inguinal---------
   --------------------------------maminensis
   Cintas gulares no bordeadas por manchitas
   multicolores; con mancha inguinal---------
   --------------------------------peruvianus

Tropidurus peruvianus peruvianus (Lesson)

1835 Tropidurus microlophus Wiegmann, Nova Acta Acad. Caes. Leop.-Carol., 17: 223, pl. 16. Type-locality: Peru.
1836 Microlophus Lessonii Duméril and Bibron, Erp. Gén., 4: 336. Type-locality: Lima, Callao, and Cobija, Peru.
1845 St.[eirolepis] xanthostigma Tschudi, Arch. für Naturg., 11: 155. Type-locality: Coastal Peru.
1876 Microlophus inguinalis Cope, Jour. Acad. Nat. Sci. Phila., (2) 8 (1875): 172. Type-locality: Valley of Jequetepeque, Peru.
1956 Tropidurus peruvianus peruvianus—Mertens, Senckenbergiana Biol., 37: 106, pl. 11, figs. 1-5; pl. 12, figs. 6-7.

   Distribution: Western foothills of Andes and coastal areas of southern Ecuador, Peru, and northern Chile.

Tropidurus peruvianus araucanus (Lesson)

1826 Lophyrus araucanus Lesson, in Duperrey, Voy. "Coquille", Reptiles, pl. 2, fig. 1. Type-locality: Biobio River, Arauco, Concepcion, Chile.
1966 Tropidurus peruvianus araucanus—Donoso-Barros, Reptiles de Chile: 143.

   Distribution: Northwestern Chile.

Tropidurus peruvianus atacamensis Donoso-Barros

1960 [Tropidurus peruvianus] atacamensis Donoso-Barros, Invest. Zool. Chilensis, 6: 69. Type-locality: Atacama Desert, Chile; further specified as Caldera, Atacama, Chile, by Donoso-Barros, Reptiles de Chile, 1966, 153.

   Distribution: Atacama Desert in region south of Antofagasta, Chile.

Tropidurus peruvianus heterolepis Wiegmann

1835 Tropidurus heterolepis Wiegmann, Nova Acta Acad. Caes. Leop.-Carol., 17: 225, pl. 17, fig. 1. Type-locality: Tacna, Peru.
1966 Tropidurus peruvianus heterolepis—Donoso-Barros, Reptiles de Chile: 134.

   Distribution: Extreme northern Chile and southern Peru.

Tropidurus peruvianus maminensis Donoso-Barros

1966 Tropidurus peruvianus maminensis Donoso-Barros, Reptiles de Chile: 150. Type-locality: Mamiña, Tarapacá, Chile.

   Distribution: Region of type locality.

Tropidurus peruvianus marianus Donoso-Barros

1966 Tropidurus peruvianus marianus Donoso-Barros, Reptiles de Chile: 148. Type-locality: Isla Santa María, Antofagasta, Chile.

   Distribution: Region of type locality.

Tropidurus peruvianus quadrivittatus (Tschudi)

1845 St.[eirolepis] quadrivittata Tschudi, Arch. für Naturg., 11: 156. Type-locality: Coastal Peru.
1966 Tropidurus peruvianus quadrivittatus—Donoso-Barros, Reptiles de Chile: 141.

   Distribution: Region of type locality.

Tropidurus peruvianus salinicola Mertens

   1956 Tropidurus peruvianus salinicola Mertens, Senckenbergiana Biol., 37: 108, pl. 12, figs.
          8-10. Type-locality: Salinas, south of Huacho, Departamento Lima, Peru.

      Distribution: Salt flats in vicinity of type locality.

Tropidurus peruvianus tigris (Tschudi)

   1845 St.[eirolepis] tigris Tschudi, Arch. für Naturg., 11: 156. Type-locality: Coastal Peru.
   1956 Tropidurus peruvianus tigris—Mertens, Senckenbergiana Biol., 37: 109, pl. 13, figs. 13-14.

      Distribution: Coastal Peru, replacing nominate race at higher altitudes.

TROPIDURUS SEMITAENIATUS (Spix)

   1825 Agama semitaeniata Spix, Sp. Nov. Lac. Bras.: 13, pl. 16, fig. 1. Type-locality: "In campis
          montosis Sincura", Bahia, Brazil.
   1885 Tropidurus semitaeniatus—Boulenger, Cat. Liz. Brit. Mus., 2: 178.
   1933 Iapinurus scutipunctatus Amaral, Mem. Inst. Butantan, 7 (1932): 65, figs. 22-25. Type-locality:
          Villa Nova (= Senhor de Bonfim), Bahia, Brazil.

     Distribution: Ceará, Rio Grande do Norte, Paraíba, Pernambuco, Alagoas, Sergipe, and Bahia, eastern
     Brazil.

TROPIDURUS SPINULOSUS (Cope)

   1862 Microlophus spinulosus Cope, Proc. Acad. Nat. Sci. Phila., 1862: 351. Type-locality: Paraguay.
   1879 Leiocephalus (Craniopeltis) variegatus O'Shaughnessy, Ann. Mag. Nat. Hist., (5) 4: 301. Type-
          locality: Cosquin, Córdoba, Argentina.
   1885 Tropidurus spinulosus—Boulenger, Cat. Liz. Brit. Mus., 2: 175.
   1930 Plica stejnegeri Burt and Burt, Proc. U.S. Nat. Mus., 78 (6): 19. Type-locality: Argentina.

      Distribution: Mato Grosso, Brazil, and Grand Chaco of Bolivia, Paraguay, and northern Argentina.

TROPIDURUS TARAPACENSIS Donoso-Barros

   1966 Tropidurus tarapacensis Donoso-Barros, Reptiles de Chile: 158, col. pl. 7. Type-locality:
          Desierto de Tarapacá, Chile, 10,000 km.

      Distribution: Region of type locality.

TROPIDURUS THERESIAE Steindachner

   1901 Tropidurus theresiae Steindachner, Anz. Akad. Wiss. Wien, 38: 195. Type-locality: Ancón, near
          Lima, Peru.
   1956 Tropidurus theresiae—Mertens, Senckenbergiana Biol., 37: 111, pl. 14, figs. 16-19.

      Distribution: Between Chancay and Lima, west coast of central Peru.

TROPIDURUS THERESIOIDES Donoso-Barros

   1966 Tropidurus theresioides Donoso-Barros, Reptiles de Chile: 155, col. pl. 7. Type-locality: Oasis
          de Pica, Tarapacá, Chile.

      Distribution: Region of type locality.

TROPIDURUS THORACICUS (Tschudi)

1845 St.[eirolepis] thoracica Tschudi, Arch. für Naturg., 11: 156. Type-locality: Coastal Peru.
1900 Tropidurus Thomasi Boulenger, Ann. Mag. Nat. Hist., (7) 6: 184. Type-locality: Eten, coast of Peru.
1959 Tropidurus thoracicus—Mertens, Senckenbergiana Biol., 37: 113, pl. 15, figs. 20-25.

Distribution: West coast of central Peru from Eten in north to Pucusana in south.

TROPIDURUS TORQUATUS (Wied)

1820 Stellio torquatus Wied, Reise nach Brasilien, 1815-1817, 1: 106. Type-locality: none specified.
1823 Agama brasiliensis Raddi, Mem. Math. Fis. Soc. Ital. Sci., 19: 59. Type-locality: Rio de Janeiro, Brazil.
1825 Agama hispida sive tuberculata Spix, Sp. Nov. Lac. Bras.: 12, pl. 15, fig. 1. Type-locality: either Rio de Janeiro or Bahia, Brazil.
1843 Tropidurus microlepidotus Fitzinger, Systema Reptilium: 72. Type-locality: Brazil.
1845 Taraguira Darwinii Gray, Cat. Liz. Brit. Mus.: 220. Type-locality: Abrolhos Inlet, Brazil.
1885 Tropidurus torquatus—Boulenger, Cat. Liz. Brit. Mus., 2: 176.

Distribution: Guianas; Brazil.

TUPINAMBIS Daudin

1803 Tupinambis Daudin, Hist. Nat. Rept., 3: 20. Type-species: Tupinambis monitor Daudin.
1820 Tutor Goldfuss (subgenus novum), Handbuch der Zoologie, Nüremberg, 2: 168. Type-species:
    Monitor americanus Goldfuss.
1822 Custa Fleming, Philosophy of Zoology, 2: 274. Type-species: Lacerta teguixin Linnaeus, by
    present designation (see below, in comments).
1826 Exypnestes Kaup, Isis von Oken, 18-19: 88. Type-species: Tupinambis monitor Daudin.
1828 Ctenodus Wagler, Isis von Oken, 21: 860. Type-species: Tupinambis nigropunctatus Spix.
1830 Podinema Wagler, Nat. Syst. Amph.: 153. Type-species: Lacerta Teguixin Linnaeus.
1830 Ctenodon Wagler, Nat. Syst Amph.: 153. Type-species: Tupinambis nigropunctatus Spix.
1831 Teguixin Gray, Synopsis Species Class Reptilia, in Griffith, Cuvier's Animal Kingdom, 9: 29.
    Type-species: Lacerta teguixin Linnaeus.
1833 Gymnogomphius Wagler, Isis von Oken, 26: 892. Type-species: Lacerta teguixin Linnaeus.
1839 Salvator Duméril and Bibron, Erp. Gén., 5: 39. Type-species: Salvator Merianae Duméril and
    Bibron.

Distribution: South America east of Andes.

Comment: We are here designating Lacerta teguixin Linnaeus as the type species of Custa Fleming,
    because this firmly fixes the generic name as a junior synonym of Tupinambis. Use of one of the
    other species assigned by Fleming to Custa could result in replacement of a well-known genus,
    such as Crocodilurus.

Content: Four species.

Key to the species	Clave de especies
1. Loreal plate divided, forming two scales-----2 Loreal plate undivided, single scale---------- ---------------------------------nigropunctatus	1. Placa loreal dividida originando dos escamas--2 Placa loreal no dividida, una sola escama------ --------------------------------nigropunctatus
2. Length of fourth toe much longer than tarsus-- --3 Length of fourth toe slightly longer than tarsus-----------------------------duseni	2. Longitud del cuarto ortejo notablemente mayor que el tarso---------------------------------3 Longitud del cuarto ortejo apenas mayor que el tarso------------------------------duseni
3. Ventral scales from collar to anus 46-50------ -----------------------------------rufescens Ventral scales from collar to anus 36-40------ -----------------------------------teguixin	3. Escamas ventrales desde el collar al ano 46-50- ------------------------------------rufescens Escamas ventrales desde el collar al ano 36-40- ------------------------------------teguixin

TUPINAMBIS DUSENI Lönnberg

1910 Tupinambis duseni Lönnberg, Ark. för Zool. 6 (9): 1, fig. 1-5. Type-locality: Paraná, Brazil.

Distribution: Known only from type-locality.

TUPINAMBIS NIGROPUNCTATUS Spix

1825 Tupinambis nigropunctatus Spix, Spec. Nov. Lacert. Bras.: 18, pl. 20. Type-locality: Brazil.

Distribution: Amazon Basin, including Brazil, Peru, Colombia, Venezuela and perhaps Ecuador; also
    Island of Trinidad.

TUPINAMBIS RUFESCENS (Günther)

1871 Tejus rufescens Günther, Proc. Zool. Soc. London, 1871: 541. Type-locality: Mendoza, Argentina.
1885 Tupinambis rufescens—Boulenger, Cat. Liz. Brit. Mus., 2: 335.

Distribution: Western Argentina from La Pampa and Mendoza to Jujuy and Salta.

TUPINAMBIS TEGUIXIN (Linnaeus)

1758 Lacerta teguixin Linnaeus, Systema Naturae, Ed. 10: 208. Type-locality: Indiis.
1885 Tupinambis teguixin—Boulenger, Cat. Liz. Brit. Mus., 2: 335.

Distribution: Northern Argentina, Uruguay, Brazil, Guianas.

Content: Two subspecies.

Key to the subspecies	Clave de subespecies
1. Heavily melanistic dorsally, dorsal pattern darkened or almost totally obscured-------------------------------------sebastiani Dorsum with strong contrasts of light and dark areas, not darkened over entire surface---------------------------teguixin	1. Dorsalmente densamente melánica, diseño dorsal oscuro o casi totalmente oscuro-------------------------------------sebastiani Dorso con fuerte contraste de áreas claras y oscuras, no oscurecido en la totalidad de su superficie------------------teguixin

Tupinambis teguixin teguixin (Linnaeus)

1768 Seps marmoratus Laurenti, Synopsis Reptilium: 59. Type-locality: Indiis.
1803 Tupinambis monitor Daudin, Hist. Nat. Rept., 3: 20. Type-locality: None given.
1820 Monitor (Tutor) americanus Goldfuss, Handbuch der Zoologie, Nüremberg, 2: 168. Type-locality: South America.
1839 Salvator merianae Duméril and Bibron, Erp. Gén., 5: 85. Type-locality: Cayenne, French Guiana; Brazil; and Montevideo, Uruguay.
1968 Tupinambis teguixin [teguixin]—Müller, Die Herpetofauna der Insel von São Sebastião (Brasilien): 31, fig. 10.

Distribution: Northern Argentina, Uruguay, Brazil, and Guianas.

Tupinambis teguixin sebastiani Müller

1968 Tupinambis teguixin sebastiani Müller, Die Herpetofauna der Insel von São Sebastião (Brasilien): 31, fig. 10. Type-locality: Isla São Sebastião, São Paulo, Brazil.

Distribution: Known only from Isla São Sebastião, Brazil.

REPTILIA: SAURIA: IGUANIDAE ★ ★ ★ ★ URACENTRON

Prepared by Richard Etheridge, San Diego State College, San Diego, California

URACENTRON Kaup

1826 _Uracentron_ Kaup, Isis von Oken, 19: 88. Type-species: _Lacerta azurea_ Linnaeus.
1829 _Doryphorus_ Cuvier, Règne Animal, Ed. 2, 2: 34. Type-species: _Stellio brevicaudatus_ Daudin.
1830 _Urocentron_ Wagler (emendation of _Uracentron_ Kaup), Nat. Syst. Amphib.: 145.
1835 _Urocentrum_ Wiegmann (emendation of _Uracentron_ Kaup), Arch. für Naturg., 1 (2): 289.
1845 _Uranocentron_ Gray (substitute name for _Uracentron_ Kaup), Cat. Liz. Brit. Mus.: 225.

Distribution: Guianas; Amazonian basin of Venezuela, Colombia, Ecuador, Peru and northern Brazil.

Content: Four species, according to most recent revision by Etheridge, Bull. Brit. Mus. (Nat. Hist.) Zool., 17, 1968, 47-64.

Key to the species

1. Dorsal scales smooth or weakly and obtusely keeled posteriorly; tail narrower and less strongly depressed, fewer than 17 scales around middle of tail------------------------2
   Dorsal scales distinctly keeled (except in small juveniles); tail wider and more strongly depressed, more than 17 scales around middle of tail-----------------------------_flaviceps_

2. Posterior dorsal scales usually at least faintly keeled; pattern green (bluish in preservative) with black crossbands, at least on neck and anterior body--------------------3
   Posterior dorsals perfectly smooth; dorsum brownish with faint lighter spots; bold yellowish mark on occipital region-----_werneri_

3. Supraoculars band-like, separated from superciliaries by single row of small scales; pattern of three narrow crossbands on neck followed by one that descends along antihumeral fold; narrow mesh-like network on dorsum of body-----------------------_guentheri_
   Supraoculars variable, seldom band-like, or, if band-like, separated from superciliaries by two rows of small scales; pattern of bold wide crossbands on neck and body, two anterior to antihumeral fold, posteriorly one or more bands may break up into a wide mesh-like reticulum----------------------------_azureum_

Clave de especies

1. Escamas dorsales lisas o ligera y obtusamente quilladas a posterior; cola más angosta y menos fuertemente deprimida, menos de 17 escamas alrededor del medio de la cola-------2
   Escamas dorsales distintamente quilladas (excepto en juveniles pequeños); cola más ancha y más fuertemente deprimida, más de 17 escamas alrededor del medio de la cola--------
   -----------------------------------_flaviceps_

2. Escamas dorsales posteriores generalmente quilladas, al menos vagamente; diseño verde (azulado en preservativo) con bandas transversales negras, al menos en el cuello y parte anterior del cuerpo--------------------3
   Dorsales posteriores perfectamente lisas; dorso parduzco con manchas ligeramente más claras; marca amarilla conspícua en la región occipital------------------------------------_werneri_

3. Supraoculares alargados, separados de los superciliares por una sola hilera de escamas pequeñas; diseño de tres bandas transversales angostas en el cuello, seguidas de una que desciende a lo largo del pliegue antehumeral; retículo de trama fina en el dorso del cuerpo----------------------------------_guentheri_
   Supraoculares variables, raramente alargados, separados de los superciliares por dos hileras de escamas pequeñas; diseño de bandas transversales anchas, conspícuas en cuello y cuerpo, dos bandas anteriores al pliegue antehumeral, a posterior una o más bandas pueden fragmentarse en un retículo de trama amplia---
   -----------------------------------_azureum_

URACENTRON AZUREUM (Linnaeus)

1758 _Lacerta azurea_ Linnaeus, Systema Naturae, Ed. 10: 202. Type-locality: Africa; in error; restricted to vicinity of Paramaribo, Surinam, by Etheridge, Bull. Brit. Mus. (Nat. Hist.), Zool., 17, 1968, 50.
1802 _Stellio brevicaudata_ Latreille, in Sonnini and Latreille, Hist. Nat. Rept., 2: 29. Type-locality: Interior of Guiana and Surinam.
1820 _Uromastyx caeruleus_ Merrem (substitute name for _Lacerta azurea_ Linnaeus), Tent. Syst. Amphib.: 56.
1826 _Uracentron azureum_—Kaup, Isis von Oken, 19: 88.
1968 _Uracentron azureum_—Etheridge, Bull. Brit. Mus. (Nat. Hist.) Zool., 17: 50.

Distribution: Guianas; also along or near Rio Amazon in northern Brazil as far west as Manaus.

URACENTRON

URACENTRON FLAVICEPS (Guichenot)

1855 Doryphorus flaviceps Guichenot, in Castelnau, Exp. Amér. Mérid., Rept.: 26, pl. 3, fig. 2. Type-locality: Sarayacu, Peru.
1871 Doryphorus castor Cope, Proc. Amer. Phil. Soc., 11 (1870): 556. Type-locality: Pebas, Peru.
1925 [Uracentron flaviceps]—Mertens, Senckenbergiana, 7: 75.
1968 Uracentron flaviceps—Etheridge, Bull. Brit. Mus. (Nat. Hist.) Zool., 17: 55.

Distribution: Western part of Amazonian basin in northwestern Brazil, southeastern Colombia, eastern Ecuador, and eastern Peru.

URACENTRON GUENTHERI (Boulenger)

1894 Urocentrum guentheri Boulenger, Proc. Zool. Soc. London, 1894: 729, pl. 47, fig. 3. Type-locality: Iquitos, Peru.
1925 Uracentron guentheri—Mertens, Senckenbergiana, 7: 75.
1968 Uracentron guentheri—Etheridge, Bull. Brit. Mus. (Nat. Hist.) Zool., 17: 53.

Distribution: Río Ucayali system in Departamento Loreto, eastern Peru, and western Amazonian basin in northwestern Brazil.

URACENTRON WERNERI Mertens

1925 Uracentron werneri Mertens, Senckenbergiana, 7: 75. Type-locality: Upper Río Orinoco, Venezuela.
1968 Uracentron werneri—Etheridge, Bull. Brit. Mus. (Nat. Hist.) Zool., 17: 55.

Distribution: Upper Río Orinoco valley in Venezuela; western tributaries of Orinoco in Colombia.

<u>URANOSCODON</u> Kaup

1811 <u>Lophyrus</u> Oppel (preoccupied by <u>Lophyrus</u> Poli, 1791), Ordnungen, Familien, und Gattungen der
      Reptilien: 27. Type-species: <u>Lacerta</u> <u>superciliosa</u> Linnaeus.
1825 <u>Uranoscodon</u> Kaup, Isis von Oken, 16: 590. Type-species: <u>Lacerta</u> <u>superciliosa</u> Linnaeus.
1825 <u>Ophryessa</u> Boie, Isis von Oken, 17: 1090. Type-species: <u>Lacerta</u> <u>superciliosa</u> Linnaeus.
1825 <u>Uraniscodon</u> Boie (emendation of <u>Uranoscodon</u> Kaup), Isis von Oken, 17: 1090.
1827 <u>Lophyrus</u> Gray (not <u>Lophyrus</u> Oppel, 1811; substitute name for <u>Uranoscodon</u> Kaup), Phil. Mag., 2:
      208.
1827 <u>Uranascodon</u> Gray (in error for <u>Uranoscodon</u> Kaup), Phil. Mag., 2: 208.
1827 <u>Ophryesa</u> Gray (in error for <u>Ophryessa</u> Boie), Phil. Mag., 2: 208.
1830 <u>Ophryoessa</u> Wagler (emendation of <u>Ophryessa</u> Boie), Nat. Syst. Amph.: 149.
1831 <u>Ophyessa</u> Gray (emendation of <u>Ophryessa</u> Boie), Synopsis Species Class Reptilia, in Griffith,
      Cuvier's Animal Kingdom, 9: 39.
1831 <u>Xiphura</u> Gray, Synopsis Species Class Reptilia, in Griffith, Cuvier's Animal Kingdom, 9: 39. Type-
      species: <u>Lacerta</u> <u>superciliosa</u> Linnaeus.

   Distribution: As for single known species.

   Content: One species.

<u>URANOSCODON</u> <u>SUPERCILIOSA</u> (Linnaeus)

1758 <u>Lacerta</u> <u>superciliosa</u> Linnaeus, Systema Naturae, Ed. 10: 200. Type-locality: "Indiis".
1802 <u>Agama</u> <u>stellaris</u> Daudin, Hist. Nat. Rept., 3: 404. Type-locality: "Batavia", from Seba,
      Thesaurus, 1, 1734-65, pl. 92, fig. 2.
1825 <u>Lophyrus</u> <u>xiphosurus</u> Spix, Spec. Nov. Lac. Bras.: 9, pl. 10. Type-locality: Solimõens, Brazil.
1825 <u>Lophyrus</u> <u>auronitens</u> Spix, Spec. Nov. Lac. Bras.: 12, pl. 13a. Type-locality: In humid areas on
      banks of Rio Amazon, Brazil.
1825 <u>Uranoscodon</u> <u>superciliosa</u>—Kaup, Isis von Oken, 16: 590.
1885 <u>Ophryoessa</u> <u>superciliosa</u>—Boulenger, Cat. Liz. Brit. Mus., 2: 111.

   Distribution: Northeastern South America.

UROSTROPHUS Duméril and Bibron

  1837 Urostrophus Duméril and Bibron, Erp. Gén., 4: 77. Type-species: Urostrophus Vautieri Duméril
       and Bibron.
  1845 Urotrophus Gray (in error for Urostrophus Duméril and Bibron), Cat. Liz. Brit. Mus.: 184.

    Distribution: Southern South America, in Chile, Brazil, Bolivia and Argentina.

    Content: Three species.

                    Key to the species   Clave de especies

  1. No collar on throat and shoulder--------------2   1. Sin collar en la garganta y·hombros-----------2
     Black collar on throat and lower half of   Collar negro en la garganta y mitad inferior de
     shoulder area------------------------torquatus   la zona de los hombros---------------torquatus

  2. Adpressed hind limb to shoulder or neck in   2. Extremidad posterior extendida hacia adelante
     males, to axilla in females; eight to nine   llega al hombro o cuello en machos, a la axila
     upper labials; seven to eight lower labials---   en hembras; ocho a nueve labiales superiores;
     -------------------------------------vautieri   siete a ocho labiales inferiores------vautieri
     Adpressed hind limb to eye-ear region; ten   Extremidad posterior extendida hacia adelante
     upper labials; nine lower labials-----valeriae   llega a la región ojo-oído; diez labiales
                                                            superiores; nueve labiales inferiores-valeriae

UROSTROPHUS TORQUATUS (Philippi)

  1861 Leiosaurus torquatus Philippi, in Philippi and Landbeck, Arch. für Naturg., 27: 295. Type-
       locality: Near Concepción, Chile.
  1861 Leiosaurus valdivianus Philippi, in Philippi and Landbeck, Arch. für Naturg., 27: 298. Type-
       locality: Valdivia Province, Chile.
  1885 Urostrophus torquatus—Boulenger, Cat. Liz. Brit. Mus., 2: 124.
  1966 Urostrophus torquatus—Donoso-Barros, Reptiles de Chile: 365, pl. 27 (col.).

    Distribution: Chile, from Chillan to Puerto Montt.

UROSTROPHUS VALERIAE Donoso-Barros

  1966 Urostrophus valeriae Donoso-Barros, Reptiles de Chile: 369, pl. 27 (col.). Type-locality: Alhué,
       Chile (from Donoso-Barros, loc. cit., p. 458).

    Distribution: Forests of Cordillera de la Costa, central Chile.

UROSTROPHUS VAUTIERI Duméril and Bibron

  1837 Urostrophus Vautieri Duméril and Bibron, Erp. Gén., 4: 78. Type-locality: Brazil; given as Rio
       de Janeiro, Brazil, by Guibé, Catalogue des Types de Lézards, Paris Mus., 1954, 51.

    Distribution: Southern Brazil, northern Argentina, eastern Bolivia.

XENOSAURUS Peters

  1861 Xenosaurus Peters, Monats. Akad. Wiss. Berlin, 1861: 453. Type-species: Xenosaurus fasciatus
       Peters [=Xenosaurus grandis grandis (Gray)].

    Distribution: Mexico to Guatemala.

    Content: Three species, two of which (arboreus Lynch and Smith and platyceps King and Thompson)
    are extralimital, according to latest revision by King and Thompson, Bull. Florida St. Mus.,
    12, 1968, 93-123.

XENOSAURUS GRANDIS (Gray)

  1856 Cubina grandis Gray, Ann. Mag. Nat. Hist., (2) 18: 270. Type-locality: Córdoba, Veracruz,
       Mexico.

    Distribution: Mexico to Guatemala.

    Content: Five subspecies, four of which (agrenon King and Thompson, grandis Gray, sanmartinensis
    Werler and Shannon and newmanorum Taylor) are extralimital.

Xenosaurus grandis rackhami Stuart

  1941 Xenosaurus rackhami Stuart, Proc. Biol. Soc. Washington, 54: 47. Type-locality: Finca
       Volcán (49 km east of Cobán), Alta Verapaz, Guatemala, 1300 m.
  1965 Xenosaurus grandis rackhami—Lynch and Smith, Tran. Kansas Acad. Sci., 68: 171.

    Distribution: Atlantic drainage in central Chiapas, Mexico, to east central Guatemala.

ALOPOGLOSSUS GRACILIS Werner

    1913 Alopoglossus gracilis Werner, Mitt. Naturhist. Mus. Hamburg, 30: 13. Type-locality: Valle del Rio Humboldt, tributario del Rio Itapocú, Santa Catarina, Brazil.

    Distribution: Known only from type locality.

    Comment: Ruibal, Bull. Mus. Comp. Zool., 106, 1952, 501, could not allocate this species generically. He suggested it might belong to Ptychoglossus.

CNEMIDOPHORUS AMIVOIDES Cope

    1894 Cnemidophorus amivoides Cope, Proc. Acad. Nat. Sci. Phila., 1894: 198. Type-locality: La Carpintera, Costa Rica.

    Distribution: Known only from type locality.

    Comment: Taylor, Univ. Kansas Sci. Bull., 38, 1956, 268, included this taxon in the synonymy of Ameiva undulata parva Barbour and Noble, 1915. If valid, this action would give amivoides priority over parva. On p. 271, Taylor indicated he was uncertain, but that this taxon appeared to belong to Ameiva, perhaps applying to a mountain form in Costa Rica. It cannot be included in this Catalogue without a name change. It cannot be put in Cnemidophorus if Taylor's action of placing it in Ameiva is valid. It appears best for the time being to list it as an unassignable name.

PANTODACTYLUS CONCOLOR Tschudi

    1847 P.[antodactylus] concolor Tschudi, Arch. für Naturg., 13 (1): 48. Type-locality: Northern Provinces of Brazil.

    Distribution: Unknown.

    Comment: This taxon was not mentioned by Ruibal in his revision of the genus Pantodactylus (Bull. Mus. Comp. Zool., 106, 1952). We are uncertain as to its proper generic allocation.

caducus (cont.)
  Scartiscus 213
caerulea
  Iguana 149
caerulescens
  Enyalioides 115
  Lacerta 94
caeruleus
  Seps 94
  Uromastyx 273
calabaricus
  Hemidactylus frenatus 142
calcaratus
  Kentropyx 151
calliscelis
  Dicrodon 107
Calliscincopus 262
Callopistes 88
camerani
  Lepidosternum 169
Camilia 108
campanae
  Liolaemus nigroviridis
    191
camura
  Amphisbaena 30
cantoris
  Peripia 161
capito
  Anolis 50
caracal
  Gecko 141
carcani
  Lepidosternon 169
carinatus
  Sceloporus 247
  Sphaerodactylus homolepis
    252
carinicaudatum
  Lepidosoma 15
carinicaudatus
  Alopoglossus 15
cariococca
  Pygopus 209
Carlia 154
carneus
  Anolis 50
carrioni
  Stenocercus 256
carruccii
  Amphisbaena 33
carvalhoi
  Amphisbaena 30
casicolus
  Sphaerodactylus 252
castanicterus
  Tretioscincus 262
castor
  Doryphorus 274
casuhatiensis
  Cupriguanus 106
catamarcensis
  Leiosaurus 156
catenata
  Agama 118
catenatus
  Enyalius 118
catenifer
  Anolis 64
caudeloti
  Gymnodactylus 161

caudiscutatus
  Gonatodes 132
  Gymnodactylus 132
ceciliae
  Gonatodes 132
Celestus 90
centralis
  Amphisbaena vermicu-
    laris 38
  Echinosaura 112
Centropyx 151
centropyx
  Cnemidophorus 107
Centrura 227
cepedii
  Scincus 199
Cephalopeltis 167
Cercosaura 91
chacoensis
  Liolaemus 181
chaitzami
  Ameiva 21
Chalcides 78
chalcidica
  Iguana 230
Chalcidolepis 39
Chalcis 78
Chamaeleopsis 101
chamaeleopsis
  Corythophanes 101
champsonotus
  Placosoma cordylinum
    229
  Prionodactylus 229
Chaunolaemus 233
chaus
  Gecko 141
cherriei
  Leiolopisma 155
  Leiolopisma cherriei
    155
  Mocoa 155
chilensis
  Liolaemus 181
chiliensis
  Calotes 181
  Liolaemus 181
chillanensis
  Liolaemus monticola 186
chiloeensis
  Liolaemus pictus 193
Chioninia 197
Chirocolus 144
chloris
  Anolis 51
chocorum
  Anolis 51
chrysochlorus
  Celestus 90
chrysolepis
  Anolis 51
  Anolis (Draconura) 60
chrysopygus
  Stenocercus 256
Chrysosaurus 170
chrysostictus
  Sceloporus 247
cinctum
  Copeoglossum 199
cipoense
  Placosoma 228

Cnemidophorus 92
Cnemidotus 17
cobanensis
  Anolis 51
Coccoëssus 43
cochabambae
  Mabuya frenata 198
cochranae
  Neusticurus 206
  Neusticurus ecpleopus
    206
coelestis
  Ameiva 260
coeruleocephala
  Lacerta 94
coerulescens
  Enyalius 115
Coleodactylus 96
Coleonyx 97
coleonyx
  Gymnodactylus 97
collaris
  Anotosaurus 71
  Gonatodes 132
Colobodactylus 98
Colobosaura 99
Colobus 78
colombianus
  Lepidoblepharis festae
    159
Coloptychon 100
columbianus
  Proctoporus 239
columbiensis
  Prionodactylus 235
completa
  Ctenosaura 105
concinnatus
  Gonatodes 132
  Gymnodactylus 132
concolor
  Ameiva bifrontata 21
  Anolis 51
  Pantodactylus 279
conspersus
  Liolaemus 189
conspicuus
  Gymnodactylus 135
constanzae
  Liolaemus 181
continentalis
  Sphaerodactylus 252
  Sphaerodactylus argus
    252
  Tropidurus 266
copei
  Anolis 49
Copeoglossum 197
Cophias 78
cophias
  Bachia 81
  Chamaesaura 80
copiapensis
  Liolaemus nigromacula-
    tus 189
copiapoensis
  Liolaemus nigromacula-
    tus 189
copii
  Alopoglossus 16
  Centropyx 152

cordylinum
  Placosoma 228
  Placosoma cordylinum
    229
cortezi
  Anolis 60
Corythaeolus 83
Corythophanes 101
Corytophanes 101
courtyi
  Liolaemus variabilis
    187
cozumela
  Cnemidophorus 93
  Cnemidophorus cozumela
    93
  Cnemidophorus deppei
    93
Craneosaura 83
Craniopeltis 264
crassicaudatum
  Scelotrema 256
crassicaudatus
  Stenocercus 256
crassulus
  Anolis 51
  Anolis crassulus 52
crassum
  Lepidosternon 168
crequii
  Liolaemus variabilis
    187
Cristasaura 83
cristata
  Agama 101
cristatus
  Corythophanes 101
  Corytophanes 101
crocodilinus
  Teius 111
Crocodilurus 102
cruciger
  Gecko 142
Cryptoblepharum 13
Ctenoblepharis 103
Ctenoblepharys 103
Ctenocercus 43
Ctenodeira 43
Ctenodon 271
Ctenodus 271
Ctenonotus 43
Ctenosaura 105
Cubina 145
Cubinia 145
cupreus
  Anolis 52
  Euspondylus 229
  Stenocercus 256
Cupriguanus 106
curicensis
  Liolaemus platei 193
curtus
  Anolis 52
Custa 271
cuvieri
  Bachia 80
  Brachypus 80
  Cephalopeltis 169
  Scolecosaurus 80
cyaneus
  Teius 94

viridissimus
  Anolis 64
viridistriga
  Centropyx 152
  Kentropyx 152
vittata
  Anadia 41
  Lacerta 152
vittatus
  Basiliscus 84
  Centropyx 151
  Cnemidophorus 95
  Gonatodes 134
  Gonatodes vittatus 134
  Gymnodactylus 134
  Hemidactylus 141
vittigerus
  Anolis (Dracontura) 58
vogli
  Ameiva ameiva 20
vulgaris
  Ameiva 19
  Amphisbaena 32
  Iguana 149

W

walkeri
  Liolaemus 179
  Liolaemus alticolor 179
Wallsaurus 145
waltersi
  Laemanctus 153
  Laemanctus longipes 153
wellbornae
  Anolis ustus 66
werneri
  Arthroseps 76
  Phrynosaura 221
  Uracentron 274
whitii
  Homonota 147
wiedi
  Amphisbaena fuliginosa 32
wiegmanni
  Dactyloa 57
wiegmannii
  Liolaemus 195
  Proctotretus 195
williamsi
  Anolis 69
williamsoni
  Kentropyx 152
woodi
  Anolis 69
  Anolis woodi 69
wuchereri
  Lepidosternon 169
  Leposternon 169

X

xanthostigma
  Lathrogecko 160
  Lepidoblepharis 160
  Steirolepis 268
Xenosaurus 277
Xestosaurus 39
xestus
  Opipeuter 216

Xiphocercus 43
Xiphosurus 43
xiphosurus
  Lophyrus 275
Xiphura 273
Xystrolepis 197

Y

yacupoi
  Ophiodes 210
yucatanicus
  Norops 68

Z

zapallarensis
  Liolaemus nigromacula-
    tus 190
zernyi
  Coleodactylus 96
zeylanicus
  Seps 19
zonatus
  Enyalius 118
  Liolaemus signifer 194